Handbook of Administrative Ethics

PUBLIC ADMINISTRATION AND PUBLIC POLICY

A Comprehensive Publication Program

Executive Editor

JACK RABIN
Professor of Public Administration and Public Policy
School of Public Affairs
The Capital College
The Pennsylvania State University—Harrisburg
Middletown, Pennsylvania

ANNALS OF PUBLIC ADMINISTRATION

Handbook of Administrative Ethics

Second Edition
Revised and Expanded

edited by

Terry L. Cooper

University of Southern California
Los Angeles, California

MARCEL DEKKER, INC.   NEW YORK • BASEL

Library of Congress Cataloging-in-Publication Data

Handbook of administrative ethics / edited by Terry L. Cooper.—2nd ed., rev. and expanded.
     p. cm. — (Public administration and public policy)
   Includes index.
   ISBN 0-8247-0405-3 (alk. paper)
   1. Civil service ethics—United States.   2. Government executives—Professional ethics—
United States.   3. Civil service ethics.   4. Government executives—Professional ethics.
I. Cooper, Terry L., 1938–   II. Series.

   JK468.E7 H36 2000 2001
   172'.2—dc21

                                                     00-060097

ISBN: 0-8247-0405-3

This book is printed on acid-free paper.

Headquarters
Marcel Dekker, Inc.
270 Madison Avenue, New York, NY 10016
tel: 212-696-9000; fax: 212-685-4540

Eastern Hemisphere Distribution
Marcel Dekker AG
Hutgasse 4, Postfach 812, CH-4001 Basel, Switzerland
tel: 41-61-261-8482; fax: 41-61-261-8896

World Wide Web
http://www.dekker.com

The publisher offers discounts on this book when ordered in bulk quantities. For more information, write to Special Sales/Professional Marketing at the headquarters address above.

Current printing (last digit):
10 9 8 7 6 5 4 3 2 1

PRINTED IN THE UNITED STATES OF AMERICA

Preface

The serious development of ethics as a field of study within public administration has been underway for only about three decades. During that time an increasing number of scholars have turned their attention and intellectual efforts toward this subject. With growing urgency, practitioners have also expressed the need for conceptual clarity, theoretical perspective, and practical techniques for dealing with ethical concerns. Since the first edition of this handbook appeared in 1994, significant progress has been made in research on administrative ethics. The circle of scholars around the world doing work on this topic has expanded considerably, the literature has grown at an increasing rate, and institutions have emerged to support these efforts.

This handbook is intended to provide an overview of what has been accomplished to date in research and theory development on administrative ethics. The chapter authors were charged with reviewing comprehensively and reflecting on the body of literature that has been generated on the subjects that they agreed to address. These overviews are intended primarily to assist scholars and students seeking access to administrative ethics as a field for their own academic studies. They are also intended to provide background information to practitioners so they may better understand, in a broader and richer context, the practical ethical problems they confront. In some areas considerable work has already been done in administrative ethics, whereas in others the topics have only begun to be explored in relationship to the administrative role. In the latter instance, the authors were asked to review literature from other fields such as sociology, psychology, and philosophy and to attempt to draw out implications for administrative ethics.

The chapter authors were asked to avoid simply advancing their own points of view and grinding their own axes; they were instructed, rather, to present first, as objectively as possible, accounts of what has been published under each of the major topics constituting the field of study. The authors' evaluative comments, presentation of their own perspectives, and recommendations about further work typically have been reserved for the later sections of each chapter. The Introduction contains a more detailed description of each of the book's seven sections and 34 chapters. Five new chapters have been added on topics not covered in the first edition, one chapter from the first edition has been completely rewritten by a new author, and most of the others have undergone varying degrees of revision, some involving extensive changes and updating, and a few with minor revisions.

ACKNOWLEDGMENTS

The preparation of this second edition has extended over a period of more than two years from the invitation to chapter authors to revise their chapters to the final publication. During that time the contributions of a number of people have helped bring it to fruition. I must first express my deep appreciation to the scholars from the first edition who have found the time in their busy lives to rewrite chapters. Revision of work done several years ago is not always the most welcomed task. However, they have been remarkably congenial, cooperative, generous, and responsive to my suggestions and requests. The new authors and coauthors for this edition have brought fresh thinking and research findings, reflecting the continued growth in the study of administrative ethics. All of these women and men have had the maturity and good sense to know when to resist the meddling of the editor and assert the prerogatives of authorship, but I have always found them open to consider editorial advice. Their self-discipline and ability to meet deadlines once again, as with the first edition, have proved those wrong who told me that an effort of this scope would drag on for much longer than I had projected, draining me of all patience and goodwill, and turning friends into enemies. I have learned much in my reading of their chapters and exchanging views with them. Their interest in administrative ethics and the insights and knowledge they display in these chapters are the best evidence of the rapid development of this subfield of public administration. Even as recently as 15 years ago it would not have been possible to find 40 scholars to write on the specialized topics covered here, and certainly not of the quality that they have manifested in this work.

I wish to express my regrets that two of the authors from the first edition, Jeffrey S. Luke and Leigh Grosenick, have passed away. Their contributions live on in this edition through the assistance of coauthors who have respectfully and appreciatively taken on the responsibility for updating the work of these fine scholars. We all will miss them in our midst.

Next, I wish to thank Diane E. Yoder for her professional handling of many of the details involved in the preparation of the manuscript for publication. She has provided invaluable assistance in reviewing the chapter manuscripts for conformance to the publisher's guidelines, communicating with the authors, and managing the flow of manuscripts to the publisher. In addition to effectively carrying out these editorial duties, Ms. Yoder has assumed the lead authorship of one of the revised chapters. Diane Yoder is a promising scholar who has not only demonstrated her ability to contribute intellectually to this edition, but also displayed the patience, fortitude, and thoroughness required to move ideas from the written word through the editorial process to publication.

To Jack Rabin I owe appreciation for inviting me to edit this second edition. I am heartened to know that our work in the first edition has been found worthy of continuation and further development.

Paige Force, the production editor at Marcel Dekker, Inc., has been a thoroughly understanding, congenial, and helpful co-worker. Her gracious manner and willingness to tolerate my delays with gentle reminders of the deadlines made the task much more manageable and enjoyable.

Finally, as always, my warmest personal gratitude and love go to my wife, Megan, and my daughter, Chelsea, who have coped with my ill temper during the stressful times that accompany a project of this magnitude. They have understood beyond any reasonable expectation as I have absented myself from them and spent too many evenings at my computer. They have seen my limits and imperfections again and again and continued to love me anyway.

Terry L. Cooper

Contents

III. Contexts of Administrative Ethics

IV. Maintaining Ethical Conduct: External Controls

VII. Administrative Ethics in Other Cultures

Contributors

Guy B. Adams Professor and Associate Director, Graduate School of Public Affairs, University of Missouri-Columbia, Columbia, Missouri

James S. Bowman Professor, Askew School of Public Administration and Policy, Florida State University, Tallahassee, Florida

John P. Burke Professor, Department of Political Science, University of Vermont, Burlington, Vermont

Gerald E. Caiden Professor, School of Policy, Planning, and Development, University of Southern California, Los Angeles, California

Ralph Clark Chandler Director, School of Public Affairs and Administration, Western Michigan University, Kalamazoo, Michigan

Terry L. Cooper Professor, School of Policy, Planning, and Development, University of Southern California, Los Angeles, California

Kathryn G. Denhardt Policy Scientist and Associate Professor, School of Urban Affairs and Public Policy, University of Delaware, Newark, Delaware

Charles J. Fox Professor, Department of Political Science, Texas Tech University, Lubbock, Texas

H. George Frederickson Professor, Department of Public Administration, University of Kansas, Lawrence, Kansas

Pamela A. Gibson Doctoral Student and Instructor, Department of Political Science and Public Administration, Virginia Commonwealth University, Richmond, Virginia

Harold F. Gortner Professor, Department of Public and International Affairs, George Mason University, Fairfax, Virginia

Leigh E. Grosenick† Professor, Department of Political Science and Public Administration, Virginia Commonwealth University, Richmond, Virginia

David K. Hart Professor Emeritus, Marriott School of Management, Brigham Young University, Provo, Utah

David W. Hart Assistant Professor, Department of Business Administration, Mary Washington College, Fredericksburg, Virginia

April Hejka-Ekins Director, Master's Program in Public Administration, and Professor, Department of Politics and Public Administration, California State University, Stanislaus, California

Paul C. Light The Brookings Institution, Washington, D. C.

Terry T. Lui Honorary Assistant Professor, Department of Politics and Public Administration, University of Hong Kong, Hong Kong

Jeffrey S. Luke† Department of Planning, Public Policy, and Management, University of Oregon, Eugene, Oregon

Donald C. Menzel Professor and Director, Division of Public Administration, Northern Illinois University, DeKalb, Illinois

Douglas F. Morgan Director and Professor, Executive Leadership Institute, Hatfield School of Government, Portland State University, Portland, Oregon

Jonathan N. Moyo Professor, Political Studies Generation Project, University of the Witwatersrand, Johannesburg, South Africa

Michael O'Neill Professor, Department of Public Management, College of Professional Studies, University of San Francisco, San Francisco, California

Jeremy F. Plant Professor, School of Public Affairs, Penn State–Harrisburg, Middletown, Pennsylvania

Gerald M. Pops Professor, School of Social Work and Public Administration, West Virginia University, Morgantown, West Virginia

Molly J. Ranney Lecturer, Department of Social Work, California State University, Long Beach, California

---

† Deceased.

Robert Roberts   Professor, Department of Political Science, James Madison University, Harrisonburg, Virginia

John A. Rohr   Professor, Center for Public Administration and Policy, Virginia Polytechnic Institute, and State University, Blacksburg, Virginia

Ian Scott   Professor, School of Politics and International Studies, Murdoch University, Perth, Australia

Anneka Marina Scranton   Adjunct Associate Professor, School of Social Work, University of Southern California, Los Angeles, California

David M. Shafer   Doctoral Student, Department of Political Science and Public Administration, North Carolina State University, Raleigh, North Carolina

Norman W. Sprinthall   Professor Emeritus, Department of Counselor Education, North Carolina State University, Raleigh, North Carolina

Debra W. Stewart   Vice Chancellor and Dean of the Graduate School, Department of Political Science and Public Administration, North Carolina State University, Raleigh, North Carolina

Camilla Stivers   Professor, Levin College of Urban Affairs, Cleveland State University, Cleveland, Ohio

Judith A. Truelson   Associate Professor, Research Services, University of Southern California, Los Angeles, California

John G. Uhr   Senior Fellow, Research School of Social Sciences, Australian National University, Canberra, Australia

Montgomery Van Wart   Associate Professor, Political Science Department, Texas Tech University, Lubbock, Texas

Curtis Ventriss   Professor, School of Natural Resources and Department of Political Science, University of Vermont, Burlington, Vermont

Jeremy David Walling   Instructor, Department of Political Science, University of Kansas, Lawrence, Kansas

Richard D. White, Jr.   Professor, Public Administration Institute, Louisiana State University, Baton Rouge, Louisiana

Dennis P. Wittmer   Associate Professor, Department of Management, Daniels College of Business, University of Denver, Denver, Colorado

Diane E. Yoder   Instructor, School of Policy, Planning, and Development, University of Southern California, Los Angeles, California

Introduction

This second edition, following the same basic structure as the first, is divided into seven major sections that include administrative ethics as a field of study, philosophical perspectives in administrative ethics, the contexts of administrative ethics, maintaining ethical conduct through external controls, maintaining ethical conduct through internal controls, administrative ethics in American society, and administrative ethics in other cultures. These have been developed through 34 chapters, the authors of which include most of the leading scholars in public administrative ethics. In several cases coauthors have been recruited to assist with the work of revision, or to take the lead role in undertaking major revisions. Seven of the chapters are wholly new for this second edition (two completely rewritten by new authors and five dealing with new topics) and 22 have been substantially revised, some very extensively. Only five chapters from the first edition have no revisions or very minor ones.

Part I, Administrative Ethics as a Field of Study, opens with my chapter, "The Emergence of Administrative Ethics as a Field of Study in the United States." As the title indicates, the focus of this volume is largely on American scholarship, although the concluding section moves beyond. In this chapter I have traced the treatment of ethics in significant pieces of public administration literature from the late nineteenth century to the present. The emphasis is on major books, articles in *Public Administration Review* and *Administration and Society,* and sessions on ethics at the national conferences of the American Society for Public Administration. This chapter includes an area of research that has become more significant, updated information on conference presentations and articles published, the launching of a new journal, and new institutional developments associated with administrative ethics.

Chapter 2, "Research and Knowledge in Administrative Ethics," by H. George Frederickson and Jeremy David Walling, deals with empirical research on administrative ethics. They adopt an appropriately broad definition of "empirical" that includes methodologically stricter positivist approaches as well as post-positivist methods such as case studies, stories, and thick description. Frederickson and Walling conclude with recommendations about the most useful research techniques for generating various categories of knowledge concerning administrative ethics. A considerable number of new references exemplifying the various approaches to research on administrative ethics have been added to update this chapter.

Diane E. Yoder and Kathryn G. Denhardt examine ethics education in public administration in Chapter 3, including a number of empirical studies that have appeared since the first edition. They begin with a review of the emergence of ethics courses in graduate programs during the 1980s, document the general agreement that has been achieved about the importance of ethics education, examine teaching methods and programs and review the empirical studies of recent years. This chapter has undergone substantial revision.

Ethics in in-service training is the subject of Chapter 4 by April Hejka-Ekins. She describes the context for the evolution of ethics training in the public sector, examines the scope of ethics training programs, reviews the types of ethics training being offered at the different levels of government, considers the effectiveness of training in ethics, and attempts to summarize what can be learned about ethics training by examining the issues related to each of these topics. This revised chapter includes extensive references to new studies.

Part II, Philosophical Perspectives in Administrative Ethics, includes six chapters. In Chapter 5, "The Use of Philosophy in Administrative Ethics," Charles J. Fox begins by noting the lack of direct uses of formal academic philosophy by administrative ethicists. Maintaining that there is no generally accepted taxonomy of administrative ethics, he uses the categories of recent philosophy to create one. Fox identifies reflections of foundationalist teleological (consequentialist) and deontological (duty-oriented) philosophical orientations in the literature of public administration ethics. He moves next to the current challenges of antifoundationalist philosophy and its manifestations in administrative ethics literature, communitarianism being the one most evident. Throughout this chapter, Fox reminds the reader of the potentially beneficial chastening effects of a more vigorous engagement with formal philosophy. This chapter remains in its original form.

In Chapter 6, "Administration and the Ethics of Virtue," David Kirkwood Hart begins with an observation that although virtue understood as character is a time-honored concern in the study of ethics that has been largely ignored in public administration ethics, it is now emerging as a topic of interest. Hart then fills in background information on the tradition of virtue ethics by tracing its history from its roots in Greco-Roman thought through Thomas Aquinas to the Renaissance and the Enlightenment, where it was joined with civic responsibility. This tradition was broken by the scientism of the twentieth century and is only recently making a comeback, becoming apparent in public administration ethics only since the 1970s. Hart then undertakes a review of the various meanings of virtue, followed by a treatment of the implications of linking virtue to technical functions. He concludes the chapter by drawing out the implications of a virtue ethic for the "virtuous administrator." This chapter has been retained in its original form.

In Chapter 7, Douglas F. Morgan's topic is ethics and the public interest. Focusing on one of the most venerable normative ethical concepts in the literature of public administration, the public interest, Morgan begins by tracing the origins of that term. He then identifies four generally shared assumptions about the public interest that pose serious difficulties for us in defining any collective good beyond individual interests. Finally, Morgan moves through the historical usages of the concept in the United States since the founding era. This revised chapter includes updated references and extensive additions to the later portions of the essay to address the reinvention of government and the new public management movement, postmodernist challenges, and the social capital movement.

Chapters 8 and 9 present two major philosophical perspectives on administrative ethics. Ralph Clark Chandler, in Chapter 8, on deontological perspectives, deals with deontological approaches to administrative ethics, those oriented toward duty to principle. He summarizes the thought of the eighteenth-century philosopher Immanuel Kant with his moral imperative, since most contemporary deontologists are characterized as "neo-Kantians." The second deontological school Chandler terms ethical and cultural relativism, which argues for duty to the principles adhered to by particular cultures. The third school Chandler refers to as "agapism," involving duty to love others. Chandler concludes with an observation that deontological thinking can serve public organizations in maintaining adherence to their mission, but that ultimately good consequences are also important. Several sections of this chapter have been extended significantly for this second edition, including the treatments of Jeremy Bentham and agapism. A new discussion of the Clinton-Lewinsky scandal has been added.

In Chapter 9, "A Teleological Approach to Administrative Ethics," Gerald M. Pops provides an overview of teleological, or consequentialist, ethics. In contrast with deontological ethics, Pops explains that this approach is not concerned with duty to principle, but to the goodness of the consequences of one's acts. These consequences have to do with nonmoral goods such as income, health care, education, or safety. After reviewing some conceptual distinctions such as "act teleology" and "rule teleology," Pops deals at greater length with one major version of this perspective, utilitarianism, which is central to much public administrative thought. He then discusses the general tendencies of public administrators to think along teleological lines. Similar to Chandler, Pops concludes with an acknowledgment that most administrators use a combination of deontological and teleological perspectives. This chapter has been extensively rewritten and now includes material on communitarianism and the Clinton scandal.

Chapter 10, "A Dream of What We Could Be: The Founding Values, the Oath, and *Homo virtutis americanus*," is a new addition to this second edition by David Kirkwood Hart. This chapter argues against postmodernist approaches characterized here as "culturalism" and for a universal status for American founding values. He characterizes this position as "originalism." This will be a controversial and provocative chapter. It makes a strong argument for the founding values as emerging from broad deliberation among the members of the founding generation rather than the ideas of a small elite and as universally valid. However, this chapter makes a case that needs to be advanced and debated among us.

Part III deals with the contexts of administrative ethics, specifically the organizational setting and the public realm in which public administration is practiced. Chapter 11, "Organizational Structure: A Reflection of Society's Values and a Context for Individual Ethics" by Montgomery Van Wart and Kathryn G. Denhardt, is a wholly new chapter on this topic. Van Wart and Denhardt acknowledge that structure has been identified by other authors as an important factor in shaping administrative conduct. However, they maintain that organization structure is not a one-way influence on conduct and argue for a more complex understanding of organization structure as a reflection of societal values. Organization structures do influence individual administrative actions as instruments of a society, but are also, in turn, influenced by individual discretion acted out within an organization. Van Wart and Denhardt develop this perspective around three concepts: paradigmatic structures, organizational systems, and organizational forms.

In Chapter 12, "Governmental Ethics and Organizational Culture," Leigh E. Grosenick and Pamela A. Gibson present an initial case for the importance of organizational culture, then review the ways in which the concept may be understood and employed for analytical purposes. They focus on the ethical dimensions of organizational culture, followed by an examination of the conflicts between culture and ethical conduct. The final portions of the chapter look at the role organizational culture has played in the literature of public administration, the treatment of organizational culture in administrative ethics books and articles, and the use of the concept for administrative ethics research. This chapter has been substantially revised with many new references, illustrations, and an important discussion of the literature on governmental reform.

Curtis Ventriss, in Chapter 13, ''The Relevance of Public Ethics to Administration and Policy,'' begins with a distinction between administrative ethics and public ethics, arguing for the latter as a broader and more appropriate perspective within which to develop an administrative ethic. Ventriss then offers some observations about the surprising lack of attention to the meaning of ''public'' in the study of public administration and moves on to a review of the literature that *does* address this important subject. He finds this material falling into four categories: classical, neoclassical, consequential, and organizational. He concludes with evaluative comments on these four schools of thought, indicating his sympathies with the classical, neoclassical, and consequential perspectives and his reservations about the organizational view. In this revised chapter, Ventriss expands his argument considerably with references from the recent literature including a treatment of postmodernism and public administration.

Chapter 14 is a new contribution for this edition by Guy B. Adams titled, ''Administrative Ethics and the Chimera of Professionalism: The Historical Context of Public Service Ethics.'' Adams begins with an assessment of the state of scholarship on administrative ethics, and then examines the relationship between professionalism and administrative ethics. Finally, he considers the possibility of a new approach to professionalism within modern society.

Part IV, ''Maintaining Ethical Conduct: External Controls,'' examines various legal and organizational devices for encouraging desired conduct. In Chapter 15, Jeremy F. Plant addresses codes of ethics. After an opening discussion of the general nature of codes along with examples, Plant deals with issues surrounding codes, reviews the research and literature on the subject, and discusses several examples of public administrative codes of ethics, including a detailed treatment of one of the most fully developed public sector codes, that of the International City Management Association. He concludes with his own critical evaluation of the strengths and limitations of codes. Plant has cited a substantial amount of new literature on codes and inserted new commentary at appropriate places in the chapter.

Chapter 16, ''From Codes of Conduct to Codes of Ethics: The ASPA Case,'' is James S. Bowman's new contribution to the second edition. Bowman argues that codes may be evolving from a compliance approach to a more reflective professional ethics orientation. He then examines the code of the American Society for Public Administration from this perspective using his own empirical research done in recent years.

''Ethics Management in Public Organizations,'' by Donald C. Menzel, is Chapter 17, another new addition to this volume. Menzel presents the concept of ''ethics management'' as a current way of understanding the integration of ethics into the management role and the organization culture. He begins by addressing the importance of managing the ethical dimensions of conduct within an organization, examining the link between ethics and performance. Menzel then moves on to discuss both formal and informal strategies for ethics management.

Chapter 18, by Robert Roberts, is concerned with "Federal Ethics Management and Public Trust." This new chapter examines the historical emergence of the public integrity structures and processes within the executive branch of the federal government and reviews the federal ethics program currently in place. Roberts concludes that these new institutions have been effective in reducing the number of conflict-of-interest controversies.

Paul C. Light begins Chapter 19, "Federal Inspectors General and the Paths to Accountability," with background on the introduction of the inspector general role into the federal government in 1978 and a brief legislative history. He then reviews definitions of accountability and examines the Inspector General Act of 1978 to discover the implied meaning of accountability therein. The remainder of the chapter deals with the monitoring role of the inspectors general and the various forms this role takes. This chapter has been updated with new references and treatment of developments since the first edition.

Chapter 20, "Whistleblower Protection and the Judiciary" by Judith A. Truelson, focuses on channels available to whistleblowers at the federal level, and means of protecting them from retribution and ostracism, but also includes a brief discussion of the state level and private sector. She concludes that since present protections are inadequate to shield whistleblowers from hostile superiors and peers, they have had to develop extralegal strategies for survival. Truelson presents a case illustrating the importance of employing all available strategies with careful and thoughtful planning. In her concluding observations, Truelson asserts the necessity to change organizational cultures if any of the attempts to mitigate the suffering of whistleblowers are to succeed. Truelson has reorganized this chapter, expanded several sections, and updated the case law and references to literature.

"Dealing with Administrative Corruption" is addressed by Gerald E. Caiden in Chapter 21. After lamenting the lack of attention to corruption ("the obverse side to public ethics"), and identifying some reasons for its unpopularity in the public administration literature, Caiden provides a working definition and discusses its significance for both the public and private sectors. He then reviews some of the efforts to break through the taboo that seems to surround the subject. The author moves next to a treatment of the key elements that must be included in any anticorruption policy and its successful implementation in an agency anticorruption program. Beyond specific legislation and programs, Caiden emphasizes the importance of a culture of public accountability throughout government as a supportive foundation for anticorruption efforts. He then reviews ten areas of the modern administrative state in which abuses are likely to occur. The author concludes with brief observations about the tendency of corruption to spread and destroy the effectiveness of governments it infects. This chapter has been significantly expanded with the inclusion of material on recent developments and new literature.

Part V, "Maintaining Ethical Conduct: Internal Controls," presents four chapters on processes and traits associated with thinking about ethical concerns, resolving ethical decisions, the nature of valuing, and personal character traits. Chapter 22, by Debra W. Stewart, Norman W. Sprinthall, and David M. Shafer, deals with moral development in public administration. After setting the historical context for the study of moral development in psychological theory and research, the authors focus on the groundbreaking work of Lawrence Kohlberg. They summarize the findings of his research on cognitive moral development and the six stages he identified as universal. Stewart and her coauthors then review the research supporting a link between the way one thinks about ethical issues and how one behaves. This is followed by a description and evaluation of an instrument designed by the authors oriented specifically to the public administrative role. Known as the "Stewart-Sprinthall Management Survey," it is based on Kohlberg's framework. They report some of their findings and discuss the usefulness of the instrument. Stewart and Sprinthall conclude by drawing out the implications of their work for public administration. This chapter has been extensively revised to include the research conducted by the authors in Poland and Russia, as well as many new references to the research literature.

Dennis P. Wittmer, in Chapter 23, "Ethical Decision-Making," emphasizes both behavioral and normative perspectives on individual decision-making by administrators. Wittmer begins with a conceptual analysis of the elements that constitute ethical situations and the ethical dimensions of situations. He then proceeds to review behavioral approaches by first examining several conceptual models found in the literature, followed by a report of empirical results from testing these models. Wittmer next treats normative perspectives that prescribe how ethical decisions should be made, discussing those found among administrative ethicists and then concluding with those associated more with traditional philosophical thought. Wittmer has added to this chapter numerous new references to the empirical research which has been published since the first edition.

In "Values and Ethics," Chapter 24, Harold F. Gortner begins by explaining how values are one of the essential elements in ethical dilemmas and then turns to a review of definitions of "value," and follows with a look at how psychology, sociology, and philosophy treat the concept. Gortner next examines the interaction of ethics and values in public administration by focusing on five categories of values central to defining the public interest: political, economic, social, bureaucratic, and professional. He then turns his attention to the functions of the public administrator and how they are influenced by values. Gortner concludes with observations about the necessity for supportive values if democratic government is to be maintained. Gortner has updated this chapter with numerous new references and has also included material on communitarianism and social capital.

In Chapter 25, "Character and Conduct in the Public Service: A Review of Historical Perspectives," Jeffrey S. Luke and David W. Hart review both psychological and philosophical definitions of character, as well as views that have emerged recently in the administrative ethics literature. In the philosophical camp, Luke summarizes the views of Aristotle, Confucius, Kant, Mill, Bentham, Dewey, and Tufts. On the psychological side, he reviews the work of Freud, Fromm, Peck and Havighurst, and Kohlberg. Unfortunately for us all, Jeff Luke has passed away since the first edition. David W. Hart has updated the chapter and rewritten its introduction and conclusion. The chapter now concludes with an argument for the need for high character in the public service.

Part VI is about administrative ethics in American society and treats four topics with particular relevance to the political and social contexts of public administration in the United States. Anneka Marina Scranton (formerly Davidson) and Molley J. Ranney deal with gender differences in administrative ethics in Chapter 26. They focus on the emerging literature on a feminine ethical perspective quite distinct from masculine views, which have been dominant. This mode of ethical thought reflects the values of relationships, caring, connection, cooperation, and concern for others. Scranton and Ranney argue that, although rooted in feminine experience, it is not exclusively a female perspective but may be adopted by males as well. They begin by describing the care model of individual ethical reasoning and then contrast it with the more traditional "justice" approach. In developing this theme, Scranton and Ranney structure their chapter around four components of ethical conduct. To assess the extent to which women actually behave consistently with the feminine perspective, they review a considerable body of empirical research findings. This chapter now includes a substantial amount of new material including theoretical perspectives, illustrative cases, and empirical research.

"Citizenship Ethics in Public Administration," Chapter 27 by Camilla Stivers, opens with a distinction between citizenship as a "status" and citizenship as a "practice." She then identifies and discusses the major ingredients in citizenship as treated in the Western philosophical tradition. The development of a citizenship perspective in public administration is treated subsequently, followed by an outline of the major features of a citizenship ethic as reflected in the public administration literature. Stivers calls attention to the tension between citizenship and the values of organizations. She concludes with recommendations about the further development of citizenship ethics. Stivers includes a number of new references and addresses the reinventing-government movement and the growing alienation of citizens during the 1990s.

Chapter 28, "Administrative Ethics and Democratic Theory," by John P. Burke, begins with reflection about the relationship between administrative ethics and democratic theory and observations about problems the former may pose for the latter. The author then reviews an array of options within the broad scope of democratic theory and draws out the implications of each for the democratic responsibility of administrators. Burke concludes with several observations about problems that remain to be worked out concerning the relationships among individual ethics, administrative ethics, and democratic theory. This revised chapter provides updated references and the further development of some specific arguments.

Michael O'Neill analyzes the ethical dimensions of nonprofit administration in Chapter 29. In this revised chapter O'Neill emphasizes the significance of differences among different organizations associated with the three sectors of American society. This leads him to outline the distinctive characteristics of nonprofit organizations and to draw out their implications for an ethic of nonprofit management. The author then concludes with comments about the underdeveloped state of nonprofit ethics as an area of study and the urgency of further research on this topic.

Chapter 30 is a new contribution to the handbook by Richard D. White, Jr., titled "Military Ethics." White begins with the assertion that military ethics is unique in that it deals with when and how war is to be fought. After a review of the history of military ethics, beginning with just war theory in the 5th century B.C. and concluding with recent scholarship, White reviews the literature on contemporary official military ethics doctrine. He concludes with a treatment of critical views of professional military ethics and his own argument for the need for a military code of ethics.

Part VII, "Administrative Ethics in Other Cultures," is an attempt to remind the reader that administrative ethics, just as the broader field of public administration, is to some extent a reflection of the context in which it occurs. While these four chapters by no means provide an adequate representation of the enormous array of the world's cultures, they do offer the reader suggestive glimpses beyond American society.

In Chapter 31, "Administrative Ethics in a Chinese Society: The Case of Hong Kong," Terry T. Lui and Ian Scott begin with the importance of contextual variables for administrative ethics and then proceed to a discussion of the spatial and temporal effects of these variables. This leads the authors to a central theme focused on the practical and conceptual relevance of administrative ethics to its context. Lui and Scott next identify and examine the specific factors that shape administrative ethics in Hong Kong: political determinants, cultural influences, and the changing environment. The authors conclude with reflections on the possibility of a new administrative ethic for Hong Kong. This chapter has been extensively revised to account for the impacts of the transition in sovereignty of Hong Kong from Britain to the People's Republic of China.

John A. Rohr offers the only truly comparative study in this section in Chapter 32, "Constitutionalism and Administrative Ethics: A Comparative Study of Canada, France, the United Kingdom, and the United States." The common point of comparison Rohr selects is the relationship between constitutionalism and public administration ethics in each of these countries. He assumes general knowledge of the United States and moves on to discuss each of the other three countries in turn, weaving in American comparisons only as appropriate points are encountered along the way. The author concludes with a summary of the significant comparative points that emerged in the study. This chapter remains in its original form from the first edition.

At the outset of Chapter 33, "Administrative Ethics in an African Society: The Case of Zimbabwe," Jonathan N. Moyo establishes colonialism and neocolonialism as the backdrop for public administration and administrative ethics throughout Africa, but suggests that administrative ethics is best understood "in the context of the rapidly changing political experience of the Continent." Moyo asserts that objective responsibility (imposed from outside oneself) has been dominant over subjective responsibility (feelings of obligation) in African administrative ethics resulting in a "law and order" orientation. The author then turns to the main focus of the chapter: Zimbabwe as an example of "imposed obligation as an *exclusive* source of administrative ethics." He concludes the chapter with a discussion of impediments to the full development of an administrative ethic in Zimbabwe and Africa in general. No revisions were made to this chapter.

Chapter 34, by John G. Uhr, "Public Service Ethics in Australia," has been extensively revised in the light of changing regime values and an evolving national identity. Uhr discusses three ethics perspectives reflected in major scholarly studies. With these as background he examines ethics as it is, ethics as it should be, and ethics as good management. Uhr then undertakes a review of the literature commenting on ethics in Australian government and a discussion of the ethics of accountability.

1

The Emergence of Administrative Ethics as a Field of Study in the United States

Terry L. Cooper
University of Southern California, Los Angeles, California

One might reasonably argue that administrative ethics has been a topic of sustained interest at least since the founding of *Public Administration Review* (PAR) in 1940 (Nigro and Richardson, 1990). One might even assert that administrative ethics has been of concern both to practitioners and scholars since the founding era of the United States (Richardson and Nigro, 1987). However, this chapter will maintain that the *study* of administrative ethics as an ongoing scholarly enterprise with the trappings of a subfield of academic inquiry does not predate the 1970s. Although there have been numerous articles dealing with administrative ethics in some way in PAR since 1940, as Nigro and Richardson have demonstrated, one does not find anything approximating a systematic and developmental treatment of the subject until the last three decades. Even during these years the study of administrative ethics has lacked sufficient emphasis on some of the elements necessary to come to full fruition as a developmental subfield. Through the 1990s the field of study has continued to develop rapidly, as reflected in the literature produced, treatment in conferences, and the creation of new institutions. Empirical research on administrative ethics has expanded, but still represents the area of the field of study needing the most development.

The primary criterion assumed here for a field of study is the existence of a group of scholars with a sustained interest in the subject, at least some of whom identify themselves as specialists. The second is a consistent flow of published materials in books, leading journals, and conference sessions devoted to the advancement of theory. This stream of literature should focus on: critically analyzing, reflecting, and building on each other's work; development of methodology for research and analysis; empirical research on specific issues, problems, and testing specific theories; and integration of theories and research findings into comprehensive frameworks. A third criterion is the establishment of academic courses in university professional education programs.

The focus of this chapter will be on the literature of administrative ethics from the late nineteenth century through the early 1990s as it has contributed to the development of a full-fledged field of study within public administration. It will examine the treatment of this subject in books, articles in PAR, *Administration & Society* (A&S), and sessions at the national conferences of the American Society for Public Administration (ASPA).[1] There is no presumption here of comprehensiveness. This chapter is offered not as an exhaustive review of the ethics literature, but a consideration of representative works that mark the significant milestones in the emergence of administrative ethics as a recognized subject of research, theory building, scholarly publication, and professional education. Since the first edition of this *Handbook of Administrative Ethics*, numerous articles have regularly appeared in other journals which have emerged as significant venues including *Public Integrity, Administrative Theory & Praxis*, the *Journal of Public Administration Research and Theory*, and the *American Review of Public Administration*.

First, the early years of public administration as a subject of study, from the late nineteenth through the middle of the third decade of the twentieth century, will be reviewed through a few classic pieces of literature. This is to demonstrate the inattention to the study of administrative ethics during that era. Then a body of literature from the late 1930s through the 1960s will be examined as forming the foundation for a field of study focusing on administrative ethics. Finally, the material of the 1970s through the early 1990s will be treated as representing the actual emergence of what may now be understood as a field of study. The most recent body of work from the early 1980s through the early 1990s will be discussed more briefly than that which came earlier since it is too voluminous to examine in detail and it is amply dealt with elsewhere in this handbook. The most recent literature, with a very few notable exceptions, will not be reviewed in this chapter since it is covered well in the revisions of those chapters that follow.

I. THE EARLY YEARS OF PUBLIC ADMINISTRATION AS A FIELD OF STUDY

Van Riper (1983) has argued persuasively that the study of American public administration predates Woodrow Wilson's famous essay (1887). He has suggested Dorman B. Eaton's (1880) examination of the British civil service, with U.S. application in mind, seven years earlier as a more appropriate point of origin.[2] Although any such specification is somewhat arbitrary, Eaton's study will be taken as a starting point here.

Upon examining Eaton's work, it is clear that he viewed civil service reform as a fundamentally ethical act. Lamenting "the long practice of making merchandise of public authority," he maintained that this practice "had vitiated and benumbed the moral sense of the English nation on the subject, so that reform had become tenfold more difficult; just as the moral sense of this nation [the U.S.] has, from like causes, become blunted to the immorality of levying assessments and bestowing office for mere partisan purposes" (pp. 23–24). Eaton saw the shift from appointment to office by a "corrupt and arbitrary king" to merit criteria based on character and competence as an advance in "justice and liberty" (p. 357). Civil service was understood, not merely as a method of conducting public business, but as "a test and expression of the justice and moral tone of a nation's politics" (p. 358).

In Eaton's work, the emphasis on the moral sense and tone of the nation, together with the identification of justice and liberty as the determinative principles were strikingly different from the emphasis on efficiency and making government more businesslike which were central to Wilson's essay (1887). In "The Study of Administration" Wilson reflected the assumptions of the American Progressive reform movement that efficiency was the hallmark of good government and the development of a scientific approach to administration was the way to achieve it. Furthermore, his work evidenced continuity with the assumptions of the Federalist philosophy of human nature which underpins the U.S. Constitution. The improvement of human nature through education and reason could not be counted on to produce ethical conduct in public affairs; authority and structural constraints on discretion were considered the primary guarantors of good government.

Although the Progressives were concerned about the unfairness of unequal treatment of the citizenry based on willingness to lend support to a political machine, they were even more disturbed by the inefficiency of those informal governments. Simply by dint of the amount of attention given to efficiency and the methods of science in the Progressive literature, one comes away with the impression that the more serious defect in machine government was thought to be its inefficiency rather than its lack of justice or liberty. Ethical conduct for the Progressives was efficient action by public servants in carrying out impartially and scientifically the policies adopted by the political leadership.

While there was a difference in emphasis on the ethics of public administration between Eaton and Wilson, both tended to view the means of achieving ethical conduct similarly. It was a matter of certain procedural reforms involving selection for public service based on job-related merit criteria instead of ties to a political boss, and promotion based on performance rather than political favors rendered. It should not be surprising then to find no call by Eaton or Wilson for the study of administrative ethics. If one assumed that ethical conduct, as well as more efficient government, could be attained through the establishment of a merit-based civil service system then the appropriate focus of study was how to accomplish these changes, not the normative content of public service ethics, or ethics training for those in the public service. What constituted ethical conduct was not a matter of great dispute, just how to secure it.

This same general orientation was reflected in Goodnow's *Politics and Administration: A Study in Government* (1900). His focus was on popular government and efficient administration. Goodnow offers no direct treatment of administrative ethics, nor are there entries in the index for terms such as "ethics," "morality," "public interest," or "common good." "Responsibility" was the only concept employed from which one might infer an administrative ethic. Goodnow's treatment of the problem of the political boss (pp. 168–198) made it clear that public administrators are responsible only for the execution of policy determined by elected officials. There was no recognition of the unavoidable discretionary power of administrators in the modern state and the policymaking role which necessarily follows. One achieved ethical administration through a merit-based civil service system controlled by "reasonable concentration and centralization" of authority; this constraint of administrative action from above made government more responsible.

Willoughby's textbook, *The Principles of Public Administration: With Special Reference to the National and State Governments of the United States* (1927), continued along similar lines. One finds there the same focus on efficiency and the quest for generic scientific principles of administration as the means of achieving it. The civil service merit system was viewed as a moral structure which would lead to ethical public administration. Ethics was not considered as an individual professional skill involving a discrete body of knowledge and analytical techniques. Rather it was subsumed under organization and personnel theory as the product of certain scientifically grounded arrangements, procedures, and rules.

There is one brief section in Willoughby's volume in which he did resort to the language of ethics in arguing for the importance of a just personnel system. He described such a system as one which "offers equal opportunities to all citizens to enter the government service, equal pay to all employees doing work requiring the same degree of intelligence and capacity, equal opportunities for advancement, equally favorable work conditions, and equal participation in retirement allowances, and makes equal work demands upon the employees'' (p. 230). Absent these conditions, loyalty, esprit de corps, and willingness to work—all of which he viewed as essential to efficiency—would be impossible to secure. However, once again Willoughby was describing system traits and the requisites of organizational efficiency. Later in the book he did mention the importance of character traits such as honesty, but Willoughby noted the difficulty of assessing these attributes, thus leaving them clearly secondary to external controls provided by the organization.

II. LAYING THE FOUNDATIONS FOR ETHICS AS A FIELD OF STUDY

Almost a decade after Willoughby's book, with the publication of *The Frontiers of Public Administration* by John M. Gaus, Leonard D. White, and Marshall E. Dimock (1936), one can see stress cracks in the dominant consensus appearing that prepared the way for greater significance for administrative ethics. In "The Meaning and Scope of Public Administration" (pp. 1–12), Dimock cautioned against "going too far in the formal separation between politics and administration" (p. 3). He then pointed out that researchers soon discover "the important differences in place, time, local tradition, and objective which need to be given their full weight" (p. 4), thus subtly calling into question the possibility of a science of administration.

John Gaus, in "The Responsibility of Public Administration" (Gaus et al., 1936: 26–44) asserted that public administrators exercise considerable discretion and raised the question concerning to whom or what are they responsible for this discretionary judgment. Responding to his own question, Gaus introduced the term "inner check" which he had borrowed from debates in the literary journals of his time. As a form of responsibility more relevant to modern government than accountability to elected officials, Gaus argued for an "inner check" consisting of obligation acknowledged by individual civil servants "due to the standards and ideals" of their profession (pp. 39–40). With this kind of argument, ethical reflection and normative judgment seem to have been only a short step away.

Dimock further reinforced Gaus' case for the existence of more administrative discretion than had been allowed previously in "The Role of Discretion in Modern Administration" (Gaus et al., 1936: 45–65). He not only observed that "the discretionary power of administrative officials has grown relative to that of courts and legislatures," but predicted that it would continue to increase (pp. 45, 64).

In the concluding chapter, "The Criteria and Objectives of Public Administration" (Gaus et al., 1936: 116–133), Dimock attacked the validity of the central value of Progressive public administration—efficiency. He noted that the highest compliment for a government in the United States is to suggest that it is efficient. Furthermore, he proclaimed: "It is no exaggeration to say that, particularly in the last fifty years, American citizens have developed an attitude toward the term 'efficiency' which is nothing short of worshipful" (p. 116).

However, according to Dimock, this was all done uncritically and efficiency had become a "slogan" (Gaus et al., 1936: 116). He was then moved to question why criteria and values are important to public administration, and finally to comment briefly on the desirability of a broader administrative philosophy that would include "the virtue of loyalty, as well as honesty, enthusiasm, humility, and all the other attributes of character and conduct which contribute to effective and satisfying service" (p. 132).

Dimock's call for an administrative philosophy, focused on the character of the individual administrator, together with his attack on the adequacy of efficient organizations, his and Gaus' claims concerning the discretion of administrators, Gaus' argument for the importance of an "inner check," and Dimock's worry about separating politics from administration, all reflect a gradual but certain tectonic shift in administrative thought which made it almost inevitable that ethics would receive major attention sooner or later.

The running debate between Carl Friedrich and Herman Finer during the years 1935–1941 further focused attention on the validity of the internal controls represented by professional values, standards, and ethics as replacements for, or complements to, the external controls of political superiors and the laws they produced. Friedrich insisted on the inadequacy of external controls to maintain responsible administrative conduct in modern complex organizations and called for the cultivation of a form of "inner check" advocated by Gaus, while Finer pointed out the weakness of internal controls in the face of human propensity for rationalization and reaffirmed the necessity for political control of administrators through laws, rules, and sanctions (Friedrich, 1935; Finer, 1936).[3] By 1940 one could discern a synthesis of the Friedrich-Finer dichotomy in *Public Management in the New Democracy*, edited by Fritz Morstein Marx.[4] Specifically, in a chapter authored by Marx, "Administrative Responsibility" (Marx, 1940: 218–251), he opined that legislative control was no longer adequate to insure responsibility (p. 237). Although he considered it, along with judicial restraint, still necessary as a foundation for responsible conduct, Marx offered a bold prescription that moved well beyond legal control:

> The heart of administrative responsibility is a unified conception of duty, molded by ideological and professional precepts; a firm determination on the part of the official to sacrifice personal preference to the execution of legislative policy and to infuse his energies and his creative impulse into his task; a wakeful consciousness of the deference he owes to the people and its vital interests. Administrative responsibility emanates from an attitude of true service. In the shaping of this attitude, the ethical outlook of the official is only one, though a very important, factor (Marx, 1940: 251).

Here one can see clearly the emergence of a role for ethics along with the more traditional instruments of political oversight and legal control. Administrative ethics involved, according to Marx, an understanding of duty that contained both ideological and professional elements, subordination of personal interests to those of the citizenry, and an obligation to the role of servant of the public.

Tugwell's article in the first volume of PAR in 1940 struck a new chord by focusing on the concept of "the general interest" as an appropriate central criterion for evaluating the planning commission of the city of New York. At an earlier time "efficiency" would have been a more likely candidate. Tugwell seemed to assume that there was sufficient general agreement about the meaning of the concept to make it useful, although his own treatment evidences only a gross distinction between individual and private interests on the one hand, and the larger interests of the city on the other. There was no real conceptual or theoretical development, only general application.

For the most part, the literature of the 1940s following Marx's edited volume was a period during which the same themes and complaints were churned over, reexamined, and digested. One sees little systematic development of a study of administrative ethics, only reaffirmation of flaws in the old formulation of the administrative role, calls for a new place for ethics, and a few tentative suggestions about the directions which should be taken in developing a professional ethic.

For example, Levitan (1942) joined the growing chorus against too firm and precise a notion of the neutrality of public servants. While affirming the need to limit the direct influence of political parties in administrative appointments and the involvement of administrators in partisan activities, he asserted the requirement of administrative loyalty to the citizenry and a devotion to democracy. He advocated education in citizenship and the American democratic tradition for the entire civil service. In this sense public administrators were obligated to political commitments.

Similarly, Caldwell (1943) resorted to historical reflection on Thomas Jefferson for a precedent for challenging administrative neutrality and affirming the political obligation of public servants. He found in Jefferson an understanding of the responsibility of the administrator to the Constitution as having priority over their accountability to the legislature. To address the problematic nature of the emerging administrative state for democratic control, he used this precedent to argue that administrators must always remember that they are "the servants of the people, not their masters" (p. 253). He concluded:

> So long as men retain a sense of social obligation and a love of personal liberty, and so long as public administrators are governed by the conceptions of service and self-restraint which Jefferson exemplified, America has nothing to fear from the expanding role of administration in the contemporary state (Caldwell, 1943: 253).

The outstanding exception to this tendency to repeat the attacks on the old consensus, call attention to discretion, and reaffirm the political and value-laden nature of public administration was a landmark article by Leys (1943). There Leys clearly linked administrative discretion with the need for greater attention to professional ethics using philosophy as the primary focus of study. In effect, he began a conceptual outline for an approach to the study of administrative ethics.

Arguing that administrative discretion is not merely the result of legislative vagueness, but a positive necessity in modern industrial society, Leys observed the need for wisdom in the exercise of discretionary power. He found the negative approach which focuses on ways of limiting discretionary judgment to be inadequate and called for greater attention to ethics. However, Leys made it clear that he was not particularly interested in codes of ethics since they tend to "prescribe standards for the administrator's own conduct" (p. 11). His concern was with administrative decisions that affect others such as citizens, departments, corporations, and subordinates. These he called policy decisions although they may be only discrete decisions in the course of one's administrative work.[5]

Leys then made his case for a philosophical foundation for administrative ethics. He explained that the philosopher's focus on how one links general standards of conduct to specific standards fits precisely the administrator's need to move from general legislation to particular actions, as well as from specific deeds to the general principle which informs them. Leys then discussed two approaches to philosophical ethics that might be employed by administrators—duty to certain values and principles on the one hand, and utilitarian concern for the consequences of one's acts on the other.[6]

Leys coupled with his argument for philosophical ethics a more complex typology of discretion than had been proposed previously. These are technical discretion, discretion in social planning, and discretion in reconciling political conflict. He concluded with an assertion that the "classical methods of ethics" should be helpful with all three forms. They would be useful in "testing the compatibility" of "technically defined rules with a settled criterion," clarifying and articulating the vague criteria which may be inherent in social planning, and in "rationalizing debate where the criteria are in dispute" (Leys, 1943: 23).

In the immediate aftermath of World War II one can still discern little real development of ethics as a field of study beyond the advances represented by Leys' article. Appleby, in a PAR article entitled, "Toward Better Public Administration" (1947) and a book called *Big Democracy* (1949) worked over the political nature of public administration, its participation in "the creation of opportunity for the fructification of moral ends" (1947: 95), its obligation to support democratic values, its duty to be responsive to the citizenry (officials are "especially responsible citizens" [1947: 99]), and its focus on the public interest. As always, Appleby said it well, perhaps better than his predecessors, but there was nothing in these works that directly contributed to the development of administrative ethics as a field of study. One might respond that Appleby's presentation of these ideas cogently and in an integrated fashion solidified the ground for administrative ethics. That may well be a valid observation, but the significance of these additions to the literature lies more in their contribution to the development of a political theory for public administration than in advancing the study of ethics.

White's third edition of *Introduction to the Study of Public Administration* (1948) treated ethics exclusively in terms of external controls under the rubric, "codes of ethics" (p. 485). He discussed codes mainly as an essential element of professionalization which is needed "to attract favorable public attention and help to raise prestige" (p. 485). He pointed to the code adopted by the International City Managers' Association as a prime example. White recognized that such codes were not fully adequate to deal with the full range of ethical concerns of administrators and gave examples of complicated situations arising out of the organizational context for which codes are not very helpful. He concluded his brief treatment of ethics by acknowledging that "We lack any general study of civil service ethics, but a subject which offers such interesting possibilities will doubtless soon be explored" (p. 489). This appears to have been the first explicit admission that administrative ethics is worthy of "general study," but that nothing up to that point amounted to such an effort.

However, greater vigor in the call for attention to administrative ethics and new momentum toward the development of ethics as a field of study in public administration began to develop in the next year with the publication of Marx's article "Administrative Ethics and the Rule of Law" (1949).[7] Marx began by observing the dependence of administrative conduct on "conscious or unconscious self-interest" and "the maturity of individual judgment and insight." The significance of the impact of administrative judgment on public policy suggested to Marx that these were not sufficient. Since they could "not be said to spring from any common agreement entered into by the civil-service profession," he asserted the need for a more "coherent body of administrative ethics" (pp. 1120–1121). Marx did not understand this lack of agreement to mean that there was no basis for arriving at such a consensus; there was "a considerable degree of uniformity" that "arises even from purely individual responses to issues of morality that recur in the occupational experience of the civil servant. The problem was that "in contrast with other professions, . . . public management has devoted less effort to evolving something in the nature of a general code of conduct" (pp. 1121–1122). Marx draws support for this assessment of the state of administrative ethics by quoting White's statement above concerning the absence of any general study of the subject.

Marx then began to outline an ethical theory for public administration by asserting that "the highest task of public administration is . . . to serve as an effective instrument in attaining the purposes of the political order" (Marx, 1949: 1127). This was not simply a revival of the politics-administration dichotomy, but a broader and deeper recognition that "administrative morality . . . acquires its inner logic from the political ideology which the machinery of government is expected to translate into social reality." He continued, "the core of all administrative ethics lies in the ideas that nourish the political system. In the United States, therefore, the morals of public management are inseparable from the egalitarian conception of popular government embedded in the American tradition" (pp. 1127–1128). This implied to Marx that administrators were not free to follow their own personal values in the course of their professional activities, but were obligated to be "conscious agents of a democratic community" and "to direct their actions toward promoting the healthy growth of a free society dedicated to the common good" (p. 1128).

This general formulation of an approach to public administration ethics anticipates arguments for regime values, founding thought, and citizenship put forth during the last two decades. It differs both from Leys' earlier advocacy for philosophy as the principal normative source for the field and the New Public Administration's preoccupation with one particular philosophical ethic—Rawlsian social equity—by grounding administrative ethics in democratic political theory and, more specifically, the American political tradition.

Marx pursued the point by identifying "civic lethargy" with the public perception that professionalized public administration had obviated the need for active citizenship. He insisted that seeking ways of stimulating civic participation in public management is a corollary of the ethical derivative stated earlier—that administrative officials are bound by duty to promote "the healthy growth of a free society" (p. 1131). Marx understood this to require a general orientation "toward a long-range concept of the general interest" (p. 1132).

Rejecting the adequacy of the external controls advocated by Finer, Marx maintained that "infinitely more important than compelling administrative officials to live up to minutely defined requirements of control is their acceptance of an ethical obligation to account to themselves and to the public for the *public* character of their actions. That is to say, they must answer for any failure to make each action breathe the general interest" (pp. 1134–1135). Furthermore, it is incumbent upon public administrators patiently to enter into the process of public consensus-building. He argued that, "the democratic process begs for time—time to establish mutual confidence, time to identify the common denominator, time to gather even the subdued relevancies, time to work out a joint conclusion." Marx recognized the tension this time-consuming process created under "budgetary pressures," but insisted on its fundamentality in the ethical obligation of administrators (p. 1141).

Sayre (1951) reinforced the perspective advanced by Marx as he reviewed the role of values at the end of the first decade of PAR's publication. He concluded that the field had moved from a focus in 1940 on becoming a science set apart from values to a point in 1950 where "the indispensable function of values in public life is now conceded on all sides" (Sayre, 1951:9). Moreover, Sayre observed that "this suggests that the basic search in the study of administration is more for a theory of government than for a science of administration'' (p. 9).

The next year brought with it the first two volumes, by Appleby and Leys, devoted entirely to administrative ethics. Appleby's *Morality and Administration in Democratic Government* (1952) attempted an integration of democratic values and bureaucracy. After developing his argument for the morality of democratic government, Appleby contended that hierarchy within organizations represents a structure of responsibility that makes administration responsive to popular will. It represents a flow of information designed to maintain accountability to democratically-arrived-at policy. Admitting that bureaucratic organizations do not always work that way, Appleby discussed the pathologies that lead them astray and offered a variety of reforms for dealing with those problems.

Appleby's book was an important one, if for no other reason than its attempt to resolve the tension between bureaucracy and democracy. However, its commitment to the priority of democratic values as the appropriate foundation for administrative ethics carried forward the position staked out by Marx, representing a substantial contribution in itself. Also, Appleby's volume unmistakably linked administrative ethics to the organizational context, an important connection sometimes forgotten by subsequent authors. Furthermore, it drew clear distinctions between public and private management. Its weakness was that it largely stopped with the organization structure and did not address significantly the situation of the individual administrator confronted with specific ethical decisions.

Leys' book of the same year (1952), *Ethics for Policy Decisions: The Art of Asking Deliberative Questions*, filled the defect in Appleby's work by providing an elaboration of the perspective first presented in his article, ''Ethics and Administrative Discretion'' (1943). While it did not deal with the organizational context, as Appleby did, nor did it distinguish between public and private sector administration, it did lay out a systematic way of analyzing and resolving the ethical problems of individual administrators, which Appleby did not.

Leys summarized an array of philosophical perspectives which one might bring to bear on ethical decisions including utilitarianism, casuistry, classical Greek thought (Plato and Aristotle), Kantian philosophy, along with the ideas of the Stoics, Hobbes, Butler, Hegel, Marx, Dewey, and linguistic analysts. He then worked through cases showing how these different philosophical approaches might be employed. The greatest deficiency of this volume was that Leys did not adopt a specifically managerial perspective, and even more specifically a *public* managerial one, but rather viewed the cases from the vantage points of the various interested parties.

During the remainder of the 1950s, administrative ethics received little attention. In the two articles dealing directly with the subject, the emphasis was largely on external controls in the spirit of Herman Finer's earlier arguments. Although it is only conjecture, one might understand this emphasis as a predictable reaction to the series of scandals which occurred in the federal government during those years. Americans typically seem to respond to serious and visible scandals by resorting to the imposition of laws, rules, and other forms of external control—the quick fix.

Moneypenny (1953) presented an argument for developing a code of ethics for public administration and referred to some efforts underway by a U.S. Senate committee. Although he acknowledged that ''conversion'' must ''take place from the inside'' if conformance is to be achieved, Moneypenny's approach to bringing about this ''conversion'' was largely through a heavily external control orientation by management (p. 186). There is no attention to the cultivation of internal professional standards and ethics as a means of securing compliance with the code.

Wood (1955) advocated an even more mechanistic control orientation in the hands of superiors. Explicitly rejecting the approach of developing professional standards as too long-run, Woods called for a shorter term solution—"the systematic employment of administrative investigatory facilities." These would be "staff devices that provide an executive with information about the personal conduct of his employees" (p. 3). The value of these mechanisms would be to expose wrongdoing from inside and preserve the reputation of the agency. Wood seems not to have recognized the pernicious possibilities of such units.

In 1962 Golembiewski raised again the concern over the relationship between ethics and the organizational context initially addressed by Appleby a decade earlier. In "Organization as a Moral Problem" (1962), he began by observing that "organizing has been considered a technical problem . . . " and then insisted, "the neglect of organization as moral problem cannot be condoned. For the man-to-man relations implied in patterns of organization have more than a technical aspect" (p. 51). Instead of turning either to the Western philosophical tradition or the American political heritage for a normative orientation, Golembiewski looked to religion by advocating "Judeo-Christian values" as the moral touchstones for organizational leadership and relations among organizational members. In contrast with traditional hierarchical, controlled-from-the-top organization theory with its view of workers as objects to be constrained and manipulated, this perspective required work that is "psychologically acceptable, generally non-threatening," allows "employees to develop their faculties," provides "room for self-determination," permits workers to "influence the environment within which they work," and does not believe "the formal organization . . . is the sole and final arbiter of behavior," but is itself subject to an external moral order (pp. 52–53).

These themes were developed further and elaborated in a subsequent book, *Men, Management and Morality: Toward a New Organizational Ethic* (1965). In this volume, Golembiewski faced fully the problems of individual freedom in an organizational society which had been identified and discussed by authors such as William H. Whyte in *The Organization Man* (1956) and Kenneth Boulding in *The Organizational Revolution* (1953). He continued to assert Judeo-Christian values as a source of optimism and individual freedom if adopted as guiding norms for organizations.

Golembiewski's focus on Judeo-Christian values as the normative foundation for an administrative ethic seems much too parochial in a time when Western values are being criticized severely as too limited for the burgeoning diversity of American society. Perhaps they were so perceived even then since they never became a major theme in public administration ethics. However, his attention to the moral importance of the organizational context was a significant and lasting contribution.

The first fully developed emphasis on the internal controls advocated earlier by Friedrich was advanced by Stephen Bailey in a PAR article entitled, "Ethics and the Public Service" (1964). Bailey focused on the personal character traits of the administrator by identifying three essential mental attitudes and three necessary moral qualities for ethical conduct. This new tack in the development of administrative ethics as a field of study was widely supported and cited. However, it did not become a major theme until much later with the emergence of a body of literature on virtue understood largely as character traits.

III. THE EMERGENCE OF ETHICS AS A FIELD OF STUDY

After another hiatus of several years, a steady stream of publications on administrative ethics began and has grown progressively in volume and depth up to the present with little interruption. The first essay in this stream was by Scott and Hart (1973). They delivered a frontal assault on the positivist assumptions that lay behind much organizational research, reflecting concerns similar to those of Golembiewski. They believed positivism, with its separation of fact and value, and its emphasis on studying only that which is observable, had led to a "neglect of metaphysical speculation" and created an "administrative crisis" (Scott and Hart, 1973: 415). This reluctance to deal with administration, and the organizations in which it is practiced, from more traditional philosophical perspectives had resulted in a lack of "metaphysical direction." Research had diminished to mere "puzzle solving," thus allowing the elite who control organizations and dominate the lives of workers to remain hidden, their values unexamined, and their use of power unexposed.

Scott and Hart called attention, as had Golembiewski earlier, to the inseparability of ethics and the organizational context of public administration. However, instead of advocating Judeo-Christian values as a normative orientation for public administration, they urged a return to metaphysical speculation.

In the next year, responding to the series of scandals associated with the Nixon administration, Waldo followed a path consistent with that of Scott and Hart. In "Reflections on Public Morality" (1974), Waldo turned to political philosophy and history to put Watergate into perspective.[8] The focus of the essay was on the relationships between public and private morality as they have varied from time to time and polity to polity. Waldo maintained that although these relationships had been a constant theme in political theory back to classical Greece and Rome, American "self-conscious public administration in its early decades avoided problems of morality. The problem to be solved was seen as a technical-scientific one: the efficient realization of ends given by agents outside the administrative sphere" (p. 275).

Sounding a hopeful note, however, Waldo observed: "For some time now, considerations of morality have been creeping into the public administration literature." Observing that some of this material was rooted in political theory and some philosophical, Waldo alluded to Scott and Hart's article calling for a return to metaphysics. He concluded with a call to develop "something in the nature of a concept of 'the public interest' that would be operational and include the entire planet (Waldo, 1974: 281).

During that same year PAR published a "Symposium on Social Equity and Public Administration" edited by Frederickson with six articles on administrative ethics. Social equity, usually of the kind advocated by John Rawls (1971), had become the central ethical concept of that loosely defined movement known as the "New Public Administration" which had emerged in the late 1960s. The symposium included articles applying social equity to personnel management (McGregor, 1974), social service productivity (Chitwood, 1974), fiscal federalism (Porter and Porter, 1974), and the use of statistics in the delivery of social services (White and Gates, 1974). However, the two essays that contributed most directly to the development of administrative ethics as a field of study were "Social Equity and Organizational Man: Motivation and Organizational Democracy" by Michael Harmon (1974) and "Social Equity, Justice, and the Equitable Administrator" by David K. Hart (1974).

In these essays by Hart and Harmon the influence of Rawls on the New Public

Administration was apparent. Both pieces were arguments for the central relevance of social equity as conceptualized by Rawls for the practice of public administration. Essentially Hart summarized Rawls' two principles of justice, developed a rationale for adopting them as foundations for an administrative ethic, and spelled out their implications for administration. Hart, more specifically, drew out of Rawls' principles what he considered to be an imperative for organizational democracy.

The strength of the New Public Administration's commitment to Rawlsian social equity lay in its specificity and application to the practice of administration. It was the first real move beyond vague arguments for the public interest or common good which tended to trail off into generalities possessing little operational value. In this issue of PAR and elsewhere, Rawls' two principles of justice were used to argue for particular policy prescriptions, thus providing evidence of the practical significance of administrative ethics and building confidence in the possibility of developing it as a field of study. Ultimately social equity was not adopted by others in the field of public administration as the central principle for an administrative ethic. However, the extensive elucidation and application of social equity in the 1974 symposium in PAR provided legitimacy, as well as both practical and intellectual status, not previously enjoyed by administrative ethics.

Another article in this issue of PAR, like Waldo's in A&S that same year, was in response to Watergate. In "Ethical Guidelines for Public Administrators: Observation on Rules of the Game" (1974), George Graham laid out what he judged to be the generally accepted norms for federal administrative conduct. These "rules of the game" reflected an ethic rooted in the nature of bureaucratic responsibility reminiscent of Appleby's (1952) treatment of that subject.

Although there has been continuing debate about the significance and impact of the New Public Administration, when one surveys the history of administrative ethics during the last hundred years it seems clear that this movement made an important contribution to the emergence of a field of study focused on ethics in public administration. It represented the first coalescing of a group of scholars around a commonly shared ethical concept—social equity—usually based on the work of John Rawls (Frederickson, 1976).

Although relatively short-lived as a movement, the New Public Administration created an ongoing debate through conference papers, book chapters, and journal articles that allowed the viability of social equity as a focus for administrative ethics to be explored in a sustained manner.[9] The result was that the once controversial suggestion that social equity had a place in the role obligations of public administrators became generally accepted. Social equity was not sustained as *the* central value for the field, but has taken its place along with other ethical principles.

Rohr recognized the contributions of the New Public Administration in his article on "The Study of Ethics in the P.A. Curriculum" (1976), but set his course in a different direction. Acknowledging that the Watergate scandals stimulated the growth of administrative ethics, he nevertheless cautioned against crediting those events for too much. Among other reasons he cited for this caveat was that we should not "neglect the solid academic foundation for ethical reflection that was laid by the 'New PA' before we knew that Watergate was anything more than an elegant apartment complex" (p. 398).

Rohr's (1976) article on ethics in the public administration curriculum was the first such piece in PAR devoted entirely to the teaching of administrative ethics, and as such it represented a signal that the study of administrative ethics had reached a new stage of development. It both reflected the rise of interest in offering courses on ethics in public administration education and provided encouragement to such activity.

In this article as well as in his subsequent book, Rohr parted ways with the New Public Administration by taking the fact of administrative discretion as his starting point, as had others before him, in calling for greater attention to ethics. After quickly rejecting political philosophy as a normative basis for administrative ethics, since it is "too demanding to be included as *part* of a course in ethics," and humanistic psychology because it is too oriented toward the individual, Rohr turned to history for his normative reference points. He advocated focusing on the "regime values" of the American political tradition (p. 399).[10] These were to be found in the U.S. Constitution, which public administrators are sworn to uphold, and its interpretations by the U.S. Supreme Court. He concluded that American regime values include, but are not limited to, freedom, equality, and property.

In the same issue of PAR as Rohr's article is another historically oriented piece by Caldwell entitled, "Novus Ordo Seclorum: The Heritage of American Public Administration" (1976). Caldwell argued similarly to Rohr that the touchstones for administrative ethics lay in the American constitutional tradition. The Constitution embodied a set of "premises" that, according to Caldwell, "seem tacitly to constitute the moral imperatives of American public life"(p. 481). They amount to a "civic religion" which is "rooted in ethical and theological concepts that became current in the 17th and 18th centuries" (p. 481). Caldwell distilled down the premises of this political faith into ten propositions which include the central doctrines which underpin the Constitution and its practical applications. They are not inconsistent with Rohr's treatment of regime values, but are somewhat broader in scope.

Wakefield (1976), in the next issue of PAR, offered a critique of the bureaucratic tendency to take refuge in the collective responsibility of the organization. She argued instead that administrators must feel personally responsible and must be held individually accountable by law and the public for their conduct if the public interest is to be upheld, corruption forestalled, and democratic government preserved.

Also during 1976, the first Professional Standards and Ethics Committee was established by the American Society for Public Administration (ASPA). Its first charge was to write a code of ethics, but the committee was divided on the importance of codes and spent some time debating what should be done. Ultimately the decision was not to work on a code, at least as a first order of business. Instead the committee chose to prepare a booklet entitled, *Professional Standards and Ethics: A Workbook for Public Administrators*, edited by Mertins (1979). This publication presented a series of themes related to ethical conduct followed by self-diagnostic questions which any public administrator ought to reflect upon and be prepared to answer to his or her colleagues, political superiors, or the public.

Although this booklet turned out to be surprisingly popular, generating considerable discussion and debate among ASPA members and students, the establishment of the committee itself may have been more important to the development of ethics as a field of study in public administration. It institutionalized an ongoing deliberative process at first focused on the handbook and its subsequent revised edition and then on the development of a code of ethics for ASPA. The committee served also to provide a regular opportunity for scholars and practitioners interested in ethics to get acquainted with each other and their work. It also became a mechanism within ASPA for planning sessions on ethics for the ASPA national conferences.

The themes originally set forth by Rohr in his 1976 PAR article were later developed further in the first edition of *Ethics for Bureaucrats: An Essay on Law and Values* (1978) and supplemented with a discussion of crucial Supreme Court cases in which regime values were treated. This volume quickly became the focus of discussion and debate over the normative foundations for public administration ethics since it was the only fully developed prescriptive proposal that had appeared in the last thirteen years.[11] It was widely adopted for classroom use and frequently cited in subsequent articles and books on ethics. Rohr can be credited with having shifted the direction of thought on administrative ethics away from philosophy of the kind recommended by Leys (1952), Scott and Hart (1973), Hart (1974), and the New Public Administration, and toward American history.

Rohr weighed into the ethics debate again in 1980 with an article in *Administration & Society* entitled, "Ethics for the Senior Executive Service: Suggestions for Management Training." Controversy swirled about the recently created Senior Executive Service (SES) over the extent to which it would be politicized by removing it from the civil service. Rohr described a management training approach which was an extension of his earlier argument for a focus on regime values. In this piece he focused on three aspects of obligation to the constitutional regime which he deemed crucial for the SES: the implications of the oath of office, institutional literacy, and appropriate responsiveness to "the political vision of a particular president" (p. 212).

Fleishman, Liebman, and Moore's (1981) *Public Duties: The Moral Obligations of Government Officials* was the product of seminars conducted over a two-year period by the Faculty Study Group on the Moral Obligations of Public Officials, sponsored by the Institute of Politics of the Kennedy School at Harvard. It provided a multi-faceted treatment of governmental ethics that covered both administrative and political roles. Generally avoiding argument for specific policies and programs intended to make government more ethical, the eleven chapter authors in this volume sought to clarify and operationalize ethical concepts, and to develop processes for arriving at ethical conclusions. The editors asserted their "renunciation of the extreme version of legalism" that relies too heavily on law and rules to assure ethical conduct in public life (p. viii). The underlying premise of the book was to make public officials consciously responsible and accountable for the ethical dimensions of their decisions, bearing fully the burden of demonstrating that their actions were directed toward public rather than private ends.

The relationship between law and ethics was also the central concern of Foster's "Law, Morality, and the Public Servant" (1981). As ethics legislation began to proliferate at every level of government during the late 1970s and early 1980s, Foster shared the opposition of Fleishman, Liebman, and Moore to an over-reliance on these mechanisms. He maintained that preoccupation with legality tended to erode moral reflection and destroy the ability to deal with ethical questions. Overdependence on law tended to reduce thinking to the moral minimum required by law. Cultivating ethical reflection was more likely to lead to moral excellence.

By 1982 the extensive use of ASPA's *Professional Standards and Ethics* workbook had generated enough suggestions for amplifying and improving it to warrant a revised edition, *Applying Professional Standards & Ethics in the Eighties: A Workbook Study Guide for Public Administrators* edited by Mertins and Hennigan. New sections were added, some old ones developed further, and suggestions for classroom use were appended.

Also in 1982, Scott, in "Barnard on the Nature of Elitist Responsibility," launched a well-honed challenge to the ethical orthodoxy of administration. In a pointed critique of Barnard's *The Functions of the Executive* (1938), Scott called into question the legitimacy of the inculcation of morals into subordinates by managers. His major concern was that the morals to be implanted were, of course, always oriented toward the good of the organization. In this fact, Scott saw ominous portents for an American form of totalitarianism.[12]

The first edition of *The Responsible Administrator: An Approach to Ethics for the Administrative Role* was also published in 1982 (Cooper, 1982). Unlike Rohr's book which argued for regime values as a normative basis for administrative ethics, this volume focused largely on descriptive analysis. It attempted to account for the kinds of ethical concerns faced by public administrators and to explain how they emerge in administrative practice. Similar to Rohr, it took the fact of administrative discretion as its starting point and argued that administrators are responsible for its exercise. It emphasized the individual administrator confronting such problems as conflicts of interest, role conflicts, and conflicts of responsibilities and presented a decision-making model for resolving them. It did acknowledge and discuss briefly the impediments to ethical conduct inherent in the organizational context of administration. To provide relevance and practical texture the book made heavy use of cases from administrative life.

Although *The Responsible Administrator* was mainly descriptive in orientation it did have some prescriptive dimensions. In arguing for a particular decision-making model for resolving ethical dilemmas, the book was methodologically prescriptive. Also, in passing references it suggested that the normative footing for public administration was to be found in the citizenship obligations of the administrator, but this perspective was left undeveloped.

During the early 1980s, the ASPA Professional Ethics and Standards Committee finally began work on a code of ethics under an agreement with the National Council of ASPA that nothing would be adopted until it had been circulated to the membership for comment and proposed revisions. It was a rocky process at best. The committee completed a draft only to have it rejected by the National Council and replaced with another document. This was sent out for comment and generated considerable reaction from ASPA members and local chapters around the nation.

Chandler addressed the difficulties in drafting a coherent code in "The Problem of Moral Reasoning in American Public Administration: The Case for a Code of Ethics" (1983). In this penetrating article, Chandler reviewed the arguments for and against a code, reflected on the reticence to engage in moral reasoning and the tendency to resolve conflicts over ethical issues politically, and presented his own arguments for a code grounded in moral philosophy and unashamed of moral rhetoric. Chandler's essay enriched the debate over a code and illuminated ASPA's travail in adopting one, but did not significantly influence the outcome which was largely the product of political compromise.

A code of ethics was adopted by ASPA in 1984 with a set of implementation guidelines to follow in 1985. Although a less than excellent document, it served to generate continuing debate among ASPA members over its meaning, proposed changes, and whether there should be some kind of enforcement mechanism. Also, the creation of the code and its adoption further served to institutionalize and legitimize administrative ethics as a significant and useful field of study. However, Bowman (1990), in "Ethics in Government: A National Survey of Public Administrators," found five years after the adoption of the code that only ten percent of the 441 responding administrators who were ASPA members indicated that they were "quite familiar with it" (p. 348). Only 57 percent had any familiarity with the code. The ASPA code was revised in 1994 resulting in a more succinct and specific statement of expected modes of conduct. Bowman (1997) then conducted a follow-up study of ASPA members and found that 79 percent indicated familiarity with the code, and that the degree of understanding of the code had risen significantly.

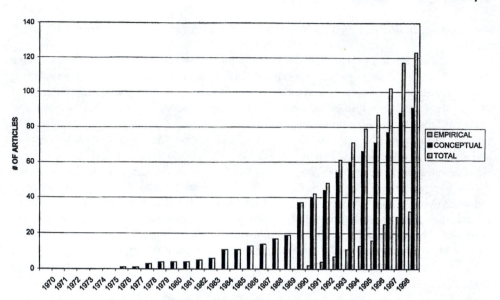

Figure 1   Cumulative number of ethics articles, 1970–1998.

From the early 1980s to the early 1990s the literature on administrative ethics began to mushroom. At least eleven new books or revised editions of previously published books came off the presses during that decade that deal directly, exclusively, and significantly with public administration ethics, not to mention those dealing with political ethics, moral philosophy, political philosophy, ethics legislation, the psychology of moral development, and business ethics that have important implications for public administration. Also, it is possible to identify a minimum of 35 articles specifically on administrative ethics published in PAR and A&S, or as chapters in books with broader themes, from 1983 until the end of 1992, the period covered in the first edition of this book.[13] Numerous other articles and book chapters have appeared in print since that time, but the limits of this chapter do not permit commentary on each of these worthy additions to the literature. Much of this more recent work is treated in greater length in one or more chapters that follow.

Menzel and Carson (1999) has provided the broad view of the trend in journal literature on administrative ethics by reviewing the articles appearing in ten public administration journals for the period 1970–1998, broken down by empirical and conceptual approaches.[14] Figure 1, displaying Menzel's findings, clearly substantiates the argument of this chapter that the origins of the field of study can be found in the mid-1970s and that the literature has dramatically expanded since that time. The total number of articles has increased at an accelerating rate from a few to more than 120 during the 28 years of his study. The number of conceptual articles is consistently greater throughout this period, but the empirical literature shows dramatic increases from about 1990 forward.[15]

IV.   COMPREHENSIVE TEXTS

Rohr's Ethics for Bureaucrats was republished in a second edition in 1989 with a new preface and some revisions of the main text. Cooper's *The Responsible Administrator* came out in a second edition in 1986, a third in 1990, and a fourth in 1998. The second edition included a new extended preface and concluding prescript, but no changes in the main text. The third involved major revisions incorporating the content of the 1986 preface into the main text, updating of information and references to literature, adding new material emphasizing the importance of the organizational context, and providing some new case studies. The fourth edition was a substantial revision of the third with some new case material, an acknowledgement of postmodern thought,and new illustrative material.

Three new comprehensive texts appeared in the late 1980s and early 1990s. They were Denhardt's *The Ethics of Public Service: Resolving Moral Dilemmas in Public Organizations* (1988), Gortner's *Ethics for Public Managers* (1991), Lewis' *The Ethics Challenge in Public Service* (1991), and Bowman's edited volume, *Ethical Frontiers in Public Management: Seeking New Strategies for Resolving Ethical Dilemmas* (1991). Denhardt's book recaps several attempts at comprehensive frameworks for administrative ethics and presents one of her own which involves an adaptation of previous efforts with new and creative twists. Gortner's is based on cases generated through interviews with civil service managers, but includes relevant references to the existing literature on administrative ethics. Both of these books give significant attention to the organizational context as a problematic environment in which administrators attempt to think and act ethically. Lewis' volume is the most practically oriented of these three sole-authored texts with numerous techniques and ''how to'' suggestions for encouraging ethical decision-making and creating an organizational environment conducive to ethical action.

Bowman's edited book provides thirteen chapters with a wide array of emphases. Interestingly, six of these deal with specific aspects of the organizational context while the other seven are a varied lot including philosophical, psychological, legal, and historical material.

As one peruses these initial comprehensive texts, several observations are relevant to the focus of this chapter. The authors reflect the concern about the impact of organizations on ethical conduct which had been growing since the late 1970s. There are also frequent attempts to orient their work in some way to democratic theory, the philosophical tradition, and the history of both the United States and American public administration. There is consciousness of an emerging stream of thought and literature on administrative ethics which the authors address and relate to their own work. Since these first comprehensive texts others have been published and are treated in later chapters of this *handbook*.

V. CONTINUING THEMES IN ADMINISTRATIVE ETHICS

Seven themes are discernible in the administrative ethics literature of the last two decades: citizenship and democratic theory, virtue, founding thought and the constitutional tradition, the organizational context, ethics education, philosophical theory and perspectives, and cognitive moral development. Each of these has tended to rise into view through specific treatments of the theme and then rather quickly become intertwined with other themes. The discussion here will focus on the seminal pieces that directly and specifically laid the foundations for each theme. Later work is treated in specific chapters that follow.

A. Citizenship and Democratic Theory

In retrospect, it seems inevitable that democratic theory and citizenship would become prominent in administrative ethics. As the politics/administration dichotomy began to break down, the question of how administration should be related to the political process came under discussion. Levitan (1942), Appleby (1947, 1949, 1952), and Marx (1949), in particular, began to connect the obligations of public administrators to democratic political theory and citizenship in a democratic state. However, the obligations and the requirements of democratic philosophy did not become a major focus until the middle 1980s. The first specific published treatment was Frederickson's article, "The Recovery of Civism in Public Administration" (1982) in which he lamented the distance that had developed between public administrators and the citizenry. He called for a renewal of civic virtue as a central value in public administration.

During 1983, Frederickson organized an invitational conference in New York on the subject, a National Conference on Citizenship and Public Service.[16] Forty-five scholars and practitioners heard eleven papers presented on the implications of the citizenship role for the practice of public administration and engaged each other in debate and deliberation. The papers were subsequently published in a special issue of PAR (in 1984, titled "Citizenship and Public Administration").

Although all of the papers might be understood in general terms as dealing with citizenship ethics in public administration, four in particular focused on administrative ethics. These were Gawthrop's "Civis, Civitas, and Civilitas: A New Focus for the Year 2000," Hart's "The Virtuous Citizen, the Honorable Bureaucrat, and 'Public' Administration," Cooper's "Citizenship and Professionalism in Public Administration," and Chandler's "The Public Administrator as Representative Citizen: A New Role for the New Century." All four addressed the attenuated role of the citizen in modern American society, the obligations of public administrators to help restore citizenship to a more vital status, and the ethical obligations of the public administrators as citizens themselves.

Cooper has published subsequently two additional items dealing directly with administrative ethics from a citizenship orientation. In 1984 his book chapter entitled "Public Administration in an Age of Scarcity: A Citizenship Role on Ethics for Public Administrators," appeared in *Politics and Administration: Woodrow Wilson and Public Administration*, edited by Jack Rabin and James Bowman. The argument here was that the norms of citizenship in the American tradition provide the most appropriate normative foundation for an administrative ethic. In 1991 Cooper developed the arguments in this paper and those in the PAR article into a book, *An Ethic of Citizenship for Public Administration* which reviews the legal and ethical traditions of citizenship in the United States, and suggests that the informal ethical tradition provides the best normative orientation for public administration ethics.

The concern for citizenship and democratic theory has tended to merge with other themes in the literature over time. It is often related to founding thought, virtue, the relationship between law and ethics and the problems of the organizational context. For example, Thompson (1992) maintained, in "Paradoxes of Government Ethics," that government ethics officials should view their responsibilities as greater than managing the flow of paper required by ethics legislation. He insisted that they should understand that they have an educational responsibility to help administrators see their obligations for the democratic process of government.

Also, Burke's (1986) *Bureaucratic Responsibility* represents a connection of democratic theory and organization structure. In that volume he attempted to deal with the relationship between the moral and political responsibilities of administrators. He expressed concern that giving exclusive or overriding attention to purely moral concerns might amount to a neglect of the administrator's institutional obligations and a failure to uphold the integrity of the larger democratic processes which public organizations are established to serve.

Denhardt's (1989) "The Management of Ideals: A Political Perspective on Ethics" developed an argument similar to Burke's. She addressed the relationship between democratic and bureaucratic ideals by suggesting that administrative ethics ought to be developed within the larger framework of political ethics. From this perspective, political activity by an administrator can be justified only "in the pursuit of democratic ideals" (p. 187).

B. Virtue Ethics

In the mid-1980s, the somewhat antiquated-sounding term, "virtue," began to reenter the vocabulary of public administration ethics. It has since become a major theme and has generally been understood as synonymous with "character." The first such piece to appear in the literature under consideration was "The Public Service and the Patriotism of Benevolence" by Frederickson and Hart (1985). In this article, the authors moved away from the emphasis in the literature of the previous decade on reasoning about ethical principles toward resolving ethical dilemmas and shifted the focus to the personal character traits that would presumably incline one to do the right thing. The specific character trait they examined was "benevolence" which they defined as "the extensive and non-instrumental love of others" (p. 547).

The publication of Pincoffs' *Quandaries and Virtues* (1986) provided impetus to the budding interest in virtue ethics. In it Pincoffs made a frontal attack on the preoccupation of ethicists with reasoning about principles to resolve ethical quandaries and constructed a cogent argument for focusing on character as a more reliable way of assuring ethical conduct.

In 1987 Cooper published "Hierarchy, Virtue, and the Practice of Public Administration: A Perspective for Normative Ethics," which advocated the use of MacIntyre's concept of "practice" to conceptualize the normative identity of the public administrator rather than the frequently adopted one of "professional." In this schema, the virtue of the administrator provides the major protection of the internal goods of public administration against corruption.

Two insightful pieces developed around fictional characters appeared in 1988 and 1989. Dobel (1988) used John Le Carre's George Smiley in "The Honorable Spymaster: John Le Carre and the Character of Espionage" to study the stresses on character traits such as moral judgment and loyalty in the shadowy world of spies where roles conflict and integrity is difficult to sustain. Harmon (1989) focused his attention on C. S. Forester's character, Horatio Hornblower, to argue that responsibility does not always call for the same action, nor is it achieved through single-minded commitment to a particular set of principles. Rather, there is often ambiguity in what a situation requires. Harmon maintained that virtues are often confronted with countervailing virtues, thus requiring an ongoing "reflective conversation about what to do next" (p. 286).

Hart, in "A Partnership in Virtue Among All Citizens: The Public Service and Civic Humanism" (1989), argued that founding thought is best understood "through the virtue-centered paradigm of civic humanism, with its attendant 'ethics of character' " (p. 101). This is a prime example of the intertwining of major themes in the literature once a particular theme has risen to prominence. The weight of this piece, however, is on examining and developing the implications of the civic humanist tradition for an administrative ethic of virtue. Its congruence with founding thought is offered as a justification for its adoption as a normative perspective.

"Administrative Responsibility Revisited: Moral Consensus and Moral Autonomy" by Jos (1990) argued against attempts to build a moral consensus among the citizenry around such concepts as social equity as futile. Instead he opted for moral autonomy for the public administrator in order to achieve responsible administration. "This," he insisted, "is primarily a matter of moral judgment and character" (p. 239).

Dobel (1990) laid out three essential commitments in "Integrity in the Public Service." These included regime accountability, personal responsibility, and prudence. He insisted that no one of these was adequate for ethical conduct in public administration, but that holding all three together "in tension while keeping some coherence" in one's actions and life amounted to public integrity. This is generally consistent with an Aristotelian understanding of virtue, or character, which emphasizes a balance of attributes within one's life rather than a list of desired traits.

Cooper and Wright (1992), in an edited volume, *Exemplary Public Administrators: Character and Leadership in Government*, presented character studies of eleven public administrators by fourteen scholars. Each of these attempted to weigh the character of some practitioner of public administration and build a case for him or her as an exemplar of virtue. The purpose of this volume was to provide an empirical test of the viability and usefulness of the concept of virtue, as well as to identify positive role models for the field.

In order to develop a continuing treatment of exemplars of virtue in public administration, the journal *Public Integrity* has invited authors to submit articles undertaking character studies of specific public administrators. These will be quite similar to those presented in Cooper and Wright. This series may provide an opportunity to cultivate interest in virtue as an aspect of administrative ethics, refine concepts associated with the study of character, and encourage consideration of a variety of analytical techniques.

C. Founding Thought and the Constitutional Tradition

Just as it now seems inevitable that democracy and citizenship would eventually form part of the foundation of administrative ethics, so also does it seem predictable that the values of the founders and the principles of the U.S. Constitution would play a similar role. When administration could no longer be separated from politics, one logical option for grounding an ethic of administration would be in the polity itself. Caldwell in 1943 turned to Jefferson for his argument that public administrators should view their fundamental responsibility to the Constitution as taking priority over their duty to legislatures. Rohr (1976, 1978) later developed this idea much further through the concept of regime values.

However, relating administrative ethics to a broader range of founding thought came into the literature later. Richardson and Nigro's article (1987), "Administrative Ethics and Founding Thought: Constitutional Correctives, Honor, and Education," was the first such treatment in the literature under consideration.[17] It attempted to establish the importance of the reemerging concept of virtue for the founders. This was intended to counter the notion that the constitutional architects were only concerned about creating mechanical constraints on the passionate self-interest which they believed were characteristic of human nature. Richardson and Nigro argued that their historical analysis revealed "a heavy reliance on the *interaction* of constitutional correctives, honor, and education to produce virtuous public officials who would serve the regime" (p. 374).

Hart and Smith (1988) developed their argument in a similar vein. In "Fame, Fame-Worthiness, and the Public Service," they argue that, contrary to prevailing scholarly opinion, the founders expressed "deep concern for the internal qualities of character of public servants'' (p. 133). They suggested that the ''desire of honorable people for 'fame' and 'fame-worthiness''' would serve as an important ''antidote to the confusions and corruptions of political power'' (p. 133). In other words, the wish to be respected would encourage public officials to conduct themselves respectably.

Richardson and Nigro (1991) returned to their reflection on founding values in ''The Constitution and Administrative Ethics in America.'' There they moderated their earlier emphasis on the centrality of virtue and a natural aristocracy of virtuous leaders in founding thought. Acknowledging that the founders recognized the power of self-interest and the propensity for factions, the authors concluded that founding thought hoped for virtue, but did not want the security of republican government to depend on it. The structural arrangements of the Constitution provided that safe foundation.

D. Ethics Education

One of the criteria for administrative ethics as a field of study set forth at the beginning of this chapter was the existence of courses on administrative ethics. Although such courses have been proliferating during recent years, there is very little in the literature under consideration concerning ethics education. Even so, it is included here because there is other material on this subject which is reviewed in Chapter 3 of this handbook by Yoder and Denhardt.

The first article on ethics education in either PAR or A&S was Rohr's (1976) previously discussed article, ''The Study of Ethics in the P.A. Curriculum.'' The second was by Hejka-Ekins (1988), entitled ''Teaching Ethics in Public Administration.'' Based on empirical research using a mailed questionnaire, the author attempted to identify how many courses in administrative ethics were being offered and by which institutions. Hejka-Ekins also included questions about the content of the courses categorized by the ethos emphasized (bureaucratic or democratic), the learning goals, and the approaches to ethical decision-making.

The only other article on ethics education in the literature under consideration was by Marini (1992), ''The Uses of Literature in the Exploration of Public Administration Ethics: The Example *of Antigone*.'' In this piece the author shows the rich possibilities for using literature, such as the Greek tragedy by Sophocles, to illuminate and vivify the dilemmas which are central to administrative ethics.

E. The Organizational Context

Echoing the earlier work of Appleby (1952), Golembiewski (1962, 1965), and Scott (1982), concern about the effects of bureaucratic organization on ethical thought and conduct has been raised regularly in more recent books and articles. Five of the comprehensive texts have dealt substantially with the organizational setting of administrative ethics (Cooper, 1982, 1986, 1990, 1998; Denhardt, 1988; Gortner, 1991; Lewis, 1991; Bowman, 1991). In addition there have been at least six new articles and a republication of Golembiewski's article (1962) followed by a revised edition of his 1965 book in 1989.[18]

The first article dealing specifically with the conflict between organizations and professional values in either of the two journals under consideration was ''Professional Values and Organizational Decision Making'' by Bell (1985). In that piece he examined the displacement of values rooted in public finance theory held by policy professionals at the U.S. Department of Housing and Urban Development (HUD) and the U.S. Office of Management and Budget (OMB) by organizational interests.

Jos, Tompkins, and Hays (1989) in "In Praise of Difficult People: A Portrait of the Committed Whistleblower" presented the findings of their empirical research on whistleblowers. It was based on a sample of 161 individuals in public service who had complained about organizational wrongdoing. Confirming prevalent impressions, they found "evidence of severe retaliation" among those who responded (p. 558). A belief in absolute moral standards held by these persons tended to make them less susceptible than others to organizational socialization.

Opposing views concerning the benevolence (Goodsell, 1985) or malevolence (Hummel, 1987) of bureaucratic organization prompted Hartwig (1990), in "The Paradox of Malevolent/Benevolent Bureaucracy," to review the literature on the subject. He concluded that the term "bureaucracy" had lost specificity of meaning resulting in conceptual confusion and differing assessments of the goodness or badness of particular organizations.

In "Trust in the Public Sector: Individual and Organizational Determinants," Carnevale and Wechsler (1992) surveyed employees at all levels of a large state agency to identify the most significant factors associated with trust formation in public organizations. Based on responses from 1279 employees, they concluded that supervisory relations and job security were most strongly correlated with trust.

Excerpts from Golembiewski's "Organization as a Moral Problem" (1962) were republished in 1992 followed by new comments from the author in "Organization is a Moral Problem: Past as Prelude to Present and Future," the reactions of Robert B. Denhardt under the title, "Morality as an Organizational Problem," and reactions from a practitioner, Jewel D. Scott, in "Past Success, Future Challenges." Golembiewski indicated that although the emphasis on Judeo-Christian values was generally accepted in 1962, it came under criticism after the publication of *Men, Management, and Morality* in 1965, both on religious grounds and on the objections of positivists. The author seemed to believe that by 1992 this religious terminology was no longer a problem. He concluded that far more techniques and supporting conditions for achieving these values in organizations exist now than was the case thirty years ago.

Denhardt (1992) characterized the original 1962 article and the book published three years later as "classics" for their challenge to the value-free notions of positivism and their illumination of the moral dimensions of organization. He placed the criticism based on positivism in historical perspective and suggested that organization theory had moved beyond the strictures of that philosophical perspective. However, while affirming the values Golembiewski identified as "Judeo-Christian," Denhardt wished he had not used that label, especially since most of them "are merely restatements of the findings of applied behavioral science" (p. 104). More significantly, Denhardt faulted Golembiewski for making the validity of the organizational values he espoused dependent on moving "the organization efficiently and effectively toward its goals." On the contrary, argued Denhardt, "organizations and their members must not be moral only where it is efficient to do so, they must be efficient only where it is moral to do so" (p. 105).

Similarly, Scott (1992) expressed appreciation for Golembiewski's insight in seeing that organizations are moral problems, but concern over the adoption of values identified as Judeo-Christian. Acknowledging that even as recently as thirty years earlier, Judeo-Christian values were dominant in American society, he opined that workplace values in 1992 "should be adjusted to adapt to and incorporate philosophies more consistent with the experience and beliefs of workers who come from backgrounds not grounded in Judeo-Christian moral and ethical beliefs" (p. 107).

In an article similar to Bell (1985) in its conclusions, Fiore, Brunk, and Meyer (1992) examined the relationships between professional ethics and entrepreneurial goals among zoological managers. Based on survey responses from 330 managers of zoos they concluded that "stress on economic goals tends to decrease support for professional ethics, whereas an increased interest in various noneconomic goals increases the level of support for professional ethics. The implication of this finding is that greater emphasis on economic motivations, such as might occur with privatization of government agencies, will likely decrease adherence to professional ethics.

F. Philosophical Theory and Perspectives

Questions concerning appropriate philosophical approaches, methodological orientations, and key concepts were the subjects of five articles in the two journals under review here. The absence of more pieces dealing with these fundamental concerns suggests a need for the future development of administrative ethics as a field of study.

Fischer (1988) was critical of both earlier positivistic approaches to public administration and more recent post-positivistic approaches to ethical discourse in "Ethical Discourse in Public Administration." In particular, he rejected Hart's focus on social equity and Rohr's use of regime values as normative foundations for administrative ethics. Instead he proposed that ethical discourse in public administration be rooted in analytical philosophy, "especially the variants of the ordinary language approach concerned with the study of the nature and rules of normative discourse in everyday affairs" (p. 16).

In "The Honorable Bureaucrat Among the Philistines: A Reply to 'Ethical Discourse in Public Administration,'" Hart (1983) offered a rejoinder to Fischer's criticism of his use of social equity. His reply was based on two contentions: first, the assumption of "a consensus about the basic social values from which the orderings of analytical philosophy would be derived," and second, Hart's conviction that public administrators are obligated to serve the values of the American regime (p. 44).

Thompson (1985) addressed the two major objections to administrative ethics as a legitimate area for study and action in "The Possibility of Administrative Ethics." These are the views that administrators should be neutral servants of their superiors and that the object of moral judgment should be the organization as a whole and no one administrator should be held morally responsible for actions of the whole when his or her conduct is only a part of the whole. He refuted these two arguments and concluded that administrative ethics is possible.

The public interest was the focus of Long's (1990) "Conceptual Notes on the Public Interest for Public Administration and Policy Analysis." In recent administrative ethics literature the concept of the public interest has not been conspicuous, but in this piece Long attempts to breathe new life into its meaning. Blaming positivism for obscuring the significance of this concept, Long maintained that "the public's shared concern with consequences is a public interest" (p. 171). He then argued for projecting and evaluating consequences "in terms of agreed-upon values" (p. 170).

In "Theoretical Foundations of Ethics in Public Administration: Approaches to Understanding Moral Action," Stewart (1991) attempted to move beyond the emotivism to which ethics had been reduced by positivism to a cognitive basis for ethical analysis. The foci of her study were the "good reasons" approaches, grounded in the ordinary language philosophy of Wittgenstein, and virtue ethics. She concluded that both were necessary in different ways for an adequate treatment of administrative ethics.

G. Cognitive Moral Development

Since the first edition of this *handbook*, research rooted in the work of Lawrence Kohlberg has emerged as a significant theme in administrative ethics. Constituting the most impressive ongoing body of empirical research in the field, the work of Debra Stewart and Norman Sprinthall, along with other collaborators, represents a systematic application and development of theories of cognitive moral development. Their research investigates the ways administrators think about ethical problems using the Stewart Sprinthall Management Survey which is structured around the six level framework developed by Kohlberg. As was Kholberg's, the work by Stewart and Sprinthall is cross-cultural, now including studies in Poland and the Russian Republic. Their work is reviewed and summarized at greater length in a subsequent chapter.

It is important to note that, although some may have thought Kohlbergian research had been invalidated by Gilligan (1982), this seems not to have been the case. Gilligan charged Kohlberg's work with being flawed by a male bias because of its orientation to principled thinking. She argued that women tend to approach ethical issues from the perspective of caring for relationships rather than principles such as justice. However, much of the research using Kohlberg's theory since Gilligan's attack has demonstrated that women are at least as principled in their thinking as men. Richard White (1999), in "Public Ethics, Moral Development, and the Enduring Legacy of Lawrence Kohlberg," provides an excellent overview of Kohlberg's thought and research, a review of the attacks on his work, the defense of his work, and an argument for the potential fruitfulness of cognitive moral development research for administrative ethics.

VI. CONFERENCE PRESENTATIONS ON ADMINISTRATIVE ETHICS

One indication of the development of administrative ethics as a field of study is the extent to which it has been treated in conference sessions. ASPA national conferences are the longest-standing professional association meetings at which administrative ethics has been discussed broadly and comprehensively, but there also have been three recent ad hoc national conferences focused on the subject, indicating its growing significance. Since discussion of the specific substance of each presentation at these conferences lies far beyond the scope of this chapter, only a cursory review of these will have to suffice.

The first ASPA conference was in 1940, but there was no indication in the conference programs of any treatment of administrative ethics until the 1952 session in Washington, D.C.[19] It was chaired by Louis Brownlow and titled generally as "Ethics in the Public Service." The next were in 1959 (1 session), 1963 (1 session), 1971 (2 sessions), 1974 (1 session), and 1975 (1 session).

Consistent with the expansion of the ethics literature under the influence of the New Public Administration in the mid-1970s, the 1976 ASPA conference in Chicago was the first to have more than two sessions on ethics; there the number jumped to five panels. The following year the number receded to two sessions, but the overall shape of the curve moves steadily upward from 1976 to 1992. There have been significant fluctuations from year to year since 1976, in part reflecting the emphases of particular ASPA presidents, but the average number of panel sessions for the last eighteen years (1982–1999) was a little more than four panels per year with peak years in 1986 (10) and 1990 (10). Thus, administrative ethics appears to have taken its place alongside more traditional topics at

ASPA national conferences as a significant subject of discussion. Each of these panel sessions has included several presentations, typically 3–5. Also, during the last 5–10 years, ethics has moved beyond the confines of panels exclusively devoted to the topic and can be found on numerous other panels dealing with such diverse topics as environmental policy, affirmative action, and financial management. Thus, it would be safe to say that the number of individual presentations at ASPA conferences has increased from about four in 1940 to an average of more than twenty per year during the last decade (see Table 1). This reflects a significant growth in research, theory development, and experimentation with applications by both scholars and practitioners since the beginning of ASPA.

Furthermore, in recent years specialized conferences focusing on ethics have provided additional arenas for the presentation and discussion of administrative ethics, and additional evidence of the growth in the field of study. Holding a national conference entirely devoted to administrative ethics would have been inconceivable until the late 1980s.

In 1989 the first national administrative ethics conference was held in Washington, D.C. under the title, "Ethics in Government: An Intricate Web." It was organized by Bayard Catron, sponsored by ASPA, and supported by nine other organizations. The meetings extended over a period of three days and included approximately 700 participants, many of whom were practitioners. Over 200 of these persons were actively involved in giving presentations, moderating sessions, or facilitating workshops. This conference demonstrated clearly the increased interest in administrative ethics and the enormous growth in the number of people actively involved in its development.

A subsequent conference, the first national "Conference on the Study of Government Ethics," was organized by George Frederickson and held in 1991 in Park City, Utah. This was a smaller invitational conference focused on scholars and practitioners interested in empirical research on administrative ethics. It was two-and-a-half days in length and involved approximately 70 participants, most of whom were scholars. Twenty papers reporting on empirically based research projects and methodology, prepared and mailed out in advance, were presented and discussed. The sense of this conference was that administrative ethics had begun to mature as a field of study with important advances beyond theoretical and conceptual development to the testing of those ideas in the field, but with a lot of empirical work yet to be done.

In 1995, a "National Symposium on Ethics and Values in the Public Administration Academy" was held in Tampa, Florida. This conference, organized by Don Menzel and James Bowman, was the first such assembly focusing on the academic setting. Approximately 130 persons attended the conference, including scholars, students, and practitioners. Topics included the ethics of teaching and research in public administration, different approaches to instruction on administrative ethics, and the relationship between scholars and practitioners. A selection of papers from the conference was published as a book entitled, *Teaching Ethics and Values in Public Administration Programs*, edited by Bowman and Menzel (1998).

From the mid-1990s to the present the number of conferences on public administration ethics world-wide has increased enormously to the point of being too numerous to mention. These have included meetings in Australia, the Netherlands, and Jerusalem. International conferences on administrative ethics are planned for Portland, Oregon and Ottawa during 2000.

The significance of this increase in conference attention and activity is that it indicates a rising level of interest and serious effort devoted to the study of administrative

Table 1 Ethics Sessions at ASPA National Conferences

Year	Place	Title	Convenor
1952	Washington, D.C.	Ethics in the public service	Brownlow
1959	Washington, D.C.	Ethics for administration	Leys
1963	Washington, D.C.	Ethics and the administrator	Leys
1971	Denver	Education for the public service: redesign of value in a time of crisis	Nigro, Sumek
1974	Syracuse	Professional and personal ethics: lessons from the Watergate scandal	Graham
1975	Chicago	Administration of state ethics laws	Ward
1976	Washington, D.C.	Professional standards and ethics	Fletcher
		Codes of ethics	Graham
		Acting upon conscience	Hartenstein
		Ethics stds. for appointed polit. execs.	Mitchell
		Approaching ethics probs.—how university helps	Stewart
1977	Atlanta	Ethical issues in public service	Rohr
		Ethics for P.A.	Gibson
1978	Phoenix	Practical considerations in ethics	Florestano
		Ethics and values in curricula	Rohr
		Strategies for social equity	Faust
		Whistleblowers	Fitzgerald
1979	Baltimore	Personal values and prof. ethics	Chandler
		Keeping anti-corruption units clean	Ruff
		Corruption, fraud, and public finance	White
1980	San Francisco	Maintaining responsible conduct	Cooper
		Admin. ethics: where are they?	Meyer
		Enforcement of ethical codes	Dwiwedi
		Ethics and values in public admin.	Clarke
		Blowing the whistle on corruption	Loman
		Comparing ethics stds.: public/private	Miller
1981	Detroit	Values/Ethics in organizations	Winn
		Admin. Responsibility: Internal/external goals	Bowman
		Teaching of ethics of public responsibility	Dwivedi
1982	Honolulu	Ethics in Govt. Act, conflict of int.	Gallas
		Ethical concerns: fraud, waste, and abuse	Blandan
		Unethical demands of elected officials	Fleagle
		Teaching ethics in P.A.	Bowen
		Ethics and intergovernmental mgt.	Cooper
		Prof. standards and ethics	Gallas
1983	New York	Ethical discourse in P.A.	Fischer
		Prof. assn. exper. with codes of ethics	Chandler
1984	Denver	Technology and ethics	F. Burke
		Ethics and lobbying	Gibbs
		Whistleblowing	Evans
1985	Indianapolis	P.A. prof.: need a higher standard?	Rabin
		Dissent and whistleblowing	Doig
		Organizational ethos and personal ethics	Catron

Table 1   Continued

Year	Place	Title	Convenor
1986	Anaheim, Calif.	Ethics and public policy	Bergeson
		Ethical issues for young professionals	Cox
		Single code of ethics for publ. serv.?	Zinke
		Issue of loyalty in public sector	S. Fox
		Applying ASPA code of ethics	Kass
		P.A. and justice	Pops
		Dissent channels	Tecumesh
		Ethical problems and ethics education	Denhardt
		State of the discipline re: ethics	Rohr
		Ethics in P.A.	Kass
1987	Boston	Ethics theories: NASA and *Challenger*	*Heisig*
		National dialogue on ethics	Brannigan
		Ethics, democracy, and teaching P.A.	Bush
1988	Portland, Ore.	Practical ethics for real-world administrators	Beaumont
		Ethics and political obligation	Schneider
		Managing ethics in human services	panel
		Ethics in practice: educ. implications	Catron
		Moral leadership: exit, voice, loyalty	Lee
		Teaching ethics in P.A.	Denhardt
1989	Miami	Guild protectionism v. prof. ethic	Fox
		Admin. theology	Dwivedi
		Ethics at govt./industry interface	Hook
		Ethics in govt.	conference
		Ethical dilemmas: Minority/women persp.	Winn
		Institutionalizing spirit of dissent	Truelson
1990	Los Angeles	Ethics decision-making in human services	Heijka-Ekins
		Fed. agency ethics training	Gilman
		Ethical strategies in public service	Lee
		Ethics in staff development	Shaumavon
		Ethics laws for local govt.	McCullough
		Is virtue enough?	Lee
		Implementing mandated ethics training	Pavlak
		Agenda for ethics reform	Denhardt
		Lessons from firing line	Beitz
		Ethics and efficiency	Winn
1991	Washington, D.C.	Managing ethics dilemmas in urban areas	Winn
		Whistleblowing	Truelson
		Ethics decision making: theory and practice	Lee
1992	Chicago	Ethical attitudes/behaviors in local govt.	Menzel
		Public opinion about corruption	Malec
		Ethics and org. design/culture/legitimacy	Denhardt
		Value conflicts and pers./org. perform.	Hook
		Ethics and mgt. in cities and counties	Menzel
1993	San Francisco	Ethics in principle	Cleary
		Ethics in practice	Cleary
1994	Kansas City, Mo.	Moral dilemma and necessity: state lottery programs	Veasey
		What is the public interest?	Thurmaier

Table 1 Continued

Year	Place	Title	Convenor
1995	San Antonio	International ethics and change	Burke
		Is our commitment to fundamental values strong enough?	Angelo
1996	Atlanta	Professional and ethical caveats regarding entrepreneurial public management	Wittmer
		On the (un)ethical side of cyberspace	Menzel
		The ethical difference	Griffith
1997	Philadelphia	The management of ethics	Bowman
		The ethics challenge	Menzel
		Author meets critics: the pursuit of absolute integrity: how corruption control makes government ineffective	Thornburgh
		Promoting ethical behavior in the public service	Lewis
1998	Seattle	Ethics issues on the edge of the next millennium	Lewis
		Ethics research evaluation	Collins
		New theory, new ethics and knowledge building in the 21st century	Miller
		Engaging change in the ethical behavior of public administrators through ethics training and the use of proactive approaches	Ford
1999	Orlando	Troubled waters: culture and ethics in the use of health care	Kirchoff
		Instilling values—managing ethics	West
		Doing ethics: the practice of teaching and applying standards	Cooper

ethics during the last two decades around the world. Ethics in public administration has moved from being largely ignored to a point at which hundreds of scholars and practitioners in a growing number of nations are devoting substantial portions of their work to its furtherance.

VII. PROFESSIONAL EDUCATION STANDARDS

One of the weakest remaining elements in developing administrative ethics as a field of study is the lack of strong curricular standards on ethics from the National Association of Schools of Public Affairs and Administration (NASPAA). NASPAA is the national accrediting association for 245 master's degree programs in public policy, public administration, public affairs, and nonprofit management in the United State. At present, the only standard dealing with ethics is under Section 4.21 of the MPA degree standards dealing with common curricular components: "The common curriculum components shall enhance the student's values, knowledge, and skills to act ethically and effectively: in the management of public service organizations." The implementation of even this standard is left largely to site visit teams and the individual programs they review for accreditation. The result is that the attention given to ethics in MPA programs varies considerably and rarely involves a required course on ethics. More often this standard is met by demonstrating that ethics is treated along with other topics in the core courses.

On several occasions, efforts have been made to strengthen the NASPAA standard to require a course entirely devoted to ethics, but to no avail. As recently as the NASPAA national conference in Boise, Idaho, in 1998, a proposal for such a requirement was soundly defeated. The irony of this particular decision was that the Boise conference had opened with a mock trial of NASPAA in which the association was found guilty of neglecting administrative ethics. Presumably, many of those who voted to indict NASPAA for inadequate attention to ethics subsequently voted against requiring a course.

While it is true, as opponents of requiring a course in ethics maintain, that the MPA curriculum is already very tight with requirements, and that finding faculty to teach a required course might be difficult, the fact remains that in the face of these problems the priorities of the academic institutions are found not to include ethics. The argument that ethics is important but can be adequately treated in a fragmented fashion in several different courses seems inconsistent with the way we teach other subjects we consider important, such as public finance, public policy, human resources management, and public management. While it is true that ethics permeates all of these areas of public administration, it does not follow that it can be adequately taught without the focused and coherent engagement only possible in a separate course.

VIII.   AN ADMINISTRATIVE ETHICS JOURNAL

In 1996 ASPA and the Council of State Governments (CSG) published the first issue of *Public Integrity Annual*, edited by James Bowman. Focusing exclusively on administrative ethics, this annual was intended to appeal to both thoughtful practitioners and academicians. In that sense it was an applied ethics venue intended to fill a gap in the periodical literature. Previously there had been no journal dedicated entirely to this field of study, and the increasing volume of ethics research in the late 1990s gave rise to a growing feeling that there was a need for an ethics journal. *Public Integrity Annual* was published again in 1997, but by 1998 the number of high quality manuscript submissions warranted converting it into a regular quarterly journal entitled *Public Integrity*. ASPA and CSG were joined by the International City/County Management Association (ICMA) in sponsoring this new publication. The statement of purpose for *Public Integrity* suggests an ambitious and encompassing scope which includes both theory and practice. The establishment of this new quarterly journal on administrative ethics represented a significant milestone in the maturation of the field of study.

IX.   NEW ETHICS ORGANIZATION

Although NASPAA seems not to be giving much support to the development of administrative ethics as a field of study, ASPA has now established a Section on Ethics, a permanent division of ASPA with its own bylaws, meetings, awards, and events. Organized by Don Menzel and James Bowman in 1997, the section had its first meeting at the ASPA national conference in Seattle in 1998. The section has grown with extraordinary rapidity to a membership of 350, one of the largest of ASPA's sections, in only three years. The Section on Ethics maintains a website, operates a listserve for its members, and publishes a very professional and substantive electronic newsletter, *Ethics Today*, with Carole Jurkiewicz as its founding editor. In addition, the section has attempted to recognize academic work in administrative ethics by establishing an award for the best student paper on ethics and public administration, and another for the best scholarly article in a public administration journal each year. Each member of the section receives a subscription to the journal, *Public Integrity*, which is included in the membership dues.

X. CONCLUSION

It seems clear that public administration ethics is a relatively new but robust, expanding, and promising field of study, showing distinct signs of maturation during the last decade. As the consensus about the nature of the administrative role began to change in the late 1930s, from one assuming the separation of politics from administration to one acknowledging the unavoidably political nature of public administrative work, the place of values and ethics began to emerge in the literature. It was another forty years before administrative ethics achieved ''take-off'' momentum as the field slowly accommodated itself to a shift from value neutrality to commitment to some form of professional ethics.

Precisely what form those ethical commitments take is still under debate, but there can be no doubt that the debate must continue. The themes discussed above reflect the different ways scholars are attempting to contribute to this process. It may well be that the debate over these themes, and others that will emerge, is the most we can expect. Codes of ethics will be adopted by associations and governmental units specifying expected norms and conduct, but the day-to-day ethical decision-making process is so complex and nuanced that a clear normative ethical consensus may never be achieved. If any consensus does emerge, it will likely be a loose and evolving one around the varying importance of these themes in different contexts.

What will keep the momentum going? What will be needed to continue the development of administrative ethics as a field of study? The following seem to be essential:

1. *Historical research* on the American political tradition, citizenship, and democratic thought will be required. There seems to be an emerging, yet still amorphous, consensus about the necessity for rooting a public administrative ethic in the values of the American regime. Since administrators are inescapably political animals, a normative political theory, rooted in the American experience, within which a normative administrative ethic can be formed appears to be an important focus of attention. To be of any real value to the field of public administration we must be able to engage practitioners in discussion about conduct, as it ought to be, within the American political tradition.

2. *Empirical research* on the world of administrative ethical conduct, as it is now in actual practice, will also be necessary.[20] The 1991 conference in Park City was a hopeful sign that empirical work was being done. It is now clear from Menzel's graph of articles (Figure 1) that the number of empirically based publications on ethics in public administration journals has been significantly increasing at an increasing rate. Conceptual articles still greatly outnumber those that are empirically based, but that will likely always be the case with a necessarily heavily normative area of study such as ethics. Ethicists and empirical methodologists need to talk to each other more and collaborate on projects that will further illuminate the factors which encourage or discourage ethical reflection and conduct in public organizations.

   3.   *Arenas for deliberation and presentation of research are* also necessary. The journals examined by Menzel and Carson (1999) have significantly increased the number of articles dealing with ethics, and a new specialized journal on administrative ethics, *Public Integrity*, is now available. Having both kinds of venues should be a major impetus for the advancement of the study of administrative ethics. For example, one of the factors contributing to the advancement of biomedical ethics has been the existence of specialized journals like *The Hastings Center Report* which provide a regular and focused venue for articles on research in that field in addition to those that appear in more general medical journals. It will be important also to maintain a stream of articles on ethics in the more general public administration journals that appeal to a broader audience to prevent the subject from becoming the esoteric province of a few specialists talking only to each other.

   Also, some kind of conference structure is needed beyond ASPA national conferences. It may be that ad hoc conferences of the kind held in 1989, 1991 and 1995 will be sufficient for a while, but eventually administrative ethics scholars and practitioners will need regularly scheduled meetings that are predictable arenas in which ideas and findings may be exposed to scrutiny and debate. The ASPA Section on Ethics seems to be the most likely candidate for providing institutional continuity for conferences of this kind. As this chapter is being revised for the second edition of this handbook, the Section on Ethics is announcing a conference entitled "Ethics 2000: Dimensions of Ethics in the New Millennium," to be cosponsored by Portland State University during May 18–19, 2000. It is being billed as the "Third Public Sector Ethics Conference," apparently to establish historical continuity with the Park City and Tampa conferences. The 1989 conference in Washington, D.C. was much more a practitioner event than these other three.

NOTES

1. Books treated will not include general texts that devote a chapter or minor portion of the volume to administrative ethics, except for four classics which are cited to demonstrate the historical emergence of ethics as a matter of concern within broad views of the field.
2. Van Riper focuses primarily on Eaton's work as a more appropriated beginning for "our modern system of public employment" (p. 482).
3. These are two illustrative examples of their debate. For a full review of the debate with references see Cooper, 1998, pp. 136–140 and 153–156.
4. In this volume, Wallace Sayre's chapter, "Political Neutrality" (pp. 202–217), continued the assault on political neutrality begun by Dimock (Gaus et al., 1936). Sayre examined the Hatch Act of 1939 and challenged its assumptions by suggesting that it amounted to depriving public servants of their citizenship and civil rights. Whenever political neutrality was called into question, the possibility of turning to ethics as one means of shaping and restraining the conduct of administrators was present.
5. Now we generally refer to these discrete acts as administrative decisions as opposed to decisions concerning policy proposals, implementation, or interpretation.
6. These are known in philosophical terms as "deontological" and "teleological" approaches to ethics.
7. Inclusion of this article is an exception to the focus on *Public Administration Review* and *Administration & Society* announced at the beginning of this chapter. It is justified as a landmark article which could not be excluded from review simply on the basis of the venue in which it appeared.
8. This article was the first specifically on ethics to be published in the journal, Administration & Society, which had been established in 1969.

9. For a sense of this material see Marini (1971) about the original Minnowbrook conference in 1968 and the special issue of PAR (1989) on the "Minnowbrook If" conference held in 1988.

10. While expressing sympathy for Hart's (1974) call for emphasis on administrative philosophy, and John Rawls's theory of justice in particular, Rohr insisted that too much philosophical background was required for such an approach to be feasible in public administration professional education.

11. The only others that had been published were Golembiewski's 1965 book advocating a Judeo-Christian ethic, Appleby's 1952 volume arguing for a bureaucratic ethic, and Leys' 1952 work prescribing a philosophical method, but no particular philosophical perspective.

12. Barnard's book was not included in this chapter since he wrote primarily from a private sector perspective. However, it is possible to make use of some of his conceptual distinctions concerning the nature of responsibility, the function of internal unwritten "codes," in public administrative ethics, and even to adapt some of his analysis of the moral functions of the executive to the values of democratic public service without also accepting the problematic nature of his assumptions about the need for a corporate managerial elite.

13. It is easily arguable that there have been more than 35 articles since some in both journals have dealt with values or broad concepts such as the public interest which are clearly relevant to administrative ethics, but do not make that connection explicitly. Also, a number of other pieces are devoted in part to ethics, but have some other emphasis. The decision with respect to this chapter was to take the conservative path of erring on the side of leaving something out in order to focus on that literature which has self-consciously treated administrative ethics.

14. The journals included *Public Administration Review, Public Administration Quarterly, American Review of Public Administration, Administration & Society, Public Productivity and Management Review, International Journal of Public Administration, Journal of Public Administration Research and Theory, Public Integrity Annual, Journal of Public Affairs Education, State and Local Government Review*.

15. Menzel and Carson (1999) provides a tabular review and assessment of the empirical articles in pp. 242–248.

16. This conference was held April 16–18, 1983 in New York City and was sponsored by ASPA, the Charles F. Kettering Foundation, and the National Academy of Public Administration.

17. This is a prime example of the intermingling of themes that began to occur soon after a particular theme achieved prominence in the literature of administrative ethics. Here founding thought and virtue are connected.

18. No further discussion will be provided for Golembiewski's revised edition since it is substantially the same as his earlier version.

19. I wish to express my deep appreciation to Glenn Chambers for his competent and generous assistance in researching the ASPA files for me concerning the presentation of sessions on administrative ethics at ASPA national conferences. He meticulously read all of the conference programs from 1940 through 1992 to find each session that was identifiably focused on ethics. I recognize that there may have been other sessions on the topic not spelled out clearly enough in the program to be able to discern them, but this method does provide a general gauge of frequency.

20. "Empirical" here is not intended to suggest positivistic social science philosophy, nor a commitment to quantitative methods. Rather it is used in its original Greek sense (*empeiros*) to refer to research that is based on experience. This might well include the full range of qualitative and quantitative methods for investigating the nature of the experienced world.

REFERENCES

Appleby, P.H. (1947). Toward better public administration. *Public Administration Review*, 7:93–99.

Appleby, P.H. (1949). *Big Democracy*. Alfred A. Knopf, New York.

Appleby, P.H. (1952). *Morality and Administration in Democratic Government*. Louisiana State University Press, Baton Rouge.

Bailey, S.K. (1964). Ethics and the public service. *Public Administration Review*, *24*:234–243.

Barnard, C.I. (1938). *The Functions of the Executive*. Harvard University Press, Cambridge, Massachusetts.

Bell, R. (1985). Professional values and organizational decision making. *Administration & Society*, *17*:21–60.

Boulding, K. (1953). *The Organizational Revolution*. Harper & Row, New York.

Bowman, J.S. (1990). Ethics in government: a national survey of public administrators. *Public Administration Review*, *50*:345–353.

Bowman, J.S. (ed.) (1991). *Ethical Frontiers in Public Management: Seeking New Strategies for Resolving Ethical Dilemmas*. Jossey-Bass, San Francisco.

Bowman, J.S. (1997). Ethics in government: from a winter of despair to a spring of hope. *Public Administration Review*, *57*:517–526.

Bowman, J.S. and Menzel, D.C. (1998). *Teaching Ethics and Values in Public Administration Programs*. State University Press of New York, Albany.

Burke, J.P. (1986). *Bureaucratic Responsibility*. Johns Hopkins University Press, Baltimore.

Caldwell, L.K. (1943). Thomas Jefferson and public administration. *Public Administration Review*, *3*:240–253.

Caldwell, L.K. (1976). Novus ordo seclorum: the heritage of American public administration. *Public Administration Review*, *36*:476–488.

Carnevale, D.G. and Wechsler, B. (1992). Trust in the public sector: individual and organizational determinants. *Administration & Society*, *23*:471–494.

Chandler, R.C. (1983). The problem of moral reasoning in American public administration: the case for a code of ethics. *Public Administration Review*, *43*:32–39.

Chandler, R.C. (1984). The public administrator as representative citizen: a new role for the new century. *Public Administration Review*, *44*:196–206.

Chitwood, S.R. (1974). Social equity and social service productivity. *Public Administration Review* (Symposium on social equity and public administration, H. George Frederickson, ed.) *34*: 29–35.

Cooper, T.L. (1982). *The Responsible Administrator: An Approach to Ethics for the Administrative Role*. Kennikat, Port Washington, New York.

Cooper, T.L. (1984). Citizenship and professionalism in public administration. *Public Administration Review*, *44*:143–149.

Cooper, T.L. (1986). *The Responsible Administrator: An Approach to Ethics for the Administrative Role*, 2nd ed. Associated Faculty Press, Millwood, New York.

Cooper, T.L. (1987). Hierarchy, virtue, and the practice of public administration: a perspective for normative ethics. *Public Administration Review*, *47*:320–328.

Cooper, T.L. (1990). *The Responsible Administrator: An Approach to Ethics for the Administrative Role*, 3rd ed. Jossey-Bass, San Francisco.

Cooper, T.L. (1991). *An Ethic of Citizenship for Public Administration*. Prentice-Hall, Englewood Cliffs, New Jersey.

Cooper, T.L. (1998). *The Responsible Administrator: An Approach to Ethics for the Administrative Role*, 4th ed. Jossey-Bass, San Francisco.

Cooper, T.L. and Wright, N.D. (eds.) (1992). *Exemplary Public Administrators: Character and Leadership in Government*. Jossey-Bass, San Francisco.

Denhardt, K.G. (1988). *The Ethics of Public Service: Resolving Moral Dilemmas in Public Organizations*. Greenwood Press, New York.

Denhardt, K.G. (1989). The management of ideals: a political perspective on ethics. *Public Administration Review*, *49*:187–193.

Denhardt, R.B. (1992). Morality as an organizational problem. *Public Administration Review*, *52*: 104–105.

Dobel, J.P. (1988). The honorable spymaster: John Le Carre and the character of espionage. *Administration & Society, 20*: 191–215.

Dobel, J.P. (1990). Integrity in the public service. *Public Administration Review, 50*:354–366.

Eaton, D.B. (1880). *Civil Service in Great Britain: A History of Abuses and Reforms and Their Bearing Upon American Politics*. Harper & Brothers, New York.

Finer, H. (1936). Better government personnel. *Political Science Quarterly, 51*:569–99.

Fiore, W.I., Brunk, G.G., and Meyer, C.K. (1992). Norms of professional behavior in highly specialized organizations: the case of American zoos and aquariums. *Administration & Society, 24*: 81–99.

Fischer, F. (1988). Ethical discourse in public administration. *Administration & Society, 15*:5–42.

Fleishman, J.L., Liebman, L., and Moore, M.H. (eds.) (1981). *Public Duties: The Moral Obligations of Government Officials*. Harvard University Press, Cambridge, Massachusetts.

Foster, G.D. (1981). Law, morality and the public servant. *Public Administration Review, 41*:29–33.

Frederickson, H.G. (1974). Symposium on Social Equity and Public Administration. *Public Administration Review, 34*(1).

Frederickson, H.G. (1976). The lineage of new public administration. *Administration & Society, 8*: 149–173.

Frederickson, H.G. (1982). The recovery of civism in public administration. *Public Administration Review, 42*:501–508.

Frederickson, H.G. and Hart, D.K. (1985). The public service and the patriotism of benevolence. *Public Administration Review, 45*:547–553.

Friedrich, C.J. (1935). Responsible government service under the American constitution. Monograph no. 7 in C.J. Friedrich et al. *Problems of the American Public Service*. McGraw-Hill, New York.

Gaus, J.M., White, L.D., and Dimock, M.E. (1936). *The Frontiers of Public Administration*. University of Chicago Press, Chicago.

Gawthrop, L.C. (1984). Civis, civitas, and civilitas: a new focus for the year 2000. *Public Administration Review, 44*:101–107.

Gilligan, C. (1982). *In a Different Voice: Psychological Theory and Women's Development*. Harvard University Press, Cambridge, Massachusetts.

Golembiewski, R.T. (1962). Organization as a moral problem. *Public Administration Review, 22*: 51–58.

Golembiewski, R.T. (1965). *Men, Management, and Morality: Toward a New Organizational Ethic*. Transaction Publishers, New Brunswick, New Jersey.

Golembiewski, R.T. (1989). *Men, Management, and Morality: Toward a New Organizational Ethic*, Revised ed. Transaction Publishers, New Brunswick, New Jersey.

Golembiewski, R.T. (1992). Excerpts from "organization as a moral problem." *Public Administration Review, 52*:95–98.

Golembiewski, R.T. (1992). Organization is a moral problem: past as prelude to present and future. *Public Administration Review, 52*:99–103.

Goodnow, F. (1900). *Politics and Administration: A Study in Government*. Russell & Russell, New York.

Goodsell, C.T. (1985). *The Case for Bureaucracy*, 2nd ed. Chatham House, Chatham, New Jersey.

Gortner, H. (1991). *Ethics for Public Managers*. Praeger, New York.

Graham, G.A. (1974). Ethical guidelines for public administrators: observations on the rules of the game. *Public Administration Review, 34*:90–92.

Harmon, M.M. (1974). Social equity and organizational man: motivation and organizational democracy. *Public Administration Review* (Symposium on social equity and public administration, H.G. Frederickson, ed.) *34*:11–18.

Harmon, M.M. (1989). The responsible actor as "tortured soul": the case of Horatio Hornblower. *Administration & Society, 21*:283–312.

Hart, D.K. (1974). Social equity, justice, and the equitable administrator. *Public Administration Review* (Symposium on social equity and public administration, H.G. Frederickson, ed.) *34*: 3–11.

Hart, D.K. (1983). The honorable bureaucrat among the Philistines: a reply to "Ethical Discourse in Public Administration." *Administration & Society, 15*:43–48.

Hart, D.K. (1984). The virtuous citizen, the honorable bureaucrat, and "public" administration. *Public Administration Review, 44*:111–120.

Hart, D.K. (1989). A partnership in virtue among all citizens: the public service and civic humanism. *Public Administration Review, 49*:101–105.

Hart, D.K. and Smith, P.A. (1988). Fame, fame-worthiness, and the public service. *Administration & Society, 20*:131–151.

Hartwig, R. (1990). The paradox of malevolent/benevolent bureaucracy. *Administration & Society*, 22:206–227.

Hejka-Ekins, A. (1988). Teaching ethics in public administration. *Public Administration Review*, 48:885–891.

Hummel, R.H. (1987). *The Bureaucratic Experience*, 3rd ed. St. Martin's Press, New York.

Jos, P.H. (1990). Administrative responsibility revisited: moral consensus and moral autonomy. *Administration & Society, 22*:228–248.

Jos, P.H., Tompkins, M.E., and Hays, S.W. (1989). In praise of difficult people: a portrait of the committed whistleblower. *Public Administration Review, 49*:552–561.

Levitan, D.M. (1942). The neutrality of the public service. *Public Administration Review*, 2:317–323.

Lewis, C.W. (1991). *The Ethics Challenge in Public Service*. Jossey-Bass, San Francisco.

Leys, W.A. (1943). Ethics and administrative discretion. *Public Administration Review*, 3:10–23.

Leys, W.A. (1952). *Ethics for Policy Decisions: The Art of Asking Deliberative Questions*. Prentice Hall, Englewood Cliffs, New Jersey.

Long, N.E. (1990). Conceptual notes on the public interest for public administration and policy analysis. *Administration & Society, 22*:170–181.

McGregor, E.B. (1974). Social equity and the public service. *Public Administration Review* (Symposium on social equity and public administration, H.G. Frederickson, ed.) *34*:18–29.

Marini, F. (1971). *Towards a New Public Administration: The Minnowbrook Perspective*. Chandler Publishing Co., Scranton, Pennsylvania.

Marini, F. (1992). The uses of literature in the exploration of public administration ethics: the example of *Antigone*. *Public Administration Review*, 52:420–426.

Marx, F.M. (1940). *Public Management in the New Democracy*. Harper & Brothers, New York.

Marx, F.M. (1949). Administrative ethics and the rule of law. *The American Political Science Review*, 43:1119–1144.

Menzel, D.C. and Carson, K. (1999). A review and assessment of empirical research on public management ethics: implications for scholars and managers. *Public Integrity, 1*:239–264.

Mertins, H. (ed.) (1979). *Professional Standards and Ethics: A Workbook for Public Administrators*. American Society for Public Administration, Washington, D.C.

Mertins, H. and Hennigan, P.J. (eds.) (1982). *Applying Professional Standards and Ethics in the Eighties: A Workbook Study Guide for Public Administrators*. American Society for Public Administration, Washington, D.C.

Moneypenney, P. (1953). A code of ethics as a means of controlling administrative conduct. *Administration Review, 13*:184–187.

Nigro, L.G. and Richardson, W.G. (1990). Between citizen and administrator: administrative ethics and *PAR*. *Public Administration Review*, 50:623–635.

Pincoffs, E.L. (1986). *Quandaries and Virtues*. University of Kansas Press, Lawrence.

Porter, D.O. and Porter, T.W. (1974). Social equity and fiscal federalism. *Public Administration Review* (Symposium on social equity and public administration, H.G. Frederickson, ed.) *34*: 36–51.

Rabin, J. and Bowman, J.S. (1984). *Politics and Administration: Woodrow Wilson and American Public Administration*. Marcel Dekker, Inc., New York.

Rawls, J. (1971). *A Theory of Justice*. Harvard University Press, Cambridge, Massachusetts.

Richardson, W.G. and Nigro, L.G. (1987). Administrative ethics and founding thought: constitutional correctives, honor, and education. *Public Administration Review*, 47:367–376.

Richardson, W.G. and Nigro, L.G. (1991). *The constitution and administrative ethics in America. Administration & Society* 23:275–287.

Rohr, J.A. (1976). The study of ethics in the P.A. curriculum. *Public Administration Review*, *36*: 398–406.

Rohr, J.A. (1978). *Ethics for Bureaucrats: An Essay on Law and Values*. Marcel Dekker Inc., New York.

Rohr, J.A. (1980). Ethics for the senior executive service: suggestions for management training. *Administration & Society*, *12*:203–217.

Rohr, J.A. (1989). *Ethics for Bureaucrats: An Essay on Law and Values*, 2nd ed. Marcel Dekker Inc., New York.

Sayre, W.S. (1951). Trends of a decade in administrative values. *Public Administration Review*, *11*: 1–8.

Scott, J.D. (1992). Past success, future challenges. *Public Administration Review*, *52*:105–107.

Scott, W.G. (1982). Barnard on the nature of elitist responsibility. *Public Administration Review*, *42*:197–201.

Scott, W.G. and Hart, D.K. (1973). Administrative crisis: the neglect of metaphysical speculation. *Public Administration Review*, *33*:415–422.

Stewart, D.W. (1991). Theoretical foundations of ethics in public administration: approaches to understanding moral action. *Administration & Society*, *23*:357–373.

Thompson, D.F. (1985). The possibility of administrative ethics. *Public Administration Review*, *45*: 555–569.

Thompson, D.F. (1992). Paradoxes of government ethics. *Public Administration Review*, *52*:254–259.

Tugwell, R.G. (1940). Implementing the general interest. *Public Administration Review*, *1*:32–49.

Van Riper, P.P. (1983). The American administrative state: Wilson and the founders—an unorthodox view. *Public Administration Review*, *43*:477–490.

Wakefield, S. (1976). Ethics and the public service: a case for individual responsibility. *Public Administration Review*, *36*:661–666.

Waldo, D. (1974). Reflections on public morality. *Administration & Society*, *6*:267–282.

White, L.D. (1948). *Introduction to the Study of Public Administration*, 3rd ed. Macmillan, New York.

White, O. and Gates, B.L. (1974). Statistical theory and equity in the delivery of social services. *Public Administration Review* (Symposium on social equity and public administration, H.G. Frederickson, ed.) *34*:43–51.

White, R.D., Jr. (1999). Public ethics, moral development, and the enduring legacy of Lawrence Kohlberg. *Public Integrity*, *1*:121–134.

Whyte, W.H. (1956). *The Organization Man*. Doubleday & Co., Garden City, New York.

Willoughby, W.F. (1927). *The Principles of Public Administration: With Special Reference to the National and State Governments of the United States*. The Brookings Institution, Washington, D.C.

Wilson, W. (1887). The study of administration. *Political Science Quarterly*, *2*:197–220.

Wood, R.C. (1955). Ethics in government as a problem in executive management. *Public Administration Review*, *15*:1–7.

2

Research and Knowledge in Administrative Ethics

H. George Frederickson and Jeremy David Walling
University of Kansas, Lawrence, Kansas

I. INTRODUCTION

Ethics is a world of philosophy, values, and morals. Administration is a world of decisions and actions. Ethics will search for right and wrong while administration must get the job done. Ethics is abstract while the practices of administration are irremediably concrete. How can ethics inform administration? How can administration inform ethics? How can the ideas of administration—order, efficiency, economy, productivity—help define ethics, and how can the ideas of ethics—right and wrong—help define administration?

One answer is research. Terry Cooper (1991: 2) reminds us that "reference has been made to the largely normative work that has dominated administrative ethics and the need to 'move beyond' that concern with prescription to a more systematic empirical approach. . . . [W]e have not yet come to grips with the relationship between these two ways of treating administrative ethics." The normative and philosophical literature in administrative ethics is, by any measure, impressive both in quantity and quality. The conduct of field-based empirical research on administrative ethics, particularly in public management, is comparatively less common. There is, as a consequence, a much smaller literature when empirical research is compared with normative discourse in public administrative ethics.

In the summer of 1991, the Section on Public Administration Research of the American Society for Public Administration and the Public Administration Ethics Network jointly sponsored the National Conference on Government Ethics Research. This conference brought together, for the first time, the leading philosophical and prescriptive ethics scholars and the empirical research scholars. Thirty-two papers were prepared for the conference, most of them reporting on field-based ethics research (Frederickson, 1993). This suggests that there is an increasing interest in empirical perspectives and a growing recognition that a carefully built and verifiable knowledge base in administrative ethics would complement philosophical and normative perspectives.

There is, however, "suspicion that the methodological requirements of empirical research ensure its irrelevance. . . . Perhaps the most fundamental concern is that the search for that which is measurable may lead empirical researchers to impoverish normatively rich concepts and hence degrade moral discourse" (Jos, 1993: 1). Following this argument, empirical research on administrative ethics would be "beside the moral point"

37

(Jos, 1993). This suspicion has particularly to do with those forms of empirical research that employ quantification. It is arguably the case, however, that even the most normative ethics scholar will employ forms of empiricism based on personal experience, case studies, stories, and the like. It follows that virtually all scholarship in the field of administrative ethics is connected to research if research is defined broadly to include the full range of epistemological perspectives. To administrative ethics scholars and researchers there are issues of both epistemology and methodology.

Researchers, following the modern positivist or behavioral cannons of social science, have come only recently to the subject of ethics in administration. The first part of this chapter will review the methods, units of analysis, and perspectives of ethics research in the positivist family. Ethics research is, however, both much older and much newer. It is older in the traditional approaches to research in administrative ethics which used history, examples, logic, and dialogue. It is newer in post-modern or post-positivist approaches to research which rely on case studies, stories, and thick description. The second part of this chapter describes this research genre. The third section of this chapter addresses especially the question of the application of ethics in administration and sets out a research agenda designed to explain how ethics and administration define each other.

In this chapter, ethics in government administration is particularly at issue. This is not because there is more or better research on government administrative ethics when compared to business or medical ethics. In fact there is less research on government administrative ethics. The reason for the focus on government ethics is found in the role or capability of government to exercise power, including administrative power, legitimated in the name of the state. When questions of right and wrong are answered by the state and enforced by public administration, ethics research is face-to-face, not with abstractions or philosophy but with the authoritative application of power. In such a context ethical questions are vital, immediate, and real.

Values are the soul of public administration (Cooper, 1990). The study and practice of public administration has never been regarded as just technical or managerial. Attempts to parse the work of government into politics and policymaking as the expression of values, on the one hand, and administration as the mere technical and value neutral carrying out of policy, on the other hand, have not succeeded. That values inhabit every corner of government is given. Those who study administration study values and those who practice administration practice the allocation of values (Waldo, 1948).

In government administration values are most often taken to mean political or policy values. Political values such as who should hold elected office and who should exercise the sanctioned power of the state connect to public administration because bureaucrats and civil servants often have extensive discretion. Policy values such as choices between spending on program A versus program B are influenced by administrators. Political and policy values and preferences such as these are often connected to matters of ethics. For example, if a police department deploys shifts and forces in such a way as to leave neighborhoods which need protection without that protection while other neighborhoods are protected, there is an issue of policy ethics. Policy ethics issues such as this are seldom the focus of study in public administration.

Values such as individual adherence to the law, honesty, following professional codes of ethics, personal morality, a commitment to constitutional principles (particularly the Bill of Rights), and ''regime values'' most often characterize the study of ethics in public administration (Denhardt, 1988; Cooper, 1990; Rohr, 1986; Bowman, 1991; Lewis,

1991; Lui and Cooper, 1997; Stewart et al., 1997). This chapter will emphasize this perspective on administrative ethics.

II. RESEARCH ON ADMINISTRATIVE ETHICS AND MODERN SOCIAL SCIENCE

The dominant approach to field research in public administration, as well as in virtually all other aspects of the study of administration, is positivist, rational, and empirical. This approach to research in administrative ethics is emerging but is still less common that interpretive-deductive treatment of ethics. In positivism, knowledge is based on natural phenomena and their properties. These properties and the relations among them can be observed or derived from the physical senses. There are in the positivist view discernable and describable patterns of order and chaos in both the physical and social worlds. Empiricism is the view that knowledge of the world can be or should be acquired by sense experience. To the rationalist, reason alone can provide knowledge of the existence and nature of things. Rationality is also used to describe the view that reality is a unified, coherent, and explicable system. Taken together positivism, rationality, and empiricism form the epistemology or theory of knowledge which guides contemporary research in science. What is to count as knowledge? What things are knowable? Can anything at all be known for certain? The positivist-rational-empirical epistemology answers all of these questions with a yes. When patterns of order in physical or social phenomena are observed, described, and verified, it can be said that it is knowledge. This knowledge is distinct from belief, values, or preferences. In logical positivism values and facts are distinct, a critically important aspect of positivism for public administration and for the study of ethics. Finally, in administrative or organizational rationality (some would say instrumental rationality) there are discernable patterns of relationships between phenomena (variables) which indicate that action A will produce result B. Individual or organizational rationality is, in this perspective, goal-oriented (usually pregiven or preconceived) behavior.

In the positivist family there are five primary methods used in administrative ethics research. The first and oldest of these methods is the use of self-reported questionnaires or surveys. Experimentation is the second major method, ordinarily involving the presentation of hypothetical ethical dilemmas to respondents. The third approach is the interview. The fourth method is the use of crime, ethics hotline data, whistleblower reports, and other data. The final method is the use of case studies. Each of these methods is described below.

What the methods have in common:

> is that researchers have not looked at performance directly, but rather they have examined such related variables as feelings, opinions, perceptions, orientations, or values held by organizational members. It is as though the difficulty and complexity of assessing ethical performance has caused researchers to solicit organization members' opinions of issues related to ethical performance rather than directly examining behavior or results (Gatewood and Carroll, 1991: 668).

It is not ethical conduct that is being studied so much as surrogate indicators of ethical views or attitudes.

A. Surveys

The use of self-administered questionnaires is probably the most common methodology in administrative ethics research. In this methodology, generally referred to as survey research, data are gathered by mailed questionnaires or increasingly by telephone. In the telephone version the data gatherer usually works from a standard instrument. Although there are some differences between self-administered questionnaires and telephone versions of survey research, the differences are not important to the purposes of this chapter.

There are a wide range of methodological issues associated with survey research including: the means by which the sample is drawn, the pretest of questions to guard against the wording of the question being predicate to the answer; the alternative forms of responses including binary, Likert scales, open-ended, and the like. Occasionally, focus groups are employed to pretest a survey instrument, to inform theory on a project, and to guide further research. As a general rule, the concern with methodology stems from the researchers' desire to be scientific and objective. They spend impressive amounts of time and energy refining questions, fine-tuning samples, and making every effort to be scientific and to present findings that are reliable, verifiable, and replicable.

The data gathered in this way are ordinarily analyzed by the use of multivariate statistics. The standard measures of central tendency, standard deviation, and tests of statistical significance and the like are employed. Especially popular is the use of Likert or other multiple-point scales to describe variables and the association of these variables by the means of multiple linear regression.

In methodological terms there is little to distinguish between survey research on administrative ethics and survey research in other fields of social science or policy analysis. What is different, of course, is the subject matter.

To illustrate the range of findings and knowledge that is based on survey research in the field of administrative ethics consider the following:

1. Attitudes toward corruption in government vary widely and depend on the nature of corruption. People judge the severity of corruption on the basis of who is involved and what is done (Malek, 1993). There are hierarchies of seriousness both in definitions of corruption and in attitudes toward it. Corruption is to some extent situationally determined. "What may be corrupt to one citizen, scholar, or public official is just politics to another, or discretion to a third" (Peters and Welch, 1978: 974). Factors such as age, socioeconomic status, residency (urban/rural; state or region), political ideology, gender, and political experience all appear to influence attitudes toward corruption in government (Malek, 1993).

2. Citizens and professionals (physicians) have different ethics. These differences are, however, more in degree than in kind and are greater or lesser depending on the particular ethical issue under consideration (organ transplants, access to health care, equality in treatment, and so on) (Overman and Foss, 1993).

3. The ethical climate of a government (city) influences the values of workers. Cities with strong ethical climates find that ethics and high organizational performance (efficiency, effectiveness, economy) are compatible. Similarly, a bureaucratic environment is compatible with high ethical values (Menzel, 1993). Furthermore, "public managers perceive the ethical climates of their organizations less favorably than do private sector managers" (Wittmer and Coursey, 1996: 568).

4. Military officers and members of Congress have somewhat different attitudes toward the legitimacy of war, the ultimate sanction of the nation-state. Military officers

tend to more favorably view war as a legitimate policy tool in international affairs than do members of Congress. Yet members of Congress are more inclined to take up the risks of war than are military officers (Tamashiro et al., 1993).

5. Research has set out the views of managers regarding the priorities of various organizational stakeholders, the perceived pressures on managers to compromise their personal principles, the influences that inhibit unethical behavior (Posner and Schmidt, 1984, 1992), and the tradeoffs between economic and ethical imperatives (England, 1975; Aldag and Jackson, 1977).

Public Managers (members of ASPA) overwhelmingly value codes of ethics in the workplace as a coherent set of work standards (90 percent). However, respondents indicate that codes of ethics must be championed by top management to prove effective among employees. In fact, "the influence of management by example, positively or negatively, is substantial" (Bowman and Williams, 1997: 520).

Citizens, politicians, and bureaucrats (in the state of Colorado) differ on the extent to which they adhere to a bureaucratic ethos (accountability, economy, competence) or a democratic ethos (compassion, the public interest, individual rights). For example, the public values bureaucratic norms more highly than bureaucrats or state legislators. As expected, politicians adhere to the aforementioned democratic ideals more than either bureaucrats or citizens. However, across all three groups, bureaucratic norms are more highly cherished. Furthermore, the hierarchy of values indicated by bureaucrats in the study indicates correspondence with traditional bureaucratic values of neutral competence, accountability, and trustworthiness (Goss, 1996). Similarly, a sample of Hong Kong middle- and senior-level managers exhibited a strong tendency toward classical bureaucratic values of neutrality, duty to the organization, respect of the law, and respect of rules and regulations (Lui and Cooper, 1997).

Research on administrative ethics using survey techniques has provided a rich and varied body of knowledge (Gatewood and Carroll, 1991). The advantages of this methodology are precision in data gathering, precision in statistical analysis and tests of statistical significance, the ability to control for contextual variables, the ability to control for attitudinal variables, the capacity for replication, and facilitation of the aggregation of knowledge. There are four primary disadvantages of ethics research based on survey techniques: First, findings from survey research are snapshots in time; second, they represent opinions and attitudes toward administrative ethics rather than behavior; third, they mask the reasons for opinions; and fourth, they do not account for the nuances of difference based on differing contingencies.

B. Experimentation

In the experimental approach to research in administrative ethics, respondents are given hypothetical problems to solve or are placed in hypothetical situations. The actual data-gathering technique is by self-administered questionnaire, by interviews or, by researcher observation of respondents. Experimentation is simply an application of survey, interview, or observation methodology coupled with hypothetical problems to be solved or dilemmas to resolve.

Often, experimental research uses vignettes or "short hypothetical cases that enable the researcher to obtain some measure of the difference between espoused ethics and likely ethical behavior" (Gatewood and Carroll, 1991: 669).

The recent research of Dennis Wittmer (1992: 451) is illustrative. He impaneled 156 subjects drawn from academic programs in public administration, business management, and engineering. These subjects dealt with an

> ethical case which involved the unfair and dishonest use of information to undercut a competitor's proposal. After acquiring a copy of a competitor's proposal from one of their ex-employees, a staff member (in a memo) requests guidance in pursuing proposed revisions that would undercut the competitor. A tradeoff is proposed that would reduce the margin of profit but improve the chances of being awarded the contract. The context is further complicated by impending layoffs unless the unit generates new revenues. The situation is considered an ''ethical'' one, principally because it involves potential harm to others as well as norms or standards of honesty and fairness.

Each respondent played the role of vice president for research, filled out an extensive background form indicating age, gender, education, and the like, and took an ethical sensitivity test and Rest's Defining Issue Test. Wittmer found that persons who ranked higher on the ethical sensitivity test were more likely to reject the staff member's recommendation.

Debra W. Stewart and Norman A. Sprinthall (1993) also do experimental research using vignettes. Their interest is in testing Lawrence Kohlberg's theory of the stages of moral development (stage 1, concern for obedience and punishment; stage 2, concern for cooperation and reciprocity in a single instance; stage 3, concern for enduring personal relationships; stage 4, concern for law and duty; stage 5, principled reasoning). Stewart and Sprinthall presented respondents with dilemmas in three domains of administrative decision-making: promotion, with attendant issues of affirmative action and patronage; procurement, with the issue of conflict of interest; and database management, with related issues of data file integrity. They measured different responses to these hypothetical dilemmas and connected these responses to stages of moral development.

There were two primary findings. First, the greatest variability in level of moral reasoning is derived from the content of the problem situation. ''If the content is familiar and there has been considerable discussion and analysis of the issues, there is a greater likelihood of higher stage moral reasoning. The opposite is also true. In unfamiliar situations where little has been discussed or processed, individuals are highly likely to employ less democratic and more self-serving reasons.'' Second, the usual factors of demography and organizational context have almost no influence on the level of moral reasons of public officials. If Stewart and Sprinthall are right, the preoccupation with codes of ethics, rules and regulations, inspectors general, and ethics officers will not be as effective in elevating our moral reasoning as will the detailed consideration of ethical issues and a careful processing of alternatives.

Stewart and colleagues (1997) applied the Stewart-Sprinthall Management Survey (SSMS) to Polish administrators and elected officials. The three vignettes described above were modified to correspond to Polish culture. An initial focus group indicated that principled reasoning was more important than adherence to law or duty. By contrast, respondents in the full study resembled Americans in their disposition toward law and duty. While the characteristics of age, role, education, and personal history were not found to produce significant differences between administrators and elected officials, female administrators were more likely to choose principled reasoning over law and duty (Stewart et al., 1997). Furthermore, females (Coast Guard) have been found to score significantly higher than males on Rest's Defining Issues Test (DIT), an instrument used to measure Kohlberg's levels of moral development (White, 1999).

The most famous, and in many ways the most important, experimental research relevant to administrative ethics comes from the field of social psychology. This research involves students, rather than administrators, which is often the case in experimental methodology. The results of two experiments (as well as many replications) are especially compelling to students of administrative ethics. Haney et al. (1973) in the famous Stanford prison experiment paid a group of students to spend two weeks in the roles of prisoners and guards. In a short time the prisoners rebelled and attempted a take-over of the "prison." When that failed they gradually became passive, lethargic, and started to experience serious emotional disturbances such as uncontrollable fits of crying or screaming. The guards gradually became more brutal. They harassed the prisoners and denigrated them and assigned them meaningless repetitive tasks. After six days the experiment was discontinued. In social psychology this experiment and subsequent replications are evidence of the strength of social roles and norms. Even when bad things happen, it is very difficult to stand apart from the group.

The Stanley Milgram experiments (1965, 1974) tested why people obey orders. In these experiments prepaid subjects were divided into two groups: those who were told they would be testing the relationship between learning behavior and punishment, and those who were presumed to be trying to learn and were to be punished if they did not. The first individuals operated a machine they believed gave an electric shock to learners when they made a mistake. Members of the other group, the learners, were in fact not shocked; they purposely make learning mistakes and feigned being shocked. The first group believed the mistakes and the shocks were real. In the experiment, the dosage of electricity was increased as learning mistakes increased. Electric dosages ranged from 15 to 450 volts. As dosage was increased learners yelled, eventually pounded on the wall, and finally became silent. In the early stages of the experiment the first group was told to please go on. As mistakes increased, they were told it was essential that they continue. Finally they were told there was no other choice and that they must go on. As a general rule, whenever this experiment is carried out, 65 percent of the first group will go all the way to 450 volts believing they have administered serious physical harm to the subjects. This body of research is taken to illustrate the propensity of persons to do as they are told and to follow orders even when it harms others. Such information could probably never be acquired by questionnaires or interviews.

The strengths and weaknesses of experimental methodology include those associated with both survey and interview techniques. The most important weakness is the surrogate nature of the research, because actual moral dilemmas are seldom as tidy as hypothetical vignettes. And the risks of being morally right and yet in career jeopardy are not present in experimental situations. Still, experimental methodology takes administrative ethics research one step nearer verifiable knowledge of individuals' moral reasoning. In addition, researchers claim that there is a consistent behavioral relationship between thought and action (Blasi, 1980).

C. Interviews

Face-to-face interviews (telephone interviews will not be considered here) are a cornerstone of research in the field of ethics in general and in administrative ethics in particular.

Interviews enable the researcher to work from a common instrument and yet to expand on particular points, clarify questions, and accommodate answers or opinions that do not fit neatly into yes/no, Likert scales, or other measured response models. Interviews enable the researcher to more fully account for variations in settings, time, and social, political, or economic contingencies. Perhaps most important, interviews are especially useful in determining the reasons for opinions, answers, or actions. When combined with self-administered questionnaires, interviews considerably enrich what is known about administrative ethics.

In administrative ethics the belief is often held that persons should be treated fairly and equally. Jennifer Hochschild's (1981) extensive research on how people feel about equality is based on extensive in-depth interviews, with a cross-section of citizens. Based on these interviews, Hochschild reached the conclusion that persons have contradictory views of equality, depending on the subject. Views of equality are not based so much on income levels, age, gender, or political ideology. They are based on the domain of life under consideration and what ought to be the definition of equality in each domain.

In the social domain (home, family, school, and community) people hold strongly to the idea of approximately equal shares which would include equal treatment of children, one spouse, equal sacrifice for the family, and equal treatment in schools and the neighborhood. When there is deviation from the commitment to equal shares it is ordinarily in the direction of, for example, giving more to the handicapped child. If persons feel they have been able generally to control their fate regarding the question of equality, they are more satisfied. If not, they are bitter and unhappy. These findings roughly accord with those of Tom R. Tyler (1990), who studies why people obey the law. His research is based on telephone interviews using a set questionnaire. He found that persons are far more likely to obey the law if they regard the law and its enforcement to be fair.

In the economic domain, following the research of Hochschild, equality should be on the basis of effort and means rather than on the basis of equal shares.

In the political domain people are of the view that political and civil rights should be fair, especially in the direction of redistribution from those who have ample to those who are poor. There is deep resentment over perceived inequality in both paying for government and receiving government services.

In all of this Hochschild found ambivalence. People recognize that their views are sometimes inconsistent and they feel anger because of not knowing who to blame and helplessness because of not knowing how to make things better. This research serves to demonstrate the capacity of the interview methodology, when used by a skilled social scientist, to plumb the details of attitudes and opinions and to enable the researcher to describe the subtleties of a subject.

Strait (1996) conducted personal interviews with twelve public employees to identify factors which might contribute to ethical violations. The sample represents a cross section of government workers, including an equal gender mix, a wide range of ages, and workers from various levels of government and different agency types (city government, military, higher education). Three common themes were found. First, respondents indicated that intense workloads might contribute to unethical behavior by providing an incentive to retaliate. Second, issues related to pay satisfaction were frequently mentioned as possibly contributing to unethical behavior. Finally, the respondents suggested that age and ethnicity might correspond with "different ethical standards" (Strait, 1996: 47). Specifically, younger employees and ethnic minorities were perceived by the respondents as being more inclined to engage in behavior they would judge to be unethical.

Lawrence Joseph (1988) conducted in-depth interviews using hypothetical examples and vignettes with fifty-eight Chicago civic and business leaders. He found varying degrees of tolerance toward government corruption depending on the nature of the corrupt act and the responsibilities of the person involved. Bribery or extortion by public officials are judged to be most corrupt while conflicts of interest or "petty" bribery are judged less corrupt. Cases that involve campaign contributions and political patronage are least likely to be considered corrupt. The police officer who takes money from drug dealers is more corrupt than the city employee who accepts money to expedite the issuance of a liquor license. Judges are held to a higher standard than police officers. Elected officials are held to a higher standard than appointed officials or merit civil servants.

The work of Douglas F. Morgan and Henry D. Kass (1993) is more closely connected to the ethics of public administrators. They interviewed in depth and several times, over an extended period, three city or county managers and three department heads from large local jurisdictions. Morgan and Kass use a technique called "focus group" in which the interviewers and the interviewees interact on particular subjects as an open dialogue rather than as researchers asking questions of respondents.

They refer to this technique as moral discourse and describe the public managers as having passed through two stages of moral development to a third stage. In the first stage, the managers are initially committed to neutral rational action which results in effective government; yet they find significant impediments to efficient and economical administration. The managers feel a moral obligation to "make things work" so that there will be effective government. While they continue to use the language of neutral competence, efficiency, and economy, they in fact mediate conflicts, temper public passions, stall precipitous action, modify ill-conceived plans. In the second stage, public managers, to make things work, involve themselves deeply in the mediation of conflicting communal values such as economic development on the one hand and environmental protection on the other. They become the "balancers of interests" and "facilitators of consensus" in a world of competing interest groups and conflict. In the final stage, the public managers freely invoke the language of the public or communal interest. They "shape the present in a manner informed by the past but with an eye to the future . . . as the lonely guardians of the larger public interest" (Morgan and Kass, 1993: 184).

Once the public managers have reached stage three they experience the "ethical crisis of role reversal." In a democracy, policy is set by those elected to represent the citizens. That policy is to be carried out by public servants. Is it morally wrong for appointed public managers to conceive of the public interest and to move government in the direction of that interest? Or, as Morgan and Kass ask, is it morally wrong if they do not? If elected officials have single narrow interests and tend to take the short view, is it morally wrong for the top city civil servants to simply let government be ineffective, inefficient, and unprepared for the future? To Morgan and Kass, the moral crisis of role reversal is resolved if the public administrator is willing to take ethical responsibility for significant intervention in both policymaking and policy implementation. In such circumstances public administrators must have, according to Morgan and Kass (1993: 187), "a moral framework that enables them to articulate a complex ordering of moral claims that are compatible with our constitutional system of government."

The Morgan and Kass example also illustrates the relative ease with which interview research facilitates interpretation and theory development. There are three weaknesses: First, there is a serious problem with replication, because each interview is a unique empirical event; second, there is the problem of verification (tape recorded interviews help);

third, there is the possibility of researcher bias in posing questions and interpreting answers; and fourth, sample size is small.

D. Data

As in most aspects of modern life there are data on many aspects of administrative ethics. There are, for example, compilations of information on codes of ethics for government employees and professional associations, background information on designated ethics officers and inspectors general in the federal government, extensive compilations on state ethics laws, information on reported incidence of whistleblowing, and the like.

Brewer and Selden (1998) utilize archival survey data generated by the Merit Systems Protection Board to examine whether whistleblowers in the federal government exhibit public service motivation (PSM). PSM is "a dynamic behavioral concept anchored in the types of behavior people exhibit rather than in the sectors in which they work" (Brewer and Selden, 1998: 416). Since the survey data were generated prior to the authors' study, the authors created indexes and variables of study around the preexisting structure of the original data. Brewer and Selden were interested in establishing differences between employees who witnessed illegal activity and reported the violation and those choosing not to report such a violation as evidence of PSM. The authors found significant differences on the variables of job security and regard for the public interest. In other words, whistleblowers place a lower value on job security and a higher value on the public interest than do nonreporting employees. Furthermore, whistleblowers are "higher performers and achievers, and they report higher levels of job commitment and job satisfaction" (Brewer and Selden, 1998: 431).

In a study of state ethics legislation, Goodman, Holp, and Ludwig (1996) examine such legislation in forty-three states. In addition to content analysis of state legislation, the authors also employ census data and data concerning state legislatures. The results suggest wide variation across states in terms of the adoption of ethics legislation. Among variables found to be insignificant in explaining such variation are level of institutionalization and state political culture. The authors conclude that "ethics legislation is a function of an ethics scandal process" (Goodman et al., 1996: 55).

Perhaps the most interesting body of data on ethics in government is compiled information on charges against and convictions of public officials for the violation of ethics laws. Holbrook and Meier (1993) conducted a study of corruption in American state governments. They define corruption narrowly as illegal activities for private gain. Their measure of corruption was the number of public officials in each state who were convicted in the federal courts of violating public corruption laws per one hundred state elected officials over a ten year period. They took this measure of convictions to be a good surrogate for the level of political corruption in a state. Using this measure as a dependent variable they tested the influence of variables such as education levels, crime rates, immigration rates, and percent of population that was urban. They found that urbanization does result in greater political corruption while greater education and immigration reduces corruption. They then tested the effects of a number of political variables on levels of political corruption and found that higher levels of party competition were a deterrent to corruption. Several measures of bureaucracy were also tested and it was found that the number of public employees and the number of gambling arrests were positively correlated with political corruption.

Most interesting in the Holbrook-Meier study is the discovery of the use of partisan and racial targeting in the prosecution of political corruption. There is no evidence that in the Carter years federal prosecutors targeted Republican states for the prosecution of possible political corruption cases. But there is statistically significant evidence that in the Reagan years the prosecution of corrupt officials was more intense in Democratic than in Republican states. In both the Carter and Reagan years, black public officials were prosecuted at a significantly higher rate than white public officials.

Holbrook and Meier found little relationship between measures of the quantity and quality of state public administration and the levels of political corruption.

The advantages of the data approach to research in administrative ethics are precision, scientific objectivity, and replicability. The disadvantages have to do with what the data do and do not represent. For example, in the Holbrook and Meier study all those convicted of violating corruption laws were lumped together in the dependent variable. We are especially interested in the difference in the corruption levels of civil servants, elected officials, and politically appointed officials, assuming that there are important differences among these different kinds of public officials. Unfortunately, the data are not disaggregated in this way. The researcher is often at the mercy of those who collect and compile the data.

E. Case Studies

Probably the most venerable methodology in social science approaches to administrative ethics is the case study. The initial case book in public policy and administration, edited by Harold Stein, was published in 1948 and included three cases on responsibility. The literature of public administration is now rich with cases, many of them on issues associated with ethics. Richard Stillman's text *Public Administration: Concepts and Cases* (1992) includes many of the best known case studies in the field. More particularly to the point is the book edited by Amy Gutmann and Dennis Thompson, *Ethics and Politics: Cases and Comments* (1984). It includes more than a dozen cases, many dealing with the most interesting ethical challenges of the day, such as the decision to use the atomic bomb, the safety of nuclear reactors, whether the public should pay for kidney dialysis, and whether there should be public spending on abortion.

In the case study methodology it is assumed that the scholar is objective. Because of this, case studies are written in a relatively straightforward fashion, after extensive research, and often with elaborate footnoting. Generally it is not acceptable to consciously introduce the bias or perspective of the researcher into the case report. The cases read, then, like a mixture of history and storytelling without embellishment. Because the subjects of the cases are almost always intrinsically interesting, the cases tend also to be interesting. They are not interesting because they include, at least in a direct way, perspective or extensive interpretation; this is left to the reader.

Although case studies are certainly not the quantitative analysis of data or the compilation of information from questionnaires or experiments, there is still an emphasis on facts, objectively, and the canons of positivist social science. Researchers who use this methodology insist on the reliability and accuracy of their cases.

The strength of the case study method is the richness of detail and the capacity of words to convey important connections between what happened and why it happened. To the reader, cases are certainly the most interesting form of research in administrative ethics. There are three chief weaknesses of the case method. First, the cases have a relatively short shelf life. The selling of the government aluminum plants after World War II was very interesting at the time. It is not interesting today. On the other hand, cases on the Challenger space accident and on the use of aborted fetal tissue in human research is very interesting now. Second, cases are unique, free-standing pieces of scholarship which are difficult to tie together for the purpose of testing or demonstrating a theory. Even when that is done there are questions as to why particular cases were selected. Finally, there are always problems with the presumed objectivity of the scholar in the researching and the writing of the case. No two scholars would report a case in exactly the same way. The replication of cases is nearly impossible.

James L. Perry (1993) recently completed an innovative use of the case methodology in his study of whistleblowing in federal government agencies. In his research the case is really an abbreviated summary with just the bare details such as the position of the whistleblower, the nature of the claim, whether there were reprisals, how long the case went on, and how the matter was resolved. He studied only those cases that were legitimate or for which there was some evidence of the veracity of the claim. these constituted fewer than half the claims. In the substantiated claims cases, in each category there is an N of over 100. He found most whistleblowers to be at the lower, non-managerial levels of government. Only one-third of them experienced reprisals, but one-third were anonymous, having blown the whistle over the telephone. Of those who were not anonymous there was a considerably higher level of reprisal. Two-thirds of the cases were resolved within a year. Based on this research, Perry finds that "whistleblowing, under existing institutional rules, has a very limited role to play in correcting specific abuses and promoting organizational change" (1993:22).

In a study of the Ethics in Government Reform Act of 1989, Roberts and Doss (1992) present a review of incremental changes in ethics controls in the federal government, including non-quid-pro-quo transfers of things of value, official acts prohibitions, supplementation-of-salary prohibitions, and interested-source prohibitions. Implementation of such reforms produced a complex web of regulations which "provide a striking example of how irrationally complex federal gift-acceptance regulations has become in the name of protecting public confidence in the integrity of government" (Roberts and Doss, 1992:266). In addition, Roberts and Doss found that President Bush's goal of "making standards . . . equitable across the three branches of the Federal Government" was not accomplished (1992:267). Congress, the Office of Government Ethics, and the judiciary all instituted disparate policies.

In conclusion, Roberts and Doss argue that the reliance on external controls has not improved public trust in public integrity. They assert: "Modern conflict-of-interest regulation, consequently, has evolved into a high stakes political game in which the participants understand the symbolic value of the restraints far exceeds their value as tools to actually rebuild public confidence in government" (Roberts and Doss, 1992:268).

Leazes (1997) utilizes a case study of an unnamed child welfare services agency to examine the privatization issue. The case examines the relationship between a public agency and the nonprofit contractor. The relationship is mediated by a child advocate officer who eventually sued the agency for its contracting. Leazes (1997) notes that "the crux of the legal issue brought by the [child advocate] was whether the state department held the private agency to a statutory requirement to report to state investigators within 24 hours all complaints of physical, sexual, or other abuse of children in a private agency's care" (401). Family court contended that the agency could not delegate the authority to interpret statutory law to a nonprofit contracting organization. Eventually, the nonprofit organization was closed. Leazes states, "The case demonstrates how public accountability can be diminished in a world where government arranges a service, but implementation is left in private hands" (405). The author found that the agency and the nonprofit organization seemed resistant to public control. Leazes concludes that "public accountability in democratic public administration must be ensured and not left passively in the hands of private administrators" (407).

Although this survey of methodological approaches to research on administrative ethics has treated each method as separate and unique, it is often the case that research is multimethodological. Several advocates of the multimethods approach (Webb et al., 1966; Jick, 1979) suggest that theoretical confidence in particular findings grow when such findings are demonstrated using more than one method. The most common combination of methods involves the use together and in a single study of self-administered questionnaires, interviews, and already available data. It is also standard to use printed or published materials and extensive interviews in the preparation of case studies.

The next section of this chapter will be a consideration of post-positivist ethics research.

III. POST-POSITIVIST RESEARCH APPROACHES TO ADMINISTRATIVE ETHICS

As indicated above, post-positivist approaches to research in administrative ethics are both much older and newer than positivist-rationalist-empirical approaches. These two approaches also have different philosophical bases. Following Harmon and Mayer (1986), these two differing philosophies of social science are "objectivist" and "subjectivist." The positivist-rationalist-empirical family of research of administrative ethics is objectivist. The post-positivist approach is subjectivist. The differences have to do with contrasting views of epistemology, the theory of knowledge, and what should count as knowledge. The objectivist perspective is that "the social world external to individual cognition is a real world made up of hard, tangible and relatively immutable structures. Whether or not we label and perceive these structures . . . they still exist as empirical entities" (Burrell and Morgan, 1979:4). In the subjectivist perspective, social structures (such as laws, rules, organizations, governments) "do not exist independent of human consciousness" (Harmon and Mayer, 1986:287). In this view "there is no objective truth 'out there' waiting to be discovered. Rather all 'reality' is socially constructed" (Kelly and Maynard-Moody, 1993:5).

In terms of methodology the objectivists base "research on systematic protocol and technique. It is epitomized in the approach and methods employed in the natural sciences, which focus upon the process of testing hypotheses in accordance with the canons of scientific rigor. It is preoccupied with the construction of scientific tests and the use of quantitative techniques for the analysis of data" (Burrell and Morgan, 1979:6–7). On the other hand, the subjective methodological approach "emphasizes a deeper understanding of social experience through the subjective frames of reference of the research subjects themselves. This . . . does not necessarily preclude a later interest in generalization. [It] 'stresses the importance of letting one's subject unfold its nature and characteristics during the process of investigation'" (Harmon and Mayer, 1986:290; Burrell and Morgan, 1979: 6–7).

The subjective perspective rejects the possibility of a value-free social science and argues instead for a social science which is value-centered. Because values are at the core of ethics, this difference in research approaches is especially important. To a post-positivist all analysis is interpretation, not an historical objective observation of the facts. Indeed facts and values (logical positivism), for the post-positivist, are not discernable. What we call values change the interpretation of observations and thus what we call facts reflect our values. The facts that positivist inquiry report, in other words, 'are inevitable artifacts of particular conceptual schemes and theoretical presuppositions' '' (Kelly and Maynard-Moody 1993: 7; Jennings, 1987:1439).

Post-positivist or subjective research methods in the study of administrative ethics include history, naturalistic inquiry, and stories. Unlike the objective study of administrative ethics which tends to focus on opinions, attitudes, and perspectives on ethics, the post-positivist approach tends to consider actual ethical behavior. Because that behavior is often associated with an actual event or incident, the purpose of the research is to describe the event and to account for or explain why it occurred and why administrative behavior was or was not ethical. This research is almost always narrative, using words as the symbols to describe events or behavior. In positivist research numbers are often used as symbols to represent reality.

A. History

History differs from case studies in that the historical researcher is expected not only to describe events but to account for why they happened. In addition the historian, and particularly the biographical historian, is expected to develop the characters of those studied and to account for their behavior. History is both fact and fact interpretation. Its great strength is the capacity to place the reader in context and to understand individual personalities, the interaction of personalities, the circumstances and events that influenced behavior, and most of all behavior. History explains directly and in detail matters of ethical behavior, unlike many of the other methodologies which are better suited to studying attitudes, opinions, and other surrogates of behavior.

Some of the best examples of the study of administrative ethics as history come in the form of biography. Robert A. Caro's detailed studies of Robert Moses (1974) and Lyndon Johnson (1982, 1990) are extraordinary examples of the richness of detail and context and the development of personality. These studies are essentially about the Machiavellian argument that "a great man cannot be a good man." Caro's work is renowned for being critical of the ethics of his subjects. An example of the opposite in history/biography is David McCullough's study of Harry Truman (1992), a tribute especially to Truman's honesty, integrity, and ethics. Another approach to ethics that uses biography is the so-called exemplars technique. With this approach, administrators with reputations for high ethics are selected in advance, studied, and presented to readers as examples of the best in ethics (Cooper and Wright, 1992).

The single best accounting of great ethical questions in the context of history is found in Richard E. Neustadt and Ernest R. May's *Thinking In Time: The Uses of History for Decision-Makers* (1986). Virtually every major American national policy issue of the middle- to late-twentieth century is placed in historical context. The authors' analyses of the Cuban Missile Crisis, the wars in Korea and Vietnam, and the Bay of Pigs incident as both policy and ethical events are extraordinary. They provide an exciting contextual examination of the ethics of many of the major policy leaders of that era: Lyndon Johnson,

Leonid Brezhnev, Martin Luther King, Malcolm X, Helmut Schmidt, Jimmy Carter, Harold Macmillan, Harry Truman, John Kennedy, Dwight Eisenhower, George Marshall, Frances Perkins, and Mary Anderson.

B. Naturalistic Inquiry or Ethnography

The naturalistic inquiry or ethnographic (descriptive anthropology) approach to social science methodology is the ultimate in post-positivist philosophy (Lincoln and Guba, 1985). This approach discounts the importance of generalizations and the determination of causality and it holds that the research attributes of being objective and value-free are not just impossible, they are undesirable. The requirements of this methodology are that the researcher not be outside the organization but inside, that values be specified and defended, that it is critical to establish trust between the researchers and the subjects, and that the reality constructed by the researcher in describing phenomena be less concerned with assumptions of causality and more concerned with the "mutual simultaneous shaping" of events.

Perhaps the best modern example of this methodology is found in *Habits of the Heart: Individualism and Commitment in American Life* by Robert Bellah et al. (1985). In their study they formed a cohesive and highly interactive research team that engaged in "active interviews" with a limited number of subjects. The researchers came to know the subjects well enough (and vice versa) to feel capable of not just reporting their words but also of interpreting their meaning. They were interested in the development of social theory and in determining the mores, consciousness, culture, and daily practices of life which constitute the "habits of the heart" of Americans. They found Americans to be separated and fragmented, individualistic, engaged in the pursuit of personal ambition and consumerism. Yet they did not find their lives to be satisfactory—a poverty of affluence. They seek a greater meaning to life in education and self-cultivation. Americans, according to Bellah and associates, have not been able to reconstruct the sense of community and common good that characterized the early settlers of this land. In broad terms they found an individual and selfish ethic rather than a community or common ethic. The report of these researchers is a mix of history, the humanities (especially literature), the words of their subjects, interpretations of those words and their likely meanings, and all of this in the context of what they call "social science as public philosophy." In this methodology the researcher takes responsibility not only for an accurate representation of reality but also for the values and issues of society. To Bellah et al., the social scientist has a responsibility to accurately describe society and also to improve society.

Another approach to naturalistic inquiry is the participant-observer. Patrick Dobel served as an appointed, unpaid member of a county ethics board. He is also a research scholar in the field of administration and ethics. Dobel provides a detailed and somewhat disheartening account of the use of ethics as a political weapon (1993). He points out that ethics and the adoption of ethics codes may have broad public support but no specific constituency or supporting interest group. Political interest in ethics is not driven by commitment to principles of ethics but by cycles of scandal and corruption. The same is true of the interest in ethics shown by the media.

By the use of naturalistic inquiry, the researcher does not worry about intervening in ongoing administrative/political processes or about being unobtrusive. This methodology is suited to observing, describing, and evaluating behavior. In order to be effective, this form of research requires high levels of trust between the observed and the observer/

participant. Perhaps equally important, it requires trust between the researcher and those reading the results of the research.

C. Stories

The stories methodology in post-positivist research is associated with the "sense-making" as opposed to the logical positivist decision-making approach to organizations (Weick, 1979; Harmon and Meyer, 1986; Maynard-Moody and Kelly, 1992). In this approach, both decisions and policy are defined not as rational actions but as after-the-fact interpretations (Lynn, 1987), stories (Stone, 1988), and arguments (Dunn, 1982). Kelly and Maynard-Moody (1993: 1) suggest that "policies themselves are largely symbolic, a way to give voice to latent public concerns: 'rather than responding to preexisting public wants, the art of policy making has lain primarily in giving voice to those half-articulated fears and hopes, and embodying them in convincing stories about their sources and the choices they represent" (Reich, 1987).

A good example of the stories approach to methodology comes from John Van Maanen (1978: 297) and his study of how young policemen are socialized.

> The novice's overwhelming eagerness to hear what police work is really like results in literally hours upon hours of war stories . . . told at the discretion of many instructors. . . . By observing and listening closely to police stories and styles, the individual is exposed to a partial organizational history which details certain personalities, past events, places, and implied relationships which the recruit is eventually expected to learn, and it is largely through war stories that the department's history is conveyed.

This process of learning and socialization continues in the early career of the policeman. "By watching, listening, and mimicking," (Van Maanen, 1978: 298) "the new policeman learns how to handle the challenges of police work: drunks, danger, the courts, the hierarchy, ambiguity" (Palumbo and Maynard-Moody, 1991: 89). Organizational stories are probably as influential as any other single factor in determining individual conduct in the organization. They combine facts, values, myths, legends, history, and useful rules-of-thumb.

The research of Steven Maynard-Moody and Marisa Kelly on stories is especially relevant to the subject of administrative ethics (1992). Their subject is the stories public managers tell about relations between civil servants or career bureaucrats and elected officials such as state legislators, mayors, or governors. In these stories "elected officials are generally negative: they are always ready to help powerful constituents but are portrayed more often as corrupt than responsive. Elected officials are often rude and self-important: they assume that government workers are hired to do their bidding" (Maynard-Moody and Kelly, 1992: 30). In these stories career civil servants are "shown as rational, diligent, expert, and concerned about the public and the proper implementation of policy. These stories describe lower-level officials as far removed from legislative politics, relying on their supervisors to preserve their independence" (Maynard-Moody and Kelly, 1992: 30).

Certainly these stories are self-serving. It is likely that stories told by elected officials would negatively characterize career bureaucrats. Still, the stories are generally believed and are often used as guides for behavior.

In the Maynard-Moody and Kelly research (1992:31) there were five stories about whistleblowing. "The singular message in these stories for would-be whistleblowers is 'don't.' Not only do supervisors demand compliance and punish dissent, but co-workers ostracize colleagues who pass information on to the press or elected officials.'' There is considerable congruence between these findings, based on stories, and the findings of other research on whistleblowing using other methodologies (Perry, 1993; Near and Miceli, 1986; Graham, 1986).

Stories are especially valuable as windows on organizational culture and bureaucratic behavior. Although they are stylized, exaggerated, and self-serving, stories enable the researcher to understand the especially difficult problem of how attitudes and beliefs affect behavior and how behavior affects attitudes and beliefs. This is the process of sense-making. For the student of administrative ethics, stories are especially informative on issues of group conformity versus doing what is right.

The post-positivist research approach to administrative ethics, with its accompanying epistemology and methodology, is not as well developed and accepted, particularly in academic settings, as is the positivist-rationalist-empirical perspective. It is growing in importance primarily because what it lacks in scientific rigor is more than compensated for by its capacity to illuminate the actual behavior of administrators.

IV. RESEARCH AND ADMINISTRATIVE ETHICS: SOME CONCLUSIONS

This chapter states at the beginning that ethics is a world of abstractions, philosophy, and values while administration is a world of specificity, application, and practice. Research was suggested as one way to bring ethics to practice and practice to ethics. It is by research that knowledge of ethical issues, attitudes toward ethics, and ethics behavior is developed. Much of this chapter has been devoted to developing the alternative theoretical premises of research and the descriptions of different research methods in administrative ethics. The remainder of this chapter will address the subject of what we need to know in administrative ethics.

What we need to know in administrative ethics is treated in four categories: knowledge of values, standards, context, and behavior. Table 1 is a summary of these categories of knowledge in terms of the capacity of the various research methodologies described in the earlier parts of this chapter to facilitate knowledge development.

A. Values

Values are any objects or qualities desirable as means or ends themselves, such as life, justice, equality, honesty, efficiency, and freedom. Values can be individual, group, community, conflicting, in hierarchies, or the objects of ambivalence or ambiguity. Values are beliefs, points of view, or attitudes. The most useful research methods by which to build a knowledge of values are surveys, interviews, history, and ethnography. As was described in earlier sections of this chapter, there is a considerable literature on the values of particular individuals such as city managers, legislators, or police officers. Less is known about the ''values'' of organizations; one cannot interview an organization. Case studies such as Herbert Kaufman's *Forest Ranger* (1960) do, however, effectively describe the values or culture of the U.S. Forest Service. Surveys and interviews are the most useful tools to assess individual values but case studies, histories, and ethnographies are the best ways

Table 1   The Most Useful Research Methods for Particular
Categories of Knowledge in Administrative Ethics

Methods used in research	Values	Standards	Context	Behavior
Positivist				
Surveys	+	+		
Experiments		+		+
Interviews	+			
Data		+	+	
Cases		+	+	
Post-positivist				
History	+	+	+	+
Naturalistic inquiry or ethnography	+		+	+
Stories			+	+

to study organizational values. When individual and organizational values are studied together, the researcher can measure value congruence.

B. Standards or Norms

Standards and norms are defined as principles of right action binding upon members of a group and serving to guide, control, or regulate proper and acceptable behavior. Standards and norms are the codification of group, organizational, community, or governmental values. Laws, regulations, codes of ethics, and rules are typical examples of standards and norms. Passing laws and making rules is probably the most common way for governments to deal with ethical problems. In recent years the Council on Governmental Ethics Laws has been very active in organizing and comparing ethics laws and regulations particularly for state and local government. There also has been extensive study of professional and governmental codes of ethics (Lewis, 1991). Surveys, documentary and historical research, and case studies have been the methods of choice for those interested in ethical standards and norms. Many governmental laws, policies, and practices were established, particularly in the Progressive era, to reduce government corruption (Frederickson, 1993). These laws and policies include stringent purchasing and contracting requirements, auditing requirements, conflict of interest prohibitions, open meetings laws, sunshine laws, and so on. Although state and local governments vary in their adoption of such laws and regulations, there has been very little research comparing jurisdictions with such requirements to those without such requirements so as to determine if such requirements in fact result in more ethical behavior (Stark, 1993). There is some evidence that there is increased corruption where such laws and regulations are not in place (Henriques, 1986; Mitchell, 1999).

The modern organizational approach to ethics could be best described as enforcement. Enforcement agencies and offices such as inspectors general, agency designated ethics officers, or the use of personal and family disclosure forms are now widely in use. This presents an opportunity for researchers, especially those using multimethodological approaches, to compare the effectiveness of laws and regulations designed to prevent corruption to offices, agencies, and policies. Paul Light's study of federal inspectors general comes the closest (1993).

C. Context

Ethical standards and behavior are always in context and context is often a powerful determinant of behavior. Context is best researched by the use of case studies, histories, stories, and ethnographies. Because contexts are unique, comparison is made difficult. Still, in the broad sense, contexts such as business/government or political/administrative are useful ways to compare differences in values, standards, and behavior. The comparative treatment of the Jews by the Danish and German career civil services is a case in point (Frederickson and Hart, 1985).

Contextual variables are often used in quantitative research to control for factors such as urban/rural or male/female. These are useful and sometimes significant determinants of outcomes.

Context is one of the most interesting factors in administrative ethics research because it gives texture, color, and depth to individuals and events. For students of ethics the knowledgeable treatment of context can bring an ethical issue or event to life.

D. Behavior

It is a paradox that research on ethics is more informing on matters of ethical values, standards, and contexts than on administrative behavior. Although the study of administrative behavior is the real reason to study ethics, it is also the most difficult part of ethics to research, to measure, and to explain. Of the four categories of knowledge of administrative ethics, the one we know the least about is behavior. This is in part because the most popular research methodologies are positivist and these methodologies are the least effective in researching behavior.

Post-positivist methods plus case studies and experimentation hold considerable promise. The biggest opportunities in ethics research have to do with behavior. This suggests that the methodological education of those who would do research in administrative ethics should include exposure to the techniques of ethnography, case studies, history, and experimentation.

REFERENCES

Aldag, R.J. and Jackson, D.W. (1977). Assessment of Attitudes Toward Social Responsibilities. *Journal of Business Administration*, 8: 65–80.

Bellah, R.N., Madsen, R., Sullivan, W.M., Seidler, A., and Tipton, S.M. (1985). *Habits of the Heart: Individualism and Commitment in American Life*. Berkeley: University of California Press.

Blasi, A. (1980). Bridging Moral Cognition and Moral Action. *Psychological Bulletin*, 88: 1–45.

Bowman, J.L. (ed.) (1991). *Ethical Frontiers in Public Management: Seeking New Strategies for Resolving Ethical Dilemmas*. San Francisco: Jossey-Bass.

Bowman, J.B. and Williams, R.L. (1997). Ethics in Government: From a Winter of Despair to a Spring of Hope. *Public Administration Review*, 57: 517–526.

Brewer, G.A. and Selden, S.C. (1998). Whistle Blowers in the Federal Civil Service: New Evidence of the Public Service Ethic. *Journal of Public Administration Research and Theory*, 8: 413–439.

Burrell, G. and Morgan, G. (1979). *Sociological Paradigms and Organizational Analysis*. London and Portsmouth, NH: Heinemann.

Caro, R.A. (1974). *The Power Broker: Robert Moses and the Fall of New York*. New York: Alfred A. Knopf.

Caro, R.A. (1982). *The Years of Lyndon Johnson: The Path to Power*. New York: Alfred A. Knopf.

Caro, R.A. (1990). *The Years of Lyndon Johnson: Means of Ascent*. New York: Alfred A. Knopf.

Cooper, T.L. (1990). *The Responsible Administrator: An Approach to Ethics for the Administrative Role* (3rd ed.). San Francisco: Jossey-Bass.

Cooper, T.L. (1991). Summary and Synthesis. Conference on the Study of Government Ethics: Park City, UT, June 12–15.

Cooper, T.L. and Wright, N.D. (1992). *Exemplary Public Administrators: Character and Leadership in Government*. San Francisco: Jossey-Bass.

Denhardt, K.G. (1988). *The Ethics of Public Service: Resolving Moral Dilemmas in Public Organizations*. New York: Greenwood Press.

Dobel, J.P. (1993). The Realpolitik of Ethics Codes: An Implementation Approach to Public Ethics. In *Ethics and Public Administration* (H.G. Frederickson, ed.), 158–176. Armonk, NY: M.E. Sharpe.

Dunn, W.N. (1982). Reforms as Arguments. *Knowledge: Creation, Utilization, Diffusion*, 3: 293–326.

England, G.W. (1975). Personal Value Systems of American Managers. *Academy of Management Journal*, 10: 53–68.

Frederickson, H.G. (1993). *Ethics and Public Administration*. Armonk, NY: M.E Sharpe, Inc.

Frederickson, H.G. and Hart, D.K. (1985). The Public Service and the Patriotism of Benevolence. *Public Administration Review*, 45: 547–555.

Gatewood, R.D. and Carroll, A.B. (1991). Assessment of Ethical Performance of Organizational Members: A Conceptual Framework. *Academy of Management Review*, 16: 667–690.

Goodman, M.R., Holp, T.J., and Ludwig, K.M. (1996). Understanding State Legislative Ethics Reform: The Importance of Political and Institutional Culture. *Public Integrity Annual*, 1: 51–57.

Goss, R.P. (1996). A Distinct Public Administration Ethics? *Journal of Public Administration Research and Theory*, 6: 573–597.

Graham, J.W. (1986). Principled Organizational Dissent: A Theoretical Essay. *Research in Organizational Behavior*, 8: 1–52.

Gutman, A. and Thompson, D. (1984). *Ethics and Politics: Cases and Comments*. Chicago: Nelson-Hall Publishers.

Haney, C., Banks, W., and Zimbardo, P. (1973). Interpersonal Dynamics in a Simulated Prison. *International Journal of Criminology and Penology*, 1: 69–97.

Harmon, M.M. and Mayer, R.T. (1986). *Organization Theory for Public Administration*. Boston: Little, Brown.

Henriques, D.B. (1986). *The Machinery of Greed: Public Authority Abuse and What to do About It*. Lexington, MA: Lexington Books.

Hochschild, J.L. (1981). *What's Fair: American Beliefs About Distributive Justice*. Cambridge, MA: Harvard University Press.

Holbrook, T.M. and Meier, K.J. (1993). Politics, Bureaucracy and Political Corruption: A Comparative State Analysis. In *Ethics and Public Administration* (H.G. Frederickson, ed.), 28–51. Armonk, NY: M.E. Sharpe.

Jennings, B. (1987). Interpretation and the Practice of Policy Analysis. In *Confronting Values in Policy Analysis: The Politics of Criteria* (F. Fisher and J. Forester, eds.), 128–152. Newbury Park, CA: Sage Publications.

Jick, T.D. (1979). Mixing Qualitative and Quantitative Methods: Triangulation in Action. *Administrative Science Quarterly*, 24: 602–611.

Jos, P.E. (1993). Empirical Corruption Research: Beside the (Moral) Point? *Journal of Public Administration Research and Theory*, 3: 359–376.

Joseph, L.B. (1988). Attitudes of Community and Civic Leaders Toward Political Corruption. A Report to the Chicago Ethics Project. Chicago: MetroEthics Coalition.

Kaufman, H. (1960). *The Forest Ranger: A Study in Administrative Behavior*. Baltimore: Johns Hopkins Press.

Kelly, M. and Maynard-Moody, S. (1993). Policy Analysis in the Post-Positivist Era: Engaging Stakeholders in Evaluating the Economic Development District Program. *Public Administration Review*, 53: 135–142.

Leazes, F.J., Jr. (1997). Public Accountability: Is It a Private Responsibility? *Administration and Society*, 29: 395–411.

Lewis, C.L. (1991). *The Ethics Challenge in Public Service*. San Francisco: Jossey-Bass.

Light, P.C. (1993). Federal Ethics Controls: The Role of Inspector General. In *Ethics and Public Administration* (H.G. Frederickson, ed.), 100–120. Armonk, NY: M.E. Sharpe.

Lincoln, Y. and Guba, E.G. (1985). *Naturalistic Inquiry*. Beverly Hills, CA: Sage Publications.

Liu, T.T. and Cooper, T.L. (1997). Values in Flux: Administrative Ethics and the Hong Kong Public Servant. *Administration and Society*, 29: 301–324.

Lynn, L.E. (1987). Managing Public Policy. Boston: Little, Brown.

Malek, K.L. (1993). Public Attitudes Toward Corruption: Twenty-Five Years of Research. In *Ethics and Public Administration* (H.G. Frederickson, ed.). Armonk, NY: M.E. Sharpe.

Maynard-Moody, S. and Kelly, M. (1992). Stories Public Managers Tell About Elected Officials: Making Sense of the Defunct Dichotomy. In *Public Management Theory*, (B. Bozeman, ed.). San Francisco: Jossey-Bass.

McCullough, D. (1992). *Truman*. New York: Simon and Schuster.

Menzel, D.C. (1993). The Ethics Factor in Local Government: An Empirical Analysis. In *Ethics and Public Administration* (H.G. Frederickson, ed.). 191–204. Armonk, NY: M.E. Sharpe.

Milgram, S. (1965). Some Conditions of Obedience and Disobedience to Authority. *Human Relations*, 18: 57–76.

Milgram, S. (1974). *Obedience to Authority*. New York: Harpers.

Mitchell, J. (1999). *The American Experiment with Government Corporations*. Armonk, NY: M.E. Sharpe.

Morgan, D.F. and Kass, H.D. (1993). The American Odyssey of the Career Public Service: The Ethical Crisis of Role Reversal. In *Ethics and Public Administration* (H.G. Frederickson, ed.), 177–190. Armonk, NY: M.E. Sharpe.

Near, J.P. and Miceli, M.P. (1986). Whistle-blowers in Organizations: Dissidents of Reformers? *Research in Organizational Behavior*, 9: 321–368.

Neustadt, R.E. and May, E.R. (1986). *Thinking in Time: The Uses of History for Decision-Makers*. New York: The Free Press.

Overman, S.E. and Foss, L. (1993). Professional Ethics: An Empirical Test for the "Separatist Theses." In *Ethics and Public Administration* (H.G. Frederickson, ed.), 121–135. Armonk, NY: M.E. Sharpe.

Palumbo, D. and Maynard-Moody, S. (1991). *Contemporary Public Administration*. New York: Longman.

Perry, J.L. (1993). Whistleblowing, Organizational Performance, and Organizational Control. In *Ethics and Public Administration* (H.G. Frederickson, ed.), 79–99. Armonk, NY: M.E. Sharpe.

Peters, J.G. and Welch, S. (1978). Political Corruption in America: A Search for Definitions and a Theory. *American Political Science Review*, 72: 974–984.

Posner, B.Z. and Schmidt, W.H. (1984). Values and the American Manager: An Update. *California Management Review*, 26: 202–216.

Posner, B.Z. and Schmidt, W.H. (1992). Values and the American Manager: An Update, (Updated). *California Management Review*, 34: 80–94.

Reich, R.B. (ed.) (1987). *The Power of Public Ideas*. Cambridge, MA: Ballinger.

Roberts, R.N. and Doss, M.T., Jr. (1992). Public Service and Private Hospitality: A Case Study in Federal Conflict of Interest Reform. *Public Administration Review*, 52: 260–269.

Rohr, J.A. (1986). *To Run a Constitution: The Legitimacy of the Administrative State*. Lawrence: University Press of Kansas.

Stark, A. (1993). Public Sector Conflict of Interest at the Federal Lavel in Canada and the U.S.: Differences in Understanding and Approach. In *Ethics and Public Administration* (H.G. Frederickson, ed.), 52–78. Armonk, NY: M.E. Sharpe.

Stein, H. (ed.) (1948). *Public Administration and Policy Development: A Case Book*. New York: Harcourt, Brace and Company.

Stewart, D.W. and Sprinthall, N.A. (1993). The Impact of Demographic, Professional and Organizational Variables and Domain on the Moral Reasoning of Public Administrators. In *Ethics and Public Administration* (H.G. Frederickson, ed.), 205–219. Armonk, NY: M.E. Sharpe.

Stewart, D.W., Sprinthall, N., and Siemienska, R. (1997). Ethical Reasoning in a Time of Revolution: A Study of Local Officials in Poland. *Public Administration Review*, 57: 445–453.

Stillman, R.J. (1992). *Public Administration: Concepts and Cases* (5th ed.). Boston: Houghton Mifflin Company.

Stone, D.A. (1988). *Policy Parados and Political Reason*. Glenview, IL: Scott, Foresman and Co.

Strait, P.B. (1996). Unethical Actions of Public Servants: A Voyeur's View. *Public Integrity Annual*, 1: 41–49.

Tamashiro, H., Secrest, D., and Brunk, G.G. (1993). Ethical Attitudes of Members of Congress and American Military Officers Toward War. In *Ethics and Public Administration* (H.G. Frederickson, ed.), 220–242. Armonk, NY: M.E. Sharpe.

Tyler, T.R. (1990). *Why People Obey the Law*. New Haven, CT: Yale University Press.

Van Maanen, J. (1978). Observations on the Making of a Policeman. In *Policing: A View from the Street* (P.K. Manning and J. Van Maanen, eds.). Santa Monica, CA: Goodyear Publishing Company.

Waldo, D. (1948). *The Administrative State*. New York: Ronald Press.

Webb, E.J., Campbell, D.T., Schwarts, R.D., and Schrest, L. (1966). *Unobtrusive Measures: Nonreactive Research in the Social Sciences*. Chicago: Rand McNally and Company.

Weick, K.E. (1979). *The Social Psychology of Organizing*, (2nd ed.). Reading, MA: Addisson-Wesley.

Wheeler, G.F. and Brady, F.N. (1998). Do Public Sector and Private Sector Personnel Have Different Ethical Dispositions: A Study of Two Sites. *Journal of Public Administration Research and Theory*, 8: 93–115.

White, R.D. (1999). Are Women More Ethical? Recent Findings on the Effects of Gender Upon Moral Development. *Journal of Public Administration Research and Theory*, 9: 459–471.

Wittmer, D. (1992). Ethical Sensitivity and Managerial Decision Making: An Experiment. *Journal of Public Administration Research and Theory*, 2: 443–462.

Wittmer, D. and Coursey, D. (1996). Ethical Work Climates: Comparing Top Managers in Public and Private Organizations. *Journal of Public Administration Research and Theory*, 6: 559–572.

3

Ethics Education in Public Administration and Affairs
Preparing Graduates for Workplace Moral Dilemmas

Diane E. Yoder
University of Southern California, Los Angeles, California

Kathryn G. Denhardt
University of Delaware, Newark, Delaware

I. INTRODUCTION

In the first edition of the *Handbook of Administrative Ethics,* Catron and Denhardt (1994) argue for "further progress in developing a shared understanding of the goals of ethics education, greater training opportunities for faculty interested in teaching ethics, and greater coverage and better coordination of ethics in the curriculum" (p. 60). In spite of those conclusions, Catron and Denhardt note that "the field of ethics education for public service [is] healthier and more vibrant today than it has been in decades" (1994, p. 60).

The same conclusions are still valid today. After examining the last eight years of work on ethics education in public administration/affairs, we find (1) general agreement on the importance and need for ethics education prevails in the field, although it has yet to be entrenched firmly in the curriculum; (2) that little consensus on the best type of substantive material or teaching methods exists; and (3) some research that documents successful teaching approaches and the effectiveness of ethics education. In other words, the more things change, the more they stay the same. As this chapter will show, ethics education in public administration/affairs is justified and increasing, and educators are experimenting with different teaching approaches. Yet, in spite of these advances, little proof exists that exposure to ethics in the graduate curriculum makes public administrators more adept at dealing with workplace moral dilemmas. Thus, the question remains: Does ethics education make a difference in the moral behavior or aptitude of public administration graduates?

The chapter begins with a brief review of the rise of ethics education in public administration programs, documents the current consensus in the field on the importance of ethics education, discusses teaching methods and programs, and reviews empirical work done in the past eight years. The chapter concludes with implications and challenges for the coming decade.

II. THE HISTORY OF ETHICS EDUCATION IN PUBLIC ADMINISTRATION AND AFFAIRS[1]

Coming to terms with ethics in professional education has been difficult for public administration. Part of the difficulty is the tenuous relationship public administration has with the concept of "profession." While public administration includes many professionals—physicians, engineers, accountants, lawyers or people who practice their given profession in an administrative and public capacity—the practice of public administration does not meet the usual profession standards of a unified theory and body of knowledge, an entrance exam that demonstrates that knowledge, and an enforceable code of ethics. Still, schools of public administration/affairs have offered graduate degrees since 1914 (Lilla, 1981).

Until the end of the 19th century, ethics was considered an integral curriculum component of institutions of higher education (IHE). As disciplines/academic fields specialized, including public administration, ethics was relegated to philosophy departments and schools of religion. Early public administration schools did not teach ethics formally; students were introduced to ethics via the prevalent democratic ethos in discussions of public administration. In fact, the study of public administration was seen as democratic *and* moral. This democratic ethos also was modeled in the leadership and scholarship of those teaching public administration. However, as scientific management and the rational-analytical tools of public policy laid claim to the public administration curriculum, the democratic ethos was overshadowed, if not replaced. The moral dimensions of public administration had, along with the ethical issues and moral questions subsumed within it, given way to economics, statistics, management, and policy analysis (Dwivedi, 1987; Lilla, 1981).

During the 1940s, however, "evidence suggests that a healthy and vital concern for administrative ethics and the democratic ethos of public administration remained" (Catron and Denhardt, 1994, p. 50). However, administrative ethics was again eclipsed by a focus on management, policy analysis, and rationality—the science of administration—in the 1950s. Science and technique replaced norms and values as the focus of public administration education, but during the mid-1960s, scholars began to see this change as a loss. Applied ethics courses found their way into the public administration curriculum a decade later, although many viewed such an approach to ethics as an extension of the rational-analytic tenor of the discipline. Lilla writes: "It is ironic that the ethics movement in public policy schools, which was born out of a reaction against economic and mathematical analysis, should adopt the same sort of scientistic approach to moral matters," (1981, p. 12).

Ethics education and the democratic ethos enjoyed a rebirth in the late 1960s and the 1970s. The new public administration sought to strike a balance between the analytic and normative dimensions of public administration, with a new focus on social equity (Frederickson, 1971). Frederickson charged that public administration/affairs programs should model the image of the public servant as an agent of change. Thus, during the 1970s, values like social equity and justice emerged as central in educating public administrators because organizational and institutional control mechanisms were viewed as unlikely to yield such outcomes (D. K. Hart, 1974; Harmon, 1974). Professional education with a normative element was viewed as the "first line of defense against unethical behavior" (Wakefield, 1976, p. 666). Curriculum change was slow and uncertain, however, so even as calls were heard to imbed ethics in the curriculum, the legacy of decades of neglect created a moral illiteracy in the field (Dwivedi, 1987). Studies in the late 1980s showed that most graduate programs were not systematically addressing ethics, and of those that were, confusion and disagreement about the goals of ethics and how ethics should be taught reigned (Dennis, 1987; Lee and Pugh, 1987).

In 1989, however, the National Association of Schools of Public Administration and Affairs[2] (NASPAA) largely settled the question of whether ethics should be taught in graduate public administration/affairs. During that year, a revised NASPAA curriculum standard went into effect, making it clear that coverage of ethics in the curriculum is essential. Standard 3.21 of NASPAA's curriculum guidelines that year says in part: "The common curriculum components shall *enhance the student's values, knowledge, and skills to act ethically* and effectively" (emphasis added). This standard was translated into a more explicit requirement in the language of the self-study report instructions used during the 1989–1991 period:[3]

> IV.C.3   Ethics in the Curriculum. Explain how the curriculum in general and specific courses in particular enhance the student's values, knowledge, and skills to act ethically: a. in the management of public and, as appropriate, third sector organizations; b. in the application of quantitative techniques of analysis; and c. with an understanding of the public policy and organizational environment.

Explicit language notwithstanding, only a small number of schools required ethics education at the close of the 1980s. Catron and Denhardt (1994) reviewed 39 self-study reports submitted to NASPAA during the 1989–1991 period and found "a significant increase in the number of courses," (p. 52). However, only 49 percent of schools offered an ethics course and only 18 percent of schools required one.

III.   ETHICS EDUCATION IN THE 1990s

The 1990s saw a general increase in the number of ethics courses taught in public administration/affairs programs. Menzel (1997a)[4] conducted a study of NASPAA-member schools granting masters of public administration degrees (MPAs) in 1995. His survey showed that:

> [E]vidence points to the fact that MPA programs moved steadily over the past 25 years toward the incorporation of ethics instruction and courses in their curriculum . . . about a dozen schools added ethics courses in the 1970s, with another 10 schools added to the list in the early and mid-1980s. . . . The adoption curve increased sharply in the late 1980s and 1990s. . . . By the mid-1990s, 78 NASPAA-member, MPA-degree-granting schools offered an ethics course (p. 225).

Interestingly, Menzel notes that no statistically significant correlation between organizational structure (i.e., a separate public administration/affairs school, department, or an institution that granted MPAs through its political science department) and ethics education was found (1997b). Menzel does not report on the respondents' reasons for why more ethics courses are offered, although he alludes to NASPAA's ethics standard. By 1997, NASPAA had adopted "mission driven" curriculum guidelines rather than "one size fits all'' guidelines. However, the guidelines still state that the ''common curriculum components shall enhance the student's values, knowledge, and skills to act ethically and effectively'' (now Standard 4.21), and the Self-Study Report Instructions continue to ask that schools specifically explain how the curriculum enhances ethical action.

We suggest that along with that standard, another impetus for the increase could be the swing back toward the democratic ethos and the normative functions of public administration. As well, other social trends may correlate with the increasing importance of ethics education in public administration/affairs. First, as Frederickson points out: ''Much of the normative and philosophical leadership of the governmental reform movement was in the universities, and so it is today with the ethics movement. Virtually every major university has an institute or center for ethics or human values'' (1993, p. 4). In other words, the increase in attention to ethics in public administration in the 1990s is simply a broader education phenomenon that follows contemporary social science. Snyder (1999) argues along the same line. She notes that changes in modern IHEs ''generally follow changes within larger society. Any particular 'moment of invention' within the history of American higher education actually developed as a product of a larger 'convergence of forces' within American politics and civil society'' (p. 1).

We argue that those changes in American politics and civil society tend to reflect the resurgence of ''family values,'' the acknowledgement of corruption in public service, and a growing distrust of public officials. However, some business scholars cite criticisms of teaching ethics in business schools that include dismissing ethics courses as a ''palliative response'' or ''knee-jerk reaction'' to business scandals (McDonald and Donleavy, 1995). The point is well taken and serves as a warning against thrusting ethics to the forefront of public administration because of real and/or perceived scandals in the profession at large.

Curriculum changes also reflect an awareness that the call to public service does not preclude what Adams and Balfour deem ''administrative evil'' (1998). Such evil is an inherent human condition that they characterize as ''those instances in which humans knowingly and deliberately inflict pain and suffering on other human beings'' (1998, p. xix). They also argue that some people can engage in evil acts without knowing they are doing anything at all. Thus, to prevent administrative evil, Adams and Balfour suggest that public administration ''develop and nurture a critical, reflexive attitude toward public institutions, the exercise of authority, and the culture at large'' (1998, p. xxix). They further argue for the reconstruction of public ethics:

> A public ethics for public administration would require that administrators be attentive
> to social and economic outcomes of public policy, as well as to their proper and faithful
> implementation. Public administrators could not ethically implement a policy that was
> overtly detrimental to the well being of any segment of the population (1998, p. 180).

We suggest that the cultivation of such an attitude, and the response to increasing distrust of public officials, can and should begin with ethics education of public administrators, as reflected in the increase in the number of ethics courses taught.

Although Menzel's data only cover MPA programs, other reviews of graduate degree programs and curricula in public administration/affairs show agreement on the need for ethics education and the lack of an adequate response to that need. The work of Brewer, et al. (1998) showed that ethics was not offered as a substantive field in doctoral programs, that no common core curriculum could be identified, and that philosophy was not one of the significant outside disciplines or fields that public administration students use. In a review of the professional doctorate in public administration (DPA), Meek and Johnson (1998) make no mention of ethics as being required in the DPA curriculum. This deficiency is punctuated by their argument that the DPA "must encompass, as an essential thread, an appreciation for the internalization of a quality of mind that can ask better questions and find better answers" (p. 58), referring to the "reflective practitioner."

Other researchers bemoan the same need. In his presidential address to the Association for Public Policy Analysis and Management (APPAM), Stokes argues that ethical analysis skills are among the top five skills needed in public administration today. He says students "need to match their commitment to public purpose with the ability to think clearly about the ethical dilemmas that can easily arise in a close, long-term relationship in which enormous resources are at stake" (1996, pp. 166–167). In identifying the needs of public policy programs, DeLeon and Steelman (1999) note that educators need to recognize the normative foundations of policy analysis, and hence require ethics training for public policy students. One of their concerns about public policy programs is the "neglect of ethics and values." They argue:

> Policy is inherently a normative practice, which is why ethics are central to the study of public policy. Only two of the top ten public policy programs reviewed (University of Georgia and Harvard) require an ethics course. We need to articulate and reinforce a basis of conduct for those who advocate on behalf of the public good. In doing so, we need to train our students to deal with the complexity of values and give them tools to assess and clarify values (DeLeon and Steelman 1999, p. 4).

Others have argued along the same vein, although less specifically. Sommers (1993) reflects generally on teaching virtues. She notes that "moral relativism" is stifling any ethical thinking or sensitivity among students. She says that the way ethics is currently taught in American IHEs reflects "an overemphasis on social policy questions" and ignores private morality. More specifically, in her presidential address to APPAM, Schall (1995) analogizes that public service is like Schön's "swamp." The swamp consists of the "important, complex, and messy problems that resist technical analysis" (p. 203). Her examples of such problems included achieving economic equity or social justice, dealing with racism, and other problems that resist the technical and rational rules and means of policy analysis and management. Schall notes that "reflective practice," the kind of skills learned in ethics training, is what students need to learn to deal with swamp problems.

Graduates of top public policy and administration graduate programs also recognize the essential nature of ethics education. In *The New Public Service*, Light (1999) reports on interviews with 1,000 people who graduated from these programs over the past two decades. Eighty-two percent of these graduates report that maintaining ethical standards had been very important to career success, yet only 48 percent felt that their graduate programs had been very helpful in teaching that skill. This gap of 34 percent was the largest gap in the list of 13 skills included in the study.

Merely identifying the *need* for ethics education begs the question: Although more schools now offer instruction in ethics, how many *require* an ethics course? Menzel's 1995 survey showed that only one of four schools offering an ethics course made it a requirement (1997a, 1997b). That is, of 134 schools that responded with usable questionnaires, 78 of them said their programs offered ethics courses, and 40 percent of respondents said they integrated ethics across the curriculum, yet only 25 percent *required* an ethics course. Menzel's study showed that larger rather than smaller programs were likely to offer ethics courses, although no correlation existed between size and requiring the ethics course. He also notes that NASPAA accreditation offered little motivation for programs to institute or require ethics courses (Menzel, 1997b).[5]

Some programs address ethics in introductory or core courses. For example, to review the content of introductory courses in MPA programs, Schachter (1993) contacted all of the NASPAA-listed institutions that award MPAs. She found that ethics was a "popular topic" like management, yet no coherence existed in the materials used to introduce ethics in such courses. Still, some scholars doubt that ethics has been firmly embedded in the public administration/affairs curriculum. Citing his own work with Menzel (c.f., Bowman and Menzel, 1998), Bowman (1998) argues "there is little evidence to suggest that faculty share an understanding of the significance of ethics in the curriculum" (p. 29). He continues:

> The curricular presence of ethics, then, is—at best—an uncertain one. It apparently has been marginalized by benign neglect and by an inferiority complex borne from an impoverished understanding of professionalism. Consequently, many students may have graduate school ideas about management but grade school notions of ethics. . . . [T]he expertise of the public administration professional with a master's degree largely consists of merely possessing technical skills (Bowman, 1998, p. 29).

Bowman even goes so far as to wonder "is the question whether ethics should be taught really 'largely settled'—or simply finessed?" (1998, p. 29). He is not the only scholar to ask such a question. Jackson (1993) reports that some critics wonder why ethics should be singled-out at all because ethics permeate every subject. Others doubt that ethics can be taught. For example, Killilea, Pasquerella, and Vocino (1995) ask if public administrators can "be trained to make decisions that are ethically correct?" (p. 19). They answer their own question:

> There is little doubt that ethics can be taught if we concern ourselves only with the issue of what is legal. . . . This education is important and factual but defines "ethics violations" simply in terms of not following objective laws and codes. Once we concede that ethics education has to extend beyond a concern for what is legal, we appear to be in the realm of moral development, indeed the realm of moral conversion. . . . It is our contention, however, that while the question of whose moral principles to follow is legitimate and essential, the question alone should not veto ethics education that goes beyond mere instruction of the law (1995, pp. 19–20).

The opposition to teaching ethics stems in part from a resistance to teach or imbue values. Although the historic mission of American IHEs included ethical training, Jennings, Nelson, and Parens (1994) argue:

> Much of [today's] faculty are on the "cultural left" and perceive the language of values . . . as the language of the "cultural right." Thus, even though the faculty embrace a set of values, they are wary of legitimating explicit values language, fearing thereby to give aid and comfort to ethical agendas they see as pernicious (1994, p. 11).

In what could be a counter to the critics who argue that it is wrong to instill values in students, Piper, Gentile, and Parks (1993) examine teaching values to business school students, arguing:

> Surely business education must be an enterprise of both the intellect and the spirit—
> an endeavor that engages one's character values, spurs one's imagination and sense

of meaning, and stimulates one's sense of responsibility and one's desire to lead and create (p. 4).

We can easily substitute "public administration" for "business" in the above quote. After reviewing three books on ethics and education in public administration/affairs, D. W. Hart (1999) argues that in spite of ethics education still being "under fire," practitioners, academics, and students all agree on the need for schools to teach ethics. He says that the problem is that "ethics education is adrift and we thus take our cues from contemporary ideology" (p. 72). He bemoans the lack of a shared moral base for ethics education: "Once again, there appears to be a yearning for a shared set of values," (p. 72).

Still, if we accept that teaching values may be an inherent or unavoidable part of a comprehensive ethics education, many critics argue that graduate school (and even college) is too late to educate students, who presumably range from their 20s–30s on average, about values. According to Piper, Gentile, and Parks, critics argue "that such students are totally formed and unchangeable" (1993, p. 5). Piper, Gentile, and Parks counter:

> We reject this assertion emphatically. These students are at a critical stage in the development of their perceptions about . . . leadership and the appropriate resolution of ethical dilemmas. . . . This is a period for inquiry and reflection; extended time is necessary to develop sufficient strength and sophistication to acknowledge the presence of ethical dilemmas, to imagine what could be, to recognize explicitly avoidable and unavoidable harms (p. 5).

Parks (1993) also argues the justification of ethics education in graduate schools:

> [Research] strongly suggests that moral development can continue into adulthood, and that particularly dramatic changes can occur in young adulthood in the context of professional school education. Surely adult moral and ethical development occurs in a variety of settings, both formal and informal, but there is now ample evidence that ethical consciousness and commitment can continue to undergo transformation at least throughout formal education. These findings fly in the face of a good deal of conventional conviction (p. 13).

We can say with some degree of confidence that ethics education can have a positive influence on the ethical awareness of individuals and on their moral reasoning and judgment, even in their 20s and 30s, so it should remain an important part of the curriculum. The task is to clarify the goals and best methods for teaching ethics, and then to see if those methods are making a difference in the ethical behavior of public administrators.

IV. CLARIFYING THE GOALS OF ETHICS EDUCATION

The goals for ethics education in public administration/affairs remain diverse and range from the general to the specific. For example, Farmer (1998) examines ethics education in public administration. He maintains that "the study of ethics requires being philosophical, rather than operating as if ethics were a mere matter of technique," (p. 34). He also warns against what he calls myopia in ethics education, noting that the inclination to teach narrow, straightforward approaches to ethics would diminish the benefit of students to handle larger moral dilemmas outside of school. He says:

> [A]dopting that approach lessens the real benefits that a more philosophical method can provide. To the extent that PA ethics ignores the philosophical and focuses too

much on seeking foundations or anchors like core values, the method is ethically short-sighted—and we have a deficiency that we can call "anchor-myopia" (1998, p. 33).

Jennings, Nelson, and Parens (1994) highlight other goals for ethics education: developing analytical skills, introducing ethical theory, developing moral reasoning, inculcating a narrow range of fundamental values, and cultivating character. In spite of what seems like a general agreement about the overall goals for ethics education (notwithstanding those who think ethics and values should not be taught at all), individual teachers vary in their goals for ethics education.

According to Dennis (1987) the most frequently stated goals of ethics education in public administration are: (a) to produce students who know how to make moral judgments (43%) and (b) to produce students who know how to make moral judgments *and* whose behavior is ethical (32%). Catron and Denhardt (1994) remind us that this type of ethics education is not only about what administrators should *not* do. They write: "Ethical behavior results not only from *knowing* what is right, but also from having the strength of character to *do* what is right" (p. 54, emphasis original).

Catron and Denhardt (1994) also note other goals that might be considered for ethics education. These include: building capacity to tolerate ambiguity and differences of opinion; conveying knowledge of democratic values and the obligations of public administrators operating in the framework of the American Constitution; developing practical understanding of the constraints on and expectations of administrators (e.g., knowledge of codes of ethics, conflict of interest statues, organizational norms and rules); developing skills in managing ethics by influencing organizational culture and bureaucratic norms; and modeling ethical conduct as a leader (see Denhardt, 1988).

Menzel's (1997b) study of ethics education underscores the wide variation in goals among ethics instructors surveyed. The top five goals for instructors (in order) included:

Developing an awareness of ethical issues and problems,
Fostering ethical conduct in public service,
Building analytical skills in ethical decisionmaking,
Cultivating an attitude of moral obligation and personal responsibility in public service, and
Stimulating moral imagination (1997b).

The goals were slightly different for *all* respondents in Menzel's survey, as seen in their top five (in order):

Fostering ethical conduct in public service,
Developing an awareness of ethical issues and problems,
Cultivating an attitude of moral obligation and personal responsibility,
Gaining greater knowledge of ethical standards in public administration, and
Building analytical skills in ethical decisionmaking (1997b).

Interestingly, both instructors *and* all respondents ranked becoming familiar with Western traditions in moral philosophy, acquiring knowledge of ethical codes, minimizing organizational corruption, and cultivating moral characters among the least important education goals (Menzel, 1997b).

This diversity in goals shows that a shared understanding of the goals of ethics education in public administration/affairs remains elusive. Indeed, part of the confusion stems in part from NASPAA's Standard—"the common curriculum components shall enhance the student's *values, knowledge, and skills* to act ethically" (emphasis added).

Catron and Denhardt (1988, 1994) offered clarification of this goal by transforming NASPAA's three key standards—values, knowledge, and skills—into action-oriented goal statements. They interpreted "knowledge" as an outcome of *education*, "skills" as a result of *training*, and "values" as an outcome *socialization*. Using these action statements, then, they offered the following ethics education goals in a statement endorsed by the Working Group on Ethics Education,[6] the Josephson Institute Government Ethics Center, the Professional Ethics Committee of the American Society for Public Administration, and the Board of the National Academy of Public Administration:

1.   Educate students in (a) the democratic values (liberty, equality, etc.) implicit and explicit in U.S. Constitutional history; (b) the role of government in dealing with conflicting social values; and (c) the ethical and philosophical underpinnings of public policy debates.

2.   Train students (a) to recognize and focus on ethical problems; (b) to develop and refine appropriate methods of moral reasoning; and (c) to be sensitive to the nuances and ambiguity of ethical situations.

3.   Socialize students (a) to appreciate public service as a noble calling and a public trust, deserving commitment to the highest standards of honor and personal integrity; (b) to appreciate the ethical dimension in decision making just as they appreciate the political, legal, and managerial dimensions; and (c) to accept the multiple and sometimes conflicting obligations of public service (Catron and Denhardt, 1988, p. 4).

Echoing the broader debate about whether values should be taught (also addressed in the previous section), Catron and Denhardt (1994) warn:

> The socialization goal perhaps causes the greatest misunderstanding and disagreement. Some people argue that ethics education cannot change the values or conduct of adults, while others view attempts to do so as indoctrination and therefore repugnant. But the goal in ethics education is not to be able to certify that students will behave ethically, nor to instill in them a new set of values. Rather, it is to model and reinforce professional norms and values, while attempting to refine and enhance the individual's powers of reflection and judgment (p. 55).

They warn that if moral foundations were not addressed and students were not taught to identify ethical dilemmas, then "new members to the profession will likely rely too heavily on values such as organizational loyalty, technical competence untempered by moral judgment, or passive obedience to authority" (Catron and Denhardt, 1994, p. 55). We add that if it is that kind of technical competence and organizational loyalty that are important for new administrators, then teaching decision techniques and ethical codes would suffice. However, in a profession where decisions have social justice, resource allocation, and other equity implications, public administrators must be armed with the ability to determine decision contingencies and social ramifications, as well as the strength to make difficult decisions and follow through with implementation. That being said, the question of how ethics best fits into the public administration/affairs curriculum must be addressed.

V.   INCORPORATING ETHICS INTO THE CURRICULUM

When Catron and Denhardt (1994) reviewed various approaches to integrating ethics into professional education, they noted that the field tended to view the question of teaching a separate ethics course versus integrating ethics across the curriculum as an "either/or" proposition, although they advocated using the best that both approaches offered. They noted that NASPAA's charge to schools to increase students' ability "to act ethically . . . in the management of public and, as appropriate, third sector organizations; in the application of quantitative techniques of analysis; and with an understanding of the public policy and organization environment," (p. 55) pointed toward integration. They argued, however, that "a separate, required course provides . . . an opportunity to give students experience in identifying ethical problems and refining skills in moral reasoning, and to help students understand the theoretical underpinnings of different approaches to ethics" (p. 55).

The either/or debate continues in the 1990s, with advocates for both integration of ethics across the curriculum and separate courses. Recall Menzel's data showed that 60 percent of schools offered an ethics course, while 40 percent of schools integrated ethics across the curriculum (1997a, 1997b). Menzel's data also showed that 71 percent of "professional schools of public administration/affairs" offered an ethics course. As for public administration/affairs deepartments, only 59 percent offered a course, and for those schools that granted MPAs within their political science department, only 53 percent had offered an ethics course (1997b). Of those who responded that they either formally or informally (with or without a stand-alone ethics course) integrated ethics, respondents mainly described an informal approach that includes ethics within the context of other course materials.

Catron and Denhardt (1994) analyzed ethics coverage in curricula using the NASPAA self-study reports. Based on their own rating scheme, they rated 18 percent of programs as good or very good coverage (e.g., conscientious and careful planning), 23 percent as adequate coverage, and 59 percent as poor or very poor coverage. They noted, however, that "overall, coverage of ethics in public administration programs is increasing," (p. 57) and argued for better training and support for faculty to further the coverage.

Also arguing for both a stand-alone course and ethics integration in core courses is Bowman (1998). He says that in spite of the difficulties of introducing or requiring a stand-alone course, integration is not enough:

> The desirability of integrating ethics into the entire curriculum, as opposed to a separate course, founders on several critical problems: faculty are primarily trained in and concerned about technical training, and the profession lacks course-specific ethics modules. The result is that there is little (if any) emphasis in course descriptions and syllabi, only an occasional mention in class discussion, and perhaps a brief add-on at the end of the term (1998, p. 30).

Bowman identifies three programs that have a combination approach: The Rhode Island Ethics Project, The University of Utah, and the University of Denver, although he does not describe these programs in detail in this particular article (1998). These programs are discussed briefly below.

A. Stand-Alone Course Instruction

Menzel (1997b) asked about the instructional methods used to teach ethics. The top five techniques used in public administration/affairs ethics instruction were: small-group discussion, case studies, decision-making scenarios, research papers, and lectures. These were followed by: role playing, self assessments, videos/movies, guest speakers, simulations, fiction/movies, biographies, field studies, and lastly, PC multimedia material.

The case-study method is very prevalent in ethics education in many fields, including public administration. Killilea, Pasquerella, and Vocino (1995) favor this method of teaching because they feel it promotes critical thinking skills, collaboration, and forces administrators to examine their values. They also note that the case-study approach does not require the consensus on moral dictates that "almost all other strategies for teaching ethics" requires. By not requiring moral consensus, the case-study approach allows for the diversity of values represented in students.

Some propose that administrative ethics can also be taught with the help of liberal arts curriculum and literature. Edmondson (1995) argues, "The liberal arts are able, however, to provide life experience vicariously. Hypothetical case studies attempt to do this, of course, but the experience they provide often reduces the involvement of the student to the intellect" (p. 228). In addition to "liberalizing" ethics courses using literary works, he also suggests that "public administration graduate program managers might consider the number of liberal arts courses prerequisite to graduate study admission" (p. 228).

Another call for the inclusion of literature comes from Richardson and Adkins (1997). They argue:

> Properly presented, the dramatic interplay within appropriate works of fiction can intrigue and immerse students in ways that surpass almost all other approaches. In the special case of administrative ethics, there are works that allow for a fulsome exploration of such topics as honor, character, law, administrative discretion, codes, political power, and even the role that more base parts of human nature (such passions as envy, anger, and hate) may inevitably play in various types of rule (p. 202).

A different approach involves inventing narratives, as suggested by Rizzo (1998). She criticizes the case-study method saying, "No matter how well written the case, students rarely find their own problems—or workplace moral dilemmas they should anticipate—in these materials" (p. 2). She suggests that "students examine fictional and non-fictional cases as precursors to writing their own problem-centered scenario" (p. 2). She says that in her experience, "students usually choose an ethical quandary common to their work experience and develop it into a narrative" (p. 2). She warns that some student-authors will write cases with one right answer or one best way to resolve it, and advises that students should have several resolution scenarios in mind. In this way, "students demonstrate their level of ability in applying general ethical principles in matters of conduct or conscience of their choosing . . . [and] integrate ethics theory and practice most effectively" (p. 6). We argue that such an approach may work well with older, more-experienced students, but may not benefit younger students or those who are new to public administration as a career.

Letcher (1998) suggests teaching "doing ethics." He suggests a "practice-oriented pedagogy" in which "'working ethically' becomes a practical accomplishment achieved through doing ethics" (p. 42). The most important part of "doing ethics" is reflective questioning. Practical tasks in Letcher's pedagogy include: applying and adopting ethical guidelines, characterizing circumstances to which guidelines apply, detailing the public service promise, and managing personal resources and time.

Another approach to teaching ethics involves using codes of ethics (Plant, 1998). Plant notes "how effective codes of ethics can be when combined with instruction in moral reasoning and the ethical dilemmas endemic to modern governance'' (p. 163). He argues that codes are valuable learning tools because they are ''real'' and are ''attempts to give expression to public values.''

Some argue that ethical awareness can be nurtured by a specific type of curriculum that demonstrates more concrete ethical concepts. Leland (1995) suggests that a prejudice reduction curriculum go beyond the typical ''ethical awareness'' that most ethics courses teach. Such a curriculum, she argues, will teach students ''to be ethical and moral leaders'' because it would ''uncover those attitudes and values which restrict a public sector manager from serving the larger public good,'' (p. 41) and overcome ''any biases which may limit [his/her] capacity to work for the public good'' (p. 42). Certainly, this is an approach that can supplement other ethics education; however, public administration/affairs schools should not rely solely on such a specific topic to teach broader ethical values and techniques.

In fact, Denhardt (1997) recommends public administration/affairs schools should approach ethics from a broader political perspective. She writes, ''approaching ethics from a political perspective permits administrators to pursue democratic ideals by exercising political judgment and participating in the political process of policy making'' (p. 1091). She also notes that such a perspective would ''emphasize results rather than procedures . . . mold and direct individual responsibility more than devise formal structures and instruments for central authority . . . [and] allow sufficient ability and discretion for administrators to act responsively in the political environment, rather than rely on controls and standardization'' (p. 1099). Mayer and Seidel (1998) echo this sentiment in their description of Johns Hopkins University's citizenship course as an approach to teaching ethics in the master's degree program.

B. Ethics Integration

Hejka-Ekins (1998) calls integration across the curriculum ''curriculum infusion'' and explains it as ''a strategy where content-appropriate information is inserted seamlessly into existing academic courses, thus reaching students where they are'' (quoting Hoeppel and Wadsworth, 1992, p. 46). In reference to the ''moral slippage of our society'' (p. 1), Lisman (1996) offers a theoretical framework for ethics integration. He argues that because of the fundamental agreement on basic values like honesty, justice, and autonomy, ethics can be integrated into case studies, with an optional service learning (i.e., community service) component. He writes: ''The overarching goal of integrating ethics into the classroom is to help students develop their capacity to engage in critical thinking about ethical issues. A secondary goal . . . is to promote moral growth through the introduction of ethics into the curriculum'' (1996, p. 67). He advocates using case studies to prompt thinking about specific problems and to provide samples of moral dilemmas with which students can practice decision-making.

As easy as it sounds, however, Walton, Stearns, and Crespy (1997) argue that for integration to be effective, three goals must be accomplished: (1) an awareness of ethical issues and problems in the field must be developed, (2) analytical decision-making skills must be built, and (3) an attitude of moral obligation and personal responsibility must be nurtured. Walton, Stearns, and Crespy (1997) offer a three-pronged strategy for integrating ethics into policy analysis courses that involves understanding basic moral philosophy, framing ethical problems via an "obligations by parties matrix," and applying the matrix.

C. Establishing a Combination Approach

Hejka-Ekins (1998) offers a comprehensive model for establishing an ethics course *and* integrating ethics throughout other courses, although she does not advocate specific details for the actual program. Her six-step model involves:

1. Identifying key stakeholders within the academic department;
2. Holding a strategy meeting to demonstrate the need for the program, gain commitment, and generate ideas;
3. Conducting a needs assessment;
4. Building a curriculum infusion plan, including designing course modules, building annotated bibliographies, collecting case studies, appointing ethics instructors, cross-training, and faculty training;
5. Building faculty capacity; and
6. Evaluating the plan.

In their Rhode Island Ethics Project, supported by the U.S. Department of Education, Killilea, Pasquerella, and Vocino (1998) found that few obstacles stood in the way of convening faculty and state agency leaders to discuss ethics and ethics education. The purpose of the project was to prepare faculty to teach ethics in core courses in the MPA program jointly offered by three IHEs. They held six day-long workshops hosted by national ethics experts and attended by eleven MPA faculty members and many state agency leaders. Faculty members provided "theory testing" and practitioners proved "reality testing." The most significant outcomes of the project include: a core ethics course institutionalized in the MPA program, a working model for teaching and studying ethics, a case anthology, and a private philanthropist's endowment of a center for ethics and public service.

One of the most interesting integration programs is found in the University of Utah's MPA program which uses an "ethics matrix" to: "structure the role of ethics in the content of MPA core courses, to nurture the development and viability of that role, and to facilitate the viewing and reviewing of relationships among those courses regarding the role of ethics" (Nelson and Van Hook, 1998, p. 37). The matrix began in 1976 and is focused around a seminar on ethics that MPA students take at the end of their coursework. This seminar is intended to integrate all coursework on ethics and link students' theoretical and practical experience with a substantial research and writing project and oral presentation. Ethics is also a component of the other courses in the MPA program by weaving themes of persons and groups, responsibilities to law and rules, administrative discretion and accountability, and conduct (Nelson and Van Hook, 1998, pp. 46–49). The matrix is supported by annual faculty retreats, faculty/practitioner seminars on ethics, and the use of faculty and resources in the university's departments of philosophy and political science.

Ozar (1998) suggests that ethics integration can be accomplished by designing an outcomes-centered curriculum, which focuses attention on learning outcomes that can be incorporated into all courses. For example, some outcomes appropriate for public sector ethics might include: awareness of values and ideals, reasoning and reflective skills, implementation of moral judgments, and motivation/conviction (Ozar, 1998, pp. 90–95). Outcomes-centered learning can be developed by: (a) asking what students need to be able to do after graduation, (b) developing ways to assess student learning of outcomes, and (c) designing appropriate teaching strategies for each outcome.

Other examples of ethics integration offer similar stories. Integration is not confined to public administration. For example, the University of Denver also restructured its Master of Business Administration (MBA) program by integrating ethics into the MBA curriculum (Wittmer, et al., 1998).

D. Who Is Teaching Ethics?

Mainzer (1991) wondered nearly a decade ago if public administration/affairs had the appropriate faculty to teach ethics. He asked: "Are there teachers who are both philosophically sophisticated (knowledgeable and subtle reasoners) and practically oriented (attuned to the problems which public administrators face)?" (p. 10). He further queried: "How can ordinary faculty usefully teach ethics to ordinary students of public administration?" (p. 10). He answered his own question, "there are too few really prepared scholars of moral philosophy, public administration, and public policy" (p. 10).

Menzel's study addressed who was teaching ethics courses (1997b). His data showed ethics courses were taught largely by full-time public administration/affairs faculty, with a large number of part-time instructors filling in. However, he warns that the demographics of who was teaching ethics courses showed racial-gender-ethnic considerations: "The survey found that fewer than one of every four ethics instructors is female and almost none are non-white" (p. 523). His data also showed that 90 percent of those teaching ethics were "drawn to it by their personal interests" (p. 523). Other reasons ethics instructors cited were being asked to teach the course and fulfilling the NASPAA requirement, although 55 percent said they taught ethics because of their research interests.

Faculty development remains an area in need of attention in ethics education. Bowman and Menzel (1998) note that faculty development and recruitment need "more work." They suggest that university and professional associations like the American Society for Public Administration (ASPA) and the American Political Science Association (APSA) can offer workshops and conferences to develop faculty capabilities. Specifically, ASPA's ethics section can provide training materials and workshops.

Having examined some instructional strategies used in ethics education, we now turn to the question of effectiveness.

VI. DOES ETHICS EDUCATION MAKE A DIFFERENCE?

A critical gap in the literature on ethics education in public administration/affairs schools involves effectiveness.[7] In Mainzer's (1991) argument for teaching "vulgar ethics," or "modes of reflection accessible to ordinary persons in our society concerning the imperfectly formulated guides to conduct" (p. 11), he notes the difficulty in teaching ethics lies in the lack of correlation to ethical behavior later in life. He argues:

> Ethics is the element most difficult to teach because we can hardly ever reasonably assume that we have succeeded in our goal: making a difference in how students will

behave in their actual public administration responsibilities. We can teach *about* goodness, but we do not know that we can teach goodness (p. 3, emphasis original).

He later concludes:

> Unable to accompany students through life, the teacher may only hope to have strength-
> ened their sense of possessing a detached, judgmental element within themselves. A
> part of one's self nourishes doubt about even actions compatible with such guides to
> behavior as statute, established policy, hierarchical command, professional standards,
> widespread approval, reassuring habit, decent self-interest, the claims of affection, or
> honorable passion (Mainzer, 1991, p. 21).

Menzel built on his 1995 survey of NASPAA-member schools by sending surveys
to randomly selected alumni of four of those schools. His purpose in surveying alumni
was to see if ethics education was making a difference (1997a, 1998). His results showed
that 74 percent of respondents reported having encountered workplace moral dilemmas.
However, only "43 percent indicated that their graduate ethics educational experience
helped them while 31 percent said it did not. One of every four said they were unsure"
(1997a, p. 227). Those who said that their ethics education made a difference commented
on values reinforcement: "Many respondents said that their ethics education, especially
as reflected in the ethics course they had taken, did not displace old or existing values
with new or different values but clarified and reinforced those that they brought to their
course of study" (Menzel, 1997a, p. 227). Others commented on how lessons in ethics
reasoning helped them reason through workplace moral dilemmas. Those who felt that
their ethics education did not help them face workplace moral dilemmas support critics
of ethics education who say that values are learned early and cannot be taught. As Menzel
writes:

> Among those who said that their ethics education did not help them deal with ethical
> dilemmas, a number of persons commented that their ethics had been molded by their
> upbringing which, for better or worse, was what mattered the most when they were
> faced with a dilemma (1997a, p. 227).

Menzel (1997a) also asked alumni to identify the factors that influenced their "ethical outlook and behavior." Family, friends, church, and interaction with coworkers ranked
among the top four in importance. The other influences dealt primarily with school influences and professional associations. Interestingly, "discussion of ethics and values in
ethics course" ranked fourth in overall importance, followed by "discussion of ethics and
values in MPA coursework as a whole." Menzel argues that, "on balance, these findings
suggest that completing a formal course of instruction in ethics is valuable even though
the respondents regard non-educational influences as more important" (1997a, p. 228).
Furthermore, some instructional technologies—case studies and decision-making scenarios—appear to increase the alumni's "self-reported ability" to resolve moral dilemmas
(Menzel, 1998). Other frequently used techniques (e.g., lecture, small group discussion)
were not significant.

Between 1995–1997, Rice, Nelson, and Van Hook (1998) sent opinion surveys to
MPA graduates of the University of Utah to examine the effectiveness of ethics education
in the MPA program. According to the authors, "some 68.1% of respondents were positive
in their assessment of 'gain' in this topical area, and 64.3% answered that they found the
area important in their careers" (p. 52). However, 20 percent of respondents were neutral
in their response and about 10 percent were negative. Some respondents (12.5%) felt that

the ethics seminar they took "helped students gain an understanding of a relevant framework for making ethical decisions" (p. 53). Other benefits included increased awareness of ethical decisions or cases and issues (8.33%), and that the seminar "built student understanding of ethics constraints and challenges facing public administrators" (7.41%), (p. 53). However, 12.04 percent of respondents said that the ethics seminar "does not—or probably does not—make students more ethical."

Such studies are welcome efforts to fill the gap in the literature on the effectiveness of ethics education. The results are mostly encouraging, yet not generalizable enough to proclaim ethics education in public administration/affairs degree programs a rousing success and advocate the mandatory inclusion of required ethics training in such programs. Still, we feel confident that studies show that ethics education—both as a stand-alone course and integrated across the curriculum—helps prepare public administration/affairs graduates for the workplace moral dilemmas they might face.

VII. CONCLUSIONS AND IMPLICATIONS

In their review of ethics in public administration, Catron and Denhardt (1994) concluded with an explanation of the diversity in education goals, course content, and curriculum integration strategies. They argued that the diversity:

> [R]eflects the necessity of choosing from among the many dimensions of ethics relevant to public administration education. . . . Second, it reflects the need to tailor an approach to ethics education that fits into an overall curriculum and program. . . . Third, of course, it represents the educational background and proclivities of those making the choices about what to include in the curriculum (p. 59).

We agree that the diversity is still appropriate; however, we conclude our review with a focus on the need for further refinement of the goals of ethics education in public administration/affairs schools and the need to understand whether or not such education makes a difference in the workplace moral dilemmas that a public administrator may face. Certainly, the gap in empirical work needs to be filled by more studies like Menzel's (1997a, 1997b). Until we can correlate workplace moral decision-making with ethics education, no guarantee exists that even if public administration/affairs schools integrate and teach ethics in the most effective manner, administrators will practice what they have learned and act ethically. Further, if education psychology studies show that graduate students cannot be taught moral values, then moral education should be addressed at an earlier stage or at the very least in undergraduate public administration/affairs or public policy programs.

We also suggest that ethics courses or integrative ethics curricula might target specific ethical behaviors and values (e.g., prejudice reduction) that might increase sensitivity to specific types of workplace moral dilemmas, rather than one-size-fits-all ethics education. Further, we recommend a continued emphasis on democratic values and suggest that public administration/affairs schools require some liberal arts training or prerequisites for students to increase their ability to ask tough questions and wade through the moral morass of the social world. Finally, to keep pace with curriculum changes and innovations, public administration/affairs faculty must be encouraged to teach and infuse ethics and must be better trained in ethics education.

NOTES

1. For a more thorough discussion of the history of ethics education, see Catron and Denhardt's chapter in the first edition of the *Handbook of Administrative Ethics*, from which this section is largely drawn.
2. NASPAA is the accrediting body for academic programs in public administration and public affairs. In addition to curriculum guidelines, it also provides important support services to academic programs. NASPAA, 1120 G Street N.W., Suite 730, Washington, D.C. 20005.
3. The self-study is the first step in the process of accreditation or reaccreditation. Following the program's own self-study is a NASPAA review of the program's eligibility and a site visit.
4. See also Menzel (1997b) and Bowman and Menzel (1998).
5. NASPAA's mission-driven guidelines are explicit about not prescribing any specific courses, or mandating amount of time spent on any subject matter.
6. The Working Group was made up of scholars and practitioners sharing a common interest in supporting and improving ethics education in public administration and affairs. For a complete list, see Catron and Denhardt (1994, p. 55).
7. It is also a gap in the literature on teaching ethics in business schools as noted by MacDonald and Donleavy (1995), who review a few of the effectiveness studies done. For example, Carlson and Burke (1988), like other scholars, have linked teaching ethics in an IHE with the "evolution of student thinking about ethical dilemmas." Such studies, however, fail to identify workplace correlations.

REFERENCES

Adams, G.B., and Balfour, D.L. (1998). *Unmasking Administrative Evil*. Thousand Oaks, CA: Sage Publications.

Bowman, J.S. (1998). The lost world of public administration education: rediscovering the meaning of professionalism. *Journal of Public Affairs Education*, 4(1): 27–31.

Bowman, J., and Menzel, D. (Eds.) (1998). *Teaching Ethics and Values in Public Administration Programs: Innovations, Strategies, and Issues*. Press. Albany, NY: State University of New York.

Brewer, G.A., Facer II, R.L., O'Toole Jr., L.J., and Douglas, J.W. (1998). The state of doctoral education in public administration: developments in the field's research preparation. *Journal of Public Affairs Education*, 4(2): 123–135.

Carlson, P.J., and Burke, F. (1998). Lessons learned from ethics in the classroom: exploring student growth in flexibility, complexity, and comprehension. *Journal of Business Ethics*, 17: 1179–1187.

Catron, B.L., and Denhardt, K.G. (1994). Ethics education in public administration. In: *Handbook of Administrative Ethics* (T.L. Cooper, ed.). New York, NY: Marcel Dekker, Inc., pp. 49–61.

Catron, B.L., and Denhardt, K.G. (1988). *Ethics Education in Public Administration and Affairs* (a monograph of the Working Group on Ethics Education). American Society for Public Administration.

DeLeon, P., and Steelman, T.A. (1999). The once and future public policy program. *Policy Currents*, 9(2): 1–9.

Denhardt, K.G. (1997). The management of ideals: a political perspective on ethics. *International Journal of Public Administration*, 20(4&5): 1091–1115.

Denhardt, K.G. (1988). *The Ethics of Public Service*. New York, NY: Greenwood Press.

Dennis, A. (1987). Teaching Ethics in Public Administration: An Analysis of Goals, Ethical Standards, and Approaches to Ethical Decision-Making. Doctoral dissertation, University of Southern California, Los Angeles, CA. (Also see her work as April Hejka-Ekins.).

Dwivedi, O.P. (1987). Moral dimensions of statecraft: a plea for an administrative theology. *Canadian Journal of Political Science*, 20: 699–709.

Edmondson III, H.T. (1995). Teaching administrative ethics with help from Jefferson. *PS: Political Science & Politics*, 28(2): 226–229.

Farmer, D.J. (1998). Against myopia: public administration and ethics. *Journal of Public Affairs Education*, 4(1): 33–38.

Frederickson, H.G. (Ed.). (1993). *Ethics and Public Administration*, Armonk, NY: M.E. Sharpe.

Frederickson, H.G. (1971). Toward a new public administration. In: *Toward a New Public Administration: The Minnowbrook Perspective* (F. Marini, ed.). Scranton, PA: Chandler Publishing Company, pp. 309–331.

Harmon, M.M. (1974). Social equity and organizational man: motivation and organizational democracy. *Public Administration Review*, 34: 11–18.

Hart, D.K. (1974). Social equity, justice, and the equitable administrator. *Public Administration Review*, 34: 3–11.

Hart, D.W. (1999). Ethics education in public affairs. *Journal of Public Affairs Education*, 5(5): 67–76.

Hejka-Ekins, A. (1998). Teaching ethics across the public administration curriculum. *Journal of Public Affairs Education*, 4(1): 45–50. (Also see her work as April Dennis.)

Hoeppel, J., and Wadsworth, E. (1992). *Prevention Across the Curriculum: Leadership in Education to Advance Prevention.* Northeastern Illinois University.

Jackson, M.W. (1993). How can ethics be taught? In: *Ethics in Public Service* (R.A. Chapman, ed.). Canada: Carleton University Press, pp. 31–42.

Jennings, B., Nelson, J.L., and Parens, E. (1994). Values on campus. *The Civic Arts Review*, 7(3): 7–13.

Killilea, A., Pasquerella, L., and Vocino, M. (1998). The Rhode Island Ethics Project: a model for integrating ethics into a master of public administration program. In: *Teaching Ethics and Values in Public Administration Programs: Innovations, Strategies, and Issues* (J. Bowman and D. Menzel, eds.). Albany, NY: State University of New York Press, pp. 21–36.

Killilea, A., Pasquerella, L., and Vocino, M. (1995). Ethics for skeptics in public administration. *Spectrum: The Journal of State Government*, 68(4): 19–27.

Letcher, R.A. (1998). Excursis: on teaching doing ethics in public service. *Journal of Public Affairs Education*, 4(1): 39–44.

Lee, D., and Pugh, D. (1987). *Codes of Ethics, Education, and the Making of a Profession.* Paper presented to the Western Social Science Association Annual Meeting, April 1987.

Leland, P.J. (1995). Beyond "ethical awareness": incorporating prejudice reduction curricula into the management classroom. *Journal of Public Affairs Education*, 1(2): 39–50.

Light, P.D. (1999). *The New Public Service.* Washington D.C.: Brookings Institution Press.

Lilla, M.T. (1981). Ethos, "ethics," and public service. *The Public Interest*, 3–17.

Lisman, C.D. (1996). *The Curricular Integration of Ethics: Theory and Practice.* Westport, CT: Praeger.

Mainzer, L.C. (1991). Vulgar ethics for public administration. *Administration & Society*, 23(1): 3–28.

Mayer, J., and Seidel, R. (1998). Citizenship and the policy professional. In: *Teaching Ethics and Values in Public Administration Programs: Innovations, Strategies, and Issues* (J. Bowman and D. Menzel, eds.). Albany, NY: State University of New York Press, pp. 103–113.

McDonald, G.M., and Donleavy, G.D. (1995). Objections to the teaching of business ethics. *Journal of Business Ethics*, 14(10): 839–853.

Meek, J.W., and Johnson, E.E. (1998). Curriculum, pedagogy, innovation: the professional doctorate in public administration. *Journal of Public Affairs Education*, 4(1): 57–63.

Menzel, D.C. (1998). To act ethically: the what, why, and how of ethics pedagogy. *Journal of Public Affairs Education*, 4(1): 11–18.

Menzel, D.C. (1997a). Teaching ethics and values in public administration: are we making a difference? *Public Administration Review*, 57(3): 224–230.

Menzel, D.C. (1997b). Teaching ethics and values: a survey of graduate public affairs and administration programs in the U.S. *PS: Political Science & Politics*, 30(3): 518–524.

Nelson, D.H., and Van Hook, P.J. (1998). Using an ethics matrix in a master of public administration program. In: *Teaching Ethics and Values in Public Administration Programs: Innovations, Strategies, and Issues* (J. Bowman and D. Menzel, eds.). Albany, NY: State University of New York Press, pp. 37–62.

Ozar, D.T. (1998). An outcome-centered approach to teaching public-sector ethics. In: *Teaching Ethics and Values in Public Administration Programs: Innovations, Strategies, and Issues* (J. Bowman and D. Menzel, eds.). Albany, NY: State University of New York Press, pp. 85–99.

Parks, S.D. (1993). Is it too late? Young adults and the formation of professional ethics. In: *Can Ethics Be Taught? Perspectives, Challenges, and Approaches at Harvard Business School* (T.R. Piper, M.C. Gentile, and S.D. Parks, eds.). Boston, MA: Harvard Business School, pp. 13–72.

Piper, T.R., Gentile, M.C., and Parks, S.D. (1993). *Can Ethics Be Taught? Perspectives, Challenges, and Approaches at Harvard Business School*. Boston, MA: Harvard Business School.

Plant, J.F. (1998). Using codes of ethics in teaching public administration. In: *Teaching Ethics and Values in Public Administration Programs: Innovations, Strategies, and Issues* (J. Bowman and D. Menzel, eds.) Albany, NY: State University of New York Press, pp. 161–177.

Rice, W., Nelson, D.H., and Van Hook, P.J. (1998). Using opinion surveys to assess ethics education in an MPA program: the Utah case. *Journal of Public Affairs Education*, 4(1): 51–56.

Richardson, W.D., and Adkins, S.R. (1997). Understanding ethics through literature: character, honor and the corruption of body and soul in King Rat. *Administration & Society*, 29(2): 201–221.

Rizzo, A-M. (1998). Inventing narratives in ethical reasoning in an administrative ethics course. *Journal of Public Affairs Education*, 4(1): 1–10.

Schachter, H.L. (1993). Graduate education in public administration: the introductory course. *International Journal of Public Administration*, 16(1): 1–13.

Schall, E. (1995). Learning to love the swamp: reshaping education for public service. *Journal of Policy Analysis and Management*, 14(2): 202–220.

Snyder, R.C. (1999). *Public administrators, public scholars, public citizens: rethinking American higher education*. Paper presented at the annual meeting of the Western Political Science Association, Seattle, WA, March 1999.

Sommers, C.H. (1993). Teaching the virtues. *The Public Interest*, 111: 3–13.

Stokes, D.E. (1996). APPAM presidential address: the changing environment of education for public service. *Journal of Policy Analysis and Management*, 15(2): 158–170.

Wakefield, S. (1976). Ethics and the public service: a case for individual responsibility. *Public Administration Review*, 3: 661–666.

Walton, J.R., Stearns, J.M., and Crespy, C.T. (1997). Integrating ethics into the public administration curriculum: a three-step process. *Journal of Policy Analysis and Management*, 18(3): 470–483.

Wittmer, D., Holcomb, J., Hutton, B., and Nelson, D.R. (1998). Reinventing the master of business administration curriculum: integrating ethics, law, and public policy. In: *Teaching Ethics and Values in Public Administration Programs: Innovations, Strategies, and Issues* (J. Bowman and D. Menzel, eds.). Albany, NY: State University of New York Press, pp. 63–84.

4

Ethics in In-service Training

April Hejka-Ekins
California State University, Stanislaus, California

I. INTRODUCTION

The current approaches to ethics training have been compared to the Eiffel Tower, which can best be understood from three perspectives. First, to grasp the intricate engineering of the tower, it must be viewed close up in order to study the "nuts and bolts" of its foundation. In terms of ethics training, this means that some advocates believe that public managers must understand the legal basis of their conduct and comply with binding regulations. Second, to comprehend the breadth and scope of the monument, the tower must be viewed from the top in order to appreciate its panoramic splendor. Similarly, some proponents believe that to be effective, ethics training must impart lofty ethical standards and a moral reasoning process that inspires administrators to do good (Block, 1991). Third, the tower needs to be viewed from a distance in order to gain a holistic view of how it fits into its surroundings. Some supporters assert that the entire organization must provide a context in which individual ethics are fostered. They claim without a holistic perspective, individual ethical conduct is otherwise problematical.

The purpose of this essay is to explore the current state of ethics in-service training in the public sector by addressing five questions: (1) What is the context for understanding the evolution of in-service ethics training in the public sector today? (2) What is the current scope of ethics training programs regarding goals, content, and methods? (3) What kinds of ethics training programs are occurring at the federal, state, local, and professional levels of public service? (4) How effective is in-service ethics training and what programs are being advocated as effective for the field? (5) What learning can be gleaned about ethics training by examining these issues?

Four themes emerge from ethics training literature which will be discussed in this chapter. First, four competing approaches currently exist in ethics training and each appears to have a certain utility in meeting the needs of public service practitioners. Second, each approach to ethics training represents a particular model with strengths and weaknesses that need to be considered in designing and implementing programs for public sector agencies. Third, this author suggests that ethics training in the public sector can best be advanced if theorists and practitioners alike recognize that a contingency perspective is needed in deciding which type of ethics training works best under what conditions. Unfortunately, the assumption is often made that there must be one best way to foster ethical conduct in public service, but ethics training not only depends upon what "ought" to happen, but also what is realistically possible. Therefore, the underlying premise of this contingency viewpoint is that the idealistic and the realistic must meld into what is possible. Thus, factors affecting contingent strategies to design effective ethics training programs will be suggested. Fourth, a critique of the existing approaches to ethics training will also be provided that points to a moral dualism that creates a neurotic component to the nature of public service in American society. A contradiction exists in attempting to educate public service practitioners according to standards of civic virtue, while the society-at-large operates according to an ethic of civic commercialism (Ventriss, 1991). Suggestions for dealing with ethics training as civic education will be offered.

Before embarking on the discussion of in-service ethics training in the public sector, a clarification of the term "administrative ethics" is in order. Kathryn Denhardt (1984: 37) has defined "public administrative ethics" as such:

> To be ethical requires that an administrator be able to independently engage in the process of reasonably examining and questioning the standards by which administrative decisions are made, at least to the extent that the decisions are legitimately made at that level of the organization. The content of the standards may change over time as social values are better understood, or social concerns are expressed. An administrator should be ready to adapt decision standards to these changes, always reflecting a commitment to the core values of our society and the recognition of the goals of the organization. The administrator will be held accountable personally, professionally, and within the organization for the decisions made and for the ethical standards which inform those decisions.

In short, Denhardt describes the ethics of public service as a process in which a public manager identifies the ethical standards involved in issues within an agency context, independently critiques those decision standards, and becomes personally and professionally accountable for the decisions rendered. Consequently, such a definition entails two aspects: a content component in terms of the ethical standards that serve as guidelines for the administrator, and a process component that establishes a method to determine and critique ethical decisions in order to act rightly. However, besides cultivating moral judgment, a second dimension is required in individual ethical conduct, which is the necessity for a person to possess the moral character to enact an ethical decision based upon a deliberative process. Seeking to live a life of integrity or acting virtuously must accompany moral judgment if ethical conduct is to take place (Cooper and Wright, 1992).

"In-service ethics training" refers to the educational approach used in order to impart the ethics of public service to practitioners within an agency context. Pedagogy includes the goals, content, and methods of instruction in ethics training; all three are the focus of debate and new developments.

II. TOWARD A TYPOLOGY FOR ETHICS TRAINING

To understand the present state of ethics training, several preliminary remarks are needed regarding the evolution of public administrative ethics. During the early 1900s the development of public service ethics at the federal level was largely minimized due to the belief by Progressive reformers, such as Woodrow Wilson, that politics and administration should remain separate. In reaction to the "spoils system" of an earlier era, a neutral, impartial civil service system was the ideal sought. Although individuals of good character were desired, ethics training was not considered a central part of a public manager's education because civil servants were thought to have little discretion in the implementation of public policy. However, with the gradual demise of the politics/administration dichotomy since World War II, scholars and practitioners have come to acknowledge that public administrators exercise significant discretionary power in their decision-making (Rohr, 1989).

Yet ever since the early debates between Carl Friedrich (1935) and Herman Finer (1972), controversy has ensued as to whether the focus of ethics on the individual level should be external or internal (Cooper, 1998). Should the emphasis be on establishing legal controls that require compliance on the part of public managers or cultivating the moral judgment within public administrators to act ethically based on some avowed professional standards or moral principles?

On the one hand, external controls, consisting of ethics legislation and codes of ethics, are viewed as essential in requiring public managers to comply at minimum with the law and at best to extol them to live up to the ethical standards of the profession. On the other hand, while external controls ground public managers in their legal obligations and highlight the ideals of the profession, the effect is largely reactive and sometimes negative because such an approach tends to convey what administrators should not do and provides mostly lip service to what they should do. For example, James Krohe (1997) contends that the compliance approach is ineffective because rules never cover every situation and subjective interpretations cause wide variations in conduct. Roberts and Doss (1992) believe that overuse of external controls diminishes the importance of individual responsibility and good judgment, which is necessary to secure public confidence and integrity in public institutions. Hence, the negative results of compliance training can dampen motivation and impede an administrator's commitment to live up to the moral idealism of the profession.

In contrast, internal controls create a different focus. First they are comprised of two components: moral judgment (which requires administrators to learn the lofty ethical standards and ethos of the profession and a method of ethical decision-making to apply those standards) and moral character (which consists of developing the virtues essential to act upon one's moral judgment). This method can lead public managers to live up to their highest potential for moral integrity in serving the public good, but it is also problematic because the field remains ambiguous as to what content and methods ought to be used to produce the desired results and whether such results are realistically obtainable.

Some theorists focus on the development of moral judgment. For example, as opposed to compliance training, Killilea, Pasquerella, and Vocino (1995), claim that ethics training should offer the opportunity to develop moral judgment because this fosters personal moral competence. Others such as Denhardt (1994) focus on character ethics as the basis for assuring ethical conduct in government. In developing virtue, theorists [such as Cooper and Wright (1992), Richardson and Nigro (1987), Frederickson and Hart (1985)] emphasize the importance of moral exemplars in public service. Their hope is to inspire public sector practitioners to emulate those who act with public honor, courage, benevolence, and integrity in the face of moral conflict or crisis.

Based on these orientations towards administrative ethics, what should be the educational purpose and anticipated outcome of in-service ethics training—adherence to external controls or development of internal controls? The response to this question parallels the classic distinctions in organization theory between bureaucratic and democratic organizations and Theory X versus Theory Y management styles (McGregor, 1957). In the former, it is obvious that the nature of human beings is viewed with suspicion and thus, external structure and control must ensure that the desired behavior is attained. In the latter, the assumption is that if individuals are properly educated they will develop the internal judgment to behave, not only properly, but exemplary. This dichotomy concerning basic assumptions about human nature has pervaded the field of ethics training, as well as the profession, and fundamentally affects its educational purposes and objectives.

For example, John Rohr (1989) makes the distinction between "low road" and "high road" ethics and criticizes both. The first is dubbed "low road" because it stresses exclusively adherence to formal rules. This type of ethics training focuses on exercises to teach participants what kinds of conduct are or are not permissible under departmental regulations. Rohr concludes that such an approach is hopelessly negative because it reduces ethics to staying out of trouble and reinforcing the trivial, while ignoring the morally significant dimensions of public service.

The second approach to ethics education Rohr terms "high road," (because it stresses social equity) which he tries to discount as either being too lofty or irrelevant to be the basis of administrative ethics. Social equity, which has its origins in the political philosophy associated with the "new public administration," is too demanding to be a part of ethics training (Marini, 1971). It is unrealistic to expect that public managers can ground themselves in the rigors of philosophy, when their focus is professional development.

Rohr also rejects humanistic psychology as a proper basis for ethics training because it encompasses all normative theories that can be applied to organization life. By humanistic psychology, he refers to theorists such as Abraham Maslow, Carl Rogers, and Lawrence Kohlberg. While their theories pertain to individuals within a societal or organizational context, public service ethics (as defined earlier) has separate considerations that are excluded from this perspective. For example, Rohr points out that humanistic psychology is concerned with individual morality; however, it does not address an inquiry into the specific role responsibilities of individual public managers nor does it attempt to distinguish between the private and public duties which stem from this administrative role.

Rohr's criticism leads him to posit regime values, based on the oath public employees take to the U.S. Constitution, as a "middle road" and the proper foundation for ethics training. While Rohr may claim that regime values are more appropriate than social equity or self actualization as the guiding ethos for public administration, it needs to be underscored that his purpose is similar to the "high road" approaches he rejects—which is to cultivate a sense of ethical acuity in public managers that places the responsibility of moral discernment upon their shoulders. Development of individual ethical awareness and moral reasoning are the goals. Hence, Rohr's comments suggest two approaches to ethics training that reflect the two basic orientations to individual administrative ethics previously discussed.

A. Compliance and Integrity Ethics

Carol Lewis (1991) clarifies Rohr's distinctions by describing two models used in ethics training, which she labels "compliance ethics" and "integrity ethics." "Compliance ethics" refers to instruction of employees regarding pertinent legal statutes or agency rules in order to gain their adherence; in other words, what employees should not do. As Lewis (1991: 9) explains: "A largely prescriptive, coercive, punitive, and even threatening route, this approach to ethics is designed to spur obedience to minimum standards and legal prohibitions. It is enforced by controls on the job that ordinarily aim at acceptable levels of risk, not flawless purity.'' In compliance or ''low road ethics,'' oversight and controls become the duties of management.

The training format for the compliance model would emphasize legal statutes and agency regulations. The purpose of training would be to impart a knowledge of those rules to the participants and to help them gain an understanding of the application of specific ethics laws to their roles as public administrators and how they would be affected. Methods of presentation would vary but often include: live lectures, video, films, case studies, panel discussions, and small group exercises and discussions. Regardless of the techniques used, rule compliance would drive the purpose and content of this training.

Examples of compliance training abound. Cody and Richardson (1992) offer an ethics guide providing a comprehensive statement of prescribed behavior for public officials, plus a discussion of the enforcement mechanisms that exist through ethics commissions and government agencies. *Ethics: An Employee Guide* (U.S. Department of the Interior, 1998), published by the Department of Interior, outlines legal standards in the areas of financial disclosure and conflicts of interest. The Office of Government Ethics includes reference publications, such as *Ethical Conduct for Employees of the Executive Branch*, as well as videotapes regarding standards of conduct, financial disclosure, and conflicts of interest (U.S. Office of Government Ethics, 1999). At the state level, state ethics commissions provide information on ethics statutes to public officials and employees, political candidates, and lobbyists regarding financial disclosure, conflict of interest, and lobbying regulations (COGEL, 1999). Even municipalities such as Chicago, Los Angeles, Seattle, and other cities have established ethics commissions to enforce legislation. This sampling at the federal, state, and local levels of government indicates a steady rise in regulatory policies aimed at governing the conduct of government officials and workers, and thus, a heavy emphasis on the use of compliance training is the instructional approach used to impart a knowledge of ethics laws, their applications, and consequences.

''Integrity ethics'' attempts to create an awareness of a public service ethos, ethical standards and values, plus a process of moral reasoning to inspire exemplary actions or ethical conduct. The emphasis is on the promotion of moral character with self-responsibility and moral autonomy as essential components. It relies on internal, positive, proactive, voluntary efforts—not external penalties, controls, or inducements. Rohr's ''high road'' and ''middle road'' categories reflect this orientation.

The curriculum concerning the integrity model of ethics training would first aim at becoming aware of the differing ethos and ethical standards that could constitute the normative basis of the field and secondly at fostering an approach to moral reasoning as suggested by Jackson (1993) or Reynolds (1995), among others. An ethos—such as regime values advocated by Rohr (1998), citizenship by Stivers and King (1998) and Box (1998), social equity by Frederickson (1997) or principles by the revised code of the American Society for Public Administration (ASPA) (Van Wart, 1996)—could constitute the ethical standards of the profession. Any of these could serve as a basis for developing ethical sensitivity. Subsequently, public managers would learn how to apply an ethical decision-making process to solve moral issues in the public workplace. As a third component, virtues may be explored by considering the lives of moral exemplars and the qualities they possess. However, the emphasis is usually on the awareness of ethical standards and the moral reasoning necessary to promote ethical conduct and individual integrity.

Perhaps a good example of an approach to the integrity model is offered by Garofalo and Geuras (1994), who argue that a delicate balance between ethics education and moral education should be the primary goal. The former refers to the process of developing analytical and critical thinking about ethical problems, while the latter approach focuses on inculcating standards of conduct and cultivating ethical behavior. According to these normative theorists, the challenge is to preserve the moral autonomy of the individual, while strengthening the potentiality for the person to act ethically. The development of a moral reasoning process and the incorporation of mental attitudes and moral qualities is preferred over indoctrination of specific standards and prescribed behaviors.

An interactive pedagogy would be used to convey integrity as suggested in the Rhode Island Ethics Project (Killilea, Pasquerella, and Vocino, 1998) in which case studies, based on the practical experience of public officials and administrators, became the basis for engaging in ethical decision-making. Professional values and standards set the basis for applying ethical decision-making to specific case study situations. Models of ethical decision-making have been suggested by numerous normative theorists, such as Brady and Woller (1996), Walton, Stearns, and Crespy (1997), and others, but one of the most widely used approaches is offered by Terry Cooper (1998), who combines the criteria of moral principles, probable consequences, and public justification in considering value conflicts. The model provides a process of moral reflection for public service practitioners to apply in weighing their objective duties and subjective values in confronting ethical dilemmas.

Lewis (1991) points out that both the "compliance model" and the "integrity model" serve certain necessary purposes but also contain basic drawbacks. Compliance training is necessary for public managers to ensure their accountability; this is essential to conducting public service. Yet it tends to discourage them from behaving above minimum standards. What is legal may not be right. Integrity training aims to encourage a high level of ethical conduct, but avoids the problem of unethical conduct, abuse, and corruption. Individual integrity training may lie beyond the capability of some.

Furthermore, because the emphasis in the compliance and integrity models deals exclusively with the individual, the critical impact of the organization on ethical conduct is largely ignored. Critics of these two approaches have questioned the appropriateness of this microlevel of analysis. Can ethics training be effective if it is aimed solely at the individual administrator? How ethical can we expect public managers to be if their public workplaces do not support, or worse yet, discourage ethical conduct? Are we setting false expectations by promoting ethics training aimed exclusively at individual public servants?

B. Fusion and Integration Ethics

To counteract the criticisms against compliance and integrity ethics, Lewis advocates "fusion ethics" which attempts to combine both into a third model—adherence to formal legal standards and cultivation of moral judgment that translates into individual ethical responsibility. As Cooper (1998) has suggested, public servants need to know and respond to their objective responsibilities of accountability and imposed obligations as well as their subjective responsibilities which reflect the development of a professional ethic grounded in personal experience.

Such an approach to ethics training would combine two curricular areas: (1) understanding legal statutes or agency regulations and the minimum standards necessary to be accountable and meet one's objective responsibilities as well as how such ethics laws would apply in practice; and (2) identification of ethical standards and values such as those embodied in the democratic ethos or a professional code of ethics, the teaching of a moral reasoning process which would help public employees apply these principles to heighten their ethical conduct, and the use of moral exemplars as role models for encouraging the practice of public service virtues. The range of techniques previously discussed for the compliance and integrity models could be similarly employed in this model.

An excellent example of the fusion approach is the ethics training program, *The Ethics Factor* (Kellar, 1988), published through the International City Manager's Association (ICMA). As a self-help manual, the focus is two-fold: (1) developing an interactive process of building knowledge of the ethics regulations as they apply to specific professional or public service practitioner groups, and (2) developing skills at ethical decision-making to enable the learner to sharpen their moral judgment in dealing with ambiguous ethical problems. Along with the practical management reader, *Ethical Insight, Ethical Action* (Kellar, 1988), a leader's guide (Hopper, 1998) outlines a pedagogy for facilitating workshops and provides self-assessments, exercises, and case studies.

At the federal level, Grosenick (1995) suggests a fusion approach to ethics training. While he acknowledges the necessity to expose public officials and employees to rules, regulations, and their legal consequences, he maintains that this does not guarantee they will understand the importance and utility of an ethical system. Ethics training should not only relate appropriate statutes and penalties to government employees but also orient them to their professional role in public service. Helping them to apply ethical principles to relevant ethical problems will better prepare them to respond ethically to difficult and changing circumstances.

Truelson (1991) also supports a fusion approach. From the compliance perspective, she recognizes the importance of imparting legal requirements to public administrators and suggests that a system of entrance and exit ethics briefings be provided to all federal employees. But she also warns that this approach alone is too restrictive and advocates an "ethical awareness package" that includes such objectives as "stimulating the moral imagination, promoting recognition of ethical issues, developing analytic skills, eliciting a sense of moral responsibility, and fostering ethical action" (p. 233). Her training techniques would be designed to enhance moral judgment by helping public managers distinguish between ethical and unethical behavior, using a professional code of ethics or ethical principles that reflect a democratic ethos, and applying an analytical method of moral reasoning through the use of case studies to promote responsible ethical conduct.

Moreover, Truelson also believes that fusion ethics must be consolidated into the agency culture. This viewpoint responds to the growing criticism that ethics training in the compliance, integrity, or fusion models are aimed exclusively at the individual level of public management. Consequently, a fourth model has begun to surface in the literature, which could be called, "integration ethics." To understand this fourth model requires shifting the primary unit of analysis most frequently focused upon in ethics training—the individual public administrator—to the organizational context in which the individual functions. Numerous administrative and organizational theorists have criticized the micro-emphasis on individual ethics in the profession and insisted that the proper unit of analysis is the organization, or at least crucial factors within the organization which affect the individual's conduct.

The emphasis on the integration model of ethics training has been advocated by various theorists since the 1980s. For example, Boling and Dempsey (1981) have argued that most ethics training focuses on individual responsibility, but they believe the emphasis should be on organizational reform. Three types of organizational change are advocated including conceptual clarification of the agency's normative guidelines, organizational protection for dissenters or whistle blowers, and ethics training that involves all members of the organization. Other normative theorists have expanded on this theme.

Bowman (1990) conducted a national survey of 750 public administrators to determine their attitudes toward contemporary ethics problems in government. Among his findings were suggestions from the respondents regarding ethics training for public managers. He indicates that a large number of respondents recommended an organizational training and development strategy that includes three elements. First, the agency mission must be defined along with the activities necessary to pursue it. Secondly, the employees need to be involved in creating an agency code of ethics. Third, top agency administrators must "walk the talk" or set the example of creating an ethical organizational climate by modeling the ethics they wish to promote.

Agreeing with Bowman, Brumback (1991) warns against ethics training that occurs in a vacuum, arguing that most preconditions for unethical behavior are situational. According to Brumback, a trained person working in the wrong organizational climate is unlikely to generate ethical conduct. Therefore, the level of analysis must include both the organization and the individual. Distinguishing between legality and ethics, he asserts that an organization-wide ethics program should be developed that encompasses both. Among its elements are the ethics factor in hiring, the ethics factor in performance management, ethics training, and an ethics program audit.

Ethics within the hiring process can be emphasized by ensuring policies and procedures are ethical, building the agency's reputation for integrity, and asking new hires to pledge a commitment to ethics through the government oath of office. In performance management the ethics factor can be incorporated into the appraisal process and managers can be asked to evaluate the ethical conduct of employees. Regarding ethics training, Brumback (1991) emphasizes developing ethical sensitivity, not so much through case studies, but by discussing the agency expectations from both a compliance and integrity viewpoint. Small group exercises and discussion are preferred over the case study approach, which can turn ethics training into an intellectual exercise or placebo. Finally, any public agency ethics program should include a periodic audit to see if all the components are working well. To gather a diagnosis and communicate the importance of ethics within the organization, the audit should include an opinion survey of the employees regarding their perceptions of the ethical climate of the agency and its ethics program.

Lewis (1991) also utilizes these organizational development strategies to construct a comprehensive agency-wide ethics program with training being one essential component. Lewis agrees with Bowman that any agency ethics program must start with the commitment of top leadership and modeling by those who set the tone and form the culture of the organization. This means executive managers must make ethics a key priority in the organization and ensure that it is integrated into every facet. Drawing on Brumback and Bowman, Lewis' intervention strategies include: developing an agency code of ethics with all levels of employees participating; adding the ethics factor in recruitment, performance appraisal, incentive and discipline systems; conducting an agency ethics audit; offering compliance and integrity training and counseling; and teaching techniques of ethical management to middle and upper levels of administration.

In other words, this integration model begins to reflect an organizational development (OD) approach to public agencies with ethics being the focal point for intervention.

Consider the well-known definition of OD offered by Beckhard (1994: 21): "[OD] is an effort (1) planned, (2) organization-wide, (3) managed from the top, to (4) increase organization effectiveness and health through (5) planned interventions in the organization's 'processes,' using behavioral science knowledge."

In this case, establishing a comprehensive agency-wide ethics program is the purpose with increased ethical conduct as the goal. Top leadership must be committed to the success of the effort, not only by supporting the plan, but by actively involving themselves in developing the ethics program, such as spearheading the development of a mission statement and an accompanying code of ethics in which all levels of the agency participate, and acting as role models for espoused ethical conduct within the organization. Planned interventions result from a diagnosis of the organizational climate using an ethics audit. Organizational changes to incorporate ethics can occur at all management levels and within the existing structure and culture of an agency. Consequently, ethics training becomes a vital part of an organization-wide endeavor in "normative-reeducation" (Chin and Benne, 1994).

Gerald Gabris (1991) echoes these sentiments by arguing that an organizational development approach to administrative ethics is essential to combat what he calls the "Machiavellian value systems" that public managers employ in practice at the organizational level. Counter to lofty ideals professed in an administrative ethos, such as regime values or social equity, or in a profession's ethics codes, public managers are in reality socialized into Machiavellian values which stress personal survival achieved through the power tactics of cunning, deceit, and manipulation. These values are exacerbated by four management practices, which Gabris identifies as a functional organization design, hierarchial authority systems, defensive routines, and socializing forces. To overcome these obstacles, the public manager faces formidable risks that can lead to lower trust, lower communication, higher risk, and lower assumption of personal responsibility. Administrative ethics among public managers is an oxymoron given the contemporary reality of organizational dynamics.

Instead, Gabris advocates that organizational development should be employed as the appropriate intervention to create the "regenerative organizational conditions" (1991: 218) necessary for administrative ethics to be practiced. He believes that high trust, high responsibility, low risk and high openness are more likely to occur through the use of OD strategies. As with the previous proponents of the integration model of ethics training, Gabris calls for diagnosis of the organizational climate and an intervention plan that creates regenerative conditions. Although ethics training is not specifically included in his discussion, it is implied that either an integrity or fusion approach fits most appropriately since OD is grounded on positive assumptions regarding human nature. Both models assume that individuals will act with integrity if the training cultivates their moral judgment through a normative reeducation process.

Building on the organization development model, Bonczek and Menzel (1994) identify six components that they believe are crucial to achieving an ethical workplace: (1) an organizational mission, that includes (2) a values statement with (3) ethical guidelines, developed by (4) a working ethics committee, that (5) creates ethical dialog and (6) provides ethics training. This dovetails with the integration approach presented by Cava, West, and Berman (1995), who advocate developing ethics codes (which employees can use by applying ethical decision-making within an organizational context of strong moral leadership) and who support ongoing ethics training at various agency levels with continuous communication occurring that focuses on ethical concerns.

Terry Cooper (1998) provides a final example of an integration approach of ethics training. Although his normative theory of administrative ethics focuses on the individual public manager and the responsibilities that ensue from defined role obligations, he also insists that responsible conduct can only be maintained if three other ethical dimensions are taken into consideration: (1) the organization's structure, which can support or impede an individual's ethical autonomy; (2) the organization's culture, which transmits the actual value context in which the public manager functions; and (3) societal expectations, which define legal boundaries for administrative discretion, the public's views of the profession, and citizens' involvement in the public planning process. Admonishing against "quick fixes" to ethical development, Cooper (1998: 258) advocates a holistic approach:

> Only a comprehensive review and treatment of the relevant aspects of an organization's structure, its personnel, training programs, formal rules and policies, prevailing informal norms, relationship to citizens, and the laws under which it operates will be fully sufficient. A long-term commitment to a plan for organization and personnel development based on such a review will produce far more significant results than sporadic efforts.

In short, the crux of the integration model rests on the conviction that ethics training delivered only at the individual level and not in conjunction with a total organization-wide program is bound to be severely limited in actually promoting ethical conduct among public managers. Only by focusing on the formal and informal aspects of the organization as well as promoting the development of external and internal controls with regard to the individual can ethics training result in any substantive effectiveness. Over the last two decades, increasingly more theorists and practitioners are maintaining that individual ethics training is severely limited without a comprehensive agency-wide ethics program.

However, in spite of the growing opinion of normative theorists in public administration that the integration model of ethics training is more likely to assure ethical conduct, it is the hardest of the four approaches to achieve. Indeed, any ethics training at all appears to be a luxury for most public service practitioners. Perhaps it is ironic that in a second survey of members of the American Society for Public Administrators regarding the revised code of ethics, Bowman (1997) found a majority of public service practitioners have not had any exposure to ethics training at all. Among many substantive findings, he states 54 percent of the public managers who responded indicate that their organization has never provided any ethics training, 22 percent state that it has only been offered once, and only 17 percent say their organization offers ethics training on a continuous basis. Whereas public managers seem to recognize the importance of an organizational approach to supporting individual ethics training, in reality ethics training of any type is still unusual in public service agencies. It appears the integration approach to ethics training remains an elusive ideal despite its growing number of advocates.

We have now investigated four models of ethics training in the public sector that have been discussed in public administration literature. A typology of the compliance, integrity, fusion, and integration models is depicted in Table 1. Five factors help to distinguish these four models: (1) whether the *focus* of analysis is aimed at the individual or both the organization and the individual; (2) whether the primary characteristic or *trait* of the approach is legal or normative; (3) whether the *expected outcome* of the training will result in public managers acting legally correct or morally right; (4) whether the *content* of the training emphasizes ethics laws, agency rules and regulations or ethical standards and ethical decision-making processes; and finally, (5) whether the *learning*

Table 1 Typology of Ethics Training Models in the Public Sector

Factor	I. Compliance	II. Integrity	III. Fusion	IV. Integration
Focus	Individual	Individual	Individual	Individual organizational
Trait	Legal	Normative	Both	Both but more normative
Outcome	Legally correct behavior	Ethically right conduct	Both	Both but more ethical idealism
Content	Ethics laws, rules and regulations	Ethical standards & decision-making processes	Both	Both but more ethical standards & decision-making processes
Learning methods	Pedagogical	Andragogical	Both	Both but more andragogical

style tends to be more pedagogical (information imparted by an expert) or andragogical (involvement of participants in their own learning).

Table 1 shows how these approaches can best be understood as points on a continuum ranging from a legalistic, microview of ethics training to a normative-reeducative, macroview of ethics training. The compliance model focuses on the individual. Legality is its primary characteristic with adherence to legally correct behavior as the expected outcome to training. The content of training entails a knowledge of ethics laws and agency rules and regulations. The dominant learning style is pedagogical because for the most part legal knowledge is imparted to participants from a trained expert, usually a lawyer.

The integrity model still focuses on the individual but its primary characteristic is normative or oriented around ethical standards based on some kind of moral idealism. The expected outcome of training is to assist public managers in developing the moral autonomy to conduct themselves in an ethically right manner. In order to accomplish this, ethical standards and a process for arriving at ethical decisions preoccupies the content of training. While the learning style can entail pedagogical techniques such as lecturing and test-taking, there is more of a tendency for trainers to create an educational process that affords participants the opportunity to become ethically sensitive to norms and values and develop a reflective capacity to apply those ethical standards in the practice of public service.

The fusion model tries to stress both the necessity for the individual public administrator to follow the law and also strive to live up to what one considers the morally right action. Thus, training would characteristically reflect both a legalistic and normative orientation that combines a knowledge of ethics legislation with high moral standards of the profession and some method for applying both to dilemmas arising in the workplace. Pedagogical and andragogical techniques may be used to achieve these goals.

The integration model changes the focus of analysis strictly away from the individual administrator and instead stresses the relationship between the organization and the individual that is essential to maintain responsible conduct. While legal obligations would be included in the training program, more emphasis would be placed on normative development that occurs within an organizational context in which the structure and climate are supportive of the individual acting along legally and ethically solid grounds. The content would tend to follow the fusion model, but this would reflect one component in an agency-wide ethics program evolved by the membership with the chief executives leading the way. Such an organizational development strategy would require a high degree of moral idealism and maturity to make a commitment to normative reeducation. Based on such humanistic value assumptions, the primary learning methods employed would be andragogical with employee participation becoming a key ingredient in the implementation of this model.

What implications does this typology have for in-service ethics training? Hartwig (1980–81) has pointed out that a "Theory X" organizational climate with an authoritative management style tends to reflect a legalistic approach to ethics, whereas a "Theory Y" organizational climate with a participatory management style would be more conducive to the integrity model or what he calls interpersonal ethics. Reflecting on our typology, four hypotheses seem to suggest themselves. (1) The more bureaucratic, closed, and structured the agency, the more it would tend to use compliance ethics in its training. (2) The more democratic, flexible, and open an organization is, the more likely it would use integrity ethics in training. (3) Organizations with mixed modes of bureaucratic and democratic elements would attempt to use fusion ethics in training. (4) Integration ethics would be least likely to be implemented because of the necessary value assumptions and the degree of commitment needed for an agency to regard it as the most effective approach to achieving a high level of ethical conduct.

In summary, this portion of the chapter has outlined four approaches to in-service ethics training in the public sector that have been derived from normative theorists in the field. Compliance ethics focuses on teaching individual public managers to follow laws and regulations. Integrity ethics instructs public managers in the ethical standards of the profession and a method of ethical decision-making to improve moral judgment and strengthen moral character. Fusion ethics attempts to combine these two approaches, and integration ethics shifts the unit of analysis to include both the individual and the organization by incorporating fusion ethics as one essential component in a comprehensive agency-wide ethics program.

III. CURRENT IN-SERVICE ETHICS TRAINING EFFORTS IN THE PUBLIC SECTOR

The next section of this essay will explore the kinds of ethics training programs that are being conducted currently in public sector organizations. Some research studies are emerging that relate directly and indirectly to ethics training and the hypotheses posited earlier. While research efforts appear to be burgeoning, huge gaps remain. A cross-section of training efforts at the federal, state, and local levels as well as in the public sector professions will be discussed in light of three questions: (1) What type of ethics training is being done? (2) How effective is the training? (3) What issues arise in using this type of ethics training approach?

A. At the Federal Level

The Office of Government Ethics (OGE) was established by the Ethics in Government Act of 1978 and was originally part of the Office of Personnel Management. OGE became a separate agency on October 1, 1989 as part of the Reauthorization Act of 1988. The mission of OGE is to foster high ethical standards for government employees and strengthen public confidence that government business is conducted with impartiality and integrity. Specifically, OGE is charged with exercising leadership in the executive branch to prevent conflicts of interest on the part of government employees and to resolve the conflicts of interest that do occur.

The director, who is appointed for five year term, is responsible for overseeing four divisions within OGE. The Office of General Counsel and Legal Policy (OGCLP) establishes and maintains a uniform legal framework of government ethics for employees, develops ethics policies for executive branch agencies and recommends changes in conflict of interest laws and other ethical statutes. Separated into three divisions, the Office of Agency Programs (OAP) is responsible for monitoring as well as providing ethics training and educational materials to executive branch agencies. The Office of Information Resource Management (OIRM) provides and promotes information technology within OGE by offering support services such as telecommunication, CD-ROM production and the OGE website. Finally the Office of Administration (OA) renders essential support to all of the OGE's operating programs.

Federal policy requires executive branch employees to engage in a minimum of one hour of ethics training annually. Each federal agency is required to select an individual employee to serve as the Designated Agency Ethics Official (DAEO), who is responsible for ensuring an agency ethics program (known as an "ethics community") is designed and implemented through the oversight of the OGE. The Program Review Division (PRD) of OAP conducts on-site reviews of agency ethics programs to determine if the agency has an adequate plan. The DAEO is responsible for sending the report to the PRD for program evaluation. The DAEO ensures that any deficiencies are corrected in 60 days.

The second division of OAP, Financial Disclosure, manages the reporting systems for 1000 presidential appointees and 125 DAEOs to ensure compliance to both public and confidential financial disclosure policies. The Education and Program Services, which represents the third division, provides support services to executive branch agencies by: developing educational materials, conducting ethics training courses (regarding standards of ethical conduct, conflicts of interest, and financial disclosure statutes), advising these agencies on compliance issues, hosting an annual government ethics conference, publishing the *Government Ethics Newsgram*, maintaining the Ethics Information Center, and other duties.

The general approach to ethics training sessions follows the compliance model. Each ethics class is three-and-one-half hours long and is team taught by a management analyst and an attorney from OGE. The learning method combines the use of lecture, video tape, slides, and case studies. The content of the classes focuses on whatever ethics legislation is in effect at the time and therefore changes to meet modifications in the law. The classes are composed mainly of the DAEOs and staff from the Inspector General offices and U. S. attorneys.

Through Information Resources and the Ethics Resource Library, ethics training materials are made available, which include videos, pamphlets, booklets, brochures, discussion outlines, and computer-based training modules. This includes "The CD-ROM," which incorporates seven ethics training subjects, in addition to current ethics legislation, executive orders, and other legal material. One example of an innovative, though highly limited, approach to the federal ethics training requirement available through OGE is an interactive video game called "Quandaries." Department employees must review at least five out of seven types of ethics statutes. The game simulates a federal career providing promotion to 15 jobs of increasing responsibility. To progress the employee has to show enough knowledge of ethics rules by resolving ethics conflicts to move to the next level.

The legislative and judicial branches have developed committees that formulate codes of conduct, and even under the executive branch the General Counsel oversees ethics compliance-oriented programs for such groups as the Department of Defense (DOD) and the National Archives and Record Administration (NARA). Yet OGE is the most outstanding example on the federal level of the compliance model of ethics training. The focus is mainly on individual executive branch employees gaining an understanding of rules and regulations as they apply to their daily work lives. The pedagogy is increasingly becoming "high tech" because it appears to be the most efficient way to fulfill the legal requirement for ethics training. While experimentation with other methods of ethics training might occasionally occur, the "nuts and bolts" approach of viewing the Eiffel Tower would seem to be the appropriate approach to ethics training at the federal level. Although the ethics workshops are evaluated by participants, Menzel and Carson (1998) indicate that no studies are available at the federal level on the effectiveness of the compliance training with regard to improving the ethical conduct of public employees. Given the low level of trust with which the public views government (Menzel, 1995) and the subsequent rise in ethics laws, it is not surprising that compliance training would be the obvious response, but even this reactive approach still appears to be minimally implemented at the federal level.

B.   At the State Level

Compliance ethics also forms the basis for ethics training at the state level. According to the Council on Governmental Ethics Laws (COGEL, 1999), all states have developed ethics commissions to deal with problems such as: conduct of political campaigns and elections, public financing of political campaigns, disclosure and regulation of campaign contributions, standards of conduct for public officials and employees, personal financial disclosures by candidates for election to public appointment and public office, registration of lobbyists, regulation and disclosure of lobbying activities, and open public meetings and records.

COGEL (1994: 1–2) conducted a 1993 study on ethics training of COGEL members. Fifty-six agencies reported on 71 programs. Thirteen agencies indicated that they had multiple training programs, while 15 agencies reported that they had no training programs. Some of the most significant results of the study are summarized as follows:

> The areas of ethics and elections are more likely to be mandated by law to do training.
> While the number trained in individual programs ranges from tens to thousands, the medians hover around 150–400.
> Likewise, while the number of sessions ranges from one to several hundred, the medians cluster around 3–10.
> Attendance is likely to be mandated for election officials but not for employees involved in campaign finance or ethics, or for lobbyists.
> Time required to present the training programs varies from 20 minutes to three days, but the median time required is two hours.
> The content of training consists mostly of imparting information and urging compliance with the law.

Almost all agencies use lecture as the primary methodology, but more than half combine case-study discussions or problem-solving with lecture. Most ethics trainers combine the use of written material with videotapes, but only a few utilize computer training.

Most agencies repeat training regularly throughout the year, especially during election periods or as requested.

Almost all the training is conducted by agency staff and only a few use outside consultants for instructors.

While most agencies believe the methods they use are effective, just over half use an assessment instrument.

Most do not know how much it costs per person to do the training or what percent of the agency's budget is being spent on training.

As with the federal government, this data certainly indicates that ethics training at the state level is overwhelmingly compliance-oriented. Occasionally an attempt is made to experiment with the other three models of ethics training. For example, the state of Washington presents ethics training programs that involve both fusion and integrated approaches. Specifically, the Washington State Executive Ethics Board (1999) indicates that learning about the state's ethics laws encompasses: educating other employees about ethics laws, teaching techniques to help employees resolve everyday ethical dilemmas, helping others to make the best ethical decisions, informing coworkers on how best to integrate ethics into the workplace, communicating how good ethics improves customer service, and serving as a valuable resource to public sector agencies. On the positive side, this certainly proves that experimentation is occurring at the state level in ethics training, even if it is piecemeal at this time.

On the negative side, several important research studies question not only the effectiveness of state ethics commissions in improving the ethical conduct of public officials, managers, and employees but also the role ethics training plays in this configuration. These studies suggest that the role of ethics training remains nebulous. Russell Williams (1996) studied the Florida Ethics Commission and compared their activities to four criteria in implementing effective external controls which include: ethics training, management audits, investigations, and controls by management. The Florida Ethics Commission accomplishes one of these criteria, the job of investigating complaints, but fails in the other three areas. In fact, the Florida Ethics Commission does little to educate public officials or administrators, having held only one ethics training conference between 1995 and their inception in 1976. Williams asserts that by reacting only to charges of ethics violations, the commission has often become a political weapon that one politician uses against another. Thus, Williams (1996: 71) believes that "the commission apparently serves more effectively as a punitive agent than as an agent of constructive change." While the commission may have undertaken a significant number of investigations, this does not necessarily improve the ethical climate of the state. In fact, from William's viewpoint, the commission may be having a negative impact.

This conclusion seems to fit research conducted by Donald Menzel (1996), who studied the complaint-making process in Florida between citizens and officeholders. He concluded that this ethics commission may actually contribute to further public distrust of government. He recommends the elimination of ethics commissions to monitor investigations and a transfer of the responsibility to local governments. In addition, Menzel calls for the creation of the office of ethics ombudsman, adoption of an "appearance" standard for conflicts of interest, and ethics education throughout the entire public education system. Indeed, one begins to wonder how many state ethics commissions are politically compromised and whether the presence or absence of compliance ethics training really makes a significant difference in curbing unethical conduct within the public sector.

California affords a second dubious example. Block (1991) indicates that when voters passed Proposition 112, they required elected officials and public managers to undergo ethics education; however, no provision was made as to the content of that training. The result was that the California legislature approached the ethics issue in two different ways: the Assembly chose the compliance model of training, while the Senate preferred the fusion model. The Josephson Institute (1999) supplied training that included some stress on legal requirements, but the infusion of core ethical beliefs and their application was also considered essential. Hence, compliance and integrity ethics were combined into the fusion model for in-service public sector ethics training in California.

However, continued politicalization appears to be the reaction to tougher ethics laws regardless of the type of training. When California passed Proposition 208, strict limits on political fund-raising and spending as well as resrictions on lobbyists were imposed. Yet as the state's top watchdog over political corruption, the Chairman of Fair Political Practices Commission told lobbyists apologetically that he believed parts of the law were unconstitutional and suggested some ways around the provisions (Morain, 1997).

Such questionable tactics undoubtedly led to a call for tighter external controls. In August of 1998, *The Sacramento Bee* reported that AB 2179 was passed by the California Legislature and signed by the governor, which extended required ethics training, not only to legislators, but also to legislative staff and lobbyists as well as 2400 high level state employees. Ethics training as a form of external control has become big business, but its actual effects—in improving the ethical climate of government or conduct of public officials and employees—remain to be proved. Indeed, the cases of Florida and California seem to indicate that with or without ethics training, the politicalization of ethics commissions themselves seems more likely than effective reform.

C.   At the Local Level

Large cities such as Burbank, Chicago, Houston, New York, Los Angeles, Seattle, San Francisco, San Jose, Washington, D.C., and even some small municipalities such as Chula Vista, California have formed their own ethics commissions. Seattle provides a poignant example of the problems that plague ethics boards. In a *Seattle Times* editorial, city ethics commissioners, Burgess et al. (1998) exhort the public to support the viability of the commission. They claim that three conditions must be met; the commission: must be independent by being empowered to aggressively and fairly enforce ethics laws, must have adequate enforcement power, and must have adequate funding to carry out its mission by hiring enough staff to do the proper job. Most of the commission's work is done through education, training, and issuing advisory opinions to city officials and employees, who inquire about ethics laws. These commissioners state that using enforcement power is unusual because when they do find problems, they are resolved through negotiated settlements. The bottom line of the editorial was to ask the public to support increased funding to carry on their operations. Interestingly, an increase in funding must come from the city and yet the commission has investigative power over the public officials who adopt the budget. The problems of the City of Seattle's Ethics Commission seem to reinforce the necessity to link ethics training (whether compliance, integrity, or fusion) into a systematic integration within the structure of government. In this case, the emphasis needs to be on autonomy, enforcement power, and adequate funding if an ethics commission is to be viable. Perhaps if these institutional arrangements are put in place, ethics training has an opportunity to make a positive impact on the conduct of government officials, managers, and workers.

Studies of local government over the past decade seem to indicate that the importance of ethics within municipalities is increasing and ethics training is on the rise. Experimentation is occurring which utilizes the integrity and fusion approaches as well as the standard compliance approach. There is some indication that even the integration model is being tried, although on a limited basis.

Donald Menzel's 1992 study of 700 public managers in local government indicated that few attended ethics training or recognized that their behavior was the subject of state ethics laws. This dovetails with a study of municipal governments and large firms, conducted by Berman, West, and Cava (1994), who explored their similarities and differences. They report that cities are less likely than corporations to implement their values through formal approaches in ethics training. Firms rely on exemplary leadership and communication, but they are no more likely than cities to adopt ethics strategies to increase their workforce effectiveness. It would appear that in the first half of the 1990s, ethics awareness and ethics training did not have a prominent place at the local government level.

But this trend seemed to reverse itself in the latter half of the decade. Willa Bruce (1998) reports the results of her study regarding a national survey of municipal clerks. She claims that significant attitudinal differences exist between those who received ethics training and those who did not. About half of those surveyed attended ethics training sessions, which the author characterizes as a fusion approach. The training consisted of an orientation to city codes and practices, continued in-service training aimed at both certification and the value of ethical behavior. She asserts that ethics training does make a difference in the respondent's ability to engage in job-related ethical decision-making and behavior. Ethics training helped public employees to become more aware of what constitutes corrupt actions and more willing to report them. Personal integrity as well as legal knowledge was enhanced. Furthermore, Bruce (1998: 247) maintains that ethics training was "a part of an overall ethos of responsibility that includes concern by citizens and commitment by both elected and appointed officials." She concludes by suggesting that education about laws and ethics will most likely have a positive effect on the conduct of local public employees.

These positive results also coincide with a 1997 survey of chief administrators in local governments of 50,000 or more. West et al. (1998) found that 85 percent of the respondents believed ethics was a high priority and that 58.5 percent of the jurisdictions provided some form of ethics training. Furthermore, 63.2 percent of the respondents reported that ethics codes had been strengthened. The emphasis on ethics also coincided with organizational revitalization in terms of productivity improvement and self-assessment of public trust. West et al. (1998: 5) state: "Although we do not claim that ethics training causes these positive outcomes, we do believe that efforts to improve government and public trust often include strategies that increase professionalism, customer orientation, and other ethics behavior."

Thus, at the local level it appears cities are beginning to take ethics and ethics training seriously. Obviously much more research needs to be done regarding the effectiveness of ethics training of all types and at all levels. However, at least there appears to be more interest in experimenting with different types of ethics training at the local level than at the state or federal levels.

D. At the Professional Level

A profession has been defined by Random House Dictionary (1987: 1544) as: "a vocation requiring knowledge of some department of learning or science [and] the body of persons engaged in an occupation or calling." Pugh (1989: 1) identifies six characteristics associated with a profession: "(1) a cast of mind (i.e., a self-awareness), (2) a corpus of theory, (3) a social ideal, (4) ethical standards, (5) formal organization to promote the standards, (6) a 'hall of fame' to recognize outstanding leaders."

A multitude of professions serve the public sector in such areas as health care, law enforcement, and social services. The espoused ethical standards of a profession are embodied in its code of ethics, and one could reasonably conclude that the type of ethics training employed by a profession will be reflected in the nature of its ethical code. If the code imparts prohibitions and an enforcement mechanism, compliance ethics is likely to prevail. If the ethics code is primarily inspirational, then integrity will be the focus, and if both dimensions are reflected in the code, then a fusion model is likely. Due to constraints in this chapter, all related public sector professions cannot be reviewed regarding their approach to ethics training. However, one example of a professional group that has been on the cutting edge of public service ethics and training that will be explored in this essay is the International City Management Association (ICMA), which has utilized all four models of ethics training in varying capacities.

Throughout its history, the ICMA has taken an active role in defining the ethical parameters of the profession. Tranter (1988) indicates that ICMA published its original code of ethics in 1924. The code has been amended numerous times since its inception to include *Guidelines and Rules of Procedure for Enforcement*. The code combines both compliance and integrity elements. With regard to the compliance approach, Hancock (1992) notes that the ICMA code has been one of the most successful to be adopted because managers are tried by their peers. When a written complaint is received by ICMA, a State Fact-Finding Committee sets up a timely investigation process and prepares a report, which is forwarded to the ICMA Committee on Professional Conduct. Violators are subject to sanctions by the ICMA Executive Board. Hence, compliance is maintained by professional enforcement.

Concerning integrity, the code also contains the highest ethical standards by which city managers are expected to conduct themselves. For example, one guideline reads (Kellar, 1988: 161): "Demonstrate the highest standards of personal integrity, truthfulness, honesty and fortitude in all our public activities in order to inspire public confidence and trust in public institutions." Another states (Kellar: 164): "Serve the public with respect, concern, courtesy, and responsiveness, recognizing that service to the public is beyond service to oneself."

In terms of ethics training, as cited earlier, ICMA has developed a "self-help" approach based on this code of ethics. This ethics training package includes a leader's guide, called *The Ethics Factor* (Hopper, 1988), an accompanying text, *Ethical Insight, Ethical Action* (Kellar, 1988) and their latest reader, *The Ethics Edge* (Berman et al., 1998). Aimed at promoting responsible conduct among city managers, the program provides three separate curricula that can be used to train new employees, supervisors, mid-level managers, top managers, and chief administrators. The curricula include: an orientation to ethics, personal ethics, and managing ethics in the workplace. Workshops can be conducted in half or full day sessions. Learning methods include exercises, case studies, discussion questions, and handouts.

While it appears that ICMA employs a fusion model of ethics training with an emphasis on both compliance and integrity, recent advances in ICMA training have led this professional group to begin advocating an integration model of ethics training that also emphasizes the importance of organizational ethics. West et al. (1998: 4) emphasize the importance of organizational ethics: "To Be effective, future ethics training must address the legal, behavioral, and policy requirements of organizations and use the best ethics training practices." The compliance aspect of ethics training is part of their legal emphasis, and integrity training is aimed at encouraging a high level of ethical conduct. However, this fusion model moves towards an integration approach because the authors further advocate that policy be linked to the ethics of the organization. The authors admit this aspect of ethics training is the least developed: "At present, ethics training is not well connected to specific policies, except in areas such as fair treatment of employees. Yet it is increasingly important that policy development and implementation are conducted in ethical ways, and also that substance of policies is ethical" (West et al., 1998: 7). This integration model focuses on organizational structure through the use of policy development as a means of supporting ethical conduct throughout the organization. No specific normative mapping is suggested but the recognition exists that the ethics training of individuals must be supported by organizational efforts to create an environment in which ethical conduct is valued, not discouraged.

Because training is based on their code of ethics, compliance rules as well as ethical standards are included. The training mode promotes development of moral judgment of individual city managers. Although one part of the curriculum includes the ethical climate of the workplace, the focus of the training remains individually oriented. The integrative model may be advocated, but at this point endeavors are experimental. Research needs to be directed toward examples of agencies that are actually integrating ethics into the fabric of the organization's structure and culture.

IV. CONCLUSION

Four approaches to ethics training in the public sector are currently being advocated by normative theorists: compliance, integrity, fusion, and integrative models. At all levels of government, the compliance model is predominantly used. This is probably because public administration is ultimately grounded in the law. The rash of scandals in government and in our society at large since the 1970s has led the public to demand more ethics legislation as the most obvious remedy for combating corruption. However, research (Williams, 1996; Menzel, 1996) casts some doubt as to whether the compliance training approach is effective in promoting ethical conduct if institutional mechanisms are not in place to ensure efficacious enforcement.

At the local and professional levels, experimentation is underway to utilize the integrity, fusion, and integration models (West et al., 1998). Particularly at the professional level, more emphasis on the integrity and fusion approaches is occurring due to a reliance on codes of ethics to define their moral parameters as well as motivate members to aspire toward professional ideals of their practice (Plant, 1994). As the most comprehensive ethics training approach, integration ethics appears to be the most difficult to enact, although often advocated (Berman, et al., 1994; Wittner and Coursey, 1996). Research studies are beginning to provide some basis for discovering what is actually occurring versus what is being purported. For example, Menzel (1992, 1995, 1996) has surveyed local and state governments as well as graduate schools regarding ethics education, while James Bowman (1990) conducted an ethics survey of members of the American Society for Public Administration (ASPA), and a subsequent survey with Russell Williams (1996). Only a few studies, such as ethics training at the state level (COGEL, 1994) and municipal level (Bruce, 1998), provide information as to who is doing the ethics training; the qualifications of ethics trainers remains uncharted territory. In short, studies of the effectiveness of ethics training are just beginning to emerge but overall they remain piecemeal with varied results.

Although a host of issues arise for debate concerning ethics training, two of the most significant problems should be addressed. First, the primary issue in ethics training focuses on what approach should be used to ethically educate public service practitioners. While integrity, fusion, and the integrative approaches have their advocates, in practice, use of the compliance model has become the foundation of ethics training. Should this be the sole approach to the ethics education of public managers? If not, to what extent should compliance drive the curriculum? How should the other training models be used either in conjunction with compliance or separate from it?

Normative theorists often argue from a linear mindset that one approach must be the best normative model. Perhaps a contingent approach to ethics training might meet with more incremental success depending upon the level of moral development (internal control) that needs to be addressed in training public service practitioners and the effectiveness of organization compliance or change (external controls) used by those overseeing the training within the institutional environment.

Concerning levels of moral maturity, Lawrence Kohlberg (1981) claimed that individuals evolve through a series of ethical stages in which each requires the mastery of the preceding ones. The preconventional stage is based on a self-orientation as to what is right. "If I want something and I can get it, then it is right." At the conventional stage individuals recognize a sense of responsibility to their group or community, and right is based on either social affiliation with others or an adherence to obeying the law. Compliance ethics is geared to help people move from the first three stages to the fourth, and in that sense such ethics training is attempting to elevate the ethical conduct of public managers to a respect for law, rather than being motivated primarily by self-interest or loyalty to a group. However, emerging research seems to be hinting that such training has little effect if institutional external controls, in the form of actual enforcement mechanisms, are not applied effectively. For example, those who would manipulate the law would learn nothing from compliance training if they are not fairly held accountable for their actions in terms of punishments and rewards.

The Seattle Ethics Commission (Burgess et al., 1998) warns us that compliance can not work if the authoritative body lacks the legal empowerment, organizational autonomy, and fiscal resources to enforce compliance measures without becoming a pawn of political manipulation. Therefore, perhaps one hypothesis worth researching would be that a decrease in illegal or corrupt behavior is more likely to occur if compliance training is conducted within the context of effective institutional enforcement. In other words, what is essential for compliance training to be effective is ensuring the proper external controls are put in place. This involves a continual struggle against the politicalization of ethics commissions and public service agencies. The extent to which this can be achieved may be dubious as suggested by Zajac's research (1996), which examined the failures of organizations to apply internal and external controls. Yet if compliance ethics is to have some effectiveness, institutional controls are a necessity.

At the postconventional level of moral development (according to Kohlberg), the individual begins to develop moral autonomy and act according to ethical principles that have universal application. Sensitivity to ethical standards, the ability to apply principles and the quality of character to act on what one discerns to be right reflects a principled level of moral maturity, which is the purpose and intent of the integrity model of ethics training. For the most part, this has been the approach of graduate ethics education. Attempts to strengthen moral judgment have been researched by Stewart and Sprinthall (1991), who found that most graduate students in public administration tend to respond to reasoning that complies with the law but resist developing principled-level reasoning. Menzel (1997) surveyed graduate schools of public administration accredited by the National Association of Schools of Public Affairs and Administration (NASPAA). A majority of the schools and alumni graduates believe that the integrity approach to ethics education helped them to become more ethically sensitive and improve their skills in ethical decision-making, but students want educators to practice what they teach. This suggests that an essential component in developing integrity ethics is the instructor's ability to exhibit moral reasoning and integrity within the organizational context of the classroom. Perhaps coupling these two research studies leads to a second hypothesis: if the instructor acts as a role model in exhibiting principled reasoning and exemplary conduct, the moral judgment of the students will increase. The integrity approach to ethics training relies on development of internal control as the means of improving ethical conduct. Therefore, the integrity of the ethics teacher is integral to the success of this method.

Yet the question must be asked: How would a principled person cope with an organization whose ethos is characterized by loyalty or self-interest? As suggested by a multitude of theorists in organizational theory and development, only an organization that incorporates a human relations management approach will be able to provide the external controls necessary to support the internal controls imparted in integrity ethics training. As with compliance ethics, we must ask the question: Does ethics training have a chance of affecting individual ethical conduct? In the case of integrity training internal controls must consist of: a humanistic management orientation with moral leadership at the forefront; and a commitment to values of trust, respect, participation, accountability, and competence that become translated into the goals, structure, rewards, and culture of the organization.

Since individuals at all levels of moral maturity exist in public service organizations, both the compliance and integrity models are incomplete. A fusion approach to ethics training could be effective for training professionals but external and internal controls would have to be successfully implemented within organizations. Enforcement mechanisms are required to correct unethical conduct, but at the same time, principled individuals must be supported through an open, trusting work climate. Otherwise the effectiveness of ethics training according to the fusion model is questionable. In short, we must honestly ask ourselves whether individual ethics training will result in any long-lasting effectiveness in the workplace unless the integrative model of developing an equitable organizational structure and supportive culture is operative.

Thus, we are left to wonder if focusing on individual ethics training (regardless of whether the content consists of compliance, integrity, or fusion ethics) has severe limitations in terms of success, unless the organization has the external controls in place to support the level of moral maturity of the individual. While a contingency approach to ethics training has been advocated by this author, it appears that the integrative model has the most potential for effectiveness, yet remains the most difficult to implement.

However, the roots of this difficulty reflect a second issue that must be acknowledged with regard to ethics training within the public sector; i.e., the double standard that exists in our society between the public and private realms. Curtis Ventriss (1991) and others have argued that political and administrative ethics operate under a "moral dualism" between high ideals of public honor and service and the ethos of the marketplace. In our private domain, we live in a culture of "civic commercialism" based on an ethic of competitive individualism, but in our public domain, we extol a culture of "civic virtue" in which we expect government officials to practice high ideals of selfless commitment to the public interest, social equity, and citizen advocacy.

Why are we surprised that individuals enter public service with the ethos of civic commercialism as their guide to behavior? The contradiction of these two ethics are illustrated in a leadership training program that Louis Zuccarello (1998) conducts for citizens who provide volunteer public service to the community. He notes that these individuals are caught in a continual tension between civic individualism and civic virtue. Further, they lack exposure to any form of ethics education or training that graduate students or practitioners may experience. Zuccarello (1998: 227) observes that Americans may know the "right" answers in theory but have trouble applying them in practice because of a pervasive attitude of "privatism" combined with "the exaggerated importance of self-interest." Yet he claims that participation in his workshop leads participants to develop moral reasoning and reconcile some of the disparities by beginning to shift their attitudes towards becoming part of a civil society.

The need for public discussion about civic ethics appears to be a frontier for the future for ethics training in the public sector. With citizens more involved in government at the local level, a shift from a culture of civic commercialism to a culture of civic virtue is the most critical direction for ethics education to take in this society. Normative theorists such as Budziszewski (1994), Menzel (1996), Dagger (1997), Berman and Bonczek (1998), among others are calling for this shift toward education for a civil society. Certainly, the four models of ethics training offer contingent approaches to improving ethical conduct among public officials and service practitioners that need further development, but a more far reaching approach to ethics training is to include active citizens who will play an increasingly important role in influencing and contributing to public service. King and Stivers (1998: 204) believe, "that not only Americans' feelings about their government, but the very future of governance in the United States, rest on the need for a more involved, active citizenry, and for active administration that has at its center the nurturance of citizenship." The term "ethics training" needs to be converted to "civic education" if we are to actually progress in forming a civil society. Citizens as well as public officials and public service practitioners need to be involved in an educational process that focuses on the cultivation of civic virtue.

REFERENCES

Beckhard, R. (1994). What is organizational development? In: *Organizational Development and Transformation: Managing Effective Change* (W.L. French, C.H. Bell, and R.A. Zawacki, eds.). Homewood, IL: Irwin, p. 21.

Berman, E.M. and Bonczek, S.J. (1998). The ethics of community building. In: *The Ethics Edge* (E. Berman, J. West, and S. Bonczek, eds.). Washington, D.C.: ICMA, pp. 216–226.

Berman, E., West, J., and Bonczek, S. (1998). *The Ethics Edge.* Washington, D.C.: ICMA.

Berman, E., West, J., and Cava, A. (1994). Ethics management in municipal governments and large firms: exploring similarities and differences. *Administration and Society*, 26(2), 185–263.

Block, A.G. (1991). Ethics training: the assembly and senate take a different approach to teaching ethics. *California Journal*, March, 112–115.

Boling, T.E. and Dempsey, J. (1981). Ethical dilemmas in government: designing an organizational response. *Public Personnel Journal*, 10, 11–19.

Bonczek, S. and Menzel, D. (1994). Achieving the ethical workplace, *Public Management*, 76(3), 13.

Bowman, J.S. (1990). Ethics in government: a national survey of public administrators. *Public Administration Review*, 50, 343–353.

Bowman, J.S. and Williams, R.L. (1997). Ethics in government: from a winter of despair to a spring of hope. *Public Administration Review*, November, 517.

Box, R.C. (1998). *Citizen Governance*. Thousand Oaks, CA: Sage Pub. CA.

Brady, F.N. and Woller, G.M. (1996). Administrative ethics and judgment in reconciling competing theories. *American Review of Public Administration*, 26(3), 309–316.

Bruce, W.M. (1998). Ethics education in municipal government: it does make a difference. In: *Teaching Ethics and Values in Public Administration Programs: Innovations, Strategies, and Issues* (J.S. Bowman and D.C. Menzel, eds.). Albany, NY: SUNY, 231–249.

Brumback, G.B. (1991). Institutionalizing ethics in government. *Public Personnel Management*, 20.

Budziszewski, J. (1994). Why we are so bad and what we can do about it: On the state of civic virtue. *International Journal of Public Administration* 17(12), 2285–2296.

Burgess, T., Dayton, P., Kim Gang, S., and Ichinaya, D. (1998). Protecting the integrity of government. *The Seattle Times*. Seattle, WA, October 19.

Cava, A., West, J., and Berman, E. (1995). Ethical decision-making in business and government an analysis of formal and informal strategies. *Spectrum: Council of State Governments*, 68(2), 68.

Chin, R. and Benne, K.D. (1994). General strategies for effecting changes in human systems. In: *Organizational Development and Transformation: Managing Effective Change* (W. French, C. Bell, and R. Zawacki, eds.). Homewood, IL: Irwin, 111–132.

Cody, M.W. and Richardson, L.R. (1992). *Honest Government: An Ethics Guide for Public Service*. Westport, CT: Praeger.

COGEL (Council on Governmental Ethics Laws). (1994). *COGEL Training Survey: The State of Training on Campaign Finance, Election, Ethics, Freedom of Information, Judicial Conduct and Lobbyist Laws*. Los Angeles, CA: COGEL, 1–2.

COGEL (Council on Government Ethics Laws). (1999). Available from the COGEL homepage (www.cogel.org).

Cooper, T.L. (1998). *The Responsible Administrator* (4th ed.). San Francisco, CA: Jossey-Bass.

Cooper, T.L. and Wright, N.D. (1992). *Exemplary Public Administrators: Character and Leadership in Government*. San Francisco, CA: Jossey-Bass, 1–7.

Dagger, R. (1997). *Civic Virtues: Rights, Citizenship, and Republican Liberalism*. New York: Oxford University Press, 194–201.

Denhardt, K. (1984). *Towards a More Ethical Public Administration* Unpublished dissertation. Lawrence, KS: University of Kansas, p. 37.

Denhardt, K. (1994). Character ethics and the transformation of governance. *International Journal of Public Administration*, 17(12), 2165–2193.

Finer, H. (1972). Administrative responsibility in democrat government. In: *Bureaucratic Power in National Power* (F. Rourke, ed.) (2nd ed.). Boston: Little, Brown.

Frederickson, H.G. (1997). *The Spirit of Public Administration*. San Francisco, CA: Jossey-Bass, 114–133.

Frederickson, H.G. and Hart, D.K. (1985). The public service and the patriotism of benevolence. *Public Administration Review*, 45(5), 547–553.

Friedrich, C.J. (1935). Responsible government service under the american constitution. Monograph No. 7 in C.J. Friedrich et al.: *Problems of the American Public Service*. New York: McGraw-Hill.

Gabris, G.T. (1991). Beyond conventional management practices: shifting organizational values. In: *Ethical Frontiers in Public Management* (J.S. Bowman, ed.). San Francisco, CA: Jossey-Bass, 205–224.

Garofalo, C. and Geuras, D. (1994). Ethics education and training in the public service. *American Review of Public Administration*, 24(30), 283.

Grosenick, L. (1995). Federal training programs: help or hindrance? *The Public Manager*, 24(4), 43.

Hancock, J.J. (1992). The ethics and essence of professional city management. *Missouri Municipal Review*, 55, 24–25.

Hartwig, R. (1980–81). Ethics and organizational structure. *The Bureaucrat*, Winter, 48–56.

Hopper, L. (1988). *The Ethics Factor: Leader's Guide*. Washington, D.C.: ICMA.

Jackson, M. (1993). How can ethics be taught? In: *Ethics and Public Service* (R. Chapman, ed.). Carleton Public Policy Series, Vol. 10. Ottawa, Canada: Carleton University Press.

Josephson Institute for the Advancement of Ethics. (1999). Homepage. Available from http://www.josephsoninstitute.org.

Kellar, E.A. (1988). *The Ethics Factor Handbook*. Washington, D.C.: ICMA.

Kellar, E.K. (ed.) (1988). *Ethical Insight, Ethical Action: Perspectives for Local Government Managers*. Washington, D.C.: ICMA.

Killilea, A., Pasquerella, L., and Vocino, M. (1998). Ethics for skeptics in public administration. *Spectrum: The Journal of State Government*, 68(4), 19.

King, S.C. and Stivers, C. (1998). *Government Is Us: Public Administration in an Anti-Government Era*. Thousand Oaks, CA: Sage Publishing, 204.

Kohlberg, L. (1981). *The Philosophy of Moral Development: Moral Stages and the Idea of Justice*. New York: Harper and Row.

Krohe, J. (1997). The big business of business ethics. *Across the Board*, VXXXIV(5), 23–29.

Lewis, C.L. (1991). *The Ethics Challenge in Public Service*. San Francisco: Jossey-Bass, 9–14.

Marini, F. (ed.) (1971). *Towards a New Public Administration*. Scranton, Pennsylvania: Chandler.

McGregor, D.M. (1957). The human side of enterprise. *Management Review*, November.

Menzel, D.C. (1992). Ethical attitudes and behavior in local governments: an empirical analysis. *State and Local Government Review*, 24(3), 94–102.

Menzel, D.C. (1995). Through the ethical looking glass darkly. *Administration and Society*, 27(3), 379–389.

Menzel, D.C. (1996). Ethics complaint making and trustworthy government. In: *Public Integrity Annual* (J.S. Bowman, ed.). Lexington, KY: Council of State Governments, 73–82.

Menzel, D.C. (1997). Teaching ethics and values in public administration: are we making a difference? *Public Administration Review*, 57(3), 224–239.

Menzel, D.C. and Carson K. (1998). Empirical research on public administration ethics: review and assessment. Unpublished article. Available at http://www.edu/-tp0deml/demhome.html.

Morain, D. (1997). California and the west: official says he is 'eviscerator' of prop 208. *Los Angeles Times*, Los Angeles, CA, June 24.

Plant, J.F. (1994). Codes of ethics. In: *Handbook in Administrative Ethics* (T.L. Cooper, ed.). New York: Marcel Dekker, 221–241.

Pugh, D.L. (1989). Professionalism in public administration: problems, perspectives, and the role of ASPA. *Public Administration Review*, 49, 1.

Random House Dictionary of the English Language. (S.B. Flexner and L.C. Hauck, eds.) (1987). New York: Random House, 1544.

Reynolds, H.W. Jr. (1995). Educating public administrators about ethics. *Annals of the American Academy of Political and Social Science*, 537, 122–138.

Richardson, W.D. and Nigro, L.G. (1987). Administrative ethics and founding thought: constitutional correctives, honor, and education. *Public Administration Review*, 47 (September/October), 367–376.

Roberts, R.N. and Doss, M.T. (1992). Public service and private hospitality: a case study in federal conflict of interest reform. *Public Administration Review*, 52(3), 260–269.

Rohr, J.A. (1989). *Ethics for Bureaucrats*. New York: Marcel Dekker, 25–95.

Rohr, J.A. (1998). *Public Service Ethics, and Constitutional Practice*. Lawrence, Kansas: University Press of Kansas.

Sacramento Bee (1998). Ethics training broadened. Sacramento, CA, August 26.

Stewart, D. and Sprinthall, N. (1991). Strengthening ethical judgment in public administration. In: *Ethical Frontiers in Public Management* (J.S. Bowman, ed.). San Francisco: Jossey-Bass, 243–260.

Tranter, R.A. (1988). Ethical problems today. In: *Ethical Insight, Ethical Action: Perspectives for Local Government Managers* (E.K. Kellar, ed.). Washington D.C.: ICMA, 147–153.

Truelson, J.A. (1991). New strategies for institutional controls. In: *Ethical Frontiers in Public Management* (J.S. Bowman, ed.). San Francisco: Jossey-Bass, 225–242.

U.S. Department of the Interior. (1998). *Ethics: An Employees's Guide*. Washington, D.C.: U.S. Department of the Interior.

U.S. Office of Government Ethics. (1999). *Ethical Conduct for Employees of the Executive Branch*. U.S.O.G.E. Homepage. Washington, D.C. Available from http://www.usoge.gov/.

Van Wart, M. (1996). The sources of ethical decision making for individuals in the public sector. *Public Administration Review*, 56(6), 525–533.

Ventriss, C. (1991). Reconstructing government ethics: a public philosophy of civic virtue. In: *Ethical Frontiers in Public Management* (J.S. Bowman, ed.). San Francisco: Jossey-Bass, 114–134.

Walton, J.R., Stearn, J.M., and Crespy, C.T. (1997). Integrating ethics into the public administration curriculum: a three-step process. *Journal of Policy Analysis and Management*, 16(3), 472–483.

Washington State Executive Ethics Board. (1999). Available at http://www.wa.gov/ethics/training.html.

West, J., Berman, E., and Bonczek, S. (1998). Frontiers in ethics training. Public Management, 80(6), 4–9.

Williams, R. (1996). Controlling ethical practices through laws and rules: evaluating the Florida commission on ethics. In: *Public Integrity Annual* (J. Bowman, ed.). Lexington, KY: Council of State Governments, 65–72.

Wittner, D. and Coursey, D. (1996). Ethical work climates: comparing top managers in public and private organizations. *Journal of Punlic Administration Research and Theory*, 6(4), 559–572.

Zajac, G. (1996). Beyond hammurabi: a public service definition of ethics failure. *Journal of Public Administration Research and Theory*, 6(1), 145–160.

Zuccarello, L. (1998). Ethics, the academy, and part-time civic leaders. In: *Teaching Ethics and Values in Public Administration Programs: Innovations, Strategies, and Issues* (J. Bowman and D. Menzel, eds.). Albany, NY: SUNY Press, 219–230.

5

The Use of Philosophy in Administrative Ethics

Charles J. Fox
Texas Tech University, Lubbock, Texas

I. INTRODUCTION: THE ESTRANGEMENT OF PHILOSOPHY FROM PUBLIC ADMINISTRATION

This chapter progresses through three tasks. First, briefly, at a high level of abstraction, a road map of Philosophy leading to administrative ethics is provided for students of public administration who may not be familiar with Philosophy (hereafter upper case "P" will be used for Philosophy as a discipline, lower case "p" will be used for generic philosophy or thoughtfulness). Second, using categories derived from the still influential analytical school within the sub-discipline of ethics in Philosophy, a taxonomy of the orthodox views in public administration ethics is developed. Third, taking note of what appears to be the cusp of a radical paradigm shift in Philosophy toward "antifoundationalism," theories clustered around communitarian ideals are explored. Concluding remarks extend the antifoundational critique to potentially innovative and more reciprocal intercourse between Philosophy and more practical arts like public administration.

The study of ethics is usually thought to be an aspect of philosophy. Two senses of "philosophy" need to be distinguished before the use of it in administrative ethics can be assessed. Generically, *philos* (love) and *sophia* (knowledge/wisdom) may be seen as the motivational spark energizing all non-trivial and extra-instrumental intellectual endeavor; the love of ideas and how they help explain our lives and the contexts in which they are lived, may be counted as an enduring part of the human spirit. Philosophy of this first sort is alive and well in administrative ethics, indeed this *Handbook* as a whole is a projection of philosophy of this first, generic, kind. Still, even by this most generous definition, philosophy is not dominant in administrative ethics. As will become clear, even less influential is academic Philosophy, which is the focus of this chapter.

The second sense of Philosophy defines a professional academic discipline. In turn, academic Philosophy is of different types. As late as 1970 it was possible to say that a schism in occidental Philosophy made sensible a neat bifurcation of Anglo-American and continental (basically French and German) traditions that could be treated separately. Although this is decreasingly true as Philosophy becomes more "postmodern," for now we need only follow the Anglo-American branch to trace Philosophical influence on administrative ethics. Anglo-American professional Philosophy has been more refined and focused than either generic philosophy or continental speculations. It is divided into specialties, and its practitioners speak to each other in codes that they have reciprocally developed about various well-defined discourses handed down to them by a lengthy and rich tradition. In both the best and worst connotations of the term they have been scholastics; their attention is often channeled into narrow areas, yet they are very bright and clever and they sometimes offer up startling insights from within the problematics that their discipline assigns them. It follows that Philosophy has several specialized branches variously divided, as in all disciplines, by the overlaying of new, sometimes unifying approaches, on historically sedimented and institutionalized areas of inquiry. Branches include: cosmology, metaphysics, ontology, epistemology, philosophy of science, linguistic philosophy or semiotics and, most important for us, ethics or moral philosophy.

Winnowing our analysis from the fragmentation of the branches to the unity of a trunk, Anglo-American Philosophy in the first three quarters of the twentieth century has been dominated by an approach called analytic Philosophy.[1] As this period parallels the development of public administration, analytic Philosophy has been also the most influential in this latter field. One could make a larger transcendent Weberian point that both public administration and analytic Philosophy are aspects of the same *zeitgeist* of industrial capitalism and high modernism.

But just as soon as one says that analytical Philosophy has been the *most* influential, one must hasten to deny very much in the way of *direct* influence. As a general rule philosophers do not *do* public administration and public administration is not directly informed by Philosophy. The Catron and Denhardt (1988, p. 10) study of syllabi used to teach graduate students in public affairs programs uncovered eight of seventy four (11%) as based on philosophical frameworks. And, the majority of these were more political theory than what we are calling Philosophy per se. Only two professors were confirmed as having philosophical training. In his survey of practitioners, Gortner (1991, p. 41) found that "[p]hilosophical or cultural concepts were never raised by any of the interviewees as they described their ethical dilemmas." The word "philosophy" appears in neither the table of contents or the workbook on ethics applying the standards of the American Society for Public Administration (ASPA) (Mertins and Hennigan, 1982), nor in the principles of ethics adopted by ASPA in 1981.

Both institutional/structural and "mental" conditions contribute to this unfortunate mutual estrangement. Even at an academic level, Philosophers and their concerns only rarely interact with public administrationists. Philosophy is normally regarded as (perhaps the preeminent) one of the humanities. Humanities, in turn, are usually housed in colleges of arts and sciences. Only one-third of public administration programs will be similarly located, and the ones that are will usually be uncomfortably attached to departments of political science (Henry, 1990). Other public administration units are either free standing or are attached to schools of business or schools of generic management. These institutional alignments reflect (and help cause) the often false perception of public administration as a (mere?) practical art, a matter of, if not vocational, at best professional, training.

These material conditions are augmented by an intellectual quasi-incommensurability. Mastering the problematics of Philosophy, and the languages used to address them, is a daunting prospect for those who spend their intellectual energies grasping other jargons. Furthermore, Philosophy still has the arrogant aura that it has, since classical times, claimed for itself as the mother of all sciences—the language umpire and arbiter of right reasoning (e.g. Dummett, 1978, p. 478). Philosophy when it captures only for itself the meaning of *philos*-sophia (the love of knowledge) and then renders it as a series of exercises in impeccable logic, has the off-putting quality of relegating other arts to the love of things less exalted.[2]

It follows that when public administration became serious about ethics, Philosophy, wherein ethics is thought to properly reside, was only gingerly approached by its leading intellectuals. And herein lies a great irony. Just at the historical moment (1970s) public administrationists looked to Philosophy for principles appropriate for founding an administrative ethics, cutting edge Philosophers had moved to question all foundations (Bernstein, 1983; Jonsen and Toulmin, 1988; MacIntyre, 1984); the Philosophers were reviving Aristoteleianism or moving to a postmodern point of view. From those ancient or postmodern points of view, public administrationists have every warrant to *do* philosophy projecting outward from the standpoint of contemporary governance. But alas, they could not have known that because Philosophers do not always communicate well beyond their kith, and obversely, public administrationists fear, scorn, or denigrate[3] venturing in Philosophy's mysterious terrain.

An encyclopedic chapter on the *use* of philosophy in administrative ethics, then, can be a blank page, a series of unrelated asides with footnotes, or (following a now classic example set by Frankena, 1973) itself an exercise in Philosophical clarification. Choosing the latter alternative, Philosophy will be *used* to array both the explicitly Philosophical views and the more implicit philosophical efforts. As will be evident this has been the primary utility of Philosophy (cf. Brady, 1988; Jennings, 1991; Denhardt, 1988, pp. 27ff; Wall, 1991; Willbern, 1984).

II. PUBLIC ADMINISTRATION ETHICS AS TYPES OF FOUNDATIONAL PHILOSOPHY

A. Introduction to a Philosophical Taxonomy

In this section we want to use Philosophical concepts derived from the analytical school of ethics to categorize public administration ethics. Aspiring to a relatively comprehensive taxonomy both overtly Philosophical stances (e.g. Hart, 1974) and tacit, even unintentional, ones will be addressed. After first justifying shoving public administrationists views into the categories without their permission, the rest of the section is devoted to "foundational" ethics. In rough chronological order of their appearance in public administration first, American utilitarianism, an essentially teleological view, is adduced. Then varieties of deontological positions are scrutinized.

As has been said, the direct influence of Philosophy on administrative ethics is difficult to substantiate. There are very few footnotes in articles and books devoted to public administration ethics that cite moral philosophers like G. E. Moore, A. J. Ayer, or H. Sidgwick. From time to time certain best-selling philosophers like J. Rawls and A. MacIntyre enjoy fleeting fame in public administration, but they are generally read as if their arguments are free-standing; the context of the tradition in which they are reacting to their philosophical opponents and interlocutors is ignored. Famous philosophers are normally appropriated only as authoritative founts of principles rather than as colleagues in dialogic discovery (cf. Cahill and Overman, 1988, pp. 14–15). And when their views are celebrated for public administration audiences, they are rarely contextualized as exemplars of particular schools or discourses.

Missing from public administration ethics is the kind of critical discourse and interchange that typifies a good rousing Philosophical controversy. Instead is found a plethora of atomistic views uncorrected by vigorous disputation. Thus from the standpoint of the intentionality of public administration authors there has been little attempt to join named Philosophical schools nor well categorized Philosophical positions. Schools and positions (like particular literatures in the social sciences), have their well known (to Philosophy) gambits, standard arguments and deficiencies, which deficiencies, at the nether edge of a paradigm, are the zones of contention and innovation. Without the focus enforced by indwelling in a rigorous discourse, novices will repeat mistakes and head down blind alleys already fruitlessly explored. To paraphrase an arrogance penned by C.D. Broad: all good fallacies go to public administration when they die and rise again as the latest discovery of the local professors (cited in Hart, 1988). To anyone imbued with a Philosophical point of view, which necessarily entails having been influenced by the cleansing accomplished by a century of analytical Philosophy, public administration ethics is a backward looking eclectic collection of eccentric and serendipitous views only rarely characterized by meticulous argumentation.

One of the premises of this chapter is that public administration ethics would benefit from a good Philosophical taxonomy whereby issues, and different stances to them, can be arrayed alongside one another. Now, philosophical taxonomies abound (see Pugh, 1991 and Wall 1991, for reviews and reworkings of the many that have been proffered). And, of course, every article in public administration ethics must begin, by force of our own protocols, with a literature review, themselves implied taxonomies. None of these taxonomies have, however, stuck (Denhardt, 1991, p. 91).[4] Rather, each attempt at taxonomy becomes a position itself and simply adds another tiny point of light, as it were, perceptually indistinguishable from the others, to the ceiling of a darkened planetarium. Perhaps using categories derived from Philosophical ethics will, because of the solidity of their consensual roots in careful analytical thought, prove less ephemeral.

Although it has been said that there is a plentitude of views, Philosophy gives us a way to unite most of them under one basic rubric. What unites virtually all ethical thought in public administration is the search for universal or quasi-universal *rules, standards*, or *principles* by which appropriate behavior may be deduced or judged; they are *foundational*. We save for Section III those views which are not foundational in the sense that we are using the term.

B. How Most Public Administration Ethics Is Foundational

The term foundationalism is of relatively recent origin, stemming from so-called postmodernist Philosophical writings (see especially Rorty, 1979; Bernstein, 1983 and 1992 are accessible secondary source interpretations). By foundationalism in Philosophy is meant something similar to (and perhaps more familiar to public administrationists) nomothetic explanation in science and logical positivist Philosophy of science. A *nomothetic* science, "seeks to establish abstract general laws for indefinitely repeatable events and processes" (Nagel, 1961, p. 547). This is also called the covering law model of explanation (Hempel, 1968). In classical Greek philosophy *nomos* understood as convention or law was opposed to *physis* variously translated as "to grow," "to be," or "what things really are" (Kerferd, 1967). Counted as nomothetic or foundational, then, is any ethical argument which takes the form of deducing the appropriate judgment or behavior located in the flux and flow of actual life (physis) from putatively higher, more general or abstract laws, principles, or standards seen as located above and outside that flow regardless of how those rules are derived.

In anticipation of Section IV, discussion of contemporary Philosophical directions, which is very much a critical reaction to all foundational ethics, these founding principles will sometimes be referred to as "vanishing referents." As will be more carefully argued in Section IV, ultimate foundational principles tend, like mirages, to vanish the closer one approaches them.

The positions described in the next section are all foundational and involve behaving or judging the behavior of others based on rules thought to entail moral obligation. Philosophers of the analytic tradition further divide such views according to how the rules are derived. Two main ways are normally distinguished: teleological or consequentialist and deontological (Frankena, 1973, pp. 14–15). Teleological views, of which utilitarianism is the paradigmatic example for American governance, are results oriented. For our purpose we need only to consider the broadly utilitarian branch of teleological or consequentialist position; this holds that an act is morally obligatory if the rule under which it is subsumed leads to the greatest overall balance of good over evil. Put overly starkly, the end justifies the means. Deontological views start the other way round. The rule is either self-justifying or is justified by some higher self-justifying principle from which lower order rules may be logically deduced. Lower order rules are of the kind: "always tell the truth," "be kind to animals." Higher order rules are of the order of the golden rule, "do unto others as you would have them do unto you," or Kant's categorical imperative "act only on the maxim which you can at the same time will to be a universal law." Higher order rules are often either the actual expression, or secular equivalent, of "because God said so."

Again, most ethical views in public administration fall under one or the other of these categories. In roughly chronological order of their appearance in public administration (since the 1880s) (cf. Nigro and Richardson, 1990) we begin with utilitarianism which in the American system of government becomes for public administration the ethics of authoritative command.

C. The Ethics of Authoritative Command as Procedural Utilitarianism

1. The Orthodox Model of Public Administration Entails an Ethics

The classical model of public administration embodying the principles of hierarchy (Weber), efficiency (Taylor) and separation of politics from administration (Wilson) has, although it is more often tacit than expressed, an ethics (cf. Plant, 1983). In the language of academic moral philosophy it is basically a utilitarian or consequentialist system. It has at least a provisional definition of the good, a foundational principle, by which it is supposed to be derived, and a theory of obligation incumbent on individual administrators.

2. The Good

As a utilitarian system, consciously designed as such by early twentieth century progressives (see Cooper, 1991, pp. 110–111), the ethics of authoritative command adheres to the phrase "the greatest good for the greatest number." In the Benthamite philosophy from which it arises, good or happiness are words we use to denote a positive ratio of pleasure to pain. Notice, this is not a very precise not substantive view of the good, it is open-ended. This leads logically to a procedural view of how it is to be achieved. To coin a phrase, it is procedural utilitarianism, which is to say that the greatest good will be achieved if proper procedures are followed.

3. Derived from "The People"

Lacking a firm grasp of exactly what happiness is, we should leave it to individuals to decide. In large part they should be free from government to pursue happiness by their own initiative in civil society. Insofar as happiness must rely on more communal arrangements, then it must be done democratically by majority rule. What is good is what we decide democratically to do to promote happiness. This view can generate considerable rhetorical power as has been recently discovered by Oliver North who ran afoul of it. As Senator George Mitchell explained to North during the Iran-Contra hearings "the American people have a right to be wrong," by which he meant really, that when policy shifts, no matter how whimsical it might appear, what used to be wrong is now right while what was right is now wrong. The people either now or in the past through more solid constitutional provisions are the standard, the sovereign. There is no higher standard by which they may be judged wrong.

4. Role of the Individual Administrator: Baseline Position

By this logic impeccably deduced by Finer (1936; 1972) bureaucrats qua bureaucrats are not to have wills of their own although they may participate in will formation through delimited (e.g. Hatch Act) political activity (i.e. voting). Bureaucrats are to shed their role in will formation once they pass through the doors of their bureaus. There, in return for security, they are to be functionaries carrying out legitimated commands from each level of superordination back up through to the representatives of the people and thence supposedly to the attentive people at the ready with their votes to approve or disapprove (the vanishing referent). There is a neat correspondence between functional role that promotes efficiency (efficiency itself being a subsidiary ethical norm relying on the validity of the rest of the construct for its own validation as means) and the ethical role: both require obedience to the rules and supervisors who bear the authoritative interpretation of rules (Dawes, 1923; Appleby, 1949). Thus, individual ethical choice is limited to choosing to follow the rules (the ethical thing to do) or to violate them by commission or omission (unethical acts). Without such hierarchical accountability, by this logic, "the people" would be deprived of the procedures to express their sovereignty and hence their current definition of the greatest good for the greatest number.

5. Current Manifestations

Since the ethics of authoritative command is simply the expression in language common to ethical studies of the classical paradigm of public administration, it shares its strengths and weaknesses. Its major strengths lie in the fact that it is still the basic official institutional view. Although the classical paradigm is tattered and worn it has not been replaced by some new coherent vision. As the unquestioned view, or foundational myth, of elected officials, the press, textbook political science, and ASPA (Mertins and Hennigan, 1982, p. 41), it is not surprising that much of the activity currently classified as ethics follows from it. Using the means available to them, the passing of laws and promulgation of regulations, officials attempt to reinforce ethical behavior by making rules that are basically designed to ensure that the other rules are followed. Some people have been unethical in that they have not followed rules. Therefore sanctions against those who violate rules must be made more stringent and the temptations to violate rules must be removed. Thus the paradigm case for this ethics is conflict of interest. One is pulled away from neutrality by an attractive force such as money wielded by special interests. We remove that force by making it illegal (ban accepting gifts), censurable (legislative ethics committees), or difficult to cash in on (legislation against immediate employment by an entity over which one once exercised regulatory power "revolving door").

6. Why Questionable

The weaknesses of the ethics of authoritative command which caused public administration scholars to search elsewhere for an ethics, come not so much from its logical structure *as an ethics* which has as much (and as little) logical power as any other foundational view. Rather the classical paradigm of "overhead democracy" (Redford, 1969) itself, which supports the ethics of authoritative command, is simply no longer credible as a description of our governmental system and the agencies which conduct its daily business. Indeed, public administrationists would not have got into the ethics business at all were it not for the erosion of the classical model. The ethics movement in public administration (Fox and Cochran 1990), comes primarily out of the recognition that public administrators exercise discretion at all levels (Rohr, 1989a, pp. 37–47) and cannot just follow rules. If written rules cannot ensure democratic accountability and right doing because there are too many of them (Fox, 1989), or they are too vague, or they cause goal displacement (Stewart, 1988; Thompson, 1988), then ethics must be internalized so that public servants will do right (see Cooper 1990, and Fox and Cochran, 1990 on the Friedrich Finer debate). Recognition of discretion and manifestos celebrating it (e.g. Wamsley et al., 1990) along with the general incredulity caused by the empirical impossibility of the politics administration dichotomy (see Rohr's [1989a] devastation of this fiction) combined to make a search for a better system of ethics imperative.[5]

7. Revisiting the Role of the Administration: Fudging the Baseline Logic

There is a kind of culture lag between theory driven academic public administration and the community of elected and appointed practitioners. At a theoretical level, academic public administration has mostly abandoned the orthodox paradigm for which the ethics of authoritative command are corollary. Accordingly, many of the efforts to develop personal ethics for individual administrators have occurred outside of procedural utilitarianism and fall within the next, deontological, section. Still, it is premature to write the obituary of the ethics of authoritative command even in academic public administration, much less as legislative strategies developed by the practitioner community. For one thing, researchers committed to description, as opposed to ethical prescription, must continue to be anchored in a reality indeed rife with command and obedience and institutionally slotted leaders and followers. For tough-minded students of administrative ethics, aware both of the implausibility of the orthodox paradigm as well as the bureaucratic realities that that paradigm is no longer capable of legitimizing, three strategies have been developed: (1) authoritative command as ideal, (2) the redundancy gambit and (3) reviving or reworking the citizen connection. These are arrayed in order of their distance from the baseline, Finer, position (subsection 1 above).

(a) Obedience to authoritative command as ideal. Strategy one is to hold out the model of authoritative command as an ideal to which we ought aspire and rededicate ourselves from our fallen state. This respectable strategy, endorsed by such prestigious political scientists as Lowi (1979), is represented in public administration ethics by the widely cited work of John Burke (1986). Burke's work may be classified as an extension to public administration ethics of Mosher's classic *Democracy and the Public Service*

(1982). Both recognize the problems with the orthodox accountability model, admit exceptions to it, then go on to reaffirm it nonetheless as the only thinkable alternative that affirms (electoral representative) democracy in a mass complex society. Because of the formula: commitment to the procedures of electoral democracy on behalf of a "public" determination of the good, obedience is still the most important rule for achieving the greatest balance of good over evil.

(b)   Redundancy gambit.   The second strategy for the cognoscenti reluctant to abandon formal chains of command reaching to the sovereignty of the people is to promote a dual system; an ethical systems redundancy. Affirmed in these views is both external and internal ethical accountability. The prescription is to follow organizational dictates (external) until and unless their implementation severely shocks the conscience of the administrator. Then the redundant, auxiliary system of personal or professional ethics may kick in. The auxiliary system may be deontologically grounded (see Section III below). This second strategy is staffed by the widely adopted Cooper (1990).[6] Other examples of this strategy are: Guy (1991), Lewis (1991), Moore (1981), Thompson (1987), and Warwick (1981). Authors will vary in emphasis across the spectrum between the poles of external and internal accountability, but more individual autonomy is affirmed than by Burke's view.

Logically subsumed under this second strategy would be the various devices by which individual conscience might find expression. These are generically cataloged by Hirschman (1970) as exit, voice, and loyalty and include whistleblowing (Bok, 1981; Glazer and Glazer, 1989; Truelson, 1986) and resignation in protest (Weisband and Franck, 1975). Said devices are promoted for the purpose of strengthening the integrity of organizational accountability, again leading back up to the sovereign people as the fount of "the good."

(c)   Revitalizing citizenship.   The third strategy for academics disillusioned with the orthodox model is to reconstitute the relationship between public administration and the sovereign people. The scheme might be called "disintermediation" because it calls for direct links between public servants and the citizens, diminishing reliance on the hierarchy of overhead democracy. It is, accordingly, the furthest away from the baseline logic of authoritative command and calls on proactive administrators to reach out and involve the citizenry. Revitalizing citizenship may be regarded as either the nethermost strategy of procedural utilitarianism (which is why it is placed here), or a form of neo-Aristotelian communitarianism (see Section IV.C below). It is a form of procedural utilitariansim insofar as it simply replaces the mechanisms of electoral representative democracy with the mechanisms of direct or "strong" democracy (for mechanisms see e.g. Barber, 1984, pp. 261–311). By this interpretation the goal of a non-substantive "good" to be pragmatically determined as we go along by majority will of the sovereign people remains untouched. Revitalizing citizenship slips the utilitarian category insofar as it becomes in itself the teleological goal of humans reciprocally defining, developing, and refining themselves in a community. The authors of what might be called the "citizen school" in public administration ethics (Adams et al., 1990; Chandler, 1984; Cooper, 1991; Fredrickson, 1982; Gawthrop 1984; and Yates 1981) are not always clear about which of these arguably contradictory branches of the road they are following. As this Philosophical matrix is being overlaid on their works it is possible that they are not sure themselves, nor are they required to be. Gawthrop and Chandler, for instance, seem to be fully within procedural utilitarianism while Cooper either dialectically combines, or vacillates between, the two views.[6]

D. Deontological Views

Many scholars of public administration are skeptical of the various attempts to either reaffirm or patch up the orthodox model. The author of this chapter has elsewhere (Fox and Cochran, 1990) classified these otherwise diverse writers as the "discretion school," (but note that strategies b. and c. under utilitarian views above also affirm varying degrees of discretion). Jennings has a similar grouping in mind under "ethics as the logic of moral reasoning" (Jennings 1991, p. 67). What unites a discretion school is the distance its authors have put between themselves and the orthodox model of overhead democracy. They have standpoints more empathetically situated with practicing administrators coming at the problematic either from "agency" perspectives (Kass, 1990; Wamsley et al. 1990) or from perspectives rooted in organizational humanism, or even from desperation about crass interest group democracy (e.g. Hart, 1988). If the "good" could not be trusted to the mechanisms of representative democracy and or hierarchical administration, can it be instilled in career bureaucrats? Are Platonic guardians a better bet than neutral functionaries? If ethical governance is not the normal output of the representative democratic accountability loop, from whence can it issue? Attempts to forge plausible answers has led authors to look for other foundational principles from which appropriate behavior may be deduced.

Positions may be classified as deontological[7] when attached to a substantive principle thought of as foundational and so compelling as to be binding or obligatory in a moral sense; rules are right and wrong on their own account or because of higher laws (these then self-validating) from which they are logically deduced rather than because of their imputed consequences. Again, to anticipate the anti-foundational views of Section IV, such abstract self-justifying principles might be considered "vanishing referents" by nonbelievers. Three authors will serve to illustrate deontological positions in public administration (Hart, 1974; K. Denhardt, 1988; and Rohr, 1989a).

1. Hart's Social Equity

Hart takes it as his task in his well wrought piece to provide philosophical foundations for "that faction of the discipline known as the 'New Public Administration'" (p. 3). Insofar as the label applies to any substantive position it means that administrators using their irreducible discretion should be proactive to promote social equity. This is done primarily by redressing the balance of power that exists in civil society which favors the wealthy, the articulate, and the well organized within the core of the state. In other words, administrators should take the part of the poor, the inarticulate, and the unorganized. This is an ethical response to the worst effects of interest group liberalism (Fredrickson, 1971). To bolster this position Hart proposes that we adopt the ethics of John Rawls' 1971 *Theory of Justice*. Rawls' position is classically neo-Kantian in its belief that right behavior can be deduced from a theoretical formula. In this case the formula is developed from an "original position," of disembodied, ahistorical, acultural minds reasoning together in a totally disinterested way. This disinterestedness is achieved because participants do not know where they might fit in the social structure for which they are developing principles of justice. Rawls ingeniously takes social contract theory to a Kantian level of abstraction. Disinterested minds, Rawls argues, would conclude that equal distribution of societal goods should occur unless inequalities benefit the least advantaged. Thus, we act ethically if our actions can be construed as beneficial to the least advantaged. From such principles, Hart believes that a moral code of obligation can be developed for public servants. Similar foundational deontological views based on justice include Pops (1991) and Fredrickson and Hart (1985).

2. K. Denhardt's Universal Moral Order

Denhardt's book stands virtually alone as the one with the most extensive intermingling of Philosophy and public administration since Leys (1952). It too offers a typology but its references are, with few exceptions, limited to foundational ethics and are generally adduced to help her build a realist abstract realm (the universal moral order) from which obligation, behavior, and judgement may be derived with some precision. Realism, in ethics, denotes a doctrine that morals and values have transcended reality beyond the mere opinions of those who hold them; realists are the natural enemy of relativists (pp. 38ff). [It should be said here parenthetically that Philosophy is filled with a maze of classification schemes and words like ''realism,'' ''idealism'' and ''objectivism.'' These terms will have different, even opposite, meanings depending on the problematic in which they occur and the school that is addressing them. Thus what is called here Denhardt's moral realism is similar to what we learned to call idealism, like Plato's forms, in our sophomore Philosophy classes, so read ''ideals are real'' (as opposed to material or empirical realities addressed by science]. She manages to find, although she admits that it has no definitive substance, and that people disagree about its principles, and that it may be *universal* only in the West, a universal moral order ''which can be understood and followed by administrators making ethical decisions'' (p. 38) (cf. Rohr's review, 1989b). Denhardt ends up simply asserting the existence of a (vanishing) referent, or her faith in same. She is driven to this conclusion because she, like many others (see e.g. Lee, 1990), believe that all alternatives, even the utilitarian views outlined above, lead to nihilism (p. 43). ''. . . [A]ny discussion of ethics must be grounded in some understanding of a moral order'' (p. 38, emphasis mine). As is usual with such views, a cartography of the ''universal moral order'' is missing as well as how exactly it might inform the daily life of administrators.

3. Rohr's Regime Norms

Perhaps the most influential attempt to derive a foundational ethics that bureaucrats might internalize to replace the ethics of authoritative command is the one associated primarily with the name of John Rohr (1986; 1989a; but see also Hart 1984; Nigro and Richardson 1990; and discussion of differences in Fox and Cochran, 1990, pp. 260–262). For the past decade and a half it has been Rohr's project to legitimize the administrative state and administrative discretion by appeal to the American Constitution and its various interpretations. The upshot of his work for ethics is that administrators should internalize principles of the Constitution which is the founding of our regime. Very much opposed to the ethics of authoritative command, Rohr believes that across the branches of government, including appointed and career administrators, all who take the ''oath of office'' have combined but also independent relationships to that common source of ethical principle which the Constitution and Supreme Court interpretations of it provide.

Rohr's argument in relation to ethics, in stark relief, is as follows:

> Public servants, elected, politically appointed, or appointed by merit take an *oath of office* to support the Constitution of the United States.

The *founding* of our regime which the Constitution embodies may be regarded as our transcendent first principle (the vanishing referent).

The Constitution is very much more important than any ephemeral electoral coalition.

Administrators owe allegiance then, to the Constitution, not necessarily the incumbent political administration of the day.

This is a plausible way to get around the politics administration bifurcation. Two aspects of privileging the Constitution make Rohr's move intellectually compelling. First, it is a proximate standard beyond which one rarely ventures; to say that something is unconstitutional is a checkmate squelch. In the American context very few arguments lead to questioning the Constitution itself; it is a powerful almost self-sustaining symbol of legitimacy. This means that reasoning back beyond or prior to the Constitution so rarely occurs that the vanishing referent, in this case the views of a particular set of men meeting in 1787, or their constituents, is seldom invoked. Second, following from the first, the Constitution stands *as if* it were natural law. That is to say an "ultimate principle underlying all legal differences, and the infallible means of reducing those differences to unity" (d'Entreves, 1965, p. 21; this is also what Denhardt means by universal moral order). Thus, Americans can count themselves as among the fortunate few who have a founding codified in a legal document and supported by a legal tradition. Political philosophers as diverse as Plato and Rousseau have recommended just such a founding to stabilize otherwise chaotic political life. It is at least fortuitous if not fortunate that the Constitution was written when it was, at the height of the enlightenment when confidence in the power of reason was at its apex. In the American context one needn't actually believe in natural law or the power of reason to reap its benefits. The Constitution channels, focuses, and delimits our considerations to manageable proportions. Everything is not up for grabs.

The upshot of Rohr's carefully argued position is a foundational deontological ethics based on the values of equality, freedom, and property. By this reasoning bureaucrats who internalize these norms and act in prudent ways in relation to them will be ethical. When the inevitable conflicts between the values occur, bureaucrats should look to the methods and "spirit" of Supreme Court jurisprudence to resolve them.

Superficially, Rohr's foundational ethics might also be classified as a form of procedural utilitarianism. The only difference would be that the sovereign people spoke once very loudly at the founding and only once and a while since then when amendments after the Bill of Rights were added. Such interpretation would miss the move that Rohr has made that makes the founding and the (quasi-realist cum natural law) realm it has established very similar to the universal moral order to which Denhardt refers and the contractarian realm of disembodied minds that Hart appropriates from Rawls. It is precisely from such variously grounded realms that deontological chains of reasoning are thought to emerge to inform practice.

III. FOUNDATIONAL ETHICS CONCLUSION

Probably most public administration ethicists sense the weakness of the ethics of authoritative command. But are the available deontological systems more credible to the phenomenological life-world, the flux and flow of decisions, micro-judgments and human relations, of day to day administration? To state the question is to entertain a negative answer;

perhaps none of us has come up with a workable coherent alternative. Contemporary (postmodern) Philosophy may be read to suggest that the failure is related to the quixotic attempt to find a calculus of foundational ethics and then find some set of principles with which to load it; that accomplished, an inexorable chain of logic may be adduced leading from principle to action or obversely from questions about what action to take, back up through the chain to the appropriate principle. But when this is tried, when administrators try to reason back from the daily flow of life to those principles, they vanish before they can get them to give up an answer. The indubitably ethical question of whether to fire, admonish, or counsel a subordinate caught in wrongdoing may be arbitrarily placed at the end of a decision tree, the first principle of which is fairness. The branches of the tree may well seem to follow, binary choice by binary choice, to rational conclusion. But then, what is fair? To justify "fair" requires a higher level principle. Should it be Rawlsian, Constitutional, or because all persons were created equal? But then, by what right, by what ineluctable principle were Rawls, the Constitution, or equality established? God says so? . . . logic requires? . . . or "we take these principles to be self-evident"? But then one must accept God, or the parallel ontological correspondence of logic and the cosmos on faith. Alas, push any logic to its foundation and one finds no presuppositionless presupposition; they vanish to another presupposition. We teeter on the brink of infinite regress— where the referent vanishes to reside in the purgatory of all a priori principles.

Reliance on vanishing referents may be more readily explained by the sociology of knowledge than either stupidity or ignorance. A sociology or genealogy of knowledge conducted on the discipline of public administration would uncover two tendencies: eclecticism and incrementalism. These help explain the attraction of the discipline to foundational ethics of various sorts.

Disappointed with the demise of the orthodox model, public administrationists went looking for a new ethics. But where can one be found? Since public administration has always been *eclectic*, borrowing from several disciplines including political science, sociology, social-psychology, and business administration, there was little compunction against picking out a hodge podge of ideas, norms, and concepts from other more integrated literatures. This approach risks confusing the "dis" placement of concepts with the misplacement of them (Ramos, 1981, pp. 60–75). In misplacement, concepts take on entirely different and skewed meanings when deprived of the context in which they were developed and to which they originally spoke. Organizational subculture and corresponding ethics, for instance, were originally thought of as something emerging from the bottom up as ways of human accommodation to top down structural imperatives (Ingersoll and Adams, 1992, Ch. 2). The concept has now evolved and been misplaced as another management tool. In ethics it finds its expression in using ethics to manipulate the organization (e.g. Pastin, 1986).

Another trait that public administration shares with other fields of study is intellectual *incrementalism*. Scholars do not radically throw out a whole set of conceptions. Rather, the tendency is to keep the basic structure and only adjust anomalous elements. For the purposes of this chapter it is important to highlight the extent to which public administration is built around a decision-making model. There are many iterations of decision-making including: input-throughput-output-evaluation-feedback systems theory; linear programming; and the budgetary process: The decision-making model assumes that decisions are arrived at through steps that either are, or look very much like, rules. It follows that the path of least resistance for public administration scholars looking for an ethics would be to bias toward those views that take a form similar to the decision-making model.[8] The procedure takes sets of moral values and, like replacing a battery pack, loads them into the old shell. Thus, students of administrative ethics think that their labors are to replace the classical model of neutral machine-like administrators. And they do this but only in the sense that they replace one set of exterior rules (authoritative command) for other (differing from author to author) ones to be internalized (cf. Jennings, 1991). Deontological ethics, then, may be seen as shifting accountability and control from obedience to political masters to obedience to ethical principles. The vanishing referent of "the people," is replaced by various other ones. The two types share a foundational form. Attempts to transcend or subtend foundationalism form the subject of the next section.

IV. ANTI-FOUNDATIONAL ETHICS IN PUBLIC ADMINISTRATION

If foundational ethics does not ring true to the flux and flow of the life-world of practitioners, where can one turn? Philosophers since the 1970s may point the way. Two current strands of Philosophy may be identified as anti-foundational: the neo-Aristotelian or communitarian strand, and that wide variety of views subsumed uncomfortably under the label "postmodern." As will be seen, only communitarian (broadly conceived) alternatives have been fully explored by public administration ethicists. These views share a critique of foundationalism viewed now as one of the more regrettable instances of arrogance of modernism. This section begins, then, by first reporting the attack on foundationalism and modernism; second, a discussion of the problem of relativism seems appropriate; third, neo-Aristotelian, communitarian ethics will be sketched followed by (fourth), public administration exemplars; fifth, positions which resemble communitarianism but stem from psychological and phenomenological sources will be outlined.

A. Critique of Modernism and Foundationalism

Although they use different language, the critique of modernist foundationalism mounted by neo-Aristotelians (e.g. MacIntyre, 1984; Jonsen and Toulmin, 1988) and post-modernists (e.g. Lacan, 1984; Rorty, 1979 and for accessible interpretations see Bernstein, 1992; Poster, 1989) are sufficiently similar to allow common treatment. Aristotelianism and its Catholic Thomism adjunct, is of course, premodern (ancient and medieval). Modernity is basically that period from the Enlightenment until, say, the 1950s (assuming for the sake of explication that there is a *post*modern condition). Exact dates cannot be provided as periods overlap and because to utter the word "modern" also entails an entire *weltanschauung* or *episteme* which includes industrialization, capitalism, triumph of science, and bureaucratic forms of organization.

Fundamental to the critique of modernity is a critique of the arrogance of reason. The Enlightenment, informed importantly by Newtonian physics, thought of the world as basically harmonious; it was like one big mechanical clock. We could not only understand the big clock of physical reality, we could also understand human society and arrange it just as harmoniously as the big clock. It was assumed that everything participated in some grand rational scheme to which all thought had access. Thus, when one speaks from the spirit of modernity about ethics, science, appropriate governmental arrangements, or anything else, one casts one's thought in the language of universals. Whenever one speaks seriously, one speaks as though the thoughts express truths which transcend the momentary, the situational, and even the cultural-historical, to verities good for now and all time. The assumption is that because we share space in some overarching rational world that we can speak for each other and to each other through this universal rational medium.

The chink in the armor of modern reason may be expressed as the problem of *vanishing referents*. Rational arguments which aspire to universal status are all based on an "indian rope trick." None are founded on a presuppositionless supposition. Follow any rational argument back up the geometrical chain of reasoning and the solidity of the referent, as it were, disappears. In the end, or the beginning, one finds things like "God," "the people," "we hold these truths to be self-evident," or "logic requires." None of these first or overarching principles passes tests established by rational thought itself as founding. Neitzche seems to have been right (MacIntyre, 1984): if God is dead or irrelevant to rational thought, nothing within rational thought can replace Him as foundational for an Archimedean (outside and above contingent and situated life) or God's-eye standpoint. There is no grammar of grammars. If one's ethics, then, as most public administrationists have done, rely on a chain of reasoning reaching to some fixed or absolutely sure entity, one will be disappointed.

B. The Metaethical Problem of Relativism

The critique of foundationalism embroils one in the realm Philosophical ethicists call metaethics. Metaethics is essentially a debate between those who come up with clever ways to justify grounds from which normative ethics (making judgments about right and wrong) can then proceed, and those who foil such attempts. Auxiliary to the debate over foundationalism is the metaethical problematic of relativism which has found its way into public administration ethics [see especially Denhardt (1988) and Lee (1990)]. As displayed above, Denhardt believes in a transcendent universal moral order, while Lee has argued for the indoctrination of students in settled professional norms. Both of these authors have taken very seriously an article by Lilla (1981) in the neoconservative opinion organ *The Public Interest*. Lilla complains that the public administration ethics movement has as its result the training of sophists, i.e. public servants expert in rationalizing their behavior by reference to complex moral arguments. Instead of being imbued with a moral compass, what he calls the "democratic ethos," students are instead delivered up to the dangers of moral relativism.

Moral relativism to those who fear it, leads by a very short road to nihilism. If values are relative to period, time, and culture, the argument goes, then there is no standard by which to judge them good or bad, or right and wrong. Certainly logical positivists (see especially Ayer, 1936) with strict empirical standards of justification for truth, express this type of relativism. Their view, called *emotivism*, considers ethical utterance as having no more truth validity than such emotive outburst as "wow," "neat-oh," or "yum yum." Pragmatists (see Bernstein, 1983 for a cogent treatment) and postmodernists go logical positivism one better and claim similar status for those scientific operations that positivists *do* believe have truth validity.

Foundationalists confronted with such heresy, go for the quick kill. They say that relativism affirms with the other hand what it has taken away with the first; the claim that there are no universals is itself a universal—trump. This is Lee's strategy. Denhardt, in addition, explains away relativism as just a misguided pluralism, which pluralism of the many can be combined in the one (universal moral order) if people just think about it properly, and *assume* that such universal moral order exists a priori, even though no one can directly describe it.

To these arguments sophisticated relativists will cry "unfair!" Only one who first believes in universals could make these arguments which beg the question; assuming in advance what ought to be the object of inquiry. If foundationalists insist on such universals as well as assuming robust ontological status for the law of contradiction, it not only proves relativism because the relativists do not do so, but makes these incorrigible self-referential thought modules (i.e. universalism and relativism) downright incommensurable, two darkened ships passing on a moonless night.

In the long run, it might be wise to distinguish between types of relativism (See Stout, 1988, Ch. 4). The emotivism (non-cognitivism) of logical positivists may be considered the extreme version. The author of this chapter has coined the phrase "entropic relativism," for such doctrines. Entropic relativism does indeed level out all values talk to literally "non-sense." "Ought not commit genocide" belongs to the same class of claims as "I like vanilla ice cream." The other sort of relativism shared by existential-phenomenologists (Fox, 1980), hermeneuticists (interpretivists) (Bernstein, 1983), and communitarians (MacIntyre, 1984) hold that not all values are equal, values are meaningful, but they are derived more from indwelling in human communities than from an abstract source of pure reason. It is this latter type of relativism that informs the collection of anti-foundationalist ethics organized under the two rubrics: communitarianism and postmodernism to which we turn.

C. Communitarian Ethics

The composite view about to be sketched has several names all signifying the same general orientation: communitarian, neo-Aristotelian, character ethics, or virtue ethics. The names all refer to a common discourse between, to name the major figures, Charles Taylor (e.g. 1985), Alasdair MacIntyre (e.g. 1984), Jonsen and Toulmin (e.g. 1988), and (to a lesser extent) Michael Walzer (e.g. 1983). Readers may be familiar with Bellah et al. *Habits of the Heart* (1985) which is rooted in communitarianism. Communitarian ethics have (1) a different (from modernist) view of the self; which (2) alters the locus and direction of ethical causality, which (3) calls forth a teleological virtue or character ethics which in turn (4) promotes an ethics typified by phronesis (practical wisdom), and casuistry for the "wicked" problems. Two additional sections follow: (5) difficulties with this standpoint will then be adduced. (6) Finally, various versions and traces of communitarian ethics will be noted in public administration ethics literature.

1. The Self

Recall that some members of the "discretion school" rebelled against the merely external controls presupposed by the ethics of authoritative command; they took the side of Friedrich in the Friedrich/Finer dispute and thought they were giving respect to autonomous individuals by substituting internal controls for external ones. From the standpoint of communitarian and postmodern philosophy, however, the substitution was only a slight modification, a marginal incremental change. Looked at more carefully, all that was accomplished was a shift from *material* external behavioral controls (command) to *ideal* external behavioral controls; the internalization of external *thought*. Communitarians (and postmodernists) protest that the "self" that such doctrines presuppose is hardly a recognizable self at all. It is an atomistic individual with no culture, no history, no situatedness and is not embodied. It is an abstract self, a disembodied reasoning being theoretically fashioned after Descartes' *cogito* . . . "I think, therefore I am." And again, to show the connection, thought, reason, and consciousness are by foundationalist lights, the essence of humanity, and because all humans are alike in relation to this essence, universals to which minds have direct access can be affirmed. Obversely, communitarianism follows Aristotle's dicta that man (sic) is a social/political animal the full development of which can only occur in a well ordered community (polis). This more robust self comes stamped by its past community experience and does not have the absolute free will assumed for abstract, atomistic, and autonomous individuals.

2. Primacy of Community

Communitarians begin not with principle nor the atomistic sovereign individual but with context. "They view human agency as situated in a concrete moral and political context and stress the constitutive role that communal aims and attachments assume for a situated self" (d'Entreves, 1992, p. 180). Individuals, it follows, do not commit good or bad acts as if in a vacuum. Nor are individuals all at once good once the appropriate moral code has been committed to memory. Causality, which in modernist patterns runs from autonomous individual consciousness-to-judgment or decision-to-act, is now conceived by communitarians as a dialectical reciprocal causality between individuals and the communal-historical context in which the individual has been formed. Indeed, without context the human individual is but an unrecognizable cipher; there is no perceivable physiognomy. An important implication of this shift in locus is to elevate the community to, if not absolute primacy, at least co-equal primacy. In contrast to the modernist paradigm where individual self-interest is assumed to be the primordial force in life magically coordinated by the invisible hand of the market and tempered subsequently by an overlay of moral obligation dictated by right reason, the community itself and other humans are a precondition for human life and happiness. It follows that other-regardingness, altruism, loyalty, community attachments and other group-based sentiments are not mere deviations from the norm of rationality. Such a view undermines rational choice theory and dominant branches of economics (for public policy implications see e.g. Stone, 1988).

3. Teleology of Virtue and Character

The cultivation of internal traits of character and virtue, then, is the task of ethics and, for that matter, these are the goals of a well ordered polis. ". . . [M]orality is internal. The moral law . . . has to be expressed in the form 'be this,' not in the form 'do this.'. . . [T]he true moral law says 'hate not,' instead of 'kill not' '' (Stephen quoted in Frankena, 1973, p. 63). Aristotle and some neo-Aristotelians go on from here to explicate an intricate taxonomy of virtues in great detail. These generally take the form of the so-called "golden mean" whereby a virtuous trait, e.g. courage, is the mean between one excess: rashness and another: cowardice. Such lists, unfortunately, lend themselves to trivialization as in the Boy Scout Code (this of course is a sin of interpretors not originators). More important is the process view of character cultivation. One does not all-at-once emerge virtuous from the womb or at puberty. As the character of the person is, by this stance, more important than any particular act, an immoral act may become the occasion for a substantial improvement in character, if that act is part of a teleological ascent toward wisdom and happiness in and with the community.

4. Casuistry and Phronesis

Casuistry, long ridiculed by modern foundationalists as no better than a popular book on etiquette, has been making a comeback especially in professional (e.g. medical) ethics. Casuistry is close in spirit to common law, where precedents evolve, cases are subsumed under them, exceptions (as in equity law) are noted and more finely wrought precedents evolve in the spirit of the former ones (Morgan and Kass, 1991, p. 300). It is more inductive than deductive. It is more organic than mechanical. It is an ongoing dialogue between cases and rules of thumb (cf. Jonsen and Toulmin, 1988, pp. 34–35). It is also called phronesis which is translated as practical wisdom. Since casuistry does not rely on some lock-step logical formula, good character and virtue are required to do it properly, and there is no guarantee that it won't be abused. Casuistry is also capable of trivialization when it is written down, and reified as an inflexible set of rules to be searched through to apply to a case at hand.

5. Problems of Communitarian Ethics

Four overlapping problems quickly surface when one begins to think through communitarianism. First, if a major problem with modernist ethics is the assumption of autonomous individualism, an abstraction of real situated individuals, the parallel problem with communitarian ethics is the assumption that communities are wholly or largely benign, also an abstraction from all known communities. Moreover, second, adopting as standpoint the ethos of a particular community allows for no transcendentally other stance from which the community can be judged unjust or oppressive. Third, communitarianism has totalitarian possibilities in that all aspects of life are gathered up, as it were, by the teleological thrust toward well ordered harmony. At best people may find this insufferably boring. Worse would be the regulation of all eccentric behavior perceived by community fussbudgets to contradict the basic direction of the teleological striving. The rights to privacy afforded sovereign individuals and the separate spheres (i.e. work, leisure, family, religion) carved out by liberal pluralism may be abrogated, for the sake of community integrity and unity. Remember too, for every misty dream of bucolic rural community in pursuit of civic virtue (Jefferson's vision) there is an equally compelling vision of the dead weight of conformity enforced by community elders (elites) and self appointed casuistrists (Mark Twain's vision). The problem may be instantly grasped by replacing the word "state" (one for all—all for one) for "community" in all preceding sentences. A fourth, related problem is that communitarianism may be essentially an idealistic stained-glass-window nostalgia no longer viable as a real option in the mass societies inexorably created by advanced and postindustrial capitalism.

D. Communitarian Ethics in Public Administration

No one in public administration has adopted or advocated communitarianism in the pure sense of adopting all four propositions in the ideal-typical form elucidated above. Eclecticism reigns also in this domain. Of the aspects, the most common is the critique of atomistic individualism and shifting the locus of causality entailed thereby. Since the insight that humans develop within contexts is not unique to communitarianism and is shared by postmodern views, all these will be lumped together when postmodernism is discussed.

The most complete articulation of communitarianism itself in the public administration literature is Norton (1988). Norton *uses* the complete doctrine, however, for relatively minor recommendations to humanize the worksite, and allow the flowering individual initiative; cooperative over command managerial arrangements are recommended. Although productivity and efficiency may also benefit, the main reason is the communitarian one: better character and development of human potential is encouraged.

The pride of place for communitarianism in public administration then, must go to Cooper (1987 and 1991).[9] Cooper acknowledges the reality of pluralism, thereby avoiding the nostalgia and totalitarian traps mentioned above. Adopting an innovative theoretical move by Cochran (1982), the concept of community is pluralized and freed from geographical jurisdiction. Thus rendered, community becomes more like an electronically augmented, communication age, affinity group. This allows a plurality of communities sharing the qualities of de Toqueville's voluntary associations seen as mediating institutions between only legal citizens and government. By "legal citizens" Cooper means minimalist citizenship consistent with atomistic passive individuals with rights and freedoms—what Sir Isaiah Berlin usefully calls negative freedom. Within these associations lies the potential for communities in the functional communitarian sense of milieux within which full ethical citizenship may be encouraged to flourish. Encouraging these communities and dialectically intermingling with them would be the citizen administrator which administrator is herself ethically nourished and co-created within "professional" communities *in* government. This requires that Cooper recapture the ideals of professionalism; the putative conspiracy against the laity and guild protectionism, illegitimately cooked up behind veils of expertise, technique, and credentialing, must be negated in favor of affirming the best aspects of professionalism as a calling to excellence within a tradition (see Fox, 1992). MacIntyre's (1984) distinction between internal and external goods of a practice is appropriated for this purpose (Cooper, 1987). Created by these theoretical moves is a complex Venn diagram of overlapping communities synergistically cocreating ethical citizens, some of whom will be also ethical citizen administrators in the virtue sense. As in Barber's (1984) strong democracy and Follett's *New State* (1965) not only would such a scheme provide for will formation and legitimize governance, but most important to communitarians, it would also encourage the full development of human potential which teleologically *requires* fulfilling the *obligation* to participate in community decisions that affect both the individual and the commonweal (Cochran, 1982, cited in Cooper 1991, p. 160). As will be seen, postmodernists part company here on grounds that these last imperatives are but another metanarrative—another linguistic power play.

Other contributors to public administration ethics are less completely immersed in the communitarian discourse. Ventriss (1991) seems headed in a similar direction to that of Cooper (1991). He laments the effects of atomistic Hobbesian individualism, affirms community interdependence and the need to recognize it and encourage it through public learning facilitated by the public service. Ventriss concludes his analysis with a call for the promulgation and spread of a public philosophy of civic virtue. Morgan and Kass (1991) access aspects of Aristotelian ethics in two senses. Their focus group of administrators reason along the lines described by the term phronesis (practical wisdom) balancing in the process the languages of "neutral competence," "pluralistic politics," and the "public interest." One might say that these administrators use phronesis to find the dialogic "golden mean" between otherwise irreconcilable extremes. Insofar as any scheme with pathological polar extremes and golden means between them may be considered Aristotelian in spirit, Harmon's (1992) and Dobel's (1990) views also qualify. Lilla's (1981) one piece, which has been cited much more often than might be expected for an exercise in neo-conservative polemics, appears to be based on some sort of character ethics which, by his lights, the venal self-serving professorate seems not to be doing enough to inculcate.

E.   Non-Aristotelian "Communitarian" Ethics

The ethical implications of White and McSwain's (1983; 1990; also McSwain and White, 1987) transformational organization theory (Harmon and Mayer, 1986, pp. 358–371) and Harmon's (1981) action theory for organizations require a niche. They are placed here because they are public administration's leading anti-foundationalists, (a view called interpretivism) and the *form* and logic of their views comes close to communitarianism even though they write from atop the shoulders of a different set of giants. White and McSwain identify themselves as Jungians (see 1983) and they have also been influenced by Berger and Luckmann, and ethnomethodology (see 1987), these latter in turn are traceable back to the phenomenologist Schutz and his mentor Husserl. Harmon is similarly influenced minus Jung but add pragmatist G. H. Mead. (For bibliography of forefathers see Harmon, 1981, pp. 46–48.)

Like communitarians, McSwain and White shift the locus of primacy away from either atomistic individuals or external verities grounded a priori elsewhere. Going the Aristotelians one better, not only are communities necessary for human development, but following Berger and Luckmann (1967), reality is itself socially constructed through the medium of language within groups. For White and McSwain the important thing is to keep the conversation going. The process is everything for reasons grounded in Jungian depth psychology, the complexity of which defeats summary explication. Suffice it to say that a good ethical environment is the same one which produces a healthy individual. Blame, judgment, and punishment may actually truncate development and stop both interpersonal and intrapersonal communication necessary for growth. Mistakes, errors, misjudgments, and malfeasance should be not so much forgiven as positively processed as occasions for individual, group, and ultimately (through a dialectic with a psychic realm called the collective unconscious), human development itself. This process is also more radically relative to group and an individual's stage of maturation, than the ideographic development of rules of thumb known to casuistry. Again, the important point is that one is not all-at-once ethical when a set of rules has been learned and properly operationalized; people are ethically *emergent* in community.

Harmon and Mayer in 1986 judged White and McSwain's Jungianism to be optimistic. This judgment should be altered in light of their more recent (1990) work. They now see society as caught up in destructive "technicism." Technicism inhibits personal growth, and they now hold out hope only for enclaves or colonies of communitarian authenticity. This too is reminiscent of more traditional Aristotelian communitarianism susceptible to nostalgia for what may have never been, and may never be.

A similar emphasis on growth, development, and maturation in public administration ethics literature is the work of Stewart (e.g. Stewart and Sprinthall, 1991; see also Chapter 18 of this *Handbook*) based on ethical stage theory of Kohlberg (1981) which is in the tradition of Erik Erikson and Jean Piaget. From a Jungian or phenomenological point of view, however, stage theory is overly simplistic.

Harmon's action theory gets to community through his primary unit of analysis which is the face-to-face encounter which in turn leads to an ethics of mutuality. Harmon wants to preserve a modicum of a voluntaristic self, which he does through the appropriation of the concept of intentionality (consciousness is never pure nor empty, it is always consciousness *of* a physical or mental object) derived from phenomenology (Harmon, 1981, pp. 38ff.; see also Fox, 1980). But voluntarism occurs within community; thus by dialectically pairing voluntarism with Mead's social determinism, Harmon's self is both active and social. This active social self finds its nexus of "we" mutuality with other active social selves in the face-to-face encounter. Ethics may, at an everyday level be read off of, and at higher levels derived from, the authenticity and equal other-regardingness of the encounter. Authenticity breeds more authenticity throughout a community thus fulfilling the "developmental" criterion of communitarian ethics. Pathologies, on the other hand, are the result of institutional structures (like hierarchy) that diminish the quantity and quality of encounters. Harmon's position may be described as sort of bottom up Rawlsianism. Social justice is not so much thought through and then applied, as it is developed through mutuality and *then* understood. Action is logically and ontologically prior to thought, and reflective thought about actions is for action (see Harmon, 1990). The upshot of Harmon's tightly woven theory is the proactive administrator whose character and virtue are insured by mutuality rather than the well ordered polis of Aristotelian vintage.

V. CONCLUSION: POSTMODERN WARRANTS FOR PUBLIC ADMINISTRATION ETHICS

This essay has a developmental sequence whereby the ethics of authoritative command was superceded by deontological stances. Deontological ethics, however, shared with the former, the same foundational structure increasingly found wanting in Philosophy. If foundationalism doesn't work, if a universal ethics can't be made credible, perhaps a more local ethics can be found. This is the hope held out by communitarian ethics and its analogues. But this hope too, may soon be dashed by the more radical anti-foundationalism of postmodernism. Since postmodern concepts have not yet really penetrated public administration ethics except to reinforce anti-foundationalism, only two additional implications from this still nascent body of thought require coverage: (1) the idea that knowledge creation is an illegitimate exercise of power and domination and (2) the celebration of otherness and difference as its corrective.[10]

Recall from the discussion of interpretivist "communitarian" ethics that not only are humans social/political creatures, but also reality is itself a social construction. Postmodern perspectives go on to "deconstruct" such constructions to find heretofore veiled, arbitrary, and thus illegitimate exercises of domination and power. "Metanarratives," as these realities are called, favor the occident over the orient, north over south, white over colored, male over female, developed over underdeveloped, and heterosexual over other sexual orientations. Metanarratives marginalize difference and otherness. Even communitarianism looks like a foundational metanarrative in this light. After all, communitarianism has an orderly idea—the teleology of human happiness which is the full development of human potential within community. Entailed thereby is the *obligation* to participate in the community or be nagged by those who *know* that that is what is best for you. Entailed also is a conception of the telos, the ideal, to which all humans "naturally" aspire, making deviants of those with other projects or inclinations. Deviants are scorned, shunned, ostracized, imprisoned and institutionalized, until they can be brought into conformity or by their example enforce the conformity by which most are chained. Thus are all ethical views reported herein rendered totalitarian. Only celebrities are allowed outrageous eccentricities.

The corrective is to adopt an ethic of "let be." Don't impose morals that are anyway only consensual and at bottom arbitrary. Celebrate otherness, difference, and cultural diversity. Postmodernism is, of course, deeply contradictory. Can we "let be" those whose ways don't let others be? At which point the postmodernist will attack the laws of contradiction as part of an occidental, Eurocentric, phallocentric, white, power play.

There is an opportunity here for public administration ethics that should not go unmentioned. With Philosophy turning away from its role as arbiter of right reason and language usage police, we may be freed to *do* philosophy from within the flux and flow of our own fragmented problematic. Because of our natural gravity which puts administrators in contact with many realities, some joyful, some painful, and too many tragic, perhaps our problematic gives unique insight into the human condition as we enter the twenty-first century. Our philosophizing may instruct Philosophy.

ENDNOTES

1. The term analytical Philosophy can have a very specific meaning relating only to a particular school of ethical philosophers (e.g. G. E. Moore, A. J. Ayer, K. Baier) generally emotivists or prescriptivists (see Gert, 1992, pp. 39–41). I mean the term more broadly and include also those philosophers who disagreed with emotivism, but nonetheless had their task set for them by analytical Philosophy.

2. It is for these reasons that John Rohr (1989a, pp. 65–66) has recommended against the philosophical fork in his "high road." His profound respect for the intricate philosophical enterprise leads him to advise against mere dabbling.

3. To some public administrationists it would seem that no more philosophical inquiry is required at all. Dalton Lee (1990), for instance, has recommended that we begin now the task of indoctrinating students headed for governmental careers in the settled professional standards of our calling. Similarly, a recent Conference on the Study of Government Ethics June 12–15, 1991, Park City, Utah, organized by H. George Fredrickson under the auspices of the Section on Public Administration Research of the American Society for Public Adminstration explicitly excluded papers devoted to Philosophical and *philosophical* theorizing. Empirical studies based on hypotheses rooted in current theory was thought to be sufficient. At the latter conference Gary Brumbeck called for the development of tests to insure that job applicants had the right ethics.

4. If there is one taxonomy that should stick, it should be that of Bruce Jennings (1991) of the Hastings Center for the Study of Ethics. I am greatly indebted to his essay.

5. Two sub-plots in the development of public administration should also be noted. First is the striving of "the establishment" in the American Society for Public Administration to adopt the mantle of professionalism. Professional associations have codes of ethics so we needed one too. Second, a code of ethics is a political response to the bureaucrat bashing of the Carter and Reagan administrations. (See Fischer and Zinke, 1989.)

6. The works of Terry Cooper are found in three of the categories developed in this chapter. In his textbook (1990) first written in the late seventies and early eighties, the redundancy strategy seems the bottom line (see p. 161). His most recent book (1991) is a more purely academically theoretical work and attempts to revitalize citizenship by communitarian means.

7. For applications to public administration ethics, we need only consider *rule* deontological theories which are the foundational ones (see Frankena, 1973, pp. 16–17).

8. Consider for instance Simon's seemingly radical challenge to the rational comprehensive method of policy decision-making. Simon shows that we can in no way fulfill the requirements of a complete scan of possible options. Then he replaces the concept of maximizing with

satisfying. The *form* of the decision process remains exactly the same (cf. Harmon and Mayer, 1986, pp. 142ff.)

9. It might reasonably have gone to Bellah et al. (1985) were it not for the fact that he and his collaborators are primarily sociologists and belong and speak to, therefore, a different literature tradition.

10. Only a very thin slice of postmodern thought is required. These oversimplified broad strokes are composites of Foucault (e.g. 1980) and Derrida (e.g. 1985). A very accessible discussion is Bernstein (1992). An introductory anthology of postmodern thought is Hoesterey (1991).

REFERENCES

Adams, G.B., P.V. Bowerman, K.M. Dolbeare, and C. Stivers (1990). Joining purpose to practice: a democratic identity for the public service, *Images and Identities in Public Administration*, (H.D. Kass and B. Catron, eds.). Sage, Newbury Park, California.

Appleby, P.H. (1949). *Policy and Administration*. University of Alabama Press, University, Alabama.

Ayer, A.J. (1936). *Language, Truth and Logic*. Golancz, London.

Barber, B. (1984). *Strong Democracy: Participatory Politics for a New Age*. University of California Press, Berkeley, California.

Bellah, R.N., R. Madsen, W.M. Sullivan, A. Swidler, and S.M. Tipton (1985). *Habits of the Heart: Individualism and Commitment in American Life*. University of California Press, Berkeley.

Berger, P.L. and T. Luckmann (1967). *The Social Construction of Reality*. Doubleday, New York.

Bernstein, R.J. (1983). *Beyond Objectivism and Relativism*. University of Pennsylvania Press, Philadelphia.

Bernstein, R.J. (1992). *The New Constellation: The Ethical-Political Horizons of Modernity/Postmodernity*. MIT Press, Cambridge, Massachusetts.

Bok, S. (1981). Blowing the whistle, *Public Duties: The Moral Obligations of Government Officials* (J. Fleishman, L. Liebman and M.H. Moore eds.). Harvard University Press, Cambridge, Massachusetts.

Brady, F.N. (1988). Ethical theory and public service, *Papers on the Ethics of Administration* (N.D. Wright, ed.). Brigham Young University, Provo, Utah.

Burke, J.P. (1986). *Bureaucratic Responsibility*. Johns Hopkins University Press, Baltimore.

Cahill, A.G. and E.S. Overman (1988). Contemporary perspectives on ethics and values in public affairs, *Ethics, Government and Public Policy: A Reference Guide* (J.S. Bowman and F.A. Elliston, eds.). Greenwood Press, Westport, Connecticut.

Catron, B.L. and K.G. Denhard (1988). Ethics education in public administration and affairs: research report and recommendations, *American Society for Public Administration*. Working Group on Ethics Education, Washington D.C.

Chandler, R.C. (1984). The public administrator as representative citizen: a new role for the new century. *Public Administration Review, 44*: 196–206.

Cooper, T.L. (1987). Hierarchy, virtue, and the practice of public administration: a perspective for normative ethics. *Public Administration Review 47*: 320–328.

Cooper, T.L. (1990). *The Responsible Administrator* (3rd ed.). Jossey-Bass, San Francisco.

Cooper, T.L. (1991). *An Ethic of Citizenship for Public Administration*. Prentice Hall, Englewood Cliffs, New Jersey.

Dawes, C.G. (1923). *The First Year of the Budget of the United States*. Harper, New York.

Denhardt, K.G. (1988). *The Ethics of Public Service*. Greenwood Press, Westport, Connecticut.

Denhardt, K.G. (1991). Unearthing the moral foundations of public administration: honor, benevolence, and justice, *Ethical Frontiers in Public Management* (J.S. Bowman, ed.). Jossey-Bass, San Francisco.

d'Entreves, A.P. (1965). *Natural Law: An Historical Survey*. Harper, New York.

d'Entreves, M.P. (1992). Communitarianism, *Encyclopedia of Ethics* (L.C. Becker, ed.). Vol. I. Garland, New York.

Derrida, J. (1985). *The Ear of the Other* (C.V. McDonald, trans.). Schocken, New York.

Dobel, J.P. (1990). Integrity in the public service. *Public Administration Review*, *50*: 354–366.

Dummett, M. (1978). *Truth and Other Enigmas*. Gerald Duckworth, London.

Finer, H. (1936). Better government personnel. *Political Science Quarterly*, *51*: 569–599.

Finer, H. (1972). Administrative responsibility in democratic government, *Bureaucratic Power in National Politics* (F. Rourke, ed.), (2nd. ed.). Little, Brown, Boston.

Fischer, F. and R.C. Zinke (1989). Public administration and the code of ethics: administrative reform or professional ideology? *International Journal of Public Administration*, *12*: pp. 841–854.

Follett, M.P. (1965). *The New State: Group Organization, The Solution of Popular Government*. Peter Smith Publisher, Inc., Gloucester, Massachusetts.

Foucault, M. (1980). *Power/Knowledge: Selected Interviews and Other Writings* (E. Gordon, ed.). Pantheon, New York.

Fox, C.J. (1980). The existential-phenomenological alternative to dichotomous thought. *Western Political Quarterly*, *33*: 357–379.

Fox, C.J. (1989). Free to choose, free to win, free to lose: the phenomenology of ethical space. *International Journal of Public Administration*, *12*: 913–930.

Fox, C.J. (1992). What do we mean when we say "professionalism?": a language usage analysis for public administration. *American Review of Public Administration*, *22*: 1–18.

Fox, C.J. and C.E. Cochran (1990). Discretion advocacy in public administration theory: toward a platonic guardian class? *Administration and Society*, *22*: 249–271. A revised and expanded version is chapter 3, in *Images and Identities in Public Administration* (H.D. Kass and B. Catron, eds.). Sage, Newbury Park, California.

Frankena, W.K. (1973). *Ethics* (2nd ed.). Prentice-Hall, Englewood Cliffs, New Jersey.

Fredrickson, H.G. (1971). Toward a new public administration, *Toward a New Public Administration* (F. Marini, ed.). Chandler, Scranton, Pennsylvania.

Frederickson, H.G. (1982). The recovery of civism in public administration. *Public Administration Review*, *42*: 501–508.

Fredrickson, H.G., and D.K. Hart (1985). The public service and the patriotism of benevolence. *Public Administration Review*, *45*: 547–553.

Gawthrop, L.C. (1984). Civis, civitas and civilitas: a new focus for the year 2000. *Public Administration Review*, *34*: 101–107.

Gert, B. (1992). Analytic philosophy and ethics, *Encyclopedia of Ethics* (L.C. Becker, ed.), Vol. I. Garland, New York.

Glazer, M.P., and P.M. Glazer (1989). *The Whistleblowers: Exposing Corruption in Government and Industry*. Basic Books, New York.

Gortner, H.F. (1991). How public managers view their environment: balancing organizational demands, political realities and personal values. *Ethical Frontiers in Public Management* (J.S. Bowman, ed.). Jossey-Bass, San Francisco.

Guy, M.E. (1991). Using high reliability management to promote ethical decision making, *Ethical Frontiers in Public Management* (J.S. Bowman, ed.). Jossey-Bass, San Francisco.

Harmon, M.M. (1981). *Action Theory for Public Administration*. Longman, New York.

Harmon, M.M. (1990). The responsible actor as "tortured soul": the case of Horatio Hornblower, *Images and Identities in Public Administration* (H.D. Kass and B. Catron, eds.). Sage, Newbury Park, California.

Harmon, M.M. (1992). The theory of countervailing responsibility, unpublished paper delivered, Public Administration Theory Network Fifth Annual Symposium, Roosevelt University, Chicago.

Harmon, M.M. and R.T. Mayer (1986). *Organization Theory for Public Administration*. Little, Brown, Boston.

Hart, D.K. (1974). Social equity, justice, and the equitable administrator. *Public Administration Review*, *34*: 3–11.

Hart, D.K. (1984). The virtuous citizen, the honorable bureaucrat, and 'public' administration. *Public Administration Review*, *44*: 111–120.

Hart, D.K. (1988). The sympathetic organization, *Papers on the Ethics of Administration*, (N.D. Wright, ed.). Brigham Young University, Provo, Utah.

Hempel, C.G. (1968). Explanatory incompleteness, *Readings in the Philosophy of the Social Sciences* (M. Brodbeck, ed.). Macmillan, New York.

Henry, N. (1990). Root and branch: public administration's travail toward the future, *Public Administration: The State of the Discipline* (N. Lynn and A. Wildavsky, eds.). Chatham House, Chatham, New Jersey.

Hirschman, A.O. (1970). *Exit, Voice, and Loyalty*. Harvard University Press, Cambridge, Massachusetts.

Hoesterey, I. (1991). *Zeitgeist in Babel: The Post-Modernist Controversy*. Indiana University Press, Bloomington and Indianapolis, Indiana.

Ingersoll, V.H. and G.B. Adams. (1992). *The Tacit Organization*. JAI Press, Greenwich, Connecticut.

Jennings, B. (1991). Taking ethics seriously in administrative life: constitutionalism, ethical reasoning, and moral judgement, *Ethical Frontiers in Public Management* (J.S. Bowman, ed.). Jossey-Bass, San Francisco.

Jonsen, A.R. and S. Toulmin (1988). *The Abuse of Casuistry*. University of California Press, Berkeley.

Kass, H.D. (1990). Stewardship as a fundamental element in images of public administration, *Images and Identities in Public Administration* (H.D. Kass and B. Catron, eds.). Sage, Newbury Park, California.

Kerferd, G.B. (1967). Physis and nomos, *The Encyclopedia of Philosophy* (P. Edwards, ed.), Vol. 6. Collier Macmillan, New York.

Kohlberg, L. (1981). *The Philosophy of Moral Development*. Harper & Row, New York.

Lacan, J. (1984). *The Postmodern Condition*. University of Minnesota Press, Minneapolis.

Lee, D.S. (1990). Moral education and the teaching of public administration ethics, *International Journal of Public Administration*, *13*: 359–389.

Lewis, C.W. (1991). *The Ethics Challenge in Public Service: A Problem-Solving Guide*. Jossey-Bass, San Francisco.

Leys, W.A.R. (1952). *Ethics for Policy Decisions*. Prentice-Hall, New York.

Lilla, M.T. (1981). Ethos, 'ethics,' and public service. *The Public Interest*, *63*: 3–17.

Lowi, T. (1979). *The End of Liberalism* (2nd ed.). Norton, New York.

MacIntyre, A. (1984). *After Virtue*, (2nd ed.). Notre Dame University Press, Notre Dame, Indiana.

McSwain, C.J. and O.F. White (1987). The case for lying, cheating, and stealing—personal development as ethical guidance for managers. *Administration & Society*, *18*: 411–432.

Mertins, H. and P.J. Hennigan (1982). *Applying Professional Standards And Ethics in the Eighties: A Workbook and Study Guide for Public Administrators*. American Society for Public Administration, Washington D.C.

Moore, M.H. (1981). Realms of obligation and virtue, *Public Duties: The Moral Obligations of Government Officials* (J. Fleishman, L. Liebman and M.H. Moore, eds.). Harvard University Press, Cambridge, Massachusetts.

Morgan, D.F. and H.J. Kass (1991). Legitimizing administrative discretion through constitutional stewardship, *Ethical Frontiers in Public Management* (J.S. Bowman ed.). Jossey-Bass, San Francisco.

Mosher, F.C. (1982). *Democracy and the Public Service*, (2nd ed.). Oxford University Press, New York.

Nagel, E. (1961). *The Structure of Science: Problems in the Logic of Scientific Explanation*. Harcourt Brace & World, New York.

Nigro, L.G. and W.D. Richardson. (1990). Between citizen and administrator: administrative ethics and *PAR. Public Administration Review, 50*: 623–635.

Norton, D.L. (1988). ''Character ethics'' and organizational life, *Papers on the Ethics of Administration* (N.D. Wright, ed.). Brigham Young University, Provo, Utah.

Pastin, M. (1986). *The Hard Problems of Management: Gaining the Ethics Edge*. Jossey-Bass, San Francisco.

Plant, J.F. (1983). Ethics and public personnel administration, *Public Personnel Administration* (S.W. Hays and R.C. Kearney, eds.). Prentice-Hall, Englewood Cliffs, New Jersey.

Pops, G.M. (1991). Improving ethical decision making using the concept of justice, *Ethical Frontiers in Public Management* (J.S. Bowman, ed.). Jossey-Bass, San Francisco.

Poster, M. (1989). *Critical Theory and Poststructuralism: In Search of a Context*. Cornell University Press, New York.

Pugh, D.L. (1991). The origins of ethical frameworks in public administration, *Ethical Frontiers in Public Management* (J.S. Bowman, ed.). Jossey-Bass, San Francisco.

Ramos, A.G. (1981). *The New Science of Organizations: A Reconceptualization of the Wealth of Nations*. University of Toronto Press, Toronto.

Rawls, J. (1971). *A Theory of Justice*. Harvard University Press, Cambridge, Massachusetts.

Redford, E. (1969). *Democracy in the Administrative State*. Oxford University Press, New York.

Rohr, J.A. (1986). *To Run a Constitution: The Legitimacy of the Administrative State*. University Press of Kansas, Lawrence, Kansas.

Rohr, J.A. (1989a). *Ethics for Bureaucrats*, (2nd ed.). Marcel Dekker, New York.

Rohr, J.A. (1989b). British and American approaches to public service ethics. *Public Administration Review, 49*: 387–390.

Rorty, R. (1979). *Philosophy and the Mirror of Nature*. Princeton University Press, Princeton.

Stewart, D.S. (1988). The moral responsibility of individuals in public sector organizations, *Ethical Insight, Ethical Action: Perspectives for the Local Government Manager* (E.K. Kellar, ed.). ICMA, Washington D.C.

Stewart, D.S. and N.A. Sprinthall (1991). Strengthening ethical judgment in public administration, *Ethical Frontiers in Public Management* (J.S. Bowman ed.). Jossey-Bass, San Francisco.

Stone, D.A. (1988). *Policy Paradox and Political Reason*. Scott Foresman/Little, Brown, Glenview, Illinois.

Stout, J. (1988). *Ethics After Babel: The Languages of Morals and Their Discontents*. Beacon Press, Boston.

Taylor, C. (1985). *Philosophical Papers*, (2 vols.). Cambridge University Press, Cambridge, United Kingdom.

Thompson, D.F. (1987). *Political Ethics and Public Office*. Harvard University Press, Cambridge, Massachusetts.

Thompson, D.F. (1988). The possibility of administrative ethics, *Ethical Insight, Ethical Action: Perspectives for the Local Government Manager* (E.K. Kellar ed.). ICMA, Washington D.C.

Truelson, J.A. (1986). Blowing the whistle on systemic corruption, Doctoral Dissertation, (unpublished). Department of Public Administration, University of Southern California, Los Angeles.

Ventriss, C. (1991). Reconstructing government ethics: a public philosophy of civic virtue, *Ethical Frontiers in Public Management* (J.S. Bowman, ed.). Jossey-Bass, San Francisco.

Wall, B. (1991). Assessing ethics theories from a democratic viewpoint, *Ethical Frontiers in Public Management* (J.S. Bowman, ed.). Jossey-Bass, San Francisco.

Walzer, M. (1983). *Spheres of Justice*. Basic Books, New York.

Wamsley, G.L., C.T. Goodsell, J.A. Rohr, P.S. Kronenberg, O.F. White, J.F. Wolf, C.M. Stivers and R.N. Bacher (1990). *Refounding Public Administration*. Sage, Newbury Park, California.

Warwick, D.P. (1981). The ethics of administrative discretion, *Public Duties: The Moral Obligations of Government Officials* (J. Fleishman, L. Liebman and M.H. Moore, eds.). Harvard University Press, Cambridge, Massachusetts.

Weisband, E. and T.M. Franck (1975). *Resignation in Protest: Political and Ethical Choices between Loyalty to Term and Loyalty to Conscience in American Public Life*. Grossman/Viking, New York.

White, O.F. and C.J. McSwain (1983). Transformational theory and organizational analysis, *Beyond Method: Strategies for Social Research* (G. Morgan, ed.). Sage, Beverly Hills, California.

White, O.F. and C.J. McSwain (1990). The phoenix project: raising a new image of public administration from the ashes of the past, *Images and Identities in Public Administration*, (H.D. Kass and B. Catron, eds.). Sage, Newbury Park, California.

Willbern, Y. (1984). Types and levels of public morality. *Public Administration Review, 44*: 102–108.

Yates, D.T., Jr. (1981). Hard choices: justifying bureaucratic decisions, *Public Duties: The Moral Obligations of Government Officials* (J. Fleishman, L. Liebman and M.H. Moore, eds.). Harvard University Press, Cambridge, Massachusetts.

6

Administration and the Ethics of Virtue
In All Things, Choose First for Good Character and Then for Technical Expertise

David K. Hart
Brigham Young University, Provo, Utah

> Virtue is natural to man inchoately . . . as there is in the will a natural appetite for the good which is in accord with reason. (St. Thomas Aquinas, in Pegis, 1948, pp. 598–599)

I. THE RESURGENCE OF THE ETHICS OF VIRTUE

Management fads come and go as the seasons: spring promises efficacy in one minute; the summer searches for excellence; the nirvana of fall lies hidden in total quality; and hard winter demands lean management. Then the cycle of the managerially chic begins all over once again. And while this is lucrative for consultants, it works a hardship on line managers and academics, who must deal with these fads. Granted, there is merit in some of the approaches, but most have little staying power, for the simple reason that they ignore the most constant and important element in effective management; the good character of the managers.

The widespread publicity about the costly ethical failures of organizational leaders during the last quarter of the 20th century gives evidence that our most critical problem is the scarcity of men and women of good character in the positions of significant leadership—whether public, private, educational, or religious. For too long, the management orthodoxy has taken as axiomatic the proposition that ''good systems will produce good people,'' and that ethical problems will yield to better systems design.

But history is clear that a just society depends more upon the moral trustworthiness of its citizens and its leaders than upon structures designed to transform ignoble actions into socially useful results. Systems are important, but good character is more important.

As a result, management scholars and practitioners are giving increasing attention to administrative ethics. Unfortunately, a review of the literature reveals a significant omission: with a few exceptions, little attention has been given to the ethics of good character, or virtue ethics (however, see Kolenda, 1988). But that neglect is turning into a resurgence, and virtue ethics is starting to receive the attention it deserves, as Terry Cooper notes:

"Virtue, or character traits that incline us toward ethical conduct, is also being recognized increasingly as an important personal attribute" (T. Cooper, 1990, p. 162; note, also, T. Cooper and Wright, 1992; and Wilson, 1991).

Following that trend, the purpose of this chapter is to argue that democracy is best served by the ethics of virtue, which should influence every administrator—public or private—in the nation.

Before proceeding, however, five cautions must be given. First, the authors cited herein often take argumentative positions. Therefore, while reference will be made to specific ideas, such references do not imply that all of their authors' arguments are equally acceptable.

Second, the management orthodoxy holds that ethics is easy, often suggesting that it requires only a remembrance of a childhood morality learned at home and in the school-yard. This is a serious mistake, because ethics is a most demanding discipline. Of ethics it may be truly said that "there's no such thing as a free lunch." It is therefore essential that those dealing with administrative ethics understand the general traditions and entailments of moral philosophy (Frankena, 1973; Raphael, 1981; MacIntyre, 1966), while those who opt for the ethics of virtue must also become familiar with that particular tradition (Geach, 1977; Wallace, 1978; Foot, 1978; Budziszewski, 1986 and 1988; Kupperman, 1991).

Third, the early virtue theorists took a broad view of the subject, including within their definitions physical, intellectual, aesthetic, and moral virtues. The purpose of human life was the achievement of excellence in all aspects of life, and then the integration of those excellences into a unique and noble character: "Wherefore you may boldly declare that the highest good is harmony of the soul; for where concord and unity are, there must the virtues be" (Seneca, in Basore; 1932, p. 121). However, this chapter is about administrative ethics, and the discussion will be limited to the moral virtues, which have most significance for organizational behavior.

Fourth, the ethics of virtue requires a moral commitment to specific—often trans-temporal, transcultural—values, as opposed to the more fashionable moral relativism (Budziszewski, 1992). This creates a serious problem for many management scholars and practitioners, who are more at ease with situational ethics: the assumption that the immediate administrative situation should dictate the ethics, because ethics is just another tool to be used to achieve organizational objectives. Machiavelli's advice in *The Prince*, while negative, applies to that attitude:

> A man who wishes to make a profession of goodness in everything must necessarily come to grief among so many who are not good. Therefore it is necessary for a prince, who wishes to maintain himself, to learn how not to be good, and to use this knowledge and not use it, *according to the necessity of the case*. (Machiavelli, in Lerner, 1950, p. 56, emphasis added)

But relativistic and situational ethics strip democracy of its reason for being, since democracy is defined by its non-negotiable values—such as the individual's rights to freedom and dignity within the context of majority rule (Hallowell, 1954).

Finally, too many of the theorists of liberalism believe that if certain political structures are in place—such as democratic elections, representative government, and laws protecting the freedom of individuals—then the civic needs of society will automatically be met. That is a mistake, as Regan observes:

> Freedom, by itself, is no guarantee that persons and societies will act wisely, and West-erners have tended to divorce the exercise of freedom from the goal of proper human development, subjective will from objective reason. As a result, *liberal societies have become indifferent to moral virtue as the foundation of private and public well-being.* (Regan, 1988, p. 342, emphasis added)

With these cautions in mind, let us turn to the ethics of virtue. The position herein is that this "particular intellectual framework, the formula which is called the 'doctrine of virtue,' was one of the great discoveries in the history of man's self-understanding, and it has continued to be a part and parcel of the European mind" (Pieper, 1966).

II. THE ETHICS OF VIRTUE

Because the ethics of virtue has such a long and distinguished history, if it is to influence contemporary management theory and practice, its advocates must get a feeling for that history. I agree with William Prior and those "who find in the ethics of virtue a superior way of thinking about moral philosophy. I also believe in the enduring merit of the writings of the ancient philosophers on this subject" (Prior, 1991). Because most of the vital questions about virtue were asked at the outset, it is necessary to become familiar with its origins in ancient Greece and Rome. (While this chapter concerns the Western tradition, there is significant work linking East and West [Yearly, 1990].)

A. An Overview of the Tradition

Although virtue was a central concern of philosophers and dramatists before Aristotle (Casey, 1990; Nussbaum, 1986), his is the name most often associated with the origins of virtue ethics. It can be argued that Aristotle's *Nichomachean Ethics* is the incunabulum of virtue ethics, the original sourcebook for a practical ethics of good character (Aristotle, in Irwin, 1985; Sherman, 1989; J. Cooper, 1986; Rorty, 1980). Because he did not limit virtue to the moral virtues, his writings on the subject take the reader into many areas: there are intellectual, physical, and aesthetic virtues. But for our purposes, it is excellence in the moral virtues that should most concern administrators.

Central to his philosophy, he argues, is the need for citizens to care for the welfare of their fellow citizens: "For while it is satisfactory to acquire and preserve the good even for an individual, it is finer and more divine to acquire and preserve it for a people and for cities" (Aristotle, in Irwin, 1985, p. 3). There is more than an intimation in his work that the virtuous individual has the talent to love the citizens of the community and, because it does exist, there also exists the obligation to develop that talent. Thus, from the outset, virtue ethics has always been marked by the moral obligation to transcend one's own self-interest.

The Roman Stoics, who were often statesmen-philosophers, made the fusion of moral virtue and political obligation into a more powerful conception of civic virtue. Isaac Kramnick defines the term as follows:

> Civic humanism [virtue] conceives of man as a political being whose realization of self occurs only through participation in public life, through active citizenship in a

republic. The virtuous man is concerned primarily with the public good, *re publica*, or commonweal, not with private or selfish ends.

He goes on to point out that "... corruption is the absence of civic virtue" (Kramnick, 1982, p. 630).

The Roman influence upon the Enlightenment is evident in so many of the writings of the age. To illustrate, one can scarcely read a dozen pages in the works of Adam Smith without finding reference to Cicero. For those changing the shape and substance of government and economics in the 18th century, he was one of the great authorities on the necessity of virtue for the good society (Wood, 1988; Rawson, 1975). And to the name of Cicero should be added the names of Seneca, Tacitus, Quintilian, and Saullust, among others. Suffice it to say that the Roman interpretations of virtue were significant to the Enlightenment, and particularly the American founding. (Wood, 1991).

Following the Roman concern with virtue ethics is St. Thomas Aquinas, who moved the concept into Christian theology and extended its influence accordingly. More significant for the modern age, however, was the interest in virtue ethics by Renaissance intellectuals, politicians, and litterateurs (Pocock, 1975). As the churches and the states ensnared themselves in disputatious tangles over secular and religious power:

> Men were turning elsewhere for moral counsel, above all to the great traditions of Greece and Rome. It is significant too that many of the humanists who led the revival of antiquity were not professional philosophers or theologians in the tradition of the medieval schools, but poets, politicians, and rhetoricians with little commitment to systematic philosophic thought. They were therefore freer to develop the implications of living in the urban and secular society of the day. (Seigel, 1973, p. 477)

They solidified the fusion of moral virtue with civic responsibility, articulating a civic philosophy of good character (Baron, 1966; Kennedy, 1980; Kristeller, 1964). Citizenship became the talisman, and the belief in the necessity for widespread virtue strengthened the cause of democracy and institutional freedom.

This trend culminated in the years of the Enlightenment, as more and more political activists saw the solution to the turmoil of Europe in civic virtue (Robbins, 1959). In particular, it found a home in colonial America, as pastors, politicians, and the press debated the extent of the distance they should take from the corruptions of Europe. The theme of civic virtue was prominent in the debates of those revolutionary years (Wood, 1991), and it reached its apex in the "debates of the Philadelphia Convention [which] are notoriously the highest point ever reached by civic humanist theory in practice ..." (Pocock, 1983, p. 239).

Unfortunately, virtue ethics did not make the transition into the 19th century. The technological and industrial revolutions in Europe and America—the context of the creation of the modern corporation, the behavioral sciences, and modern organization (Scott and Hart, 1989)—turned the attention of moral philosophers to other ideas and ideals. For them, it now seemed that the "social geometers" of Saint-Simon had the answers (Manuel, 1956), and the illusion of a simple "science" of morality, quantifiable in all of its aspects, came to dominate the scene.

The new breed of administrative theorists of the 20th century continued along those lines, as modern organizations consolidated their power, and new technologies lured political philosophers to the techniques of empiricism and quantification (Wolin, 1960 and 1969). In all of this, virtue received short shrift. Evidence of its neglect is nowhere more clearly demonstrated than in the prestigious volumes of *The Encyclopedia of Philosophy*, which does not even list "virtue."

So it is that when the defenders of the paradigm (Kuhn, 1973) of the modern management orthodoxy consider administrative ethics, they most often do so within the framework of a morality of rules, which are attached to organizational positions, and ignore the issue of the moral character of the incumbents. This is intentional, because it corresponds to the cardinal rule of the management orthodoxy that an organization must never allow itself to be dependent upon individuals. Thus, managers intentionally design organizational positions so that they require only persons acting as functions (Cleveland, 1972, pp. 25–26). Positions are structured so that they can be filled by anyone with the requisite training who can follow the functional rules laid down in the job description. The same attitude carries over to ethics, and administrative ethics has become synonymous with an "ethics of rules," rather than an "ethics of character" (Kekes, 1988).

Yet it is strange, in this age so completely dominated by modern organizations, that virtue is seldom used —or even mentioned, for that matter—by organizational theorists and practitioners. Modern organization, and the techniques of management, are largely creatures of capitalism (Scott and Hart, 1989; Chandler, 1972). The seminal philosopher of capitalism, Adam Smith, was adamant and eloquent in his claim that virtue was essential for his ideal economic and political systems, because "the love of virtue [is] the noblest and the best passion in human nature" (Smith, in Raphael and Macfie, 1982, p. 309; Phillipson, 1983; Hope, 1989).

But, as the century draws to a close, the sterility and unhelpfulness of ethics-as-rules has become increasingly clear (Scott and Hart, 1991). Into this ethical vacuum have come a new set of theorists and practitioners who are turning once again to an ethics of good character and virtue (Budziszewski, 1986 and 1988; Pincoffs, 1986; Wilson, 1991).

Interestingly, public administration, rather than business administration, led out in supporting the work of the theorists of virtue. The point of origin was the Minnowbrook Conference, held in the late 1960s in upstate New York. That conference was a catalyst, and the 1970s witnessed an increasing interest in an ethics of virtue applied to public administration. The exemplars have been Dwight Waldo and Paul Appleby, among others. Among those whose papers, articles, anthologies, and books touch upon the ethics of virtue are H. George Frederickson, Ralph Chandler, Michael Harmon, Gary Wamsley, John Rohr, Kathryn Denhardt, Terry Cooper, and Patrick Dobel. This is not to say that they are all virtuists, but rather that they acknowledge the singular importance of good character for public administration.

B. The Dimensions of Virtue

Because the ethics of virtue has been out of fashion for so long, it will be useful to review some of its fundamental aspects. The space available allows for only a cursory overview, but there are some good books available that cover things in full (Wallace, 1978; Budziszewski, 1986).

We must begin with a definition. As virtue was such an important concept for the Enlightenment, a good place to begin is with Dr. Samuel Johnson's *A Dictionary of the English Language* (1755). Virtue is defined there as "1. Moral goodness," and "2. A particular moral excellence." In those times, such goodness and excellence referred more to qualities of character, rather than to obedience to moral rules. Put another way, virtue ethics—then and now—places primary emphasis upon the development of internal qualities of character, and only secondarily upon obedience to external moral rules. Thus, the ethics of virtue is generally used as synonymous with an ethics of good character (Kupperman, 1991).

In our time, the *Oxford English Dictionary* defines virtue as: "Conformity of life and conduct with the principles of morality; voluntary observance of the recognized moral laws or standards of right conduct; abstention on moral grounds from any form of wrongdoing or vice." It is most important to note the emphasis upon the "principles" of morality, and "voluntary observance." In an ethics of virtue, the principles are superior to the rules, because the former require thought and intentionality, as opposed to simple obedience, when they are applied to actual situations.

In the processes of thinking about the principles, individuals exercise their intellect and direct their passions in such a way that they progress ethically. Thus, moral thought is essential to the development of good character, and goodness is a result of internal imperatives to do right, rather than conformity to the external rewards and sanctions of moral rules (Arendt, 1971). For that reason, all organizations should be principle-oriented, rather than rule-oriented, to encourage the greatest development of virtuous character. This idea was expressed well by a minor presidential candidate in the mid-19th century who stated his platform as: "Teach them correct principles and let them govern themselves." That is the essence of the ethics of virtue applied to the administration of organizations.

The phrase, "voluntary observance," is also essential because, as most of the philosophers of virtue recognized, virtue cannot be compelled: the good character of the virtuous man or woman must be achieved voluntarily. One of the proven truisms of moral life (as virtually all parents of adolescents will attest) is that individuals must go beyond the prescriptions of others, to learn for themselves. In other words, virtue ethics does not yield to social engineering.

To expand upon the definitions given above, it must be noted that most virtuists believe that it is only through a life of virtue that persons can become fully human. Yves Simon, commenting about St. Augustine, argues that "virtue is the good quality of the soul by which we live rightly . . . not in pursuit of our various occupations but as human beings" (Simon, 1986, pp. 91–92). In the same vein, Philippa Foot believes that the "virtues are in general beneficial characteristics, and indeed ones that a human being needs to have, for his own sake and that of his fellows" (Foot, 1978, p. 3). A most distinctive aspect of the ethics of virtue, then, is that the virtues are essential for the full realization of our human-ness.

The term commonly used by virtue ethicists these days is "human flourishing." That is the intention behind Peter Geach's belief that "men need virtues to effect whatever men are for," which also means that we must "determine the end and the good of man" (Geach, 1977, p. 13). The virtues are not just psychological traits, helpful in utility maximization, or good interpersonal relationships, or achieving organizational goals. Rather, they are essential aspects of innate human nature: the precondition for the attainment of human flourishing and genuine community.

I will discuss the basics of the ethics of virtue in six categories: the cardinal virtues; moral excellence; moral action; moral intentionality and voluntarism; moral reinforcement and refreshment; and living the best life.

1. The Cardinal Virtues

We must begin with the substantive content of the virtues. The history of moral and political philosophy teems with moral prescriptions, and their multitude causes many to despair of ever achieving a consensus. But the virtues are few in number, and represent the essential aspects of our common, transcultural, transtemporal, human nature. One of the constant chores of virtue theorists has been deciding which of the virtues are "cardinal," and which are derivative.

"By a set of cardinal virtues is meant a set of virtues such that (1) they cannot be derived from one another and (2) all other moral virtues can be derived from or shown to be forms of them" (Frankena, 1973, p. 64). For those who would be virtuous, the task of choosing among the multitude of moral principles is simplified by the process of elimination: select those virtues from which all of the auxiliary virtues are derived. Among the numerous virtues, only a few can be considered cardinal virtues.

From the earliest times, the cardinal virtues were considered to be prudence, justice, fortitude, and temperance—the necessary predicates for human flourishing. By the Middle Ages, three theological virtues—faith, hope, and charity—were added for the benefit of the Christian faithful, giving a total of seven virtues (Pieper, 1966; Geach, 1977). Contrasted to them were the seven deadly sins, generally considered to be: pride, envy, sloth, intemperance, avarice, ire, and lust.

In order to facilitate the discussion, and with apologies to those who have written extensively about each of the virtues, the table below presents the definitions of the four cardinal virtues from the *Oxford English Dictionary*.

Prudence	"Ability to discern the most suitable, politic, or profitable course of action, esp. as regards conduct; practical wisdom, discretion."
Justice	"The quality of being (morally) just or righteous; the principle of just dealing; the exhibition of this quality or principle in action; just conduct; integrity, rectitude."
Fortitude	"Moral strength or courage . . . Unyielding courage in the endurance of pain or adversity."
Temperance	"The practice of restraining oneself in provocation, passion, desire, etc.; rational self-restraint."

A profile of a virtuous individual, then, would look something like this: he or she would believe deeply in the principles of moral truth (justice), but not to the extent of fanaticism or intolerance (temperance). Nonetheless, he or she would refuse to compromise on their principles (fortitude), but would also choose strategies that would maximize the acceptance of those principles (prudence). Such an individual could be termed a "practical idealist," because at every point, the cardinal virtues are to guide action in practical affairs.

A problem becomes immediately apparent, because the cardinal virtues are not sufficiently substantive. For instance, in the Western tradition, justice is assumed to have a generally accepted meaning, stemming from Plato's writings. But justice is relative to a prior set of values. Thus, the Nazis could claim, based upon their claim of a higher value of racial superiority, that they had a system of justice and that the Jews were treated justly (the procedures were observed). We would argue, correctly I believe, that such an interpretation of justice is in error and is malignant. But there can be a question, and similar questions can be raised about the other cardinal virtues.

Addressing themselves to that dilemma, some virtue theorists have added contenders to the list of cardinality, foremost among which is "benevolence." However, the trend since the Enlightenment has been in the other direction. For instance, Frankena opts for only two cardinal virtues:

> However, many moralists, among them Schopenhauer, have taken benevolence and justice to be the cardinal moral virtues, as I would. It seems to me that all of the usual virtues (such as love, courage, temperance, honesty, gratitude, and considerateness), at least insofar as they are *moral* virtues, can be derived from these two. (Frankena, 1973, pp. 64–65).

To illustrate this trend toward simplification, I shall present my interpretation. I have reduced the cardinal virtues to two: eudaimonism and benevolence. They have been chosen, first, because they add a needed content and, second, the four cardinal virtues can be derived from them.

Thus, the first cardinal virtue is "eudaimonism." It is a most complex concept, elegantly discussed by David L. Norton in his book, *Personal Destinies* (Norton, 1976; see also Kekes, 1989 and 1990). Norton provides the moral philosophy undergirding A.H. Maslow's hierarchy of needs, which culminates in self-actualization (Maslow, 1970). He brings together both the moral philosophy and the psychology of self-actualization, into a modern statement of eudaimonism: "Literally, eudaimonia is the condition of living in harmony with one's . . . innate potentiality, 'living in truth to oneself' " (Norton, 1976, p. 216).

This conception of eudaimonism holds that all individuals are born with unique potentialities and the purpose of life is to actualize them in the world. These potentialities involve, first, moral virtues and, second, our unique individual talents. With respect to morality, eudaimonism cannot involve harming either self or others, as the prefix "eu," or "good," makes clear.

The second cardinal virtue is "benevolence," or the love of others. The philosophers of virtue of the Scottish Enlightenment gave great emphasis to the concept of benevolence, as essential to all of their prescriptions for the good society (Roberts, 1973; Bryson, 1945). They ranged from Francis Hutcheson's belief that benevolence was *the* cardinal virtue (Scott, 1900; Jensen, 1971), through David Hume's greatly overlooked emphasis upon its importance (Roberts, 1973; Broad, 1930), to Adam Smith's moderating benevolence down to a more workable sympathy (Roberts, 1973; Morrow, 1969). Also, one should not overlook the arguments for benevolence by the 18th century English cleric, Bishop Joseph Butler (Butler, in Darwell, 1983; Penelhum, 1985).

They correctly understood that without some form of benevolence, most of their aspirations for a good society—as well as for democracy and free enterprise—would not be realized. A strong argument can be made, following Hutcheson, that benevolence is actually the single most important virtue, from which all others can be derived. For instance, the benevolist would argue that one is morally obligated to develop one's unique talents as a gift to the loved others.

I do not go that far, but I do make eudaimonism and benevolence co-equal—with neither derivable from the other. The other virtues can be derived from them. For instance, justice may be derived from benevolence; fortitude and temperance from both eudaimonism and benevolence; and prudence from eudaimonism. The purpose of this personal account is not to argue that others should accept my conception of the cardinal virtues. Rather, it has been presented to suggest the range of possibilities available to virtue theorists. The important point is that the virtues exist innately, as potentialities, within each individual and they push for actualization in the life of the individual.

Most virtue theorists would argue that, given the primordial importance of the virtues, they are the only solid ethical foundation upon which to construct a social, economic, or political system. I agree. With respect to administration, the virtues should be the foundation of all ends, policies, and practices. This is not to say, however, that virtue alone is sufficient for governance. To the contrary, humans need the back-up of well-designed institutions. Thomas Paine, for instance, placed the origins of government in "the inability of moral virtue to govern the world . . ." (Paine, in Foner, 1948, p. 6). This does not mean that moral virtue is unnecessary, for it is of primary importance. But, given the vagaries of human commitment, wisdom suggests a back-up.

2. Excellence of Moral Character

Another of the definitions of virtue from the *Oxford English Dictionary* is "A particular moral excellence; a special manifestation of the influence of moral principles in life or conduct." In the literature, moral virtue almost always refers to continuous efforts to achieve moral excellence in those areas that are essential for living a good life. These virtues are an ineradicable aspect of the innate moral nature of all individuals, and they carry with them the imperative for actualization in the moral actions of everyday life.

As noted, virtue relies upon internal imperatives, rather than upon external rules and controls. This means that for an individual to be virtuous; he or she must—intentionally, voluntarily, and constantly—be in the process of creating a noble character. For that reason, the ethics of virtue has often been made synonymous with an ethics of good character (Thomas, 1989; Wilson, 1991). Although there are some who argue that there is some difference between the two (Kupperman, 1991), the older identification of virtue and good character is, I think, valid—to say virtue ethics is also to say character ethics (French et al., 1988). This means that the single most important activity of an individual's life is the creation of a morally excellent character. The answer to the question of "why" is what makes virtue ethics so unique.

3. Homo Virtutis and the Active Life

The classical virtue theorists have no problem with that "why," because for them the answer was found in innate human nature. The Latin root of virtue is "vir," or "man," and virtue refers to those aspects of the moral personality that are essential for a fully human life: one cannot be fully human unless one is virtuous (Thomas, 1989). That being the case, human beings—so often tabbed as "homo economicus" or "homo faber"—may well be more correctly termed "homo virtutis."

While virtue theorists differ about some of the specific virtues, most of them base their ideas upon the validity of homo virtutis. The defining fact of human-ness is that the imperatives toward the actualization of the virtues is, if you will, our life-force—an inherent drive toward a unique personal identity. As Casey writes:

> This ethic is founded on virtues which constitute personhood, and . . . an ethic of the
> virtues significantly, although not entirely, overlaps with an ethic of persons. In valuing
> others for possessing the traditional virtues, one implicitly recognizes and values their
> personhood. (Casey, 1990, p. vii)

While the imperative toward virtue exists as innate within us, its realization requires enormous effort, in thought, feeling, and action. Since no one can achieve complete virtue, the quest is never-ending and moral progress can never cease. For that reason, the ethics of virtue recommends that happiness comes from learning to love the *processes* of a virtuous life rather than the chimera of *achievement*. David Norton's term for a virtuous life is "integrity," the "consummate virtue," which is characterized as "the process . . . by which a diversity is made into a singular thing . . ." (Norton, 1976, p. 8). For him, moral integrity is the

> Integration of separable aspects of the self—notably faculties, desires, roles, life-shaping choices—into a self-consistent whole. Second, it implies "wholeness as completeness" by which it is distinguishable, for example, from fanaticism and monomania. The third dimension of meaning may be preliminarily described as a deeper kind of honesty, and it is this dimension that has prominence in popular usage, as for example when newspapers demand "integrity" of politicians and business managers. (Norton, 1991, pp. 82–83)

Nature has implanted in all the imperatives to virtue, and a life of virtue, with its never-ending exertions and tribulations, is our ideal home. Into the bargain is the fact that life is never more fully experienced than in virtuous action, for action is essential. For some philosophers, the highest condition of human life is the contemplative life. But virtue theory is action-oriented, and Adam Smith caught this perfectly: "The most sublime speculation of the contemplative philosopher can scarce compensate the neglect of the smallest active duty" (Smith, in Rafael and Macfie, 1982, p. 237).

4. Moral Intentionality and Voluntarism

To be actualized, however, virtue requires both intentionality and voluntarism, because they are aspects of our human nature. First, individuals are born with the need to understand the "why" of things and, second, they are, born with the need to be free.

Intention requires moral thoughtfulness prior to moral action. This means that the intellect and the passions are consciously directed toward producing good in the world, and intentionality has always been the hallmark of good character. But because intention cannot be seen nor measured, it is overlooked: "That the world judges by the event, and not by the design, has been in all ages the complaint, and is the great discouragement of virtue" (Smith, in Raphael and Macfie, 1982, pp. 104–105).

Virtue theorists argue that while fortune can up-end action, it cannot affect the intentions of the virtuous individual—thus making intention safe from the vagaries of the world. As Seneca wrote: ". . . Fortune can snatch away only what she herself has given. But virtue she does not give: therefore she cannot take it away" (Seneca, in Basore, 1928, p. 61).

Because nature designed humans for freedom, all moral action had to be marked by voluntarism. The reason is simple: the only thing a good act that is compelled tells us about a person's character is that he or she gives into fear. The only way freedom has any meaning in society is when individuals do good because they want to do good. Therefore, virtue theory must reject all forms of moral determinism and moral compulsion, whether they are theological (e.g., all humans are tainted by original sin), cultural (all humans are the product of cultural forces over which they have little control), or political (the state must compel citizens to be virtuous).

Thus Foot correctly argues that "the disposition of the heart is part of virtue," and that the heart will not be compelled (Foot, 1978, p. 4). Individuals must *choose* virtue. Compulsion means that virtue will not become a part of the individual's character. Further, they must act upon their beliefs intentionally, in the old prescription: do the right thing for the right reason. Good character is the product of free moral choice. Virtue is the sine qua non of any economic, administrative, or political system that professes to promote human freedom.

All of this raises two troublesome issues about moral mistakes, and non-virtuous ends. Since the virtues are considered to be transtemporal and transcultural, what should we think about virtues employed in pursuit of mistaken or repugnant ends? The question demonstrates that *moral wisdom* is essential to the ethics of virtue.

To illustrate, Stanley Kubrick's black comedy *Dr. Strangelove* (1963) is built around a moral mistake. A demented general lies to his crews (the United States is under nuclear attack), and launches his bombers into an attack on the Soviet Union. The U.S. President and the Soviet Premier eventually get things sorted out, and the bombers are either recalled or shot down—save one. It has sustained battle damage and its radios are out. Allowing for a little satire, the crew is extremely courageous in pressing the attack in their patched-up ship. Unfortunately, the Soviets have just activated a "doomsday machine" that will destroy the world if a nuclear bomb is exploded. Thus, while the audience cheers the courage of the bomber crew, they are also appalled by what will happen if their virtue (fortitude) wins out.

Extreme care must be taken, then, to ensure that virtue is never deployed by a moral mistake. Moral wisdom (derived from benevolence) must be one of the highest obligations of leadership, to ensure that virtue directs the choice of all organizational ends and procedures. We cannot allow the virtue of honorable subordinates to be despoiled by moral mistakes.

The other problem is the deployment of virtue in the service of morally repugnant ends. A good friend once challenged my arguments for virtue with a question. "What about the German soldiers at Stalingrad," he asked, "who climbed out of their frozen holes time and again to press home an attack, or to rescue wounded or trapped comrades?" As to courage and comradeship, their behavior was exemplary—and yet it was in the service of Nazism.

Obviously, villainous leaders can use the virtue of the citizens in the service of morally repugnant ends—but only if they deceive those virtuous citizens. Also, villainous individuals can sometimes be courageous. Because my friend is an exemplar of moral wisdom, I've thought seriously about his question, and have come to a conclusion. Even though those German soldiers were brave, they were still brave in the service of an evil government—a fact that was not hidden from them—and that invalidates their virtue. Recent evidence indicates that those soldiers were not as free of ideology as some would like to believe (Bartov, 1991).

This raises the issue of virtue and followership. Virtue requires that followers *always* question the ends to which their actions are to be directed, and never allow their virtue to be used to advance morally wrong causes.

Granted, in both of the illustrations given above, the soldiers were obedient to the laws of their nation, but true virtue should not be based upon national law, if such law violates virtue. The illustrations are dramatic, of course, but let us remember the business and union leaders, the professors and prelates, and the public servants of the 1950s who defended, used, and enforced racist and sexist laws. Virtue ethics demands that all individuals—leaders and followers alike—think and act in terms of a morality of individuals that transcend all social, economic, and political systems.

5. Moral Reinforcement and Moral Refreshment

Once attained, good character does not exist in a vacuum: it needs both reinforcement and refreshment. Thus, V. M. Hope rests his theory of virtue upon virtuous reciprocity:

> The real good of virtue, then, only appears when a virtuous person is being fair to
> another who agrees in finding equality good . . . the good of his virtue to him, apart
> from maintaining his rights, is as a means towards encouraging virtue in others so that
> he and they and other virtuous people can enjoy moral fellowship in the future. (Hope,
> 1989, p. 147)

I agree with Adam Smith that virtuous action is sufficient in and of itself, ultimately requiring nothing more than self-approbation (Smith, in Raphael and Macfie, 1982, p. 117). But he also understood that even the strongest among us will tire, and needs the reinforcement of virtuous others from time to time. For that reason, virtue theorists praise gratitude. This is fairly well understood and accepted. Thus it is that one's own courageous actions can bolster the flagging courage of another, or that another's magnanimity can invigorate our own magnanimity. We need moral exemplars (Cooper and Wright, 1992).

But there is another dimension that is seldom remarked upon, and that is the need for the periodic refreshment of the spirit.

To illustrate, in the spring of 1992 I presented a paper at the Geneva Environmental Meetings. The political situation in the United States was profoundly dispiriting, with a corresponding impact upon my attitude toward my work. But a presentation by, and conversation with, Dr. James Lovelock, the author of the Gaian environmental philosophy, turned things around. Not only was the spirit refreshed, my orientation toward my work took a new turn. This emphasized again the extreme importance of the refreshment that comes from *moral friendship* among the committed.

6. Living the Best Life

Finally, what is the purpose of living a life of virtue? As William Prior puts it:

> Greek ethics speaks to us in a different voice . . . The primary question the Greeks
> sought to answer was not, "What actions are universally morally right?" but "What
> is the best sort of life for human beings to live?" (Prior, 1991, p. 1)

The virtuists assert that there is a quality added to human life from living virtuously. For them, virtue is the essential element in that life humans should live. Furthermore, their answer to that "primary question" strikes at the central assumption of the management orthodoxy.

Where that orthodoxy speaks first of the efficient achievement of organizational goals, and structures work accordingly, virtue theory speaks first of the quality of life within the organization. The management orthodoxy ignores the issue of the good life—perhaps if it did address it, the sterility of organizational life would be exposed. E. F. Schumacher, calling for the humanization of work, is worth quoting at length:

> That soul-destroying, meaningless, mechanical, monotonous, moronic work is an insult
> to human nature which must necessarily and inevitably produce either escapism or
> aggression, and that no amount of "bread and circuses" can compensate for the dam-
> age done—these are facts which are neither denied nor acknowledged but are met with
> an unbreakable conspiracy of silence—because to deny them would be too obviously
> absurd and to acknowledge them would condemn the central preoccupation of modern
> society as a crime against humanity. (Schumacher, 1973, p. 35)

Virtue theory argues that such a situation need not exist, and that an insistence upon virtue as the basis for all organizational theory and practice would solve the problem. It makes the good life its first concern, arguing that it is the very purpose of life. Thus,

Aristotle writes ". . . why not say that the happy person is the one who expresses complete virtue in his activities, with an adequate supply of external goods, not for just any time but for a complete life?" (Aristotle, in Irwin, 1985, pp. 26–27).

For virtue theorists, that is human flourishing, and "our concept of a human being is deeply tied to a conception of human flourishing" (Thomas, 1989, p. 56). Such flourishing is moral, since an immoral person cannot flourish, and it requires the integration of all the virtues into a complete human character (a fragmented character cannot flourish). It is the purpose of all organizations to provide both the framework and the conditions for that endeavor.

The path to the good life cannot be described in clear and rational steps. The process is similar to Adam Smith's distinction between justice and benevolence: justice requires obedience to the law—benevolence requires more. To make his point, he likened justice to the rules of grammar, and benevolence (the highest state) to an appreciation of the "sublime" in writing (Smith, in Raphael and Macfie, 1982, pp. 175–176). Strict obedience to the rules of grammar or a heightened appreciation of literature do not produce great works.

Such appreciation for "elegance or sublimity" in writing requires an almost indescribable appreciation of the aesthetics of literature. This may seem impossibly vague, but it is understood by all who love great literature. The same principle applies to morality: one can follow the moral rules, and for that they deserve a certain "cold esteem." But something lies beyond, something Smith terms "superior prudence." He writes:

> This superior prudence, when carried to the highest degree of perfection, necessarily supposes the art, the talent, and the habit or disposition of acting with the most perfect propriety in every possible circumstance and situation. It necessarily supposes the utmost perfection of all the intellectual and of all the moral virtues. It is the best head joined to the best heart. It is the most perfect wisdom combined with the most perfect virtue. (Smith, in Raphael and Macfie, 1982, p. 216)

That summarizes both the noble character of virtue theory, and the qualities needed for the good life.

7. Conclusion

To conclude: (1) all individuals are born with an innate imperative to virtue; (2) virtue is necessary to be fully human; (3) the cardinal virtues must be intentionally cultivated; (4) they must emerge in intentional, voluntary moral action; and (5) they require unending moral improvement—"use it or lose it." Virtue, then, is made manifest in the character, rather than in the obedience, of the individual, which leads to a community of self-governing individuals.

III. JOINING EXCELLENCE IN VIRTUE WITH EXCELLENCE IN FUNCTION

The virtuist interpretation of democracy presumes that its citizens prefer leaders who are virtuous as well as technically competent. But that presumption leads to a formidable problem: how can organizations (social, economic, and political) be set up to ensure that men and women possessing both virtue and technical competence will wind up in the key leadership positions?

The process begins with the following proposition about choosing leaders: *always choose first on the basis of good character and then on the basis of technical expertise.* While good character is the most important qualification for any office, technical ability is also necessary if we are to have robust organizations. An individual may have the moral character of Mother Teresa, but that, alone, would not qualify her to be the director of the Office of Management and Budget (OMB). The problem is depicted below:

		A	B
Functional Expertise (F)	1	V+ F+	V− F+
	2	V+ F−	V− F−

Virtue (V)

The east-west dimension is the measure of functional expertise (F); the north-south dimension is the measure of virtue (V). For any organizational position, the rankings would be as follows: the optimum individual would be Cell 1A (or V+F+); second best would be Cell 2A (or V+F−); third would be Cell 1B (or V−F+); and worst would be Cell 2B (or V−F−).

The reason for listing Cell 1A as best is simple: they make better leaders. To illustrate, I would place the following presidents as exemplars of each cell:

Cell 1A: Washington, Jefferson, Lincoln, Truman
Cell 2A: Hoover, Carter
Cell 1B: Lyndon Johnson, Nixon
Cell 2B: Harding

Given the wild and wooly way presidential elections are conducted in the United States, we have been extremely fortunate in the large number of 1As we have elected—and the surprisingly small number of 2Bs.

The ideal for our society, then, would be a presidential contest between Washington and Jefferson, or Lincoln and Truman. Regardless of the outcome, all citizens would be winners. The same circumstances are true for any position of leadership—agency head, CEO, dean. Filling a position of leadership should, ideally, always involve a choice between two 1As. The organizational problem is how to structure all organizations, public and private, to ensure that we are led by those in Cell 1A?

The solution begins in giving as much attention to the development of good character as we do to the development of technical expertise. Some admirable people argue that virtue cannot be taught, but I strongly disagree. History is quite clear that virtue can be taught and learned. Our problem is that we have let that aspect of education die out, for reasons too lengthy to discuss here. Worse, the management orthodoxy only validates things that can be measured, we have created very incomplete measures for choice—such as SATs, GMATs, and LSATs in education. Thus, we have let our abilities to evaluate good character atrophy.

As individuals come up for promotion, or seek our votes, the first question must invariably be that of the good character of the candidate. Yves Simon discussed this distinction in some detail, illustrating his choice with the following example. Two students are competing for one fellowship: one is of "average intelligence but extremely strong good will;" the other is undeniably brilliant, "but with a considerably weaker, somewhat disordered will."

> On the basis of my own observations, I am inclined to favor the young man with the strong will over the one with the brilliant mind, which may well be his by accident, so to speak. A brilliant mind at the mercy of an unstable will is something rather disquieting; the average intelligence supported by a disciplined will seems to me much more promising. (Simon, 1986, p. 27)

The reasoning behind his choice is that, in the long run, the student with strong good character will most probably become a good philosopher, while the brilliant student will be susceptible to the will of others—which can be good or bad. The virtue theorist would argue that his judgment is applicable in all areas of life.

Experience tells us that virtuous character is reliable, no matter what the job, or the pressures. By placing good character first, we protect ourselves in two ways. First, the virtuous individual will not seek positions for which he or she is not qualified. Therefore, we avoid the problem we have created in contemporary organizational practice: we have made the leadership position available to the aggressive rather than to the good (or even the technically competent). Second, the virtuous will not be moved and shifted by expediency: their moral course will be clear and undeviating.

Of course, we should not expect too much in the way of virtue—saints are few and far between. As George Orwell wrote, "Most people wish to be good, but not all of the time" (Shelden, 1991, p. 356). But we should weight things in favor of the virtuous.

IV. THE VIRTUOUS ADMINISTRATOR

We come at last to the issue of the virtuous administrator within the modern organizations of contemporary society. To begin, such administrators must make virtue the central aspect of their character, allowing it to guide all of their organizational behaviors. But that is not enough, for virtuous leaders need—and have the obligation to sponsor—virtuous subordinates. It is a very unique relationship, perhaps the ultimate system of checks and balances.

To illustrate, James Madison wrote of that relationship in a public setting:

> I go on this great republican principle, that the people will have virtue and intelligence to select men of virtue and wisdom. Is there no virtue among us? If there be not, we are in a wretched situation. No theoretical checks—no form of government can render us secure. To suppose that any form of government will secure liberty or happiness without any virtue in the people, is a chimerical idea. If there be sufficient virtue and intelligence in the community, it will be exercised in the selection of these men. So that we do not depend on their virtue, or put confidence in our rulers, but in the people who are to choose them. (Madison, in Padover, 1953, pp. 48–49)

Madison did not have a great deal of confidence in the prevalence of citizen virtue, but he was unwavering in his belief as to its importance. The issue here, however, is that followers could choose leaders based upon their qualities of character—and the ideal guarantee against abusive leaders is followers of virtue.

Madison understood that in large and complex organizations there will always be too many issues and relationships for individuals to comprehend. Therefore, there must be a profound trust among all members—leaders, colleagues, followers—that none of them will use their expertise to take advantage of the others. The common tie binding organizational members together is virtue, because all can understand virtue. The division of labor, whether hierarchical or lateral, will always be moderated by virtue, which is the only guarantee against the "tyranny of expertise" so vividly described by Robert Michels (Michels, 1915).

Therefore, virtuous administrators will always be conscious of the moral obligation of promote virtue—among themselves and their subordinates. They must *never* try to force virtue upon others, nor exercise any degree of compulsion—virtue must be voluntary. Instead, they must advocate an education in virtue from the earliest ages, and follow that up with policies, programs, and practices that will promote virtue. Finally, they must consciously try to become exemplars of the virtue that guides all of their actions. Let me conclude this section with David Hume:

> General virtue and good morals in a state, which are so requisite to happiness, can never arise from the most refined precepts of philosophy, or even the severest injunctions of religion; but must proceed entirely from the virtuous education of youth, the effect of wise laws and institutions. (Hume, in Miller, 1985, pp. 54–55)

CONCLUSION

Administrative ethics is finally beginning to receive the attention it deserves and in that context, virtue is making an impressive comeback. But we are still at the early stages of seeing virtue incorporated into administrative theory and practice. The most impressive support for the concept has come in public administration, and it is beginning to appear in business administration—reversing the usual trend of who borrows from whom. But that is as it should be, since public administration has a strong background in political philosophy.

Furthermore, both as a teacher and as a consultant, it has been my experience that most people are very receptive to virtue and the ethics of good character. Nonetheless, virtue will not have much of an impact upon organizational life unless the leadership gets involved. Unfortunately, Sorel's observation, made in 1906, is as valid today as it was then: ". . . people of the higher classes have always considered that they had less need of moral discipline than their subordinates . . ." (Sorel, 1906, p. 219).

Leaders—whether elected officials, agency heads, CEOs, or university presidents—too often protest that they are "too busy" to spend time reading books, or going to classes. They tend to take their own ethical commitments for granted, not realizing that of all the disciplines necessary for running an organization, none demands as much effort as ethics. Further, the ethics of virtue is even more demanding, because it requires individuals to intentionally shape their moral character around virtue.

But the greatest barrier is the fact that the ethics of virtue stands in opposition to the management orthodoxy. First, virtue does not allow for any compromise of its basic principles, while the management orthodoxy views ethics as instrumental to organizational success. Second, virtue requires serious study and intensive thought, whereas the management orthodoxy reduces ethics to platitudes that promise a quick and easy fix for ethical problems. Third, virtue places the quality of human lives above organizational success, while the management orthodoxy reverses the order.

For those reasons, acceptance of the paradigm of administrative virtue will require the displacement of the orthodox paradigm of management that is now dominant. Paradigmatic shifts are not easy, but they are essential for progress (Kuhn, 1970). Hopefully, the pervasive failures of the management orthodoxy that precipitated the multiple domestic crises of the 1980s will lead to a serious reconsideration of what we are doing. The father of "total quality management," W. Edwards Deming, was blunt in his assessment: "The basic cause of sickness in American industry . . . is [the] failure of top management to manage" (Deming, 1986, p. ix). And, I would add, to manage virtuously.

But out of the stupidities of those bad times has come a growing seriousness about administrative ethics, and the comprehension that ethics must be the foundation upon which all management is practiced. It has been argued herein that of all the ethical systems, the ethics of virtue is most congenial to our human nature.

So, those who believe in the ethics of virtue must persuade the leaders, practitioners, and theorists alike, to take virtue seriously. When they are persuaded, we can then get on with the much easier task of applying virtue to all of our goals, policies, and practices. Given the staggering problems that confront all nations, as the 21st century rolls onto the scene, we would do well to follow the advice of that excellent man of virtue, Cicero:

> But those whom Nature has endowed with the capacity for administering public affairs should put aside all hesitation, enter the race for public office, and take a hand in directing the government; for in no other way can a government be administered or greatness of spirit be made manifest. (Cicero, in Miller, 1913, p. 75)

REFERENCES

Arendt, H. (1971). Thinking and Moral Considerations. *Social Research, 38*: 417–446.

Baron, H. (rev.ed.; 1966). *The Crisis of the Early Italian Renaissance: Civic Humanism and Republican Liberty in an Age of Classicism and Tyranny*. Princeton University Press, Princeton, New Jersey.

Bartov, O. (1991). *Hitler's Army: Soldiers, Nazis, and War in the Third Reich*. Oxford University Press, New York.

Basore, J.W. (trans.) (1928). Seneca. On Firmness, *Moral Essays*, Volume I, Loeb Classical Library. Harvard University Press, Cambridge, Massachusetts.

Basore, J.W. (trans) (1932). Seneca. On the Happy Life, *Moral Essays*, Volume II, Loeb Classical Library. Harvard University Press, Cambridge, Massachusetts.

Broad, C.D. (1930). *Five Types of Ethical Theory*. Routledge & Kegan Paul, London, England.

Bryson, G. (1945). *Man and Society: The Scottish Inquiry of the Eighteenth Century*. Augustus M. Kelley Publishers, New York.

Budziszewski, J. (1986). *The Resurrection of Nature: Political Theory and the Human Character*. Cornell University Press, Ithaca, New York.

Budziszewski, J. (1988). *The Nearest Coast of Darkness: A Vindication of the Politics of Virtues*. Cornell University Press, Ithaca, New York.

Budziszewski, J. (1992). *True Tolerance*. Transaction Books, New Brunswick, New Jersey.

Casey, J. (1990). *Pagan Virtue*. Clarendon Press, Oxford, England.

Chandler, A.D., Jr. (1977). *The Visible Hand*. Harvard University Press, Cambridge, Massachusetts.

Cleveland, H. (1972). *The Future Executive*. Harper & Row, New York.

Cooper, J.M. (1986). *Reason and Human Good in Aristotle*. Hackett Publishing Company, Indianapolis, Indiana.

Cooper, T.L. (3rd. ed; 1990). *The Responsible Administrator*. Jossey-Bass, San Francisco, California.

Cooper, T.L. and Wright, N.D. (eds.) (1992). *Exemplary Public Administrators: Character and Leadership in Government*. Jossey-Bass, Publishers, San Francisco.

Darwell, S.L. (ed.) (1983). Bishop J. Butler, *Five Sermons Preached at the Rolls Chapel and A Dissertation Upon the Nature of Virtue*. Hackett Publishing Company, Indianapolis, Indiana.

Deming, W.E. (1986). *Out of the Crisis*. Massachusetts Institute of Technology, Cambridge, Massachusetts.

Etzioni, A. (1964). *Modern Organizations*. Prentice-Hall, Englewood Cliffs, New Jersey.

Foner, P.S. (ed.) (1948). *The Life and Major Writings of Thomas Paine*. The Citadel Press, Secaucus, New Jersey.

Foot, P. (1978). *Virtues and Vices*. University of California Press, Berkeley, California.

Frankena, W.K. (2nd ed.; 1973). *Ethics*. Prentice-Hall, Englewood Cliffs, New Jersey.

French, P.A., Uehling, T.E., Jr., and Wettstein, H.K. (eds.) (1988). *Ethical Theory: Character and Virtue*, Midwest Studies in Philosophy, Volume XIII. University of Notre Dame Press, Notre Dame, Indiana.

Geach, P.T. (1977). *The Virtues*. Cambridge University Press, Cambridge, England.

Hallowell, J.H. (1954). *The Moral Foundation of Democracy*. University of Chicago Press, Chicago.

Hope, V.M. (1989).*Virtue by Consensus: The Moral Philosophy of Hutcheson, Hume, and Adam Smith*. Clarendon Press, Oxford, England.

Irwin, T. (trans.) (1985). Aristotle's *Nicomachean Ethics*. Hackett Publishing Company, Indianapolis, Indiana.

Jensen, H. (1971). *Motivation and the the Moral Sense in Francis Hutcheson's Ethical Theory*. Martinus Nijhoff, The Hague, Netherlands.

Kekes, J. (1988). *The Examined Life*. Pennsylvania State University Press, College Station, Pennsylvania.

Kekes, J. (1989). *Moral Tradition and Individuality*. Princeton University Press, Princeton, New Jersey.

Kekes, J. (1990). *Facing Evil*. Princeton University Press, Princeton, New Jersey.

Kennedy, G.A. (1980). *Classical Rhetoric and Its Christian and Secular Tradition from Ancient to Modern Times*. University of North Carolina Press, Chapel Hill, North Carolina.

Kolenda, K. (ed.) (1988). *Organizations and Ethical Individualism*. Praeger, New York.

Kramnick, I. (1982). Republican Revisionism Revisited. *American Historical Review*, 87: 630.

Kristeller, P.O. (1964). *Eight Philosophers of the Italian Renaissance*. Stanford University Press, Stanford, California.

Kuhn, T.S. (2nd ed., 1970). *The Structure of Scientific Revolutions*. University of Chicago Press, Chicago.

Kupperman, J.J. (1991). *Character*. Oxford University Press, Oxford, England.

Lerner, M. (ed.) (1950). Machiavelli's *The Prince and The Discourses*. The Modern Library, New York.

MacIntyre, A. (1966). *A Short History of Ethics*. Macmillan, New York.

MacIntyre, A. (1981). *After Virtue*. University of Notre Dame Press, Notre Dame, Indiana.

Manuel, F.E. (1956). *The New World of Henri Saint-Simon*. Harvard University Press, Cambridge, Massachusetts.

Maslow, A.H. (2nd ed.; 1970). *Motivation and Personality*. Harper & Row, New York.

Michels, R. (1915). *Political Parties* (E. and C. Paul, trans). Dover Publications, New York.

Miller, E.F. (ed.) (1985). David Hume, *Essays: Moral, Political, and Literary*. Liberty Classics, Indianapolis, Indiana.

Miller, W. (trans.) (1913). Cicero's *De Officiis*, Loeb Classical Library. Harvard University Press, Cambridge, Massachusetts.

Morrow, G.R. (1969). *The Ethical and Economic Theories of Adam Smith*. Augustus M. Kelley Publisher, Clifton, New Jersey.

Norton, D.L. (1976). *Personal Destinies: A Philosophy of Ethical Individualism*. Princeton University Press, Princeton, New Jersey.

Norton, D.L. (1988). Moral Minimalism and the Development of Moral Character in *Ethical Theory* (French, *et al.*, eds.). University of Notre Dame Press, Notre Dame, Indiana.

Norton, D.L. (1991). *Democracy and Moral Development*. University of California Press, Berkeley, California.

Nussbaum, M.C. (1986). *The Fragility of Goodness: Luck and Ethics in Greek Tragedy and Philosophy*. Cambridge University Press, Cambridge, England.

Padover, S.K. (ed.) (1953). *The Complete Madison: His Basic Writings*. Harper & Brothers, New York.

Pegis, A.C. (ed.) (1948). *Introduction to Saint Thomas Aquinas*. The Modern Library, New York.

Penelhum, T. (1985). *Butler*. Routledge & Kegan Paul, London, England.

Phillipson, N. (1983). Adam Smith as Civic Moralist, in *Wealth and Virtue: The Shaping of Political Economy in the Scottish Enlightenment*, (I. Hont and M. Ignatieff, eds.). Cambridge University Press, Cambridge, England, pp. 179–202.

Pieper, J. (rev. ed., 1966). *The Four Cardinal Virtues*. University of Notre Dame Press, Notre Dame, Indiana.

Pincoffs, E.L. (1986). *Quandaries and Virtues: Against Reductivism in Ethics*. University Press of Kansas, Lawrence, Kansas.

Pocock, J.G.A. (1975). *The Machiavellian Moment: Florentine Political Thought and the Atlantic Republican Tradition*. Princeton University Press, Princeton, New Jersey.

Pocock, J.G.A. (1983). Cambridge Paradigms and Scotch Philosophers, in *Wealth and Virtue* (I. Hont and M. Ignatieff, eds.). 235–252.

Pocock, J.G.A. (2nd ed.; 1989). *Politics, Language, and Time*. University of Chicago Press, Chicago, Illinois.

Prior, W.J. (1991). *Virtue and Knowledge: An Introduction to Ancient Greek Ethics*. Routledge, London, England.

Raphael, D.D. (1981). *Moral Philosophy*. Oxford University Press, New York.

Raphael, D.D. and Macfie, A.L. (eds.) (1982). Adam Smith's *The Theory of Moral Sentiments*. Liberty Classics, Indianapolis, Indiana.

Rawson, E. (1975). *Cicero*. Cornell University Press, Ithaca, New York.

Regan, R.J. (1988). Virtue, Religion, and Civic Culture, *Ethical Theory* (French, *et al.*, eds.), 342–351.

Robbins, C. (1959). *The Eighteenth-Century Commonwealthman*. Harvard University Press, Cambridge, Massachusetts.

Roberts, T.A. (1973). *The Concept of Benevolence: Aspects of Eighteenth-Century Moral Philosophy*. Macmillan, London, England.

Rorty, A.O. (ed.) (1980). *Essays on Aristotle's Ethics*. University of California Press, Berkeley, California.

Schumacher, E.F. (1973). *Small Is Beautiful*. Harper & Row, New York.

Scott, W.R. (1900). *Francis Hutcheson*. Augustus M. Kelley Publishers, New York.

Scott, W.G. and Hart, D.K. (1989). *Organizational Values in America*. Transaction Books, New Brunswick, New Jersey.

Scott, W.G. and Hart, D.K. (1991). The Exhaustion of Managerialism in the Twentieth Century. *Society*, 28: 39–48.

Seigel, J.E. (1973). *Virtu* In and Since the Renaissance, *Dictionary of the History of Ideas*, Volume IV (P.P. Wiener, ed.). Charles Scribner's Sons, Publishers, New York.

Shelden, M. (1991). *Orwell*. Harper Collins Publishers, New York.

Sherman, N. (1989). *The Fabric of Character: Aristotle's Theory of Virtue*. Clarendon Press, Oxford, England.

Simon, Y.R. (1986). *The Definition of Moral Virtue* (Vukan Kuic, ed.). Fordham University Press, New York.

Sorel, G. (1906). *Reflections on Violence*, (T.E. Hulme, trans.). Collier Books, New York.

Thomas, L. (1989). *Living Morally: A Psychology of Moral Character*. Temple University Press, Philadelphia, Pennsylvania.

Wallace, J.D. (1978). *Virtues and Vices*. Cornell University Press, Ithaca, New York.

Wilson, J.Q. (1991). *On Character: Essays*. The AEI Press, Washington, D.C.

Wolin, S.S. (1960). *Politics and Vision*. Little, Brown, Boston, Massachusetts.

Wolin, S.S. (1969). Political Theory as a Vocation. *American Political Science Review*, 63.

Wood, G.S. (1991). *The Radicalism of the American Revolution*. Alfred A. Knopf, New York.

Wood, N. (1988).*Cicero's Social and Political Thought*. University of California Press, Berkeley, California.

Yearley, L.H. (1990). *Mencius and Aquinas: Theories of Virtue and Conceptions of Courage*. State University of New York Press, Albany, New York.

7

The Public Interest

Douglas F. Morgan
Portland State University, Portland, Oregon

American public administration is the bearer of a tradition of practices that reflect continuous debate about the proper role of the career public service in promoting the public interest. Yet, within this debate there are "continuities of conflict" (MacIntyre, 1984, p. 222) which, when properly understood, are critical to active and responsible participation of the career public service in our system of democratic governance. The historical analysis that follows identifies these major "continuities of conflict" with two goals in mind: first, to illustrate that there is a lively body of tradition within American public administration which anchors *praxis* to the pursuit of the larger public interest; and, second, to demonstrate that the recovery of this narrative is vital to guiding the exercise of administrative discretion and maintaining the health of our democratic polity (Morgan and Kass, 1991).

I. INTRODUCTION: THE ORIGINS OF THE PUBLIC INTEREST

> Ambition must be made to counteract ambition. The interest of the man must be connected with the constitutional rights of the place. It may be a reflection on human nature that such devices should be necessary to control the abuses of government. But what is government itself but the greatest of all reflections on human nature? If men were angels, no government would be necessary. If angels were to govern men, neither external nor internal controls on government would be necessary. (Rossiter, 1961: Federalist #51)

Publius' famous observations in *Federalist* #51 reflect the victory of a new universe of English political discourse that by the end of the seventeenth century had stood 1500 years of tradition on its head. This new discourse begins with the private interests of individuals rather than with some teleological *summum bonum* as the basic building block upon which to construct a stable and prosperous political order. In the process of lowering the standards against which to measure political regimes, the "public interest" became a commonly accepted way of talking about the public good.

Prior to the outbreak of the English civil wars in the 1640s, the term "public interest" was not in wide use. Instead, terms like the "common good" or "public weal" were invoked when referring to the good of the larger political whole. While these terms were never defined with much precision, they always assumed the desirability of subordinating particular individual interests to a larger set of communal values. Sometimes these values were religious in nature, such as doing God's will or, more generally, living a morally virtuous life. Sometimes these public values were more secular in nature, such as keeping the domestic tranquility or doing one's patriotic duty against foreign enemies to insure the safety of the nation (Gunn, 1969; Hirschman, 1977).

During the Civil War period the English vocabulary underwent dramatic changes as various parties challenged the dominant religious, economic, and political orthodoxies in the name of promoting and/or liberating the private interests of the people. The majority of these critics rejected the traditional view that the common good could be defined apart from the interests of the individual members of the community. Instead of seeing the common good as a check on private interests and a moral guide for the cultivation of human virtue, they argued that the common good was *derivative from* rather than *constitutive of* private interests. This turnabout in thinking occurred as partisans of the new orthodoxy saw the salutary role private interests could play in constructing a stable political order. While "interest still remained a term of abuse to describe the motivations of wicked governors," by the end of the 17th century the language of interest had become such a dominant centerpiece of public discourse that the "public interest" supplanted "the common good" as the characteristic way of talking about the good of the polity (Gunn, 1969, pp. 36, 44; Hirschman, 1977, pp. 3–66).

As with the previous use of terms like the "common good" and "public weal," "public interest" lacked considerable precision. However, in 17th-century England it is possible to identify at least two major patterns of thinking about the public interest, each of which has its counterpart in both the tradition and practice of American public administration (Hirschman, 1977, pp. 20–47).

A. The Interest-Balancing Approach

The debate over religious toleration during and after the English Restoration spawned a variety of tracts advocating a multiplicity of religious sects as the best way to secure the public peace. As Dr. Jeremy Taylor, chaplain to Charles I, observed, "[i]f you persecute heretics or discrepants, they unite themselves as to a common defence. If you permit them, they divide themselves upon private interest . . ."(in Gunn, 1969, p. 156). When applied to the traditional estates of the monarchy, clergy, and nobility, this argument stripped these institutions of their ascriptive status and reduced them to critical, but not necessarily exclusive, interests that needed to be balanced in order to secure the public peace.

B. Public Interest as the Promotion and Protection of Private Interests

As parties came to recognize the importance that self-interest could play in balancing off religious and political differences, they similarly came to see the importance of self-interest in promoting the economic prosperity of the nation-state. Appeals to charity, to altruism, or some *summum bonum* were abandoned in favor of the more secure ground of private gain. As one of Hobbes' critics observed in a clever parity, ". . . for FEAR of catching cold, I took the shoes, and for FEAR he should never see me again he took my money" (in Gunn, 1969, p. 214). By the end of the 17th century, the English debate over free trade, mercantilism, and enclosure had produced a widespread belief that the public economic interest consisted of, and resulted from, the individual pursuit of private economic gain (Gunn, 1969, pp. 205–265). These beliefs, when coupled with the religious and political utility of protecting private interests, set the stage for arguing that the public interest *requires* the protection of private interests.

From these historical beginnings, we have inherited a legacy that embodies four important assumptions about the public interest. First, the public interest can not be defined without taking into account the private interests of subjects. Second, the existence of the public interest is a matter of artificial creation, an instrumental contrivance, rather than something that is "laid up in the heavens" or has universal moral status like the "common good" and "public weal." Third, the main goal of government is to secure a proper identity of interests between rulers and ruled rather than actively and aggressively to cultivate the intellectual and moral virtue of its subjects. Finally, interest is not seen as the ideal foundation of government, just the best possible. As William Penn observed, "interest has the security though not the virtue of a principle. As the world goes, it is the secure side" (in Gunn, 1969, p. 187).

The legacy of these assumptions about the public interest creates a central dilemma for our present day system of democratic governance: how can we appeal to a higher and commonly shared sense of ethical duty within a society almost exclusively devoted to the protection and promotion of individual liberty? This question is made even more difficult to answer in our own age of "hyper-pluralism" where the proliferation of single-issue interest groups further undermines our capacity to think and act in the name of a larger community of shared values and interests (Morrow, 1987; Roelofs, 1991; Bellah, et al., 1986, 1991; Bell, 1973; Mulgan, 1994).

In this chapter we will proceed historically to examine the dominant approaches that have been used since the founding of our nation to give meaning to the public interest. How do we know the public interest when we see it? What ethical values inform and guide its definition? What role can and should career administrators play in bringing this public interest to fruition? Starting with the founding debates, we will explore the Federalist and Antifederalist notions of how best to reconcile the pursuit of private interest with the public good, and then proceed to identify the conceptions of the public interest that have been dominant within various periods of our history.

As we will discover in our review of this history, career public administrators inherit a legacy of at least three major continuities in conflict. First, there is conflict over the proper *ends* to be served by democratic governance. While there is nearly universal consensus that the public interest requires the protection of individual liberty, there is considerable disagreement whether this liberty consists of merely leaving citizens alone or providing them with some minimum threshold of economic and social equality. Second, there is conflict over the appropriate *form* democratic governance should take. Should its legitimacy be judged against the standards of majoritarianism, competition among various interest groups, or the communitarian democratic tradition? Finally, there is conflict over the appropriate *balance* between the claims of science and the claims of majoritarian sentiment in guiding both policy development and implementation. As we will see, in all of these conflicts there is an important role to be played by career public administrators in helping to shape and define the public interest.

II. THE FOUNDING DEBATE: THE PUBLIC INTEREST AS PROCEDURAL V. SUBSTANTIVE JUSTICE

The meaning of the public interest in the United States has been largely shaped by our founding dialogue about the meaning of self government.[1] This debate can be easily divided into two broad schools of thought. As we will see in the following discussion, one school contends that differences of opinion about the public interest have everything to do with the promotion of substantive democratic values, particularly equality of condition.[2] The other contends that the public interest is mainly a debate over the procedural values which should govern the determination of the common good.

The first school of thought sees the public interest as a substantive tug of war between those who wish to promote greater equality and those who fear that such action will come at the expense of individual liberty (Beard, 1913; Jensen, 1940; Ferguson, 1961; Main, 1960). The second school sees the public interest as an attempt to achieve a procedural and structural balance among three major sources of danger that threaten to undermine a regime of ordered liberty (Brown, 1963; Boorstin, 1953; Diamond, 1977, 1981; Hartz, 1955; MacDonald, 1958; Thach, 1969): abuses of authority by public officials, excesses by tyrannical majorities, and the incapacity of government to develop and implement competent public policy. Finding procedural correctives to guard against these three sources of democratic danger is viewed as problematic. For example, too much protection against usurpation may deprive government of the energy necessary to forestall the dual dangers of governmental incompetence and the excesses of tyrannical majorities. Consequently, striking the right procedural balance is viewed as decisively important for promoting the public interest.

A. The Public Interest as a Substantive Debate Over Democratic Ends

Since the publication of Beard's *Economic Interpretation*, historians have engaged in a prolonged debate over the degree to which our Constitution reflects democratic as opposed to antidemocratic impulses.[3] According to Beard and his supporters, the Constitution resulted from economic pressures by a financial elite to stem the egalitarian tide set in motion by the Declaration of Independence and the Articles of Confederation (Beard, 1913; Jensen, 1940; Ferguson, 1961; Main, 1960). During the Revolutionary War period the small farming and debtor interests dominated at the increasing expense of what Beard calls "personalty interests," i.e., money, public securities, manufacturing, and trading/shipping interests.[4] Because of the inflationary pressures of the war and the weakness of the Articles of Confederation, the personalty interests conspired to stem the democratic economic tide by forming a new and much less egalitarian national government. The result, according to Beard and his followers, was a Constitution that "was essentially an economic document based upon the concept that the fundamental private rights of property are anterior to government and morally beyond the reach of popular majorities" (Beard, 1913, p. 324).

Those who opposed Beard's economic interpretation did so on two main grounds: (1) his science was flawed, and (2) he failed to recognize the significance of the underlying liberal democratic consensus that was shared by all sides of the debate.

The "flawed science" argument drew on microhistorical analysis of the financial holdings by the founding generation to undermine Beard's simple distinction between personal and real property (MacDonald, 1958; Brown, 1963). This analysis pointed out that there was a much broader ownership of personalty than was admitted by Beard (even by men like Elbridge Gerry who opposed the Constitution!), that existing property qualifications were modest and did not seriously impair the ability of the citizenry to vote, and, finally, that there was agreement by many radical democrats that some of the popular excesses under the Articles of Confederation and the majoritarian state constitutions needed tempering.

The most persistent criticism of the Beardian thesis has come from the "consensus" historians like Daniel Boorstin and Louis Hartz who have emphasized the uniqueness of the American culture with its absence of feudalism, rigid class distinctions, and deep ideological divisions (Boorstin, 1953; Hartz, 1955). By the late 1950s and 1960s the dominant interpretation of the founding debates emphasized the libertarian goals of both the Revolution and the Constitution. As Hannah Arendt has observed, what set the American Revolution apart from all other revolutions before and after was its singular focus on *Constitutio Libertatis*. Simply stated, the purpose of the American Revolution was to make the new nation safe for freedom, not to achieve an already widely existent social and economic equality (Arendt, 1963, Chap. 4).

The libertarian interpretation of the Constitution emphasizes negative over positive freedom (Berlin, 1969). By "negative freedom" is meant "freedom from interference, from being pushed around, restricted, locked up" (Held, 1984, p. 124). The libertarian view reminds us that our form of government was not established to cultivate human excellence (either moral or intellectual) or the advancement of the rich and well-born. This does not mean that those who are aristocratic or oligarchic in spirit are not able to cultivate their respective excellences. They are permitted to do so, but only because liberty is defined negatively as the value of preserving the pursuit of individual interests (Diamond, 1977, pp. 45–49). This is how the libertarian interpretation of the founding debates is turned from a dialogue over democratic ends into a debate over means to preserve liberties.

B. The Public Interest as a Debate Over Procedural Balance

In order to successfully constitute liberty the founders had "to reconcile the advantages of democracy with the sobering qualities of republicanism . . . to render a democratic regime compatible with the protection of liberty and the requisites of competent government" (Diamond, 1981, pp. 8, 9). While many scholars agree on the primacy of the libertarian goals of the American Constitution, there are vast differences of opinion over *how* the ends of democratic government can best be achieved. The question of how best to secure freedom turns on *which* of the following are thought to be most dangerous to democratic government: too much government, too little government, or incompetent government. These dangers were a vital part of the everyday experiences of the founding generation. They began during the early days of the Revolutionary period with the excesses of King George. They were quickly followed by the excesses of majoritarianism represented by the Shay's Rebellion. Neither experience prepared the founding generation adequately to cope with the General George Washington Problem, namely, the incapacity of government to marshal the resources necessary to fight a successful war.

1. The King George Problem

Usurpation of authority by having too much power at the center was an easy lesson for the colonists to learn. This lesson was reflected in each of the newly adopted state constitutions which concentrated governmental power in the popularly elected legislative branch (New York remained an exception with strong powers reserved to the executive branch; Thach, 1969, Chap. 2). The joys resulting from giving "all power to the people" soon ended, however, in the face of rising concerns for majority tyranny and incompetent government.

2. The Shay's Rebellion Problem

The excesses of popular government soon manifested themselves as state legislatures bowed to the majority pressures of the debtor classes to suspend contract obligations in the face of severe war-induced inflation. Many realized that such actions undermined the kind of long-term certainty necessary for economic growth and development. By the time there was a call for a constitutional convention to revise the Articles of Confederation, there was considerable sentiment favoring checks on the unrestrained power of the populace. This sentiment was reinforced by the wartime experience of attempting to conduct coordinated battle against the British with an all-powerful legislative branch.

3. The George Washington Problem

The constant inability of General Washington to acquire the necessary arms and supplies to successfully conduct the war demonstrated the need for a much greater unity of command. It was nearly impossible to conduct coordinated battle under the superintending authority of a committee. Not only was a strengthened executive branch necessary to guard against the ''Shay's Rebellion Problem,'' it was also necessary to ameliorate the ''George Washington Problem.''

In summary, for the founding generation, the public interest was problematic because each of the three major sources of danger to liberty could not be corrected without making the others worse. There was an irreconcilable three-way tension among the need for government competence, popular sovereignty, and the preservation of minority rights. For the Federalists too little governmental power at the center *and* majority tyranny were far more deleterious to the public interest than the Antifederalists' fear of too much power at the center. The dilemmas of the founders are well-captured by the following beatitudes.

The Founding Beatitudes

Too much power begets usurpation, to which majority rule is a corrective;
Too much majority rule begets majority tyranny, to which separation of powers and checks and balances is a corrective;
Too much separation of powers and checks and balances begets incompetent government, to which unity at the center is a corrective.
Too much unity at the center begets usurpation.

—Douglas Morgan

C. Continued Relevance of the Founding Debate

While the strong version of the Beardian thesis—that the Founders' holdings of securities dictated their beliefs and actions—has long been discredited, the weaker version of his thesis is very much alive. We continue to draw on the egalitarian and populist impulses of the Revolutionary War period to support contemporary arguments favoring greater democratization in the form of both more equality of social condition and greater citizen participation. These views have taken on new life within public administration in the last two decades, as some scholars and students of the American administrative process have argued that career administrators should become more active agents of expanded social equity and citizen participation (Marini, 1971; Adams et. al., 1990; T. Cooper, 1991; Fox and Miller, 1994; King and Stivers, 1998; Box, 1998).

While some scholars of the administrative process draw on the substantive egalitarian tradition of the founding period to guide the discretionary exercise of administrative authority, others draw on the procedural approach to the public interest to support a similar kind of role being played by career administrators. For example, John Rohr has argued that the career public service has taken on the balancing role originally intended to be performed by the U.S. Senate (Rohr, 1987, 1986). Now that the Senate is popularly elected, it can not carry out the mediating role originally intended for it by the framers of the Constitution nearly as well as the professional bureaucracy. He has argued that this balancing role goes beyond procedural considerations to include balancing substantive democratic values such as liberty, property, and equality (Rohr, 1989).

III. THE FEDERALISTS: THE PUBLIC INTEREST AS THE REGULATION OF THE PASSIONS

The Federalists and Antifederalists present us with two competing conceptions of the public interest. For the Federalists the public interest was primarily a matter of regulating the passions and interests; for the Antifederalists, the public interest required the cultivation of republican virtues. While the Federalists were certainly not indifferent to the impact that the formation of character had on public life, they did not believe the Constitution could or should make government dependent on the continued existence of personal virtue or its active cultivation. For the Federalists a healthy and long-lived democratic polity could be created by mitigating the adverse effects of undesirable popular passions at the base of the system and by manipulating the structures and duties of public office at the top of the system so that ambitious and qualified leaders could be turned loose to pursue their self-interest without having to worry very much about the larger public good. Fortunately for the friends of liberty, argued the authors of *The Federalist Papers*, the science of politics, like most other sciences of the day, had improved sufficiently to make this difficult task possible (Rossiter, 1961, #9).

A. Controlling the Adverse Effects of Popular Passions

One of the more salutary discoveries of the "new science of politics" was how to establish liberty over a vast expanse of territory and simultaneously to guard against majority tyranny. Previous to 1787 all democratic regimes had fallen prey either to the mob or the precipitous centralizing tyranny of a large standing army. Both fates, Madison argued, could be avoided by "enlarging the orbit." By this he meant the incorporation of a multiplicity of interests within a larger territorial whole. Consolidating the 13 colonies into a common geographic area would have a three-fold advantage. First, the larger orbit (assuming open access to commercial diversity) would increase the multiplicity of interests. Second, the large size would make it more difficult for any one interest to see what it had in common with others. Finally, the sheer expanse of territory would make it difficult to undertake common action by a tyrannous majority. In short, a large and commercially diverse territory with open access to development would fragment opinion, multiply sects, and balkanize the formation of interest groups. For the first time in history government could be protected from tyranny by both a single ruler and the majority, and do so in a manner that preserved the full essence of a democratic regime.

B. Structuring the Duties of Public Office to Maximize the Salutary Influences of Personal Interest

Madison observed in Federalist #51 that the "new science of politics" must discover a way of making government safe from the usurpation of authority, without at the same time discouraging the best and the brightest from offering themselves up as candidates. The secret of achieving these dual objectives was to structure the duties of public office so that "the interest of the man [is] . . . connected to the constitutional rights of the place." The application of this principle is painstakingly and brilliantly illustrated in Federalist #72 where Publius makes an extensive argument against limitations on eligibility for reelection.

> One ill effect of the exclusion would be a diminution of the inducements to good behavior. There are few men who would not feel much less zeal in the discharge of a duty when they were conscious that the advantage of the station with which it was connected must be relinquished at a determinate period, than when they were permitted to entertain a hope of *obtaining*, by *meriting*, a continuance of them. . . . [T]he desire of reward is one of the strongest incentives of human conduct; or that the best security for the fidelity of mankind is to make their interest coincide with their duty. . . .
>
>   Another ill effect of the exclusion would be the temptation to sordid views, to peculation, and, in some instances, to usurpation. An avaricious man who might happen to fill the office, looking forward to a time when he must at all events yield up the advantages he enjoyed, would feel a propensity not easy to be resisted by such a man to make the best use of his opportunities while they lasted, and might not scruple to have recourse to the most corrupt expedients to make the harvest as abundant as it was transitory; though the same man, probably, with a different prospect before him, might content himself with the regular perquisites of his situation, and might even be unwilling to risk the consequences of an abuse of his opportunities. His avarice might be a guard upon his avarice. Add to this that the same man might be vain or ambitious, as well as avaricious. And if he could expect to prolong his honors by his good conduct, he might hesitate to sacrifice his appetite for them to his appetite for gain. But with the prospect before him of approaching and [sic] inevitable annihilation, his avarice would be likely to get the victory over his caution, his vanity, or his ambition. (Rossiter, 1961, #72, pp. 437–438)

For the Federalists the best that could be hoped for under a properly constructed system of government was displacement of the lower passions of avarice and vanity by the higher motivations of ambition and honor. If the duties and terms of office could be structured to appeal to the ambitious, then individuals would be encouraged to launch long-term projects that would be conducive to the public good. Projects like the "New Deal," the "Fair Deal," the "Great Society," and the "New Frontier" give one a place of honor in the annals of history.

C. Consequences of the Federalist View of the Public Interest for Administrative Service

The Federalist vision of the public interest provides us with a model of public service reminiscent of the classical Roman tradition, a tradition where honor and devotion to *res publica* are high callings, where grand and ambitious public ventures are encouraged, and where the doers of such grand deeds are held in high esteem (Green, 1993). However, what decisively separates the Federalists' vision from their classical forebears is a truncated view of public life in which the state becomes an instrument of negative rather than positive freedom. Government would serve as a regulatory agent for promoting peace and prosperity without assuming any responsibility for cultivating virtue or even the minimum qualities of character that they believed government needed to survive. The Federalist framers seemed to have assumed that institutions in the private sector, such as families, churches, schools, etc., would produce individuals of high character and that "American democracy would seek out and reward the 'natural aristocracy' with public trust. Whether these expectations of the Founders were reasonable then or remain so now is a grave matter for inquiry . . ." (Diamond, 1979, pp. 71–72; also see Richardson, 1997).

The Federalist model of public service was employed by George Washington in staffing his administration. He appointed public servants who could successfully pass a "fitness of character test." This test required that individuals possess impeccable personal integrity and have high standing in their local communities. Through this fitness-of-character test Washington sought to appoint public servants who "would give dignity and luster to our National Character . . ." (in White, 1948, p. 259).

IV. THE ANTIFEDERALISTS: THE PUBLIC INTEREST AS REPUBLICAN VIRTUE

Fear of excessive individualism and the loss of community has been a major theme of American politics since our founding. However, over the past three decades we have witnessed a dramatic resurgence in the communitarian impulse with the publication of a corpus of literature which has challenged the popular and long-held notion that our constitutional principles are simply Lockean in origin. According to the Lockean thesis, popularized by Louis Hartz and his followers, those who framed the American Constitution assumed that nothing more than the rational pursuit of self-interest was necessary to achieve a well-ordered and long-surviving regime of liberty (Hartz, 1955). This thesis has been challenged by a growing body of literature which argues that a second tradition held powerful sway over the minds of the founding generation (Bailyn, 1967; Wood, 1969; Pocock, 1975; Kendall and Carey, 1970; McWilliams, 1973). This tradition drew upon classical republicanism and the Puritan biblical tradition to provide "a conceptualization and vocabulary of citizenship" which created "a fairly well developed theory of community . . . alongside Hobbesian-Lockean individualism" (De Maio, 1980, p. 3). The animating principle of the theory of community was civic virtue, or the "willingness of the individual to sacrifice his private interests for the good of the community" (Wood, 1969, p. 68; T. Cooper, 1991, especially chapters 1–3).

There is a considerable difference of opinion among those contributing to this new emphasis on a communitarian tradition as to whether it was a major contribution (Storing, 1981, p. 3) or only minor (Diamond, 1977, pp. 49–68); whether it was "derailed" by the founding generation (Kendall and Carey, 1970, p. 72) or simply misunderstood as to what its preservation required (Yarbrough, 1979, pp. 85–87, 93–95). Despite these subtleties of interpretation, all of the various disputants agree on the inadequacy of a regime based only, or even mainly, upon the promotion of private self-interest. Such a regime is left without "a convincing and generally accepted theory of political obligation" (Kristol, 1978, p. 79; Box, 1998; King and Stivers, 1998).

The resurgence of interest in the communitarian roots of our body politic traces its origins to the Antifederalist tradition. There are two versions of this tradition. The strong version claims that the Antifederalists attempted to reclaim the classical republican belief that the perfection of our full potential as human beings requires active participation in public affairs and the cultivation of the civic virtues that this participation necessitates. The weak version of the Antifederalist tradition argues that the commitment to republican virtue is intended to serve as a corrective to excessive individualism rather than provide a genuine and serious alternative to the large commercial republic favored by the Federalists.

A.   The Weak Version of the Antifederalist Tradition: Republican Virtue as a Corrective to Excessive Individualism

Both the history and practice of free government had convinced the Antifederalists that liberty could not be maintained over a large and extended territory like the United States. There was the obvious danger arising from a large standing army that would be needed to protect the frontiers from invasion by greedy and envious foreign powers. But more importantly, a large territory could not cultivate the right kind of citizen virtue. The energies of the people would be mobilized to increase their trade and commerce in the service of what Patrick Henry in the Virginia ratifying convention characterized as "grandeur, power and splendor," rather than in guarding their liberties. "[T]hose nations who have gone in search of grandeur, power and splendor have also fallen a sacrifice, and been the victims of their own folly. While they acquired those visionary blessings, they lost their freedom" (Storing, 1981, Vol. V, p. 214). What was needed most was a vigilant temperament, and this was thought to exist especially among those in "middling circumstances," who, according to Melancton Smith in New York, "are inclined by habit, and the company with whom they associate, to set bounds to their passions and appetites." The substantial yeomanry of the country were thought to be "more temperate, of better morals, and less ambition, than the great" (Storing, 1981, Vol. VI, p. 158).

In short, for the Antifederalists the public interest was inseparable from right living. It was a habit of virtue cultivated by yeomanry circumstances. Such circumstances fostered the essential republican virtues of moderation, vigilance, industry, and thrift. But this leaves open the question of whether active participation in public life by all citizens was viewed as necessary for human happiness. Cincinnatus at the plow, like George Washington at Mount, Vernon, may dutifully and temporarily abandon his station to heed the call of public service, but is his public service necessary to fulfill his full potential as a human being? Abandoning the plow may be useful for the republic, much like the Jacksonian argument in favor of rotation in office, but is it necessary for Cincinnatus? The weak version of the Antifederalist argument in favor of republican virtue would say no, while the strong version would say yes.

For Alexis de Tocqueville there was little question which of these two versions of the Antifederalist tradition Americans had adopted as he observed community life in his travels throughout the United States during the Jacksonian period. De Tocqueville was struck by the enormous "daily small acts of self-denial" which lead every American "to sacrifice some of his private interest to save the rest" (de Tocqueville, 1969, p. 131). He was so immensely impressed by the vibrancy of voluntary associations, religious sects, and organized acts of self-help that he was moved to conclude that the "science of association is the mother of science; the progress of all the rest depends upon the progress it has made. . . . If men are to remain civilized or to become so, the art of associating together must grow and improve in the same ratio in which the equality of conditions is increased" (de Tocqueville, 1969, p. 517). Because this communitarian impulse emanated from the enlightened pursuit of one's own self-interest, de Tocqueville dubbed this republican habit of virtue, "self-interest rightly understood," to distinguish it from the older aristocratic tradition which considered virtue to be an end-in-itself.

B. The Strong Version of the Antifederalist Tradition: Community as Way of Life

There is a stronger version of the argument in favor of republican virtue that takes it bearings primarily from a classical republican interpretation of the Jeffersonian tradition. According to this interpretation, while Jefferson shared most of Locke's natural right views, he rejected the a-social assumptions associated with the Lockean state of nature. He accepted the classical Greek assumption that human beings, by nature, are social creatures whose full virtue can only be perfected within an organized human community (Peterson, 1960, p. 94). Only in such communities could the "inherent moral instinct . . . to establish and cultivate fraternal ties" be developed to its full capacity. According to this interpretation of Jeffersonianism, the pursuit of happiness meant "public activity" that grew out of a commonly shared sense of "public well-being" (T. Cooper, 1991, p. 82).

This strong version of republican virtue falls considerably short of the view of public life celebrated by Pericles in his famous "Athenian Funeral Oration." For Pericles Athens provided a public stage where the living deed and the spoken word could produce the greatest achievements of which human beings were capable. The Athenian polis inspired "men to dare the extraordinary" (Arendt, 1958, p. 184), and in so doing perfect their distinctive natures. Thus, while both Pericles and Jefferson view humans as naturally social creatures who need to participate in public life to perfect their natures, for Jefferson this participation is a way to obviate selfishness and instill duty to others, not to produce grand words and glorious deeds.

C. Consequences of the Antifederalist View of the Public Interest for Administrative Service

The Antifederalists have left us with a legacy of public service that has served as a precedent for some of the more important features of our modern-day career civil service. First, the Antifederalists insisted that agents of the republic be comprised of those with modest means, neither rich nor poor. This feature is preserved in the open access of our competitive merit system which sets minimal technical qualifications that are job specific. Second, the Antifederalists argued that public agents were to be drawn from the local community and have knowledge of local circumstances. Our federal civil service system follows this practice by hiring local employees to administer national programs or by having such programs administered by state and local public officials rather than federal employees. Finally, by comparison to those employed in the private sector our career public servants display those qualities of prudent judgment and modest expectations which the Antifederalists believed were so essential in moderating unreflective, overly bold, and self-serving ambitious initiatives undertaken by elected public officials.

V. JACKSONIAN DEMOCRACY AND UTILITARIANISM: THE PUBLIC INTEREST AS SIMPLE MAJORITY RULE

Jacksonian democracy seized upon the majoritarian impulse of the Antifederalist and Jeffersonian traditions and over time came to identify the voice of the people with democratic government itself. Four Jacksonian principles helped to mold and shape this utilitarian view of the public interest: energetic use of presidential power, plebiscitarian executive leadership, direct democracy, and a strong belief in limited government.

A. An Energetic Executive

Jackson went well beyond both his Federalist and Republican predecessors to strengthen the executive function of governance. He extended the veto power "to include mere differences of opinion concerning the expediency of legislation." He exercised unrestrained use of his removal power. And he exercised popular leadership over a mass political party movement (White, 1954, p. 22). However, the uniqueness of Jackson's contributions to our understanding of the public interest arises from the way in which he combined an energetic use of executive authority with a strong commitment to direct democracy and a belief in limited government.

B. Plebiscitarian Executive Leadership

Jackson was the first president to articulate the novel theory that the president was a direct representative of the people, rather than an agent of a larger constitutional order. He recommended the direct election of the president in his first annual message to Congress, so that "as few impediments as possible should exist to the free operation of the public will" (Richardson, 1911, Vol. II, p. 448; in White, 1954, p. 23). He returned to this view in his famous "Protest" message to the Senate justifying his right to dismiss William Duane, Secretary of the Treasury, for his refusal to remove deposits in the U.S. Bank. In electing him president, Jackson claimed the people had conferred upon him "the entire executive power" of government (Richardson, 1911, Vol. II, p. 85; in White, 1954, 37). Carried to its logical conclusion, this view would turn executive subordinates into mere ministerial agents of the chief executive's interpretive authority, thus saving them from having to exercise independent responsibility.

C. Rotation in Office

President Jackson converted the Antifederalist and Jeffersonian suspicion of long-term government service into an operating principle called "rotation in office." The rule of frequent rotation of government officials was based on the two-fold argument that over time power tends to corrupt and that everyone possesses the necessary qualities to rule over others. Jackson believed that public employees needed to be constantly reminded that office is not a species of property but "an instrument created solely for the service of the people." Too much time in office allows individuals to "divert government from its legitimate ends and make it an engine for the support of the few at the expense of the many." We need not worry about frequent personnel changes, since "the duties of all public offices are, or at least admit to being made, so plain and simple that men of intelligence may readily qualify themselves for their performance" (Richardson, 1911, Vol. II, p. 448; original speech by Jackson on Dec. 8, 1829).

D. Limited Government

Jackson used the vigorous exercise of his administrative leadership to check "bigness" in all of its forms. His attack upon the National Bank was evenhanded; he attacked big business with equal vigor and for the same reasons. He believed unshackled business competition was "the best guaranty of the prosperity of the country. . . . If the door is thrown open to every competent man, the public wants will be attended to" (U.S. House Committee on Commerce, 1837; quoted in White, 1954, p. 448).

E. Consequences of the Jacksonian View of the Public Interest for Administrative Service

Throughout the founding period and well into the republican era there was a healthy separation between public service and the people. Both the Antifederalist and Jeffersonian traditions viewed administrative agents with suspicion, a potential vested interest pushing aristocratic values. For the Federalists, the separation between public service and the people was necessary to foster energetic and visionary leadership while guarding against majority whims and ignorance. This separation was accomplished through such devices as indirect elections, opportunities for extended terms of office, and adequate powers of office to resist encroachment by another branch of government. The Jacksonian period brought this wall of separation down. But in doing so, it left the administrative function of government with two countervailing propensities. One emphasized the subordination of administrative agents to a popularly elected chief executive who embodied the will of the people. The other propensity emphasized a representative bureaucracy that directly reflected the will and energy of the people throughout all levels of the administrative process. This tension between bureaucracy as active agent and bureaucracy as neutral minion was brought more fully into conflict during the Populist and Progressive periods (Cook, 1996, Chaps. 3 and 4).

VI. POPULIST REFORM: THE PUBLIC INTEREST AS NEUTRAL COMPETENCE

A. The Moral Basis of Populist Reform

Toward the end of the 19th century moral reformers turned their attention from the cause of abolitionism to the abuses of the Jacksonian spoils system. In contrast to the Federalists, there was no desire on the part of the reformers to manipulate human passions and interests to serve higher public purposes (Storing, 1964). Instead, reformers sought to throw the rascals out "by muckraking and otherwise arousing the public to vote. The intent was to place honorable candidates in public office. The logic was that good candidates would implement good policies" (Stever, 1988, p. 30).

While the first wave of late nineteenth century reformers emphasized the special moral qualities necessary for public service, their Populist successors accepted the Jeffersonian assumption that ordinary citizens possessed the knowledge, the will, and the moral character to make democratic government work. All that was needed to correct the ills of the day was some institutional safeguards to insure that good policies and good people would not become corrupted over time. The passage of the Pendleton Act of 1883 and the creation of a public service merit system institutionalized the best thinking of the day about the relationship between personal ethics and the public interest. Career administrators would be appointed and promoted on the basis of written qualifications to perform the job, not on the basis of friendship or partisan political loyalty. Thus, the primary concern during the first two generations of moral and Populist reformers was to make government less corrupt, not more efficient. The moral reformers would accomplish this through the selection of virtuous officeholders while the Populists would reduce corruption by relying on the initiative, referendum, recall, shorter terms of office, and similar instruments of popular accountability.

B. The Populist Legacy

The Populist legacy guides much of our modern-day thinking about how best to protect the public interest from the unacceptable influences of private self-interest. Conflict of interest legislation, financial disclosure laws, open government requirements, and various Hatch-Act regulations at the state and local levels of government testify to the seriousness of our continuing commitment to protect the neutral competence of our public servants (Morgan and Rohr, 1986; Rohr, 1981). Like the turn-of-the century Populist reforms, these measures are aimed at protecting against moral corruption rather than promoting greater government efficiency.

VII. PROGRESSIVE REFORM: THE PUBLIC INTEREST AS SCIENTIFIC MANAGEMENT OR MORAL UPLIFTING?

The Populist Era reaffirmed the long-standing American rule-of-law principle that public office is never to be used to promote or acquire personal gain. But if discretionary choices by career administrators are not to be governed by personal relationships, political favoritism, and personal visions of the public good, what ought to fill the discretionary vacuum? If politics is taken out of administration, what is left? In short, what precisely is meant by "neutral competence"? What values should guide, inform, and check this competence? The Progressives gave two kinds of answers to this question, one drawing on the scientific impulse within Progressivism and the other drawing on the pragmatic side of the movement. James Stever has respectively labeled these two strains as "organic idealism" and "pragmatism" (Stever, 1990).

A. Progressive Visions of the Public Interest

The Progressives took seriously Woodrow Wilsons's call for the establishment of public administration as a separate field of study and for many of the same reasons (T. Cooper, 1991, Chap. 4). "The object of administrative study is to rescue executive methods from the confusion and costliness of empirical experiment and set them upon foundations laid deep in stable principles" (Wilson, 1978, p. 10). These stable principles were, of course, the principles of an empirically grounded positive science. It is this science, according to Wilson, "which shall seek to straighten the paths of government to make its business less unbusiness-like, to strengthen and purify its organization and to crown its duties" (Wilson, 1978, p. 5).

This scientific approach to managing the public's business was made possible by two coincidental developments. First, the long period of constitution-making that preoccupied the founding generation and the abolitionists had come to an end. Essential governance principles had been successfully established, thus bringing closure to shrill public debate over the *ends* of our democratic government. Now attention could focus on questions of *how* to achieve results. A second factor contributing to the call for a new science of administration was the increased complexity of urbanized life. As Wilson observed, "[t]here is scarcely a single duty of government which was once simple which is not now complex . . ."(Wilson, 1978, p. 5).

There is another strain of the Progressive Movement that goes well beyond the desire to use career administration to increase governmental efficiency. This strain draws on the close kinship between American Pragmatism and the reform agenda of the Progressive Movement (Stever, 1988, chap. 3). Underlying both movements was a vision of human nature that could reach its full potential only if the agents of government would serve as exemplars, as tutors, as goads to moral and intellectual excellence. As Herbert Croly, one of the intellectual leaders of the Progressive Movement, observed:

> [the] common citizen can become something of a saint and something of a hero, not by growing to heroic proportions in his own person, but by the sincere and enthusiastic imitation of heroes and saints, and whether or not he will ever come to such imitation will depend upon the ability of his exceptional fellow-countrymen to offer him acceptable examples of heroism and saintliness. (Croly, 1964, p. 454)

This larger moral vision of the Progressive Movement transforms the practice of public administration from a merely scientific and technical enterprise into what Stever calls a "polity profession." By "polity" Stever means a profession that is composed of the most knowledgeable members of society (in contrast to the rich and powerful) who have regular institutionalized control over policy and exercise this control for the larger public good (Stever, 1988, p. 31). In short, the task of "speaking truth to power" was more than a matter of making things work, or making things work efficiently (Wildavsky, 1980). It was a matter of keeping the democratic system on moral course by at least role-modeling the appearance of virtue, if not cultivating its actual practice.

B. The Progressive Legacy

The Progressive Era has left career public administrators with two seemingly different roles to play in fostering the public interest. One emphasizes the purely instrumental role of scientifically managing public organizations and of using state-of-the-art techniques in policy development and implementation. The other emphasizes the moral leadership role career administrators play in elevating public discourse and in fostering human development. The purely instrumental role harkens back to the earlier Antifederalist and Jacksonian visions of an administrative process that simply and mainly facilitates the implementation of the community's will. The moral leadership role within the Progressive tradition is reminiscent of the Federalist vision of an administrative elite that protects the democratic system from unenlightened impulses of the masses. But the moral goal of both the Federalists and Progressives was primarily instrumental and utilitarian, falling far short of the Antifederalist concern for the cultivation of personal and civic virtue.

What tended to get lost during the Progressive Era was the problematic character of our democratic system of governance. Good science ended up being pitted against morality without harnessing the two poles of the debate to a consideration of what was needed to ensure a system of majority rule that produced both efficient *and* morally enlightened governance. The Progressive concern for efficiency turns out on second examination to resemble "cardboard competence" rather than knowledge; its concern for role-modeling resembles "cardboard virtue" rather than personal goodness.[5] The Post-

Progressive Era has left American public administration with considerable differences of opinion as to exactly how and why it can get beyond these cardboard standards.

VIII. POST-PROGRESSIVE CRITIQUES: THE PUBLIC INTEREST IN SEARCH OF A NEW IDENTITY

The Progressive Movement left us with a legacy of "positive government" staffed by an elite corps of technically trained career administrators. But what peculiar competence should this corps possess? What should be its unique contributions to the public interest? What moral principles should guide the exercise of its discretionary judgment? The following four answers have been give to these questions in this century.

1. Career administrators should be strictly governed by the principles of positive science.
2. Career administrators should become masters of interest group politics.
3. Career administrators should promote both procedural and substantive values that are unique to their role within our American constitutional system of governance.
4. Career administrators should preserve a proper balance among the private, non-profit, and public spheres.

A. The Behavioral Revolution and Positive Science: The Public Interest as Myth

The Progressive Movement promoted a conception of the public interest that was exquisitely suited to the extreme claims of both logical positivism and the subsequent scientific revolution in the social sciences. Early twentieth century logical positivism greatly simplified our thinking about the relationship between ethics and the public interest. By drawing a clear line of separation between questions of fact and questions of value, terms like "ethics" and the "public interest" were transformed into useless tools of analysis. Both were value laden terms which reflected personal taste, opinion, and preference. When something was said to be in the public interest, it was a way of legitimizing one's personal preference under the guise of psuedo-objectivity. As one of the more outspoken critics of this practice observed, the "public interest . . . may at times fulfill a 'hair shirt' function . . .; it may also be nothing more than a label attached indiscriminately to a miscellany of particular compromises of the moment. In either case, 'the public interest' neither adds to nor detracts from the theory and methods presently available for analyzing political behavior" (Schubert, 1982, p. 223). In short, the public interest is just another political datum which makes no operational sense as an organizational or analytical concept. This view had some important implications for our approach to the study and practice of public administration.

In the eyes of science much of what had traditionally passed for administrative principles were little more than proverbs that had acquired the status of pseudo-science. Like the term "public interest," administrative principles such as "span of control," "centerlization," "hierarchy," etc. were nothing more than terms of art, filled with contradictions, and of little use as guides to action (Simon, 1957, p. 44). By subjecting these administrative proverbs to the rigors of science, the practice of administration could more efficiently allocate the public's scarce resources. This efficiency would not only result from a more systematic assessment of policy alternatives but from a better documentation of the organizational, financial, and human resources necessary for achieving success. Much of the public administration literature of the 1950s and early 1960s is greatly influenced by Simon's efforts to accomplish these goals of enhancing efficiency through improved approaches to administrative decision-making (Simon et al., 1950; March and Simon, 1958).

B. The Public Interest as "Interest Group Liberalism": A Return to Procedural Democracy

The American tradition of interest group pluralism provides another framework from which to assess the contributions of career administrators to the public interest. This tradition "replaces enlightened and public-spirited policies with the compromises resulting from interest group conflict" (Morrow, 1987, p. 164). Administrative institutions become active arenas for the facilitation of this compromise with career administrators serving as both instigators and agents. This facilitation role has led students of the administrative process to opposite conclusions about how the public interest is best served. One vision emphasizes the pathological consequences that result from unchecked and unguided administrative influence over the policy process. The other vision emphasizes the contributions administrators make to the ends of both balanced public policy and democratic governance.

Those who emphasize the pathological consequences of interest-group liberalism point to the fact that the difficulty of reaching compromises at the legislative level frequently produces law without policy (Lowi, 1979). In the face of vague and ambiguous laws, the administrative setting becomes a free-for-all battle for control over the American public policy process. Of course, there are those who can succeed well in this kind of environment. Generally they are those who have acquired special policy expertise (Heclo, 1978) or those who are part of an iron-triangle alliance among special interests, bureaus of government, and subcommittees of Congress (Freeman, 1965). The critics of this approach to policymaking emphasize the limited access of a few participants who are relatively far removed from the direct influences of the electoral process. In this kind of environment there is a danger that the public interest will become corrupted by the excesses of both partisan extravagance and technocratic arrogance.

Several steps have been taken over the past three decades to ameliorate these kinds of potential abuses of the public interest. First, through the aggressive efforts of Kenneth Culp Davis (Davis, 1971), increased use has been made of the administrative rule-making process to guard the bureaucracy from the arbitrary and capricious behavior of individual administrators (P. Cooper, 1983; Kerwin, 1999). Second, legislative bodies at the federal and state levels have taken more aggressive steps to bring administrative agencies under greater scrutiny. This is reflected in Sunshine legislation, freedom of information and right to privacy acts, and the protection of whistleblowers who speak out against agency wrongdoing. Finally, during the 1970s Congress began to heed the advice of many of its critics and write laws that were much more specific in their content (Levine and Wexler, 1981).

C. The Public Interest as Administrative Stewardship: The Legitimacy Movement in Public Administration

Those who worry about the pathological consequences of interest-group liberalism on the public interest have tended to seek procedural correctives that check the discretionary judgment of career administrators. However, there is another side to interest-group liberalism which emphasizes the need for balanced democratic government operating within a "rule of law" framework of constitutional governance. Starting with this framework, many students argue that career administrators have an opportunity, if not an obligation, to actively use their discretion in a statesmanlike manner to promote the public interest. This approach has been labeled the "legitimacy movement," largely because its proponents are preoccupied with legitimating the exercise of extensive administrative discretion within a rule of law system that gives little explicit recognition of the right for administrators to serve as stewards of the public interest (McSwite, 1997).

Proponents of the "stewardship model" have been challenged by their critics to provide public interest standards that allow us to distinguish acts of administrative statesmanship from acts of tyrannical abuse, to distinguish pathological abuses from discretionary actions that "really" serve the public interest. At least two kinds of response are provided by proponents of the "stewardship model." One emphasizes some version of universal standards of basic human decency. The other looks to the standards that are inherent in our unique structure of public authority.

1. The Basic Decency Response

In the 1960s and 1970s much of the writing and research on bureaucratic organizations refocused our attention on some elemental facts about large complex organizations: they can be oppressive (Scott and Hart, 1979); through co-opting behavior they can lose sight of their mission (Lowi, 1979); and the principle of hierarchy itself undermines the realization of full human potential (Hummel, 1987; Thayer, 1978).

The refocus of attention on the dysfunctional dimensions of organizational life spawned a variety of correctives that drew their strength from our Western humanist tradition. At the center of this tradition is a belief that human beings want and can do what is right and decent if free to do so. For the humanist reformers the major problem was a lack of organizational freedom or opportunity, not a fatally flawed will. Two steps were necessary to unleash the morally good potential of human beings. First, moral exhortation would sharpen the sensibilities that large complex organizations had dulled over the years. Second, massive restructuring of authority relationships in public organizations was in order. The moral exhortation phase promoted a variety of traditional humanist values, including benevolence (Frederickson and Hart, 1985), integrity (Benjamin, 1990), and equity (Hart, 1974, 1983, 1984, 1987). The New Public Administration movement of the late 1960s represents the most successful and far-reaching efforts to institutionalize the moral exhortation phase of the transformation of administrative values (Marini, 1971).

Since good people cannot succeed for long in hostile environments, considerable attention has been placed on the transformation of authority structures in large complex organizations. These efforts have been largely aimed at reconciling the tension between the pursuit of individual self-interest and the greater public good (Thayer, 1978; Likert, 1961; McGregor, 1967). The infatuation with theories Y and Z and with the works of Deming (1982) are examples of our continuing attempts to transform the work environment into the kind of place where human potential can be unleashed. Such efforts rest on the assumptions that moral excellence in public life can be improved to the extent that the moral excellence of individuals can be released.

2. The Uniqueness of Public Authority Response

A second response by proponents of the "stewardship model" to its critics is to emphasize the distinctive public interest values that are inherent in the American structure of public authority. The advocates of this view begin with Aristotle's assumption that the morally virtuous citizen will be the same as the morally virtuous person *only in the best regime*. In short, the moral excellence of a political system reflects the peculiar virtues it has chosen to promote and defend. Viewed in this light, the morally virtuous public servant must be judged by the procedural and substantive values that are unique to its unique system of governance. For American public servants, what are these values? More importantly, what unique contributions can career administrators make to the furtherance of these values? These questions are the starting point for further inquiry by proponents of the "stewardship model."

The most expansive stewardship scholars argue that career administrators are responsible for our democratic "enterprise as a whole." This includes responsibility for "the more encompassing web of offices, processes and institutions that define the explicit obligations the official accepts" (Burke, 1986, p. 42; Morgan, 1996). In charging administrators with responsibility for the whole, the question arises as to what distinguishes the moral responsibility of career administrators from other public officials, such as judges and elected officeholders? Two kinds of answers have been given to these questions in recent years, one emphasizing the unique *structural* role administrators now play within our constitutional system of governance and the other emphasizing the promotion of *substantive* democratic values.

The administrative function of governance is clearly different from both the legislative and judicial functions. Out of these differences scholars have sought to construct a special stewardship role for the American career administrator. One such view sees administrators as balance wheels with responsibility to use their "statutory powers and professional expertise to favor whichever participant in the process needs their help at a given time to preserve the intent of the Constitution" (Wamsley et al., 1987, p. 314). But what makes administrators better suited to serve this role of balance wheel than officials in the legislative and judicial branches of government? This question is similar to the one faced by John Marshall in *Marbury v. Madison* when confronted with the need to justify why the judgment of the Supreme Court was superior to the judgment of the executive and legislative branches in deciding when a law was unconstitutional.

Many scholars answer this challenge by citing the unique features of the administrative setting itself (Terry, 1995). For one thing, the implementation process provides an opportunity for career administrators to structure and facilitate an on-going dialogue with citizens in what has been characterized as "public encounters" (Goodsell, 1981). Providing the *conditions* for healthy public discourse between the government and its citizens plays a decisive role in maintaining a community of shared meaning (T. Cooper, 1991; J. White, 1990; Fox, and Miller, 1994; McSwite, 1997; Box, 1998; King and Stivers, 1998).

Other scholars emphasize those unique qualities of the bureaucratic setting itself, such as the rules of evidence, burden of proof, etc., which give career administrators "a special kind of prudence, or what Aristotle called phronesis, that enables them to coalesce considerations of workability, acceptability, and fit'' (Morgan, 1990, p. 74; also see Jennings, 1990; Spicer, 1995; Cook, 1996; and Vinzant and Crothers, 1998).

Another way of carving out a unique stewardship role for the career public service is to see what it can contribute to the perpetuation of our system of constitutional governance, especially given the substantial changes it has undergone since 1787. One of the leading advocates of this view, John Rohr, has argued that the career public service now performs a role originally intended by the founders to be played by both the U.S. House and Senate. Senatorial attributes like duration, expertise, and stability have been eroded by electoral changes. ''In a word, today's Senate is not the sort of institution the Federalists wanted and the Anti-Federalists feared. The closest approximation . . . can be found in the career civil service, especially at its higher levels.'' Rohr also argues that with its merit system and affirmative action policies, the American bureaucracy serves to curb the excessive filtering and refining which the Antifederalists feared would undermine the representative function of the House of Representatives. In short, ''the administrative state with its huge career public service, heals and repairs a defect in the Constitution of the United States'' (Rohr, 1987, p. 142; Rohr, 1986; Morgan, 1996).

In summary, there are at least three versions of the argument that career public administrators make a distinctive contribution to the public interest by virtue of the *structural role* they occupy within our democratic system. Some emphasize the conditions administrators can provide for healthy dialogue between citizens and officials; others emphasize the exercise of a peculiar administrative prudence; others emphasize the opportunity for the administrative branch to correct the defects of some of our other political institutions. None of these formulations appear to be mutually exclusive or in any way contradictory.

Some go beyond these structural contributions to the unique role that administrators can make to the public interest by promoting substantive values that are at the core of our Constitution. Liberty, property, and equality are examples of the kind of values that some expect career administrators to promote through the exercise of their discretion (Rohr, 1989; Adams et al., 1990). Whether one grounds the unique moral contributions of the American public service in structural or substantive values, proponents of the ''stewardship model'' view career administrators as partners in our constitutional democracy.

D. Restoring Democratic Balance: Restricting Administrative Influence Over the Public Interest

The notion that the public interest is best served by viewing administrators as equal partners in democratic governance has been seriously challenged in the last decade by the following three developments: (1) the ''reinvention of government'' initiative; (2) postmodern public administration theory and the discourse movement; and (3) the rediscovery of ''social capital.''

1. The Reinvention of Government and the New Public Management Movement

Perhaps the most serious recent challenge to strong administrative influence in shaping the public interest has come from the reinvention of government movement. This initiative (Osborne and Gaebler, 1992; Executive Office, 1993) has been spawned by a variety of diverse developments in the 1990s that include growing scarcity of public resources, disaffection with government programs, unfunded federal mandates, and changes in the ideological landscape. Taken together, these changes have resulted in defunding, deregulation, decentralization, and devolution of greater responsibility for service provision to the private and nonprofit sectors.

The most important implication of these changes for career administrators is a shift away from an emphasis on legal accountability and a shift toward more emphasis on private marketplace principles in assessing administrative action. One of the major goals of "reinvention" is to liberate career administrators from a variety of bureaucratic constraints and introduce greater market economy incentives into public organizations. These private market assumptions have been invoked to create one-stop shopping, to place greater emphasis on customer satisfaction, to push for more outsourcing and contracting-out, to increase internal rewards for high performance, and to develop system-level assessment programs to measure outcomes and performance. These changes represent what has come to be called "New Public Management" (Box, et al., 1999; Terry, 1998).

Critics of New Public Management (NPM) claim that the movement displays a cavalier disregard of the multiple and complex political goals that have traditionally been central to our rule-of-law system. The most important of these include: meeting the needs of the most vulnerable members of our society (Smith and Lipsky, 1993), maintaining simultaneous legal accountability to both legislative and executive structures of authority, balancing the need for individual citizen access and responsiveness with the need for collective action, and facilitating citizen-centered governance that is informed and guided by wisdom and expertise (Moe, 1994; Moe and Gilmour, 1995; Box, et al., 1999). NPM's focus on altering the *instruments* of governance constitute what some call "tool tropism" (Jun and Gross, 1996) and, worse, a "*faux* democracy" that obscures the problematic nature of the conflicting democratic ends that the tools of governance are intended to serve (Box, et al., 1999). These critics fear that public service professional may be "co-opted by the market-based model," thus undermining their capacity to serve as "potential sources of meaningful social and institutional change" (Box et al., 1999, p. 5).

2. The Postmodern Challenge to the Public Interest: The Discourse Movement

A somewhat gentler criticism of the notion that administrators should serve as stewards of the public interest has been provided by what has come to be called the "discourse movement" in public administration. This movement draws its intellectual raison d'être from the work of postmodern public administration theorists (Fox and Miller, 1994; Farmer, 1995; McSwite, 1997; McSwite, 1998). Using the assumptions and tools of continental critical theorists and phenomenologists, members of the discourse movement deny the possibility and legitimacy of using the "public interest" as a meaningful category of *initial* analysis. This claim is based on a combination of the following assumptions.

1. Human beings acquire meaning only through direct experience in the world.
2. To the extent that direct experience is mediated by universalisms, canonical metanarratives, institutional, and natural law-like symbols, at best individual liberty/freedom is impaired both in terms of understanding and action. At worst, individuals are oppressed through the use of these "trumping categories" (Fox and Miller, 1994; McSwite, 1998).
3. The only accessible and legitimate medium for creating shared experience, understanding, and action is language.

Perhaps the most important consequences of these assumptions for administrative practice is that the public interest has to be socially constructed through a dialogical process that is open and free from all forms of oppressive constraints. To start a dialogue with any assumptions about what the "public interest" means undermines the only source of legitimacy, namely, agreement through open discourse. The goal is to create a dialogue "in which we all talk, and we all listen, and we all get to be in on coming up with what we do next" (McSwite, 1997, p. ix). To make this happen requires some basic rules of dialogue that include the following kinds of simple "warrants for discourse": people must speak sincerely and authentically; they must address what is relevant to the current focus of the discussion; they must be attentive and feel no sense of coercion; they must be willing and able to make a substantive contribution to the dialogue (Fox and Miller, 1994).

Some advocates of the discourse movement are trained political scientists who are primarily interested in the policy consequences of their position. Others are trained psychologists who are more interested in the interpersonal consequences of dialogue for building agreement at the small group and organizational level (compare McSwite, 1997 with Fox and Miller, 1994; and King and Stivers, 1998). Both groups place a high value on membership in communities of shared meaning. Both groups concede an important role for administrators in initiating, facilitating, and maintaining the rules of proper civic dialogue. But by comparison to "stewardship theorists," discourse theorists concede a more limited role for administrators in creating and maintaining a community of shared meaning.

3. The Social Capital Movement

Most of the conditions that have spawned the New Public Management movement are also responsible for a quite different initiative that is sometimes called the "social capital movement"(SCM). SCM is composed of an unlikely confluence of social critics from the right and left wings of the political spectrum. They have one major goal in common that has far reaching significance for the role of public administrators in shaping the public interest. Proponents of SCM believe that the health of democratic governance depends on the health of civic institutions (Fukuyama, 1995; Putnam, 1993, 1995; Symposium, 1999). This belief is used by political conservatives to argue for less government and more reliance on the "thousand points of light" that exist within the voluntary and nonprofit sectors of local community life (Etzioni, 1993, 1995). The left end of the SCM spectrum argues that professional career administrators have a major role to play in local institution-building. In fact, some believe that the primary role of career administrators is to use their discretionary authority to assist local communities in identifying, assembling, and using their institutional civic assets for community development purposes (Kretzmann and McKnight, 1993; Symposium, 1999).

Whether one falls at the strong or weak end of the government interventionist spectrum, SCM has three important implications for the role of public administrators in shaping the public interest. First, it has refocused attention away from individual citizen participation to the symbiotic consequences of institutional activities within the community. Second, it has broadened the notion of citizenship so that it includes almost any activity that affects the well-being of the community. Finally, it has deepened the meaning of citizenship so that it includes more than just the knowledge and skills to make the formal institutions of government work. It also includes the knowledge and skills necessary to make communities work. Taken together, these consequences of SCM require administrators and citizens *together* to refocus attention on the larger democratic ends that local institutions serve. When viewed in this way, the role of public administrators is redirected back to its Athenian roots where collective governance is hardly distinguishable from the task of living together as a whole (Morgan and Vizzini, 1999, especially, pp. 51, 59).

CONCLUSION

We conclude on a theme with which we began this chapter. The public interest is necessarily problematic in liberal democratic systems of government which place such high priority on individual freedom. Efforts to define the public interest on substantive grounds must necessarily restrict the pursuit of this freedom. Such consequences frequently produce procedurally defined governance and impoverished public dialogue about the character of the public interest.

   We have been saved from such fate in large part because of a constitutional system of governance which seeks to protect liberty from a wide variety of dangers, including usurpation of authority by government officials, the tyranny of the majority, and incompetent administration. These dangers have spawned a healthy tradition of correctives that call for contradictory responses: greater citizen participation versus less citizen participation; more scientific expertise versus more common sense; the promotion of greater equality of condition versus the promotion of equality of opportunity; encouraging the proliferation of competing interests versus preventing their co-optation of governmental processes by privilege, power, and money. As we have seen from the preceding historical analysis, there is a well-defined body of public discourse and a recognized role to be played by the career public service in helping to ameliorate these various dangers of democratic governance. We are blessed by a rich tradition that permits career administrators actively to participate with the other branches of government in helping to define and shape the public interest. Because this tradition is well bounded by what Alastair MacIntyre (1984) calls "continuities in conflict," we are also blessed by a tradition which helps to protect us from administrative excesses.

ENDNOTES

1. Professor John Rohr reminds me that the Federalists and Antifederalists do not speak of a "public interest." Instead, they make use of terms like public good, the general interest, or in the case of the U.S. Constitution, the general welfare. The reason for this may have to do with the founding generation's tendency to speak of the collective well-being of the community as though it possessed some kind of objective status. This objective quality tends to get lost when the more subjective term, interest, is used. This speculation is supported by the founding generation's tendency to reserve the use of the word interest for private, and usually partial, expressions of opinion (see especially Rossiter, 1961, *Federalist* #10, #51).

2. In the 1960s the equality debate shifts to the language of equity, as defenders of compensatory policies argue that formal legal equality undermines fairness (equity).

3. For excellent reviews of this debate see: Gordon Wood, 1973, pp. vii–xv; Leonard Levy (ed.), 1969; Goldwin and Schambra (eds.), 1980.

4. "Personality" is defined by Beard as liquid personal property in the form of land, money, public securities, slaves, and business investments in the mercantile trade, manufacturing, and shipping. Non-personalty is defined by Beard as debtors, yeoman farmers, and propertyless artisans and mechanics.

5. I wish to thank Professor Craig Brown, recently retired from the University of Illinois, Sanga-
    mon State, Springfield, Illinois for suggesting the terms cardboard "virtue" and cardboard
    "competence."

REFERENCES

Adams, G., Bowerman, P.V., Dolbeare, K., and Stivers, C. (1990). Joining purpose to practice: a
    democratic identity for the public service. In *Images and Identities in Public Administration*
    (H.D. Kass and B. Catron, eds.). Sage Press, Newbury Park, California, pp. 219–240.

Arendt, H. (1958). *The Human Condition*. Doubleday, Anchor, New York.

Arendt, H. (1963). *On Revolution*. Viking Press, New York.

Bailyn (1967). *The Ideological Origins of the American Revolution*. Belknap Press, Cambridge,
    Massachusetts.

Beard, C.A. (1913). *Economic Interpretation of the Constitution of the United States of America*.
    Macmillan, New York.

Bell, D. (1973). *The Coming of Post-Industrial Society: A Venture in Social Forecasting*. Basic
    Books, New York.

Bellah, R., Madsen, R., Sullivan, W.M., Swidler, A., and Tipton, S.M. (1986). *Habits of the Heart:
    Individualism and Commitment in American Life*. Harper and Row, New York.

Bellah, R., Madsen, R., Sullivan, W.M., Swidler, A., and Tipton, S.M. (1991). *The Good Society*.
    Alfred Knopf, Inc., New York.

Benjamin, M. (1990). *Splitting the Difference: Compromise and Integrity in Ethics and Politics*.
    University of Kansas Press, Lawrence, Kansas.

Berlin, I. (1969). *Four Essays on Liberty*. Oxford University Press, London.

Boorstin, D. (1953). *The Genius of American Politics*. University of Chicago Press, Chicago.

Box, R. (1998). *Citizen Governance: Leading American Communities into the 21st Century*. Sage
    Publications, Thousand Oaks, California.

Box, R., Marshall, G., Reed, B.J., and Reed, C. (1999). New public management, *faux* democracy,
    and the challenge to democratic governance. Paper presented at the Annual Public Adminis-
    tration Theory Network Conference, Portland, Oregon, March 11–12, 1999.

Brown, R.E. (1963). *Reinterpretation of the Formation of the American Constitution*. Little Brown,
    Boston, Massachusetts.

Burke, J.P. (1986). *Bureaucratic Responsibility*. The Johns Hopkins University Press, Baltimore,
    Maryland.

Cook, B. (1996). *Bureaucracy and Self-Government: Reconsidering the Role of Public Administra-
    tion in American Politics*. The Johns Hopkins University Press, Baltimore, Maryland.

Cooper, P.J. (1983). *Public Law and Public Administration*. Mayfield Publishing Co., Palo Alto,
    California.

Cooper, T. (1991). *An Ethic of Citizenship for Public Administration*. Prentice Hall, Englewood
    Cliffs, New Jersey.

Croly, H. (1964). *The Promise of American Life*. Capricorn Press, New York.

Davis, K.C. (1971). *Discretionary Justice: A Preliminary Inquiry*. University of Illinois Press, Ur-
    bana, Illinois.

De Maio, G. (1980). Religion, republicanism and the American founding. Paper presented to the
    NEW/APSA Seminar, Citizenship: Ancient and Modern. Washington, D.C., August 26–27.

de Tocqueville, A. (1969). *Democracy in America* (J.P. Mayer, ed.). Doubleday, Garden City,
    New York.

Deming, W.E. (1982). *Quality, Productivity and Competitive Position*. M.I.T. Press, Cambridge,
    Massachusetts.

Diamond, M. (1977). Ethics and politics: the American way. *In: The Moral Foundations of the
    American Republic* (R.H. Horowitz, ed.). University Press of Virginia, Charlottesville, Vir-
    ginia.

Diamond, M. (1981). *The Founding of the Democratic Republic*. F.E. Peacock Publishers, Inc., Itasca, Illinois.

Etzioni, A. (1993). *The Spirit of Community: Rights, Responsibilities and the Communitarian Agenda*. Crown Publishers, New York.

Etzioni, A. (1995). *Rights and Responsibilities: The Communitarian Agenda*. St. Martin's Press, New York.

Executive Office of the President (1993). National Performance Review, *From Red Tape to Results: Creating a Government That Works Better and Costs Less*. U.S. Government Printing Office, Washington, D.C.

Farmer, D.J. (1995). *The Language of Public Administration: Bureaucracy, Modernity and Post-modernity*. University of Alabama Press, Tuscaloosa, Alabama.

Ferguson, E.J. (1961). *The Power of the Purse: A History of American Public Finance, 1776–1790*. University of North Carolina Press, Chapel Hill, North Carolina.

Fox, C.F. and Miller, H.T. (1994). *Postmodern Public Administration: Toward Discourse*. Sage Publications, Thousand Oaks, California.

Frederickson, H.G. (1982). The recovery of civism in public administration. *Public Administration Review*, 42: 501–508.

Frederickson, H.G. and Hart, D.K. (1985). The public service and the patriotism of benevolence. *Public Administration Review*, 45: 547–553.

Freeman, J.L. (1965). *The Political Process: Executive Bureau-Legislative-Committee Relations* rev. ed. Random House, New York.

Fukuyama, F. (1995). *Trust: The Social Virtues and the Creation of Prosperity*. The Free Press, New York.

Goldwin, R. and Schambra, W. (eds.) (1980). *How Democratic is the Constitution?* American Enterprise Institute, Washington, D.C.

Goodsell, C.T. (ed.) (1981). *The Public Encounter: Where State and Citizen Meet*. Indiana University Press, Bloomington, Indiana.

Green, R.T. (1993). Prudent constitutionalism: Hamiltonian lessons for a responsible public administration. *International Journal of Public Administration*, 16: 165–187.

Gunn, J.A.W. (1969). *Politics and Interest in the Seventeenth Century*. University of Toronto Press, Toronto.

Hart, D.K. (1974). Social equity, justice and the equitable administrator. *Public Administration Review*, 34: 3–11.

Hart, D.K. (1983). The honorable bureaucrat among the philistines. *Administration and Society*, 15: 43–48.

Hart, D.K. (1984). The virtuous citizen, the honorable bureaucrat, and public administration. *Public Administration Review*, 44: 116–117.

Hart, D.K. (1987). Public administration: the thoughtless functionary, and feelinglessness. In: *Revitalizing the Public Service* (R.B. Denhardt and E.T. Jennings, Jr., eds.). University of Missouri-Columbia Press, Columbia, Missouri.

Hartz, L. (1955). *The Liberal Tradition in America: An Interpretation of American Political Thought Since the Revolution*. Harcourt, Brace and World, New York.

Heclo, H. (1978). Issue networks in the executive establishment. In: *The New American Political System* (A. King, ed.). American Enterprise Institute, Washington, D.C., pp. 90–124.

Held, V. (1984). *Rights and Goods*. Free Press, New York.

Hirschman, A.O. (1977). *The Passions and the Interests: Political Arguments for Capitalism Before Its Triumph*. Princeton University Press, Princeton, New Jersey.

Hummel, R. (1987). *The Bureaucratic Experience*, 3rd edition. St. Martin's Press, New York.

Jennings, B. (1991). Taking ethics seriously in administrative life: constitutionalism, ethical reasoning and moral judgment. In: *Ethical Frontiers in Public Management* (J.S. Bowman, ed.). Jossey-Bass Publishers, San Francisco.

Jensen, M. (1940). *The Articles of Confederation: An Interpretation of the Social-Constitutional History of the American Revolution*. University of Wisconsin Press, Madison, Wisconsin,

Jun, J. and Gross, B. (1996). Tool topism in public administration: The pathology of management fads. *Public Administration Theory and Praxis*, 18: 108–118.

Kendall, W. and Carey, G.W. (1970). *Basic Symbols*. Louisiana State University Press, Baton Rouge.

Kerwin, C. (1999). *Rulemaking: How Government Agencies Write Law and Make Policy*, 2nd edition. Congressional Quarterly Press, Washington, D.C.

King, C. and Stivers, C. (1998). *Government is Us: Public Administration in an Antigovernment Era*. Sage Publications, Thousand Oaks, California.

Kretzmann, J. and McKnight, J. (1993). *Building Communities From the Inside Out*. Center for Urban Affairs and Policy Research, Northwestern University, Chicago, Illinois.

Kristol, I. (1978). *Three Cheers for Capitalism*. Mentor, New York.

Levine, E.L. and Wexler, E. (1981). *P.L. 94–142: An Act of Congress*. Macmillan, New York.

Levy, L. ed. (1969). *Essays on the Making of the Constitution*. Oxford University Press, New York.

Likert, R. (1961). *New Patterns of Management*. Harper, New York.

Little, J. (1999). The new normativism and the discourse movement: another perspective. *Administrative Theory and Praxis*, 21: 128–133.

Lowi, T. (1979). *The End of Liberalism: The Second Republic of the U.S.* 2nd ed., W.W. Norton and Co., New York.

MacDonald, F. (1958). *We the People: The Economic Origins of the Constitution*. University of Chicago Press, Chicago, Illinois.

MacIntyre, A. (1984). *After Virtue*. University of Notre Dame Press, Notre Dame, Indiana.

McGregor, D. and Argyris, C. (1957). *Personality and Organization*. Harper and Row, New York.

McGregor, D. (1967). *The Professional Manager*. McGraw Hill, New York.

McSwite, O.C. (1997). *Legitimacy in Public Administration: A Discourse Analysis*. Sage Publications, Thousand Oaks, California.

McSwite, O.C. (1998). The new normativism and the discourse movement: A meditation. *Administrative Theory and Praxis*, 20: 377–381.

McWilliams, W.C. (1973). *The Idea of Fraternity in America*. University of California Press, Berkeley, California.

Main, J.T. (1960). Charles A. Beard and the constitution: a critical review of Forrest McDonald's "*We the People*," with a rebuttal by Forrest McDonald. *William and Mary Quarterly*, 17: 82–110.

March, J.G. and Simon, H.A. (1958). *Organizations*. John Wiley and Sons, Inc., New York.

Marini, F. (1971). *Toward a New Public Administration*. Chandler, Scranton, Pennsylvania.

Moe, R.C. (1994). The "Reinventing Government Exercise": misinterpreting the problem, misjudging the consequences. Public Administration Review, 54: 111–122.

Moe, R. and Gilmour, R. (1995). Rediscovering principles of public administration: the neglected foundation of public law. *Public Administration Review*, 55: 135–146.

Morgan, D.F. (1996). Institutional survival in a postmodern age: administrative practice and the American constitutional legacy. *Administrative Theory and Praxis*, 18: 42–56.

Morgan, D.F. (1990). Administrative phronesis: discretion and the problem of legitimacy in our constitutional system. In: *Images and Identities in Public Administration* (H.D. Kass and B.L. Catron, eds.). Sage, Newbury Park, California.

Morgan, D.F. and Kass, N.D. (1991). Legitimating Administrative Discretion Through Constitutional Stewardship. In: *Frontiers in Public Management* (J.S. Bowman, ed.), pp. 286–307. American Society for Public Administration, Washington, D.C.

Morgan, D.F. and Rohr, J.A. (1986). Traditional responses to administrative abuse. *Administrative Discretion and Public Policy Implementation* (D. Hibbeln and D.H. Shumavon, eds). Praeger Press, New York, pp. 211–232.

Morgan, D.F. and Vizzini, D. (1999). Transforming customers into citizens: some lessons from the field. In: Sympsium: community capacity, social trust and public administration. *Administrative Theory and Praxis*, 21: 51–61.

Morrow, W.L. (1987). The pluralist legacy in American public administration. In: *A Centennial History of the American Administrative State* (R.C. Chandler, ed.). The Free Press, New York.

Mulgan, G. (1994). *Politics in an Antipolitical Age*. Polity Press, Cambridge, Massachusetts.

Osborne, D. and Gaebler, T. (1992). *Reinventing Government: How the Entrepreneurial Spirit is Transforming the Public Sector*. Addison-Wesley, Reading, Massachusetts.

Peterson, M.D. (1960). *Thomas Jefferson and the Nation: A Biography*. Oxford University Press, New York.

Pocock, J.G.A. (1975). *The Machiavellian Moment*. Princeton University Press, Princeton, New Jersey.

Putnam, R. (1993). *Making Democracy Work: Civic Tradition in Modern Italy*. Princeton University, Princeton, New Jersey.

Putnam, R. (1995). Tuning in, tuning out: the strange disappearance of social capital in America. *PS: Political Science and Politics*, December: 664–683.

Richardson, J.D. (1911). *A Compilation of the Messages and Papers of the Presidents*, 11 vols. Bureau of National Literature, Washington, D.C. (N.B.: 1897 original has 18 vols. Paged in one sequence.)

Richardson, W. (1997). *Democracy, Bureaucracy and Character*. University of Kansas Press, Lawrence, Kansas.

Roelofs, M. (1991). *The Poverty of American Politics*. Temple University Press, Boston, Massachusetts.

Rohr, J.A. (1981). Financial disclosures: power in search of policy. *Public Personnel Management*, 10: 29–40.

Rohr, J. (1986). *To Run a Constitution: The Legitimacy of the Administrative State*. University of Kansas Press, Lawrence, Kansas.

Rohr, J. (1987). The administrative state and constitutional principle. In: *A Centennial History of the American Administrative State* (R.C. Chandler. ed.). Free Press, New York.

Rohr, J. (1989). *Ethics for Bureaucrats: An Essay on Law and Values*, revised. Marcel Dekker, New York.

Rossiter, C. (ed.) (1961). Hamilton, A., Madison J., and Jay, J. *The Federalist Papers*. Mentor, New American Library, New York.

Schubert, G.A. (1982). *The Public Interest. A Critique of the Theory of a Political Concept*. Greenwood Press, New York.

Scott, W.G. and Hart, D. (1979). *Organizational America*. Houghton Mifflin Company, Boston, Massachusetts.

Selznick, P. (1992). *The Moral Community*. University of California, Berkeley, California.

Shafritz, J.M. and Hyde, A.C. (1978). *Classics of Public Administration*. Moore Publishing Co., Oak Park, Illinois.

Simon, H.A. (1957). *Administrative Behavior, A Study of Decision-Making Processes in Administrative Organizations*, 2nd ed. The Macmillan Company, New York.

Simon, H.A., Smithburg, D.W. and Thompson, V.A. (1950). *Public Administration*. Alfred A. Knopf, Inc., New York.

Smith, S. and Lipsky, M. (1993). *Nonprofits for Hire: The Welfare State in the Age of Contracting*. Harvard University Press, Cambridge, Massachusetts.

Spicer, M. (1995). *The Founders, The Constitution, and Public Administration: A Conflict in Worldviews*. Georgetown University Press, Washington, D.C.

Stever, J.A. (1988). *The End of Public Administration: Problems of the Profession in the Post-Progressive Era*. Transnational Publishers, New York.

Stever, J.A. (1990). The dual image of the administrator in progressive administrative theory. *Administration and Society*, 22: 39–65.

Storing, H.J. (ed.) (1962). *Essays on the Scientific Study of Politics*. Holt, Rinehart and Winston, Inc., New York.

Storing, H.J. (1964). Political parties and the bureaucracy. In: *Political Parties and the Bureaucracy* (R. Goldwin, ed.). Rand McNally, Chicago, pp. 137–158.

Storing, H.J. (ed.) (1981). *The Complete Anti-federalists*, 7 volumes. University of Chicago Press, Chicago.

Symposium: community capacity, social trust and public administration. (1999). *Administrative Theory and Praxis*, 21: 10–119.

Terry, L. (1995). *Leadership of Public Bureaucracies: The Administrator as Conservator*. Sage Publications, Inc., Thousand Oaks, California.

Terry, L. (ed.) (1998). Symposium: leadership, democracy and the new public management. *Public Administration Review*, 58: 189–231.

Thach, C. (1969). *The Creation of the Presidency: 1775–1789*. Johns Hopkins University Press, Baltimore.

Thayer, F.C. (1978). Materialism and humanism: organization theory's odd couple. *Administration and Society*, 10: 86–106.

Vinzant, J.C. and Crothers, L. (1998). *Street Level Leadership: Discretion and Legitimacy in Front-Line Public Service*. Georgetown University Press, Washington, D.C.

Wamsley, G., Goodsell, C., Rohr, J., Stivers, C., White, O., and Wolf, J. (1987). The public administrator and the governance process: refocusing the American dialogue. In: *A Centennial History of the American Administrative State* (R.C. Chandler, ed.). Free Press, New York.

White, J.D. (1990). Images of administrative reason and rationality: the recovery of practical discourse. In: *Images and Identities in Public Administration* (H.D. Kass and B.L. Catron, eds.). Sage, Newbury Park, California.

White, L.D. (1948). *The Federalists: A Study in Administrative History, 1789–1801*. The Free Press, New York.

White, L.D. (1954). *The Jacksonians: A Study in Administrative History*. Macmillan, New York.

Wildavsky, A. (1980). *Speaking Truth to Power: The Art and Craft of Policy Analysis*. Little Brown, Boston.

Wilson, W. (1978). The study of administration. In: *Classics of Public Administration* (J.M. Shafritz and A.C. Hyde, eds.). Moore Publishing Company, Inc., Oak Park, Illinois.

Wood, G.S. (1973). *The Confederation and The Constitution: The Critical Issues*. Little Brown, Boston.

Wood, G.S. (1969). *The Creation of the American Republic, 1776–1787*. University of North Carolina Press, Chapel Hill, North Carolina.

Wright, D. and Hart, D. (1996) The "public interest": what we are now leaving our posterity. *Administrative Theory and Praxis*, 18: 14–28.

Yarbrough, J. (1979). Republicanism reconsidered: some thoughts on the foundation and preservation of the American republic. *The Review of Politics*, 41: 61–95.

8

Deontological Dimensions of Administrative Ethics Revisited

Ralph Clark Chandler
Western Michigan University, Kalamazoo, Michigan

> An action done from duty has its moral worth, not in the purpose to be attained by it, but in the maxim in accordance with which it is decided upon: it depends, therefore, not on the realization of the object of the action, but solely on the principle of volition in accordance with which, irrespective of all objects of the faculty of desire, the action has been performed.
>
> Immanuel Kant

I. INTRODUCTION

Deontological ethics are ethics of duty or principle, while teleological ethics are ethics of results or consequences. Within this simple distinction are colorations of ethical thought and traditions of inquiry and action that plumb the depths of human experience and illustrate fundamental differences in how modern American public administrators view and practice moral responsibility. Although our purpose here is to discuss deontological ethics, it is impossible to do so without preliminary reference to the other side of the same ethics coin. Teleological ethics are derived from the Greek *teleos*, meaning complete or final, itself coming from *telos*, meaning completion or end. Hence the knowledge, *logos* (or *ology*), of the *telos* is the knowledge of the utility of natural processes or occurrences for overall natural design.

The idea of utility is a key one for understanding teleological ethics. The two primary manifestations of teleological ethics in philosophy are utilitarianism (elaborated by Jeremy Bentham and John Stuart Mill) and what professional philosophers call egoism (elaborated by Niccolo Machiavelli and Max Weber). Egoism holds that the right thing to do is what increases my own good, or that everyone really wants what is best for themselves. Given the demonstrable logical deficiencies of egoism, however, egoists move easily from personal consequences of action to consequences of action for everyone, or utilitarianism.[1] Thus, consequential ethical action exists along a continuum from one's interest in power and influence (perhaps for a humane end—Machiavelli), to one's interest in the honor of executing conscientiously the order of superior authority (a disguised act of ego—Weber), to "this sacred trust—that the greatest happiness of the greatest number is the foundation of morals and legislation" (Bentham), to the role of the public servant as an impartial, disinterested, and benevolent instrument as he or she maximizes such common values as human dignity or national security. Mill bent the continuum into a circle when he concluded in *On Liberty* (1859) that "Liberty consists in doing what one desires."

Bentham (1748–1832) coined the word "deontology," but his use of it is directly opposite to the current usage inspired by Kant. The ultimate aim of deontology, as of legislation, in Bentham's view, is to motivate behavior that maximizes community happiness. While the law's basic technique is to *alter* the shape of individual interests with threats of punishment, the technique of deontology is to mobilize reasons of private interest already available to the agent. Thus, the focus of Bentham's utilitarianism was primarily social and institutional, not personal and private. His theory has a decidedly technocratic character, being designed as a framework to guide the legislator who seeks rationally and humanely to restructure social behavior and institutions.

Even when Bentham belatedly turned his attention to personal morality in his book, *Deontology* (published in 1834), the technocratic character of his thought remained. He advocated a *strategic* version of the egoist doctrine. Human beings are more likely in any particular case to be moved by considerations of their own private interest than by any other motive, he claimed, especially when they exercise power over others. The only safe assumption for the legislator or political constitution writer to make is that people will act only to advance their private ("sinister") interests. The aim of law and social order, according to Bentham's "duty-and-interest-junction" principle is to provide individuals with adequate motives, through the threat of sanctions, to comply with the dictates of the utility principle, thereby securing artificially a convergence of individual self-interest and utilitarian duty.

Bentham sums up what has been called his psychological hedonism in the following paragraph from volume one of *Deontology*, interestingly subtitled "The Science of Morality."

> It is, in fact, very idle to talk about duties; the word itself has in it something disagreeable and repulsive; and talk about it as we may, the word will not become a rule of conduct. A man, a moralist, gets into an elbow chair, and pours forth pompous dogmatisms about *duty*—and *duties*. Why is he not listened to? Because every man is thinking about *interests*. It is a part of his very nature to think first about interests, and with these the well-judging moralist will find it for *his* interest to begin. Let him say what he pleases,—to interest, duty must and will be made subservient.[2]

When one understands teleological ethics compared to deontological ethics, it is easier to understand why over half the nation believed that Lieutenant Colonel Oliver L. North was an honorable man. As deontologist John W. Nields, Jr., a House of Representatives committee chief counsel, kept pressing North in terms of ethical principles with questions such as "Did you ever say, 'You can't do that, it's not true and you cannot commit the President of the United States to a lie'?" North kept replying evenly, and, for him, honestly, "I don't believe that I ever said that to anyone, no." Nields, a lawyer and constitutionalist, was thinking of ethics in terms of principles of truth. North, a professional military officer, was thinking of ethics in terms of consequences. For Nields, doing right or wrong involved personal decisions that were right or wrong *in themselves*. North, like any good Weberian public servant, was deriving honor from serving the interests of the president. Like a good Machiavellian, he would lie for the prince if he had to. And like a good utilitarian, he was doing the greatest good for the greatest number of Americans. Hence, in terms of teleological ethics, Oliver North was a moral man.[3]

Deontologists tend to be not only lawyers and constitutionalists, but also, public administrators, particularly those who regulate something and those who are interested in codes of ethics; religionists, particularly those who believe in the prescriptions of the Ten Commandments and the Sermon on the Mount, not to mention the duties described by Catholic scholastics such as St. Thomas Aquinas; and philosophers holding to the categorical imperative of Immanuel Kant. What each of these types of ethical thinking has in common is that somewhere near at hand there is a statement of agreed-upon or settled values.

Some people think the word deontology is a negative form of ontology, which refers to one's idea of basic reality. Examples of this misunderstanding of deontology are that deontology is represented by Jean-Paul Sartre's belief in the incoherence of reality and Simone de Beauvoir's conclusion that there can be no connective tissue between one situation or moment of experience and another. In *The Ethics of Ambiguity*, de Beauvoir cannot quite bring herself to accept either "the contingent absurdity of the discontinuous" or "the rationalistic necessity of the continuous." Thus the real world is "bare and incoherent" and every situation has only its particularity."[4] Sartre sums up the existentialist position regarding ontology by saying resolutely: "Ontology itself cannot formulate ethical precepts. It is concerned solely with what is, and we cannot possibly derive imperatives from ontology's indicatives."[5]

Such opinions about ontology do not necessarily represent deontological ethics, although, as we will see, the situational component of existentialism contributes notably to a major school of deontological ethical thought. The *de* in deontological is not negative, as is often true in English, but is whole with *deon*, coming from the Greek verb stem *deont-*, to bind. *Deon* is also influenced by *dei*, (it is necessary) from *dein* (to need, want, or lack). Hence, *deon* refers to that which is binding or needful. It is then a short step to deont*ology* as the knowledge or study of moral obligation or commitment.

Since present day deontological ethicists such as Dennis F. Thompson are rightly referred to as neo-Kantians, it is useful for us to understand what we can of the philosophy of Immanuel Kant (1724–1804). Kantianism, ethical and cultural relativism, and what William K. Frankena calls agapism are the three principal single-rule theories of deontological ethics. They are called single-rule theories because, unlike multiple prima facie rule theories that bring in consequences (because obligation or rightness is a partial function of many different kinds of consequences), single-rule deontological theories do not make obligation a function of consequences at all. This is why professional philosophers refer to such views as formalistic.

Single-rule theories sometimes demand special attention in administrative practice. As Terry L. Cooper has pointed out, an issue may be so unique, so complex, or so profound in teleological terms that the practitioner has no choice but to review the deontological *principle* that is implicit in certain routine norms of conduct.[6] Since a deontological principle is a general law or rule that guides action, and is often expressed in a statement concerning the conduct or state of being that is required for the fulfillment of a value, the deontological principle explicitly links a value with some general procedure and practice. Both substantive and procedural due process of law, for example, are values in American political theory, jurisprudence, and administrative practice. To reflect due process as an organizing value, however, we would need a deontological principle which could show us what pattern of action would comply with this value. A common form of the due process principle, for example, is that "law must be just, fair, and equal," and it should not be "oppressive, fanciful, or biased.'' Under this principle, therefore, all accused persons have the protections of the Bill of Rights and the guarantees of the Fourteenth Amendment. They are constitutionally and politically equal.

In a multiple prima facie rule theory, different from a single-rule theory, the United States government may borrow $1 billion from Saudi Arabia, for example, to keep up its legal obligation to pay social security benefits to older Americans. It promises to pay the money back. We cannot conclude, however, that the money will be paid back no matter what else is true. Saudi Arabia is wealthy and does not need the money right away. The United States in the meantime comes to the aid of Saudi Arabia in the Persian Gulf War. Since the American government cannot repay the $1 billion *and* defend Saudi Arabia against Iraq, we cannot say the United States is categorically obliged to pay back the loan. The prima facie obligation to pay one's debts is colored by the consequences of other moral obligations, in this case to defend a militarily weaker friend. Single-rule theories are less forgiving than multiple prima facie rule theories, and the most rigorous of all single-rule theories was devised by Kant.

II. KANTIANISM

Bernard Rosen summarizes Kant's views as follows:

1. Consequences (ends attained by actions) are not the determinants of moral obligation.
2. The moral worth of an action (that it is right or the fulfillment of an obligation) is a function of the direct rule (principle of volition or maxim) from which the action is performed.
3. The direct moral rule must be chosen independently of any desire to achieve an end, or even from any desire regarding the rule itself.
4. The indirect moral rule that determines the direct moral rules cannot have any particular actions or moral rules described within it.
5. The form of the indirect moral rule is, as stated by Kant, ''I ought never to act except in such a way that I can also will that my maxim should become a universal moral law.''[7]

In terms of our Saudi loan example, therefore, we must all pay our debts lest it become a universal law that none of us will.

The indirect rule that Kant calls the categorical imperative can be written as follows:

If any person *a* performs an action from a direct rule R, where R (1) is willed by person *a* and (2) can be willed to be a universal law of nature, then R is a rule of moral obligation.[8]

In *The Moral Law*, Kant tries to illustrate the rule that is categorical and imperative with reference to lying. He says that I, a moral actor, should not be content with the maxim that getting out of difficulty by a false statement should hold as a universal law because, even though I can will to lie, I can by no means will a universal law of lying. My maxim, as soon as it was made a universal law, would be found to annual itself. I should therefore reject the unethical practice of lying to get myself out of trouble because it cannot fit as a principle into a possible enactment of universal law.

It can be argued that lying comes close to being a universal law in America as some 91 percent of 2,000 randomly selected people recently admitted that they lied regularly at work and at home.[9] The same survey, which promised anonymity to the respondents on every page as it sought "total honesty," also reported that only 13 percent of Americans believe in all Ten Commandments, most workers admit to goofing off about seven hours a week, and half say they regularly call in sick when they are not. And what if public officials perceived to be icons of morality are exposed at some later time to be living a lie? Does the disclosure that former Supreme Court Justice William Brennan accepted $140,000 in cash and gifts from a developer while serving on the Court mean that he was living a lie when he wrote the splendid opinion of the Court upholding freedom of expression in *Texas v. Johnson*? Was Clark Clifford living a lie as he wisely and unselfishly advised Democratic presidents from Truman to Carter? What is lying anyway? Is it the same thing as a mistake? Do good people do bad things? Do bad people do good things? Do good people do good things for bad reasons? Do bad people do bad things for good reasons?

Some of the most ingenious explanations in the language are employed by executive department operatives to help Kant prohibit lying from becoming a universal law. In the Reagan administration, for example, the president's aides argued that it did not matter whether some of his stories were literally true. Ronald Reagan's numerous misstatements of fact, his confusion about details, and his repeated anecdotes about supposed welfare cheats that no one was ever able to confirm, all contained a larger truth, they said. Others might prefer the description of the phenomenon of lying by John Foster Dulles, who said simply it was a necessary art.

If it is in fact true that over 90 percent of us lie, including moral icons, then there must be some kind of truth to be perceived *under* the lies, and thus Kant would be saved for deontological ethics. Was there a Bill Clinton *under* the fling with Gennifer Flowers? Did he handle the exposé better or worse than Gary Hart handled his? Had Slick Willie learned anything? What do my antennae tell me about his fundamental relationship with Hillary? Did he just come right out and lie about Gennifer? (No.) Was he bigger than the indiscretion? (Yes.) What was his *character*? Had he been to Delphi and conferred with the gods? In such processes of unconscious moral reasoning, the American people really make their ethical tabulations. Such tabulations were obvious in the Clinton-Lewinsky affair that preoccupied the nation in 1998 and early 1999. The public's approval rating of how President Clinton was doing his job remained in the sixtieth and seventieth percentiles despite lurid revelations about his relationship with White House intern Monica Lewinsky and the fact that he lied to a federal grand jury about it. The American people kept saying they knew something about the president that his detractors did not know about or did not properly value. What was it?

One of the factors involved is what we can only call developing historical sophistication. We know now about George Washington's love letters to his neighbor's wife, Sally Fairfax. We know about: Thomas Jefferson and Sally Hemings; Franklin Roosevelt and Lucy Mercer; Dwight Eisenhower and Kay Sommersby; John Kennedy and Judith Exner; and at least ten other documented presidential extramarital affairs. Most of them leave the Clinton-Lewinsky assignation as fairly small potatoes in comparison. We have Ralph David Abernathy's description of Martin Luther King's womanizing in his celebrated biography, *And the Walls Came Tumbling Down*. The nation has been forced to examine questions of moral ambiguity which we had been able to avoid earlier in our history in an ignorance-is-bliss condition. We have had to consider whether sex is the final measure of the value of a man or woman.

The fact that Americans are not single-rule ontologists is further illustrated by a remark Arthur Schlesinger, Jr. made in the midst of the Clinton-Lewinsky episode. "We have no moral obligation to answer truthfully a question someone has no right to ask," he said. By and large the American people agreed with him, although the agreement took the form of "that is a personal matter that has nothing to do with how the president is doing his job." Single-rule ontologists have never dealt with the significant effect of manners on their ethical position. The fact that the American people tend to be situationists does not mean that deontological principles are abandoned, however. It just means they are not Kantian. The world of democratic politics and public administration is more complicated than Kant found at the University of Konigsberg in the late 18th century.

As we move toward the second great school of deontological ethics, from Kantianism to ethical and cultural relativism, let us stop off briefly at the White House to consider the relations between presidential press secretaries and reporters. It has generally been admitted in recent years that government has a right to lie in some circumstances because of the consequences of not lying. Is this also a defeat for Kant and a triumph, not for relativism, but for teleological ethics?

In October 1962, during the Cuban missile crisis with tensions rising and questions flying thick and fast, Kennedy administration spokesman Arthur Sylvester authorized a press release from the Pentagon that read: "A Pentagon spokesman denied tonight that any alert has been ordered or that any emergency military measures have been set in motion against Communist-ruled Cuba." Further, the spokesman said, "The Pentagon has no information indicating the presence of offensive weapons in Cuba."

The first sentence may have been technically correct, but the second was false, a government-planted lie at a time when Kennedy had made the decision to confront Khrushchev. When Sylvester had to stand tall for his lie to reporters at a dinner meeting of the New York chapter of Sigma Delta Chi later that year, he said he had come down on the side of the "Lying Baptists" against the "Truthful Baptists." His reference was to a dispute between two groups of Baptists that had erupted at Long Run, Kentucky, in 1804. The issue was whether a man with three children who had been captured by marauding Indians was justified in lying to the Indians in order to conceal the fact that a fourth child was hiding nearby.

The "Lying Baptists" said the father had a right to lie, thus to save the child. The "Truthful Baptists" disagreed, saying that, no matter what the consequences, the truth should be told. This debate paralleled an example Kant himself gave when he argued that even if one tells a man escaped from an asylum where his intended victim is, and even if the man finds and murders him, at least only one sin has been committed, murder, not two, lying as well. Kant said that truthfulness cannot be avoided by any person, no matter how serious "may be the disadvantage accruing to himself or another."

The Lying Baptists have held the high ground in Washington since World War II. Historical examples abound.[10]

> November 25, 1957: Dwight Eisenhower, sixty-seven years old and recently recovered from both a heart attack and abdominal surgery, is in his office. He tries to pick up a document, and cannot. He tries to read it, and fails. The words, he later says, seemed literally to run off the top of the page. He tries to get up, and nearly falls down. He tries to tell his secretary what is wrong, but she cannot make any sense of what he is saying. His physician realizes almost immediately that Eisenhower has suffered a stroke.

The president has developed " a chill," the press office tells reporters. It is not until twenty-four hours later that the nation is told that the president is seriously ill.

December 7, 1971: Henry Kissinger is briefing the press on the government's position on the India-Pakistan war. "First of all, let's get a number of things straight," he begins. "There have been some comments that the administration is anti-Indian. This is totally inaccurate." A briefing paper has been handed out at the start of the session. The first sentence reads: "The policy of this administration towards South Asia must be understood. It is neither anti-Indian nor pro-Pakistan."

A month later, Jack Anderson publishes the transcript of a meeting attended by Kissinger on December 3, just four days before the briefing for the press. "I am getting hell every half-hour from the president that we are not being tough enough on India," Kissinger is quoted as saying. "He wants to tilt in favor of Pakistan."

April 22, 1980: Jody Powell, President Carter's chief spokesman, is talking with Jack Nelson, Washington bureau chief for the Los Angeles Times. No military operation is being planned to rescue the hostages in Iran, Powell tells him. A blockade might be feasible, somewhere down the road, but a rescue mission just would not make any sense.

The newspapers with Nelson's story, which says that the Carter White House considers a rescue operation impractical, are still scattered around the living rooms of Los Angeles when the members of the Delta Team board airplanes for the raid on Teheran.

October 24, 1983: Larry Speaks, the White House spokesman, is asked by reporters whether U.S. troops have landed on Grenada. He checks with a member of President Reagan's national security staff, and relays the response. "Preposterous," he says, and goes on to deny that any invasion is planned.

The landing takes place the next day.

Even reporters who are consistently deceived by White House spokesmen and who once overwhelmed Ron Nessen, President Ford's press secretary, with sarcastic applause when he began a response to a question by saying, "to tell you the truth," agree with Philip Geyelin of the *Washington Post* that "the president has an inherent right—perhaps even an obligation in particular situations—to deceive." But Geyelin and his colleague go to great lengths to define what those *particular situations* are. Even though most of them have never read Joseph Fletcher's *Situation Ethics*, they back off and down from consequences to such deontological terrain as principles, equity, fairness, and justice. They and their counterparts in public administration do not get as far as love as the only moral imperative, but they write openly of the debilitating costs of deception and the pragmatic moral responsibility of distinguishing between honest lies, inadvertent lies, half-truths, and flat-out lies. There are reasonable bounds of dishonesty, they say, just as there are bounded ethics.[11]

Immanuel Kant is not a bounded ethics man. He and the neo-Kantians of the new ontological ethics are straight shooters. When Dennis F. Thompson writes of the ethics of the DIME (Denver Income Maintenance Experiment), for example, and observes that Kant would have counseled the Department of Health, Education, and Welfare (HEW) officials to ignore all the serpentine calculations about what politicians might do, and present Congress with the proposal they believed to be morally right, and the result would be that *congressmen* would bear the moral responsibility for whatever happened to the families involved. "There is a lot to be said for this approach," concludes Thompson. Why? As a moral being I can bear responsibility only for my own decisions. Others can bear the blame I have saved myself from. Ethical egoists begin to chortle at this point and existentialists less tough-minded than Sartre think once again about jumping off the next bridge or perhaps fleeing to Christianity, as did Albert Camus, in despair of human nature.

III. ETHICAL AND CULTURAL RELATIVISM

Ethical and cultural relativists deny the existence of absolutes, which they understand as categorical direct moral rules such as the Ten Commandments. In teleological ethics, utilitarianism also offers a direct rule that governs all of morality (i.e., to increase the overall good). More precisely for relativists, it is the specific characteristics of directed moral actions to which they object. The general characteristic of increasing the overall good must be contrasted with the specific characteristics in the Ten Commandments, killing, for example. Relativists want the freedom to select which action among those available will increase the overall good. Killing, lying, and stealing are places to start.

As a normative ethical theory, relativism appears as a direct moral rule theory and then as an indirect moral rule theory.

> *Direct Ethical Relativism*: If a person *a* of culture C performs an action that is believed by the majority of people of culture C to be right or obligatory, then that action is right.
> *Indirect Ethical Relativism*: If any proposed direct moral rule R is believed by the majority of people to be a direct moral rule, the R is a direct rule.[12]

One finds empirical views most often being put forward in defense of ethical relativism, because opinions vary from culture to culture. The Eskimos in their traditional culture think it is right to put an aged parent on an ice floe and push it out to sea. But we do not. European culture had one way to respond to the challenge of the environment, but the Quakiutal Indians had another. When we learn moral rules we learn them from our parents or in school or church. The child is caused to hold certain views by cultural and societal pressures. He or she then enters every decision-making situation encumbered with a whole apparatus of prefabricated rules and regulations. Not just the spirit but the letter of the law reigns. The law's deontological ethical principles, codified in rules, are not merely guidelines or maxims in the Kantian sense of illustrating the situation; the are *directives* to be followed. Solutions are preset, and you can look them up in a book—a Bible, a Constitution, a statute book, or a procedures manual, for example.

The great weakness of ethical and cultural relativism as a deontological theory is that it does not account for moral disagreements *within* a culture. Identifying subcultures within cultures does not adequately account for historical instances in which whole cultures have changed moral opinions without any significant outside influence. In the case of the moral attitude toward slavery in England and the United States, for example, people within the culture argued that keeping slaves was morally wrong, and they carried the day. In this weakness of ethical and cultural relativism, however, lies the slumbering giant of empirical research and evaluation that is known as *situationism*.

Those who argued that the American involvement in Desert Storm was morally wrong, supposing ethical relativism to be correct, would have been making a simple error about public opinion in 1991. In that year the vast majority of Americans believed the war to be morally justified. In 1993, however, even the most enthusiastic supporter of the military action to oust Saddam Husseain from Kuwait agrees that evidence can be presented to show it was a mistake after all. Why? The situation changed. What is moral appears to depend on the situation rather than on such absolutes as American national interest or the directives of the president or the United Nations, which may be the results of political casuistry anyway. Situation ethics, growing first out of theology, has become the great challenge to Kantianism within deontological ethical theory and both egoism and utilitarianism outside deontology in teleological ethical theory.

The seminal work in situation ethics was Joseph Fletcher's book of that title, published in 1966.[13] Fletcher points out that all major Western religious traditions—Judaism, Catholicism, and Protestantism—have been legalistic. In the best deontological tradition, they have spelled out single-rule ethical theories that established systematic orthodoxy. In ancient Judaism, for example, under the post-exilic Maccabean and Pharisaic leadership, the Torah and its oral tradition, the halakah, established 613 precepts, amplified by an increasingly complicated mass of Mishnaic interpretations and applications. In such a legalist religion, as in public administration, statutory and code law inevitably piles up, ruling upon ruling, guideline upon guideline, because the complications of life and the claims of mercy and compassion, not to mention fairness and justice, accumulate an elaborate system of exceptions and compromises in the form of rules for breaking the rules. The current guidelines of the otherwise simple code of ethics of the International City Management Association goes to five single-spaced pages of careful, some would say tortuous, explanations of what the tenets of the code really mean.

Abraham J. Heschel has lamented the tragic death of the prophets' ethos—living by love as norm, not program—before the pyramiding of codes from Covenant to Pentateuch to Midrash and Mishna to Talmud. The prophets, he says, cared not for what the rabbis called pilpul, a hairsplitting and logic-chopping study of the letter of law, but in sensitively seeking "an understanding of *the situation*."[14]

Modern Catholicism has tried to disentangle itself from the web that chokes its weavers by devising an ingenious moral theology that resorts more and more to a casuistry that appears to evade the very laws of right and wrong laid down by such late medieval deontologists as St. Thomas Aquinas. Anyone who has sought the annulment of a marriage in the Roman Catholic Church understands the process. In Fletcher's words, "Love continues to plead mercy's cause and to win at least partial release from law's cold abstractions. Casuistry is the homage paid by legalism to the love of persons, and to realism about life's relativities."[15]

In many ways Protestantism has outdone both Judaism and Catholicism by its puritanical predisposition to let cry, *Fiat justitia, ruat caelum*! (Do the right even if the sky falls down.) Mark Twain called such a person a good man in the worst sense of the word. In the United States the Protestant tradition of legalistic *revelation*, as opposed to Catholic *reason*, has formed secular alliances for the laws that challenge equity and fairness at every turn. Classical ethics and jurisprudence tell us the more statutory the law, the greater need of equity and fairness. As statutes and administrative regulations are applied to actual situations, latitude is necessary for doubtful or perplexed consciences. Does the rule apply in this case? Which of the several rules that might apply is the rule I should actually follow? Is this example of corruption petty enough that I should ignore it?

Take the example of Tricia Nixon's wedding cake. In 1971 the White House claimed that Tricia's wedding cake was based on an old family recipe that had been in Mrs. Nixon's recipe box for years. But when the White House released the recipe, scaled down to family size, there was a problem. Housewives and amateur cooks all over the country, including food writers for several newspapers and magazines, rushed to test it. The result was a porridge-like glob that overflowed the baking pans and messed up ovens. After a good deal of hemming and hawing about the fact that most recipes for pound cake call for whole eggs, while this one called only for the whites, the truth finally came out. The cake was actually created by the White House pastry chef. One of the ethical concerns written about at the time was that if the White House would lie to us about Tricia's wedding cake, it would probably lie to us about Cambodia as well. The larger truth is that Tricia's wedding was the wrong moral battle to fight. Sissela Bok probably draws the line too close when she argues, in *Lying: Moral Choice in Public and Private Life*, that it is dangerous to let public officials get away with even minor lies. Frederickson has a better perspective:

> Regime legitimacy is a function of fairness and equity and some level of official benev-
> olence in the administration of the law. To the extent that petty or grand corruption
> detract from fairness, equity, and benevolence, they reduce regime legitimacy. The
> larger deontological issue here is the identification of fairness, equity, and official be-
> nevolence as high-order ethical principles.[16]

While situationism is one response to the legalism of single-rule deontology, another is antinomianism, which holds that moral decisions are random, unpredictable, erratic, and anomalous. Making moral decisions is a matter of spontaneity. They are unprincipled, purely ad hoc, and casual. Antinomians are anarchic (i.e., without rule). Whereas *moral* decisions are extemporized for antinomians, they often make common cause with teleologists in public administration. Many policy analysts tend to be moral antinomians because the results they measure are often measured only in terms of efficiency and have no ethical dimension. Cost-benefit analysts and game theorists, as well as market model devotees, frequently maintain that they receive professional guidance from outside the internal moral constraints—some would say hangups—imposed by the imperial superego of deonotological ethics. Ironically, however, they, in their own way, are *pnuematikoi* in the classical Greek sense (i.e., they are spirit-possessed), but they are also possessed by the singular spirit of logical positivism. They clearly distinguish between the values that drive deontological ethics and the facts that they can verify empirically.

IV. AGAPISM

The third and last form of single-rule deontological theory is agapism. Rosen says it takes two forms.

> *Direct Agapism*: If any person *a* performs an action of love, then that action is right.
> *Indirect Agapism*: If any person *a* acts on a proposed direct moral rule R that is
>   likely to increase the amount of love in the world, then R is a direct moral
>   rule.

Agapists argue that there is only one source of rightness—love. If someone performs an action out of love, then it is right whatever the consequences. Joseph Fletcher summarizes the view in these words:

Nothing is inherently good or evil, except love (personal concern) and its opposite, indifference or actual malice. Anything else, no matter what it is, may be good or evil, right or wrong, according to the situation.[17]

Professional philosophers hold agapism to be quite deficient, suffering from the same ills as utilitarianism. How does one properly distribute justice in the name of love, for example? Neither agapism nor utilitarianism can distinguish between distributive and retributive justice. The latter concerns theories of punishment, and the former theories of the morally proper manner of distributing the relatively scarce things of value. What are "things of value" in terms of social benefit, good, utility, or disutility? If right action is one that increases the benefit or value for the greatest number, utilitarianism would have to allow that it is morally permissible to kill nonproductive elderly people in the name of justice, while agapists would love them deeply as the ice floe on which they were placed slipped out to sea. For agapism to work as a deontological ethical theory it must move from single-rule to multiple prima facie rule, so that out of a sense of love one cannot torture someone else until he recants what you take to be heresy.

Professional philosophers do not understand agapism as well as theologians and public administrationists do. There is irony here, for the three forms love took in the Greek language, *eros, philia*, and *agape* are the bedrock of ancient Greek philosophy. Plato (430–347 B.C.) and the Platonic tradition concentrated on *eros* as the desire common to us all, the desire for the vision of true good and beauty. Plato incorporates his depiction of *eros* into his metaphysical philosophy, orienting it toward a transcendent reality where good and beauty hold eternal sway. We start by loving the beauty attached to a particular body, he said, and eventually love the same beauty in all bodies which possess it (*Symposium*, 210–212b). When we see beauty in the world, we are "reminded of true beauty" (*Phaedrus*, 248e). Each beautiful face or form represents finally a summons from beyond the realm of finitude, and so our love is left unsatisfied unless we recognize its divine origin. This summons means that the character of our love varies with the quality of the object loved. It bids us to aspire upward, to go beyond gratifying sensual appetite, to live by the vision of beauty that addresses our longing for a higher world of home. Objects of love can include not only beautiful persons, but beautiful philosophical theories, political constitutions, and administrative arrangements, which is why Plato devotes both the *Republic* and the *Laws* to these theories, constitutions, and arrangements.

In yet another rendering of love in Greek, *philia*, Aristotle (384–322 B.C.) writes of a love we can have only for persons and not for things. "Let loving be defined as wishing for anyone the things which we believe to be good, for his sake but not for our own, and procuring them for him as far as lies in our power" (*Rhetoric*, II, 4). The love so defined is a matter of the fondness and liking of *philia*, in contrast with the desire and longing of *eros*. *Philia* transcends even spiritualized egocentrism.

The Greeks gave *philia* a wider application than friendship has for us. There is a form of civic friendship, for example, that bonds members of the political community, and a friendship that parent and offspring naturally feel for one another. All these relations have in common the wish for good things for the other's sake.

Aristotle elaborates the meaning of *philia* in Books VIII and IX of *The Nicomachean Ethics*. Among the claims he makes are the following:

1. The state of attained reciprocity is to be especially valued. In this state, each wishes good for the other for the other's sake, and each is aware of the other's wish.

2. There are three lovable objects: the good, the pleasant, and the useful. Those who enjoy the highest kind of friendship are not only good but also pleasant and useful to each other.

3. The highest kind of friendship can be realized only infrequently, because it sets stringent conditions. It involves a familiarity that demands time and opportunity, and ongoing contact. It also involves choice, so that the mutual love required follows ''not as a result of feeling but as a result of character'' (VIII, 5). Persons with the requisite good character are themselves rare.

4. Certain revelations are constitutively unequal, yet excellence accrues when the parties conform to these inequalities, such as father to son, elder to younger, man to wife, and ruler to subject. Those who are better and more useful should be loved more than they love.

5. Our special bonds of attachment establish particular expectations and create peculiar vulnerabilities. The possibility of injustice increases with the closeness of the relation. ''It is a more terrible thing to defraud a comrade than a fellow citizen, more terrible not to help a brother than a stranger'' (VIII, 9).

6. While friendship goes beyond goodwill, goodwill can have moral value even when reciprocity is not attained. Goodwill is ''a kind of inactive friendship'' (IX, 5). Loving is more essential to friendship than being loved.

7. Self-love is to be commended, insofar as the self is committed to virtue. ''It is for himself most of all that each man wishes what is good'' (VIII, 7). The true lover of self does not succumb to wealth, honors, and bodily pleasures, thus gratifying the appetite, but instead assigns to himself only the things that are noblest and best.

To find an elaboration of *agape* one does not look to Greek philosophy, but to the books of the New Testament. *Eros* is noticeably absent there, and *philia* appears only infrequently. Jesus refers to two commandments on which ''depend all the law and the prophets.'' They are ''to love God with all your heart, soul, and mind, and to love your neighbor as yourself'' (Matthew 22: 37–40 and Mark 12: 29–31). Jesus links Deuteronomy 6:5 and Leviticus 19:18,

> You shall love the Lord your God with all your heart, and with all your soul, and with all your mind (Deuteronomy 6:5).
>   You shall not take vengeance or bear a grudge against any of your people, but you shall love your neighbor as yourself: I am the Lord (Leviticus 19:18).

While the order of the commandments must not be reversed, Jesus said the second is ''like'' the first. Love of neighbor shares in the seriousness of a divine command. As Christianity moved out from its moorings in Judaism, it reflected more and more the Greek thought whose language was its vehicle of dissemination. Augustine (354–430 A.D.) confessed that our hearts are restless until they find rest in God, recalling not only the psalmists' *thirst* (Psalms 42 and 63), but also the Platonic unsatisfied *eros* summoned from beyond the realm of finitude and the Neoplatonic desire for union with God. Thomas Aquinas (1225–1274) treated charity in the *Summa Theologica*, II-II, q. 24, a. 12, in a way that appropriated and revised Aristotle's account of *philia*. The love which is charity involves mutual communication, a friendship between God and ourselves.

Yet *agape* possesses features that distinguish it from the desire and longing of *eros* and the fondness and liking of *philia*, features that themselves influence subsequent moral reflection in the West and relate directly to the deontological dimensions of administrative ethics. The seven claims of Aristotle provide a convenient structure for their discussion.

1. Interpreters of the second commandment value the state of attained reciprocity, agreeing that such reciprocity requires each party to wish good for the other's sake. Yet certain Biblical passages generate pressures toward greater inclusiveness. One passage enjoins a love that extends beyond relations of understanding safe, assured reciprocity: "For if you love those who love you, what reward have you? Do not even the tax collectors do the same?" (Matthew 5: 46 and Luke 6:32–34). Neighbor-love should then at least include *unilateral* efforts on the agent's part to establish and enhance personal relations marked by closeness and social relations marked by concord. *Agape* does not await, anticipate, or demand a response in kind, though it may compatibly desire and hope for such a response, and regard attainment as the fruition it seeks. Furthermore, we are to love not only our friends but also our enemies (Matthew 5:43).

2. Normative pressures toward inclusiveness prompt certain extrapolations of the second commandment. What a person does in particular should not determine by itself whether he or she is cared about *at all*. This case remains independent both in its genesis (the neighbor need not know who the lover is) and continuation (the neighbor may not cease to be the lover's enemy). The neighbor should be regarded as irreducibly valuable prior to doing anything in particular that marks him or her off from others. We cannot restrict our love—*agape*—to those we find lovable only insofar as they are good, enjoyable, or useful.

3. Interpreters of the second commandment modify Aristotle's account of *philia* in order to do justice to normative pressures toward inclusiveness. Agape must set boundaries within which the highest friendship comes into its own, and must go beyond the limits such friendship may impose. The boundaries include moral prohibitions against doing anything whatever to those outside the friendship for the sake of friendship. To go beyond the limits it may impose includes active promotion of the well-being of neighbors where the conditions for the highest kind of friendship cannot, for various reasons, be met.

4. Relations between father and son, elder and younger, ruler and subject possess their own exigencies. All involved should honor impartial guidelines that attend to what every neighbor's well-being requires or prohibits. We must pursue as much equality as possible, answering the question of which differences among neighbors are morally relevant. Differential treatment pertains to different needs. There is preferential treatment for the poor, for example, and appeals to merit based on the differential exercise of an equal liberty.

5. Aquinas maintains that we ought to love some neighbors more than others, in our affections as well as outwardly (II-II, q. 26). He allows that we should love all equally out of charity, wishing all the same generic good—everlasting happiness—and loving each person, including the enemy, to some degree. Yet he accords preference to ourselves, to those nearer to God, and to those bound to us by ties of consanguinity and marriage.

6. The goodwill *agape* involves permanent stability on the agent's part. Permanence means persistence in the face of obstacles. Even when the agent does not approve of the neighbor's behavior, it still makes sense to talk of regarding the neighbor as worthwhile and of caring about what happens to him or her. The

agent ought to be "for" the neighbor, whatever the particular changes in him or her, for better or for worse.

7. Self-love is positively valued as revering one's identity and particular life, a life non-interchangeable with others' lives. To be concerned about one's own flourishing is a substantive religious and moral claim along with concern about neighbors. The enemy of self-love is sloth more than pride. Self-love is normal, reasonable, and prudent. It is neither particularly praiseworthy nor necessarily blameworthy. The second commandment interpreted as "you shall love your neighbor as you now love yourself" can serve as a model for what neighbor-love means. We then transform prudential reasoning into moral reasoning by invoking some variant of the golden rule.

The influence of agapism on the seminal deontological thinkers can hardly be over-estimated. John Stuart Mill (1806–1873) wrote, for example, that "in the golden rule of Jesus of Nazareth we read the complete spirit of the ethics of utility. To do as you would be done by, and to love your neighbor as yourself, constitute the ideal perfection of utilitarian morality."[18] R.M. Hare holds that "utilitarianism is the extension into philosophy of the Christian doctrine of agape."[19] Even Kant, especially Kant, believed that human beings possess incomparable worth. He wrote in 1788: "Two things fill the mind with ever new and increasing admiration and awe the oftener and more steadily we reflect on them: the starry heaven above me and the moral law within me."[20] This moral law reaches into the infinite and is the ground of the dignity of human nature.

V. CONCLUSION

Despite the difficulties associated with the three main single-rule deontological theories, the everyday world of the practicing public administrator is still built around the principles, precepts, and regulations that deontological ethics encourage and sometimes prescribe. The reform movement saw to that. The procedural controls that characterize professional public administration in America have been notably successful in limiting corruption, assuming the American administrative class were inclined toward it. The psychological fact is that most people prefer to work in deontologically unambiguous circumstances, where there are no mixed messages and where one is expected to do what is right and honorable. Each individual conscience plays a role in keeping an organization deontologi-cally sound. Indeed, if there were too many members of an organization who heard the still, small voice of God, as the antinomians and agapists sometimes do, no code of ethics, deontological or teleological, could save the organization from what happens when angels fall. As a practical matter, organizations must appeal to the deontological consciences of their members, because they have no better way to defend the organization's reputation.

To rely exclusively on each individual's sense of right and wrong is to take other risks, however, because of the pitfalls of relativism. While the assumptions of Kantianism really do apply to American civil servants—they value civic virtue highly—it is also true that American public administrators are generally inexperienced in the processes of moral reasoning. They are not always able to make the necessary situational adjustments to Kant's categorical imperative. Codes of ethics are helpful as deontological tools, but they cannot substitute for dealing personally, courageously, responsibly, and creatively with the moral ambiguity that is the stuff of administrative life. Educators can play an important role at this point in better equipping administrators to recognize and handle ethically marginal situations. Alfred North Whitehead once said, however, that simple-minded notions of right and wrong are the chief obstacles to understanding. Deontological ethics will maintain the notions of right and wrong for their serviceable value, but the wise citizen will remember that universal obligation attaches not to particular judgments of conscience but to acts willing both the present and consequential good.

REFERENCES

1. The deficiencies of both psychological and ethical egoism, as well as direct and indirect utilitarianism, are described in Chapters 2 and 3 of Bernhard Rosen, *Ethical Theory: Strategies and Concepts* (Mountain View, CA: Mayfield Publishing Company, 1993). Rosen also provides a brilliant description of rule deontology in Chapter 4.
2. Jeremy Bentham, *Deontology* (Edinburgh: William Tart, 1834), pp. 10–11.
3. See Carol W. Lewis, *The Ethics Challenge in Public Service* (San Francisco: Josey-Bass Publishers, 1991), p. 90.
4. Simone de Beauvoir, *The Ethics of Ambiguity* (New York: Philosophical Library, Inc., 1948), pp. 4, 122.
5. Jean-Paul Sartre, *Being and Nothingness*, translated by Hazel Barnes (New York: Philosophical Library, Inc., 1956), p. 153.
6. Terry L. Cooper, *The Responsible Administrator*, 3rd ed. (San Francisco: Josey-Bass Publishers, 1990), pp. 10–11.
7. Bernhard Rosen, *Ethical Theory: Strategies and Concepts* (Mountain View, CA: Mayfield Publishing Company, 1993) p. 153.
8. Bernhard Rosen, *Ethical Theory: Strategies and Concepts* (Mountain View, CA: Mayfield Publishing Company, 1993) p. 154.
9. Stephen J. Bronczek, "Ethical Decision Making: Challenge of the 1990s–A Practical Approach for Local Governments," *Public Personnel Management*, Vol. 21, No. 1 (Spring 1992), pp. 75–76.
10. See Anthony Marro, "When the Government Tells Lies," *Columbia Journalism Review*, Vol. 19 (March/April 1985), pp. 29–41.
11. H. George Frederickson introduces the idea of bounded ethics in his pathfinding conclusion to *Ethics and Public Administration* (New York: M.E. Sharpe, 1993), p. 249.
12. Bernhard Rosen, *Ethical Theory: Strategies and Concepts* (Mountain View, CA: Mayfield Publishing Company, 1993), p. 160.
13. Joseph Fletcher, *Situation Ethics: The New Morality* (Philadelphia: The Westminster Press, 1966). See also Harvey Cox (ed.), *The Situation Ethics Debate* (Philadelphia: The Westminster Press, 1968). The latter work is a collection of twenty-eight reviews and estimates of situation ethics and "a sharp reply" by Joseph Fletcher.
14. Abraham J. Heschel, *The Prophets* (New York: Harper and Row, 1962), p. 225.
15. Joseph Fletcher, *Situation Ethics: The New Morality* (Philadelphia: The Westminster Press, 1966), p. 19.
16. H. George Frederickson, *Ethics and Public Administration*, (New York M.E. Sharpe, 1993, pp. 248–249.
17. Joseph Fletcher, "Love Is the Only Measure," *Commonweal* (January 14, 1966), cited in Bernard Rosen, *Ethical Theory: Strategies and Concepts* (Mountain View, CA: Mayfield Publishing Company, 1993), p. 168.
18. John Stuart Mill, *Utilitarianism*, edited by J.B. Schneewind, (New York: Collier, 1965), p. 292.
19. R.M. Hare, *Moral Thinking: Its Levels, Method, and Point* (Oxford: Clarendon Press, 1981), p. 129.
20. Immanuel Kant, *Critique of Practical Reason*, translated by Lewis White Beck (Indianapolis: Dobbs-Merrill, 1956), p. 166.

9

A Teleological Approach to Administrative Ethics

Gerald M. Pops
West Virginia University, Morgantown, West Virginia

A teleological approach to making ethical judgments is one that adopts a criterion of consequence or result as the standard of what is morally right and wrong. This philosophy of ends is quite uncomplicated at first blush. The ultimate reference is to the comparative amount of benefit produced or expected to be produced—the goodness or badness of the consequences of the decision (as this may be determined by the actor) drives the choice. The end, consequence, or result is itself a nonmoral good.

This definition implies, although it does not state, the obverse; that a teleological approach does not concern itself with a priori reasoning, that is, a preoccupation with the morality of means (first principles and procedures) that could be employed.

Teleologists differ markedly over what kinds of goods are to be measured and which serve as consequentialist values. Are we to measure lives saved? Profit achieved? Levels of satisfaction, pleasure, or fulfillment? Acquisition of knowledge or power? The nature of the final "product" may be important to the individual teleologist, but not to the definition of teleology.

In the context of public administration, teleologists often have in mind such values as the achievement of public policy goals and the related services that are delivered (health care, education, national defense, and so forth), satisfaction of citizen demands, or (on the darker, Machiavellian side) the acquisition and maintenance of personal influence.

But what if the consequences we hope to gain by our decision are valued by us precisely because of their inherent moral quality—an end such as the broadening of public participation or some other result regarded as just? Does the fact that the result also constitutes a moral good convert the teleological to the deontological? If knowledge is the result being sought, who can judge what part of it is "moral" and what part "nonmoral"? In such cases, distinguishing teleological reasoning from deontological reasoning is made more difficult.

Beyond this distinction, teleologists may be classified as ethical egoists and utilitarians. Ethical egoists act in a way which will promote the personal welfare of the actor, usually but not necessarily implying less than optimal consequences for other persons (the actor may believe it is in his long-term self-interest to be considerate of the interests of others). In contrast, utilitarians act in such a way as to bring about the greatest general good, or the greatest net balance of good over evil for society as a whole.[1] Of the two schools, utilitarianism is the more favored and appealing among philosophers.

> The Principle of the Common Good is the basic principle of the philosophy of utilitarianism, which is probably the most influential moral theory in the recent history of western philosophy. It received its classic formulation in the nineteenth century by Jeremy Bentham and John Stuart Mill. According to utilitarianism, being moral means doing what will bring about the greatest good for the greatest number of people. Everyone must be considered; then the moral thing to do is what is most helpful to the greatest number. (Clark, 1986:9)

I. UTILITARIANISM

The principle of utility requires measuring and aggregating (at least in rough quantity) the relative benefits and burdens to an entire community of people of some specific act or rule. The goal is to maximize the net balance of good over evil (the "greatest good") for as many members of the society as is possible (the "greatest number"). Consequences may be judged as relatively good or bad from the perspective of the decision-maker or of a broader social consensus (the "agency" or the "general public," for example).

Frankena (1972:34–43) describes three types of utilitarian reasoning: act utilitarianism, general utilitarianism, and rule utilitarianism. In act utilitarianism, the act itself is judged for its actual or expected consequences (i.e., what are likely to be the consequences for the community if I, in this specific case, take this action?). For the administrator, this may be an inefficient criterion to adopt, for it requires the actor to reckon benefits and burdens of every action in a series of actions that are more or less similar. General utilitarianism poses the question: What would be the consequences for the community if everyone were to act similarly to the actor, in this case? The criticism here is that it is simply unrealistic to expect everyone to act the same, particularly under the circumstances of imperfect information. Rule utilitarianism directs our attention to the aggregate of consequences flowing from the consistent application of a rule. The relevant question becomes: Which rule, applied in this and similar cases, will promote the greatest general good? According to Frankena, rule utilitarianism is probably the more sensible than the other forms, as its consistent application is likely to produce optimal consequences with the least decision costs, despite the fact that any particular act may produce a less-than-optimum or even harmful result. Also, it makes unnecessary the recalculation of net good on every occasion, thus simplifying action and improving efficiency.

Regardless of the type of utilitarianism employed, the issue of the actor's responsibility for accurate calculation and prediction of consequences arises. Utilitarian calculations rest on a prediction of actual consequences flowing from the decision. The actor is by necessity limited to those factors that are currently available and knowable in predicting outcome, and perforce prevented from assessing consequences produced by factors not currently knowable or so uncertain as to defy prediction. What then is the actor's ethical responsibility? Making an error (as judged by the actual consequences) is said to be not unethical, but circumstances may alter this judgment. For example, it is probably a defense to a charge of unethical conduct that the actor had insufficient time to make an accurate assessment of factors that could have, had sufficient analysis been done, been seen to influence the result (Rosen, 1978:90–93). The better view, Rosen asserts, is to apply the rule of the reasonable man familiar to the courts: a moral obligation to predict and calculate the influence of decision factors arises only if the administrator could have reasonably predicted their consequences. Consequences should be thought of in terms of what is likely to occur given knowledge that is current and reasonably available (given the constraints of time, expense, and the analytical tools at hand).

The clear implication in this discussion is that the problem of accurate prediction of consequences should be separated from the problem of moral choice. But ought they to be separated? To be sure, it is often very difficult to measure benefits and burdens in advance of their occurring, and this difficulty is severely compounded in the field of public policy choice where multivariate interdependencies and unforeseen second-order interactions abound. So difficult, in fact, that the extreme difficulty of prediction is often posed as a serious objection to the use of utilitarian logic for most policy and many management decisions. However, the ethical question still remains, undiminished: Should the public administrator strive, regardless of difficulty and limited vision, to bring about the best result? And, in democratic administration, what moral compass guides the thinking determining what consequences are best?

This question takes on additional luster when the decision is within the province of an actor who is identified with a professional field that putatively bears on the decision to be made. Greater knowledge of decision variables and mastery of cause-effect analysis is asserted. What if the assertion is made unaccompanied by the professional actor's confidence that he or she has better tools for prediction than the lay administrator? Is this not a moral lapse?

Let us now turn the question around. Is a generalist administrator, lacking professional knowledge that seems appropriate to a decision situation, ethically bound to seek, assess the applicability of, and then use the services of staff or consultant professionals to increase the likelihood that consequences might be better foreseen? As a professional generalist, the administrator may be properly expected to possess special knowledge related to staffing, budgeting, coordinating the activities of work units, planning, and other management functions, and to be ethically required to improve skills in these areas if they are lacking. Is it unreasonable to expect that same administrator to recognize that a particular professional expertise is needed if they are not schooled or even familiar with the nature and claims of such profession?

Utilitarian logic also requires that net good be calculated relative to "the greatest number." Although this proviso is explained as meaning all members of a given society or community (from the family through the entire planet), we are still left in some doubt about the boundaries of the society. If we have in mind the United States, do we take "community" to mean citizens only? How about resident aliens? Do we take into account the welfare of future generations? And, given our ripening understanding of the interdependence of nations and ecological systems, should consequences expected to occur in other nations, or in animal populations, or to natural elements within important ecological systems be included in our reckoning (Pops, 1997)?

Luke (1991) cogently observes that the rapid development of global and interorganizational interdependencies and the impact of present (particularly environmental) decisions on future generations have irrevocably raised the focus of administrative ethics from managerial to policy ethics, particularly at the executive level. Executives require longer time horizons for effective planning and implementation. Technology has shortened geographic and social distance. The global economy integrates capital markets. Environmental issues, once perceived as local or national in scope, have escaped their boundaries and become global. Government and institutional managers must now take into account geographic interconnections, functional interdependence which blurs the separation of powers of executive from the judicial and legislative branches, and temporal interconnectedness that ties together past, present, and future generations. Obviously, in such an environment the "greatest number" is an amorphous and moving target.

II. THE ASCENDENCY OF INDIVIDUAL CHOICE AND THE COMMUNITARIAN RESPONSE

The last quarter of the twentieth century seemed like a steady parade of teleological theory development, punctuated by the logic of free markets and growth in the value of individual choice as the prime criterion of deciding the goodness of consequences. This movement seems to have begun with public choice theory (Buchanan and Tullock, 1967). Derived in large measure from utilitarianism, public choice theory centers upon serving individual preferences as the basis for political and administrative action. It is also concerned with minimizing the costs of collective action. The goal of maximizing individual preferences is the major teleological element. Methods for enlarging personal and free choice—selling off government assets, privatizing the production of public services, identifying and responding to the "customers" of government services, and facilitating negotiation among contending private and public interests in lieu of legislating end states—become the preferred consequences of government action.[2]

Public choice theorists recognized that individual preferences will often conflict, and that managing conflict, rather than imposing government will to achieve legislated ends or suppressing private opposition, should provide the primary guideline for administrative policymaking, organizational design, and agency operations (Harmon and Mayer, 1986).

> In organizing for collective action, the objective is to construct decision-making arrangements—which is to say, organizations—that produce the least possible infringement on individual liberty and hold the organizing costs to a minimum, and at the same time produce results with which everyone involved can live. (Harmon and Mayer, 1986:247)

Following public choice theory, the task of government is to invent the means to aggregate individual choices and give them voice and articulation. Ostrom (1974) took up the challenge by relating concepts of individual citizen choice maximization to the ethical obligations of administrators, thus constructing an ethic of administrative behavior.

> The practitioner of American public administration, if he is to contribute to the viability of a democratic society, must be prepared to advance and serve the interests of the individual persons who form his relevant public. His service is to individual persons as users or consumers of public goods and services and not to political masters. . . . While he is obliged to respect governmental authority, [the public official] in a democratic society is not a neutral and obedient servant to his master's command. . . . Each public servant in the American system of democratic administration bears first the burden of being a citizen in a constitutional republic. (Ostrom, 1974:131)

Ostrom's reasoning includes four elements. First, authority should be divided so as to limit political power. Second, administration should be seen as part and parcel of politics. Third, multiorganizational arrangements should promote healthy competition among government agencies. Fourth, administrators should strive to maximize efficiency by seeking least-cost alternatives to meet the preferences of the consumers of government services. The latter requires full information to citizen-consumers and their participation to allow administrators to rank preferences. His model public organization is consistent with an ethic of individual choice and includes a decentralized organizational structure in which authority is fragmented, strong inputs from citizen advisory committees and broad access for the public to information possessed by government agencies are encouraged, and agency decision processes are made vulnerable to challenge in other forums.

The logic and language of free-market economics and teleological reasoning now dominate the American public organization landscape. The theme was echoed in the keystone book of the decade, Osborne and Gaebler's Reinventing Government (1992), in its paeans to competition and entrepreneurialism, empowerment, management by mission instead of rule and results instead of inputs, and to consumer choice as the guiding star of government purpose. March (1992) sees a trend toward a new vision of society and governance. It is a vision that measures itself by voluntary exchanges and rational self-interest, "a conception of political entrepreneurship in which political brokers arrange voluntary exchanges among political actors" (March, 1992:225). Behavior is seen to be the result of "conscious choices among alternatives of action" and "choices are made on the basis of individual comparisons of the personal value of each alternative's consequences" (March, 1992:226). Many operating principles—such as, due process, ensuring the integrity of decision-makers through civil service protection, comparable worth as a new basis for determining government compensation, and negotiated grievance systems— once familiar in our public service settings have faded into the background and seem increasingly arcane and the stuff of legal actions rather than the driving force behind daily decisions.

Communitarian theory is a seawall to the flood tide of individual choice theory and market logic. Etzioni (1996) and others pose the healthy community as the goal of public decision-making rather than the maximization of individual choice. They systematically attack the individualistic paradigm in which all values are acceptable and are to be tolerated, and that government's job is to enlarge and protect individual preferences. But does this theory development represent a return to deontological reasoning or a new set of values to define the goodness or badness of the results of government decisions (i.e., a new teleological analysis)? A review of the themes in *The New Golden Rule* (Etzioni, 1996) lead to the conclusion that both are intended. On the teleological side, the new consequences to be pursued are a healthy citizenry, environmental protection, lower crime, and community-strengthening activity. On the deontological side, process values such as megalogues (linking of multiple public dialogues), and greater civility in discourse ("rules of engagement") are stressed. "The last thing that a democracy needs is for people to vote their raw feelings, their first impulses, before having a chance to reflect on them and discuss them with others" (Etzioni, 1996:115). In the end, the main thrust is teleological. The only laws that will be *effective* (a teleological word) will be those based on a moral consensus valuing a certain type of social outcome. Communitarianism seeks solutions to social problems that enhance community well-being. While improved process is important, even essential, it is the consequences of social discourse that motivate communitarians.

III. WHY ADMINISTRATORS ARE COMPELLED TO MANAGE BY RESULTS

As Martin Shapiro (1988) makes clear, public administration has steered an unsteady course between conequentialist and deontological philosophies over the past half century. Using the development of administrative law as his text, Shapiro sees the Warren era (late 1950s to mid-1970s) as "highly compatible with the brand of ethics that conceived of values as essentially matters of personal preference" (Shapiro, 1988:11). This period was followed in the late 1970s and 1980s by a shift in court doctrine, led by the Court of Appeals of the District of Columbia, imposing a deontological style of decision-making closely tied to "administrative due process" in which contentions of all parties to administrative forums must be heard and their concerns addressed in the decision, alternatives made clear and analyzed, and statements of reasons required. The focus was upon the process and not the result. But Shapiro goes on to argue that the administrative response was the construction of a "technological smokescreen" to satisfy the courts on process grounds so that results-oriented strategies could be pursued. This period was followed during the Rehnquist era by a return to agency discretion and a relaxation of court-imposed process constraints, allowing the agencies more latitude in pursuing policy goals.

It is a truism that public administrators are agents of constitutions and laws, that they reside primarily in politically subordinate agencies, and they must necessarily be concerned with legislative mandates, in addition to executive and judicial directives and rules. The deontological basis of public administration is thus secured. Nonetheless, each step in the administrative policy process (policy formulation, program development, and program implementation) is a part of the political process (Appleby, 1949; Mazmanian and Sabatier, 1983), in which agencies and public administrators are political actors. Being accountable to all three branches of government thus involves far more than following the rules and assuming subordinate postures. Rohr (1986) tells us that public administration is the balance wheel in the pull and tug between the branches and the mix of values they represent, and that public administrators bring to the balancing act their own values and forms of reasoning. And, of course, much of that reasoning springs from technocratic orientations—getting things done effectively. Accountability is a complex task; it is a product of following the rules, getting results, and projecting a positive image of having certain values (competence, justice, efficiency, responsiveness, and so on).

In order to be effective, public organizations must survive by acquiring new resources—financial, human, and political. Successful acquisition of resources depends on a demonstration of real and potential achievements to persuade those with influence that further support is justified. This demonstration includes the appearance of good results, which counts for a lot in a competitive world that rewards positive image. The acquisition of political influence is thus a critical driving force in the ethical reasoning of public administration. This is an old theme. Niccolo Macchiavelli, the notorious fifteenth century Florentine administrator, argued that power and personal survival are the proper goals of government administrators and not the doing of good deeds or the following of rules. The latter put the administrator at a disadvantage in a world of self-interested power seekers (Machiavelli, 1950; Gabris, 1991).

Osborne and Gaebler (1992) underline the need for government functionaries at all levels to focus on results relative to mission and goals, and the subordination of administrative processes (particularly civil service regulation and protection) to serve this need. The emphasis is on making decisions that serve client populations and institutions (called "customers''), conditioning administrative behavior to serve this population, and using private sector methods (including contracting-out) that increase efficient delivery of services.

These reasons for taking a teleological approach to administrative ethics are compelling. There are, moreover, other important reasons for favoring teleologic values having to do with the mindsets and learned behaviors of persons who typically enter the public service. Public administrators, many of them idealists that worry about the welfare of the commonweal and many others as professionals associated with their special training (bridges, cures, environmental cleanup, etc.), are arguably more concerned with the health of the society and where it is going than the average citizen or business manager. It is likely in many cases that this concern with the collectivity is the major reason they choose public service careers. This mindset dictates a concern with the results of their activity.

IV. TWO ILLUSTRATIONS

In the year in which this essay was written, it was not an auspicious time for deontological ethics in America. We recently witnessed the disquieting events involved in a successful impeachment of the president and an unsuccessful effort to convict and remove him from office. These events contain within them the reasonable certitude of a president lying under oath, of carrying on an illicit relationship in the Oval Office with an intern, and perhaps (with less certitude because of the intricacies of judicial interpretation) suborning perjury in a federal court. Yet the president's approval ratings throughout the period of these events ran in the 70 percent range and actually increased during the trial on the impeachment! The refrain sung by the administration during these sad events was the same: the economy is strong, the country is not involved in war, the events alleged or proven did not undermine the security of the nation or the constitution. The message of the president's surprising immunity to mortal wounding is clear—it is the results that count! No amount of deontological reasoning, most of it coming from his Republican opponents in the House of Representatives, dented the popular view that the president was being unfairly targeted. Neither the well supported charges of perjury, nor of systematic lying to administrative staff and supporters, nor of immoral behavior, nor of the use of character attacks from the White House designed to discourage potential adverse witnesses, seemed to matter much in forming American public opinion. It is not how you behave, it is what comes from your actions that is most important.

The second illustrative case of the ascendency of teleological ethics in government is drawn from another level of government, from another era, and from the administrative realm. It is drawn from events occurring in Skokie, Illinois in 1978 involving a dispute over the attempt of a group of neo-Nazis to stage a lawful demonstration in this Chicago suburb. In this effort, the right-wing group was supported by the American Civil Liberties Union (ACLU). The ACLU is committed to the defense of individual liberties contained in the Bill of Rights, the very hallmark of American deontological principles. The right of any individual or group, however unpopular or ill-intentioned, to speak is among these revered rights. Freedom of speech is a leading light in the ranks of deontological ethics.

In the Skokie case, the neo-Nazis sought a permit from village officials to parade through the streets of Skokie, an atypical Chicago suburb composed largely of Jewish-European survivors of the Holocaust and their families. The explicit purpose of the right-wing group was to foment tension and to gain media attention in the expected confrontation with community residents. When the city raised obstacles to gaining the permit, the

ACLU, in line with its traditional principles, took up the cause of the would-be-marchers. The ACLU argued that the right to free speech guaranteed the same privileges for the unpopular as well as those in the mainstream and that the right to speak could not be overridden by the threat of violence posed by those who hear the speech—the so-called "heckler's veto" (The New Republic, 1978). Its decision to enter into the controversy was costly. About 25 percent of the members of the heavily-Jewish membership dropped their ACLU membership (Time, 1978).[3] The exodus clearly stems from the primary importance ascribed to the ethics of consequence (peaceable, formerly persecuted people being made to suffer indignities, public embarrassment, and perhaps violence at the hands of a group of unconscionable bullies), overwhelming the deontological ethic represented by the constitutional principle of free speech.[4]

To bring the matter home to the public administrator, consider the thought processes of the town manager of Skokie. He has a decision to make. The law is clear—the city cannot discriminate in its issuance of parade permits on the basis of the beliefs of the participants. Should he allow practical consequences to dissuade him? There are a number of reasons to decide in the affirmative:

1. He wishes to serve the citizens of the city. These do not include the Nazis.
2. He believes that the Nazis can find other means and other places to express themselves, in a way that is less hurtful to people he knows, cares for, and works for.
3. He wishes to keep his job. If he acts to prevent the march, he will be a local hero and shift bad-guy status to the courts who may well enjoin him, upon ACLU prompting, from refusing to issue the permit.

Given these practical considerations, it is not surprising when a public administrator acts in the manner of the Skokie manager. Yet, to admit that one does not take moral principles and rules seriously is not something we should expect to hear or encourage. A public administrator must be concerned with the legitimacy of his or her actions as well as with outcomes. Thus, the administrator will often speak the language of deontological ethics while at the same time searching for devices to justify favoring a good result where it is seen to conflict with principle.

1. She will attempt to justify actions by arguing ethical relativism.
2. He will play the legal card, obfuscating rules through imaginative interpretation. He may seek to substitute "not doing anything illegal" for "being ethical."
3. She will play the professional card, deferring to expert advisors within or outside the agency, to justify an action seemingly in conflict with the rules.
4. He will act quietly or secretly, seeking the counsel of few, putting little into writing and avoiding public forums.

V. A PRACTICAL MERGER

Inevitably, the public administrator is concerned, and should be concerned, with both deontological and teleological reasoning. Thompson (1992:25) tells us: "Because other issues are more important than ethics, ethics is more important than any issue." This enigmatic statement needs clarification. Thompson (1992:25) continues:

> Ethics is not a primary goal of government in the way that, say, national defense, economic prosperity, or public welfare are. These and other public policy goals are intrinsic to government: they are part of the reason that government is established and maintained. Ethics is mainly instrumental to government: its main purpose is to contribute to the other, intrinsic goals of government.

Although policy goals (outcomes) are paramount, ethical rules of conduct provide the preconditions for the making of good public policy. For this reason they are indispensable to good policymaking because they increase the likelihood that officials will make decisions on the merits of issues rather than on the basis of personal gain or political advantage, and help to create and maintain citizen confidence in government.

The importance of this merger of deontological and teleological reasoning becomes clear when the nature of "the good result" is further explored. Teleological ethics takes in a wide range of human values. Desired results with a nonmoral content include personal power, organizational power, pleasure, knowledge, virtue, love, freedom, and beauty. A consequence is defined as a positive one whether the decision is nobly or selfishly approached, organizationally or personally defined, or rationally or irrationally reasoned. There are also desired results with a decidedly moral content of a kind that affects the rules for how government should function, and thus of special interest to public administrators as means as well as ends. These results are: achieving public policy goals, reaching agreement, agency survival, and a participative society.

A. Policy Goal Achievement

The form of consequence most frequently claimed is the achievement of policy objectives that are well defined by law or political leadership. Those actions or rules that can achieve "the will of the people" must be chosen; those that work against that will must be opposed or bypassed. This type of reasoning involves a clearly instrumental view of rules and principles, enshrining rationality and efficiency as the prime criteria. Rationalists dislike process rules that distract administrative actors from achieving goals or make reaching those goals more difficult or expensive.

B. Agreement

In politics, a consensus for action among major stakeholders is in itself a positive consequence, as well as a means to the attainment of a policy result. The logical consequences of this truth is that agreement using means not compatible with the rules may be attempted to be justified on the basis that it makes reaching the policy result more likely (for example, buying off an opponent). Utilitarianism to a practical public administrator means that the emphasis must be upon a result that will maximize the interests of a collectivity of major stakeholders and a process that will make that result more likely. By promoting an interactive process of stakeholder interaction, most especially negotiation, a utilitarian administrator seeks to forge a broad, lasting agreement.

C. Organizational Survival

A less openly claimed but commonly sought consequence of administrative decision-making practices is survival. This ethical posture is well served by couching survival motives in terms of the need for stability, seen as necessary for the operation of government processes and the ultimate achievement of policy goals. Machiavelli (Skinner and Price, 1988) stated that the essential goal of the government official, be he prince or advisor, is the achievement and maintenance of power. Almost any action, be it deceit, brutality, or departure from rules may be justified on the grounds that it is necessary to maintain stability in a social order that would otherwise be chaotic and dangerous. No reasonable chance exists for obtaining policy goals unless those in power can feel secure in the continuance of their influence.

D. Participatory Process

In one sense, participation is a means, a principle, and an accepted a priori rule having no direct relationship to consequences. In another sense, achieving such a process is a major outcome sought in a tolerant and democratic political system—thus it may be defined as a desirable consequence. In this sense the distinctions between deontological and teleological reasoning becomes blurred. It would appear to be incumbent upon those who espouse teleological ethics to specify the results they desire and give opportunity to others to debate, oppose, or modify the same.

VI. IMPLICATIONS OF THE ASCENDANCE OF TELEOLOGICAL ETHICS

If I am correct in my conclusion that teleological reasoning now prevails in public administration, certain things are likely to follow. First, there occurs an elevation of techniques that foster our abilities to predict, or at least to appear to predict, consequences of administrative and policy decisions. Further, administrators will attempt to spell out these consequences in terms of the major stakeholders and participants in policy and administrative processes. Policy analysis has developed as a "science" precisely because it promises this type of rational analysis of consequences as a basis for decision-making. Advances have been made, however, in taking into greater account such first principles as justice and freedom as decision criteria.

A second possible implication is that public organizations will face hard choices between promoting experimentation and favoring system stability. These are competing consequences that trigger different sets of teleological values. Gabris (1991) argued that the price of putting positional power, status, and stability of institutional arrangements first is to lower the plane of governmental excellence. Osborne and Gaebler (1992) would agree. The danger is that organizational cults and special environments will produce climates that promote a naked survival/power ethic. If Gabris' fear is realized and a Machiavellian style of teleological ethics is legitimized, certain results can be expected. Organizational mediocrity will dominate and people will be encouraged to find comfortable niches in the system. Any attempt to radically change will threaten personal survival and will be resisted. It would be much more prudent to go along and to play the game. Practices such as whistle-blowing will be treated harshly. System stability, not excellence, could emerge as the central value.

VII. CONCLUSION: AN ARGUMENT FOR ETHICAL INCLUSIVENESS

Certainly, the use of teleologic ethics unrestrained by principles or rules carries dangers for public administrators. Thompson (1992) is persuasive that certain deontological principles relative to fairness and democratic process (public access and openness, legality and due process, and so forth) must be incorporated. The fact that these "process values" may also be seen as ends or consequences suggests that a theory of ethics truly concerned with both consequences and first principles is both possible and necessary. It makes perfect sense for public administrators who must work within the framework of law and who are also charged with reaching effective and efficient results to balance utility, rights, justice, and self-interest.

A generation ago, Emmette Redford (1969) told us that "democratic morality" necessarily includes the condition that administrators respect the opinions and concerns of others. Giving people what we think they should have denies them respect. Satisfying citizens is an important step toward effective goal achievement. A long step toward ensuring responsiveness to citizens is to involve them in significant discourse and to include them in proceedings from which decisions emerge that are likely to affect them (Thibaut and Walker, 1978). But democratic morality also requires that we make every attempt to deliver the goods the lawmakers have promised.

NOTES

1. "Thus, an act is right if and only if it or the rule under which it falls produces, will probably produce, or is intended to produce at least as great a balance of good over evil as any available alternative; an act is wrong if and only if it does not do so" (Frankena, 1963:13).
2. Is this not a "moral good"? Is maximization of individual preferences sought because it actually improves the lives of people in the community, or because it is simply assumed that enlargement of free choice itself improves the lives of people? Is more free choice an end or a means?
3. ACLU membership fell from 270,000 in 1976 to 200,000 in June, 1978.
4. Why, asked William Kunstler, a leading legal defender of the dispossessed, should a liberal organization defend the rights of would-be tyrants, when right-wing extremists crush free speech when they assume power (*The New Republic*, 1978)?

REFERENCES

Appleby, P.H. (1949). *Policy and Administration*. University, AL: University of Alabama Press.
Buchanan, J.M. and Tullock, G. (1967). *The Calculus of Consent: Logical Foundations of Constitutional Democracy*. Ann Arbor: The University of Michigan Press.
Clark, R.W. (1986). *Introduction to Moral Reasoning*. St. Paul, MN: West Publishing.
Etzioni, A. (1996). *The New Golden Rule*. New York: Basic Books.
Frankena, W.K. (1963). *Ethics*. Englewood Cliffs, NJ: Prentice-Hall.
Gabris, G.T. (1991). Beyond conventional management practices: shifting organizational values. In: *Ethical Frontiers in Public Management: Seeking New Strategies for Resolving Ethical Dilemmas* (J.S. Bowman, ed.). San Francisco: Jossey-Bass, pp. 205–224.
Harmon, M.M. and Mayer, R.T. (1986). *Organization Theory for Public Administration*. Boston: Little, Brown, Ch. 9.

Luke, J.S. (1991). New leadership requirements for public administrators: from managerial to policy ethics. In: *Ethical Frontiers in Public Management* (J.S. Bowman, ed.). San Francisco: Jossey-Bass, pp. 158–182.

Machiavelli, N. (1950). *The Prince and the Discourses*. New York: Random House.

March, J.G. (1992). The war is over, the victors have lost. *Journal of Public Administration Research and Theory*, 3: 225.

Mazmanian, D.A. and Sabatier, P.A. (1983). *Implementation and Public Policy*. Glenview, IL: Scott, Foresman.

Osborne, D. and Gaebler, T. (1992). *Reinventing Government: How the Entrepreneurial Spirit is Transforming the Public Sector*. Reading, MA: Addison-Wesley.

Ostrom, V. (1974). *The Intellectual Crisis in American Public Administration* (revised ed.). University, AL: University of Alabama Press.

Pops, G. (1997). Seeking environmental equity and justice. *Korean Review of Public Administration*, 2:69–96.

Redford, E.S. (1969). *Democracy in the Administration State*. New York: Oxford University Press.

Rosen, B. (1978). *Strategies of Ethics*. Boston: Houghton Mifflin.

Shapiro, M. (1988). *Who Guards the Guardians? Judicial Control of Administration*. Athens, GA: The University of Georgia Press.

Skinner, Q. and Price, R. (1988). *Machiavelli: The Prince*. Cambridge, England: Cambridge University Press.

The New Republic. (1978). Springtime for Skokie, April 22, pp. 5–8.

Thibaut, J. and Walker, L. (1978). *A theory of procedure. California Law Review*, 66:541.

Thompson, J.D. (1967). *Organizations in Action*. New York: McGraw-Hill.

Thompson, D.F. (1992). Paradoxes of government ethics. *Public Administration Review*, 52:254–263.

Time. (1978). The high cost of free speech, June 26, p. 63.

10

A Dream of What We Could Be
The Founding Values, the Oath, and Homo virtutis americanus

David K. Hart
Brigham Young University, Provo, Utah

> Thus, the hurry of spirits, that ever attends the eager pursuit of fortune and a passion for splendid enjoyment, leads to forgetfulness; and thus the inhabitants of America cease to look back with due gratitude and respect on the fortitude and virtue of their ancestors, who, through difficulties almost insurmountable, planted them in a happy soil.
>
> Mercy Otis Warren (1805)

> Nothing then is unchangeable but the inherent and unalienable rights of man.
>
> Thomas Jefferson (1984)

I. INTRODUCTION

At the outset of his massive *A History of the American People*, the British historian, Paul Johnson (1997), assessed the moral worth to humankind of the 400 years of America. His book, which is neither a diatribe nor paean of praise, begins with the important and controversial assertion that:

> The *creation* of the United States of America is the greatest of all human adventures. No other national story holds such tremendous lessons, for the American people themselves and for the rest of mankind. (Johnson, 1997:3, emphasis added)

His claim stems, I believe, from two fundamental assumptions. First, he apparently believes in the moral universality of the founding values, articulated as natural rights, which belong to all individuals, in all times and in all cultures. Second, he applauds the continuous efforts of the American people—uneven as their efforts may sometimes seem to be—to incorporate these values into the organizations, processes, and relationships of everyday life. It is those values and that quest—more than the physical and even the social environments—that has given such a unique cast to American history. More specifically, it has been the constant attempt to intentionally embody those fundamental values into all aspects of American national life which makes American history so useful to democrats everywhere and everytime. It contains lessons, both positive and negative, for all who believe that every individual *qua* individual possesses specific and transcendent "inalienable'' rights which, when actualized, are the necessary prerequisite for achieving a fully human life.

A caveat. I am fully aware of how controversial these assertions are and, therefore, I ask the reader to bear with me for the sake of argument. The point of view expressed herein is my interpretation of the traditional point of view—which is under heavy attack recently. Also, it is certainly a point of view that is no longer academically fashionable. However, fashion is irrelevant. The real question is: do the founding values represent moral universals? I believe they do and, thus, this chapter is written *a priori*: that the principles undergirding the founding values are timeless, universal and belong to all individuals, regardless of time or cultures. Most of the founders (of the United States) believed that of them and believed, further, that they would (and should) provide the continuing foundation for American government, for its public service, and, further, as the moral center for living a fully human life.[1] While written for a somewhat different argument, the historian, Linda Kerber—in *Women of the Republic: Intellect and Ideology in Revolutionary America*—stated that expectation extremely well:

> The political revolution had been an act of faith. Believing as they did that republics rested on the virtue of their citizens, Revolutionary leaders had to believe not only that Americans of their own generation displayed that virtue, but that Americans of subsequent generations would continue to display the moral character that a republic required. (Kerber, 1986:199)

To argue thus is not to claim that America, as a nation, or that Americans, as a people, are superior to other nations or other peoples—this is not an exercise in chauvinism. It is obvious that, in some areas, we have failed to fully actualize the ideal of a ''republic of virtue,'' but those failures do not invalidate the ideal. It is fair, I believe, to hold that throughout our history we have morally succeeded more often than we have failed. But because the ideal of the republic rests upon such excellent moral principles, it makes our failures all the more glaring and inexcusable.

Having stated that caveat, it is now necessary to state the purpose of this chapter. In this chapter, it is argued, first, that the most fundamental commitment, the one that legitimizes all that follows, for a career in the American public service—a career distinguished by moral integrity—is taking the *oath*, whether spoken or implied, of fidelity to the Constitution and, by extension, to the founding values. Second, that oath binds the public servants to the pure ideal of the founders: the creation and maintenance of a republic of virtue, a republic legitimized by the extensiveness and intensiveness of the virtue of all individual citizens. Third, they believed that because they had the good fortune to live in America, unburdened by the heavy hand of European aristocratic tradition, they had all that was necessary for the creation of such a republic of virtue. Because of that good fortune, they inherited the moral obligation to become exemplars of a republic of virtue. They had, in other words, the obligation to be the ''city on a hill'' for democrats everywhere. Finally, in order to make all of this work, each individual had the moral obligation to make themselves into men and women of good character. But, because of the enormously rich potentials—both material and spiritual—of this land, it would have to be a uniquely American character, the creation of *homo virtutis Americanus*.

II. THE PUBLIC SERVICE AND THE OATH

We begin with the oath of office—spoken or implied[2]—to the Constitution and, therefore, to the founding values. The argument that the oath of allegiance to the Constitution also includes a commitment of fidelity to the founding values is familiar, but it was stated particularly well by John Rohr. In place of "the founding values" he presented his conception of "the regime values," but the intention is similar. "Because the Constitution of the United States is the preeminent symbol of our political values, an oath to uphold the Constitution is a commitment to uphold the values of the regime created by that instrument. *Thus the oath of office provides for bureaucrats the basis of a moral community that our pluralism would otherwise prevent*" (Rohr, 1989: 70, emphasis added). In a very important sense, the oath of office is not only the foundation for one's bureaucratic career, but also a reward for that public service.

There are many reasons for asserting that the oath of office was (and is) the primary moral obligation of the public service, the foundation of all that is to occur in the career of the American bureaucrat. Historically, the "founding generation"—along with so many of the men and women of the Enlightenment—placed great reliance upon the political and social function of the covenant of an oath, as Gordon Wood has noted:

> The patriots were indeed trying to destroy the ligaments of the older society and to reknit people together in new ways. All revolutionaries in the eighteenth century were fascinated with oath-taking and the need to find some republican substitute for the personal fealty and loyalty that subordinates felt toward their superiors in a monarchical society. Whig committees sought . . . to make the oaths "a touchstone of public virtue. . . ." This oath-taking was so solemn and ceremonious because the revolutionaries knew that something important was happening. They were creating new social bonds by making individuals swear a "new attachment to the body of the people" . . . . (Wood, 1991: 214–215)

To them, an oath was not only important because it set the moral foundation for all that was to follow in a career in the public service, but also because it was one of the highest moral expressions congruent with our mutual human nature.

Unfortunately, our discipline has neglected—in research, in research agenda, and in practice—the study (and the implementation) of the moral significance of the oath, a situation that must be rapidly rectified. However, it is not the purpose of this chapter to write a disquisition about the nature of oaths (although it is a project that will be undertaken soon). Suffice it to say, I accept the premise that the oath is of critical importance not only for the public service but for our collective sense of *civitas*. But, since the concern here is for public administration, it will be emphasized that the oath commits public servants to specific and essential moral obligations throughout their careers.

Briefly, *Black's Law Dictionary* defines an oath as "Any form of attestation by which a person signifies that he is *bound in conscience* to perform an act faithfully and truthfully. . . . An oath [of allegiance is when] a person promises and binds himself to bear true allegiance to a particular sovereign or government" (Black, 1979: 966, 967, emphasis added). Correctly understood, then, swearing an oath is one of the most fundamental moral commitments a man or a woman can make ("bound in conscience"), and the act of so swearing obligates the individual to conform to a higher moral standard than is required of ordinary citizens.

Further, one's essential moral integrity requires that there can be *no* evasion of one's covenant to "support and defend" the Constitution, and the founding values, nor can the public servant be slothful in meeting his or her moral obligation to make of oneself a man or a woman of good character. For such individuals, the oath grounds their moral beliefs in the founding values, which gives moral meaning, purpose, legitimacy, and significance to their civic thoughts and actions. To violate one's oath, therefore, is unthinkable since it is destructive to his or her proper functions as public servant and damaging, perhaps irreparably, to one's moral integrity, running the risk of the alienation of meaninglessness (Schacht, 1970: 161–204). In the familiar passage from *A Man for All Seasons*, the playwright, Robert Bolt, has Sir Thomas More explaining to his daughter why he cannot violate his oath: "When a man takes an oath, Meg, he's holding his own self in his own hands. Like water. . . . And if he opens his fingers *then*—he needn't hope to find himself again. Some men are capable of this, but I'd be loathe to think your father one of them" (Bolt, 1962: 140; see also Martz, 1990). Thus, an oath is not only a pledge of fealty to a government, but also an attestation of one's moral trustworthiness, both to self and to others, since trustworthiness is essential to both good government and to the fully human life. In this sense, it can be rightfully argued that the oath transcends, in moral importance, the law itself.

Finally, both as a people and as a discipline, we have become too cavalier about the moral obligations taken on swearing fidelity through the oath. At the worst, too many bureaucrats-to-be look upon the oath as just another routine triviality of bureaucratic red tape. Somewhat better, and probably more prevalent, is the notion that a "swearing an oath" is synonymous with "making a promise." It is anything but that, as Rohr makes clear: "The difference between [an oath and a promise] is that oaths are reserved for human activities of the highest order: marriage, citizenship, the healing arts, the pursuit of justice, divine worship, and so forth. Promises can be serious or somewhat trivial" (Rohr, 1986: 190).

The oath is, in fact, *the* moral promise the public servant makes to herself, to her colleagues, and to the citizens of the republic. The founders intended the oath to be a sacred covenant that would never be entered into thoughtlessly or evasively. As argued previously (Wright and Hart, 1996; Hart and Wright, 1998), the first duty of public servants is to be the guardians and guarantors of the founding values to the citizens of the republic. Essential to that obligation is the necessity of both understanding and believing in those founding values, as they constitute the moral *a priority* of this nation.

III. ORIGINALISM VS. CULTURALISM: BATTLE OF *A PRIORITIES*

This leads to an urgent and singular dilemma facing public administration today. Usually the quandaries confronting our discipline are of a familiar variety: from controversies over specific policies or the extent of "legitimate" governmental intervention into the private sector, on to the more mundane issues of funding or matters concerning internal departmental organization and management. What that range of problems share in common is that they ultimately originate from, and are legitimatized and resolved by, reference to the moral principles of the founding values, which public bureaucrats are oath-bound to follow. Although it is not much discussed, inherent in our pledge of fidelty to those founding values is the issue of whether those "self-evident" and "unalienable" values have a universal moral validity, transcending time and culture, or whether they are simply culturally determined, to be changed at our whim, or our convenience. The presumption is that they are moral universals and this is borne out by the great civil rights crusades we have witnessed, from women's suffrage to the citizenship rights of ethic minorities. Their demands were always couched in the language of moral universality.

The point is that the *a priori* status of the founding values has not been significantly challenged in our past, with the exception of the antebellum years before the Civil War. Issues are always with us, but what faces us now is a rare and extremely important problem: the rise of an alternative moral *a priority* to the founding values. As recently as, say, twenty years ago, it was safe to assume there was a consensus about both the content and the importance of the founding values for society, the economic system, the political system, and the public service in the United States, at all levels. Further, it was also assumed that most individuals headed for the public service would have been at least moderately schooled in the history, ideas, and ideals of the Constitution. Finally, it was also assumed, at least for some, that they had chosen a career in the public service in order to serve the ideals of the Founders and the Constitution. Unfortunately, that is no longer a warranted assumption. We are now confronted with a battle of the *a priorities*.

Public administration is balkanized about the validity and moral status of the founding values. A new contender to the status of the moral *a priority* of our nation is on the scene and captured large numbers of academicians, many public servants, and significant chunks of the media—a contender flying the flag of "post-modernism," or some variant on the term. To further complicate matters, most of the young people preparing for careers in the public service are quite uninformed about both the history of the Constitution and the moral content of the Founding values. Thus, many public administration scholars and practitioners—from the ahistorical young to their disillusioned elders—proceed into an increasingly complex future ill-equipped to deal with this battle of the *a priorities*.

To repeat, then, the most urgent civic task facing public administration—scholars and practitioners alike—concerns the moral status of the founding values: specifically, whether those values are moral universals or just another set of culturally determined propositions which should be accorded no special status, and can be laid aside for the *a priority* of post-modernism.

A. Two Confederations: The Culturalists and the Originalists

The confrontation today is between two loose confederations which, for the sake of this argument, will be termed the "Culturalists" and the "Originalists." Further, on using either term, each should be read as "American culturalists" and "American Originalists."

On the one hand, the Culturalists cluster loosely around the moral *a priority* of multiculturalism, or post-modernism, or political correctness, or some other allied movement. While Culturalism is plagued by internecine warfare, they do share, roughly, the same moral *a priority*: although ostensibly committed to moral and cultural relativism, in fact their arguments have hardened into a single, fairly monolithic ideology based upon the assumption of the social construction of reality.

On the other hand, the Originalists cohere loosely around the traditional belief that the founding values represent moral universals that embody those natural rights belonging to all human beings, rights transcending both time and cultures. Thus, reality should be constructed from that moral universal. For most of our history, the guiding a priority for the public service has been some variation of Originalism, and that paradigm is still dominant. However, Culturalism has made some deep incursions.

The literature of this debate is voluminous and only an abbreviated argument can be presented here. A few comments are necessary since, I believe, it is the intention, explicit or implicit, of the Culturalists to displace Originalism as the defining and legitimizing *a priority* of American government, economics, and society.

1. Culturalism

Culturalism is derived originally from the work of a few mid-20th century European intellectuals. Most prominent is the French *quintette* of Claude Levi-Strauss, Roland Barthes,

Michel Foucault, Jacques Lacan, and Jacques Derrida (Sturrock, 1979). Perhaps the most well-known overviews of Culturalism are Frederic Jameson's *Postmodernism, or, The Cultural Logic of Late Capitalism* (1991), and Richard Rorty's *Achieving Our Country: Leftist Thought in Twentieth-Century America* (1998). To that list, however, must be added the works of Herbert Marcuse (1889–1979), the German philosopher, Martin Heidegger (1889–1976), and Karl Marx.

Obviously, the term "Culturalism" does not adequately reflect the variety of positions (and oppositions) within the movement. However, they also share two further propositions, propositions that are antithetical to the founding values: first, the belief that the contingent morality stemming from each unique culture (a *volksgeist*) is morally superior to the presumed universality of the founding values, and, second, militant hatred of all things American.

The belief in the moral superiority of cultural, racial, and gender identities is built upon a belief in the reality of such volksgeists. This argument has recently been advanced and defended by the French philosopher, Alain Finkielkraut, in his book *The Defeat of the Mind* (1996). Briefly, the concept of the volksgeist is most frequently associated with the work of the German philosopher, J.G. Herder (1744–1803), in his opposition to the values of the Englishment. It refers to the presumed reality of a collective "spirit" (or "mind") of a people, which expresses itself in their unique values, languages, folklore, folk art, and folk music (Berlin, 1991: 359–435; see also Barnard, 1965). Finkielkraut (1996: 6, 9) writes: "Nothing had higher authority for Herder than the plurality of collective souls. All supranational values, whether legal, aesthetic, or moral, had lost their sovereignty. . . . He had universal values condemned in the court of diversity." The idea of a volksgeist was seized upon by many German intellectuals after the German defeat in the Napoleanic wars. They consoled themselves by venerating all things purely German, which were, of course, embodied in a Germanic volksgeist. That version of the concept was intensely nationalistic, and Finkielkraut argues that it was employed by Heidegger—a doyen of Culturalism.

Thus, taken within the context of an underlying volksgeist, the recent controversies about such things as Ebonics, or the overriding importance of the preservation of the cultures of the designated minorities, the legal battles about cross-racial adoptions, or the demands for ideological purity among individual members of such minorities—along with many other things—are more understandable.

The point is that among Culturalists such folk identities are superior to any other means of identity, particularly any that rely upon presumed and objective moral universals. Specifically targeted are the moral universals of the founding values, tainted as they are with the ideas and beliefs of the Enlightenment.

But it goes further and it is just a short step to the Culturalists' vocal and militant hatred for all things American and, particularly, the founding values. As the political scientist, James Ceaser (1997:1), summarizes ". . . the literary critics, philosophers, and self-styled postmodern thinkers . . . have made the very name 'America' a symbol for that which is grotesque, obscene, monstrous, stultifying, stunted, leveling, deadening, deracinating, deforming, rootless, uncultured, and—always in quotation marks—'free.'" Their contempt for the founding values is caught in the comment of a political scientist, to the effect that "the ruling paradigm, which, since the inception of the United States, has said that genocide is good, racism is better, and exploitation of women and the poor is the best way to go" (Dent, 1999: 27–28).

To conclude, such beliefs virtually negate the moral commitments within the oath—

again, whether spoken or implied—that is to define and delimit the careers of American public servants. American Culturalism is, in the most fundamental way, the antithesis of American Originalism.

2. Originalism

The paradigm of the founding Values has provided the traditional moral foundation for American government since the inception of the republic. As a sidebar, it should be noted that the term Culturalism can be used without a national adjective, since it refers to a transnational human condition. On the other hand, the term Originalism requires the adjective "American" because the claim of universal moral validity for the founding values locks it into the American experience.

To return to the argument, the Originalists believe that—even with the obvious and tragic oversights—the founders essentially "got it right." For them, the founding values articulate specific universal (and, thus, unalienable) rights that belong to *all* individuals, regardless of cultures and time. They regard the Enlightenment sensibilities of the founders as sound, and are respectful of their endeavors, in spite of some failures to achieve the ideal. However, they often disagree, sometimes strenuously, among themselves about the moral status and correct interpretations of the founding values.

To illustrate, Daniel Walker Howe, in his excellent book, *Making the American Self: Jonathan Edwards to Abraham Lincoln* (1997), argues that the prominent debate about whether it was the intent of the founders to establish a "republican" or a "liberal" government is a distinction more one of our making then of theirs. He continues: "*To them, what was important was that their political ideas, republican and liberal alike, were true*. The pedigree of the principles, showing how and by whom their truth had first been perceived, was a secondary matter" (Howe, 1997: 10–11, emphasis added). The Originalists, for the most part I believe, would agree: the founders were searching for nothing less than the moral universals upon which a "republic of virtue" could be established.

Recently, it seems that even a hint of Originalism triggers a firestorm of outrage, often quite *ad hominem*, from the Culturalists. Even so, both sides generally agree that all political systems must rest upon "certain basic starting points—foundations—that will lend coherence and rigor to political theory and activity" (Seery, 1999: 460).

Therefore, the clash between the moral *a priorities* of Originalism (moral universals) and Culturalism (moral relativism) has become the most important issue facing contemporary public administration. This is not just another "ho-hum, blue sky," academic squabble, for the triumph of Culturalism would necessitate nothing less than the displacement of the traditional Originalist paradigm. Further, the Culturalists cannot be simply ignored, since their ideas have gained currency—in both content and methodology—in many academic disciplines, university administrations, a large number of governmental agencies, and a good segment of the media (Himmelfarb, 1999). In all probability, at some point in the reasonably near future, we will have to decide whether or not to exchange the Originalist *a priority* for the Culturalist *a priority*.

Whether one agrees or disagrees with the moral tenets of Culturalism, I argue that because its tenets reject, first, the existence of self-evident moral universals and, second, the worth of all things American, the oath still binds public servants to support and defend the Constitution and, by extension, the Founding values. That being the case, the substitution of the *a priority* of Culturalism for the *a priority* of Originalism would require nothing less than a new Constitution for the United States. Presently, we face a fundamental and morally incongruent disjunction so acute that it must produce extensive alienation, and even nihilism. The resolsution of the issue of the opposing *a priorities* is of the greatest importance.

This chapter is written, in aid of genuine civic discourse, from an Originalist point of view: that moral universals do exist, that the Founders were essentially correct in identifying and articulating them and, thus, the primary, oath-bound obligation—explicit or implicit—of every American public servant is the actualization of those Founding values in the laws, the organizations, and the lives of all citizens. While most Culturalists believe that the injustices of our national life begin with the Founding values, I argue that our moral failures have come about from ignoring those Founding values.

Finally, as I write I can almost hear the collective grinding of Culturist teeth. For that I am genuinely sorry, for it is not my intention to be confrontational—argumentative, yes, but confrontational, no. Productive discourse about the moral foundations of this nation requires civic discourse rather than ideological combat: civility will serve us better than *ad hominem* brass knuckles and a verbal cosh.

It is not the purpose of this chapter to discuss, in any depth, my interpretation of the substance of the founding values. That has been begun elsewhere (Wright and Hart, 1996; Hart and Wright, 1998) and will be continued in a forthcoming book about the public interest. The purpose here is to discuss two very important topics: the process by which the Founders "discovered"[3] the Founding values, and the moral obligations stemming from their ideal of a republic of virtue.

IV. THE FOUNDING GENERATION, THE FOUNDING DISCOURSE, AND A GOVERNMENT *FROM* THE PEOPLE

I must begin with another caveat: one writes an essay such as this with trepidation. While I have tried hard to be faithful to the intentions of the Founders, it is still me who chooses, reads, and interprets the historical records. They are seen through the lens of my moral beliefs, I weight the significance of various interpretations, and the historic personages encountered are evaluated in comparison with my heroes and villains. This is, of course, the problem faced by anyone who attempts to study and interpret the past. Therefore, one must periodically stop and question how faithful to the original intent is one's interpretation, and make course corrections when needed. The colonialist historian, Richard Bushman, deftly summarized the problems all of us face at the outset of his excellent book about the development of political thinking and commitment in colonial Massachusetts, from 1691 to the Revolution. "Dealing with both religion and politics, I found myself working at a level of generality far removed from actual events and people. The connections were so abstract that probably no one in the eighteenth century comprehended them, and I was in danger of creating a mythical colonial mind with no real existence" (Bushman, 1992: 3). That concern led Bushman to consider and reconsider his focus, with stellar results. Those problems—innumerable, endemic, and inherent—will always be there, and the best one can do is to always try for objectivity. But when writing about values, unless one is willing to settle for "contingency ethics," in the end he or she must take a stand.

Three fundamental problems are always perplexing. First, one must constantly try to understand the moral, political, economic, and social context of the Founding generation and, at the same time, avoid the sin of imposing upon them our own ideological passions and sensibilities, in order to condemn them for their proleptic failures. Second, the problem of context is further complicated by our ever-changing language. As one tries to comprehend their ideas and intentions, one constantly encounters key words from that age (such as "enthusiasm") that have quite different meanings today. Such words must, as accurately as possible, be translated into terms comprehensible to this generation. This leads to the third problem: in attempting to make the ideas and beliefs of the Founders relevant to our time, it is often necessary to use modern words that hadn't even been invented at the time (such as "actualization"). As a result, Samuel Johnson's *A Dictionary of the English Language* (1755) has received quite a beating, more so than my old partner *The Oxford English Dictionary.*

To return to the argument, one of the most egregious misinterpretations of the founding of the republic is that it was an elitist manipulation for the self-benefit of those elites—but that assertion oversimplifies and distorts what happened during those extraordinary years. The founding of the American republic originated within an unprecedented, colonies-wide public discourse—*a Founding discourse*—that took place roughly between 1750 and 1805. But it was not, in any conventional sense of the word, an elitist discourse, for it involved significant numbers of the colonial population. That discourse formed the broad, popular base upon which the republic was founded. For that reason, I believe it is more accurate to define the *Founders as the Founding generation*—and from hereon, the two terms will be used synonymously.

A. The Founding Generation

The term "the Founders" has long been the most popular identification for the central characters in the creation of the American nation. Since the earliest days of the republic, however, there have been some who have argued that term "the Founders" referred to a coterie of men of wealth and property, and that "the Founding" was little more than an elitist arrogation of power to consolidate, advance, and protect the status of their socioeconomic class.

In the final quarter of the 20th century, that elitist argument has been transmogrified into the hyper-elitism of the ideology of Culturalism. While other factions still argue for some variation of elitism, Culturalism has taken that argument much further than the relatively simple conceptions of the past. Now it is argued that the Founding was engineered by a powerful economic and patriarchal cabal of white males of Northern European extraction, men with imperious ambitions and the obsession to concretize their hegemony of power, status, and wealth, regardless of the cost to others. Their plans also included the repression of racial and ethnic minorities, women, and people who belonged to strange religions. In short, they argue that the Founders were an unsavory lot.

That is an unwarranted assumption. Granted, the Founders may not have been Madison's angels, but they were far from villains. For the most part, they were good and accomplished men who wanted to bring into being a republic of virtue, wherein the ultimate authority would be the people themselves. There is not space to write, to any extent, about the arguments that the source of the supreme authority lay with the people, and nowhere else. Symbolic of those arguments is the following comment from James Madison, in the record of the Constitutional convention, August 31, 1787, where he is recorded as stating emphatically that "The people were in fact, *the fountain of all power*, and by resorting to them, all difficulties were got over" (Farrand, 1966: Vol. II, p. 476, emphasis added).

Thus, if the people were the "fountain of all power," those who could change constitutions, then it stands to reason that they did, indeed, participate in the Founding discourse, and that their ideas were treated with the same respect as accorded to the more famous.

To make the question more specific, who were the Founders as individuals and what did they do to earn that appellation? The traditional qualification for being awarded the status of a Founder was significant *practical* participation in the drafting of the enabling documents, their ratification, and, finally, the establishment of the new government. In other words, the Founders were the practical men of affairs who shepherded the new nation into being. That being the case, their numbers were not large and it should be possible to draw up a complete duty roster of their names, using that practitioner criterion.

But here we encounter problems. When reasonably well-educated individuals are asked to name the Founders, most of them are hard-pressed to identify more than, say, a half-dozen. Usually the nod is given to Washington, Jefferson, John Adams, Madison, Franklin, and Hamilton. But what about George Wythe, Benjamin Rush, James Wilson, John Dickinson, and George Mason, to name but a few others? By the criterion of practical creation, they certainly qualify as "Founders."

But, it is argued, the practitioner criterion ignores an overriding fact about the Founding discourse. The more I read about those years, the more convinced I become that the republic was born in the hearts and minds of the people, the men and women of the colonies. Therefore, it is argued that *since the new republic was the product of that discourse, it is more accurate to identify the Founders as those who participated in that Founding discourse.* From this point on, the "Founders" will be used as synonymous with those who participated in the Founding discourse. Thus, the names of so many of the formerly excluded—especially the names of some women (such as Mercy Otis Warren) and some minority individuals—are given their rightful status as Founders of the American Republic.

As that discourse surged and rolled through the colonies—and later through the nation—men and women from all segments of life were caught up by the intelligence of it all: from self-styled Virginia aristocrats, impecunious Massachusetts ministers, New York merchants, New England patriarchs, publishers of newspapers, and representatives from the farms and the mills and Jefferson's "sturdy yeomanry." Of course, most of the participants simply read the pamphlets and editorials, occasionally penned one or two, listened to the speeches and the sermons, and then debated the ideas with their peers in places of public gathering. As Bailyn wrote: "This nationwide debate, *in which every community and every politically conscious person participated*, was a sequel to everything that had come before and it was preface to what was to follow" (Bailyn, 1992: viii, emphasis added).

That makes the American Founding much more than the machinations of an elite: it can be fairly argued that the events of the American Founding, in the broadest sense, were the product of the people. A great many men and women in the colonies were caught up in that unique discourse about the moral foundations, the appropriate ends, and the best structures for their ideal of government. And so to the list of the Founders must be added names like that of the physician, John Perkins, of the pastor, John Tucker, as well as David Rice, Nathanael Emmons, and Zephaniah Swift Moore, among many, many others. As the ideas that led to "the Founding" were sorted out in that discourse, they set the foundations and guidelines for their ideal society and its government—an ideal that could be achieved in practice. To overstate a bit, the ideal was of the people themselves.

B. The Search for Moral Universals

It is the usual practice, of those who write about the ideas of the Foundling Fathers, to focus upon one or another famous political philosopher, and attribute to him the greatest influence upon the Founders. But they were not in search of philosophic antecedents, as Bailyn made clear:

> But the spokesmen of the Revolution—the pamphleteers, essayists, and miscellaneous commentators—were not philosophers and they did not form a *detached intelligensia*. They were active politicians, merchants, lawyers, plantation owners, and preachers, and they were not attempting to align their thought with that of major figures in the history of political philosophy *whom modern scholars declare to have been seminal*. (Bailyn, 1992: vi, emphasis added)

Nonetheless, academicians remained undeterred, and so we find books—often excellent books—about the pre-eminence of Locke or Montesquieu or Burlamaqui or the Scots, or whomever. Undeniably, many of the Foundners were profoundly influenced by one or two philosophers (one of the most cited philosophers, Lord Kames, has unfortunately attracted little attention). But what seems to have had the most profound influence upon the Founders was the Founding discourse itself, wherein they hammered out and refined their ideas.

What, then, were they after? In his excellent book, Daniel Walker Howe caught their ambition. Referring to our contemporary debate as to whether the Founding discourse favored "liberalism" or "republicanism," he concluded that the "distinction between the two philosophies is more one of our making than of theirs. To them, *what was important was that their political ideas, republican and liberal alike, were true"* (Howe, 1997: 10, emphasis added). This is the most important part of the Founding discourse: the search for those transcultural, transtemporal self-evident rights. Regardless of how much modern scholars, and especially the Culturalists, loathe the Founding values, or how vehemently they dismiss the possibility of the existence of objective moral universals, that was what the Founders were after. It was upon such a moral foundation that they proposed to build a new nation.

What is more, when the new republic came into being, they believed they had, indeed, founded it upon moral universals. Therefore, if we wish to discover the *intent* of the Founders, we cannot ignore their quest to find such universals and, as they did, we must give fair hearing to the arguments for such moral universals.

To conclude, the actual "Founding" emerged from, and was shaped by, the conscious attempt of a large number of the people—obviously, the exact numbers cannot be calculated, but they were sufficient to invalidate the charge that the Founders were an "elite"—to redefine themselves as the avatars of a new republic, of a new democratic reality.

C. "The Great Enemy of All Sane Idealism Is the Notion that the Ideal Belongs to the Future."

The Founding generation engaged in a discourse that aimed at presenting the ideal form of government for a people who would be free. But, unlike so many idealists, they hoped to live in the ideal new republic they envisioned. The section heading is a quotation from the British absolute idealist, Bernard Bosanquet, and is from his Gifford Lectures of 1911

(Bosanquet, 1912: 136). While the passage is part of his very complex social philosophy, nonetheless, it expresses what the Founders had in mind. The ideal was not something to be constantly deferred to the future, for the ideal belongs to *now*. The Founders believed that, properly understood, that the achievement of an ideal republic, a republic of virtue, was attainable.

Having—miraculously, it seemed—triumphed in their revolution over Great Britain (Bobrick, 1997; Draper, 1996), and having survived the confusions of the mid-1780s and the Articles of Confederation, fortune seemed to be on the side of the Americans. That seemed even clearer with the writing and adoption of the Constitution, from which emerged—almost in a blaze of glory—the new republic. As Page Smith wrote, "Two thousand years of political theorizing and practical experience crystallized in Philadelphia in the summer of 1787 in the most brilliant sustained intellectual and oratorical achievement of history" (Smith, 1980: xvi). That "oratorical achievement," seen as a more dramatic and public version of the Founding discourse, revealed the civic mind of the people.

To illustrate, Thomas Jefferson's very familiar statement about his intentions as he wrote the Declaration of Independence is much more than a modest disclaimer. In a letter to Henry Lee, dated May 6, 1825, Jefferson reflected back on his state of mind at that time, about his desire "to place before mankind the common sense of the subject." He wrote: "Neither aiming at originality of principle or sentiment, nor yet copied from any particular and previous writing, it was intended to be *an expression of the American mind*, and to give to that expression the proper tone and spirit called for by the occasion" (Jefferson, 1984: 1501, emphasis added). His knowledge of "the American mind" was fairly come by. Jefferson went further than the books he constantly read, the endless discussions he was part of, the vast correspondence he carried on—he also went to the people to determine what they believed. Thus, before he left Virginia in the spring of 1776, to join the Congress meeting in Philadelphia, he "went to great pains to sound out local sentiment before he left home and became convinced that nine tenths of the people in the upper counties favored independence" (Malone, 1948: 217). He was not engaging in a pre-Gallup effort at survey research, but attempting to understand the civic mind of the American people. And, as nowhere else, that civic mind was revealed in the Founding discourse.

The Founders had no interest whatsoever in creating a vast metaphysical system of ethics that would explain the universe to God and man, with added instruction about how it should be run. The idealism of the Founders was of the here and now. Although not referring specifically to them, Adam Smith did describe their attitude. "The administration of the great system of the universe, however, the care of the universal happiness of all rational and sensible beings, is the business of God and not of man. . . . The most sublime speculation of the contemplative philosopher can scarce compensate the neglect of the smallest active duty" (Smith, 1790: 237).

At the very heart of that countrywide moral colloquy, was the most difficult and important question of all: what was the moral status of those Founding values? Were they simply transient values, given shape and dimension by the extant culture, which could be changed to suit whims, seasons, or circumstances? Or were they—as the Founders believed—moral universals which transcended all cultures and times, and established the rights of all individuals, in all places and at all times? Dale Wright and I have argued, in previous essays, that the Founders—for the most part—believed in the moral universality of the Founding values (Wright and Hart, 1996; Hart and Wright, 1998), and I will not revisit that argument here. Suffice it to say, and with some notable exceptions, the Founders wanted more than just a change of government: they wanted to create and live in their vision of the ideal society—a republic of virtue—that they had been working toward.

D. Securing the Founding Values in Trust for All of Humankind

As the colonies moved through time closer and closer to the fateful summer of 1776, the discourse began to reflect their belief that they were engaged in something unique, that they were building a "city on a hill," to which the world could look to as an example of democratic redemption. As John Adams wrote: "This liberties of *mankind* and the glory of human nature is in their keeping. . . . America was designed by Providence for the *theatre* on which man was to make his true figure, on which science, virtue, liberty, happiness, and glory were to exist in peace" (as quoted by Bailyn, 1992: 20, emphasis added).

By the end of the French and Indian War there was a growing awareness of this "American exceptionalism." It was not a belief in the inherent superiority of the American people over other peoples but, rather, a belief that, because of a good fortune that had placed them on this continent, at this time, that they were obligated—*in the name of all of humankind*—to create a new nation, built upon virtue, that would be exemplary to all peoples everywhere. In other words, the Founding of the republic extended the moral obligation of being exemplars to all the peoples of the world. They believed that "never was there a People whom it more immediately concerned to search into the Nature and Extent of their Rights and Privileges than does the people of America at this Day" (Wood, 1969, quoting Rossiter, p. 5). This was certainly John Adams' belief, as he observed in a note to Richard Henry Lee, in January of 1776:

> You and I, my dear friend, have been sent into life at a time when the greatest lawgivers of antiquity would have wished to live. How few of the human race have ever enjoyed an opportunity of making an election of government, more than of air, soil, or climate, for themselves or their children! When, before the present epocha, had three millions of people full power and a fair opportunity to form and establish the wisest and happiest government that human wisdom can contrive? I hope you will avail yourself and your country of that extensive learning and indefatigable industry which you possess, to assist her in the formation of the happiest governments and the best character of a great people. (Adams and Adams, 1946: 57)

In addition to the moral obligation to all of humankind that came from their good fortune, the Founders also recognized an additional dimension to that obligation. History was replete with individuals who had spoken in defense of the same values that were, ideally, to be at the center of American life—both public and private. It was the obligation to so secure those values that they would not be swept away at the turn of fortune's card. In other words, we had to be exemplars of the permanence of the Founding values.

On the whole, Americans generally viewed the Founding values as the *sine qua non* of social, economic, and political progress and stability for all nations that would be democratic. Futhermore, they were to be "working" values, referred to regularly for the guidance of the state, its public servants, and its citizens. As Gordon Wood has written, "they sought constantly to recur to those first principles that overlay the workings of politics, agreeing with young Alexander Hamilton that 'the best way of determining disputes, and of investigating truth is by ascending to elementary principles'" (Wood, 1969: 5).

Thus, they wanted to secure those *original* principles for the people and from the depredations of tyrants and tinkering politicians. While the revolutionary turmoil was still with them, Thomas Jefferson—in "Notes on the State of Virginia," 1784—warned of a major threat to their new nation. Since every ordinance established by their governments would be contested by someone, public doubts would arise about the moral worth of both the ordinances and the government that brought them into being. Therefore, "is it not better to remove that doubt by placing it on a bottom which none will dispute?" The "bottom" was, of course, provided by the Founding values. He articulated a future task for the Founders: "But . . . when peace shall be established, and leisure given us for intrenching within good forms, the rights for which we have bled, let no man be found indolent enough to decline a little more trouble *for placing them beyond the reach of question*" (Jefferson, 1984: 250–251, emphasis added).

The Founding values were to serve as the immutable foundation for the republic, and all institutions, processes, and rights were to depend upon them, throughout time. In other words, they were the "first principles" to which the people should always repair when political questions arose.

This attitude toward the first principles was popularly accepted until well after the Civil War. For instance, in a letter to Henry Pierce and others, written on April 6, 1859, Abraham Lincoln concluded with praise for the Founders, in general, and Jefferson, in particular, for placing the Founding values beyond the reach of self-interested triflers:

> All honor to Jefferson—to the man, who, in the concrete pressure of a struggle for national independence by a single people, had the coolness, forecast, and capacity to introduce into a merely revolutionary document, *an abstract truth, applicable to all men and all times*, and so to embalm it there, that to-day, and in all coming days, it shall be a rebuke and a stumbling-block to the very harbingers of re-appearing tyranny and oppression. (Lincoln, 1980: Vol. 2, p. 19, emphasis added)

The reason for the praise was the belief that those Founding values were the *sine qua non* of freedom and, as such, they transcended all cultures and all times.

V. *HOMO VIRTUTIS AMERICANUS* AND THE VISION OF A REPUBLIC OF VIRTUE

Some time ago a student, a Chinese citizen, stopped me after a class about the Founding values. She was an excellent student, but not at all familiar with American history. She asked for the title of the best book about the Founding values, certainly a reasonable request. Since I knew she would read the book, and since no title came immediately to mind, I said I would provide her with a title at the beginning of our next class period. I immediately began looking for a title; I then deployed my research assistant; I starting calling friends who were colonial historians; and then I panicked. I couldn't find such a book—a devastating blow to one's vanity. Two days later, I was more than a little embarrassed when I had to tell the young lady that I couldn't find a single book dealing exclusively with the Founding values and, to the best of my knowledge, I didn't think one had been written.

As I think about it, the lack of such a book is singularly unfortunate, for the obvious reasons. But a further problem struck me: the lack of a scholarly book about the Founding values displays not only an apparent lack of interest in the subject. Furthermore, it also masks the extremely important fact that, in spite of our worship of "practical experience" as the be all and end all of life, America, more than any other nation, came into being because of an unprecedented moral and political public discourse. That Founding discourse provided us with the foundation for our national value system, established our specific political forms, and shaped the course of our practical political experience—a fact seldom appreciated by the public. Yet there is, to the best of my knowledge, no single scholarly book dealing specifically with those values.

To summarize before getting to the main point: the people discovered, in the Founding discourse, a set of moral universals—based upon our common human nature—that they believed to be valid for all individuals, across cultures and through time. From that, it was understood that the purpose of human life was the attainment of a progressive happiness. History clearly demonstrated that living a fully human life was synonymous with living a life of virtue, and the Founding generation discussed virtue endlessly. Such virtue was not an abstraction, but the reality of everyday life, when virtue was actualized in good character. Finally, just as happiness was the end of human life, so also the end of government was the attainment of happiness for the polity—which could only be attained through a republic. John Adams, in his *Thoughts on Government*, written in January of 1776, summarized it as follows:

> We ought to consider what is the end of government, before we determine which is the best form. Upon this point all speculative politicians will agree that the happiness of society is the end of government, as all divines and moral philosophers will agree that the happiness of the individual is the end of man. . . . All sober inquirers after truth, ancient and modern, pagan and Christian, have declared that the happiness of man, as well as his dignity, consists in virtue. . . . If there is a form of government, then, whose principle and foundation is virtue, will not every sober man acknowledge it better calculated to promote the general happiness than any other form? . . . They [Sidney, Harrington, Locke, etc.] will convince any candid mind that there is no good government but what is republican. (Adams and Adams, 1946: 51, 52)

Reduced to its simplest statement, the general intent of the Founders was the creation and maintenance of a republic of virtue.

Furthermore, in order to attain that ideal, such virtue had to be the dominant normative feature of both public and private life. John Adams had that in mind when, on April 16, 1776, he wrote to Mercy Otis Warren:

> Public virtue cannot exist in a nation without private virtue, and public virtue is the only foundation of republics. There must be a positive passion for the public good, the public interest, honor, power, and glory, established in the minds of the people, or there can be no republican government, nor any real liberty; and this public passion must be superior to all private passions. (Adams and Adams, 1946: 57–58)

The Founders' ideal republic of virtue required the intentional and voluntary expression of individual good character as the norm in all human institutions and relationships (public or private). The Founding values, then, were never to be limited to the conduct of government: rather they were to serve as the moral foundation of all economic, educational, social, and religious institutions. This was a central theme in the great Founding discourse. As James Madison made clear in a speech to the Virginia Ratifying Convention on June 20, 1788:

But I go on this great republican principle, that the people will have the virtue and intelligence to select men of virtue and wisdom. Is there no virtue among us? If there be not, we are in a wretched situation. No theoretical checks—no form of government can render us secure. To suppose that any form of government will secure liberty or happiness without any virtue in the people is a chimerical idea. If there be sufficient virtue and intelligence in the community, it will be exercised in the selection of these men. *So that we do not depend on their virtue, or put confidence in our rulers, but in the people who are to choose them.* (Madison, 1999: 398, emphasis added)

This leads to the first conclusion of this chapter. It is commonplace for academicians to abbreviate the version of innate human nature in which they believe. It takes the form of a variation off of our identification as a species: *homo sapiens*. For many economists, the familiar term is *homo economicus*; for some sociologists, it is *homo laborans*, and so it goes. I believe that the argument can be made that the moral and political philosophy of many of the Founders was based upon their belief that nature (and "Nature's God") gave to humankind the innate need to be men and women of virtue—or *homo virtutis*. In other words, our natural home is found in virtue. To my knowledge, they never used that term or, at least, I have never run across it. But so many of their writings are based upon that *a priority*.

Thus, it is as *homo virtutis* that all human beings share a generic moral nature. But the Founders were men and women of considerable wisdom, and they deeply appreciated the human need for diversity, as well as for individuality. Many of them, or their ancestors, had come to the colonies in order to maintain their diversity. Therefore, in order to emphasize that fact, I believe that they would not have stopped with the species-identification of *homo virtutis*. I believe they would have taken one further step and written it as *homo virtutis Americanus*—the addition of our geographical and cultural identity in the last word of the term, a fact which is seldom appreciated by the public.

The concept of "national character" is no longer fashionable, but it still has relevance. The final word—*Americanus*—necessitates a consideration of our human diversity. An equivalent ending could be used for the Scots, or the French, or the Indians, or the Chinese, or whatever. The first two words, then, leave us with a cross-cultural, transtemporal moral nature. The third word incorporates the obvious and invaluable cultural pluralism—provided that pluralism is congruent with, and does not offend, our innate natural rights.

VI. CONCLUSION

The second conclusion of this chapter takes us back to the oath of office that every career public servant must take (explicitly) or abide by (implicitly). They voluntarily bind themselves to support and defend the Constitution—which includes also the Founding values that undergird the enabling documents. The Constitution is the symbol of the whole of the Founding values.

Obviously, public servants must be faithful to those first principles, but no laws, no checks and balances, no separations of power will completely protect the public. For that reason, the oath took on added meaning for the Founders, as "a touchstone of public virtue" (Wood, 1991: 215). Public servants must, upon their "sacred honor," support and defend the Founding values. The significance of the oath for the Founders can be seen in the works of Montesquieu, who wrote about the Romans. "Such was the influence of an oath among those people, that nothing bound them more strongly to the laws. They often did more for the observance of the oath than they would ever have performed for the thirst of glory or for the love of their country'' (Montesquieu, 1748: 118, emphasis added). So, to the list of signal characteristics of a republican government must be added the extreme importance the Founders attached to the oath—an importance that we should give it today.

As we move into the 21st Century, less attention is paid to the importance of the oath of office, which is unfortunate. My second conclusion for this chapter involves a serious reconsideration of the meaning of the oath. When taken in good faith, most public servants try to abide by its necessarily broad injunctions. But I recommend that we take a major step forward. I have argued that the Founders gave an enormous amount of attention to the necessity for each individual in the republic to intentionally, vigorously, and progressively to become a man or a woman of good character—which is a defining characteristic of a republic. Furthermore, they incorporated that imperative into their ideal, a republic of virtue.

I suggest that we not only take the oath very seriously, but that we extend our sworn obligations a step further. We should, intentionally and voluntarily, include within the oath the moral obligation to, first, consciously work on becoming men and women of good character, to the end of trying to actualize the ideal of the Founders to become a republic of virtue. It seems to me that such an attempt would not only be consistent with the intent of the Founders, but that it would also return to the public service the dignity and moral esteem it deserves.

NOTES

1. Obviously, the Founders failed in some areas: most notably with slavery and the failure to extend those rights to all individuals, regardless of race or gender. But they must be judged within the context of the late 18th century. They were trying to cut their way through the customs of centuries and what seemed *avant-garde* to them now seems to some to be moral nonfeasance. But we must take great care not to read history backwards, to condemn them for not thinking as their critics now think. Furthermore, many of those revolutionary writers condemned slavery in the strongest words possible and acted upon those beliefs. To illustrate, in 1794 an attorney, Theodore Dwight, denounced the cynical double-standard of the slave owners who, for public consumption, argued that they were the praiseworthy "caretakers" of a people who could not care for themselves but, in reality, these slave owners destroyed the lives of untold men, women, and children to advance their own economic interests:

   The labours of the poet, the historian, the legislator, and the divine, have often presented [slavery] in the strongest, and most odious colours. Still the evil exists; the Interest alone has been able to withstand the united force of imagination, of eloquence, of truth, and of religion. I say interest alone; for I will venture to assert, that when it shall cease to be for the interest if [sic] mankind, to torture their fellow creatures in this wicked commerce, not one solitary individual will be found trafficking in human flesh. (Dwight, 1794: 885)

   But the most succinct condemnation of slavery was made by Lincoln on April 6, 1859, when he wrote: "This is a world of compensations; and he who would *be* no slave, must consent to *have* no slave. Those who deny freedom to others, deserve it not for themselves; and, under a just God, can not long retain it" (Lincoln, 1980: Vol. 2, p. 19, emphasis in the original).

2. As is well-known, the great majority of public servants, at all levels of government, are not required to take an oath of office. It has been held, however, that such an oath is implied in accepting a position in the public service. Be that as it may, it is a situation that should be corrected and, just as all members of the military services swear an oath upon joining, all public servants should take the same oath that the highest level of civil servants take—whether elected or employed—as a condition for the public service.

3. My commitment to the possibility of ''discovering'' the universality of values dates back nearly 45 years. Beginning in my senior year in college I had a brief love affair with constitutional law. During Christmas vacation that year, I was trying to dazzle my father with my newly acquired legal ''sophistication.'' Dad was an attorney with the best legal mind I've ever encountered. He was also built along the lines of Mt. Rushmore, with a dignity to fit. We were very close. I started a discussion about the Supreme Court in the mid-1930s and, especially, about the swing vote of Mr. Justice Roberts. In trying to explain his behavior, I parroted a line I thought quite witty: ''Dad, at that level of law-making the most relevant factor is whether or not the justice had his morning cup of coffee!'' Instead of the expected chuckle, my Father became instantly serious and, gesturing with his right hand (the sure sign of an authoritative pronouncement) he said: ''Kirk, don't *ever* forget that at that level, law is *never* 'made,' it is always 'discovered!' '' For years thereafter—at home, on the trout streams of Idaho, or out hunting pheasant—my father and I discussed, in increasing depth, the meaning and implications of the word ''discover.'' I came by my commitment early and have studied it long.

REFERENCES

Adair, D. (1974). *Fame and the Founding Fathers: Essays by Douglass Adair* (T. Colburn, ed.). Institute of Early American Studies, Williamsburg, VA.

Adams, J. (1962). *Diary and Autobiography of John Adams* (L. H. Butterworth, ed.). Harvard University Press, Cambridge, MA, in four volumes.

Adams, J. and Adams, J.Q. (1946). *The Selected Writings of John and John Quincy Adams* (A. Koch and W. Peden, eds.). Knopf, New York, NY.

Bailyn, B. (ed., 1993). *The Debate on the Constitution*. The Library of America, New York, NY, in two volumes.

Bailyn, B. (1992). *The Ideological Origins of the American Revolution*, 2nd ed. Harvard University Press, Cambridge, MA.

Bailyn, B. (1990). *Faces of Revolution: Personalities and Themes in the Struggle for Independence*. Knopf, New York, NY.

Bailyn, B. (1968). *The Origins of American Politics*. Vintage Books, New York, NY.

Barnard, F.M. (1965). *Herder's Social and Political THought: From Enlightenment to Nationalism*. Clarendon Press, Cambridge, England.

Berlin, I. (1991). Herder and the Enlightenment. In *The Proper Study of Mankind* (H. Hardy and R. Hausheer, eds.). Farrar, Straus and Giroux, New York, NY.

Black, H.C. (1979). *Black's Law Dictionary*, 5th ed. West Publishing, St. Paul, MN.

Bobrick, B. (1997). *Angel in the Whirlwind: The Triumph of the American Revolution*. Simon & Schuster, New York, NY.

Bolt, R. (1962). *A Man for All Seasons*. Vintage Books, New York, NY.

Bosanquet, B. (1912). *The Principle of Individuality and Value*. Macmillan, London, England.

Bushman, R.L. (1992). *King and People in Provincial Massachusetts*. University of North Carolina Press, Chapel Hill, NC.

Bushman, R.L. (1967). *From Puritan to Yankee: Character and the Social Order in Connecticut, 1690–1765*. Harvard University Press, Cambridge, MA.

Ceaser, J.W. (1997). *Reconstructing America: The Symbol of America in Modern Thought*. Yale University Press, New Haven, CT.

Cohen, L. (1980). *The Revolutionary Histories: Contemporary Narratives of the American Revolution*. Cornell University Press, Ithaca, NY.

Colbourn, T. (1965). *The Lamp of Experience: Whig History and the Intellectual Origins of the American Revolution*. Liberty Press, Indianapolis, IN.

Cooper, T.L. (1998). *The Responsible Administrator: An Approach to Ethics for the Administrative Role*, 4th ed. Jossey-Bass, San Francisco, CA.

Dent, Jr., G.W. (1999). Political discrimination in the curriculum: A case study. *Academic Questions*, 12: 24–31.

Draper, T. (1996). *A Struggle for Power: The American Revolution*. Times Books, New York, NY.

Dwight, T. (1794). An oration, spoken before the Connecticut society, for the promotion of freedom and the relief of person unlawfully holden in bondage. In Hyneman, C.S. and Lutz, D.S. (eds.), *American Political Writing during the Foundation Era, 1760–1805*.

Farrand, M. (eds., 1966). *The Records of the Federal Convention of 1787*, Rev. ed. Yale University Press, New Haven, CT, in four volumes.

Finkielkraut, A. (1996). *The Defeat of the Mind.* Columbia University Press, New York, NY.

Hart, D.K. and Wright, N.D. (1998). The civic good: The public interest of civic humanism. *Administrative Theory and Praxis*, 20: 406–421.

Himmelfarb, G. (1999). *One Nation, Two Cultures.* Knopf, New York, NY.

Howe, D.W. (1997). *Making the American Self: Jonathan Edwards to Abraham Lincoln*. Harvard University Press, Cambridge, MA.

Hyneman, C.S. and Lutz, D.S. (eds., 1983). *American Political Writing during the Founding Era: 1760–1805*. Liberty Fund, Indianapolis, IN, in two volumes.

Jameson, F. (1991). *Postmodernism, or, The Cultural Logic of Late Capitalism*. Duke University Press, Durham, NC.

Jefferson, T. (1984). *Thomas Jefferson: Writings* (M. Peterson, ed.). The Library of America, New York, NY.

Johnson, P. (1997). *A History of the American People*. HarperCollins, New York, NY.

Johnson, S. (1755; 1979). *A Dictionary of the English Language*. Times Books, London, England.

Kenyon, C.M. (1962). Republicanism and radicalism in the American Revolution: An old-fashioned interpretation. *The William and Mary Quarterly*, 19: 153–182.

Kerber, L.K. (1986). *Women of the Republic: Intellect and Ideology in Revolutionary America*, 2nd ed. Norton, New York, NY.

Koch, A. (1961). *Power, Morals, and the Founding Fathers*. Cornell University Press, Ithaca, NY.

Kurland, P. and Lerner, R. (eds., 1987). *The Founders' Constitution*. University of Chicago Press, Chicago, IL, in seven volumes.

Lincoln, A. (1980). *Abraham Lincoln: Speeches and Writings* (D.E. Fehrenbacher, ed.). The Library of America, New York, NY, in two volumes.

Lutz, D.S. (ed., 1998). *Colonial Origins of the American Constitution: A Documentary History*. Liberty Fund, Indianapolis, IN.

Madison, J. (1999). *James Madison: Writings* (J.N. Rakove, ed.). The Library of America, New York, NY.

Maier, P. (1997). *American Scripture: Making the Declaration of Independence*. Knopf, New York, NY.

Malone, D. (1948). *Jefferson the Virginian*, Vol. I. Little, Brown, Boston, MA.

Martz, L.L. (1990). *Thomas More: The Search for the Inner Man*. Yale University Press, New Haven, CT.

Montesquieu, Baron De (1748). *The Spirit of the Laws* (T. Nugent, trans). Hafner Press, New York, NY.

Ott, H. (1993). *Martin Heidegger: A Political Life*. BasicBooks, New York, NY.

Paine, T. (1948). *The Life and Major Writings of Thomas Paine* (P.S. Foner, ed.). The Citadel Press, Secaucus, NJ.

Peckham, H.H. (ed., 1978). *Sources of American Independence: Selected Manuscripts from the Collections of the William L. Clements Library*. University of Chicago Press, Chicago, IL, in two volumes.

Ramsay, D. (1789). *The History of the American Revolution.* Liberty Fund, Indianapolis, IN, in two volumes.

Robbins, C. (1959). *The Eighteenth-Century Commonwealthman.* Harvard University Press, Cambridge, MA.

Rohr, J.A. (1989). *Ethics for Bureaucrats: An Essay on Law and Values,* 2nd ed. Marcel Dekker, New York, NY.

Rohr, J.A. (1986). *To Run A Constitution: The Legitimacy of the Administrative State.* University of Kansas, Lawrence, KA.

Rorty, R. (1998). *Achieving Our Country: Leftist Thought in Twentieth-Century America.* Harvard University Press, Cambridge, MA.

Sandoz, E. (ed., 1991). *Political Sermons of the American Founding Era: 1730–1805.* Liberty Fund, Indianapolis, IN.

Sandoz, E. (1990). *A Government of Laws: Political Theoery, Religion, and the American Founding.* Louisiana State University Press, Baton Rouge, LA.

Schacht, R. (1970). *Alienation.* Anchor Books, Garden City, NY.

Schutz, J.A. and Adair, D. (eds., 1966). *The Spur of Fame: Dialogues of John Adams and Benjamin Rush: 1805–1813.* The Huntington Library, San Marino, CA.

Seery, J.E. (1999). Castles in the air: An essay on political foundations. *Political Theory,* 27: 460.

Smith, A. (1790). *The Theory of Moral Sentiments* (D.D. Raphael and A.L. Macfie, eds.), 6th ed. Liberty Fund, Indianapolis, IN.

Smith, P. (1980). *The Shaping of America,* Volume III. McGraw-Hill, New York, NY.

Sturrock, J. (ed., 1979). *Structuralism and Since: From Levi-Strauss to Derrida.* Oxford University Press, New York, NY.

Trenchard, J. and Gordon, T. (1755, 1995). *Cato's Letters* (R. Mamowy, ed.). Liberty Fund, Indianapolis, IN, in two volumes.

Waldo, D. (1984). *The Administrative State: A Study of the Political Theory of American Public Administration,* 2nd ed. Holmes & Meier, New York, NY.

Warren, M.O. (1805). *History of the Rise, Progress and Termination of the American Revolution— interspersed with Biographical, Political and Moral Observations.* Liberty Fund, Indianapolis, IN, in two volumes.

Washington, G. (1997). *George Washington: Writings* (J. Rhodehamel, ed.). The Library of America, New York, NY.

West, T.G. (1997). *Vindicating the Founders: Race, Sex, Class, and Justice in the Origins of America.* Rowman & Littlefield, Lanham, MD.

Wood, G.S. (1991). *The Radicalism of the American Revolution.* Knopf, New York, NY.

Wood, G.S. (1969). *The Creation of the American Republic: 1776–1787.* W.W. Norton, New York, NY.

Wood, G.S. (1966). Rhetoric and reality in the American Revolution. In McGiffert, M. (ed., 1993), *In Search of Early America.* The Institute of Early American History and Culture, Williamsburg, VA.

Wright, L.B. (1975). *Tradition and the Founding Fathers.* University Press of Virginia, Charlottesville, VA.

Wright, N.D. and Hart, D.K. (1996). The public interest: What we are not leaving our posterity. *Administrative Theory and Practice,* 18: 14–28.

Zuckert, M.P. (1996). *The Natural Rights Republic.* University of Notre Dame Press, Notre Dame, IN.

11

Organizational Structure
A Reflection of Society's Values and a Context for Individual Ethics

Montgomery Van Wart
Texas Tech University, Lubbock, Texas

Kathryn G. Denhardt
University of Delaware, Newark, Delaware

I. INTRODUCTION

The decade of the 1990s was an era of rapid change in government with the ''new public management'' encouraging competition, devolution, contracting out, privatization, entrepreneurial government, and other reforms that brought fundamental changes to many structures and processes of government. These reforms and innovations reflected changing values and belief systems about what government should do and how it should operate, and had the effect of fundamentally altering governmental structures in many cases. And, though less widely recognized, these innovations and structural changes resulted in profound ethical implications as well.

The clear lessons from the 1990s seems to be that value changes cannot occur without accompanying structural changes, and that structure changes necessarily involve value changes. All value changes—whether leading to structural changes or caused by structural changes—affect the rules about unacceptable behavior and our notions of ideal behavior. In other words, these changes affect our fundamental sense of ethics. This chapter will explore how value systems affect organizational structures, how organizational structures affect value systems, and what this means for administrative ethics today.

Organizational structure is widely believed to be a key determinant of the values that frame ethical decision-making. For example, Terry Cooper (1990: 161) identifies structural aspects as one of four major value-ethical determinants: organizational structure, organizational culture, individual attributes (in which he includes professional norms), and societal expectations. Although organizational structure is not always identified as a separate factor, broader organizational and bureaucratic roles are defined as major determinants by most generalist researchers (see, for example, Gortner, 1991: 75–81; Lewis, 1991: 23; Pugh, 1991; Posner and Schmidt, 1994; Van Wart, 1996a; Warwick, 1981). Even scholars who do not catalogue the major factors or focus on other aspects of ethics usually comment on organizational issues such as structure. Sociologists such as Robert

Merton have long recognized the profound influence of organizations and their role in institutionalizing values for good or ill (Merton, 1968); communitarians such as Bellah often incorporate organizations and institutions in their vision of community as "an indispensable source from which character is formed" (Bellah et al., 1991: 6); and management specialists such as Robert Golembiewski note that "it is in organizations, if anywhere, that our values will be achieved, that individual freedom will be attained" (Golembiewski, 1965; 4). Furthermore, empirical research has also demonstrated the importance of organizational structure (Pugh, et al., 1969; Jackall, 1988; Victor and Cullen, 1988).

Nevertheless, the relationship between organizational structure and administrative ethics is complex and difficult to isolate, especially in relation to public organizations. On the one hand, the structure of public organizations reflects social values, especially through authoritative public judgements such as laws and legislative oversight. The legal and social elements should have a powerful effect on organizational structure because a public agency's mission is to act as an agent of the public interest in a democratic system. From this perspective, ethical behavior requires understanding and acting upon social legal values, many of which are embedded in various administrative structures. On the other hand, public organizations also provide a context for the discretionary actions of individual administrators. Administrators are themselves a key source of information for society and lawmakers and thus are a part of the authoritative decision-making process; and no social/ legal guidelines in an organization can be so specific, or structures so articulated and rigid, that extensive interpretation (discretion) will not be necessary. Thus, discretionary administrative actions allow room for, and even demand, individual choice and judgment. Therefore, ethical behavior requires an understanding of one's own values and motivations which affect the decisions one makes and contributes to inside the administrative structure (Brown, 1990) and occasionally outside it (Bowman et al., 1984).

Organizational structure has at least three major aspects, only two of which will be covered in this chapter: paradigmatic structures, organizational systems, and organizational forms. *Paradigmatic structures* involve public administration as macrolevel elements of the political system and the implementation of democratic theory (Van Wart, 1998: 192). At this broad level of analysis, public administration may emphasize a strict system of administrative accountability to voters through a hierarchical chain of command consisting of appointed and elected officials (the traditional American paradigm). It may also emphasize public administration as the fulcrum of communication and decision-making in the political system (the French and Japanese public administration models). Or, it may emphasize administrative responsiveness, not only to elected officials and citizens, but also directly to market forces (the new public management model being advocated around much of the world). Debate currently rages about which of these abstract structural paradigms is the most effective, but this debate will not be reviewed here since it is largely captured in the next two more mid- and microlevel aspects. (Also, this volume alludes to this debate in many other chapters.)

Organizational systems provide the overarching structural constraints on, controls of, and (to some degree) powers of, not only individual agencies, departments, divisions, units, centers, sections, and so on, but also entire government systems. We will examine two systems-as-structures in this chapter. One of the best known and most coherent is a civil service system, which applies to entire governments, be they federal, state, county, or city. The second example—a system of accountability—is really an amalgamated system or composite of many small subsystems that cover seven different types of control and discretion.

The third level of analysis is the narrowest and is the *organizational form* that individual agencies, departments, and divisions assume. Organizational form or design determines how work is divided up and how it is coordinated in formal structures (Mintzberg, 1979). The two primary general theories of organizational form will be examined here. The first emphasizes internal organizational characteristics and proposes five ideal forms (Mintzberg, 1979); and the second emphasizes environmental characteristics, identifies four ideal forms, and is generally known as the "competing values framework." An important purpose of examining these organizational systems and forms is to establish their general value biases, which are critical not only for scholars, but for contemplative practitioners involved in organizational design.

The preceding discussion about organizational design (and the implicit values in those designs) assumes their proper functioning. However, organizational structures often do not function well. Thus, there is also the critical issue of maladministration since organizational systems and forms (that is, types of organizational structures) frequently have substantial weaknesses. There are two major types of maladministration. First, organizational systems and forms can operate poorly because they are violated through wrongdoing such as corruption or various types of administrative abuse or ignorance (Caiden, 1991). When these bureaucratic pathologies are rampant, Petrick and Quinn suggest that there is a culture of collective connivance (Petrick and Quinn, 1997). See also Chapter 21 on administrative corruption. A second important bureaucratic pathology does not involve explicit wrongdoing; rather, it involves problems with the fundamental organizational system or form. These type-of-organization problems can occur because of the excesses to which systems and forms are prone over time. Regulatory excess is an example (Howard, 1994). Type-of-organization problems can also occur because of fundamental shifts in the environment in which an agency or department operates. Stated differently, a new social consensus about what government does or how it does it requires a fundamental rethinking of organizational systems and forms as well. For example, social welfare policy changes requiring "workfare" necessitate organizational reorganization to place more recipients in jobs and generate new values about the importance of requiring work in exchange for benefits. Similarly, the new social consensus to demand more accountability (or different types of accountability) of public employees requires shifts in civil service systems. Although environmental changes are articulated in legislation to some degree, many changes must be administered by the organizations themselves, especially at the process and case levels. Fundamental shifts in systems and forms are common today and require deep understanding of the value shifts and the appropriate adjustment of ethical systems that should be made.

The paradox of organizational structure is that at its ideal it perfectly reflects the values of society, the authorized mandates of the political legal system, and individual administrators' legitimate judgments in discretionary matters. Yet this ideal is both fragile and transitory because society is fragmented with no one set of values perfectly capturing the whole. The political legal system changes constantly with evolving social tastes, and individual and professional value promptings get neglected in some cases or become overweening in others. Yet no matter how well or how poorly values and ethics of organizational structures fit a political tradition, environmental demands for efficiency and effectiveness, or employee sensibilities of right and wrong, they are extraordinarily powerful in determining the *authorized* values and ethical context.

In this chapter, we will next examine the values and ethics inherent in organizational systems. We will do the same with organizational forms. Then we will examine the traditional question in this area: What is the relationship of bureaucratic pathologies to organizational structure? Finally, we will conclude with a section on a more contemporary question: What are the ethical ramifications of making changes to an organizational structure?

II. VALUES AND ETHICS INHERENT IN ORGANIZATIONAL SYSTEMS

When governments set up constraints that affect most or all of their individual agencies, departments, or boards, they are setting up systems to guide and control those entities. For example, the general parameters of compensation are not left up to the discretionary decisions of individual agencies. Rather, legislative bodies generally approve fairly specific compensation plans or schedules, guidelines for use in individual cases, and annual adjustments for inflation, raises, and merit. The values in such systems are both explicit (e.g., the monetary amounts) and implicit (e.g., pay relationships between the private and public sector, between the elected officials and careerists, and among grade levels assigned to various positions and among agencies). These tightly monitored systems have relatively few ethical problems involving outright violations of authorized systems such as bogus positions (pay without work), false classification, or gross overcompensation. Problems are more likely to arise involving administrative abuse such as overclassification or featherbedding (making work for friends or supporters). The chronic ethical problem in compensation for legislators and political executives is determining what the right pay scale is and then authorizing it. This ethical problem can become intense for individual administrators charged with getting the work done if and when the compensation falls well below the market and positions turn over frequently, are filled with inadequately trained recruits, or go unfilled altogether.

Two examples of organization systems-as-structures follow: systems of staffing and systems of accountability.

A. Systems of Staffing

The confusion about the correct values to use in staffing (recruitment and hiring) in the public sector in the nineteenth century are well known (Mosher, 1982). Three personnel systems—based on appointment, rules, or elections—are typical in the United States and most Western-style nations. In the nineteenth century, appointment-based systems were extensive and rule-based systems were far less frequent and informal. Spoils appointments (rewarding political supporters with positions) and nepotism (positions for family and personal friends) were common, and often legally permissible, practices. Senator Marcy of New York stated on the floor of the U.S. Senate in 1832 what many politicians believed: "To the victor belong the spoils."

Because of the abuses and excesses of the public sector appointment-based system, the rules-based civil service reform movement developed after the Civil War, finally getting a secure foothold with the Pendleton Act of 1883. Social values changed (government was becoming too large and technically complex for the amateur administrators still advocated in the Jacksonian period) which required a formal system deemphasizing appointment-based staffing practices. The new civil service system eventually replaced selection procedures for all but the most senior appointments with rule-based staffing processes. Recruitment and candidate certification for entry and middle management positions were completely removed from politicians' control through the use of nonpartisan, independent civil service commissions, and even the hiring supervisors could generally only select from the top three candidates to reduce managerial cronyism (even if more were certified as meeting eligibility requirements).

Staffing systems—and their concomitant values—are some of the most important organizational structures in the public sector, and discussions about violations of, abuses of, and changes to them can provoke heated debate. Each of the three competing strategies has its strengths and weaknesses. Election as a strategy for personnel selection focuses on democratic values (e.g., broad participation, equality of participation, openness). Those selected through this strategy normally have policy positions or chief executive roles. The election process allows the most visible of public-sector employees to be directly controlled by the voters. Appointment as a strategy today focuses on values of competence (but not necessarily expertise), policy affinity (which often translates into political loyalty), and personal acquaintance (preference for those known by the appointing official). As a strategy, it is generally reserved for senior advisors to elected officials, for senior administrators of agencies, advisory boards, and commissions. Because voter control is indirect and poorly articulated, most appointments require confirmation processes to assure that candidates for positions are sufficiently qualified (competent) for the positions to which they are nominated (normally by senates, boards of supervisors, and city councils). Rule-based selection gives precedence to merit principles (technical qualifications and competitive selection), but also incorporates seniority (experience and organizational loyalty) and representativeness (fairness among various groups in society). As society, through law, adjusts or changes these strategies over time (e.g., increasing the number of presidential appointments, turning some county "row" officers into appointed officials, or extending civil service requirements to groups not formerly covered), the values of incumbents are expected to change as are the ethical constraints in the modes of selection.

B. Systems of Accountability

Accountability systems are invariably a combination of formal and informal controls which reflect different values and which locate the responsibility of ethical decision-making in different domains. Accountability systems structure what is to be done, how it is to be done, and who is to do it. As with civil service systems, the values reflected by the various types of controls in accountability systems diverge greatly, leading to radically different ethical mechanisms in some cases. Seven types of control over or through administration are identified here (Van Wart, 1996b). They are laws, rules, public opinion, virtue, professional norms, competition, and comparison.

As a category, laws are defined here as legislative actions and their judicial interpretation. Laws have always been a powerful type of ethical control. Examples include "ethics legislation" (e.g., laws regarding conflict of interest, financial disclosure, discrimination, nepotism, future and "outside" employment, gifts, private use of public resources, and so on) as well as legislation on information access, open meetings, employee political activity, competitive bidding, whistle blowing, and financial authorization. The strengths of such laws include setting clear social standards of behavior, democratic accountability, openness, and due process. Some of the weaknesses of legal regulation may be rigidity (requiring excessive conformity), confusing minimum standards for ethical behavior (encouraging ethical minimalism), stifling creativity and experimentation, and proliferation of statutes (the "there-ought-to-be-a-law" syndrome).

The second type of control are rules defined as stipulated organizational actions and philosophies. Examples include organizational controls through financial authorization processes, internal audits, agency personnel procedures, codes of conduct, supervisory and executive supervision, and authorization requirements. Rules have similar (though not identical) strengths and weaknesses as laws of which they are an extension to some degree. Although there has been considerable discussion of these strengths and weaknesses (for example: Davis, 1969; and Howard, 1994), that debate will not be reviewed here.

A third control is exercised by public opinion through civic sentiments and their effects on political and administrative processes. Public opinion is reflected through voting preferences, as well as through the media, complaint mechanisms (legislative, administrative, and judicial), citizen review and policy boards, hearing processes, and citizen surveys. The value of public opinion lies in the public's fundamental sovereignty, its reasonableness and pragmatism in the long term, and its distrust of excessive power of any type. Its weaknesses include its tendency to fragment into splinter groups along self-interested lines, its short-term changeability, and its superficial understanding of the particulars of complex systems and solutions.

Virtue, our fourth category of control, refers to the character and values of the individuals who work in the public service. It is exemplified by internal philosophies of self-restraint, trustworthiness, belief in the dignity of citizens, and actions demonstrating diligence, competence, excellence, commitment, and optimism. The strengths of virtue include its fundamental necessity for honest government, the dignity it affords those who work in the public's behalf, and its tendency to elicit the best, rather than the minimum, from individuals. Its weaknesses include its variability among individuals and over time, fundamental concerns about private interpretation of the public good (for example, making a wide exception to provide benefits to a person who is clearly ineligible on technical grounds), and concerns about reliance on virtue (discretion) giving way to abuse of power.

The next control mechanism, norms, here refer to professional standards. Examples include expectations of education and training, notions about the proper use of expertise, standards of acceptable practice that are not agency specific, and credos and codes of ethics emphasizing the aspirational aspects of professionalism. The strengths of professional norms as structures influencing ethical behavior include the emphasis on high levels of knowledge and training, and the tendency to encourage best practices as standard practices (thereby raising the bar for good practice over time). Their weaknesses include excessive resource demands when lesser standards would do (such as requiring a doctor when a physician's assistant would do) and the tendency to be self-serving by the professional group, especially when legally codified (such as by limiting admission to the field to maintain employment demand).

A sixth mechanism, competition, refers to the option of public choice. The expansion of vouchers in public school systems is meant to increase competition among schools and/or among public and private systems. Accountability is to the "market" rather than to decrees or people. Examples include public-public competition, public-private competition, contracting out, public corporations, and resorting to privatization. Although competition has always been a significant structural element in American public-sector organizations (especially contracting out), it has recently gained a new robustness with the popularity of market discipline and models. Its strengths are its "invisible hand" (provision of financial restraint through microeconomics), its compatibility with the basic capitalistic economic system, and its widespread popular support as an axiom underpinning

U.S. government. Its weaknesses as a structural element include its incompatibility with government as the provider of last resort (e.g., welfare), state coercion and police action (i.e., the authorized use of force), public security (confidentiality of records), and multiple goal attainment (e.g., regulating, serving, and educating simultaneously).

The final mechanism, comparison, refers to contrasts of management and financial performance between entities. For example, activity-based costing (rather than line-item costing) allows for the cost of a service such as an average ambulance run to be compared with private providers. It is related to competition but is a less rigorous way of curbing excess. It is often viable where competition is not, and it, too, is enjoying great popularity as techniques such as benchmarking become commonplace. Examples include cost accounting (comparative unit costing), public review of comparable data, and tougher assessments of system performance and goal attainment over time. The strengths of comparison include its capacity to educate, its fairness when similar measures are used, its ability to motivate improved performance, and its adaptability as a mechanism. Its weaknesses include the incomparability of things (ultimately everything is different), the difficulty of finding and maintaining similar measures across agencies to compare meaningfully, the cost of creating and maintaining the data, and the misuse of data by the uninformed or politically motivated.

Thus, organizational systems—both staffing and accountability—are powerful structures which profoundly affect the values to which organizations adhere. The rise in use and vigor of rule-based merit systems in the 20th century completely altered the government landscape by creating technically competent and putatively "neutral" organizational structures which could be expanded during the New Deal era. Contemporary efforts to curb the perceived excesses of civil service and tenure systems as organizational structures will likewise have an enormous effect on their values. In a similar fashion, changes in the emphasis of accountability mechanisms, such as the decreased reliance on rules, whether through "empowerment" or entrepreneurial government initiatives, and increased reliance on competition, will also have a major impact on the values and sensibility regarding what are perceived to be ethical practices. If systems are the general structures for a series of agencies or departments, forms (to which we next turn) are the specific structures for them.

III. VALUES AND ETHICS INHERENT IN ORGANIZATIONAL FORMS

Just as organizational systems are formulated to operationalize the values of society and forcefully mandate ethical behavior for the individuals working within those systems, so too do organizational forms operationalize values and set ethical parameters for employees. One only has to imagine the differences between a government agency with its standard emphasis on public control and internal stability, and a privately owned company whose owner might, for example, take substantial risks or use employees to provide personal services. Such practices are not allowed in public sector forms. In a medical partnership, the partners are only directly responsible to other partners, not to a legislative body. An advertising agency may create and dissolve ad account teams with alacrity, as well as hire and fire frequently, but pay large salaries. Organizational forms determine both the formal and informal values and ethics, such as the appropriateness of profit making and the reliance on strict hierarchical protocols. A discussion highlighting the values of the different forms of organizations follows.

Weber's classic discussions on bureaucracy ([1904] 1930, 1947) dominated the literature for decades. However, scholarship on the types or forms of organizations blossomed in the 1960s and 1970s. Lawrence and Lorsch (1967), James Thompson (1967), Khandwalla (1977), Child (1974), Hall (1972), and Pugh et al. (1969) were some of those who worked to connect systematically the environment and different organizational forms. Some scholars articulated the nature and utility of non-hierarchical models such as Toffler (1970), Galbraith (1971, 1973), and Davis and Lawrence (1977). Simon explained the impact and importance of information systems and technology on organizational form (1973, 1977). Many scholars highlighted the challenges and opportunities of bureaucracies in various public and private settings such as Blau and Scott (1962), Hummel (1977), Etzioni (1961), Victor Thompson (1961), Argyris (1957, 1973a, 1973b), Burns (1971), and Perrow (1970). Two major taxonomies emerged in the course of this period of productivity. Henry Mintzberg's *The Structuring of Organizations* (1979) became a standard treatment in most textbooks about management, and Quinn and Rohrbaugh (1981) were among another group who articulated an alternative, if complementary, perspective that is also much used today. Mintzberg emphasized the technical aspects of organizational design, whereas Quinn, Rohrbaugh and others emphasized the values and culture inherent in organizational forms. We will briefly discuss both here.

Mintzberg's taxonomy divides organizations into five basic types: simple structures, machine bureaucracies, professional bureaucracies, divisionalized forms, and "adhocracies." Each emphasizes a different part of the organization. Simple structures emphasize the role of a strong leader whose direct control is evident throughout the organization, no matter whether that supervision is considered authoritarian or charismatic. Organizations with simple structures tend to be either small or new. A common example in government is the offices of major elected officials such as presidents, governors, or members of Congress. Machine bureaucracies emphasize the role of standardization of work processes and technical experts who design and follow rules carefully. Many government agencies fall into this category with their reliance on laws and rules, and their tendency toward mass production techniques. The professional bureaucracy emphasizes the professionalization of the line workers who coordinate through the standardization of skills. Professional training means that operatives have greater discretion in decision-making than most production workers because the complex nature of their work requires sophisticated distinctions calling for independent judgment. Common examples include medical practices, universities, and law firms. Divisionalized forms emphasize coordination through the standardization of outputs, no matter where a service or product is produced. The field offices in divisionalized systems tend to adopt the standards of the central office, only making local adjustments in nonessential areas. Many federal and state agencies exhibit this type of conglomerate or multidivisional form. Adhocracies (organizations whose internal structures are highly flexible and often reorganized around specific projects) emphasize coordination through collaboration and mutual adjustment. They are best suited to environments that are both complex and dynamic, and that call for constant entrepreneurialism. Work processes tend not to be highly standardized so that creativity can be enhanced. Examples of adhocracies are ad agencies, task forces, and professional organizations that do large batch projects such as engineering and architectural firms.

Implicit in Mintzberg's work is a contingency model which promotes organizational design based on the nature of the environment and the nature of the work, but which also accounts for organizational tradition and leadership. Of course the selection of an organizational type involves the prioritization of many values. For example, if high degrees of external control, efficiency, and standardization are deemed the most important values, then a machine bureaucracy makes sense. However, if customization or decentralization (to suit local needs) become more valued and there is a willingness to relax standardization and efficiency standards somewhat, then the organization may move toward the professional bureaucracy or adhocracy. Employee "empowerment" will tend to have the same effect. Machine bureaucracies undergoing great changes and needing charismatic leadership may take on more of the characteristics of a simple structure with strong executive direction and oversight. These are just a few of the typical trends in government which have the effect of diversifying organizational forms.

Maintaining organizational forms implicitly involves maintaining a set of values; changing an organizational form involves changing the underlying values as well. The tension among values is clear today as public organizations themselves are seeking greater autonomy for entrepreneurialism and decentralization of decision-making (empowerment), while legislative bodies continue to focus on rules adherence and efficiency, and have a heightened interest in cost containment, privatization, and downsizing. All this while the public clamors for more personalized treatment, quality assurances, and service options. The ethical implications for individual employees are enormous too. If an individual believes that entrepreneurialism is called for and acts accordingly, but the organization maintains strict work standardization policies, a well-intentioned activity may be labeled inappropriate at minimum or even unethical.

Quinn and Rohrbaugh (1981; Hall and Quinn, 1983) label their framework the "competing values approach." It superimposes a series of dichotomous, competing values to create four organizational types based on environments, associated cultures, and leadership styles. From an environmental perspective, one axis is created by dividing conditions that call for stability and control from those that call for flexibility and change. A second axis is created by those conditions calling for an internal focus versus those calling for an external focus. This results in four types of organization. Figure 1 illustrates the competing values framework.

The hierarchical bureaucracy is the result of stable conditions, an emphasis on control, and an internal focus on process. It is suited to the public sector with its stable funding and monopolistic characteristics, requirements for procedural equity, and external regulation. Values typically emphasized in hierarchical bureaucracies include technical knowledge, factual decision-making, employee security, and a conservative leadership style.

In the competing values framework, a second type of organization is the rational bureaucracy which also thrives in a stable environment where there is relatively little product change. However, in a rational bureaucracy there is an external focus caused by

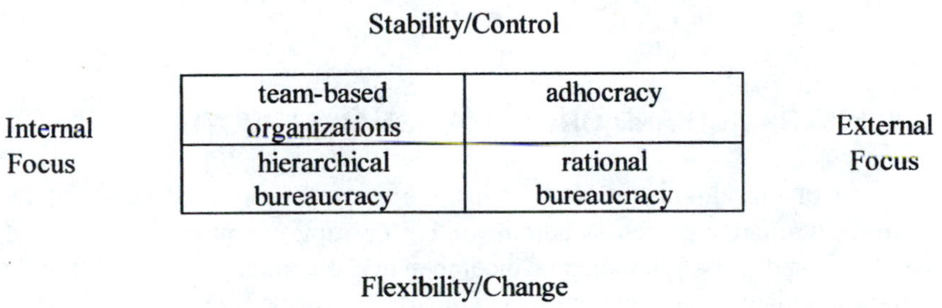

Stability/Control

	team-based organizations	adhocracy	
Internal Focus	hierarchical bureaucracy	rational bureaucracy	External Focus

Flexibility/Change

Figure 1 The competing values framework.

competition among a small number of rivals (such as typified in many American industries in the 1950s through the 1970s). In such organizations, strong leaders can direct most changes (because the pace of change is slow), coordinated by a handful of senior managers and design experts. Both bureaucratic types highly value classical cost efficiency through mass production practices, but hierarchical bureaucracies are more directed by external control while rational bureaucracies are more affected by the market. Values emphasized typically in rational bureaucracies include competence, decisiveness, employee achievement, and a directive and goal-oriented leadership style.

Adhocracies are more appropriate, according to the competing values approach, when product change is frequent and the competitive environment remains keen. Adhocracies are flexible and able to handle constant change more readily because structures are assembled and dismantled to suit specific projects or challenges. Tom Peters has been a major project management advocate (1992, 1994) in the private sector. The creation of virtual organizations within large companies has been an effort to reduce the scale of organizations while increasing the responsiveness and accountability in a dynamic market. Values emphasized typically in adhocracies include adaptive skills, intuitive knowledge, employee flexibility, and risk-oriented or inventive leadership styles.

A group or team approach is often used when there is a lot of product or service change calling for flexibility, but competition is not keen. This is becoming far more common in the public sector with its stable funding sources but where mission and operation changes are increasingly necessary because of increased demands for service customization. For example, TQM (and variant quality management approaches) inevitably calls for cross-functional teams to solve problems as well as to redesign systems for rapidly changing environments. Values emphasized typically in team-based cultures include informal status in the group, participative decision-making, feelings of affiliation and attachment among employees, and a concerned and supportive leadership style.

Both the Mintzberg and competing values approaches help us understand the values associated with the deep structures of organizational forms. The importance of such analysis is magnified in an era experimenting extensively with changes in form. Although it seems unlikely that hierarchical bureaucracies will be largely abandoned for other relatively pure organizational types, it does seem likely that many bureaucracies will take on more hybrid characteristics than in the past. Given the importance of organizational structures to almost all organizational activity, the next question centers on the relationship of poor and dysfunctional organizational performance (maladministration) to values and ethics. In other words, when organizations perform optimally, then the values and ethics that they operationalize in their structures are perfectly expressed. However, when organizations suboptimize or when the gap between formal structures and actual behavior becomes significant, espoused values and ethics are diminished or violated altogether. It is to this important topic that we next turn.

IV. MALADMINISTRATION AND ORGANIZATIONAL STRUCTURE

Two primary forms of maladministration exist in reference to organizational structure. The first is outright wrongdoing such as administrative corruption, substantial forms of administrative abuse, and gross ignorance or incompetence. Examples of administrative corruption include nepotism, fraud, theft, graft, and misuse of property or resources. Examples of administrative abuse or ignorance include illegal discrimination, illegal political activities by administrators or political manipulation of administration by elected officials, rule breaking, managerial egotism, featherbedding, gross incompetence (doing a job for which one is unqualified), and gross ignorance (failing to learn about critical organizational constraints such as laws). (Chapter 17 on administrative corruption focuses on this topic at length.) Yet as Gary Brumback states, "government scandals notwithstanding, corruption is not the primary problem" when talking about the problems of ethical management in advanced democracies (Brumback, 1991, p. 362).

The second form of maladministration is due to organizational dysfunction, which although less blatant than corruption or gross incompetence, is more common and collectively more important in the United States and many other countries. Such dysfunction has numerous causes and symptoms which create an environment of blurred values and unnecessary ethical ambivalence.

Organizations have many interests to defend and balance, and it is easy for them to allow one set of interests either to wane or become excessively emphasized. One lighthearted jab at the excesses of bureaucratic organizations includes Parkinson's Law that work expands to fill the time available for its completion (Parkinson, 1957) which underscores the real problem in bureaucracies of creating appropriate performance accountability for public workers. Another example is the Peter Principle which states that employees tend to be promoted to their level of incompetence (Peter and Hull, 1969). Anyone who works with managers knows that many of them are promoted based on technical competencies rather than managerial training or interpersonal skills which are necessary for supervisory success.

The list of serious organizational excesses, commonly called bureaupathologies, is long and much commented upon. Robert Merton (1940) discussed goal displacement in which the organization's goals are replaced by conformity to rules. This causes bureaucratic rigidity and red tape. Boulding examines the tendency for "organizational hardening" to sap the best energies of workers and the organization itself over time (1953, p. 85), a theme that echoed Marx's alienation critique of modern work nearly a century earlier and predating others such as Robert Denhardt (1981) and Kathryn Denhardt (1988). Victor Thompson (1961) focused on the tendency of many bureaucrats to dominate and control others, inside and outside the organization. This is largely done through rule-mongering which requires subordinates to follow detailed strictures or to get permission for minor deviations for exceptional cases. Michel Crozier (1964), in studying two French agencies, discovered that their formalistic behavior did not allow them to adapt or learn well. Ralph Hummel (1977) examined the effects of a lifetime of working in a bureaucratic setting which results in a "truncated" personality characterized by technical and legalistic manias and a lack of humanistic values. The public choice critics have pointed out the budget maximizing behavior of bureaucrats (Niskanen, 1971; Migue and Belanger, 1974). Gawthrop (1984) argues that organizations often become "shields" for a variety of inappropriate actions, from covering up egregious wrongdoing (Adams and Balfour, 1998) to overlooking minor but significant inefficiencies and mistakes.

From Merton's early critique in the 1940s through the critiques in the early 1990s, however, the major complaint has been about excesses of the particular type of organization—the hierarchical bureaucratic structure. In the 1990s there has been a pronounced increase in the amount of discussion about changing the fundamental organizational type (generally a relatively pure type of hierarchical bureaucracy) to different types altogether (e.g., a team-based organization, a rational bureaucracy, or an adhocracy) or at least to a less extreme type of bureaucracy. The same environmental shifts that began to influence the restructuring of the private sector in the 1980s were beginning to affect the public sector by the 1990s (Barzelay, 1992; Osborne and Gaebler, 1992). Organizations were called on to be less rule-oriented and more employee-focused, customer-focused, and/or flexible (Guy Peters, 1994). This value shift, to the degree that it actually occurs, not only has structural implications, such as the possible devolution of authority, but related ethical implications too, such as the ethical appropriateness of reasoned variation (discretion) instead of absolute rule conformity.

In sum, then, at least five categories of organizational dysfunction exist. The first category includes ethical lapses. Such lapses occur when the employees, units, or clients disregard organizational/legal rules for personal gain, preference, and power. When they become serious and/or routine, we refer to them as administrative corruption. A second category includes motivation-psychological problems which are consequences of poor attitudes, bad morale, lack of cohesiveness and vision, and weak performance discipline, among others. A third type of dysfunction includes capacity-capability problems that emerge when individual employees do not have the capability to perform current or future responsibilities, or when a unit or the organization does not have the capacity to fulfill its current or future mission. A fourth type of dysfunction includes structure-systems problems that arise when the organization's fit with its environment or mandate is poor, there is a poor fit among the system components, or there are inappropriate incentives (ineffective or perverse). A fifth type of dysfunction includes accountability problems that may result from too little accountability, which permits ethical lapses (or worse, outright administrative corruption), or too much accountability, which tends to lead to administrative red tape and rigidity. However, as discussed earlier in this chapter (under systems of accountability), an organization can be dysfunctional because it has the wrong balance of accountability or control types. For example, the organization's philosophy may be one putatively emphasizing teams and yet all control may be hierarchically enforced (rather than through peers), or moderate risk-taking may be encouraged in the rhetoric of the organization and yet any perceived mistake may result in a new rule or policy.

All the categories of organizational dysfunction tend to stem from either poor value articulation or poor value inculcation/education. They all significantly reduce the organization's efficiency and effectiveness for the public and all tend to make the organization a less enjoyable and fulfilling place for employees to work in. Value clarification becomes an ethical imperative because people cannot do the right thing unless they know what it is and want to do it, both collectively and individually. Similarly, value clarification becomes a managerial imperative because people cannot do the efficient and effective thing unless they know what it is and want to do it, both collectively and individually. Yet the importance of value-clarification consensus building, and values training, should not disguise its complex and difficult nature, especially in an era of value changes.

Because of the perception of the high incidence of various types of maladministration in public organizations today, there has been an increasing external and internal pressure to change organizational structures. It is the value and ethical ramifications of such changes in organizational structure where we conclude.

V. THE RAMIFICATIONS OF CHANGES IN ORGANIZATIONAL STRUCTURE

At their best, changes in organizational structure in the past have tended either to refine them or to reduce their excesses. These refinements and minor improvements were generally to relatively similar structural organizations. The bulk of the time the system of staffing would be heavily rule-based civil service systems, the system of accountability would emphasize laws and rules, and the form would be a relatively pure type of hierarchical bureaucracy. Today, however, there is much discussion and experimentation (sometimes radical) with all elements of organization structure—both the systems and forms.

The implications of such structural changes are enormous. Society's needs, as fuzzily but nonetheless powerfully expressed by the new global economy, are heavily affecting the public sector. The scope of government, the means of government, and the systems of government are all being questioned and changes are occurring in many places. The general inclination toward less government (Yergin and Stanislaw, 1998), for example, is expressed in privatization initiatives, downsizing, competition, more rigorous comparative performance measurement systems, and increased use of market mechanisms in government.

In turn, organizations' needs affect the lives of their employees. The opportunities and challenges are both impressive. On the positive side, the public sector (on the whole) is a more exciting place, more complex, less rigid, more inventive, more responsive, faster moving, more focused, and more quality oriented. Examples include one-stop customer service centers, law enforcement personnel who give citations with grace and courtesy, convenient electronic tax returns, rigorous cost containment in routine services such as garbage collection, customer surveys, empowered problem-solving teams, and job enlargement because of devolution.

There is a negative side as well to all this change. The public sector often does a far poorer job of representing the most disenfranchised in the past. Change is often poorly planned, frenetic, and thus unsuccessful (Caiden, 1999). In order to be more responsive to more constituencies, sometimes the public sector fails to please anybody. Old accountability systems which are slow to change are often at odds with newer structural changes. New philosophies of quality and efficiency often naively discount old political realities and sometimes seem to threaten democratic theory itself. While teams, flexibility, and entrepreneurialism (both customer and market orientations) may seem like good antidotes to the excesses of the hierarchical bureaucracies that once dominated the public sector, at what point do they weaken too much the traditional democratic chain of command from voters to elected officials to the civil service? How will civil servants know what to do when values compete? Will it give them too much discretion, or alternatively, unfairly place too much responsibility and possible blame on them? The savings and loan debacle provides a sobering reminder that system changes that are poorly designed are expensive indeed, turning a *somewhat* overly cautious and circumscribed industry into a *wildly* audacious and unrestrained one in a relatively short time span. The public sector is ultimately a public treasure and misplaced enthusiasm for change could result in a costly diminution of the public sector that would take a generation or more to fix.

The clear lesson from the 1990s seems to be that value changes cannot occur without accompanying structural changes. Conversely, structure changes necessarily involve value changes. And all value changes affect the rules about unacceptable behavior and our notions of ideal behavior, which is to say our fundamental sense of ethics. What is not so clear is how much to modify our old structures, in what ways, and when? Further, when these changes are occurring, which enduring values do we want to carefully maintain stemming from our Constitution and our cherished traditions such as a politically neutral civil service, and which values is it time to change, and to what new values and structures?

REFERENCES

Adams, G. B., and Balfour, D. (1998). *Unmasking Administrative Evil*. Thousand Oaks, CA: Sage.

Argyris, C. (1957). *Personality and Organization*. New York: Harper.

Argyris, C. (1973a). Some limits of rational man organization theory, *Public Administration Review*, 43:253–267.

Argyris, C. (1973b). Organizational man: Rational and self-actualizing, *Public Administration Review*, 43:354–357.

Barzelay, M. (1992). *Breaking through Bureaucracy*. Berkeley: University of California Press.

Bellah, R. N., Madsen, R., Sullivan, W. S., Swidler, A., and Tipton, S. M. (1991). *The Good Society*. New York: Alfred A. Knopf.

Blau, P. M., and Scott, R. (1962). *Formal Organizations*. San Francisco: Chandler.

Boulding, K. E. (1953). *The Organizational Revolution: A Study in the Ethics of Economic Organization*. Chicago: Quadrangle Books.

Bowman, J. S., Elliston, F. A., and Lockhart, P. (1984). *Professional Dissent: An Annotated Bibliography and Resource Guide*. New York: Garland, 1984.

Brown, M. T. (1990). *Working Ethics: Strategies for Decision Making and Organizational Responsibility*. San Francisco: Jossey-Bass.

Brumback, G. B. (1991). Institutionalizing ethics in government, *Public Personnel Management*, 20(3):362.

Burns, T. (1971). Mechanistic and orgasmic structures, in D. S. Pugh (ed.), *Organizational Theory*. New York: Penguin.

Caiden, G. E. (1991). What really is public maladministration? *Public Administration Review*, 51: 486–493.

Caiden, G. E. (1999). Administrative reform: Proceed with caution, *International Journal of Public Administration*, 22:815–832.

Child, J. (1974). What determines organization, *Organizational Dynamics*, 2:2–18.

Cooper, T. L. (1990). *The Responsible Administrator: An Approach to Ethics for the Administrative Role*, 3rd edition. San Francisco: Jossey-Bass.

Crozier, M. (1964). *The Bureaucratic Phenomenon*. Chicago: University of Chicago Press.

Davis, K. C. (1969). *Discretionary Justice*. Baton Rouge: Louisiana State University Press.

Davis, S. M., and Lawrence, P. L. (1977). *Matrix*. Reading, MA: Addison-Wesley.

Denhardt, K. G. (1988). *The Ethics of Public Service*. New York: Greenwood Press.

Denhardt, R. B. (1981). *In the Shadow of Organization*. Lawrence, KS: The Regents Press of Kansas.

Etzioni, A. (1961). *A Comparative Analysis of Complex Organizations*. New York: Free Press.

Galbraith, J. R. (1971). Matrix organization designs, *Business Horizons*, 24:29–40.

Galbraith, J. R. (1973). *Designing Complex Organizations*. Reading, MA: Addison-Wesley.

Gawthrop, L. C. (1984). *Public Sector Management, Systems, and Ethics*. Bloomington: Indiana University Press.

Golembiewski, R. T. (1965). *Men, Management, and Morality: Toward a New Organizational Ethic*. New York: McGraw-Hill.

Gortner, H. F. (1991). *Ethics for Public Managers*. New York: Praeger.

Hall, R. H. (1972). *Organizations: Structure and Process*. Englewood Cliffs, NJ: Prentice-Hall.

Hall, R. H., and Quinn, R. E. (eds.) (1983). *Organization Theory and Public Policy*. Beverly Hills: Sage.

Howard, P. K. (1994). *The Death of Common Sense: How Law Is Suffocating America*. New York: Random House.

Hummel, R. (1977). *The Bureaucratic Experience*. New York: St. Martin's.

Jackall, R. (1988). *Moral Mazes: The World of Corporate Managers*. New York: Oxford University Press.

Khandwalla, P. N. (1977). *The Design of Organizations*. New York: Harcourt Brace Jovanovich.

Lawrence, P. R., and Lorsch, J. W. (1967). *Organization and Environment*. Cambridge, MA: Harvard University Press.

Lewis, C. W. (1991). *The Ethics Challenge in Public Service*. San Francisco: Jossey-Bass.

Merton, R. K. (1940). Bureaucratic structure and personality, *Social Forces*, 18:560–568.

Merton, R. K. (1968). *Social Theory and Social Structure*. New York: The Free Press.

Migue, J. L., and Belanger, G. (1974). Towards a general theory of managerial discretion, *Public Choice*, 17:24–43.

Mosher, F. C. (1982). *Democracy and the Public Service*. 2nd ed. New York: Oxford University Press.

Mintzberg, H. (1979). *The Structuring of Organizations*. Englewood Cliffs, NJ: Prentice-Hall.

Niskanen, W. A. (1971). *Bureaucracy and Representative Government*. Chicago: Aldine-Atherton.

Osborne, D., and Gaebler, T. (1992). *Reinventing Government*. Reading, MA: Addison-Wesley.

Parkinson, C. N. (1957). *Parkinson's Law*. Boston: Houghton Mifflin.

Perrow, C. (1970). *Organizational Analysis*. Belmont, CA: Wadsworth.

Peter, L. J., and Hull, R. (1969). *The Peter Principle*. New York: William Morrow.

Peters, G. (1994). New visions of government and the public service, in P. W. Ingraham and B. S. Romzek (eds.), *New Paradigms for Government: Issues for the Changing Public Service*. San Francisco: Jossey-Bass, pp. 295–321.

Peters, T. (1992). *Liberation Management: Necessary Disorganization for the Nanosecond Nineties*. New York: Fawcett-Columbine.

Peters, T. (1994). *The Pursuit of WOW! Every Person's Guide to Topsy-Turvey Times*. New York: Vintage.

Petrick, J. A., and Quinn, J. F. (1997). *Management Ethics: Integrity at Work*. Thousand Oaks, CA: Sage.

Posner, B. Z., and Schmidt, W. H. (1994). An updated look at the values and expectations of federal government executives, *Public Administration Review*, 54:20–24.

Pugh, D. S., Hickson, D. J., and Hinings, C. R. (1969). An empirical taxonomy of work organizations, *Administrative Science Quarterly*, 14:115–126.

Pugh, D. L. (1991). The origins of ethical frameworks in public administration, in J. Bowman (ed.), *Ethical Frontiers in Public Administration*. San Francisco: Jossey-Bass.

Quinn, R. E., and Rohrbaugh, J. (1981). A competing values approach to organizational effectiveness, *Public Productivity Review*, 5:122–140.

Simon, H. A. (1973). Applying information technology to organizational design. *Public Administration Review*, 33:268–278.

Simon, H. A. (1977). *The New Science of Management Decision*. Englewood Cliffs, NJ: Prentice Hall.

Toffler, A. (1970). *Future Shock*. New York: Bantam Books.

Thompson, J. D. (1967). *Organizations in Action*. New York: McGraw-Hill.

Thompson, V. A. (1961). *Modern Organization*. New York: Alfred A Knopf.

Van Wart, M. (1996a). The sources of ethical decision making for individuals in the public sector, *Public Administration Review*, 56:525–534.

Van Wart, M. (1996b). Trends in the types of control of public organizations, in J. Bowman (ed.), *Public Integrity Annual*. Lexington, KY: Council of State Governments, pp. 83–97.

Van Wart, M. (1998). *Changing Public Sector Values*. New York: Garland.

Victor, B., and Cullen, J. B. (1988). The organizational bases of ethical work climates, *Administrative Science Quarterly*, 33:101–125.

Warwick, D. P. (1981). The ethics of administrative discretion, in J. L. Fleischman, L. Leibman, and M. H. Moore (eds.), *Public duties: The Moral Obligations of Government Officials*. Cambridge, MA: Harvard University Press.

Weber, M. ([1904] 1930). *The Protestant Ethic and the Spirit of Capitalism* (translated by T. Parsons). New York: Scribner's.

Weber, M. (1947). *The Theory of Social and Economic Organization* (translated by A. M. Henderson and T. Parsons). Glencoe, IL: Free Press.

Yergin, D., and Stanislaw, J. (1998). *The Commanding Heights: The Battle Between Government and the Marketplace That Is Remaking the Modern World*. New York: Simon & Schuster.

12

Governmental Ethics and Organizational Culture

Leigh E. Grosenick and Pamela A. Gibson
Virginia Commonwealth University, Richmond, Virginia

> The substantial difficulty that is certain to be countered by public management stems not from its inability to think of or design new organizational structures or stipulate new processes of interaction but primarily from its inability to overcome the ethical inertia of its past and to change the ethical values of its present (Gawthrop, 1984).

Academic and consultant approaches to the understanding of applied ethics and the development of new values based in governmental organizations are dominated by assumptions and theories of organizational development and moral maturity that focus upon either the moral capacity of the individual to make organizational decisions based upon ethical principles; or the ability of a leader to reweave the moral fabric of an organization to reflect the ethics of "professional citizenship." Noted, but mostly ignored in these approaches, is the presence of *organizational culture*, a ubiquitous presence that can stymie the attempts of individuals to refocus their decisions, or leaders to remake the organizations. The brief attention that has been given to organizational mores takes the form of retrospective storytelling in which either pathologic behavioral manifestations of a culture result in unquestionably unethical acts being committed and the audience is simply forewarned to not repeat such mistakes, or the tale is of a happy and productive collective that can be duplicated with sufficient perseverance by the leadership to instill change. In any attempt to change the values of an organization, whether it is through the education of its participants in moral principles, or the imposition of leadership committed to higher ethical principles, the contents of the existing organizational culture must be dealt with directly for positive change to occur. Any efforts which disregard culture not only risk suppression of positive change but may also unintentionally perpetuate negative cultural norms, beliefs, and values. Ignoring culture in attempting to refocus the values orientation of an organization is similar to ignoring causes and treating symptoms allowing underlying disease to spread and intensify.

An organization's culture is composed of the ". . . *basic assumptions* and *beliefs* that are shared by members of the organization, that operate unconsciously, and that define in a basic 'taken-for-granted' fashion an organization's view of itself and its environment" (emphasis in original) (Schein, 1985: 6).

The organizational culture perspective has become an important way of analyzing organizational processes, procedures, and the effects of routines on the organizational environment. It also assists in understanding the psychological elements of organizational participant commitment to the group. It is the basis for the current private sector emphasis upon values as the key to employee creativeness, loyalty, and productivity. If the organizational culturists are correct in their analyses of the effect of culture upon an organization, the road to a reorientation of an organization's values is beset with problems of implementation and adaptation. This is a hard lesson that has been learned quickly by some American businesses that are attempting to incorporate the ''Japanese approach'' by infusing into their organizational cultures values that emphasize quality. They ignore or minimize the underlying and critical elements of the present organizational culture that aid in the success or failure of any imposed change. Differences in Eastern and Western cultures allow, encourage, and resist differing values. Therefore, adoption or adaptation of values requires consideration of much more than, say, a goal of greater profit margins.

American public sector organizations are beginning to examine and apply private sector quality principles to governmental services. Unfortunately, however, the bottom lines are different in the private and public sectors, and government has yet to solve the problem of how to turn indifferent citizens into satisfied customers through private sector quality approaches to service delivery (Frederickson, 1993; Theobald, 1997). It appears that the most scholarly public administration advice on how to accomplish this conversion is to pump ethics into the governmental system, assuming that the wholesale re-education of governmental operatives and leaders will result in a kindlier, more values-oriented public service that will deliver quality programs and services.

Most of the scholarly examinations and evaluations of organizational change efforts in private sector organizational environments offer very little support for the effectiveness of a focus upon leadership as the prime element in creating the values-driven organization. Although leadership is important, it must be directed toward reorienting the organization's culture to facilitate the emergence of appropriate ethical values as the basis for organizational decisions. There is little recognition in public administration of the relationship between leadership and cultural change—even strong leadership fails when confronted by strong organizational cultures with different values.

I. ORGANIZATIONAL CULTURE FROM AN ANALYTICAL PERSPECTIVE

To understand the relationship between ethics and organizational culture in both theoretical and applied perspectives, one must first understand the breadth and depth of the concept of organizational culture. Dr. Stephen Ott has provided an excellent review and analysis of the relevant theory and research which provides the basis for our present understanding of this social construct (Ott, 1989). Ott describes the organizational culture perspective as meaning ''. . . two different but related things.'' The first is that similar to societal culture, *organizational culture* consists of ''. . . shared values, beliefs, assumptions, perceptions, norms, artifacts and patterns of behavior. It is the unseen and unobservable force that is always behind organizational activities that can be seen and observed.'' Secondly, the *organizational culture perspective* is an analytical perspective comprised of ''. . . a collection of theories that attempt to explain and predict how organizations and the people in them act in different circumstances'' (Ott, 1989:1).

These theoretical approaches lead Ott to observe that organizational culture:

1. Is similar to societal culture;
2. Has content;
3. Is a force behind organizational activity;
4. Energizes organizational members to act;
5. Is a unifying theme that expedites meaning, direction, and mobilization of organizational members; and
6. Is a control mechanism which encourages or prohibits behaviors.

Also, this perspective challenges most of the prevailing academic systems and structural theories of organization as "... using the wrong lenses to look at the wrong organizational elements in ... attempts to understand and predict organizational behavior" (Ott, 1989: 50).

To organize the findings of the organizational culture theories and studies, Ott draws upon the definitions provided by Schein (1981, 1985) and Keesing (1974). Keesing notes that there are two schools of cultural anthropology that have influenced organizational cultural studies. One is the *adaptationist* approach which focuses upon the directly observable, tangible items in a culture—speech, writing, the uses of tools, transmission of knowledge, and related items. The other is the *ideationalist* approach which is based upon common beliefs, knowledges, meanings, and other patterned ways of thinking in social groupings.

Adaptationists count the visible in organizations, especially the patterns of language that are employed, develop trends and patterns, and derive cultural meaning from the contents of visible things in the organization environment. Thus, the intensity of the presence of the visible object will be the basis for generalizing about the role and importance of cultural elements. This approach lends itself to the more traditional social science analytical techniques, especially statistical and trend analysis techniques.

Ideationalists interpret organizational factor responses to questions about values and mores in the group, or they observe interaction patterns and rituals to derive common elements and patterns of interaction. These observations are either interpreted by the subjects or by the observers and cultural meaning is ascribed to the resulting patterns.

Schein develops a paradigm of the essential elements of culture joining the adaptationist concepts to the ideationist approach by suggesting a three-level interactive continuum of major organizational culture elements. This paradigm is based upon the degree of visibility of each of the phenomena in an organizational setting.

Level 1 (the most visible) is called the *artifacts and creations level*. It consists of technology, art, and the visible and audible behavior patterns of a group. It is the level at which the adaptationists work. level 2 (partially visible to any observer) joins the adaptationists and the ideationalists in the realm of *values*. This mid-level describes phenomena that are viewable and testable in the physical and social environment, but require interpretation by the observer. Level 3 (generally not visible), the foundation of the Schein ranking, is the *basic assumptions level*. Among the elements that Schein includes are the organization's assumptions about: (1) its relationship to its environment; (2) the nature of its reality, time, and space; (3) the nature of human nature; (4) the nature of human activity; and (5) the nature of human relationships.

Organizational culture researchers have investigated the elements at each of these analytical levels. In providing a perspective on the discrete elements of organizational culture, Ott has developed a list of the elements of organizational culture and classified them according to the Schein paradigm (Ott, 1989: 63–64). In further refining the Schein approach, Ott divides Level 1 into Parts A and B. Level 1A artifacts relate to the technology and art in an organizational culture. Level 1B, labeled *patterns of behavior*, designates familiar management tasks, visible and audible behavior patterns, and norms as common cultural artifacts (Ott, 1989: 62).

The listing of the subjects of organizational cultural inquiry in Table 1 is derived from the Ott analysis and is presented in this format for an easier recognition of the relationship of the levels of organizational culture to the elements of inquiry that comprise each level. In analyzing the most pertinent research in the organizational culture arena, Ott uses the 66 principal authors and studies which have contributed to an understanding of various aspects of the organizational culture concept. Each is classified according to the level of organizational culture addressed. From this massive body of investigation and speculation, Ott derives what he calls "functional agreement across the literature about four functions that can be viewed as the core of a functional definition of organizational culture." These are:

1. It provides shared patterns of cognitive interpretations or perceptions, so organization members know how they are expected to act and think.
2. It provides shared patterns of affect, an emotional sense of involvement and commitment to organizational values and moral codes—of things worth working for and believing in—so organizational members know what they are expected to value and how they are expected to feel.
3. It defines and maintains boundaries, allowing identification of members and nonmembers.
4. It functions as an organizational control system, prescribing and prohibiting certain behaviors.

There is no agreement on a fifth function:

5. *Organizational culture strongly affects organizational performance* (emphasis added) (Ott, 1989:68).[1]

Ott contends that organizational culture is "a social force that *controls patterns of organizational behavior by shaping members' cognitions and perceptions of meanings and realities, providing affective energy for mobilization and identifying who belongs and who does not*" (emphasis his) (p. 69). However, without more discriminating discrete research and an improvement of investigative methods in organizational culture research methods, Ott concludes that there are many questions about organizational culture left to be answered.

Ott's analysis is valuable for the integrating role that it plays in examining a wide body of literature, synthesizing the findings, noting the gaps in the various approaches, and recommending research strategies. For the serious researcher of American governmental ethics, the theoretical and behavioral perspective that is offered serves as a guide to ways in which the organizational culture perspective can be utilized in understanding the role of ethics in organizational decision-making and service delivery. For the organizational development consultant who is pursuing ethical development as a means for improving quality, the organizational culture perspective provides ways of understanding an organization and where ethical development can be most usefully employed in changing the organization's view of itself and its role in the governance and service delivery process.

Table 1 Typology of Elements of Organizational Culture

Level 1A Artifacts		
Art	Language	Ceremonies
Patterns of communication	Heroes	Historical vestiges
Translation of myths into action and relationship	Organizational anecdotes	Links between language, metaphor, and ritual
Material objects	Myths	Physical arrangements
Organizational scripts	Organizational stories	Traditions
Symbols	Jargon	Celebrations

Level 1B Patterns of behavior		
Attitudes	Behavior regularities	Custom
Rites	Shared expectations	Management practices
Patterns of interaction	Links between language, metaphor, and ritual	Ways of doing things
Manner	Norms	Ritualized practices
Habits	Rituals	Informal system of rule
Style	Traditions	

Level 2 Beliefs and values		
Attitudes	Intersubjective meanings	Beliefs
Patterns of shared beliefs	Patterns of cognitive processes	Source of norms, rules, attitudes, customs
Level of consensus	Core	Organizational ethic
Ethos	Feelings	Identity
Ideologies	Justifications for behavior	Knowledge
Patterns of meaning	Meaning	Mindset
Being	Philosophy	Practical syllogisms
Purpose	Sentiments	Commitment to excellence
Way of thinking	Tacit understandings	Values
Basic or core values	Patterns of shared values	Vision, way, worldviews

Level 3 Assumptions		
Assumptions people live by	Glue that holds an organization together	Organizational scripts (transactional analysis)
Patterns of basic assumptions	Mindset	Identity
Being	Philosophy	Core
Way	Spirit	Enactment
Worldview		

Unclear elements (difficult to classify)		
Organizational climate	Core	
Roots	Quality of perceived specialness, way, worldviews	

Source: From Ott (1989).

II. THE ETHICS ELEMENT IN ORGANIZATIONAL CULTURE

Ethics, values, moral codes, and ideologies are important in the organizational culture paradigm. Ott concludes that these Level 2 elements are central to understanding culture. He observes that: ethics, values, and morals provide the justification for what people do in the organization; and it would not be possible to understand the most visible levels of the organization, its artifacts (Level 1A) and patterned behaviors (Level 1B) without ". . . knowing the beliefs and values that drive them'' (Ott, 1989: 41).

This idea of the centrality of ethics and values to organizational culture and, by extension, to organizational performance is the key concept in the recent spate of popular management literature that emphasizes the role of values in the development of quality (Ouchi, 1981; Pascale and Athos, 1981; Peters and Waterman, 1982; Iococca, 1984; Peters and Austin, 1985; Leavitt, 1986; Walton, 1986; and others). An arbitrary choice to represent this approach is William G. Ouchi's *Theory Z* (1981). On the surface, the Ouchi essay can be seen as a partially academic analysis of one kind of organizational culture and a partially consultant pitch for the development of organizational working philosophies that encompass the primary values of caring and cooperation at all levels and in all parts of the organizational environment. It is Ouchi's linking of culture to organizational performance that is especially appealing. He argues that measured by several economic indicators and by corporate reputations for quality products and services, the most successful companies are those that are the most values-holistic with regard to employees and other organizational stakeholders. This means that the culture of the group is based upon common assumptions and identities with others who are engaged in the same quest, and that individual identity with the group rests upon the value of what the group does. This identification allows common beliefs, norms, ethics, and patterned interactions to function in the organizational decision process. It also affects the organizational structure, the technical processes of the organization, and even the physical aspects of the space occupied by the organization. In the marketplace, the content of the assumptions of a rich organizational culture usually reflect a common agreement on the value of the organization's product to society; a commitment to service to maintain that quality; and the honorable treatment of individuals, both within the organization and without, as essential human participants in the corporate endeavor. This is what Peters and Waterman meant when they observed that to be successful in the marketplace, an organization must be "hands-on and values-driven" (1982: 278–291).

Leadership is important in the development, maintenance, and adaptation of organizational culture. One long-ignored leadership theory that has emerged from a fifty-year hibernation addresses directly the relationship between leadership and ethics, values, and norms. Although it is grounded in the hierarchy concept of classical organization theory, it observes that the leader is the developer, expediter, and guardian of organizational norms and values, hence its ethics and moral behaviors.

During the 1980s, chapter 17 of Chester Barnard's 1938 classic, *The Functions of the Executive*, was exhumed. Its claim is that the executive can (should, must) control the moral codes of the organization. Scott (1982) notes that Barnard's claims for moral leadership in the organization is directed toward the organizational processes only and not to the basic values structure of the organization. There is a significant difference between leading and applying morals to process and, on the other hand, developing and maintaining basic values in the organization. Leadership, which does not appear in the listing of elements that have been examined in the structured research in organizational culture, continues to be hailed as the crucial variable in the changing or reorienting of organizational cultures (e.g., Fairholm, 1991; Leavitt, 1986).

Surveys of public sector managers (Bowman, 1990; Bowman and Williams, 1997), have consistently expressed the significance attributed to leadership in establishing and fostering the ethical climate of organizations. Both positive acts of advocacy, publicity, and celebration, as well as negative leadership behaviors of neglect, hypocrisy, and exhortation serve to cultivate, in the opinion of the respondents, a climate to support or sabotage the value structure of the organization. However, there are enough examples of strong leadership failing to change the value structure of organizations to question the claim (Ott, 1989; Pastin, 1986).

In the private-sector values literature, leadership is seen as essential in the maintenance or changing of organizational culture (Ouchi, 1981: 89). As ethics and morals are examined within a cultural context, leaders are seen as persons who hold strong ethical and moral beliefs. Thus, although leadership is recognized as a maintenance or change variable in the organizational culture literature, it is treated as a process variable. The major difficulty with the present interpretation of the leadership variable in the popular organizational culture and change literature is that some of the popularizers of the values thesis suggest that all an organization needs is a leader who has a strong sense of ethics and a commitment to moral management in order to redirect or change organizational culture and organizational character. Although this assumption may sell leadership books and managerial training, gaining control over the organizational culture is not usually as easy as it is depicted in the leadership literature. It seems to depend upon whether the existing organizational culture is weak or strong, and how smart and determined a leader is to confront organizational cultures with new values and ethics.

So far the case for leadership alone impacting upon organizational culture significantly has not been made.

III. THE CLASH OF ETHICS AND ORGANIZATIONAL CULTURE

The interface between ethics and organizational culture is of interest to Mark Pastin, a philosopher who studies and advises business corporations, and approaches the ethics and culture phenomena from a decidedly different perspective than the anthropologists, applied psychologists, and organizational sociologists who dominate the organizational culture field. Pastin (1986) is one of the few applied academic consultants who advocate organizational change by confronting the organization's Level 2 and Level 3 norms and belief systems. For Pastin, "[e]thics is not only the heart of organizational culture, it is also the fulcrum for producing change. Since ethics is the fulcrum for changing culture, changing culture without ethics is akin to changing a tire without a jack" (1986: 128). The recognition of the primacy of ethics in organizational environments places Pastin in general agreement with the organizational culture analysts about the importance of ethics and values. Pastin goes a step further, however, in classifying both organizational cultures and organizational ethics as either weak or strong. For analytical purposes this allows Pastin to determine the effort required for changes in ethics to impact and change cultures. His conclusion is that strong organizational cultures are generally impervious to changes in ethics where new ethics are introduced at Level 1B (visible patterns of behavior level). A strong belief system (Level 3, the invisible assumptions of the organization level) will not integrate values at the operating level (Levels 1A and 1B, artifacts and patterns of behavior level). Strong organizational cultures must be approached at the base, its "worldview," if change is to occur. Pastin observes that strong cultures can easily defeat even the most determined efforts of capable leaders to introduce changes in cultural assumptions. Thus, even the most enlightened, determined police chief may not be able to succeed in affecting the behavior of the street level operatives in the department by introducing ethical codes and new, strong behavioral rules.

Weak organizational cultures, which are generally found in new or totally reorganized organizations, have not developed strong beliefs which dominate operating processes and value premises. This type of organization can absorb new value premises and fashion operating procedures that are based upon imported values. In infusing organizations with new ethical propositions, Pastin (1986) advocates behavioral strategies that soften the behavioral controls of culture and by enhancing the role of ethics as the essential element in the organizational social contract. In terms of the Schein paradigm, Pastin would support organizational strategies that focus on Level 2 ethics and values, pushing these values downward to dominate the basic social contract. Where positive values and ethical behavior expectations are a part of the base of the organization, they will be reflected visibly in the organization's procedures and policies.

As the heart of organizational culture, ethics becomes for Pastin the "forum . . . in which organizations argue fundamental changes in their bylaws (ground rules)" (1986: 132). In strong organizational cultures these Level 2 and 3 ground rules are so ingrained in the Level 1A and 1B practices that they are beyond alteration by simply adopting a new code of ethics, establishing conflicting behavioral rules of conduct, or training the entire work force in ethical principles. To accomplish any change, the focus of the discussion of organizational ground rules, and any alterations in those standards, must take place at the less visible organizational culture levels. Strong organizational cultures abound in public administration. Current organizational efforts to reform the personnel practices of the Federal Bureau of Investigation and the agency-wide ethics improvement effort of the Internal Revenue Service are two visible examples of attempts at organizational change through ethics training and Level 1B policy implementation. A more public and vivid example is the U.S. Navy "Tailhook" incident that dramatically illustrates how organizational culture dominates behavior and resists change. In a one-hour press briefing on the C-SPAN network (September 24, 1992), Acting Secretary of the Navy Sean C. O'Keefe continually referred to "cultural problems" as the root cause of both the sexual harassment incident and a lax investigation by the Navy's Office of Naval Investigation. On September 25, 1992, the *Washington Post* featured O'Keefe on the front page with a caption under his picture which said, "the larger issue is a cultural problem." Eight years later, following the resignation of the Secretary of the Navy, Lawrence H. Garrett, the early retirement of Admiral Frank B. Kelso, and 50 navy and marine corps pilots having been fined or disciplined, there is still "a defiant tone" from some members. As one member, retired from the military, noted: if the standards applied to the Tailhook investigation had been applied to the conduct on V-J Day, "my goodness, we would have court-martialed everyone in the military" (*The New York Times*, 1999).

These tightly bureaucratic, professionally-dominated agencies have developed worldviews, norms, and values in their organizational cultures that are the unquestioned basis of the ground rules which govern the patterns of internal and external interaction. Needing to change the ground rules, these reform attempts amount to only an organizational ethics "facelift." The underlying social contract structure probably remains untouched. According to Pastin, that strategy will not work. Organizational participants—

leaders, managers, professionals, and operatives—must examine and understand the behavioral power of their basic assumptions, their social contracts, if real change is to occur.

Thus, no matter how ethically appealing are new standards or how morally strong a leader may be, attempts to alter behavior by introducing different ethical standards may cause disruption without effecting change. Similarly, without identifying and confronting the cultural variables that are inhibiting the absorption of new ethical standards, even organization-wide ethics educational efforts may be wasted. If this is so, and Pastin's evidence is ample, the "values-driven" organizational tactics prescribed by the popular literature, the notion that leaders can do it all without strategically employing ethics changes, and the idea that rational organizational actors will change the organization's ethics if they are made aware of importance of ethics, is highly speculative.

Pastin's observations on the strength of organizational cultural assumptions (Level 3) provides a needed addition to the organizational culture literature. This approach enables one to fit the ethics, values, and morals elements of organizational culture into a perspective that is useful in both understanding the role of organizational culture and how the use of ethics can contribute to organizational change in any organization, private or public. The combination of emphasis upon the assumptions level of culture and the strength of those assumptions requires the consideration of the entire cultural paradigm in understanding the relationship between culture and organizational action.

Organizational researchers have adopted, challenged, and significantly extended Schein's theory (Hatch, 1993; Schultz, 1994) to incorporate greater dynamic interplay between and among the levels he introduced to examine organizational culture.

One of the few recent works in public administration literature to address Level 3 cultural assumptions and organizational values is Van Wart's *Changing Public Sector Values* (1998). He extends the Schein and Ott cultural framework to philosophical and macropolitical questions and makes an important contribution to theoretical concerns regarding metaethical questions; however, research attending to these foundational cultural elements in the public sphere and ethics remains insufficient.

IV. PUBLIC ADMINISTRATION, ORGANIZATIONAL CULTURE, AND ETHICS

American public administration suffers from a lack of attention to organizational culture. The seminal works of Phillip Selznick's *TVA and the Grass Roots* (1949), Peter M. Blau's *The Dynamics of Bureaucracy* (1955, 1963), and Herbert Kaufman's *The Forest Ranger* (1960) provide our introduction to organizational culture in the public sector literature. The more recent "reinventing government" literature (Osborne and Gaebler, 1992; Osborne and Plastrik, 1997) extends greater attention to the multilevel variables of the Schein paradigm and suggests a slow but certain awakening to organizational culture in public, case-study research. Each study provides glimpses of organizational culture through the analysis of the development of an organization's policy apparatus and an evaluation of the structured patterns of interactions within the agencies that were analyzed.

With reference to Ott's adaptation of the Schein paradigm (Table 1), the Selznick and Kaufman approaches are macro in execution, devoting a great deal of effort to the Level 1B phenomena, noting management practices, behavioral regularities, ways of doing things, patterns of interaction, norms, style, and (especially in *The Forest Ranger*) the strength of the traditions of this governmental agency. Neither of these works is particularly concerned with ethics, but both touch upon the Level 2 elements. Shared values and beliefs, ideologies, and ways of thinking are explored in relation to the function of each organization. Kaufman's examination of professionalism in binding together the far-flung field operations of the U.S. Forest Service is a good example of linking Level 2 variables to the visible characteristics of the organization. His analysis provides an understanding of the ground rules of the Forest Service and why it did things the way it did.

Blau's approach more closely links the essentials of organizational operations (Level 1A and B) with the values and the shared belief systems of Level 2 variables in organizational culture. In one of the agencies studied, the introduction of new work measurement methods produced an adjustment in the behavior of the lower level employees studied. In another agency the practice of not reporting bribe attempts underlined the tacit understandings and norms of the work group. Both of these are Level 2 variables in the organizational culture paradigm. What would now be considered ethical concerns, and these could be examined from the culture perspective, are treated as organizational norms. The message conveyed is an organizational culture message. Both agencies could be conceived of as having strong cultures which guide behavior at the street operating level. In Pastin's terms, the strong culture at the service delivery level is armor against the sorts of fundamental changes desired by management. In the case of the bribe offers, even behaviors required by law are immune to change.

Osborne and Gaebler, in *Reinventing Government* (1992), continue the argument that alterations in Level 1A and 1B variables may effect change in public sector organizations. They gesture to Level 2 and 3 variables in their closing remarks when calling for a "new paradigm" in perceptions and expectations of governmental services. However, it is in *Banishing Bureaucracy* (1997) where Osborne and Plastrik offer sweeping "prescriptive" measures to exact such change. They are clearly aware that all strategies which alter the observable elements of an organization invoke temporary change unless significant attention is granted to the values and worldviews of organizational members. They note leaders' and employees' predispositions, or in Ott's framework, Level 3 assumptions, are the most essential for change to take place and the most resistant to it.

Their formula calls for three approaches to changing organizational culture at its foundational core. The first two approaches, "changing habits and touching hearts" revert to Level 1A and B activities—changing ritualized practices, symbols, stories, and style— to effect change. The third strategy, "winning minds," speaks to the more intangible underpinnings that sustain change by suggesting such tools as "surfacing the given" unspoken assumptions of its membership and building a shared vision of the organizational image. They cite a new entrepreneurial culture in one Virginia city as an example of successful cultural transition. It is left to others to debate the desirability of such a design for governmental organizations.

The current wave of reform literature acknowledges the vital part organizational culture can play in institutionalizing change. Now the cultural assumptions of the reformers are being subjected to examination for how they identify government's deficiencies to date and frame their proposed remedies (Light, 1995; Peters, 1996). Realignment (Gilman, 1999) and reinvigorating (Gawthrop, 1999)—not reinventing—the democratic principles specific to public organizations will have a greater chance of success because the significance of the current organizational culture is addressed.

These governmental organizational culture studies contribute to an understanding of some of the elements of organizational culture as they affect behavior in the governmental organization. They are usually cited by organizational culture writers and researchers when organizational culture phenomena are analyzed. However, their lasting impacts upon public administration appear to be minimal. The organizational theory concerns of public administration do not attach much importance to the impact of culture upon the organization.

In addition to the research-based examinations of individual governmental agencies and departments, essays by Hummel (1977, 1982, 1987), Scott and Hart (1979), and Gawthrop (1984) provide speculative views of bureaucratic culture, views that could be the basis of research in governmental culture. Hummel's interpretation of bureaucratic culture is the most general and the most closely related to the mainstream of the organizational culture approach. In *The Bureaucratic Experience* (1982), the second chapter, "Bureaucracy as the New Culture," evaluates the capitalistic system and the Weberian rational bureaucratic system of both the private and public sectors as "normless" and without a culture (pp. 60–98). This condition is antithetical to societies based upon values and with expectations that the organizational structures in those societies will reflect those values. For Hummel, the values of policy and procedural control directed toward the maximization of power lead to meaningless lives and activities. Bureaucracy as an organizational form corrupts itself and society by its lack of human-centered norms, values, and ethics.

Scott and Hart (1979) pursue a similar theme by emphasizing the totalitarianism of the organization; the manipulative role played by the power-holders (the "significant people"); the organizational values maintenance role of the professionals; the powerlessness of the lower level participants (the "insignificant people"); and the resulting "values-neutral" organizational forms that depend entirely upon the values of the powerful for any meaning to the individual. In organizational culture terms, Scott and Hart observe perverse Level 2 values, norms, and ethics which result in value-neutral policies, behaviors, and artifacts of organizational activity. They speculate that organizational change can occur through the efforts of the powerful and the professional, but that such change must be based upon positive individual values (as opposed to organizational maintenance values) becoming operative at Level 2 and being reflected in the observable activities of organizations. In this approach, the organization must exhibit a culture that reflects productive human values; the neutrality of organizational value structures are too easily manipulated and emptied of the values that give meaning to life.

While maintaining the organizational neutrality thesis, Gawthrop (1984) narrows the focus to the governmental organization and the nature of the public-regarding ethics of governmental organizations. The Level 2 elements that Gawthrop identifies as contributing to "an ethics of civility" in public organizations is a ". . . a mechanistic ethics that stresses the notion of equity primarily in quantitative terms" (p. 139). Included in the definition are the norms, values, and beliefs in procedural due process, an avoidance of public policy debates that focus on long-term ends and procedural legalism. The result is a systems ethic that reduces all the functions of the organization to "the lowest common denominator quality" in the provision of quantities of public services. Gawthrop labels this approach as "reductionist," measured by political gains and losses, with little concern for personal notions of worth. The neutrality thesis is underscored by Gawthrop's observation that "if we are lucky, prudent pragmatists will apply the ethics of civility in a manner that at least approximates the conventional notions of decency, honesty, and integrity" (p. 145). The alternatives are "nihilistic, ethical monstrosities" (p. 145).

The void suggested by value-neutral organizational systems has lead some to warn of the maladaptive cultures which have and can continue to replace them. Caiden (1991) calls them "bureaupathologies" which infuse organizations with cultural illnesses at all levels leading to an undercurrent of evasive dysfunction. Adams and Balfour, in *Unmasking Administrative Evil* (1998), note severe cases evident in an organizational context which promotes a technical-rational approach to decision-making cradled in a scientific-analytical mindset. From the more obvious (i.e., unmasked) example of the great efficiency and effectiveness of the German bureaucracy to implement the "final solution" to a more convoluted one in which former Nazi scientists made the NASA space race a success, they reveal that organizational goals and systems are not value-free and can, in fact, disguise and perpetuate unintentional immorality. The organizational culture can encourage a moral inversion in which employees rationalize and justify actions by allowing organizational process to supercede the normative context of their behavior. Guy also cautions "contradictory norms give rise to unethical behavior . . . individuals adapt their personal values to make them compatible with the organizations" (1990:97).

The cultural essayists' perspectives on the relationship of ethics, values, and norms to organizational outputs reflect pessimism about prevailing organizational culture assumptions and values in governmental environments. Without reference to the organizational culture approach, each speculates that if the Level 2 and Level 3 elements identified as important in organizational culture can be reoriented to more human-centered values, changes can occur in the Level 1A and 1B characteristics of organizations. In this, they join the consultants and organizational change scholars. This movement for values change is evident in the private sector with; the emphasis upon values, norms, and ethics as the driving forces in organizations; and change applications that are intended to humanize organizational activities through the elimination of hierarchies, more cooperation, and very fundamentally, a re-education of persons to understand that the content of the operating assumptions, beliefs and values, and ethics are essential to the production of quality products and services.

V. ORGANIZATIONAL CULTURE IN THE PUBLIC ADMINISTRATION ETHICS LITERATURE

Educators and researchers who are interested in the ethics of American public administration have not embraced the organizational culture perspective to any substantial degree. The contemporary public administration interest in, and concern about, ethics probably began with Stephen Bailey's 1964 essay in the *Public Administration Review*. Bailey speculated about the discretion inherent in the governmental administrator role and how ethics was a necessary element in the exercise of administrative decision-making. This theme gradually attracted more attention to the role of ethics in a professional environment. The result has been a gathering of the public administration intellectual community to examine, reflect, and propose various paradigms for an understanding and advancement of ethical thought within the profession. Bailey's choice of emphasis, the individual administrator, may have influenced greatly the path of public ethics scholarship. This focus tends to detract from the organizational context in which the administrator exercises discretion and generates value paths for others in the group.

Secondary priming of the public ethics well was provided by public reactions to Watergate and a gaggle of political and administrative scandals which emerged under the Nixon administration and continued unabated through the Reagan presidency. The national government, most of the states, and many local governments have responded to a growing concern about the ethics of government by enacting ethics codes, developing principles of operating ethics, and prescribing rules for the ethical conduct of governmental employees. Prominent governmental scandals and the governmental reaction to them, especially in the development of training programs, have awakened the concern of scholars and consultants. This awakening has produced a number of essays and training materials that are directed specifically toward the governmental ethics problem.

It is difficult to identify precisely the major contributors to the American public administration ethics literature; there are a number of scholars who have contributed. If ethics course textbooks are considered, the following are important: Rohr (1978, 1989), Cooper (1982, 1986, 1990, 1998), Denhardt (1988), Guy (1990), Bowman (1991), Sternberg and Austern (1990), Timmins (1990), Gortner (1991), and Lewis (1991). Professional journals contain an increasing number of reflections and the results of studies of ethical problems in public organizations. Influential among the contributors are: Chandler (1983); Thompson (1985), Frederickson and Hart (1985), Bowman (1990), and Cooper (1987). In this body of thought and recommendations several organizational culture elements are treated extensively, but in isolation from the organizational culture context.

Only Cooper devotes a meaningful part of his essay to the organizational culture context of public sector ethics (1998: 183–90). Citing Schein (1985) and Kilmann (1984), and noting that the Los Angeles County Sheriff's Department has been seriously using organizational culture concepts to intervene in its culture (Preimsberger and Block, 1986), Cooper concludes that cultural intervention can be very effective. Cooper's observation about organizational culture is that it"... exercise[s] powerful influence over the conduct of employees apart from, and sometimes in opposition to, the formal rules, regulations, procedures, and role authority of the managers" (p. 183). This recognition of the strong organizational culture and its possible immunity to ethical change leads Cooper to recommend several ways of recognizing the phenomenon and attending to it through appropriate leadership activity.

Carol Lewis', *The Ethics Challenge in Public Service* (1991), contains an appendix questionnaire which Lewis has labeled Agency Ethics Audit (p. 202–203). This audit asks for data and impressions about agency ethics policy. The information from this instrument reflects the Level 1B visible behaviors that are the starting point for a values, norms, and ethics investigation of a public organization. However, Lewis does not explain the audit or offer any guidelines for its application.

The public administration ethics textbook analysts divide rather neatly among those who provide thoughtful insights into the basic values ethics of the public service (Rohr, 1978, 1989; Denhardt, 1988; Gortner, 1991) and those who present difficult cases and policy problems with suggested ethical solutions (Guy, 1990; Sternberg and Austern, 1990; Timmins, 1990; and Lewis, 1991, 1993). In all of these writings, the recommendations for change are directed toward organizational culture Levels 1A and 1B. Without much regard to the actual composition of the Level 2 elements or the organizational ground rules at Level 3, the general approaches that are advocated for change in governmental organizations are the education of organizational operatives in public sector ethics and stimulating managers and executives to lead ethics reform. While this may seem logical and appropriate, the problem of the strength of organizational culture—especially in large, long-established public agencies, the non-public backgrounds of political appointee executives, and the short tenure of political-administrative leaders—may preclude any change in the values and ethical nature of a public agency, no matter who wants to see ethical change or how strong is the appeal to values which are considered essential in maintaining public virtue.

VI. THE ORGANIZATIONAL CULTURE RESEARCH ELEMENT

Essential to the organizational culture approach is an appropriate research methodology. Ott notes that research in organizational culture generally rejects the logical-positivistic, highly quantifiable data approaches that dominate the social sciences (Ott, 1989: 90). Organizational culture research is primarily qualitative, hands-on, and requires digging around in the organization. Ott mentions the following as the principal general methods of investigating the various levels of organizational culture:

1. Wandering around and looking at physical settings (Level 1A);
2. Rummaging through historical records (Level 1A);
3. Content analyzing publications (Level 1A);
4. Learning from organizational charts (Level 1A);
5. Listening to spoken words (Level 1A, 1B, 2, 3);
6. Listening to myths, stories, sagas, and legends (Level 1A, 1B);
7. Administering paper and pencil instruments (Level 1B, 2);
8. Combinations of the foregoing using a clinician and an insider (Level 3); and
9. Combinations of the foregoing by an outsider with an ethnographic perspective (Level 3) (Ott, 1989: 106–127).

Each investigative method has been utilized to understand aspects of organizational culture. Each configures cultural elements in certain patterns for analysis by the investigator.

Research in organizational culture requires those organizational analysis skills that enable the investigator to document the relationship of the Level 1A and 1B visible outputs to the Level 2 values. This approach is commonly associated with industrial and applied psychology, or organizational sociology, and applying research skills not ordinarily found in the policy-oriented research trends in public administration. The ethnographic research is in the domain of the cultural anthropologists, even further removed from public administration analytical approaches.

In conducting organizational research to determine the ethical content of an organization's culture, the most appropriate methods for determining the degree to which the elements are present seem to be listening (method 5); analyzing organizational stories or examining its records (method 6); and the administration of paper and pencil tests (method 7). Ott reprints Alexander's *Organizational Norms Opinioniare* (1977) and Harrison's *Questionnaire for Diagnosing Organizational Ideology* (1975) as examples of the paper and pencil test approach (Ott, 1989: 126–137). Each instrument asks organizational participants to respond to questions about the organization's norms and ideologies. Scales are constructed to provide profiles of the organization based upon respondent interpretations of various decisions, procedures, and behaviors in the organization. From the results of these organizational participant surveys, the clinician can develop perceptions of the Level 2 and 3 elements of organizational culture.

This approach can be fruitfully employed in evaluating the presence or absence of ethical elements, norms, and values in governmental organizations. The results are quantifiable and subject to statistical analysis, if that is appropriate. For governmental organizations, ethics researchers can examine the official values of codes, rules, and subject interpretations about how approved behaviors are managed. Typically, the items ask the respondents to evaluate the degree to which some ethical principle or behavior is present (or absent) in the various operations of the agency.

The opinions of the organizational respondents can be arrayed in various ways. Through either statistical correlation or induction, the researcher can develop analyses indicating any patterns in the presence, absence, or corruption of the various elements of ethics that are under study. The findings can be further verified through a secondary survey asking the respondents about the accuracy of the patterns that emerge from the responses to the questionnaires.

The use of self-scoring analytical instruments is in its infancy in examining the ethical elements in public organizations. There is an increase in using the pencil and paper technique with public organization executives and managers. Although this is a start in examining the ethical cultures of public organizations, the view from the top about the organization's ethics may be quite different from that of the street level bureaucrat. Few studies have turned inward to the operative point of citizen contact in the organization for any data that would reveal operating norms and values. Cooper's mention of the Los Angeles County Sheriff's Department is one of a very few examples of this approach in government.

Several experiments with paper and pencil technique have begun to show promise. Carnevale and Wechsler (1992) surveyed employee attitudes and perceptions to identify individual and organizational determinants of trust formation in public systems. Menzel's local government studies utilized a Likert-type instrument to examine values attitudes in two municipal settings (Menzel, 1993, 1995). These researchers are searching for a way to capture organizational climate. Both approaches demonstrate that it is possible to target the values, norms, and ethics of government organizations and identify discrete value patterns in governmental organizations. Having the ability to do this type of analysis is of tremendous value if organizational leaders want to change the value systems. The presence of patterned data can provide starting points for education and the development of new policies.

Recent research on organizational cultures typically involve ethnographic observations, interviews, and participation (Hatch, 1993; Schultz, 1994) in order to obtain sufficient relevant information; however, these methods require extensive amounts of time and money.

The difficulties in performing organizational ethical analyses are those problems that are inherent in organizational culture research generally. Ott lists a number of them, including the necessity for applying multiple research strategies, the difficulty of generalizing and hypothesizing using qualitative research approaches, ascertaining the content of Level 3 variables can be costly and time-consuming, and the lack of acceptance of qualitative research results by the logical-positivistic research community (Ott, 1989: 125–26). One additional difficulty that Ott does not mention is that digging around in the organization, especially if the investigator is seeking values, can be threatening to managers and executives. While many executives support ethics training and will welcome assistance in developing codes, requests to take the ethical temperature of the organization's culture may be refused. Executive confidence in the researcher and the need for intrusion in the organization must be built by the researcher.

Despite these difficulties, understanding an organization's cultural base before attempting to change a governmental agency's values assumptions can be an efficient way of directing change in the values system. The present popular trend of emphasizing ethics through the top-downward imposition of codes, working philosophies, values principles, rules, and the creation of formal ethical systems has created some optimistic expectations that these structural artifacts can achieve a quick ethics transplant. However, if there is a strong competing set of values, the new organ has a high rate of organizational rejection. Structured organizational cultural research can identify the extent to which values already exist and determine their strength in the culture. It can also provide the base measurements from which the effectiveness of change methods can be evaluated. The ways in which ethics and values are being introduced to governmental organizations always include the Level 1B elements that are visible manifestations of organizational cultural elements. Structured investigations using the principal methods of cultural research can establish whether or not the organizational operatives or other stakeholders see these values in organizational methods, management, and output. A more accurate understanding of these elements can make change strategies more effective. Quality organizational culture research can provide a sharpening of the assumptions that currently underlay the educational and training efforts to change governmental value systems through wholesale education and training programs, and through the creation of ethics-oriented, formal, control mechanisms.

VII. CONCLUDING OBSERVATIONS

Reflecting upon organizational culture in public administration will not greatly assist those scholars and researchers who are seeking the fundamental working values and ethics of public service—Rohr (1989); Denhardt (1988). The cultural approach will be of only limited assistance in solving discrete cases—Guy (1990); Timmins (1990); Sternberg and Austern (1990). However, for the increasing number of ethics activists who are engaged directly in changing the values orientation of public agencies and training public professionals, an understanding of organizational culture and the employment of organizational culture research methods is crucial for any success in the endeavor—Cooper (1998); Gortner (1991); Lewis (1991). Recognizing the importance of the organizational culture context has been essential for any successes that private sector organizations have had in developing quality products and services, and in creating the truly values-based organization. For these successes to be repeated in public sector environments, especially insofar as planned cultural change orients public organizations toward the operationalization of democratic values, organizational culture must be an important consideration.

If one considers only the elements that Pastin emphasized—the assumptions, ground rules, and social contracts that form the basis of culture—it becomes quite clear that the educational efforts in public administration (and the opportunities that public administrationists have to train public employees) must be directed less toward creating ethical codes and behavioral rules and more toward engaging public administration organizational actors in discussions about the basic ethical assumptions of public service. The social contract of public service is quite different from the social contract of those engaged in selling widgets. If public ethics and values are to become essential elements in the operations of public agencies, public organizational cultures must be recreated to include the assumptions of democracy and citizenship. This is only possible if the organizational culture concept is understood.

NOTE

1. The reader interested in specific approaches is urged to consult the bibliography in Ott (1989: 199–217). A very useful and contemporary introduction to both the range of concerns in concep-

tualization and research is Frost, et al. (1985) and Schultz (1994). The bibliography in Frost is especially good for a sampling of research techniques. The bibliography in Schultz provides extensive study of the culture concept in organizational theory (1994:171–179). Sources familiar or useful to public administration scholars in understanding the concept and research approach include the following: (1) For Level 1—artifacts—Edelman (1964), and Smircich (1983); (2) Level 1B—patterns of behavior—Goffman (1967), and Ritti and Funkhouser (1982); (3) Level 2—beliefs and values—Barnard (1938), and Selznick (1957); and (4) Level 3—basic assumptions—Sathe (1985), and Schein (1985). In addition, the public administration reader will benefit from Etzioni (1975) where all levels are addressed in context. A review of the 1981 *Annual Handbook for Group Facilitators* is also useful for effective research instruments. For the seminal work in the field, Jaques (1952) should be consulted.

REFERENCES

Adams, G.B. and Balfour, D.L. (1998). *Unmasking Administrative Evil*. London: Sage.

Alexander, M. (1977). Organizational norms opinionaire. In *The 1977 Annual Handbook for Facilitators* (J.W. Pfeifer and J.E. Jones, eds.). LaJolla, CA: University Associates, pp. 81–88.

Bailey, S.K. (1964). Ethics and the public service. *Public Administration Review*, 24(4):234–243.

Barnard, C. (1938). *The Functions of the Executive*. Cambridge, MA: Harvard University Press.

Blau, P.M. (1955, 1963). *The Dynamics of Bureaucracy*. Chicago: University of Chicago Press.

Bowman, J.S. (1991). *Ethical Frontiers in Public Management: Seeking New Strategies for Resolving Ethical Dilemmas*. San Francisco: Jossey-Bass.

Bowman, J.S. (1990). Ethics in government: A national survey of public administrators. *Public Administration Review*, 50(5):345–353.

Caiden, G.E. (1991). What really is public maladministration? *Public Administration Review*, 51(6): 486–493.

Carnevale, D.G. and Wechsler, B. (1992). Trust in the public sector: Individual and organizational determinants. *Administration and Society*, 23(4):471–495.

Chandler, R. (1983). The problem of moral reasoning in American public administration: The case for a code of ethics. *Public Administration Review*, 43:32–39.

Cooper, T.L. (1981, 1986, 1990, 1998). *The Responsible Administrator*. San Francisco: Jossey-Bass.

Cooper, T.L. (1987). Hierarchy, virtue and the practice of public administration. *Public Administration Review*, 47(4):320–328.

Denhardt, K.G. (1988). *The Ethics of Public Service*. New York: Greenwood Press.

Edelman, M. (1964). *The Symbolic Uses of Politics*. Urbana: University of Illinois Press.

Etzioni, A. (1975). *A Comparative Analysis of Complex Organizations* (rev. ed.). New York: Free Press.

Fairholm, G.W. (1991). *Values Leadership: Toward a New Philosophy of Leadership*. New York: Praeger.

Frederickson, H.G. (1993). *Ethics and Public Administration*. London: M. E. Sharpe.

Frederickson, H.G. and Hart, D.K. (1985). The public service and the patriotism of benevolence. *Public Administration Review*, 45(5):547–553.

Frost, P.J., Moore, L.F., Lundberg, C.C., and Martin, J. (eds.). (1985). *Organizational Culture*. Beverly Hills, CA: Sage.

Gawthrop, L.C. (1984). *Public Sector Management, Systems, and Ethics*. Bloomington, IN: Indiana University Press.

Gawthrop, L.C. (1999). Public entrepreneurship in the lands of oz and uz. *Public Integrity*. 1(1): 75–86.

Gilman, S.C. (1999). Public sector ethics and government reinvention: Realigning systems to meet organizational change. *Public Integrity* 1(2):175–192.

Goffman, I. (1967). *Interaction Ritual*. Garden City, NY: Anchor Books.

Gortner, H.F. (1991). *Ethics for Public Managers*. New York: Praeger.

Guy, M.E. (1990). *Ethical Decision Making in Everyday Work Situations*. Westport, CT: Quorum Books.

Hatch, M.J. (1993). The dynamics of organizational culture. *Academy of Management Review*, 18(4): 657–694.

Hummel, R.P. (1977, 1982, 1987). *The Bureaucratic Experience*. New York: St. Martin's Press.

Harrison, R. (1975). Diagnosing organization ideology. In *The 1975 Annual Handbook for Group Facilitators* (J.E. Jones and J.W. Pfeifer, eds.). LaJolla, CA: University Associates, pp. 101–107.

Iococca, L. (1984). *Iococca: An Autobiography*. Toronto: Bantam Books.

Jaques, E. (1952). *The Changing Culture of a Factory*. New York: Dryden Press.

Kaufman, H. (1960). *The Forest Ranger*. Baltimore: Johns-Hopkins University Press.

Keesing, R.M. (1974). Theories of culture. *Annual Review of Anthropology*, 3:73–79.

Kilmann, R.H. (1984). *Beyond the Quick-Fix*. San Francisco: Jossey-Bass.

Leavitt, H.J. (1986). *Corporate Pathfinders. Building Vision and Values into Organizations*. Homewood, IL: Dow-Jones-Irwin.

Lewis, C.W. (1993). Ethics codes and ethics agencies: Current practices and emerging trends. In *Ethics and Public Administration* (H.G. Frederickson, ed.). Armonk, NY: M.E. Sharpe, pp. 136–157.

Lewis, C.W. (1991). *The Ethics Challenge in Public Service: A Problem-Solving Guide*. San Francisco: Jossey-Bass.

Light, P.C. (1995). *Thickening Government: Federal Hierarchy and the Diffusion of Authority*. Washington, D.C.: The Brookings Institution and the Governance Institution.

Menzel, D.C. (1993). The ethics factor in local government: An empirical analysis. In *Ethics and Public Administration* (H.G. Frederickson, ed.). Armonk, NY: M.E. Sharpe, pp. 191–204.

Menzel, D.C. (1995). The ethical environment of local government managers. *American Review of Public Administration*, 25(3):247–262.

The New York Times (1999). August 23, p. 12.

Osborne, D. and Plastrik, P. (1997). *Banishing Bureaucracy: The Five Strategies for Reinventing Government*. Reading, MA: Addison-Wesley.

Osborne, D. and Gaebler, T. (1992). *Reinventing Government: How the Entrepreneurial Spirit Is Transforming the Public Sector*. Reading, MA: Addison-Wesley.

Ott, J.S. (1989). *The Organizational Culture Perspective*. Chicago: Dorsey Press.

Ouchi, W.G. (1981). *Theory Z: How American Business Can Meet the Japanese Challenge*. Reading, MA: Addison-Wesley.

Pascale, R.T. and Athos, A.G. (1981). *The Art of Japanese Management: Applications for American Executives*. New York: Simon and Schuster.

Pastin, M. (1986). *The Hard Problems of Management: Gaining the Ethics Edge*. San Francisco: Jossey-Bass.

Peters, B.G. (1996). *The Future of Governing: Four Emerging Models*. Lawrence, KS: University Press of Kansas.

Peters, T. and Austin, N. (1985). *A Passion for Excellence: The Leadership Difference*. New York: Random House.

Peters, T. and Waterman, R.H., Jr. (1982). *In Search of Excellence: Lessons from America's Best Run Companies*. New York: Harper and Row.

Preimsberger, D.T. and Block, S. (1986). Values, standards, and integrity in law enforcement: An emphasis on job survival. *Journal of California Law Enforcement*, 20(1):10–13.

Ritti, R.R. and Funkhouser, G.R. (1982). *The Ropes to Skip and the Ropes to Know: Studies in Organizational Behavior* (2nd ed.). New York: John Wiley & Sons.

Rohr, J.A. (1978, 1989). *Ethics for Bureaucrats: An Essay on Law and Values*. New York: Marcel Dekker.

Sathe, V. (1985). *Culture and Related Corporate Realities. Text, Cases, and Readings on Organizational Entry, Establishment, and Change.* Homewood, IL: Irwin.

Schein, E.H. (1981). Does Japanese management style have a message for American managers? *Sloan Management Review*, 23:55–68.

Schein, E.H. (1985). *Organizational Culture and Leadership*. San Francisco: Jossey-Bass.

Schultz, M. (1994). *On Studying Organizational Culture*. New York: Walter de Gruyter.

Scott, W.G. (1982). Barnard on the nature of elitist responsibility. *Public Administration Review*, 42(3):197–201.

Scott, W.G. and Hart, D.K. (1979). *Organizational America: Can Individual Freedom Survive Within the Security it Promises?* Boston: Houghton-Mifflin.

Selznick, P. (1949). *TVA and the Grass Roots*. Berkeley, CA: University of California Press.

Selznick, P. (1957). *Leadership in Administration: A Sociological Interpretation*. New York: Harper & Row.

Smircich, L. (1983). Organizations as shared meanings. In *Organizational Symbolism* (L. R. Pondy, P.J. Frost, G. Morgan, T.C. Dandridge, eds.). Greenwich, CT: JAI Press.

Sternberg, S.S. and Austern, D.T. (1990). *Government, Ethics, and Managers: A Guide to Solving Ethical Dilemmas in the Public Sector*. New York: Praeger.

Theobald, R. (1997). Enhancing public service ethics: More culture, less bureaucracy? *Administration and Society*, 29(4):490–505.

Thompson, D.F. (1985). The possibility of administrative ethics. *Public Administration Review*, 45(5):555–561.

Timmins, W.M. (1990). *A Casebook of Public Ethics and Issues*. Pacific Grove, CA: Brooks/Cole.

Walton, M. (1986). *The Deming Management Method*. New York: Perigee Books.

The Washington Post, September 25, 1992, p. 1.

Van Wart, M. (1998). *Changing Public Sector Values*. New York: Garland Publishing.

13

The Relevance of Public Ethics to Administration and Policy

Curtis Ventriss
University of Vermont, Burlington, Vermont

"We commonly face two problems in our moral life: deciding what is the right thing to do and having the moral strength to do it" (R. T. Sullivan, 1989).

I. INTRODUCTION

Paul Appleby, in his discussion of the relationship between morality and administration, made the following perceptive observation worth noting:

> The problems [philosophers] set out to solve are intellectual and abstract, not the specific problems faced by social operators. . . . Made as full-bodied as possible, their formulations still would be designed to illuminate the field of action, not to relieve its captains of responsibilities. We therefore beg the more general questions which philosophers ruminate; we begin by assuming democracy (1952:28).

What is particularly salient about this statement is how he links the discussion of ethics directly to the discussion of a democratic ethos in the modern polity. We need an ethics, Appleby seems to be arguing, that is not articulated as "abstract ideals," but rather as an integral part of a democratic mindset that can help administrators or policy analysts in determining the substantive content of their actions. Putting aside for the moment the pragmatic and operational merits of Appleby's insight, he seems to overlook a more obvious point: that it may be the *public* role and *public* purpose of political and administrative action that is becoming increasingly more abstract in promoting and serving the goals of democratic citizenship. The emphasis on "public" here is not merely a matter of semantics, but rather a reminder that any ethical inquiry cannot be separated from the "publicness" of the administrator's role and public obligation to the citizenry. While the meaning of the "public" is often regarded as an ambiguous term devoid of any practicality, it nevertheless lies at the very core of what public administrators do and for whom. As one scholar put it:

> . . . as many are beginning to understand, [we cannot] separate our view of social problems from our view of the public. They are inexorably linked. This is precisely why we call issues that we confront public problems and the actions we take public policies. Lingering behind every policy action is some conception of the public, regardless of how broad or pedantic that view may be (Ventriss, 1987:35).

Saying this, it makes sense to distinguish between *public* ethics and *administrative* ethics. Guy Adams (1992), for example, has recently argued that administrative ethics is best understood as historically linked to the growth of professionalism which began during the progressive era. It was during this period, Adams maintains, that scientific expertise and technical rationality became legitimized under the banner of public service ideals—ideals that codified functional values as commensurate with organization goals. In other words, administrative ethics—whether couched in terms of internal or external controls—tends to promote a client-centered approach because it is unable to scrape away the instrumental residue of expertise and technical rationality. Conversely, public ethics has been defined as a normative examination of the prevailing political ethos or of the national character (McCollough, 1991; Sellars, 1970). Taking a somewhat different view, Albert Jonsen and Lewis Butler (1975) have defined public ethics in relationship to how it can help policymakers determine the following factors: ''(1) articulation of relevant moral principles in the policy problem; (2) elucidation of proposed policy options in light of relevant moral principles; and (3) displaying ranked order of moral options for policy choice'' (McCollough, 1991:16). Thomas McCollough (1991) has tried to integrate these two perspectives of public ethics by proposing that what is needed is a critical reflection that transcends individualism—a public ethic that locates moral responsibility in the self. Thus, as McCollough states later, ''public ethics . . . embodies and makes concrete the kind of public conversation that can humanize policy making'' (1991:80). For purposes of analysis, I will argue that public ethics is a normative approach to public affairs that stresses the tradition of democratic citizenship in light of the administrator's (or policy analyst's) role and obligation to serve and promote the public interest.

This chapter will discuss the merits of public ethics and the relevant literature that highlights its contribution to administrative ethics. The point of this chapter, among other things, is that the publicness of administrative ethics can help frame the debate—or at minimum broaden the debate—about the discussion of ethics in public affairs, particularly in regards to public administration and public policy.

II. THE REDISCOVERY OF THE "PUBLIC" IN PUBLIC ADMINISTRATION: TOWARD A RECONCEPTUALIZATION OF ETHICS IN PUBLIC AFFAIRS

There is probably nothing more surprising (or perplexing) in the field of public administration than the lack of any serious discussion of the relevance of ''public'' in public administration. One would think that such an obvious omission is peculiar given the field's apparent relationship to such salient issues as civic duty, public purpose, and citizenship. George Frederickson, recognizing this serious omission, has wrestled with how we might define the meaning of the public. It is worth quoting him at length (1989:2–3):

> The classic meaning of public derives from two sources or roots. The first is the Greek word *pubes*, which was their term for maturity. Maturity in the Greek sense means both physical and emotional or intellectual maturity, to include moving from selfish concerns or personal self-interest to seeing beyond one's self to understand the interest of others. It implies an ability to understand the consequences of individual actions on others. Public, as the derivative, means moving to an adult state, understanding the relationship between the individual and other individuals, and an ability to see connections.

The second root word is the Greek word, koinon, from which the English word common is derived. The Greek word koinon derives from the second Greek word, komm-ois, meaning to care with. Common and caring with both imply the importance of relationships.

Maturity and seeing beyond one's self seems to indicate that the word public can be both a *thing*, as in the case of a public decision, and a *capacity*, as in the case of the ability to function publicly, to relate to others, to understand the connection between one's action and the effects of those actions on others. Adding the words common and caring with to maturity makes the case even stronger that public means not only working with others, but looking out for others.

I pushed this point a little further by stating that the meaning of the public denotes more than just a capacity and maturity, it also implies the understanding that—

... public actions are by definition interactive, and can have a variety of public consequences or impacts, [and thus] the public must act in a public learning capacity in the formulation and deliberation of policy actions—a deliberation based on the mutual sharing of information and knowledge between the public and governmental institutions. At the heart of any theory of the public, then, is the conception of political education, which implies, as Tocqueville recognized so well "the transformation of commitments, the cultivation of the public virtue." One can only cultivate public virtues, Tocqueville believed, by participating in public life. This is precisely why he saw the jury system, town meetings, and other citizen-based institutions as educative vehicles to engage the public in its responsibilities as citizens. What is hinted at here should not be more directly stated: The capacity, the maturity, and the learning process of the public must be inexorably linked with the activities of public administration to facilitate a political educative process between the public and the administrators. The theory we have been so desperately looking for may be only a process: an asymptotic...exercise in deliberative public learning, a public learning that jointly links public administration and the public in furthering their [ethical] capacity, maturity, and knowledge (Ventriss, 1987:37).

It should be noted that both of these scholarly articulations of the public do not assume that the meaning of the public is somehow synonymous with the notion of the state or the government. Rather, the conception of the public is to be understood as related to a political community or, as the Greeks put it, a "polis." According to Deborah Stone (1988:25), a political community (or polis) has the following characteristics:

It is a community;
It has a public interest, if only as an idea about which people fight;
Most of its policy problems are common problems;
Influence is pervasive, and the boundary between influence and coercion is always
        contested;
Cooperation is as important as competition;
Loyalty is the norm;
Groups and organizations are the building blocks;
Information is interpretative, incomplete, and strategic;
It is governed by the laws of passion as well as of matter; and
Power, derivative of all those elements, coordinates individual intentions and actions
        into collective purposes and results.

These views of the public, if correct, directly imply that individuals of a state have to live a public life to be truly citizens (Mathews, 1988:52). A public, according to David

Mathews (1988:52), will manifest the following characteristics: "(1) set directions for the community and the country; (2) give legitimacy to governments by building the common ground they need if they are to operate; (3) generate the political will needed to act on major issues; and (4) transform private individuals into a public, or citizens." A public, therefore, is a community of citizens who attempt to understand the substantive interdependency of social and political issues in the community, and who maintain a critical perspective on the ethical implications of governmental policymaking. In part, this is what Robert Ezra Park (1904:20) had in mind when he asserted that "when the public ceases to be critical, it dissolves or is transformed into a crowd." A public ethic, as part of administrative ethics, is concerned with normative issues as they affect the political community— concerns of governmental action that can foster rather than hinder the public discussion of societal and ethical *consequences*.

While this discussion of a public (and a public ethic) as a part of the normative discourse of politics seems conceptually vacuous, Richard Flathman (1966) has tried to give it some practical importance. Flathman contends that the public interest is not, as E. Herring (1936) or Schubert (1960) concluded, a matter of individual judgment or merely a label attached to a miscellany of particular compromises of the moment, but instead is a useful concept if we employ some normative criteria to ethical policymaking. That ethical standard, according to Flathman, is if a policy can adhere to his notion of universalizability, "determining so far as possible the foreseeable consequences of a [policy's] adoption and evaluating those consequences in terms of community values" (Long, 1990:175). Norton Long (1990:175), speaking in favor of Flathman's contribution to our understanding of a public ethic, posed the following example of why Flathman's concept of universalizability is so important to public administration:

> The bottom line is the evaluation of consequences in terms of agreed on values. Generalization is a way of determining whether a policy serves the appropriate public. Thus the Department of Housing and Urban Development program in Richard Lee's New Haven, which . . . consumed more money per capita than had ever been spent before or would ever be spent since, was a Potemkin Village masquerading as a National urban policy. Generalization would have shown that as a national urban policy it was radically unaffordable and was (absent demonstrable means of replicating its supposedly desirable results at vastly reduced costs) in no way justifiable as an experiment whose results might have no general value. Generalizability is a test that the pork barrel cannot pass.

The critical issue here is that if Flatham is correct in his argument, there is a moral obligation to determine the impact of a policy's interdependence on the public (Ventriss, 1991). In short, the public administrator has an ethical responsibility to assess the consequences of policy options that are often hidden and have indirect costs and, more importantly, how the externality of policy choices can have a variety of impacts on different publics (Ventriss and Luke, 1988).

Thus, the public is a public space in which citizens of the republic hold each other responsible for what we know and value (McCollough, 1991). Moreover, administrators and policy analysts are accountable not only to one another, but to the citizenry for the public good and to help communities, as public spaces, to flourish in order to develop the citizenry's skills and moral imagination in addressing important policy issues. As McCollough (1991) has emphasized, this is at the heart of what it means to seek a public ethic.

Let us now turn to a review of some of the pertinent literature pertaining to that subject and the differing perspectives in articulating the publicness of administrative ethics.

III. ADMINISTRATIVE ETHICS AND THE NATURE OF THE PUBLIC: A LITERATURE REVIEW

Given the recent proliferation of literature on administrative ethics, I have, for the purposes of this chapter, constructed a typology to capture the differing normative descriptions that deal specifically with public ethics. To be sure, no literature review can be completely exhaustive. Rather, my attempt here is to outline the dimensions of varying ethical viewpoints and the similarities and differences among such approaches. Typologies, of course, also run the theoretical risk of placing a theorist in one conceptual camp, so to speak, when in fact the theorist may overlap into several typological classifications. Like Brent Wall (1991:137), when theorists straddled categories, "I placed them in the class that seemed to best capture the essence of their position."

Notwithstanding some of the inherent difficulties associated with conceptual typologies, I constructed five classifications organizing the literature. They are: (1) the classical perspective on public ethics as represented by Hannah Arendt, Alberto Ramos, and Aladair MacIntyre; (2) the neo-classical view or republican view of public ethics as emphasized by such thinkers as David Hart, Terry Cooper, William Richardson, Lloyd Nigro, William Sullivan, Guy Adams, and Dan Balfour; (3) the consequential approach to public ethics which is reflected in the works of John Dewey, Benjamin Barber, and Richard Flathman; (4) the organizational view of public ethics that is characterized by theorists such as Dennis Thompson, John Burke, Jim Bowman, John Rohr, Kathryn Denhardt, and Montgomery Van Wart; and finally (5) a postmodern view of ethics as exemplified in the erudite works of Michael Harmon, Charles Fox, and Hugh Miller. By far, the majority of modern theorists of public administration would fall under the rubric of the organizational perspective. This is hardly surprising given the managerial emphasis inherent in public administration. However, under each typology there are subgroupings that indicate different strains of thought. This is particularly evident in those grouped in the last category. Saying this, I will now discuss in turn the different views concerning the publicness of administrative ethics.

A. Classical View

From a classical view, public ethics is a normative inquiry by citizens in a political community who deliberate freely on policy issues that transcend issues of an utilitarian concern or of administrative efficiency and expediency. Public ethics thus is part and parcel of ethical citizenship and the creation of public spaces where substantive deliberations can take place free from operational constraints. This is a public space where citizens can act rather than behave. Alberto Ramos (1981:45) speaking directly to the field of public administration made the following distinction between behavior and action:

> Behavior is a mode of conduct predicated upon functional rationality or utilitarian reckoning of consequences, a capacity, as Hobbes correctly pointed out, that the human individual has in common with other animals. Its cardinal category is expediency. *Behavior is accordingly void of generally valid ethical content. It is a mecanonmorphic type of conduct dictated by external imperatives*. It can be appraised as functional or effective. It is completely included in a world solely determined by efficient causes.
>
> In contradiction, action is proper to an agent who deliberates about things because he is conscious of their intrinsic ends. *By acknowledging such ends, action is an ethical mode of conduct*. Social and organizational effectiveness is an incidental, not cardinal

dimension of human action. Human beings are bound to act, to make decisions and choices, because final, not only efficient causes, have a bearing upon the world at large. This action is predicated upon utilitarian reckoning of consequences only by accident at best.

Behavior, Ramos claims, is a term that denotes conformity to commands that are externally imposed. Moreover, because organizations are what he (1981:44) calls cognitive systems "organizational members generally internalize these systems and thus unknowingly become unconscious thinkers." Ramos (1981:44) concludes, in the next breath, that contemporary organizational thinkers tend to ignore this point and thus attempt to "articulate the cognitive system inherent in a particular type of organization (read: formal organization) as a normative cognitive system in general." What Ramos thinks we are suffering from in our deliberations about the role of public administration in society is the inability to understand what he refers to as the "behavioral syndrome." He defines this as "a socially conditioned mood affecting individuals' lives when they confuse the rules and norms of operation peculiar to episodal social systems with rules and norms of their conduct at large" (1981: 46).

While not explicitly saying so, Ramos is calling for a "public" ethics in the classical sense of the word that forces theorists to make a distinction between the substantive and the formal meaning of organization. Ramos, no doubt, is borrowing heavily from Aristotle and other classical thinkers in his analysis of the political realm and how it has been distorted by the rise of a market-centered mentality characteristic of industrialized countries. This distortion is, to a certain degree, also reflective in our language that supports an epistemological permissiveness that leads to what he states is a crypto-political phenomenon; that is, "a disguised normative dimension of the established power configuration" (1981: 4). Putting aside whether Ramos' analysis is correct or not, anyone even slightly familiar with Hannah Arendt's philosophical works can see her strong influence on Ramos' thinking. For purposes of comparison, let us now explore her conceptualization of public ethics.

When Hannah Arendt (1963; 1965) arrived in Jerusalem in 1961 to observe the trial of the notorious Nazi war criminal Adolf Eichmann, she sat quietly in the back of the courtroom scribbling down her thoughts that would later appear in a series of articles for the *New Yorker*. Arendt's analysis of this trial provoked an immediate storm of controversy, not only because of her interpretation of this legal proceeding, but because Eichmann symbolized to many the archetypical figure who tried to administer the "Final Solution." When one strips away Arendt's somewhat clumsy way of explaining her views, one central theme emerges over all the others: Eichmann's terrifying acts against humanity was an exercise in the banality of evil in that Eichmann seemed completely incapable of independent, critical thought. Specifically, what frightened Arendt the most about Eichmann was his thoughtlessness—a total lack of thought or substantive reflection that did not make him pause once when he was committing unjust and cruel acts. He signified, moreover, the "socialized man" who had no conceptualization of the meaning and purpose of citizenship and who exhibited no strong passions or beliefs. Arendt (Kaleb, 1983: 74) somberly concludes that Eichmann (for what he really represents) is merely the scary caricature of "the average mass-man as philistine." Eichmann's mentality, however, represents something more troubling than we would like to admit to ourselves: that the private individual devoid of any notion of citizenship is, in many respects, the perfect cog:

> He has driven the dichotomy of private and public functions of family and occupation, so far that he can no longer find in his own person any connection between the two. When his occupation forces him to murder people he does not regard himself as a

murderer because he has not done it out of inclination but in his professional capacity. Out of sheer passion he would never do harm to a fly (Arendt, 1978: 234).

In short, this person is *behaving*—he is not *partaking in action*. "He did not need to close his ears to the voice of conscience, as judgment had it, not because he had none, but because his conscience spoke with a respectable voice, with the voice of respectable society around him" (Arendt, 1965: 126). In a similar manner as Ramos, Arendt also makes a distinction between human behavior and political action. She (1958) contends that behavior is to a large extent controllable, predictable, and manipulative. Furthermore, behavior represents a conformity to a mass society—a mass society subject to bureaucratic management that attempts to control (and eliminate) any uncertainty that may arise when individuals try to freely act in their capacity as citizens. Conversely, action is the medium for freedom and speech to shape one's destiny and, equally important, is the vehicle to reveal—and express—one's individuality. Put in other terms, it is a substantive public forum in which to display one's uniqueness and potential for greatness within the political community. It is for this reason that she goes to great theoretical lengths to connect action with spontaneity, uncertainty, and unpredictability. While this may sound peculiar to our modern ears, at the heart of her analysis is the meaning of citizenship and how it has become usurped by the rise of society.

Given this controversial perspective, it is not surprising that Arendt is adamant in her view that governmental management can never be regarded as part of the public realm—for to do so would be to substitute political action for administration which would only result in the enfeeblement of citizenship. Concomitantly, any effort to introduce action into governmental organizations would not only politicize administration and potentially injure its instrumental ends, but it would inevitably do irreparable harm to the political realm. This is why, in part, she (1958: 49) states that "no activity can become excellent if the world does not provide a proper place for its exercise." The non-utilitarian nature of action just has no "public place" in which to fully flourish in governmental organizations; the world of rational administration simply cannot account for individuality or the plurality of individuals. Thus, we cannot realistically expect governmental organizations, regardless of how we might clothe them in normative garments, to permit public spaces free from contrived superordinated prescriptions. The unqualified usage of administrative ethics, Ramos (1981: 125) and Arendt would maintain, "is itself an indication of the undimensional character of current organizational theory and practice."

It is worth noting that the main difference between Ramos' and Arendt's thinking on this matter is that Arendt does not directly relate ethical purposes with action; rather "the supreme achievement of action is existential, and the stakes are seemingly higher than Moral ones" (Kateb, 1983: 31). Action is valued as an end in itself and is judged only by its greatness—a greatness that facilitates the achievement of human excellence within a political community. However, she (1965: 27) is quick to point out that a political community is also an ethical community because it must be predicated on the normative goals of mutual concern, friendship, and trust. Ramos, on the other hand, calls for what he terms organizational delimitation which specifies that a formal organization's cognitive system should match its objectives. Whether we like it or not, Ramos believes we cannot avoid the following simple (and undeniable) reality: contemporary formal organizations are based on a rationality system that is functional and contrived, not substantive. To ignore this simple truth, he surmises, is to partake in "the transvaluation of reason— leading to the conversion of the concrete into the abstract, of the good into the functional, and even of the ethical into the a-ethical" (Ramos, 1981: 5). For Ramos (1981: 46) this drives him to the only conclusion that he can draw: "The good man in turn is never a completely socialized man; rather he is an actor under tension, yielding to, or resisting social stimuli on *the grounds of his ethical sense.*" For what it is worth, this statement merits some pondering.

Another variation of this emphasis on a classical approach to ethics is Aladair MacIntyre's (1981) thought-provoking work, *After Virtue.* MacIntyre's contribution to our discussion is his perceptive distinction between "practices" and "institution." Practice, MacIntyre (1981: 175) writes, is inherently a cooperative endeavor (or activity) "through which goods internal to that form of activity which are appropriate to, and partially definitive of, that activity, with the result that human powers to achieve excellence, and human conceptions of the ends and goods involved, are systematically extended." There is a lot packed in this awkwardly phrased sentence that has salient implications for public administration in general and ethics in particular.

First, MacIntyre argues that while the game of football, chess, and the inquiries of physics, biology, and history are practices, such things as playing tic-tac-toe and throwing a football are clearly not. His point here is that practice is distinguished by its striving for excellence; that is, goods internal to a practice. "In other words, we have to accept as necessary components of any practice with internal goods and standards of excellence the virtues of justice, courage and honesty" (1981: 178). He (1981: 175) is not splitting hairs here, but rather raising the critical point that practice, if properly understood, is also an "achievement of what is good for the whole community who participate in the practice."

But his general argument is made even stronger by comparing it to what he terms "external goods." He claims that external goods are those things emphasized by institutions. These include such external goods as money, status, and power—goods which are valued because they are objects of competition. He is eager to remind us that practice cannot, and should not, be confused with institutions. The paradox, he says, is that "no practices can survive for any length of time unsustained by institutions" (MacIntyre, 1981: 181). The obvious danger is that as a result of this relationship the ideals of practice can be contaminated by the acquisitiveness of institutions. This is why he (1981: 181) feels it necessary to state that "without justice, courage and truthfulness, practices could not resist the corrupting power of institutions." Institutions (read: bureaucracies), therefore, are Janus-faced—they help sustain practice but they can also distort its ideals. Saying this, one may fairly ask what this theoretical discussion about practice has to do with public administration?

Terry Cooper (1987: 322), in his desire to apply MacIntyre's views to the practice of public administration, raises the following salient point: "Public administrators need to determine which human attributes are most likely to advance the internal goods which are defined as essential to the practice and protect them from organizational pressures, to the extent possible." This is only plausible, Cooper acknowledges, if public administration itself is not captive of external goods, or put in slightly different terms, by an instrumental orientation. Cooper maintains that public administration is instrumental only in a particular sense. The reason is simple: public administration should not be viewed as solely dominated by functional rationality (and all that this type of rationality entails) because "the role of the public administrator as a fiduciary for the citizenry gives rise to certain internal goods and virtues associated with carrying out the trust inherent in that role" (Cooper, 1987: 315). Public administrators, for example, have an explicit *public* role and *public* responsibility to pursue the public interest which implies an obligation to authorizing procedures as well as to colleagues to enhance standards of excellence. Certainly, Cooper's insights add an interesting twist to the issue of the "publicness" of ethics in public affairs in comparison to Ramos and Arendt. MacIntyre provides Cooper with a way of rescuing public administration away from the pessimism somewhat inherent in the arguments presented by both Ramos and Arendt. There indeed can be an ethic of virtue for the practice of public administration without elapsing into a kind of ethical dualism.

In sum, MacIntyre's message to us is clear enough: anything less than the rediscovery practice in public administration will ultimately result in the diminution of the field as a practice devoted to the *public interest*, and hence would surrender whatever claim it had in serving a truly public role to be in reality nothing more than a professional bundle of technical skills and knowledge at the service (and mercy) of the state. Under these circumstances, there would be no category (or need) for "practice," let alone heroes.

These three thinkers have given us different theoretical (and practical) cuts at the way we can rethink the meaning of ethics in public affairs. Because of their theoretical affinity to Aristotle and other classical thinkers, I have grouped them under the rubric of promoting a classical view of public ethics, even given their varying viewpoints on this subject. We need to turn our attention to a slightly different (and more modern) version of this approach which I call the republican approach to public ethics.

B. Republican/Neo-Classical View

When David Hart (1984) wrote his paper for the *Public Administration Review* symposium on "Citizenship and Public Administration," he struck a theoretical nerve in many who believed that public administration must reformulate itself congruent with the philosophy of the founding fathers. Hart's underlying assumption is blunt, and to the point: the values of public administration must be commensurate with the natural law values of our founding fathers or the field's *raison d'etre* is lost. Following the lines of John Rohr's work in ethics, Hart (1984: 111–112) called for a strict adherence to American regime values:

> In the United States, those values are the natural law values upon which the Republic was predicated . . . the American regime values. They must be the basis for all public administration policies and practices. The Founders established the new republic upon the conviction that the American regime values were (and are) true principles, necessary for individual happiness (correctly understood) regardless of time, place, or culture. By the oaths of office we give and by our dependence upon legal precedence, we acknowledge that we are bound to those regime values by the terms of the original contract. Therefore, we must understand them in the same terms as the Founders.

Several years later after Hart first wrote these words, William Richardson and Lloyd Nigro echoed this same sentiment by arguing for a "cultivation of public virtue" predicated upon the founding fathers' thinking. In their own words, they (1987: 374) concluded that "our reading of Founding intentions reveals a heavy reliance on the interaction of constitutional correctives, honor, and education to produce virtuous public officials who serve the regime." According to this analysis, the founding fathers are important because of their emphasis on republican *public* virtues as related to both governmental leadership and the citizenry. What Richardson and Nigro do not mention is that this confidence in the cultivation of moral virtues for all citizens was tempered by the founding fathers' need to develop a set of complex institutional arrangements to appropriately check "passion" in the political process and to abate any abuse of power.

Notwithstanding the tension between "reason" and "passion" in the founding fathers' thinking, David Hart (1984: 9) argues that the founders viewed the individual in a certain manner that has a critical message to us today:

> The most fundamental assumption of the . . . Founders was that each individual's life is of infinite and irreplaceable worth. Believing that it is obvious that they would not devise any moral philosophy, theology, political, or economic system that subsumed the individual within the larger whole: any instrumental use of the individual was anathema. It was to the service of this belief in the absolute preciousness of each individual's life that all organizations were to be devoted.

Hart is not quite ready to end his analysis here. He pushes his point to further argue that the founders assumed the existence of a "moral sense," a natural law that determines the rightness or wrongness of moral action. In a later work, Hart and Wasden (1990: 757) put a little more spice in this argument by stating how far we have ventured from the path of our founders: "the management orthodoxy is displacing civic idealism as the foundation of public administration, which redefines the primary purposes of the profession." To rediscover this civic idealism, or civic humanism as he sometimes calls it, requires from the public administrator a sense of justice, honor, and a love of the public one serves.

However, when one analyzes Hart and Wasden's (1990: 759) point carefully, they are trying to nudge public administration back (or some may say forward) to the idealism of civic humanism that began in the 19th century. They recognize that this theoretical posturing will most likely fall on deaf ears, particularly since the moral psychology of the field is comfortably embedded in ethical relativism and, more importantly, since most administrators have been socialized to take the values of the organization as a given. This is symptomatic of a field that is trying hard to emulate the perceived efficiencies of business administration (read: management orthodoxy). Yet, this misguided emulation has come with a hefty price tag: "the loss of the uniqueness of public service; a diminished conception of the individual; and the irrelevance of good character for public leadership" (Hart and Wasden, 1990: 763). In other words, how can we realistically expect public administrators to act in the public interest when the management orthodoxy minimizes the development of exemplary moral character? In particular, can we really expect the highest ethical standards from our public administrators when a Faustian bargain has already been struck: the general acceptance of the organizational imperative for the civic ideal of democracy. To correct this process, Hart and Wasden (1990: 770) assert, will require nothing less than these dramatic changes:

> First, the basic subject of all public administration education, whether in universities or in agencies of government, must be the political philosophy of civic humanism. Both scholars and practitioners must be well-schooled in the subject. Second, all management goals, procedures, and techniques must be intentionally modified to promulgate civic virtue. Functional effectiveness must be interpreted in terms of the entailments of virtue. Thus, public administrators must re-write the management books and create a unique and distinctive "public" administration.

One can claim that this view is nothing more than an overly romantic notion of the founders' real thinking on such notions as civic virtue, civic life, and community. It can be further argued that when one strips away the civic language to describe the Founders' views, the proponents ignore a more fundamental issue that Tocqueville (1969) perceptively raised: the founders tried to create a precarious moral balance between civic community and economic individualism which is based upon a contradiction, an opposition of two distinct moral visions of political life. Here Tocqueville senses something that warrants serious attention: it is difficult to preserve civic virtue and civic life when threatened by the ubiquitous influence of an utilitarian capitalism that by definition promotes—and encourages—an untrammeled self-interest onto all spheres of social and political existence.

Unfortunately, Tocqueville's warning to us on this issue is never directly addressed by either Hart or Richardson and Nigro. More directly concerned with this warning is Terry Cooper who has articulated his views on both administrative ethics and citizenship in the following books: *The Responsible Administrator* (1990) and *An Ethic of Citizenship for Public Administration* (1991). Echoing a similar theme as Robert Bellah and his colleagues (1985), Cooper wants to bring citizenship itself into the process of governmental operations and policymaking. This view, he contends, is embodied in the tradition of antifederalism, Puritan thought and community, and the Jeffersonian philosophy of government. Taken together, these perspectives reflect an ethical dimension of citizenship along these lines: "(1) the dignity of the individual citizen; (2) the consensual nature of authority; (3) a concern for the common good; (4) the importance of civic virtue; and (5) the experience of participation in government as not only a right and obligation of citizenship, but also as education for citizenship" (Cooper, 1991:91–92). Even more important than the acknowledgment of this tradition for an ethical view of citizenship, is Cooper's recognition of a public-private continuum in a democratic society. In fact, Cooper (1991: 171) traces the etymology of the word public and concludes that "its most fundamental denotations are the shared, communal, universally accessible dimensions of collective life, as well as those things that have general impact upon the interests of all, the realm of interdependence." Cooper maintains that a democratic political community, which is critical for any democratic government, incorporates a complex interdependence of the full public-private continuum which ranges from the personal and intimate (private) to the fraternal and associational (quasi-public) to the organizational economic and political (public). In the same manner as Tocqueville, Cooper is troubled by the declining importance of mediating structures that stand between the individual and the state. What Cooper (1990:196) is attempting to do is advocate a citizen administrator who "bears responsibility for acknowledging, respecting and supporting the existence of a community of communities that includes the affiliational, organizational, economic, and political portions of the continuum."

Another perspective that also takes Tocqueville's critical observations seriously is William Sullivan (1986) in his book, *Reconstructing Public Philosophy*. Sullivan's underlying assumption is relatively simple; namely, that the administrative apparatus of the state has contributed to the degradation of both civic life and public virtue as the result of being part and parcel of modern liberalism. Sullivan argues forcefully that modern liberalism has negated the development of a coherent public discourse adequate to the complexities we face in political life. Consequently, public virtues have become essentially drained of their moral significance because they are tightly wrapped around the individualist *ethos* of liberalism. Thus, it should come as no surprise, Sullivan adds, that the moral and political perspective of liberalism is inherently instrumental in its view of political and social life. He (1986: 26) explains it this way:

> Thus the moral and political outlook of liberalism is instrumental in its view of political and social life. It identifies value with what is useful to the individual. Human beings are conceived of as self-interested individuals driven by passions to fulfill their needs by means of rational calculation and planning. This view of human nature is in turn

supported by the notion that reason is a tool of analysis, taking apart the elements of a situation or entity so as to reorganize it for greater usefulness. The logical goal of liberal rationality is scientific social engineering that will be able to bring about a perfect adjustment of needs and wants.

Sullivan contends that as a society we rarely question the basic assumptions of liberalism that exalts the primacy of self-interest and the public (and private) institutions that often perpetuate those interests—indeed, gives those interests legitimacy as an integral (and normal) part of the political and institutional process. According to Sullivan, here is the real rub: "liberal individualism cannot provide a convincing conception of a common good" (Sullivan, 1986: xiii). While Sullivan's analysis may sound unduly critical, it does raise some basic issues that cannot be so easily disregarded. That is, it may be futile to promote public ethics in our public institutions without reconstructing a new public philosophy that is somehow predicated on the values of interdependency (and quality of social relations) as well as mutual concern that transcends an utilitarian perspective on public affairs. Only with this new outlook can we see "the value of politics as the moral cultivation of responsible selves" (Sullivan, 1986: 21).

The theoretical similarities between Tocqueville and Sullivan are readily apparent. Like Tocqueville, Sullivan is concerned with how our liberal capitalist society can generate public conformity to its instrumental dictums and why, given this fact, it is so crucial to buffer this influence on civic life. Not surprisingly, Sullivan believes we need an associated life to cultivate meaningful citizenship that can counter, pressure, and restrain the forces of modern liberalism. For Tocqueville, as with Sullivan, public virtue is cultivated only when citizens participate in public affairs—a civic participation that can develop a sense of shared responsibility and mutual concern. In a similar vein, Clark Cochran (1982) has proposed what he calls "the theory of communal pluralism" and Benjamin Barber (1984) has developed his notion of strong democracy to highlight the importance of political community to the notion of the common good.

Although not explicit on this point, Sullivan is calling for both internal and external checks to unethical, or moral questionable practices, of public institutions. Sullivan, for instance, is calling for an external check in the respect that public institutions have a *moral obligation* to provide public forums for civic participation that can promote an ethical bond between public administrators and the communities they serve. Of course, this sounds like an old song that most public administrators may no longer want to sing. This is not Sullivan's argument, however. He is calling for a *mutual educative process* between the citizenry and public institutions—in a similar manner as Mary Parker Follett (1965)— that can restructure what he (1986: 225) so aptly calls, "a new ordering of the ecology of social relationships." Only with this educative process, Sullivan reiterates, can we begin to build a truly moral culture of the polity. The internal check, given what has already been stated, is quite obvious: without a renewed "public" philosophy of our public institutions we will be doomed to doing ethical patchwork—and sloppy patchwork at that— which leaves untouched the liberal architecture of our modern polity that is hardly structured for a civic renewal. Perhaps, Sullivan is asking too much from us. Regardless of the idyllic tone of his arguments, Sullivan poses a challenge to theorist and practitioner alike that ethics in public affairs inherently involves issues of a much broader intellectual landscape (and changes in that intellectual landscape), than just an operational set of administrative guidelines.

Another perspective that exhibits a civic republican view of public ethics is the provocative and disturbing book, *Unmasking Administrative Evil*. Guy Adams and Dan

Balfour (1998:xxv) contend that "a central theme of the modern psyche is the emphasis on the value of technical rationality and attendant narrowing of the concepts of reason, professionalism, ethics, and politics." This view, in part, is reminiscent of Alberto Ramos' critique of modern rationality and its deleterious impact on social and human affairs. Adams and Balfour do not blink when they argue, in polemic terms not often heard in the literature of public administration or public policy, that when technical rationality is linked to the modern bureaucracy, "the result is an unintentional tendency toward dehumanization and the elevation of technical progress and processes over human values and human dignity" (1998:xxv). Some may assert that this perspective is overly Weberian in tone—a tone too pessimistic, if not exaggerated, in drawing certain controversial conclusions. Because they believe that public administration (in general terms) is predicated upon technical rationality and, equally as important, because modern public (and private) organizations are deeply embedded in an instrumental-technical culture, administrative evil is sometimes masked. In fact, they indicate, "because administrative evil wears many masks, it is entirely possible to adhere to the tenets of public service ethics and participate in a great evil, and not be aware of it until it is too late (or perhaps not at all)" (1998: 4). To be sure, their assertion will make many in public administration and public policy rather uncomfortable. What Adams and Balfour are pointing to is a process that can be opaque and subtle which they call a moral inversion. Moral inversion, they claim, occurs when administrative evil has been redefined as something good, thus "ordinary people can all too easily engage in acts of administrative evil while believing that what they are doing is not only correct, but, in fact, good" (1998:xx).

In perhaps the most controversial part of the book, they raise the issue—which has been ignored in the field—concerning the relationship of public administration to the horrors of the Holocaust:

> The historical record shows that the Holocaust was not the departure from the practice of modern, technical-rational administration, but, instead represents one of its inherent . . . possibilities. The public service facilitated the killing process from ghettoization, to desportation to slave labor and systematic killing, to the disposal of millions of bodies. If the final solution evolved, there was nothing that is normally considered part of modern public administration—professional education and expertise, ethical standards, scientific methods, bureaucratic procedures, accountability to elected officials, and so on—that could prevent or resist the genocide of the Jews. Public administrators were both willing and helpless in the face of great evil. Today, they remain just so because administrative evil wears a mask (Adams and Balfour, 1998:71).

According to their line of logic, and given the moral vacuity of administrative ethics, we offer little to the contemporary public servant other than to leave voluntarily when confronted with serious ethical violations within the organization or the state. But too often—and there is the real fear of Adams and Balfour—the public servant instead of resisting evil becomes merely a helpless victim, or worse yet, a willing accomplice.

As a bulwark against this process, they propose a public ethics that can both recognize the different masks of administrative evil as well as to resist becoming an instrument of policies and procedures that might engender eruptions of evil. What they are proposing is, in effect, a communitarian ethic that anchors public ethics to a critical and active notion of citizenship. In other words, we need a public ethics that can sustain communities and a "strong democracy" based upon a participation citizenry in order to foster a critical perspective on the ethical implications of governmental policymaking. Echoing Terry

Cooper's notion of a citizen-administrator, Adams and Balfour see a major responsibility for this role as guarding against policies that would undermine the role and purpose of democratic citizenship in the community. But strong communities, they correctly conclude, do not and can not guarantee the elimination of administrative evil. In the end, they offer the hope that administrative evil will find it difficult to mask itself where there are citizen administrators attempting to strengthen the role of democratic citizenship in the polity.

Some may argue that Adams and Balfour put too much theoretical weight on the role of instrumental rationality in comparison to other factors that could contribute to what they describe as administrative evil. Moreover, in their obsequious emphasis on instrumental rationality, critics could further claim that they have given us only a schematic and highly partial presentation of those societal and historical factors that can lead to administrative evil. Yet, even if these critics have validity concerning Adams' and Balfour's epistemological difficulties, they have drawn our attention to a disturbing and insufficiently studied aspect of the field: the role of public administration and its relationship to administrative evil and how, perhaps, a renewed stress on public ethics may serve as a way of adverting the emergence of evil in public and social affairs. In a time where we have seen the human carnage in Bosnia, Cambodia, and Rwanda, it is a message we can hardly afford to ignore. Such is the challenge of Adam's and Balfour's book and, by inference, the neo-classical perspective.

C. Consequential View

This perspective, for the most part, is characterized by its recognition of the multiplicity of publics and the unintended direct consequences of public acts on the political community. As John Dewey (1927) reminds us, interactions create consequences, which, in turn, "give rise to a public with a shared interest in controlling those consequences" (Long, 1990:171). The public interest, in other words, is the public's shared recognition of consequences and the substantive impact those consequences can have on community life. For Dewey—as well as for Benjamin Barber and Richard Flathman—the state has grown more remote from the citizenry to the point that we are witnessing what Dewey called the "disintegrating public." We are in the ironic situation in which "we have inherited local town-meeting practices and ideas . . . but we live and act and have our being in a continental national state" (Dewey, 1988:22). At the heart of Dewey's concern was a haunting question: how do we as a public normatively address the issue of the consequences of interdependence without a vital notion of community? Dewey is, to be sure, touching upon one of the essential points of a democratic polity: that is, the "problem of citizenship in a large scale, increasingly complex nation state" (Cooper, 1991:2). Dewey (1927:86) posed the issue in this manner:

> Our concern at this time is to state how it is that the machine age in developing the Great Society has invaded and partially disintegrated the small communities of former times without generating a Great Community. The facts are familiar enough; our special affair is to point out their connections with the difficulties under which the organization of a democratic public is laboring.

What the Great Society did not, and could not, accomplish is the successful transformation into the Great Community. The result, according to Dewey, was predictable: a public that is too diffused for any conjointed actions which can have enduring consequences. Subsequently, this diffused public "generates its own group of persons especially affected [by public acts], with little to hold these different publics together in an integrated whole" (Dewey, 1988:29).

The problem of citizenship posed by Dewey is directly addressed by Benjamin Barber (1984) in his book *Strong Democracy*. Borrowing heavily from Dewey, Barber articulates a different theoretical cut at trying to foster ethical citizenship. He contends the real problem stems from our incessant attachment to the "liberal democracy" view of citizenship which he refers to as "thin democracy." Thin democracy is basically a political bargaining system that promotes private interests over the common good. It is, in short, a "zoo-keeping function" that sets constraints on antisocial behavior that can hinder the common good. Under this arrangement, he surmises, it is no wonder that liberal democracy de-emphasizes the role of the citizen as an active participant in the policy process. Barber contrasts this definition of liberal or thin democracy with "strong democracy." Barber (1984:132) defines strong democracy as "politics in the participatory mode where conflict is resolved in the absence of an independent ground through a participatory process of ongoing, proximate self-legislation and the creation of a political community capable of transforming dependent, private individuals into free citizens and partial and private interests into public goods."

One may ask what relationship does strong democracy have with the role of public administrators? If we can assume that public administrators are stewards of the democratic process, Barber (1984:156) provides an answer: the central task of a democratic polity is "to invent procedures, institutions, and forms of citizenship that nurture political judgment" which is facilitated by the ongoing process of democratic talk, deliberation, and public action. Political judgment, he tells us, is the "idea of public seeing," a process which is always provisional and open to constant normative refinement (Ventriss, 1985). To foster the kind of deliberative democratic talk that is necessary in addressing the normative implications of policy issues, we need to initiate a public language as opposed to a private (technocratic) language—a commitment that helps citizens transcend the focus on the "I" to include the "we." Barber is insistent that only strong democracy can confront the issue of accountability to the public good. To Barber, citizenship implies accountability because it promotes civic virtue through an educative process. "To rule well they need first to rule. To exercise responsibility prudently they must be given responsibility" (Barber, 1984:237). Here the influence of both Dewey and Tocqueville is apparent in that accountability and civic virtue are achieved when citizens learn to deliberate through practice, thus inculcating the substantive values to accommodate the public interest.

Like Dewey, Barber recognizes the focus of modernity on citizenship. What is needed is the formulation of a citizens' agenda. This agenda means incorporating a national initiative and referendum process, a national system of neighborhood assemblies, a civic videotex service, a civic communication cooperative, and an universal citizen service system, to name a few. "To a large extent, Barber turns the problems of modernity on their head: instead of viewing modernity as always an obstacle to participation, he perceives that the characteristics of modernity (particularly technology) can be retooled to promote ideals of a strong democracy" (Ventriss, 1985:439).

The role of the publicness of administrative ethics, as seen through the eyes of Barber's conceptual lens, is nothing short of engaging the citizenry in ways that will enhance the achievement of a strong democracy and the civic values that this entails. This is clearly a call to develop the "public" side of public administration

Since Richard Flathman's thinking has already been discussed, I will only briefly highlight some of his ideas as applied to this category. Flathman (1966) wants to promote what he calls the "politics of public interest." He understands, although he is not explicit on this point, that policy action often takes place in an increasingly intersectoral environment and that public agents for the common good have an obligation to not only account for the visible costs of policy action but, more importantly, for the less apparent (or visible) costs borne by some groups and that can be passed on to other groups who may not have any direct recourse. Hence, there is a moral obligation to assess the impact of a policy's interdependency on the public. Flathman, by inference, is calling upon public administrators to identify the unintended and indirect outcomes or other normative consequences in which the organization exists. In this sense, Flathman's notion of the "universalizability principle" requires of the administrator or policy analyst to focus on the public interdependence of policy acts and to deliberate on past, present, and future policy choices that can lead to human betterment rather than merely developing instrumental approaches to implement enacted policies.

D. Postmodern View

Postmodern thought is primarily an attempt to provide an imaginative and comprehensive critique of modernity—a modernity that is predicated upon the enlightenment philosophy of historical progress and modern reason (Foucault, 1977). The literature is vast on this subject, so no attempt will be made here to repeat what has already been written before. For our purposes here, I want to first focus on Charles Fox's and Hugh Miller's mordant work, *Postmodern Public Administration* (1995).

Fox and Miller's lucid work is both a critique of the "orthodoxy" (as they call it) of public administration and public policy as well as an effort to formulate a postmodern approach in constructing a discourse theory for public affairs. Fox and Miller describe what they mean by postmodern and the thinkers who have articulated its basic theoretical premises:

> [Derrida, Lyotord, Foucault, Baudrillard and others] . . . are united by their skepticism toward these typically modern claims to what used to be called universalism or essentialism but is now gathered up under foundationalism or metanarratives . . . examples of such metanarratives include logical positivism in philosophy, the material dialectic in Marxism, and structural functionalism and systems theory in . . . sociology and political science (1995:44).

From this they surmise—albeit with acknowledging the partial validity of postmodern thinking—that there is no stable common reality apart which truth claims can be verified and redeemed and, secondly, that there is a growing refracted and "incommensurable series of realities [being] constructed by multiple subcultural fragments" (1995:43). In the next breath, they do not wince when they assert that even issues like governance and citizen participation "are all rendered problematic under postmodern conditions" (1995: 43).

Given this reality, Fox and Miller posit the following question: "Under these circumstances what should we do next?" (1995:4). In answering this question, they critique what they refer to as the loop model of democracy (procedural democracy), the Blacksburg manifesto, and the communitarian view that has grown more influential in the field. The real challenge confronting us, Fox and Miller maintain, is "to seek a new framework that can withstand the postmodern conditions, [and] on the other hand, can claim congruence with democratic ideals'' (1995:7).

This new framework is grounded in a discourse theory that is based, in part, on Hannah Arendt's and Jurgen Haberman's conceptualization of public spaces. Their real purpose is to construct a nonfoundational framework from which public discourse and, subsequently, public spaces can endure. In order to ensure that ''public discourse'' can actually take place, Fox and Miller presuppose certain conditions necessary for its validity: sincerily in speech (condemning false promises and insincere claims), situation-regarding intentionality (discussing issues in regards to a concrete situation), willing attention (as opposed to apathy and coercion), and substantive contribution (the public articulation of policy issues).

The question that needs posing is whether the postmodern thinking they lean on—with all the usual disclaimers—can provide ethical insights that are useful to administrators or policy analysts? Can a normative framework be developed when even ''meaning itself is up for grabs'' and conceptual notions of social reality are clothed in the garments of the contingent, the nonessential, the fragmentary, and the ephemeral? Although Fox and Miller have articulated a perspective that is theoretically intriguing and challenging to the issue of public ethics, they tend to stumble over a more basic point that has been eloquently argued by Jeffrey Issac:

> Our choice is not between absolute foundations or no foundations, between overblown narratives or just plain narratives, but between conviction resting on warranted but contingent principles and those based on grounded assertions or prejudices. Questions about human nature and the human good are central to politics, even if they can never be answered once and for all nor in a theoretically neutral way. The effort to avoid them is disingenuous, for if we do not take them up explicitly, we are likely simply to smuggle them with our arguments through the back door (1992:8).

How they would respond to the assertion is, of course, open to speculation, but someone who has tried to reframe the theoretical inquiry—from a somewhat different angle—is Michael Harmon. Harmon's analysis in his book, *Responsibility is Paradox*, is, one could argue, the most theoretically sophisticated examination of responsibility in recent memory. Saying this, what exactly is Harmon's contribution to issue of responsibility and, more specifically, to public ethics?

Harmon has emphasized a conceptual point that is often ignored in our elaboration on ethics: the saliency of personal responsibility. But he does not stop here. He contends that responsibility itself is inherently a paradoxical idea in that it denotes two different meanings; that is, the meaning associated with moral agency and answerability to legitimate political authority. According to Harmon, there are two kinds of paradoxes which he calls antinominal (good) paradox and schismogenic (bad) parodox. A schismogenic paradox, he insists, is a part of the rationality process associated with Western societies that tries to excoriate the inherent tension between opposing principles, thus resulting in predictable pathologies. An antinominal paradox, on the other hand, is an integral part of the human condition—a process whereby the individual struggles to unify inner opposites which ''defines the dynamic of the individuals quest for wholeness and individuation'' (1995:76). It is within the context that he introduces personal responsibility ''as referring to action that (a) is informed by self-reflexive understanding and (b) emerges from a context of social relationships wherein personal commitments are regarded as valid bases for moral action'' (1995:81). He openly acknowledges that personal responsibility is grounded in the notion of subjectivity, a subjectivity that modern rationalism dismisses as fundamentally irrelevant. Here he launches into a critique of "rationalism" that divorces public life as separate from personal responsibility; that distrusts emotivism being expressed in public life; that equates the narrative with the instrumental values of efficiency and effectiveness; that equates accountability with administrative control; that assumes responsibility is congruent to the actions of authoritative ends; and finally, that assumes that there is such a thing as responsible conduct that can lead to "correct" ethical solutions. He, moreover, forcefully articulates the limitations of rationalism in regards to how it tries to resolve the paradoxes of obligation, agency, and accountability. Although he offers no recommendations or specific guidelines to help the administrator of policy analysts (that was not his purpose), he does, at the end of the book, suggest that we link personal responsibility (moral agency) as part of a self-reflexive process to Alasdair MacIntyre's notion of practice. Because some have misinterpreted his meaning on this point, he has revisited this issue by clarifying that "a self-reflexive exercise of moral agency, rather than being a solitary, intellectual activity, is only achievable in the context of social relationship. Making, which is to say acts of freedom, is intimately associated with answering, being accountable to others by means of continuing dialogue" (1996:606).

I have hardly been exhaustive with all aspects of Harmon's percipient analysis of responsibility. In respect to public ethics, what is important about Harmon's exegete concerning the idea of responsibility is his focus on relating personal responsibility to social practice. This relationship is particularly interesting given that he negates—reminiscent of many of those associated with postmodern thinking in the field like O.C. McSwite (1997)—the existence of foundational truths. Borrowing directly from McSwite's contention against any pretensions to some foundational truth, Harmon states that "modernism's enchantment with the enlightenment's 'man of reason,' serves chiefly to disguise, though with increasing transparency, power moves by some to impose their self-saving versions of it upon others" (1996:607). What Harmon, and for that matter Fox and Miller, may be doing is confusing foundations with foundationalism. Joseph Margolis, for example, has raised exactly this poignant issue: "Human inquiry [can] pursue universal conditions without universalism, foundations without foundationalism, [and] essentials without essentialism" (1986:38). What Margolis is hinting at here is the view that we need not surrender any search for foundations in public life, but rather we need to understand that such a search will always be partial and incomplete. It is for this reason, to a large degree, that Hannah Arendt, who was very aware of both historical contingencies and limitations of knowledge in public affairs, could without any hesitation argue that we need new political principles in our precarious age that can provide a means of rethinking our approach to ethics and politics. Camus, I think, said it best:

> We know that we live in a contradiction, but we also know that we must refuse this contradiction and do what is necessary to reduce it. Our task as men [and women] is to find the few principles that will calm the infinite anguish of free souls. We must mend what has been torn apart, make justice imaginable again in a world so obviously unjust, give happiness a meaning once more to people poisoned by the misery of the century (1968:135–136).

While postmodern approaches in public administration (and public policy) have not exerted quite the influence many would have liked, they do—and this is especially exemplified in the works of Harmon, and Fox and Miller—focus our attention on the necessity to reframe a deliberative discourse with the citizenry that engages the field with public affairs in all its ambiguity.

E. Organizational Perspective

Since this perspective incorporates such a wide range of different theorists, a few words are in order to clarify the nature of this approach in relationship to the publicness of administrative ethics. First, unlike the other views presented here, the characteristics of organizational life and the pressures that such a life entails are more concisely addressed in this category. This includes such dilemmas as the problem of dirty hands, many hands, and no hands. Concomitantly, it involves the legal and constitutional obligations of administrators who implement programs or policies and, as a related issue, Stephen Bailey's (1965:293) idea of the essential moral components that administrators need to promote: "optimism, courage, and fairness tempered by charity." This is not to imply that the theorists in this category are not concerned with issues of ethical citizenship, civic virtue and community, but rather that their frame of reference is anchored more in the dilemmas posed by bureaucratic practices that can hinder ethical decision-making within the organizational context. Probably more than anything else this organizational view acknowledges—at least more explicitly than the other approaches to publicness—that administrators generally exercise policy discretion and that this "discretion requires autonomy of judgment and action that may at times be at odds with the interests and purposes of other legitimately involved in the policy process" (Burke and Pattenaude, 1988:227).

Dennis Thompson (1985), for example, has questioned whether the possibility of administrative ethics can be realistically achieved when one is confronted with the stark realities or ethics of organizational life. Thus the critical issue, according to Thompson (1980), is how to preserve the idea of personal responsibility against the strong pressures of organizational life. Political ethics, he reasons, is really the attempt "to provide a link between actions of the individual and the structures of organizations" (Thompson, 1980: 6). Following up on this related theme is John Burke's (1986) book *Bureaucratic Responsibility*. Burke somewhat broadens Thompson's ideas to argue that responsibility to the public interest must be understood within the context of how individual responsibility is linked to the institutions of a democratic polity and public consent. He (1986:217) recognizes that "any attempt at reconciling bureaucracy and democracy through analysis of individual responsibility is admittedly ambitious in scope." Burke (1986) further asserts that a purely moral assessment is unlikely to give sufficient weight to the institutional (and legal) obligations of public officials. He calls for an "active sense of administering . . . [which] means acting on responsibilities to protect the integrity of broader democratic processes and the institutional, and especially the administrative enterprise as a whole" (1986:183). The publicness of the administrator's role is by adhering to these broader democratic processes.

Kathyrn Denhardt (1988, 1989, 1991), on the other hand, is concerned with the administrator who has a responsibility to make personal moral assessments. She (1988) concludes that organizational controls such as supervision and rules cannot act as a substitute for individual normative judgments. Denhardt (1988:26) has attempted to resuscitate—or breath a little more substantive life—into the meaning of administrative ethics by proposing the following definition: "Administrative ethics is the process of independently critiquing decision standards, based on core social values which can be discovered, within reasonable organizational boundaries, which can be defined, subject to personal and professional accountability."

Moreover, Denhardt has made the interesting observation that there has been too little focus on the role of ethics in an organizational setting. The key to responsibility, she maintains, is understanding the dynamic relationship of the individual to the organization structure. This prompts her to consider possible organizational reforms commensurate with her views on administrative ethics. She argues for "developing an organizational conscience; altering an organization's division of task; protecting the ethical individual who violates organizational policies and procedures; and raising the level of ethical discussion as part of organizational practice" (1988:140). She pushes this point even more by advocating that through the educational process, students and practitioners alike must become acquainted with the basic language of philosophy. She pulls no punches in claiming that "the notion that public administrators must become philosophers as well as managers will meet some resistance, but is nevertheless important if public administration is to become more ethical" (1988:184). The "publicness" of ethics is captured in this new role for the public administrator.

John Rohr would find this claim, as sympathetic as he would be to it, as not feasible in the real world of administrative practice. He (1978) proposes, in comparison to what he states is the high road and low road to ethics, a middle road that is more consonant to the expectations of public administrators and how they are educated to perform their public duties and roles. He suggests that administrative ethics be grounded in the values of the American people and maintains that such "regime values" can be discovered in major Supreme Court opinions and other historical writings that can provide a substantive foundation for ethical decision-making. He argues that when an administrator takes an oath to uphold the Constitution "that brought this regime into being and continues to state symbolically its spirit and meaning" (1978:67), this obligates the administrator to adhere to the guiding principles of constitutional regime values. In a later work, Rohr (1986) declares that constitutional regime value should be viewed as more than just an ethical framework for decision-making, but as maintaining an attitude that instructs a certain perspective on the public role of the administrator. Regime values thus serve as a way of better informing ethical choice and of serving the public interest. Needless to say, this assumes that the regime values of equality, freedom, and property are truly reflective of the whole spectrum of values of our democratic society. It is interesting to note that the Agency Perspective, as it is called, put forward in the Blacksburg Manifesto (in which Rohr was a co-author) encompasses a much broader set of values in addressing the issue of public governance and the public interest (Wamsley et al., 1990). The proponents of this approach openly advocate an institutionally grounded Minnowbrook Perspective that recognizes the importance and efficacy of public institutions. Furthermore, Wamsley and his co-authors believe that one cannot solely depend on individual responsibility as the basis for new action and social change. In contrast to the Minnowbrook view, the Blacksburg perspective recognizes "the need to work to change values and to bring about social change from both ends of the structural-individual continuum" (Wamsley et al., 1990: 21). Wamsley's group real theoretical purpose, among other things, is to revitalize the concept of the public interest. They (1990:40) define the public interest as a combination of several habits of mind in formulating public policy:

> attempting to deal with the multiple ramifications of an issue rather than a select few; seeking to incorporate the long-range view into deliberations, to balance a natural tendency toward excessive concern with short-term results; considering competing demands and requirements of affected individual and groups, not one position; proceeding equipped with more knowledge and information rather than less; and recognizing that to say that the public interest is problematic is not to say it is meaningless.

While the Blacksburg Manifesto tried to define the public interest within an agential perspective, the American Society for Public Administration sanctioned a book edited by

James Bowman (1991) called aptly the *Ethical Frontiers in Public Management* which is clearly an organizational view to administrative ethics. This is particularly evident in Part Three of this book that tries to balance strategies for both the institutional and individual level analysis. For example, Gerald Gabris (1991) argues that because of the pervasive Machiavellian valve system in organizations, an organizational development approach is essential in establishing new value patterns within the organization, thus promoting both ethical action and organizational change. With a few exceptions, most of the authors in this book rarely question the role of professionalism, citizenship, community, and the inherent tension between democracy and bureaucracy as an integral part of redefining administrative ethics and the role of public administration in forging a civic culture for renewing the field's conception of the public interest. Even the calls for a constitutional stewardship, as Douglas Morgan and Henry Kass (1991) put it, seem to take the organization as a historical given thus attempting to situate ethics solely within the domain of administrative practice. By and large, no serious mention is made by these authors to critically examine modern liberalism which underlies much of the administrative milieu. Darrell Pugh, much to his credit, is one of the few theorists in this book to raise the following salient issue: "the bureaucratic ethos is the consequence of modern capitalism and not that of republican, constitutional self-governance" (1991:24). Pugh (1991:26) concludes somberly that "although the field has claimed to reject the politics/administration dichotomy—replacing its emphasis on the word administration with an emphasis on the word *public*—the operational values have remained bureaucratic."

Finally, some thoughts on Montgomery Van Wart's book, *Changing Public Sector Values* (1998), that tries to create "a field of public administration values, a field that currently does not exist in a recognizable forum" (1998:xix). However, he actually is trying to create something more: a major contribution to the science (his word) of values for public administration. Notwithstanding the ambitious nature of Van Wart's analysis, he notes that ethics is but a subfield of values, hence the challenge of the administrator acting on correct values. These values, he concludes, come from five major sources: individual values, professional values, organizational values, legal values, and public interest values. Van Wart continues to build upon this perspective by emphasizing the cultural perspective of values, which, as he maintains, are the broader values of the overall society and culture in which the administrator is embedded. This is the closest he comes in explicitly acknowledging the intrinsic importance of public ethics.

At the end of the book, he states that "the term ethical . . . signifies someone who is an exemplar of ideal behavior. This means that the individual not only complies with the general legal and organizational norms but also "achieves a high standard of excellence and works hard to fulfill social, organizational and altruistic ideals" (1998:316). Within this context, he argues that the administrator has the added responsibility "to understand values, to find value consensus, and to monitor and control value consistency" (1998:317–318). Thus, the need of developing "the art of values management" (1998: 319). This art of values management, Van Wart asserts, is especially vexing in an era of value competition, complexity, and change.

What is so interesting about this book is how it differs so much from other views of public ethics, particularly that of the classical and neo-classical perspective of public ethics. One can only imagine what Guy Adams and Dan Balfour would say about Van Wart's theoretical construct as a means of unmasking administrative evil. As ambitious as Van Wart's analysis seems to be, this examination still begs a question that is so characteristic of the organizational perspective to public ethics: the difficulty in mitigating the functional rationality that is such an integral part of organizational life.

Against this theoretical backdrop, there have been vocal voices that have warned the field about the power of organizational socialization and loyalty—a story somewhat echoed in the works of Ralph Hummel (1987), Robert Denhardt (1981), and William Scott and David Hart (1979), to mention only a few. As varied as the approaches are in addressing administrative ethics within the organizational setting—as the discussion of the different theorists discussed here indicate—the vexing challenge they all, to a large extent, must confront was posed by Alberto Ramos (1981:72):

> . . . the citadel of todays' organizational scholarship is like a tower of Babel. The confusion of tongues is almost deafening. The source of much of this confusion is the distinctive language which has emerged as a consequence of the ascendance of economizing criteria into the social fabric at large, and the diffusion of the political into the social.

IV. CONCLUSION

I have tried to present here the variety of theoretical views related to the publicness of administrative ethics. I have refrained, as much as possible, from stating my own opinions on the shortcomings and merits of each approach. Before I discuss these points, I will say at the outset that I am openly sympathetic to the views presented by those who fall under the rubric of the classical and consequential perspective on ethics. Concomitantly, I lean heavily towards some of the theoretical positions stated in the neo-classical or republican perspective, particularly in regards to the works of Terry Cooper and William Sullivan. I have some rather strong reservations about many of the theories and issues raised in the organizational perspective, mainly because few in this category analyze administrative ethics as a reflection of the ideological dimensions of professionalism in public administration and public policy (Adams, 1992; Fischer and Zinke, 1989; Fox 1992; Ventriss, 1992).

This is not to say that the organizational perspective has not added much to our understanding of the complexity of ethical decision-making. It certainly has, as evident in the lucid works of such scholars as Rohr and Burke. My point is that they do not go far enough in reconceptualizing the publicness of administrative ethics as it pertains to the relationship of citizenship to the administrator or the policy analyst. The negative baggage of professionalism, moreover, is given only scant attention by most of the theorists who adhere to this organizational approach. This is hardly surprising since most of the debates about administrative ethics in public administration and public policy are, as Guy Adams is quick to remind us, rather "problematic because they assume that current practice, though flawed, is in one sense fundamentally just" (Adams et al., 1990:231). More on this later.

The attractiveness of both the classical, neo-classical, and consequential approach to public ethics is the explicit focus on citizenship and its normative relationship to the political community. The first two perspectives are quite concise on this point. The representative thinkers, for example, in the classical category are heavily influenced by Aristotle. In particular, McIntyre's contribution, I think, is clear: we need to redefine our notion of professionalism that is more commensurate with his views of practice. In some respects, this view is related to Edmund Pincoffs's book, *Quandaries and Virtues* (1986) when he argues that moral judgment is part and parcel of moral character and virtue.

Ramos and Arendt, on the other hand, force the field to re-examine the importance of establishing public spaces where ethical action rather than behavior can take place. Some might accuse them of placing artificial barriers between action and behavior and reintroducing the questionable assumption that the political and administrative can be separated. However, I think they raise an intriguing question that cannot be so easily be brushed aside: are we naive to expect that public organizations can promote and sanction ethical action when their fundamental goals are grounded in pursuing instrumental and calculative ends? Is it not more realistic to argue, I believe Arendt and Ramos would maintain, that the pursuit (and attainment) of ethical ends should belong to other ''public'' realms where human activity is not under superimposed operational constraints? This vexing issue, to a large extent, was behind Ramos' call for a social system delimitation approach that would have us design different enclaves that would meet the individual's multidimensional needs. If nothing else, this is an interesting challenge to the field of public administration.

The neo-classical view, in many respects, builds upon some of the critical elements presented in the classical category. Yet, I must state that I am somewhat troubled by those theorists who believe that our ''ethical ethos'' must be linked to the philosophical views of our founding fathers. I do not at this time want to enter the debate dealing with the differences between the Federalists' new science of government (that was influenced strongly by such philosophical thinkers as David Hume) and the Anti-Federalists who adhered to the more traditional republican view of government. I think it is fairly accurate to say that, by and large, most public administration theorists have tended to overlook the Manichean vision that dominated our founding fathers' thinking (Ventriss, 1991; Kammen, 1973). Michael Kammen has maintained that his Manichean view manifested in our founding fathers' thinking has resulted in a moral dualism that is still present in our political fabric today: ''the conflict between high ethical standards and the ethos of the marketplace'' (1973:110). I am still puzzled by why, for the most part, so little attention is given to what Joseph Tussman (1960) warned us about over thirty years ago: in a liberal political universe dominated by possessive individualism, competition, and bargaining, should it really surprise us that there is hardly any incentive for citizens and administrators alike to act as morally autonomous agents? In response to Tussman's observation, William Sullivan's plea for a new public philosophy is perhaps where we need to be focusing more of our theoretical attention in coming to terms with the ''publicness'' of public administration and its normative role in shaping societal affairs.

The consequential approach, on the other hand, has important relevance to us not only because of its emphasis on community and citizenship, but because this approach acknowledges the issue of public interdependency and the saliency of having an active public for meaningful, effective participation in public affairs. While Flathman does not directly address this issue, it is clearly stated in the works of both Dewey and Barber. Collectively, their various perspectives open the theoretical door for public administration to develop a public learning and public language approach that can permit us ''to be experimental and constantly to reestablish concrete links with the public that are not merely procedural in nature, but experientially substantive in content'' (Ventriss, 1987: 42). What I believe would be interesting—both from a theoretical and a practical perspective—is the integration of the classical, neo-classical, and consequential views on public ethics and how that may prompt us to redefine public administration's theoretical linkages to the meaning of the public. Some, in my opinion, like Adams and Balfour have come close to achieving this goal, but none have quite succeeded.

The postmodern thinking that has captured the attention of many scholars in public administration represents, I think, a major contribution to public ethics in that it exposes the multiple forms of "otherness" and "differences" depicted in race, class, gender, knowledge, and, of course, subjectivity. More importantly, as scholars in this vein try to develop a "nonfoundational framework" for ethical inquiry, which is often expressed in lofty abstractive terms, they do present a direct challenge to modern liberalism.

The salient issue that nags, however, at this perspective with its broad attack on any (and every) perceived "metanarrative," is not only a mode of thinking unencumbered by the instrumental calculi of liberalism or logical positivism (or any other "ism"), but also a mode of thinking which offers little assistance in addressing Hannah Arendt's challenge when we find ourselves in dark times: "that human dignity [itself] needs a guarantee that can only be focused in a new political principle" (1963:ix). Unfortunately, postmodern thinking in public administration, for the most part, leaves us with little encouragement to initiate any such search. That in itself should give us pause about some of the unintended consequences of postmodern thought, irrespective of many of its contributions to our understanding of the historical vicissitudes we face in society.

I have left my final parting comments to the organizational perspective. Many might argue that I have painted too many scholars in this group with the same broad theoretical brush, so to speak. It is obvious that there are vast differences between what Kathryn Denhardt proposes and the arguments raised by Burke. I have tried to be careful in addressing those differences. My general reservation about this broad group, notwithstanding some of their critical contributions to administrative ethics, is that they seem to make an assumption, albeit not explicitly, which I find somewhat disturbing: they assume that the state and the public are one and the same and because public administration serves the needs of the state (as it must), it also serves the needs of the public. What concerns me is that the organizational perspective never seriously questions the legitimacy of the state and the field's relationship to it. Even raising such an issue makes us nervous—as it should. My point is this: before we can confront the meaning of the public, particularly in regards to administrative ethics, we must examine the changing role of state and at the same time explore the normative implications of the field's relationship to public institutions which may be promoting the prevailing arrangement of societal power. Peter Nettl (1969:22) has argued this point which is worth repeating: "that science, rationality, bureaucracy, and power are not just random concepts but stand in a tight causal chain."

While the debates will continue to rage on about what constitutes administrative ethics and how the public administrator can best serve the public interest, I think (perhaps naively some many contend) that redefining our view of the public will be a critical step in concomitantly redefining the administrator's civic purpose and normative role in "doing" public administration. In the process of redefining public administration's normative relationship to the publicness of the administrator's public obligation and role, we might just find ourselves in a new substantive political universe—to use a poetic phrase from Carol Sternhell (1984:559)—"shooting planets into stars."

REFERENCES

Adams, G.B. (1992). Enthralled with modernity: the historical context of knowledge and theory development in public administration. *Public Administration Review*, 52:363–373.

Adams, G.B., Bowerman, P.V., Dolbeare, K.M., Stivers, C.M. (1990). Joining purpose to practice:

a democratic identity for the public service. In *Images and Identities in Public Administration* (H.D. Kass and B.L. Catron, eds.). Sage Publication, Newbury, California, pp. 219–240.

Adams, G.B. and Balfour, D.L. (1998). *Unmasking Administrative Evil*. Sage Publication, Newbury, California.

Appleby, P.H. (1952). *Mortality and Administration in Democratic Government*. Louisana State University Press, Baton Rouge, Louisana.

Arendt, H. (1978). *The Jew as Pariah*. Grove Press, New York.

Arendt, H. (1965). *On Revolution*. Viking Press, New York.

Arendt, H. (1963). *Eichmann in Jerusalem: A Report on the Banality of Evil*, Viking Press, New York.

Arendt, H. (1958). *The Human Condition*. University of Chicago Press, Chicago.

Bailey, S.K. (1965). The relationship between ethics and public service. In *Public Administration and Democracy: Essays in Honor of Paul Appleby* (R.C. Martin, ed.). Syracuse University Press, Syracuse, New York.

Bailey, S.K. (1962). The public interest: some operational dilemmas. *Nomos V.*, pp. 96–106.

Barber, B.R. (1984). *Strong Democracy*. University of California Press, Berkeley, California.

Bellah, R.N., Richard, M., Sullivan, W.M., Swidler, A., Tipton, S.M. (1985). *Habits of the Heart: Individualism and Committment in American Life*. University of California Press, Berkeley, California.

Bowman, J.S. (ed.) (1991). *Ethical Frontiers in Public Management*. Jossey-Bass, San Francisco, California.

Burke, J.P. and Pattenaude, R.L. (1988). Professional expertise in politics and administration. In *Ethics, Government, and Public Policy*. (J.S. Bowman and F.A. Elliston, eds.). Greenwood Press, New York.

Burke, J.P. (1986). *Bureaucratic Responsibility*. Johns Hopkins University Press, Baltimore, Maryland.

Camus, A. (1968). *Lyrical and Critical Essays*. Knopf, New York.

Cochran, C.E. (1982). *Character, Community, and Politics*. University of Alabama Press, University, Alabama.

Cooper, T.L. (1991). *An Ethic of Citizenship for Public Administration*. Prentice Hall, Englewood Cliffs, New Jersey.

Cooper, T.L. (1990). *The Responsible Administrator*. Jossey-Bass, San Francisco, California.

Cooper, T.L. (1987). Hierarchy, virtue, and the practice of public administration: a perspective for normative ethics. *Public Administration Review*, 47:320–328.

Cooper, T.L. (1986). *The Responsible Administrator: An Approach for the Administrative Role*. Kennikat Press, Port Washington, New York.

Denhardt, K.G. (1991). Unearthing the moral foundations of public administration: honor, benevolence, and justice. In *Ethical Frontiers in Public Management* (J.S. Bowman, ed.). Jossey-Bass, San Francisco, California, pp. 91–113.

Denhardt, K.G. (1989). The management of ideals: a political perspective on ethics. *Public Administration Review*, 49:187–192.

Denhardt, K.G. (1988). *The Ethics of Public Service*. Greenwood Press, New York.

Denhardt, R.B. (1981). *In the Shadow of Organization*. The Regents Press of Kansas, Lawrence, Kansas.

Dewey, J. (1988). The eclipse of the public. *Kettering Review*, Fall Edition:21–30.

Dewey, J. (1927). *The Public and its Problems*. Swallow Press, Chicago, Illinois.

Fischer, F. and Zinke, R.C. (1989). Public administration and the code of ethics: administrative reform or professional ideology? *International Journal of Public Administration*, 12:841–854.

Flathman, R.E. (1966). *The Public Interest: An Essay Concerning the Normative Discourse*. Wiley, New York.

Follett, M.P. (1965). *The New State*. Peter Smith, Gloucester, Massachusetts.

Foucault, M. (1977). *Language, Counter-Memory, Practice*. Cornell University Press, New York.

Fox, C.J. (1992). What do we mean when we say professionalism: a language usage analysis for public administration. *American Review of Public Administration*, 22:28–38.

Fox, C. and Miller, H. (1995). *Postmodern Public Administration*. Sage Publications, Newbury, California.

Frederickson, G.H. (1989). Finding the public in public administration. Department of Public Administration, University of Kansas, Lawrence, Kansas, pp. 1–24.

Gabris, G.T. (1991). Beyond conventional management practices: shifting organizational values. In *Ethical Frontiers in Public Management* (J.S. Bowman, ed.). Jossey-Bass, San Francisco, California, pp. 205–224.

Harmon, M.M. (1996). Harmon responds. *Public Administration Review*, 56:604–610.

Harmon, M.M. (1995). *Responsibility as Paradox: A Critique of Rational Discourse on Government*. Sage Publications, Newbury, California.

Harmon, M.M. (1990). The responsible actor as the tortured soul: the case of Horatio Hornblower. In *Images and Identities in Public Administration* (H.D. Kass and B.L. Catron, eds.). Sage Publishers, Newbury, California.

Hart, D.K. and Wasden, C.D. (1990). Two roads diverged in a yellow road: public administration, the management orthodoxy, and civic humanism. *International Journal of Public Administration*, 13:747–775.

Hart, D.K. (1984). The founders, the Scots, and moral sense. Institute of Public Management, School of Management, Brigham Young University, Provo, Utah.

Herring, E. (1936). *Public Administration and the Public Interest*. McGraw-Hill, New York.

Hummel, R.D. (1987). *The Bureaucratic Experience*. St. Martin's Press, New York.

Issac, J.C. (1992). *Arendt, Camas, and Modern Rebellion*. Yale University Press, New Haven, Connecticut.

Jonsen, A.R. and Butler, L.H. (1975). Public ethics and policy making. *Hastings Center Report*, 5: 20–27.

Kammen, M. (1973). *People of Paradox*. Vintage, New York.

Kass, H.D. (1990). Stewardship as a fundamental element in images of public administration. In *Images and Identities in Public Administration*, (H.D. Kass and B.L. Catron, eds.). Sage Publishers, Newbury, California.

Kateb, G. (1983). *Hannah Arendt: Politics, Conscience, Evil*. Rowman and Allanheld, New York.

Long, N.E. (1990). Conceptual notes on the public interest for public administration and policy analysts. *Administration and Society*, 22:170–181.

MacIntyre, A. (1981). *After Virtue: A Study in Moral Theory*. University of Notre Dame Press, Notre Dame, Indiana.

Margolis, J. (1986). *Pragmatism Without Foundations: Reconciling Realism and Relativism*. Basil Blackwell, Oxford.

Mathews, D. (1988). Afterthoughts. *Kettering Review*, Fall Edition:51–54.

McCollough, T.E. (1991). *The Moral Imagination and Public Life*. Chatham House, Chatham, New Jersey.

McSwite, O.C. (1997). *Legitimacy in Public Administration: A Discourse Analysis*. Sage Publications, Newbury, California.

Morgan, D.F. and Kass, H.D. (1991). Legitimizing administrative discretion through constitutional stewardship. In *Ethical Frontiers in Public Management* (J.S. Bowman, ed.). Jossey-Bass, San Francisco, California, pp. 286–307.

Nettl, P. (1969). Power and the intellectuals. In *Power and Consciousness* (C.C. O'Brien and W.D. Vanech, eds.). New York University Press, New York, pp. 5–16.

Park, R.E. (1904). *The Crowd and the Public*. University of Chicago Press, Chicago, Illinois.

Pincoffs, E.L. (1986). *Quandaries and Virtues*. University Press of Kansas, Lawrence, Kansas.

Pops, G.M. (1988). Ethics in government: a framework for analysis. In *Ethics, Government, and Public Policy* (J. G. Bowman and F.A. Elliston, eds.). Greenwood Press, New York.

Pugh, D.L. (1991). The origins of ethical frameworks in public administration. In *Ethical Frontiers in Public Management* (J.S. Bowman, ed.). Jossey-Bass, San Francisco, California, pp. 9–33.

Ramos, A.G. (1981). *The New Science of Organizations*. University of Toronto Press, Toronto, Canada.

Richardson, W.D. and Nigro, L.G. (1987). Administrative ethics and founding thought: constitutional correctives, honor, and education. *Public Administration Review*, 47:367–376.

Rohr, J.A. (1986). *To Run a Constitution: The Legitimacy of the Administrative State*. University Press of Kansas, Lawrence, Kansas.

Rohr, J.A. (1978). *Ethics for Bureaucrats*. Marcel Dekker, New York.

Schubert, G. (1960). *The Public Interest: A Critique of the Theory of a Political Concept*. Free Press, Glencoe, Illinois.

Scott, W.G. and Hart, D.K. (1979). *Organizational America*. Houghton Mifflin, Boston, Massachusetts.

Sellars, J. (1970). *Public Ethics: American Morals and Manners*. Harper and Row, New York.

Sternhell, C. (1984). Human all too human. *Nation*, 67:558–559.

Stone, D.A. (1988). *Policy Paradox and Political Reason*. Harper Collins Publishers, New York.

Sullivan, R.J. (1989). *Immanuel Kant's Moral Theory*. Cambridge University Press, New York.

Sullivan, W.M. (1986). *Reconstructing Public Philosophy*. University of California Press, Berkeley, California.

Tocqueville, A. (1969). *Democracy in America*. (translated by G. Lawrence). Doubleday Anchor Books, New York.

Thompson, D.F. (1985). The possibility of administrative ethics. *Public Administration Review*, 45:555–561.

Thompson, D.F. (1980). Moral responsibility of public officials: the problem of many hands. *The American Political Science Review*, 74:903–987.

Tussman, J. (1960). *Obligation and the Body Politic*. Oxford University Press, New York.

Van Wart, M. (1998). *Changing Public Sector Values*. Garland Publishing, New York.

Ventriss, C. (1992). The ideology of professionalism. *International Journal of Public Administration*, 15:525–536.

Ventriss, C. (1991). Reconstructing governmental ethics. In *Ethical Frontiers in Public Management* (J.S. Bowman, ed.). Jossey-Bass, San Francisco.

Ventriss, C. (1987). Two critical issues of American public administration. *Administration and Society*, 19:25–47.

Ventriss, C. (1985). Emerging perspectives on citizen participation. *Public Administration Review*, 45:433–440.

Ventriss, C. and Luke, J. (1988). Organizational learning and public policy. *American Review of Public Administration*, 18:337–357.

Wall, B. (1991). Assessing ethical theory from a democratic viewpoint. In *Ethical Frontiers in Public Management* (J.S. Bowman, ed). Jossey-Bass, San Francisco, California, pp. 135–157.

Wamsley, G.L., Bacher, R.N., Goodsett, C.T., Kronenberg, P. S., Rohr, J.A., Stivers, C.M., White, O.F., Wolf, J.F. (1990). *Refounding Public Administration*. Sage Publications, Newbury Park, California.

14

Administrative Ethics and the Chimera of Professionalism
The Historical Context of Public Service Ethics

Guy B. Adams
University of Missouri-Columbia, Columbia, Missouri

> . . . the modern world calls into existence certain conceptions of morality, but also destroys the grounds for taking them seriously. Modernity both needs morality, and makes it impossible.
>
> —Ross Poole, 1991, p. ix.

It is common knowledge that professionalism is on the rise in public administration in the United States (Mosher, 1982; Stillman, 1987; Lynn, 1996). Since one of the distinguishing features of a profession, nearly always cited in the literature, is a code of ethics (e.g., Greenwood, 1957), increasing professionalization in the public service is viewed, at worst, as benign for the state of public service ethics, and at best, as a highly positive development. In this chapter, the relationship between professionalism and ethics is examined in its historical context; and the argument is made that the association of ethics and professionalism is oxymoronic, and indeed that professionalism itself is like the chimera of Greek mythology—an imaginary monster compounded of incongruous parts.

The historical context may be construed as consisting of many elements, but perhaps none are as significant as the culture at large within which American public administration is practiced, researched, and taught. Today, the culture at large is one of *modernity* (Turner, 1990; see also Bernstein, 1985; Bauman, 1989; and Rabinbach, 1990). Intellectual strands of modernity reach back to the sixteenth and seventeenth centuries and beyond, but as the defining characteristic of our own culture, modernity coalesced only within the last one hundred years. Our culture of modernity has, as one of its chief constituents, *technical rationality* (Barrett, 1979). Technical rationality is a way of thinking and a way of living that emphasizes the scientific-analytical mindset and the belief in technological progress. Technical rationality has been crucial to the development of professionalism. In the development of modernity in the United States, technical rationality and professionalism emerged in fully visible, contemporary form during the Progressive Era (1896–1916). I elaborate further on the emergence and development of technical rationality and professionalism below, but first an overview of the argument seems in order.

In this chapter, I examine first the state of ethics scholarship in public administration and then how the intersection of ethics and professionalism has been treated. The focus on professionalism leads directly to the Progressive Era during which, it is argued, the current relationship of professionalism and ethics in public administration first became fully visible. The development of technical rationality and professionalism, along with the emphasis on science, are closely examined. Next, I show how the early tension within the professions between advocacy and science was resolved in favor of the latter, and how codes of ethics emerged as compensation for the erosion of moral ground within the professions. Both the moral vacuity and the anti-democratic tendency of modern professionalism are discussed. Recent, repeated calls for professionalism and for more "rigorous" and "scientific" research in public administration echo themes of technical rationality and are closely linked to the legitimation problems of public administration in the American context. Finally, I address the prospects for a new professionalism in the context of our present cultural circumstances within modernity. First, however, the argument begins with a discussion of ethics in the public administration literature.

I. ETHICS SCHOLARSHIP IN PUBLIC ADMINISTRATION

Attention to ethics in the field of public administration has never been greater. The last decade has seen the creation of an Ethics Section within the professional association, the American Society for Public Administration (ASPA); three national symposia on ethics research in the public service; along with an impressive set of book-length treatments of the topic (Bowman, 1991; Cooper, 1994; Cooper and Wright, 1992; Frederickson, 1993; Gortner, 1991; Lewis, 1991; Madsen and Shafritz, 1992; Mertens, et al., 1994; Reynolds, 1995; Pasquerella, et al., 1996; Adams and Balfour, 1998; see also, Cooper, 1996; Dobel, 1992; Marini, 1992; Plant, 1997; Rosenbloom, 1992; and Stewart, 1991). The 1980s saw the adoption of a code of ethics and the staging of a national conference by ASPA, as well as a spate of other books and articles (Amy, 1984; Bowman, 1990; Brown, 1986; Burke, 1986; Denhardt, 1988; Fischer, 1983; Fox, 1989; Frederickson and Hart, 1985; Jackson, 1984; Lane, 1988; Lee, 1990; McSwain and White, 1987; Rohr, 1989; Yarwood, 1985; among others).

More significantly, the current attention to ethics in public administration builds on a sustained record of scholarship, which reaches back to the last wave of ethics concern, prompted by the Watergate scandals of the early 1970s. Ralph Clark Chandler (1984), Terry L. Cooper (1990), David K. Hart (1974), and John A. Rohr (1978) are perhaps most prominent among public administration scholars, whose attention to ethics spans at least three decades. There have been other important pioneers within public administration ethics (e.g., Appleby, 1952; Bailey, 1964; and Leys, 1943). Indeed, as documented in a *Public Administration Review* article (Nigro and Richardson, 1990), attention to ethics in that journal has been continuous, albeit with ebbs and flows, since its inception in 1940.

The Friedrich (1940) and Finer (1941) debate of that time is still a useful way of describing the ethics terrain in public administration (Stewart, 1985b). Finer argued for a version of ethics that emphasized *external* standards and controls—laws, rules, regulations, and codes. By contrast, Friedrich maintained that ethics was of necessity a matter of *internal* standards of conduct—a moral compass which would guide the public administrator through the morass of ethical dilemmas. The Finer position of external controls is most compatible with a view of the public administrator as a neutral functionary who carries out, in Max Weber's phrase, *sine ira ac studio* (without bias or scorn), policy decisions made in the political sphere or by those in higher echelons of the organizational hierarchy. One author has gone so far as to argue that both an ethic of neutrality (decisions from politics) and an ethic of structure (decisions from higher up) preclude administrative ethics altogether because they deny the legitimacy of administrative discretion (Thompson, 1985, 1992; see also, Ladd, 1970). The public administration literature on ethics has swung quite noticeably in the Friedrich direction (Fox and Cochran, 1990; Cooper, 1990; Green, 1994; Van Wart, 1996), and now arguments in that literature are primarily over just which ethical grounds might justify administrative discretion. Prominent among the arguments for administrative discretion are: (1) justice-based claims, usually following Rawls (Hart, 1974); (2) citizenship (Cooper, 1991; Stivers, 1994); (3) American regime values (Rohr, 1978; 1998); (4) stewardship (Kass and Catron, 1990); (5) conservation (Terry, 1995); and (6) countervailing responsibility (Harmon, 1995), among others. Before turning to the public administration literature which addresses ethics and professionalism, a brief discussion of the more general literature on professional ethics will help set the stage.

A. Professional Ethics

Professional ethics has commanded considerable attention in the academic literature (Baumrin and Freedman, 1983; Bayles, 1981; Callahan, 1988; Caminisch, 1983; Goldman, 1980; Gorlin, 1986; Haskell, 1984; Kultgen, 1982; among others). Still, the literature on professional ethics represents a rather small subset of a much larger literature dealing with professionalism *per se*. This larger literature for the most part omits ethical considerations altogether. Perhaps the most significant branch of this larger literature on professionalism typically discusses the professions as social institutions, adopting a stance of moral neutrality (e.g., after structural-functional sociology). Within the smaller literature on professional ethics, by far the larger portion is concerned with the ethics of a *particular* profession, for example, medical ethics. A much smaller portion of the literature on professions deals with professional ethics in general. The results of this mixed attention are described by Kultgen (1988:7):

> The authors take the structures of society and the professions as givens and debate the rules that should govern the relations between individual professionals and individual clients or employers. They ignore the impact on these micro-ethical issues of macro-ethical issues, such as the corporate responsibilities of professions and defects in their organization and practices. They describe the obligations of moral professionals in a moral society, but ignore their obligations in an immoral or at least imperfect society, where in fact they must act.

While the larger culture is often not dealt with, there is a fine-grained attention to ethical issues surrounding the *individual* professional's relationship with an *individual* client, thus reflecting the deeply embedded cultural value of individualism.

Other authors have addressed the *ideological* dimension of professionalism and professional ethics (Kultgen, 1982; Larson, 1977). Their focus is on how professionalism embodies certain social values, as well as certain social distributions of status and wealth, all at the expense of other possible configurations, and how even professional ethics seems to reinforce the social and economic position of the profession. There has been some attention to the ideological dimension of professional ethics in the public administration literature (Fischer and Zinke, 1989; Fox, 1992; Olufs, 1985; and Ventriss, 1992). Much of the public administration literature, however, does not focus on the ideological dimension of professional ethics.

B.   Ethics and Professionalism in Public Administration

It is almost an article of faith in the literature that professionalism imbues its practitioners with a *public service ideal* and a *code of ethics*—that is, internalized standards (after Friedrich). To this way of thinking, professionalism itself becomes the basis for a version of virtue or character ethics (Stewart, 1985a; see also Green 1994; Cooper, 1987; and MacIntyre, 1984). On the other hand, professionalism can also offer a grounding for the external version of ethics (after Finer). Professions have codes of ethics and they also often have some method of peer control in which ethics and standards are enforced and, in the extreme, in which the serious transgressor can be drummed out of the profession (Kernaghan, 1980).

At the same time, much of the activity in the world of public administration practice has been directed at external controls. The promulgation of additional laws and regulations has dominated our response to the moral slough of the 1990s, much as it did in the post-Watergate times. Foster (1981), among others, has called into question the common practice of equating law and ethics, or worse, substituting the former for the latter.

The depth and breadth within the public administration literature on ethics is to be applauded. Yet, it is quite unclear whether such theoretical formulations make an appreciable difference in the *internal* standards and norms of practicing public administrators. Here the distinction suggested by Chris Argyris (1990) between *espoused theory* and *theory-in-use* seems relevant. Espoused theory is, roughly, what we say we do while our theory-in-use informs our actual behavior.

Professional ethics appears in the public administration literature in both forms—espoused theory and theory-in-use (Pugh, 1989; Bruce, 1996; Plant, 1997; Bowman and Williams, 1997). At the level of espoused theory, one of the clearest associations of ethics and professionalism is found in an article by Kearney and Sinha (1988:575):

> In a sense, the profession provides the professional administrator with a Rosetta Stone
> for deciphering and responding to various elements of the public interest. Professional
> accountability as embodied in norms and standards also serves as an inner check on
> an administrator's behavior. . . . When joined with a code of ethics or conduct and
> the oath of office, professionalism establishes a value system that serves as a frame
> of reference for decision making . . . and creates a special form of social control condu-
> cive to bureaucratic responsiveness.

The response of both in-career and pre-career MPA students to discussions of professionalism reinforce this perspective. There is a clear consensus that the preferred role model for both aspiring and current public servants is that of the professional. Students and practitioners alike do not see this choice as eschewing ethics, quite the contrary; they see the role model of professional as satisfying the need for a system of ethical standards. To be professional is to be ethical.

Thus, the association between professionalism and ethics is a strong one within public administration. The association is probably stronger within our theory-in-use than within our espoused theories, which show a good deal more variety and depth of ethical thinking. But the question arises: from where does this association of professionalism and ethics come, and what are the implications of this historical juxtaposition? Answers may be found in the Progressive Era in the United States, when modernity coalesced.

II.   THE PROGRESSIVE ERA

The dominant image of the Progressive Era, the period from 1896–1916, is perhaps still the age of reform. The Progressive Era was a time of popular outrage against the depredations of big business, against social ills, against exploitation of all kinds. The result was a wave of progressive reform: child labor legislation, minimum wage, women's suffrage, direct election of senators, trust busting, as well as eliminating patronage, instituting clean government, and regulating industry. The image obscures as much as it reveals.

In the Progressive Era, Jeffersonian language, emphasizing a laissez-faire, limited government, was used by conservative business men (especially small business men; Weinstein, 1968). The reformers, on the other hand, used Hamiltonian language, promoting an active, assertive national government in the service of not just economic aims, but social principles as well. The Progressive aim was a Hamiltonian national government in the service of Jeffersonian ideals. In many instances, this was altered in practice to become a Hamiltonian national government with Jeffersonian rhetoric in the service of commercial interests. Gabriel Kolko (1963) aptly called this age of "reform," the "triumph of conservatism."

Far-sighted corporate leaders actively sought government regulation in order to eliminate unnecessary competition and to rationalize the economy as far as possible. Clientele agencies such as the Department of Commerce, which was formed in 1913, straightforwardly served their "client's" interests. Regulatory agencies, created in response to public outcry, often became, for all intents and purposes, client agencies of the regulated (Kolko, 1963).

There has been considerable attention paid in the public administration literature to the Progressive Era (Caiden, 1984; Chandler, 1987; Karl, 1987, 1976; Stever, 1988; Stillman, 1991; and Ventriss, 1987). This period of time is widely acknowledged as the beginning of public administration as a field of study, with Woodrow Wilson, a prominent Progressive himself, almost universally cited as the founder of modern public administration (Walker, 1990; see also Link, 1964). The legacy of the Progressive Era for contemporary thought in public administration in general and ethics in particular is considerable. I want to argue here that the conception of professional ethics which pervades our theory-in-use in public administration and which tends to drive out moral reasoning dates from this period of time as well. But first the idea that the Progressive Era is important for contemporary public administration needs some elaboration.

The basic outlines of the modern welfare-liberal state came together in the Progressive Era, rather than much later as the conventional wisdom has it. As Weinstein puts it (1968:ix): ". . . the political ideology now dominant in the United States, and the broad programmatic outlines of the liberal state (known by such names as the New Freedom, the New Deal, the New Frontier and the Great Society) were worked out and, in part, tried out by the end of the First World War." A similar argument, made in part by Skowronek (1982; see also Lustig, 1982; and O'Toole, 1984), holds for public administration. The basic parameters and trajectory of the field became visible during the Progressive Era, and the evolution of public administration since that time, both in practice and in thought, has not deviated significantly from that framework.

Skowronek analyzes the reconstitution of the federal government during this period, reaching back to the end of reconstruction in 1877 for the beginnings of this process. This transformation began as patchwork efforts to repair first one area and then another, often in response to the political pressure brought to bear by one or another socially powerful group. These efforts often went awry (Nelson, 1982). After the watershed election of 1896 between Bryan and McKinley, however, a more systematic reconstruction was undertaken. Thus, the federal government, according to Skowronek, was reconstructed during the Progressive Era to serve new goals and interests that were growing more and more important. The themes of this reconstruction were (1) the promise of a new democracy, (2) the embrace of corporate conservatism, (3) the lure of professionalism, and (4) the quest for administrative rationality (Skowronek, 1982:18). The latter two themes in particular bear further investigation.

III. MODERNITY AND TECHNICAL RATIONALITY

Beginning in the Progressive Era, technical rationality was applied to the social world and placed on the political agenda. In the context of modernity, technical rationality is the convergence of the scientific-analytical mindset and technological progress (Turner, 1990). It is quite similar to "functional rationality" as it was described by Karl Mannheim (1940). Mannheim saw functional rationality as the logical organization of tasks into smaller units, originally in the interest of efficiency. Mannheim contrasted this with "substantive rationality," the ability to understand the purposeful nature of the whole system of which a particular task is a part. Technical rationality is also closely akin to the notion of "instrumental reason" as it was discussed by Max Horkheimer (1947). Instrumental reason is the narrow application of human reason solely in the service of instrumental aims. Until the modern era, reason was conceived as a process incorporating ethical and normative concerns as well as the consideration of merely instrumental aims. In the public administration literature, similar points have been made by Alberto Guerreiro-Ramos (1981).

A. The Confluence of Science and Technology

A confluence of two streams occurred during the Progressive Era (1896–1916) which unleashed a flood of ideas and practices into the social and political world (Wiebe, 1967: 145–163). One of the two streams emerged from the recent history of epistemology in Western culture. This first stream is the scientific-analytical mindset that was the particular legacy of seventeenth century enlightenment thinking. The second stream was the product of the Great Transformation of the nineteenth century and comprised the technological progress characteristic of this period of industrialization with its unparalleled succession of technological developments. The two streams combined to provide the physical, tangible embodiment of the sheer power of scientific thinking. What could have been more plausible than to apply technical rationality to the social world in order to achieve science-like precision and objectivity? It was no accident that Frederick Taylor found a ready audience for the notion of scientific management during the Progressive Era (Noble, 1977; Merkle, 1980; Haber, 1964). Technical rationality became the vehicle of hope in the social and political world, and created a wave that before World War II prompted new professionals, managers, behaviorists, social scientists, and industrial psychologists toward a world view in which human conflicts appeared as problems fit for engineering solutions (Bendix, 1956; see also Ellul, 1954). At the close of the twentieth century, as William Barrett states (1979: 229):

> ... it would be silly for anyone to announce that he is "against" technology, whatever that might mean. We should have to be against ourselves in our present historical existence. We have now become dependent upon the increasingly complex and interlocking network of production for our barest necessities.

B. Technical Rationality and Professionalism

The scientific-analytic mindset and technological progress which combined during the Progressive Era unleashed a powerful current of technical rationality and professionalism. Impressed by the tremendous achievements of science and technology in the physical world, the Progressives naturally wanted to apply them in the social and political world, to achieve science-like precision and objectivity in these spheres as well (Bendix, 1956; Graebner, 1987).

Technical rationality led irresistably to specialized, expert knowledge, the very life-blood of the professional, and concomitantly to the proliferation of professional associations in the latter half of the nineteenth and early part of the twentieth centuries (Larson, 1977). Without the legitimacy derived from specialized knowledge, the professional could not have gained the social status nor the autonomy and control over the practice of the profession, which are the ultimate goals, even if sometimes unstated, of every profession (Friedson, 1971). But the compartmentalization of knowledge demanded by technical rationality also inevitably led to a context-less, or timeless, practice: Witness the lack of historical consciousness across the professions and disciplines. The practice of a profession with little or no sense of context has precluded meaningful engagement with the larger ethical and political concerns of society (Guerreiro-Ramos, 1981).

The modern model of professionalism was conceived and tried out in the Progressive Era. The development of professional associations of all kinds began in the mid-nineteenth century, at first more rapidly in England and then burgeoning in the United States (Larson, 1977:246). The characteristics of professions, which are fully visible by the turn of the century, include a professional association, a cognitive scientific base, institutionalized training (usually within higher education), licensing, work autonomy, colleague control, a public-service ideal, and a code of ethics (Larson, 1977:208). Larson emphasizes the connection between the development of professionalism and the broader process of modernization, which she describes as (1977:xiii), ". . . the advance of science and cognitive rationality and the progressive differentiation and rationalization of the division of labor in industrial societies."

IV. PROFESSIONALISM, TECHNICAL RATIONALITY, AND ETHICS

The evolution of professional associations in the latter half of the nineteenth century, as well as during and just after the Progressive Era, reveals much about the current state of professional ethics, in public administration as well as other fields and disciplines. Put simply, science—the scientific-analytical mindset—won out over reform and advocacy (Furner, 1975). Advocacy and reform, although in differing versions, were an integral part of the ethos of most professions until the turn of the century, and can be traced back to the prominence of moral philosophy in college curricula in ante-bellum America (Bryson, 1932).

Thomas L. Haskell, in *The Emergence of Professional Social Science*, traces the history of the old American Social Science Association (ASSA), founded in 1865, as it confronted what he calls a "crisis of professional authority" (1977:vi). Reform and advocacy coexisted, albeit somewhat uneasily, with science and objectivity during most of the latter half of the nineteenth century within the ASSA. Members of the ASSA came not only from the academy, but also included practitioners interested in charity work and in prison reform among other causes. Many were involved in the Social Gospel, Chatauqua, and urban reform movements as well (Ross, 1979:118). David Rothman's *The Discovery of the Asylum* (1971) is a good example of the reform roots of those who later turned to a rising professionalism during the latter half of the nineteenth century. Increasingly, however, the professional associations moved to become more and more separate, academic, and scientific (Ross, 1991), leaving the practitioners behind and advocating a different brand of reform. Thus, in the professional organizations, the tensions grew and eventually choices had to be made. Haskell places the crucial turning point during the "watershed decade" of the 1890s.

In his founding address to the American Economic Association (AEA) in 1886, Richard Ely (1982) attempted to preserve both directions, yet he called prominently for the scientific study of economics. The founding AEA platform captured the ambiguity as well (Ely, 1982:282):

> We regard the state as an educational and ethical agency whose positive aid is an indispensable condition of human progress. . . . we hold that the doctrine of laissez-faire is unsafe in politics and unsound in morals. . . .

> We hold that the conflict of labor and capital has brought to the front a vast number of social problems whose solution is impossible without the united efforts of Church, state and science.

The formation of the AEA in the 1880s, along with the American History Association and the American Statistics Association, was indicative both of the growing specialization of the social sciences and of the fatal contradiction in the ASSA. By the time the American Political Science Association and the American Sociological Association were founded in 1903, the demise of the ASSA was becoming inevitable. Franklin H. Giddings of Columbia University made it clear to the ASSA as early as their 1894 meeting that social science, as they had conceived it, was dying, and its heir was to be *scientific* sociology (Haskell, 1977:204). The comments of Albion W. Small, the founding editor of the *American Journal of Sociology* and chair of the Sociology Department at the University of Chicago, about the ASSA are representative (1916:729): ". . . it represented humanitarian sentiment more distinctly than a desire for critical methodology."

Outside the academy, a similar process was occurring in a variety of professional associations formed in the nineteenth century, including dentists (1840), medical doctors (1847), pharmacists (1852), architects (1857), civil engineers (1867), lawyers (1878), and accountants (1887). The American Medical Association, reorganized in 1903 under the banner of scientific medicine, is representative. The AMA's Council on Medical Education, relying on visits to medical schools by Abraham Flexner, set about to insure the conformity of medical education to the principles of "scientific medicine." Larson notes that this process was characterized by (1977:163), "the same general principles that guided the general movement of reform in the nineties and in the first decades of the twentieth century: centralization, consolidation into larger units, efficient management by experts, and the inevitable accent on technology . . ." Reform became equated with science and technical expertise. Flexner's conclusions—"fewer and better doctors"—were firmly and colorfully stated (Larson, 1977:163), "the priveleges of the medical school can no longer be open to casual strollers from the highway." Flexner operationalized this dictum by recommending that the 131 medical schools in the United States be cut down to the 31 which could teach on the "modern, scientific bases" (Larson, 1977:163).

A. The Demise of Reform and Advocacy and the Emergence of Ethics

As the Progressive Era drew to a close, professionalization had come to mean predominantly the increasing reliance on science and the scientific-analytical mindset, and the growing specialization and expertise of the professions. It also meant the sloughing off of reform and advocacy as a trademark of professionalism. I want to suggest here that the tenets of advocacy and reform, when they were part and parcel of the ethos of professionalism as they were in the latter half of the nineteenth century, represented a large part of the substance of both the *public service ideal* and the *ethical standards* of the professions. Their loss left a technically expert, but morally impoverished professionalism—a void which the proliferation of codes of ethics has attempted to fill. The chimerical quality of modern professionalism thus becomes fully apparent.

In 1919, an "Interprofessional Conference" was held in Detroit, the purpose of which was (King, 1922), "to liberate the professions from the domination of selfish interest, both within and without the professions, to devise ways and means of better utilizing the professional heritage and skill for the benefit of society and to create relations between the professions looking toward that end." The promulgation of codes of ethics for each profession was the widespread avenue of choice to fulfill the conference's aims, as papers written for this extraordinary conference attest. These papers, along with twenty-two codes of ethics, were later collected in the May, 1922 issue of the *Annals of the American Academy of Political and Social Science*, under the title, "The Ethics of the Professions and of Business." These codes of ethics range in date of adoption from 1904 to 1922 (with a single exception), all but the one after what Haskell (1977) called the watershed decade of the 1890s. The single exception is an early code of ethics adopted in 1852, which captures in its preamble the ambivalent motivations of the professions more explicitly than one sees in later times (King, 1922):

> The American Pharmeceutical Association, composed of Pharmaceutists and Druggists throughout the United States, feeling a strong interest in the success and advancement of their profession in its practical and scientific relations, and also impressed with the belief that no amount of knowledge and skill will protect themselves and the public from an undue competition, and the temptations to gain at the expense of quality, unless they are upheld by high moral obligations in the path of duty, have subscribed to the following Code of Ethics for the government of their professional conduct.

This early code was revised in 1922. An article in the same volume of the *Annals*, by Willam C. Beyer (1922:152–157), Assistant Director of the Bureau of Municipal Research in Philadelphia, suggests, under the title, "Ethics in the Public Service," that public administration would do well to follow the lead of the other professions and adopt a code of ethics. This would not occur until 1984 (Chandler, 1984). The first public service code of ethics, of course, was adopted by the International City Management Association in 1924 (Besuden, 1981).

Of over twenty professions represented at the Interprofessional Conference, and later in the *Annals*, the only one that had neither a code of ethics nor aspirations for one was the ministry. The reasoning for this absence of a code of ethics in the ministry was well explained by S. Z. Batten (1922:147): "The various professions have their codes and standards. Why is it that the ministry, which is supposed to represent the highest ideals, has no such formulated and recognized code. . . . The ministry is regarded as a calling rather than a profession . . . such a professional code of ethics would cast discredit upon the very idea of the ministry." While the ministry obviously has a rather different kind of advocacy integral to its practice, it was not subject to the same powerful movement toward scientific expertise and technical rationality, which drove out advocacy and reform in the other professions represented at the conference, and which created the moral vacuum that codes of ethics attempted to fill.

B. The Moral Vacuity of Modern Professionalism

The model of professionalism consistent with modernity drives out moral reasoning. Ethics becomes a chimerical accoutrement of professionalism. This oxymoronic relationship accounts for the confusion which arose within the professions over behavior which benefits a profession and ethical behavior. John Kultgen, in his *Ethics and Professionalism*, states (1988:212):

> Codes contribute to the professional project in two ways. The professional ideology maintains that every genuine profession has an ethic. An occupation's code conveys the impression that this is true for it and hence that it is a profession. Second, the code formulates what leaders of the profession would have the public think its operative ethic is. This is intended to instill trust in its actual practices.

The same emphasis on scientific method and procedure that impacted the political sphere, making more difficult a meaningful democratic politics, has also narrowed the conception of ethics within professionalism. Writing in 1922, the architect, Robert Kohn, expressed the moral vacuity of modern professionalism quite clearly (1922:4):

> Nothing is more evident than that today the inexpert is listened to more frequently, perhaps more trustfully than the expert, on questions of public policy. Even when the expert speaks officially as representative of his particular professional body, he is weak because of the suspicion as to his motives. The right technique, that is to say the technique best qualified, can be brought to bear upon our government affairs only when the professions as professions join together . . .

As both MacIntyre (1984) and Poole (1991) have argued, modernity has produced a way of thinking—an epistemology—that renders moral reasoning necessary but superfluous.

C. The Anti-Democratic Dimension of Modern Professionalism

By the Progressive Era, science came to mean the application of scientific method (Wiebe, 1967:147): "Science had become a procedure, or an orientation, rather than a body of results." For many progressives, this view toward science had its parallel with politics, which also came to be viewed increasingly as procedural. Woodrow Wilson and Charles Merriam are two examples of progressives who saw a harmonious link between the proceduralism of science and that of politics (on Wilson, see Van Riper, 1983; for Merriam, see Karl, 1974).

Politics, especially in its democratic versions, had to undergo considerable revision in order to be made compatible with this new emphasis on science and procedure. Herbert Croly's writing (1909) is particularly revealing of this resolution. The new requirements for professionalism, the demands for expertise, the growing calls for a politics/administration dichotomy, the adage that there is "no Republican way to build a road," all rendered the greater democratic involvement of people in politics more and more problematic (Hanson, 1985). This tension between a meaningful democratic politics on the one hand, and a professionalized, scientized, expert administration on the other, has commanded attention in the public administration literature since the turn of the century. It was central to Waldo's *The Administrative State* (1984), and indeed, to most of his later writing. It has been noted more recently by Barry D. Karl (1987), among others (see O'Toole, 1987; Caiden, 1984; Redford, 1969), and has a central place in the recurring and persistent discussion of the legitimacy and identity of public administration (Adams et al., 1990; Wamsley and Wolf, 1996; McSwite, 1997).

V. MODERNITY, PROFESSIONALISM, AND LEGITIMATION PROBLEMS

Recent discussions of legitimacy in public administration are simply the latest versions of attempts to reconcile the tensions between democracy and administration endemic to a liberal state (Stillman, 1991; McSwite, 1997). These tensions date from the American founding, but they are brought to the forefront and exacerbated by modernity and become more prominent during and after the Progressive Era.

A strong current in recent public administration literature imagines various alternative scenarios—many of them seeking an ethical foundation for the exercise of administrative discretion—in which public administration can be accorded (more or better) legitimacy within the American state (Kass and Catron, 1990; Wamsley, 1990; Wamsley and Wolf, 1996; McSwite, 1997). While it is natural for a field to discuss its role and place in the larger culture, particularly when that role and place have become as profoundly problematic as they have in the United States in the last several decades, the legitimacy of that field is fundamentally a social and political construction (O'Toole, 1990; Waldo, 1988). Various professions, and perhaps especially the most successful ones, do certainly contribute to their own social legitimacy—the history of the American Medical Association and the import of the Flexner Report of 1910 on medical education and practice is but one prominent example (Larson, 1977:162–163). However, legitimacy, it seems clear, is far more significantly a product of complex social, political, and economic forces, as other legitimation claims within public administration make clear.

A. Professionalism and Scientific Rigor in Public Administration

Most prominent in public administration literature are legitimation claims which call for increased professionalization (Kearney and Sinha, 1988; Henry, 1990; Cigler, 1990; Nalbandian, 1990) and research-based expertise (McCurdy and Cleary, 1984; Perry and Kraemer, 1986; Houston and Delevan, 1990; Lynn, 1996). These legitimation claims are in keeping with the themes of modernity and represent an orthodoxy in public administration that became fully visible in the Progressive Era and has continued, albeit with ebbs and flows, to the present (Adams, 1992).

While professionalism is most concerned with the *practice* of public administration, it is also of serious concern to academics in the field for reasons spelled out clearly in historical perspective by Larson (1977:136), in discussing the Progressive Era:

> The unification of training and research in the modern university is a particularly significant development. As graduate and professional schools emerged at the top of the educational hierarchy, the professions acquired not only an institutional basis on which to develop and standardize knowledge and technologies; they also received university training, a most powerful legitimation for their claims to cognitive and technical superiority and to social and economic benefits.

Of course, public administration is still poorly organized as a profession in comparison to law or medicine, for example, and is unlikely, in the American context where government has consistently been viewed as little better than a necessary evil, to achieve the degree of professionalization to which many clearly aspire. Perhaps this should be counted as a positive state of affairs (Kultgen, 1988:127): "The economic practices of other professions approximate those of medicine in proportion to controls available to the professional association. . . . That some professions have not acted as blatantly in self-interest as the American Medical Association reflects limitation of power rather than an effulgence of good will toward humanity."

For a discipline to be well organized, it must have a scientific knowledge base. The calls for greater scientific rigor in public administration follow this credo which gained ascendancy during the Progressive Era (Perry and Kraemer, 1986; Houston and Delavan, 1990). Sounding very much like turn-of-the-century sociologists promoting "scientific sociology," this literature compares public administration research to the (McCurdy and Cleary, 1984:50), "criteria that conventionally define careful systematic study in social science."

B. Legitimation in Public Administration: A New Professionalism?

Modernity exacerbates the question of a legitimate role for public administration within the American state. The tension between a meaningful, democratic politics and an expert, specialized administration, embedded in our nation's founding and intensified greatly by the flowering of technical rationality nearly one hundred years ago, remains at the forefront of any possible legitimation claim for public administration in the American state. Professionalism, as it has developed in this century, resolves this tension by abandoning democratic politics and rendering moral reasoning groundless. However, some have proposed new models of professionalism (Baum, 1983; Mitchell and Scott, 1987; Rohr, 1985; Hart, 1984). Most noteworthy of these efforts is Terry L. Cooper's (1991; see also, 1987) vision of a new professionalism based on *citizenship*. Understanding public administration as a *practice*, following MacIntyre (1984), Cooper argues for a more public-centered version of public administration, one that strongly emphasizes the tradition of democratic citizenship. Conceptions of public administration which call for stronger democratic practices—drawing both politics and ethics back into the center of discourse—of necessity call for revisions in professionalism (Adams et al., 1990; Wamsley and Wolf, 1996; McSwite, 1997). But what are the prospects of such cultural revisionism?

VI. THE CULTURAL BONDAGE OF MODERNITY

Social theorists have long emphasized that culture is a social construction and, as such, is a product of human interaction over time; they caution against reifying culture, that is, treating it as though it were a phenomenon of nature, a part of physical reality, or otherwise an object arising from non-human sources (Berger and Luckmann, 1967; see also, Harmon, 1981). No one, however, should leap to the conclusion that culture is therefore easily malleable or readily amenable to new constructions.

Our culture is a culture of modernity, and technical rationality and professionalism are part and parcel of the modern age. They represent a part of the "first language" of American culture (Bellah et al., 1985). This first language makes public and moral commitments difficult in the American cultural context, a point given strong emphasis here (White, 1992). The authors of *Habits of the Heart* (Bellah et al., 1985) note that images of community are available, though not easily articulated, within most Americans' experience. This they refer to as a second language, which can be remembered—albeit with some difficulty—and spoken, but cannot be as "natural," as much "second nature" as one's first language, the language of one's culture. Second languages, which offer us different versions of professionalism and ethics, are certainly available but the difficulty of displacing one language—that is, one context of meaning—with another is not to be underestimated.

Given a culture which renders moral reasoning problematic, one can still, according to MacIntyre, perform well or poorly in ethical terms (1983:356):

> One of the best ways to ensure . . . perform(ing) badly is to refuse to admit one's own involvement in radical moral imperfection and to see this as a condition in others which justifies perpetual moral indignation in oneself. Another equally good way is to use the recognition of radical moral imperfection as a moral alibi to excuse complacent satisfaction with the status quo.

The latter moral alibi might well serve as a motto for the decade of the nineties. MacIntyre's recommendations for coping ethically in such circumstances represent good advice for those of us who rest uneasy with a public administration enthralled with professionalism and technical rationality (1983:357–358). First is the expansion of one's time horizon—both back into history and forward into the future—the former in order to understand the historical and cultural roots of our current predicament, and the latter in order to provide a place in the equation, however tenuous, to our daughters and sons and to their progeny. The second aspect is the overcoming of role fragmentation in which, for example, one's administrative role is safely compartmentalized from one's role as democratic citizen. People, after all, do lead whole lives. And the third is the importance of publicity—the importance of making visible the activities of public administration, both to those inside organizations and to the public at large. One might describe this advice cumulatively as a rather paltry and tenuous ethics, but perhaps that is all that is available to us in this country in this age of modernity.

REFERENCES

Adams, G.B. (1992). Enthralled with modernity: The historical context of knowledge and theory development in public administration. *Public Administration Review*, 52:363–373.

Adams, G.B. and Balfour, D.L. (1998). *Unmasking Administrative Evil*. Sage Publications, Thousand Oaks, CA.

Adams, G.B., Bowerman, P.V., Dolbeare, K.M., and Stivers, C. (1990). Joining purpose to practice: A democratic identity for the public service. In: *Images and Identities in Public Administration*, (H.D. Kass and B.L. Catron, eds.). Sage Publications, Newbury Park, CA, p. 219–240.

Amy, D.J. (1984). Why policy analysis and ethics are incompatible. *Journal of Policy Analysis and Management*, 3:573–591.

Appleby, P. (1952). *Morality and Administration in Democratic Government*. Louisiana University Press, Baton Rouge, LA.

Argyris, C. (1990). *Overcoming Organizational Defenses*. Addison-Wesley, Reading, MA.

Bailey, S.K. (1964). Ethics and the public service. *Public Administration Review*, 24:234–243.

Barrett, W. (1979). *The Illusion of Technique*. Anchor Doubleday, Garden City, NY.

Batten, S.Z. (1922). The ethics of the ministry. *Annals of the American Academy of Political and Social Science*, 101:147–151.

Baum, H.S. (1983). *Planners and Public Expectations*. Schenkman Publishing, Cambridge, MA.

Bauman, Z. (1989). *Modernity and the Holocaust*. Cornell University Press, Ithaca, NY.

Baumrin, B. and Freedman, B. (eds.). (1983). *Moral Responsibility and the Professions*. Haven Publications, New York.

Bayles, M.D. (1981). *Professional Ethics*. Wadsworth Publishers, Belmont, CA.

Bellah, R.H., Madsen, R., Sullivan, W.M., Swidler, A., and Tipton, S.M. (1985). *Habits of the Heart: Individualism and Commitment in American Life*. Harper and Row, New York.

Bendix, R. (1956). *Work and Authority in Industry*. Harper and Row, New York.

Berger, P. and Luckmann, T. (1967). *The Social Construction of Reality*. Anchor Doubleday, Garden City, NY.

Bernstein, R. (ed.). (1985). *Habermas and Modernity*. MIT Press, Cambridge, MA.

Besuden, W. (1981). The profession's heritage: The ICMA code of ethics. *Public Management*, 63: 2–5.

Beyer, W.C. (1922). Ethical frontiers in public service. *Annals of the American Academy of Political and Social Science*, 101:152–157.

Bowman, J. (1990). *Ethical Frontiers in Public Management: Seeking New Strategies for Resolving Ethical Dilemmas*. Jossey-Bass, San Francisco.

Bowman, J.S., and Williams, R.L. (1977). Ethics in government: From a winter of despair to a spring of hope. *Public Administration Review*, 57:517–526.

Brown, P. (1986). Ethics and education for the public service in the liberal state. *Journal of Policy Analysis and Management*, 6:56–68.

Bruce, W. (1996). Codes of ethics and codes of conduct. *Public Integrity Annual*, 1:13–22.

Bryson, G. (1932). The emergence of the social sciences from moral philosophy. *International Journal of Ethics*, 42:304–323.

Burke, J.P. (1986). *Bureaucratic Responsibility*. Johns Hopkins University Press, Baltimore, MD.

Caiden, G.E. (1984). In search of an apolitical science of American public administration. In: *Politics and Administration: Woodrow Wilson and American Public Administration* (J. Rabin and J.S. Bowman, eds.). Marcel Dekker, New York.

Callahan, J.C. (ed.). (1988). *Ethical Issues in Professional Life*. Oxford University Press, New York.

Caminisch, P.F. (1983). *Grounding Professional Ethics in a Pluralistic Society*. Haven Publications, New York.

Chandler, R.C. (1984). The problem of moral reasoning in American public administration: The case for a code of ethics. *Public Administration Review*, 43:32–39.

Chandler, R.C. (ed.) (1987). *A Centennial History of the American Administrative State*. Free Press, New York.

Cigler, B.A. (ed.). (1990). Public administration and the paradox of professionalism. *Public Administration Review*, 50:637–653.

Cooper, T.L. (1987). Hierarchy, virtue and the practice of public administration: A perspective for normative ethics. *Public Administration Review*, 47:320–328.

Cooper, T.L. (1990). *The Responsible Administrator*. Jossey-Bass, San Francisco.

Cooper, T.L. (1991). *An Ethic of Citizenship for Public Administration*. Prentice Hall, Englewood Cliffs, NJ.

Cooper, T.L. (ed.). (1994). *Handbook of Administrative Ethics*. Marcel Dekker, New York.

Cooper, T.L. (1996). The paradox of responsibility: An enigma. *Public Administration Review*, 52: 599–604.

Cooper, T.L., and N.D. Wright, (eds.). (1992). *Exemplary Public Administrators*. Jossey-Bass, San Francisco, CA.

Croly, H. (1909). *The Promise of American Life*. Macmillan, New York.

Denhardt, K.G. (1988). *The Ethics of Public Service*. Greenwood Press, Westport, CT.

Dobel, J.P. (1992). The moral realities of public life: Some insights of fiction. *American Review of Public Administration*, 22:127–143.

Ellul, J. (1954). *The Technological Society*. Vintage, New York.

Ely, R. (1982). Report of the organization of the American economic association, 1886. In: *Political Thought in America* (M.B. Levy, ed.). Dorsey Press, Homewood, IL.

Finer, H. (1941). Administrative responsibility in democratic government. *Public Administration Review*, 1:335–350.

Fischer, F. (1983). Ethical discourses in public administration. *Administration & Society*, 15:5–42.

Fischer, F. and Zinke, R.C. (1989). Public administration and the code of ethics: Administrative reform of professional ideology? *International Journal of Public Administration*, 12:841–854.

Foster, G.D. (1981). Law, morality and the public servant. *Public Administration Review*, 41:29–34.

Fox, C.J. (1989). Free to choose, free to win, free to lose: The phenomenology of ethical space. *International Journal of Public Administration*, 12:913–930.

Fox, C.J. (1992). What do we mean when we say professionalism: A language usage analysis for public administration. *American Review of Public Administration*, 22:29–46.

Fox, C.J. and Cochran, C.E. (1990). Discretionary public administration: Toward a platonic guardian class. In: *Images and Identities in public administration* (H.J. Kass and B. L. Catron, eds.). Sage Publications, Newbury Park, CA.

Frederickson, G. (1993). *Ethics and Public Administration*. M.E. Sharpe, Armonk, NY.

Frederickson, H.G. and Hart, D.K. (1985). The public service and the patriotism of benevolence. *Public Administration Review*, 45:547–553.

Freidrich, C.J. (1940). Public policy and the nature of administrative responsibility. In: *Public Policy* (C. J. Freidrich and E.S. Mason, eds.). Harvard University Press, Cambridge, MA.

Friedson, D. (ed.). (1971). *The Professions and Their Prospects*. Sage Publications, Beverly Hills, CA.

Furner, M.O. (1975). *Advocacy and Objectivity: A Crisis in the Professionalization of Social Science*. University Press of Kentucky, Lexington, KY.

Goldman, A.H. (1980). *The Moral Foundations of Professional Ethics*. Rowman and Littlefield, Totowa, NJ.

Gorlin, R.A. (ed.). (1986). *Codes of Professional Responsibility*. Bureau of National Affairs, Washington, D.C.

Gortner, H.F. (1991). *Ethics for Public Managers*. Greenwood Press, Westport, CT.

Graebner, W. (1987). *The Engineering of Consent: Democracy and Authority in Twentieth Century America*. University of Wisconsin Press, Madison.

Green, R.T. (1994). Character ethics and public administration. *International Journal of Public Administration*, 17:2737–2764.

Greenwood, E. (1957). Attributes of a profession. *Social Work*, 2:45–50.

Guerreiro-Ramos, A. (1981). *The New Science of Organization*. University of Toronto Press, Toronto, Canada.

Haber, S. (1964). *Efficiency and Uplift: Scientific Management in the Progressive Era, 1890–1920*. University of Chicago Press, Chicago, IL.

Hanson, R.L. (1985). *The Democratic Imagination in America: Conversations with Our Past*. Princeton University Press, Princeton, NJ.

Harmon, M.M. (1981). *Action Theory for Public Administration*. Longmans, New York.

Harmon, M.M. (1995). *Responsibility as Paradox: A Critique of Rational Discourse on Government*. Sage Publications, Thousand Oaks, CA.

Hart, D.K. (1974). Social equity, justice and the equitable administrator. *Public Administration Review*, 34:3–11.

Hart, D.K. (1984). The virtuous citizen, the honorable bureaucrat and "public" administration. *Public Administration Review*, 44:111–120.

Haskell, T.L. (1977). *The Emergence of Professional Social Science*. University of Illinois Press, Urbana, IL.

Haskell, T.L. (ed.). (1984). *The Authority of Experts: Studies in History and Theory*. University of Indiana Press, Bloomington, IN.

Henry, N. (1990). Root and branch: public administration's travail toward the future. In: *Public Administration: State of the Discipline* (N. Lynn and A. Wildavsky, eds.). Chatham House Publishers, Chatham, NJ.

Horkheimer, M. (1947). *The Eclipse of Reason*. Oxford University Press, New York.

Houston, D.J. and Delevan, S.M. (1990). Public administration research: An assessment of journal publications. *Public Administration Review*, 50:674–681.

Jackson, M.W. (1984). Eichmann, bureaucracy, and ethics. *Australian Journal of Public Administration*, 43:301–307.

Karl, B.D. (1974). *Charles E. Merriam and the Study of Politics*. University of Chicago Press, Chicago, IL.

Karl, B.D. (1976). Public administration and American history: A century of professionalism. *Public Administration Review*, 36:489–504.

Karl, B.D. (1987). The American bureaucrat: A history of a sheep in wolves' clothing. *Public Administration Review*, 47:26–34.

Kass, H.D. and Catron, B.L. (1990). *Image and Identity in Public Administration*. Sage Publications, Newbury Park, CA.

Kearney, R.C. and Sinha, C. (1988). Professionalism and bureaucratic responsiveness: Conflict or compatability. *Public Administration Review*, 48:571–579.

Kernaghan, K. (1980). Codes of ethics and public administration. *Public Administration*, 59:207–223.

King, C.L. (1922). The ethics of the professions and of business. *Annals of the American Academy of Political and Social Science*, 101:1–148.

Kohn, R.D. (1922). The significance of the professional ideal: Professional ethics and the public interest. *Annals of the American Academy of Political and Social Science*, 101:1–4.

Kolko, G. (1963). *The Triumph of Conservatism: A Reinterpretation of American History, 1900–1916*. Free Press, New York.

Kultgen, J. (1982). The ideological use of professional codes. *Business and Professional Ethics*, 1: 53–69.

Kultgen, J. (1988). *Ethics and Professionalism*. University of Pennsylvania Press, Philadelphia.

Ladd, L.M. (1970). Morality and the ideal of rationality in organizations. *The Monist*, 54:488–516.

Lane, L.M. (1988). Individualism, civic virtue and public administration: The implications of American habits of the heart. *Administration & Society*, 20:30–45.

Larson, M.L. (1977). *The Rise of Professionalism*. University of California Press, Berkeley.

Lee, D. (1990). Moral education and the teaching of public administration ethics. *International Journal of Public Administration*. 13:359–389.

Lewis, C.W. (1991). *The Ethics Challenge in Public Service*. Jossey-Bass, San Francisco.

Leys, W.A.R. (1943). Ethics and administrative discretion. *Public Administration Review*, 3:10–23.

Link, A.S. (1964). *Woodrow Wilson and the Progressive Era, 1910–1917*. Harper and Row, New York.

Lustig, R.J. (1982). *Corporate Liberalism: The Origin of Modern American Political Theory, 1890–1920*. University of California Press, Berkeley.

Lynn, L.E. (1996). *Public Management as Art, Science and Profession*. Chatham House Publishers, Chatham, NJ.

MacIntyre, A. (1983). Why are the problems of business ethics insoluble? In: *Moral responsibility and the professions* (B. Baumrin and B. Freedman, eds.). Haven Publications, New York.

MacIntyre, A. (1984). *After Virtue*, 2nd ed. University of Notre Dame Press, Notre Dame, IN.

Madsen, P. and Shafritz, J.M. (1992). *Essentials of Government Ethics*. Meridian, New York.

Mannheim, K. (1940). *Man and Society in an Age of Reconstruction*. Harcourt, Brace and World, New York.

Marini, F. (1992). Literature and public administration ethics. *American Review of Public Administration*, 22:111–126.

McCurdy, H.E. and Cleary, R.E. (1984). Why can't we resolve the research issue in public administration? *Public Administration Review*, 44:49–55.

McSwain, C.J. and White, O.F. (1987). The case for lying, cheating and stealing: Personal development as ethical guidance for managers. *Administration & Society*, 18:411–432.

McSwite, O.C. (1997). *Legitimacy in Public Administration: A Discourse Analysis*. Sage Publications, Thousand Oaks, CA.

Merkle, J.A. (1980). *Management and Ideology*. University of California Press, Berkeley.

Mertins, H. Jr., Burke, F., Kweit, R.W., and Pops, G.M. (1994). *Applying Professional Standards in the Nineties*. American Society for Public Administration, Washington, DC.

Mitchell, T.R., and Scott, W.G. (1987). Leadership failures, the distrusting public, and the prospects of the administrative state. *Public Administration Review*, 47:445–452.

Mosher, F.C. (1982). *Democracy and the Public Service*. Oxford University Press, New York.

Nalbandian, J. (1990). Tenets of contemporary professionalism in local government. *Public Administration Review*, 50:654–662.

Nelson, M. (1982). A short ironic history of American national bureaucracy. *Journal of Politics*, 44:747–778.

Nigro, L.G., and Richardson, W.D. (1990). Between citizen and administrator: Administrative ethics and PAR. *Public Administration Review*, 50:623–635.

Noble, D.F. (1977). *America by Design*. Alfred A. Knopf, New York.

Olufs, D.F. (1985). The limits of professionalism. *Public Administration Quarterly*, 9:26–46.

O'Toole, L.J., Jr. (1984). American public administration and the idea of reform. *Administration and Society*, 16:141–166.

O'Toole, L.J., Jr. (1987). Doctrines and developments: Separation of powers, the politics-administration dichotomy, and the rise of the administrative state. *Public Administration Review*, 47:17–25.

O'Toole, L.J., Jr. (1990). Legitimacy, legitimation and public administration: Rejoinder to Stever. *Public Administration Review*, 46:215–226.

Pasquerella, L., Killilea, A., and Vocino, M. (1996). *Ethical Dilemmas in Public Administration*. Praeger Publishers, Westport, CT.

Perry, J.L. and Kraemer, K.L. (1986). Research methodology in the public administration review, 1975–1984. *Public Administration Review*, 46:215–226.

Plant, J.F. (1996). Public ethics in squalid times: Codes of ethics and the deeming truth. Paper delivered at the National Conference on Public Service Ethics and the Public Trust St Louis, MO.

Plant, J.F. (1997). Using codes of ethics in teaching public administration. In: *Teaching Ethics and Values in Public Administration: Program Innovations, Teaching Strategies, and Ethical Issues* (Bowman, J.S. and D.C. Menzel, eds.) SUNY Press, Albany, NY.

Poole, R. (1991). *Morality and Modernity*. Routledge, Chapman and Hall, London.

Pugh, D.H. (1989). Professionalism in public administration: Problems, perspectives, and the role of ASPA. *Public Administration Review*, 49:1–8.

Rabinbach, A. (1990). *The Human Motor: Energy, Fatigue and the Origins of Modernity*. Basic Books, New York.

Redford, E.S. (1969). *Democracy in the Administrative State*. Oxford University Press, New York.

Reynolds, H.W., Jr. (1995). Symposium: Ethics in American public service. *The Annals of the American Academy of Political and Social Sciences*, 537:1–213.

Rohr, J.A. (1978). *Ethics for Bureaucrats*. Marcel Dekker, New York.

Rohr, J.A. (1985). Professionalism, legitimacy and the constitution. *Public Administration Quarterly*, 8:401–418.

Rohr, J.A. (1989). British and American approaches to public service ethics. *Public Administration Review*, 49:387–390.

Rohr, J.A. (1998). *Public Service, Ethics and Constitutional Practice*. University Press of Kansas, Lawrence, KS.

Rosenbloom, D.H. (1992). The Constitution as a basis for public administrative ethics. In: *Essentials of Government Ethics* (P. Madsen and J.M. Shafritz, eds.). New American Library, New York, pp. 48–64.

Ross, D. (1979). The development of the social sciences. In: *The Organization of Knowledge in Modern America* (A. Oleson and J. Voss, eds.). Johns Hopkins University Press, Baltimore, MD, pp. 107–138.

Ross, D. (1991). *The Origins of American Social Science.* Cambridge University Press, New York.

Rothman, D.J. (1971). *The Discovery of the Asylum: Social Order and Disorder in the New Republic.* Little Brown, Boston, MA.

Skowronek, S. (1982). *Building a New American State: The Expansion of National Administrative Capacities, 1877–1920.* Cambridge University Press, Cambridge.

Small, A. (1916). Fifty years of sociology. *American Journal of Sociology,* 21:724–731.

Stever, J.A. (1988). *The End of Public Administration: Problems of the Profession in the Post-Progressive Era.* Transnational Publishers, Dobbs Ferry, NY.

Stewart, D.W. (1985a). Ethics and the profession of public administration: The moral responsibility of individuals in public sector organizations. *Public Administration Quarterly,* 8:487–495.

Stewart, D.W. (1985b). Professionalism vs. democracy: Friedrich vs. Finer revisited. *Public Administration Quarterly,* 9:13–25.

Stewart, D.W. (1991). Theoretical foundations of ethics in public administration: Approaches to understanding moral action. *Administration & Society,* 23:357–373.

Stillman, R.J. (1987). *The American Bureaucracy.* Nelson Hall, Chicago.

Stillman, R.J. (1991). *Preface to Public Administration: A Search for Themes and Directions.* St. Martins Press, New York.

Stivers, C. (1994). Citizenship ethics in public administration. In: *Handbook of Administrative Ethics* (T.L. Cooper, ed.). Marcel Dekker, New York.

Terry, L.D. (1995). *Leadership of Public Bureaucracies: The Administrator as Conservator.* Sage Publications, Thousand Oaks, CA.

Thompson, D.F. (1985). The possibility of administrative ethics. *Public Administration Review,* 45:555–561.

Thompson, D.F. (1992). Paradoxes of government ethics. *Public Administration Review,* 52:252–259.

Turner, B.S. (ed.) (1990). *Theories of Modernity and Postmodernity.* Sage Publications, London.

Van Riper, P. (1983). The American administrative state: Wilson and the founders, An unorthodox view. *Public Administration Review,* 43:477–490.

Van Wart, M. (1996). Sources for ethical decision making for individuals in the public sector. *Public Administration Review,* 56:525–533.

Ventriss, C. (1987). Two critical issues of American public administration. *Administration and Society,* 19:25–47.

Ventriss, C. (1992). The ideology of professionalism in public administration: Implications for education. Paper presented to the National Conference on Teaching Public Administration, Charleston.

Waldo, D. (1984). *The Administrative State,* 2nd ed. Holmes and Meier, New York.

Waldo, D. (1988). The end of public administration? A review. *Public Administration Review,* 48:929–932.

Walker, L.N. (1990). Woodrow Wilson, progressive reform and public administration. In: *The Wilson Influence on Public Administration* (P.P. Van Riper, ed.). American Society for Public Administration, Washington, DC.

Wamsley, G.L. (1990). *Refounding Public Administration.* Sage Publications, Newbury Park, CA.

Wamsley, G.L. and Wolf, J.F. (eds.). (1996). *Refounding Democratic Public Administration: Modern Paradoxes, Post Modern Challenges.* Sage Publications, Thousand Oaks, CA.

Weinstein, J. (1968). *The Corporate Ideal in the Liberal State, 1900–1918.* Beacon Press, Boston.

White, J.D. (1992). Taking language seriously: Toward a narrative theory of knowledge for administrative research. *American Review of Public Administration,* 22:75–88.

Wiebe, R.H. (1967). *The Search for Order, 1877–1920.* Hill and Wang, New York.

Yarwood, D.L. (1985). The ethical world of organizational professionals and scientists. *Public Administration Quarterly,* 8:461–486.

15

Codes of Ethics

Jeremy F. Plant
Penn State–Harrisburg, Middletown, Pennsylvania

I. INTRODUCTION

Codes of ethics are systematic efforts to define acceptable conduct. To their supporters they are a means of providing guidance to public officials on doing good and avoiding evil (Rohr, 1991). They instill confidence in government and elevate the standards of administrative behavior in public organizations (Kernaghan, 1974). They provide guidance to decision-makers dealing with situations where values may be in conflict (Lewis, 1991). They are a means of defining ethical conduct for public professionals by linking occupational standards with the context of public action (Bruce, 1996).

Codes may be written or unwritten, but it is the written codes that are enforceable and that provide a measure of accountability to the public (Chandler, 1989). Written codes can be promulgated by a jurisdiction or level of government, by a profession, by an organization, or by an association representing a class of organizations (Benson, 1991). Codes may be general or specific, aspirational and idealistic, or coercive and legalistic (Chandler, 1983; Lewis, 1991). They may be a list of 10 golden rules to hang on a wall, or they may be part of an elaborate system of education and training, enforcement, and continuous revision (Menzel, 1997).

Codes of ethical conduct have been part of public administration since the International City Managers' Association promulgated the first major code in 1924 (Stillman, 1974; Pugh, 1991; Plant, 1991; Charles and Cagle, 1997). The first codes were professional codes that bound public officials to standards of conduct defined by professional associations. In 1958, by a concurrent resolution Congress enacted a code of conduct for federal executive branch employees. In 1961, President Kennedy strengthened the code by executive order. In the 1970s, the Watergate scandal triggered a wave of code-making, especially in state and local governments and the public service professions (Denhardt, 1988; Pugh, 1991). The Ethics in Government Act of 1978 reinforced the notion that ethical conduct was an aspect of public management (Plant and Gortner, 1981; Walter, 1981; Gilman, 1991).

Today, state governments provide the setting for the most intense codification of ethical conduct of public officials (Hays and Glessner, 1981; Lewis and Gilman, 1991; Blake, 1998). By 1989, 36 states had enacted codes and set up ethics commissions to enforce them (Burke and Benson, 1989). Such "codes" usually focus on proscribed activities, disciplinary actions, and means of compliance; they rarely express ideals or provide a way

309

for public administrators to engage in moral reasoning. Blake (1998) characterizes the state government ethics codes as "dramatically skewed in the low-road direction" (p. 457).

Codes of ethics have been a source of controversy in public administration since the International City Managers' Association adopted its code in 1924 (Stillman, 1974; Pugh, 1991). The adoption of a code of ethics for the American Society for Public Administration in 1984 came after many years of heated debate over whether a code: was needed, was feasible given the diversity of roles performed by public professionals, and was enforceable (Chandler, 1982, 1983; Pugh, 1989, 1991; Bowman, 1990; Van Wart, 1996). Current debate on codes centers on a number of issues, including: *locus*—should the organization, the profession, or an agency of the state be the point of enactment and promulgation; *philosophical underpinning*—should the code be grounded in moral philosophy (Hart, 1983), law and constitutional theory (Rosenbloom, 1992; Rohr, 1985, 1986), the faith in science (Plant, 1988), or professional responsibility (Freedman, 1978; Gewirth, 1989; Mount, 1990); *specificity*—should the code be detailed and highly specific to work performed, or broad and subject to interpretation (Lewis, 1991); and *enforceability*—is the code a statement of ideals, or a quasilegal constraint that will carry penalties for noncompliance (Charles and Cagle, 1997)?

This chapter will discuss the issues surrounding codes of ethics for public professionals, survey the research and major writings on codes, and examine a few illustrative codes drawn from government agencies and professional associations. Codes are coming into the forefront of the discussion of public sector ethics for several compelling reasons. First, there is an explosion of codification going on in society (Plant, 1991; Lewis, 1991; Bruce 1996), explained in part by the growing importance of legalistic approaches to administration (Rosenbloom, 1992), in part by the penetration of the professionals into government, bringing with them the values and oftentimes the codes of ethics operationalizing their value systems (Bayles, 1989; Jos, 1995). Second, there is a sense of declining public trust in and support for traditional approaches to managing the public's business, leading to a variety of approaches designed to convince a wary public that government is honest, accountable, and caring. In this sense, codes are akin to quality improvement programs, reinvention exercises, and public relations exercises where the public is considered the "customer" of government. Third, the complexities facing public decision-makers continue to increase, making Mosher (1968: 218) seem prophetic in his diagnosis of the problem of contemporary public management:

> In the future, merit will increasingly be measured by professionals against criteria established by the professions and by the universities which spawn them. It will depend in part upon technical and cognitive qualifications in the fields of specialization. The danger is that these will be too large a part of the criteria. Truly meritorious performance in public administration will depend at least equally upon the values, the objectives, and the moral standards which the administrator brings to his decisions, and upon his ability to weigh the relevant premises judiciously in his approach to the problems at hand. His code can hardly be as simple as the Ten Commandments, the Boy Scout Code, or the code of ethics of any of the professions; his decisions usually will require some kind of interpretation of public and public interest—explicit, implicit, even unconscious.

II. DEFINING CODES OF ETHICS: SYSTEMS OF LAW OR SYSTEMS OF MORALS

Webster's Third New International Dictionary (Gove, 1961) provides a curious beginning for our study of codes. Code derives from the Latin *codex*, meaning tree trunk. Tree trunks were split and waxed by the ancients, and upon them were inscribed systems of law. As the dictionary entry suggests, we are not so clear today as to the nature of the phenomenon of codes. Webster's lists three major meanings: a written collection of laws; a collection or system of rules that are not law, but morally binding; and a system of symbols for meaningful communication.

Codes of ethics in public administration usually include elements of all three meanings. They often include a statement of ideals, canons of action consonant with the ideals, *Enforcement* and binding means of enforcing behavior within the boundaries established by the code (Kernaghan, 1974; Chandler, 1983). Their use of rhetoric is a signal that the code is a symbolic statement binding adherents to larger issues of the public interest, professional and personal identity, or standards of right conduct (Chandler, 1989).

There is a large measure of agreement that codes of ethics for public officials differ fundamentally from codes of businesses, nonprofit organizations, and trade associations (Benson, 1991) because of the need for the public to assume that its guardians are held (or holding voluntarily) to a higher standard than others in society. Thus, the value of codes cannot be measured solely by their effectiveness in guiding good behavior and avoiding evil.

They exist as political statements (Rohr, 1991) that the public's business is being conducted fairly, honestly, and competently. In this, their value is not to catch miscreants or even guide the behavior of bureaucrats through the thickets of administrative discretion. They serve to extol the values of democracy and increase the level of public trust in government.

Confusion over the three possible meanings—legal systems, moral systems, or symbolic means of communicating—is at the heart of the discussion of codes in public administration. Is the purpose of the code of ethics to create a new body of administrative law to constrain public officials in the name of public accountability (Walter, 1981; Plant and Gortner, 1981; Lewis and Gilman, 1991; Dobel, 1993)? Or is law unacceptable as a source of ethical guidance, providing a set of moral minimums (Foster, 1981; Cooper, 1990, 1992)? Should we look at codes as ways in which association and communication outside the coercive character of law and state power is facilitated (Besuden, 1981; Pugh, 1991)? Or a way for leaders and managers to communicate more effectively with other roleplayers in the organization (Barnard, 1938; Denhardt, 1988)?

Public administration's stance toward codes of ethics reflects the ambiguity of its standing as a profession, as an intellectual discipline, and as an advocate of high standards of service to the public (Cigler, 1990; Jos, 1995). It lacks the occupational specificity and licensure power of other public professions and, as a field combining practice with research and scholarship, has had to absorb a growing body of knowledge about ethics in public service and an often spirited dialogue about how to construct the proper ethical framework to guide the field (Cooper, 1994; Frederickson, 1993; Menzel and Carson, 1998). It is to this dialogue within the field that we now turn.

III. CODES OF ETHICS IN PUBLIC ADMINISTRATION LITERATURE

Codes of ethics do not figure prominently in the literature of public administration prior to the 1970s. This reflects the general disinterest among scholars in the field with the subject of administrative ethics (Cooper, 1994; Menzel and Carson, 1998). Ethical conduct was a product of the management of hierarchical government organizations (Finer, 1941; Appleby, 1952), or of the choice process by which altruistic, public-minded individuals chose careers in the public sector (Cassinelli, 1962). Appleby (1952) and Bailey (1965) chose to discuss ethical conduct of individuals in the public sector in terms appropriate to the dominant theme of management discretion for the public interest. Appleby stressed organizational mechanisms and Bailey moral qualities of administrators, but each eschewed formal systems of codified conduct.

The cursory treatment of ethics in public administration derived in large measure from the technocratic emphasis of the field that reflected American progressivism and bureaucratic rationalism (Pugh, 1991; Fox, 1992; Adams, 1993). Public administration's ability to reason was limited to technique and structure, divorced from traditional approaches to ethical reasoning: normative political theory and moral philosophy. The field also had made a conscious effort to maintain a distance from jurisprudence, making it difficult to deal with the demand for codification and enforcement of ethics in ways that smacked of the law.

The orthodox picture of public administration was rational managers pursuing predetermined policy objectives through disciplined organizational hierarchies in the executive branch of government. This simple notion of the field began to be challenged in the 1960s and 1970s. Mosher (1968) argued convincingly that government is in fact a collection of professionals, with all the baggage that comes from professionalism: credentialism, a limited view of the public interest, and also notions of good conduct—right and wrong—that are grounded in the culture of the professions, not abstract notions of the public interest or the accountable public agency. Many adhered to codes of ethics promulgated by their profession; the challenge was to adapt such professionalism to the particulars of public service. Watergate (National Academy, 1974) challenged the ideas of Appleby and Bailey that either organization or personal values provide guarantees of good conduct. The clamor for greater systems of ethics was sounded but more in the world of practice than among scholars in public administration, who remained divided on the merits of codes (Kernaghan, 1974).

Rohr (1978) began the process of creating ethics as a major topic of inquiry in the field with his incisive book *Ethics for Bureaucrats*. Rohr combined moral reasoning and normative political theory (as well as solid grounding in jurisprudence) to come up with an approach to ethical conduct that stressed doing good, not just staying out of trouble. Dismissing codes as part of the "low road" that reduces ethical behavior to "staying out of trouble" (p. 54), he argues for greater reasoning by bureaucrats exercising necessary discretion. The key is the internalization of "regime values," understood by seeing how judicial decisions interpret the meaning of the key values of equality, freedom, and property in contemporary situations. The freedom of inquiry required of ethical bureaucrats is incompatible with the revealed truths or simple homilies of a code.

Rohr's dismissal of codes—either those contained in the personnel manual or those brought into government through the professions—reflected the growing interest among scholars of the field in finding ways to help public administrators be independent moral agents, not simply technocrats finding efficient ways of implementing policy directives. Public administration clung to the notion of administrative discretion as a possibility to do good and also to enable individuals in public hierarchies to achieve greater levels of personal fulfillment and enlightenment (Gawthrop, 1984). Codes seem to limit, not liberate; find minimum and not optimal levels of ethical conduct; and reinforce the coercive power of law and organizational leaders.

The American Society for Public Administration in the late 1970s and early 1980s debated the merits of a code of ethics for the society. In part in response to the post-Watergate public interest in ethics, in part because professional associations were engaged in codification of ethics in the late 1970s (Arnold and Plant, 1994), and in part reflecting the academic ferment on issues of ethics and morality in administration, the ASPA debate stimulated discussion on the merits of ethical codes in general and for ASPA in particular. Chandler (1982, 1983) produced the most comprehensive analysis to date on the subject of codes. Carefully noting the arguments for and against codes, Chandler (1983) lets the reader decide which camp to join, although the argument seems to favor the affirmative.

Codes, Chandler notes, are distrusted for three major reasons: first, that we should resist moralizing and be practical about accepting moderate levels of immorality in life; second, that procedures to develop consensus and debate on issues are hindered by rigid codification of right and wrong; third, that the tradition of bureaucratic neutrality considers it moral to avoid moral judgments and view governance as a technical exercise. Arrayed against these arguments are three arguments in favor of codes: objectivism, which recognizes the existence of transcendent values and an ultimate ground of being; the argument from community, which posits that judgments about right and wrong are community decisions, that "the community is the arbiter of what is ethical" (p. 34). The third argument is from courage, from the positive value of agonizing over decisions and actions. In Chandler's words, "Sin-talk is admittedly old-fashioned, restrictive, and somewhat embarrassing, but if this is the only reason that the parlance of idealism is rejected, we also put ourselves out of touch with a rich classical tradition which sought for moral unity and a higher law in conversation that has little to do with sin" (p. 34).

Chandler's essay opened up a number of important issues implicit in ASPA's deliberation of a code. First, by noting the general movement toward professional codes in society—a statement that appears to have been overstated somewhat for the strictly public professions—Chandler challenged ASPA to undertake what is commonly thought to be an attribute of any true profession, a code. Second, by noting arguments for and against a code, Chandler noted a number of normative positions—from political theory and philosophy—from which to argue. Thus, any debate (such as ASPA's) over codification had to be analyzed to see what arguments were mobilized by groups backing either a pro or con position on the issue. Third, by aligning bureaucratic neutrality within the camp of those arguing against codes, he implicitly raised the value of codes for those in the field who for one reason or another dislike traditional bureaucratic theory and its constructs.

Despite Chandler's balanced approach, writers in the field of public administration ethics remained unconvinced that codes of ethics were important or advisable. Gawthrop (1984) associated codification of behavior with the idea that "through the detailed specification of what is wrong public administrators and managers can be counted on to do what is right. Therefore, if public sector administrators do not violate an explicitly stipulated wrong, they must be doing what is right" (p. 142). Stewart (1985) noted the debate within public administration over codes of ethics and the question "to what extent should the individual be cast as a moral actor" in the work setting (p. 487). Dismissing arguments against assigning moral responsibility to individuals within organizations from three bases—role expectations, systems theory, and executive accountability—Stewart does not address how and to what extent codes are desirable or effective in facilitating moral judgment of public administrators.

Chandler (1989) argues that emphasis on the substance of codes and other forms of ethical discourse leads one to forget the moral force of written and spoken words:

> The thread is not in the combinations one can discern in the variegated quilt. It is in the symbolic power of words. They inspire, they set a tone, and they create expecta-

tions. They are rallying points for conceptual clarity. With them we tell others who we are. Both the precepts and the codes, which try to translate words into habits of action, are images of what professional public administrators think we should live up to. Thus, ethical discourse brings order, direction, and idealism to public service (p. 617).

Codes of ethics have received a fair degree of attention in general texts on ethics in public administration. Cooper (1990) considers codes examples of external control, "collectively imposed on individuals by organizations, professional associations, or political jurisdictions" (p. 129). However imposed, they are seen nonetheless as elements of professional life, going further than laws in projecting ideals and tailoring model behavior to situations, a mechanism for clarifying values and binding individuals to broader group and public values (Cooper, 1990: 143). Their weaknesses are their vagueness, which inhibits operationalization, the protectionism of the professional groups that promulgate them, and their lack of adequate means of ensuring compliance (p. 144).

Denhardt (1988) views the interest in codes of ethics from a historical perspective, seeing them as a reaction to corruption during Watergate and a response in general to the realities of administrative discretion (pp. 127–128). She takes a moderate view of their usefulness, indicating their potential to guide some actions and make social values relevant to administrators. But her abbreviated treatment of the subject, without clarifying her identification of codes either with law or with professionalism, implies that codes are not fundamental to her understanding of the ethical problems of public administrators.

Lewis (1991) views codes as legalisms enacted by political jurisdictions and stresses the variety of approaches and motivations for enactment among states and local governments. Her chapter on codes is the fullest treatment of the subject in the public administration ethics literature. She notes three options in drafting a code: intricate rules with complex enforcement procedures; blanket prohibitions that are simple but inflexible; and a vague approach that contains no explicit rules, standards, or prohibitions. She identifies three realistic objectives of a code: to encourage high standards of behavior, to increase public confidence in government, and to assist individual decision-making (p. 143). An unreasonable expectation is the idea that codes can somehow make flawed souls moral:

> Codes do not improve the moral climate in the true meaning of the phrase, despite sincere wishes and wrongly placed bets. . . . Agency codes may alter behavior via coercion, by outlawing a range of behaviors, but they target only enforceable, minimal taboos. Ethics codes do not prevent conflicts of interest—these are inherent in public service (p. 143).

Codes should therefore try to assist the moral practitioners in understanding how to function within the bounds of acceptable behavior, although she notes that they may contain aspirational principles as well as disciplinary rules.

Gortner (1991a) takes a generally negative view of codes, seeing them as "belaboring the obvious" (p. 142). In this view he is supported by his methodology, which consisted of indepth interviews with 42 retired federal managers. These individuals had very few good things to say about codes of ethics, either agency promulgated or developed by professional associations to which they belonged. As one interviewee said:

> I perceived myself as a professional. (I have always perceived myself as ethical.) But the professional code of ethics, although on my wall, I perceived as a motherhood statement without all that concrete meaning for me. It belabored the obvious. I never recall having tested a decision on that code of ethics. But I try to make "professional"

decisions. I believe the frame of reference attached to professionalism is appropriate for public managers as they try to serve the larger society (p. 142).

Scholars in the field are beginning to examine codes using more empirical approaches, arguing not just for the merits of a code, or the relevance of codes to a particular approach to ethics, but how codes actually influence behaviors and outcomes. To date, the efforts are scattered. Dobel (1993) has produced an excellent case study of one community's decision to implement a code focusing on the politics of code development and implementation. But we lack the body of research findings necessary to begin creating descriptive theories of codes of ethics as determinants of action. Bowman (1990) surveyed public administrators on their views of ethical codes. He found that general codes of conduct, such as the ASPA code, need to supplemented by agency-specific codes, that codes are seldom used in daily management decisions, not often a subject of discussion with colleagues, and not always taken seriously by top management (p. 349). In his view, the ASPA code had not succeeded in penetrating the public workplace:

> To summarize, five years after the passage of the ASPA ethics document, these practitioners (56 percent of whom have been members five or six or more years) have some acquaintance with it, but over 40 percent admitted they have none. Among those indicating familiarity (57 percent), just 10 percent claimed substantial knowledge of the Code, while a majority reported general familiarity and over one-third said that they "had heard of it" (p. 349).

Codes of ethics as a subject for research remain of marginal interest to most scholars of public administration. Rohr (1990) surveyed the interests of 27 scholars in the field of administrative ethics; none indicated that codes of ethics were a major research interest. Hejka-Ekins (1988) found few professors used codes of ethics in teaching ethics in the classroom. In the essays on ethics edited by Bowman (1991) delivered at ASPA's 1989 Conference on Ethics, several showed an interest in codes, particularly Gabris, Pugh, and Truelson (1991). But the dominant themes of research and writing on ethics in the field seemed likely to remain focused on discretion (Rohr, 1990), civic humanism (Hart, 1983; Hart and Wasden, 1990), and the moral exemplar (Cooper and Wright, 1992; Hart, 1992). Bok's (1978) statement was still heeded: "There is little help to be found in the codes and writings on professional ethics (p. xvii). . . . The codes must be but the starting point for a broad inquiry into the ethical quandaries encountered at work" (p. 246).

Things began to change dramatically in the early 1990s. More and more scholars began to see ethics as a subject for empirical research (Bowman, 1990; Frederickson, 1993; Menzel, 1992; Menzel and Carson, 1998). Codes of ethics provided a good subject for empirical research (Bruce, 1996). Research focused on attitudes toward codes by those practitioners operating under their constraints (Bruce, 1996), or on their enforcement (Charles and Cagle, 1997). Interest also began to emerge on the global context of ethics and the comparison of national experiences with codes (Kernaghan, 1993). The adoption of the ethics code by the leading professional association in the field, the American Society for Public Administration, and its revision in the 1990s has allowed an ongoing dialogue in the field on the proper language for a general ethics code for public professionals (Van Wart, 1996; Bowman, 1997). Printed on the back cover of the leading journal in the field, the *Public Administration Review*, the ASPA Code has become a familiar pillar of the association.

As more and more jurisdictions legislate codes of conduct for their employees, much of the discussion of codes centers on the differences between codes of conduct promulgated by political agencies, and codes of ethics developed by professional associations (Lewis, 1991; Bruce, 1996). While it is easy to identify the locus of codification—association or political body—it is still tricky to differentiate professional codes of ethics from codes of conduct. In wording there may be little difference, although it is expected that codes of ethics state values or aspirations to do good that are in contrast to the "don't do this" approach of codes of conduct. Enforcement of violations is stressed more in codes of conduct than their professional counterparts, although no simple pattern emerges. Both share the goal of serving as what Bruce (1996) calls a "quality assurance statement to society" (p. 23), but the codes of conduct, if vigorously enforced, do so with a scorecard mentality—success measured by the number of abuses found and disciplined—rather than the preventive approach favored by professional associations.

The 1990s also saw most other professional fields and disciplines struggling to keep up with the demand for systematic approaches to ethical conduct and discourse relevant to their undertakings. The "ethics explosion" of the times has allowed public administration to benefit from a growing literature on ethics in other professions, especially the professions that practice in the public arena. It is to a brief review of this literature that we now turn.

IV. PUBLIC PROFESSIONS AND CODES OF ETHICS

Much of the discussion in the literature of public administration has assumed that the roles performed by public professionals involve management and program implementation, in keeping with the Weberian/Wilsonian constructs that have defined the field since its inception. That is, the twin concerns of organizational efficiency and public accountability frame the work of administration and hence the ethical dilemmas. The focus is on balancing personal and professional identities and on serving the public interest and not special or personal interests (Griffith, 1962). Codes of ethics are viewed in light of this definition of what work in the field is and how the field views itself.

One of the first public professions to focus on ethical issues associated with its work was policy analysis. Since the 1960s, policy analysis has developed a significant body of literature. Policy analysts apply scientific method to questions of policy design, policy choice, and evaluation. Their natural role is in advising policymakers—speaking truth to power—and not managing programs and agencies. The literature of policy analysis is intertwined with that of public administration, as is the work, but like the work it is separate enough to consider separately.

If we can assume that the roles of administrators require codes stressing benevolence (Denhardt, 1994), honesty, and commitment to the public, the roles played by policy analysts stress the conflict between service and loyalty to political superiors and a commitment to methodological purity and basic honesty (Leys, 1968; Benveniste, 1984). Several scholars in policy analysis have addressed the issue of codes of ethics for policy analysts.

Policy analysis is an amalgam of political science, economics, and various substantive fields that provide insight into public problems. Although, as a group, policy analysts are widely dispersed in society and divergent in background and education. Amy (1984) finds no compelling logical reasons why policy analysis cannot engage in ethical discourse. Repeating a litany of arguments against codes—that ethical analysis is subjective, unnecessary because of political checks, unnecessary because the field agrees upon utilitarian values, may lead to personal biases injected into analysis, or is simply impractical and too abstract to operationalize—Amy suggests that political realities, not logic, work against the use of codes or a more general interest in moral reasoning in policy analysis. Analysts work for clients who don't want substantive criticism, an argument that sounds suspiciously like the politics-administration dichotomy reworded. But Amy's most cogent argument is that, for better or worse, policy analysis is cast into a "technocratic ethos" (p. 582) which makes it impossible to advance arguments in any language other than positivism to politicians who themselves are uncritical believers in a economics-laden technocratic approach to public issues. Amy concludes by suggesting that, "without a significant shift away from the current technological style of policy analysis or an increased emphasis placed on ethical and ideological issues in American politics, ethical inquiry is unlikely to become an integral part of policy analysis" (p. 588). Benveniste (1984) makes a similar argument from the perspective of policy analysis' evolving professionalism.

Although he makes the argument that codes of ethics have economic value by legitimating the work of professionals, Benveniste finds the profession of policy analysis unlikely soil for codes to take root. Practical considerations of power, not moral reasoning, are the lifeblood of policy analysis, as evidenced by this quote: "In searching for the truth, should experts lean toward the truth that helps the 'Prince' who hires them or toward the truth that protects the public interest" (p. 563)? Truth is presumably defined in relation to power. Thus Benveniste's arguments against a code of ethics are logical: (1) policy analysis has a diversified professional base of policy experts with a variety of backgrounds; (2) the hiring agent is powerful (the Prince) unlike those who hire professionals in society; (3) analysts themselves are comfortable in their role and don't need the protections and status provided by codes; and (4) there is a "disenchantment" with the over-regulation of professions in society (p. 563).

Brown (1986) finds most current codes of ethics in the public sector inappropriate to policy analysts, since they deal with conflicts of interest and personal enrichment rather than role deviance (p. 58). Nonetheless, he finds a code of conduct potentially useful for a number of reasons. Codes can restore a civic vocabulary, a perspective on analytical techniques, provide a challenge to students (most of whom in policy analysis are preservice and inexperienced) to test their assumptions and presuppositions, put policy debates into a useful context and remove the abstract games sense of much policy work, and identify areas of consensus that can guide analysis (p. 62).

A code of ethics for the profession of policy analysis may thus be impossible to craft and implement. However, many other professions have succeeded in developing codes that combine a concern for substantive policy issues with issues of personal conduct, basic moral qualities, and a concern for the public interest. A literature on the subject of professional ethics codes is burgeoning and is useful to students of public administration in clarifying the role that codes of ethics play in: the practice of specific professions (Davis, 1991; Harrington, 1996; Chiampou, 1992; Banks, 1998); the legal standing of codes (Chiampou, 1992; Landry, 1997); or the impact of organization-specific codes on professional conduct (Dean, 1992; Montoya, 1994; Cassell, 1997). The almost universal use of company-specific codes in large business corporations has fostered an intense interest in the use and importance of ethics codes in corporate life (Kaye, 1992; L'Etang, 1992).

Much of the literature on professional and business codes of ethics, however useful it is in providing general understanding of codes and their usefulness in producing desired outcomes, diverges from that of public administration either in its inattention to the philosophical underpinnings of ethics codes or the differences between the public and private theaters of action. A more fruitful source of insights is provided by the literature on public professional associations, many of which have a long and rich involvement in ethical issues, as well as a strong historical connection to the field and practice of public administration. Let us turn now to one of the oldest and most significant of these associations, the International City/County Management Association, and review its 75 years of experience with a code of ethics.

V. THE CASE OF ICMA

The connection between ethics and public professionalism has provided public administration with one of its most cherished accomplishments, the ICMA Code of Ethics. First adopted in 1924, the code has been revised several times, in 1938, 1952, 1969, 1976, 1987, and 1998. In addition to changes in wording, guidelines were included in 1972 to help interpret the code; these were rewritten in 1978 to relate to specific provisions of the code (Besuden, 1981). The ICMA Code is balanced by a Declaration of Ideals, adopted so that management would be humane, equitable, and committed to democratic values. The Code of Ethics with guidelines is illustrated in Table 1.

Codes of ethics are assumed to be required of any mature profession (Chandler, 1983; Gortner, 1991b; Arnold and Plant, 1994). Codes are part of a professionalization process that includes the creation of associations to help individual practitioners communicate; relationships with government, universities, and other groups in society to advance professional interests and policy preferences; certification and credentialism, restricting entry to qualified professional practitioners and specifying how work is to be performed; and lifelong opportunities for professional and individual growth.

Codes of ethics developed in the professional context to specify and clarify acceptable conduct. This was done with a variety of goals in mind: to augment education that was vocational or technical in nature and did not help the practitioner deal with the conflict of values or the need for a public service orientation; to help the professional group achieve a higher level of self-conscious identity (Stillman, 1974; Arnold and Plant, 1994); to reach high levels of professional conduct and work performance; and to achieve a higher degree of legitimacy in the eyes of clients, fellow professionals, government, and the public (Hudson Institute, 1990).

The locus of code-making was the professional association in most cases. Professional associations in the United States date from 1857, with the formation of the National Education Association, but their period of greatest growth was the Progressive Era, from 1880 to 1930. From the outset, the advancement of public professionalism was the goal of most associations. In this process of professionalization and legitimization, statements of ideals, standards of performance, and codes of ethics were fundamental, stressing usually the particular responsibility of the public professional to serve the public in an honest, informed, and disinterested manner (Karl, 1963).

Professional associations intent upon codifying good behavior typically tried to find ways to relate the work of the practitioner to unexamined ethical directives derived from societal values and democratic theory. The code was as much a statement of professional identity and separateness as it was a carefully reasoned approach to doing good and avoiding evil. Stillman (1974) provides a through analysis of the ICMA code. He sees it as a step toward professionalization. In his words, "the code should not be taken too literally but rather as a general expression of the ethical ideals of the new association" (p. 37). Nevertheless, Stillman uses the changes of the code, in 1938, 1952, and 1969, as

Table 1 ICMA Code of Ethics with Guidelines

The ICMA Code of Ethics was adopted by the ICMA membership in 1924, and most recently amended by the membership in May 1998. The Guidelines for the Code were adopted by the ICMA Executive Board in 1972 and most recently revised in July 1998.

The purposes of ICMA are to enhance the quality of local government and to support and assist professional local administrators in the United States and other countries. To further these objectives, certain principles, as enforced by the Rules of Procedure, shall govern the conduct of every member of ICMA, who shall:

1. Be dedicated to the concepts of effective and democratic local government by responsible elected officials and believe that professional general management is essential to the achievement of this objective.

2. Affirm the dignity and worth of the services rendered by government and maintain a constructive, creative, and practical attitude toward local government affairs and a deep sense of social responsibility as a trusted public servant.

   Guideline
   Advice to Officials of Other Local Governments.   When members advise and respond to inquiries from elected or appointed officials of other local governments, they should inform the administrators of those communities.

3. Be dedicated to the highest ideals of honor and integrity in all public and personal relationships in order that the member may merit the respect and confidence of the elected officials, of other officials and employees, and of the public.

   Guidelines
   Public Confidence.   Members should conduct themselves so as to maintain public confidence in their profession, their local government, and in their performance of the public trust.

   Impression of Influence.   Members should conduct their official and personal affairs in such a manner as to give the clear impression that they cannot be improperly influenced in the performance of their official duties.

   Appointment Commitment.   Members who accept an appointment to a position should not fail to report for that position. This does not preclude the possibility of a member considering several offers or seeking several positions at the same time, but once a *bona fide* offer of a position has been accepted, that commitment should be honored. Oral acceptance of an employment offer is considered binding unless the employer makes fundamental changes in terms of employment.

   Credentials.   An application for employment should be complete and accurate as to all pertinent details of education, experience, and personal history. Members should recognize that both omissions and inaccuracies must be avoided.

   Professional Respect.   Members seeking a management position should show professional respect for persons formerly holding the position or for others who might be applying for the same position. Professional respect does not preclude honest differences of opinion; it does preclude attacking a person's motives or integrity in order to be appointed to a position.

   Confidentiality.   Members should not discuss or divulge information with anyone about pending or completed ethics cases, except as specifically authorized by the Rules of Procedure for Enforcement of the Code of Ethics.

   Seeking Employment.   Members should not seek employment for a position having an incumbent administrator who has not resigned or been officially informed that his or her services are to be terminated.

Table 1 Continued

4. Recognize that the chief function of local government at all times is to serve the best interests of all of the people.

    Guideline
    Length of Service.   A minimum of two years generally is considered necessary in order to render a professional service to the local government. A short tenure should be the exception rather than a recurring experience. However, under special circumstances, it may be in the best interests of the local government and the member to separate in a shorter time. Examples of such circumstances would include refusal of the appointing authority to honor commitments concerning conditions of employment, a vote of no confidence in the member, or severe personal problems. It is the responsibility of an applicant for a position to ascertain conditions of employment. Inadequately determining terms of employment prior to arrival does not justify premature termination.

5. Submit policy proposals to elected officials; provide them with facts and advice on matters of policy as a basis for making decisions and setting community goals; and uphold and implement local government policies adopted by elected officials.

    Guideline
    Conflicting Roles.   Members who serve multiple roles—working as both city attorney and city manager for the same community, for example—should avoid participating in matters that create the appearance of a conflict of interest. They should disclose the potential conflict to the governing body so that other opinions may be solicited.

6. Recognize that elected representatives of the people are entitled to the credit for the establishment of local government policies; responsibility for policy execution rests with the members.

7. Refrain from all political activities which undermine public confidence in professional administrators. Refrain from participation in the election of the members of the employing legislative body.

    Guidelines
    Elections of the Governing Body.   Members should maintain a reputation for serving equally and impartially all members of the governing body of the local government they serve, regardless of party. To this end, they should not engage in active participation in the election campaign on behalf of or in opposition to candidates for the governing body.

    Elections of Elected Executives.   Members should not engage in the election campaign of any candidate for mayor or elected county executive.

    Elections.   Members share with their fellow citizens the right and responsibility to exercise their franchise and voice their opinion on public issues. However, in order not to impair their effectiveness on behalf of the local governments they serve, they should not participate in any political activities (including but not limited to fundraising, endorsing candidates, and financial contributions) for representatives to city, county, special district, school, state, or federal offices.

    Elections in the Council-Manager Plan.   Members may assist in preparing and presenting materials that explain the council-manager form of government to the public prior to an election on the use of the plan. If assistance is required by another community, members may respond. All activities regarding ballot issues should be conducted within local regulations and in a professional manner.

    Presentation of Issues.   Members may assist the governing body in presenting issues involved in referenda such as bond issues, annexations, and similar matters.

8. Make it a duty continually to improve the member's professional ability and to develop the competence of associates in the use of management techniques.

Table 1 Continued

Guidelines

Self-Assessment.   Each member should assess his or her professional skills and abilities on a periodic basis.

Professional Development.   Each member should commit at least 40 hours per year to professional development activities that are based on the practices identified by the members of ICMA.

9. Keep the community informed on local government affairs; encourage communication between the citizens and all local government officers; emphasize friendly and courteous service to the public; and seek to improve the quality and image of public service.

10. Resist any encroachment on professional responsibilities, believing the member should be free to carry out official policies without interference, and handle each problem without discrimination on the basis of principle and justice.

Guideline

Information Sharing.   The member should openly share information with the governing body while diligently carrying out the member's responsibilities as set forth in the charter or enabling legislation.

11. Handle all matters of personnel on the basis of merit so that fairness and impartiality govern a member's decisions, pertaining to appointments, pay adjustments, promotions, and discipline.

Guideline

Equal Opportunity.   Members should develop a positive program that will ensure meaningful employment opportunities for all segments of the community. All programs, practices, and operations should: (1) provide equality of opportunity in employment for all persons; (2) prohibit discrimination because of race, color, religion, sex, national origin, political affiliation, physical handicaps, age, or marital status; and (3) promote continuing programs of affirmative action at every level within the organization.

It should be the members' personal and professional responsibility to actively recruit and hire minorities and women to serve on professional staffs throughout their organizations.

12. Seek no favor; believe that personal aggrandizement or profit secured by confidential information or by misuse of public time is dishonest.

Guidelines

Gifts.   Members should not directly or indirectly solicit any gift or accept or receive any gift—whether it be money, services, loan, travel, entertainment, hospitality, promise, or any other form—under the following circumstances: (1) it could be reasonably inferred or expected that the gift was intended to influence them in the performance of their official duties; or (2) the gift was intended to serve as a reward for any official action on their part.

It is important that the prohibition of unsolicited gifts be limited to circumstances related to improper influence. In *de minimus* situations, such as meal checks, some modest maximum dollar value should be determined by the member as a guideline. The guideline is not intended to isolate members from normal social practices where gifts among friends, associates, and relatives are appropriate for certain occasions.

Investments in Conflict with Official Duties.   Member should not invest or hold any investment, directly or indirectly, in any financial business, commercial, or other private transaction that creates a conflict with their official duties.

In the case of real estate, the potential use of confidential information and knowledge to further a member's personal interest requires special consideration. This guideline recognizes that members' official actions and decisions can be influenced if there is a conflict with personal investments. Purchases and sales which might be interpreted as speculation for quick profit ought to be avoided (see the guideline on ''Confidential Information'').

Table 1 Continued

Because personal investments may prejudice or may appear to influence official actions and decisions, members may, in concert with their governing body, provide for disclosure of such investments prior to accepting their position as local government administrator or prior to any official action by the governing body that may affect such investments.

Personal Relationships.   Member should disclose any personal relationship to the governing body in any instance where there could be the appearance of a conflict of interest. For example, if the manager's spouse works for a developer doing business with the local government, that fact should be disclosed.

Confidential Information.   Members should not disclose to others, or use to further their personal interest, confidential information acquired by them in the course of their official duties.

Private Employment.   Members should not engage in, solicit, negotiate for, or promise to accept private employment, nor should they render services for private interests or conduct a private business when such employment, service, or business creates a conflict with or impairs the proper discharge of their official duties.

Teaching, lecturing, writing, or consulting are typical activities that may not involve conflict of interest, or impair the proper discharge of their official duties. Prior notification of the appointing authority is appropriate in all cases of outside employment.

Representation.   Members should not represent any outside interest before any agency, whether public or private, except with the authorization of or at the direction of the appointing authority they serve.

Endorsements.   Members should not endorse commercial products or services by agreeing to use their photograph, endorsement, or quotation in paid or other commercial advertisements, whether or not for compensation. Members may, however, agree to endorse the following, provided they do not receive any compensation: (1) books or other publications; (2) professional development or educational services provided by nonprofit membership organizations or recognized educational institutions; (3) products and/or services in which the local government has a direct economic interest.

Members' observations, opinions, and analyses of commercial products used or tested by their local governments are appropriate and useful to the profession when included as part of professional articles and reports.

---

metaphors for the ferment within the profession of city management. The 1938 code enshrined a Taylorian vision of the city manager as technocrat; the 1952 changes moved the manager away from a strict interpretation of the policy-administration dichotomy to that of community leader and political realist; the 1969 version tried to embrace changing societal values on issues of equity.

ICMA has since 1924 tried to make its code useful to practitioners. In 1972 guidelines were included to help interpret the meaning of the canons of the code. For example, canon 4 of the code, on service, is worded in general terms: "Recognize that the chief function of local government at all times is to serve the best interests of all of the people" (ICMA, 1998).

What does this mean? The guidelines indicate that a minimum of two years of service is anticipated when a manager takes a position, unless, of course, the manager loses the confidence of the council or has "severe personal problems." It is the responsibility of the manager, not the jurisdiction hiring her/him, to ascertain clearly the terms of employment prior to arrival.

Not all of the twelve canons have guidelines for assisting managers in understanding the code. As might be expected, the most detailed guidelines concern the behavior proscribed by the canons stating ''seek no favor'' and ''be dedicated to the highest ideals of honor and integrity.''

As well as the guidelines for interpreting the code, ICMA utilizes a Declaration of Ideals to complement the negative and coercive aspects of the code. Adopted by the membership on the basis of a recommendation of the ICMA Committee on Future Horizons of the Profession, the declaration is a result of a concern that management be humane as well as economical, equitable as well as efficient, and dedicated to democratic government as well as efficacious policy.

The ICMA code is part of a system of behavior that includes the code, the declaration, and methods of enforcing and updating the association's stance on good behavior. ICMA members take the code seriously (Frederickson, 1989); as one ICMA staff member put it, they ''guard the code jealously.'' To what can we attribute the success of ICMA in professionalizing around a code of ethics?

First, as Stillman (1974) has shown, the association sees the need to review the code on a regular basis for relevance and appropriateness. It is not a static statement of golden rules or unchanging professional norms, but a guide to proper behavior under the conditions and operative management philosophies of the day. It changes with the times.

Second, it is understood by the members and enforced. At any time, between 30 and 35 complaints are active, with three-member state fact-finding teams handling investigations. A standing Committee on Professional Conduct acts upon the reports of the state teams, assisted by staff (who generally keep a low profile in all ethics matters). In FY 1998, there were ten private censures, two public censures, one membership bar, and fourteen dismissed cases resulting from alleged ethics code violations. The two public censures resulted from involvement with a political campaign and inappropriate abandonment of a manager position to take another job. The membership bar case involved falsification of information on a resume.

Enforcement of the code is costly in several ways. It requires a good deal of staff and members' time to investigate charges. The possibility of liability for investigators, staff, or the association requires that ICMA set up a self-insurance fund to guard against possible legal challenges to its rulings. Also, roughly 70 percent of the time of a fulltime ICMA staff member is dedicated to code enforcement. Traditionally a role played by the associate or executive director, it is now entrusted to a staff individual with a background in law.

A cost that is harder to measure is the personal pressure on other ICMA members to enforce the ethical rules of the association. Since most jurisdictions have only one or a small number of ICMA members, a manager or assistant manager from another jurisdiction often is required to file the complaint with the association. The great majority of alleged violations come to the attention of ICMA in this fashion. It is probable also that, given the central position of the code in the life of the association, a number of potential violations are resolved informally, member to member.

ICMA does not certify managers and hence cannot bar individuals from employment; city councils are free to hire the applicant that they prefer regardless of background or professional membership (Besuden, 1981). But a number of sanctions can be taken under the code that make it much more than a toothless tiger. These sanctions range from the mildest penalty, a private letter of censure, to public censure—newspapers and media in the community of the offending manager are informed by ICMA of action taken, i.e., suspension or expulsion. The ICMA also enforces sanctions against members who are found guilty of professionally relevant misdeeds in courts of law.

ICMA members were surveyed by the staff in 1990 to identify ways of ensuring that the code be current, realistic, and accepted. Two major areas of concern were identified. First, the code needs to be the basis of a system of training and education for members, using case studies, training sessions, articles in association journals, anything that can translate the abstract into the actual for members. Second, the association needs to provide more assistance to the state committees to assist in investigations and ethics enforcement. The staff assistance given to ethics attests to the seriousness with which city managers approach the subject of ethics.

Given ICMA's interest in maintaining the legitimacy of its code by periodic updates, what of the future? One interesting possibility under consideration is a more encompassing code of ethics for all the major players in local governance, including not only professional managers but also elected officials, citizens, and researchers and consultants under contract to a jurisdiction. Such a code would probably not supplant the enforceable professional code of the association so much as complement it, much as the Declaration of Ideals did in the 1980s. But it would provide a more comprehensive sense of the local government as part of a community (Newland, 1984; Frederickson, 1989) and not a technical or political artifice placed atop the life of the polis. It would also bring to the attention of more than the members of ICMA the importance of ethical guidelines in local governance. One respondent to the survey noted that "ICMA should promote and publicize the fact that the city management profession has had a code of ethics for sixty years or so." Another said, "Local elected officials are always surprised by the Code of Ethics. I think we have to make ethics information part of our normal interaction with them [elected politicians]" (ICMA, 1990b). The most recent changes, in 1998, received a 90 percent vote of approval from voting members and made changes in Tenet 7 to reinforce the idea that members should not engage in any political activity.

VI. PROFESSIONAL CODES AND PROFESSIONAL ASSOCIATIONS

ICMA's experience with a written, enforced code of ethics is pronounced among associations representing public professionals in many respects: the length of time the association has pursued ethics as a major concern, the importance attached by members to the code as a statement of professional conduct and ideals, and the attention given it in the literature of the field. Other associations representing public professionals have also considered codes of ethics, although none has the wealth of experience or duration of interest of ICMA. Plant (1991) surveyed the 102 associations included in the Directory of National Associations of State and Local Government compiled by the Academy for State and Local Government (1989). Each association was asked if it had an official code of ethics for its membership. Out of 90 associations responding, only 26, or 29 percent, had codes; another four had a variant, such as bylaws or a constitutional statement that was the equivalent. Roughly two-thirds of these associations did not have a code.

Why don't all public official associations have codes? First, it is important to understand the associations that represent public officials. Some represent elected officials or politically appointed staff, whose basis of selection and temporariness of office make professional codes unlikely and inappropriate. Other associations represent professions solidly grounded in the professional life of occupations that unlike ICMA are found outside as well as inside government: accountants, physicians, lawyers, nurses, and so on. Others represent professions traditionally associated with the public service, but with employment possibilities outside government that raise serious issues of conflict of interest or the revolving door phenomenon, such as city planners or chiefs of police.

The analysis of the survey showed that four types of associations are most likely to have a formal code: (1) engineering associations, including such public sector associations as the American Association of State Highway and Transportation Officials (AASHTO), the Institute of Transportation Engineers, and the American Public Works Association; (2) associations representing professionals in administration of justice or regulatory activities using the law as an enforcement approach; (3) associations with a clearly public sort of professionalism, including ICMA, the American Planning Association/ American Institute of Certified Planners, the Government Finance Officers Association, the International Personnel Management Association, and the American Society for Public Administration; and (4) associations representing professionals in education, of which six had codes that closely resembled one another (Plant, 1991).

Little has been written about association codes of ethics other than ICMA. An exception is the profession of public planning (Marcuse, 1976; Howe and Kaufman, 1979). Slater (1983) examined the planning profession's experience with codes and compared them to that of the city managers. Like ICMA, the American Planning Association and its certifying agent, the American Institute of Certified Planners, has had a long history of involvement with codes of ethics (Howe and Kaufman, 1979), but it was not until 1970 that a moribund code and approach to implementation was replaced by a commitment to a strong code identifying six canons of ethics and fourteen rules of discipline. The code was rewritten in 1982 with 28 statements organized into four major issue areas: responsibility to the public; responsibility to clients and employers; obligation to the profession and colleagues; self responsibility (p. 4). As is the case with ICMA, the planning profession uses the code as a means to educate members on situations that involve ethical choice, such as how to judge the admissibility of contacts with prior or new employers, how to work with citizen groups, conflicts of interest, and many other common job-related situations. Slater concludes that a narrow and technical approach to planning facilitates an enforceable approach to ethics. Kaufman (1981) argues that "many contemporary planners are increasingly recognizing the ethical basis of choices they must make about a wide range of complex issues involved in their work" (p. 196). He argues that the interest of the planning profession in an upgraded code of ethics is symptomatic of ethical issues, especially those involved with discretionary judgment, that are hard to codify.

As more and more professional associations adopt codes of ethics, the question of the binding character of privately-adopted association codes (often with enforcement procedures) on public employees is raised. This can be seen as a type of privatization, or even agency-shop situation, in which association membership is not required for employment, but adherence to codes developed by association is. For example, the State Historical Society of Iowa, the historical division of the Department of Cultural Affairs, includes in its work rules (1987) section VII entitled "Codes of Ethics." This section states that "The State Historical Society of Iowa subscribes to all codes of ethics adopted by appropriate professional organizations and expects its employees to abide by those standards" (p. 6). Listed are the codes of the American Library Association, the Society of American Archivists, the American Association of Museums (including special codes for curators and museum registrars), the American Institute of Conservation, the Educational Press Association, and the National Society of Fund Raising Executives. Copies of the relevant codes are included in the work rules. This appears to be an extreme example of a government agency relying upon professional associations for ethical codes, but as more and more professional associations representing public professionals promulgate such rules, it is an easy and oftentimes efficacious alternative to creating by statute codes of conduct for government employees and public mechanisms for their enforcement (Menzel, 1992).

The proliferation of professional codes, and the requirement that a public employee be familiar with the rules of those operative within a particular professional milieu, may be less onerous than the Iowa example suggests. Most codes attempt to take the basic themes of ethics in government and apply them to the work of their profession. How to deal with the public, what constitutes the actuality or perception of conflicts of interest, what constitutes personal honesty in the work setting, what constitutes improper relations with private interest—these form the key to understanding almost all codes. Very rarely do they engage in true moral reasoning, or invent new approaches to define ethical behavior in political or organizational settings. Usually from 5 to 15 canons identify ethical behavior, combining positive statements of ideal behavior and examples of improper or proscribed behavior.

The fear that professions may use their certification and monopoly power to evade ethical constraints—either external or internal—has given rise to the issue of "the separatist thesis" (Freedman, 1978; Gewirth, 1989; Overman and Foss, 1991). The separatist thesis of professional ethics argues that the professional's objective of providing valued services justifies using means that violates basic ethical rules in order to prevent the violation of other, more important, moral rights out of necessity or derived from the rules of an institution (Gewirth, 1986: 283). The separatist thesis applied to the professional work of public agencies raises the critical factor of the monopoly position of government in providing many services and the nonvoluntary, client status assumed by individuals who come into contact with the agency. Truly moral action by professionals requires that individuals not be used as means to greater social ends, or even deprived of what Gewirth calls their right to be "agents, that is, to control their own lives and effectively pursue and sustain their own purposes without being subjected to domination and harm from others" (p. 288).

Codes of ethics promulgated by public official associations are a potential force for reminding professionals that the separatist thesis is incompatible with public service. To accomplish this, they are required to state the particular ethical constraints that come from public service, and by stating that while service to clients is the goal, actions that are politically unacceptable, however efficacious, lessen the public trust in government and violate the basic social contract of citizen and government in a democracy. In other words, some of the language of professional codes that seems to identify common truths and values may in fact help to remind the professional that special status, and the freedom of action that accompanies it, are not possible in public sector situations.

VII. CONCLUSIONS

Codes of ethics are becoming a fact of life for more and more public employees. They may be seen as a manifestation of societal demands for accountability and the need to apply basic values to the work of professions and public organizations. These two major forces, professionalization and the public's demand for formal accountability and standards of conduct, have been converging in the two and half decades since Watergate. An approach to codes of ethics that sees the code as part of a process of training and education for the public servant, a basis for creating valid public expectations of honest, competent, and public-interested behavior, and a way to express public service ideals as well as a means to regulate individual behavior, is becoming the standard. Codes do little to examine in any analytical way basic values such as honesty, public service, or personal integrity. Their main value is in interpreting basic societal standards of right and wrong for the milieu of work in the public service.

It is logical to assume, however, that professional codes developed, promulgated, and enforced by professional associations will be better avenues for heightened ethical self-awareness than codes developed by statute and made binding on employees as a condition of employment. Association life is a form of citizenship, in which duties and obligations are identified and opportunity for meaningful participation is present. As the examples of the ICMA and AICP illustrate, codes of ethics of associations are rarely set in stone. The healthy association is continually learning from its experience with its code and making changes in procedure or substance. Such change, it should be noted, is different than changes in public law, in which the employee has little opportunity for involvement and in which, by implication, he/she is the problem to be corrected by the imposition of laws, work rules, and other coercive measures.

Relying entirely upon professional associations for codes of ethics, however, is risky. Codes are often seen by associations as vehicles to enhance the standing of the profession or organization for economic gain by the fostering or furthering of relationships with stakeholders. Consider for example the instrumental language in a report on associations issued by the Hudson Institute: ''Association codes of ethics and professional standards provide information that generally enhances consumers' trust in the reliability, quality, and safety of goods and professional services. Association performance and safety standards improve quality, reliability, and interchangeability among products and services'' (1990: 117).

Donabedian (1993) applies a similar argument in analyzing the contribution of professional accounting codes of ethics in producing trust. Using a mathematical model, he probes the exit costs of professionals and the authority of associations to impose standards through codes. Assuming the need for societal trust in the probity of professionals, his work suggests that civil courts will replace association-based disciplinary efforts if there is an ''inner erosion'' (p. 109) of the profession's enforcement power.

Such an analytical approach, couched in economic logic, is far from traditional justifications for codes of ethics. These justifications emphasize the code: as a statement of basic moral principles, such as courage, honesty, loyalty, and commitment; as a map to operationalizing principles in the specifics of governance activities; or as a regulator of the behavior of members (Kernaghan, 1974; Chandler, 1983). Research is needed to examine how much of the code-making since the 1970s has been motivated by economic motives and how much by moral reasoning.

The literature of public administration is moving to a more systematic and informed discussion of ethics (Bruce, 1996; Van Wart, 1996). The need in the literature now is not to discover codes, but to understand the basis of codifying and the differences in form and effect between codes emanating from public professionalism and those that are efforts of the state to satisfy public and elite demands for accountability and control of subordinate behavior. The topic of codes fits into at least two major areas of the field, professionalism and administrative ethics. Are codes seen as a necessary attribute of any true profession, or are they means by which moral reasoning can be brought to bear on public decisions? Are they efforts to regulate behavior, or ways to help individuals improve their ability to reason in moral categories? What are appropriate expectations for codes in cleansing the public sector? When someone is found guilty of a transgression of a code, is the code to be credited with protecting the public interest, or held deficient by not properly guiding and motivating the offending individual? Are codes created by law and imposed on employees without an opportunity to participate in their crafting and enforcement true codes of ethics, or top-down management control devices?

Ethicists in public administration have not been fond of codes. By their formalism, their preachiness, their legalisms, codes in the opinion of many fall far short of the goal of creating a new civic perspective to replace the old progressive constructs of public service and the public interest (Ventriss, 1989). By stressing constraints on behavior many feel codes fail to create character and leadership in the service of the public (Cooper, 1990). By stressing situationalism and realism they avoid asking whether there are eternal, essential, universal values that transcend contextualism and situationalism (Becker, 1941; Fox, 1992). It is unlikely that, in the eyes of their critics, any code will be the best vehicle for elevating the ethics of the public service. Foster's criticism of codification (1981) is still a valid criticism of all formal efforts to regulate behavior and limit discretion:

> There is an ingrained bias in nearly all modern and modernizing societies that *less discretion*, and therefore by association *more law*, is the ideal normative state. But, discretion lies at the very heart of moral behavior. Difficult moral decisions can only be made by the individual who has the discretionary authority to treat each situation in its own merits (p. 31).

But it is clear that some codes are better than others as a way of educating public servants on how to do good and avoid doing evil in serving the public. Studies indicate that the typical American public servant does not hold views on the role of government or acceptable behavior very different from that of the average citizen (Bowman, 1990; Lewis, 1990). What is perhaps needed most, and which seems to be burgeoning, is a body of descriptive theory of codes that will look at the wave of codification since the 1970s, put it into historical perspective, and balance it with normative constructs of virtue, character, and public service. Hart (1992) puts it well when he reminds us that all public servants operate under a code of sorts in their duty to honor the Constitution:

> The common normative link among all public servants is that they have sworn an oath, in one form or another, to support and defend the Constitution. Today, we have lost the significance of what it means to swear an oath. In its most basic expression, it means that public servants have a greater obligation than those in the private sector to be men and women of good character, prepared at all times to sacrifice personal gain for the public interest (p. 26).

This is the lasting significance of all codes of ethics: how they can lift individual public servants above the "do's and don't's" of ordinary organizational life to give meaning and reality to the highest values of a democratic society. That few now do is no reason to abandon the hope that codes, with their powerful mixture of affirmational language, work-relevant guides to proper and improper behavior, and participatory mechanisms for enforcement, evaluation, and rewording, have an important place in the evolution of ethical thinking in public administration.

REFERENCES

Academy for State and Local Government. (1989). *Directory of National Associations of State and Local Government*. Washington: Academy for State and Local Government.

Adams, G.B. (1993). Ethics and the chimera of professionalism: The historical context of an oxymoronic relationship. *American Review of Public Administration*, 23:117–139.

Amy, D.J. (1984). Why policy analysis and ethics are incompatible. *Journal of Policy and Management*, 3(3):573–591.

Appleby, P.H. (1952). *Morality and Administration in Democratic Governance*. Baton Rouge, LA: LSU Press.

Arnold, D.S., and Plant, J.F. (1994). *A Bridge Across One Hundred Years: Public Official Associations in America*. Fairfax, VA: George Mason U. Press.

Bailey, S.K. (1965). The relationship between ethics and public service. In *Public Administration and Democracy: Essays in Honor of Paul Appleby* (R.C. Martin, ed.). Syracuse, NY: Syracuse U. Press, p. 283–298.

Banks, S. (1998). Codes of ethics and ethical conduct: A view from the caring professions. *Public Money & Management*, 18:27–30.

Barnard, C. (1938). *Functions of the Executive*. Cambridge, MA: Harvard University Press.

Bayles, M.D. (1989). *Professional Ethics*, 2d ed. Belmont, CA: Wadsworth.

Becker, C.L. (1941). *New Liberties for Old Freedom and Responsibility*. New Haven, CT: Yale U. Press.

Benson, G.C.S. (1991). Codes of Ethics: A Need for Research. *Mimeo*.

Benveniste, G. (1984). On a code of ethics for policy experts. *Journal of Policy Analysis and Management*, 3(3):561–572.

Besuden, W. (1981). The profession's heritage: The ICMA code of ethics. *Public Management* 63(March):2–5.

Blake, R. (1998). The nature and scope of state government ethics codes. *Public Productivity & Management Review*, 21(June):453–459.

Bok, S. (1978). *Lying: Moral Choice in Public and Private Life*. New York, NY: Vintage Books.

Boulmetis, J., and Russo, F.X. (1991). A question of ethics. *Leadership*, (Winter):15–18.

Bowman, J.S. (1977). Ethics in the federal service: A post watergate view. *Midwest Review of Public Administration*, 11:3–20.

Bowman, J.S. (1990). Ethics in government: A national survey of public administrators. *Public Administration Review*, 16:345–353.

Bowman, J.S. (1991). *Ethical Frontiers in Public Management*. San Francisco, Jossey-Bass.

Bowman, J.S. (with R.L. Williams) (1997). Ethics in government: From a winter of despair to a spring of hope. *Public Administration Review*, 57:517–526.

Braun, P. (1987). The critical role of the states in the ethics process. *Public Management*, 69(August):6–8.

Brenner, S. and Brenner, E.M. (1977). Is the Ethics of Business Changing? *Harvard Business Review*, 55(January/February):59–61.

Brown, P. (1986). Ethics and education for public service in a liberal state. *Journal of Policy and Management*, 6:56–68

Bruce, W.P. (1996). Codes of ethics and codes of conduct: Perceived contribution to the practice of ethics in local government. *Public Integrity Annual*, 13–30.

Burke, F., and Benson, G. (1989). State ethics codes, commissions and conflicts. *State Government Review*, 105(5):195–198.

Cassell, C. (1997). Opening the black box: Corporate codes of ethics in their organizational context. *Journal of Business Ethics*, 16:1077–1093.

Cassinelli, C.W. (1962). The public interest in political ethics. In *The Public Interest* (C.J. Friedrich, ed.). New York, NY: Free Press, p. 44–53.

Chandler, R.C. (1982). The problems of moral illiteracy in professional discourse: The case of the state of principles of the american society for public administration. *American Review of Public Administration*, 16:369–386.

Chandler, R.C. (1983). The problem of moral reasoning in American public administration: The case for a code of ethics. *Public Administration Review*, 43:32–39.

Chandler, R.C. (1989). A guide to ethics for public servants. In *Handbook of Public Administration* (J.L. Perry, ed.). San Francisco, CA: Jossey Bass, p. 602–618.

Chandler, R.C. (1991). Summary and Synthesis. Conference on the Study of Government Ethics, Park City, UT, Mimeo.

Charles, R.A. and Cagle, M.C. (1997). Ethical codes with teeth: Professional practices commissions. *Public Integrity Annual*, 85–94.

Chiampou, K.M. (1992). Environmental Public Policy and the NAEP Code of Ethics. *Journal of Environmental Regulation*, 1:291–296.

Common Cause, A Model Ethics Law for State Government. (1989). Washington, D.C.

Cooper, T.L. (1990). *The Responsible Administrator*, (3rd. ed.). San Francisco, CA: Jossey-Bass.

Cooper, T.L. (1994). The emergence of administrative ethics as a field of study in the United States. In *Handbook of Administrative Ethics* (T.L. Cooper, ed.). New York, NY: Marcel Dekker, Inc., p. 3–30.

Cooper, T.L., and Wright, N.D. (1992). *Exemplary Public Administrators: Character and Leadership in Government*. San Francisco, CA: Jossey-Bass.

Cowan Commission. (1989). Ethics and Excellence in Government. Los Angeles, CA.

Davis, M. (1991). Thinking like an engineer: The place of a code of ethics in the practice of a profession. *Philosophy & Public Affairs*, 20:150–167.

Dean, P.J. (1992). Making codes of ethics "real." *Journal of Business Ethics*, 11(4):285–290.

Deming, R. (1987). I'm manager's Manager. Public Management, 9(July):2.

Denhardt, K.G. (1988). *The Ethics of Public Service* New York, NY: Greenwood Press.

Dobel, J.P. (1993). The realpolitik of ethics codes: An implementation approach to public ethics. In *Ethics and Public Administration*, (Frederickson, H.G., ed.). Armonk, NY: M.E. Sharpe.

Donabedian, B. (1993). Accounting self-regulation and the enforcement of professional codes. *Journal of Accounting & Public Policy*, 12:87–112.

Finer, H. (1941). Administrative responsibility in democratic government. *Public Administration Review*, 1:335–350.

Fischer, F. (1983). Ethical discourse in public administration. *Administration and Society*, 1(2):5–42.

Foster, G.D. (1981). Law, morality and the public servant. *Public Administration Review*, 41:29–33.

Fox, C.J. (1992). Pragmatism and Power: The Philosophy That Can't Say No. Paper presented to the Annual Conference of the American Society for Public Administration, Chicago, April 15.

Frederickson, H.G. (1989). *Ideal and Practice in Council-Manager Government*. Washington: International City Management Association.

Frederickson, H.G., ed. (1993). *Ethics and Public Administration*. Armonk, NY: M. E. Sharpe.

Freedman, B. (1978). A meta-ethics for professional morality. *Ethics*, 89:1–19.

Gabris, G.T. (1991). Beyond conventional management practices: Shifting organizational values. In *Ethical Frontiers in Public Management* (J.S. Bowman, ed.). San Francisco, CA: Jossey-Bass, p. 205–224.

Gawthrop, L. (1984). *Public Sector Management, Systems, and Ethics*. Bloomington, IN: Indiana University Press.

Gewirth, A. (1989). Professional ethics: The separatist thesis. *Ethics*, 96:282–300.

Gilman, S.C. (1991). The U.S. Office of Government Ethics. *The Bureaucrat*, 20:13–16.

Gortner, H.F. (1991a). *Ethics for Public Managers*. New York, NY: Praeger.

Gortner, H.F. (1991b). How public managers view their environment: Balancing organizational demands, political realities, and personal values. In *Ethical Frontiers in Public* Management, (J.S. Bowman, ed.). San Francisco, CA: Jossey-Bass, p. 34–63.

Gortner, H.F. and Plant, J.F. (1990). Ethics and Public Personnel Administration. In *Public Personnel Administration: Problems and Prospects*, 2d ed., (S.W. Hays and R.C. Kearney, eds.). Englewood Cliffs, NJ: Prentice-Hall, p. 243–260.

Gove, P.B., editor-in-chief (1961). *Webster's Third New International Dictionary of the English Language, Unabridged*. Springfield, MA: G & C Merriam Company.

Graham, G. (1974). Ethical guidelines for public administrators. *Public Administration Review*, 34: 90–93.

Griffith, E.S. (1962). The ethical foundations of the public interest. In *The Public Interest*, (C.J. Friedrich, ed.). New York, NY: Free Press.

Harmon, M., and Mayer, R. (1986). *Organization Theory for Public Administration*. Boston, MA: Little, Brown.

Harrington, S.J. (1996). The effect of codes of ethics and personal denial of responsibility on computer abuse judgments and intentions. *MIS Quarterly*, 20:257–278.

Hart, D.K. (1983). The honorable bureaucrat among the Philistines: A reply to "Ethical Discourse in Public Administration." *Administration and Society*, 15:43–48.

Hart, D.K. (1992). The moral exemplar in organizational society. In *Exemplary Public Administrators: Character and Leadership in Government*, (T.L. Cooper and N.D. Wright, eds.). San Francisco, CA: Jossey-Bass, p. 9–29.

Hart, D.K. and Wasden, C.D. (1990). Two roads diverged in a yellow wood: Public administration, the management orthodoxy, and civic humanism. *International Journal of Public Administration*, 13:747–775.

Hays, S.W. and Glessner, R.R. (1981). Codes of ethics in state government: A nationwide survey. *Public Personnel and Management Journal*, 10:48–55.

Hejka-Ekins, A. (1988). Teaching ethics in public administration. *Public Administration Review*, 48:885–891.

Hirschman, A. (1970). *Exit, Voice, and Loyalty*. Cambridge, MA: Harvard U. Press.

Howe, E. and Kaufman, J. (1979). The ethics of contemporary American Planners. *Journal of the American Planning Association*, 45:243–255.

Hudson Institute. (1990). The Value of Associations in American Society. Washington, D.C.: American Society of Association Executives.

International City Management Association. (1990a). ICMA Fact Sheet.

International City Management Association. (1990b). Response to Ethics Survey. Report of the ICMA Ethics Workshop, 1991.

International City/County Management Association. (1998). ICMA Code of ethics with guidelines. Washington, DC: International City/County Management Association.

Jamal, K. and Bowie, N.B. (1995). Theoretical consideration for a meaningful code of professional ethics. *Journal of Business Ethics*, 14:703–714.

Jos, P.H. (1995). Administrative practice and the waning promise of professionalism for public administration. *American Review of Public Administration*, 25:207–229.

Josephson Institute. (1990). *Preserving the Public Trust: Principles of Public Service Ethics, Standards of Conduct and Guidelines for Government Decisionmaking*. Marina Del Rey, CA: Josephson Institute.

Josephson, M. (1991). Politics in the year 2000. *Ethics: Easier Said Than Done*, 13/14: 78–80.

Karl, B.D. (1963). *Executive Reorganization and Reform in the New Deal: The Genesis of Administrative Management, 1900–1939*. Chicago, IL: University of Chicago Press.

Kaufman, J.L. (1981). Ethics and planning: some insights from the outside. *Journal of the American Planning Association*, 47(2):196–199.

Kaye, B.N. (1992). Codes of ethics in Australian business corporations. *Journal of Business Ethics*, 11:857–862.

Kernaghan, K. (1974). Codes of ethics and administrative responsibility. *Canadian Journal of Public Administration*, 1(7):524–541.

Kernaghan, K. (1993). Promoting public service ethics: The codification option. In *Ethics in Public Service*, (R. Chapman, ed.). Edinburgh, UK: University Press, p. 15–31.

Landry, T.L. (1997). Ethics code: A public policy exception to employment at will. *Ohio CPA Journal*, 56:36–38.

Lee, D.S. (1990). The difficulty with ethics education in public administration. *International Journal of Public Administration*, 13:181–205.

L'Etang, J. (1992). A Kantian Approach to Codes of Ethics. *Journal of Business Ethics*, 11:737–744.

Lewis, G.B. (1990). In search of the Machiavellian milquetoasts: Comparing attitudes of bureaucrats and ordinary people. *Public Administration Review*, 50:220–227.

Lewis, C.W. (1991). *The Ethics Challenge in Public Service: A Problem Solving Guide*. San Francisco, CA: Jossey-Bass.

Lewis, C.W., and Gilman, S.C. (1991). Ethics Codes and Ethics Agencies: Emerging Trends. Conference papers of the Conference on the Study of Government Ethics, Park City, UT, June 12–15.

Leys, W.A.R. (1968). *Ethics for Policy Decisions: The Art of Asking Deliberative Questions*. Westport, CT: Greenwood Press.

Lilla, M.T. (1981). Ethos, "Ethics," and Public Service. *The Public Interest*, 63:3–17.

Long, N. (1976). The Three Citizenships. *Publius*, 6:13–32.

Madsen, P., and Shafritz, J.M. (1992). *Essentials of Government Ethics*. New York, NY: Meridian Books.

Marcuse, P. (1976). Professional ethics and beyond: Values in planning. *Journal of the American Institute of Planners*, 42:264–273.

Menzel, D.C. (1992). Ethics attitudes and behaviors in local governments: an empirical analysis. *State and Local Government Review*, 24:94–102.

Menzel, D.C. (1997). Teaching ethics and values in public administration: Are we making a difference? *Public Administration Review*, 57:224–230.

Menzel, D.C. and Carson, K. (1998). Empirical Research on Public Administration Ethics: A Review and Assessment. Paper delivered to the 59th Conference of the American Society for Public Administration, Seattle, May.

Montoya, I.D. (1994). A comparative study of codes of ethics in health care facilities and energy companies. *Journal of Business Ethics*, 13:713–717.

Mosher, F.C. (1968). *Democracy and the Public Service*. New York, NY: Oxford U. Press.

Mount, E. Jr. (1990). *Professional Ethics in Context, Institutions, Images, and EmRathy*. Westminster: J. Knox Press.

National Academy of Public Administration. (1974). *Watergate: Implications for Responsible Government*. New York, NY: Basic Books.

National Municipal League. (1979). Model State Conflict of Interest and Financial Disclosure Law.

Newland, C. (1984). *Public Administration and Community: Realism in the Practice of Ideals*. Washington, D.C.: Public Administration Service.

Overman, E.S., and Foss, L. (1991). Professional ethics: An empirical test of the "Separatist Thesis." *Journal of Public Administration Research and Theory*, 1:131–146.

Plant, J.F. (1988). The use of quantitative analysis in the public sector. In *Ethics Government, and Public Policy* (J.S. Bowman and F. Elliston, eds.). New York, NY: Greenwood Press, p. 247–265.

Plant, J.F. (1991). Public Official Associations and Codes of Ethics. Conference paper, Conference on the Study of Government Ethics, Park City, Utah, June 13.

Plant, J.F., and Gortner, H.F. (1981). Ethics, personnel management, and civil service reform. *Public Personnel Management Journal*, 10:3–10.

President's Commission on Federal Ethics Law Reform. (1990). *To Serve With Honor: Report and Recommendations*. Washington, D.C.: Government Printing Office.

Pugh, D.L. (1989). Professionalism in public administration: Problems, perspectives, and the role of ASPA. *Public Administration Review*, 49:1–8.

Pugh, D.L. (1991). The origins of ethical frameworks in public *administration*. In *Ethical Frontiers in Public Management*, (J.S. Bowman, ed.). San Francisco, CA: Jossey-Bass, p. 9–33.

Rohr, J.A. (1976). The study of ethics in the public administration curriculum. *Public Administration Review*, 36:398–406.

Rohr, J.A. (1978). *Ethics for Bureaucrats*, New York, NY: Marcel Dekker.

Rohr, J.A. (1985). Professionalism, legitimacy, and the constitution. *Public Administration Quarterly*, 5:461–486.

Rohr, J.A. (1986). *To Run a Constitution: legitimacy and the Administrative State*. Lawrence, Kansas: University Press of Kansas.

Rohr, J.A. (1990). Ethics in public administration: A state-of-the-discipline report. In *Public Administration: The State of the Discipline*, (N.B. Lynn and A. Wildavsky, eds.). Chatham, NJ: Chatham House, p. 97–123.

Rohr, J.A. (1991). Keynote Address to the Conference on the Study of Government Ethics, Park City, UT, June 12.

Rosenbloom, D.H. (1992). The constitution as a basis for public administration ethics. In *Essentials of Government Ethics* (P. Madsen and J.M. Shafritz, eds.). New York, NY: Meridian Books, p. 48–64.

Slater, D. (1983). Ethical Responsibilities of Professional Societies: Planners and Managers. Paper presented to the Annual Conference of the American Society for Public Administration, New York City, April.

State Historical Society of Iowa. (1987). Work rules effective 2 November 1987 (mimeo).

Stewart, D. (1985). Ethics and the profession of public administration: The moral responsibility of individuals in public sector organizations. *Public Administration Quarterly*, 8:487–495.

Stillman, R.J., II (1974). The rise of the city manager: A public professional in local government. Albuquerque, NM: University of New Mexico Press.

Truelson, J.A. (1991). New strategies for institutional controls. In *Ethical Frontiers of Public Management*, (J.S. Bowman, ed.). San Francisco, CA: Jossey-Bass.

U.S. Congress. (1958). Codes of Ethics for Government Services: Concurrent Resolution of the U.S. Congress 85th Congress, 2d sess.

Van Wart, M. (1996). The sources of ethical decision making for individuals in the public sector. *Public Administration Review*, 56:525–533.

Ventriss, C. (1989). Toward a public philosophy of public administration: A civic perspective of the public. *Public Administration Review*, 49:173–179.

Wakefield, S. (1976). Ethics and the public service: A case for individual responsibility. *Public Administration Review*, 36:661–666.

Walter, J.J. (1981). The Ethics in Government Act, conflict of interest laws, and presidential recruiting. *Public Administration Review*, 41:659–665.

Warwick, D.P. (1980). *The Teaching of Ethics in the Social Sciences*. Tarrytown, NY: Hastings Center.

Yarwood, D. (1985). The ethical world of organizational professionals and scientists. *Public Administration Quarterly*. 6:461–486.

16

From Codes of Conduct to Codes of Ethics
The ASPA Case

James S. Bowman
Florida State University, Tallahassee, Florida

I. INTRODUCTION

Peering into the 21st century, it is clear that ethics will continue to be one of the principle public policy issues of contemporary times—and not without reason. Yet if the scandals of the post-Watergate era exposed weaknesses in ethical behavior, they also revealed strength. People may have lost confidence in the way the political system is operated, but surveys show that they have not lost faith in the system itself (Zajac, 1997). Nonetheless, the putative failure to meet the special ethical demands of the public sector has fed anti-government sentiment, led to downsizing, and fueled the drive toward reform.

While much of this activity reflects a fundamental precept of American political ideology—the mistrust of power—citizens seem to be requiring that officials live up to the ideals of public service. People have shown an increased intolerance of the notion that everything in government—agencies, legislatures, the White House itself—is up for sale: be it influence-peddling, embezzlement, the Lincoln bedroom, or campaign contributions. "Accountability," "performance management," and "reinvention" have become buzzwords, sometimes encased in legislation, in an effort to promote integrity. In fact, written ethical standards—long seen as key to encouraging right behavior—are an integral part of such attempts, most notably the 1991 Federal Sentencing Guidelines that mandate their use in government and business (Ferrell et al., 1998).

This chapter shows how public service canons may be evolving from an emphasis on regulatory, compliance codes of conduct to developmental, reflective codes of ethics. The initial section briefly reviews the history of public sector codes, their strengths and weaknesses, and how they have been informed by two competing philosophies. The central portion builds upon these two theories by probing the dimensions of a professional ethos and the critical role that a code holds in that approach. To demonstrate the utility of the ethos, a newly-promulgated standard is examined and applied to a management case; this is followed by a discussion of the roles a professional association can play to promote ethical conduct. The penultimate section builds upon that analysis by exploring ways to cultivate a professional ethos. The chapter concludes with implications for theory and practice.

II. BACKGROUND

Both the oldest and newest codes in American public administration were developed by professional groups—the International City/County Management Association in 1924 (modestly amended in 1998) and the American Society for Public Administration in 1984 (reformulated in 1994). As discussed in the previous chapter, within government itself a variety of activities have taken place at the federal level; notably, during the last half century most states and many local governments (in the wake of Watergate) adopted standards of their own. None of these public administration initiatives unify the field to the extent that the Hippocratic Oath seems to do for medicine. However, while codes are not everything, they are decidedly more than nothing (Lewis, 1991: 140). Like a marriage vow, they will not prevent sickness and death, corruption and wrongdoing, but they can transform the context within which these events occur. By providing a basis for personal and public expectations, they offer perspective—a way of thinking when confronting dilemmas of public service. The real question is not so much whether codes *qua* codes are effective, but rather how they are developed and what accompanies them.

Two traditions, first reflected in the landmark Freidrich-Finer debate over 50 years ago, have informed the development of ethical standards in public administration (Pugh, 1991). The bureaucratic ethos (which includes efficiency, efficacy, expertise, loyalty, and accountability) is grounded in Weber's model of bureaucracy, Wilson's politics-administration dichotomy, and Taylor's scientific management. The democratic ethos (which embraces regime values, citizenship, the public interest, and social equity) is based on Rohr's constitutional values, Cooper's responsible administrator, Lippman's public interest, and Rawl's social equity.

The dominant bureaucratic approach focuses on mechanisms of external control, the moral minimum. Laws, rules, and regulatory codes of conduct detail what a public servant must do to avoid punishment and stay out of trouble. Florida's code, for instance, includes multiple subjects (e.g., financial disclosure, gifts, adverse personnel actions, investigatory procedures, prohibitions and penalties, and additional requirements) in 30 pages of double-column, single-spaced text in the state's statutes; a comparable, if less complex, local government example is shown in Table 1. A negative ethic based on criminal law, this tradition emphasizes conformity to standards; a code is typically used in a reactive manner to order and evaluate behaviors by stipulating a basis for detection and discipline.

In contrast, the democratic, developmental approach relies on cultivating internal controls, the moral maximum. It is concerned not only with adherence to law, but also the protection and advancement of the public interest. As illustrated by aspirational codes of ethics (Table 2), the emphasis is on the cultivation of virtues, integrity, and character. A positive, idealistic ethic, it seeks to enable responsible conduct; the public servant is not seen as a bureaucratic functionary, but rather as a moral agent capable of transcending particular interests in pursuit of the larger social good. When used proactively, such a code serves as a standard to foster awareness, education, and decision-making.

Jay Black (1995:30) describes the significant differences between these two approaches and their conception of human nature.

Table 1 Regulatory Code: City of Carbondale, Illinois (excerpts)

Pecuniary Interests in Contracts

(b) Any elected or appointed member of the governing body and any person serving on a municipal advisory panel or commission or nongoverning board or commission may, however, provide materials, merchandise, property, services, or labor, if:

(1) the contract is with a person, firm, partnership, association, corporation, or cooperative association in which the interested member of the governing body of the municipality or advisory panel or commission member has less than a 7 1/2% share in the ownership;

(2) in the case of an elected or appointed member of the governing body, the interested member publicly discloses the nature and extent of the interest before or during deliberations concerning the proposed award of the contract;

(3) in the case of an elected or appointed member of the governing body, the interested member abstains from voting on the award of the contract (though the member shall be considered present for the purposes of establishing a quorum);

(4) the contract is approved by a majority vote of those members presently holding office;

(5) the contract is awarded after sealed bids to the lowest responsible bidder if the amount of the contract exceeds $1500 (but the contract may be awarded without bidding if the amount is less than $1500); and

(6) the award of the contract would not cause the aggregate amount of all contracts so awarded to the same person, firm, association, partnership, corporation, or cooperative association in the same fiscal year to exceed $25,000.

(c) In addition to the exemption in subsection (b), an elected or appointed member of the governing body and any person serving on a municipal advisory panel or commission may provide materials, merchandise, property, services, or labor if:

(1) the award of the contract is approved by a majority vote of the governing body of the municipality (provided that, in the case of an elected or appointed member of the governing body, the interested member shall abstain from voting);

(2) the amount of the contract does not exceed $2000;

(3) the award of the contract would not cause the aggregate amount of all contracts so awarded to the same person, firm, association, partnership, corporation, or cooperative association in the same fiscal year to exceed $4000;

(4) in the case of an elected or appointed member of the governing body, the interested member publicly discloses the nature and extent of his interest before or during deliberations concerning the proposed award of the contract; and

(5) in the case of an elected or appointed member of the governing body, the interested member abstains from voting on the award of the contract (though the member shall be considered present for the purposes of establishing a quorum).

(d) A contract for the procurement of public utility services by a municipality with a public utility company is not barred by this Section by one or more members of the governing body being an officer or employee of the public utility company, or holding an ownership interest in no more than 7 1/2% in the public utility company, or holding an ownership interest of any size if the municipality has a population of less than 7500 and the public utility's rates are approved by the Illinois Commerce Commission. An elected or appointed member of the governing body or a nongoverning board or commission having an interest described in this subsection (d) does not have a prohibited interest under this Section.

(e) Nothing contained in this Section, including the restrictions set forth in subsections (b), (c), and (d), shall preclude a contract of deposit of moneys, loans, or other financial services by a municipality with a local bank or local savings and loan association, regardless of whether a member of the governing body or a nongoverning board or commission of the municipality is interested in the bank or saving and loan association as an officer or employee or as a holder of less than 7 1/2% of the total ownership interest. A member holding an interest described in this subsection (e) in a contract does not hold a prohibited interest for purposes of this Ad. The interested member of the governing body or a nongoverning board or commission must publicly state the nature and extent of the interest during deliberations concerning the proposed award of the contract but shall not participate in any further deliberations concerning the proposed award. The interested member shall not vote on the proposed award. A member abstaining from participation in deliberations and voting under this Section may be considered present for purposes of establishing a quorum. Award of the contract shall require approval by a majority vote of those members presently holding office. Consideration and award of a contract in which a member is interested may only be made at a regularly scheduled public meeting of the governing body of the municipality.

Source: Center for Personnel Research (1996: 15 16).

Table 2   An Aspirational Code (The Athenian Oath)

We will ever strive for the ideals and sacred things of the city, both alone and with many; we will unceasingly seek to quicken the sense of public duty; we will revere and obey the city's laws; we will leave this city not only not less, but greater, better, and more beautiful than it was given to us.

> The first . . . seems to reflect a world of neurosis if not outright paranoia. The fundamental assumption appears to be that people are inherently flawed, and morally primitive; that they have inadequate independent judgment and a need to be led by authority figures through the decision-making process; that they respond to threats and fear of punishment; that their natural inclination is to take advantage of any and all opportunities to abuse others and misuse their power.

> [The second] . . . reflect(s) a quite different universe. The lofty and abstract standards set down in them indicate a faith in one's fellow beings, a recognition that inherently decent people are trying to do better, a sense that gentle reminders of our lofty goals are more effective means of achieving an ethical society than are base-level, punishment-oriented rules and guidelines. Finally, (these) codes admit to our imperfections, and generally offer positive "thou shalt" suggestions that will make the world a better place in which to live.

Both the bureaucratic ethos of minimal expectations and external controls, as well as the democratic ethos of maximum expectations and internal controls, are subject to deficiencies, most notably in the area of compliance. Such problems occur for two reasons, intrinsic and extrinsic (Brien, 1996: 22–23). Intrinsic factors pertain to the features of the measure itself as it can be suffocated by detail (regulatory conduct codes) or trivialized by vagueness (aspirational ethics codes). Either way, such documents may lack internal authority. Extrinsic factors are evident when there is inadequate socialization and institutionalization of code values. Leaders and employees may not genuinely believe that the standard embodies concerns important to their duties and it may not be part of the organizational infrastructure. In short, codes can be rendered ineffective either because they are poorly designed and/or badly implemented.

For these reasons, published ethical precepts are often problematic. While couched in the language of high principle, they either reduced complicated problems to a set of rigid, narrowly-circumscribed behaviors based on the lowest common denominator or are written at such a high level of abstraction as to have little practical value. Charles Levy's harsh judgment of codes as "unrealistic, unimpressive, and widely unknown or ignored guides to wishful thinking" (quoted in Vogelsang-Coombs and Bakken, 1988:85) remains a widely-held critique applicable to those based on either ethos.

It follows that empirical evidence reveals that codes are seldom used in decision-making, are not often a subject of discussion, and are not always taken seriously by top management (e.g., Bowman, 1990). Indeed, not only do bureaucratic outnumber democratic approaches, but a majority of managers report that their agencies have no consistent approach whatsoever to ethics. Stated differently, although there is no lack of argument over codes, codism appears to prevail. To avoid this fate, a dialectical process can produce a synthesis of the bureaucratic and democratic ethos: the professional ethos.

III. PROFESSIONAL ETHOS

Professional administrators, as discussed below, are coming to recognize that the development of an operational system of public service ethics necessitates the reconciliation of the bureaucratic and democratic ethos.[1] The nub of the problem is this: the bureaucratic model contracts moral responsibility (by limiting it to one's position in the hierarchy), whereas the democratic model expands it (by placing an enormous burden on the individual to master political philosophy). If the former definition of responsibility is too crabbed, then the latter conception, however laudable, is too ambitious. It follows that a third premise for public service ethics—a professional ethos—warrants exploration. The development of professional excellence is at least as important as an understanding of bureaucratic and democratic ethos; indeed, it is informed by them. This section will briefly examine the classic attributes of a profession, provide a definition of a *compleat* professional, and explore two key dimensions of the professional ethos.

A. Attributes of a Profession

A series of well-known traits (specialized competency; autonomous exercise of this competence; commitment to a career in this competency as well as a service orientation, professional association, and an ethical standard to encourage competency) are central to a professional ethos. In fact, adoption of a code is an external hallmark testifying to the claim that the group recognizes societal obligations that transcend self-interest. Yet if it is to be assumed that a credo should guide (if not govern) professional life, ethical requirements often represent the weakest link among all the characteristics noted (Pugh, 1991: 9).

In the federal government, for instance, the existence of the 1958 Code of Ethics for Government Service brought no mention during the long Watergate inquiry in the 1970s.[2] Indeed, few Congressional offices displayed it and it is likely that a large majority of the federal work force was not aware of the dictum; this included personnel in the Office of Personnel Management responsible for dealing with employee grievances, as well as representatives of relevant public interest groups (Bowman, 1981). A 1979 effort to have it posted in government offices was unsuccessful partly because only eleven copies were available in the entire federal establishment; even the United States Supreme Court had difficulty obtaining a copy of the document to hang in its chambers. In 1980 a law was passed to reprint, distribute, and post the code. More recently, as noted earlier, several empirical studies in the early 1990s revealed that codes were of little consequence to public servants in their work (e.g., Gortner, 1991; cf., Rowe and Hug, 1990).

B. The Complete Professional

An important reason for this state of affairs is that the field, seduced by the bureaucratic ethos and overwhelmed the democratic ethos, has focused on instrumental values over substantive values—the triumph of technique over purpose. Yet since ethical concerns are the soul of modern public administration (Frederickson, 1997), the compleat professional requires more than mere technical skill. He or she is not simply a professional because of expertise, but also because of adherence to high moral standards.

It follows that with power comes responsibility; *ought* implies *can* for that is what moral responsibility means. The scandals of the 1990s offer an opportunity to examine the norms of the profession and to rediscover an authentic professional ethos. The classical definition and vow of a professional demands both technical ability and moral character. Competence is not an end in itself, but refers to the capacity to realize particular values; being competent is not the same as having competencies (MacLagan, 1998: 175–176).

When someone is recognized as a "real professional," it is acknowledged that he or she has something to profess and the skill with which to do so. He or she is admired not only because the person knows what to do, but also why it must be done. "We do not expect professionals simply to act in a particular way, we also expect them to *be* a particular kind of person" (Gellerman et al., 1990: 8; original emphasis). Technical and moral accountability is inherent in the work; it is an obligation as well as a duty of a high and noble calling. As symbolized by the oath of office, such an ethos places professionals in a leadership position to renew the foundations of trust in democracy.

C. Dimensions of the Ethos

The professional ethos has two features: the internal, which has its roots in each individual professional, and the external in the credo of a professional organization (Newton, 1981: 45–46). Taken alone, neither personal conscience nor professional code is sufficient as an ethic. The internal is apt to be a set of competing, individual feelings, whereas the external may be consensual, but not necessarily compelling, collective statements. Indeed, the initially inchoate moral nature of the internal dimension is an important reason that led practitioners to create a profession.

And the two dimensions work together uneasily since the essence of conscience is to resist a priori rules, which is precisely what codes aim at doing. However, a profession must develop a code for the simple reason that its competence, which cannot be readily evaluated by the laity, requires that its exercise be evaluated by those qualified to do it. Thus it falls to the profession to define standards of ethical behavior. "The articulation of the professional ethos," Lisa Newton observes, "is what makes a profession a moral enterprise and distinguishes it from any other job category" (1981: 50). Codes provide a basis for, a codification of, professional responsibility. This articulation, in dialectical fashion, likely will inform and test personal conscience which in turn will lead to a dialogue about the code, a process that is the crux of the professional ethos.

Such a process is difficult in a secondary, "umbrella" profession like public administration not only because it consists of a multiplicity of primary professions (e.g., engineering, military, accounting, medicine, law), but also because it is but one of many political actors and influences affecting the profession. Thus, for instance:

> The passage of the 1883 Pendleton Act (which abolished the spoils system and established the merit system), the embrace of Woodrow Wilson's "politics/administration dichotomy," and the subsequent adoption of scientific management firmly established a nonpartisan civil service based on merit. Public servants were responsible for the execution of policy and were not expected to exercise discretion in decision making; ethics was a product of rules and regulations, not necessarily of professional judgment. Although World War II, Vietnam, and Watergate all called this view into question, the neutrality of the civil service remained a powerful force in government. Ethical concerns, while important, could be regarded as an administrative matter as virtuous

conduct was to be achieved by procedural reforms in the merit system (Bowman, 1998: 159–160).

Although there are interesting differences in emphasis, the resulting codes historically focused on efficiency, economy, and administrative principles at the expense of justice, equity, and the public interest (Chandler, 1983). Following the bureaucratic ethos and the politics-administration dichotomy, it seemed to be moral to avoid morality.

In summary, by building upon the traditional attributes of a profession, as well as the classical meaning of the professional role and the internal-external dynamic of the professional ethos, it becomes possible to discern an ethic that bridges the bureaucratic ethos and the democratic ethos and the challenges that it confronts. This is illustrated by the newly-revised code of the American Society for Public Administration (ASPA).

IV. THE ASPA CODE

Since a standard of technical and ethical practice is inherent in the very concept of professional life, an association of professionals is well-positioned to develop the implications of that conception. Acting alone, the success of individual managers will be limited, in part, by the fact that administrators do not show the same understanding of their place in the public sector as, for instance, lawyers (Martinez, 1998: 705). Further, the departments for which they work, whatever their administrative powers, most often have an inconsistent passive and/or reactive approach to ethics or no strategy at all (Bowman, 1990; Bowman and Williams, 1997). Indeed, improvement often originates in forces external to organizations. Yet in American government, neither lawmakers nor professional schools are likely to fulfill this role. The former are captivated by the bureaucratic ethos and the latter reach small percentage of public administrators.

Taken together, professional organizations represent a wide variety of highly-trained personnel and as such have the potential to capitalize on powerful human impulses for moral thought and action (Wilson, 1993). Their codes articulate implicit expectations and standards otherwise left unspoken and uncritically accepted. It is well-known, in fact, that executives regard codes as the most valuable way to promote ethics, perhaps because they are seen as an important indicator of professionalism. Only three percent of public administrators are satisfied that, ''there is no real need for codes of ethics in work organizations'' (Bowman and Williams, 1997: 54). There is little dispute, then, that codes meet a perceived demand. This section examines the ASPA code by reviewing perceptual data on its use, interpreting a case study, and discussing various roles that a professional association can perform to nourish ethics.

A. Code Utility

In 1984, ASPA adopted a 12-point code of ethics (complemented by a set of detailed guidelines in 1985) which was subsequently revamped into five overarching principles in late 1994 (Table 3).[3] While the former reflected the bureaucratic ethos by emphasing efficiency and economy (e.g., Pugh, 1991; Vogelsang-Coombs and Bakken, 1988), the latter manifests a professional ethos by focusing on administrative discretion in decision-making and excellence in public service (Van Wart, 1996). Survey data from ASPA prac-

Table 3 1994 ASPA Code

The American Society for Public Administration (ASPA) exists to advance the science, processes, and art of public administration. The Society affirms its responsibility to develop the spirit of professionalism within its membership, and to increase public awareness of ethical principles in public service by its example. To this end, we, the members of the Society, commit ourselves to the following principles:

1. Serve the Public Interest
2. Respect the Constitution and the Law
3. Demonstrate Personal Integrity
4. Promote Ethical Organizations
5. Strive for Professional Excellence

Principles

1. **Serve the Public Interest**
   Service to the public is beyond service to oneself. ASPA members are committed to:
   1. Exercise discretionary authority to promote the public interest.
   2. Oppose all forms of discrimination and harassment, and promote affirmative action
   3. Recognize and support the public's right to know the public's business.
   4. Involve citizens in policy decision making.
   5. Exercise compassion, benevolence, fairness, and optimism.
   6. Respond to the public in ways that are complete, clear, and easy to understand.
   7. Assist citizens in their dealings with government.
   8. Be prepared to make decisions that may not be popular.

2. **Respect the Constitution and the Law**
   Respect, support, and study federal and state constitutions and laws that define responsibilities of public agencies, employees, and all citizens. ASPA members are committed to:
   1. Study and work within authorizing legislation and regulations as established.
   2. Work to improve and change laws and policies that are counterproductive or obsolete.
   3. Eliminate unlawful discrimination.
   4. Prevent all forms of mismanagement of public funds by supporting audits, investigative activities, and establishing and maintaining strong fiscal and management controls.
   5. Respect and protect privileged information.
   6. Encourage, protect and facilitate whistle-blowing and other legitimate dissent activities in government.
   7. Promote constitution principles of equality, fairness, and due process.

3. **Demonstrate Personal Integrity**
   Demonstrate the highest standards in all activities to inspire public confidence and trust in public service. ASPA members are committed to:
   1. Maintain truthfulness and honesty and to not compromise them for advancement, honor, or personal gain.
   2. Ensure that others receive credit for their work and contributions.
   3. Zealously guard against conflict of interest or its appearance: e.g., nepotism, improper outside employment, misuse of public resources or the acceptance of gifts.
   4. Respect superiors, subordinates, colleagues, and the public.
   5. Take responsibility for their own errors.
   6. Behave in ways that do not suggest that official acts are driven by partisanship.

4. **Promote Ethical Organizations**
   Strengthen organizational capabilities to apply ethics, efficiency, and effectiveness to service to the public. ASPA members are committed to:
   1. Approach all duties with open communication, creativity, and dedication.
   2. Institutional loyalty not preceding the public interest.
   3. Establish procedures that promote ethical behavior and hold individuals and organizations accountable for their conduct.
   4. Provide a formal means of dissent and safeguards against reprisal.
   5. Merit employment that protects against arbitrary and capricious actions.
   6. Organizational controls that encourage and promote accountability.
   7. Encourage organizations to adopt, distribute, and periodically review a code of ethics as a living document.

5. **Strive for Professional Excellence**
   Strengthen individual capabilities and encourage the professional development of others. ASPA members are committed to:
   1. Provide support and encouragement to upgrade competence.
   2. Accept as a personal duty the responsibility to keep up to date on emerging issues and potential problems.
   3. Encourage others, throughout their careers, to participate in professional activities and associations.
   4. Allocate time to meet with students and provide a bridge between classroom studies and the realities of public service.

Source: American Society for Public Administration, Washington, D.C.

titioner members in 1989 (n = 441) and 1996 (n = 446), summarized in this section, cutlines the important attitudinal differences toward these old and new standards.[4]

Nearly eight of ten (79 percent) administrators claimed code familiarity in 1996 contrasted to 58 percent in 1989. Moreover, their degree of acquaintance surpassed that found earlier as most said they either "have a general familiarity" or "are quite familiar" with the code as opposed to indicating that "I have heard of it." These results indicate that the depth and breadth in awareness of the ASPA statement increased substantially in a short period of time. Perhaps this is partly due to the 1994 revision process and its frequent reprinting in *Public Administration Review*. No longer is a very large segment of the membership "either unaware or has but a passing acquaintance with" the code as reported in the previous study.

To be productive such a measure, arguably, should meet at least two criteria: acceptability and enforceability. Most administrators in 1996 (90 percent versus 70 percent in 1989) affirmed that the "code provides an appropriate set of standards" to guide public managers. There is, nonetheless, recognition that more tailored policies are needed for different workplaces. Thus some two-thirds in both surveys suggested that for the ASPA mandate to be truly effective, it "must be supplemented by an agency-specific code," a finding that suggests a possible role for the Society. The test of acceptability is, of course, whether or not the ideals embodied in the document are actually practiced. In another considerable shift, a total of 80 percent (69 percent in 1989) reported that they either "often" (65 percent versus 38 percent earlier) or "occasionally" (20 percent versus 34 percent previously) use the code and/or its principles on the job.

A 1996 open-ended question provided some depth to the findings as managers were asked to describe an ethical dilemma in their agency, and whether or not the code helped them; approximately one-half found it helpful and one-half did not. Among the former, most of the written comments focused on its value in providing a benchmark for interpreting the public interest, dealing with conflicts of interest, and coping with improper influences on decision-making by elected officials. Among the latter, administrators stated that: other standards were used; the ASPA document contained incompatible provisions; the credo did not deal with specific issues; or that it was not applicable because the respondent was caught in the middle with no authority to resolve the issue.

Most of the 1996 sample, in short, either often or occasionally used the code in their work. Further, nearly two thirds (65 percent) stated that it is used "fairly often by their agency in daily management," with another one-fifth (20 percent) saying "occasionally," 7 percent "seldom," and 5 percent "never." In stark contrast, almost two-thirds (65 percent) indicated in 1989 that the earlier code was "seldom" used (one-fourth "occasionally," and approximately one-tenth "often"; the "never" option did not appear previously).

Turning to enforceability, over 90 percent agreed that in order for the code to be given weight, it must first be taken seriously by top management—apparently something that is taking place in a number of agencies. Interestingly, in proportions similar to the earlier survey, a plurality (38 percent) endorsed giving ASPA power to enforce the measure (31 percent were undecided; 24 percent disapproved). Hesitancy on the part of members to do this may stem from questions about whether a general professional society has legitimacy to affect sanctions and whether they could be feasibly implemented.

To summarize, 1996 respondents had a substantial acquaintance with the ASPA ethics document. Not only that, but they and many of their agencies also use it in daily management. If one standard of an effective credo is acceptability, then the ASPA's code is well on its way to achieving that criterion.[5] Concerning enforceability, many recognize the features that such a statement should contain (such as congruence with employee values, confidential reporting mechanisms, and sanctions for noncompliance; data not reported above). Like the earlier study, however, the membership remains split over granting ASPA compliance power.

One way to interpret these findings is to recall the distinction between codes of conduct and codes of ethics made previously (Bruce, 1996). Rule-based conduct codes are most often found in statutes or executive orders. Directive and top-down in approach, they are typically imposed on (and often resented by) employees with no advice for effective implementation, training and development, or recognition of the importance of leadership modeling. Attempting to convert the realm of ethics into the realm of law, this coercive, quick-fix strategy usually reduces ethics to legalism by focusing on both the lowest common denominator and penalties for deviations. The strategy does little to promote a philosophy of excellence or to engender a sense of personal responsibility. Worse, it does not work. The incidence of problems is not significantly reduced (Bruce, 1996: 29; Paine, 1994). In contrast, codes of ethics demand more than simple compliance; they mandate the exercise of judgment and acceptance of responsibility for decisions rendered—the real work of ethics. Acknowledging the ambiguities and complexities of public service, ethics codes offer interpretative frameworks to clarify decision-making dilemmas.

The reluctance to grant genuine sanction authority may now be understood. Enforcement and sanctions emphasize avoidance of improper behavior—something already more than adequately covered in law—and, as such, fit snugly with an anti-government climate. Well aware of the drawbacks to conduct codes, survey respondents nonetheless provide widespread support for the ASPA ethics code. What is needed, the managers seem to say, is not more punitive minimalist ethics and the despair they tend to create.

The ASPA statement is one of the few attempts to reinforce the legitimacy of public administration, articulate government service as a public trust, and attend to the need to take administrative discretion seriously. Ethics, Richard Green (1994: 2142) writes, then becomes an ''integrative foundation for everything (managers) do and are,'' rather than a burdensome constraint. In short, the code provides positive moral authority. It clearly indicates the importance of the principles that it embodies. As such, the point is precisely not to levy discipline. An overwhelming majority of respondents, in fact, concur that the precepts—as now written—are appropriate and use its principles.

B. A Case Study

Ethical dilemmas in management are pervasive; both in appearance and reality, they are part of being a public servant. To illustrate the functional nature of the ASPA mandate, consider the 1996 survey responses to the following hypothetical, but realistic, downsizing scenario:

> Bob has heard from his manager that their organization's staff will be downsizing; it could be as little as 5 percent or as much as 30 percent. However, the supervisor told Bob that ''we're all under strict orders to keep it quiet'' so that the agency's best employees will not seek other jobs.
>
> Ron (one of the finest professionals in Bob's unit), upon hearing the downsizing rumors, told Bob that he was sure that he could get another job at a new business if a reduction in force occurred. However, their openings will close soon. Ron asked

Bob, "Will there by layoffs?" and "Should I get another job now?" Does the ASPA code assist you in thinking about this problem?
1 yes n = 231/54.4%   (No Answer n = 106/24.9%)
2 no n = 88/20.7%
Please explain your response:

Nearly three-fourths of the sample (74.9 percent) responded; 72 percent of those managers who responded agreed that the code assisted them, while the balance said it did not. Most explained their answer by commenting on how it either helped or did not help them to consider the broad issues raised and/or justify their solution to the case itself. The analysis below is facilitated by Kohlberg's (1981; also see Stewart and Sprinthall, this volume) well-known theory of moral development to explain differences in the way respondents react to the code.[6]

1. Code as Helpful

While the case was seen as an "interesting," "good," "tough," and "complex" dilemma by the managers, one opines that "it is important to pose these issues so that when situations arise, decision-makers can proceed against some background instead of in a vacuum" (an experienced administrator from the Northeast). In focusing on how the ASPA measure assisted them in thinking about the general problem, these observations were offered:

> The code addresses the responsibility of an employee as well as the organization to behave ethically (a division director in a large Wisconsin city).
>
> It helps me to think about my responsibilities to the organizations. But it doesn't help me to release the conflict between them and what seems to be unethical behavior on the organization's part. It's a dilemma—how to be ethical in an unethical environmental situation (a mental health services assistant director in a town near Chicago).
>
> It provides a checklist of obligations that should be considered in thinking about the problem. In ethical dilemmas, there is usually no singular, correct answer. Ethical decision-making often requires weighing several, sometimes contradicting principles (a department director in a California city).

The association's statement, in short, provides a starting place or springboard for pondering specific issues. As a senior advisor to a high U.S. Office of Personnel Management official notes, "I don't think that the code can (or should) focus on specific cases; however, it presents a conceptual framework for setting boundaries in ethical decisions." Thus, "although the code doesn't tell you how or what to answer, it gives you plenty of guidance as to how you can best handle the situation," according to a local official from Alabama.

The case, in other words, provides not only a test of the code's utility, but also a test of one's beliefs. It can assist in reflecting on the problem and, in so doing, the credo's guidance (combined with personal beliefs) can help to actually resolve it. Accordingly, many respondents found the standard to be practical in developing solutions to the case proper. "It allows you to do," said a division director in a department of Los Angeles city government, "what is right." But what is right? The sample had definite, but different, answers to this question.

For some, the employee should be told nothing since the measure requires that confidential information be respected and protected. "No comment," "I am not authorized to discuss rumors", "I am not in a position to confirm or deny", and "The decision is yours alone" are among the suitable responses for these administrators. "Bob is duly obligated,'' says a New York city public health director, ''to give an honest answer, which is, I don't know.'' A federal middle manager notes that:

> Section V of the code (accepting duty to keep up issues) prepares managers/professionals to counsel on overall societal trends. Section I (serving public interest) encourages serving beyond self and ''agency.'' The correct response is to say ''I don't know what level of reduction may happen, but some is inevitable. Ron, you must take personal responsibility for the choice. There are no guarantees, no easy personal decisions, in such matters.''

In brief, these officials (about one quarter of those who tackled the case) exemplify Kohlberg's stage four: the appropriate approach is to follow orders and say as little as possible.

For others (some 25 percent), the answer to the dilemma was also straightforward: the employee should be told everything.

> ASPA's code essentially reflects that managers and agency employees should deal with each other openly and fairly. This type of information should not be withheld from subordinates for any purpose, especially organizational convenience or expediency (a state of Alabama department director).
>
> Yes, Duh! (The code helps; tell him what you know.) See sections 1(3) (right to know) and 4(1) (open communication). This is not privileged information (Section 2[5]) (a West Virginia correctional institutional manager).
>
> Sections 1 (Serve the Public Interest), 3 (Demonstrate Personal Integrity), and 5 (Strive for Professional Excellence) all have relevance; if you can't keep your best people unless you lie, you don't deserve them (a program officer, U.S. Department of State).

These administrators, then, believe that the bottom line is unambiguous truth telling; people's needs must be put ahead of organizational needs. If an agency cannot or will not be fair, open, and democratic and since employees outnumber executives, then individual rights prevail *à la* Kohlberg's stage five.

Finally, still other managers (approximately 50 percent) sought a win/win solution by weighing conflicting elements in the code; such creativity, when based on ethical values, is illustrative of Kohlberg's stage six. For them, it is possible to respect privileged information while simultaneously respecting employees. Thus the principle of promoting ethical organizations through open communication (Section 4) will assist Bob in dealing with his manager (discussing rumors in the first place is inappropriate), while demonstrating personal integrity (Section 3) will help Bob deal with Ron (telling Ron and not the entire staff is improper). It follows that, for these respondents, Bob could tell Ron that he himself has heard rumors too, and that since they must be dealt with, he (Bob) will seek clarification from his supervisor—something only top management can provide.

2. Code as not Helpful

As for the one-fourth of the sample who found the code not to be useful, they too commented on the ASPA statement proper as well as its applicability to the case. Concerning the former, these administrators indicated that they would rely on their own values, personal philosophy, common sense, good manners, and feelings to do what is right regardless of what the code says. A transportation planner in a large Florida city wrote, ''It is good to know that others are concerned about ethics in government, but I don't think I would stop to review the code before I acted on this situation. Personal ethics apply to both the organization and fellow workers.'' These are, then, subjective matters in which no written standard can be very effective.

Perhaps one reason for this viewpoint is that the managers found that the ASPA's document could be interpreted one way or another because of its competing values. Since its internal contradictions make decision-making impossible, everything still comes down to personal ethics.

> Codes, especially such broadly-worded ones like ASPA's, are not like procedures or manuals that guide someone through to a decision. Their value lies in establishing a tone or climate within an organization. The code is too cluttered with self-evident principles (e.g., 2[3], eliminate discrimination; 2[4], prevent mismanagement of public funds), with policy mandates (e.g., affirmative action), and simplistic formulas (e.g., 1[5]). Fewer, more personal standards like those in Section 5 (strive for excellence) would be more effective (a New York local administrator).

Concerning the case specifically, the responses paralleled those just given—i.e., the scenario was a personal, not a professional, dilemma and/or because of differing obligations, the code provides no solution. A management analyst from a California city believed that the standard ''is of no real help (as) no code could cover 100 percent of the situations 100 percent of the time.'' A city manager in Kansas concurred, saying that ''after reading the case, I scanned the code, and nothing struck me as a clear guide.'' A mayor of a Northeastern town summarized these views by stating that while ''the case is a real problem, . . . codes are just words.''

Attempting to characterize these respondents, using Kohlberg's framework, is difficult (no doubt in-depth interviews would provide a richer database than questionnaire replies). Clearly, freely-chosen principled values that rise above self-interest define the latter stages of moral development. Officials in government can seldom rely solely on personal values when authoritatively allocating values. Available data, however, reveal that criticisms of the code too easily rely on personal values without any indication of the foundation upon which these values are built. Thus rejecting the document (as mere words that contain conflicting obligations) could reflect a failure of moral imagination and a belief in simplistic solutions based on individual, or perhaps group, needs indicative of Kohlberg's earlier levels of development.

C. Professional Association Roles

Since ASPA expects its members to exemplify code principles, what can be done to support them in making ethical judgments? These partially-overlapping association roles were identified in a multiple-choice question: advocate, consultant, and evaluator. Nearly 6 of every 10 members (57.2 percent in the 1996 survey) believed that ASPA should serve as an advocate to promote the public service. This includes activities such as drafting ethics legislation, offering training, and/or speaking out when officials act (un)ethically. Over one-quarter of the sample (28.7 percent) saw the ASPA in a consulting mode: developing agency-specific codes and encouraging their adoption through technical assistance, convening symposia, and/or creating training curricula. A small group (6.1 percent) preferred that the association act in the capacity of an evaluator: appraising organizational programs and rating them against code standards, tracking unethical practices, and publicizing (un)ethical conduct. Finally, most of those responding to the open-ended choice (5.8 percent) approved either a combination of the roles or all three of them.

I believe that ASPA should adopt a gradual process by first becoming an advocate, then a consultant, and finally an evaluator, much like the current law enforcement agency accreditation process (a Florida law enforcement investigator).

Start by promoting, be available to consult, and evaluate upon request (the finance director and tax administrator of an Ohio city).

All organizations are in need of roles 1, 2, and 3 at sometime in their growth; ASPA should adapt to their needs (a budget analyst in a Maryland county).

In short, a large majority of these administrators support ASPA's ethics initiatives and would like them extended in an advocacy, consulting, and/or evaluative mode.

To conclude this section, the survey responses revealed that most managers found the code to be beneficial in thinking about the larger issues represented by the case as well as in developing differing strategies to deal with it. A minority of the sample, however, believed that the code in general is not practical (personal values predominate in decisions; it contains incompatible ideas), and, therefore, is no help in solving the scenario. Yet what is important is not that the ASPA statement is an imperfect instrument, but rather that dilemmas arise precisely because duties conflict. Both trivial and significant, these conflicts will be resolved by repairing to some standard. In seeking to assist decision-makers, the ethical values in the code clearly are critical for most of the respondents. In fact, most back ASPA's ethics activities and would like to see them augmented. Consistent with Kohlberg's views, many respondents reflect the "conventional" stage of morality, although there is some evidence that preconventional stages may be evident. More interestingly, a striking one-half of the sample arguably manifested postconventional morality characteristics by searching for creative solutions to the downsizing case; these were based not only on code principles, but also on enlightened self-interest and transcendental values.

V. CULTIVATING A PROFESSIONAL ETHOS

However one assesses the views of the survey participants, it is evident that codes are not strong enough to insure genuine progress—no one approach to ethics will be equally effective since people are on different moral planes. Instead, achievement of a professional ethos needs to be seen as developmental experience, one in which written standards play a significant part. That is, effective professional practice, in addition to technical knowledge, requires reflective knowledge in those areas of practice not readily susceptible to technical solutions (Schon, 1987).

Since professions see themselves from the outset as moral communities, the professionalization of the public service in the latter half of the 20th century (Mosher, 1982) provides the capacity to create an epistemology of reflective practice. For this practice to thrive, both professional associations and government agencies that employ their members have key responsibilities in creating a moral support system for people. Stated differently, although ultimate responsibility for actions rests with individual professionals, promoting ethical conduct is not solely the duty of the individual.

As a guardian of professional principles, the professional organization has a collective moral duty independent of individual members. This can be discharged not only by developing a code, but also by creating peer groups to ensure that the profession does not hypocritically publish a code and then vanish when problems arise.

The data reported in the previous section seem consistent with the notion that associations like ASPA need to stand ready to honor exemplary practices as well as to respond to code violations. The former shows profession-wide respect for its own standards—to serve humankind—and can be affirmed (''professed'') by identifying those who model the profession's highest ideals, an action that reaches far beyond the person or organization recognized (e.g., Table 4). The latter involves national, regional, and local support for individuals under pressure as well as to provide appropriate sanctions and rehabilitation for wayward employers and employees (Walton, 1999: 4). The necessary infrastructure to perform these roles includes association dues, national committees, and local chapters with websites, listservs, phone dues, and roving ''circuit riders'' to make the code come alive, to reinforce its values, and to provide assurance that members and the organizations that employ them adhere to technical standards and moral principles (Table 5).

If professional codes are seen as hypotheses for critical debate, not final dogma, it is also true that organizations who hire association members are contestable. That is, inspirational ideals in the code can buttress agency culture and be adapted to organizational

Table 4 ASPA Professional Responsibility Exemplary Practices Award

The American Society for Public Administration's Professional Responsibility Exemplary Practices Award pays tribute to an individual or organization which has made outstanding contributions to responsible professional ethical conduct.

Eligibility

An award will be presented annually to an individual or organization representing the following categories:

> Employees at all levels of public service, including local, state and federal governments, international and non-profit organizations. Nominees should have responsibility for accomplishing or causing to be accomplished significant programs or projects within their areas of responsibility to the ultimate benefit of the general public.

Nominational Procedures

Nominations will be accepted from individuals, professional groups, the business community, non-profit organizations and educational groups. Nominations must be received no later than February 1, be typewritten and follow the format described below:

1. A cover letter stating the name, address, and telephone number of the nominee, the nominator and three references that can attest to the nominee's performance.
2. A narrative, not exceeding five pages in length explaining the basis for the nomination.

The nomination should be sent to: Professional Responsibility Exemplary Practices Award Selection Committee, American Society for Public Administration, 1120 G Street, N.W., Suite 700, Washington, DC 20005.

Presentation of Award

The award will be presented at the annual ASPA National Conference.

Note: In late 1999, a proposal, put forth by the journal *Public Integrity*, to modify this award and add the International City/County Management Association and The Council on State Governments as sponsors was approved.

Table 5   Making the Code a Living Document

The International City/County Management Association . . . supplements its code of ethics with a web site, publications, and . . . a kind of "circuit-rider" service whereby experienced, retired . . . managers are made available to come to the aid of professionals in their field who find themselves under attack or pressure in ways which seem, in their best judgment, to require violation of the ICMA code of ethics. This practice . . . accomplishes two sorts of peer backup and group moral solidarity usually missing from professional associations—the immediate, and sometimes visible help of an "outsider" to bring weight to bear on the seriousness of the code of ethics, and also (an) informal system of communication by which harmful consequences wrought by a city council or county commission would very likely come to be known nationally among the members of the ICMA. Thus a sort of informal sanction exists when would-be violators of the code come to find out just how wide and interested is the larger population of city and county managers now aware of the consequences they had planned to cause.

Source: Walton, 1999: 5–6.

strategy. To make codes a living document, to align their values with existing power structures:

> an agency-specific code, using the profession's code as a catalyst, should be developed with maximum participation on the part of employees;
> the "home grown" credo should:
> be prefaced with a letter by the agency's leadership that puts it in the context of the department's traditions and mission statement, summarizes its rationale, and personally commits the signer(s) to its precepts;
> include guidance on its use including implementation procedures, case materials and study resources, and commonly-asked questions and answers;
> be integrated into the personnel system, from recruitment through training to evaluation; and
> provide the basis for the agency to undergo periodic ethical audits to identify contemporary issues confronting it.

In the absence of a synergistic, comprehensive approach an organization that takes incremental measures, paradoxically, may be worse off then one that does nothing at all. "A half of a loaf," writes *Ethics Today*, "is not better than none at all" (1997: 7) because of the hypocrisy that such a strategy tends to engender. Alternatively, a robust strategy likely will produce another paradox: organizational tensions and the number of observations of misconduct may increase—not because this approach is dysfunctional, but because it enhances the ability to perceive and recognize wrongdoing (Ethics Resource Center, 1994).

In summary, effective practice of public service includes professional associations which develop and implement codes that empower employees and employers to use them as models for their own ethics initiatives—efforts that at least in the short run are not without contradiction. By reflecting individual and group values, codes, as a foundation of a broader quality assurance program, will be meaningful to all concerned. To be sure, it is better to have moral people ready to make ethical judgments than to rely on a program. But equally sure, an initiative created and operated by members of the organization can and will be helpful. Cultivating a professional ethos does not simply mean trying to do the right thing. It means trying to be the kind of person and organization who does the right thing. A comprehensive program that encourages the practice of virtue, which like anything else improves with repetition, can only help to achieve that end.

VI. CONCLUSION

"Ethics," Bayard Catron and Kathyrn Denhardt opine, "is central to the identity and legitimacy of public service" (1994: 56); the profession of government is only as good as its ethics. The centrality of ethics is undeniable as managerial decisions test one's values when they affect people's lives, distribute resources, and require judgment in so doing. Such discretion demands decisions that are both procedurally and morally sound. Professional practice requires not only the technical ability to analyze problems, but also the capacity to grasp those problems in a manner consistent with professional principles of role responsibility and personal integrity (Bowman, 1998). Stated differently, a concern for the "bottom line" of technical skill must be complemented, if not superseded, by the "top line" of ethical responsibility—the essence of the professional ethos.[7]

Public service magnifies these considerations in two ways. First, many government problems are not "tame" or technical ones that have straightforward solutions (e.g., how to build a highway); rather, they are "wicked" or political ones (Harmon and Mayer, 1986) that have only imperfect, temporary solutions (e.g., where to build a highway). The challenge is that officials must attempt to "correct" wicked problems in order to make them manageable. Second, whatever decisions are made come to be seen as "moral and absolute," as they publicly represent both the symbolic and real authoritative allocation of values in a society. It is in government that ethical standards are found to a degree unknown in most other professions. Achieving these standards is both complex and simple and epitomizes the professional ethos. In the end, public administration, David Hart reminds us, "is not only (or even most importantly) a kind of technology but instead it is a moral endeavour"(1984: 116).

ACKNOWLEDGMENT

The author gratefully acknowledges Montgomery Van Wart for his review of a draft of this work.

NOTES

1. While those associated with each ethos do not necessarily take an "either-or" approach, the premise of their position usually is one or the other school.
2. This paragraph is adapted from Bowman (1981: 62).
3. The Professional Ethics Committee of the 10,000-member association (approximately 90 percent of whom are practitioners) prepared a preliminary draft, which was reviewed by the ASPA's National Council, earlier that year. It was subsequently published in ASPA's newsletter at large for comment by the membership. When revised, it was unanimously adopted by the council.
4. This, and parts of the following subsections, are adapted from Bowman and Williams (1997:

521–523) and include additional case analysis. For an exegesis of the new code, see Van Wart (1996).

5. Over two-thirds of the sample (69 percent) in fact favored having the following statement (with a signature line) placed on the association's membership application and annual renewal forms: "I fully support and will abide ASPA's Code of Ethics."

6. This well-known theory consists of three levels of moral development with two overlapping stages in each one. The preconventional level emphasizes self-interest and is comprised of obedience/punishment and instrumental exchange stages (the world is seen, respectively, as a prison and a marketplace). The conventional level, characterized by group norms, includes interpersonal conformity and social system maintenance stages (the world is viewed as an exclusive club in the former and as a inclusive society regulated by law and order in the latter). The postconventional or principled level focuses on one's enlightened conscience/independent philosophy derived from social contract and individual rights (stage five) or universal ethical principles (stage six). The world is interpreted through freely and responsibly chosen cultural or, more likely, transcendental principles quite apart from narrow self-interest, the views of others, or the strictures of authority figures. The divergent responses to the case in the text do not mean that the code is useless as participants differ based on their level of cognitive development. Rather, as discussed in a subsequent section, such variations suggest a role for professional associations in encouraging their members to think about ethics.

7. The worst form of incompetence is not knowing how to do something, but not knowing why it is to be done; an irresponsible manager is at least as dangerous as a technically deficient one.

REFERENCES

Black, J. (1995). Minimum standards vs. ideal expectations. *Quill* 83 (November/December):26–29.

Bowman, J.S. (1998). The professional edge. In: *The Ethics Edge* (E. Berman, J. West, and S. Bonczek, eds.). International City/County Management Association, Washington, DC, pp. 159–163.

Bowman, J.S. (1990). Ethics in government: A national survey of public administrators. *Public Administration Review*, 50(3):345–353.

Bowman, J.S. and Williams, R.L. (1997). Ethics in government: From a winter of despair to a spring of hope. *Public Administration Review*, 57(6):517–526.

Bowman, J.S. (1981). The management of ethics: Codes of conduct in organizations. *Public Personnel Management*, 10(1):59–66.

Brien, A. (1996). Regulating virtue: Formulating, engendering, and enforcing corporate ethical codes. *Business and Professional Ethics Journal* 15(1):21–52.

Bruce, W. (1996). Codes of ethics and codes of conduct. *Public Integrity Annual*, 1:13–22.

Catron, B. and Denhardt, K. (1994). Ethics education in public administration. In: *Handbook of Administrative Ethics* (T. Cooper, ed.). Marcel Dekker, New York, pp. 3–30.

Center for Personnel Research. (1996). *Personnel Practices: Ethics*. International Personnel Management Association, Alexandria, VA.

Chandler, R. (1983). The problem of moral reasoning in American public administration: The case for a code of ethics. *Public Administration Review*, 43(1):32–39.

Ethics Resource Center. (1994). *Landmark Survey*. ERC, Washington, DC.

Ethics Today. (1997). A little knowledge. 2(1):6–7.

Ferrell, O.C., LeClair, D.T., and Ferrell, L. (1998). The federal sentencing guidelines for organizations: A framework for ethical compliance. *Journal of Business Ethics*, 17:353–363.

Frankel, M. (1989). Professional codes: Why, how, and with what impact? *Journal of Business Ethics*, 8:109–115.

Frederickson, H.G. (1997). *The Spirit of Public Administration.* Jossey-Bass, San Francisco, CA.

Gellerman, W., Frankel, M. and Ladenson, R. (1990). *Values and Ethics in Organization and Human Systems Development.* Jossey-Bass, San Francisco, CA.

Gortner, H. (1991). *Ethics for Public Managers.* Greenwood Press, Westport, CT.

Green, R. (1994). Character ethics and public administration. *International Journal of Public Administration,* 17(12):2137–2164.

Harmon, M.M. and Mayer, R.T. (1986). *Organizational Theory for Public Administration.* Little, Brown, Boston.

Hart, D.K. (1984). Virtuous citizen, the honorable bureaucrat, and ''public'' administration. *Public Administration Review,* 44(2):111–120.

Kohlberg, L. (1981). *Essays in Moral Development.* Harper and Row, New York.

Lewis, C. (1991). *The Ethics Challenge in Public Service.* Jossey-Bass, San Francisco, CA.

MacLagan, P. (1998). *Management and Morality.* Sage, Thousand Oaks, CA.

Martinez, J.M. (1998). Law versus ethics: reconciling two concepts of public service ethics. *Administration and Society,* 26(6):690–722.

Mosher, F. (1982). *Democracy and Public Service,* 2nd ed. Oxford, New York.

Newton, L. (1981). Lawgiving for professional life: Reflections on the place of the professional code. *Business and Professional Ethics,* 1(1):41–53.

Pugh, D.L. (1991). The origins of ethical frameworks in public administration. In: *Ethical Frontiers in Public Management* (J. S. Bowman, ed.). Jossey-Bass, San Francisco, CA, pp. 9–33.

Paine, L. (1994). Manage for organizational integrity. *Harvard Business Review,* 72(2):106–117.

Rowe, L.A. and Hug, R.W. (1990). City manager perceptions of the ICMA Code of Ethics. In: *The Ethics Edge* (E. Berman, J. West, and S. Bonczek, eds.). International City/County Management Association, Washington, DC, pp. 129–144.

Schon, D.A. (1987). *Educating the Reflective Professional.* Jossey-Bass, San Francisco, CA.

Van Wart, M. (1996). Sources for ethical decision making for individuals in the public sector. *Public Administration Review,* 56(6):525–533.

Vogelsang-Coombs, V. and Bakken, L. (1988). The conduct of legislators. In: *Ethics Government and Public Policy* (J.S. Bowman, ed.). Greenwood, Westport, CT, pp. 79–102.

Walton, C. (1999). Where the code meets the road: Professional ethics and the need for sanctions. Paper presented at the Association for Practical and Professional Ethics Eighth Annual Meeting, Washington, DC, February 26–27 [Forthcoming in 2000, *Public Integrity* 2(4)].

Wilson, J.Q. (1993). *The Moral Impulse.* Free Press, New York.

Zajac, G. (1997). Reinventing government and reaffirming ethics: Implications for organizational development in the public service. *Public Administration Quarterly,* 20:385–404.

17

Ethics Management in Public Organizations
What, Why, and How?

Donald C. Menzel
Northern Illinois University, DeKalb, Illinois

Ethics management in public organizations? Can there be such a thing? Can we talk about managing ethics in the same breath or manner in which we talk about managing budgets, policies, or people? The answer is a resounding yes! Indeed, the single act of developing and adopting a code of ethics, as Bowman (1981) documented nearly twenty years ago, is managing ethics in the workplace. Thus, ethics management is not a new enterprise; it is an old enterprise. What is new about it is how we think about it. If we think about it as a systematic and consistent effort to promote ethical organizations, as Article IV of the American Society for Public Administration (ASPA) Code of Ethics declares, then there is such a thing as ethics management.[1] Ethics management, however, does not mean ''control.'' It is not the act, single or plural, of controlling co-workers' behaviors or thinking about ethics in the workplace. Rather, it is the cumulative actions taken by managers to engender an ethical sensitivity and consciousness that permeates all aspects of getting things done in a public service agency. It is, in short, the promotion and maintenance of a strong ethics culture in the public workplace.

This chapter explores what ethics management is, why it is important, how it is approached, and how specific techniques and approaches do or do not work in public organizations. This chapter argues that ethics management is vital to well-functioning public organizations and presumes that public managers can become effective ethics managers, although many may not understand how to do so.

I. WHY IS ETHICS MANAGEMENT IMPORTANT?

The ''why'' question of ethics management is, in a sense, relatively new. Ethics has never received the attention that the hallmark values of efficiency, economy, and effectiveness have in modern public administration scholarship or practice. This is due largely to the assumptions of 19th-century civil service reformers like Woodrow Wilson who declared in his famous essay of 1887 that we must clear ''the moral atmosphere of official life by establishing the sanctity of public office as a public trust . . . [thereby] opening the way for making it businesslike" (Wilson, 1887:20). Administrators, so presumed Wilson and his intellectual successors over the decades, were expected to be men and women of high moral character and integrity. "The ideal for us," he argued, "is a civil service cultured and self-sufficient enough to act with sense and vigor . . ." (1887:24). Thus there was little reason to be concerned about the need to add a fourth "e"—ethics—to the holy trilogy of efficiency, economy, and effectiveness. But times change and ethics has become academic talk and shop talk. Indeed, it is increasingly common to find public administration graduate programs offering ethics courses and public organizations providing in-house ethics training.

At first blush one might think this trend is a result of an increasing incidence of wrongdoing in government. Thus the "why" of ethics management might be tied to stamping out wrongdoing! Upon closer examination, however, there is a more compelling explanation—a growing recognition by private and public sector managers that productive, high performing units are value driven units that place ethics high on their list of values. Insofar as such a link exists between ethics and organizational performance, prudent managers and scholars have focused on understanding and studying the dynamics of the ethical workplace and the role that professional associations and ethics codes and pronouncements play in the scheme of things.

Studies of the ethics-performance linkage in the public administration literature began to appear in the early 1990s. Burke and Black (1990), for example, conducted an exploratory study of organizational ethics and productivity by surveying 69 executives and managers, approximately one-third of whom were from the public and nonprofit sectors. Their findings did not demonstrate a conclusive empirical link between ethics and performance but did motivate them to recommend that agencies should create "a leadership group focused on identifying ethical concerns and productivity measures" (1990: 132). Bruce (1994) also used survey research to study the ethics of municipal clerks. Municipal clerks, she found, are a highly ethical group who feel that city employees are basically ethical and highly productive. She contends that managers and supervisors have a "substantial influence on employee ethics and, by extension, on organizational performance" (Bruce, 1994:251).

Menzel (1992, 1993, 1995) has also probed the ethics-performance link. He surveyed different populations—city and county managers in Florida and Texas, and city and county employees in two Florida local governments. One study (Menzel, 1993) question included: "Do ethical climates of public organizations reinforce or detract from organizational values such as efficiency, effectiveness, excellence, quality, and teamwork?" He hypothesized that as the ethical climate of an organization becomes stronger, organizational performance values such as efficiency, effectiveness, teamwork, excellence, and quality will be strongly supported. The findings led him to accept the hypothesis that an organization's ethical climate has a positive influence on an organization's performance.

Similar findings are reported by Berman and West (1997) in their study of the adoption of ethics management strategies in cities. City managers participating in the study report that "commitment to workforce effectiveness and the adoption of pay-for-performance policies are associated strongly with ethics management practices." And, "efforts to decrease absenteeism and to adopt a customer-orientation also are significantly associated with ethics management" (Berman and West, 1997:26).

Other studies (Menzel, 1996a) have focused on the organizational consequences of ethics-induced stress in the public workplace. Menzel defined ethics-induced stress as a form of cognitive dissonance between an employee's personal ethics and the ethics climate found in the employee's workplace. He asked: Does ethics-induced stress lower employee productivity? Does it result in less job satisfaction? Greater conflict? More employee turnover? Drawing on surveys of city and county managers in Florida and Texas, he found strong statistical associations between managers' high levels of ethics-induced stress and impaired organizational performance. Specifically, as the level of ethics-induced stress increases, job satisfaction decreases, organizational conflict increases, and employee turnover is greater.

Again, why is ethics management important? After all, government is not in the business of producing ''ethics.'' Rather, it is in the business of providing necessary and desired public goods and services such as roads and transportation, social security, education, national security, and protection from: air, water, and ground pollution; and persons and firms who would harm us intentionally or unintentionally. ''Ethics,'' as Dennis F. Thompson (1992:255) reminds us, ''is not a primary goal of government . . . [it's] mainly instrumental to government.'' Nonetheless, Thompson and others believe that ethical government is vital to effective and democratic government. ''Ethics may be only a means to an end, but it is a *necessary* means to an end'' (Thompson, 1992). In other words, well meaning public managers and policymakers cannot presume that effective public policies and organizations are achievable in an ethical vacuum. Indeed, such a vacuum is likely to swallow up even the most well conceived plans, policies, and day-to-day operations of government.[2]

II. ETHICS MANAGEMENT: WHO PRACTICES IT?

Public administration practitioners live with ethical and unethical realities day-in and day-out. This places them in the unique position of being able to practice ethics management and, on occasion, to experience the consequences of ethics management. But do they practice ethics management? And, if they do, how do they do it? To answer these questions, the author searched practitioner journals such as *The Public Manager, PM: Public Management*, and publications issued by the International City/County Management Association.[3] The assumption was made that if practitioners do ethics management then there should be some evidence of what and how they do it in practitioner publications.

In searching through *PM: Public Management* (January 1990–December 1998), a total of seven articles were found, among the more than 400 articles published, that focused on ethics.[4] At first glance, the relatively small number of articles published on the subject of ethics suggest that public managers neither practice nor give much systematic attention to ethics management. The numbers, however, are misleading inasmuch as the authors of the articles published in *PM: Public Management* and ICMA books have much to say about what ethics management is and what managers should do to strengthen the ethical cultures of their organizations. Gary B. Brumback (1998), for example, identifies four key components of ethics management: hiring, performance, training, and auditing. Hire the ''right'' people, he admonishes. But who knows how to hire the right people? Should some kind of ethics screening be conducted? Yes—Brumback asserts. Here are his suggestions:

1. Review background investigation policies and procedures to determine if they are ethical, can be improved, and are used for the right (seductive) jobs.
2. Build the agency's reputation for integrity . . . and then stress that reputation to recruits.

3. Do not use surreptitious screening and explain the policy to recruits.
4. Ask new hires to pledge a commitment to ethics in government in the oath of
    office (Brumback, 1998:66).

Once hired, Brumback contends, "factoring ethics into the process of managing
performance is the best way to ensure that work objectives are achieved in an ethical
manner, and that other on-the-job behaviors are ethical" (Brumback, 1998:66). Performance evaluations can and should include an ethics dimension. Assertions that "ethics
is not performance" or "ethics is too subjective to be measured" are bogus arguments,
he believes.

Ethics management should also emphasize training programs. Employees throughout a public organization are vulnerable to ethics lapses from time to time. Thus, a continuous, ongoing ethics training program amplifies the message that ethics matters. "Above
all," Brumback (1998:68) asserts, "tell people what the preconditions of unethical behavior are, what the bottom line of ethics is, and what the agency and each individual can
do to make ethics a work habit."

Another component in managing ethics in public organizations is the ethics audit.
An ethics audit, whether based on a survey of employees or an assessment of occupational
vulnerability, should be conducted periodically. Bonczek (1998), a city manager with 20
years experience, strongly supports the use of an ethics audit to let employees know the
positive as well as the negative effects of their efforts. He also believes that managers
should "review with their employees all decisions on ethical issues, asking, What did we
do right? What did we not do that we should have done? What should we do in future,
similar situations?" (Bonczek, 1998:78). He encourages managers to use weekly staff
meetings "to review all discussions and decisions for ethical implications" (Bonczek,
1998:78). Bonczek fully believes that a strong ethical climate in a public organization has
a positive influence on organizational performance and productivity.

The admonishments above are directed primarily at the "how" of ethics management which, in brief, urges managers to practice integrity and embrace ethical principles.
Donald G. Zauderer (1994), for example, asserts that integrity includes taking risks to:
oppose unjust acts (don't just go along); communicate truthfully (do not intentionally
deceive others); deal fairly (don't provide others with special advantages or disadvantages
because of their affiliations or positions); honor agreements (keep your commitments);
accept personal responsibility when things go right or wrong; forgive individuals for mistakes or wrongdoing (don't hold grudges or strive to get even); exhibit humility (avoid
unbridled ambition and emphasizing rank and status differences); respect the dignity of
individuals by giving earned recognition (don't treat employees as simply vehicles for
getting the work done); and celebrate the ability and good fortune of others (suppress
envy).

The Council for Excellence in Government (1992–1993) urges every individual in
government to recognize that public service is a public trust and that he/she must accept
two paramount obligations: (1) to serve the public interest and (2) to perform with integrity. Furthermore, top leaders in public organizations must advocate and exemplify these
core values and obligations. Subordinates' performances, the council asserts, should be
evaluated in light of these standards. Organizational leaders should also make every effort
to insure that their organization recruits others with strong ethical values to work in the
organization.

Chris Wye (1994) shares the council's view of the role that top leaders should assume in promoting ethical public organizations. "At every level in the organization, but especially at the top," Wye (1994:45) contends, "effective leadership is an essential ingredient for maintaining the highest standards of ethical conduct in an organization." Nonetheless, Wye worries that the present course of action in the United States has been to focus on the "moral minimum," not the "moral maximum." Through the use and reliance on laws and regulations, certain types of unacceptable behavior have been proscribed which become the default for defining the moral minimum for acceptable behavior. "Shouldn't we," he asks, "spend at least some time encouraging good behavior?"

Professor James S. Bowman's (1990; Bowman and Williams, 1997) surveys of public administration practitioners are also suggestive for understanding what ethics management is and how prevalent it is in the public sector. When he asked public managers in 1989 if their agencies had a consistent approach toward dealing with ethical concerns, nearly two-thirds said their organizations did not have a consistent approach. When he asked the same question in 1996, he found that a smaller (58 percent) yet still large percentage of respondents replied in the same fashion—"my agency does not have a consistent approach toward dealing with ethical concerns." Do these responses suggest that there is little ethics management in the public sector? Possibly, but not necessarily. Consider the findings reported by Berman West, and Cava (1994) and Berman and West (1997).

In 1992, Berman, West, and Cava surveyed more than 1000 directors of human resource agencies in municipalities with a population over 25,000 in order to find out what ethics management strategies are employed, how they are implemented, and how effective they are. Their findings confirmed Bowman's findings about the lack of a consistent approach—if consistent means "formal." A minority of cities surveyed reported using formal ethics management strategies while a majority claim that their city relied primarily on leadership-based strategies—an informal strategy.

Berman, West, and Cava (1994) found four categories of ethics management—two they label as formal, one informal, and one a combination of formal-informal.

> *Formal* ethics management strategies involve mandatory employee training, use of ethics as a criterion in the reward structure, and the adoption of organizational rules that promote the ethical climate, such as requiring financial disclosure and approval of outside activities. *Informal* ethics management strategies involve reliance on role models and positive reinforcement and are behaviorally based (Berman et al., 1994: 189).

Code-based and regulatory-based strategies are the two formal strategies used by a large number of cities. Adopting a code of ethics or establishing guidelines for standards of conduct would be considered part of a code-based strategy. Advocates of codes typically presume that codes contribute to a healthy organization and thus a higher performing organization. Bowman's (1990; Bowman and Williams, 1997) surveys of practitioner members of the American Society for Public Administration show that practitioners strongly embrace codes and believe that they have a positive influence on organizational life. Bruce's research (1996) also adds to the believed real-world impact of codes. Her study of members of the International Institute of Municipal Clerks found that clerks "rank a code of conduct as the most powerful way a city can prevent corruption" (Bruce, 1996: 29). Using ethics as a criterion in hiring and promotion or requiring approval of outside employment would constitute part of a regulatory-based strategy. Leadership-based strategies, such as demonstrating exemplary moral leadership by senior management, constitutes an informal ethics management strategy. Employee-based strategies that incorporate ethics training, protect whistle-blowers for valid disclosures, or solicit employees' opinions about ethics constitute a mixed strategy.

Does reliance on an informal strategy, which most cities claim to do, result in ineffective ethics management? Not necessarily. Berman, West, and Cava's research indicates that moral-leadership strategies are more effective than regulatory- or code-based strategies in enabling cities to achieve ethics management objectives such as avoiding conflicts of interest, reducing the need for whistle-blowers, and fostering fairness in job assignments.

III. OTHER RESPONSES TO ETHICS FAILURES

Ethics are important in public organizations. Yet, ethics lapses and failures can and do occur. When this happens, what else might be done? At the macro level, codification of acceptable behavior in the form of *state law or local ordinance* is common practice. Many states and cities, for example, have opted for ethics laws and regulatory bodies or boards. A recent count found that 38 states have established ethics offices or commissions. Many cities, including mega-cities Los Angeles and Chicago, have established ethics commissions to investigate real and alleged cases of wrongdoing. The United States government has also taken action, having established the Office of Government Ethics (OGE) with the passage of the Ethics in Government Act of 1978. Now, some twenty years later, nearly 15,000 full and part-time ethics officials can be found in the federal executive branch (Gilman and Lewis, 1996:521).

These efforts have not gone unnoticed by academic investigators. Several investigators have attempted to assess what difference ethics laws and commissions make in states and communities. Williams (1996), for example, studied the Florida Commission on Ethics to assess the agency's effectiveness in training public officials, conducting ethics audits, investigating complaints, and encouraging an ethical climate by management. Based on unstructured interviews with commissioners and archival records of the agency, he concluded that the Florida Ethics Commission was largely ineffective in all four areas. "Unfortunately," Williams (1996:71) asserts, "the commission apparently serves more effectively as a punitive agent than as an agent of constructive change."

Menzel (1996b) also studied the Florida Commission on Ethics but from a different vantage point—the view from the street. He surveyed persons who had filed ethics complaints (legally referred to as complainants) and public officials (legally referred to as respondents) who were the objects of complaints. He asked three questions:

1. What is the relationship between how an ethics complaint is handled and citizen trust or distrust in government?
2. Do persons who file ethics complaints have a positive or negative experience? Are those experiences satisfactory and therefore build trust and confidence in government? Or are those experiences unsatisfactory and therefore contribute to the erosion of public trust and confidence in government?
3. What are the outcomes of the ethics complaint making?

Menzel's study involved mail surveys of 303 complainants (144 responded) and 555 respondents (161 responded) in the time period of 1989–1992. Among other things, he found that complainants were much more likely to say they were dissatisfied with the outcome of the complaint they filed than were respondents who were the object of the complaint. Furthermore, neither complainants nor respondents differentiate process outcomes from substantive outcomes. How you are treated and how things turn out, regardless of whether you are the person filing a complaint or the person who is the object of the complaint, seem to go hand in hand. Finally, he concluded that "the ethics complaint-making process in Florida may be widening rather than closing the trust deficit" (Menzel, 1996:80).

IV. TRUST BUILDING AS ETHICS MANAGEMENT

Closing the trust deficit is a legitimate and needed activity within and between agencies and the community. But how? How does one build trust within a public organization? How can one build trust in the community? These are important questions, and there is some literature that is helpful in answering them. Carnevale and Wechsler (1992), for example, have built a model of organizational trust that combines characteristics of the individual (e.g., gender, salary, efficacy, etc.) and the organization (e.g., in-group status, fairness of rewards and punishment, ethical environment, etc.) Their data involved a survey of more than 1000 employees of a state agency responsible for issuing driver licenses. Among other things, they found that the willingness of employees to place trust in their organization depended on how they were treated by the organization. "Individuals who perceive the organization as ethical in its treatment of themselves and others," they assert, "will report higher levels of organizational trust" (Carnevale and Wechsler, 1992:480).

Building trust in one's community is likely to be more challenging than building trust in one's organization, as a recent study by Berman (1996) suggests. Berman sought to find out how much trust there is among local government officials and community leaders, what municipal strategies are employed to increase trust levels, and how socioeconomic conditions may influence perceptions of trust in local government. He surveyed city managers and CAOs (Chief Administrative Officers) in 502 cities with a population of more than 50,000 to obtain their perceptions of trust levels. His findings indicated that "community leaders have only moderate levels of trust in local government" but that cities with a council-manager form of government experience a significantly higher level of trust than do cities with the mayor-council form of government (Berman, 1996:33).

Berman identifies three principal trust-building strategies—communication, consultation and collaboration, and minimizing wrongdoing. Communication strategies emphasize providing information about the city's programs and performance. Consultation/collaboration strategies involve engaging community leaders via partnerships, meetings, panels, and so forth. Minimizing wrongdoing strategies emphasize the adoption of ethics codes, providing ethics training, and so forth. Strategies vary from community to community and no single one appears to be more effective than the other. However, there is some evidence that "using a range of strategies by local officials increases trust, even though the impact of individual strategies is modest" (Berman, 1996:34). Socioeconomic conditions, Berman concludes, have an influence on trust levels. Positive conditions in a community such as high economic growth and cooperation among local groups inspire trust in government. "Negative community conditions, such as economic stagnation, low income levels, racial strife and high levels of crime reduce economic and political resources . . . for dealing with community problems" and contribute to a distrust of government (Berman, 1996:34).

V. BUILD ETHICS INTO THE ORGANIZATIONAL CULTURE

How can managers build ethics into their organizational cultures? Alas, the quick answer is "not easily!" Creating and sustaining an ethical workplace takes many hands and much time. It's not that public organizations are staffed with unethical workers but that we have over the years fallen prey to a series of false assumptions about the role and place of ethics in public agencies. So, if one wants to build ethics into the organizational culture, one must first dismiss the following false assumptions.

A. Ethical Values Are Personal and Are Not Expressed Within the Organization

Part of the mythology of working in the public sector is that employees should not act on their values and beliefs because to do so would undermine their ability to be fair and impartial. In other words, its okay to have personal values and ethics but don't bring them to the workplace! This approach will breed ethical complacency and eventually contribute to ethical lapses within one's organization.

B. Ethical People Always Act Ethically Regardless of What Goes on in the Organization

President John F. Kennedy once said, "the ultimate answer to ethical problems in government is honest people in a good ethical environment." Notice that it takes two things—ethical people and a good ethical environment! To assume that ethical people will not experience ethical lapses is a false assumption. Recruiting ethical people to public organizations is certainly an important first step but is not in and of itself sufficient to assure that ethical government will result. Ethical employees need ethical support or reinforcement in the workplace. How this might be done is the subject of another essay.

C. Ethics Discussions in Public Organizations Contribute Little, if Anything, to Productivity, Morale, or Problem Solving

Another false assumption. Many mangers likely believe that it is nice to talk about ethics in the workplace but that such talk matters little when it comes to getting the job done. Indeed, time devoted to ethics discussions or formal training might be viewed as a major distraction from time that could be devoted to providing public services in a more cost-effective fashion. There is growing empirical evidence that there is a significant correlation between the presence of a strong ethical climate in an organization and the emphasis the organization places on values such as efficiency, effectiveness, quality, excellence, and teamwork. It is sometimes said that "ethics is good business." This maxim is just as appropriate for public service organizations—ethics makes for excellent public service.

As managers, it is important to develop strategies that encourage dialogue on issues with ethical implications and to provide an approach to establishing an ethical workplace. The creation of a shared value system based on ethical principles requires meaningful and serious dialogue through an inclusive, not an exclusive, process. The involvement of employees in ethics training and development seminars that allow for questions and confrontations will give individuals the confidence needed to take action, resolve problems, and raise productivity.

D. Ethics Cannot Be Learned, Taught or Even Discussed in Any Meaningful Way

There is a widespread belief that ethics are acquired or not acquired as a youngster and therefore any effort to teach or learn about ethics as an adult is fruitless. A corollary is that one can only learn ethics through the crucible of personal experiences. These views reduce ethics in the workplace to whatever values and life experiences workers bring to the workplace and is hardly reassuring to managers who wish to build ethics into their organizational culture.

Neither ethical persons nor ethical workplaces are entirely products of past experiences whether personal or organizational in nature. This "naturalist" view of how an ethical sense is acquired or transmitted must be rejected. Rather, ethical behavior must be viewed as learned behavior which can be relearned and modified, if needed.

Ethical behavior is learned behavior and managers can build organizational processes and strategies that contribute to this learning effort. Ethics initiatives (e.g., placing ethics stories in newsletters) and training, for example, may not create ethical employees, but they can facilitate decisions that reflect organizational values and purpose. When ethics training is successful, employees become aware of ethical choices and have the knowledge and resources to choose and carry out the right choices.

E. Creating and Distributing a Written Ethics Policy Eliminates Any Further Responsibility of the Organization or Its Leaders

False! False! False! While it is important to have ethics guidelines and to provide those guidelines to employees, this action alone will fall short of guiding behavior and can do little to change it, when such change is needed. Building ethics into the organizational culture is not a one shot event. It is a continuous happening that finds expression in many ways. A written ethics policy or statement of principles is an important beginning point and no organization should be without one. Equally important, however, are the ethical and moral cues sent out by the top management. Top managers who do not "walk the ethical talk" will soon experience a credibility gap that employees will see as hypocrisy— "do as I say, not as I do." James Madison, one of the writers of the Constitution, put it plainly: "No government, any more than an individual, will long be respected without being truly respectable."

F. Appearing to Do Wrong and Actually Doing Wrong Are Different Matters

Factually true but "so what" when it comes to building ethics into the organizational culture. The belief that a person's ethics should be judged not by appearance but by facts does not reflect the power of perception. Appearing to do wrong when we actually have done nothing wrong may have the same negative impact as doing wrong, or an even greater one. The appearance of impropriety erodes employee and public trust in public agencies and weakens the principles of accountability. It may, for example, be legal for a manager to invest in a business that does not do business with his or her agency, but he or she will have difficulty convincing a skeptical public and workforce that he is not using the power of his position for personal gain. The appearance of impropriety is inescapable, regardless of the reality. Appearances do matter!

Beyond dismissing the six false assumptions above, managers can and should rely on both formal and informal strategies to strengthen the ethical environment of their agencies. Managers need not run through a daily ten page ''to do'' and ''not to do'' checklist to achieve the ethical workplace. There is no algorithm or methodically correct manner to building ethics into the organizational culture. Still, the literature reviewed in this chapter strongly suggests that managers should take a systemic and comprehensive approach toward building ethical organizations. Evidence collected to date, although limited, suggest that incorporating a wide range of practices into the total fabric of an organization is most likely to have a lasting imprint on ethical life in public organizations. Managers who encourage employees to participate in professional associations, devise creative ways for ethical behavior to be rewarded, establish an ethics conscience via a committee or statement of principles in their organization, provide for ethics training or dialogue, and ''walk-the-talk'' are likely to enjoy the benefits of a sustained ethical workplace.

Organizations with integrity are places where human beings with integrity carry out their daily duties with pride and respect for others. This view is especially embraced by practitioners whose contributions were examined in this chapter. Character, integrity, moral competency, and exemplary behavior are words and phrases that one finds threaded throughout the practitioner literature.

The why, what, and how of ethics management in public organizations have been explored in this chapter. There is no magic elixir or formula for achieving the ethical workplace, but there are ways and means to strengthen the ethical environments of public organizations. It seems rather foolish if not outright dangerous to fail to employ those ways and means to build public organizations with integrity.

ACKNOWLEDGMENTS

The author would like to thank Mazen Gonder Nagi, a Ph.D. student at Northern Illinois University, for research assistance. A previous version of this paper was presented at the 60th Annual Conference of the American Society for Public Administration, held in Orlando, Florida, April 10–14, 1999.

NOTES

1. The Code of Ethics of the American Society for Public Administration, Article IV, Promote Ethical Organizations states: ''Strengthen organizational capabilities to apply ethics, efficiency and effectiveness in serving the public. ASPA members are committed to:
   a. Enhance organizational capacity for open communication, creativity, and dedication.
   b. Subordinate institutional loyalties to the public good.
   c. Establish procedures that promote ethical behavior and hold individuals and organizations accountable for their conduct.
   d. Provide organization members with an administrative means for dissent, assurance of due process, and safeguards against reprisal.
   e. Promote merit principles that protect against arbitrary and capricious actions.
   f. Promote organizational accountability through appropriate controls and procedures.
   g. Encourage organizations to adopt, distribute, and periodically review a code of ethics as a living document.''
2. The means-ends argument may have been most clearly illustrated by the Congressional proceed-

ings to impeach and remove President Clinton from office. The president's ethical if not moral imbroglio brought the presumed work of government to a standstill for the better part of a year.

3. The International City/County Management Association also publishes monographs from time to time focusing on ethics. In 1988, for example, the ICMA published *Ethical Insight/Ethical Action*, an edited volume (Kellar, 1988) with 15 chapters. Only one chapter dealt with ethics management, and it did so in an indirect manner. Most chapters focused on ethical decision-making from the perspective of the individual manager. A decade later, in 1998, the ICMA published a second edited volume *The Ethics Edge* (Berman, West, and Bonczek, 1998). This book, which has 20 chapters, contains about 10 chapters that address directly or indirectly the "what, why, and how" of ethics management.

4. It should be noted that *PM: Public Management* has published an ethics column every month since July 1992. The column reports on unethical situations managers can find themselves in and provides advice on how to deal with them. The December 1998 issue, for example, describes a situation in which a county administrator lunched with several members of the elected city council to discuss problems of mutual interest. The problem? He didn't consult with his elected body before meeting with the city officials. Was this ethical? The County Chairwoman didn't think so. The December issue also presented a situation facing a town manager who was offered a job from a company that had recently moved its headquarters to her community. The rub— she had developed excellent working relationships with the firm's leaders during the relocation negotiations which led to the firm wanting to hire her. Was the town manager's decision to accept the job ethical?

REFERENCES

Berman, E.M. (1996). Restoring the bridges of trust: Attitudes of community leaders toward local government. In: *Public Integrity Annual*. Council of State Governments, Lexington, KY, pp. 31–49.

Berman, E.M., and West, J.P. (1997). Managing ethics to improve performance and build trust. In: *Public Integrity Annual*. Council of State Governments, Lexington, KY, pp. 23–31.

Berman, E.M., West, J.P., and Bonczek, S.J. (eds.) (1998). *The Ethics Edge*. International City/County Management Association, Washington, D.C.

Berman, E., West, J.P., and Cava, A. (1994). Ethics management in municipal governments and large firms: Exploring similarities and differences. *Administration & Society*, 26:185–203.

Bonczek, S.J. (1998). Creating an ethical work environment: Enhancing ethics awareness in local government. In: *The Ethics Edge* (E.M. Berman, J.P. West and S.J. Bonczek, eds.). International City/County Management Association, Washington, D.C., pp. 72–79.

Bowman, J.S. (1981). Ethical issues for the public manager. In: *A Handbook of Organization Management* (W.B. Eddy, ed.). Marcel Dekker, New York.

Bowman, J.S. (1990). Ethics in government: A national survey of public administrators. *Public Administration Review*, 50:345–353.

Bowman, J.S. and Williams, R.L. (1997). Ethics in government: From a winter of despair to a spring of hope. *Public Administration Review*, 57:517–526.

Burke, F., and Black, A. (1990). Improving organizational productivity: Add ethics. *Public Productivity and Management Review*, 14:121–133.

Bruce, W. (1994). Ethical people are productive people. *Public Productivity and Management Review*, 17:241–252.

Bruce, W. (1996). Codes of ethics and codes of conduct: Perceived contribution to the practice of ethics in local government. In: *Public Integrity Annual*. Council of State Governments, Lexington, KY, pp. 23–39.

Brumback, G.B. (1998). Institutionalizing ethics in government. In: *The Ethics Edge* (E.M. Berman,

J.P. West and S. J. Bonczek, eds.). International City/County Management Association, Washington, D.C., pp. 61–71.

Carnevale, D.G., and Wechsler, B. (1992). Trust in the public sector: Individual and organizational determinants. *Administration & Society*, 23:471–494.

Council for Excellence in Government. (1992–1993). Ethical principles for public servants. *The Public Manager*, 21:37–39.

Gilman, S.C., and Lewis, C.W. (1996). Public service ethics: A global dialogue. *Public Administration Review*, 56:517–524.

Kellar, E.K. (ed.) (1998). *Ethical Insight Ethical Action*. International City/County Management Association, Washington, D.C.

Menzel, D.C. (1992). Ethics attitudes and behaviors in local governments: An empirical analysis. *State and Local Government Review*, 24:94–102.

Menzel, D.C. (1993). The ethics factor in local government: An empirical analysis. In: *Ethics and Public Administration* (H.G. Frederickson, ed). M.E. Sharpe, Armonk, NY, pp. 191–204.

Menzel, D.C. (1995). The ethical environment of local government managers. *American Review of Public Administration*, 25:247–262.

Menzel, D.C. (1996a). Ethics stress in public organizations. *Public Productivity & Management Review*, 20:70–83.

Menzel, D.C. (1996b). Ethics complaint making and trustworthy government. In: *Public Integrity Annual*. Council of State Governments, Lexington, KY, 73–82.

Thompson, D.F. (1992). Paradoxes of government ethics. *Public Administration Review*, 52:254–259.

Williams, R.L. (1996). Controlling ethical practices through laws and rules: Evaluating the Florida commission on ethics. In: *Public Integrity Annual*. Council of State Governments, Lexington, KY, pp. 65–72.

Wilson, W. (1887). The study of administration. Reprinted in *Political Science Quarterly*, 2:56.

Wye, C. (1994). A framework for enlarging the reform agenda. *The Public Manager*, 23:43–46.

Zauderer, D.G. (1994). Winning with integrity. *The Public Manager*, 23:43–46.

18

Federal Ethics Management and Public Trust

Robert Roberts

James Madison University, Harrisonburg, Virginia

From the colonial period of American history through today, the problem of maintaining public trust in federal government agencies has confronted the nation (Locke, 1995: 14–24). Despite some extremely bleak periods (Summers, 1993), the last forty years has seen federal agencies and departments make considerable progress in the development of ethics programs designed to protect public trust in government. The chapter argues that the executive branch ethics program deserves much of the credit for the improved ethical climate in federal agencies and departments. The federal executive branch ethics management program has proven exceptionally effective in reducing the frequency of conflict-of-interest controversies involving federal employees and officials.

Interestingly, public administration ethics scholars have not welcomed the evolution of public ethics codes and conflict-of-interest focused public ethics programs. They criticize public ethics codes for typically dealing with only a limited number of ethical issues; where a financial conflict-of-interest raises questions regarding the ability of a public official or employee to perform their public duties in an impartial manner. In contrast, many public ethics scholars argue that public ethics programs should focus their efforts on persuading public managers to ''weigh the ethics of the programs and policies they set in motion'' (Cohen and Eimicke, 1995: 107).

The sharp difference of opinion over the usefulness of public ethics codes has complicated the process of reaching a consensus over the best strategy for protecting public confidence in public institutions. An objective analysis of public ethics codes and ethics programs that focus upon the ethical implications of public policy decisions provide strong evidence that both types of ethics programs help public employees and officials to resolve ethical problems directly related to the performance of official duties.

I. THE EVOLUTION OF THE FEDERAL EXECUTIVE BRANCH PUBLIC INTEGRITY MANAGEMENT SYSTEM

Annually, a relatively small number of federal employees and officials come under investigation for possible violations of criminal public corruption statutes (Miller, 1992). Today, the Federal Bureau of Investigation, the Public Integrity Section of the United

States Department of Justice, United States Attorneys, and independent counsels exercise responsibility for investigating and prosecuting possible violations of these criminal public corruption prohibitions involving federal employees and officials (Roberts and Doss, 1997: 88–91). However, from the beginning of this republic, the vast majority of public ethics controversies have not involved allegations of *criminal* wrongdoing. Despite this fact, it took until the early 1960s for the White House and federal agencies and departments to begin putting in place a formal executive branch ethics management program designed to reduce the number of public ethics controversies involving federal employees and officials.

Long before a series of 1950s political ethics scandals persuaded the Kennedy White House to establish an executive branch ethics program, a small number of federal agencies experimented with administrative ethics codes as a method of protecting public trust in government. For instance, Postmaster General Amos Kendall, in 1829, created a model ethics code of conduct for postal employees. Kendall's code "included a long list of rules governing work habits, office conduct, the use of government property, and personal morals" (Roberts, 1988:8). Kendall believed that the post office's credibility depended, in part, upon his employees remaining above reproach in the performance of their official duties as well as in their private lives. The commitment of Kendall to high ethical standards in government proved to be much more the exception than the rule.

From the early 1830s through the 1880s, public corruption scandals involving federal departments multiplied like rabbits (Summers, 1987). By the end of the Civil War, critics focused on the "spoils system" as one of the primary causes for the collapse of ethical standards in federal agencies and departments (Roberts, 1988: 19–21). And reformer-minded individuals and groups came to regard civil service reform as the best hope of restoring integrity to management of federal departments (Roberts, 1982: 105–125).

Decades of struggle culminated in the passage of the Pendleton Act of 1883 which authorized the establishment of an executive branch merit system. Equally significant, the act provided for the establishment of the Civil Service Commission and delegated it responsibility for protecting the integrity of the process for selecting members of the new merit system. The Pendleton Act made it a crime punishable by "a fine up to $1000 or imprisonment up to a year or both" for any commissioner or public employee to engage in any "collusion or corruption in the administration of the examinations" used to select individuals for merit system positions (Van Riper, 1979: 9). The passage of the Pendleton Act of 1883 represented the beginning of a long road back from a low point in federal public service ethics (Mosher, 1982: 65). Public corruption prevention and civil service reform went hand in hand.

From 1900 to 1950, the nation experienced an unprecedented explosion in the size and power of the federal government. With the proliferation of federal agencies and programs, came the necessity to delegate to a new generation of federal employees and officials increased discretion to formulate and implement solutions for pressing national problems (Rosenbloom, 1994: 3–36). By the end of the 1930s, a growing number of Americans began to raise legitimate questions regarding the accountability of federal officials and the agencies that employed them. As explained by Kenneth F. Warren, "the Brownlow Commission's 1937 recommendations for procedural reform, along with reports by the American Bar Association on the state of administrative law, and the 1941 report of the Attorney General's Committee on Administrative Procedure, inspired Congress after World War II to draft and unanimously pass the Administrative Procedure Act of 1946"

(Warren, 1996: 183). The passage of the Administrative Procedure Act did little to stop growing public concern over the perceived ability of powerful special interests to influence federal decision-makers.

During the early 1950s, a series of public ethics controversies involving close associates of President Harry Truman and a number of high-profile federal agencies (Dunar, 1984) led many Americans to doubt the impartiality of federal employees and officials. During the fall of 1951, the Senate subcommittee on Labor and Public Welfare issued a report titled *Proposals for Improvement of Ethical Standards in the Federal Government*. The report urged federal agencies and departments to adopt new codes of ethics to prevent federal employees and officials from becoming involved in situations that tend "to make public officials consciously or unconsciously partial in handling issues which come before them" (U.S. Senate, Committee on Labor and Public Welfare, 1951: 11). In addition, the report argued that conflict of interests often "create a suspicion of bias even where it may not exist; they tempt public officials to put personal interests ahead or in conflict with the public interest; or they are damaging or unfair to members of the public" (U.S. Senate, Committee on Labor and Public Welfare, 1951: 11).

Throughout the 1950s, a battle swirled around the future of federal ethics reform. Defenders of the administrative state argued that, without a major overhaul of the way federal agencies and departments resolve ethics controversies involving their employees and officials, public support for major federal programs would continue to erode. On the other hand, critics of existing federal ethics restrictions argued that confusion regarding the scope of public ethics prohibitions deterred some individuals from accepting government positions and made it extremely difficult for individuals with private sector backgrounds to move back and forth between government and the private sector. By the close of the 1950s, the search intensified for a new approach to federal ethics management that would reduce the number of ethics controversies without making it impossible for federal agencies and departments to recruit and retain essential personnel.

A. Presidential Ethics Reform and the Standards of Ethical Conduct for Government Officers and Employees

In 1960, the Association of the Bar of the City of New York issued a report titled *Conflict of Interest in Federal Service*. The report called for a major overhaul of the system for regulating conflict-of-interest situations involving federal employees and officials (Association of the Bar of the City of New York, 1960). The report did not find a crisis in federal service ethics. To the contrary, it found that the vast majority of federal employees and officials tried to do the right thing. However, a confusing web of outdated criminal conflict-of-interest statutes did little to protect public trust in government and had proven next to impossible to enforce. Equally important, the report expressed serious concern that the existing system made it difficult to recruit essential personnel for political and career positions.

To deal with these problems, the Association of the Bar of the City of New York threw its full support behind the issuance of new administrative ethics rules to supplement revised criminal bribery and conflict-of-interest prohibitions (Association of the Bar of the City of New York, 1960: 8). In other words, the report argued that reliance upon criminal bribery and conflict-of-interest statutes hindered efforts to protect public confidence in the impartiality of executive branch decision-making. According to the report, a new administrative ethics program offered the best opportunity for protecting public support for government policies and programs without making it even more difficult to recruit full-time career and political employees as well as part-time employees.

From the spring of 1961 through the close of 1968, the Kennedy White House and then the Johnson White House directed efforts to put in place a new executive branch ethics program. No one in the Kennedy or Johnson White House viewed the new ethics program as a solution to the unethical problems faced by federal employees and officials. Both administrations saw the new ethics program as helping to reduce the number of instances where ethics controversies disrupted the formulation and implementation of public policies and programs. Both administrations saw the new ethics program as a way to reduce reliance upon criminal ethics restrictions as the primary tool for assuring the objectivity and impartiality of actions taken by federal employees and officials.

Through the 1960s, the Kennedy and Johnson administrations issued a series of directives and executive orders establishing new non-criminal ethics guidelines for federal employees and officials (Gilman, 1995: 71). Interestingly, the Civil Service Commission Chairperson, John Macy, played a pivotal role in the development and implementation of the new ethics policies and proved instrumental in the development and the subsequent implementation of the new ethics guidelines (Macy, 1971: 249–256). This fact helps to explain why the new guidelines reflected a much more progressive approach for the resolution of ethics controversies.

In this 1971 book, titled *Public Service: The Human Side of Government*, Macy explained why the Kennedy and Johnson administrations pursued their ethics reform agenda. "Although the federal standards are by no means ideal and must be reevaluated frequently to assure that they match the requirements of the times," stressed Macy, "they do constitute a valid starting point for other jurisdictions. Such standards can emphasize for the benefit of the public the strong intention of the public administrators that the affairs of government be conducted openly, honestly, and impartially" (Macy, 1971: 256).

Not surprisingly, the first directives sought to clarify ethics rules governing the conduct of high-level presidential nominees and appointees. Executive Order 10939 directed:

> All heads of departments and agencies, full-time members of boards and commissions appointed by the president, and members of the White House staff not to accept any fee, compensation, gift, payment of expenses, or anything of monetary value, or create the appearance of, or resulting in (1) use of public office for private gain, (2) an undertaking to give preferential treatment to any person, (3) any loss of complete independence and impartiality, (4) the making of a Government decision outside official channels and (5) any adverse effect on the confidence of the public in the integrity of the Government (Roberts, 1988: 84).

The Kennedy White House subsequently directed all federal agencies and departments to require all federal employees and officials to comply with similar ethics guidelines.

On May 9, 1965, President Johnson issued Executive Order 11222, "Prescribing Standards of Ethical Conduct for Government Officers and Employees" (Newland, 1967: 158). Of great significance, Executive Order 11222 delegated to the United States Civil Service Commission day-to-day responsibility for overseeing the implementation of the new ethics code by federal agencies and departments (Gilman, 1995: 71).

The new executive order differed in three significant respects from the earlier Kennedy standards of conduct order. In the first place, the order directed all federal employees and officials to avoid any action that "might result in, or create the appearance of (1) using public office for private gain; (2) giving preferential treatment to any organization or person; (3) impeding government efficiency or economy; (4) losing complete independence or impartiality of action; (5) making a government decision outside official channels; or (6) affecting adversely the confidence of the public in the integrity of the Government'' (Gilman, 1995: 71). Second, the order gave the Civil Service Commission the authority to require tens of thousands of federal employees to file confidential financial disclosure statements. Third, the order directed every federal agency and department to appoint an individual to oversee ethics programs within individual federal agencies and departments.

Of equal importance to the future evolution of the executive branch ethics program was the requirement that every federal agency and department appoint a Designated Agency Ethics Official (DAEO) to implement the Executive Order 11222 at the agency and department level. Over time, agency and department DAEOs assumed primary responsibility for reviewing confidential financial disclosure statements for conflicts of interest problems, fashioning remedies for actual and potential conflicts of interest, and for issuing agency standards of conduct. As explained by John Macy, Executive Order 11222 ''encouraged individuals faced with problems involving sensitive judgments to seek counsel'' (Macy, 1971: 253). To facilitate effective ethics problem solving, President Johnson directed Chairman Macy ''to work with each department and agency head to designate within his organization qualified persons who could provide guidance and interpretation in specific situations'' (Macy, 1971: 253).

Looking back more than three decades, little doubt remains that the actions taken by the Kennedy and Johnson administrations succeeded in reducing the dependence on criminal statutes as the primary method for guaranteeing the impartiality of decisions made or actions taken by federal agencies and officials. By the end of the 1960s, federal agencies and departments came to depend upon the new standard of conduct regulations as the primary tool for resolving conflict-of-interest problems involving federal employees and officials.

B.   The Public Integrity War and Public Ethics Reform

Through the 1960s and early 1970s, the executive branch ethics program received little public or media attention, until the Watergate scandal. In the aftermath of the Watergate scandal, Congress and public interest groups placed the blame for the scandal on inadequate ethics regulations rather on the character flaws of a group of individuals who proved unable to distinguish between right and wrong. A consensus quickly developed that Congress needed to enact new ethics measures designed to prevent the repeat of Watergate.

Other critics of Washington ethics used the Watergate scandal to push a much broader reform agenda. Critics of federal regulatory agencies argued that powerful special interests exercised too much influence over federal regulatory policies. They placed part of the blame for this situation on former federal officials leaving key regulatory agencies to become lobbyists for regulated industries and enterprises (Roberts and Doss, 1997: 63–85). To deal with the so-called ''revolving door'' problem, reformers urged Congress to enact new restrictions on former high-level federal officials lobbying their former agencies.

The aggressive lobbying campaign culminated in the passage of the Ethics in Government Act of 1978 (Roberts, 1988: 147–162). Today, the Ethics in Government Act of 1978 has come to symbolize a turning point in the management of federal public service ethics. In the first place, the act established procedures for the appointment of special prosecutors (now independent counsels) to investigate allegations of criminal wrongdoing made against certain high-level executive branch and White House officials (Carroll and Roberts, 1988–1989: 437–438).

Second, the act established within the Office of Personnel Management a new United States Office of Government Ethics (USOGE) headed by a presidential nominee. Congress delegated to OGE responsibility for coordinating ethics policy through agency-designated ethics officials (DAEOs) (Gilman, 1995: 72). Third, the act put into place a far reaching public financial disclosure system for high-level officials in all three branches of the federal government (Carroll and Roberts, 1988–1989: 439–440). Fourth, Congress enacted a number of new restrictions on former high-level federal officials lobbying their former agencies after leaving federal agencies and departments. Yet, the Ethics Act left unchanged the vast majority of public corruption statutes and executive branch ethics standards.

Although the Ethics Act added only a few new ethics restrictions, Watergate ushered in an unprecedented period of scrutiny of the on- and off-duty conduct of federal employees and officials. Investigative reporters looked behind every door in Washington for the next Watergate scandal. From 1981 through 1988, a significant number of Reagan nominees and appointees found themselves caught up in public ethics controversies (Gilman, 1995: 73). Not unexpectedly, many Reagan administration officials blamed their predicament on political opponents who used ethics allegations as a way to destroy the reputations of honest public servants (Garment, 1991: 83–107). Many incorrectly thought that the Ethics in Government Act had significantly tightened federal ethics laws and rules. On the other hand, Reagan administration critics blamed the situation on the failure of these officials to follow well established ethical rules or guidelines (Kurtz, 1986: 11–13).

Neither the Reagan administration officials who faced intense scrutiny for their conduct nor the critics of Reagan administration ethics understood that Watergate had set back efforts to decriminalize federal ethics management for at least two decades. The enactment of an independent counsel law and the establishment of the Public Integrity Section of the Department of Justice pumped new resources into public corruption investigations (Roberts and Doss, 1987: 88–94). Badly damaged by its failure to uncover the Watergate conspiracy, the Federal Bureau of Investigation developed the capacity to conduct elaborate public corruption stings.

From the Watergate scandal through much of the 1980s, the executive branch ethics program found itself caught between groups arguing for more aggressive criminal investigations of federal officials and those complaining about the use of ethics allegations to discredit honest public servants. These factors, along with a lack of resources, made it extremely difficult for the Office of Government Ethics to make any significant progress in improving the effectiveness of the executive branch ethics program.

C. The Professionalization of Federal Ethics Management

Early in 1989, the executive branch ethics program received help from an unlikely source. Wishing to avoid a repeat of the ethics scandals that had damaged the reputation of President Reagan, President Bush took immediate steps to evaluate the effectiveness of the executive branch ethics program. In late January 1989, President Bush established the President's Commission on Federal Ethics Law Reform (Roberts and Doss, 1997: 133). President Bush directed his ethics commission to take a close look at federal ethics regulation in all three branches of the federal government. To the dismay of some observers, President Bush appointed Washington insiders who had strong views regarding the direction of the federal ethics program (Clinton, 1989: 10).

The March 1989 report of the Bush ethics commission turned out to be remarkably similar to the 1960 report of the Association of the Bar of the City of New York. The commission found that the vast majority of federal officials and employees experienced few ethics problems. At the same time, the report found that certain federal criminal conflict-of-interest statutes significantly complicated the process of recruiting individuals for career and political positions. Instead of significantly tightening executive branch ethics rules, the report argued that the same ethics rules should apply to members of Congress and executive branch employees and officials. In particular, the commission criticized Congress for requiring executive branch employees to comply with much stricter gift acceptance and financial conflict-of-interest laws than members of Congress (Roberts and Doss, 1997: 134). Finally, the report recommended the relaxation of a small number of ethics rules in order to ease the burden of ethics rules on federal employees and officials (President's Commission on Ethics Law Reform, 1989).

Shortly after the president's ethics commission released its report, President Bush issued Executive Order 12674 which replaced President Johnson's 1965 Executive Order 11222. The new standards of conduct order increased the number of fundamental principles of ethical conduct from six to fourteen and "changed the standards-of-conduct framework from a model program, with agencies writing their own variations, to a single, comprehensive set of standards applicable to the entire executive branch" (Gilman, 1995: 73). Equally significant, the order delegated to the Office of Government Ethics responsibility for assuring government-wide implementation of the uniform ethical guidelines. The issuance of Bush's standards of conduct executive order provided the OGE the authority to restructure the federal executive branch ethics program. Between 1990 and 1994, the Office of Government Ethics issued hundreds of pages of ethics-related regulations (Ethics Resource Library, 1999). More important, over the next five years, Congress significantly increased the budget of the ethics office which permitted OGE to expand federal executive branch ethics programs.

The Bush White House ethics reform program did not stop with the issuance of the new executive branch standards of conduct executive order. When Congress passed the Ethics in Government Reform Act of 1989, they included a number of ethics initiatives which the Bush White House demanded in return for supporting a congressional pay increase (Roberts and Doss, 1997: 139–141). With little fanfare, Congress agreed to expand the authority of federal agencies to accept travel reimbursements from nonfederal sources to defray the cost of travel by federal employees and officials. Congress also agreed to allow federal employees and officials to defer capital gains on financial holdings sold to comply with federal conflict-of-interest rules. Congress also agreed to place new restrictions on the right of members of Congress to accept honoraria from nonfederal sources. Although the Ethics Reform Act did expand the scope of federal "revolving door" restrictions and prohibited all federal executive branch employees and officials from accepting honoraria, the Ethics Reform Act did not significantly tighten ethics restrictions on federal employees and officials.

II. THE FEDERAL ETHICS MANAGEMENT PROGRAM TODAY

As discussed previously, the federal executive branch ethics program has taken some 40 years to evolve. The main ethics management topics include: (1) gifts from outside sources, (2) gifts between employees, (3) conflicting financial interests, (4) impartiality in performing public duties, (5) seeking outside employment, (6) restrictions on former employees, (7) misuse of position and (8) outside activities (USOGE, 1993b). The ethics program relies upon criminal and administrative conflict-of-interest sanctions to protect public confidence in the impartiality and objectivity of actions taken by federal officials and employees.

Since the passage of the Ethics in Government Act of 1978, the Office of Government Ethics has issued hundreds of pages of regulations defining the scope of administrative and criminal ethics prohibitions. During early 1993, USOGE (1993a) took the major step of issuing uniform standard of conduct regulations for the eight program topic areas. The Office of Government Ethics issued the uniform standard of conduct regulations in an effort to establish minimum standards of conduct for all federal employees and officials. Written in an easily understandable question and answer format, the regulations went a long way toward reducing confusion with respect to major areas of federal ethics regulation. In issuing the standards of conduct rules, the USOGE took great care to draft the regulations to reduce the impact of federal ethics rules on the day-to-day operations of federal agencies and departments. Yet, the complexity of the new regulations required a significant increase in agency and department resources devoted to ethics education, training, and enforcement.

A. Gifts from Outside Sources and Travel Reimbursements

Setting clear and workable policies governing the acceptance of private hospitality by federal employees and officials has constituted the most difficult undertaking for the executive branch ethics management program (Roberts and Doss, 1992: 260). Federal gift acceptance prohibitions take two different approaches for distinguishing between permissible and impermissible gifts. One rule prohibits federal employees and officials from accepting gifts from certain sources. A second rule prohibits federal employees and officials from accepting gifts from nonfederal sources motivated by official acts performed by the federal employee or official.

The executive branch, administrative, prohibited-source rule states that federal employees and officials may not accept anything of value from persons or organizations that (1) seek a particular action from their agency, (2) does business or seeks business with their agency, (3) are regulated by the employee's agency, or (4) "have interests that may be substantially affected by" the performance or nonperformance of the employee's official duties (USOGE, 1993b: 5). The prohibited-source rule requires federal employees to inquire into the relationship between any source of a potential gift and the federal employee's official activities.

To reduce the impact of the prohibited-source rule on the routine activities of federal employees and officials, USOGE regulations established a category of permissible gifts or gift "exclusions" (USOGE, 1993b: 6). Gift acceptance exclusions permit federal employees to accept "soft drinks, coffee, donuts, and other modest items of food and refreshment when not offered as part of a meal," and "items of inherent value such as plaques and certificates and items which federal employees pay full market value for" (USOGE, 1993b: 6). In addition to items treated as "gift exclusions," federal gift acceptance rules allow federal employees to accept "certain unsolicited gifts with a value of $20 or less per occasion (but not cash gifts and not gifts that add up to over $50 in value in any year from any single source" (USOGE, 1993b: 6).

Prior to the passage of the Ethics in Government Reform Act of 1989, federal law prohibited the vast majority of federal agencies and departments from accepting travel reimbursements from private sources to cover the travel expenses of federal employees. To remedy this situation, the Ethics Reform Act granted the General Services Administration the authority to issue regulations permitting all federal agencies and departments to accept travel reimbursements from nonfederal sources (USOGE, 1997a: 1). For instance, a corporation would like to host a conference to examine ways to reduce air pollution by commuters. The new law permits the corporation to pay the travel and lodging costs of Environmental Protection Administration officials invited to the conference.

To guard against possible conflict-of-interest problems, the law requires all federal agencies and departments to certify, prior to the acceptance of any payments, that the acceptance of a travel reimbursement would not lead a reasonable person to ''question the integrity of agency programs or operations'' (USOGE, 1997a: 1–2). The establishment of government-wide agency gift acceptance authority constituted a major relaxation of executive branch ethics rules.

Besides being subject to the prohibited-source gift acceptance rule, federal employees and officials must comply with the federal illegal-gratuity statute (Roberts et al., 1996: 1). The illegal-gratuity statute prohibits federal employees from accepting anything of value from a nonfederal source for the performance of official acts or duties. Despite the fact that the provision became law in 1962, considerable controversy still continues over the scope of the illegal-gratuity statute. It would take the Supreme Court to resolve the dispute.

On the one hand, some experts argued that the statute prohibited federal employees and officials from accepting all ''non quid pro quo'' gifts motivated by the position held by the federal employee or official. In other words, the illegal-gratuity statute prohibited private sources from providing federal employees and officials a wide variety of private hospitality (Greenhouse, 1998: A18). On the other hand, other ethics experts argued that illegal-gratuity statute only prohibited federal employees and officials from accepting private hospitality from private sources if the federal employee knew that a particular action taken by the employee motivated the gift (Greenhouse, 1998: A18).

Prior to the criminal prosecution of former Secretary of Agriculture, Mike Espy, for accepting illegal-gratuity from companies regulated by the Department of Agriculture, few Americans ever heard of the illegal-gratuity statute (Greenhouse, 1998: A18). In late 1998, a federal jury rejected this broad interpretation of the statute put forward by independent counsel Donald Smaltz. After the verdict, members of the federal jury publicly criticized independent counsel Donald Smaltz for bringing the charges without being able to prove that Espy had done something in return for the gifts (Miller, 1998: A1).

On April 27, 1999, in *United States v. Sun-Diamond Growers of California*, the Supreme Court rejected the broad interpretation of the illegal-gratuity statute supported by the Department of Justice and independent council Donald Smaltz. The Court held that ''in order to establish a violation of 18 U.S.C. & 201(c)(1)(A), the Government must prove a link between a thing of value conferred upon a public official and a specific 'official act' for or because of which it was given'' (*U.S. v. Sun-Diamond*, 1999, 526 U.S. 398). In rejecting the argument that the illegal-gratuity statute prohibited all private hospitality of federal officials, Justice Scalia pointed to gift acceptance regulations issued by the Office of Government Ethics which permitted executive branch employees and officials to accept certain types of private hospitality. As Justice Scalia explained, ''we are frankly not sure that even our more narrow interpretation of 18 U.S.C. & 201(c)(1)(B) will cause OGE's assurance of nonviolation if the regulation is complied with to be entirely accurate; but the misdirection, if any, will be infinitely less'' (*U.S. v. Sun-Diamond*, 1999).

The criminal ban on nonfederal sources supplementing the salaries of executive branch employees and officials constitutes the final type of gift acceptance ban. Originally enacted in 1917, the salary supplementation prohibits nonfederal sources from supplementing the salaries of executive branch employees. For instance, a major corporation may not pay the difference between what an executive earned and his or her salary as a cabinet secretary. However, the Supreme Court ruled in the 1990 case of *Crandon v. United States* that the ban did not apply to payments made prior to the date individuals legally become an executive branch employee or official (*Crandon v. United States*, 1990). Prior to the decision, the Department of Justice had ruled that the salary supplementation ban also applied to payments made to individuals prior to the date they became a federal employee or official.

B. Gifts Between Employees

A separate ethics policy regulates gifts between federal employees. As a general rule, federal employees may not provide superiors gifts or accept gifts from superiors. In addition, federal employees may not accept gifts ''from non-subordinates who receive less pay'' than another federal employee (USOGE, 1993b: 8). Much like the exemption provisions of the prohibited-source gift acceptance policy, federal ethics regulations permit certain types of gifts between subordinates and superiors, and between superiors and subordinates. The first exception permits gifts ''given on an occasional basis'' to express appreciation for private hospitality. The second exception permits federal employees to give or accept certain small gifts ''recognizing special, infrequent events such as a marriage, illness, the birth or adoption of a child, and a retirement, resignation or transfer'' (USOGE, 1993b: 9).

Like the outside gift acceptance rules, the gift-between-employees rules demonstrate sincere effort by USOGE to adopt flexible ethics rules which do not unreasonably interfere with social activities that occur routinely in all types of organizations.

C. Conflicting Financial Interests

Without question, the regulation of conflicting financial interests has proven the most difficult federal executive branch ethics rule to enforce. As part of the 1962 revision of federal criminal conflict-of-interest laws, Congress enacted a new criminal conflicting-financial-interests statute (Roberts, 1988: 101–102). At the urging of the Kennedy White House and federal agencies and departments, Congress exempted from coverage so called ''special government employees'' from coverage under the statute; individuals employed for less than 135 days in any 365-day period by a federal agency or department (Roberts, 1988: 97). The action reduced the problem of paid or unpaid experts or consultants being unable to work on certain projects because of the fact that they held certain financial interests.

On the other hand, the statute established a sweeping financial conflict-of-interest rule for the vast majority of executive branch employees and officials. Section 208 of title 18 of the United States Code prohibits executive branch employees or officials ''from participating personally and substantially in certain matters'' in which federal employees have a financial interest (USOGE, 1993b: 11). The fact that the statute treated the financial interests of a spouse, minor children, and business partners of an employee as the financial interests of the employee further complicated enforcement of the law. Despite the fact that the statute did not require executive branch employees and officials to sell any financial holdings, the law constituted a major broadening of executive branch ethics rules.

From the enactment of the measure through today, the disqualification rule has forced executive branch ethics officials to put in place a sophisticated system for detecting and resolving financial conflicts of interest. As discussed earlier, President Johnson's Executive Order 11222, required thousands of federal employees to file confidential disclosure statements (Newland, 1967: 158–180). Then in 1978, the passage of the Ethics in Government Act required high-level federal officials to file annual public financial disclosure statements (Carroll and Roberts, 1988–1989: 439–440). The Ethics in Government Reform Act of 1989 also directed the Office of Government Ethics to put in place a new confidential financial reporting system (Gilman, 1995: 73). Besides a comprehensive financial disclosure system, federal agencies and departments have come to rely upon a mix of remedies to resolve actual and potential financial conflicts of interest. Remedies include (1) recusal or disqualification, (2) divestiture, (3) or obtaining a statutory waiver (USOGE, 1995: 18).

Although executive branch employees and officials historically used disqualification as the primary method for resolving financial conflict-of-interest problems (Moore, 1987: 1962–1967), disqualification created a number of serious management problems. First, an employee or official who disqualified himself or herself might not be able to do the job the agency or department hired the employee or official to do. Second, disqualification required ethics officials to spend a vast amount of time determining what matters were and were not covered by the disqualification rule. Throughout the 1960s, 1970s, and 1980s, federal agencies and departments complained about the loss of expertise and the administrative burden resulting from the disqualification policy (Moore, 1987: 1962–1967).

When Congress passed the new financial conflict-of-interest statute in 1962, it clearly anticipated that the president would make periodic use of new waiver authority to deal with situations where federal agencies and departments badly needed the services of certain individuals where requiring the individual to disqualify himself or herself or sell off certain financial holdings would destroy the effectiveness of the employee or official or work a hardship on the employee or official (Murdock, 1990: 502–525). Interestingly, presidents have made infrequent use of waiver authority to resolve the financial conflict-of-interest problems of federal employees and officials. At the urging of the Bush White House, Congress included liberalized waiver authority among the provisions of the Ethics Reform Act of 1989 (USOGE, 1999: 12).

Between the enactment of the 1962 federal conflict-of-interest law and the passage of the Ethics Reform Act of 1989, federal agencies and departments looked for a more effective way to resolve financial conflict-of-interest problems. Recusal or disqualification could seriously reduce the effectiveness of key agency or department officials and employees. Agencies and departments found waivers difficult to obtain. Consequently, federal agencies and departments looked for a more effective way to resolve financial conflict-of-interest problems. As part of the Ethics Reform Act of 1989, Congress empowered the Director of the Office of Government Ethics with the authority to issue certificates of divestiture permitting executive branch employees and officials to roll over capital gains resulting from the forced sale of financial interests (Roberts and Doss, 1996: 49–60). Between 1990 and today, the director of the USOGE has issued hundreds of certificates of divestiture to both political appointees and career federal employees (Roberts and Doss, 1996: 49–60).

After decades of struggling with the issue of how to enforce financial conflict-of-interest rules without working an undue hardship on executive branch employees and officials, it appears that agency ethics officials now have sufficient flexibility to effectively resolve the financial conflict-of-interest problems of federal employees and officials.

D. Impartiality in the Performance of Official Duties and the Appearance of Impropriety Standard

As discussed earlier, the Kennedy White House issued the first executive branch ethics directive requiring federal employees and officials to avoid even the appearance of impropriety in the performance of official duties (Roberts, 1988: 84). President Johnson's 1965 standards-of-conduct executive order included an appearance-of-impropriety rule standard among its provisions. From the 1960s through the early 1980s, federal agencies and departments periodically disciplined federal employees and officials for violating the appearance-of-impropriety rule (Brownstein, 1985: 640). During this period, the Merit Systems Protection Board had upheld the authority of federal agencies and departments to enforce the rule (Dickenson, 1985: A17).

Between 1981 and the end of 1988, the ethics problems of a number of Reagan administration officials led to the development of intense interest in the appearance-of-impropriety policy (Roberts and Doss, 1997: 123–128). Critics of the conduct of Reagan appointees demanded that agency ethics officials or the Director of the USOGE discipline Reagan appointees for their conduct (Moore, 1987: 1984). During the 1985 confirmation battle over nomination of Edwin Meese III for Attorney General, the Director of the USOGE argued "that the executive order requiring federal employees to avoid any action 'which might result in, or create the appearance of impropriety' is only 'aspirational in nature'" (Dickenson, 1985: A17). The statement ignited a firestorm in Washington (Brownstein, 1985: 639). Democratic members of Congress attacked the USOGE Director for advocating the weakening of executive branch ethics rules. Yet, the debate did little to deal with legitimate concerns over the fairness of enforcing an appearance-of-impropriety rule.

Issued on April 12, 1989, President Bush's standards-of-conduct executive order included a new test for applying the appearance-of-impropriety rule to the on- and off-duty activities of federal employees and officials. "Employees shall endeavor to avoid any action creating the appearance that they are violating the law or the ethical standards set forth in the Standards of Ethical Conduct," states principle 14. "Whether particular circumstances create an appearance that the law or these standards have been violated shall be determined from the perspective of a reasonable person with knowledge of the relevant facts," concludes principle 14 (USOGE, 1995: 9). The Bush White House saw the tightening of the appearance-of-impropriety rule as a way to protect federal employees and officials from unwarranted attacks.

Subsequently, the USOGE issued guidelines delegating to federal agencies and departments primary responsibility for interpreting and enforcing the impartiality rule. The rule states that if an employee determines that a reasonable person would not question the employee's impartiality, then the employee "may participate in the matter, unless the agency designee reaches a different conclusion" (USOGE, 1995: 20). In an April 27, 1997 letter to a United States Senator regarding a possible violation of the appearance-of-conflict rule by a federal official, Stephen D. Potts, Director of the OGE explained the difficulty of applying the appearance-of-conflict standard on a case-by-case basis. "We recognize that some might find section 2635.502 of our Standards of Conduct troubling as applied in an individual case," stressed Director Potts. "On the other hand," continued Potts, "we have been aware that 'appearance of conflict' has been used as the weapon of choice in Washington for years. We developed these rules to afford some protection to the employee who, in good faith, takes appearance into some consideration, but who decides on a course of conduct susceptible to second-guessing" (USOGE, 1997b: 2).

E. Outside Employment and Public Service

Federal standards-of-conduct regulations also require all federal employees and officials to pay careful attention to possible financial conflicts of interest that might result from job-hunting, job discussions, and outside employment (USOGE, 1995: 23). Several criminal statutes and standard-of-conduct regulations deal with a number of outside employment related issues.

First, executive branch ethics rules permit most federal employees and officials to engage in a wide range of outside activities. These include "paid employment and civic, charitable, religious, and community service work performed without compensation" (USOGE, 1995: 29). However, a federal employee "may not engage in an outside activity if the rules dealing with conflicting financial interests or the appearance of a loss of impartiality would require the employee's disqualification from matters so central or critical to the performance of the employee's official duties that his ability to perform the duties of his position would be materially impaired" (USOGE, 1995: 29). Consequently, federal agencies and departments have broad discretion to monitor and regulate the outside employment of their employees and officials.

Second, federal criminal statutes prohibit federal employees from representing a person or organization before a department, agency, or court, or serving as an expert witness with or without compensation. Specifically, the laws prohibit federal employees and officials from representing private parties with respect to particular matters pending before federal agencies or departments or before federal courts (USOGE, 1995: 29–30).

At the urging of the Kennedy White House, Congress with its 1962 revision of federal bribery and conflict-of-interest laws exempted from the in-service representation ban so-called "special government employees." To qualify for the special government employee exemption, the employee must not work for a federal agency or department for more than 130 days out of a 365 day period (Roberts, 1988: 97–99). Federal law also permits federal employees to represent themselves, their parents, their spouse, their children, and certain others "whom the employee serves in a specific fiduciary capacity, such as a guardian" (USOGE, 1995: 29).

Third, federal law now places limits on the amount of outside income certain executive branch employees and officials may receive. Beginning in the early 1960s, presidential ethics directives imposed a ban on federal employees and officials receiving compensation "from any source other than the Government for teaching, speaking or writing that relates to the employee's official duties" (USOGE, 1995: 31). However, the "official duties" outside compensation ban did not apply to compensation received for teaching, speaking, and writing for matters unrelated to the employee's official duties.

The Ethics Reform Act of 1989 made a major change in the rule. The act prohibited all federal employees and officials from receiving any honorarium for teaching, speaking, or writing for matters related or unrelated to the employee's official duties. The action touched off a firestorm of criticism from groups representing career federal employees and officials. Career employees argued that the ban deterred federal employees and officials from writing articles and giving talks and thus violated their First Amendment right to freedom of speech and association. The government defended the prohibition on the grounds that it helped to protect public trust in government.

Subsequently, federal employee organizations sought to strike down the constitutionality of the new honorarium ban. In the 1995 case of *United States v. National Treasury Union*, the Supreme Court ruled that the ban violated the First Amendment rights of federal employees and officials below the grade of GS-16 (*U.S. v. National Treasury Employees Union*, 1995). Significantly, the decision left in place the authority of Congress to regulate outside appearances, speeches, and written articles of high-level federal officials.

Fourth, federal law places a cap on the outside earned income received by certain types of executive branch employees and officials. The Ethics in Government Act of 1978 established the first federal outside income limit. The act prohibited ''certain non-career federal employees'' whose basic pay is equal to or greater than the annual rate of basic pay for positions classified above GS-15 ''from accepting more than 15% of their salary in additional earned outside income'' (USOGE, 1995: 32). In 1989, President Bush issued E. O. 12674 which prohibited presidential appointees to full-time noncareer positions from ''accepting any outside earned income during their Presidential appointments'' (USOGE, 1995: 32). As a result of these actions, federal law now prohibits most presidential appointees from accepting any outside income. Critics of outside income prohibitions continue to argue that they work an undue hardship on individuals who enter federal service without substantial private resources. Despite such criticism, outside income restrictions have become a permanent part of the executive branch ethics program.

Fifth, executive branch ethics rules heavily regulate the employment negotiations of federal employees and officials with prospective private sector employers. Specifically, section 208 of title 18 of the United States Code prohibits all executive branch employees and officials from participating in any particular matter that would affect the financial interest of a prospective employer (USOGE, 1995: 23). As a result of the prohibition, federal employees who seek employment outside of the federal government must carefully examine their duties and responsibilities to make sure that they do not involve the prospective employer.

F. Restrictions on Former Employees

Of the major types of executive branch ethics rules, restrictions on former federal employees and officials have experienced the greatest change over the last forty years. Although Congress enacted the first restrictions on the activities of former federal employees during the 1870s, Congress did not move to enact effective revolving-door prohibitions until the early 1960s (Roberts, 1988: 16). As discussed earlier, ethics reformers used the Watergate scandal to persuade Congress to enact a number of new revolving-door restrictions for former high-level federal officials (Common Cause, 1977). The Ethics in Government Reform Act of 1989 also made minor adjustments to existing revolving-door restrictions (Roberts and Doss, 1997: 140).

Today, executive branch employees and officials find themselves subject to a number of revolving-door prohibitions designed to prevent former federal officials from using their government contacts to obtain preferential treatment for their clients or other special interests. The permanent switching-sides statute, section 207 of title 18 of the United States Code, prohibits all former executive branch employees and officials from representing "another person or organization before a Federal department, agency, or court on certain matters in which the former employee participated personally and substantially while working for the Government" (USOGE, 1995: 24). A second post-employment statute prohibits former federal employees from representing "another person or organization before a Federal department, agency, or court on certain matters which were pending under the employee's supervision during the last year of [the employee's] government service" (USOGE, 1995: 24). A third restriction prohibits all former executive branch employees, for a period of one year after leaving government service, "from engaging in activities related to certain trade and treaty negotiations" (USOGE, 1995: 25).

Between 1978 and 1990, Congress enacted a number of revolving-door restrictions which only apply to former high-level executive branch officials. The 1978 Ethics Act established a new one-year, cooling-off period which prohibited "covered" officials from contacting their former employers on behalf of a client with regard to any particular matter pending in the official's former agency. The Ethics Reform Act of 1989 imposed additional "one year restrictions on the activities of former senior and very senior Government employees" (USOGE, 1995: 25). Finally, on January 20, 1993, President Clinton issued Executive Order 12834 which covered senior noncareer executive branch officials appointed by the president, vice president, or an agency head after the date of the order. The Executive Order requires these appointees to sign an agreement restricting their "representations before or to agencies served by the appointees with those agencies" for a period of five years after leaving the federal government (USOGE, 1995: 25). The Clinton Executive Order also imposes a lifetime restriction on covered appointees from undertaking certain activities before federal agencies and departments "on behalf of foreign governments and foreign political parties" (USOGE, 1995: 25).

Much like outside earned income restrictions, the debate continues over the need for criminal revolving-door restrictions. Supporters of revolving-door restrictions argue that they help to shield federal employees and officials from being pressured by former federal officials to provide special interests preferential access to executive branch officials. Critics of the restrictions argue they do little to stop influence peddling and simply make it more difficult to recruit individuals to serve in government. Interestingly, it appears that former federal officials have learned to live under the new generation of revolving-door rules. Presidents Carter, Reagan, Bush, and Clinton seemed to have little difficulty recruiting high quality individuals to staff key policymaking positions. The so-called revolving-door problem no longer seems a crisis that threatens to destroy public confidence in government.

III. EXTERNAL CONTROLS AND PUBLIC SERVICE ETHICS

In 1993, the ethics programs in the executive branch required the help of "144 DAEO's who employed 14,399 individuals in full-time and part-time capacities" (Gilman, 1995: 74). Federal employees and officials spend countless hours filling out public and confidential financial disclosure forms which agency ethics officials review for conflict-of-interest problems. Every year federal agencies and departments conduct numerous ethics seminars designed to familiarize employees and officials with ethics rules and requirements.

Despite the expansion of the executive branch ethics program, few public ethics scholars view external ethics rules as the best way for guaranteeing ethical behavior on the part of public employees and officials. After completing a review of the literature of public service ethics, Jerry Plant of Pennsylvania University concluded that, "writers in the field of public administration ethics remained unconvinced that codes of ethics were important or advisable" (Plant, 1994: 225). "Ethicists in public administration," writes Plant, "have not been fond of codes. By their formalism, their preachiness, their legalism, codes in their opinion fall far short of the goal of creating a new civic perspective to replace the old progressive constructs of public service and the public interest" (Plant, 1994: 237).

The ambivalence of public ethics scholars to legal codes of public service ethics results from the belief that compliance with ethics codes does little to guarantee that public administrators will act in an ethical manner in the formulation and implementation of public policy. As David H. Rosenbloom and James D. Carroll argue in *Toward Constitutional Competence: A Casebook for Public Administrators*, "[j]ust as public administrators need to know how to interpret statistical regression and cost-benefit analysis, they must often have knowledge of the constitutional rights of their subordinates and the individuals on whom their official actions bear directly" (Rosenbloom and Carroll, 1990: 2). In a 1995 article entitled "Ethics and the Public Administrator," Steven Cohen and William B. Eimicke argue that "[public administrators] must therefore make personal value and moral judgements about the types of activities they are willing to perform. These judgements should not be made casually, and when taken seriously, they can require profoundly disturbing choices" (Cohen and Eimicke, 1995: 106–107). Simply put, public administrators have a moral obligation not to participate in the implementation of public policies that violate fundamental rights; even if the law or the courts have not recognized those rights. In other words, critics of ethics regulation believe that the preoccupation with the enforcement of ethics rules does little to improve ethical decision-making in government.

A 1993 American Bar Association study of the executive branch ethics program argued that "ethics is in danger of becoming an elaborate legalistic ritual, in which the application of multi-part tests substitutes for the internalization of values, and the establishment of multi-level clearance processes replaces the development of a supportive institutional culture" (ABA, Committee on Government Standards, 1993: 290). On the other hand, Michael Martinez (in a 1998 *Administration & Society* article) strongly endorsed the adoption of a strong code of ethics for public administrators:

> At a minimum, a strong code of ethics must require, with appropriate enforcement mechanisms (i.e., private and public letters of reprimand, monetary fines, and expulsion from the profession in rare, egregious circumstances), that public administrators act in accordance with the public interest and democratic values as those ambiguous terms are defined through codified rules and guidelines published by the independent board of public administrators in consultation with practitioners, scholars, and the public. In short, a code of ethics "with teeth" that also allows for a private sense of ethics is the most practicable means of ensuring that public servants behave responsibly (Martinez, 1998: 722).

IV. MYTH AND REALITY: THE EXECUTIVE BRANCH ETHICS PROGRAM

From 1961 to the end of 1968, United States Civil Service Commission Chairman, John Macy, pushed vigorously for the expansion of the executive branch ethics program (Gilman, 1995: 71). Macy understood that as the size and power of the federal government increased, public servants would find themselves under increased pressure to do the wrong thing from special interests seeking preferential treatment. He also understood that an effective executive branch ethics program could prevent situations that would raise questions regarding the impartiality and objectivity of decisions made by federal employees and officials.

For far too long, a debate has raged over the usefulness of public-service ethics codes as a tool for instilling a sense of ethical responsibility in the hearts and minds of public servants. Like the canon of ethics for lawyers, public-service ethics codes serve an important role in preventing public servants from becoming involved in situations which will raise serious questions regarding their impartiality and objectivity (Martinez, 1998: 690). A close examination of the executive branch ethics program reveals that it has evolved into an effective program to help federal employees and officials to avoid situations which might lead some members of the public and the media to question the impartiality and objectivity of actions taken by federal employees and officials.

REFERENCES

ABA Committee on Government Standards. (1993). Keeping faith: Government ethics and government ethics regulation. *Administrative Law Review*, 45:288–340.

Association of the Bar of the City of New York. (1960). *Conflict of Interest and Federal Service*. Harvard University Press, Cambridge, MA.

Brownstein, R. (1985). Agency ethics officers fear Meese ruling could weaken conflict laws. *National Journal*, 17(March 23):639–642.

Carroll, J.D. and Roberts, R. (1988–1989). "If Men Were Angels," assessing ethics in government act of 1978. *Policy Studies Journal*, 17(Winter):435–447.

Clinton, Z. (1989). Watchdogs that purr: How not to set up an ethics commission. *The New Republic*, 200:10–12.

Cohen, S. and Eimicke, B. (1995). Ethics and the public administrator. *Annals*, 537:96–108.

Common Cause. (1977). *Serving Two Masters: A Common Cause Case Study of Conflicts of Interest in the Executive Branch*. Common Cause, Washington, D.C.

Crandon V. United States. (1990). 494 U.S. 152.

Dickenson, J.R. (1985). Meese hearings over, but not forgotten, ethics chief's opinion causes concern. *Washington Post*, April 2: A17.

Douglas, P.H. (1952). *Ethics in Government*. Harvard University Press, Cambridge, MA.

Dunar, A.J. (1984). *The Truman Scandals and the Politics of Morality*. University of Missouri Press, Columbia, MO.

Ethics Resource Library. (1999). United States Office of Government Ethics. URL: *http://www.usoge.gov/usoge006.html#orders*

Frederickson, G.H. and Frederickson, D. (1995). Public perceptions of ethics in government. *Annals*, 537:163–172.

Frier, D.A. (1969). *Conflict of Interest in the Eisenhower Administration*. Iowa State University Press, Ames, IA.

Garment, S. (1991). *Scandal: The Crisis of Mistrust in American Politics*. Times Books, New York.

General Services Administration. (1993). Acceptance of Payment from a Non-Federal Source for Travel Expenses, 41 C.F.R. 301-1 and 304-1.

Gilman, S. (1995). Presidential ethics and the ethics of the presidency. *Annals*, 537:58–75.

Greenhouse, L. (1998). Justice agrees to resolve dispute out of Espy case regarding law on gifts. *New York Times*, November 3:A18.

Huddleston, M.W. and Sands, J.C. (1995). Enforcing administrative ethics. *Annals*, 537:139–149.

Kurtz, H. (1986). Reagan's people, issues of propriety: Deaver case revives questions about senior officials' conduct. *Washington Post*, April 27:A1, A11–13.

Locke, H.G. (1995). Ethics in American government: A look backward. *Annals*, 537:14–24.

Macy, J.W. (1971). *Public Service: The Human Side of Government*. Harper and Row, New York.

Manning, B. (1964). The purity potlatch: An essay on conflict of interest, American government, and moral escalation. *The Federal Bar Journal*, 24:239–256.

Martinez, M. (1998). Law versus ethics: Reconciling two concepts of public ethics. *Administration & Society*, 29:690–722.

Miller, N. (1992). *Stealing from America: History of Corruption from Jamestown to Reagan*. Paragon House, New York.

Miller, B. (1998). A harsh verdict for Espy's prosecutor; jurors say independent counsel wasted tax dollars, didn't make a case. *Washington Post*, December 5:A1.

Moore, J.W. (1987). Cop on ethics beat caught in a cross fire. *National Journal*, 19:1984.

Moore, J.W. (1989). Hands off: To avoid conflict-of-interest questions, many of President Bush's appointees are holding on to corporate stocks but are disqualifying themselves from issues involving specific firms. *National Journal*, July 1:1678–1683.

Mosher, F.C. (1982). *Democracy and the Public Service*. Oxford University Press, New York.

Murdock, E.J. (1990). Finally, government ethics as if people mattered: Some thoughts on the ethics reform act of 1989. *The George Washington University Law Review*, 58:502–525.

Newland, C. (1967). Federal employee conduct and financial disclosure. *Record of the Association of the Bar of the City of New York*, 22:158–180.

Plant, J.F. (1994). Codes of ethics. In *Handbook of Administrative Ethics* (T. Cooper, ed.). New York, Marcel Dekker, p. 221–241.

President's Commission on Ethics Law Reform. (1989). *To Serve with Honor: Report of the President's Commission on Ethics Law Reform*. Government Printing Office, Washington, D.C.

Principles of Ethical Conduct for Government Officers and Employees. (1990). Executive Order 12731, October 17.

Principles of Ethical Conduct for Government Officers and Employees. (1989). Executive Order 12674, April 12.

Revolving Door Proposal Strikes a Nerve. (1978). *Broadcasting*, 20:44.

Roberts, R. (1982). Conflict-of-interest and the federal service. In *The Centenary Issues of the Pendleton Act of 1883: The Problematic Legacy of Civil Service Reform*. (D.H. Rosenbloom, ed.). Marcel Dekker, New York, p. 105–125.

Roberts, R. (1988). *White House Ethics: The History of the Politics of Conflict of Interest Regulation*. Greenwood Press, Westport, CT.

Roberts, R. and Doss, M.T. (1992). Public service and private hospitality: A case study in federal conflict-of-interest reform. *Public Administration Review*, 52:260–270.

Roberts, R. and Doss, M.T. (1996). Recruitment of American presidential nominees and appointees: Divestiture and deferred taxation of gain. *The Journal of Social, Political and Economic Studies*, 21:49–69.

Roberts, R., and Doss, M.T. (1997). *From Watergate To Whitewater: The Public Integrity War*. Praeger, Westport, CT.

Roberts, R., Doss, M.T., and Hammond, J. (1996). Lobbyists beware: The rise of the illegal-gratuity statute. *The Journal of Social, Political and Economic Studies*, 21:383–420.

Rosenbloom, D.H. (1994). The evolution of the administrative state and transformation of administrative law. In *Handbook of Regulation and Administrative Law* (D.H. Rosenbloom and R.D. Schwartz, ed). Marcel Dekker, New York, pp. 3–36.

Rosenbloom, D.H. and Carroll, J.D. (1990). *Toward Constitutional Competence: A Casebook for Public Administrators*. Prentice Hall, Englewood Cliffs, NJ.

Skidmore, M.J. (1995). Ethics and public service. *Annals*, 537:25–36.

Summers, M.W. (1993). *The Era of Good Stealing*. Oxford University Press, New York.

Summers, M.W. (1987). *The Plundering Generation: Corruption and Crisis of the Union 1849–1861*. Oxford University Press, New York.

U.S. Senate, Committee on Labor and Public Welfare. (1951). Report of the Subcommittee on Labor and Public Welfare on *Ethical Standards in Government*, 82nd Cong., 1st Sess.

United States v. National Treasury Employees Union. (1995). URL: *http://laws.findlaw.com/US/000/010314.html*.

United States v. Sun-Diamond Growers of California. (1999). 526 U.S. 398.

United States Office of Government Ethics. (1995). *Do it Right: An Ethics Handbook for Executive Branch Employees*. United States Office of Government Ethics, Washington, D.C.

United States Office of Government Ethics. (1999). Ethics Program Topics. URL: *http://www.usoge.gov/usoge003.htm*, February 16.

United States Office of Government Ethics. (1998). Executive Branch Financial Disclosure, Qualified Trusts, and Certificates of Divestiture, 5 CFR Part 2635.

United States Office of Government Ethics. (1998). Interpretation, Exemption and Waiver Guidance Concerning 18 U.S.C. 208 (Acts Affecting a Personal Financial Interest) 5 CFR 2640.

United States Office of Government Ethics. (1997a). *Gifts of Travel and Other Benefits*. United States Office of Government Ethics, Washington, D.C.

United States Office of Government Ethics. (1997b). Letter to a United States Senator, April 27.

United States Office of Government Ethics. (1993a). *Standards of Ethical Conduct for Employees of the Executive Branch*. 5 C.F.R. Part 2636.

United States Office of Government Ethics. (1993b). *Take the High Road: An Ethics Booklet for Executive Branch Employees*. United States Office of Government Ethics, Washington, D.C.

Van Riper, P. (1979). Americanizing a foreign invention: The pendleton act of 1883. In *Classics of Public Personnel Policy* (Thompson, F.J., ed.). Moore Publishing Company, Oak Park, Illinois, pp. 9–15.

Walter, J.J. (1981). The ethics in government act, conflict of interest laws and presidential recruiting. *Public Administration Review*, 41:659–665.

Warren, K.F. (1996). *Administrative Law in the Political System*, 3rd ed. Prentice Hall, Upper Saddle River, NJ.

19

Federal Inspectors General and the Paths to Accountability

Paul C. Light
The Brookings Institution, Washington, D.C.

No story did more to raise the visibility of the federal inspectors general (IGs) than the 1989 HUD scandal.* The Housing and Urban Development IG was in the papers almost daily, whether revealing new details about "Robin HUD," testifying before Congress about $300,000 consultants, such as former Interior Secretary James Watt, who had used their influence to win housing projects for high-priced clients; or continuing the investigation of the apparent political slush fund that operated out of the HUD secretary's office. Suddenly, the IG was frontpage news.

Not all of the headlines were positive, however. Simply put, some in Washington believed the IG had missed the story. Seeking answers to a scandal that went to the very top of the agency, Congress and the press also asked about the IG. As *Time* asked in its story on "The Housing Hustle," "How could such a scandal remain uncovered for so long? The answer lies partly in the fact that no one was looking."[1] By implication, that "no one" included the HUD IG, a point argued by Rep. Christopher Shays (R-CT) in the following exchange with HUD IG Paul Adams during the House investigation hearings:

> Mr. Shays: . . . My impression of the IG's office was that you looked at wrongdoing, found it out, and then you made sure something was done about it . . .
>
> Mr. Adams: First of all, Mr. Shays, the investigation was ongoing, so we didn't have the final report nor did we have the final audit. We did report it to Congress in our September 30, 1988, report, semiannual report to Congress, that we had problems and it was an ongoing effort.
>
> Mr. Shays: You are missing my point here. I am talking in general. See, I have a lot of faith, historically have had a lot of faith in the concept of an IG's office. My understanding is we have an IG's office so we wouldn't have the kind of problems we are uncovering, and I, frankly, this is—you know, I am not going to be shocked any more, I am simply not going to be because nothing is going to shock me . . .
>
> My point, though, is it your job to make sure this doesn't happen, isn't it? That is the whole reason why we have the IG's office. And once you uncover it, to make sure it doesn't happen again.[2]

---

* The author wishes to acknowledge the input and encouragement of the Governance Institute and its president, Robert A. Katzmann, in the work from which this paper is drawn.

Whatever one thinks of Shays' comment—and the research from which this chapter is drawn suggests his interpretation of the legislative history is mostly incorrect—his comment sets the stage for asking about the IG's role in assuring accountability in government.[3]

I. AN INTRODUCTION TO THE CONCEPT

The fact that an IG was even available to take the blame was due to the Inspector General Act of 1978. Passed against nearly uniform executive branch opposition, the bill created Offices of Inspector General (OIGs) in 12 departments and agencies, adding to the two statutory OIGs that already existed—one in Health, Eduction, and Welfare (about to be divided into the departments of Health and Human Services and Education) and the other in Energy. By 1998, the concept had been expanded to cover 57 departments and agencies, including 30 entities headed by agency-appointed IGs and 27 headed by presidentially-appointed and Senate-confirmed IGs.

The basic thrust of the IG Act was remarkably simple. It merely consolidated what were then dozens of separate, often scattered audit and investigation units into single operations headed by a presidential appointee. In giving new impetus to the search for accountability, the act clearly envisioned greater resources for the IGs, a hope clearly expressed throughout the legislative process. Thus, as the number of OIGs continued to grow, so, too, did the staff and resources. Despite staff cuts across the nondefense agencies of government, the OIGs actually grew by almost 25 percent over the 1980s.

II. AN ABBREVIATED LEGISLATIVE HISTORY

Compared to most of the bills that passed in 1978, however, the Inspector General Act was almost invisible. Reorganizing the varied audit and investigation units of 12 departments and agencies into single-headed Offices of Inspector General was hardly the stuff of which major floor debates are made. Indeed, the more one reads into the IG statute, the more mundane the language.

Yet, whether mundane or complex, barely visible or controversial, there is no question Congress gave the IGs broad powers.[4] Under statute, the IGs were to provide direction for conducting audits and investigations both including and *relating to* the programs and operations of their establishments. They also had a long list of ancillary duties: review existing and proposed legislation and regulations for impacts on economy and efficiency; coordinate relationships between the department or agency and other federal agencies, state and local governments, and nongovernmental entities, and, most importantly, promote the general economy, efficiency, and effectiveness of their departments and agencies.[5] The IGs clearly had plenty of mandate to pursue all three paths to accountability discussed below. The question was not *if* they had the power, but *whether* they would use it.[6]

As noted earlier, the IG Act was merely an organizational device for unifying two simple functions, audit and investigation, into one unit. However, what made the IG Act much more significant was the decision to protect those new units through at least three devices.

First, even though each IG was to be a presidential appointee, and removable without cause, each was to be selected "without regard to political affiliation and solely on the basis of integrity and demonstrated ability in accounting, auditing, financial analysis, law, management analysis, public administration, or investigations.'' Further, each IG, not the president nor the head of the establishment, was to appoint an assistant IG for Audit and an assistant IG for Investigations and have full authority to undertake whatever audits and investigations each deemed necessary to ferret out fraud, waste, and abuse.

Second, every IG was to have access to all ''information, documents, reports, answers, records, accounts, papers, and other data and documentary evidence'' needed for an audit or investigation, the right to request assistance from within the agency and information from across government, the authority to subpoena documents (but not witnesses or testimony), the right to hire and fire staff, and ''direct and prompt'' access to the secretary or administrator whenever necessary for any purpose. Moreover, neither the head of the establishment nor the second in command was to prevent or prohibit the IG from ''initiating, carrying out, or completing any audit or investigation, or from issuing any subpoena during the course of any audit or investigation.''

Third, every IG was bound by a two-fold, dual-channel reporting requirement. One was a relatively simple semi-annual report to the head of the department or agency. Automatically forwarded *unchanged* to Congress within 30 days, each report was to include a description of every significant problem, abuse, and deficiency the IG encountered in the previous six months, as well as lists of recommendations and results. The other was a letter report to the head of the department or agency to be used only in the event of ''particularly serious or flagrant problems, abuses, or deficiencies.'' This much shorter report was also to be transmitted *unchanged* to Congress, but within 7 days. Hence, the term ''7-day letter.''

Together, these two reporting requirements constituted an unique dual-channel authority. As Margaret Gates and Marjorie Knowles argue, ''The inspector general is the *only* executive branch presidential appointee who speaks directly to Congress without clearance from the Office of Management and Budget. . . . This ability to speak directly to Congress provides a potential source of substantial clout for an active inspector general.''[7]

III. EXPANDING THE CONCEPT

Clearly, the single most important issue confronting the drafting of the 1978 IG Act was independence. Questions regarding the dual reporting arrangement and removal clause were being asked at the Department of Justice and in the White House. At the November 7, 1977, Cabinet meeting, Domestic Policy Advisor Stuart Eizenstat recorded the following notes regarding the weekly cabinet briefing from OMB Director James McIntyre. The only people recorded in Eizenstat's notes were Attorney General Griffin Bell and Carter (J.C.) himself:

1.   Gov't Operations passed Reorg. Plan 2.
2.   Inspector Generals bill. Cut out part re. report to Congress and other objectionable items.
     J.C.: Less restrictive than one in HEW and DOE. Not think it's onerous. Good to have it uniform.
     Bell: Unconstitutional re. no removal w/o Congress rep.
     J.C.: Good to have if under my control.[8]

The two-minute conversation reveals but the tip of the executive branch opposition, including the Departments of Agriculture and HUD, both of which had their own *nonstatutory* IGs at the time.[9] As Elsa Porter, then assistant secretary for administration at Commerce, would later write, the opposition resided in the dual reporting line and the adversarial relationship it created:

> It boggles the mind! Had the legislation merely created the IG's in GAO's image and left them as the agency's relatively independent auditing and investigating arm, reporting to the head of the agency, I think the model might work. But in forcing dual allegiance (and, therefore, dual dependency) of the IG to both the Executive and the Congress, the legislation creates an enormous problem of trust for the IG's to overcome. Put another way, it plants the seeds of distrust.[10]

This nearly uniform executive branch opposition was further reinforced by Justice Department concerns about the dual reporting channel as "an impermissible infringement on the prerogatives and responsibilities of the Executive."[11] Additionally objecting to the bill as a dilution of the president's authority under the "Take Care" clause of the Constitution, Justice took aim at three specific provisions:

> (a) *Transmittal of information to Congress without clearance or approval*. Section 4(e) of the bill provides that the information required by the bill shall be transmitted to Congress without further clearance or approval. This clearly conflicts with the President's power to control and supervise all replies and comments from the Executive Branch to Congress . . .
>
> (b) *Power of Removal*. Section 2(c) provides that, while the President would have the power to remove an Inspector General, he must communicate his reasons for removal to both Houses of Congress. We believe that this restriction, even as limited as it is, constitutes an unconstitutional infringement on the unqualified power of the President to remove officers of the Executive Branch . . .
>
> (c) *Budget submission*. Section 5(a)(5) would provide that if an Inspector General deems that a budget request for his office has been reduced so as to affect adversely the performance of his duties, he is to inform Congress without delay. This provision is an obvious interference with the disciplined order necessary for effective functioning within the Executive Branch. Does it not constitute a typical example of encouraging, in James Madison's words, the joining of high Executive officers "in cabal" with Congress?

Justice also objected to what it saw as a congressional usurpation of executive functions, ignoring the General Accounting Office's once-prominent role as the chief accounting agency of government under the 1921 Budget and Accounting Act. "In our view," the Justice Department counsel wrote, "the continuous oversight of Executive agencies contemplated by the bill is not a proper legislative function but is rather a serious distortion of our constitutional system."[12] Further, according to Justice, the semi-annual reports violated the president's constitutional privilege to withhold information:

> Congress has other legitimate, and fully effective, means of acquiring the information which the bill seeks to make available to Congress. Congressional committees are quite vigilant in seeking the information they require, and the consistent policy of the Executive Branch has been to cooperate as fully as possible with Congressional requests for information. In addition, Congress may utilize the General Accounting Office as it wishes in order to obtain information on government programs. We believe that these methods have proven fully adequate in the past, and hence no overriding need can be asserted to justify this more intrusive form of inquiry.[13]

Ironically, this opposition was neutralized by one of the president's own appointees, HEW Secretary Joseph Califano. His department had lived comfortably with a statutory IG for two years, and Califano saw nothing to worry about. Juxtaposed against eight days of complaints, Califano's testimony had a singular impact. As James Naughton, the subcommittee's counsel would later explain, Califano and his highly respected IG, Thomas Morris, were held in reserve until the ninth and last day of the hearings when their endorsement would make the greatest counter-point. Witness the following exchange.

> Mr. Fountain: Mr. Secretary, has your Office of Inspector General, as established by statute, in any way impaired your efforts to carry out HEW's mission?
> Mr. Califano: No, it has not, Mr. Chairman. It has actually helped greatly.
> Mr. Fountain: Has the existence of a statutory Office of Inspector General in any way inhibited your capability to investigate problem areas in departmental programs and operations?
> Mr. Califano: No. Again, it has helped.
> Mr. Fountain: Has Mr. Morris at any time refused or failed to carry out any request you have made for investigations or audits of particular programs?
> Mr. Califano: No—despite the fact that I keep calling him up and asking him to do more. It is all underway.
> Mr. Fountain: Have you had any significant problems, in your judgment, which are due to the provisions of law establishing your Office of Inspector General?
> Mr. Califano: No, Mr. Chairman.[14]

Despite Califano's later aside in the hearing that the White House opposed certain features of the emerging bill, particularly the reporting and appointment clauses, the die was cast. It was as if the first eight days of testimony mattered naught.

IV. THE MERITS OF COMPROMISE

Ultimately, the debate surrounding the 1978 IG Act is best viewed as a political dispute between separate institutions sharing power. This was not an issue to be resolved through discussion of legal precedents, but balancing of presidential and congressional interests.

There is little doubt, for example, that Congress was quite willing to test the envelope of separation of powers that year, enacting a provision in the 1978 Civil Service Reform Act creating an Office of Special Counsel to investigate merit system violations with the explicit authority to "transmit to the Congress on the request of any committee or subcommittee thereof, by report, testimony, or otherwise, information or views on functions, responsibilities, or other matters relating to the Office, *without review, clearance, or approval by any other administrative authority.*"

More visibly, Title VI of the 1978 Ethics in Government Act created an independent counsel mechanism for investigating and, if appropriate, prosecuting high-level criminal complaints. Not only were these independent counsels to be appointed by a special court (the Special Division), which also determines the counsel's prosecutorial jurisdiction, they would be removable, other than by impeachment and conviction, "only by the personal action of the attorney general and only for good cause, physical disability, mental incapacity, or any other condition that substantially impairs the performance of such independent counsel's duties."[15] In the event of such action, the attorney general is required to report to both the Special Division and the Senate and House Judiciary Committees "specifying the facts found and the ultimate grounds for such removal."[16]

Table 1 Expansion of the IG Concept, 1976–1990

Date	Statute	Establishment
		Presidentially appointed IGs
1976	P.L. 94-505	Health, Education, and Welfare
1977	P.L. 95-91	Energy
1978	P.L. 95-452	Agriculture, Commerce, Housing and Urban Development, Interior, Labor, Transportation, Community Services Administration, Environmental Protection Agency, General Services Administration, National Aeronautics and Space Administration, Small Business Administration, Veterans Administration
1979	P.L. 96-88	Education
1980	P.L. 96-294	U.S. Synfuels Corporation
1980	P.L. 96-464	State
1981	P.L. 97-113	Agency for International Development
1982	P.L. 97-252	Defense
1983	P.L. 98-76	Railroad Retirement Board
1986	P.L. 99-399	U.S. Information Agency
1987	P.L. 100-213	Arms Control and Disarmament Agency
1988	P.L. 100-504	Justice, Treasury, Federal Emergency Management Administration, Nuclear Regulatory Commission, Office of Personnel Management
1989	P.L. 101-73	Resolution Trust Corporation
1989	P.L. 100-193	Central Intelligence Agency
		Non-presidentially appointed IGs
1988	P.L. 100-504	ACTION, Amtrak, Appalachian Regional Commission, Board of Governors of the Federal Reserve System, Board for International Broadcasting, Commodity Futures Trading Commission, Consumer Product Safety Commission, Corporation for Public Broadcasting, Equal Employment Opportunity Commission, Farm Credit Administration, Federal Communications Commission, Federal Deposit Insurance Corporation, Federal Election Commission, Federal Home Loan Bank Board, Federal Labor Relations Authority, Federal Maritime Commission, Federal Trade Commission, Government Printing Office, Legal Service Corporation, National Archives and Records Administration, National Credit Union Administration, National Endowment for the Arts, National Endowment for the Humanities, National Labor Relations Board, National Science Foundation, Panama Canal Commission, Peace Corps, Pension Benefit Guaranty Corporation, Securities and Exchange Commission, Smithsonian Institution, Tennessee Valley Authority, United States International Trade Commission, United States Postal Service
1993	P.L. 103-82	Corporation for National and Community Service
1993	P.L. 103-204	Federal Deposit Insurance Corporation
1994	P.L. 103-296	Social Security Administration
1994	P.L. 103-325	Community Development Financial Institutions Fund
1998	P.L. 105-206	Treasury Inspector General for Tax Administration

Source: Fred Kaiser, "Inspectors General: Establishing Statutes and Statistics," Congressional Research Service, The Library of Congress, Memorandum, November 12 1998; each P.L. number refers to the act that contained the respective amendment to the 1978 act or separate statute (CIA).

These provisions were sustained by the Supreme Court in *Morrison v. Olson*, a case pitting Independent Counsel Alexia Morrison against former assistant attorney general, and investigatory target, Theodore Olson.[17] Writing for the seven-member majority in 1988, Chief Justice Rehnquist dismissed the idea that the independent counsels were an invasion of executive prerogative. First, Congress had not created for itself a role in the removal of executive officials other than its established powers of impeachment and conviction. Second, and more importantly, Congress had not violated separation of powers in creating the independent counsel mechanism.

The point of this brief discussion is not to construct a Supreme Court case that has never arisen, but to suggest that the compromises on the 1978 IG Act were motivated not by a fear of constitutional challenges, but by real politics. Neither chamber of Congress showed any reluctance whatsoever to create novel reporting arrangements and restrictive removal clauses, whether in the IG acts, the Civil Service Reform measure, or the Ethics in Government Act.

Indeed, despite continuing executive branch opposition, the IG concept was an idea whose time had surely come. As Table 1 shows, starting with HEW in 1976, Congress expanded the concept *13* times over the next 15 years. Inspectors general were added to the newly created Department of Energy in 1977; Agriculture, Commerce, Housing and Urban Development, Interior, Labor, Transportation, the Community Services Administration, Environmental Protection Agency, General Services Administration, National Aeronautics and Space Administration, Small Business Administration, and Veterans Administration in 1978; State in 1980; Defense in 1982; Justice, Treasury, and a host of "federally funded entities," what most would call small agencies in 1988. With expansion to the Central Intelligence Agency in 1989, IGs existed in virtually every corner of government.

By 1990, the total number of presidential IGs—those appointed by the president with Senate confirmation—stood at 27, while the number of small agency IGs—those appointed by the agency head without Senate confirmation—stood at 34. Two of the early IGs, Community Services and U.S. Synfuels, were forced out of business when their agencies were abolished in the early days of President Ronald Reagan's administration.

This expansion of the IG concept may have been inevitable. Once an IGship was established at HEW in 1976, it was easily transferable to the new Department of Energy and the spin-off Department of Education. And once the concept achieved its breakthrough velocity in the 1978 government-wide bill, it was bound to spread to the inner-Cabinet of Justice, Treasury, State, and Defense.

Ultimately, what makes the IG Act important in the history of administrative reform is not its expansion to virtually all departments and agencies of government, nor its uniqueness in the pantheon of legislation that emerged in the Vietnam and Watergate era. Rather, the IG Act is most important for its blend of three approaches to accountability: (1) efforts to assure compliance with detailed rules of administrative behavior, (2) creation of incentives for improved performance, and (3) investments in the basic capacity of government and its employees to do their jobs effectively.

V. PATHS TO ACCOUNTABILITY

Prior to the 100th Congress in 1977, and for much of the history that has followed, the definition of accountability has been clear: limit bureaucratic discretion through compliance with tightly drawn rules and regulations. As Francis Rourke argued at the time:

The reformers of the 1960s and the 1970s seem bent not on extending but on curtailing the independence of bureaucratic organizations. They argue that bureaucracies represent formidable concentrations of power in contemporary society, and that executive agencies should be brought back within the political system and made more accountable. If traditional efforts at reform could be described as an attempt to depoliticize the administrative process in the United States, the reform movement in our day seems rather aimed at repoliticizing administration—at least in the sense of restoring public control over previously independent agencies.[18]

To this day, it is a definition well supported in public administration scholarship. As Dennis Palumbo and Steven Maynard-Moody argue, "There are two separate dimensions to accountability that must be kept distinct. One pertains to the substance of the concept, and the other pertains to the methods of achieving accountability. Most of the literature deals with the latter, but the former is just as crucial."[19]

So noted, how scholars define their methods of accountability still reveals much about their underlying views of the concept. Indeed, even a cursory review of contemporary public administration textbooks suggests that the dominant definition is one of command-and-control. Accordingly, accountability is seen as the product of limits on bureaucratic discretion, limits that flow from clear rules (commands), and the formal procedures, monitoring, and enforcement to make them stick (controls). Palumbo and Maynard-Moody, for example, summarize the two methods of bureaucratic accountability as follows:

One is *external*; this involves controls by legislatures through such mechanisms as legislative oversight, by the courts through review of decisions and administrative law, or by citizen participation. The second method is through *internal* controls; this includes development of professional standards and ethics, the use of rules, whistle-blowers, representative bureaucracy, and opening up administrative proceedings.[20]

The problem with the control definition, however, is that it creates an artificial trade-off between accountability and values such as creativity and innovation. Addressing the potential cost of accountability, for example, the late Frederick Mosher argued as follows:

I begin with the premise that accountability any more than any other single value is not an absolute. If everyone were held accountable for everything he did or tried or thought or imagined, this would be a pretty sterile, dull, and static world. Accountability is not commonly associated with invention or novelty or serendipity, but rather with carrying out assignments, which are more or less specifically defined, honestly, efficiently, effectively, and at minimal cost. Thus, at the very outset, there is a conflict between the value associated with accountability and the values of originality, experimentation, inventiveness, and risk-taking.[21]

Defined in such command-and-control terms, the search for accountability breeds just these kinds of trade-offs. However, this is not the only definition in the field. James Fesler and Don Kettl, for example, divide accountability into two dimensions: "One is accountability; faithful obedience to the law, to higher officials' directions, and to standards of efficiency. The other is ethical behavior; adherence to moral standards and avoidance even of the *appearance* of unethical actions."[22]

Moreover, after examining a familiar inventory of methods for achieving faithful obedience and ethical behavior, they end up rejecting the conventional compliance path to accountability: "In the end, we come back to the recruitment and retention of individuals dedicated to public service, respectful of its call for bureaucratic accountability and ethical behavior, and both knowledgeable about and committed to the constitutional, democratic system.''[23]

VI. A BROADER DEFINITION

This broader definition of accountability is particularly appropriate for understanding the rise of the 1978 IG Act. With a new democrat in the White House, the Watergate scandal receding from memory, and the Iran hostage-taking still two years away, the accepted definition of accountability widened momentarily to include questions of both improving performance and building capacity, a conclusion evidenced in other bills enacted that year. The Civil Service Reform Act, for example, contained a very clear commitment—albeit never fully funded—to performance pay, merit bonuses, and greater stewardship of the government's human capital, while the Ethics in Government Act created a financial disclosure process that, while heavily laden with compliance measures, still envisioned presidential appointees coming into office with a greater incentive to perform in the public's interest.

Enactment of the 1978 IG Act involved at least three implied definitions of accountability—a first that would find a time-honored place on the list of traditional *compliance* mechanisms cited by Palumbo and Maynard-Moody, a second that would rest in the *performance* devices cited by Fesler and Kettl, and a third in a broader mandate to advise Congress and the president on how to improve the *capacity* of government.

Before turning to the role of monitoring in each path to accountability, it is important to note that the choice of one type does not necessarily exclude the need for a second or third. Compliance accountability is not inconsistent with performance incentives or capacity building, and may be essential for assuring the fairness and equity that sometimes influence employee confidence in performance systems.

Nevertheless, it is useful to consider each definition separately. In part because of raw budget pressure, in part because of political incentives, Congress and the president may have created an artificial trade-off among the three, substituting compliance accountability for performance systems and capacity building. Moreover, as Table 2 suggests, the three involve very different targets, mechanisms, and timetables.

To compare the three methods, start with the *point of intervention*. Under a compliance model, intervention awaits the activity. Although compliance also assumes some preactivity deterrence effect, it is primarily a tool for catching mistakes after they have occurred. In contrast, both performance- and capacity-based accountability rely on establishing impacts before activities occur.

The three definitions tend to also involve different primary *targets*, ranging from individuals and accounts at one end of a continuum, to accounts and programs toward the middle, and agencies and government as a whole at the other end. Accepting the imprecision of this continuum, it seems reasonable to place compliance at the individual and account end of the range, performance in the middle, and capacity building at the agency and government-wide opposite. Inspector general investigations, for example, focus quite clearly on individual violations, whether perpetrated by beneficiaries, contractors, or federal employees. So do most federal pay-for-performance plans.

There is no such lack of precision regarding the *primary mechanisms* for achieving change. The common currency of compliance accountability is rules and regulations, whether dealing with procurement, travel, personnel, paperwork, or specific policy. These

Table 2 Aspects of Accountability

Characteristic	Accountability from		
	Compliance	Performance	Capacity
Point of intervention	Post-activity	Mixed pre- and post-activity	Pre-activity
Primary targets	Individuals and accounts	Individuals and programs	Agencies and governments
Primary mechanism	Rules	Incentives	Technologies
Role of sanctions	Negative	Positive	Positive
Role of management	Supervision and discipline	Goal-setting and reinforcement	Advocacy and stewardship
Role of oversight	Detection and enforcement	Evaluation and bench-marking	Analysis and design
Complexity of strategy	Simple	More complex	Most complex
Durability of effects	Short-term	Intermediate	Long-term

rules are reinforced through cumbersome signature and approval systems. In contrast, performance accountability emerges from the establishment of incentives, the most familiar of which are the pay-for-performance provisions of the Civil Service Reform Act; capacity building focuses on technologies, broadly defined to include people and the tools they work with. In addition, capacity building also includes both program and organizational redesign—that is, the development of workable programs and responsive structures.

Nor is there any lack of clarity regarding the role of *sanctions* in each type of accountability. Compliance accountability places its emphasis on negative sanctions, whether formal or informal. Medicare providers who violate the rules can be disbarred; contractors who cheat can be fined; employees who steal can be prosecuted. Performance accountability puts its focus instead on positive sanctions, notably bonuses and awards, although members of the Senior Executive Service created under the Civil Service Reform Act can also receive sabbaticals. The problem with such positive sanctions, at least as implemented during the 1980s, is one of inadequate funding. Without funding, pay for performance has a hollow ring. Capacity-based accountability does not involve formal sanctions per se, but can be seen as a similarly positive approach to performance incentives. Increases in training budgets, purchase of state-of-the-art technology, and so forth can be powerful inducements for organizational effectiveness.

According to Table 2, the three types of accountability involve different roles for managers and overseers. Capacity building views the *role of management* as one of advocacy and stewardship. Managers are responsible for both securing and maintaining the tools and resources to achieve effectiveness. By comparison, performance accountability requires goal-setting and reinforcement, while compliance accountability requires tight supervision and needed discipline. The *role of oversight* is equally distinct along each path. Compliance accountability demands detection of violations and enforcement of sanctions, performance demands evaluation of effectiveness and benchmarking (which Janet Weiss defines as "the results achieved by the very best organizations doing the same work,"), and capacity building demands analysis and design.[24]

The *complexity* of the strategy for achieving change also varies under the three definitions. Compliance and performance accountability are both relatively simple concepts to implement, while capacity building is much more complex. It is one thing to hold individuals accountable to clearly stated rules and regulations, quite another to find and train a new generation of public managers.

Finally, the *durability* of each approach flows from these earlier characteristics. When accountability resides in rules, not the individual or organization, it must be constantly reinforced. When it resides in incentives or organizations, it is more easily remembered. Individuals do the right thing not because they fear detection, but because the incentives and organization lead them, usually on a longer timeframe. This is not to argue that compliance is somehow less valid than capacity building; rather that each one has differing staying power.

This list of differences does not mean that there is an inherent trade-off among the three approaches. If Congress saw such a trade-off, as some scholars do, it is not apparent in the statute. The IGs were to play a role in all three, working to ensure conformity with internal rules and regulations (compliance), economy and efficiency across a wide range of programs and activities (performance), and more general effectiveness in the management and operation of their departments and agencies (capacity building).[25]

Alas, much as Congress wanted the three goals to co-exist—compliance reinforcing performance, capacity reinforcing compliance—many IGs were forced to choose. Bluntly put, the IGs have become much more instruments of retrospective, or backward looking, compliance than catalysts for either performance incentives or capacity building.

VII. MONITORING TOWARD ACCOUNTABILITY

Whatever the type of accountability, whether tracking down cheaters or assessing the prospects for efficiency, the IGs have but one tool at hand: *monitoring*. They were to look, not act, recommend, not implement. The IGs were not created as line, or operating, officers of their departments and agencies, nor were they given any powers to suspend, or otherwise interfere with program activities. Monitoring can be exercised through traditional financial compliance audits, highly individualized criminal investigations, program evaluations, or policy analyses, but it relies on others for action.

Instead, what they were given was complete access to information—information that Congress wanted, too, but information nonetheless. The IGs were free to audit, investigate, review, assess, analyze, evaluate, oversee, and appraise every problem, abuse, deficiency, and weakness relating to the programs and operations of their establishments, but were specifically prohibited from accepting any program operating responsibilities. Ironically, even as Congress began its hearings on ways to reduce paperwork imposed on the private sector, it signalled its willingness to impose an ever-increasing level of regulatory and reporting requirements on executive agencies and their employees. So, too, did Presidents Carter and Reagan, and their Offices of Management and Budget.

Ironically, at the same time Congress and the president increased the regulation of government's employees, the private sector began to embrace the quality management philosophy of W. Edwards Deming with its focus on designing quality into a product at the front end of the process, instead of inspecting it at the back end. Although all of Deming's 14 points toward quality may be relevant to federal management improvement, point three is most relevant to the IGs: cease dependence on mass inspection. As Mary Walton explains, ''American firms typically inspect a product as it comes off the line or at major stages. Defective products are either thrown out or reworked; both are unnecessarily expensive. In effect, a company is paying workers to make defects and then to correct them. Quality comes not from inspection but from improvement of the process.''[26]

This does not mean quality eschews measurement. Quite the contrary. Implementation of Deming management is highly dependent on statistical process control, and the careful performance monitoring that allows managers, not inspectors, to track and tune the process. What makes monitoring different under Deming is its role in the management process. Unlike the American public sector, where monitoring is sometimes an end in itself, and is almost always part of individual performance review, Deming views monitoring as valid only for checking the progress of an overall management plan. Monitoring is never to be used for assessing employee blame. Indeed, evaluation by performance, merit rating, or annual review is one of Deming's seven deadly diseases blocking quality in manufacturing.[27]

Obviously, the federal government is not a private entity. No matter how much its managers want to manage, the fact that they work for a public organization creates a demand for bureaucratic responsibility, or accountability. The fact that government revenues are raised through coercion, not consumer choice, places a special burden on public agencies, as does the exercise of sovereign powers. The question, then, is not *whether* to create systems of individual and agency-wide compliance, but *how* to link those systems to performance and capacity building. Simply put, compliance cannot be a substitute for basic investment in human capital and state-of-the-art workplace technologies, careful design of more workable policy, or organizational restructuring to better leverage administrative resources. If compliance monitoring does feed into capacity building, it is useless.

Unfortunately, as Table 3 suggests, even before the IGs launched their first audit or investigation, the incentives favored compliance.

To compare the three kinds of monitoring, start with the essential product of any monitoring system, *findings*—that is, the written conclusions that emerge from audits, investigations, inspections, program evaluations, and so forth. The three approaches to accountability clearly generate very different kinds of findings.

First, compliance monitoring produces a very high volume of findings, the kind that turn into long semi-annual reports to Congress and the president, while capacity monitoring often yields far less. After all, how many times can an IG make the finding that an

Table 3 Aspects of Monitoring

Characteristic	Monitoring toward		
	Compliance	Performance	Capacity-building
Findings			
Volume of findings	High	Moderate	Low
Visibility of findings	High	Low	Low
Ease of measurement	High	Moderate	Low
Credit-claiming yield	High	Low	Low
Recommendations			
Dollars and resources	Low	Moderate	High
Goal consensus	High	Moderate	Low
Jurisdictional neatness	High	Low	Low
Time to implement	Low	Moderate	High

agency's financial system is antiquated or that government is underinvesting in training? One reason is targets—individual targets can be expected to yield more findings than agency-wide or government as a whole. Another is the durability of effects—short-term effects produce "opportunities" for similar findings in the near future.

Second, compliance monitoring generates greater visibility. Although the story may be the same time after time, the names change. Congress, the president, and the media appear to have much greater interest in the products of compliance monitoring than performance or capacity monitoring. Whatever the reason, there appears less of a market for findings on government capacity, perhaps because the findings have become so familiar.

Third, compliance is much easier to measure. It is quite simple to know when an employee or contractor breaks a rule, provided, of course, those in charge of monitoring have the resources to fully audit or investigate a target. At the individual level, it is often difficult to establish reasonable performance indicators. At the organizational level, it is much more difficult to know whether an organization is failing by some objective measure. Part of the problem may be remedied by current work to develop broad performance indicators for government, whether for outcome-based budgeting or school reform. Part of the problem will continue to reside in the inherent difficulty of "evaluating their outputs in relation to the cost of the inputs to make them," as Anthony Downs argues.[28]

Finally, findings clearly vary in their credit-claiming potential. Members of Congress and presidents who seek to show their success in fighting the war on fraud, waste, and abuse, will find compliance monitoring much more helpful than capacity monitoring. There always appears to be room in the paper or time on the news for yet another story on fraud, waste, and abuse.

Findings are not the final IG product, however. Most lead to at least some *recommendations for improvement*—that is, the broad proposals for change that emerge from patterns in audits, investigations, and so forth. Once again, compliance monitoring yields more attractive results politically.

First, not only are most compliance-based recommendations likely to be cheaper to implement—add more rules and regulations—they are easier to staff, sometimes simply by adding more resources to existing monitoring units. In contrast, performance and capacity-based recommendations are much more likely to be expensive. Fixing the federal pay-for-performance system, for example, means money, and lots of it. Rebuilding the antiquated financial management systems that populate the federal government would also be expensive, as would writing new software, recruiting the new, and retraining the old.

Second, there is a high degree of political consensus surrounding the simple goal of most compliance recommendations to punish the cheaters and abusers. Republicans and democrats rarely disagree; liberals and conservatives have plenty of common ground. But when the issue is one of paying employees for successful performance, or recruiting the best and brightest to government, those agreements quickly break down. Why not the mediocre? Why pay for something government workers should automatically produce? Third, implementing performance and capacity-building recommendations runs into the problem of messy jurisdictions both in OMB and on Capitol Hill. It is exceedingly difficult, for example, to deal with pay for performance in, say, the Federal Aviation Administration without raising questions about the Veterans Administration (VA). Creating a special pay category for police officers in the Federal Park Service inevitably generates questions about security staff at the National Aeronautics and Space Administration (NASA). Not only are performance and capacity recommendations more expensive literally, they raise tough problems about committee lines and budgetary accounts.

Finally, recommendations for improving the capacity of government take a longer time to implement. A new compliance rule can be drafted in a month or two, a new audit started immediately. To the member of Congress who wants something to take home, the best the capacity builders can say is "it takes time." In an era of tight budgets and political tension, time is exactly what government lacks.

Yet, if compliance monitoring is often good politics, it is also part of a historically dominant paradigm of government management. According to the three basic characteristics of the "bureaucratic paradigm," as Michael Barzelay and Babak Armajani argue, government can be seen as a system of authority:

> Specific delegations of authority define each role in government. Officials carrying out any given role should act only when expressly permitted to do so, either by rule or by instructions given by superior authorities in the chain of command.
>
> In exercising authority, officials should write formal rules and procedures and apply them in a uniform manner. The failure to obey rules should be met with an appropriate penalty.
>
> Experts in substantive matters—such as engineers, lawyers, enforcement personnel, and social service providers—should be assigned to line agencies, while experts in budgeting, accounting, purchasing, personnel, and work methods should be assigned to centralized staff functions.[29]

Here, accountability is the responsibility of those who fashion the rules. Drawing upon the foundation of Max Weber's classic model of bureaucracy and Frederick Taylor's scientific management method, workers have no role in accountability except to do exactly what they are told, particularly if supervisors are always watching.[30] Nevertheless, the fact that the IGs capture more fraud, waste, and abuse year after year may suggest that this compliance monitoring approach cannot succeed without linkage to systematic management improvement.

Indeed, Barzelay and Armajani envision a second way of achieving results. The fundamental assumption of their post-bureaucratic paradigm reflects "the notion that government organizations should be customer-driven and service-oriented." According to this alternative view,

> A recurring aspiration of public managers and overseers using these concepts is to solve operational problems by transforming their organizations into responsive, user-friendly, dynamic, and competitive providers of valuable services to customers. Thinking in terms of customers and service helps public managers and overseers articulate their concerns about the performance of the government operations for which they are accountable.[31]

Within this "service" paradigm, improvement flows from understandings of the interaction between government and its customers. In this paradigm, the IGs are led toward a nontraditional definition of monitoring, one that emphasizes citizen satisfaction, process design, and negotiation. Unlike traditional audit and investigation, in which failure and success are easily measured by the bright line of long-held standards and formal-legal boundaries, the post-bureaucratic paradigm envisions a very different kind of monitoring clearly focused on "product" design and continuous improvement. It is a very different conceptualization indeed.

It is not yet clear whether Congress and the president are ready to embrace this postbureaucratic paradigm. There is no doubt, for example, that Vice President Al Gore's reinventing government campaign envisioned a very different role for the IGs. Not only did Gore's first reinventing government report criticize the IGs for creating a climate of fear in their agencies, it rejected the basic premise of the war on waste that had generated so much IG attention in the 1980s: "The standard by which they are evaluated is finding error or fraud," the report argued. "The more frequently they find mistakes, the more successful they are judged to be. As a result, the IG staffs often develop adversarial relations with agency managers—who, in trying to do things better, may break rules."[32]

The IGs clearly responded to the signals, even to the point of drafting a vision statement that promised to become "agents of positive change striving for continuous improvement in our agencies' management and program operations, and in our own offices." Toward that general mission, the IGs committed themselves to:

Each work with our agency head and the Congress to improve program management;

Maximize the positive impact and ensure the independence and objectivity of our audits, investigations, and other reviews;

Use our investigations and other reviews to increase government integrity and recommend improved systems to prevent fraud, waste, and abuse;

Be innovative and question existing procedures and suggest improvements;

Build relationships with program managers based on a shared commitment to improving program operations and effectiveness;

Strive to continually improve the quality and usefulness of our products; and

Work together to address government-wide issues.[33]

Five years after making the commitment, it was not clear just how much progress the IGs have made in changing toward the proactive, performance accountability they had promised. Part of the problem is that the IGs were subject to the same downsizing pressure that reduced total federal civilian employment by nearly 400,000 jobs between 1993 and 1998.

There is no doubt that the IGs noticed the cuts. According to a 1996 survey of 53 of 57 IGs by Kathryn E. Newcomer, nearly 62 percent of the IGs viewed the lack of resources and staff as the most important challenge facing their office.[34] Even if IGs wanted to redeploy staff to a more proactive stance, the staff cuts forced hard choices about which master to serve: the congressionally-mandated war on waste or the presidentially-supported proactive approach. Presidents may come and go, but Congress remains undeterred in its hunger for the kind of hearings that produce headlines on government mismanagement.

Nevertheless, there is at least circumstantial evidence of a change in IG fortunes during the mid to late 1990s. The IGs became less visible on Capitol Hill, particularly once the Republican party recaptured the House. Once a favorite source of testimony at the House subcommittee level, the IGs were sharply devalued by the new majority. As Table 4 shows, the IGs testified 520 times from 1989–1994, with the bulk of their appearances coming at the House subcommittee level. In the first two years under the Republican majority, IG testimony declined only slightly to 133, but in the next two years, IG appearances declined dramatically, falling to just 45 appearances total.

There are several possible explanations for the declining visibility. A first explanation is that the new Republican majority simply began to doubt that the IGs were reliable sources of the kind of hard-hitting reports on fraud, waste, and abuse that make for good subcommittee hearings. This explanation would fit well with the notion that the IGs were, indeed, changing direction to a more cooperative, proactive approach to fraud prevention.

Table 4 Inspectors General on Capitol Hill, 1989–1997

Locale	Nomination	Appropriation	Program	General Oversight	Total
1989–1990					
House	0	41	59	11	111
Senate	10	10	27	10	57
Full committee	10	2	12	4	28
Subcommittee	0	49	74	17	140
1991–1992					
House	0	42	73	4	119
Senate	4	6	33	4	47
Full committee	4	0	21	2	29
Subcommittee	0	48	85	4	137
1993–1994					
House	0	47	78	14	139
Senate	3	9	30	5	47
Full committee	3	0	22	2	27
Subcommittee	0	56	86	17	159
1995–1996					
House	0	38	62	1	101
Senate	8	0	24	0	32
Full committee	6	1	16	0	23
Subcommittee	2	37	70	1	110
1997–1998					
House	0	27	17	1	45
Senate	2	1	7	0	8
Full committee	2	2	8	0	10
Subcommittee	0	26	16	1	43
1989–1998 totals (percent)					
House	0 (0)	195 (88)	289 (68)	31 (62)	515 (73)
Senate	22 (100)	26 (12)	121 (32)	19 (38)	188 (27)
Full committee	20 (91)	5 (2)	79 (19)	10 (20)	144 (16)
Subcommittee	2 (9)	216 (99)	331 (81)	40 (80)	589 (84)
1977–1988 totals (percent)					
House	0 (0)	53 (58)	74 (63)	39 (59)	176 (52)
Senate	46 (100)	46 (42)	44 (37)	27 (41)	163 (48)
Full committee	46 (100)	0 (0)	25 (21)	18 (27)	89 (26)
Subcommittee	0 (0)	109 (100)	93 (79)	48 (73)	250 (74)

A second, more compelling explanation is that the Clinton administration allowed a significant number of IG posts to stand vacant. Congressional committees can hardly be faulted for not inviting IGs to testify when there are no IGs to invite. As of March 1998, for example, there were eight vacancies among the 27 presidentially-appointed IG posts, the largest number of vacancies in a single quarter since Reagan fired all of the IGs en masse in an effort to demonstrate presidential control at the start of his first term.

Absent more detailed information from the congressional consumers of IG information, it is impossible to know which explanation might hold. It is clear, however, that the IGs celebrated the twentieth anniversary of the 1978 act with some discomfort. Although they may have embraced elements of reinventing government, the IGs remain creatures of two branches. To the extent they are viewed as too close to Congress, they lose their credibility as sources of advice on how executive agencies might prevent problems before they occur, but to the extent they are viewed as too close to the executive branch, they lose their most visible opportunities for highlighting problems that need to be fixed through legislation. It is, as one IG once argued, like straddling a barbed-wire fence.

VIII. CONCLUSION

Surveying investments made in IG staffing, oversight, OMB central clearance, and a host of other devices for limiting administrative discretion, Congress and the president appear to have favored the short-term approach. Much as one can appreciate the effort to attack the perceived causes of fraud, waste, and abuse in a time of great budget stress, perhaps the National Academy of Public Administration (NAPA) was right in its 1984 call for deregulating federal management. According to the NAPA panel,

> Checks and balances are essential in our form of government, and there have been enough examples of abuse of power to make this clear. The question, therefore, is not whether they are needed, but how much of such protection is required and how it can be brought to bear without impairing effectiveness. The Panel believes that the accumulation of such protections has, in total, become excessive and has often been represented as the answer to poor management in situations where the emphasis should more realistically have been on strengthening management.[35]

More to the point of the IG concept, many of these statutes envision, in fact, demand, an explicit role for the IGs. These roles include auditing the new financial statements required under the Chief Financial Officers Act, responding to citizen-initiated suits under the False Claims Amendments, and investigating complaints under the Program Fraud and Civil Remedies Act. One might even argue that the IGs provided an excuse for Congress and the president to create more rules than they otherwise could have.

Not only do the IGs monitor compliance in much of what government does by way of program delivery, procurement, and financial management, they are also the key enforcers of a growing inventory of sanctions, from disbarment of Medicare providers to administrative recoveries—and have become the leading investigators of white collar crime against the government. Alongside the political pressures leading toward compliance accountability, the legislative agenda may give the IGs little opportunity to do much else.

Yet, the IGs' increasing focus on compliance monitoring involves much more than legislative mandates. It reflects the politics surrounding passage of the original statute, the lessons that emerged from the difficulties getting started under Carter, the incentives that unfolded in the Reagan administration's war on waste, the priorities that came with the growing number of investigators-turned-IGs, and the independence that arose from the natural evolution of the IG organizations, all forces that continue to support compliance as the dominant model for assuring ethics in government.

ENDNOTES

1. Nancy Traver, "The Housing Hustle," *Time*, Vol. 133, No. 26, June 26, 1989, p. 19.
2. See House of Representatives, Committee on Government Operations, Subcommittee on Em-

ployment and Housing, *Abuses, Favoritism, and Mismanagement in HUD Programs*, Hearings, One-Hundred-First Congress, First Session, Washington, D.C.: U.S. Government Printing Office, 1989, Part 1, p. 499.

3. See Paul Light, *Monitoring Government: Inspectors General and the Search for Accountability*, Washington, D.C.: Brookings Institution, 1993.

4. See Kurt Muellenberg and Harvey Volzer, "Inspector General Act of 1978," *Temple Law Quarterly*, Vol. 53, No. XX, 1980, pp. 1049–1066, for a general introduction to the IG concept.

5. For those still in doubt about the IG mandate, the negotiations between the House and Senate en route to final passage reveal further insights into hoped-for impacts. Of greatest interest was the Senate's definition of the IG audit function, a definition designed to assure that audit had a strong role in the new offices, but one that was dropped because conferees saw it, and its companion definition of investigations, as unduly narrow. According to this lost section, the audit function was to include, but not be limited to,

   1. The traditional examinations of financial transactions normally expected in an audit unit,
   2. Broader reviews of the "management, utilization, and conservation of resources," including "procedures, whether officially prescribed or informally established, which are ineffective or more costly than justified;" "the performance of work which serves little or no useful purposes;" "inefficient or uneconomical use of equipment;" "overstaffing in relation to the amount of work to be done;" and "wasteful use of resources;" and
   3. Even broader reviews of program results, asking whether "the program or activity is meeting the objectives established by the Congress or the establishment;" whether "the establishment has considered alternatives to achieve desired results at a lower cost;" and also reviewing "the relevance and validity of the criteria used . . . to judge effectiveness in achieving program results," "the appropriateness of the methods followed by the entity to evaluate effectiveness in achieving program results;" "accuracy of the data accumulated; and the reliability of the results obtained."

6. See Margaret Gates and Marjorie Fine Knowles, "The Inspector General Act in the Federal Government: A New Approach to Accountability," *Alabama Law Review*, Vol. 36, No. 2, Winter, 1985, pp. 473–514.

7. See Margaret Gates and Marjorie Fine Knowles, "The Inspector General Act in the Federal Government: A New Approach to Accountability," *Alabama Law Review*, Vol. 36, No. 2, Winter, 1985, p. 475.

8. These notes come from Eizenstat's files and are dated November 7, 1977. My thanks for the access and insights.

9. U.S. House of Representatives, Committee on Government Operations, Subcommittee on Intergovernmental Relations and Human Resources, *Establishment of Offices of Inspector General*, Ninety-Fifth Congress, First Session, Washington, D.C.: U.S. Government Printing Office, 1976, pp. 23, 122; hereafter referred to as House 1978 IG Act Hearings.

10. Elsa Porter, untitled speech, December 1, 1980, p. 3; author's files.

11. Department of Justice, *Memorandum on Constitutional Issues Presented by H. R. 2819*, reprinted in House 1978 IG Act Hearings, pp. 831–49.

12. Department of Justice, *Memorandum on Constitutional Issues Presented by H. R. 2819*, reprinted in House 1978 IG Act Hearings, p. 844.

13. Department of Justice, *Memorandum on Constitutional Issues Presented by H. R. 2819*, reprinted in House 1978 IG Act Hearings, pp. 848–49.

14. House 1978 IG Act Hearings, pp. 468–69.

15. 28 U.S.C. 596(a)(1).

16. 28 U.S.C. 596(a)(3).

17. 108 S.Ct. 2597 (1988); for various interpretations of the decision, see Earl C. Dudley, Jr., "*Morrison V. Olson*: A Modest Assessment," *American University Law Review*, vol. 38, no. 2, Winter, 1989, pp. 255–74; Eric Glitzenstein and Alan B. Morrison, "The Supreme Court's

Decision in *Morrison V. Olson*: A Common Sense Application of the Constitution to a Practical Problem,'' *American University Law Review*, vol. 38, no. 2, Winter, 1989, pp. 359–93; Morton Rosenberg, ''Congress's Prerogative Over Agencies and Agency Decisionmakers: The Rise and Demise of the Reagan Administration's Theory of the Unitary Executive,'' *The George Washington Law Review*, vol. 57, no. 3, January, 1989, pp. 627–703.

18. Francis Rourke, ''Bureaucratic Autonomy and the Public Interest,'' in Carol Weiss and Allen Barton, eds., *Making Bureaucracies Work*, Beverly Hills: Sage Publications, 1979, 1980, p. 103.

19. Dennis Palumbo and Steven Maynard-Moody, *Contemporary Public Administration*, New York: Longman, p. 254.

20. Dennis Palumbo and Steven Maynard-Moody, *Contemporary Public Administration*, New York: Longman, p. 255; emphasis in original; for a similar list and approach, see B. Guy Peters, *The Politics of Bureaucracy*, New York: Longman, 1989, third edition.

21. Frederick Mosher, ''Comment by Frederick C. Mosher,'' in Bruce L. R. Smith, and James D. Carroll, eds., *Improving the Accountability and Performance of Government*, Washington, D.C.: Brookings Institution, 1982, p. 72.

22. James Fesler and Donald Kettl, *The Politics of the Administrative Process*, Chatham, NJ: Chatham House, 1991, p. 317.

23. James Fesler and Donald Kettl, *The Politics of the Administrative Process*, Chatham, NJ: Chatham House, 1991, p. 335; see also D. Kettl, ''Micromanagement: Congressional Control and Bureaucratic Risk,'' in P. Ingraham and D. Kettl, eds., *Agenda for Excellence: Public Service in America*, Chatham, NJ: Chatham House Publishers, 1992, pp. 94–112.

24. Janet Weiss, ''Making Public Managers More Receptive to New Ideas,'' paper prepared for the University of California, Berkeley, conference on innovations, May, 1992, p. 13; Weiss argues that ''Measuring performance against the performance of other agencies facing similar problems, and especially against those regarded as leaders in the field, provides a demanding standard of accomplishment.''

25. For a discussion of the conflict between democratic values and efficiency, see Douglas Yates, *Bureaucratic Democracy: The Search for Democracy and Efficiency in American Government*, Cambridge, MA: Cambridge University Press, 1982.

26. Mary Walton, *The Deming Management Method*, New York: Perigee Books, 1986, pp. 34–35.

27. Mary Walton, *The Deming Management Method*, New York: Perigee Books, 1986, p. 36.

28. Anthony Downs, *Inside Bureaucracy*, Boston: Little, Brown, 1967, p. 30.

29. Michael Barzelay with Babak Armajani, *Breaking Through Bureaucracy: A New Vision for Managing in Government*, Berkeley, CA: University of California Press, 1992, p. 5.

30. See Max Weber, ''Bureaucracy,'' in H. H. Gerth and C. W. Mills, eds., *Max Weber: Essays in Sociology*, New York: Oxford University Press, 1946; see also Frederick Taylor, *Principles of Scientific Management*, New York: Harper & Row, 1911.

31. M. Barzelay and B. Armajani, *Breaking Through Bureaucracy: A New Vision for Managing in Government*, Berkeley, CA: University of California Press, 1992, p. 6.

32. Al Gore, *Creating a Government that Works Better & Costs Less*, Report of the National Performance Review, Washington, D.C.: U.S. Government Printing Office, 1993, pp. 31–32.

33. President's Council on Integrity and Efficiency and the Executive Council on Integrity and Efficiency, *Inspectors General Vision Statement*, Washington, D.C.: PCIE/ECIE, 1995.

34. Kathryn E. Newcomer, ''The Changing Nature of Accountability: The Role of the Inspector General in Federal Agencies,'' *Public Administration Review*, vol. 57, no. 3, March/April 1998, p. 135.

35. National Academy of Public Administration, *Revitalizing Federal Managers: Managers and Their Overburdened Systems*, Washington, D.C.: National Academy of Public Administration, November, 1983, p. 3.

20

Whistleblower Protection and the Judiciary

Judith A. Truelson
University of Southern California, Los Angeles, California

Whistleblowers have become indispensable agents of accountability by exposing huge cost overruns at the Pentagon, numerous environmental hazards and many other instances of government malfeasance. In particular, since Watergate, federal government employees have played a vitally important role in exposing fraud, waste, and abuse by blowing the whistle on wrongdoing in the government bureaucracy. Since 1986, amendments to the False Claims Act have returned $1.8 billion to the U.S. Treasury that would have been lost to fraud but for the actions of individual whistleblowers. Too often though, these bureaucracies have undermined and punished whistleblowers for focusing unfavorable publicity on their misdeeds.

In 1978 Congress attempted to defend government whistleblowers by passing the Civil Service Reform Act of 1978 (CSRA) to protect and thus encourage federal employees to report government agency misconduct, and later the Whistleblower Protection Act of 1989 (WPA) to enhance the protection available to federal employees who disclosed government fraud, waste, and abuse. The difficulties associated with protecting whistleblowers under the provisions of CSRA and WPA have illustrated the limitations to legal regulation imposed by bureaucratic resistance (Dworkin and Near, 1987) and now suggest that no legal defense can be wholly successful in protecting whistleblowers.

This chapter examines judicial interpretation of whistleblower protection in the United States, particularly in relation to CSRA and WPA and concludes that those charged with interpreting and implementing the Whistleblower Protection Act are failing to meet the proper standard Congress set to safeguard and promote whistleblowing. The current scheme of whistleblower protection needs to be expanded and better enforced. Partly for this reason, whistleblowers have had to develop extra-legal survival strategies for dealing with bureaucratic blockages to legal intent. The focus of this chapter is primarily on developing the rationale for better whistleblower protection through involvement of the judiciary, rather than simply relying on the executive branch to police itself. This chapter primarily emphasizes whistleblowing at the federal government level, but some of this analysis may apply to the private sector as well. The chapter presents arguments for giving whistleblowers who have been subjected to retaliation the unmitigated right to press their claims in federal district court as well as arguments for combating bureaucratic resistance to whistleblowing through "antigag" provisions and prevention of adverse personnel actions at the middle-management level.

I. DEFINING WHISTLEBLOWING

The definition of whistleblowing implicit in the CSRA and the WPA covers most ways in which whistleblowing may occur. These federal laws regard whistleblowing as any disclosure of information by an employee which the person reasonably believes evidences a violation of any law, rule, or regulation; or gross mismanagement, a gross waste of funds, an abuse of authority, or a substantial and specific danger to public health or safety (CSRA, s. 2302(b)(8)). The information disclosed does not have to be accurate in every detail in order to be treated as a protected whistleblower disclosure. All that is required is that, when the disclosure is made, the individual has a reasonable basis to believe that the information disclosed evidences one or more of these kinds of wrongdoing. When such a disclosure is made, a federal agency is prohibited from taking or threatening to take a personnel action—defined at section 2302(a)2 to include an appointment, promotion, transfer, or decision concerning pay—against the individual because of the disclosure.

With only two exceptions, an individual does not have to disclose the information to any particular person or to make the disclosure within his or her own agency in order to be protected. Disclosures can be made to anyone, a co-worker, a supervisor, Congress, the press, or the Special Counsel. The two exceptions are defined at s. 2302(b)(8)(A) as disclosure of information specifically prohibited by law and disclosure of information specifically required by executive order to be kept secret in the interest of national defense or the conduct of foreign affairs. In order for an individual to receive protection, information of these two kinds must be disclosed to the Special Counsel, the inspector general (IG) of an agency, or to another employee designated by the head of the agency to receive such disclosures.

Anonymity may affect both the nature of the whistleblowing act and the credibility with which it is received (Elliston, 1982: 167–169). The positive side of remaining anonymous is that whistleblowers may protect their careers. But anonymity often limits whistleblowers in what they can expose because they have to ensure that the leaked documentation is explanatory and can stand on its own merits without their public explanation. The anonymous whistleblower has often been subsequently traced.

II. JUDICIAL INTERPRETATION OF WHISTLEBLOWER PROTECTION

There have been three stages in the interpretation of substantive constitutional rights for whistleblowers. During the first stage, which lasted until the early 1950s, the Supreme Court took a "private sector vision" maintaining that employers can condition employment at will. In the second stage, which lasted from the early 1950s until the late 1960s, the Court's analysis reflected an "individual rights vision" recognizing in particular that public sector employers are subject to constitutional limits. In the third stage, which began in the late 1960s and continues today, the Court has maintained the analysis developed in the private sector stage applying it, though, with a "public policy vision" which emphasizes the importance of protecting the public interest (Developments in the Law, 1984: 1738–1739).

A. Private Sector Vision: Employment-at-Will

The common law doctrine of employment-at-will means that an employment contract for an indefinite time period is presumed to be terminable at will—either party may terminate the relationship at any time and for any reason (Wood, 1977: 134). This contractual proposition is based on the legal presumption that without specific agreement as to the duration of employment, the only consideration on which the contract obligation is based is pay. Second, the formation of the relationship depends upon the concept of freedom of contract—just as no employee should be forced to do particular labor, so no employer would be forced to hire a particular laborer or keep that laborer employed. As a result, an at-will employee is defenseless against the threat of dismissal and vulnerable to employer coercion and caprice (Blades, 1967: 1404).

Under the employment-at-will doctrine, the constitutional position of the public employee has been essentially identical to that of its private sector counterpart. The public employer no more violated the Constitution when it placed conditions upon employment than the private employer did. It has been a case of a "right-privilege" distinction, which held that a public employee has a constitutional right to government largess.

B. Individual Rights Vision

Despite the dominance of the common law precept of termination-at-will in the private sector during the 1950s and early 1960s, the Court began to recognize that, as citizens, employees might retain their constitutional rights against employers. First Amendment protection of the speech of public employees has depended on an application articulated in *Pickering v. Board of Education* (1968) in which the Court forbade the discharge of a school teacher for speaking out on matters of public interest. While *Pickering* recognized the interests of both the employee and the public in the speech of public employees, it stated that these interests must be weighed against the interests of the government's efficient administration. Although the Court has expressed its consideration of the public policy through the balancing of state and individual interests prescribed by the individual rights version, the weight attached to the state interest in efficiency has suggested a resurgence of the private sector vision. The lingering power of the private sector vision has been apparent in the *Connick v. Myers* (1983) case which upheld a restriction on First Amendment rights in the interest of government's effective and efficient fulfillment of its responsibilities to the public (Developments in the Law, 1984: 1748).

During the 1960s and early 1970s, the involvement of the Supreme Court in matters concerning federal employee rights to their jobs increased. The ideal of federal employment as a "property interest" began to gain credence in 1964 (Baran, 1979: 101–102). Related to the property concept, various types of benefits, provided by the government, including public employment, should be protected and received as a right (Reich, 1964: 733–735). The Supreme Court allowed that once workers gained a federal job on a permanent basis, they could be deprived of it only for certain reasons and only by certain methods, which satisfied amendments of the Due Process Clause of the Fifth Amendment (Lowry, 1976: 1, 15).

C. Public Policy Vision

The "public policy vision" suggests that the right of an employer to discharge an at-will employee should not apply when an employee is acting or speaking for the public good.

Although the public policy exception is still evolving, courts thus far have applied it to discharges involving three broad categories. In the first category, a particular statute exists which gives a right to the discharged employee but not a corresponding remedy. In this case, a plaintiff seeks an implied remedy through a public policy exception. In the second category, a statute defines a public policy that the employer has breached, but the statute fails to express either a right or a remedy for the discharged employee. The plaintiff in such a situation seeks judicial implication of both the right not to be discharged and a corresponding remedy. Finally there may be no legislative expression of a public policy to cover the circumstances of the discharged employee. Again judicial implication of a right and a remedy is sought. The problem here is that in such a situation the entire weight of defining public policy is shifted to the judiciary (Conway, 1977: 787–788). *Frampton v. Central Indiana Gas Co.* (1973) exemplified the first category approach. In this case, an employee was discharged one month after she filed a workmen's compensation claim against her employer. Her action for damages alleged that the termination was in retaliation for the filing of the claim. The workmen's compensation law involved in *Frampton* prohibited employers from using any "device" to escape liability for its provisions. The court read "other device" broadly so as to include retaliatory discharge (Conway, 1977: 789).

The California decision of *Petermann v. International Brotherhood of Teamsters* (1959) set the precedent for the second category of public policy exceptions by employing both a right and a private remedy which went beyond the employment relationship to include the need for truthful testimony. Petermann alleged that the only reason for his termination from the Teamsters Union was his refusal to commit perjury before a state legislative committee investigating union wrongdoing. Citing no authority in the *Petermann* decision, the California Court of Appeals in a unanimous opinion held that the right of an employer to discharge an at-will employee must be limited "by consideration of public policy." The court reasoned that state perjury laws reflected a public policy that testimony should be truthful within the legal system. Given this interpretation, failure to permit plaintiff's cause of action was viewed as equivalent to encouraging criminal conduct and defeating the clear interest of the state.

In the absence of any relevant statute respecting the right of an employer to discharge an employee, court interpretations must be used to entertain an action for wrongful discharge. Courts in such a position have responded in one of two ways; they have either modified the doctrine of termination-at-will or they have created a narrowly defined exception to its precepts (Conway, 1977: 793). For example, in *Monge v. Beebe Rubber Co.* (1974), the New Hampshire Supreme Court modified the concept of termination-at-will. In *Monge*, the plaintiff alleged that she had been discharged for having refused the advances of her foreman. The lower court award for damages for malicious discharge and breach of employment contract was upheld in a court of appeal.

The Oregon decision of *Nees v. Hocks* (1975) exemplified the narrowly defined public policy exception approach. Rather than excising the power to discharge for "bad" cause, the Oregon Supreme Court defined a narrow public policy exception to the termination-at-will doctrine (Conway, 1977: 798). In *Nees*, an at-will employee was terminated for serving on a jury. On appeal, the Oregon Supreme Court upheld the awarding of compensatory and punitive damages for a wrongful discharge stating that there are circumstances in which an employer discharges an employee for such a socially undesirable reason that the employer must respond in damages for any injury done. In summary, the establishment of a public policy exception to the termination-at-will doctrine represents a private concern becoming a public concern. By its operation, the private employment relationship, with the employer's right to terminate the relationship, becomes subordinated to the public interest (Conway, 1977: 798).

The Wisconsin Supreme Court decision of *Hausman v. St. Croix Care Center* (1996) is a recent example of the continuing precedent to narrowly define the public policy exception. Under Wisconsin common law, employers generally may terminate at-will employees for good cause, for no cause, or even for cause morally wrong, as long as that decision does not violate the various statutes and ordinances governing employment (e.g., Title VII, ADEA, ADA, WFEA). However, the courts have recognized exceptions to the employment at-will doctrine, including a common law claim for wrongful discharge when an employee's termination violates a "fundamental and well-defined public policy."

When the court announced its opinion in *Hausman*, allowing two former employees to proceed with a lawsuit against their nursing home employer, it declined to recognize a broad whistleblower exception; however, the court clearly recognized a new type of wrongful discharge claim. Hausman, a registered nurse, and Wright, a social worker, were terminated after repeatedly reporting their concerns about patient care and mistreatment to management and eventually to governmental officials. Neither of the plaintiffs were told to overlook poor patient treatment or asked not to make reports of suspected abuse. Accordingly, the trial court and the court of appeals dismissed their claims because neither had been terminated for refusing a command or instruction of the employer that violated public policy.

Until the decision in *Hausman v. St. Croix Care Center*, such public policy wrongful discharge claims were only recognized when an employee was terminated for refusing a command or instruction of the employer to violate a public policy. In Hausman, the court recognized a new kind of wrongful discharge public policy claim, in which an employee who was terminated for fulfilling a statutory duty, as opposed to refusing the employer's request to violate the law, may maintain a claim against the employer.

The Wisconsin Supreme Court first noted that Hausman and Wright could have been prosecuted for failing to report suspected patient abuse under Section 940.295(3) of the Wisconsin Statutes, which makes it a crime to knowingly permit another person to abuse a patient or resident. The court then reasoned that employees who act in response to such a statutory command should be protected from termination for fulfilling their legal obligation. In light of the Hausman decision, employers must be cautious about terminating employees, in heavily regulated industries such as health care, who have made internal or official complaints. If the employee was legally obligated to report suspected abuse or unsafe conditions, a genuine, distinct reason for the termination is essential to avoid liability for wrongful termination (Sholl, 1998).

Because there is no comprehensive federal law that prohibits employers from retaliating against whistleblowers, some states have adopted common law remedies, under the public policy exception to the termination-at-will doctrine. Although a definition of "public policy" is clearly essential to a court's decision whether to invoke the public policy exception, developing a coherent doctrine of "public policy" has long been a source of judicial difficulty and confusion. Typically courts have defined the concept in extremely broad terms as, for example, what is right and just for the collective citizens of the state. Many courts have reached remarkably narrow results in applying this concept to whistleblower cases for wrongful discharge. In *Adler v. American Standard Corp.* (1971), an employee was fired after reporting to company officials that his supervisors were falsifying business records and taking bribes. The court held that the mandate of public policy was not sufficiently clear in this case to give the plaintiff a recognizable claim (Protecting,

1983: 1947). Similarly, statutory language for such acts as National Labor Relations Act (NLRA) and Occupational Safety and Health Act (OSHA) has been interpreted to deny protection to employees in situations where they reported in good faith what they believed to be violations of a statute (Solomon and Garcia, 1980: 282). More recently, however, this precedent is changing. In *Kulch v. Structural Fibers, Inc.* (1997), in Ohio an at-will employee was discharged or disciplined for filing a complaint with the Occupational Safety and Health Administration concerning matters of health and safety in the workplace was entitled to maintain a common-law tort action against the employer for wrongful discharge/discipline in violation of public policy pursuant to *Greeley v. Miami Valley Maintenance Contrs., Inc.* (1990) and its progeny.

III. STATUTORY WHISTLEBLOWER PROTECTIONS

The creation of numerous federal and state remedies has enhanced the rights and ability of employees to disclose employer violations of law and public policy. CSRA, WPA, and the False Claims Act are most noteworthy among federal statutes for the protection they afford; yet the current scheme of whistleblower protection is incomplete and lacks uniformity.

A. Federal Statutes

1. CSRA

With the passage of CSRA, a whistleblower provision for the first time offered whistleblowers broad statutory protection from arbitrary actions. Congress forged this new statute in such a way as to protect whistleblowers while simultaneously reducing the likelihood that whistleblowing would become the only legitimate personnel action (Vaughn, 1982: 619). The basic underlying principle is that appointments to, and retention in, the federal civil service should be based on fitness and merit. Toward this end, section 2301 of the CSRA enumerates nine principles to be followed in the management of federal personnel. These principles are designed to protect career employees against improper influences of favoritism in the hiring, promotion, or dismissal processes and to ensure that personnel management would be conducted without discrimination (U.S. Congress, 1978: 18). The ninth principle concerns the protection against reprisal of employees who speak out about government wrongdoing.

The CSRA changed the structure of the civil service system by abolishing the U.S. Civil Service Commission and establishing the Office of Personnel Management and the Merit System Protection Board (MSPB), including the Office of Special Counsel (OSC). Precluding independent lawsuits by individual claimants, CSRA attempts to provide comprehensive protection to whistleblowers through the establishment of MSPB and OSC. MSPB is the primary interpreter of the powers of the OSC. Yet both share the common objective and responsibility for insuring that personnel practices in the federal government are consistent with merit system principles. When the OSC receives information which evidences a violation of law, rule, or regulation; mismanagement, gross waste of funds, abuse of authority, or a substantial and specific danger to public health or safety, it is required to review the allegation and transmit it promptly to the appropriate agency head. The OSC also has the responsibility directly to investigate prohibited personnel practices, including violations of the Hatch Act and to bring actions against employees who have engaged in prohibited personnel practices. The MSPB has authority to discipline any person who has engaged in prohibited personnel practice, including the power of removal, reduction in grade, debarment from the civil service, or civil penalties up to a $1,000 (U.S. Congress, 1978: 6–7).

At the time that Congress enacted the whistleblower provision, interpretations of the First Amendment heavily weighed the government interest in efficient government. Congress, therefore, legislated against weaknesses in the First Amendment standard through use of a number of specific terms such as "disclosure," and "reasonably believes," as well as specification of types of agency conduct that must be implicated, and requirement that release of information should not be prohibited by law (Vaughn, 1982: 640–641).

The whistleblower provision contains two important measures for ensuring meaningful application of the concept of personal responsibility. First, the provision allows outside review of allegations against the agency and requires that an agency respond to any substantial allegation of impropriety or wrongdoing. Second, the whistleblower provision adopts one of the few systems for imposing external accountability upon agency officials. The principal modification to existing civil service procedures is that a person outside the agency may initiate disciplinary proceedings against agency officials (Vaughn, 1982: 667).

2. WPA

Since CSRA has not always provided the broad protection initially intended, WPA was enacted to enhance the protection available to federal employees who disclose government fraud, waste, and abuse. The Whistleblower Protection Act of 1989 was enacted to strengthen and improve protection for whistleblowers. Its provisions include:

- separation of the OSC from the MSPB. The OSC is now an independent federal agency;
- reduction of the burden of proof that reprisal occurred as a consequence of whistleblowing;
- provision to whistleblowers of the right to appeal OSC decisions to the MSPB if they did not obtain relief through OSC;
- expansion of the definition of a whistleblower-related, prohibited personnel practice to include a threat to take or fail to take a personnel action.

Some of these changes increase the Special Counsel's powers, others clarify or refocus the Special Counsel's role, while still other provisions curtail Special Counsel powers when they potentially interfere with whistleblower protection. Making the Special Counsel independent of the MSPB is important symbolically as well as practically. OSC is responsible for investigating employee complaints of whistleblower reprisal and initiating corrective and disciplinary actions when reprisal is found. Given the ability of many bureaucrats to "cover their footprints," this separation could help to identify the source of any resistance to whistleblowers. This role clarification is important for future congressional oversight as well.

The more favorable burden of proof with respect to certain aspects of whistleblowing should assist the Special Counsel in bringing whistleblower cases to court. Because OSC was seeking corrective action in a very small percentage of whistleblower cases, the 1989 act gave employees the right to appeal to MSPB for relief. The 1989 act now allows employees to appeal to MSPB after first going to OSC if either (1) OSC had terminated its efforts on their cases, or (2) OSC had failed to complete its efforts within 120 days after the employee filed a complaint with OSC. This right of appeal to MSPB, known as an individual right of action (IRA), has been important in assuring employees that, if they did not obtain relief through OSC, they could go to MSPB for a hearing and adjudication.

Lastly, the definition of whistleblower reprisal has been expanded to include employers threatening to take or not take a personnel action against employees. The former Special Counsel suggested this addition as a way of assisting OSC in providing additional or expedited assistance to whistleblowers. OSC has attempted to spread the word about employees' rights to be protected from reprisal by participating in federally sponsored seminars and workshops, even though the law does not require OSC to do so. In fact, no legal requirement exists in the whistleblower statute (5 U.S.C. 1201 et seq.) for agencies to inform employees about their right to protection from reprisal for whistleblowing. Yet agency and department heads are held responsible under 5 U.S.C. 2302(c) for preventing prohibited personnel practices, including whistleblower reprisal (sec. 9, pp. 1–2).

WPA does not directly cover employees in private industry. Yet a close reading of WPA indicates that Congress may have included an inadvertent form of protection for the employees of government contractors. A non-federal employee may be afforded protection against retaliation should a government contractor fear an adverse response from its contracting agency (Israel and Lechner, 1989).

3. False Claims Act

In 1863, at the urging of Abraham Lincoln, Congress enacted the Civil False Claims Act, including the *qui tam* provision, as a weapon to fight procurement fraud. This law has also been known as the ''Lincoln Law'' and the ''Informer's Act.'' *Qui tam* is an abbreviation from the Latin ''qui tam pro domino rege quam pro sic ipso in hoc parte sequitur'' meaning ''who as well for the king as for himself sues in this matter.'' Although this act was designed to entice whistleblowers to come forward by offering them a share of the money recovered, very few people took advantage of the law between 1863 and 1986, primarily because of the many obstacles to whistleblowing built into the act and the many judicial rulings making it difficult to enforce the law.

Due to determined leadership by Senator Charles Grassley, and renewed interest in the prevention of fraud and waste, the False Claims Act (33 U.S.C.3730(h)) was amended in 1986 to increase the whistleblower's share of the recovery to a maximum of 30 percent. The amended act also increases the powers of relators in bringing qui tam lawsuits and the damages and penalties that are imposed on defendants. As a result of the 1986 amendments, qui tam actions have increased dramatically and have been the most effective and successful means of combating procurement and program fraud. The type of cases filed as *qui tams* generally revolve around false claims that are either directly or indirectly presented to the government for ''payment or approval.'' These false claims can be generated through the submission of false records; statements or other presentations made to the government, which result in mischarging, false negotiation, product and service substitution, and false certification of entitlement for benefits. Whistleblower protection is one of the most important provisions of the False Claims Act. If whistleblowers experience retaliation for using the False Claims Act, they are allowed to file a separate claim against their employers. If whistleblowers can prove that their employers engaged in retaliatory actions, they are entitled to reinstatement with full seniority, two times the amount of back pay owed, interest on back pay, and compensation for damages sustained as a result of discrimination, including litigation costs and attorney fees. Since 1986, *qui tam* recoveries have exceeded $1 billion with most of the successes involving fraud in defense and health care programs.

4. Other Federal Statutes

The creation of federal rights for whistleblowers has enhanced the ability of employees to disclose employer violations of law, although the patchwork nature of these remedies has hindered aggressive litigation and enforcement of whistleblower protection provisions. Corporate whistleblowers may, however, sometimes be protected by anti-retaliation provisions of one of a variety of federal statutes, although the protection afforded by these statutes is not comparable to that afforded by CSRA, WPA, and the False Claims Act for other public sector employees and private sector employees.

Each potential whistleblower case must be evaluated on the basis of who the employer is, what the disclosure concerns, and in which state the whistleblowing occurred, since each federal whistleblower statute has its own filing provisions, its own statute of limitations, and its own administrative or judicial remedies. Each federal statute generally includes its own definition of what kind of speech rights the statute protects, the statute of limitation for filing an action under the law, and its own administrative or judicial rules for adjudication of the claim. Even though each statute is different, courts and administrative agencies regularly apply the case law and legal analysis developed under one statute in interpreting other statutes.

The broadest protection for whistleblowers is virtually identical anti-retaliation provisions of Title VII of the Civil Rights Act of 1964 (Title VII) and the Age Discrimination in Employment Act (ADEA) which provide the broadest protection for whistleblowers. Prohibited retaliation is not limited to discharge, but encompasses as well all actions inconsistent with the employer's usual procedures as well as reprisals outside the scope of the employment relationship such as the filing of a retaliatory lawsuit.*

Other federal labor statutes furnish a different measure of protection from retaliation. The National Labor Relations Act (NLRA) shields any employee from retaliation who has filed charges or given testimony in proceedings under the NLRA. In contrast to Title VII and ADEA, however, general protection is not afforded to employees opposing illegal employer practices. NLRA protection is extended only to those participating in NLRA proceedings. National Labor Relations Board (NLRB) decisions have further limited protections to exclude managerial employees (Malin, 1983: 295).

The Fair Labor Standards Act (FLSA) is a second major piece of federal employment legislation containing an anti-retaliation provision. Protecting all persons, not just employees from retaliation, as with NLRA, FLSA's provisions are applicable whether or not the employer is otherwise subject to FLSA jurisdiction. FLSA protects such issues as complaints to the employer about alleged violations, threats to file suit or initiate an administrative complaint, and refusals to give false testimony. Employees are under no risk that their complaint ultimately will be found to be lacking in merit; instead they are protected from reprisal as long as they entertain an objectively reasonable, good faith belief that the employer is violating the act (Malin, 1983:278–279).

The Occupational Safety and Health Act (OSHA) is another piece of federal legislation to incorporate an anti-retaliation provision. OSHA has been broadly interpreted to encompass not only the filing of complaints with OSHA but also complaints to the employer, complaints to other agencies regulating workplace safety, and retention of council to rectify unsafe working conditions. OSHA also affords an employee a right to refuse

---

* 29 USC, 621-634 (1976 & Supp. IV 1980); USC, 623(d) (1976).

hazardous work under certain specified and limited circumstances. Generally, OSHA will intercede on behalf of an employee if it is established that the employee or his or her representatives engaged in a protected activity, and that the employers committed a discriminatory act against the employee and that there was a connection between the protected activity and the discriminatory act (Solomon and Garcia, 1980: 279–280). The Federal Mine Safety and Health Act, Longshoremen's and Harbor Workers Act, and the Atomic Energy Act may be included in the same category with OSHA with respect to anti-retaliatory provisions.

Environmental laws represent yet another kind of statute with anti-retaliatory provisions. Examples include the Toxic Substances Control Act, the Superfund, the Water Pollution Control Act, the Solid Waste Disposal Act, the Clean Air Act, the Atomic Energy and Energy Reorganization Acts, and the Safe Drinking Water Act (Solomon and Garcia, 1980: 278–279).

B. State Statutes

Michigan was the first jurisdiction to provide statutory whistleblower protection for both private and public employees in 1981. Since then, ten other states have followed suit. These states include: Connecticut, Hawaii, Louisiana, Maine, Minnesota, New Hampshire, New Jersey, New York, Ohio, and Rhode Island. Twenty-five additional states have enacted whistleblower protection statutes which protect only state and local government employees: Alaska, Arizona, California, Colorado, Delaware, Florida, Illinois, Indiana, Iowa, Kansas, Kentucky, Maryland, Missouri, New Hampshire, North Carolina, Oklahoma, Oregon, Pennsylvania, South Carolina, Tennessee, Texas, Utah, Washington, West Virginia, and Wisconsin.

The Michigan Whistleblowers' Protection Act (MWPA), which has served as a model for much of this state legislation, forbids employers, both public and private, from taking reprisals against employees who have given information to authorities concerning suspected violations of the law or who were about to give such information. The law protects those who have already reported violations in addition to those who are about to report any violations. The law specifically prohibits the firing or the threatening of employees, or discrimination against employees with regard to compensation, terms, conditions, locations, or privileges of employment because they reported, or were about to report, violations of the law. Employees are likewise protected if they are requested to participate in an investigation, hearing, or inquiry (Barcia, 1988:2). Many of the state whistleblower laws specify that employees will be protected if they report violations of federal or state regulations or statutes. Whistleblowing employees may be required to make their disclosures in good faith (New Hampshire, New York, Pennsylvania, Texas); to have reasonable cause to believe that a violation has occurred (California, Iowa, Maryland, Maine, New Jersey); and, to disclose a violation to a public body, usually a governmental body or law enforcement agency (California, Connecticut, Hawaii, Minnesota, New Jersey, New York, Ohio, Rhode Island, Wisconsin) (Westman, 1991: Appendices A and B).

IV. WHISTLEBLOWER ADVOCACY AND SUPPORT

Several private organizations such as the National Whistleblower Center, the National Whistleblower Legal Defense and Education Fund, and the Nader groups have as their goal the initiation of organizational reform and the protection of whistleblowers. The Project on Government Oversight (POGO) and Government Accountability Project (GAP) are two of these organizations which are particularly dedicated to the provision of both formal and informal assistance and referral services to whistleblowers. The Project on Government Oversight (originally named the Project on Military Procurement) has been instrumental in exposing spare parts overpricing, falsification of the weapon testing process, cost over-runs in weapon systems, fraudulent procurement processes and faulty weaponry. POGO takes the responsibility of ensuring whistleblowers of confidentiality and will help whis-tleblowers to decide whether to go to the press, the Congress, the Department of Defense (DoD) or to file a false claims suit. POGO launched the Military-Industrial Complex Initia-tive (MICI) in 1996 which investigates abuses in the defense budget. POGO's methods include networking with government investigators and auditors whose findings have re-ceived little attention, working with whistleblowers inside the system who risk retaliation, and performing independent investigations into problematic areas. Several lawyers work-ing with the project will act as unpaid advisors to the whistleblowers and lawyers in the investigation process of a lawsuit. POGO seeks to expose wrongdoing and to initiate reform while providing the maximum protection possible for whistleblowers (Stewart et al., 1989: 26–27; Project, 1999).

Like POGO, GAP helps defend whistleblowers against reprisals, assists them in pursuing their defense more effectively, and offers informal assistance and referral services when formal representation is not possible. In addition, GAP also advocates stronger free speech laws and teaches the law of dissent through scholarly works and law school clinical programs. GAP has concentrated on certain issues such as safety hazards from commercial and military facilities, and meat and poultry inspection. Whistleblowers with ongoing issue campaigns receive priority representation, since work on these cases complements assistance to other clients whose cases are pending. GAP also advises public agencies and legislative bodies about management policies and practices that help government deal more effectively with substantive whistleblower disclosures, while protecting the jobs and identities of those who provide this information (Kippen, 1990).

Private organizations like POGO and GAP play a major role in promoting govern-ment accountability. But, due to the quantity of requests for their help and their own limited resources, they are able to support only a few of the whistleblowers that seek their help. Also, since POGO and GAP are anxious to maintain their perfect record of no lost whistleblower jobs, they tend to support only those whistleblowers with very strong cases. Despite the support of such public interest groups though, the individual whistleblowers alone still bear the burden of proof, the court costs, and delays. But, the major problem in relying on public interest groups as arbiters of organizational retaliation is that they are primarily reactive. Even if a support network could be developed to effectively protect all whistleblowers from retaliation, until it is developed, a great deal of damage—some perhaps irreversible—can and is being done.

V. INEFFECTIVENESS OF WHISTLEBLOWER PROTECTION

The reasons for the ineffectiveness of whistleblower protections at the federal level can primarily be attributed to statutory and judicial review limitations such as exacting stan-dards of proof; limited action on planned remedial follow-up, abolition (or restriction) of constitutional remedies (U.S. GAO, 1993); and other administrative and procedural deficiencies. In addition, systemic or bureaucratic failures such as lack of confidentiality and lack of investigator objectivity compound the problems with whistleblower protection.

A. Statutory and Judicial Review Limitations

1. CSRA

Potentially, CSRA gave federal employee whistleblowers an alternative to costly legal action in protecting themselves and meant that the MSPB could take strong disciplinary action against superiors and other public employees who victimized whistleblowers. In practice, this legislation has been weakly enforced. Congress, federal employee representatives, and the GAO have all been critical of the Special Counsel for failing to provide adequate protection to whistleblowers, of the MSPB's exacting standards of proof of reprisal action, and the failure of the Special Counsel to convince the MSPB to take the necessary disciplinary action against victimizers (U.S. GAO, 1985: 4). In a comparative analysis of 1980 and 1983 data from fifteen federal organizations, a MSPB study concluded that the CSRA whistleblower protections have had no ameliorative effect on employee expectations or experience in regard to reprisals (U.S. MSPB, 1984: 7).

The MSPB set a significant precedent for the adjudication of federal employee appeals by adopting the Supreme Court's controversial "but for" test set forth in *Mt. Healthy Board of Education v. Doyle* (1977) to evaluate evidence of reprisal in cases where an employee alleges an action constitutes reprisal and the agency counters that such action is taken for valid management reasons. The employee must first show that the conduct was protected and that his conduct was a motivating factor in the adverse decision. If the employee can meet this burden, the public employer must show by a preponderance of the evidence that it would have reached the same decision, even in the absence of the protected conduct. The "but for" text established in *Mt. Healthy* seeks to balance the two competing interests in an employment context—that of the employee as well as that of the employer. Thus it can serve well to evaluate and protect the rights of the employer and employee in an individual employment context where two reasons, one prohibited, the other legitimate, are advanced. It was intended to discourage abuse of the whistleblower provision by not giving status to those who would have received disciplinary action if they had not engaged in whistleblowing (Weidberg, 1983: 110). Between 1979 and 1984, only sixteen out of more than 1500 complaints by federal employees (against what they considered unjustifiable reprisals for whistleblowing activities) met CSRA's exacting standards of proof and resulted in any corrective or disciplinary action; that is, only one in a hundred cases (U.S. GAO, 1985: 18).

2. WPA

Specifically, under prior law, the Special Counsel had to prove that whistleblowing was a significant or motivating factor in retaliating against the whistleblower. The 1989 act now requires that the whistleblower prove only that whistleblowing was a factor leading to the adverse personnel action. The act changed the standard for proving causal connection by requiring proof that the retaliation was a "contributing" factor in the personnel action, rather than a "significant" factor. According to a Senate Governmental Affairs Committee report, showing that an agency official who took a personnel action knew of the disclosure and that the personnel action occurred within a period of time such that a reasonable person could conclude the disclosure was a factor in the action would be sufficient to prove a connection. The committee believed that this more liberal interpretation should be applied because most reprisal cases are built on circumstantial, rather than direct, evidences (U.S. House, 1987). Yet, between 1996 and 1998, favorable actions were obtained in only 159 out of 2180 matters having to do with whistleblower reprisals (U.S. MSPB, 1998: 11).

B. Restriction of Constitutional Remedies

1. CSRA

The fundamental problem with CSRA is that it took basic constitutional rights from civil service and has entrusted protection of these rights to the Special Counsel who has been more concerned with bureaucratic rather than individual welfare. Previous federal workers had access to the courts to challenge First Amendment reprisals, where they could pursue suits for punitive damages in jury trials before their peers. In effect, Congress abolished constitutional remedies when it passed the 1978 statute. Further, the Supreme Court held in *Bush v. Lucus* (1982) that whenever a CSRA remedy is available, the constitutional remedies are not.

2. WPA

Under the 1989 statute, whistleblowers are still burdened by the weakest remedy and are still not entitled to a jury trial by their peers, or to punitive damage remedies that Americans—even convicted felons—can receive when the government violates their constitutional rights. Other than the Supreme Court, they can only appeal an adverse bureaucratic decision to one appellate court, the Federal Circuit, which has a track record of ruling against whistleblowers and whose precedents inhibit freedom of speech. Since the Federal Circuit was created in 1982, it has allowed the MSPB's decision to stand—either through dismissal of the case or affirmation of the board's decision in 92 to 97 percent of the MSPB cases reviewed (U.S. MSPB, 1999: 7). Whistleblowers will continue to be at the mercy of OSC and MSPB, whose abuses led to passage of the new law in the first place. In short, WPA is no stronger than the will of OSC and MSPB to enforce it (Fisher, 1991).

C. Procedural and Administrative Deficiencies

1. CSRA

The most conspicuous vacuum in CSRA's remedial provisions concerns the OSC. Since its creation, the OSC has turned down between 93 and 99 percent of whistleblower cases without attempting any disciplinary or corrective action (U.S. MSPB, 1998: 11). The Special Counsel has deliberately emphasized the prosecuting role as opposed to its obligation of offering assistance to individual employees who felt they had been unjustly penalized for speaking out (U.S. GAO, 1985: 4). After Mary Wiesman became Special Counsel in September 1986, there was a decided shift toward remedial action on behalf of federal employees who were subjected to discipline as a result of protesting against unlawful personnel practices. But, even though her office more than doubled the number of remedial actions in her first nine months of office, they still total well below fifty such actions a year (U.S. MSPB, 1987: 2–3).

2. WPA

Even though WPA was intended to strengthen and improve protection for whistleblowers, more employees have been experiencing reprisals for whistleblowing and have been finding proof of cases reported to OSC as difficult now as it was before the act was passed. The number of whistleblower complaints, and corrective and disciplinary actions have increased under the 1989 act, but the increases have generally been proportionate to increases in the volume of complaints filed. About the same percentage of reprisal complaints filed with OSC for periods studied before and after the 1989 act's passage have resulted in corrective action. The principal reason remains the lack of sufficient evidence to establish the link between the employee's whistleblowing and the reprisal (U.S. GAO, 1992). According to an MSPB report, based on response to a 1992 survey of federal employees (an update of the board's 1983 study of whistleblowing in the federal government), more federal employees say they are blowing the whistle on what they consider to be illegal and wasteful activity in the federal government, but an increasing number also are experiencing threats and reprisals for their actions. The 1992 data showed that 18 percent of those who responded (13,432 federal workers) claimed they had observed or obtained evidence of one or more activities that they believed were illegal or wasteful compared to 23 percent in 1983. Half who had witnessed an illegal or wasteful act also said they blew the whistle on the wrongdoing as compared to 30 percent in 1983. Just over a third (37 percent) who reported an illegal or wasteful activity said they had experienced or had been threatened with reprisals compared to the 24 percent recorded in the 1983 survey. The survey also indicated that some federal managers may have skirted the law by developing more subtle forms of retaliation such as shunning by co-workers and verbal harassment against those who report illegal acts or waste. The report concluded that government cannot hope to achieve its goals of greater efficiency and effectiveness unless employees are willing to bring workplace problems into the open and are encouraged to work to resolve them and managers are more receptive to the disclosure of such information (U.S. GAO, 1993).

3. Other Federal and State Statutes

The federal government has passed whistleblower protection provisions tucked into various federal statutes to shield employees who help to enforce those laws. But these statues (such as ADEA, FLRA, OSHA and the False Claims Act) suffer from procedural and administrative deficiencies, which inhibit their whistleblower protection provisions. Further, none cover corporate employees for all public policy dissent, only for an employer's violation of the particular statute at issue. For example, since OSHA alone can bring action, if OSHA decides that cases are not meritorious and refuses to proceed on behalf of employees, those employees do not have the option of pursuing their own claims under the act. Moreover, for many of the anti-retaliation provisions, an employee who has been the target of discrimination has only 30 days within which to file a complaint. OSHA officials identify this short filing period, which many applicants fail to meet, as the cause of most case dismissals. While the employee has a very short filing period, once the complaint is filed, the employee may encounter significant delays in the determination of the case. Compounding the backlog problem for the employee pursuing a claim, there is no requirement that the employee be reinstated or that the employer discontinue the allegedly discriminatory conduct while the case is pending. Furthermore, the penalties for violations are too weak to deter violative employer conduct (Solomon and Garcia, 1980: 283–285).

Filing suit against such statutes can also be tricky in other ways. These cases can run into five or six figures in costs and fees. Whistleblowers will also have to go public in filing suit, risking the chance that they will become permanently blackballed in their field. Another problem with filing suit under these statutes is that government regulations are sometimes written loosely and vaguely so as to inadvertently encourage abuses. Congressman Berkely Bedell's experience with the now infamous $435 hammer illustrates this problem. After the congressman was tipped off to the overpriced hammer by a whistleblower, he asked the Navy to audit the program and find the fraud. The Navy came back and said that the price for the hammer was exorbitant but legal, because the Navy used government approved purchasing and estimating systems (Stewart et al., 1989: 26).

Although a majority of states have passed some sort of legislation to protect whistleblowers, the current protection is insufficient and lacks uniformity. Some states offer protection to only public sector employees. Among those states that do offer statutory protection to private sector whistleblowers, the protections and procedures of the statutes differ (Boyle, 1990: 825). MWPA, for example, imposes no requirement that in appropriate circumstances employees should utilize internal channels before publicly blowing the whistle, it fails to give employers the initial opportunity to correct their own violations. Moreover, nowhere does the act explicitly protect employees pursuing internal channels from retaliation. MWPA also fails to protect employees who report violations to the federal government even though this will usually be the most appropriate course of action for violations of federal law. MWPA is also ambiguous about the degree to which employees must point to specific statutes or regulations that employers have allegedly violated (Malin, 1983: 304–306). Most states also do not have provisions for penalizing any wrongdoings. As exceptions to the rule, Maine, Michigan, Texas, and Wisconsin laws impose mandatory fines to violators. Violation of the statutes in California is punishable both by a fine and imprisonment, with stiffer fines to an errant corporation. Disciplinary actions, including discharge, are imposed in Connecticut and Indiana to an employee found making a false report. Violators of Kansas and Oklahoma law are disqualified, for a specified period, from holding supervisory positions in state employment (Employment, 1987: (505) 24).

D. Bureaucratic Problems with Whistleblower Protection

The Inspectors General Act of 1978 attempted to structure into each agency an accountability mechanism in the office of the Inspector General (IG) by which employees of an agency could make a public interest disclosure relating to the agency and could be protected against reprisal for making these disclosures in accordance with the procedure. According to the General Accounting Office (GAO), congressional reviews, and other commentary and research, there are several recurring systemic problems with confidentiality and investigator objectivity (Glazer and Glazer 1989; Truelson 1986). Confidentiality is a problem inherent in the system because it is difficult for whistleblowers to strike a balance between providing sufficient information to support allegations and giving away details that identify themselves. Even with OSC support, when the agency targeted by whistleblower charges has investigated itself, good faith responses have been the exception rather than the rule. It has not been uncommon for an IG to investigate the whistleblowers rather than their charges.

VI. OVERCOMING PROBLEMS THROUGH WHISTLEBLOWER STRATEGIES

The whistleblowers' quest for vindication has usually begun with three basic goals: first, to have some formal body, such as the courts or an investigating committee, officially declare that the initial charges are true; second, to have one's name cleared; and, third, to recover what was taken away during the retaliation period. They seek reinstatement, eligibility for promotion, serious work assignments or some financial compensation, and the right to find another position without prejudice (Glazer and Glazer, 1989: 171). In order to achieve these goals, particularly in view of the shortcomings of whistleblower channels and protections, successful whistleblowers have used carefully planned and executed strategies in their struggles for personal vindication (Miceli and Near, 1992; Jos, 1989; Johnson and Kraft, 1990; Bok, 1989; Nader et al., 1971). Credibility, skill in preparing documentation, choice of support, and timing of survival tactics are techniques which have afforded whistleblowers considerable advantages in this struggle.

The following case illustrates the successful use of these tactics. Richard Nuccio's protests began in 1993, when he first discovered CIA violations of human rights in Central America. In a high profile resignation in 1997, Nuccio left his Bureau of Inter-American affairs post denouncing both the CIA (for covering up its connection to atrocities in Guatemala) and Bill Clinton's White House (for failing to defend him and his reputation when the CIA stripped Nuccio of his top-security clearance in December of 1996), a move that effectively ended his promising diplomatic career. Nuccio wrote, in a letter to President Clinton, that he was leaving the administration "unwillingly" because of a three-year CIA campaign to penalize him for providing the name of a CIA asset in Guatemala to then Representative (now Senator) Robert Torricelli. It was Torricelli, not Nuccio, who subsequently gave the name of Colonel Julio Alpirez to the *New York Times*, along with information that the CIA had covered up its connection to the colonel that was involved in the torture and murder of both an American citizen (innkeeper Michael Devine) and Guatemalan rebel leader Efraim Bamaca (the husband of American Jennifer Harbury). The *Times* story, "Guatemalan in Killings Tied to CIA," set off a scandal which forced the CIA to conduct a full review of its so-called liaison relationships with human rights violators like Aspires, as well as an internal investigation of wrongdoing inside the agency.

Nuccio appealed, arguing that his communications with Torricelli were authorized and protected under the law. But his appeal was denied. His disclosures were criticized as jeopardizing not only the security and integrity of U.S. intelligence sources but also its methods and activities. In early March 1997, other intelligence sources leaked word to the *Washington Post* and the *New York Times* that as many as 100 CIA "assets" had been dropped from the agency's covert payroll because of human rights violations and other criminal behavior. Nuccio quickly became a cause celebre. Although he was portrayed in some news reports as a hero and martyr, he was actually a reluctant player in the drama. The person who actually forced the cover-up into the open was Jennifer Harbury, a Harvard-educated lawyer and widow of the late Guatemalan rebel leader Efraim Bamaca. She argued that her husband had not committed suicide on the battlefield, as the Guatemalan government claimed, but had been captured alive and had been seen in secret detention by two companeros who later escaped.

In 1993 and 1994, Nuccio's job overseeing the Guatemalan peace negotiations also made him the key State Department official responsible for the Harbury case. While some found Harbury's claims about her husband credible, Nuccio disparaged her story to all who would listen. But in late October 1994, Nuccio came across a May 1993 CIA intelligence report based on Guatemalan military sources, which explicitly supported Harbury's position that her husband had been seen alive in detention. On November 1, 1994, Nuccio and deputy assistant secretary of state, Ann Paterson, met with three CIA officials. When pressed, the CIA officials refused to identify the source for the cable. Possibly, Nuccio's most important contribution toward ending the cover-up occurred then, when he pressed the buttons in the State Department that forced the CIA to provide additional information about Bamaca's fate. On January 25, 1995, a CIA intelligence report quoted a Guatemalan official as stating point blank that "Commandante Everardo was killed by Colonel Julio Roberto Alpirez."

The CIA station chief in Guatemala withheld this report from the U.S. ambassador, the State Department, and the White House for more than a week. The apparent reason was that once Alpirez's name appeared in Washington, the CIA would have to admit that he was a longstanding CIA "asset." Even more troubling, his identification would reveal that while on the CIA payroll, Alpirez was implicated in the murder of an American citizen, Devine. Despite a near rupture in U.S.-Guatemalan relations over the Devine killing, the CIA covered up its connection to Alpirez. According to a later report by Clinton's Intelligence Oversight Board, the CIA's failure to inform Congress was "a dereliction of responsibility and a violation of its statutory obligation." As the most prominent administration spokesman on Guatemala, Nuccio feared that when the story broke, he would be perceived as another Oliver North. He remembers thinking that they've been trying to cover this up and nobody will believe that I wasn't a participant. Nuccio decided to share the information with Torricelli for that reason.

On March 22, 1995, an irate Torricelli wrote a letter to the President, which was given to the *New York Times*, accusing the CIA of harboring a criminal element that was out of control. A subsequent Justice Department investigation exonerated Nuccio of any criminal wrongdoing. The Justice Department concluded that Nuccio's disclosure is not a violation of the law protecting the names of secret CIA agents because Torricelli was cleared to receive the classified information pursuant to his membership on the House Permanent Select Committee on Intelligence. Moreover, Nuccio's communication with Congress was ostensibly protected by the 1912 LaFollette Act which states that the right of employees to petition Congress or a member of Congress or to furnish information to either House of Congress, or a committee or member thereof, may not be interfered with or denied (Kornbluh, 1997).

Although Nuccio won this battle, he lost the war in the sense that he was left vindicated but without a security clearance, which effectively blocked his advancement within the foreign policy establishment. His decision to go to work in the office of the legislator in whom he once confided, Senator Toricelli, may afford him an even more powerful position to push for disclosure of human rights abuses.

With the help of people in government, the press, and public interest groups, whistleblowers have successfully aired significant social issues. To increase the chances for successful whistleblowing, GAP has recommended that whistleblowers: (1) be assured of family support for whatever action is taken; (2) assess the potential for working within the system; (3) attempt discretely to learn of others who are upset about the wasteful or fraudulent activity in question; (4) be on good behavior with the administrative and support staff; (5) keep a careful record of events as they unfold; (6) identify and copy all supporting records; (7) get a lawyer or talk to a non-profit watchdog organization (Stewart et al., 1989). The influence of allies like GAP though has rarely extended to control of hiring and firing. Public pressure can defend those who stay on the job, but cannot ensure reinstatement for those who leave, or are fired (Nuccio's is one case in point).

VII. FUTURE PROSPECTS

Critics of present U.S. whistleblower protection have proposed model whistleblower legislation at the federal level which would set forth and standardize the nation's response to the moral, ethical, and legal issues related to whistleblowing and would eliminate conflicting state and federal court rulings and inconsistencies in coverage for different kinds of employees for different kinds of disclosures. These proposals have particularly emphasized provision for criminal and civil penalties, as opposed to civil penalties only, and compensatory and punitive damages in order to encourage individuals to take responsibility for incidents that otherwise would be written off as the actions of a corporate or government entity (Boyle, 1990: 828–829). For example, Senator Grassley has proposed whistleblower protection in the 105th Congress for airline employees which sets forth civil penalties for violation of employee protections and contains an anti-gag provision allowing disclosures (to Congress or to an authorized official of an executive agency or to the Department of Justice) that are essential to reporting a substantial violation of law. This bill takes what has been learned with WPA and seeks more practical and meaningful protections. Above all, Grassley attempts to ensure that these whistleblower protections involve the judiciary (i.e., the right to press claims in federal district court). The "anti-gag" amendment seeks to counteract infringement of free speech rights of government workers, as illustrated in Nuccio's case (Insight, 1998).

There is growing support for the idea of integrating ethical awareness and a sense of moral responsibility into agency culture through such means as development and distribution of organizational codes of ethics, ethics workshops, and improvement of internal dissent channels (Truelson 1991; Boyle, 1990: 829–830). This emphasis on organizational policy could serve to maximize the societal benefits of whistleblowing while minimizing its costs. Administrative values of guardianship, trust, competence, and discipline from this perspective are viewed as integral to moral and professional concerns with justice, fairness, honor, and the public interest. It has been suggested that an existing coordinating unit such as the Office of Government Ethics (OGE) or a possible new unit such as a federal ombudsman office could train public managers in strategies designed to expand ethical awareness and a heightened sense of individual ethical responsibility. Yet, such ethical awareness would have to become part of the organizational culture through ethics training and peer pressure (Truelson, 1991: 226).

While OGE might serve the function of ensuring training consistency and promoting inter- and intra-agency communication of ethics issues, there may be advantages in creating a new unit that could also serve some ombudsmanlike functions including: coordination of external bureaucratic accountability mechanisms by referring federal employees to the proper agency official or office to lodge their complaints; mediating timely and voluntary solutions when public employee complaints are lodged with these agencies; counseling federal employees on strategy and possible outcomes for invoking the services of these agencies; and educating federal employees on the services offered by the IG, OSC, and the MSPB. In view of the fragmentation of the U.S. ethical system, such an office would offer the advantage of providing a degree of coordination presently lacking while also inquiring into major variations and breakdowns in the system and recommending improved techniques. Ultimately, though, the key to the acceptance of whistleblowing as a legitimate means for improving public sector performance lies in changing the administrative culture.

VIII. CONCLUSION

The beginning of the 21st century presents an unprecedented opportunity to overhaul the concept of institutional control of administrative responsibility by switching emphasis from external sanctions (too late to prevent wrongdoing) to development of organizational cultures sensitive to possible wrongdoing, somewhat like an antenna forewarning of impending misconduct. Obviously both internal and external institutional controls need to be combined and coordinated in a more systematic fashion, but just as important, internal institutional controls need to be defined in terms more of professional pride than of pure adherence to legal guidelines. Organizational cultures in the public sector need to emphasize that both the spirit as well as the intent of the law should be followed, and the public's expectation of public norms should be met as well as the organization's perceptions of its own norms.

CASES

Adler v. American Standard Corp., 291 Md. 31, 432 A. 2d 464 (1971).
Bush v. Lucus, 458 U.S. 1104 (1982) and 462 U.S. 367, 1114 (1983) and 76 L Ed 2d 648 (1983).
Connick v. Myers, 461 U.S. 138 (1983).
Frampton v. Central Indiana Gas Co., 260 Ind. 249, 297 N.E. 2d 425 (1973).
Frazer v. MSPB, 672F 2d 150 (D.C. Circuit 1983).
Greeley v. Miami Valley Maintenance Contrs., Inc., 49 Ohio St.3d 228, 551 N.E.2d 981 (1990).
Hausman v. St. Croix Care Center, 96-0866, 207 Wis 2d 402, 558 N.W. 2d 893 (1996).
Kulch v. Structural Fibers, Ohio St. 3d (1997).
Monge v. Beebe Rubber Co., 114 N.H. 130, 316 A. 2d 549 (1974).
Mt. Healthy Board of Education v. Doyle, 429 U.S. 274 (1977).
Nees v. Hocks, 272 Or. 210, 536 P. 2d 312 (1975).
Petermann v. International Brotherhood of Teamsters, 174 Cal. App. 2d 184, 344 P,. 2d 25 (1959).
Pickering v. Board of Education, 391 U.S. 563 (1968).

REFERENCES

Baran, A. (1979). Federal Employment—The Civil Service Reform Act of 1978—Removing Incompetents and Protecting "Whistleblowers," *Wayne Law Review*, 26:97–118.

Barcia, J.A. (1988). Update on Michigan's Whistleblowers' Protection Act. *Detroit College of Law Review*, 1988:1–8.

Blades, L.E. (1967). Employment at will vs. individual freedom: On limiting the abusive exercise of employer power. *Columbia Law Review*, 67:1404–1435.

Bok, S. (1989). Blowing the whistle. In: *Public Duties: The Moral Obligations of Government Officials* (J.L. Fleishman, L. Liebman, and M.H. Moore, eds.). Harvard University Press, Cambridge, MA, pp. 147–169.

Boyle, R.D. (1990). A review of whistle blower protections and suggestions for change. *Labor Law Journal*, 41:821–830.

Conway, J.W. (1977). Protecting the private sector at will employee who blows the whistle: A cause of action based upon determinants of public policy. *Wisconsin Law Review*, 1977:777–812.

Developments in the Law—Public Employment. (1984). *Harvard Law Review*, 97:1611–1800.

Dworkin, T.M. and Near, J.P. (1987). Whistleblowing statutes: Are they working? *American Business Law Journal*, 25:241–264.

Elliston, F.A. (1982). Anonymity and whistleblowing. *Journal of Business Ethics*, 1:167–177.

Employment-at-Will: Whistleblowing. (1987). In *Individual Employment Rights Manual, BNA Labor Relations Reporter* (Bureau of National Affairs). Washington, D.C.

Fisher, B. (1991). The Whistleblower Protection Act of 1989: A false hope for whistleblowers. *Rutgers Law Review*, Winter: 355–416.

Glazer, M.P. and Glazer, P.M. (1989). *The Whistleblowers: Exposing Corruption in Government and Industry*. Basic Books, New York.

Insight on the News. (1989). February 2, 14:9.

Israel, D. and Lechner, A. (1989). Protection for whistleblowers. *Personnel Administrator*, 34:106.

Johnson, R.A. and Kraft, M.E. (1990). Bureaucratic whistleblowing and policy change. *Western Political Quarterly*, 43:849–874.

Jos, P.H. (1989). In praise of difficult people: A portrait of the committed whistleblower. *Public Administration Review*, 49:552–561.

Kippen, A. (1990). GAP's in your defense. *The Washington Monthly*, 22:28–36.

Kornbluh, P. (1997). Empire Strikes Back: How the CIA Got Its Man. [Online] Available: *http://www.consortiumnews.com/archive/story27.html* [July 21, 1999].

Lowry, J.B. (1976). Constitutional limitations on the dismissal of public employees. *Brooklyn Law Review*, 43:1–30.

Malin, M.H. (1983). Protecting the whistleblower from retaliatory discharge. *Journal of Law Reform*, 16:277–318.

Miceli, M.P. and Near, J.P. (1992). *Blowing the Whistle: The Organizational and Legal Implications for Companies and Employees*. Lexington Books, New York.

Nader, R., Petkas, P.J., and Blackwell, K. (1971). *Whistle Blowing: the Report of the Conference on Professional Responsibility*. Grossman Publishers, New York.

Project on Government Oversight. (1999). [Online] Available: http://www.pogo.org [July 21, 1999].

Protecting Employees At Will Against Wrongful Discharge: The Public Policy Exception (1983). *Harvard Law Review*, 96:1931–1951.

Sholl, R.K. (1998). Terminated Nursing Home Employees Who Reported Patient Abuse May Bring ''Wrongful Discharge'' Claim, Wisconsin Supreme Court Rules. [Online] Available: *http://www.rbvdnr.com/Articles/lab/hausman.htm* [July 12, 1998].

Solomon, L.D. and Garcia, T.D. (1980). Protecting the corporate whistleblower under federal anti-retaliation statues. *Journal of Corporation Law*, 5:275–297.

Stewart, J., Devine, T., and Rasor, D. (1989). *Courage Without Martyrdom: A Survival Guide for Whistleblowers*. Government Accountability Project and Project on Military Procurement, Washington, D.C.

Truelson, J.A. (1986). *Blowing the Whistle on Systemic Corruption*. Ph.D. Dissertation, University of Southern California, School of Public Administration, Los Angeles.

Truelson, J.A. (1991). New strategies for institutional controls. In: *Ethical Frontiers in Public Management: Seeking New Strategies for Resolving Ethical Dilemmas*. (J.S. Bowman, ed.). Jossey-Bass, San Francisco.

U.S. Congress, House Committee on Post Office and Civil Service. (1987). *Whistleblower Protection Act of 1987, H.R. 25*, U.S. Government Printing Office, Washington, D.C.

U.S. Congress, Senate Committee on Governmental Affairs. (1978). *The Whistleblowers; A Report on Federal Employees Who Disclose Acts of Governmental Waste, Abuse, and Corruption*. U.S. Government Printing Office, Washington, D.C.

U.S. General Accounting Office. (1985). *Whistleblower Complaints Rarely Qualify for Office of the Special Counsel*. U.S. Government Printing Office, Washington, D.C.

U.S. General Accounting Office. (1992). *Determining Whether Reprisal Occurred Remains Difficult.* GAO, GGD-93-3, October 27.

U.S. General Accounting Office. (1993). *Whistleblowing in the Federal Government: An Update.* U.S. Government Printing Office, Washington, D.C.

U.S. Merit Systems Protection Board, Office of Merit Systems Review and Studies. (1984). *Blowing the Whistle in the Federal Government.* U.S. Government Printing Office, Washington, D.C.

U.S. Merit Systems Protection Board, Office of the Special Counsel. (1987). *Testimony of Mary Wieseman, Special Counsel, before the Civil Service Subcommittee of the House Committee . . . Concerning the Whistleblower Protection Act of 1987.* mimeographed, 10 March, 1987.

U.S. Merit Systems Protection Board, Office of the Special Counsel. (1989–1991). *Report to Congress on the U.S. Office of the Special Counsel.* U.S. Government Printing Office, Washington, D.C.

U.S. Merit Systems Protection Board, Office of the Special Counsel. (1998). *Report to Congress on the U.S. Office of the Special Counsel.* U.S. Government Printing Office, Washington, D.C.

U.S. Merit Systems Protection Board, Office of Merit Systems Review and Studies. (1999). *Celebrating 20 Years: Building a Foundation for Merit in the Twenty-first Century.* U.S. Government Printing Office, Washington, D.C.

Vaughn, R.G. (1982). Statutory Protection of Whistleblowers in the Federal Executive Branch. *University of Illinois Law Review*, 1982:615–667.

Weidberg, L.P. (1983). Whistleblower Protection under the Civil Service Reform Act. *Federal Bar News & Journal*, 30:106–112.

Westman, D.P. (1991). *Whistleblowing: The Law of Retaliatory Discharge.* BNA Books, New York.

Wood, H.G. (1877). *A Treatise on the Law of Master and Servant.* John P. Parsons, Albany, New York.

21

Dealing with Administrative Corruption

Gerald E. Caiden
University of Southern California, Los Angeles, California

I. INTRODUCTION

Most societies have their taboos, topics which are rarely mentioned in polite conversation. In some, money matters are discouraged, particularly how one makes it or spends it. In others, sex and related cohabitation matters are frowned on. In a few, death and the rituals accompanying the disposal of the dead are infrequently heard. In many, until quite recently, corruption of any kind was taboo although it is a fact of life everywhere and a way of life in many countries around the globe. When the subject is now raised, people still pause over how much they can reveal or excuse away, even those who are morally principled, free of taint, and responsible for condemning corrupt practices or any conduct that departs from expected norms. A few recent examples of such ostrich-like behavior by people who ought to know better illustrates this reticence.

At the Sixth International Conference on Public Service Ethics held in the Netherlands in June 1998, a senior executive of a multinational corporation producing and selling alcoholic beverages explained how his organization was strict on enforcing ethics within and tried to curb anything unethical that might be associated with its brand name. He was questioned about his company's policy in employing child labor, paying kickbacks to secure contracts, and failing to take sufficient responsibility for discouraging customers who might overindulge in his company's products. He replied that his company followed local laws and practices in the countries where it operated. He pointed out that the country where his company's headquarters were located allowed kickbacks as a legal business tax deduction as did other European countries (a practice now condemned by the Council of Europe). While his company regretted any overindulgence and indeed opposed such behavior, he declared that his company could not be society's conscience although it strongly supported government attempts to reduce intoxication. In this, his company considered itself one of the industry's leaders. Did it have a responsibility for setting a moral example? Only if that benefited its image and business.

While that conference was being held, the world's economy was reeling from revelations about the extent of corruption among the elites of some of the touted models of economic development for poor countries that had made such progress in just a few decades. These countries and others (including Brazil, Indonesia, Japan, Malaysia, Mexico, South Korea, Thailand, Venezuela, and members of the former Soviet Union) had been suddenly and unexpectedly confronted with: a run on their currencies; the drastic decline of their stock exchange prices; the collapse of several major financial organizations; the flight of investment capital; the loss of business confidence; the upsurge of inflation; the spread of unemployment without any or adequate social safety net; and the reversal of large numbers of people back into poverty accompanied by new violence and threatened social upheaval.

A major contributory factor had been the prevalence of corrupt business and official practices that had hidden the real dangers to their economies, siphoned off sizable investments and earnings into conspicuous consumption, kept in operation grossly inefficient and outdated producers and determined in large measure public policy which enabled them to cover up the risks and social consequences involved. How could they have prospered with such corruption? How had such corruption been hidden for so long? From whom had it been secreted? Who had run off with the money that had been lost? The elites had known, had taken little if any action to discourage corruption, had even justified it, had profited from it, had publicly lied about it, and had managed in large part to extricate themselves from major damage to themselves. They were still in positions where they could aid villains to escape the consequences of their actions, spread or divert the blame, extract themselves with minimal losses, and even rescue the worst offenders with their largesse and international connections. They rarely shared the fate of the mass of newly unemployed and their dependents. For them, it was largely business as usual and it mattered little to them whether the country could have prospered even more without so much corruption.

Representatives of some of the world's principal financial, banking, and management consulting organizations involved in the economic development of some of the hardest-hit countries attended the Second Conference on Public Sector Management in Transitional and Developing Societies held in Washington, D.C., in November 1998 where some of this background was discussed. But most of the formal agenda was devoted to improving governance around the world. One session was devoted to the topic of fiscal transparency and priorities for improving government budget systems. At the session, the principles of the proposed Fiscal Transparency Code devised by the International Monetary Fund (IMF)—to establish minimum compliance by countries seeking future IMF assistance and to emphasize clarity of roles and responsibility, public accountability of information, open budget preparation, execution and reporting and independent assurances of integrity, all worthy endeavors—were discussed. They demanded processes and information that not even the most sophisticated countries could meet, let alone international agencies, including the IMF itself. The true state of public sector financial management in some poor countries had been revealed only the previous day in a newspaper article which began as follows:

> Strapped for cash and smarting from the prodding of the World Bank to restructure its economy, the Cameroon government leapt in 1993 at the suggestion by a foreign expert that it start collecting tolls on major highways.
>
> Tollbooths sprang up on the roads linking the country's major towns, accompanied by howls of anguish from the traveling public.
>
> The measure proved so lucrative that the government introduced tolls on some heavily traveled dirt tracks. The booths were burned down by outraged citizens in the rebellious, English-speaking northwest of the country, where there are no paved roads at all.

Five years later, a World Bank official concedes that the toll brings in money—but little, if any, of it reaches the public treasury. The purpose of this road fee, which was to enhance revenue collection, was defeated almost as soon as it was implemented.

There has never been a real accounting of the revenue from the tolls because these large amounts of ready cash are immediately appropriated by ministers, security officers, junior functionaries—even the tollbooth collectors. (Wamey, 1998)

How was the somewhat idealistic IMF's code to deal with such prevailing conditions without tackling corruption first? Where should the international community start and what should have priority? Would IMF exhortations change anyone's behavior? Like the three monkeys who see no evil, speak no evil, and hear no evil, this may isolate international bodies from being involved, but it hardly deals with the rampant corruption that obviously exists in the governance of so many applicants to the IMF.

Perhaps this inability to confront corruption is partly attributable to convenient organizational and cultural blindness or amnesia, and lack of sensitivity to ethical issues in executive education and training. After all, rarely in the past have public administration textbooks mentioned—let alone analyzed—corrupt practices. Yet much preventable maladministration could be minimized if they were identified, if their persistence were accounted for, and if effective preventive measures were indicated. By eliminating the worst abuses, good practices should expand. Unfortunately, by concentrating on the defects of public administration, research on corruption paints a somewhat distorted picture. Researchers who persist in uncovering corruption often find themselves "persona non grata" in both official circles and academia because they supposedly tarnish public administration and stain public officials. Nonetheless, these researchers believe that the mainstream has not been critical enough of obvious deficiencies and lapses in public business and too much self-censorship has been exercised in exposing official misconduct.

In the past decade or so, all this has now been acknowledged certainly by academia which has shifted course (with the change in climate in public and official circles) toward administrative corruption whose dysfunctions have become too obvious to ignore. As a result, recent textbooks have been revised accordingly; new journals such as *Corruption and Reform* (later incorporated into *Crime, Law & Social Change*), *TI Newsletter, Accountability,* and *Public Integrity,* have appeared since 1990 to cater to the specialization of public ethics and corruption; and a new industry has been established just to deal with the teaching of public ethics and the investigation of corrupt practices. Governments with corruption problems have been coming into the open and asking for help wherever it can be found. They now sponsor and finance conferences and meetings on the subject. The international community echoes this new frankness as seen by: the passage of United Nations General Assembly Resolutions A/RES/51/59 and A/RES/51/601 in early 1997 against corruption; statements made by international leaders condemning corruption; the success of Transparency International in provoking remedial action; increased technical assistance in dealing with corruption; the publicity given to anti-corruption conferences; and concerns shown by world business leaders expressing the need to reduce corrupt business practices and venality. The last decade of the twentieth century saw an abrupt turnaround in international attitudes which now promise practical steps in reducing judicial and administrative corruption. The former taboo has probably now been removed at least in international circles but the question remains whether it will stay on the agenda and whether the new initiatives will spread towards all the relevant social, political, and economic actors.

But do all these bodies have the same thing in mind? What public malpractices do they consider as constituting conduct unbecoming public officials? What exactly is administrative corruption? The most commonly used definition that captures its flavor is

> Behavior which deviates from the normal duties of a public role because of private-regarding (family, close private clique), pecuniary or status gains; or violates rules against the exercise of certain types of private-regarding influence. This includes such behavior as bribery (use of rewards to pervert the judgment of a person in a position of trust); nepotism (bestowal of patronage by reason of ascriptive relationship rather than merit); and misappropriation of public resources for private-regarding uses. (Nye, 1967: 966).

It includes all abuses of public role for private advantage that deviate from expected norms. Added to this are all abuses of public position, business and other extraneous improprieties that influence official acts and the special category of organized crime that causes deviations in administrative conduct than otherwise would have been the case. More specifically, most definitions include the following categories of administrative corruption:

> treason; subversion; illegal foreign transactions; smuggling
> kleptocracy; privatization and personalization of public resources; larceny and stealing
> misappropriation; forgery and embezzlement; account padding
> diverted funds; misuse of funds; unaudited revenues; skimming
> abuse and misuse of coercive power; intimidation; undeserved pardons and remissions; torture
> non-performance of duties; desertion; parasitism
> deceit and fraud; misrepresentation; cheating; and swindling
> perversion of justice; criminal behavior; false evidence; unlawful detention; frame-ups
> bribery and graft; extortion; illegal levies; kickbacks
> tampering with elections; vote-rigging
> misuse of inside knowledge and confidential information; falsification of records
> unauthorized sale of public offices, loans, monopolies, contracts, licences and property
> manipulation of regulations, purchases, and supplies; bias and favoritism
> tax evasion; profiteering
> influence peddling; favor-brokering; conflict of interest
> improper gifts and entertainment; ''speed'' money; blackmail
> illegal surveillance; misuse of and tampering with mails, telecommunications, and computers
> cronyism; junkets
> misuse of official seals, stationery, residences, and perquisites
> protecting maladministration and cover-ups; perjury.

Given such an extensive list, no administrative systems, public or private, can be entirely free of corruption. Some types are quite serious and endanger whole societies, and in this era of globalization they also have the potentiality of harming the whole world. Others are trivial and unimportant, hurting only a small circle and in no way life-threatening. The best that can be expected is that corruption takes minor, unimportant, non-recurrent forms (i.e., isolated occurrences that trigger automatic, institutionalized fail-safe devices that minimize potential damage).

Only long established democracies appear to be relatively free but even in them scandals occur involving even the most venerated institutions. Elsewhere, public officials routinely plunder the public purse and abuse their official positions (Mellow, 1991). Although it would be desirable to tackle all forms of corruption at once, it is more likely that they have to be tackled individually with emphasis on the most dysfunctional forms. Prior attention will have to be given to countries that obviously suffer more than others, particularly the less developed where systemic corruption handicaps their efforts to improve the living standards of their people. Furthermore, serious attention has to be paid to whether priority should be put on the law, on independent institutions, on enforcement, on investigation and publicity, on individual integrity, on organizational safeguards, on public education, on example and leadership, or on the costs not only of corruption but also of remedial action and anti-corruption campaigns (which in the larger scheme of things may not rank high in priority).

Because administrative corruption takes so many forms and arises from so many different causes, there are no simple formulas to deal with it. But one thing is certain—administrative reform cannot be separated from other kinds of corruption, whether economic, legal, political, social, cultural, professional, even religious, but especially political (Heidenheimer et al., 1989). The one feeds on the others and they are all linked. If the public would not tolerate corruption, then any revelation of wrongdoing would be accompanied by swift and stiff retaliatory measures and failure to take such action would provoke an immediate outcry. Corruption would be rare. The possibilities of being caught would be high, the penalties would be severe and the potential gains would be most problematical. To succeed would require much ingenuity and the effort would hardly be worthwhile. But where people are passive, if not self-indulgent, in corrupt practices, then public officials might as well get their share of the pickings. Scandals would not stir up much action and those temporarily sacrificed would eventually be restored to grace and compensated for any inconvenience suffered. Whistleblowers would not make much of an impression; they would make news only for one day and then fade into oblivion.

Likewise, administrative corruption contaminates everyone who comes into contact with it. People who are not resolute or strong enough to deal with it will probably turn a blind eye if they don't take advantage of it, knowing that they will probably be protected and shielded by the corrupt. Somehow it will be arranged that accusers and whistleblowers will be ostracized and isolated if not silenced, incriminating evidence lost and possible prosecutors bought off. The public has little choice except to go along or just do without whatever they seek, which in poor countries means worse suffering and too often further deprivation and possibly certain death. The public, sooner or later, has to take the initiative, to take matters into their own hands and bypass public agencies altogether, which since the late 1980s is becoming less rare. Otherwise, the public has to rely on public officials to clean their own house, especially law enforcement officers willing to prosecute corrupt office holders. Dirty hands (i.e., those who are corrupt) cannot do this; they only spread the contamination.

Thus, dealing with administrative corruption involves many different parties. First, the public must be unwilling to tolerate it in any form. They must be willing through civic action to protest against corrupt practices, to boycott corrupt organizations, to expose corrupt administrators wherever located and to reform corrupt practices wherever found. Second, public leaders have to forego the advantages of their special social position to plunder the modern administrative state and to use their public offices for private gain. They must impose the same discipline on all public officers and ensure that even the potentially corrupt are screened out of any position of public trust. Third, more action is needed to treat infected administrative bodies and to combat likely contamination from clear sources of infection. Fourth, additional anti-corruption specialists capable of monitoring public activities, particularly those areas most vulnerable to corruption, and of devising measures to minimize the occurrence of corrupt practices are required. They are still not adequately trained and equipped. All these measures presuppose freedom of information and free mass media willing to investigate and report corruption without fear or favor. Altogether, this is a tall order for most countries and it should not be a surprise if few come close. Without increased efforts in these directions, corruption will continue to present serious challenges to the integrity, well-being, and stability of the global society in which all are victims of its distortions of power, governance, incentives, and desserts.

II. REMOVING THE TABOO ON CORRUPTION

Corruption is nothing to be proud about. It is not something to which people readily admit. It is embarrassing and probably criminal, certainly bordering on the illegal. Whatever the reason, the taboo on corruption still persists in many countries although in the past decade that taboo has been undermined if not vanquished altogether. Where the taboo still prevails, corruption is not something that respectable folk talk about, at least not publicly. All know that it exists but nobody can be sure to what extent or who is guilty. By its very nature, corruption is a secret activity and those who indulge will not readily admit that they do. Suspicion is not enough; there has to be clear and irrevocable evidence. But such evidence is difficult to obtain without resorting to exceptional methods of investigation. Given any skilled lawyer's ability to create reasonable doubt, conviction is difficult. Even so, every so often major scandals erupt and public inquiries uncover additional damaging evidence. But again there is no way of knowing whether such evidence is representative or exceptional. Nobody is sure just what to include or exclude or where corruption stops and something else (e.g., incompetence, ignorance, unwitting collusion) takes over. Some forms are outlawed while others are not. Likewise, some forms can be prosecuted while others cannot. Such confusion reinforces natural reluctance to raise the subject.

Because of such doubts, researchers have tended to shy away from the subject, preferring to deal with something more precise and clear. They may fear too that some of the moral opprobrium surrounding the whole topic might rub off on them or their work. In any event, informants are few and their reliability suspect. Who can tell whether they are holding back and hiding information or whether they are exaggerating and making it up or whether they are misguided, lying, self-indulgent, vengeful, guessing, or mentally ill? Those in positions of public trust, even when they know the truth, sometimes believe that it is in everybody's best interests to deny any knowledge of corruption if only to retain public confidence in public institutions, to uphold the reputation of their organizations, and to indicate that they personally know of no corrupt practices in their immediate jurisdiction. Many also claim that they have their own ways of dealing with corruption that do not involve public disclosure; indeed, premature disclosure might defeat countermeasures. They may not be able to reveal all they know because of overriding constitutional, legal, and official restrictions. They may fear victimization if they act. Self-censorship may be at work because of an unwillingness to get mixed up with unpleasant things that lead they know not where.

But as long as the existence of corruption is denied, it can hardly be tackled. Just because people will not talk about it openly does not mean that it will go away of its own accord or that the public, which is at the receiving end, is unaware of its presence. It cannot be hidden long. Whoever participates knows of it. So do all those who know some participants even if they do not themselves indulge. Reassurances and denials alike only confirm popular assumptions about official hypocrisy and untrustworthiness and prompt the thought that the situation must be worse than commonly supposed. As long as corruption cannot be discussed openly, rumor will replace fact. Once admitted, silence no longer condones. People are put on notice that corruption will no longer be disregarded or secreted away, but it will be tackled. The public will not feel so reluctant to talk about it or express their concerns. The innocent will feel exonerated and encouraged that they will be supported. The guilty must watch their step: they are put on the defensive, unable to find institutional supports or comfort. In these ways, the symbolic recognition of the existence of corrupt practices changes the atmosphere of all administration, public and private, and creates a climate conducive to investigation and rectification. But open admittance may encourage scandalmongers, demoralize the falsely accused, and make administrators unduly conservative lest unjust accusations be leveled at them by those who enjoy muckraking seemingly for its own sake.

As far as the public sector is concerned, the taboo seems to be breaking down. Public leaders, mass media and citizen associations seem more willing to discuss corruption openly. The way was led in official circles by a hardy band of researchers, investigators, and anti-corruption professionals who succeeded in overcoming such inhibitions and broke through the taboo barrier. Formally, they have met since 1983 under the banner of the International Anti-Corruption Conference (IACC) and over the years they have received increasing government sponsorship and subsidies from international agencies with gatherings held in Europe, Asia, South America, and the ninth and latest in South Africa (held in Durban, October 1999). These gatherings were held in countries where corruption was acknowledged as a major obstacle to national development (e.g., China in 1996, Mexico in 1993, and Peru in 1997). The IACC publishes its proceedings, although it is still difficult for those not attending to obtain copies. Perhaps the most significant statement to come out of these IACC meetings was that issued as the Lima Declaration which was a bold statement about the dysfunctions of official corruption and a list of some 40 specific actions that ought to be taken at international, regional, national, and local levels to reduce corruption. It looked forward to "a new millennium of ethics and integrity" (United Nations Development Programme, 1998: 174).

Anti-corruption specialists can be found associated with such organizations as INTERPOL, the International Political Science Association, the International Institute of Administrative Sciences, and most importantly the United Nations Criminal Justice Department (UNCJD) in Vienna which issues anti-corruption manuals. The UNCJD has played a major part in getting more and more countries to associate themselves with United Nations efforts in crime prevention and criminal justice designed to get member countries to

> (a) review the adequacy of their criminal laws, including procedural legislation, in order to respond to all forms of corruption and related actions designed to assist or to facilitate corrupt activities . . . (b) devise administrative and regulatory mechanisms for the prevention of corrupt practices or the abuse of power, (c) adopt procedures for

the detection, investigation and conviction of corrupt officials; (d) create legal provisions for the forfeiture of funds and property from corrupt practices; and (e) adopt economic sanctions against enterprises involved in corruption. (United Nations, 1990: 4)

The culmination of United Nations efforts came with the passage of General Assembly Resolutions A/RES/51/59 (January 28, 1997) and A/RES/51/601 (February 21, 1997), parts of which are worth quoting in full.

51/59. *Action against corruption*:

The General Assembly,
Concerned at the seriousness of problems posed by corruption, which may endanger the stability and security of societies, undermine the values of democracy and morality and jeopardize social, economic, and political development,
Also concerned about the links between corruption and other forms of crime, in particular organized crime and economic crime, including money-laundering,
Convinced that, since corruption is a phenomenon that currently crosses national borders and affects all societies and economies, international cooperation to prevent and control it is essential, . . .
1. *Takes note* of the report of the Secretary-General (E/CN.15/1996/5) on action against corruption submitted to the Commission on Crime Prevention and Criminal Justice at its fifth session;
2. *Adopts* the International Code of Conduct for Public Officials annexed to the present resolution, and recommends it to Member States as a tool to guide their efforts against corruption; . . .
9. *Also requests* the Secretary-General . . . to provide increased advisory services and technical assistance to Member States, at their request, in particular in the elaboration of national strategies, the elaboration or improvement of legislative and regulatory measures, the establishment or strengthening of national capacities to prevent and control corruption, as well as in training and upgrading skills of relevant personnel; . . .
11. *Requests* the Commission on Crime Prevention and Criminal Justice to keep the issue of action against corruption under regular review.

51/191. *United Nations Declaration against Corruption and Bribery in International Commercial Transactions*:

The General Assembly,
Recalling its resolution 3514 (XXX) of 15 December 1975, in which it . . . condemned all corrupt practices, including bribery, in international commercial transactions, reaffirmed the right of any State to adopt legislation and to investigate and take appropriate legal action . . . against such corrupt practices, and called upon all Governments to cooperate to prevent corrupt practices, including bribery, . . .
Welcoming the steps taken at the national, regional and international levels to fight corruption and bribery . . .
1. *Adopts* the United Nations Declaration against Corruption and Bribery in International Commercial Transactions, the text of which is annexed to the present resolution; . . .
8. *Also requests* the Secretary-General to prepare a report . . . on the progress made towards [its] implementation; . . . and on measures taken in accordance . . . to promote social responsibility and the elimination of corruption and bribery in international commercial transactions.

Following their adoption, the Vice President of the United States organized a conference in Washington, D.C. in February 1999 at which practical methods of tackling corruption in the public sector were reviewed. The conference's resolutions were submitted to the Group of Eight (G-8) for approval in June 1999 at Cologne and the principles and practices against corruption were incorporated into the United Nations Global Program against Corruption. The Vice President also convened a conference following the implementation of the Anti-Bribery Convention of the Organization of Economic Cooperation and Development (OECD) in February 1999 to criminalize the bribery of foreign government officials, a convention that had taken eight years to negotiate, to urge all OECD members to adopt it as barely half had done so.

Even before the passage of the UN resolutions, hardly a month had passed when somewhere around the globe there had not been a conference or meeting of experts where corruption and anti-corruption measures had been discussed and if anything the pace has since quickened. At these gatherings, the same references kept cropping up. The same sources, particularly four leading books by Heidenheimer et al. (1989), Klitgaard (1988), Noonan (1984), and Rose-Ackerman (1978); these books were quoted repeatedly together with their authors' updated commentaries. The same theories were used. Although the literature may still be too incestuous, it does provide fairly acceptable definitions, classifications, boundaries, and tenable criteria for distinguishing between good and bad practices, normal and abnormal, significant and insignificant, and major and minor forms. Today's attendees diligently sift through newly available evidence and check and recheck sources to reduce second-hand references, hearsay, and unsubstantiated charges.

Unfortunately the water has been muddied by the successful efforts of world media to break down the taboo on corruption outside official circles. Long before diligent research efforts had begun to bear fruit, mass media in the free world and also in the unfree world had grown bolder in their public criticism of corruption and less forgiving of disgraced public officials. They had devoted more resources to investigative reporting. As a result, the private lives of public officials have become more of an open book. The public have seemingly wanted to know more about government scandals. The taboo on corruption has been increasingly relaxed until anything now seems fair game for the gossipmongers. Nothing is sacred anymore. The more that public authorities do to try to protect their secrets, the more vulnerable they become. The more they try to retain their credibility, the more their indiscretions are glorified and the more suspicious and doubting the public becomes and people become more willing to believe in wrongdoing in official circles. Whistleblowers increasingly take risks to reveal what they claim to know and to challenge officialdom in court when victimized for their exposures. Indeed, since the Watergate affair and the forced resignation of the president, mass media has thrown down the gauntlet to corrupt public leaders and institutions. In their wake, a veritable corruption information industry has sprung up. Corruption stories regularly appear in the world's serious newspapers while the less reliable sensational press rakes up what it can. Television now considers corruption newsworthy as it is wherever telecommunications can escape censorship, a factor that does not inhibit worldwide computer networks.

Even the business world has jumped on the bandwagon, stirred by the publication by the CEO Institutes of International Media Partners Inc. in its September/October 1991 issue of its *CEO/International Strategies* devoted to corruption. Soon after, the world was rocked by the Bank of Commerce and Credit International (BCCI) affair which exposed money laundering on a grand scale by the corrupt in high public positions. But the main channel of the anti-corruption campaign has been the establishment of Transparency International (TI), founded in Berlin in 1993 by Peter Eigen, a former World Bank officer who had been so upset by what he had seen on his job that when he was ordered to stop his anti-corruption antics, he retired to establish TI to combat international bribery through quiet diplomacy. Business bribery contaminates all contracting and seduces public figures into being financially rewarded for their contacts, introductions, influence, and intervention, if not directly then through their relatives and friends. The Foreign Corrupt Practices Act 1977 had prohibited the bribery of foreign officials by American business and TI was partly responsible for getting the European Union to adopt similar measures in 1998, measures that will apply to any new members who have been warned in advance to reduce their corruption before entry. TI has generally been instrumental behind the scenes and through its quarterly newsletter to expose official corruption and to get international organizations and countries to commit themselves to combating corruption.

Transparency International, with branches in over seventy countries, has received international blessing in both the business and official worlds. In partnership with the United Nations, it has assumed a leading role in the IACC and in partnership with the World Bank it has been involved in the bank's anti-corruption programs. The World Bank, which once maintained a taboo on corruption, has changed its tune as have so many other international organizations, following the collapse of the taboo in the former Soviet Union and elsewhere. Possibly such a reversal would have taken place anyway as it had already occurred in the United Nations Development Programme, in the Organization for Economic Cooperation and Development, and in major donors of international technical assistance, all of which have taken on new responsibilities for anti-corruption measures. There are few countries left which can hold out against the eroding of the taboo on corruption or can resist pressure to combat all kinds of corrupt practices. Although talking about corruption is a far cry from actually doing something about it, it is a necessary prelude to adopting an effective anti-corruption policy.

III. DETERMINING AN ANTI-CORRUPTION POLICY

Once people feel freer to publicly acknowledge corruption in their midst, then it becomes possible to discuss what needs to be done. History shows that something can indeed be done, for countries have succeeded in reducing corruption across the board and in specific areas of governance. But history also shows that unless continuous efforts are maintained for detection and prevention, corruption returns and persists. The cynical deny anything can be done for all attempts at containment eventually fail. Corruption, they claim, is an integral part of human nature. It will always flourish in the right circumstances. As long as individuals believe they can benefit from corruption, they will be tempted to indulge. Attempts to control corruption resemble the activities of King Canute defying the waves: they are so much wasted effort. Instead, a better strategy would be to recognize that corruption exists for good reason. It performs functions not always detrimental to a society or possible by legal means. Harness the propensity to corruption for good rather than evil. See it akin to market forces that indicate unmet social needs and shortcomings, fill certain gaps in societal transfers and incentives, and reward enterprise and initiative. In any event, corruption is largely a cultural phenomenon, related to avarice, scarcity, non-accountability, and inadequate deterrents. In short, concentrate on reducing greed, equating supply and demand for goods and services, and improving mechanisms for public accountability and self-policing. Then corruption should be manageable.

If corruption did not have such devastating effects on the global society, perhaps people could be more complacent and less concerned about devising an effective anti-corruption policy. But throughout the ages, people have recognized corruption for what it is and for its untold harm—destroying empires, destabilizing society, distorting distribution, wasting precious scarce resources, undermining social cohesion, discrediting public institutions and reducing the quality of life for its innocent victims. As disease attacks the physical body, so corruption attacks the moral spirit. Both result in rot, decay, and eventual premature death to the collectivity (and to those who compose it) that sheer numbers cannot overcome. Corrupt societies cannot go far for they build on shifting sand. Their investments are wasted and their efforts bear little fruit. Their end is suicidal, certainly fratricidal. Dramatic as all this sounds, even the mightiest have fallen when unable or unwilling to contain corruption, sacrificing the whole to the ambitions of a few.

Civilization could never have come this far if people were as corrupt as the cynics believe. Certainly there would not be so many variations among localities and communities, clearly indicating that there are wide differences in anti-corruption policies. At the one extreme, there are weak government policies that do little to contain it and allow it to flourish. At the other, there are strong government policies that tackle it at many different levels and in many different forms. None work perfectly. None deal with every aspect. All that can be offered is a general menu which does include specific items for which precise recipes can be altered to individual taste. Nevertheless, there are certain basic elements that need to be present if administrative corruption is to be reduced.

Countries that pledge themselves to the United Nations resolution on international cooperation for crime prevention and criminal justice in the context of development have available to them a handy revised UNESCO code of practical measures against corruption originally prepared for the Eighth UN Congress on the Prevention of Crime and the Treatment of Offenders held in Cuba in August 1990 (United Nations, 1990). It covers basic penal laws, administrative and regulatory mechanisms, procedures for the prosecution of suspected corrupt administrators, and the legal provisions for the expropriation of financial rewards derived from corrupt practices. Implementing such measures would go far to reduce the incidence of administrative corruption. To this detailed guide which is continuously revised and updated have been added several more, notably those issued by: Transparency International (1995); the United Nations Department of Development Support and Management Services in conjunction with the International Organization of Supreme Audit Institutions (1996); the United Nations Development Programme (1997b, 1998) and its Programme for Accountability and Transparency (1998, 1999); the World Bank (1998); and Development Alternatives, Inc. (1998) which add elaborations. There can be no excuse for not knowing what to do. The issue is not so much *what* to do but *how* to do it, where to start, what measures to adopt, how those measures might reinforce one another, and so on. Also important is the will to continue to combat corruption under difficult and adverse circumstances.

A. Moral and Trustworthy Leaders

If the obvious explanation for the ubiquity of corruption is that human beings are by nature sinful and untrustworthy, then only the fittest, meaning the most moral, should occupy positions of public trust. This entails that, first, able and virtuous people must be attracted to public service and kept there without too great a personal sacrifice on their part (i.e., adequate status and compensation); second, careful selection of all incumbents of positions of public trust should include strict checks on background and character (i.e., references and investigation); third, there has to be instant removal of public officials for breaches of public codes of ethics (i.e., purges and dismissals for cause). On taking office, public leaders have to leave behind them attachments to traditional folkways and pledge themselves to serving the public interest without fear or favor. Thus, *el hombre nuevo* of Castro's Cuba

> would dedicate his life to the needs of the revolution, to fellow Cubans and to humanity as a whole. He was to be self-disciplined, hard working, ascetic and incorruptible. He was therefore to be free of egotism, selfishness and materialism and would especially not indulge in the three principal malpractices that were undermining the revolution: privilege taking, *amiquismo* [cronyism] and black marketeering. (Theobald, 1990: 150)

Similar entreaties are found elsewhere. One of the latest efforts along these lines has been the Social Controllership Program in Mexico under which all citizens were encouraged to play an active part in improving government services and rooting out corrupt practices by monitoring and auditing government actions. The Social Controllership Program was linked to the much broader National Solidarity Program to guarantee that resources allocated to improving living conditions actually reached the people for whom they were intended in a timely and direct fashion and applied as originally earmarked (Program National De Solidaridad, 1992). It was a community effort to ensure honest, fair, and competent public administration. This was what people expected of their leaders and public servants even if they did not always get it. Alas, corruption has remained so entrenched that the program has had little impact, like so many others of its kind, in producing more trustworthy public leaders.

B. Appropriate Social Regulation

Another universal cause of corruption is the existence of social controls that nobody wants (i.e., the administrative state intervenes in areas of social conduct which nobody thinks it should). Here, government intervention is ill-advised and inappropriate. Outward conformity is achieved at the cost of sullen resentment and much collusion between the public and public employees, who alike feel no moral compulsion to obey. Simply put, the government should get out of where it ought not to be. It should not do what it cannot do and it should get rid of social controls which are inoperable and undesirable. Although nobody likes any interference in their personal affairs, there are probably areas where the administrative state may well have overstepped the mark.

C. Regular Law Revision

As Bracey has long pointed out:

> Related to the problems of laws that people don't want to obey are the problems of laws that people can't obey . . . laws . . . often the result of piecemeal legislation designed to cope with a specific situation and then incorporated into a general rule. Given the fact that many . . . are vague, anachronistic and internally contradictory . . . there results a situation which makes it impossible for the most earnestly law-abiding citizen to conduct his lawful business in a lawful manner. (Bracey, 1976: 17–18)

A good example was the abundance of elaborate and complex rules within the administration of the European Union which was inciting fraud and corruption (Tutt, 1989). It has since tried to simplify and update its rules. Probably within every governmental system, scores of rules, regulations, instructions, and orders have outlived their usefulness or raison d'etre but they tend to stick even though they diverge sharply from current attitudes. In effect, they have become unenforceable. Such laws should be removed and replaced. Law revision should be institutionalized so that all laws are reviewed regularly. Public officials who find they cannot enforce laws should suggest workable alternatives and lobby for the necessary changes. What may push officialdom into law revisions are the new laws designed to encourage the development of performance-based management and accountability systems such as the Government Performance and Results Act of 1993.

D. Curbing Public Monopolies

Public agencies can exploit their monopoly position no less than their private sector counterparts. Their propensity to corruption can be reduced in several ways. The public can be offered alternatives by breaking up public monopolies and providing genuine competition among different suppliers of public goods and services. Where a certain degree of monopolization is unavoidable, full public accounting should be required. Besides tighter political, legal, financial, and policy controls, public monopolies (like all other public agencies) should be subject to performance and value-for-money audits that assess their legality, morality, productivity, sensitivity, and effectiveness. Every effort should be made to install independent and effective complaint-handling mechanisms so that people can know how often public agencies are subject to complaint, how many complaints are justified, and what is being done to prevent their recurrence. Of course, the omnipotence of all officialdom should be minimized through public participation, freedom of information, civil rights enforcement, and democratization generally.

E. Open Democratic Government

Closed nondemocratic government obviously has the highest propensity for corruption because it can most hide corrupt practices. To ensure government in the sunshine, the following are minimum requirements:

> The executive branch is subject to close supervision by a responsible and responsive legislature and to overrule by an independent judiciary;
>
> Free elections are conducted by reliable and untainted commissions, held regularly, in which parties and candidates are limited in what they can spend on campaigns;
>
> All potential and current officeholders are properly screened and obliged to reveal possible conflicts of interest;
>
> All public agencies are subject to external audit and the scrutiny of free mass media and obligated to publish annual performance accounts;
>
> All public proceedings are open wherever possible with minutes and transcripts readily available at nominal cost;
>
> All public business is conducted by rules similar to the U.S. Administrative Procedures Act;

> All public contracts are subject to competitive tender and to independent appeal and review;
> All public agencies are governed by a general anti-corruption apparatus that includes adequate penal laws, complaint offices, inspectorates, hotlines, and whistle-blowing protection.

To further reduce opportunities for corruption, no public employees should be judges in their own case or placed in position where they are obviously confronted with divided loyalties and conflicts of interest. Discretion should be limited by set guidelines, performance standards, and designated targets. All decisions should be accompanied by explanations and on review and appeal judged according to prevailing conventions. Wherever possible, feasible legal redress and compensation should be provided where wrongdoing is proven.

F.   Professional Career Positions

Install career administrators who are carefully screened, tested, and selected, specially prepared and trained, adequately remunerated and who adhere to professional ethics and standards. They usually know whether or not a job is being properly done and where wrongdoing is likely to occur. They are disciplined and can generally regulate themselves. They take pride in a job well done. They know what is correct conduct and can exercise beneficial peer group pressure. Experienced public administrators know the tricks of the trade and where fellow practitioners are likely to go wrong and how they cover their tracks. But knowledge and ability are insufficient if they operate in a weak culture of public accountability and an inhospitable operating environment.

G.   Competent Administration

When things work in a mess, nobody knows what is going on. Anything can be hidden amid the chaos; anyone halfway clever can get away with almost anything. System, order, and regularity are essential for the detection of abuses. Good routine procedures soon reveal irregularities, exceptions, bottlenecks, subterfuges, and even sabotage. Regularly paid employees are not impelled to retain revenues in their possession just in case they do not get paid. If they have to record all transactions, give receipts for all monies received and produce accounts for everything, they cannot hide much or divert much to irregular channels. Fully occupied officials have little time on the job to attend to their private business. Staff who are rotated regularly cannot easily maintain their cliques and informal working arrangements. Competent administration is in itself a deterrent to corruption. An ongoing administrative reform program is essential to reduce overbureaucratization and specific bureaupathologies that aid corrupt practices. Naturally, any such reform program should include effective banking and financial regulations and machinery to prevent capital flight, tax and customs evasion as well as money laundering together with the many anti-corruption measures outlined in several easily accessible international manuals.

H.   Integrity

When all is said and done, there is no substitute for the personal integrity of each and every member of society. A crucial factor is the global fostering of a democratic ethos.

Another is the global fostering of a universal ideology of community service. Last but by no means least is the global fostering of professional and organizational codes of ethics. For the public sector, the International Association of Schools and Institutes of Administration (IASIA) and its parent body, the International Institute of Administrative Sciences (IIAS), have taken a leading part since 1978 in framing suitable codes. This has led in turn to the global fostering of public service ethics education and training through IASIA's ethics working groups. Outside the public sector, multinational corporations around the world have developed their own in-house codes which they make publicly available on request together with information on their ethics training programs (Caiden, 1992). These ethics programs work well, providing all the other pieces of the anti-corruption puzzle are in place and the policy adopted is activated through an effective anti-corruption program. For public sector agencies, these programs are somewhat more complex than for their counterparts elsewhere simply because of their *public* nature.

None of these measures is easy to translate into specific conditions. It requires strongly committed leaders to shoulder the task, a task that may take several generations to accomplish successfully. Transforming the public sector, indeed what amounts to the ethical framework of a society, cannot be done overnight and is unlikely to achieve idealistic goals. The difficulties entailed can be seen in reviewing just six of the current major international concerns in dealing with corrupt practices. The first concern is business bribery. Little seems to get done without some form of "economic rent," gift, favor, or other reciprocal return. Transparency International has achieved some success in getting business bribery outlawed. But passing laws is easy compared to their effective enforcement and grappling with extra-legal contrivances to get around the laws. This so-called "gray" corruption causes the most headaches in combating corruption.

The second concern is money laundering which is closely related to business bribery and to gray corruption in the public sector. The corrupt have to put their ill-gotten gains somewhere. Huge amounts of hot money slosh around the globe daily (Caiden 1997: 10) and "no financial institution and no country are immune" (CRIME, 1996: 1). A significant portion of the world's financial assets is controlled by corrupt and corrupted agents who use their wealth and power to suborn governments and influence public policy and management.

The third concern is the operations of transnational crime, particularly the activities of crime syndicates and drug cartels which include terrorism, sexual slavery, black market trade in arms and nuclear materials, counterfeiting, computer tampering, environmental crimes, and trafficking in endangered species. Some of the most serious involve drug trafficking and the creation of narco-democracies effectively controlled by drug kingpins who manipulate political systems and exploit banking systems with impunity, free of effective investigation or prosecution, and instead submitting to a rigged plea bargaining system that leaves their assets intact and merely slaps them on the wrist (Caiden, 1997: 11).

The fourth concern is the growing influence of money in political life through the direct buying of politicians and political parties by way of campaign contributions in exchange for expected favored treatment, the purchase of commercial space and time to influence the electorate, the concentration of mass media ownership, the ability of well-placed insiders to secrete their manipulation of mass media through public funding and the use of privileged information, asset stripping in the guise of privatization, and tax avoidance and evasion.

The fifth concern is kleptocracy itself wherein government is viewed as just another avenue for entrepreneurship and public office is a means of self-enrichment. Public officials rob the public treasury; steal; embezzle; run rackets and conduct private business from public premises; award relatives and friends government monopolies and lucrative public contracts; and generally live well at public expense. Anyone dealing with kleptocracies has to pay ransom and must devise means of hiding the fact from others.

The sixth concern is the situation of the non-governmental organizations (NGOs) which have become increasingly popular as an alternative to delivering public goods and services from either governmental bodies or business companies. Unfortunately, NGOs are not subject to the same public scrutiny as these other organizations. They are largely responsible and accountable only to themselves. While many are honorable and above reproach, others are mere fronts for aggrandizers and criminals rewarding themselves handsomely for puny results.

Frequent revelations of wrongdoing in these six areas make the public cynical about government, public institutions, and organizational elites. Everyone seems just to be out for self benefit. All organizations are made to look rotten. Every public official is made to appear with dirty hands. Worse still, nothing seems to change. But this impression is quite wrong and is a gross distortion of reality. Great strides have been made and are being made to combat corruption in public office and to reduce misconduct. Since the mid-1990s, complacency has been replaced by activism urged by frustrated citizens, powerful pressure groups, aggressive victims, and responsive politicians jumping on a populist bandwagon.

IV. INSTITUTING AN AGENCY ANTI-CORRUPTION PROGRAM

As the ingenuity of the corrupt is boundless, a general anti-corruption policy has to be accompanied by special protective measures in every public agency, particularly those most prone to corruption. Yet rarely have administrative manuals provided for the identification, investigation, and prosecution of corrupt practices. So for each public agency special anti-corruption manuals are being devised to provide workable definitions, identify corruption-prone areas, and indicate preventative measures. Undesirable acts are not hard to identify and there is usually much agreement about them. They can be spotted by watchful supervisors, special investigators, outside experts, and alert citizens. They can be detected from statistical records, random file selection, trends in complaints, and confidential interviews. Some model manuals exist and are publicly available, notably the *Internal Control Guidelines* published by the U.S. Office of Management and Budget (OMB) and the anti-corruption manual for police departments put out by the Criminal Justice Center at the John Jay College of Criminal Justice in New York. Others are confidential in-house documents, to which access is restricted although there is usually little in them that really merits confidentiality or departs dramatically from the more accessible manuals.

The OMB's manual, for instance, recommends that agency policymakers undertake vulnerability assessments by looking at the general control environment, the inherent risk of corruption among its activities, and the adequacy of current control safeguards. Is the agency too permissive of corruption by not being committed enough to strong internal control, by inappropriate reporting relationships, by employing incompetent and dishonest people, by insufficiently limiting authority, by poorly specified and ineffective budgeting and reporting procedures, or by inadequate financial and management controls? Is the agency at risk: by having too vague or complex aims; over involvement with third party beneficiaries; by dealing in cash; because of approving applications, licenses, and such;

because it has a history of corruption; or as a result of working under tight time constraints? Are existing safeguards and controls adequate to contain corruption?

Robert Klitgaard's *Controlling Corruption* (1988) is probably still the best practical guide to instituting an agency anti-corruption program, based as it is on his experience in countries where corruption can be said to be a way of life. Besides thinking about what should be done to deal with corruption, Klitgaard includes several elaborate cases of anti-corruption programs in tax bureaus, police stations, customs agencies, procurement agencies, and service delivery. They involve bribery, speed money, extortion, kickbacks, and fraud. The cases illustrate both unsuccessful and temporarily successful programs for stimulating creative thinking in specific contexts. Klitgaard also provides a general framework for policy analysis:

1. Select agents for their honesty and capability by screening out the dishonest and networking to find dependable agents.
2. Change the usual bureaucratic pattern of incentives and disincentives by rewarding honesty and integrity and penalizing corrupt behavior in a deterrent manner (i.e., take the profits out of corruption).
3. Collect information that increases the possibilities of detection by improving auditing and management information systems, strengthening information sources (auditors, investigators, whistleblowers, ombudsmen, anti-corruption bodies) both inside and outside the agency, and changing the burden of proof to the potentially corrupt.
4. Restructure relationships to reduce vulnerability by inducing competition, reducing discretion, rotating people, changing the nature of the agency's activities to render them less vulnerable, and organizing clients into anti-corruption lobbying forces.
5. Change attitudes about corruption by using training, educational programs, and personal example, promulgating codes of ethics and changing agency culture (Kligaard, 1988: 94–95).

In all this, it is important to (a) distinguish between "ostensible" and "strategic" issues, (b) cultivate political support, (c) mobilize the public, (d) break the agency's corruption culture, (e) use positive as well as negative means, (f) link measures to the agency's main mission, and (g) find and support Mr. Clean (Klitgaard, 1988: 183–186).

Over the past decade since the appearance of Klitgaard's classic, several agencies have produced their own detailed guidelines of how they and others deal with corrupt practices in very practical ways. These manuals are circulated at the many meetings held around the world on combating corruption. Serious investigators and students should have little difficulty obtaining them. But Klitgaard has since warned that implementing anti-corruption measures requires

> Breaking the culture of corruption and irresponsibility, which means frying "big fish" in public.
> Strengthening systems to prevent corruption and inefficiency, which means information and incentives.
> Involving the public and civic organizations in the campaign for responsibility and efficiency. (Price-Waterhouse, 1991: 10).

In short, much depends on tackling weak cultures of public accountability in general and boosting the role and effectiveness of independent supreme audit institutions. Indeed, in recent years international attention has been focused increasingly on fostering the democratic ethos in countries where it does not exist or is very weak, strengthening the ideology of community/public service, furthering institution building and capacity building, including incentives for institutional adjustment and the attendant risk-taking, and inculcating a culture of public accountability and transparency. Variable success with reforms in governance to reduce corruption has cautioned reformers but has also spurred them to greater efforts and strengthened their resolve.

V. STRENGTHENING A CULTURE OF PUBLIC ACCOUNTABILITY

The weaknesses of governments in dealing with corruption was illustrated in the early 1990s by the collapse of the international empires ruled by Robert Maxwell and by the exposure of the Bank of Commerce and Credit International (Caiden, 1992). Large sums of public and private monies were put at risk and probably lost simply because international financial dealings were unregulated altogether or poorly regulated. In these and other cases, auditors from the world's leading firms did not know what was going on and did not make it their business to know. If they did know, they so feared losing profitable accounts that they did not report observed wrongdoings and their own private misgivings and kept their own firms in the dark. Worse still, some allegedly connived in corrupt practices and helped scheme large-scale frauds. Thus professional auditors themselves were deceived, indifferent, careless, incompetent, fearful, unethical, and even criminal, not exactly the right cast to combat corruption. A culture of public accountability was weak or entirely absent in their organizations and professional associations, and among themselves too. It is not a question of sloppy accounting and auditing but of deliberate evasion of professional obligations and exploitation of gaps and ambiguities in professional standards and practices, in this case, those of the International Federation of Accountants.

Unfortunately, other major professions and their professional governing bodies have failed to live up to their own codes of ethics when it comes to self-policing because they too lack a strong culture of public accountability. They have failed to discipline even outrageously corrupt offenders. For example, medical and legal practitioners who have connived at defrauding the welfare state have not been deprived of their professional status. Even practitioners who have performed miserably and certainly been guilty of gross misconduct have been allowed to continue to practice with merely a warning or weak slap on the wrist. Professional disciplinary bodies frequently appear soft on their delinquent members and this is true of the public sector too. They seem to have replaced public accountability (meaning accountability to the public) with professional accountability (meaning accountability to the profession), to safeguard professional self-interests in corrupted, certainly distorted, and biased self-policing systems. They want to be answerable to themselves only and they possess enough power and influence to get their way (Caiden, 1988).

The theory of public accountability tells us what this means. When people answer only to themselves without the risk of sanctions, they do whatever they want often at terrible cost to everyone else. For this reason, institutional checks and safeguards are established to ensure that everyone is answerable to someone else. If others take a dim view of what individuals do, then they are supposed to say so and insist on corrections. In the public realm, "those who exercise the power of the state are obligated to answer for their actions whether those actions are taken individually or collectively, even when the legality of such actions is not in doubt'' (Jabbra and Dwivedi, 1988: 3). Answerability enables the community to assess whether or not state power has been properly (i.e., politically, legally, morally, and professionally) exercised; that state power has not been used solely for personal gain and self-promotion without advancing the collective benefit, the common weal, the public interest; and that state power and its exercise have not brought disgrace on the community. It is for the community to judge whether wrongdoing has been done and to decide what to do about it. Power holders must remember that they personify the state; they must honor and dignify the state; and they must devote themselves to the public's business. Should they fail, they are removable and replaceable.

It is not the theory of public accountability that is in question but its implementation, particularly failure to inculcate a culture of public accountability. With the advent of the organizational society and the emergence of the modern administrative state, public agencies (and private organizations too) wield considerable power and their aggrandizement has seen them exhibit authoritarian, tyrannical, and totalitarian traits. They can override external controls and treat the public with contempt. Those who govern them internally, secure in their isolated, cozy niches, are quite distant from operations and they can easily become divorced from the realities at the point of impact with their clients and the general public. Full of their own self-importance and buttressed by elite privileges, these public agencies do not really feel accountable to anyone but themselves. They learn how to evade external controls, escape responsibility, persuade others to go along with them, and bully those reluctant to do so. Some matters are so technical that only they can decide. But nobody, not even these agencies, can possibly keep track of everything and everyone. So it is possible that things can get out of hand, as if no one was in control. Even in the best of organizations, things occasionally get out of hand. Although scapegoats are sacrificed to assuage public opinion, the root causes that give rise to such events are not touched.

Unfortunately, there are several areas in the modern administrative state where no matter who may be replaced, nobody is really in charge, and things are so disorganized that abuses are bound to occur. No one is answerable (i.e., no one is responsible).

A. Unregulated International Exchanges

The Maxwell and BCCI scandals in the early 1990s and more recently the financial scandals in Africa, Latin America, and Asia and gross improprieties in Italy, Romania, Russia, Turkey, and the Ukraine have revealed how prone to fraud and corruption international financial exchanges are because there is no one really in charge. The same applies to weaponry, narcotics, and the like where no international constraints on trade exist, or if they do they are unenforceable. Privateers are not the only ones who flourish. Governments are also involved as are public agencies and public employees. Much money can be made but no one is answerable as to how it is made and who makes it. To reduce corruption, the international community has to put these houses in order by enforcing effective restrictions.

B. Self-Governing International Agencies

In the past half century or so, numerous international bodies (such as the World Health Organization and the International Monetary Fund) have been established to further global objectives and to provide public goods and services at an international level. These now have a life of their own. While they are supposed to be accountable to member countries and answerable to the United Nations, they are quite free to run their own internal affairs. Indeed, they have become so accustomed to being independent that they are virtually self-governing. While they have been relatively free of public scandal, questions can be asked whether they may have become self-serving and to that extent corrupted institutionally. Many of their activities are conducted in secret and even their auditors state that they suffer from mismanagement, patronage, and sinecurism. They are long overdue for overhaul and reform. Only recently has the United Nations been willing to take the initiative to clean house.

C. Rogue Regimes

It has been disappointing that so few of the newly independent states that have come into existence in the past fifty years have been democratic. Among them are several rogue regimes that have defied civilized norms. They have also fostered international and domestic corruption (Mellow, 1991). These are the notorious kleptocracies where public officials consider public monies to be their own personal property. Yet they have received much international aid and they continue to do so even though it is well known that the aid is diverted and only enriches their rulers. In 1991, for the very first time some aid was denied to a kleptocracy in Africa (Kenya), but little aid has yet been publicly cut off to any rogue regime anywhere else. More recently the international community has begun to take more concerned action to penalize kleptocracies and refrain from acting roguishly itself.

D. Secret Activities

The public cannot hold anyone responsible for things that they do not know about. Many government activities are conducted in secret, particularly national security, intelligence gathering, research and development, diplomacy, taxation records, and health records. Wherever secret activities are, there is room for abuse and corruption. Denied access, the public has to rely on intermediaries such as trusted mass media reporters with privileged access, secret or secretive supervisory and investigatory bodies, and occasional courageous whistleblowers. Often the rules governing access are contradictory, arbitrary, and vague. Even partial secrecy inhibits public accountability because public employees can hide things from the public, and members of the public cannot find out whether they have been mistreated. Secret deals smack of corruption; otherwise, why aren't they revealed?

E. Collaborative Government

Public agencies rarely act alone; they are part of an elaborate cooperative network. Powers and responsibilities are shared. One agency performs activities on behalf of another and one level of government will share activities with another. In multilayered governmental systems (and most are), it is most difficult to untangle the maze of complex interrelations among the parties. No single body can be charged with the whole. Such broad, diffuse systems invite conspiracy, deceit, fraud, irresponsibility, and evasion of public accountability as no single locus of authority can be identified. On the other hand, they can act as elaborate systems of mutual checks and balances. It is when they are subverted that the trouble occurs; for although everyone in general is answerable, no one in particular is, and corruption often occurs by default. The problem is compounded when, ''As the result of constitutional permissiveness, the legislative and executive departments have increasingly lost out (or abdicated) to private and quasi-governmental institutions to conduct core government functions. Public accountability has been lost in this exchange" (Craig and Gilmour, 1992: 46).

F. Contracted Functions

Government by contract is increasingly popular as it relieves public agencies of much detailed management and relieves them of specialized operations. In effect, the private sector shares public functions and the delivery of public goods and services. In the newer forms of contracting, the end product cannot be spelled out in detail and the contractor's performance cannot be clearly evaluated. Such contracting allows private groups who are foreign to public sector norms to exert considerable influence over important public decisions. Surveillance is too large and complex and "the more avenues there are for exacting accountability, the more difficult it seems to pinpoint responsibility for seeing that it is executed" (Mansfield, 1975: 334–335). The close intermingling of public and private poses several unsolved ethical, legal, and even constitutional questions (Seidman, 1975: 97).

G. Privileged Status

Public accountability means little where public agents are given privileged status not to be held accountable, answerable, or liable for their actions. For example, the doctrine that the crown (i.e., state) can do no wrong dies slowly. Governments still retain a privileged legal position to evade prosecution for alleged wrongdoings. The public does not have access to all allegations which are never systematically exposed. Corrective action is fragmented and inconclusive. Thus, the public believes "that a double standard exists in the catching and punishing of high level wrongdoers . . . [who] abuse their public trusts, get away with it for long periods or entirely, or if caught, finally escape serious punishment" (Kieffe, 1980: 17). Even low level public employees escape because their poor clients have little or no access to the legal system; the poor cannot afford to go to court and they are effectively shut out of legal redress. Only the rich can enforce their rights against improper government infringement. The unprivileged suffer and take for granted that the public in public accountability excludes them.

H. Entrepreneurial Public Management

Debureaucratization not only embraces privatization but also entrepreneurial public management or at least more enterprising public employees. It means giving public sector managers greater freedom of action, greater independence, greater self-initiative in this bold endeavor to make public management more businesslike. Managers of public enterprises have always had wide latitude in conducting their business and the result has been mixed, to put it generously. Exempt from the normal civil service controls and public service restrictions, they have not always used their freedom virtuously. On the contrary, several have conducted public enterprises as if they were their own personal fiefdoms bereft of any iota of a culture of public accountability. The same dangers lurk in other entrepreneurial public management should it fail, like so many state-owned businesses, to be responsive to their particular client/consumers and to the public at large. Greater operating flexibility compromises the customary strict standards of public accountability. The risk may well be worth taking. The enhanced propensity to corruption may be offset by cost saving and more productive public agencies but it also may involve wiping one's hands of public responsibility.

I. Self-Policing

Among the professions, self-policing does not seem to be working as well as it should. This does not mean that it could not be tried elsewhere. Given complaints of over-regulation and the heavy overhead costs of government policing, experiments are under way to give self-policing a chance as a halfway house between over- and under-regulation of business. Prevention of wrongdoing is seen as being better than cure. More effective self-policing would prevent corruption from occurring in the first place and would detect it earlier, before business firms got into deep trouble with regulatory agencies. If businesses could show that they had effective prevention programs in place before an offense occurred, then as an incentive their penalties might be reduced. In short, make self-policing more profitable for business. Such is the thinking behind: U.S. federal laws on white collar and business crime, the Defense Industry Initiatives on Business Ethics and Conduct audited by the industry's Ethics Resource Center, the Voluntary Protection Programs run by the Occupational Safety and Health Administration, and at the local level the Silver Platter Award scheme of Camden County in the State of New Jersey (Caiden, 1992; Sigler and Murphy, 1988). At first eligible businesses were slow to join and employees of the firms that did join claimed that they were not taken as seriously as they should have been and that there was still too much window dressing. Attempts to extend such programs into particularly corruption-prone industries met with little success. But since then, there has been much more progress made which suggests that self-policing works where people want it to work (i.e., where a strong culture of public accountability already exists). But where more effective self-policing is really needed it is likely to be resisted because of a weak culture of public accountability. Here strong public regulation is all the more imperative, but even that will not suffice to combat corruption emanating from organized crime.

J. Organized Crime

Typically, organized crime is seen as illegal business activity operating in the underground economy and in black markets far away from public sector operations (with the exception of law enforcement). But organized crime goes where the money is, and as these days considerable money can be made from the public sector, organized crime has not been far behind in suborning public agencies well beyond law enforcement. For many decades, organized crime has dominated several regions around the world and taken over several trades and occupations in big cities. To conduct any business, public or private, has meant dealing with organized crime and paying tribute out of the public purse. The situation grew so intolerable in New York that the city administration started some public enterprises in asphalt and cement because it discovered that it could produce these products cheaper for itself than pay the tribute demanded by the organized crime interests that dominated their manufacture and supply.

New York is by no means the only place where organized crime corrupts everything it touches. Organized crime corrupts the political system and law enforcement agencies. It hides behind legitimate business fronts to penetrate the public sector and scoop what it can from public contracts, grants, and subsidies. It controls unions in the public as well as private sector. It monopolizes trades and industries that public agencies have to use. It delays public works. It controls ports and harbors. It forces public employees to provide high paying no-show jobs and other sinecures. By these and other means, organized crime manipulates the allocation of public resources and deprives other members of society from getting their just desserts.

Thus, an anti-corruption program is insufficient in itself to reduce corruption. It needs to be accompanied by the more complex mission within society of improving the culture of public accountability, which in turn requires a strengthening of personal integrity everywhere and greater honesty in conducting public business and personal transactions. No organization can be exempted, for the actions of one influence the actions of others. Some corruption problems are fairly obvious and not so difficult to tackle as compared to corruption problems that are well hidden and fail to capture public awareness. But no solution is easy to implement. No solution completely resolves a corruption problem. Few solutions, assuming they are appropriate, last beyond the vigilance needed to see that they remain effective. There are few quick fixes where corruption is major and serious. Effective remedies may take decades, if not generations, to institutionalize and will depend on so many different parties taking their roles seriously until they become routine, dependable, and efficient. Progress on a grand scale cannot be measured in just a few short years; one has to compare improvements over the long haul. Fortunately, the weaker and minor forms of corruption are much easier to deal with, and relatively quick and immediate success in tackling these forms of corruption can and do encourage reformers to take on the more serious and major forms.

VI. CONCLUSION

The bottom line is fairly obvious. No matter what external and internal controls exist, no matter how they are enforced, corruption is a particularly viral form of bureaupathology. Once it enters the life stream of an administrative system, it quickly spreads to all parts even if it goes undetected for a long time. If untreated, it will eventually destroy the effectiveness of the infected area. Even if treated in time, there is no guarantee that it will be eliminated altogether. It is highly contagious, debilitating, and costly to treat. Current strategies only aim at containment and minimization. It is tackled until it becomes impractical, uneconomic, and unwise to go further. The ingenious are always a step ahead. Only personal integrity wards off the disease. Responsible administrators, backed by the wide range of instruments previously outlined, know what they have to do repeatedly in the never ending fight against corruption. They realize, like Rieux in Camus's *The Plague*,

> that the plague bacillus never dies or disappears for good: that it bides times . . . ; and that perhaps the day would come when, for the bane and the enlightening of men, it would rouse up its rats again and send them forth to die in a happy city. (Camus, 1948: 278)

SELECTED BIBLIOGRAPHY

Ades, A. and di Tella, R. (1996). The causes and consequences of corruption: a review of recent empirical contributions. *IDS Bulletin*, 27(2): 6–11.

Alam, A.S. (1995). A theory of limits on corruption and some applications. *Kyklos*, 48(3): 419–435.

Andvig, J.C. and Moene, K.O. (1990). How corruption may corrupt. *Journal of Economic Behavior and Organization*, 13(1): 63–76.

Anechiario, F. and Jacobs, J.B. (1996). *The Pursuit of Absolute Integrity: How Corruption Control Makes Government Ineffective*. Chicago: University of Chicago Press.

Ayittey, G.B. (1992). *Africa Betrayed*. New York: St. Martin's Press.

Berkman, S. (1996). The impact of corruption in technical cooperation projects in Africa. *International Journal of Technical Cooperation*, 2(2): 208–223.

Bracey, D.H. (1976). *A Functional Approach to Police Corruption*. New York: John Jay School of Criminal Justice.

Brademas, J. and Heimann, F. (1998). Tackling international corruption; no longer taboo. *Foreign Affairs*, 77(5): 17–22.

Cadot, O. (1987). Corruption as a gamble. *Journal of Public Economics*, 33(2): 223–244.

Caiden, G.E. (1988). Toward a general theory of official corruption. *Asian Journal of Public Administration*, 10(1): 3–26.

Caiden, G.E. (1992). Public disillusion and organizational self-policing. Fifth International Anti-Corruption Conference, Amsterdam.

Caiden, G.E. (1997). Undermining good governance: corruption and democracy. *Asian Journal of Political Science*, 5(2): 1–22.

Caiden, G.E. (1998). The essence of public service professionalism. United Nations Seminar on Public Service Ethics, Thessalonica, Greece.

Caiden, G.E. and Caiden, N.J. (1994). Administrative corruption revisited. *Philippines Journal of Public Administration*, 38(1): 1–16.

Caiden, G.E. and Caiden, N.J. (1995). More on official misconduct. *Indian Journal of Public Administration*, 41(3): 371–382.

Camus, A. (1948). *The Plague*. New York: Random House.

Canadian Centre for Management Development. (1996). *Values and Ethics in the Public Service*. Discussion Paper, Ottawa.

Carino, L.V. (1989). *Bureaucratic Corruption in Asia: Causes, Consequences and Control*, Quezon City, The Philippines: JMC Press.

Celarier, M. (1997). Corruption: the search for the smoking gun. *Public Fund Digest*, 8(1): 37–45.

Chapman, R.A. (ed. 1993). *Ethics in Public Service*. Edinburgh: Edinburgh University Press.

Clague, C. (ed. 1997). *Institutions and Economic Development: Growth and Governance in Less-Developed and Post-Socialist Countries*. Baltimore, MD: The Johns Hopkins University Press.

Craig, B.H. and Gilmour, R.S. (1992). The constitution and accountability for *public* functions. *Governance*, 5(1): 46–57.

CRIME (1996). United Nations Newsletter on Crime Prevention and Criminal Justice, 24/25.

Crime, Law & Social Change (1997). Special issue on corruption in contemporary politics. *Crime, Law & Social Change*, 27(3–4): 169–314.

Development Alternatives, Inc. (1998). *Combating Corruption in Developing and Transitional Countries: A Guidelines Paper for USAID*. Bethesda, MD: DAI.

Dey, H.K. (1989). The genesis and spread of economic corruption: a micro-theoretical interpretation. *World Development*, 17(4): 503–511.

Diamond, L., Linz, J. and Lipsett, S.M. (1995). *Politics in Developing Countries: Comparing Experiences with Democracy*, 2nd edition. Boulder, CO: Lynne Rienner Publishing.

Doig, R.A. (1995). Government and sustainable anti-corruption strategies: a role for independent anti-corruption agencies. *Public Administration and Development*, 15(2): 151–166.

Eigen, P. (1996). Combating corruption around the world. *Journal of Democracy*, 73: 158–168.

Elliot, K.A. (1997). *Corruption and the Global Economy*. Washington, D.C.: International Economics. *Finance and Development* (1998). Fighting corruption worldwide. *Finance and Development*, 35(1): 3–17.

Flatters, F. and Bentley, W.L. (1995). Administrative corruption and taxation. *International Tax and Public Finance*, 2(3): 397–417.

Gambetta, D. (1993). *The Sicilian Mafia*. Cambridge, MA: Harvard University Press.

Geddes, B. and Neto, A. (1992). Institutional sources of corruption in Brazil. *Third World Quarterly*, 13(4): 641–661.

Gel, R. and Rich, R. (1989). On the economic incentives for taking bribes. *Public Choice*, 61: 269–275.

Georges, C. (1992). Confessions of an investigative reporter. *The Washington Monthly*, 24(3): 36–43.

Gould, D.J. (1980). *Bureaucratic Corruption and Underdevelopment in the Third World: The Case of Zaire*. New York: Pergamon Press.

Hampton, M. (1996). *The Offshore Interface: Tax Havens in the Global Economy*. Basingstoke, England: Macmillan.

Handelman, P. (1995). *Comrade Criminal*. New Haven, CT: Yale University Press.

Heywood, P. (ed.) (1997). Political corruption. *Political Studies*, 45(3): 417–658.

Heimann, F. (1995). *Should Foreign Bribery Be a Crime*? Berlin: Transparency International.

Heidenheimer, A.J., Johnston, M., and LeVine, V.T. (1989). *Political Corruption*. New Brunswick, NJ: Transaction Books.

Henderson, K. (1995a). *Internal Controls*. Berlin: Transparency International.

Henderson, K. (1995b). *Whistleblowers*. Berlin: Transparency International.

Huberts, L.W. (1998). What can be done against public corruption and fraud: Expert views on strategies to protect public integrity. *Crime, Law & Social Change*, 29: 209–224.

Husted, B. (1994). Honor among thieves: a transaction-cost interpretation of corruption in third world countries. *Business Ethics Quarterly*, 4(1): 17–27.

International Chamber of Commerce. (1996). Extortion and bribery in international business. Transactions Document 193/15, Paris.

Jabbra, J.G. and Dwivedi, O.P. (1988). *Public Service Accountability*. West Hartford, CT: Kumarian Press.

Jagananthan, N.V. (1986). Corruption, delivery systems and property rights. *World Development*, 14(1): 127–132.

Johnston, M. (1993). 'Micro' and 'macro' possibilities for reform. *Corruption and Reform*, 7: 189–204.

Johnston, M. and Hao, Y. (1995). China's surge of corruption. *Journal of Democracy*, 6(4): 80–94.

Kaufmann, D. and Siegelbaum, P. (1997). Privatisation and corruption in transitional economies. *Journal of International Affairs*, 50(2): 419–459.

Kaufmann, D., Pradhan, S. and Ryterman, R. (1998). New frontiers in diagnosing and combating corruption. *Public Management Forum (PMF)*, 4(6): 1–5.

Khan, M. (1996). A typology of corruption transactions in developing countries. *IDS Bulletin*, 27(2): 12–21.

Kieffe, J.A. (1980). The case for an inspector general of the United States. *The Bureaucrat*, 92: 11–17.

Klitgaard, R. (1988). *Controlling Corruption*. Berkeley: The University of California Press.

Klitgaard, R. (1991). Strategies for reform. *Journal of Democracy*, 2(4): 86–100.

Klitgaard, R. (1997). Cleaning up and invigorating the civil service. *Public Administration and Development*, 17(3): 487–509.

Kong, T.Y. (1996). Corruption and its institutional foundations: the experience of South Korea. *IDS Bulletin*, 27(2): 48–55.

Langeth, P. and Stagenhurst, R. (1997). The role of the national integrity system in fighting corruption. Washington, DC. Economic Development Institute, The World Bank.

Leiken, R. (1997). Controlling the global corruption epidemic. *Public Finance Digest*, 3(1): 47–59.

Lim, S.G. (1998). Integrity with empowerment: challenges facing Singapore in the 21st century. *Asian Journal of Political Science*, 6(2): 132–139.

Little, W. and Posada-Carbo, E. (eds.) (1996). *Political Corruption in Europe and Latin America*, Basingstoke: Macmillan.

Lotspeich, R. (1995). Crime in transitional economies. *EuroAsia Studies*, 47(4): 555–589.

Manion, M. (1996). Corruption by design; bribery in Chinese enterprise licensing. *Journal of Law, Economics and Organization*, 12: 167–195.

Mansfield, H. C. (1975). Independence and accountability for federal contractors and grantees. In *The New Political Economy: The Public Use of the Private Sector* (B.R.L. Smith, ed.). New York: John Wiley and Sons, pp. 334–335.

Manzetti, L. and Blake, C. (1996). Market reforms and corruption in Latin America: new means for old ways. *Review of International Political Economy*, 3(4): 662–697.

Mauro, P. (1995). Corruption and growth. *Quarterly Journal of Economics*, August:681–712.

Mauro, P. (1997). Why worry about corruption? *Economic Issues*, 6: 1–12.

Mbaku, J. (1994). Bureaucratic corruption and policy reform. *The Journal of Social, Political and Economic Studies*, 19(2): 149–175.

Mbaku, J. (1999). Corruption cleanups in developing societies: the public choice perspective. *International Journal of Public Administration*, 22(2): 309–346.

Mellow, C. (1991). The wages of sin. *CEO/International Strategies*, 4(5): 24–26.

Mitchell, R.H. (1996). *Political Corruption in Japan*. Honolulu: University of Hawaii Press.

Moody-Stuart, G. (1994). *The Good Business Guide to Bribery*. Berlin: Transparency International.

Noonan, J.T. (1984). *Bribes*. New York: Macmillan.

Nye, J.S. (1967). Corruption and political development: a cost-benefit analysis. In *Political Corruption* (A.J. Heidenheimer et al., eds.). New Brunswick, NJ: Transaction Books, pp. 963–983.

Organisation for Economic Cooperation and Development. (1998). *Survey on Anti-Corruption Measures in the Public Sector in OECD Countries*. Public Management Service/PUMA, Paris.

Pope, J. (1996). *The TI Source Book*. Berlin: Transparency International.

Price-Waterhouse (1991). *Recent Activities in Controlling Fraud and Corruption in Government*. Washington DC: Price-Waterhouse.

Program National De Solidaridad. (1992). *The Social Controller Program*. Mexico City: Asesoria De Communicacion.

Programme for Accountability and Transparency/PACT. (1998). *Biannual Reports*. New York: Global Secretariat, United Nations Development Programme.

Rachin, R. (1996). State failure in India: fiscal implications of the black economy. *IDS Bulletin*, 27(2): 22–30.

Rasmunen, E. and Ramseyer, M. (1994). Cheap bribes and the corruption ban: a coordination game among rational legislators. *Public Choice*, 78(3–4): 305–327.

Reed, S.R. (1996). Political corruption in Japan. *International Social Science Journal*, 149: 395–405.

Rose-Ackerman, S. (1978). *Corruption: A Study in Political Economy*. New York: Academic Press.

Rose-Ackerman, S. (1997a). Corruption, inefficiency and economic growth. *Nordic Journal of Political Economics*, 24: 3–20.

Rose-Ackerman, S. (1997b). The role of the World Bank in controlling corruption. *Law and Politics in International Business*, 29: 93–114.

Rosenn, K. and Downes, R. (eds.) (1999). *Corruption and Political Reform in Brazil*. Coral Gables, FL: North-South Center Press.

Seidman, H. (1975). Government-sponsored enterprise in the United States. *The New Political Economy: The Public Use of the Private Sector* (B.R.L. Smith, ed.). New York: John Wiley and Sons, p. 97.

Shleifer, A. and Vishny, R. (1993). Corruption. *Quarterly Journal of Economics*, 108(3): 599–617.

Sigler, J. and Murphy, J. (1988). *Interactive Corporate Compliance*. Westport, CT: Greenwood Press.

Skidmore, M. (1996). Promise and peril in combating corruption: Hong Kong's ICAC. *Annals of the American Academy of Political and Social Science*, 547: 118–130.

Smith, B.R.L. and Hague, D. (1971). *The Dilemma of Accountability in Modern Government: Independence versus Control*. London: Macmillan.

Stapenhurst, R. and Kpundeh, S.J. (eds.) (1997). *Fighting Corruption: Lessons of Experience*. Washington, DC: Economic Development Institute, The World Bank.

Theobald, R. (1990). *Corruption, Development and Underdevelopment*. Durham, NC: Duke University Press.

Thompson, D. (1980). Moral responsibility of public officials: the problem of many hands. *American Political Science Review*, 74: 905–916.

Transparency International. (1996). *A National Integrity Source Book for Building More Transparent and Accountable Government*. Berlin.

Tutt, N. (1989). *Europe on the Fiddle: The Common Market Scandal*. London: Helm.

United Kingdom Audit Commission. (1993). *Protecting the Public Purse: Probity in the Public Sector*. London: Her Majesty's Stationery Office.

United Nations. (1989). *Corruption in Government*. TCD/SEM.90/2 INT 89, R 56. New York: Department of Technical Cooperation for Development.

United Nations. (1990). *Crime Prevention and Criminal Justice in the Context of Development: Realities and Perspective of International Co-operation*. Document A/CONF. 144/8, Vienna: Crime Prevention and Criminal Justice Division.

United Nations. (1997). *Promotion and Maintenance of the Rule of Law and Good Governance: Action Against Corruption*. New York: Report of the Secretary-General E/CN.15/1997/3.

United Nations/INTOSAI. (1996). *The Role of SAIs in Fighting Corruption and Mismanagement*. New York: Department of Development Support and Management Services, and Vienna: the International Organisation of Supreme Audit Institutions.

United Nations Development Programme. (1997a). *Reconceptualizing Governance*. Discussion Paper 1. New York: Bureau for Policy and Programme Support.

United Nations Development Programme. (1997b). *Corruption and Good Governance*. Discussion Paper 3. New York: Bureau for Policy and Programme Support.

United Nations Development Programme. (1998). *Corruption & Integrity Improvement Initiatives in Developing Countries*. New York and Paris: the OECD Development Centre.

United Nations Development Programme (1999). *Fighting Corruption to Improve Governance*. New York: United Nations Development Programme.

Van Rijckeghem, C. and Weder, B. (1997). Corruption and the role of temptation: do low wages in the civil service cause corruption? Working Paper. Washington, D.C.: International Monetary Fund.

Wamey, J. (1998). Cameroon's corruption seen as near universal. *The Washington Times*, November 5, A19.

Ward, P.M. (1989). *Corruption, Development and Inequality: Soft Touch or Hard Graft*. London: Routledge.

Werner, S.B. (1983). New directions in the study of administrative corruption. *Public Administration Review*, 43(2): 146–154.

Williams, R. (1987). *Political Corruption in Africa*. Aldershot, England: Gower.

White, G. (1996). Corruption and market reform in China. *IDS Bulletin*, 27(2): 40–47.

World Bank. (1996). *Guidelines for Procurement under IBRD Loans and IDA Credits*. Washington, DC: World Bank.

World Bank. (1997a). Helping countries control corruption: the role of the World Bank. Washington, DC: World Bank.

World Bank. (1997b). *The State in a Changing World: World Development Report 1997*. Oxford: Oxford University Press.

22

Moral Development in Public Administration

Debra W. Stewart, Norman W. Sprinthall, and David M. Shafer
North Carolina State University, Raleigh, North Carolina

I. INTRODUCTION

This chapter reviews the treatment of moral development in the public administration literature. In contrast to most chapters in this volume, this chapter introduces literature and methodologies that may appear far afield from public administration. A faithful rendering of the theoretical background for moral development theory ranges from developmental psychology to theories of social justice. The actual application of moral development theory to public administration ethics is an important but still emerging initiative in the field. A prime objective of this chapter is to assess its potential as an approach for learning more about how public administrators make moral choices and for strengthening their capacities for ethical decision-making. Since the overall framework for our work has been derived from research in behavioral science, we will provide a detailed review of that material, then indicate how we have adapted the approach for public administration, outline our findings, and close with a discussion of implications and continuing issues.

II. DIRECTING CONSTRUCTS: BEHAVIORAL SCIENCE ROOTS

The framework for our theory and research in public administration has been derived and adapted from behavioral science. For many years psychology had avoided questions of values and ethics as a result of the predominance of the behavioristic paradigm. The very early research of Hartshorne and May in the 1920s and 1930s dispelled all the myths of character training and education. They found that none of the common approaches made any difference at all. Boy Scouts, Girl Scouts, religious education, exhortations, and similar programs designed to promote habits and traits of honesty and resistance to temptation had no effects. Cheating and similar behavior appeared to be normally distributed (the psychologists' usual *deus ex machina*) around a node of moderate cheating. As a result, research on character traits disappeared from the behavioral science scene. Instead, virtue, values, and ethics were viewed in the context of positive reinforcement in a Skinnerian sense. This indicated that values were in fact relativistic. Skinner illustrated the view when he compared psychology to other sciences: "physics and biology study things without reference to their value, but the reinforcing effects of things are the province of behavioral science" (1971, p. 104). In other words, individuals are simply schedules of behavioral reinforcement. Society and its leaders decide which values to shape through reinforcement and control, shades of Stanley Kubrick's *Clockwork Orange*.

As a result, the question of values seemed trapped in a cul de sac. Either fixed personality traits and virtues bore no relationship to behavior, or values were totally outside of individual control, externally determined by society's reinforcers. The emperor of character traits not only had no external clothes but was nude inside as well. While behavioral science as a whole struggled with such relativism vis à vis values and ethics, Kohlberg and his colleagues (working first at the University of Chicago and later at Harvard) revised the entire approach to the study of values which then became the basis for our own framework.

Kohlberg first demonstrated both theoretically and empirically that values and ethics were neither "born" nor made. Traits were not fixed, nor were they shaped, externally. Following in the path of theorists such as John Dewey, J.M. Baldwin, and Jean Piaget, Kohlberg suggested that values and ethics were *developed* as a result of the interaction between the person and the environment. Thus he replaced the idea of fixed traits of, for example, honesty versus dishonesty with a framework of levels or stages of development. Secondly, he replaced the Skinnerian idea of the person as an empty organism with the concept of cognitive structure. This indicated that individuals cognitively construct their own interpretation of values over time from interactions with the environment. For example, Piaget found that children construct their own systems for understanding physical concepts such as time, space, and causality. Children and adolescents were not midget-sized adults but rather had a uniquely developing set of stages of intellectual growth. Kohlberg, then, found parallel sets of stages of moral and ethical development, a kind of staircase of cognitive systems which persons used as a basis for choices and behavior when confronted with value dilemmas.

It is important to understand the background for the framework and particularly the current state of the art as our basis for value stages in public administration. The Kohlberg research started with cross-sectional studies of males, then shifted to longitudinal studies of both males and females, and then shifted again to include studies in different countries. There are now more than 5000 empirical studies in support of the assumption (Rest and Narvaez, 1994).

The current framework represents a sequence of stages of value and ethical development and includes the following propositions about values:

1. Stages are qualitatively distinct systems of value choices.
2. The stages form a hierarchy.
3. The sequence is invariant.
4. The system transcends cultures in urban societies.
5. The system is gender neutral.
6. There is a consistent relationship between stage and moral behavior.

A stage model implies that different systems of cognitive process are qualitative, as different worldviews or paradigms which an individual uses for decisions in complex situations. The stages are presented along with brief descriptions in Table 1. In the case

Table 1   Kohlberg's Stages of Moral Growth

Basis of judgment	Stage of development	Characteristics of stage
Preconventional moral values reside in external, quasi-physical happenings, in bad acts, or in quasi-physical needs rather than in persons and standards	Stage 1	Obedience and punishment orientation; egocentric deference to superior power or prestige, or a trouble-avoiding set; objective responsibility
	Stage 2	Naively egoistic orientation; right action in that instrumentally satisfying one's own and occasionally others' needs; awareness that value is relative to each person's needs and perspectives; naive egalitarianism and orientation to exchange and reciprocity
Conventional moral values reside in performing good or right roles, in maintaining the conventional order, and in meeting others' expectations	Stage 3	Orientation to approval and to pleasing and helping others; conformity to stereotypical images of majority or natural role behavior, and judgment by intentions
	Stage 4	Orientation to doing one's duty and to showing respect for authority and maintaining the given social order for its own sake; regard for earned expectations of others
Postconventional moral values are derived from principles that can be applied universally	Stage 5	Contractual-legalistic orientation; recognition of an arbitary element in rules of expectations for the sake of agreement; duty defined in terms of contract, general avoidance of violation of the will or rights of others, or of the majority will and welfare
	Stage 6	Orientation to conscience or principles, not only to ordained social rules but to principles of choice appealing to logical universality and consistency; conscience is a directing agent, together with mutual respect and trust

of a concept like honesty, instead of a continuum from great dishonesty to comprehensive honesty, the Kohlberg system transforms such continua to a vertical hierarchy. Thus, at the lowest stage, the frame of reference which the person employs is either the giving or receiving end of physical force for honest or dishonest behavior. Such a frame is qualitatively different from the next stage when such decisions are driven by concerns for materialistic gain or loss. Honesty at this level is a matter of dollars and cents. The succeeding stages follow the same process, each as a transformation, a different worldview on the concept of honesty. Each stage as a result can be considered as more morally adequate from the standpoint of the "moral point of view." A word about the underlying philosophical perspective of moral development research will put principled reasoning in context.

To find the most ethically adequate solution to a moral quandary, one must don the cap of the independent, disinterested observer's posture labeled by Baier (1958) as "the moral point of view." Sometimes called the "good reasons" approach to moral philosophy, this perspective emerged in the 1950s in reaction to a realistic view that equated ethical choice with personal preference (see Stewart, 1991). The good-reasons approach contains these elements: that ethics resides in the cognitive realm; that one can reach ethical decisions through reasoning; and that the final justification for a claim can appeal to a principle outside of the person making it or the argument being made (Gewirth, 1978; Stewart, 1991). But while the "moral point of view" does provide a court of appeal for inevitable conflicts of interest (Baier, 1958), an explicit methodology is needed for deciding what moral principles should be held and how competing claims among values should be resolved (Stewart, 1991). John Rawls provides the methodology that undergirds Kohlberg's stage model.

Rawls (1971) begins by acknowledging that though society is a "cooperative venture for mutual advantage, it is typically marked by a conflict as well as by an identity of interests" (p. 4). Conflicts of interest occur because people are not neutral as to how the benefits produced by their cooperation are distributed, each desiring a larger share (p. 4). Rawls concluded that there are principles of justice that allow choosing among different processes for deciding advantages. From an "original position" in which one would choose principles without knowing one's own place in the future society, Rawls claims two principles would be chosen. "The first requires equality in the assignment of basic rights and duties, while the second holds social and economic inequalities . . . are just only if they result in compensating benefits for everyone, and in particular for the least advantaged members of society" (Rawls, 1971, pp. 14–15).

What Kohlberg adopted from Rawls is the broad heuristic for working through ethical quandaries and a substantive set of justice principles. The implicit assumption in Kohlberg is that the individual operating at the highest stage of moral reasoning takes into account those considerations addressed in John Rawls' property-structured society. The "justice as fairness" ethic described by Rawls corresponds to the Kohlberg "postconventional" stage (Kohlberg, 1984, pp. 301–303; Hennessy, 1979, p. 219). Since the 1970s, Rawls' work has dealt largely with how "justice as fairness" can provide a framework for understanding the conceptual underpinnings of modern constitutional democracies and the individual's relationship to the democratic order (Rawls, 1985; Cohen, 1989; Arneson, 1989; Stewart and Sprinthall, 1991). Most recent assessments of Kohlberg suggest that his major contribution was in fact to illuminate the organization and practice of democratic community (Reed, 1997).

From this philosophical underpinning, Kohlberg developed the moral development stage framework. Following in the tradition of developmental researchers, Kohlberg emphasized what can be termed a grass-roots inductive method. Subjects were asked to reason out loud as to how they would resolve dilemmas involving questions of ethics and values. Then, examining the different clusters of reasons, the hierarchical framework itself was literally constructed. Thus the format was taken from an inductive process of seeking a synthesis of different groups of reasons which the research subjects offered. Stepping back from the framework, it is easy to see the underlying, almost Platonic, framework for values and ethics vis à vis concepts of justice; for example, Thrasymachus and might makes right (stage 1), unlimited self seeking (stage 2), Glaucon and helping one's friends (stage 3), laws as "second best" (stage 4), and the equal sharing of benefits and burdens of distributive justice (stages 5 and 6). The main point here is that the system was derived from research subjects of both sexes and from over 50 different countries. The longitudinal studies have confirmed the assumptions derived originally from cross-sectional research.

There are a number of controversial aspects of the scheme which require special emphasis: (1) cross-cultural universality, (2) gender differences, (3) adult development, and (4) the relationship of stage and behavior.

Cultural anthropologists in general have maintained that cultural values are relativistic. Each culture or society is like a snowflake, different and distinct, and cannot be compared to other cultures. In fact such comparisons are usually criticized as examples of cultural bias. Thus, there have been criticisms (Simpson, 1974; Baumrind, 1986) that the stage scheme is just such an example. Kohlberg and associates have responded by transposing the standard dilemmas, with the aid of ethnologists, into culturally relevant issues in some 50 different countries. The stage sequence has been cross-validated in all industrialized societies and even in tribal/feudal cultures for the first four stages (Gielen, 1991). While there was an absence of principled reasoning in these later cultures, for reasons still under investigation, the general framework for industrialized societies is intact. This, of course, is an important point since our own investigation will proceed from studies in this country to comparative studies with other industrialized societies.

Both the interview system of Kohlberg and objective versions of the survey developed by James Rest's Defining Issues Test (DIT) have been successfully employed in different industrialized societies. Snarey (1985) and others have translated the interview method and the objective version has been adapted for use in German-speaking countries (The Moralisches-Urteil Test; Lind, 1995).

On the gender question, a major controversy was created by the charge of Gilligan (1982) who claimed the entire cognitive developmental scheme of Kohlberg was biased against women. Her criticism, in fact, reached national prominence through her book of case studies and one of her own research investigations. Her point was that there was a woman's voice that is not captured by Kohlberg. Since that time, however, reviews by Rest (1986) and a meta-analysis of research by Walker (1986)—which included both the interview method and the objective version with some 10,000 subjects—yielded correlations of almost zero (.04) by gender and stage. Also, since the studies noted above were all cross-sectional, Lee and Snarey (1988) performed a meta-analysis on longitudinal data with 625 subjects. There were no gender differences by stage of moral development from either assessment technique. Thus, the research reviews in general disprove any charge of gender bias in assessment of moral-ethical reasoning as it pertains to levels of capacity to reason at principled levels. In fact, and somewhat ironically, much of the most recent research with large-sized samples from adult professionals in fields such as medicine, veterinary medicine, accounting, and dentistry indicates a consistent trend for women to be at a somewhat *higher* level of moral development than males (Rest and Narvaez, 1994). If research in allied fields confirms these trend differences, we may need to stand the earlier research on its head. If you hold educational and professional backgrounds constant and the gender ratio moves more toward equality of representation, then females may consistently reason at a higher level of ethics than their male cohorts. Given such an extensive research base, there will be no case for charging a bias against males.

A third question of significance concerns adult growth. Originally it was suggested by most cognitive-developmental researchers that the last stage (in a qualitative sense) was complete by early adulthood. However, these researchers (Piaget, Kohlberg, and others) all made the same fortuitous mistake. They conducted longitudinal research. By assessing the same persons over substantial time spans they found that at least some adults continued to move to higher stages. There was no arbitrary age during adulthood after which further development was no longer possible. These studies also indicated the critical nature of the environment. The context (e.g., colleagues and the nature of the career role responsibilities) was extremely important in providing opportunities for discussion and analysis of any important professional ethical problems which the adults faced, such as a doctor wrestling with euthanasia or a business manager faced with knowledge of bribery by a peer. Kohlberg (1984) in particular also found examples of adult professionals (such as trial lawyers who refused to examine issues at a principled level) who remained stabilized without regard to issues of fairness and equity. These examples indicate that the process of ethical growth, then, is possible for adults in general and probable in certain contexts. The developmental truism throughout the life span is the same. Growth depends upon appropriate interaction.

Armon (1998) has shown that adults in general may face moral dilemmas in their own interpersonal relationships as well as in the workplace and can develop a more comprehensive ethical framework as a result of systematic discussion and reflection. Without such opportunities, however, adults may prematurely stabilize in levels of ethical reasoning. We will discuss this latter issue more fully in the section on implications for programmatic intervention. At this point, the main issue is to underscore the potential for adult development.

III. ETHICAL REASONING AND BEHAVIOR: NARROWING THE GAP

In all that has preceded this section an effort has been made to outline the philosophical-psychological rationale for a developmental model to comprehend the question of human development vis à vis ethical reasoning. The crucial question, however, has not been answered. What, if any, is the connection between the concepts and real world behavior? If we cannot answer this then we would be forced to accept the stinging criticism of Haan (1983) who opined that moral reasoning was "nothing more than reified adulterations of intellectualized restatements of interactional morality . . . (requiring) special intellectual training . . . (and derived from) the intellectual's phobic reactions to social uncertainty" (p. 246).

In earlier research on this question, the results were somewhat ambiguous. The research employing general assessments of ethical reasoning (e.g., generic moral dilemmas) had consistently shown positive trends. Yet there were still troublesome gaps in the findings, particularly the attempt to generalize the results to adults. Much of the research employed college students, creating an obvious issue of how adults actually might behave in similar situations. Also the few studies with adults (such as the famous Milgram research on obedience to authority) were conducted with relatively small samples (Kohlberg, 1984). As a result, it was somewhat problematic to claim that general ethical reasoning bore a strong and consistent relationship to behavior in the real world of adults.

Research on this important issue has shifted in focus away from general assessment of reasoning (e.g., should Heinz steal a drug to save his wife's life?) to reasoning levels that were directly relevant to adults in particular professions. The shift to such real-life moral reasoning, in the view of some researchers [such as Krebs et al. (1997), Armon (1998), Rest and Narvaez (1994)], is an important step in the direction of reducing the unexplained variance between prediction and behavior in ethically conflicted situations. Table 2 displays some of the more recent research focused on adults in particular professions illustrating the connection between ethical reasoning and actual professional performance.

As Table 2 indicates, there are a series of important relationships between reasoning levels and professional performance across a wide variety of groups, doctors, accountants, dentists, nurses, teachers, and so on. The results are consistent in two ways. Effective performance is associated with higher stages of reasoning and incompetent professional behavior is directly related to lower levels of ethical thought. Cognition and ethical behavior are significantly and functionally related.

Finally, it is important to point out that higher stages are not always "better." In discussing adaptation of decision theory models to ethical choice in administration, Brady and Woller (1996) have made the point that there are situations where decision-makers should fall back on the "rules" and not be responsive to changing conditions. Still other situations demand rules be abandoned. This mixed model facilitates a holistic decision process. For example, if tasks call for repetitive and rote-like activities, then less complex stages are more adaptive. The same would hold for training tasks as opposed to educative experiences. This is one more example of the developmental interactive hypothesis. More complex stages are adaptive (and better) when the tasks require complex thought and democratic behavior. Also (shades of Socrates and the dissatisfied pig), higher stages are

Table 2 Relationships Between Ethical Reasoning and Professional Performance

Group	Researcher(s)	Outcomes
Medical doctors	Self and Baldwin (1994)	Higher levels of reasoning, M.D.s more likely to (1) match treatment to needs of patients,* and (2) meet commitments for research
Orthopedic surgeons	Baldwin, Adamson, Self and Sheehan (1994)	Higher levels of reasoning associated with fewer claims of malpractice
Accountants and auditors	Ponemon and Gabhart (1994)	Higher levels of reasoning associated with fraud detection and willingness to "blow the whistle": lower levels associated with under-reporting
Nurses	Duckett and Ryden (1994)	Higher levels of reasoning was the most important predictor of competent clinical practice
Dentists	Bebeau (1994)	Low levels of reasoning virtually excluded adequate clinical performance
Teachers	Chang (1994)	Higher levels predicted greater empathy, respect for student rights, more flexible teaching methods, more objective and greater student achievement gains

*In fact these researchers noted that a high level of moral reasoning, "virtually excludes the possibility of being a poor performer, and conversely, that a low level of moral reasoning virtually excludes the possibility of performing well" (Self and Baldwin, 1994, p. 151).

not necessarily happier. In fact, at the more complex levels of thinking and feeling, individuals are more aware of injustice and the lack of equity, hardly a condition conducive to contentment.

There have been a few post facto studies of the behavior and reasoning of elected officials which support the systematic research noted above. For example, at the time of Watergate, statements by those involved in the scandal were coded according to moral stage level including those of Nixon, Porter, Magruder, and Krogh (Kohlberg and Candee, 1984). All were rated exclusively at stages 3 and 4 on the scale while Archibald Cox's statements (and presumably Elliot Richardson's) were at stage 5. One supposes the same analysis could be instructive of these relationships if a study were made of contemporary examples of unethical political behavior. Such a study, of course, is not conclusive since many of the requisite research conditions are not possible. As case studies, however, such research does add further credence to the contentions at hand, namely that stage predicts behavior when the expectations or context calls for democratic decision-making and ethical behavior.

Given the philosophical framework, together with the multiple research studies underscoring the importance of ethical reasoning levels in relation to adult behavior in a variety of professions, it seems obvious that a field as central to the public welfare as public administration merits investigation. Cohen and Eimicke (1995) have reminded us that one of the central issues in administrative ethics is how to guide administrative behavior in situations where there is no clear legal guidance. Our first steps in addressing that issue will be described next in the creation of an assessment technique embedded in the content of issues specifically related to our field.

IV. THE METHODOLOGICAL CHALLENGES: ADAPTING A STAGE SYSTEM TO PUBLIC ADMINISTRATION

In thinking about adapting the scheme of stages to the tasks of the public administrators, two issues had to be confronted. First, whether public administrative tasks require the ability to understand the ethical dimension of decision-making; second, whether ethical, yet practical, reasoning can be measured empirically in a sequence of stages. We accepted the assumption that public administrative decisions did have an ethical dimension, perhaps for obvious reasons. As to whether it could be measured empirically in a sequence of stages, we were sensitive to the question of context in measurement. If a dilemma is directly relevant to a person's professional work activity, does the person reason differently from their reasoning with respect to general or abstract moral dilemmas? Since earlier research suggested that the closer the issue to a person's immediate role responsibility the greater the dissonance and the more varied the responses, the Stewart-Sprinthall Management Survey (SSMS) was developed to feature ethical dilemmas typically experienced by public administrators as they acted in their professional roles.

The content of the dilemmas was created based on several years of problem-solving discussions which Stewart conducted with executives in a public sector executive development program. The three dilemmas in the instrument represent real-world issues that administrators actually experience. In terms of the discussion above about abstract moral dilemmas versus professionally relevant ones, the SSMS dilemmas are specific to the

Table 3 Comparing Principled Reasoning and Stage 4 on DIT and SSMS Tests, P Scores Compared to Stage 4 Scores* (N = 34)

	DIT	SSMS
P score	41%	38%
Stage 4	34%	48%
P score range	(7–83)	(17–70)

*P scores = scores on principled reasoning; Stage 4 scores = scores on reasoning indicating a "concern for law and duty."

public administration context and in accord with recent research in other professions, as noted.

The second part of the instrument provides a series of rationales for resolving such dilemmas. In each case, respondents choose from twelve alternatives the reasons that best fit how they would solve the problems. The alternative "reasons" that are suggested as possibly important in solving each dilemma were constructed to parallel different Kohlberg levels or stages as those stages were displayed in Table 1. For example, for the first dilemma, concerning promotion, a respondent who chooses "Does Bob's sense of fairness require that he resist this patronage intrusion whatever the costs to his future effectiveness?" as an important reason would be selecting an answer that represents the highest stage in the scheme. On the other hand, selecting "Doesn't Bob need to consider how to pay for his daughter's college tuition if he is fired?" would be congruent with the lowest levels. The alternative choices on the SSMS were created by Sprinthall on the basis of his extensive background in applying the Kohlberg approach to research and practice. The content validity of the choice issues were supported by ratings of professional colleagues and advanced graduate students skilled in comprehending Kohlberg theory.

The concurrent validity of the instrument was first tested with two samples of graduate students in public administration who completed both the SSMS and the Defining

Table 4 Comparing All Stages of Moral Reasoning on the DIT and SSMS Tests of Public Administration Graduate Students, All Stage Scores Compared (N = 50)

Stage	DIT	SSMS
1 and 2	5%	5%
3	11%	5%
4	33%	47%
P	41%	39%
Meaningless	7%	3%
P score range	(0–83)	(17–70)

Reproduced from Stewart and Sprinthall, Chapter 11 in James Bowman, Ed. *Ethical Frontiers in Public Management.*

Table 5 Intercorrelation Matrix for DIT and SSMS

Score	SSMS story 1	SSMS story 2	SSMS story 3	SSMS total
DIT	.34	.24	.34	.42
SSMS story 1	1.00	.24	.20	.67
SSMS story 2		1.00	.30	.65
SSMS story 3			1.00	.76
SSMS total				1.00

Reproduced from Stewart and Sprinthall, Chapter 11 in James Bowman, Ed. *Ethical Frontiers in Public Management*, 1991.

Issues Test (DIT) (Rest, 1986), which is the most widely used general measure of moral judgment. The SSMS was patterned after the DIT but with the context-specific dilemmas and alternative "answers" relevant to content. Table 3 reproduces an earlier report of a comparison across the stages for the first sample (N = 34) that showed on the SSMS the differences between principled and nonprincipled reasoning with the same degree of accuracy as assessed through the DIT. The range of scores on both instruments was also highly similar. The test-retest reliability of the SSMS was computed by the Cronbach Alpha Technique (the results showed that r = +.63 for stage 4 and r = +.66 for P score, highly congruent with DIT results).

The only point of difference was the tendency of public administration graduate students to use stage 4 (concern for law and duty) more frequently on the SSMS than on the DIT. Similar results, displayed in Table 4, were generated from a second sample (N = 50). The distribution of principled versus nonprincipled thought was the same but again the selection of stage 4 was more common with the SSMS than with the DIT.

In a further assessment of the similarities and differences between the SSMS and the DIT, an intercorrelation matrix was constructed. Table 5 shows a moderately positive overall correlation between the SSMS total score and the DIT total score. All three individual stories intercorrelated positively with the DIT total score.

V. FINDINGS FROM SAMPLES OF PUBLIC ADMINISTRATION PRACTITIONERS

Between spring 1988 and spring 1992, Stewart and Sprinthall administered the SSMS to a total of 485 public managers in the United States, including a sample of local government managers attending executive management programs in North Carolina (N = 136), a sample of North Carolina city and county managers and assistant managers (N = 190), a sample of North Carolina budget officers (N = 55), and a sample of Florida city and

Table 6 Principled Reasoning by Gender (Florida)

Male	38% (n = 94)
Female	40% (n = 9)

Source: Stewart and Sprinthall, 1994.

Table 7 Principled Reasoning by
Race (Florida)

White	38% (n = 99)
Non-white	40% (n = 4)

Source: Stewart and Sprinthall, 1994.

county managers and assistant managers (N = 104). Our study in post-Communist Poland replicated, to a large degree, our studies of public administrators in the United States. From December 1993 through January 1994 we secured complete interviews with 289 public administrators and 196 elected officials in 12 towns in Poland. Presently, we are conducting a pilot study in Russia, administering the SSMS instrument at the Russian Academy of Civil Service (RACS) in Moscow. Using a sample of 100 civil servants representing a broad spectrum of functional areas and regions in Russia, we will pilot test the SSMS instrument in the Russian context. Here we attempt to summarize our major findings to date.

The first question asked in the United States probed the system of ethical reasoning that local public officials evoked when confronted with ethical quandaries in their work lives. In a wide variety of U.S. samples, the fourth stage of reasoning (law and duty) had emerged as the primary system of reasoning selected by public administrators (Stewart and Sprinthall, 1991, 1993, 1994). Looking for factors that might produce variation in this outcome, in each of our samples we explored the impact of demographic variables, organizational structural factors, and organizational context. Much to our initial surprise we found no impact that could be attributed to demographic characteristics of the respondents. Neither gender, race, education, nor age was significantly related to a moral reasoning stage for any of our samples of U.S. officials. Similarly, we found no variation in reasoning stages that could be linked to the organizational variables such as level of responsibility, job function, or line versus staff role. Finally we considered whether various features of the context within which a manager functioned might impact capacity to engage in moral reasoning at different levels. Here again we found no variation that could be attributed to type of jurisdiction (city versus county) or the size of jurisdiction. Finally, in spite of the generally recognized importance of ethics codes, we found no relationship between the existence of codes in a jurisdiction and capacity of incumbents to select principled reasoning as a practical guide to ethical decision-making (Gilman, 1996; Van Wart, 1996). Tables 6 through 15 present mean principled reasoning scores for U.S. respondents for selected variables.

With the emergence of democracy in Eastern Europe in the early 1990s, our research interest turned to exploring the moral reasoning orientation of these newly enfranchised decision-makers. We expected to find that Polish local officials brought to power in 1990

Table 8 Principled Reasoning by
Education (Florida)

Less than BA	42% (n = 2)
BA or more	38% (n = 30)
MA or more	38% (n = 71)

Source: Stewart and Sprinthall, 1994.

Table 9   Principled Reasoning by
Age (Florida)

25–30	33% (n = 3)
31–40	38% (n = 27)
41–50	38% (n = 47)
51 or older	39% (n = 25)

Source: Stewart and Sprinthall, 1994.

Table 10   Principled Reasoning by Level
of Responsibility (Florida)

Manager	36% (n = 70)
Assistant manager	41% (n = 33)

Source: Stewart and Sprinthall, 1994.

Table 11   Principled Reasoning by Job Function
(North Carolina)

Budget officers	39% (n = 55)
City and county managers	38% (n = 190)

Source: Stewart and Sprinthall, 1994.

Table 12   Principled
Reasoning by Line versus Staff
Position (North Carolina)

Line	38% (n = 203)
Staff	39% (n = 112)

Source: Stewart and Sprinthall, 1993.

Table 13   Principled Reasoning
by Jurisdictional Context
(Florida)

City	38% (n = 84)
County	39% (n = 19)

Source: Stewart and Sprinthall, 1994.

Table 14   Principled Reasoning by
Size of Jurisdiction: North Carolina
Cities (n = 204)

Less than 10,000	40%
10,000–25,000	39%
Greater than 25,000	38%

Source: Stewart and Sprinthall, 1993.

Table 15 Principled Reasoning
by Code of Ethics in Jurisdiction
(Florida)

Code	37% (n = 51)
No code	39% (n = 52)

Source: Stewart and Sprinthall, 1994.

would demonstrate a strong choice for principled reasoning when selecting among bases for decision-making in morally ambiguous situations. This assertion was motivated by the belief that the principled rhetoric of the transition from communism to democracy would inform the practice of government in post-Communist Poland. However, the most striking finding of the Polish study was that local officials in newly democratic Poland paralleled almost precisely their counterparts in the United States, with their distinct preference for law and duty as the basis for decision-making. Overall, the average score for the Polish officials across the board was 47 percent for law and duty, while the average law and duty scores for public administrators in the United States were 48 percent in one sample and 47 percent in a second sample. The same was true in Poland for principled reasoning (stages 5 and 6) with a P score of 34.6 percent. P scores in U.S. samples were 38 percent and 39 percent, basically the same (Stewart et al., 1997, p. 449). We hypothesize a significantly lower preference for the use of "law and duty" and "principles" as the basis for decision-making in Russia in part because former "nomenklatura" still dominate in the Russian civil service (Kotchegura, 1997).

As in the U.S. research, we then considered the extent to which demographic, organizational, or context variables might influence an official's capacity to reason at various levels. In terms of organizational variables in Poland we considered only level of responsibility and found no impact of this variable on moral reasoning choice. Nor did we find any difference that could be attributed to the context variable of rural versus urban setting across our 12 jurisdictions in Poland. On the demographic variables of age and education, as in the United States, no differences in moral choice could be attributed to variation across these factors. Neither in Poland did we find differences in moral reasoning that could be associated with intensity of religious involvement, a variable not examined in the United States but historically important in the Polish culture. However, in Poland the demographic variable of gender did make a difference (Stewart et al., 1997, pp. 449–450).

As noted above, in our U.S. studies gender did not differentiate the decision models preferred. For example, in our sample of Florida city and county managers and assistant managers, 38 percent of the men (n = 94) and 40 percent of the women (n = 9) reasoned at the principled level. However, in Poland we found a distinct gender effect, with women (representing 33 percent of the population interviewed) pulling strongly toward principled reasoning and men oriented toward "law and duty" to explain issues they would consider in solving an ethical quandary (Table 16). For the total sample, females scored at a higher level than males on P scores (female mean = 36.9 percent; male mean = 33.5 percent; p = .02). Also, women were slightly lower on "law and duty" reasoning than their male counterparts (Stewart et al., 1999).

We hypothesize a similar gender effect in Russia, where women are comparatively marginalized in decision-making roles (much as they are in Poland), now that the communist requirement for representation has been eliminated.

Table 16 Moral Reasoning Stage Scores by Gender in
Poland

Gender	Stage 4 (law and duty)	Stage 5/6 (principled)
Female (n = 158)	45.8	36.9
Male (n = 324)	47.2	33.5
	p = .17	p = .02

Source: Reproduced from Stewart, Sprinthall, and Siemienska, 1999.

One additional feature to our research in Poland in contrast to that in the United States was that we included in the sample elected as well as appointed local officials, allowing us for the first time to compare the pathway to position in relationship to moral reasoning. As indicated in Table 17, the results are strikingly similar for the elected (n = 196) and the appointed officials (n = 289). For example, the total scores for principled reasoning (P score) are 34.7 for elected officials and 34.5 for appointed officials. Similarly, the total scores for "law and duty" reasoning (stage 4) are 45.8 and 47.4, respectively, indicating no real differences between the two groups on the two major dimensions of ethical reasoning (Stewart et al., 1997, p. 449). This finding is consistent with a recent literature review that reported similar value structures for elected and appointed officials in the United States (deLeon, 1994).

In the course of our studies in the United States and Poland it became clear that, while there were no differences that could be explained in terms of most of the variables considered (with the exception of gender in Poland), there did appear to be differences across ethical domains. As noted earlier, the individual dilemmas in the survey deal with three domains of administrative decision-making: friendship in promotion; procurement, with concern of conflict of interest; and database management, with concerns of data file integrity.

As indicated in Table 18, in both the United States and Poland, principled reasoning was the preferred choice when balancing competing claims in a promotion decision. It declined in importance with the friends story and was least important in the data case. Thus not only is the reasoning choice the same overall, but also the components assessed in those different stories. This result indicates that the samples in the two countries were not simply following a response set in selecting their answers. On the contrary, their choices varied according to the differences among the dilemmas presented in the stories,

Table 17 Three Story Results for the Stewart-Sprinthall Management Survey:
Combined Totals for Elected, Appointed, and Combined Groups in Poland

	Elected (N = 196)	Appointed (N = 289)	Combined (N = 485)
1 & 2	5.8	4.9	5.3
3	4.2	4.1	4.1
4	45.8	47.4	46.7
P	34.7	34.5	34.6
M	5.9	5.5	5.5

Cronbach's Alpha Stage 4 = +.63, P = +.66

Table 18 Comparing P Scores by Story of Polish and U.S. Samples

Score stories	Principled reasoning, Poland (N = 485)	Principled reasoning, U.S.* (N = 136)
Promotion	48%	52%
Friends	38%	43%
Data re-creation	17%	22%

*Local government managers in North Carolina. Reproduced from Stewart, Sprinthall, and Siemienska, 1997, p. 449.

from the most familiar, a promotion, to the least familiar, a computer simulation (Stewart et al., 1997, p. 449).

Domain effects have been described in other ethics studies. For example, Hochschild (1981) has found that different beliefs about distributive justice prevail in different domains of life. People may use equalitarian norms when addressing issues in the political or socializing domain, but shift to differentiating norms in the economic domain. However, the most compelling explanation in our case comes from Rest's (1986) finding that the factors required to engage in principled reasoning develop as a result of experience in dealing with controversial issues and in taking action. This means that when dealing with issues that have not been "hashed out" and are personally evoking (close to real life) that levels employed will be lower than that assessed through more familiar dilemmas.

The promotion story raised issues that have been thoroughly worked through in most public sector organizations with the competing claims of "merit" and "equity" broadly discussed. The procurement dilemma, with its focus on "conflict of interest" is also a standard topic in agency training programs, though not the central focus that promotion policies have been in the last decades. The third story, on recreating a data set, is the least familiar story of the three. The problem itself is one occasioned by a technology not well known to most respondents. It is unlikely that most public managers would have the benefit of discussions either in the agency or in society that would provide background for making a decision.

VI. DISCUSSION OF SSMS STUDIES

From this initial work in developing and testing the SSMS, several important points emerged. First, the finding that, as a whole, public managers studied were pulled toward the "law and duty" response rather than distributing responses more evenly across non-principled reasoning options* suggests a tendency to address ethical issues exclusively in

---

* Graduate students in general (Rest, 1986, p. 107) score about 10 points higher on principled reasoning than our graduate students in public administration on the DIT. Also, adults in general score about 6 points higher on the P score than our administrators. This indicates that our PA managers are more likely to identify "law and duty" versus principled reasoning than other graduate students or adults in general.

The question we can't really answer from our studies to date relates to the possible regional effect. Sapp (1985) has shown that adults in the south and southeast have very low P scores (e.g., about 30 P, which is equal to high school students) and are much more likely to choose stage 4 or 3. Further research applying the SSMS to other regions will shed light on this issue.

terms of adherence to agency rules—John Rohr's "low road" in administrative ethics (Rohr, 1989). Several factors may motivate this outcome. It may be that the occupational emphasis in the SSMS stories pulls respondents in an upward direction, since Kohlberg has shown that a shift from stage 3 to stage 4 is usually the result of increased occupational responsibility. It could also be that public administrators are drawn to law and regulation for protection in their precarious political worlds and that such behavior holds across democratic systems. Finally, it could reflect the grip that the Wilsonian dichotomy has on the culture of public administration: a dichotomy which casts ideal public administrators as unwavering implementors of the politically forged law. In the final section of this paper we consider this pulling toward "law and duty" reasoning as one of the unresolved issues in moral development approach.

A second point is that across all of the samples of public administrators considered to date the factors of function and level of responsibility, organizational context, and demography (save gender) have had virtually no influence on level of moral reasoning. That level of responsibility makes no difference may be particularly surprising and disturbing. Luke (1991) has argued that public executives need to manifest a broader ethical vision that recognizes interconnectedness and operates on a larger time frame. But public executives in these studies are no more able to identify principled reasons than middle level or first-line managers. Even ethical codes in place in the jurisdiction appear to make no difference. Moral reasoning levels in public administration seem independent of these factors that have at times explained variation in moral judgment in private sector management (see Stewart and Sprinthall, 1993).

The third point relates to the gender differences that did emerge in our study of Polish local officials. As these local officials struggled to build and operate new institutions, women more strongly favored a model of ethical reasoning characterized by a concern for abstract principles of social cooperation than their male counterparts. While this gender difference has not appeared in recent U.S. studies of men and women in public management roles, we have noted elsewhere (Stewart et al., forthcoming) that it highlights an opportunity for Poland that was lost to our country in the formative days of the modern administrative state. Female participants in this contemporary Polish "reform" may be positioned to find approaches to governing that are more sensitive to the complex balancing required by the modern democracies than their male counterparts.

A fourth finding points to the emergence of differences across ethical domains. The greatest variability in level of reasoning across all samples is derived from the content of the problem situation. Unfamiliar situations where the ethical nuances have not been discussed or processed by individuals are likely to elicit less principled and more self-serving reasons. Likewise with familiar content, that has enjoyed the benefit of considerable discussion, there is a greater likelihood of principled reasoning. It merits emphasis that discussion is critical here. Familiarity with the issue alone is not sufficient. While ethical domains do make a difference, we hypothesize at this point that the difference is a function of how familiar and "processed" the content is for the public administrator and that this difference holds cross-culturally.

A fifth conclusion to be drawn from our SSMS studies speaks to public administration education. Given the low rate at which our samples of respondents selected principled reasoning, there is an opportunity for curriculum development both here and abroad. Especially since objective recognition measures like the SSMS may actually overestimate by one stage the level subjects might employ in a real situation (Kohlberg, 1984), developing a student's capacity to actually function at a principled reasoning level could be a goal of public administration curricula. Of course, this does require examining the point made above regarding regime values. In both graduate and professional in-service education, focusing dialogue on issues of ethical controversy and involving participation and challenge can facilitate the growth process even in a complex area like ethical reasoning (Thoma, 1984).

At the same time, it is necessary to add a note of urgency to this entire question. It is very clear that if major ethical questions do not receive direct and intensive attention during graduate education, there is little hope of improving both ethical reasoning and behavior of professional administrators. Recent research focused on the effect of professional education for medical doctors, veterinary medical doctors, dentists, and accountants has yielded troublesome findings. These graduate programs in general either had no effect upon principled reasoning or appeared to reduce and inhibit the development of higher order reasoning (Ponemon and Glazer, 1990; Self et al., 1993). In fact, when Ponemon and Glazer (1990) then examined the effect of actual employment after graduate school they found that the partners in accounting firms had lower scores than new hires, and those who were promoted had lower scores than those not promoted. All leading to the conclusion that we cannot expect increases in ethical reasoning and behavior if we follow current procedures either in graduate school or during professional practice. The only exception to this gloomy outlook is the work of Bebeau (1994) and her associates at the University of Minnesota graduate program in dentistry. She created an intensive (45 hour) program focused on ethical issues specific to dentistry. Not only was the program successful in increasing ethical reasoning scores of the students but also in improving their ethical behavior. In fact, that program has been selected by the State Professional Board as a requirement for practicing dentists who violate the Dental Practice Act.

The lessons drawn from all this are obvious. Standard professional and graduate programs may avoid or actually inhibit the development of higher order (i.e., principled) reasoning. For graduate training to work effectively in this domain, there must be a significant portion of the curriculum focused on content relevant ethical material, presented in a dialogic format. The method of instruction must recognize the use of small groups, led by trained discussion leaders—a slow and often circuitous process as the students confront their own ethical reasoning patterns. The same would hold for professional in-service programs. Brief one-day or weekend seminars are inadequate. In fact, one prominent adult development theorist, Daniel Goleman (1995), noted in an interview with David Gergen on P.B.S. that industries in this country were simply wasting literally billions of dollars on such so-called leadership training programs. Recognizing the challenge that this intensive approach to ethics presents to public administrators in the United States is substantial. In the overwrought world of the Polish public administrator, it is daunting. In the Russian situation, it may be simply unrealistic. Still, these more intensive methods are clearly requisite to producing growth in moral reasoning.

VII. IMPLICATIONS OF MORAL STAGE THEORY APPROACH IN PUBLIC ADMINISTRATION: CONTINUING ISSUES

The first, and in some sense the most basic, continuing issue in assessing the moral stage theory approach in public administration relates to whether the underlying assumption of ''principled reasoning'' as the normative ideal is the right assumption for public administration. The challenge comes in two forms: one suggesting that it cannot be right because the conditions necessary for the emergence of principled reasoning do not prevail in modern public sector organizations; the second indicating that even if principled reasoning were feasible it points public administration in the wrong direction.

On the critical point of feasibility, we do know what conditions support the emergence of post-conventional thinking. According to Gielen these include:

> Living in a structurally complex society,
> Exposure to schooling at least through late adolescence,
> Exposure to competing complex value systems which include certain abstract considerations,
> A high level of formal operations (e.g., the ability to conceptualize issues theoretically), and
> Exposure to highly generalized and abstract role-taking opportunities (Gielen, 1991, p. 46).

While there can certainly be debate about the extent to which these conditions prevail across all of public administration practice, it is true that these conditions increasingly describe the context in which democratic government in the United States operates today. The differences are most probably aligned with differences in level of responsibility within the organization, with the conditions being met more uniformly at the upper echelons of decision-making. But public administrators increasingly find themselves in a veritable crucible of competing claims as organized and vocal citizens with divergent agendas demand governments smooth the bumpy roads of modern life. The opportunities for abstract role-taking, for example, on the part of the public managers will only increase as the complexity of our society and its problems increase. This does not, of course, translate into a situation where all public administrators will take advantage of these opportunities.

On the related point of whether or not principled reasoning is desirable, the argument is more complex. One could argue that while moral development theory might provide a service in teaching children and young adults how to think with moral clarity, public administration by its very nature must eschew the postconventional ideal. Reasoning in this ideal form embraces values and principles that are applicable and valid apart from the authority of the group and the person holding the principle (Weber and Green, 1991). The independence and disinterestedness inherent in principled reasoning or ''the moral point of view'' decouples the practitioner from the vital world of practice. But is it not the public administrator's duty to faithfully implement the law as it comes to him/her rather than to reject it in favor of his/her own conclusion about what some abstract principle of justice requires in a particular situation? One could argue that principled reasoning (according to Kohlberg and Rest) exceeds the boundaries of legitimate authority in public administration.

The counterargument is that, in the real world, law cannot and should not prescribe all decisions by managers. Effective exercise of administrative discretion is central to effective government. As Denhardt has noted, the ethical administrator has a responsibility to utilize personal moral assessments. In an earlier work we argued that ''principled reasoning'' is the ideal model for utilizing that personal discretion.

> In a just and fair society organized on democratic principles, the laws and rules that emerge from democratic government and practice have a kind of moral authority that is recognized in principled reasoning and is distinct from blind allegiance to policies, practices, and rules (Denhardt, 1988, pp. 109–110).

It is the capacity to assimilate the legitimate regime values of fairness and justice, while maintaining the autonomy to recognize conditions mandating dissent, that marks the morally mature administrator. Hence, the resistance to principled reasoning suggested in our preliminary data is a matter of some concern.

The second continuing issue relates to whether this type of research results mainly in identifying either the moral acrobats, or worse, the moral cynics and implies no essential relationship to good practice in public administration. The argument can be approached from different perspectives.

One perspective criticizes the use of the dilemma technique as a way to assess moral reasoning. The real world is not a multiple choice problem and asking people to respond in the abstract as if they were simply critical spectators does not reflect real life. In Nagel's famous words there is a problem with "the view from nowhere" (Nagel, 1986). The counterargument is that this is the precise justification for developing context-specific dilemmas. The use of dilemmas, sometimes called "difficult situations" has increasingly been used in ethics research in business management as well as in public administration research and training (Liedtka, 1991, p. 555). This dilemma presentation forces the respondent to ground his reflection on values in a concrete, specific decision context (Liedtka, 1991, p. 555). In other words, if the dilemma is properly structured it represents much more than "a view from nowhere."

A second related perspective in this same genre of stage theory criticism has been offered by Lapsley (1996). In his view, the postconventional (stages 5 and 6) levels provide a picture of an extremely "thin self," much disembodied from feelings and operating as a cold, calculating version of Immanuel Kant (or perhaps a Mr. Spock from *Star Trek*). Instead Lapsley suggests that we turn to a more Aristotelian version which broadens the conception of self and character to include personality traits including concepts such as virtue and identity. Whether this criticism is valid, of course, will depend both upon extensive theoretical development and research inquiry of such a moral personality as well as our current conception of the Kohlberg Model. The research evidence, thus far, does provide a reasonable defense against the charge of a disembodied self at the principled level. Only at that level did the subjects "care enough" and possess the ego strength to protect an apparent victim from authoritarian abuse. Also, the definition of principled thought and behavior in our scheme is certainly parallel to Stephen Bailey's (1965) framework of the moral qualities of effective public administrators. In any case, stage theory with particular significance to the principled level will continue to require theoretical validation if it is to continue to serve as a general directing construct for work in public administration. At some level, the "moral cynic/moral acrobat" charge can only be addressed by further empirical research.

This brings us to the implications for further research and, specifically, on the SSMS instrument itself not only for construct validation but for all forms of validity including content, concurrent and predictive. To date the results do support both the content and concurrent validity of the dilemma cases themselves and the issues involved in the different stage levels of the responses. The data base from the four pools of subjects indicates both the relevance of the dilemmas and the consistent sequencing of reasoning levels across the different dilemmas. Also, there is substantial consistency in one sample between our instrument and the well-researched general measure. In fact it may be that our instrument will provide the type of content credibility which Harold Gortner has called for. He says we "must focus, or translate, discussions about these general (ethical) subjects in ways that are directly related, or useful, to managers. As one interviewee noted, 'It really doesn't matter to me what Confucius said—unless I am dealing with a problem in the Chinese community.'" (Gortner, 1991, p. 57). Obviously, as we refocus the content toward generic philosophy of deontology and utilitarianism we will very likely begin to render the obvious obscure. Instead, we need to continue the effort at content relevance and the accuracy of the issue choices as representing stage levels.

From the standpoint of content and concurrent validity then, continued effort is required. We have accomplished an ethnographically appropriate translation of the SSMS, case dilemmas themselves, and issues, into Polish. The resulting research provides solid cross-cultural comparisons between administration here and in the newly democratic Poland. We are moving toward a more difficult challenge in the translation of the SSMS into Russian and implementation of the same research design in the Russian Federation, a fundamentally different political and cultural context. However, research underway will allow assessment of the robustness of the instrument on this challenging environment.

By far the most important research agenda will be the question of predictive validity, namely: how do administrators actually behave in real dilemma situations and what is the link between behavior and stage? This also relates to one of the most substantial continuing issues in moral development research generally. Fullinwider has argued against Kohlberg that the moral development stages are really just stages in the theoretical sophistication that don't necessarily speak to actual moral judgment (Fullinwider, 1989, p. 335). In a like vein, Jennings makes the distinction between two different problems in professional ethics: (1) seeing the right thing to do or "knowing" and (2) being motivated to behave in the right way or "doing" (Jennings, 1991, p. 562). As we have pointed out earlier in this text, the current linkages are either indirect, as in Kohlberg stage and behavior, or based on post hoc case studies, such as the Watergate group affair.

The only direct evidence of the bridge between public administration, moral development, and behavior we have been able to find was from a study by Gortner. He reported that managers often employed, "terms surprisingly near to those developed by Kohlberg—as rules of thumb about how and when a person could be trusted to carry out specific kinds of assigned tasks" (Gortner, 1991, p. 47). As a result, Gortner has suggested that some managers, intuitively at least, do employ such levels in evaluating the performance of subordinates according to their ability to reason and believe at a principled level. This, quite obviously, would be a significant contribution to our understanding of the stage-behavior connection.

Such predictive validation studies could shed light on the opposite question, namely: how firmly have public administrators accepted and perhaps even internalized the law and duty model? Again Gortner poses the question in the context of a real life dilemma, a principled administrator attempting to deal with a staff which regards "any deviation from cumbersome and sometimes outdated procedural requirements as illegal" (Gortner, 1991, p. 53). Detailing such real world behavioral relationships between stage and performance would add immeasurably to what is admittedly the most complex question which behavioral scientists face. We plan to progress slowly yet cumulatively on this question.

Finally, the educative implications are direct. If we know how developmental stage relates to ethical behavior, then we have the agenda for instruction. There is no need to harp upon the current series of ethical lapses evident in government at every level to underscore the need. The problem is clear but the solutions vary. One approach is that of the federal Office of Government Ethics. By statute, every agency is required to designate an ethics officer and these appointments numbered 140 in 1998. The Designated Agency Ethics Officers (DAEOs) are empowered in turn to further develop a staff to assist them in their work. As of the most recent survey in 1998, there were 9174 ethics officials, 400 of whom were full time, working in the federal agencies to provide counsel and advice on questions of ethics. We, however, do not view this as a transforming solution since the procedure still leaves segments of the huge day-to-day operation untouched. We have all had enough experiences with organizations to agree with the quip, "Where there's a wile, there's a way." Also, in reviewing the examples cited (Priest, 1992), there seems a clear focus on issues such as perks (which are admittedly sensational) and favors but little attention on the larger issues of the ethical responsibilities of agencies to carry out their mandates. To us, the current focus alone seems far too concrete and limited.

In the first edition of this volume we proposed the creation of formal yet practical educational programs to foster ethical reasoning and behavior. Our advice remains unchanged, though we are more fully aware of the obstacles to action in less stable democracies than the United States. We suggest a seamless connection between graduate and in-service professional training. Continuity is critical (yet is missing from most current systems) if we are to advance the ability to identify and act upon principles. Gerald Pops (1991) clearly has this in mind when he calls for less emphasis on conventional administrative law as a first step to reclaim the decision-making process. In its place we would offer extensive experience through dialogue and case studies from a developmental stage framework. Rest (1986) has already proved the educational point for dilemmas in general. We need to create a context relevant curriculum in the same model. The need to move forward in ethics education in graduate public administration is recognized in the curriculum standards articulated by the National Association of Schools of Public Affairs and Administration. Its Committee on Peer Review and Accreditation reviews the performance of candidate programs for curricular evidence of "curriculum components . . . [that] enhance the student's values, knowledge and skills to act ethically and effectively" (Commission on Peer Review and Accreditation, NASPAA, 1997). In the long run, we see this approach as essential to preventing either the spread of moral cynicism or the ascendence of amoral behavior as the norm for public administrators.

There are multiple definitions for a profession such as public administrator. The one we like best is perhaps the simplest, the practice of a learned art in the public interest. A developmental framework may make it possible to achieve such goals.

REFERENCES

Armon, C. (1998). Adult moral development, experience and education. *Journal of Moral Education*, 27(3): 345–370.

Arneson, R.J. (1989). Introduction. *Ethics*, 99: 695–710.

Baier, C. (1958). *The Moral Point of View: A Rational Basis of Ethics*. Ithaca, NY: Cornell University Press.

Bailey, S.K. (1965). The relationship between ethics and public service. In R. C. Martin (ed.), *Public Administration and Democracy: Essays In Honor of Paul Appleby*. Syracuse, NY: Syracuse University Press.

Baldwin, D.C. Jr., Adamson, E., Self, D. J. and Sheehan, T. J. (1994). Moral reasoning and malpractice: A study of orthopedic surgeons. Unpublished manuscript, American Medical Association.

Baumrind, D. (1986). Sex differences in moral reasoning: Response to Walker's (1984) conclusion that there are none. *Child Development*, 57: 511–521.

Bebeau, M. (1994). Influencing the moral dimension of dental practice. In J. Rest and D. Narvaez (eds.), *Moral development in the professions*. Hillsdale, NJ: Erlbaum, pp. 121–146.

Brady, N. and Woller, G. (1996). Administration ethics and judgements of utility: Reconciling the competing theories. *American Review of Public Administration*, *26*(3): 309–326.

Chang F.Y. (1994). School teachers' moral reasoning. In J. Rest and D. Narvaez (eds.), *Moral development in the professions*. Hillsdale, NJ: Erlbaum, pp. 71–84.

Cohen, J. (1989). Democratic equality. *Ethics*, *99*: 727–751.

Cohen, S. and Eimicke, W. (1995). Ethics and the public administrator. In H. Reynolds, Jr. (ed.), *The Annals of the American Academy of Political and Social Science: Ethics in American Public Service*, Volume *537*. Thousand Oaks, CA: Sage Publications, Inc., pp. 96–108.

Commission on Peer Review and Accreditation, NASPAA. (1997). *Standards for Professional Master's Degree Programs in Public Affairs/Policy/Administration*. Washington, D.C.: NASPAA.

deLeon, L. (1994). The professional values of public managers, policy analysts and politicians. *Public Personnel Management*, *23*(1): 135–152.

Denhardt, K.G. (1988). *The Ethics of the Public Services Resolving: Moral Dilemmas in Public Organization*. New York: Greenwood Press.

Duckett, L.J. and Ryden, M.B. (1994). Education for ethical nursing practice. In J. Rest and D. Narvaez (eds.), *Moral development in the professions*. Hillsdale, NJ: Erlbaum, pp. 51–69.

Fullinwider, R. (1989). Moral conventions and moral lessons. *Social Theory and Practice*, *15*(3): 321–338.

Gewirth, A. (1978). *Reason and Morality*. Chicago, IL: University of Chicago Press.

Gielen, V. (1991). Research on moral reasoning. In L. Kuhmerker (ed.), *The Kohlberg Legacy*. Birmingham: REP, pp. 18–38.

Gilligan, C. (1982). *In a Different Voice*. Cambridge, MA: Harvard University Press, p. 173.

Gilman, S. (1996). Ethics and reinvention: Public management in contemporary democracy. *The Public Manager*, *25*(2): 45–48.

Goleman, D. (1995). *Emotional intelligence: Why it can matter more than I.Q.* New York: Bantam Books.

Gortner, H. (1991). How public managers view their environments: Balancing organizational demands, political realities, and personal values. In J. S. Bowman (ed.), *Ethical Frontiers in Public Management*. San Francisco: Jossey-Bass, pp. 34–63.

Haan, N. (1983). An interactional morality of everyday life. In N. Haan, R. Bellak, P. Rabinow and W. Sullivan (eds.), *Social Science as Moral Inquiry*. New York: Columbia University Press, p. 218–250.

Hennessy, T.C. (1979). An interview with Lawrence Kohlberg. In T. Hennessy (ed.), *Value/Moral Education*. New York: Paulist Press.

Hochschild, J.L. (1981). *What's Fair? American Beliefs about Distributive Justice*. Cambridge, MA: Harvard University Press.

Jennings, B. (1991). The regulation of virtue: Cross-currents in professional ethics. *Journal of Business Ethics*, *10*(8): 561–568.

Kotchegura, A.P. (1997). The Russian Civil Service Legitimacy and Performance. Paper presented to the International Conference, Civil Service Systems in Comparative Perspective. Bloomington, IN, April 5–8.

Kohlberg, L. (1984). *Essays on Moral Development*, Vol. II. New York: Harper and Row.

Kohlberg, L. and Candee, D. (1984). The relationship of moral judgment to moral action. In L. Kohlberg (ed.), *Essays on Moral Development*, Vol. II. New York: Harper and Row, pp. 498–581.

Krebs, D., Denton, K. and Wark, G. (1997). The forms and functions of real-life moral decision-making. *Journal of Moral Education*, *26*(2): 131–146.

Lapsley, D. (1996). *Moral Psychology*. Boulder: Westview Press.

Lee, L. and Snarey, J. (1988). The relationship between ego and moral development: A theoretical review and empirical analysis. In D. Lapsley and C. Power (eds.), *Self, Ego, and Identity: Integrative Approaches*. New York: Springer-Verlag, pp. 151–178.

Liedtka, J. (1991). Organizational value contention and management mindsets. *Journal of Business Ethics*, *10*(7): 543–557.

Lind, G. (1995). *The psychology of moral competence*. Hillsdale, NJ: Erlbaum.

Luke, J. S. (1991). New leadership requirements for public administrators: From managerial to policy ethics. In James S. Bowman (ed.), *Ethical Frontiers in Public Management*. San Francisco: Jossey-Bass.

Milgram, S. (1974). *Obedience to Authority*. New York: Harper and Row.

Nagel, T. (1986). *The View from Nowhere*. New York: Oxford University Press.

Ponemon, L.A. and Gabhart, D.R.L. (1994). Ethical reasoning research in the accounting and auditing professions. In J. Rest and D. Narvaez (eds.), *Moral development in the professions*. Hillsdale, NJ: Erlbaum, pp. 101–120.

Ponemon, L.A. and Glazer, A. (1990). Accounting education and ethical development. *Issues in Accounting Education*, *5*(Fall): 21–34.

Pops, G. (1991). Improving ethical decision-making using concepts of justice. In J. S. Bowman (ed.), *Ethical Frontiers in Public Management*. San Francisco: Jossey-Bass, pp. 261–285.

Priest, D. (1992). Suddenly "being taken seriously" at Office Government Ethics. *The Washington Post*, June 15.

Rawls, J. (1971). *A Theory of Justice*. Cambridge, MA: Belknap/Harvard University Press.

Rawls, J. (1985). Justice as fairness; political, not metaphysical. *Philosophy and Public Affairs*, *14*(3): 223–251.

Reed, D.R.C. (1997). *Following Kohlberg: Liberalism and the Practice of Democratic Community*. Notre Dame, IN: Notre Dame University Press.

Rest, J.R. (1986). *Moral Development*. New York: Praeger.

Rest, J. and Narvaez, D. (1994). *Moral Development in the Professions*. Hillsdale, NJ: Erlbaum.

Rohr, J.A. (1989). *Ethics for Bureaucrats: An Essay on Law and Values*. 2nd edition. New York and Basel: Marcel Dekker, Inc.

Sapp, G. (1985). *Handbook of Moral Development*. Birmingham: REP.

Self, D.J. and Baldwin, D.C. (1994). Moral reasoning in medicine. In J. Rest and D. Narvaez (eds.), *Moral development in the professions*. Hillsdale, NJ: Erlbaum, pp. 147–162.

Self, D.J., Baldwin, D.C. and Olivarez, M. (1993). Teaching medical ethics to first year students. *Academic Medicine*, *68*(5): 383–385.

Simpson, E. (1974). Moral development research: A case study of scientific cultural bias. *Human Development*, *17*: 81–106.

Skinner, B.F. (1971). *Beyond Freedom and Dignity*. New York: Knopf.

Snarey, J. (1985). Cross-cultural universality of social-moral development. *Psychological Bulletin*, *97*(2): 202–232.

Stewart, D.W. (1991). Theoretical Foundations of Ethics in Public Administration. *Administration and Society*, *23*(3): 357–373.

Stewart, D. and Sprinthall, N. (1991). Strengthening ethical judgment in public administration. In J. S. Bowman (ed.), *Ethical Frontiers in Public Management*. San Francisco, CA: Jossey-Bass, pp. 243–260.

Stewart, D. and Sprinthall, N. (1993). Impact of demographic, professional and organizational variables and domain on the moral reasoning of public administrators. In H. George Frederickson (ed.), *Ethics and Public Administration*, Chapter 11. Armonk, NY: M.E. Sharpe.

Stewart, D. and Sprinthall, N. (1994). Moral Development in Public Administration. In Terry L. Cooper (ed.), *Handbook of Administrative Ethics*. New York: Marcel Dekker, Inc., pp. 325–348.

Stewart, D., Sprinthall, N., and Siemienska, R. (1997). Ethical reasoning in a time of revolution: A study of local officials in Poland. *Public Administration Review*, *57*(5): 445–453.

Stewart, D., Sprinthall, N. and Siemienska, R. (1999). Women and men in the project of reform: A study of gender differences among local officials in two provinces in Poland. *American Review of Public Administration*.

Thoma, S. (1984). Do moral education programs facilitate moral judgment? *Moral Education Forum*, *9*: 20–24.

Van Wart, M. (1996). The sources of ethical decision making in the public sector. *Public Administration Review*, *56*(6): 525–533.

Walker, L. (1986). Sex differences in the development of moral reasoning: A rejoinder to Baumrind. *Child Development*, *57*: 522–526.

Weber, J. and Green, S. (1991). Principled moral reasoning: Is it a viable approach to promote ethical integrity? *Journal of Business Ethics*, *10*(5): 325–334.

23
Ethical Decision-Making

Dennis P. Wittmer
University of Denver, Denver, Colorado

I. INTRODUCTION

If one accepts Herbert Simon's (1948) proposition that a science of administration is fundamentally about decision-making, and if one believes that all decisions have an ethical dimension, then the study of administration necessarily involves an understanding of ethical decision-making. Using a different tact, the well-being of organizations, their members, and society are affected by the ethical decisions made by those charged with leading and guiding these organizations. Acknowledging this proposition provides the basis both for the importance of understanding ethical decision-making behavior and for developing management strategies and policies to promote ethically sound decision-making in organizations.

Both of the above arguments point to the importance of increasing our understanding and knowledge of ethical decision-making. One important approach is normative or prescriptive, providing frameworks to guide and justify managerial decision-making. Yet, decisions are a product of various factors, such as organizational climate or reward structures. Hence, there is also a need for a behavioral understanding of ethical decision-making.

The purpose of this chapter is to provide a general overview of both normative and behavioral approaches to ethical decision-making. The focus will be on administrative or managerial decision-making, although important general theories in normative ethics will also be discussed. The focus will also be on individual decision-making, rather than organizational and group decision-making.

The structure of the discussion will begin with a conceptual analysis of what constitutes an ethical situation and the ethical dimensions of situations. As critical as such conceptual clarification would seem to be, this analysis is often missing or given very cursory treatment in research concerning ethical decision-making.

The second major section will be an overview of behavioral or descriptive approaches to ethical decision-making. This section is divided into two parts. The first part of this section is a discussion of several conceptual models that are prominent in the management literature. Focusing on managerial decision-making, these models portray the "world as it is." The second part is a discussion of some of the most important empirical results from testing various relationships of these behavioral models.

The third major section is a discussion of normative or prescriptive approaches to ethical decision-making. They are theories about how the "world should be." The first part of this section will focus on public administration theorists. While many recent public administration scholars (e.g., Bowman, 1991; Denhardt, 1988; Burke, 1986; Chandler, 1983; Frederickson and Hart, 1985) have made important contributions in the area of ethics, those discussed represent some of the most recent efforts that focus more directly on decision-making. The other part of the normative section summarizes standard philosophical approaches to ethical decision-making, theories which should not be overlooked in any overview of ethical decision-making.

II. ETHICAL DECISION-MAKING SITUATIONS

Ethical decisions are presumably made in "ethical situations" which have "ethical dimensions." But what is an ethical situation, and what are the dimensions of situations that make situations "ethical?" Researchers have generally not given sufficient attention to clarifying these basic concepts, although typically there is at least some implicit assumption that it involves choice as to what is "right or wrong" (e.g., Ferrell and Fraedrich, 1991). Unfortunately such definitions are vague and in need of much further clarification. Evaluating how to invest liquid assets may be a decision about what is "right or wrong" *economically*, but not *ethically*.

What makes managerial situations ethical? What are ethical dimensions of decision-making situations? Some classical ethical theory may be useful in illuminating these concepts. Aristotle understood that ethics was fundamentally about choice (decisions) and the pursuit of the good or happiness. Moral virtue (*arete*) is viewed by Aristotle as making choices that are in accordance with a principle of choosing the "mean." Moreover, the good life for Aristotle and the Greeks was to be achieved only in the political and social environment of the city-state. Thus, moral virtue for Aristotle can be understood as behaviors, decisions, and choices which are in accordance with principles that would produce happiness.

Some of this Aristotelian theory may help to illuminate the ethical dimensions of decision situations. Consistent with this Aristotelian focus on principles of conduct that promote individual happiness and social life, most contemporary accounts maintain that an ethical situation involves, as a necessary condition, that decisions or contemplated behavior will have a significant impact on the welfare of oneself and other humans (e.g., Velasquez, 1992; Barry, 1986), although some have extended that which should be considered to include animals (Singer, 1975; Regan, 1983) and even the physical environment (Commoner, 1971; Frankena, 1979; Blackstone, 1980).

Typical of researchers in ethical decision-making, Jones (1991) adopts a broad conception of an ethical or moral situation, stating that "the action or decision must have consequences for others and must involve choice, or volition" (p. 367). Again, such a broad conception is insufficient to delimit ethical decision situations from nonethical decisions. Indeed, all management decisions can be said to affect others and involve choice. Some (e.g., Norton, 1987) have argued that since all decisions fit this criteria, there are no morally neutral acts. For example, an apparent nonethical decision to order pencils for the office will have some consequences for others. Perhaps one employee mildly prefers the feel of a different brand of pencils. However, this fact alone would not be sufficient to warrant calling this an ethical decision. Every managerial choice will affect others in some way, but by itself this fact does not make a situation ethical, since this would have the consequence of trivializing ethical considerations and not distinguishing ethical decisions from any other decisions. Such examples indicate why ethical situations or decisions are thought to involve significant impact on others.

These criteria of (1) significant impact on the welfare of others and (2) choice do seem to exclude some decision situations from being ethical. How one understands and defines "significant" and "welfare of others" are critical and debatable. What also defines an ethical situation are the particular norms, standards, or principles relevant in guiding decisions. Moral standards and principles would include fairness, honesty, justice, human dignity, and integrity, among others. Such values and principles, then, could be seen as constituting the ethical dimensions of situations, and a situation could be thought of as ethical to the extent that these values and principles are relevant and deserve consideration in a particular situation. Buchholz (1992) defines an ethical decision as "a decision where questions of justice and rights are serious and relevant moral considerations" (p. 47). Such a definition is consistent with the above analysis, but unless all of morality reduces to justice and rights, it may be more useful to include a broader range of other norms, standards, and principles (e.g., honesty, truthfulness, generosity, integrity, among others).

One might respond that these ethical values always deserve consideration. This is, no doubt, true and perhaps makes a fundamental point about moral principles. They are, in an important respect, the first principles of social organization and control. Other organizational values and principles may also be relevant and may guide decision-making (e.g., control the external environment in order to preserve organizational resources), but ethical principles are generally thought of as overriding when conflicts occur. As Cooper (1998) says, "Doing ethics, then, involves thinking more systematically about the values that are embedded in choices we otherwise would make on practical or political grounds alone" (p. 8). Recognizing and adhering to basic ethical standards and principles is fundamental to cooperative social life. Thus, "moralities are best understood as special forms of social control" (Baier, 1965, p. v).

Yet, in many situations ethical standards are not at issue or in jeopardy of being compromised. Accordingly, we would not consider such situations to be ethical. While adherence to ethical standards and principles is always expected (and in that sense all situations are ethical), unless a situation more directly and explicitly requires or involves considerations of ethical standards and principles, we would not describe the situation as an ethical one.

The above analysis indicates the importance of various elements in understanding ethical decision situations: choice; right and wrong; cooperative social life; having significant impact on others; and justice, rights, and other particular standards and principles. For purposes of this discussion, an *ethical situation* is taken to be essentially one in which *ethical dimensions are relevant and deserve consideration in making some choice that will have significant impact on others*. Ethical dimensions are those norms and principles that "provide the basic guidelines for determining how conflicts in human interests are to be settled and for optimizing mutual benefit of people living together in groups" (Rest, 1986, p. 1).

III. DESCRIPTIVE APPROACHES TO ETHICAL DECISION-MAKING

When a man sets out to solve a problem, he embarks on a course of mental activity more circuitous, more complex, more subtle, and perhaps more idiosyncratic than he perceives. . . . Dodging in and out of the unconscious, moving back and forth from concrete to abstract, trying chance here and there, soaring, jumping, backtracking, crawling, sometimes freezing on point like a bird dog, he exploits mental processes that are only slowly yielding to observation and systematic description (Braybrooke and Lindblom, 1970, p. 81).

Such was one view of the state of research in decision-making and policy evaluation, as seen over 20 years ago. We are still only beginning to understand and analyze systematically ethical decision-making behavior. While normative ethics is important for providing principled and coherent frameworks for ethical decision-making, actual decisions are a result of various factors. An improved understanding of these behavioral factors can be important for such issues as the design of organizations, the selection and training of managers and administrators, and the necessary support mechanisms to promote ethical decision-making.

A. Descriptive Models of Ethical Behavior

In the past five years several conceptual models have been proposed for understanding ethical/unethical decision-making behavior in managerial and organizational contexts. While behavioral research in managerial ethics is quite limited, there is a growing awareness among management scholars of the importance of understanding the process and determinants of ethical behavior and decision-making. What follows is a brief summary of several of the most recent conceptual models, which is followed by a summary of some of empirical results of testing aspects of these models.

1. Person-Situation Interactionist Model

Linda Trevino (1986) has proposed a "person-situation interactionist model" to explain ethical decision-making behavior in organizations. Trevino's model posits cognitive moral development of an individual as the critical variable in explaining ethical/unethical decision-making behavior. Other individual variables (e.g., locus of control, ego strength, field dependence) and situational variables (e.g., reinforcement contingencies, organizational culture) are also theorized to moderate an individual's level of moral development in explaining ethical decision-making.

Trevino's theory is important for several reasons. First, it clearly recognizes the complexity of ethical decision-making and the numerous factors affecting decision-making in managerial contexts. Decisions are a product of numerous factors, and some researchers have focused on one or more of these influences. For example, Hegarty and Sims (1978, 1979) suggested that unethical decision-making results from a combination of personality, value orientation, and reward and punishment structures in the organization. Trevino's model, however, was one of the earliest efforts to present a systematic model of these various influences. Second, while recognizing the complexity, her model is illuminating because it simplifies and groups the expected influences on ethical decision-making. Her model organizes moderating factors into individual variables (e.g., ego strength and locus of control) and situational variables (e.g., immediate job context and organizational culture). Third, while the theory offers a behavior model, it clearly recognizes the importance of cognitive processes in explaining ethical behavior. The kind of thought process employed in resolving problematic situations is conceived of as critical in understanding ethical decision-making.

2. Clarkson Group

A group of researchers from Clarkson University represents another recent effort to develop a theoretical framework for understanding ethical behavior in organizations. Their model views ethical behavior as a function of individual characteristics and environmental influences, but as mediated through an individual's decision-making process.

Both the Trevino and Clarkson models are similar in viewing ethical behavior to be a product of individual and environmental influences. However, the Clarkson group (Bommer et al., 1987) expands the Trevino model, both internally and externally. Their model expands the Trevino model externally by including environmental influences outside the organization. The Clarkson model expands external influences to include numerous environments (work environment, government/legal environment, social environment, professional environment, and personal environment). Internally, the theory is expanded by articulating an individual decision process as mediating both environmental factors and individual attributes, such as level of moral development.

The decision process of an individual is seen as one in which individuals acquire a vast amount of information. The information is synthesized and analyzed, filtering out much of the information. The decision-maker constructs a model of what is going on and this drives an appropriate solution. For example, when presented with a proposal to have employees tested for drug use, a manager might filter the information and construct a model of the situation as primarily an invasion of privacy. Because of this construct, he or she might then decide to reject the proposal.

Besides generally expanding the variables and factors included in a behavioral model of ethical decision-making, the Clarkson model is important because it makes explicit the importance of perception (and implicitly information) to the decision process and outcomes. Information about either the nature of the situation or the character of the environment is seen as selectively filtered by a manager or decision-maker. Cognizant of the literature challenging rational decision-making models, the authors emphasize the subjective nature of the filtering process and individual differences in perceptual orientation.

3. James Rest (Four Component Model)

Another important contribution to the development of an ethical decision-making model is the work of James Rest, a moral psychologist who has developed the Defining Issues Test, a measure of cognitive moral development. Rest (1984, 1986) has proposed a four-component model for understanding moral behavior or psychology.

Rest's approach to the complexity of moral behavior is to ask the following question: "When a person is behaving morally, what must we suppose has happened psychologically to produce that behavior?" (Rest, 1986, p. 3). His answer is a theory that individuals work through four psychological processes to produce the ethical behavior. These components include: (1) ethical interpretation or perception of situations in terms of alternative courses of actions and the effects on the welfare of those involved or affected; (2) ethical judgment or formulation of what would be the morally right course of action (that is, reasoning to some conclusion about the ethically right action); (3) selection or actual choosing of the moral values and actions; and (4) implementation or executing the moral course of action; which the behavioral follow-through or "doing" of what is determined to be morally right.

Consider the case of a local government administrator who receives a request to hire the son or daughter of a loyal party member and financial contributor. While the position is covered by civil service and while there are a number of competent and qualified applicants, the administrator knows there are ways around the civil service rules. Following Rest's model, the first stage is perception or interpretation. How does the administrator see the situation? Who will be affected by the decision, and what will be the consequences on others? Is the situation seen as one involving fairness? If the administrator conceives of several possible courses of action, the second stage involves reasoning to some judgment or formulation of what is the right course of action. In this case one might determine that the right course of action will be to hire the party member's child because the greatest good for all affected can be achieved. On the other hand, one might reason that a person on the civil service list deserves the job and would be harmed by giving the job to the party member's family. Moreover, to give it to the party member would violate a basic rule of fairness. At the third stage the administrator makes some selection. Moral and ethical values are often in conflict with other values, such as career advancement or party loyalty. Having judged that the ethically right course of action would be to preserve fairness and follow civil service rules, one may not choose the ethical value(s) over other competing values. Some intention is formed in this stage. Finally, according to Rest, there is the actual execution or implementation of the judgment and intention. What will be the actual behavior or follow-through? Rest contends that proper functioning in all components is necessary for achieving moral behavior, and that research and moral education will be enhanced by adopting a process model. While similar in some respects to prescriptive or normative models of ethical decision-making, Rest offers this model as descriptive of the psychological process involved in producing ethical/unethical behavior.

4. An Issue Contingent Model of Ethical Decision Making

One of the most recent models of ethical decision-making for individuals in organizations is that developed by Thomas Jones (1991). Jones provides a synthesis of ethical decision-making models and adds another important construct, the ''moral intensity'' of the moral issue itself.

The basic idea has intuitive appeal. Jones argues that ethical decision-making is affected by various aspects of the kind of situation and problem confronting the decision-maker. For example, individuals are likely to be more concerned about ethical issues that affect people close to the decision-maker. Or decision-makers are likely to react differently to issues that involve injustices of an immediate sort, rather than those that involve distant or long-term effects. In other words, decision-making behavior is contingent on features of the ethical issue confronting the decision-maker. Yet, Jones argues that previous decision-making models have not explicitly included these factors.

Jones introduces moral intensity as the construct capturing various features of the issue. Moral intensity is conceived as multidimensional and includes magnitude of the consequences, social consensus, probability of effect, temporal immediacy, proximity, and the concentration of effect. For example, moral proximity is one dimension of an issue. So, selling dangerous chemicals in the United States may have greater moral proximity than selling the same chemicals to countries in the Middle East. What is most significant about his model is the notion that aspects of the situation itself, independent of the individual or the general decision-making environment, influence ethical decision-making outcomes.

5. General Model

Drawing upon the conceptual and theoretical models discussed, a general model of ethical decision-making behavior by managers is presented (see Figure 1). The model conceives

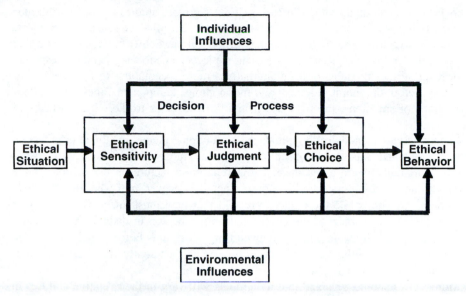

Figure 1 General behavioral model for ethical decision-making.

of ethical decision-making as a function of an individual's cognitive decision processes, as influenced by various individual attributes (such as self-esteem, age, or gender) and various environmental factors (such as organizational reinforcements, organizational culture, or professional standards) (Wittmer, 1992).

Ethical decision making = f (ethical decision processes, individual attributes, environmental factors)

To illustrate, consider a manager who is presented with a copy of a competitor's proposal and must decide whether to use this information to improve one's own proposal and undercut the proposal of the competitor. Applying the model, the decision will depend, in part, on how sensitive the manager is to ethical issues such as honesty and fairness in the particular situation and whether the manager sees the use of the information as an instance of stealing or inappropriate behavior. The decision will also depend on the moral reasoning employed. For example, one might make the judgment that using the information is appropriate since it is highly unlikely that one will be "found out" and using the information will benefit all those in the organization. On the other hand, one might reason that using the proposal is wrong on the grounds that it violates certain social expectations.

Besides sensitivity and reasoning, environmental factors would be expected to influence the final decision, such as organizational pressure or rewards to generate resources for his or her unit. At the same time, individual factors may influence a final decision, such as self-esteem or ego strength of the individual. The decision then is viewed as a product of cognitive decision processes as well as individual attributes and environmental forces.

An important qualification should perhaps be made at this juncture. Moral behavior, indeed most behavior, is extremely complex, and while the model in Figure 1 provides a logical or conceptual framework, the general model should not be understood as a rigid, linear process. The different components may overlap in time and may influence one

another. For example, as discussed in Rest (1986), there are studies to support the idea
that the reasoning process or decision selection process may influence sensitivity. Subjects
may use defensive strategies to deny feelings of obligation. Schwartz (1977) found that
as the costs of moral actions became more clear, subjects came to deny personal responsibility or reappraised situations to make alternatives more acceptable. Rest argues that as
subjects engaged in the moral judgment and moral choice components, they altered their
interpretations of situations, in effect desensitizing themselves to the ethical aspects of
the situation.

In another classic study of the influence of situational factors in ethical or prosocial
behavior (Darley and Batson, 1973), seminary students (those with the highest expressed
standards of morality) were given the task of preparing a lecture on the parable of the
Good Samaritan or on job opportunities for graduates. However, half were told they had
ample time to prepare, while the others were told that they must hurry. On the way to
deliver the lecture, all subjects were confronted with a person in distress. Significantly
more of the subjects who were under perceived time constraints failed to help the person
in distress. Rest interprets this as an example of how engaging intently in the action component influenced their sensitivity to a new ethical situation.

Moreover, it should be noted that individuals will vary in their relative abilities in
each of the component areas. Being very sensitive to the ethical issues and being able to
provide convincing reasoning about what ought to be done does not guarantee the intention
or motivation to make decisions based on ethical values or to follow through in action.
For example, a sibling who articulates the legitimate right of privacy for others in the
family may, nevertheless, not be able to restrain themselves from infringing on their sib-
lings' rights in particular situations.

B. Empirical Studies of Ethical Decision-Making Behavior

As seen in the behavioral models discussed above, in one form or another, various individual characteristics and environmental forces are thought to influence ethical behavior. For
example, in terms of environmental influences, Trevino uses situational moderators (i.e.,
focusing on organizational and job variables) while the Clarkson group proposes various
environments as influencing decisions. Various studies have been conducted to test the
theorized relationships. The next section will discuss studies focusing on individual variables followed by a discussion of studies related to environmental variables. Two summa-
ries of this body of research provide valuable overviews (Fritzsche, 1997; Ford and Richardson, 1994).

1. Individual Characteristics

(a) Cognitive Moral Development. An individual's level of cognitive moral development (or moral reasoning) has been the single, most important individual characteristic studied in the theoretical and empirical research related to moral psychology. Based
on the pioneering work of Piaget (1932), Kohlberg (1969, 1984)—the most well-known
theorist of cognitive moral development—proposed a six-stage theory of moral reasoning
or differences in the kinds of reasons individuals employ in resolving moral dilemmas.

According to Kohlberg, moral thinking progresses from more self-centered kinds
of justifications to more principled and universal kinds of reasoning. The theory is structured as three levels of moral development, with each level consisting of two stages. It
is maintained that individuals pass sequentially, invariantly, and irreversibly from lower
to higher stages, although not all persons ever reach the highest stages of moral reasoning.

In fact, Kohlberg has estimated that only 20 percent of adults ever display the highest stages of moral reasoning (Kohlberg and Delfenbein, 1985).

In the first level (preconventional) individuals focus on external rewards, obedience to authority, and personal exchanges or deals. The second level of reasoning (conventional) is characterized by conformity to expectations of one's family or peer group or by adherence to the rules and conventions of the larger society. At the third level (postconventional or principled) one finds the recognition that rules and values may be relative to groups, yet the importance of upholding basic individual rights, and ultimately the appeal to self-chosen universal rules. Development progresses toward greater autonomy and universality in one's moral thinking.

While cognitive moral development deals with how people reason about ethical problems, moral development has been related to individual ethical decision-making and ethical behavior in organizational and managerial contexts. Trevino and Youngblood (1990) tested students in an experimental, *in-basket* design. Cognitive moral development was found to be a significant predictor of ethical decisions. In another study of ethical decision-making (Stratton et al., 1981), students were asked to recommend whether or not to pad an expense account. All students who recommended padding the expense account used reasons categorized in the first three stages of moral development, while students who recommended against padding used reasoning in stages four through six.

Besides managerial decision-making situations, moral development has been found to be significantly related to various other ethical and prosocial behaviors: for example, cheating (Malinowski and Smith, 1985), helping behavior (Kohlberg and Candee, 1984), and whistleblowing (Brabeck, 1984).

In a comprehensive and critical review of empirical studies relating moral judgment and moral behavior, Blasi (1980) reported that 57 of 75 studies showed a statistically significant relation between moral judgment and behavior, although the strengths of the relationships were generally moderate (correlations of approximately .30). In a review of studies relating the DIT (an instrument measuring moral development) to behavioral measures, there was a pervasive and modest relationship in approximately 30 studies reviewed (Thoma, 1985). Thus, empirical studies tend to support the proposition that cognitive moral development is related to decision-making and ethical behavior.

(b) Locus of Control. Another individual characteristic studied in managerial decision-making is locus of control, which is conceived as the relative perception of how much control an individual feels over events in one's life. As originally conceived by Rotter (1966), individuals are located on an internal/external scale. Internal types are more inclined to view outcomes such as reinforcements as more contingent to one's own efforts and behavior, while an external type views outcomes as more a result of luck, chance, fate, or powerful others. Relating this characteristic to ethical decision-making in a managerial context, Trevino and Youngblood (1990) reported locus of control as having the strongest direct effect on ethical/unethical decision outcomes, with the internal types related to more ethical decision-making. Hegarty and Sims (1978, 1979) included locus of control as a variable in several laboratory decision-making experiments. Decision tasks such as kickback payments were examined, and in two of the three experiments locus of control was found to be related to unethical decision outcomes.

In addition to managerial decision-making behavior, locus of control has been related to other moral behaviors: whistleblowing (Dozier and Miceli, 1985), as well as resistance to social pressure, willingness to harm another person if directed by an authority, helping behavior, and cheating (Lefcourt, 1982). Other related variables are ego strength (a kind of self-confidence in acting consistently with personal values and beliefs) and field dependence (how much individuals rely on information and attitudes from others in their environment).

(c) Age. As reported in Ford and Richardson (1994), there have been a number of studies examining the relationship of age and ethical behavior. They found eight studies, with only three finding significant relationships, and of those the results were mixed. Thus there is limited empirical support for age being related to ethical behavior and decision-making.

(d) Experience or Years of Employment. The evidence is mixed here as well, but Fritzsche concludes that "age and/or tenure also appear to have some bearing on the ethics of decision making" (1997, p. 62). In one study (Harris, 1990), tolerance for unethical behavior decreased as the years of service increased. In another study (Kelley et al., 1990), researchers age 50 and over and with ten or more years of experience perceived themselves as more ethical. Thus, some studies indicate experience (and hence age, which is highly intercorrelated with experience) is related to ethical decision-making. Ford and Richardson (1994) find some studies where years of employment is related to decision-making behavior, but generally they feel the support is mixed, concluding that "further study is warranted on both age and employment related factors" (p. 211).

(e) Gender. Another characteristic receiving increasing attention is the role gender plays in ethical decision-making. Gilligan (1982) has suggested that women tend to define themselves in terms of relationships in which they are involved, making decisions that will maintain those relationships. Thus, decisions may be based more on caring and fostering cooperative relationships, rather than the application of rules and principles of justice, which is the focus of Kohlberg's approach to moral development. Barnett and Karson (1989) found that gender did have an effect on the decisions made in response to hypothetical scenarios. For example, women were more likely to keep (rather than dismiss) an employee for the summer when the employee was not motivated or competent but was the child of close friends who had asked that the child be hired for the summer. Overall, the results here are mixed. Ford and Richardson (1994) find that gender is reported more than another variable. They report 14 studies, seven of which indicate that females are likely to act more ethically. The other seven studies show no impact of gender. Fritzsche (1997) reports two other studies that support females being more ethical (Akaah, 1989; Arlow, 1991), while other studies show mixed results (e.g., Powell et al., 1984; Fritzsche, 1988). While the results are mixed, there are a number of studies that support the idea that women are more ethical in decision-making (e.g., Banerjee et al., 1996; Franke et al., 1997). Like most of the other variables, gender differences require more systematic study.

(f) Machiavellianism. One other interesting variable that has been related to ethical decision-making is Machiavellianism, a measure of preference for manipulative behavior. Hegarty and Sims (1978, 1979) found that Machiavellianism explained significant variance in ethical behavior. Singhapakdi and Vitell (1990) found that more Machiavellian managers tended to perceive ethical problems as less serious and were less likely to take corrective action.

(g) Other Individual Variables. Various other individual characteristics have been related to ethical behavior and decision-making in organizational managerial contexts.

Other individual characteristics that have been studied in relation to ethical behavior and decision making in managerial and organizational contexts include: personal value systems (England, 1967); personal ethical philosophy (Fritzsche and Becker, 1984); economic value orientation and foreign nationality (Hegarty and Sims, 1978, 1979); and motivational orientation (safety and esteem) (Ward and Wilson, 1980).

What can we conclude from the empirical research on individual variables as related to ethical decision-making? While there is limited support in most cases, we can say that more ethical decision-making behavior tends to be associated with those who have higher levels of moral development, who have a greater sense of personal control, who are older and more experienced, who are female, and who are not as manipulative in their behavior.

2. Environmental Variables

Besides individual attributes, various environmental variables are thought to influence ethical decision-making and the behavior of managers. While environment can be thought of as including a wide range of influences (social, legal, organizational, professional, and personal), most of the empirical research on ethical behavior in management has focused on the organizational or immediate job environment.

(a) Reward (and Punishment) Structures.   One of the most obvious factors influencing ethical decision-making concerns the organizational sanctions, or rewards and punishments. In one of their decision-making experiments, Hegarty and Sims (1978) found that extrinsic reward explained the greatest amount of variance in unethical behavior. In another laboratory study of decision-making and direct reinforcement (Trevino et al., 1985), subjects whose ethical behavior was punished or whose unethical behavior was rewarded were more likely to make unethical decisions. Ethical decisions were more likely to occur when unethical behavior was punished. In yet another decision-making experiment, Trevino and Youngblood (1990) studied the effect of indirect learning, which is based in social learning theory, and they found that vicarious reward had an indirect influence on ethical decision-making. Other studies have found a relationship between sanctions and ethical decision-making (Fritzsche and Becker, 1983; Hunt et al., 1984; Laczniak and Inderrienden, 1987).

(b) Significant or Referent Others.   Another important and intuitively obvious environmental variable would be the behavior and attitudes of others in the organization or one's peer group. This has been studied as the influence of significant others or referent others in organizations. In a survey of practicing marketing managers, Zey-Ferrell et al. (1979) found that perceptions of peer behavior was a significant predictor of their own self-reported ethical behavior. In fact, peer behavior was found to be more strongly related to ethical/unethical behavior than the subjects' own beliefs or what they thought management believed. In a later study, Zey-Ferrell and Ferrell (1982) expanded referent others to include individuals outside the organization, such as clients. In another survey of the perceptions and self-reported ethical behavior of two groups of practicing advertisers (ad agency account executives and corporate clients), it was found that the perceived behavior of referent groups again was strongly related to ethical behavior of subjects, and for both groups intraorganizational relationships were more important than interorganizational relationships.

(c) Organizational Policies and Codes of Conduct.   Another organizational factor expected to influence ethical/unethical decision-making concerns the policies and codes of the organization. The articulation of clearly stated organizational policies is considered important in providing guidance to decision-makers. In one of their decision-making experiments, Hegarty and Sims (1979) found that the presence of an organizational ethics policy reduced unethical decision behavior. On the other hand, at the organizational level of analysis, Mathews (1987) analyzed 485 top corporations in terms of the relationship of corporate codes of conduct and illegal corporate activity. He found that the existence of codes was not related to the number of legal violations. Ford and Richardson (1994) report nine studies examining the relationship of codes or policies to ethical decision-making and ethical perception. They conclude that codes or policies are "consistently and significantly related to ethical behavior" (p. 216). The greatest effect, however, seems to occur when policies are accompanied by good communication and clear sanctions.

(d) Top Management Commitment.   The results of Mathews' study would not come as a surprise to many who believe that a serious commitment of top management, as well as appropriate sanctions, must accompany any organizational code of conduct for it to have a positive effect on ethical decision-making and behavior. In a decision-making study using students as subjects, the influence of stated organizational concern was examined as a major independent variable on ethical decision-making. It was found that only when the existence of a code and top management concern was combined with sanctions (dismissal for unethical conduct) was there a significant effect on ethical decision-making (Laczniak and Inderrieden, 1987). In one of their decision-making experiments, Hegarty and Sims (1979) found that when subjects were given a letter from the corporate president supporting ethical behavior, ethical decision-making behavior increased while unethical decision-making decreased. Ford and Richardson (1994) report that a number of studies follow the results of Brenner and Molander (1977) and Baumhart (1961). In these studies Harvard Business Review readers were asked what they believed most influenced their own ethical behavior. The highest ranked factor was the behavior of superiors.

(e) Ethical Work Climates.   Other factors that have been studied in more recent years are organizational culture and climate, and ethical work climates. Victor and Cullen (1987, 1988) developed a typology that was empirically tested. Following the idea that organizational culture involves shared beliefs, customs, and values, they conceive of ethical climate as the "shared perceptions of what is ethically correct behavior and how ethical issues should be handled" (Victor and Cullen, 1987, p. 52). Their empirical studies produced five dimensions of ethical climates: caring, law and code, rules, instrumental, and independence. More recent work has examined the effect of sector (i.e., public or private sector) on ethical climates, concluding that "public managers generally perceive the ethical climates of their organizations less favorably than do their private sector counterparts" (Wittmer and Coursey, 1996). Akaah (1989) determined that healthier ethical environments would improve the likelihood that marketing professionals would make ethical decisions.

(f) Other Environmental Variables.   Besides the factors reported above, other environmental variables have been examined in terms of their impact on ethical decision-making and ethical behavior: for example, opportunity (Zey-Ferrell et al., 1979; Zey-Ferrell and Ferrell, 1982) and scarcity-munificence in the environment (Staw and Szwajkowski, 1975); ethics training programs (Delaney and Sockell, 1992); structural factors such as formalization, centralization, and controls (Ferrell and Skinner, 1988); and organizational size (Browning and Zabriskie, 1983; Murphy et al., 1992; Weber, 1990).

What can we conclude from this body of empirical research? Generally there is support that ethical decision-making is affected by the behavior of peers and associates, by the actions of supervisors and top management, by the existence of policies and codes of conduct, by rewards and punishments, and by the general atmosphere or climate of the organization.

IV. NORMATIVE THEORIES, MODELS, AND DECISION PROCESSES

Managers and administrators can benefit from a better understanding of the behavioral determinants of ethical/unethical decision-making. However, administrators are also often in search of guidance or frameworks for determining what the "ethically right" course of action is. Confronted with uncertainty in an ethical situation, the administrator searches for the ethically correct and responsible solution. One considers the alternative courses of action. What values are of highest priority? Whose interests deserve greatest consideration? What is ethically right?

Normative or prescriptive theories offer guidance as to what should be done and what course of action is ethically right. An administrator searches for some principle to guide his or her decision or reasons that will justify his or her decision. While adopting this perspective might be seen as exhibiting a rationalist bias, this would seem to be the very nature of administration and moral decision-making. This is especially true for the public administrator, who must be prepared to defend decisions to policymakers and the general public. Consider the difference between personal preferences and following principles. One's desire for a particular flavor of ice cream does not require any justification beyond personal preference. However, if an administrator decides to monitor the electronic mail of agency employees, he or she must be prepared to provide reasons that go beyond personal preference. Whether for guidance or justification, administrators confront ethical decisions by engaging or consulting reason.

Moral or ethical decision-making, then, involves considered analysis of the situation and the appropriate standards, norms, and principles that apply to the situation. Why are principles necessary? Principles or general rules provide guidance and justification for actions. Perhaps more fundamentally, to make decisions and act on the basis of principles is to bring coherence, consistency, and predictability to one's life and role of administrator. Principled decision-making avoids arbitrariness, capriciousness, and unpredictability. As agents in a social community, we generally value such traits in ourselves and others. Indeed, we demand such traits of those responsible for managing our public institutions. While there may be disagreement as to the correct principle in a situation, we do expect principled decision-making, in the sense of consistency, coherence, and non-arbitrariness.

A. Normative Models in Public Administration

1. Rohr and Regime Values

One of the most widely cited normative approaches for guiding public administrators in their ethical decision-making is a framework presented in John Rohr's (1989) *Ethics for Bureaucrats: An Essay on Law and Values*. Rohr offers a general framework for both the ethical education of public managers and for deriving principles to guide administrators in their decision-making.

The subtitle, *An Essay on Law and Values*, reveals the key elements of Rohr's model. Guidance and justification in making ethical decisions is found in "regime values," as reflected fundamentally in the Constitution and in the laws that interpret the priorities of regime values, which can be discovered through important decisions of the Supreme Court.

Rohr rejects grounding decision-making in philosophical theory (abstract and often unhelpful for addressing specific problems), in specific agency rules and procedures (often not appropriate to new situations), or individual conscience (often too variable). Instead, the law and broader values of the society, the "regime," are viewed as providing guidance specifically for administrators whose role is to uphold those values and laws. It is perhaps not surprising that the first edition (1978) was published in the wake of Watergate, a time when the highest leaders behaved in disregard of the law, the Constitution, and fundamental values of the society.

At the risk of oversimplifying this important normative framework, the following propositions are fundamental in achieving ethical decision-making, according to Rohr.

1. Public administrators have significant discretion, such that they govern and set public policy, and their decisions have important ethical dimensions and impact on society.
2. Public administrators have a responsibility to be guided by regime values in their decision-making. Regime values are basically those public and political values that have endured in our society. "These values are normative because they are regime values, and bureaucrats have taken an oath to uphold the Constitution that brought this regime into being and continues to state symbolically its spirit and meaning" (Rohr, 1989, p. 76).
3. The Constitution and decisions of the Supreme Court provide guidance in identifying the meanings of these evolving regime values and in determining the balancing of these values in specific situations.

2. Cooper and Dynamic Process

Terry Cooper is Aristotelian in his approach to administrative ethics in that he believes that administrators become ethical by making ethical decisions. Also, as for Aristotle, the ultimate aim of administrative ethics for Cooper is taken to be action, with both theory and experience being essential to accomplish that end. "Without the illumination born of the marriage of abstract thought and practical experience, it is impossible to see where we are going" (Cooper, 1998, p. 2).

For Cooper an operational ethic is developed by each administrator through the decisions that one makes over a period of time. Cooper's framework is, moreover, predicated on the assumption that the skill in making ethical decisions can be learned and cultivated by understanding and practicing a dynamic process of decision-making. Hence, Cooper's particular approach to normative ethics focuses on the process dimension of ethics, rather than the content dimension (Denhardt, 1988).

What, then, is this normative decision-making process? Ethical decision-making is presented as a sequence of steps that moves from perception that there is a problem to a state of resolution. Each stage of the process is discussed briefly in the context of a problem presented in an introductory text in public administration (Straussman, 1990).

Perception (of an ethical problem). One cannot expect administrators to make ethically sound decisions if they do not even see the situation as ethical. Consider a situation where psychiatrists in a municipal hospital are working several hours less than their contract indicates. The administrator must first see that this is a situation involving ethical dimensions and standards.

Describing (the situation).   Basic to any resolution is some description and understanding of the situation. This is obvious but often complicated. For Cooper
the goal is to describe the situation as objectively as possible, although information may be limited and fragmented. There may also be differing perspectives as to what are relevant facts. In the psychiatrist example, a description
might include the contracted number of hours, the number of hours generally
worked, how many psychiatrists engage in the practice, the availability of
other psychiatrists in the local labor force, and whether efforts have been made
to address the issue.

Defining (the ethical issues).   Involved in this stage of the process is an articulation
or specification of the actual ethical issues and values involved in the situation.
Cooper has found that public managers have difficulty in this stage, in part
because managers have a tendency to describe the situation in nonethical
terms. Just what are the principles and values involved? For example, for our
case, principles might include fulfilling obligations to an employer, being fair
with other employees, meeting the needs of the public, and maintaining honesty and integrity.

Identifying (alternatives).   Cooper argues that the temptation is to make the alternatives too limited, often taking an either-or perspective. For example,
either fire the psychiatrists or ignore their behavior. It is important to brain-
storm and expand the alternatives. In the case of the psychiatrists, perhaps a
renegotiated contract is possible, or perhaps the administrator could hold a
general meeting, focusing on total quality management and responsibilities of
employees.

Projecting (consequences).   This is a critical part of the process of getting to an
ethical solution. Both positive and negative consequences should be projected.
As an aid Cooper suggests creating a written grid, with alternatives written
on the left and the negative as well as positive consequences on the right of
each alternative. The skill needed here is moral imagination or what John
Dewey (1922) thought of as "dramatic rehearsal." In short, it is the deliberative process, requiring an open and exploring mind. In the psychiatrist case,
one might consider the probability that the psychiatry staff might quit if confronted about the lost hours. What will happen to client care if the practice
is ignored? What will be the likely impact on employee morale if the practice
continues?

The process leading to selection of a course of action involves four interactive aspects of the analysis. One is identifying the moral rules that apply to the alternatives. The second consideration is the rehearsal of defenses, which is essentially the extent to which one could defend each of the alternatives. This is
especially important for the public administrator, who must not only be prepared to justify a course of action to members of the organization, but also
to policymakers and to the general public. Another consideration is the appropriateness of more general ethical principles. For example, what will maximize
the good for all affected by the decision regarding the psychiatrists. Finally,
and not least in importance, the decision-maker must consider anticipatory
self-appraisal, which is reflection on how consistent the alternatives are with
one's image of oneself.

Selecting (a course of action).   As a result of the contemplated consequences and the rehearsal of what will be the most defensible alternative, the administrator decides on a course of action.

Resolution. Having started with the perception that there is a problem or the need to do something, this is the end state that should result from the other stages in the process. It is important to note that Cooper is quite pragmatic about this state of resolution. "As neither a perfect balance of duty and consequences nor a supremely rational alternative that provides complete emotional satisfaction is often available, resolution is ordinarily an approximate state" (Cooper, 1998, p. 27). In other words, the solution should "satisfice."

We have outlined and described Cooper's ethical decision-making model at some length, since it is one of the few efforts among public administration scholars to provide such a comprehensive and systematic analytical model. Moreover, he believes that if employed regularly, an "intuitive" decision-making skill will develop. Even though the process has been presented as a linear schema, it should be noted that for Cooper this is *not* an entirely linear *or* rational process. Rather it is both cognitive and affective in nature.

3. Justice as "Metaguide"

Another recent approach is found in *The Case For Justice: Strengthening Decision Making in Public Administration* by Gerald Pops and Thomas Pavlak. As indicated in the title, Pops and Pavlak (1991) argue that administrative decision-making should be linked and guided specifically to principles and procedures of justice. Administrators face no shortage of rules and guidelines. "What is needed is a 'metaguide' for administrative decision making . . ." (p. xv). Justice is seen as an integrative normative principle and guide for administrators. "Because justice is a fundamental and widely shared value that can be understood and practically applied, we argued that it has considerable merit as a normative premise for administrative decision making in public organizations" (p. 169).

Pops and Pavlak conceive of justice as incorporating other public administration values such as the public interest, social equity, and efficiency, and for this reason they view their framework as superior to other ethical decision-making frameworks in public administration. Justice is viewed as a "meaningful alternative to the technical rationality paradigm, including those based on concepts of social equity, ethics and virtue, and administrative agency" (Pops and Pavlak, 1991, p. 169).

In a chapter, "Making Just Decisions," Pops and Pavlak (1991) present criteria for just administrative decisions. "Broadly speaking, administrative decisions are considered just to the extent that they (1) produce just outcomes (distributive justice) and (2) are produced by a process that is regarded as fair (procedural justice)" (p. 72). The remainder of the chapter is a specification and discussion of the various aspects encompassed by distributive and procedural justice. These are summarized below.

(a) Outcome (Distributive) Justice.   Decisions are just if they are:

1. Accurate or correct.   Decisions must fit the facts of the case. For example, merit increases should be made to those who, in fact, have performed better.
2. Rationally related to public policy decisions.   Decisions should attempt to achieve the policy purposes of legitimate political authority.
3. Do not violate the formal principle of justice.   The formal principle of justice requires that like cases be treated alike. In other words, administrators must be consistent.
4. Reflect a balance between adherence to rules and the exercise of discre-

tion. Reflected here is the difficult challenge of maintaining uniformity of treatment while using discretion to respond to unique circumstances. It is difficult but justice requires it.

5. Serve client needs. The concern is that client interests can be displaced by the organization's or the administrators' interests, resulting in unjust outcomes.

6. Balance fairness to individuals and social ends of policies. Just outcomes will balance these two goods. Efficient goal attainment is important for society, such as using social security funding to meet individual resource needs. At the same time, resources must be used to insure that individuals have a process to insure fairness in the system. There are tradeoffs that must be balanced to achieve a proper balance.

(b) Process (Procedural) Justice. Decisions are just if there is:

1. Equality of access. A just process would insure that all stakeholders have equal access to decision forums, information, and other factors affecting decisions.

2. Neutrality. A just process implies that decision-makers are not biased in their consideration of situations.

3. Transparency. The idea here is that to be just, decisions must not be closed or have a false appearance of openness. Rather, stakeholders should have meaningful participation.

4. Efficiency. A just process will be one that yields timely decisions, for instance. A just process is also one that is efficient while also being accurate.

5. Participation and humaneness. In the broadest of terms this criterion is simply one that emphasizes respect for the dignity and worth of participants and those affected by decision outcomes. People are accorded value and worth in a just process.

6. Right to appeal. Serious avenues of appeal in decision-making insures greater procedural justice. When appeals are discouraged or difficult to use, there is an increased likelihood of inaccurate or unfair decisions.

4. Decision-making Tools

While Pops and Pavlak move in a reductionist direction, viewing justice as a single, unifying guide to decision-making, Carol Lewis offers a more eclectic and pragmatic approach to ethical decision-making. In *The Ethics Challenge in Public Service* (1991) Lewis includes a section entitled "Tools for Personal Decision Making," in which she discusses various models, theories, and frameworks that may be appropriate for improving ethical decision-making. Ethical reasoning and decision-making is conceived as a form of problem-solving. In her chapter, "Strategies and Tactics for Managerial Decision Making," Lewis, in fact, develops her own hybrid normative, analytical framework by drawing from three other models: Nash (1981, 1990), Rion (1990), and Cooper (1998).

As a result of her practical, managerial orientation, Lewis offers various aids, checklists, and tools for assisting managers in getting to a satisfactory and ethically responsible decision. For example, a hybrid checklist is offered that includes the following considerations.

Decision-making checklist:

1. Facts (including law). It is critical that the decision-maker collect information about relevant facts so as to achieve an informed and complete understanding of the problem.

2. Empathy.   This involves an attempt to put oneself in others' shoes. There are usually various parties affected by decisions, and it can be useful to try to appreciate their positions.

3. Underlying causes.   Considering the causes of important features of situations can help one define the problem more clearly. To what extent has the problem been caused by the decision-maker, others, or external events?

4. Stakeholders and responsibilities.   It is also important to assess the various stakeholders involved. Who will be affected by the decision? Who matters in the situation?

5. Motives and objectives.   To the extent this is possible, it can be useful to assess the objectives and motives of important players in the situation. It can also help for the decision-maker to reflect on his or her own objectives in the situation.

6. Possible results.   Like Cooper's phase of projecting consequences, this aspect involves employing one's imagination to imagine the consequences of various decision outcomes. How will others be affected? Is one comfortable with predicted outcomes?

7. Potential harm (stakeholders).   One of the basic moral injunctions is to avoid doing harm. Thus it is important to consider harm that may result for the various stakeholders affected.

8. Participation.   In view of an understanding of the situation by working through items in the checklist, one should consider who should participate in the decision process and in what form.

9. Long-term time frame and anticipated change.

10. Disclosure and publicity.

11. Appearance and communication.   Items 9 through 11 all focus on testing contemplated decisions against change. For example, how will the organization be affected in the long run? What will be the appearance of the decision to the public?

12. Universality and consistency.   Here the decision-maker considers what decision will be consistent with previous policies and exhibit uniformity in treatment.

The checklist provides an example of the kind of managerial aid that is typical of Lewis' pragmatic approach. Specifying alternative courses of action, managers employ various tools to come to some resolution. "Using a decision-making model open to contending viewpoints and values, managers tool up for fact-finding, accommodation, and selective trade-offs that lead to informed, principled choices" (Lewis, 1991, p. 101). This statement contains many of the same elements (e.g., fact-finding) as those frameworks already discussed. Moreover, it supports the notion that ethical decision-making is essentially principled by searching for appropriate reasons and considerations relevant to the situation. What is perhaps most distinctive of Lewis' approach is the practical orientation designed to assist managers.

5. Gortner's Framework

Yet another recent effort to provide managers with a framework for ethical decision-making is found in Harold Gortner's (1991) *Ethics for Public Managers*. In a chapter, "Analyzing and Resolving Ethical Dilemmas," Gortner proposes a series of questions to guide a decision-maker. These are summarized below.

A Framework of Analysis:

Is the problem an ethical dilemma? Positive responses should follow from the following, if the problem is ethical:

1. Are important values in conflict in the case?
2. Can those values be identified, and/or must additional effort be made to discover them?
3. Is it necessary to analyze, calculate, or reason about which of the competing values must be served?

The following areas and questions should then be assessed in arriving at an ethically sound decision:

I. The law. What can relevant laws tell me about what I am expected to do in this case?
II. The philosophical and cultural setting. Can I learn important factors about the situation by examining the basic philosophical and cultural elements that create ethical perceptions and determine what responses are acceptable?
III. Professions and professionalism. Does my professional training or my broader sense of "professionalism" help me to understand what I should do?
IV. Organizational dynamics. Is the organization in which I work, or my relationship with that organization, a part of the problem?
V. Personal aspects. What do I need to know about myself in order to adequately deal with this ethical dilemma?

Gortner explores in greater detail sub-questions for each area. He offers the areas and questions as a procedure that will insure that the problem is considered from critical viewpoints, thereby "guaranteeing analytical and intellectual rigor" (p. 149).

B. A Common Thread: Social Contract and Social Values

Other public administration researchers and scholars continue to advance perspective on administrative ethics (e.g., Cava et al., 1995; Brousseau, 1995; Van Wart, 1996). The above sketch offers a representative view of some of the most recent frameworks concerning ethical decision-making for public administrators and managers. There are important differences in emphasis, content, and method in those approaches presented. Yet there also appears to be a common thread that ties these frameworks together. Generally the guidance and justification for these theories seems to be grounded in a kind of social contract orientation or the set of prevalent and agreed-upon social values. Morality is generally viewed as the set of rules or values that promote social living, and government is seen as an instrument for enforcing and maintaining these rules, values, and laws. Public administrators, then, have responsibilities for making decisions that will fulfill public purposes in accordance with these time-tested values and norms. In Plato's terms, public administrators are the "guardians" of society.

For example, for Rohr ethical decision-making should be grounded in the regime values of the Constitution, as given more practical meaning through decisions of the Supreme Court. For Pops and Pavlak, decision-making should be guided by administrative justice, both procedural and distributive, as developed over the history of American public administration. Indeed, the authors quote Madison, "Justice is the end of government. It is the end of civil society" (*Federalist Papers*, 51).

However, this generalization is not to imply a kind of simple-minded "law and order" framework. Indeed, these approaches regard seriously the need for independent judgment and decision-making. The mere following of rules and directives is inadequate if one is to be an ethical administrator. However, when called upon to make independent judgments, basic values and principles of the society offer legitimate and justified guidance for administrators. More specifically, these are typically the values of a democratic society, including the value and participation of individual citizens, equality, freedom, and private property.

C. Philosophical Theories and Decision Rules for Ethical Decision-making

Another approach for guiding and justifying ethical decision-making involves the search for a general decision rule that can be used when confronting ethical situations and problems. Moral philosophers have attempted to develop and defend such general normative theories of ethics. While each of the major classical theories contains important insights, none is without important weaknesses. Nevertheless, awareness of the major theories can be helpful in illuminating ethical problems and arriving at acceptable and reasoned solutions. The purpose here will be only to sketch the major elements of the most dominant philosophical theories, providing a simple framework of questions that might be used by decision-makers.

1. Utilitarianism, a Consequentialist Orientation

The basic idea of utilitarianism is very simple. Morality is viewed as fundamentally about developing rules and practices that will produce as much happiness as possible in the world. Therefore, decision-makers should be guided by one principle, the principle of utility: choose that course of action that will produce the greatest balance of happiness over unhappiness. This involves taking into account the interests and consequences for all affected by the decision. Choices that maximize happiness constitute the ethically right things to do.

It is useful to note that this "modern" theory of morality was developed by philosophers who were social reformers in a turbulent time of European history. The theory was formulated by Jeremy Bentham (1748–1832) and John Stuart Mill (1806–1873) at a time when the modern nation-state was emerging and when ideas of "freedom, equality, and fraternity" were spreading. Old ethical frameworks were being challenged (e.g., duty to God or faithfulness to abstract rules that had little perceived connection to achieving a happy life). New orientations and values were promoted, including the equality and value of all individuals (and their happiness) in determining social policy. Happiness was the end and all individuals and their interests were weighted equally, especially in determining public policies and social rules.

For utilitarians actions and practices are not inherently right or wrong; it all depends on the consequences. Hence this is a consequentialist theory, with rules and decisions being ethically justified in terms of the actual or predicted consequences. Such a decision rule seems particularly suited to public administrators, who are charged with creating and implementing policies in the broader public's interest. Moreover, it is a reasonable guide for many decisions, such as how to spend limited funding for highway improvement, the

level of air pollution to tolerate in urban areas, or even the extent of prohibitions on smoking in public places. Moreover, as a theory it seems to fit the way we commonly make personal decisions and choices.

However, as a decision rule it has limitations and weaknesses. These can generally be categorized as (1) difficulties related to the measurement and calculation of happiness, (2) problems related to the just distribution of happiness, and (3) the violation of basic moral rights while yet maximizing the "greatest happiness for the greatest number." For example, policies that inflict unhappiness on a minority such as migrant workers might produce greater happiness for most of society through lower prices and a plentiful supply of food, or consider a decision not to promote a loyal and productive employee over one who might have not worked as hard but could have more utility to the organization. In the latter case, utilitarian decision criteria would seem to leave out an important element of ethical decision-making, individual desert (Rachels, 1986).

2. Formalism and Universal Rules, a Duty Orientation

Another approach for guiding and justifying ethical decisions looks to the form of the principle to be adopted in guiding decisions, rather than the consequences of the alternative courses of action. A major figure in developing and defending this approach is Immanuel Kant (1724–1804). While Kant's theory is notoriously complicated and his writing difficult to understand, the basic principles are rather intuitive and often used in our moral reasoning. Kant proposed a general procedure for deciding what our ethical or moral duties were when confronting ethical decisions. This general rule is called the categorical imperative: "Act only according to that maxim by which you can at the same time will that it should become a universal law" (Kant, 1959, p. 39).

By "maxim," Kant means a principle of action. So, the test is whether one's principle for action could be universalized. Kant distinguished hypothetical imperatives as those that are conditional; that is, they depend on the existence of particular desires and wishes. For example, if one wants to be an excellent administrator, then he or she ought to work on certain skills such as planning, directing, and coordinating. Categorical imperatives or moral duties, according to Kant, are not conditional but rather "oughts" that are binding on all rational agents. The categorical imperative provides a procedure for determining one's moral duties. This procedure is generally thought to include two tests:

Universalizability: Are one's reasons such that they would be good reasons for anyone in similar situations?

Reversability: Would one be willing to accept the rule or reasons, even if one reversed positions or roles in the situation (in effect, a version of the Golden Rule)?

A second formulation of the categorical imperative is perhaps even more intuitive: "Act so that you treat humanity, whether in your own person or that of another, always as an end and never as a means only" (Kant, 1959, p. 47). The second formulation simply calls for decisions that respect the dignity of other people, which for Kant is because "rational nature exists as an end in itself" (p. 47).

A classic example of applying the categorical imperative is to consider whether lying is justified. Lying is the practice of intentionally misleading. Consider whether it would be right to minimize, by misleading or lying about, the extent of the Savings and Loan bailout in an election year, perhaps on the grounds that such action would maintain political stability and public trust, protecting important officials from an irrational public reaction. Employing Kant's criteria, such a principle of action could not be justified. It would not be treating other rational agents as ends; rather it would be manipulative of citizens who are held to have equal worth in our democratic system. Nor would one be willing to accept the rule if the roles were reversed and the administrator were in the citizen's position. Finally, it is not universalizable in that the practice is self-defeating, since if adopted as a practice, we would not be able to believe our leaders.

Naturally, there are criticisms of this theory. It may be argued that the theory is too abstract, vague, and unhelpful in specific situations. Others may object to the view that moral rules are absolute, allow for no exceptions, and may never be violated. The theory also does not provide guidance when there are conflicts of duties. Discussions of these kinds of criticisms can be found in various introductory ethics books (e.g., Velasquez, 1992; Rachels, 1986; Taylor, 1975) or in more comprehensive analyses of Kant's ethical theory (e.g., Wolff, 1969; Paton, 1967; Beck, 1960).

Nevertheless, the basic idea of the formalist approach may provide useful guidance for administrators. The core idea is one of duty to principle, consistency, and rationality. In deciding what to do, one should search for reasons that other rational decision-makers would find acceptable. One then has a duty to act in accordance with such principles. This point is connected to always acting with respect for other persons, since they also are rational agents.

Moreover, it has also been argued that Kant's theory provides a basis for why people have basic moral rights (Velasquez, 1992; Dworkin, 1978; Vlastos, 1964). Moral rights are taken as those entitlements to freely pursue their interests as they choose, and such rights can be grounded in the common rationality of persons. A more thorough discussion of Kant and other duty-based approaches can be found in Ralph Chandler's chapter in this volume entitled "Dimensions of Administrative Ethics Revisited" (Chapter 8).

3. Justice

Another important consideration (especially for public administrators) in making ethically sound decisions concerns considerations of social justice, in particular distributive justice or how benefits and burdens should be distributed. In fact, to be guided by conceptions may be thought of as a deontological orientation, since it involves duty to principle, the principle of justice.

There are various and competing principles or theories that provide guidance and justification for how benefits and burdens in society should be shared, and each perspective may be relevant for making administrative decisions. For example, one criterion would be having equal shares based on citizenship (e.g., voting, public education, or equality before the law). Another criterion is that shares ought to be distributed on the basis of contribution (e.g., productivity in the workplace). A just distribution can also be conceived on the basis of ability and need (e.g., providing a social safety net to meet basic needs). These various principles apply in differing social circumstances, so that no one principle can be said to provide guidance and justification for making ethical decisions. In *A Theory of Justice*, however, John Rawls (1971) has provided the most significant contribution in developing a comprehensive theory of social justice. The important point here is that ethical decision-making often calls for a principle concerned with social justice.

4. Questions to Guide Decision-makers

This brief discussion of major philosophical theories provides different orientations for general standards and principles to guide decision-makers. These different theories can be summarized as questions that decision-makers might ask when confronting ethical situations (Velasquez, 1992).

1. What decision will maximize the social utility (i.e., produce the greatest happiness for those affected)?
2. Does the decision respect the moral rights of those affected? Is the dignity of other persons respected?
3. Does the decision distribute the benefits and burdens justly?

Affirmative answers to these questions are strong indicators that an ethically defensible decision has been made.

V. CONCLUSION: REFLECTIONS ON ETHICAL KNOWLEDGE

At the outset of this chapter it was argued that the study of administration and managerial decision-making is essentially concerned with matters of ethics. Being an effective administrator and making sound decisions, then, requires ethical knowledge. We have discussed two rather different approaches or directions in furthering ethical knowledge, and both would seem to be important for administrators.

DeGeorge (1990) offers a definition of ethics that may be useful for seeing the place of both descriptive and normative orientations. Ethics can be conceived as the study of morality; it is "a systematic attempt to make sense out of individual and social moral experience" (p. 14).

One form that this may take is to understand better the factors and influences that affect ethical decision-making. This would seem to be especially important for administrators who are responsible, not only for making ethical decisions themselves, but for creating the environment and policies that will foster and promote ethical decision-making in their organizations. Thus, knowledge about stages of moral development can be useful for understanding the kinds of reasons that will be persuasive to different individuals in the organization. Understanding how to increase ethical sensitivity can be useful for improving ethical decision-making. Or understanding the impact of implementing codes of ethical conduct without adequate support from top administrators or without adequate sanctions for violations can be invaluable for an administrator who wants to improve ethical conduct in the organization. Such knowledge is essentially descriptive, behavioral, and scientific. Thus, a major section of this chapter was designed to introduce the reader to this growing body of ethical knowledge.

Yet, some will say such knowledge is not ethical knowledge at all. It does not inform us as to what is right and good in our conduct and decision-making. It does not tell us what ends or purposes to pursue. This is, of course, precisely why normative ethics is also critical for the administrator. In fact, DeGeorge goes on in his definition of ethics to say that making sense of moral experience involves "determining the rules that ought to govern human conduct, the values worth pursuing, and the character traits deserving development in life" (p. 14). Here a normative orientation is clearly articulated. To reflect on these questions and pursue answers is a fundamental part of human experience. It is also fundamental for administrators who are charged with guiding important social institutions. Hence, a substantial part of this chapter was devoted to various normative theories articulated by public administration scholars and philosophers. They all provide normative frameworks for judging decision-making, whether the Constitution and regime values, justice, or some other process is employed. While the survey of frameworks exhibits differences, there is a common recognition that administrators should be engaged in a search for such a normative framework and that decision-making should involve such ethical considerations.

The extent to which ethical knowledge can be attained is as debatable as particular ethical theories. Yet the link between knowledge and action should be kept in focus. Action that is not informed by knowledge runs the risk of being misguided or misdirected, and knowledge that is unconnected with action may lack significance and value. As theoretical as this discussion may be, it is hoped that improved understanding and knowledge will lead to more ethical behavior and decision-making, for as Aristotle said, "we are inquiring not in order to know what virtue is, but in order to become good, since otherwise our inquiry would have been of no use" (Aristotle, 1941).

REFERENCES

Akaah, I.P. (1989). Differences in research ethics judgements between male and female marketing professionals. *Journal of Business Ethics*, 8(5): 375–381.

Aristotle. (1941). Nichomachean Ethics: In *The Basic Works of Aristotle* (R. McKean, ed). New York: Random House.

Arlow, P. (1991). Personal characteristics in college students' evaluations of business ethics and corporate social responsibility. *Journal of Business Ethics*, 10(1): 63–69.

Baier, K. (1965). *The Moral Point of View*. New York: Random House.

Banerjee, D., Jones T.W., and Cronan, T.P. (1996). The association of demographic variables and ethical behavior of information system personnel. *Industrial Management and Data Systems*, 96(3): 3–11.

Barnett, J.H., and Karson, M.J. (1989). Managers, values, and executive decisions: An exploration of the role of gender, career stage, organizational level, function, and the importance of ethics, relationships and results in managerial decision-making. *Journal of Business Ethics*, 8: 747–771.

Barry, V. (1986). *Moral Issues in Business*. Belmont, CA: Wadsworth.

Baumhart, R. (1961). Problems in review: How ethical are businessmen? *Harvard Business Review*, 39(July–Aug): 6–9.

Beck, L.W. (1960). *A Commentary on Kant's Critique of Practical Reason*. Chicago: University of Chicago Press.

Blackstone, W.T. (1980). The search for an environmental ethic. In *Matters of Life and Death* (T. Regan, ed.). New York: Random House.

Blasi, A. (1980). Bridging moral cognition and moral action: A critical review of the literature. *Psychological Bulletin*, 88: 1–45.

Bommer, M., Gratto, C., Gravander, J., and Tuttle, M. (1987). A behavioral model of ethical and unethical decision making. *Journal of Business Ethics*, 6: 265–280.

Bowman, J.S. (1991). *Ethical Frontiers in Public Management*. San Francisco: Jossey-Bass.

Brabeck, M. (1984). Ethical characteristics of whistle blowers. *Journal of Research in Personality*, 18: 41–53.

Braybrooke, D., and Lindblom, C. (1970). *A Strategy of Decision*. New York: Free Press.

Brenner, S.N., and Molander, E.A. (1977). Is the ethics of business changing? *Harvard Business Review*, 55(Jan–Feb): 57–71.

Brousseau, P.L. (1995). Ethical dilemmas: Right vs right (Ethical decision making for public administrators). *Journal of State Government*, 68(winter): 16–23.

Browning, J., and Zabriskie, N.B. (1983). How ethical are industrial buyers? *Industrial Marketing Management*, 12: 219–224.

Buchholz, R.A. (1992). *Business Environment and Public Policy* (4th ed.). Englewood Cliffs, NJ: Prentice-Hall.

Burke, J.P. (1986). *Bureaucratic Responsibility*. Baltimore, MD: Johns Hopkins University Press.

Cava, A., West, J., and Berman, E. (1995). Ethical decision-making in business and government: An analysis of formal and informal strategies. *Journal of State Government*, 68(Spring): 28–37.

Chandler, R.C. (1983). The problem of moral reasoning in American public administration: The case for a code of ethics. *Public Administration Review*, 43(1): 32–39.

Commoner, B. (1971). *The Closing Circle*. New York: Alfred A. Knopf.

Cooper, T.L. (1998). *The Responsible Administrator: An Approach to Ethics for the Administrative Role* (4th ed.). San Francisco: Jossey-Bass.

Darley, J., and Batson, C. (1973). From Jeruselum to Jericho: A study of situational and dispositional variables in helping behavior. *Journal of Personality and Social Psychology*, 27: 100–108.

DeGeorge, R.T. (1990). *Business Ethics*. New York: MacMillan.

Denhardt, K.G. (1988). *The Ethics of Public Service*. Westport, CT: Greenwood Press.

Delaney, J.T., and Sockell, D. (1992). Do company ethics training programs make a difference? An empirical analysis. *Journal of Business Ethics*, 11: 719–727.

Dewey, J. (1922). *Human Nature and Conduct*. New York: Holt, Rhinehart, and Winston.

Dozier, J., and Miceli, M.P. (1985). Potential predictors of whistleblowing: A prosocial perspective. *Academy of Management Review*, 10: 823–836.

Dworkin, G. (1978). *Taking Rights Seriously*. Cambridge, MA: Harvard University Press.

England, G.W. (1967). Personal value systems of American managers. *Academy of Management Journal*, 10: 53–68.

Federalist Papers. (1962). New York: New American Library.

Ferrell, O.C., and Fraedrich, J. (1991). *Business Ethics: Ethical Decision Making and Cases*. Boston: Houghton Mifflin.

Ferrell, O.C., and Skinner, S.J. (1988). Ethical behavior and bureaucratic structure in marketing research organizations. *Journal of Marketing Research*, 25(Feb): 103–109.

Ford, R.C. and Richardson, W.D. (1994). Ethical decision making: A review of the empirical literature. *Journal of Business Ethics*, 13: 205–221.

Franke, G.R., Crown, D.F., and Spake, D.F. (1997). Gender differences in ethical perceptions of business practices: A social role theory perspective. *Journal of Applied Psychology*, 82(6): 920–935.

Frankena, W.K. (1979). Ethics and the environment. In *Ethics and Problems of the 21st Century* (K.E. Goodpaster and K.M. Sayre, eds.). Notre Dame, IN: University of Notre Dame Press.

Frederickson, H.G., and Hart, D.K. (1985). The public service and the patriotism of benevolence. *Public Administration Review*, 45(5): 547–553.

Fritzsche, D.J. (1988). An examination of marketing ethics: Role and decision maker, consequence of decision, management position and sex of the respondent. *Journal of Macromarketing*, 8(3): 29–39.

Fritzsche, D.J. (1997). *Business Ethics: A Global and Managerial Perspective*. New York: McGraw-Hill.

Fritzsche, D.J., and Becker, H. (1993). Ethical behaviour of marketing managers. *Journal of Business Ethics*, 1: 291–299.

Fritzsche, D.J., and Becker, H. (1984). Linking management behavior to ethical philosophy—an empirical investigation. *Academy of Management Journal*, 27: 166–175.

Gilligan, C. (1982). *In a Different Voice: Psychological Theory and Women's Development*. Cambridge, MA: Harvard University Press.

Gortner, H.F. (1991). *Ethics for Public Managers*. New York: Greenwood Press.

Harris, J.R. (1990). Ethical values of individuals at different levels in the organizational hierarchy of a single firm. *Journal of Business Ethics*, 9(9): 741–750.

Hegarty, W.H., and Sims, H.P. (1978). Some determinants of unethical behavior: An experiment. *Journal of Applied Psychology*, 63: 451–457.

Hegarty, W.H., and Sims, H.P. (1979). Organizational philosophy, policies, and objectives related to unethical behavior: A laboratory experiment. *Journal of Applied Psychology, 64*: 331–338.

Hunt, S.D., Chonko, L.B., and Wilcox, J.B. (1984). Ethical problems of marketing researchers. *Journal of Marketing Research*, 21: 304–324.

Jones, T.M. (1991). Ethical decision making by individuals in organizations: An issue-contingent model. *Academy of Management Review*, 16: 366–395.

Kant, I. (1959). *Foundations of the Metaphysics of Morals* (L. W. Beck, trans.). Indianapolis, IN: Bobbs-Merrill.

Kelley, E.K., Ferrell, O.C., and Skinner, S.J. (1990). Ethical behavior among marketing researchers: An assessment of selected demographic characteristics. *Journal of Business Ethics*, 9(8): 681–688.

Kohlberg, L. (1969). Stage and sequence: The cognitive-developmental approach to socialization. In *Handbook of Socialization Theory and Research* (D.A. Goslin, ed.). Chicago: Rand McNally, pp. 347–380.

Kohlberg, L. (1984). *Essays on Moral Development, Vol. II (The Psychology of Moral Development)*. New York: Harper and Row.

Kohlberg, L. and Candee, D. (1984). The relationship of moral judgment to moral action. In *Morality, Moral Behavior and Moral Development* (W. M. Kurtines and J. L. Gerwirtz, eds.). New York: John Wiley, pp. 52–73.

Kohlberg, L., and Delfenbein, P. (1985). The development of moral judgments concerning capital punishment. *American Journal of Orthopsychiatry*, 45: 619.

Laczniak, G.R., and Inderrieden, E.J. (1987). The influence of stated organizational concern upon ethical decision making. *Journal of Business Ethics*, 6: 297–307.

Lefcourt, H.M. (1982). *Locus of Control: Current Trends in Theory and Research* (2nd ed.). Hillsdale, NJ: Erlbaum.

Lewis, C.W. (1991). *The Ethics Challenge in Public Service: A Problem Solving Guide*. San Francisco: Jossey-Bass.

Malinowski, C., and Smith. (1985). Moral reasoning and moral conduct: An investigation prompted by Kohlberg's theory. *Journal of Personality and Social Psychology*, 49: 1016–1027.

Mathews, M.C. (1987). Codes of ethics: Organizational behavior and misbehavior. In *Research in Corporate Social Policy: Vol. 9, Empirical Studies of Business Ethics and Values* (W.C. Frederick and L.E. Preston, eds.). Greenwich, CT: JAI Press, pp. 107–130.

Murphy, P.R., Smith, J.E., and Daley, J.M. (1992). Executive attitudes, organizational size, and ethical issues: Perspectives on a service industry. *Journal of Business Ethics*, 11: 11–19.

Nash, L.L. (1981). Ethics without the sermon. *Harvard Business Review*, 59: 70–90.

Nash, L.L. (1990). *Good Intentions Aside: A Manager's Guide to Resolving Ethical Problems*. Boston: Harvard University Press.

Norton, D.L. (1987). *Moral minimalism and the development of moral character*. Unpublished doctoral dissertation, University of Delaware.

Paton, H.J. (1967). *The Categorical Imperative: A Study in Kant's Moral Philosophy*. New York: Harper and Row.

Piaget, J. (1932). *The Moral Judgment of the Child*. New York: Free Press.

Pops, G.M., and Pavlak, T.J. (1991). *The Case for Justice: Strengthening Decision Making and Policy in Public Administration*. San Francisco: Jossey-Bass.

Powell. G.N., Posner, B.Z., and Schmidt, W.H. (184). Sex effects on managerial values systems. *Human Relations*, 37(11): 909–921.

Rachels, J. (1986). *The Elements of Moral Philosophy*. New York: McGraw-Hill.

Rawls, J. (1971). *A Theory of Justice*. Cambridge, MA: Harvard University Press.

Regan, T. (1983). *The Case for Animal Rights*. Berkeley, CA: University of California Press.

Rest, J.R. (1984). The major components of morality. In *Morality, Moral Behavior, and Moral Development* (W. Kurtines and J. Gerwitz, eds.). New York: Wiley.

Rest, J.R. (1986). *Moral Development: Advances in Research and Theory*. Westport, CT: Praeger.

Rion, M. (1990). *The Responsible Manager: Practical Strategies for Ethical Decision Making*. New York: Harper Collins.

Rohr, J.A. (1989). *Ethics for Bureaucrats: An Essay on Law and Values*. New York: Marcel Dekker, Inc.

Rotter, J.B. (1966). Generalized expectancies for internal versus external control of reinforcement. *Psychological Monographs: General and Applied*, 80(1): 1–28.

Schwartz, S.H. (1977). Normative influences on altruism. In *Advances in Experimental Social Psychology* (L. Berkowitz, ed.). New York: Academic Press.

Simon, H. (1948). *Administrative Behavior*. New York: Free Press.

Singer, P. (1975). *Animal Liberation*. New York: New York Review Books.

Singhapakdi, A., and Vitell, S.J. (1990). Marketing ethics: Factors influencing perceptions of ethics problems and alternatives. *Journal of Macromarketing*, (Spring): 4–18.

Staw, B.M., and Szwajkowski, E. (1975). The scarcity-munificence component of organizational environments and the commission of illegal acts. *Administrative Science Quarterly*, 20: 345–353.

Stratton, W.E., Flynn, W.R. and Johnson, G.A. (1981). Moral development and decision-making: A study of student ethics. *Journal of Enterprise Management*, 3: 35–41.

Straussman, J. (1990). *Public Administration* (2nd ed.). New York: Longman.

Taylor, P.W. (1975). *Principles of Ethics: An Introduction*. Encino, CA: Dickenson.

Thoma, S.J. (1985). *On improving the relationship between moral reasoning and external criteria: The utilizer/nonutilizer dimension*. Unpublished doctoral dissertation, University of Minnesota, Minneapolis.

Trevino, L.K. (1986). Ethical decision making in organizations: A person-situation interactionist model. *Academy of Management Review*, 11: 601–617.

Trevino, L.K., Sutton, C.D., and Woodman, R.W. (1985). *Effects of reinforcement contingencies and cognitive moral development on ethical decision-making behavior: An experiment*. Paper presented at the annual meeting of the Academy of Management, San Diego.

Trevino, L.K., and Youngblood, S. (1990). Bad apples in bad barrels: A causal analysis of ethical decision making behavior. *Journal of Applied Psychology*, 75.

Van Wart, M. (1996). The sources of ethical decision making for individuals in the public sector. *Public Administration Review*, 56 (Nov–Dec): 525–532.

Velasquez, M.G. (1992). *Business Ethics: Cases and Concepts*. Englewood Cliffs, NJ: Prentice-Hall.

Victor, B., and Cullen, J.B. (1987). A theory and measure of ethical climate in organizations. In *Research in Corporate Social Performance* (W.C. Frederick and L.E. Preston (eds.). pp. 51–71.

Victor, B., and Cullen, J.B. (1988). The organizational bases of ethical work climates. *Administrative Science Quarterly*, 33(Mar): 101–125.

Vlastos, G. (1964). Justice and equality. In *Social Justice* (R. Brandt, ed.). Englewood Cliffs, NJ: Prentice-Hall.

Ward, L. and Wilson, J.P. (1980). Motivation and moral development as determinants of behavioral acquiescence and moral action. *Journal of Social Psychology*, 112: 271–286.

Weber, J. (1990). Managers' moral reasoning: Assessing their responses to three moral dilemmas. *Human Relations*, 43(7): 687–702.

Wittmer, D.P. (1992). *Ethical Sensitivity and Managerial Decision Making: An Experiment*. Unpublished doctoral dissertation, Syracuse University.

Wittmer, D.P., and Coursey, D. (1996). Ethical work climates: Comparing top managers in public and private organizations. *Journal of Public Administration Research and Theory*, 4: 559–572.

Wolff, R.P. (ed.). (1969). *Kant: Foundations on the Metaphysics of Morals, with Critical Essays*. Indianapolis, IN: Bobbs-Merrill.

Zey-Ferrell, M., and Ferrell, O.C. (1982). Role-set configuration and opportunity as predictors of unethical behavior in organizations. *Human Relations*, 35: 587–604.

Zey-Ferrell, M., Weaver, K.M., and Ferrell, O.C. (1979). Predicting unethical behavior among marketing practitioners. *Human Relations*, 32: 557–569.

24

Values and Ethics

Harold F. Gortner
George Mason University, Fairfax, Virginia

I. INTRODUCTION

Since the time of Descartes, Western intellectual endeavor has focused on the twin pillars of reason and empiricism—logic combined with fact or experience. In a world committed to scientism, such an approach to "knowing" and developing knowledge is to be expected. We humans are the only animals capable of the high levels of abstract reasoning that allow us to bend the environment and to use or change raw materials to dramatically alter our existence. Science allows us, within limits, to control our destiny.

At the same time, we are the only animals capable of controlling our behavior, understanding the concept of right or wrong judgements, and placing differing values on ideas and deeds. As Nietzsche noted, man is "the beast with red cheeks"—only human beings are capable of shame. Humans are "moral" beings. This ultimately leads to our concern with ethics, the study of the general nature of morals and the specific moral choices to be made by the individual in his or her relationship with others (*The American Heritage Dictionary of the English Language*, 1982). Here is added to the two aforementioned pillars of human intellect, reason and empiricism, a third—values—with which many scholars and practitioners feel uncomfortable.

Ethics and values are inextricably intertwined; values are at the core of moral choices, and an understanding of the role of values in choices clarifies many of the issues related to ethics in public administration. This is especially brought home in the more extreme situations referred to as ethical dilemmas when public administrators are forced to choose between competing and mutually exclusive values. In ethical dilemmas, "Two or more competing values are important and in conflict. If you serve one value you cannot serve another, or you must deny or disserve one or more values in order to maintain one or more of the others" (Gortner, 1991: 14).

Administrative ethics are regularly and hotly debated, and one of the major causes of disagreement is the diversity of values held by those involved in the discussion. The issues cannot be ignored or avoided because they are major factors in determining fair and equitable treatment for all citizens and for continuing trust in government. Therefore, ethics in public life—for administrators as surely as for politicians and citizens-at-large— has been a central issue of analysis at least since Plato argued for philosopher kings to rule society. Although they are sometimes couched in different terms, the same questions are raised today that Machiavelli raised while instructing *The Prince*. Should a leader be honorable or ruthless? Moral or amoral? Passionate or professional? Assertive or responsive? Do the ends ever justify the means? Can an individual be amoral or immoral in his private life and an exemplary leader of society? As these questions are debated, administrators regularly must face situations where they have no clear answer as to what is "right" or "wrong." Yet they must make decisions and take actions while facing a cacophony of reactions and demands from politicians, peers, clientele, special interest groups, and the general citizenry, all of whom see the issues from divergent viewpoints and with opposing values. Often the public administrator cannot reach a personal, internal agreement on what is the best action or decision in the case being faced. There is, in other words, an ethical dilemma.

In the arena of ethics, scientific analysis alone often does not work effectively. Administrative ethical dilemmas require that one also become conversant with the role of values. Therefore two major questions are addressed in this discussion: What are values and where do they come from? How do public administrators understand and use values when dealing with ethics and ethical dilemmas?

II. VALUES: THEIR DEFINITION IN A MULTIFACETED WORLD

To understand what values are and where they come from it is necessary to borrow freely from several disciplines including psychology, sociology, philosophy, and history. In each field we shall briefly synthesize the definitions of, and the questions about, values raised by scholars in a way relevant to our discussion of public administrative ethics and the political world within which public administrators work. Likewise, by combining these disciplines' contributions to understanding and using values, it is possible to develop a relatively comprehensive perception of the central role values play in public administrators' ethical thoughts and actions.

Administrators work in a world of facts and values (and a lot of surmises because these two elements are often confused or unclear). There is no bridge between these two elements; they are different and play disparate roles in the world of decision-making. Facts are the raw data that serve as the knowledge base for decisions. There is debate about what is factual. If facts are accepted as such, there cannot be conflict over them—they simply exist. As David Hume (in Selby-Bigge, 1978) puts it, facts are the "is" and "is not" of the world. In that case, everyone accepts the information as a given from which the debate then springs as values come into play. In other words, once facts are accepted the discussion begins as to how facts can be used—or the appropriateness of facts in any specific case.

On the other hand, values, assuming the existence of more than one set, are always a matter of conflict between individuals or groups. Hume, for example, describes values as the "oughts" and "ought nots" of the world. What are values, and why do we assume the existence of multiple, competitive sets of values in a political environment? The philosopher William Frankena, notes that the word "values" is used in the narrower sense to refer to that which is considered good, desirable, or worthwhile, while in a broader sense value refers to "all kinds of rightness, obligation, virtue, beauty, truth, and holiness" (1967: 229–230). At the same time, the anthropologist, Clyde Kluckhohn, says that: "A value is a conception, explicit or implicit, distinctive of an individual or characteristic of a group, of the desirable which influences the selection from available modes, means, and ends of action'' (1962: 395).

Thus, each individual or group has a set of values related to various people, objects, ideas, and actions; value is also placed on future events and states of being as well as current reality or perception. These values, often taken for granted and regularly unconsidered, determine how situations are perceived and judged, what decisions are made, and which actions are taken. Because of the variation in values existing between individuals or groups there is societal conflict—in one of its controlled forms it is known as politics—and public administrators work in the ensuing environment. Psychology, sociology, and philosophy can help us to ask and answer specific questions that clarify our responses to the basic questions of what values are, where they come from, and how public administrators understand and use them.

A. Psychology

How do individuals perceive themselves? How does this personal perception affect the way the individual thinks about and resolves ethical dilemmas? Psychologists, who study the mental processes and behavior of individuals, say that the answer to the first question is built around the "understanding of self" and "motivation." How we see ourselves, who we think we are, is an essential element in answering the second question, in determining what we perceive in the world around us and how we react to it. As Brewster Smith notes,"Our metaphors and myths about the microcosm of personhood enter intrinsically into constituting who we are as persons as well as providing the ground for our valuing . . . and for our actions toward ourselves and others" (1991: 46).

Thus, how people comprehend themselves, which also affects their understanding of the selfhood of others, determines their values in general and their attitudes and behavior toward others. For instance, whether people see themselves as "origins" or "pawns" (i.e., where they see the locus of control in their lives) plays a major role in determining their conceptualization and explanation of human experience and behavior (De Charms, 1968; Rotter, 1966). If individuals control their lives, they are truly moral creatures with the ability to choose between good and bad; if others, outside of themselves, control their lives, then people cannot be held accountable for their attitudes and actions. While radical behaviorists might offer the second, external control theory,[1] it is not accepted by those who believe that humans must make moral choices. Instead, the "self" is viewed as controlling the actions of the individual through a chain of events or occurrences. This chain starts with the twin elements of values and beliefs, which are in part created by, and in part energized by, motives and attitudes, and ends with behavior or action in the social context (see Figure 1).

Erik Erikson, one of the leaders in the field of developmental psychology, argued that individuals advance through eight stages of development or socialization, each one occurring at a different period in life (Gale, 1969). As individuals advance they become more secure in their understanding of themselves, knowledgeable about their values and analytic skills, and, therefore, sophisticated in dealing with the complexities surrounding ethical dilemmas. The achievement of full self-development, which does not occur in all individuals, is critical to working successfully in a democratic setting where there are no authoritarian directions for thought and behavior.

Likewise, Lawrence Kohlberg (1976) studied the development of moral maturity, and found that an individual advances through six stages of sophistication in understanding

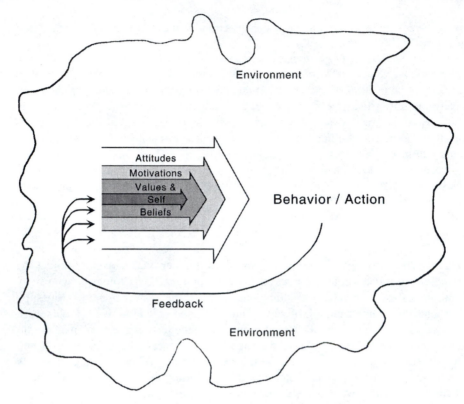

Figure 1   Causality of behavior/action.

and handling ethical issues. The most immature individuals are basically self-centered and amoral, worrying only about being caught and/or punished. As individuals advance in moral maturity they move through a stage during which their values and moral decisions are determined by those around them, from peers to officials. Finally, the most mature individuals develop personal moral standards based on self-chosen values and principles applied in a universalistic manner.[2]

Finally, Kiersey and Bates (1984) use the ideas of Jung (1923) to develop "character and temperament types" that help us to understand how people comprehend and analyze problems, and how they tend to be motivated and behave in their work or private environment. These types are based on how individuals perceive situations and make judgements. Perception is accomplished through sensing (the use of the senses for perception with a focus on observable facts) or intuition (the use of hunches and insight to perceive possibilities, meanings, and the relationships inherent in situations). Once the information is assimilated through the perceiving process, judgements are made by thinking (the use of logical and cause/effect analysis) or feeling (the use of personal values and convictions as the criteria for judgements). The result is a set of four personality types: (1) Dionysian—impulsive, active, and short-term oriented; (2) Epimethean—duty-bound and group-service oriented; (3) Promethean—seeker of competence, questioner of authority, and pursuer of new information; and (4) Apollonian—searcher for self and immersed in the process of "becoming."

Erikson's and Kohlberg's models of human development, and the personality types of Kiersey and Bates, help to answer many of the questions about how individuals develop values and how they use them in handling ethical problems. First, the models help one to understand his or her personal values; and, second, through this understanding a public administrator can deal with the numerous other characters that are part of any ethical dilemma. Alongside the development of values is the growth of a set of beliefs (based on perceptions of and feedback from experience as well as reason—however mature or immature they may be) about the world and how individuals fit into that world. From the combination of values and beliefs comes the overall perception of the world; in other words, what can be done and what is worth doing.

While considering the interaction of values and ethics it is necessary to examine also the issue of motivation. When discussing an ethical faux pas we often wonder out loud, "What on earth motivated him or her to do that?" Motivation combined with action equals behavior. Some behavior is based on conscious reasoning—it is purposive; such intentional behavior, often referred to as "conduct," is the means to a particular end. At the same time, some behavior may be the result of unconscious drives, in which case it is difficult to assign moral attributes to the resulting actions.

There is great debate about this concept of drives and their semiconscious or unconscious state. Such subliminal drives, to the extent that they exist, are beyond the control of individuals, thus of administrators. The only thing that can be done is to increase the recognition of subliminal drives and bring a larger portion of them into the conscious where they can be examined and appropriately included in the overall calculation for proper conduct.

Abraham Maslow (1954), who studied the question of motivation, has organized the concept in a way that allows it to be used in everyday discussion of behavior. His "hierarchy of needs" (physiological, security, affiliation, esteem, self-actualization), while open to debate, still proves useful to individuals wishing to understand the link between motivation, behavior, and ethics. Looking at the five levels of needs, it appears that, to the extent ethical issues arise at the physiological and security levels of motivation, they originate internally but are subject to external manipulation through the use of physical reward and punishment. Social or cultural factors have the greatest chance of influencing values while one is seeking affiliation and esteem. Values are once again primarily internally generated, but also internally satisfied, at the level of self-actualization. As one moves from the lower levels up to esteem and self-actualization, there appears to be a correlation with the development of moral maturity as described by Kohlberg.

Self-understanding, and an understanding of others, based on these psychological premises allows one to comprehend his or her own capability as well as the capability of others to deal with values in a personal, clear, comprehensive, yet sophisticated manner. As individuals work at differing levels of understanding, divergent approaches to ethical dilemmas inevitably occur. In many cases ethical dilemmas cannot be dealt with unless at least one of the participants understands the different levels of maturity and sophistication being acted out in the situation.

The answers that psychology gives to the two basic questions—What are values and where do they come from? and How do individuals understand and use values when dealing with ethics and ethical dilemmas?—are necessary, but not sufficient, to allow a meaningful dialogue about values. Throughout the answers given by psychologists, there are references to parents, peers, and significant others, and the influence they have on the individual. This means that it is necessary to turn to sociology for further information related to values and ethics.

B. Sociology

How does social experience influence human values? Sociologists point out that values are not strictly individual, but, to quote Thomas McCullough,

> Values . . . are communal. They are public in that they are standards transcending individual taste, carrying a claim to be recognized by the community. They can be discussed, analyzed, ordered, justified in a rational discourse. A meaningful discussion about values presupposes a common lifeworld, a shared cultural context within which persons respect one another and care about ideas and values as determinants of their life together (1991: 19).

Values, therefore, are standards of desirability, couched in terms of good or bad, beautiful or ugly, pleasant or unpleasant, appropriate or inappropriate, that come about (at least in part) through socialization. Beyond the basic values related to survival, individuals develop standards of the desirable through social experience. Initially values are inculcated through the approval and disapproval of parental caretakers; the learning of what is good, proper, or right continues through the reinforcement of peers (those with whom individuals identify in various ways) and the explicit requirements and prohibitions of formal and informal authorities. Ultimately, individuals may turn inward to develop their own set of values; however, they have been permanently influenced by their society and their experiences by the time such internalization of values takes place.

It is possible to see how the socialization process affects behavior, but just as surely socialization also affects values which in turn help to determine behavior. When examining the socialization process, one must consider the values being inculcated, the agents participating in the socialization process, and the techniques and practices used to carry out the process.

All of this leads, according to Robin Williams, to the development of values that can be measured somewhat objectively by observing four forms of behavior:

1. Choice—although this is difficult because choice often involves a complex network of issues or factors;
2.   Directions of interest—to what people pay attention;
3. Verbalization—what people avow or disavow; and
4. Social sanctions—reward or punishment by the group or society (1970: 444–447).

The measurement of these four forms of behavior all require inference to move from observed action to the values that they reflect; therefore cross-cultural inferences are truly tricky. Cultural sensitivity and sophistication is an inherent requirement of any attempt to measure behavior and, from that behavior, to make judgements about the values of individuals in a society. Such understanding is critical, however, because these values become part of a society's culture—the socially shared and transmitted knowledge, represented through behavioral and material artifacts, concerning both what does exist and what ought to exist. Values are a central part of the "what ought to exist" and help determine one's perception of both reality and the ideal. Thus sociology adds a second, group-based dimension to values that, added to the individual-based dimension of psychology, helps to clarify what values are, how they are developed, and how values are used when dealing with ethical dilemmas.

C. Philosophy

Eventually we move from the descriptive to the normative, or to remember David Hume's dichotomy, we shift from the "is" to the "ought" (in Selby-Bigge, 1978: 469–470). We cannot avoid going beyond asking what values people hold and how they developed them. We ask "What values should people hold?" The answer to this question definitely influences how people understand and use values. Philosophy, the critique and analysis of fundamental beliefs as they come to be conceptualized and formulated, asks what values people ought to hold and examines the clarity and consistency of the ethical principles that issue from individuals as they work out the complex matter of combining values, beliefs, and action. Thus, philosophy constantly helps us to answer the question of how clearly we recognize and deal with values and ethical issues as they arise.

Philosophy wrestles with the basic question raised earlier when talking about the self. Are individual decisions and actions the result of free will or are they the predetermined reaction to greater, external forces? There are phrases in every language insinuating that people cannot control their actions or their fate ("God willing," "Insh'Allah," "Ikata ganai," "Que sera, sera"), and predestination has been a central tenet of some Christian theologians and philosophers. On the other hand, unless we agree with Kant (Beck, 1985) that the will is free, no moral order is possible and moral discussion is idle chatter.

It is necessary, however, to ask the question, "How free?" because psychology and sociology argue that there are limits to freedom created by individual capabilities, group/social pressures, and, therefore, intellectual capacity. Thus, free will must be defined with recognition of the limitation generated by external factors that often exist without our awareness of their presence.

Of equal importance to the debate about free will is the issue of whether the determination of "right" and "the good" is relative or absolute. Teleologists (naturalists) argue that actions or rules may be determined as right by comparing them to observable phenomena. Do actions satisfy desires (hedonism), produce pleasure for the greatest number (utilitarianism), or foster historical progress (Marxism)? The teleologists ground "ethical action in human nature and the fulfillment of biological and social needs" (Kernaghan and Langford, 1990: 23), and accept an action or rule as right if it tends to produce desired results. Such an approach opens the way for differences in people and societies and the consideration of relativism based on culture and differing values or expectations.[3]

Utilitarianism, arguing that action should be chosen on the basis of the production of the greatest net balance of good over evil consequences, has proved to be the most potent of these arguments in the English-speaking world because, according to Braybrooke and Lindblom, it

> is the school toward which most social scientists are inclined. . . . There are historical reasons for this inclination: Important branches of social science, among them economics and sociology, grew out of utilitarian preoccupations. There is also a natural convergence in preoccupations between utilitarianism and social science. Utilitarianism, after all, insists more strongly than any other ethical theory on forcing moral judgements to the test of facts—the facts of social science (1970: 205).[4]

Deontologists (absolutists), on the other hand, do not accept observable phenomena as valid measures of what is right or good. Rather, they find support for statements of what is right or good in a priori laws and reason (Kant), divine law (St. Augustine and St. Thomas Aquinas), or intuition (Sidgewick and Ross). Justification or condemnation, or decisions as to rightness or wrongness, stand on their own without reference to the results of an action. The biggest problem with this approach of course is determining on what authority one accepts a judgement of rightness or goodness. It is not so difficult to reach agreement on locus of authority when dealing with one culture or one religion; however, we live in a multicultural, multireligious world. South Pacific Islanders, Middle Easterners, Asians, and Americans will turn to different authorities. Is the ultimate authority the Jews' Jehovah, the Christians' Jesus, or the Muslims' Allah? Even when dealing with a single religion and a fracturing issue like abortion, which interpretation of individual rights and the value of each individual life do we accept, and the God of which Christian gives us the truth? As M. Brewster Smith suggests, "the older certainties are moot. There are liberating advantages to our intellectual and moral situation just as there are heavy human costs" (1991: 188).

"The judgements we make are necessarily relative to our knowledge, our social situations" (Kalish and Collier, 1981: 88–89). That does not, however, deny the possibility that there still is some absolute standard that makes an act a good act. It simply means that we must look beyond the situation at hand and return to more basic elements in our judgement of current actions. This means that our values also must be rooted ultimately in those absolutes that determine right and good.[5]

Actually, many people feel uncomfortable with both philosophical camps. Kalish and Collier make a special note of this problem.

> Absolutism can be demanding and restrictive: it may leave little room for individual differences in temperament, ability, or upbringing; it may require an acceptance of supernaturally revealed divine laws or a belief that human reason is strong enough to comprehend a universal, natural law or morality. Relativism can mean that people have no ultimate guidelines—that, whatever you do, the only moral error you can make is not being attentive enough to your own feelings (1981: 89).

Thus, philosophy adds clarity to our questions as to where values come from and what role they play in ethical conduct. But philosophy does not answer the most fundamental question about the worth of values, nor does it prove the ultimate validity of definitions of "right" and "wrong," especially when we move down from the conceptual, theoretical level of thought to the practical and action-oriented level of administrative action.

D. History

Finally but briefly, it is necessary to recognize that values are influenced by any people's history. When applying the other disciplines to any particular people, it is necessary to also be aware of their history. The predominant operant values in the political system of the United States, for example, exist to a great extent because of the individuals who originally settled the colonies. Many, if not most of them, were fleeing religious persecution or looking for a chance to escape from the bottom of the European social system; thus, the social class system of Europe was not reproduced in America. Likewise, the fact that the American Revolution occurred at the height of the Enlightenment determined the values that were central to the debate over whether to revolt. As Robert Ferguson notes in his book, *The American Enlightenment*, two related features influence the writers arguing for the revolution. "First, and to an unusual degree, the leaders of the Revolution believe in ideas as intrinsic repositories of meaning. Second, the source of these ideas depends heavily on the international context of the Enlightenment" (Ferguson, 1997: 33). To an equal degree the structure of the Constitution was influenced by the "Enlightenment values" of the founding fathers. Suffice it to say that other events of that and later days further shaped America's values in relation to the political system.

Ultimately, one must grapple with the questions raised by all four disciplines (psychology, sociology, philosophy, and history) in order to use the total information for the public good and to comprehend the importance of values to ethical public administration occurring in a political environment. Values held by public administrators are developed through a combination or an interaction, of self, society, and situation. Those values must be questioned, examined, and challenged regularly and thoughtfully if public administrators are to operate "in the public interest."

III. VALUES RELATED TO PUBLIC ADMINISTRATION

Public administration, as a field of study, is an electric enterprise; however, it has a special affinity with political science. According to democratic theory (notice, an assumption in favor of this set of values is made) public administrators are presumed to share the values of the larger society and, at the same time, have an individually developed and deeply rooted commitment to the concepts of representative government. Therefore, any discussion of public administrative values must start from this basis. It must also be noted that the discussion is based on political values of the United States of America. Democratic values are interpreted and applied differently in each society purporting to operate its government under such standards. Likewise, the democratic values that are emphasized within a society change over time. In addition, it is necessary to reiterate that the discussion involves sets of values—so many sets that writers often refer to the constellation of values held by individuals and societies. However, at the risk of oversimplification, it should be noted that these numerous values have three primary functions:

1. They are relevant to selectivity in perception by increasing or decreasing the likelihood that a stimulus will be perceived;
2. They influence the interpretation of the outcome of responses, so that some outcomes become positive and others negative; and
3. They provide nonspecific guidelines for the selection of goals (Triandis, 1980: 209).

Other functions obviously exist, and the relevance and subtle texture of values throughout society must not be lost; but, at the same time, the issues of perception, interpretation, and action are central to the enterprise of formulating and implementing public policy. In order to appreciate the interaction of values and ethics in public administration, let us examine five sets of values—political, economic, social, bureaucratic, and professional—that play a primary role in the never-ending attempt of public administrators, as individuals and as a group, to serve in the public interest.

Western political values are grounded in the long history of political thought beginning with the Greeks and moving through the world influenced by the Roman Empire and the Judeo-Christian religious tradition. In particular, the values of the United States governmental system are drawn from the debates of the French and English political philosophers that were occurring at the time of the American Revolution. The basic parameters of the American debate were created by Hobbes, Hume, Locke, Montesquieu, Rousseau, and their compatriots. The values of "life, liberty, and the pursuit of happiness" were stated as major reasons for the actions of the revolutionary leaders. The present result of those initial values, plus history, according to Seymour Martin Lipset (1990: 212) is a "classically liberal, Whig, individualistic, antistatist, populist" political society. This cluster of terms that all support or reinforce one another (and reinforce what they stand for) helps to create one perspective of the political values that influences thought and action in the world of public administration.

Thus, one basis for American political thought is individualism. According to this perspective, all other values start from "the concept of man as an autonomous individual, whose actions are the product of choice and purpose" (Barry, 1987: 4), and from the agreement on the inherent worth of each person. This equality of worth demands a political system that guarantees equality of rights or liberties and protects minority political opinion. A democratic form of government (direct or representative) is valued to the extent that it guarantees individual rights, and in order to guarantee individual freedom, governmental power—especially that of the central government—is limited. Thus the founders of the national government in the 1780s argued for the separation of powers as a system of checks on the natural tendency for power to coalesce. Finally, one of the surest ways to limit governmental authoritarianism is to insist upon the careful adherence to due process. Other political values could be included here; however, it is possible to extrapolate from these most basic values to the longer list over which debate regularly occurs.

There are countervailing values in American society. Alongside the individualistic, materialistic values, there exists a set of communitarian values (Bellah et al., 1985; Cooper, 1991; Etzioni, 1993). According to Etzioni, "(c)ommunitarians maintain that the concept of shared values is pivotal for social thinking . . . (and these) values are handed down from generation to generation rather than invented or negotiated" (1996: 91–93). In other words, "humanness" is demonstrated only through interactions with others, and this means we must take into account their needs and desires. Individuals can only excel within a larger community that sets many of the limits on development and "the good life." As Herbert Simon (1973) points out, absolute freedom often serves as a limitation on human development; creativity often achieves its apex when occurring within boundaries created by nature and society.[6]

Within the political realm, the ongoing debate between individualist and communitarian philosophies has actually heated up during the last decade. Michael Sandel (1996) argues that the values by which America works have changed during this century. According to Sandel, the nation's values have changed from a republican (communitarian) political theory that values citizen involvement in spelling out the common good for the community to a liberal (individualist) political theory that places an emphasis on individual rights and focuses on fair procedures rather than the ends they produce (Sandel, 1996: 4–7). He argues that this change in values lies at the heart of many current complaints about democracy and is the cause of the feeling that we are losing control of the forces that govern our lives. Of course, his thesis is challenged by many scholars, as would be expected (Allen and Regan, 1998).

In another piece of major research exploring democracy in Italy, Putnam (1993) attempts "to explore empirically whether the success of a democratic government depends on the degree to which its surroundings approximate the ideal of a 'civic community' "

(87). In his now famous *Bowling Alone* article (1995) and in subsequent writing, Putnam has projected his findings about Italy onto the United States and he asserts that an erosion of *social capital*[7] is occurring in our democracy. This means that people's values are changing, with less emphasis or importance placed on civic or communitarian values. At the same time, Everett Ladd (1996) uses a variety of survey data to contradict Putnam's thesis. The point is not who is right, but that the debate is occurring because it shows that values are an important element in American politics. Such debate does, however, require that public administrators remain familiar with the dominant values, or the rhetoric of politicians that attempts to capture the public's political support, so that they can work and communicate in the current vernacular.

It is equally necessary for public administrators to be cognizant of, and responsive to, the fluctuation of social values even when the goals of public service remain constant. Sensitivity to social values can be maintained through examining public opinion polls, interviewing in depth individuals or groups (Bellah et al., 1985), and by watching people in action. The central American social values, according to extensive research by Robin Williams (1970), are: achievement and success, activity and work, humanitarianism, efficiency and practicality, progress, material comfort, equality, and freedom. It is easy to note the overlap here, the fact that many of these values reinforce one another. But it is also obvious that these social values sometimes conflict with themselves and especially with political values.

Milton Rokeach (1973) asked various groups in the United States to rank a set of 20 values in order of importance as guiding principles in their lives. While there was some agreement in the rankings, differences became noticeable as sex, income, education, occupation, race, religion, political identification, and certain behavioral characteristics were taken into account. In other words, there may be broad agreement on broad values or sets of values, but there is disagreement on the importance or centrality of these values in one's life.

Max Weber (1947) talks of "value pluralism" and notes that ultimately the possible attitudes towards life are innumerable and irreconcilable; however, as pointed out by Durkheim (1966), we do arrive at some unity in our values through "collective sentiments and collective ideas." In the modern post-Enlightenment society, that unity is built around individualism, centering on liberty and equality, which is the major link that binds everyone together and has penetrated all American social and political institutions. Thus, sociologists have found support for the political beliefs mentioned above; however, as Lukes (1991) notes, "Weberian value pluralism can manifest itself through divergent interpretations of abstract Durkheimian (collectively held) values. Thus 'liberty' and 'equality' unite us at a very high level of abstraction: what divides us is the interpretation of what they mean" (65–66).

Economic values are influencing many people in the United States. Many individuals believe that goals developed in the political and social realms can be best achieved through the maintenance of a laissez faire, capitalist economic system. They are convinced that both theory and experience support the idea, originally presented by Adam Smith (1998), that the economic system should be allowed to work under the concept of "the unseen hand." The interesting aspect of this issue is to determine to what extent the unseen hand can exist and how much government interference is necessary in the economic sphere of our lives. Those economists who believe most strongly in a market answer for all problems would remove government from almost all aspects of everyday life, therefore limiting public policy to deal only with the most public of goods and leaving all other decisions

Table 1   Comparative Value Systems*

Social values
Humanitarianism
Security, comfort
Equality
External conformity
Efficiency, practicality

Bureaucratic values
Technical competence and specialization (defined by superiors)
Goals externally established
Impersonality in actions
Rationality, stability
Career in organization
Hierarchical obligation and accountability

Economic values
Rationality, scientism
Efficiency
Measurability of values in material terms
Quantifiability of goals
Minimal interference with the market forces

Democratic values
Individual worth and dignity
Personal achievement
Minority rights
Liberty, freedom
Efficacy, empowerment

Professional values
Expertise (defined by members of profession)
Rejection of self-interest in actions
Autonomous decisions
Beneficence for clients
Recognition, identification by community
Commitment to "life's work"
Social obligation, self-regulation within profession

* Only representative values are noted here in order to emphasize the similarities and differences that exist between the value clusters of any individual or group. Likewise, only five sets of values are included; others
  could easily be added.

to "economic individuals." Those economists who favor more state intervention in society
believe that the market forces often fail to achieve the best possible distribution of goods
and services, and that it cannot include many important values in the price mechanism.
In fact, McCullough (1991) believes that economic criteria "do not function very well
as critical standards for the evaluation of public policy." For example, many issues in the
health and welfare areas, he argues, "can be addressed only in the context of community"
(McCullough, 1991: 134). At the same time these critics of a primarily laissez faire system
would point out that the blessings promised under totally unrestrained capitalism have
often fallen prey to malfeasance and rapaciousness, thereby requiring some restraints from

government. Even Adam Smith, in his *Theory of Moral Sentiments* (1997), argued that moral sentiments would constrain and influence the market. It would appear that Smith is admitting that, when determining the ends and means of public policy, many of the important values do not have an economic base. Their value is based on other-than-economic factors. Thus it appears that the economic theory one holds is generated, to a great extent, by clusters of other more basic values (e.g., "individualism, materialism, or anti-statism" and "communitarianism, egalitarianism, or statism").

In addition to political, social, and economic values, public administrators' perceptions and actions are colored by two other sets of values—bureaucratic values and professional values. Much has been written elsewhere about bureaucratic values, so that subject will be left unexplored here. But it is necessary to deal with the values subsumed within the concept of *professionalism*, the values and accompanying frame of mind central to the traditional professions. Included in these values are, at a minimum, a belief that members must have: (1) expertise in the knowledge and skills of the profession; (2) autonomy in action and decision-making related to clients; (3) identification with others in the profession; (4) commitment to a life's work in the field; (5) a sense of obligation to render unselfish, neutral service; and (6) a belief in self-regulation by members of the profession (Filley, House, and Kerr, 1976).

These values, while generally supporting an emphasis on democratic decisions and actions within the profession, and a great deal of individual flexibility in carrying out one's duties, do not accept any sense of egalitarianism between members of the profession and those they serve. Nor do professionals accept the idea of external control over the decisions and actions taken within their field of special competence. Thus while it is assumed that professionals are interested in serving the public and the public interest, how that can best be accomplished often leads to conflicts between professionals and the organizations in which they serve or the larger society. Central to this conflict is the problem of who the professionals see as their clients, whether those clients are representative of the public, and whether actions taken for the clients are in the public interest. Professional values can and do come into conflict with the political, social, and economic values spelled out above. Such conflict is a normal part of public administrative life, and within sensible limits this conflict or tension between values is a valuable ethical check on individual actions. All of these values interact within public administration and influence administrators' decisions and actions.

IV. VALUES, THEORIES, AND ACTIONS

How do values affect the work of public administrators? After thinking about the major functions carried out by public administrators, we will examine the interaction of values, theories, and actions with a special emphasis on the interactions that regularly occur between public administrators, politicians, and private sector administrators.

Broadly stated, the functions of public administrators can be categorized as falling into two fields—policymaking and policy implementation. In the policymaking arena public administrators play an important role in the political process as the goals of society are established; on the policy-implementation side public administrators decide how government and society will attempt to accomplish the established goals.

Numerous works describe the policymaking process and the roles and powers of the bureaucracy in that system (Gilmour and Halley, 1994; Kelman, 1987; Koven et al.,

1998). Public administrators are often experts in the subject being addressed, primary actors in defining the issue, and controllers of the nexus between issues, politicians, and constituents. In addition, public administrators are activists, playing a significant part in creating the goals of society. Successful public administrators recognize their multiple roles and prepare for them. They do not accept the statement of Charles G. Dawes that they are the people who "are down in the stokehole of the ship of state, and are concerned simply with the economical handling of fuel" (1970: 95).

Likewise, public administrators play a critical role in the implementation of public policy (Wilson, 1989). The interpretation of legislative intent and the achievement of that intent through the regulatory process, the establishment of rules and procedures, and the overseeing of day-to-day operations are as critical to success in attaining goals as was the original writing of the enabling act. Good intentions in legislation, however specifically or generally stated, mean little without their implementation.

Not only must public policy activities be carried out in a multicurrent, eddying environment, the internal dynamics of public administration usually involve group activities. Success in the public policy arena comes not from lone deeds performed by heroic figures. In most cases each individual has input, but no one person definitively determines or resolves, stops or starts, decisions or actions. It is for this reason that the concept of "systemic problem" exists. While the individual is important when talking about public policy, it is critical to remember the group nature of most ethical issues. The group nature of most ethical decisions, however, does not let the individual public administrator off the hook. Instead it requires one more level of sensitivity to the nature of the political environment in which daily activity occurs. One of the calculations required of anyone who feels ethical unease in a group process (whether making a decision or carrying out an action) must be to what extent she or he can affect the issue under consideration given the nature of the other actors involved in the process.

When dealing with any part of the policy process and regardless of the systemic nature of most issues, both personal and organizational actions are based on theory (assumptions about causation) and that theory is based on values (what one believes to be "good"). Not only must public administrators be sensitive to the importance of values in their own decisions, they must also dig below the surface of issues and become aware of the core values held by the other major societal or political actors with whom they must interact. For example, three major groups of actors (though far from the only three) involved in any policymaking or implementing process are members of the private sector, politicians, and public administrators. These three groups often experience conflict because they do not realize that they are operating from different "basic value sets" that determine their perception of the world, the definition of the problem, the alternatives that are possible, and their perception of fairness.

> The basic value, the bottom line for business is *profit*;
> Politicians value *power*, and
> Public administrators value the *public interest*.

These three specific, potent, divergent, and defining values serve as the basic elements, or delimiters, in calculations by these three groups. Each group uses its basic value as the starting place for all other calculations of utility or appropriateness while formulating, implementing, and evaluating public policy. A failure to recognize these differing values can lead to serious miscommunication; the use of the same words in different ways that leads to "talking past one another" can create grave misunderstandings. While all parties should be aware of this problem of differing base values, public administrators cannot afford to ignore this fact because they are the ones who will be held accountable for the success or failure of the policies and programs that result from the negotiations.

The central question, then, for public administrators is: What can we do to guarantee that values are properly considered as public decisions are made? One of the major tasks that must be assumed by public administrators is that of articulating for everyone the values that are involved in any public issue. Clear articulation of values is important, yet it infrequently happens in the complex world of public policy. As Mary Maxwell notes, thinking about groups and issues has an inherent "muddle factor" because of the complexity involved, and "fuzziness about values creates an atmosphere that is easily exploited" (1991: 29). Even those who have given serious thought to the values involved in a particular policy stance or administrative action often obfuscate these issues, for whatever reason, when going to others for support or to explain actions. Therefore, public administrators, in order to do their job of educating their peers, political bosses, and clients, often have to carry out the task of "the social scientist" by engaging in clarification and analysis of values (Reich, 1988). The steps in this task include:

1. Articulating the various ultimate principles used in the political argumentation and note the values attached to those principles;
2. Deriving the secondary principles that follow logically from each of those first principles;
3. Enumerating the values which, while not logically deducible from the principles, are logically compatible with them;
4. Listing those values which are not logically compatible with the given principles;
5. Noting, insofar as possible, the consequences (intended and unintended) of adhering to each value; and
6. Making sure that all parties in the debate are aware of the principles and values involved and who holds them.

Obviously, a large number and variety of values are involved when dealing with any public issue. In addition to the competing values of the various interacting groups, the public administrator must determine which of three levels of values (see Table 2) are

Table 2 Levels of Values to be Articulated or Clarified

Macro
Social (individualist, equal opportunity)
Political (democratic, limited government)
Economic (modified capitalist, market)

Middle
Organizational (bureaucratic, entrepreneurial, collegial)
Professional (expertise, autonomy, commitment, public service)
Community (regionalism, ethnicism)
Constituency (clients, interest groups, politicians, parties)

Micro
Individual (personal security, success)
Primary groups (acceptance, esteem of family/friends)

being examined, and if individual actors are operating at different value levels the difficulty of meaningful communication is further diminished. If one communicator is thinking about the issue as a "macro" problem while a second is dealing with the issue as a "micro" problem, it can be assumed that those two individuals are using the same words to mean totally different things. If you combine into a matrix the different competing values noted in Table 1 and the levels of values shown in Table 2, the complexity of the policy discussion and resolution becomes painfully apparent.

Public administrators can play an important role (even though non-partisan) in the larger debate because of the unique qualities of their positions. The handling of ethical dilemmas requires digging into the value bases of the parties in the dispute, making them clear to all, and then allowing the decision process to work to its normal conclusion. Public administrators may be uncomfortable with some of the decisions made within the political system and some of the actions they ultimately have to take. But if they make sure the relevant values are brought into the open and discussed, they can be much more secure in the thought that the public, or their political bosses, have made the decision on which action is being taken from an informed position. Likewise, if public administrators practice the clarification and analysis of values in those situations where they must take action without specific prior guidance, those decisions will be made from a well-informed position.

Along with articulation goes sensitization. One cannot articulate values without developing sensitivity to one's own values and those of others. Articulation will also help others to become more sensitive to the variation in values within the larger society. At the same time, increased sensitivity to others' values does not require the acceptance of them. One can be sensitive to the values of others while disagreeing with their definition of good and bad, right and wrong. Sensitivity, however, can help in developing mutual understanding, in creating a respect for the perceptions and ideas of others even though there is disagreement, and ultimately, in finding ways to solve the seemingly unresolvable. Resolution of policy and administrative conflicts or ethical dilemmas becomes a greater possibility. New answers can sometimes be found because "Sensitization . . . can lead to the emergence of new values, and . . . Socratic self-confrontation . . . can lead to the reordering of . . . values and behavior toward more inclusive, self-chosen patterns of consistency" (T. Smith, 1991: 16).

Clarifying values is an important element in maintaining accountability to the people for administrative conduct. Through examination of values also goes growth. Those who wish to develop to higher levels of ethical maturity, or to maintain a current high level, must challenge their current values and beliefs. Sometimes that challenge will lead to change; if that change is based on careful consideration of the numerous factors underlying the values and moral stances, such change will usually be positive. However, such challenge will not always change those values and beliefs. Reinforcement of current beliefs is also useful because the challenges that occur will come from various directions and have different foci. In such cases the challenge will broaden the base for holding the values and beliefs. Ultimately, openness to challenge and a willingness to evenhandedly consider new ideas is required at all times or else there is no guarantee that the values and beliefs are based on anything other than personal biases.

In situations involving ethical dilemmas (which postulate the presence of conflicting values), public administrators must present both the image and reality of scrupulous fairmindedness. This means respecting data, maintaining norms of openness, explicitness, and full disclosure, seeing problems in their complexity, weighing evidence carefully and objectively, and never settling for the shoddy "simple and sovereign" theories or remedies (Meltsner, 1976; T. Smith, 1991). Of equal importance is the recognition and acceptance of the deepest values of democracy. Public administrators cannot act expeditiously, judiciously, and successfully without understanding the panoply of values inherent in society and the individual.

V. CONCLUSION

We live in a period when self-interest and capitalist/entrepreneurial values are in the ascendance. Altruism and communitarianism are recognized but often considered naïve. It is a period that might be referred to as "individualism run rampant." Caution in the acceptance of easy answers is the watchword for public administrators. A recognition that the answers to important questions seldom come from one theory or philosophy is critical to avoiding oversimplification in dealing with human and social problems. Society downplays values and wants facts, but it is impossible to operate in a *democratic* world without values or where values are purely self-generated and self-interested. In such a situation every individual creates what M. Brewster Smith calls an "assumptive world."

> Each of us takes our own assumptive world for granted; that *is* our reality. So when we find ourselves in irreconcilable disagreement about matters like euthanasia or abortion or capital punishment, we get exasperated, sometimes to the point of violence, by our opponents' inability to listen to reason. Of course, they *do* reason, even if they don't listen, but they reason from unarguably different premises (1980: 321–322).

The political world cannot continuously operate in such an environment. Integrative solutions, solutions where both sides find a satisfactory solution with neither side sacrificing anything of value, are rarities in the best of times and impossible in such surroundings (Follett, 1973). Compromise must be possible but cannot exist when opposing sides will not listen. Everyone must recognize the interconnection of values and ethics. The fact that values will differ between equally sincere, honorable, moral people must also be accepted. An understanding of the centrality of values to all types of ethical dilemmas, personal, organizational, social, and political, and the conflicts surrounding them, will allow progress to be made toward achieving a workable accommodation in creating and implementing public policy that allows productive activity to continue. Such an understanding allows public administrators to accomplish their ultimate goal of serving all the citizens of the state while achieving the public interest.

NOTES

1. Radical behaviorism suffers also from its inability to adequately answer the question of where those attitudes and behaviors inculcated into people came from in the first place.
2. Kohlberg's framework of moral development is discussed at length, by Stewart, Sprinthall, and Shafer, in Chapter 22 of this volume.
3. Teleological perspectives are discussed at greater length, by Pops, in Chapter 9 of this volume.
4. There are also numerous arguments against using utilitarianism. Barbour (1980), for example, in his discussion of technology, environment, and human values, notes that utilitarianism has several inherent weaknesses, including, but not limited to, the facts that:

    utilitarianism is often anthropocentric, referring only to human beings, often focusing on presently existing persons;

    utilitarianism has difficulty attempting to quantify the greatest good so that comparison between alternatives can take place; and

in utilitarianism only the total goal is calculated and not its distribution.

5.   Deontological perspectives are described at greater length by Chandler, in Chapter 8 of this volume.

6.   Simon (1973: 350) says:

> All the evidence from the fine arts suggests that unlimited freedom is not the best condition for human creativity. The Gothic cathedrals were created not out of unlimited freedom, but out of the stern physical constraints imposed by gravity acting upon masonry walls, and the equally severe social constraints of the Catholic liturgy. Man creates best when he operates in an environment whose constraints are commensurate with the capacities of his bounded rationality. More constraint restricts his creativity, less throws him into confusion and frustration.

7.   "Social capital," according to Putnam (1993: 167) "refers to features of social organization, such as trust, norms, and networks, that can improve the efficiency of society by facilitating coordinated actions."

REFERENCES

Allen, A. L., and Regan, M. C., eds. (1998). *Debating Democracy's Discontent: Essays on American Politics, Law, and Public Philosophy.* New York: Oxford.

The American Heritage Dictionary of the English Language. (1982). Boston: Houghton Mifflin.

Barbour, I. G. (1980). *Technology, Environment, and Human Values.* New York: Praeger.

Barry, N. P. (1987). *On Classical Liberalism and Libertarianism.* New York: St. Martin's Press.

Beck, L. W., trans. (1985). Immanuel Kant's *The Critique of Practical Reason.* New York: Macmillan.

Bellah, R. N., Madsen, R., Sullivan, W. M., Swidler, A., and Tipton, S. M. (1985). *Habits of the Heart: Individualism and Commitment in American Life*, University of California Press, Berkeley.

Braybrooke, D., and Lindblom, C. E. (1970). *A Strategy of Decision: Policy Evaluation as a Social Process.* New York: Free Press.

Cooper, T. L. (1991). *An Ethic of Citizenship for Public Administration.* Englewood Cliffs, NJ: Prentice-Hall.

Dawes, C. G. (1970). The first year of the budget of the United States. In *The Administrative Process and Democratic Theory* (L. C. Gawthrop, ed.). Boston: Houghton Mifflin.

De Charms, R. (1968). *Personal Causation: the Internal Affective Determinants of Behavior.* New York: Academic Press.

Durkheim, E. (1966). *The Rules of Sociological Method*, 8th ed. Glencoe, IL: The Free Press.

Etzioni, A. (1993). *The Spirit of Community: Rights, Responsibilities, and the Communitarian Agenda.* New York: Crown Publishers.

Etzioni, A. (1996). *The New Golden Rule: Community and Morality in a Democratic Society.* New York: Basic Book/HarperCollins.

Ferguson, R. A. (1997). *The American Enlightenment: 1750–1820.* Cambridge, MA: Harvard University Press.

Filley, A. C., House, R. J., and Kerr, S. (1976). *Managerial Process and Organizational Behavior.* Glenview, IL: Scott, Foresman.

Follett, M. P. (1973). *Dynamic Administration: The Collected Papers of Mary Parker Follett* (Elliot M. Fox and L. Urwick, eds.). London: Pitman.

Frankena, W. (1967). Values and valuation. In *Encyclopedia of Philosophy* (P. Edwards, ed.). New York: Macmillan.

Gale, R. F. (1969). *Developmental Behavior: A Humanistic Approach.* New York: Macmillan.

Gilmour, R. S., and Halley, A. A., eds. (1994). *Who Makes Public Policy: The Struggle for Control Between Congress and the Executive.* Chatham, NJ: Chatham House Publishers.

Gortner, H. F. (1991). *Ethics for Public Managers.* New York: Greenwood Press.

Jung, G. (1923). *Psychological Types.* New York: Harcourt Brace.

Kalish, R. A., and Collier, K. W. (1981). *Exploring Human Values: Psychological and Philosophical Considerations.* Monterey, CA: Brooks/Cole.

Kelman, S. (1987). *Making Public Policy: A Hopeful View of American Government.* New York: Basic Books.

Kernaghan, K., and Langford, J. W. (1990). *The Responsible Public Servant.* The Institute for Research on Public Policy and the Institute of Public Administration of Canada, Halifax, Nova Scotia.

Kiersey, D., and Bates, M. (1984). *Please Understand Me: Character and Temperament Types.* Del Mar, CA: Prometheus Nemesis.

Kluckhohn, C. (1962). Values and value orientations in the theory of action. In *Toward a General Theory of Action* (T. Parsons and E. A. Shils, eds.). New York: Harper.

Kohlberg, L. (1976). Children's perceptions of contemporary value systems. In *Raising Children in Modern America: Problems and Perspective Solutions* (N. Talbot, ed.). Boston: Little, Brown.

Koven, S. G., Shelley, M. C., II, and Swanson, B. E. (1998). *American Public Policy: The Contemporary Agenda.* New York: Houghton Mifflin.

Ladd, E. C. (1996). The data just don't show erosion of America's "social capital." *The Public Perspective,* June/July: 1–22.

Lipset, S. M. (1990). *Continental Divide: The Values and Institutions of the United States and Canada.* New York: Routledge.

Lukes, S. (1991). *Moral Conflict and Politics.* Oxford: Clarendon.

Maslow, A. (1954). *Motivation and Personality.* New York: Harper.

Maxwell, M. (1991). *Moral Inertia: Ideas for Social Action.* Niwot, Colorado: University of Colorado Press.

McCullough, T. E. (1991). *The Moral Imagination and Public Life: Raising the Ethical Question.* Chatham, NJ: Chatham House.

Meltsner, A. J. (1976). *Policy Analysis in the Bureaucracy.* Berkeley: University of California Press.

Putnam, R. D. (1993). *Making Democracy Work: Civic Traditions in Modern Italy* (with R. Leonardi and R. Y. Nanetti). Princeton, NJ: Princeton University Press.

Putnam, R. D. (1995). Bowling alone: America's declining social capital. *The Journal of Democracy,* 6 (January): 65–78.

Reich, R. B. (1988). *Policy Making in a Democracy.* The Power of Public Ideas. Cambridge, MA: Ballinger.

Rokeach, M. (1973). *The Nature of Human Values.* New York: Free Press.

Rotter, J. R. (1966). Generalized expectancies for internal versus external control of reinforcement. *Psychological Monographs,* 80 (1: Whole No. 609).

Sandel, M. J. (1996). *Democracy's Discontent: America in Search of a Public Philosophy.* Cambridge, MA: Harvard University Press.

Selby-Bigge (ed.) (1978). David Hume's *A Treatise of Human Nature,* 2nd ed. (with revisions and variant readings for second edition by P. H. Nidditch). New York: Oxford.

Simon, H. A. (1973). Organization Man: Rational or Self-Actualizing? *Public Administration Review,* 33 (July–August) 346–353.

Smith, A. (1997). *The Theory of Moral Sentiments, or, An essay; a dissertation on the origin of languages.* Washington, DC: Regnery.

Smith, A. (1998). *An Inquiry into the Nature and Causes of The Wealth of Nations: A Selected Edition* (K. Sutherland, ed.). New York: Oxford.

Smith, M. B. (1980). Attitudes, values, and selfhood. In *Nebraska Symposium on Motivation, 1979: Beliefs, Attitudes, and Values* (H. E. Howe and M. M. Page, eds.). Lincoln: University of Nebraska Press.

Smith, M. B. (1991). *Values, Self, and Society: Toward a Humanist Social Psychology*. New Brunswick, NJ: Transaction Publishers.

Smith, T. (1991). *The Role of Ethics in Social Theory: Essays From a Habermasian Perspective*. Albany: State University of New York Press.

Triandis, H. C. (1980). Values, attitudes, and interpersonal behavior. In *Nebraska Symposium on Motivation, 1979: Beliefs, Attitudes, and Values* (H. E. Howe and M. M. Page, eds.). Lincoln: University of Nebraska Press.

Weber, M. (1947). *The Theory of Social and Economic Organization* (A. M. Henderson and T. Parsons, eds. and trans.). New York: Free Press.

Williams, R. M., Jr. (1970). *American Society: A Sociological Interpretation*, 3rd ed. Alfred New York: Alfred A. Knopf.

Wilson, J. Q. (1989). *Bureaucracy: What Government Agencies Do and Why They Do It*. New York: Basic Books.

25

Character and Conduct in the Public Service
A Review of Historical Perspectives

Jeffrey S. Luke
University of Oregon, Eugene, Oregon

David W. Hart*
Mary Washington College, Fredericksburg, Virginia

With the recent indiscretions of high-ranking officials in the United States, the age-old issue of the role of character in leadership is once again being raised. One of the issues being debated is whether there is a public and private character in individuals, and more specifically, whether one's private activities affect the ability to lead. Yet it is quickly apparent that one of the central problems surrounding this issue today is the fact that it is not clear what we mean by the term "character." The question of what citizens want with respect to the moral character of its public servants is a complex one. There is less and less agreement on the nature of character and its role in public leadership. This chapter provides a preliminary discussion of character and its crucial role in public administration by reviewing two major approaches to the study of character—philosophy and psychology. Given the conclusions of the work in these two disciplines, we end the chapter with a discussion on why good character is particularly necessary in public leadership. To begin, however, it is helpful to understand character in the context of public administration.

I. CHARACTER IN PUBLIC ADMINISTRATION

Public administration as a discipline grew out of political science at a time when political science was well-grounded in political philosophy. In the evolutionary process of creating

---

* I was invited by Terry Cooper to prepare this chapter for the second edition of this book. Jeff Luke, the original author of this chapter included in the first edition, has unfortunately passed away since that time. Although I did not personally know him, I am familiar with his work and know that he will be sorely missed by the academy. In an effort to preserve the integrity of this piece I have made relatively few substantive changes to the content outside of the introductory and concluding statements (which reflect his more recent work).

a unique discipline, much of the substantive content and tradition of moral discourse of political science was left behind. As a result, we have lost touch with much of the moral foundation that underlies the discipline of public administration—and we too are having trouble articulating the problems of character in the public service (see Lilla, 1981; Chandler, 1983; Brady, 1988; and to a lesser extent Wright, 1988; Wilson 1993 and 1995). It is perhaps most evident in the lack of a substantial literature on the topic of character and its relationship to the public service. In fact, character and its qualities are seldom mentioned or directly addressed. Except for references to a specific set of virtues or personality traits that particular authors suggest as characteristic of administrators of high moral standing, there have been relatively few systematic treatments of character and its qualities in public administration. Yet there has been a growing movement in recent years that is placing more emphasis on the importance of this issue. Here we briefly discuss a few of the more influential works in this area.

A. Stephen K. Bailey's Essential Attitudes and Moral Qualities of a Public Administrator

One of the first to outline the qualities of character in a moral public administrator was Stephen K. Bailey (1965; see also 1964) who suggested that the various ethical dilemmas facing public administrators require three specific mental attitudes and three unique moral qualities. The essential attitudes include: (1) a recognition of the moral ambiguity of all individuals and of all public policies, (2) a recognition of the contextual forces which condition moral priorities in the public service, and (3) a recognition of the paradoxes of procedures. These cognitive characteristics must be matched by three essential moral qualities: (1) optimism, (2) courage, and (3) fairness tempered with charity. Together, these six characteristics might be considered as the elements of good character for individuals in the public service.

B. Kathryn Denhardt's Moral Foundations of Public Administration

Kathryn Denhardt arrives at another definition of character, less intentionally than Bailey, but with equal succinctness and clarity. As virtue returns to currency in the teaching of ethics in public administration, she describes the essential moral foundations of the field to facilitate our teaching of the appropriate virtues, values, and ethical commitments of the profession. In her analysis (1991; see 1988 for a broader discussion), she identifies honor, benevolence, and justice as the core moral foundations. Honor "is the preeminent virtue" and is a quality of character that is fundamental because "it is the basis on which public confidence rests" (Denhardt, 1991:103). It includes such characteristics as magnanimity, or great-mindedness, as well as honesty and acting consistently with high standards. Benevolence, the disposition to promote the welfare of others, implies sympathy, enthusiasm, and a strong commitment to service. It is essentially the regard for the interests of others as more important than one's own personal or parochial interests. The third essential virtue is justice, or the respect for, and commitment to, the dignity and worth of each individual. This means not only ensuring that the equality, dignity, and worth of individuals is not violated by others, but also goes as far as to guarantee that informed participation in the governing process is permitted and even promoted.

C. Terry L. Cooper's Responsible and Exemplary Public Administrator

Terry Cooper also describes several qualities that an administrator of good character must possess. In "Hierarchy, Virtue, and the Practice of Public Administration" (1987), he applies a framework presented by Alisdair MacIntyre (1984) in *After Virtue*. Cooper discusses the internal and external goods of the practice of public administration and then presents 20 specific virtues that directly relate to three broad "realms of obligation" of public servants. These realms include (1) the obligation to pursue the public interest, (2) the obligation to authorizing processes and procedures, and (3) the obligation to colleagues. He attaches anywhere from five to nine virtues to each of these obligations.

Cooper (along with N. Dale Wright) furthered the argument for good character in the public service with the publication of *Exemplary Public Administrators* in 1992. The book goes beyond theories and speculation on the nature of character in public administration and applies them to specific exemplars that devoted their lives to the public service. By examining the lives of moral exemplars one is able to extrapolate the qualities necessary for persons of good character in public administration.

D. David K. Hart's "Benevolent Bureaucrat" and "Moral Exemplar" in Public Administration

As with Bailey, Denhardt, and Cooper, David K. Hart assumes that public administration is unique and different from business in fundamental ways. Public servants have a "higher purpose" that requires not only a different set of personal characteristics but also a higher set of moral qualities (1984). In fact, he argues that public administration is essentially a "moral endeavor" that requires special moral obligations and unique moral character. These include "superior prudence," moral heroism, caring or love for humanity, trust in the citizenry, and a continuing quest for moral improvement. Superior prudence, based on Adam Smith's writings, is defined as incorporating and then transcending one's duty as a virtuous citizen and seeking a higher honor that is directed toward greater and nobler purposes than individual achievement. The key to this ideal, Hart concludes, "lies in the will—the self-command—of the individual public administrator" (1984:119). This self-directed, superior prudence is the essence of being an honorable bureaucrat, and requires four additional duties or characteristics. Moral heroism is required for a public administrator to maintain one's moral convictions, particularly when forced to oppose an unjust or immoral policy. Caring is essential, requiring the capacity to care for the citizens within one's jurisdiction, consistently considering the best interests of the individuals who constitute the public he or she serves. By treating the public as virtuous citizens, the honorable bureaucrat trusts and depends on the trustworthiness of citizens. This requires the capacity to take moral risks. The fourth duty or characteristic is the quest for moral nobility, or noblesse oblige, which is the continuing drive to improve, develop, and refine one's moral qualities. This is particularly required the higher one rises in public service because the individual's moral character must become more developed at higher, successive levels of responsibility.

In a later essay, "The Moral Exemplar in an Organizational Society," Hart (1992) emphasizes that acting morally, both intentionally and voluntarily, is essential for moral character in public administration. Such moral actions are exemplary when they proceed from genuine qualities of character. He further defines exemplary public administrators of good character with four distinguishing elements (p. 15). First, good moral character is not a sometime thing; it is a constant aspect of the personality of the exemplary administrator. Second, he or she must act intentionally, voluntarily, and freely with no compulsion from rules or superior organizational authority. Third, the exemplary administrator must be relatively faultless—not perfect in all things but striving toward it. Finally, the exemplar's actions are not frivolous, and must result in "real good, even in failure" (p. 15).

The work of the four individuals mentioned above is representative of the important work that focuses on the qualities of character of public administrators. Clearly there are many others that have contributed to the literature in this area as well.[1] In any case, most of these discussions use virtue as the medium for discussing character and often use the terms interchangeably. As Kupperman notes "it is tempting to think of character as simply the sum of virtues" (1991:102). It is not enough, however, to identify good character from a collection of good virtues. Character is not a "bag of virtues" (Kohlberg, 1981a); they are deep-seated dispositions born *from* our character, not *creating* character (see David K. Hart's chapter in this volume for more detail on virtue). Key questions remain, however. If an individual with exemplary character is not simply someone who possesses a master virtue, or set of virtues, what then describes a person of good or strong character? It is our experience that most writers on this topic do not differentiate between good and strong character, a distinction necessary to better understand the unique moral obligations and character of individuals committed to the public service. What are the enduring tendencies of one who manifests a moral character? How does a strong character differ from a good character? To answer these questions, the following review provides key philosophical and psychological discussions of character and highlights the defining characteristics in each. A preliminary framework is then offered to illuminate the characteristics of an individual executive or administrator of high character in the public service.

II. PHILOSOPHICAL PERSPECTIVES ON CHARACTER

Plato described character as the naked soul, the real self after death, stripped bare of external qualities such as beauty, rank, power, or wealth.[2] Aristotle identified character as enduring attitudes, sensibilities, and beliefs and the resulting habituated patterns of actions (Sherman, 1989 and 1997) and feelings (Larmore, 1987). More recent philosophical definitions similarly focus on character as a unification of a person's tendencies through time and the expression of habitually dominant tendencies organized into one's fixed character (Dewey and Tufts, 1925). One's style of thought and action in matters of importance is critical as well (Kupperman, 1991). It is, as Coles emphasizes, the "way-down-deep truth of a person" (1981). In most cases, however, character is seen as the ways in which we most commonly think or act and is embedded in the "actions of everyday life crises, confrontations, projects, and work" (Hart, 1992:26). The following review summarizes the conclusions of a select few to assist articulating an exemplary or high character for public service.

A. Aristotle: A "Fabric" of Character

Much of Aristotle's moral theory focuses on the question about how one can live a good life, which is to say, how one can attain happiness. Simply put, happiness is a matter of good character. Thus, an individual with good character seeks the good life, cares about the virtues that lead to a good life, and continually attempts to deepen his or her commitment and ability to lead a good life (Sherman, 1989). Aristotle's focus on the development and refinement of the virtues, and one's pursuit of the good life, would imply that a person of good character would possess one or several key virtues or, as he called them, "excellences" (*arete*).

Unlike Plato, however, Aristotle did not attempt to establish a list of cardinal virtues, or states of character that typify the good or virtuous person. In *The Nicomachean Ethics*, he did suggest that there are some natural virtues, for example, innate inclinations for some toward justice, courage, and temperance (1980). These are isolated capacities, he argued, that need proper development ("habituation") to reflect truly virtuous behavior (Sherman, 1989). He also compiled a list of virtues that were characteristic of a Greek citizen: for example, self-control, generosity, magnificence, high-mindedness, gentleness, friendliness, truthfulness, and wittiness (Hauerwas, 1981). Because of different individual temperaments and the widely varying circumstances requiring virtuous behavior, he did not develop a list of core virtues of good character. More important, it was not enough for an individual of good character to have the right virtue, even if one could be isolated; one also had to have the capacity and practical wisdom to know when and how to exhibit them (Sherman, 1989). From Aristotle's perspective, virtue is the ability to choose and reason correctly, and the individual with good character knows how to act and feel in ways that are appropriate to each circumstance while still faithful to the ultimate moral values that underlie a true *polis*.

For Aristotle, then, good character is more than possessing the virtues that guide a good life. Virtues are modes of conduct and result from actualizing good character rather than the reverse (having ethical virtues which then lead to good character) (Sherman, 1989). In other words, it is not the possession of virtues or excellences (*arete*), but excellent actions that distinguish good character. And this "excellent" activity is not one type of action that can be isolated, extracted, or repeatedly practiced to form good character (like being kind). Just actions, for example, are contextually defined and vary considerably from other just actions "in terms of judgment, emotion, and behavior" (Sherman, 1989: 178). The one commonality in persons of good character is that they possess practical reason, the foundation of "excellent activity," which consists of moral perception, choice making, and collaboration.

Moral perception is recognizing and identifying morally salient features in concrete, practical situations. This first stage of practical reason involves perceiving ethical salience and the perceptual judgments of moral relevance. This is critical for Aristotle, because before one decides how to act, one must recognize that the situation requires some action. Second, once a situation is identified as requiring action, a choice is made regarding how and in what way to act. The deliberation and reflection characteristic of the good person is a special sort of deliberative preference called *prohaires*, or reasoned choice. Reasoned choice involves two aspects that distinguish it from more instrumental notions of preference. First, it is a choice based on more than achieving a single goal. It involves balancing several goals in a complex, interdependent network of long-term and short-term goals. A second distinction is that feelings and emotions propel reasoned choice. Emotions are themselves integral to moral response and directly influence what one determines as morally relevant. A person of good character is emotionally engaged, Aristotle suggests, and action motivated by the right principle but lacking in the right feeling or emotion does not express virtue (Sherman, 1989).

The third element of practical reason is collaboration. The well-being of the person of good character is inextricably tied to the well-being of others. Individuals survive, prosper, and grow through significant interaction with the environment. Society in general, and the polis in particular, is characterized by interdependence. Friendships, intimate relations, familial relationships, and civic friendships result in "the ends of life being shared, and similarly the resources for promoting it . . . [in fact] there is no moment of self-sufficiency which marks full independence from others" (Sherman, 1989:6). As a result, a person of good character must engage in collaborative or collective action to pursue the good life.

For Aristotle, practical reason and the resultant virtues of good character are learned through repetition and successive trials that vary according to the different circumstances and stages of development of each individual. Virtues are "implanted in us neither by nature nor contrary to nature; we are by nature equipped with the ability to receive them, and habit brings this ability to completion and fulfillment" (Aristotle, 1980:1103a, 23–25). The acquisition of practical reasoning similarly occurs through a form of habituation (*ethismos*), a refinement of perception, reflection, feeling, and action through repeated efforts. Habit is thus crucial in forming good character. It is a non-mechanical repetition, one more like the virtuosity of a craftsperson or musician than that of an assembly-line worker. Through such habit, "actions become effortless but careful and attentive" (Hardie, 1980:104). Thus, the process of seeing, reacting, and understanding, inherent in practical reasoning become almost second nature as an enduring pattern of thought and action. In short, Aristotle believed that "(t)o have character requires the integration of different ends and interests in a unified life over time" (Sherman, 1989:6). Such character takes on a certain coherence or fabric of character. Rather than a manifestation of separate, isolated virtues, it is a fabric of several uniquely constituted virtues, resulting from the habituation of practical reasoning—moral perception, passions, and deliberation and action toward long- and short-term goals—woven together in one's character over a lifetime.

B. Confucius: *Chun-tzu* as Exemplar of Good Character

In many ways, Confucius' notion of good character is similar to Aristotle's. First, both agree that moral judgment cannot be guided by following some general principle or rule (Kupperman, 1991). Second, one cannot isolate central or characteristic virtues that distinguish one of good character. Rather, virtues and vices together form an interrelated personal system over life that reveals moral character. Third, both assume that some perfect notion of good character is unreachable. As a result, developing good character is a process of self-cultivation that continues throughout one's life. Underlying or perhaps motivating this life-long process of character formation is a well-considered moral commitment—Aristotle's person of good character cares about virtues, finds pleasure in the thought and pursuit of noble ends, which deepens his or her commitment and the ability to lead a good life (Sherman, 1989). Confucius similarly suggested that people of good character have a sincere commitment to the ideal, which involves daily examination of the ethical impact of one's action and which stimulates a "constant and unceasing process of self-cultivation" that significantly transforms the moral agent's conduct throughout life (Cua, 1992).

The person of good character in Confucian ethics is best articulated as the *chun-tzu* or exemplary individual. The sage in Confucian thought, a *sheng-jen*, is a perfect man of moral concern, however, and is not considered a realistic or practical goal for an individual, but rather as an ideal character. Confucius once remarked that he had no hope of meeting a sage but he would be happy meeting a chun-tzu (Cua, 1992). Chun-tzu, while not perfect, were exemplary persons who embodied a deep moral concern for humanity—called *jen*—in their lives and conduct. A salient feature in Confucian ethics, chun-tzu served as standards, models, or examples of moral competence for others. They embodied three elements of good character that distinguished them as exemplary: li, yi, and jen.

1. Li

The chun-tzu is skillful in managing his or her conduct in accord with the li (the accepted rules, norms, or precepts of established morality). These accepted practices provide a moral tradition, or set of formal prescriptions and rules for behaving. Moral competence of li can be learned like any skill or technique. What differentiates persons of good character from others is their use of yi, or reasoned judgment. The exemplary individual easily acquires the minimum mastery of accepted moral practices, the li, but he or she must also have a flexible attitude and a reasonableness to deal with exigent cases and changing circumstances. Obedience to the moral precepts of li is not enough for a chun-tzu.

2. Yi

Moral precepts, however effectively taught, are always subject to interpretation in changing circumstances. Yi is required either when the environment changes and no specific rule applies or when an individual experiences a conflict of principles or obligations. This then becomes a matter of exercising yi, an individual sense of rightness in relation to the li or moral tradition, which is the preeminent quality of a chun-tzu in coping with the indeterminate, problematic situations of human life (Cua, 1992). As a result, Confucius rejected the development of a hierarchy of rules for such conflict out of fear of developing an ethical edifice. Such a system could not be developed for all cases and exceptions and would deprive individuals of the opportunity "to think for themselves in the light of their own experience, circumstances and aspirations" (Cua, 1992).

3. Jen

In people of good character, reasoned judgment (yi) is first and foremost guided by an extensive concern for others (jen). Jen focuses on "caring for one's fellows," or more specifically, on a growing sensitivity to the suffering, happiness, and well-being of others, as well as an expanding awareness and concern for all humans and non-humans (Cua, 1992). It is also based on the Confucian understanding that all human lives are intertwined. Ethical action by a person of good character revolves around the interdependence between personal well-being and societal well-being that leads to a sense of shared destiny with others. Thus, to have this concern for others is to understand the importance of being a member of a larger moral community. This translates into an appreciation and respect for others, for individual styles of life and for the general well-being of others. As Mencius notes, "there are alternative paths to the pursuit of jen" (Cua, 1992:54). Thus, jen includes respect for customary rules of proper conduct and (li), an interdependence or "reciprocity of moral wills" (Cua, 1992:54), which are guided by a sincere concern for others. For Confucius, jen provides a broad theme for one of good character—rather than a set of prescriptions for conduct on how to specifically care for others, it allows the exercise of individual interpretation in light of one's experience.

C. Deontology and Utilitarianism: Character as Impartial Reason

Deontology and utilitarianism are two of the better known traditions in modern moral philosophy. Although both theories address the nature of character, it is in a much less explicit way than Aristotle and Confucius. Kant and Bentham (associated with deontology and utilitarianism, respectively) typically do not directly address the role of character in their pursuit of a "fully explicit decision procedure for settling moral questions" (Larmore, 1987:ix). In both, the individual's character—the general form or structure of human personality, the personal concerns and commitments of persons with moral character, and the conditions under which good lives are lived—does not play a major role in understanding moral choices. In these theories of moral conduct, the individual's "personality was caused to disappear behind the excessively optimistic Enlightenment view that right action will follow, no matter what one's overall character is like, so long as one recognizes and accepts the right general-purpose principle" (Flanagan, 1991:181). This reflects the utilitarian rule of pursuing the greatest good for the greatest number, or Kant's categorical imperative which stipulates that there is a significant relation between an action being morally right and its being in accordance with a rule that can be generalized or universalized for everyone.

1. Kant's Transcendence of Personal Feelings

The decision procedures of Kant emphasize broad general maxims that are impersonal and place minimal requirements on character. He starts with the assumption that all individuals have desires, feelings, and appetites, and that they are rational—they can discern what is right action. An individual of good character—a person of "moral worth" in Kant's terms—exercises his or her will in the rational, self-control of their desires, feelings, and appetites in order to pursue the right action. There is a clear separation of appetite, desire, or inclinations from reason and duty in persons of moral worth.[3] Acting right out of a sense of inner satisfaction—for example, helping others because it feels personally satisfying—is not the kind of action that has moral worth. Only when one acts "from duty and without inclination, then for the first time his action has genuine moral worth" (Kant, 1898:346–347). Here, persons of good character transcend their personal feelings and inclinations to follow rationally imposed principles or duties that are universally generalizable to all human beings (Munzel and Felicitas, 1998).

To do the right thing out of principle, versus desire, recognizes that such action could be an objective right, principle, or duty that could be an obligation on other individuals. Kant's categorical imperative states that people of moral worth act in such ways that the principles of their actions could be universal laws for everyone else. These principles become an internalized sense of duty that transcends self-interest. The principle most deeply sustained by a person of moral worth is the Good Will. Kant (1898:329) states that

> (n)othing can possibly be conceived, in the world or out of it, which can be called Good without qualification, except a Good Will. Intelligence, wit, judgment, and the other talents of the mind, however they may be named, or courage, resolution, perseverance as qualities of temperament are individually good and desirable in many respects; but these gifts of nature may also become extremely bad and mischievous, if the will which is to make use of them and which, therefore, constitutes what is called character, is not good. It is the same with the gifts of fortune. Power, riches, honor, even health . . . inspire pride and often presumptions if there is not a Good Will to correct the influence of these on the mind.

2. Utilitarianism's Character of Consequences

Decision procedures lie at the heart of the ethical theory of utilitarianism, as they do in the moral theory of Kant. The foundation of utilitarianism lies in the concept that each individual is a "felicific calculator," or one capable of minimizing pain and maximizing pleasure, in that order (Halevy, 1928). On the societal level, the good of society is based on each individual determining his or her own good. The result is the greatest good for the greatest number. Moral worth thus resides in the consequences or actual outcomes achieved by one's action and not in the principle or will of the individual as argued by Kant. The motive or the will to do something makes no difference in determining the morality of the act.

This approach to character derives first from Bentham's principle of utility: actions are right and good when they result in increased happiness and diminished misery to conscious beings. Bentham argues that moral individuals make moral decisions on the basis of their impact on producing pleasure and happiness. Pleasure is evaluated according to seven measures: intensity, duration, certainty, propinquity (nearness), fecundity (likelihood of leading to other pleasures), purity (likelihood of not leading to pain), and extent (the number of persons to whom the act extends or are affected by it) (Bentham, 1989). Thus, a person of good character has the education, sensitivity, and steady willingness to apply rational utilitarian calculus prior to making moral decisions. Pursuing these ends requires intelligent forethought, analysis, and advance planning as well as resoluteness and perseverance. Although a person of good character may occasionally act in accordance with a particular rule or maxim, he or she nevertheless begins by applying a utilitarian calculus in all cases in which he or she deliberates and chooses a particular action (Smart, 1973; see Railton, 1988 for an interesting alternative).

Here, utilitarianism joins deontology in seeking to overrule or transcend the individuals' emotions with the cognitive process of rational calculation. One's dispositions or motives are mere abstractions, "a kind of fictitious entity," and are unimportant in utilitarian theory. The moral worth of internal motives or dispositions is not relevant except in relation to the consequences to which the motives lead. Utilitarianism insists that individuals become aware of the moral worth of their impulses and motives on the basis of the results they create, and must control these impulses, no matter how good the impulse feels to the individual, in order to reach morally good results (Dewey an Tufts, 1925). Thus, a person of good character in the utilitarian perspective is one who controls his or her internal impulses, dispositions, and states of mind in order to direct them to outcomes that provide the greatest amount of pleasure to the greatest number of human beings.

D.　Dewey and Tufts: Moral Conduct and Character

Dewey (1922) and Dewey and Tufts (1925) seem to integrate the explicit definitions of good character by Aristotle and Confucius with the less explicit elaboration of character emerging in more recent philosophies:

> For Kant's fixed and absolute separation between the self of inclination and the self of reason, we substitute the relative and shifting distinction between those factors of self which have become so definitely organized into set habits that they take care of themselves, and those factors which are more precarious, less crystallized, and which depend therefore upon conscious acknowledgment and intentionally directed affection (similarly recognized in Aristotle and Confucius). The consciousness of duty (Kant's

influence) grows out of the complex character of the self; the fact that at any given time it has tendencies relatively set, ingrained, and embodied in fixed habits, while it also has tendencies in process of making, looking to the future, and taking account of unachieved possibilities (a focus on consequences prescribed by utilitarians). The former gives the solid relatively formed elements of character; the latter, its ideal or unrealized possibilities. Each must play into the other; each must help the other out (1925: 362).

Dewey and Tufts focus on moral conduct and the requisite character of a moral agent. The two main aspects of conduct are character and circumstance. Character is "whatever lies behind an act in the way of deliberation and desire" (1925:203) and encompasses the "inner" side, or the will, dispositions, motives, and inclinations. Circumstance includes the outer side, the external conditions, the past and present consequences, and the effects of behavior. Conduct is the result of character acting in the context of particular external conditions and circumstances in one of three ways:

1. Instinctive Activity: unconscious impulses, hereditary reflexes, and fundamental needs.
2. Deliberative Choice: action by conscious direction, desire or choice; the process of deliberation and valuation; "action under the stress of attention, with conscious intervention and reconstruction" (1925:12).
3. Habit: habitual activities acquired through prior deliberation and action; the "organization of consciously directed conduct into habits and a self of higher order" (1925:13).

A distinguishing mark of their definition of character is reliance on habit as the foundation of forming strong character. Habits, or tendencies to act or respond, develop over time and are results of prior deliberations and choices that have become "more or less automatic habits" (Dewey and Tufts, 1925:203). Habits are thus formed through a gradual process of selection, as a result of deliberative choice, valuation, and attention. It is important to note that habit is not conceived as a routine, mechanical response to an external condition. Rather it is a consistent way of thinking about something, similar to what Allport (1968) called a "schemata of value," where decisions about certain values, on specific issues, automatically flow.[4] Yet it is the consecutiveness and consistency among habits that constitute a strong character. Dewey and Tufts (1925:38) argue that strong character requires the "interpenetration of habits. Of course interpenetration is never total. It is most marked in what we call strong characters. . . . A weak, unstable, vacillating character is one in which different habits alternate with one another rather than embody one another." Strength of habit is a result of continual deliberation, choice, reflection, and then integration into the self as habit, "due to reinforcement by the force of habits which it absorbs into itself" (Dewey, 1922:38).

If a strong character requires an interpenetration of habits, then what distinguishes a good character? Goodness of character, according to Dewey and Tufts, is related to the "habitual dispositions" of a person "as manifested in the tendencies (habits) which cause certain consequences, rather than others, to be considered and esteemed—foreseen and desired" (1925:263). One of good character thus has developed a habit of greater thoughtfulness about the future, about consequences of actions. They emphasize that the "great need of the moral agent is thus a character which will make him as open, as accessible as possible, to the recognition of the consequences of his behavior" (p. 262) and that "our chief moral business is to become acquainted with consequences" (p. 464). This requires conscious deliberation of consequences of past actions, holding oneself account-able in subsequent reflection for careless acts or acts omitted through negligence, and the capacity to alter modes of action based on this reflection.

Although we have covered only the most basic discussions, certain important themes emerge from philosophy; these will be considered later. The work done in psychology on the nature of character also makes important contributions to our understanding as well. Thus, a brief overview of relevant work on character is necessary before reaching any conclusions about character in the public service.

III. PSYCHOLOGICAL PERSPECTIVES ON CHARACTER

Psychological investigations into character, beginning with William James, have tied char-acter into various conceptions of personality and focus on dispositions that are central to an individual. Character in the Freudian tradition similarly refers to an individual's "typi-cal or habitual pattern of responding to instinctual or interpersonal forces" (Gibson et al., 1989:1139). Historically, character from the psychological perspective includes patterns of behavior and actions consistent through time, that are motivated by internal dispositions that characterize and define the individual, particularly in contrast to other people.

Most current psychological theorists agree that character closely resembles personal-ity, but that character is the deeper, more fundamental part of the self that is different from two other basic components of personality—(1) temperaments (personality traits) and (2) intellectual capacity. Psychologists now recognize that character has moral quali-ties and can be defined in terms of those internalized dispositions "that are subject to moral evaluation within a society" (Hogan, 1973:219). Gordon Allport argued that "character is personality evaluated"; it is a "moral center within ourselves that is quite simply there."[5] Thus, character could be viewed as the "persisting patterns of attitudes and motives which produce rather predictable kind and quality of moral behavior" (Peck and Havighurst, 1960:164). Character contains moral dimensions that the concept "personality" lacks. Character thus generally encompasses certain forms or patterns of thought and action that are characteristic of a person, particularly those qualities that constitute the individual as a moral being. Fromm, Peck and Havighurst, and Kohlberg have all made important contributions to the understanding of character from a psychological perspective.

A. Fromm's "Productive Orientation"

For Fromm, the underlying basis of character was in how a person related him- or herself to the world. Individuals relate to the world by acquiring and assimilating things, and by relating him- or herself to others (Fromm, 1947). Thus, character is the relatively perma-nent form in which human energy is engraved or canalized as the result of assimilation and socialization during the childhood years. "Once energy is canalized in a certain way, action takes place 'true to character' "(1947:59). Character thus provides consistent and reasonably patterned sets of behaviors. Our actions are not determined by genetically instinctual patterns; one's character system or orientation could be considered the human substitute for the innate instinctive apparatus found in other animals.

Fromm identified two general types of character, non-productive and productive orientations. Within the non-productive, he identified four types: the receptive orientation (the person who feels the source of all good lies outside oneself and will be received from some external source); the exploitive orientation (what one wants lies outside and must be taken from there); the hoarding orientation (security is based on hoarding and saving); and the marketing orientation (where an individual experiences him- or herself as a buyer, seller, and a commodity to be sold).

The productive orientation is Fromm's fully developed character, and refers to a fundamental attitude much broader than material productivity. It is a mode of relatedness in all realms of experience or productive, healthy, developing modes of relating to the external world (Fromm, 1947). One major theme is "productive love," which includes care, responsibility, and respect and knowledge of others. A second theme is "productive thinking," which encompasses depth of reason (the ability to see the essence of things and processes) and objectivity (ability to see things as they are and not as one wishes them to be).

Character orientation is significantly determined by the socioeconomic and political structure of the society in which one is raised. The external environment has a critical impact on character since a person is influenced by the way individuals relate to one another. And since the environment is never the same for two people, there will be variations in individuals manifesting a particular orientation. Thus, an individual never fully embodies a single orientation, but is a blend or combination of several, yet there is usually a dominant orientation that characterizes a person. These behaviors are rooted deeply and are "changeable only if a fundamental change in a person's character takes place" (Fromm, 1947:61).

B. Peck and Havighurst's Rational-Altruistic Character

In what is arguably the best empirical assessment of character development, Peck and Havighurst (1960) integrated the developmental aspects of Freud's stage-concept theory with a focus on moral aspects of character in a longitudinal study of adolescents. They viewed character as a special aspect of personality, measurable on a Maturity of Character Scale (which used several instruments over seven years). For these adolescents, four particular aspects of personality were found to be significantly related to maturity of character:

1. Moral Stability: includes such things as conformity to expectations of the community at large, age mates of the opposite sex, and expectations of parents, especially one's mother;
2. Ego Strength: perceptual capacities of observation and insight, realism in appraising self and others, psychological autonomy, maturity of emotional reaction, and internal consistency or integration of the personality system;
3. Superego Strength: the degree that behavior is effectively guided by some set of inner moral principles; and
4. Spontaneity: spontaneity, empathy, and good feelings about same-sex peers and one's father.

In addition, Peck and Havighurst found that these individuals often progressed through a set of five basic character types, a hierarchy of ascending moral maturity that characterized high or low manifestations of the above personality elements. Their stage-theory is consistent with Piaget's theory of the moral development of children, which suggests that individuals' behavior and actions are first ruled by adult constraints. This evolves into the moral realism of uncritical conformity to external rules, and then matures into a personal morality where individuals examine and validate or change their own moral decisions. Like Fromm, Peck and Havighurst used categories to capture the essence of character as one progresses through the stages of moral development.

1. *Amoral characters* are people of low character that follow their own whims, urges, and impulses, regardless of the effects on other people. There are no internalized moral principles and no conscience. They consider themselves the center of the universe and see other people or objects as means for self-gratification. Spontaneity was also found to be high in this character type.

2. *Expedient characters* are similarly self-centered, but only consider the welfare and reactions of others in order to achieve personal ends. They may behave in ways that are morally suitable, but only so long as it suits their purpose. Expedient characters consider themselves the center of the universe as well but differ from amoral characters because they are generally more aware of the advantage of conforming to expectations in the short run in order to achieve long-term self-interest.

3. *Conforming characters* attempt to conform to all the rules of the particular group or situation of which they are a part. They follow one general rule—do what others do and what they say one should do. They define "right" as acting within proper rules and codes of conduct, but there are no abstract principles or maxims such as honesty, responsibility, etc. As such, conformists depend on external rules and sanctions to behave in a manner dictated by the moral code.

4. *Irrational-conscientious characters* are on the same level of maturity, and are no more autonomous than conformers—they live by absolute rules, but they are derived from the established dictums of one's parents. Principles consist mainly of "don'ts," are rigidly internalized, and rule one's behavior. They are not capable of questioning internalized rules or evaluating to see if they serve a genuinely moral purpose. The internal conscience is essentially a reflection of the injunctions of one's parents.

5. *Rational-altruistic characters* are on the highest level of moral maturity. They are rational because they assess new actions and behaviors and their effects realistically in light of some internalized moral principles derived or learned from social experience. They observe situations, see implications beyond the immediate, and can mentally experiment to help decide on the right choices of action. In addition, they do not pursue a principle for its own sake, without regard for its consequences; they are concerned with the real effects of each action, and not with abstract rules or labels such as honesty, truth, etc. Actions are seldom justified by referring to abstract principles or rationalizations. One is altruistic because he or she is sincerely interested in the welfare of others, as well as him- or herself. They can recognize how other people feel; in fact, one is able to feel as others do, or project how one would feel if in their position, without completely identifying with them and losing one's own perspective. In the studies, these individuals were the only ones that regularly showed both good intentions and thoughtful, sensitive judgment in how they treated others. In general, these individuals act on rational moral principles, rather than on absolute dictums or rules, because they have a high regard for people. In addition, they are very spontaneous and open to continued growth and development.

Peck and Havighurst also discovered that three central threads run through the character-type sequence. First, they noted an increasing ego strength from the amoral to the rational-altruistic character. This means an increase in internal integration of the various personality elements, perceptual capacities of observation and insight, increasing psychological autonomy, and a stronger sense of self that frees one from arbitrary outer pressures or from irrational inner pressures.

Second, there was an increasing strength of conscience that showed an increasingly firm, increasingly internalized set of moral principles (not rules) which act as a guide to one's behavior and action. As a result, Peck and Havighurst were able to distinguish four qualitatively different forms of conscience. The most primitive form was a set of harsh, crude, ''don'ts.'' The next level was rule conformity, with authority residing outside of oneself. Third consisted of an organized body of internalized moral rules, minimally influenced by others' rules and unable to be internally questioned or tested. Last, ''rational-altruistic'' conscience was characterized by a firm set of internalized principles, accessible to rational questions and testing, which changes and deepens as new experiences are encountered, new action is tested, and consequences are assessed and reflected back into the deliberations.

The third central theme revealed in this longitudinal study of moral development is the capacity to love. For example, the amoral and expedient character types essentially feel unloved and are nearly incapable of unselfish affection for others. The rational-altruistic person, on the other extreme, is both well-loved and also loving, warm, and spontaneously affectionate.

Peck and Havighurst conclude that character can be defined in terms of action patterns and emotion-laden attitudes that tend to become habituated. Further, there is an empirically defined character that tends to persist through the years. Further, they emphasize, one's character is learned during the first ten years of life, shaped primarily by interactions with one's parents. The character of an individual ''is the direct reproduction of the way his parents treat him'' (1960:178). In other words, character is developed in growing children through the emulation of the behavior and attitudes of their parents.

C.   Kohlberg's Moral Stages and the Ethic of Justice

Perhaps the most discussed theory of moral development is that of Lawrence Kohlberg. He disagreed with earlier philosophical attempts to identify character traits of morally mature individuals, as a ''bag of virtues.'' He argued that the various lists of virtues that had emerged in philosophical discussions were arbitrary, the definitions of the virtues were relative to the particular culture from which they emerged, and they were psychologically vague (Kohlberg, 1984). In addition, when he first published his theory in 1954 there was little evidence of unified character traits in the moral behavior of children (this same dilemma is also what inspired Peck and Havighurst to conduct their classic study).

Kohlberg preferred a morality of principles, particularly the principle of justice, and argued that justice is the only master virtue, the only principle for resolving moral conflict (Kohlberg, 1981a). The morally mature adult is one who reasons with, and acts on the basis of, abstract principles of justice to arrive at ''right action'' (Kohlberg, 1981a). From this perspective, character is ''defined solely in terms of cognitive structures, or ways of thinking and judging'' (Kohlberg, 1981b:4).

Moral conduct is related to levels of judgment and follows a hierarchical sequence of developmental stages or levels in which an individual progressively moves toward basing moral judgment on concepts and principles of justice (see Stewart and Sprinthall's chapter in this volume for further detail on this model).[6] The highest level of moral reasoning is the postconventional, autonomous, or principled level. This level initially had two distinct stages focusing on fairness and justice: the first emphasizes respect for others' rights, equality, and mutual obligation, relativism of personal values and the need for procedural rules in reaching consensus. The second stage emphasizes principles of conscience that are comprehensive, consistent, universal, and abstract (much like Kant's categorical imperative) rather than concrete (like the Ten Commandments). One is guided at this level "by universal ethical principles that all humanity should follow" (Kohlberg, 1981a:412).

Although Kohlberg did not specifically describe how one with moral character would behave or act, several characteristics are evident. First, individuals with moral character would be independent, autonomous, purely rational decision-makers (similar to Kant's implied notion of moral character). In resolving interpersonal and social conflicts, moral choice is fundamentally the cognitive application of a general rule or principle of justice. Kohlberg states that "moral judgments are not reducible to, nor directly expressive of, emotive statements, but rather describe reasoning or reasons for action where reasons are different from motives" (1984:215). One who is guided by the general principle of justice is impartial and disinterested, a stance that requires an individual to abstract oneself from particular attachments—for example, from one's personal history, relationships, and physicality—in order to make crucial moral decisions (Bluestein, 1991).

This particular image of the morally mature individual that resolves moral dilemmas through the reasoned, impartial application of justice, has been the center of many criticisms of Kohlberg's theory. Ross (1991) argues that this characterizes a morally mature person not only as disinterested, but also as isolated and disembodied. Loevinger's (1987) and Gilligan's (1982) studies of women highlight additional aspects in making moral choices, particularly the concern for relationships, interpersonal responsibility, and an ethic of care as the ultimate value or principle, rather than an ethic of justice.

IV. "HIGH" CHARACTER: STRENGTH AND GOODNESS

Given the review of the nature of character above, two major conclusions can be drawn. First, it is clear that character is more than a master virtue or the sum of individual, discrete virtues. This is the conclusion of both the philosophers and psychologists discussed in this chapter. From either a psychological perspective or a philosophical framework, it seems difficult to identify one feature that is essential to a person of moral character. Thus, exemplary character can be best understood as a process that requires multiple habits or competencies.

The second major conclusion is that character emerges from a morality of feelings as well as a morality of thought. Peck and Havighurst concluded that "intellect and emotion are essential components" (1960).[7] Aristotle's practical reasoning relied on both deliberation and passion. Character appears to require both an ethic of reason and an ethic of care. This departs, however, from both Kohlberg and Gilligan, who argue that moral reasoning is oriented around either justice or caring, with most individuals primarily focusing on one orientation to the exclusion of the other. For Gilligan it is a set of moral criteria focusing on concern for relationships and others. For Kohlberg, it is a focus on principled reasoning and justice. Gilligan even suggested that these two orientations were fundamentally incompatible (1986). Yet at least one empirical investigation indicates that "most individuals use a considerable mix of both orientations—with no clear preference or focus" (Walker et al., 1987:856). Even Max Weber argued that "neither ethic should be rejected; we must learn to live with both, and with the conflicts between them" (quoted in Larmore, 1987:xiii).

At the personal level, knowing the difference between right and wrong is not enough; caring about the difference is also required for moral character. It is not enough to have the capacity to reason abstractly about rules or consequences. Moral character requires the capacity for empathy, caring about how the well-being of people is affected by one's breach or observance of those rules (see, for example, Gilligan, 1982; Noddings, 1984; Bluestein, 1991) and the consequences of one's actions. A two-pronged approach to character thus emerges: one of impartial reason of rights, justice, and consequences (e.g., Kant, Bentham, and Kohlberg) and one of human concern, empathy, and love (e.g., Confucius, Peck and Havighurst, and Gilligan). Put another way, character and community are related (see Cochran 1982 as well).

One could also conceive of these differing approaches in terms of strength versus goodness of character. Strength of character can be simply understood as strength of will (McDougall, 1927) or consistence of habit; however, one with strong will can pursue either goals that are self-centered or goals that are directed to the greater well-being of others. Goodness of character (capacity for caring, empathy, and jen) typically considers the impact of an action on others, but if there is no strength of character, the individual will be swept away with a variety of immediate good deeds with little recognition of longer-term commitments and responsibilities. Although specific manifestations of moral character vary from one person to another, a person of exemplary character has a character that is both strong and good. We argue that both these components are required for good character. We refer to this combination of strong and good character as "high" character and believe it is particularly important for those in the public service. Before explaining, however, further discussion of strength and goodness of character is necessary.

A. Strength of Character

First and foremost, character strength requires the individual to understand the accepted rules and norms of the community or profession. These standards (Confucius called them the li) provide the customary practices that must be considered (see Pugh, 1991, for an elaboration of the li of public administration). But blind obedience to such codes can actually clog and stunt the growth of a strong character. The moral dilemmas and choices facing an individual in the public service can require considerably more reflection and deliberation than encompassed in a code, a set of rules or principles. As Bailey noted several years ago, there is an inherent moral ambiguity in all public policies, there are rich and often conflicting contextual forces in the political and economic environment, and there are "paradoxes of procedures" in the public service (1965). A rigid, literal insistence on formal rules or principles will not work, and can even backfire sometimes (see Harris, 1997 for more).

Aristotle's practical reasoning or Confucius' yi is thus required in moral judgment and includes the ability to see interrelations among the various elements in a real-life situation. It also includes the ability to generalize and apply a principle in terms appropriate to the situation, to foresee the results of any action he or she takes (Peck and Havighurst, 1960), to consider and think critically about multiple perspectives, and the capacity to make connections through time (Bluestein, 1991). These multiple competencies inherent in practical reasoning or yi are based on three specific core elements of a strong character: ego strength, capacity for high levels of abstraction, and identity-conferring commitments.

1. Ego Strength

Ego strength has several important benefits with regard to character. First, it allows one to ensure a form of self-control that "by holding in check impulses excited by what is immediately present, allows the cognitive harvest of our reasoning powers to have an effect on what to do" (Coles, 1981:121). It was also the first common theme that Peck and Havighurst (1960) found in their analysis of adolescent moral behavior. Similarly, Loevinger's (1987) empirical studies of moral development showed that ego strength or "impulse control" was a significant element in character development. Furthermore, a person of weak ego, or weak character, may be impulsive and yield to temptations quickly. For them "the future means nothing more than the expectancy of immediate pleasure" (Allport, 1955:76).[8] Second, ego strength provides the inner security to allow one to engage in critical self-reflection. This includes the reflective examination of values and internalized moral principles that, upon experience, need modification and redirection (Peck and Havighurst, 1960). Finally, ego strength provides the self-respect and self-regard often necessary to do what is morally right. Acting morally is "sometimes so disruptive of social rhythms as to be acutely embarrassing" (Kupperman, 1991:172). Someone without ego strength tends to be an extreme conformist who habitually does what others expect of him or her. Ego strength is the prerequisite for what Hart (1984) calls "moral heroism" or moral courage.

2. High Levels of Abstraction

Being able to resist temptation and immediate pressures for conformity requires one to think and plan beyond the moment, more specifically the ability to think in the long-term and to consider multiple perspectives (see Jaques, 1976 for an elaboration on abstraction). This capacity is particularly noticeable in individuals of strong character. They have developed what Dewey and Tufts refer to as a "habit of greater thoughtfulness in the future" (1925:464), the "intelligent forethought of ends and resolute endeavor to achieve them" (p. 246). There is a focus on the future gains and impacts of one's actions rather than on the immediate consequences of the act. This setting of future intentions commits an individual to long-term projects, people, and other forms of connection. In addition, it also constrains more immediate actions. Focusing on the future does not allow one to be indifferent to the present; a future intention requires appropriate immediate strategies to attain future goals (Sherman, 1989). Such long-term thinking establishes and maintains connection among what to others could seem to be entirely separate and unconnected projects, actions, or behaviors (Kupperman, 1991).

3. Identity-Conferring Commitments

At its deepest level, morality is a motley collection of ultimate commitments (Larmore, 1987). For some, developing and pursuing commitments is the essence of will or will power in that it "displays great energy and steadfastness along certain lines of action" (McDougall, 1927:79). Others define the ability to hold to commitments as integrity (Bluestein, 1991; see also Dobel, 1988 and 1990). Either way, strong character is tied to having commitments. First, it involves a commitment to moral or virtuous conduct. Being committed to moral conduct means not merely having different goals from someone whose commitment to virtuous conduct is wavering or shallow. Second, faithful commitments are made to such things as principles, causes, ideas, and people, which eventually become core commitments that reflect what is most important to individuals, and thus attain a ''privileged status'' in their lives (Bluestein, 1991). Core commitments reflect an individual's centrally important values and become identity-conferring commitments (Taylor, 1985) which contribute to one's identity, make us what we are, and place constraints on our actions.

A person with weak character may feel prompted to act contrary to one's core commitments or may allow other people's expectations to easily overwhelm one's own shallow commitments. One with weak character typically has only very tentative loyalties to anything, relationships or causes (Kupperman, 1991). Some individuals, though strongly tempted to abandon their commitments, resist temptation by sheer effort of will; nevertheless, this too is not strong character. Even with intense or competing desires, individuals with strong character have such strong will and firm commitments that they do not have to make much of an effort at self-control (Bluestein, 1991). However, on-going core commitments do require continuous choice and reaffirmation; they create integrating and unifying connections throughout one's life, resulting in a sense of personal integrity as well as a ''situation-resistant interconnectedness of lived experience'' (Kupperman, 1991:143). Whatever the commitment, the person with strong character is someone who cares deeply. Indifference is incompatible with the possession of strong commitments. The object of one's caring is the essence of one's goodness of character.

B. Goodness of Character

Yet, having strong character does not guarantee having good character. One with strong commitments to monstrous goals or harmful ends may not necessarily exhibit a particularly good character. Similarly, strong self-regard or ego strength does not ensure goodness of action; one may merely act with a strong will to satisfy one's long-term self-interests, regardless of the impact on the well-being of others. In discussing moral character, goodness must also be a preeminent consideration (Kupperman, 1988). It is the intent to do good or ill to other people that is the subject of debate among many ancient and modern philosophers. For many, it is development of self-control in order to ensure the well-being of others that is the hallmark of an ethical person. In discussing exemplary character in the public service, one must include the feelings, attitudes, and dispositions toward others' well-being. As society becomes more complex, Hart notes, citizens are less able to be involved in self-governance and ''must rely upon others to care enough to represent them fully'' (1992:117). Thus, goodness of character requires an ''allocentric'' versus ''autocentric'' perception (Schactel, 1959), care and *jen*, or the active concern for the well-being of humans and non-humans, and prosocial behaviors such as empathy (Kohn, 1990) and love (Peck and Havighurst, 1960). These qualities go beyond traditional definitions of altruism and incorporate a concern for others that is fundamentally based on a sense of connectedness and interrelatedness with other people.

1. Allocentric Perception

Goodness of character requires first a shift in one's attention away from a preoccupation with self-interest. Walker Percy (1980) called this the ''great suck of self,'' or the tendency for self-absorption, to pull toward one's own thoughts, own pleasure, or personal self-interests. Schactel referred to this preoccupation with self the ''autocentric'' perception,

> where objects are perceived from the perspective of how they will serve a certain need of the perceiver, or how they can be used by him for some purpose, how they can be avoided in order to prevent pain, displeasure, injury or discomfort . . . the predomi-

nating feature of the perception is not the object in its own right, but those of its aspects which relate to the perceiver's more or less conscious feelings of the need or purpose which the object is to serve (1959:83).

Care and concern for others based on a strong sense of self-regard (or ego strength) is called an "allocentric" perception. This is "where the emphasis is on what the object is like. . . . The perceiver usually approaches or turns to the object actively and either opens himself toward it receptively, figuratively, or literally, takes hold of it, tries to grasp" it (Schactel 1959:167). When applied broadly, the allocentric perspective engenders a broad concern for the good of people one has never met. At an interpersonal level, it represents interactions between persons characterized by mutual reciprocity and concern for others' interests.

2. Care and Jen

One of the aims of good character is the care, concern, development, and flourishing of others (Flanagan, 1991). The interest and capacity to care about others and the natural world shifts attention away from one's self and are closely related to good character. Although care has many definitions (see Bluestein 1991) it is best understood for our purposes as "caring about" rather than "caring for," and has two key aspects. The first is non-personal care, which focuses on aspects of the world in a detached way. This is similar to jen, which is Confucius' conception of the greater, active concern for the welfare and well-being of humans and non-humans. A person who embodies jen has steady preferences and concern for such things as amelioration of suffering, and respect for diversity of individual life plans and styles of life within a moral community. Personal care, on the other hand, focuses on specific persons rather than on persons as instances of a general type, and can be seen in the tender care of someone we love. Care is different and distinct from commitment: one can "care about a wide diversity of things—people, ideas, causes—but one may not necessarily be committed to them. People care about the objects of their commitment, but not everything or everyone people care about is an object of their commitment" (Bluestein, 1991:38).

3. Prosocial Skills: Empathy and Love

Prosocial skills refer to actions undertaken by individuals by deliberative choice (voluntarily and intentionally) to benefit someone else (Eisenberg, 1982). Prosocial, however, stands for a wide diversity of actions. Kohn (1990) argues that empathy is one of the underlying foundations of most prosocial skills, and that these are revealed most clearly in recent studies on moral development. Gilligan (1982) found, in her classic book, *In a Different Voice*, that women view moral dilemmas in terms of relationships and are more likely to make moral decisions based on their care and sensitivity to the needs of others. Women reason differently than men when confronted with a moral problem. Female reasoning tends to be based on relationship rather than individuality, attachment rather than autonomy, and the injunction of care rather than the injunction of respect for the rights of others (Ross, 1991). This sense of relatedness and empathy is one of the key criteria in moral choices by women. (See Scranton and Ranney's chapter on gender differences in this volume for a more extensive discussion of this topic.) Other empirical investigations, however, indicate that men also use this orientation (see, for example, Walker et al., 1987). Peck and Havighurst (1960) specifically found that empathy and love are highly characteristic of the rational-altruistic moral character of adolescent boys.

Empathy is the capacity to appreciate another's attitude from his or her point of view. Kohn (1990) described it as a "feeling into" rather than a "feeling with," and is different from sympathy, which is "feeling for." It is both an active and receptive way of understanding others, even if they are not present, or if one does not know them (Eisenberg and Strayer, 1987; Held, 1993; Okin, 1989). One aspect of empathy is perspective taking, which is the process by which an individual imagines the "ways another individual thinks about, feels in response to, or literally sees the world" (Kohn, 1990:101). A second aspect of empathy is relatedness; it is based on a model of relatedness that recognizes a connection with others, an interdependence that "ripples out concentrically from our loved ones to those we know to everyone else" (Kohn, 1990:266). This definition does not emerge from a traditional sense of altruism—an individual helping another individual without consideration for personal gain. Rather, it is a predisposition to help those "with whom we feel a personal connection for reasons that are neither egoistic nor altruistic" (Kohn, 1990:266). It is empathy based on the jen conceptions of interconnections, a sense of connectedness with other people, rather than an empathy of separate, autonomous individuals. In other words, it is based on "how can I help us?" rather than "how can I help you?"

The theme of love also typifies one of good character. Peck and Havighurst found that as one develops morally, he or she becomes more able to love others (and also becomes more loved by others). Individuals with good character experience some sense of connectedness with other people, are able to feel an active concern for the well-being of others, and can form personal attachments with selected individuals. They can love in a genuinely constructive way, not making excessive demands on those he or she loves, and can love others unconditionally without insisting on anything in return. He or she can express affection warmly and spontaneously, within specific cultural constraints, and shows both "good intentions and accurate judgment in their treatment of other people" (Peck and Havighurst, 1960:172).

Thus, high character is a product of both the strength of one's character, as well as the goodness of that same character. Although there are diverse routes to the achievement of high character, common to them all is the ability of individuals to free themselves from the contingencies of the present and to project into the future the implications of their essential "identity-conferring" moral commitments. Furthermore, people of high character must possess, to a great degree, the power of self-command. In other words, they can trust themselves to act upon their moral commitments in the future, regardless of the conditions of that future—a much-desired quality in a public servant. As Adam Smith wrote: "The most perfect knowledge, if it is not supported by the most perfect self-command, will not always enable him to do his duty" (Smith, 1976:237).

Obviously, the attainment and maintenance of high character requires an integration of reason and emotions. Dewey and Tufts (1925:83) emphasize that "(a)dequate thoughtfulness is possible only when there is sympathetic interest in others." This quality of character is often referred to as benevolence and consists of the capacity for and interest in an allocentric care for others, as well as the critical qualities of empathy and love. Thus, high character is a lofty and difficult goal—a goal never to be attained, since it is a life-long process. And, the constant striving for high character should be the most distinguishing of the public life.

As noted throughout the chapter, the psychological evidence supports the fact that the attainment of high character is a quest, rather than a destination, a quest that never ends. Certainly, a great number of moral philosophers support the same conclusion:

that the search, attainment, and progress of high character constitutes the very definition of the good life. The important point here is that once an individual attains high character, he or she cannot back off and let it rest at that. To put it colloquially, "use it or lose it."

By now it is clear that character is powerfully shaped in the first decade of life, which has led to extensive work about character formation and childhood (through adolescence). We also know that those of high character have a continuing openness to new experiences, along with an inherent disposition to "continue to grow, to experiment, to incorporate new facts and to develop new depths of understanding" (Peck and Havighurst, 1960:10). Thus, character growth comes from an individual's decision—which must be both intentional and voluntary—to constantly expand one's understanding of the moral purposes of one's life, a deliberate enlargement of one's areas of moral concern.[9]

In conclusion, let us look at some of the unique reasons why high character is critical for the public service and public leadership more specifically.

V. THE NEED FOR "HIGH" CHARACTER IN THE PUBLIC SERVICE

The final question to be answered in this chapter is why character is relevant in public leadership and administration. In order to answer this question, one must have a basic understanding of the context of public administration.

Much of the work of public administration focuses on addressing public issues and problems—which differs significantly from other generic administrative or management processes. In other words,

> Public problems are interconnected, they cross organizational and jurisdictional boundaries, and they are interorganizational. No single agency, organization, jurisdiction, or sector has enough authority, influence, or resources to dictate visionary solutions. Thus, contemporary strategies for organizational leadership are less effective in addressing public problems in an interconnected world (Luke, 1998:xiv).

The interconnected nature of public administration thus requires unique skills and competencies of its leaders. These requirements differ from those of other sectors (i.e., business, not-for-profit). For example, dealing with interconnected problems raises issues of shared power and fragmentation of authority (Bryson and Crosby, 1992). Luke states that

> (p)ublic leadership is essentially a transorganizational leadership process of focusing attention and mobilizing or catalyzing a diverse set of individuals and agencies to address a public problem. It is a type of leadership that evokes collaboration and concerted action among diverse and often competing groups toward a shared outcome. A leadership that evokes collaboration rather than followership can create a critical mass of action that has a long-term impact on addressing public problems. This type of public leadership can be characterized as catalytic rather than heroic or visionary. While corporate leadership hinges on influencing followers over whom one has legitimate authority, (public) leadership stimulates action among people over whom one has little or no authority (1998:33).

Given this, there are several reasons why good character is necessary in public leaders (both elected and bureaucrat).

First, public leaders have an obligation as stewards of the common good. Critical to this is a deep concern for others. As discussed throughout the chapter, the capacity to care for others is a key attribute of high character. Many of the issues and problems that public servants confront on a daily basis focus on the well-being of citizens. As such, leaders must have the strength and goodness of character to not lose sight of that overarching goal in day-to-day administration. As Luke (1998:228) puts it, "(i)t is not enough to have the capacity to reason abstractly about systemic interconnections and ripple effects. Strong character requires caring about how the well-being of people is affected by one's actions."

In a related way, high character is required of public leaders because one must have a sense of connectedness and relatedness with the parties directly and indirectly affected by the issues with which one is involved. This includes the ability to see things from multiple perspectives, which is particularly important in the interconnected world of public administration. Also known as empathy, this process of imagining the way another "thinks about, feels in response to, or literally sees the world" (Kohn, 1990:101) is critical to successful negotiations (Fisher et al., 1994). Leaders that have this ability are more likely to find common interests and thus agreeable outcomes and solutions.

Third, public leaders of high character also have integrity and the corresponding quality of interpersonal trust. These are clearly valued in any leader, but they are especially helpful to public leaders. Integrity, or the consistent action resulting from a well-ordered set of commitments and beliefs (Dobel, 1990) is the foundation of trust. Trust refers to the capacity to depend on and place confidence in the actions of others.[10] Although integrity and trust is the foundation of almost all social interaction, it is fundamental to public leadership because it is "the underlying foundation for cooperative, collaborative, and collective efforts to address interconnected public problems" (Luke, 1998:233). Most work of public leaders and administrators involves cooperation and collaboration; thus trust and, subsequently, character play prominent roles in public leadership.

The purpose of this chapter has been to provide a basis for discussing the role and importance of character in the public service. By reviewing the philosophical and psychological approaches to character, one starts to see the most important aspects of character emerge. Good or high character requires both strength and goodness of character. One must have multiple habits or competencies in long-range thinking, strong core commitments that are "identity-conferring," an active concern for the well-being of humans and non-humans, empathy, and the ability for "perspective taking." Although conduct is influenced by norms and standards of one's community and profession, individuals of high character examine and reflect on ends, consider the consequences of their actions on others, cultivate and embody certain feelings of caring and empathy, and emphasize the collective interests of the group, organization, community, or jurisdiction. Because of the nature of public administration, these are clearly necessary qualities of effective public leaders.

Psychological studies also show that character is shaped by external influences that are most powerful in the first decade of life. Individuals may have actually developed their core character by the time they are morally reflective adults. Yet these same psychological studies indicate that those who have high character (strong and good) have a continuing openness to new experience and a tendency to continue to grow and refine one's character. Growth in character essentially results from an expansion of ends and an enlargement of one's circle of concern. This continual transformation of self is dependent on conditions of internal readiness as well as environmental factors such as exemplary role models with whom one has direct contact. Nevertheless, it is apparent that high character is a lifelong process of self-education.

Finally, character is such an integral part of the self that it would be difficult, if not impossible, to distinguish between one's private and professional character. Effective public leadership over the long-term will require leaders of high character. Thus, more emphasis needs to placed on electing, appointing, and hiring public servants of good character. How that will happen is the subject of other important work, yet the debate needs to grounded in an understanding of character and its place in the public service.

NOTES

1. See especially the work of William D. Richardson (1997; Richardson and Nigro, 1987; and Richardson et al., 1999) and J. Patrick Dobel (1988; 1990; 1998), as well as Galston (1988) and Davis (1988) for more of this work as it relates to the public service.
2. See *The Republic* and *Laws* for Plato's views on character. Otherwise, consult Dewey and Tufts (1925), or Strauss (1975) for more.
3. Nancy Sherman (1997) argues that this line is not as distinct as previously thought. She makes a compelling argument that Kant's moral theory has surprising similarities to that of Aristotle's.
4. Allport explains that it is a special attentiveness or accessibility to certain types of stimuli, standing predilections and aversions, with an acquired predisposition to ways or general modes of response, rather than the mere recurrence of specific, particular acts (Allport, 1968).
5. This quotation, attributed to Gordon Allport, comes from the lecture notes of Robert Coles (1981, 1989), a student of Allport at Harvard.
6. Kohlberg argues that children operate at the preconventional level while most adults function at the conventional level. Few people reach the postconventional level of mature reasoning. In response to many critics, he revised his theory several times. For example, he revised stage 6, because he found it so rare in adults, and made it an advanced form of stage 5 (Kohlberg, 1978). Stage 6 now figures merely as a hypothetical ideal. Yet, he also suggested the existence of a stage 7, a contemplative state of reasoning characterized by non-ego and non-dualism (Kohlberg, 1973). For general discussions and critiques see: Kohlberg, 1981a; Rich and De-Vitis, 1985; Modgil and Modgil, 1985; and Flanagan, 1991. For discussion of the measurement process, see Kohlberg, 1981b. See Stewart and Sprinthall (1991 and 1993) for measurement strategies for public administrators.
7. This is an age-old debate and there is a vast literature on the topic. See Cooper (1999) for a thorough overview of this issue, and May, Friedman, and Clark (1995) and Sabini and Silver (1998) for recent and representative work in this area.
8. An interesting side benefit is suggested by Mischel and Gilligan (1964), who found that children who chose a delayed, larger reward over a smaller, immediate reward were significantly less likely to cheat.
9. This quality of high character was known by the term magnanimity in the 18th century.
10. See the special issue on trust in and between organizations in the *Academy of Management Review* (1998, vol. 23, number 3) for an excellent overview.

REFERENCES

Adams, G. and Balfour, D. (1998). *Unmasking Administrative Evil*. Sage Publications, Beverly Hills, CA.

Allport, G. (1937). *Personality: A Psychological Interpretation*. Holt, New York.

Allport, G.W. (1955). *Becoming: Basic Considerations for a Psychology of Personality*. Yale University Press, New Haven.

Allport, G. (1968). *Person in Psychology: Selected Essays*. Beacon Press, Boston.

Aristotle. (1980). *The Nicomachean Ethics* (D. Ross, trans.). Oxford University Press, New York.

Bailey, S.K. (1964). Ethics and the public service. *Public Administration Review*, 24:234–243.

Bailey, S.K. (1965). The relationship between ethics and public service. In: *Public Administration and Democracy: Essays in Honor of Paul Appleby* (R. Martin, ed.). Syracuse University Press, Syracuse, NY, pp. 283–298.

Bentham, J. (1989). The principle of utility. In: *Vice and Virtue in Everyday Life* (C. Sommers and F. Sommers, eds.). Harcourt Brace Jovanovich, Orlando, FL.

Bluestein, J. (1991). *Care and Commitment: Taking the Personal View*. Oxford University Press, New York.

Bowman, J. (1990). Ethics in government: a national survey of public administrators. *Public Administration Review*, 50:345–353.

Brady, F.N. (1988). Ethical theory and the public service. In: *Papers on the Ethics of Administration* (N.D. Wright, ed.). Brigham Young University Press, Provo, UT, pp. 225–243.

Bryson, J.M. and Crosby, B.C. (1992). *Leadership for the Common Good*. Jossey-Bass, San Francisco.

Chandler, R.C. (1983). The problem of moral reasoning in American public administration: the case for a code of ethics. *Public Administration Review*, 43:32–39.

Cochran, C. (1982). *Character, Community, and Politics*. University of Alabama Press, Tuscaloosa, AL.

Coles, R. (1981). On the nature of character: field notes. *Vice and Virtue in Everyday Life* (C. Sommers and F. Sommers, eds.). Harcourt Brace Jovanovich, Orlando, FL.

Cooper, J. (1999). *Reason and Emotion*. Princeton University Press, Princeton, NJ.

Cooper, T. (1987). Hierarchy, virtue, and the practice of public administration: a perspective for normative ethics. *Public Administration Review*, 47:320–328.

Cooper, T. and Wright, N.D., eds. (1992). *Exemplary Public Administrators*. Jossey-Bass, San Francisco.

Cua, A.S. (1992). Competence, concern, and the role of the paradigmatic individuals (chun-tzu) in moral education. *Philosophy East and West*, 42:49–68.

Davis, M. (1988). Civic virtue, corruption, and the structure of moral theories. In: *Midwest Studies in Philosophy, Volume XIII* (P.A. French, T.E. Uehling, and H.K. Wettstein, eds.). University of Notre Dame Press, Notre Dame, IN, pp. 352–366.

Denhardt, K. (1988). *The Ethics of Public Service: Resolving Moral Dilemmas in Public Organizations*, Greenwood Press, New York.

Denhardt, K. (1991). Unearthing the moral foundations of public administration. *Ethical Frontiers in Public Management* (J. Bowman, ed.). Jossey Bass, San Francisco.

Dewey, J. (1922). *Human Nature and Conduct*. H. Holt and Co., New York.

Dewey, J. and Tufts, J.H. (1925). *Ethics*. Holt and Company, New York.

Dobel, J.P. (1988). Personal responsibility and public integrity. *Michigan Law Review*, 86:1450–1453.

Dobel, J.P. (1990). Integrity in the public service. *Public Administration Review*, 50:354–365.

Dobel, J.P. (1998). Political prudence and the ethics of leadership. *Public Administration Review*, 58:74–81.

Eisenberg, N. (1982). *The Development of Prosocial Behavior*. Academic Press, New York.

Eisenberg, N., and Strayer, J. (1987). *Empathy and its Development*. Cambridge University Press, Cambridge.

Fisher, R., Kopelman, E. and Schneider, A. (1994). *Beyond Machiavelli: Tools for Coping with Conflict*. Harvard University Press, Cambridge.

Flanagan, O. (1991). *Varieties of Moral Personality: Ethics and Psychological Realism*. Harvard University Press, Cambridge.

Fromm, E. (1947). *Man for Himself: An Inquiry into the Psychology of Ethics*. Rhinehart and Co., New York.

Galston, W. (1988). Liberal virtues. *American Political Science Review*, 82:1277–1290.

Gibson, D.R., Malerstein, A.J., Ahern, M., and Jones, R.D. (1989). Character structure and performance on the MMPI. *Psychological Reports*, 65:1139–1149.

Gilligan, C. (1982). *In a Different Voice*. Harvard University Press, Cambridge.

Gilligan, C. (1986). Remapping the moral domain: new images of the self in relationship. In: *Reconstructing Individualism: Autonomy, Individuality and Self in Western Thought* (T.C. Heller, M. Sosna, and D. Wellbery, eds.). Stanford University Press, Stanford, CA.

Halevy, E. (1928). *The Growth of Philosophic Radicalism*. Macmillan, New York.

Hardie, W.F.R. (1980). *Aristotle's Ethical Theory*. Clarendon Press, Oxford.

Harris, G.W. (1997). *Dignity and Vulnerability: Strength and Quality of Character*. University of California Press, Berkeley.

Hart, D.K. (1984). The virtuous citizen, the honorable bureaucrat, and "public" administration. *Public Administration Review*, 44:111–119.

Hart, D.K. (1992). The moral exemplar in an organizational society. In: *Exemplary Public Administrators* (T.L. Cooper and N.D. Wright, eds.). Jossey Bass, San Francisco, pp. 9–29.

Hauerwas, S. (1981). *A Community of Character*. University of Notre Dame Press, Notre Dame, IN.

Held, V. (1993). *Feminist Morality*. University of Chicago Press, Chicago.

Hogan, R. (1973). Moral conduct and moral character: a psychological perspective. *Psychological Bulletin*, 79:217–232.

Hunt, L. (1997). *Character and Culture*. Rowman and Littlefield Publishers, Lanham, MD.

Jaques, E. (1976). *A General Theory of Bureaucracy*. Halsted Press, New York.

Kant, I. (1898). *Fundamental Principles of the Metaphysics of Morals* (T.K. Abbott, trans.). Liberal Arts Press, New York.

Kierkegaard, S. (1962). *The Present Age*. Harper and Row, New York.

Kohlberg, L. (1973). Stages and aging in moral development: some speculations. *The Gerontologist*, 13:493–502.

Kohlberg, L. (1978). Revisions in the theory and practice of moral development. In: *Moral Development* (W. Damon, ed.). Jossey Bass, San Francisco.

Kohlberg, L. (1981a). *Essays on Moral Development: Volume 1*. Harper and Row, New York.

Kohlberg, L. (1981b). *The Meaning and Measurement of Moral Development*. Clark University Press, Worcester, MA.

Kohlberg, L. (1984). *Essays on Moral Development: Volume 2*. Harper and Row, New York.

Kohn, A. (1990). *The Brighter Side of Human Nature: Altruism and Empathy in Everyday Life*. Basic Books, New York.

Kupperman, J.J. (1988). Character and ethical theory. In: *Midwest Studies in Philosophy, Volume XIII* (P. A. French, T.E. Uehling, and H. K. Wettstein, eds.). University of Notre Dame Press, Notre Dame, IN, pp. 115–125.

Kupperman, J.J. (1991). *Character*. Oxford Press, New York.

Larmore, C.E. (1987). *Patterns of Moral Complexity*. Cambridge University Press, Cambridge.

Lilla, M. (1981). Ethos, "ethics," and public service. *The Public Interest*, 63:3–17.

Loevinger, J. (1987). *Paradigms of personality*. W.H. Freeman & Co., New York.

Luke, J. (1991). New leadership requirements for public administrators: from managerial to policy ethics. In: *Ethical Frontiers in Public Management* (J. Bowman, ed.). Jossey Bass, San Francisco.

Luke, J. (1998). *Catalytic Leadership*. Jossey-Bass, San Francisco.

MacIntyre, A. (1984). *After Virtue: A Study in Moral Theory*. University of Notre Dame Press, Notre Dame, IN.

May, L., Friedman, M., and Clark, A. (1995). *Mind and Morals: Essays on Cognitive Science and Ethics*. MIT Press, Cambridge, MA.

McDougall, W. (1927). *Character and the Conduct of Life*. G.P. Putnam's Sons Publishers, New York.

Mischel, W. and Gilligan, C. (1964). Delay of gratification: motivation for the prohibited gratification and response to temptation. *Journal of Abnormal and Social Psychology*, 69:411–417.

Mogdil, S. and Mogdil, C. (1985). *Lawrence Kohlberg: Consensus and Controversy*. Falmer Press, New York.

Munzel, F., and Felicitas, M. (1998). *Kant's Conception of Moral Character*. University of Chicago Press, Chicago.

Noddings, N. (1984). *Caring: A Feminine Approach to Ethics and Moral Education.* University of California Press, Berkeley.

Okin, S.M. (1989). Reason and feeling in thinking about justice. *Ethics*, 99:240–253.

Peck, R.F. and Havighurst, R.J. (1960). *The Psychology of Character Development.* Wiley and Sons, New York.

Percy, W. (1980). *The Second Coming.* Farrar, Straus & Giroux, New York.

Plato. (1986). *The Republic* (B. Jowett, trans.). Prometheus Books, Buffalo, NY.

Pugh, D.L. (1991). The origins of ethical frameworks in public administration. In: *Ethical Frontiers in Public Management* (J. Bowman, ed.). Jossey Bass, San Francisco.

Quinton, A. (1983, 1989). Character and culture. In: *Vice and Virtue in Everyday Life* (C. Sommers and F. Sommers, eds.). Harcourt Brace Jovanovich, Orlando, FL.

Railton, P. (1988). How thinking about character and utilitarianism might lead to rethinking the character of utilitarianism. In: *Midwest Studies in Philosophy, Volume XIII* (P.A. French, T.E. Uehling, and H. K. Wettstein, eds.). University of Notre Dame Press, Notre Dame, IN, pp. 398–416.

Rich, J.M. and DeVitis, J.L. (1985). *Theories of Moral Development.* Thomas Publishers, Springfield, IL.

Richardson, W.D. (1997). *Democracy, Bureaucracy, and Character: Founding Thought.* University of Kansas Press, Lawrence, KS.

Richardson, W.D., Martinez, J.M., and Stewart, K. (1999). *Ethics and Character: The Pursuit of Democratic Values.* Carolina Academic Press, Durham, NC.

Richardson, W.D., and Nigro, L.G. (1987). Administrative ethics and founding thought: constitutional correctives, honor, and education. *Public Administration Review*, 47:167–176.

Ross, M.E. (1991). Feminism and the problem of moral character. *Journal of Feminist Studies in Religion*, 5: 47–64.

Sabini, J., and Silver, M. (1998). *Emotion, Character, and Responsibility.* Oxford University Press, New York.

Schactel, E.G. (1959). *Metamorphosis: On the Development of Affect, Perception, Attention, and Memory.* Basic Books, New York.

Sherman, N. (1989). *The Fabric of Character: Aristotle's Theory of Virtue.* Clarendon Press, Oxford.

Sherman, N. (1997). *Making a Necessity of Virtue: Aristotle and Kant on Virtue.* Cambridge University Press, New York.

Smart, J.J. (1973). Utilitarianism. *Utilitarianism: For and Against* (J. J. Smart and B. Williams, eds.). Cambridge University Press, Cambridge.

Smith, A. (1976). *The Theory of Moral Sentiments.* Liberty Classics, Indianapolis, IN.

Stewart, D.W. and Sprinthall, N.A. (1991). Strengthening ethical judgment in public administration. In: *Ethical Frontiers in Public Management* (J. Bowman, ed.). Jossey Bass, San Francisco.

Stewart, D., and Sprinthall, N. (1993). The impact of demographic, professional, and organizational variables and domain on the moral reasoning of public administrators. In: *Ethics and Public Administration* (H.G. Frederickson, ed.). M.E. Sharpe, Armonk, NY, pp. 205–219.

Strauss, L. (1975). *The Argument and the Action of Plato's Laws.* University of Chicago Press, Chicago, IL.

Taylor, G. (1985). *Shame and Guilt.* Clarendon Press, Oxford.

Thomas, L. (1989). *Living Morally: A Psychology of Moral Character.* Temple University Press, Philadelphia.

Walker, L.J., de Vries, B., and Trevethan, S. (1987). Moral stages and moral orientation in real-life and hypothetical dilemmas. *Child Development*, 58:842–858.

Wilson, J.Q. (1993). *The Moral Sense.* The Free Press, New York.

Wilson, J.Q. (1995). *On Character.* The AEI Press, Washington, DC.

Wright, N.D. (1988 *Papers on the Ethics of Administration.* Brigham Young University Press, Provo, UT.

26

Gender Differences in Administrative Ethics

Anneka Marina Scranton
University of Southern California, Los Angeles, California

Molly J. Ranney
California State University, Long Beach, California

I. INTRODUCTION: THE FEMININE ETHICAL PERSPECTIVE AND FEMINIST THEORY

Sandra Hale, former Commissioner of Administration for the state of Minnesota and winner of the prestigious Ford Foundation Award for Innovation in Government, once described to me an incident at a large public personnel conference sponsored by a leading university. After a long series of panel speakers, a woman in the audience brought up her concern that individual competition reduced cooperation and teamwork; why were the speakers so focused on increasing competition? All four male panelists, academic experts, proceeded to describe her as "naive" and "soft"; they clearly felt confident that their position was superior to that of the unfortunate woman's. As the woman was being publicly embarrassed, Sandra stood up and spoke in her defense. Sandra (with whom I had discussed this chapter just the night before) gently suggested that there was perhaps a communication gap that might be related to gender. The public discussion ended, and the panel moved on to other questions. Several men came up later to privately thank Sandra for her comments and to inquire into the issue of a gender gap.

This incident dramatically illustrates the "different voice" (Gilligan, 1982) of women administrators, a voice that is alien, and perhaps highly threatening, to traditional male managers. The so-called "feminine" ethical perspective is emerging in the literature as a significant and powerful alternative to the highly individualistic approach which has dominated management philosophy. The feminine mode of ethical decision-making is based upon the maintenance of relationships, upon the importance of cooperation, connection, and concern for others. The activity of caring, within the concrete context of administrative behavior, is central to this morality. Responsibility to meet the needs of others lies at the core of the feminine perspective.

The author wishes to express her sincere appreciation to Debra Stewart and Robin Derry for their kind support and assistance, reflecting the feminine ethic of care.

The feminine perspective may or may not reflect the morality of a majority of women. There has been much recent debate around the empirical validity of gender differences. Although this chapter will briefly summarize the limited empirical findings, this author will argue that the feminine perspective is important to public administrators whether or not it is empirically linked to gender because it offers the *potential* of an alternative ethical framework for administrative behavior. The morality of care is significant to our moral discourse "not by gender but by theme" (Gilligan, 1982, p. 2). The feminine philosophy, whether articulated exclusively or even primarily by women, may increasingly challenge the mainstream approach to administrative ethics, an approach developed and sustained almost exclusively by men.

Whether the articulation of the feminine perspective will lead to actual changes in individual administrative behavior will depend, "feminists"* argue, upon changes in the structure and culture of organizations. As our incident illustrates, women who speak out (even to ask a question) in a different voice are often ignored, embarrassed, or dismissed by organizational leaders. Only the intervention of a powerful and highly respected woman rescued our female conference participant from further criticism. "Feminist," as opposed to "feminine," theorists argue that the power structure and traditional culture of bureaucratic organizations must be radically altered before the different voice of feminine morality can be heard (Kanter, 1977; Ferguson, 1984). Feminists take the alternative feminine morality and move the core issues of care and connection to the organizational level; they make the personal political. They argue for greater equality, diversity, participation, and cooperation within public bureaucracies. Feminist theorists attack all forms of competition, domination, and subordination that weaken or destroy genuine human relationships. Again, feminism is not equated with inherent differences between the philosophies of men and women; it is raised up as an alternative framework which has the potential to liberate both men and women within the corporate environment.

This chapter will begin with a discussion of the feminine or "care" mode of individual ethical reasoning. The care perspective on ethical decision-making will be contrasted with the traditional "justice" approach (Gilligan, 1982). The significance of the feminine challenge to individual rights philosophy will be discussed. Further, the care perspective on moral reasoning will be linked to virtue theory. Virtues traditionally attributed to women such as kindness, caregiving, and compassion will be emphasized. Some potential changes in administrative behavior that would result from the adoption of the feminine perspective on ethical reasoning and the promotion of feminine virtues are described. These hypothetical styles of administrative behavior are contrasted with existing studies of actual gender-based differences in ethical reasoning, values, and behavior among managers. It should be clear to the careful reader that women managers do not, on balance, act in a feminine manner.

The apparent discrepancy between theoretical and actual gender differences will be analyzed from a feminist perspective. Turning to the structural and cultural barriers to feminine behavior, I will summarize the feminist critique of traditional public and private bureaucracies. Finally, I will describe alternative feminist organizations that foster feminine values. These alternative organizations are committed to inclusiveness, diversity, and

---

* Following Ferguson (1984), this author will distinguish the feminist perspective on social ethics which calls for organizational and societal change and the feminine perspective which poses an alternative individual ethic.

empowerment—both within the organizational setting and within the political environment; they promote organizational and social change (Martin, 1990).

   This chapter thus focuses upon the four components of ethical behavior proposed
by Cooper (1990, p. 161): individual attributes, organizational structure, organizational
culture, and societal expectations. Individual attributes, primarily ethical decision-making
and personal virtues, along with societal expectations of individual behavior, are discussed
under the feminine perspective. Organizational culture, essentially organizational norms
and standards, and organizational structure are presented from a feminist approach. Actual
ethical conduct appears, I will hypothesize, to be more heavily influenced by organizational variables than by individual and societal values. I will conclude, therefore, with a
call for increased attention to the feminist critique of traditional organizational structure
and culture. The feminization of American public administration would require more than
a recognition, or even acceptance, of individual differences; it would require a transformation of our public organizations.

II. THE FEMININE PERSPECTIVE ON INDIVIDUAL MORALITY

The feminine perspective emphasizes the distinctive moral reasoning processes and virtues
that appear to be linked to gender in American society; this perspective is clearly related
to popular stereotypes of women as more nurturing and caring than men. The different
voice attributed to women is granted equal (and in some instances, preferred) status—
overcoming the strong bias within the ethical literature towards the male or justice position, the tendency in philosophy and psychology to "equate male with human" (Gilligan,
1987, p. 31). Responsibility toward particular others is, it is argued, a legitimate criteria
for ethical decision-making; caring is a noble endeavor.

A. Individual Attributes: Moral Reasoning

The debate over the legitimacy of a distinctively feminine perspective began essentially
in the early 1980s with the work of Carol Gilligan. Gilligan, a former student of Lawrence
Kohlberg, contested Kohlberg's theory of moral development, arguing that it was based
exclusively upon male development. She noted that women had generally scored poorly
on Kohlberg's scale, appearing immature in their moral reasoning. Women did not often
reach the highest level of moral development—the principled stage. Perhaps, Gilligan
hypothesized, the problem lay not with women but rather with the theoretical model of
development.

   According to Kohlberg (1976, 1981), individuals move through six stages of moral
development. At the highest stage, individuals come to recognize both their own right to
autonomy and the "natural" rights of others; they achieve a morality of "justice." Moral
maturity is based upon the acknowledgment of personal liberty and upon respect for the
dignity of other individuals. The equal rights of all members of society are acknowledged.

   Within the Kohlberg schema, therefore, mature moral decisions are made rationally
and are based upon abstract principles. Universal moral principles, centered upon the
dignity and the freedom of the individual, are the criteria for just decision. The individual
is granted the right to self-determination, to the pursuit of one's own interests, as long as
one does not interfere with the rights of others. In summary, the morally mature person,
within the justice perspective, is an "autonomous moral agent who discovers and applies

a set of fundamental rules through the use of universal and abstract reason'' (Kittay and Meyers, 1987, p. 3).

Carol Gilligan's research, however, led her to challenge the implicit assumptions of the justice perspective (1982, 1987). Women, she argues, also can pass through six stages of moral development, but they move towards a different ethical perspective—one based ''not on the primacy and universality of individual rights, but rather on . . . a very strong sense of being responsible to the world'' (1982, p. 32). In the Gilligan schema, the six stages are grouped into three levels. At the first level, the child is concerned with personal survival and strength; the focus is thus on meeting one's own needs. Upon moving to the second level, the girl rejects selfish behavior and becomes concerned with being part of the group. Conforming to rules and social norms becomes central to morality. Girls focus on being responsible and good to others.

Gradually, the social pressures to sacrifice self become too onerous, and the young woman begins a search for personal ''truth.'' Retrieving the judgmental initiative, the woman begins to ask whether it is selfish or responsible, moral or immoral, to include her own needs within the compass of her care and concern'' (1982, p. 82). The mature individual comes to understand the value of nurturing both self and others, of being responsive to the (often conflicting) demands of all those in her web of relationships. The well-being self, by stage six, is understood to be linked to the well being of others.

Women's morality is thus based upon connectiveness, upon ongoing interpersonal attachment and upon relationship. For women, the social world is ''comprised of relationships rather than of people standing alone, a world that coheres through human connection rather than through systems of rules'' (p. 29). Therefore, women seek to avoid hurting others and to respond in a caring and loving fashion to those around them. Doing the right thing depends upon the interpersonal context, upon the concrete needs of others in the situation—not upon the abstract principles of equality and reciprocity.

From the ''care'' perspective, therefore, the mature individual acknowledges not only his or her own desires, but also the needs and hopes of those in one's ''web of relationships.'' Self and others are perceived as interdependent; ''Women regard their selves as selves in relationship'' (Kittay and Meyers, 1987, p. 8). Caring for others also nurtures the relationships that sustain the self. ''Thus the logic underlying an ethic of care is a psychological logic of relationships, which contrasts with the formal logic of fairness that informs the justice approach'' (Gilligan, 1982, p. 73). The individual comes to ask not, ''What is right?,'' but ''How can I respond in a caring fashion?'' The individual seeks to prevent harm to others, to provide care, and to maintain connectiveness.

Gilligan has thus articulated two hypotheses about moral development: (1) that the care perspective is a distinctive moral voice, differing from the justice perspective and (2) that the care perspective reflects the ethical concerns of women, i.e., that there is a gender difference in ethical reasoning (Friedman, 1987; Derry, 1989). Both hypotheses are controversial, but the gender difference hypothesis has produced the greatest debate. Empirical studies (Friedman, 1987) have not supported the gender difference hypothesis. Yet, although a wide variety of studies have produced disconfirming evidence, there continues to be a great deal of support for Gilligan's hypothesis within the feminist community. Even researchers who find the disconfirming studies valid have commented that Gilligan's perspective ''resonates with their own experience as women'' (Greeno and Maccoby as quoted in Friedman, 1987, p. 93). Increasingly, scholars are seeking explanations for the apparent discrepancy between the results of Gilligan's own research and subsequent research. Turning away from the developmental approach, they are beginning to address the context of decision-making—the impact of environmental factors (Derry, 1989). Overall, it appears that the gender difference hypothesis will be under debate for some time to come.

For the purposes of this chapter, Gilligan's first hypothesis—that there are two distinctive modes of moral reasoning—is of greatest importance. Her work grants a moral perspective, based upon a recognition of interpersonal responsibility (rather than individual rights), new legitimacy. Marilyn Friedman (1987) argues that Gilligan has uncovered the "*symbolically* female moral voice and has disentangled it from the *symbolically* male moral voice" (p. 96). She believes that within our society moral work is divided, by and large, between men who are responsible for public justice and women who are responsible for private caregiving. "The genders have thus been conceived in terms of special and distinctive moral projects" (p. 94). Therefore, we assume, perhaps erroneously, that women are innately more concerned with care than justice. Carole Patemen (1984) also emphasizes that the association of women with the private domestic sphere and men with the public sphere of economics and politics leads to distinctive moral perspectives.

Seyla Benhabib has analyzed the dichotomy between justice and care in our society from a psycho-social perspective (1987). She argues that men, in leaving the nurture and care of their mothers and the security of the family, attempt also to distance themselves from the private morality of care. Benhabib states that:

> The split between the public sphere of justice, in which history is made, and the atemporal realm of the household, in which life is reproduced, is internalized by the male ego . . . I want to suggest that contemporary universalist theory has inherited this dichotomy between autonomy and nurturance, independence and bonding, this sphere of justice and the domestic, personal realm. (1987, p. 163)

Within the public sphere, men move towards relationships with the "generalized" other, relationships built upon norms of formal equality and reciprocity. These norms dominate political and economic institutions. Relationships to the "concrete" other, to actual friends and family members, are linked to the subordinate private realm, i.e., to the "women's sphere."

Other scholars have noted that this apparent division of moral labor by gender does not exist in many other cultures. For example, Robert Coles' studies of Eskimo culture provide some evidence of the care perspective dominating both male and female thinking (Coles, 1977). Sandra Harding has commented on the "curious coincidence" of feminine and African moralities (1987). Harding notes the many similarities between traditional African and modern feminist thinking and proposes a common source—oppression. Other scholars have linked the so-called feminine perspective to minority and subjugated groups within American society (Tronto, 1987).

The importance of these studies lies in the challenge to the universality of the justice position. The assumption, inherent in Kohlberg's work, that the rights perspective is the highest form of morality—applicable at all times, in all places—is under attack. The work of Carol Gilligan and subsequent theorists legitimizes an alternative framework— a framework that may be called the feminine or care perspective. Whether or not the care perspective is empirically linked to women in our society at this time is not the fundamental issue. The care perspective demands that the fundamental values of nurturing and caregiving be recognized and raised up in our society. It asks that the moral work attributed to women no longer be considered second class or subsidiary to the male work of protecting individual rights. "Gilligan's work implies the need to take women's experience seriously and to build feminist moral theory" (Kittay and Meyers, 1987, p. 13). Feminine moral theory thus recognizes the essential moral work of loving and caring that must be done in our society—work that can, in theory, be done by men or women. It recognizes the legitimacy and importance of interpersonal relationships and connections, granting relationships and connections equal moral status with individual rights.

In summary, the feminine perspective emphasizes (1) interpersonal responsibility and relationships rather than rights and rules, (2) concrete situations rather than formal and detached reasoning, and (3) the activity of care rather than abstract and universal principles (Tronto, 1987, p. 648). The feminine mode is reflexive, responding with love to particular others, rather than rationally predicting and assessing outcomes. The emphasis is upon inclusion and connection. Individuals recognize and respond to the web of their relationships, to the needs and concerns of concrete others. Whether or not individual women actually make ethical decisions based upon the feminine mode of reasoning may depend upon the context of the specific decision and upon the dominant culture.

B. Individual Attributes: Active Virtues

Recent feminine theorists have emphasized that women, beyond framing moral decisions differently, naturally behave in a more caring and nurturing fashion than men. Feminine virtues such as compassion, charity, and kindness are linked to the experiences of women as caregivers. Women learn through their work as primary caregivers to the dependent, most importantly through their work as mothers, to respond emphatically to the needs of others. Thus women, through their ongoing work of mothering and nurturing, acquire "active virtues" (in Hume's terms) rooted in deep emotional commitment and concern for particular others.

The concept of moral virtues, based upon the disciplined development of moral character, can, of course, be traced back to Aristotle. David Hume, in particular, has been called "the women's philosopher" because his concept of active virtues closely parallels the modern feminine approach. For Hume, morality is not obedience to universal law but rather cultivation of proper character traits through close interpersonal relationships, character traits "grounded in emotional and personal concern" (Kittay and Meyers, 1987, p. 8). Virtue is based upon the experience of sharing and caring, upon the pleasure of human company, and upon the maintenance of personal relationships.

Recent feminine scholars have stressed the importance of the mothering role in developing the active virtues of kindness and compassion. Nancy Chodorow, in *The Reproduction of Mothering* (1988), argues that because women provide primary child care, girls and boys develop differing capacities for caring and loving relationships. Girls become more skilled in and committed to interpersonal relationships. Boys, striving for independence and autonomy, repress their sensitive and sharing sides. Chodorow overturns the traditional superiority of autonomy and self-reliance, stressing the importance of relational skills for both sexes.

Virginia Held (1987) also asserts that mothering provides a unique opportunity for the development of active virtues. Mothering, she says, is not the only activity that generates commitment to concrete others.

> But mothering may be one of the best contexts in which to make explicitly clear why
> familiar moral theories are so deficient in offering guidance for action. And the variety

of contexts within mothering, with the different excellences appropriate for dealing with infants, young children, or adolescents, provide rich sources of insight for moral inquiry. (p. 118)

Caring for children is based upon natural warmth, empathy, and commitment; it is active love. Mothers respond automatically to the perceived needs of the child; action is grounded in emotion, not based upon abstract reasoning. Mothers learn to trust their emotions and empathetic instincts. They become increasingly sensitized to the concrete concerns and problems of others, increasingly skilled in caring and compassionate behavior.

In her book, *Caring: A Feminine Approach to Ethics and Moral Education* (1984), Nel Noddings provides an elaborate and elegant analysis of the relationship between the feminine work of caregiving and the development of active virtues such as kindness, compassion, and commitment. Emphasizing the natural goodness of the caring person, she develops a feminine morality rooted in "receptivity, relatedness, and responsiveness." Feminine morality is based upon "the sentiment of natural caring" demonstrated particularly by mothers and upon "the remembrance" of being cared for; "This memory of our best moments of caring and being cared for sweeps over us as a feeling—as an 'I must'— in response to the plight of the other and our conflicting desire to serve our own interests" (pp. 80–81). Experiences of mothering and being mothered are transferred to other interpersonal situations.* Women learn through their caring actions, becoming evermore receptive to opportunities to help others and evermore responsive to the needs of those around them.

Noddings concludes that the "mother's voice," the feminine spirit of caring, should be reasserted in contemporary philosophy. She, along with the previously noted scholars, condemns the presumed superiority of masculine virtues such as courage, self-reliance, independence, patriotism, and abstract benevolence. Commitment to immediate others, shown through gentleness, sympathy, thoughtfulness, self-sacrifice, generosity, and kindness, is the basis for active feminine virtues.

Feminine virtues, based upon experiences of caring and being cared for, are clearly linked to societal expectations and traditional gender roles. As described by recent scholars, feminine behavior reflects the private or domestic sphere—a sphere traditionally viewed as belonging to women. Chodorow, Held, and Noddings all recognize that men could—and, in fact, should—cultivate the virtues of caregiving.† By linking the caring virtues to women, they are raising up the importance of, indeed the nobility of, the caregiving work done most frequently in our society by women. Mothering, in particular, is viewed as a practice that promotes moral excellence. These scholars encourage women to recognize receptivity and responsiveness as moral strengths. Clearly, these theorists believe that the virtues of kindness, compassion, and generosity are superior virtues, superior to virtues traditionally associated with the public work of men. The cultivation of feminine virtues is, they argue, desirable for both men and women; a truly "kinder and gentler" society would enhance the quality of life for all citizens.

---

* Noddings believes that altruistic or prosocial behavior, helping others even at risk to our own self-interest, is "innate," latent in each human being. However, she argues that it is not "instinctive" as some scientists believe. Altruistic behavior must be learned through the experiences of caring relationships (see 1984, pp. 79–85).

† Indeed, in Sweden, for example, men are increasingly the primary caregivers—taking more sick child care leave than women.

C. Societal Expectations

In addition to the virtues cultivated through experiences of caregiving, women, it can be argued, display different ethical behavior patterns as a result of societal norms and expectations. Sexual stereotypes certainly remain strong in American culture and may influence individual behavior. Women are often expected to be kinder, warmer, gentler, and more cooperative than male colleagues in organizational settings. Further, in order to cope with hostile masculine corporate cultures, women may develop enhanced skills in networking and mutual support.

Popular stereotypes of gender differences continue to link women with qualities which some authors call ''communal.'' These qualities include: ''a concern for the welfare of others, the predominance of caring and nurturant traits; and to a lesser extent, interpersonal sensitivity, emotional expressiveness, and a gentle personal style'' (Friedman, 1987, p. 95). Women are expected to be more sympathetic and self-sacrificing, more concerned and generous. Women are commonly viewed as more intuitive, more emotional, and more passive while men are expected to be rational, controlled, and dominant. Female workers are expected to be more cooperative and considerate while male employees are understood to be more competitive and decisive (Kanter, 1977; Friedman, 1987; Rosener, 1995).

Although these stereotypes may appear trite and antiquated, there is strong social science data that they still exist in American culture (Friedman, 1987) and may continue to influence female behavior. As Friedman argues, there continues to be a clear distinction between the moral work associated with women, that is the symbolically female, and the moral work attributed to men, that is the symbolically male. Cultural myths and expectations continue to impact organizational life.

Some feminine scholars emphasize that cooperative and nurturing behavior could enable women to more effectively cope in the competitive economic and political spheres. Given women's historical role as primary caregivers, women have learned to assist one another in meeting responsibilities, have learned to work cooperatively. Women's kinship and networks have enabled individual women to survive grueling and competing demands around work and family. Connection and collaboration have been central to women's collective experience. As Lenz and Myerhoff eloquently state:

> Woman's historic responsibility for protecting life has endowed her with a set of adaptive characteristics; a strong nurturing impulse that extends to all living things; a highly developed capacity for intimacy that fosters her need for relatedness; a tendency to integrate rather than separate; an ability to empathize; a predilection for egalitarian relationships together with a resistance to hierarchy; . . . and a preference for negotiation as a means of problem solving, which springs from her antipathy to violence. (1985, pp. 4–5)

As more and more women enter the political and economic spheres, some scholars anticipate a transformation of the workplace. Women's presumed preference for cooperation over competition could alter corporate cultures and structures. Feminine commitment to friendship and collaboration is seen as a positive alternative to competitive masculine managerial behavior (Lenz and Myerhoff, 1985). Women's ability to network and to provide mutual support may become crucial to their survival in male-dominated organizations and may produce new subcultures within traditional organizations. Perhaps most dramatically, women's commitment to family caregiving could produce a more flexible and humane working environment for men and women, a working environment with flextime, on-site child and elder care, and preventative health care.

Under ideal conditions, feminine scholars believe, women conforming to both societal expectations and individual values, will bring significant changes to our public organizations. Acting in ways that are clearly more caring and more cooperative than their male counterparts, women employees (particularly administrators) may humanize American bureaucracies and corporations. Focusing upon the concrete needs of others and upon opportunities to promote interpersonal relationships, living out the feminine virtues of kindness, compassion, and generosity, and responding to cultural pressures to act more cooperatively and more intuitively, women could transform the public sphere.

> The willingness to listen and the quality of caring and comforting that exists in many women comes through in their work, sometimes without being aware of it, as they go about their daily tasks in the business and professional world. The cumulative effect of such empathetic behavior does not show up in organizational blueprints or financial statements; but in building small, often imperceptible bridges between home and work, this aspect of feminization is performing a function essential to the health of the American workplace. (Lenz and Myeroff, 1985, p. 92)

D. The Behavior of Female Administrators

Given this cohesive body of theoretical literature around feminine values and virtues, we would expect to find substantial behavioral differences between male and female administrators. Thus far, however, the empirical studies do not support such sharp differences. Unfortunately, there has been very little quality research done in the field; further, the few studies available to us were conducted (with one or two exceptions) in private corporate settings, not in public bureaucracies. The results of the few existent studies have been somewhat conflicting. In general, scholars have reached the tentative conclusion that there are no substantive gender differences in the moral reasoning or behavior of administrators within traditional settings (Stewart and Sprinthall, 1991; Derry, 1989).

From the feminine perspective, we would anticipate that women administrators would be more concerned with affiliation, cooperation, and nurturance. They would focus on the process, rather than the outcome, of executive decisions—consulting with and including a wide range of employees in the decision-making process. Women's power should be, in Follett's terminology, shared power (power with) rather than authoritarian power (power over) (1978). Women administrators should certainly be more caring and nurturing towards subordinates. Women executives would, theoretically, be committed to maintaining friendships and networks. Finally, women are expected to be more committed to their family relationships and caregiving responsibilities, unwilling to abuse their families for the sake of career advancement. In summary, feminine theory argues that female administrators are concerned with collaboration, friendship, connection, kindness, and caregiving—in contrast to men who are committed to productivity, competition, self-reliance, personal power, and success (Grant, 1988).

Extant empirical studies simply do not support these theoretical gender differences; indeed, there is some evidence that women, lacking power and confidence in hierarchical organizations, can be more aggressive and ruthless than male colleagues (Kanter, 1977). It is certainly possible that women enter traditional organizations with different moral perspectives and values. A study by Betz, O'Connell, and Shepard (1989), for example, found that women business school students were more concerned with relationships and helping people while male students were more interested in making money and advancing their careers. Interestingly, the men in this study were two times as likely to say that they would engage in unethical behavior such as insider trading.

Once holding executive positions, however, women and men do not differ markedly in their modes of moral reasoning or their actual ethical behavior. A study by Stewart and Sprinthall (1991) of active public administrators, for example, found no differences in moral reasoning; their results "show quite clearly that males and females are virtually the same in numbers who identify principled reasoning" (p. 5). An in-depth study of 20 women and 20 men randomly selected from managers of a Fortune 500 company reached a similar conclusion (Derry, 1989). Nearly all the executives in this study analyzed moral dilemmas from a justice perspective. Derry hypothesizes that "Smart business players should figure out early on which mode is most credible within their work environment" (p. 860). So that even if gender differences exist prior to or outside of employment, "the work environment imposes certain modes of reasoning" (p. 860).

Women apparently learn to adapt to traditional corporate cultures which are based upon a contractual model. Female managers are rewarded for "following the rules, making fair decisions"; they are clearly not rewarded for "being caring, building strong relationships at work, or alleviating others' burdens" (p. 859). Gender differences in preferred modes of reasoning and values may be, Derry suggests, "context specific."

Rosabeth Kanter argued that the values and behavior of women managers are primarily a function of the rewards and punishments imposed by traditional corporate cultures (1977). In her pioneering book, *Men and Women of the Corporation*, Kanter states that "what appear to be 'sex differences' in work behavior emerge as responses to structural conditions, to one's place in the organization" (p. 262). She believes that there is "great overlap between men and women in their work behavior and attitudes. Every statement that can be made about what women typically do or feel holds true for some men" (p. 262). Apparent differences reflect women's relative powerlessness and their status as token minority members in management. Women managers who develop "a man's way of thinking," who become tough, aggressive, and even abusive, do so in order to survive in the male-dominated environment. The stereotype of controlling and nasty women bosses, the "bitches," "is a perfect picture of people who are powerless. Powerlessness tends to produce those characteristics attributed to women bosses" (p. 202).

More recent studies support Kanter's argument that "differences based upon early socialization and other role requirements will be overridden by rewards and costs associated with occupational roles" (Betz, O'Connell, and Shepard, 1989, p. 322). Women, it appears, adapt to the demands of the corporate environment and culture, sometimes compromising their values in order to compete successfully with men. A survey of 260 matched corporate managers found virtually no difference in the value systems of men and women (Powell, Posner, and Schmidt, 1984). Differences that did exist ran counter to expectations of feminine thinking. Interestingly, women "rated high productivity, efficiency, strong leadership, and organizational stability as more important than did men" (p. 197); women also rated ability, ambition, and skill as more important leadership traits than did male managers. Female managers even placed greater emphasis on career advancement and expressed less concern over work/family conflicts. The authors hypothesize that women managers who have reached the same level as men their own age are probably more aggressive and career-oriented.

A study of 160 women executives and leaders concluded that women are becoming "better adapted" to competitive business environments; young women are "understanding the rules of the game before they start playing'' (Collins, Gilbert, and Nycum, 1988, p. 40). Women are becoming, according to this study, more and more like their male colleagues. As one co-author stated: ''I believe that the nurturing image may be part of the emotional baggage of the over-forty female manager, but the under-forty female manager is expected to be as much or as little a nurturer as a man in a comparable slot'' (p. 56). Further, as a result of overt and covert sexual discrimination, female managers may need to be more ruthless, political, and selfish than men, according to these authors.

Survival and success in mainstream hierarchical organizations (such as those broadly found in public administration) apparently require women to conform to the dominant masculine culture. As Derry concludes, ''general gender differences do not carry over into strong organizational cultures'' (1989, p. 859). Differences that may exist outside of the work world disappear in traditional organizations.

Gender differences, conforming to our expectations, however, may emerge in less constrained settings, in organizations where women possess either greater autonomy and power or where operating norms and rules are more flexible. Case studies of feminist organizations (to be discussed in depth later) offer examples of women leaders clearly exhibiting feminine reasoning and behavior. An interesting study of female elected officials recently released by the Eagleton Institute finds that women are clearly more committed to caring for the vulnerable in our society and promoting healthy families (1991). Women officeholders, who act with broad discretion and autonomy, may apply their feminine values to their work.

A study of four powerful women executives found that women who do reach the top of the organizational pyramid are able to implement feminine values (Helgesen, 1990). Observing these leaders throughout the work day, Sally Helgesen found that they were committed to nurturing their employees and empowering others. The women focused on the ecology of leadership, maintaining multiple relationships, sharing information, and promoting networks. These women CEOs perceived themselves as at the center of ''webs of inclusion''; for example, Frances Hesselbein, chief executive of the Girl Scouts, designed a circular organizational chart with positions ''represented as circles, which are then arranged in an expanding series of orbits'' (p. 44). Helgesen quotes Anita Roddick, founder of Body Shop, describing her principles as ''principles of caring; making intuitive decisions; not getting hung up on hierarchy or all those dreadfully boring business-school management ideas; having a sense of work as being part of your life—not separate from it; putting your labor where your love is; being responsible to the world in how you use your profits; and recognizing the bottom line should stay at the bottom.'' The rare women with meaningful power can assert these feminine values.

Although Sally Helgesen does not specifically assess the difference between male and female managers in her second book, *The Web of Inclusion* (1995), she does provide several case studies that describe the nontraditional management styles of leading women in both for-profit and non-profit organizations. The innovations described in her book are, significantly, initiated primarily by women. Women create web-like structures that facilitate participation and inclusion. For example, Julia Mast at *The Miami Herald* persuaded her CEO that the ''key to achieving pluralism was for management to listen to and learn from employees'' (p. 103). ''The issue of diversity,'' she wrote, ''brings forth profound issues of loss, personal values and belief systems, acceptance, self-esteem, anger, fear, uncertainty, power and control'' (p. 103). She created a highly participatory web of discussion across divisions to promote maximum inclusion for women and minorities. Similarly, Julie Anixter forged a training process within her company that was ''much more organic, more reflective of the networked, integrated shape of our company and our work . . . very web-like'' (p. 183). She recognized that promoting ongoing learning required constant creativity and flexibility.

Hegelson describes women who brought an entirely new management philosophy to large organizations—enhancing customer satisfaction and employee morale. Joyce Clifford at Boston's Beth Israel hospital is seen as a ''guru for leaders seeking ways of transformation'' (p. 132) for her work in empowering front-line nurses. Totally breaking down the traditional (and masculine) medical hierarchy, Clifford granted nurses autonomy and responsibility for medical care of the patients. She decentralized the formal structure, added multiple lines of communication, and redefined the roles of all staff members. The response in terms of patient satisfaction and care were extremely positive. Similarly, Gerry Laybourne revolutionized the management of Nickelodeon when she took over. She created a flexible team that ''included kids in our web, putting them at the center of everything we do'' (p. 223). She emphasized process and participation, ''letting the organization evolve in response to people'' (pp. 243–244). The result was a dramatic rise in the network's market share. Hegelson argues that these women, among others, represent the effective use of feminine ''heart and hearth'' values to enhance productivity in competitive industry settings. Judy Rosener (1995) makes a similar point, arguing that women managers are ''America's Competitive Secret.'' The willingness of women to share power, to use ''power with'' rather than ''power over,'' improves the responsiveness of front-line workers to customers and stakeholders. She states that women's ''interactive style is particularly effective in flexible, nonhierarchical organizations of the kind that perform best in a climate of rapid change'' (p. 11).

Judy Rosener uses profiles of managers to demonstrate that women tend to ''feel comfortable with ambiguity, to be inclusive rather than exclusive, and evaluate performance in both qualitative and quantitative terms'' (1995, p. 201). Rosener asserts that women do have unique managerial styles that are not necessarily superior to men but are definitely different. Women managers tend to create a more flexible work environment where people do not have to feel they have to fit into one model or style of management.

A study of 153 advertising personnel/CPAs and 86 business school professors found that women were more concerned than men with avoiding job discrimination and enhancing job satisfaction with challenging, meaningful tasks (Thumin et al., 1995, p. 399). Conversely, men were found to place a higher priority than women on hiring high-caliber employees. Gender differences were not found on the corporate values of customer service, ethical behavior, and product quality with both groups rating these as very important. The authors attribute the concern women have with job discrimination and satisfaction to the historical emphasis the women's rights movement has had on removing barriers in the workplace and in creating challenging jobs for women (p. 396).

A meta-analysis of 20,000 respondents in 66 samples found that women are more likely than men to perceive a specific hypothetical business practice as unethical (Franke, Crown, and Spake, 1997, p. 920). Social role theory was used as the theoretical guide for the meta-analysis. Gender differences were found to be the largest among student samples, with these differences declining as the amount of work experience increased. The strongest moderator of gender differences in ethical perceptions was the type of behavior involved in the evaluated practice. For example, women were found to be more critical than men of rule breakers and those who had misused insider information (p. 926). Additionally, gender differences were greater among perceptions of nonmonetary issues than monetary. The authors suggest that men are more likely to recognize an ethical problem if money is involved.

Wahn's (1998) study of Canadian human resource professionals found that women had a higher level of continuance commitment than men. Contrary to popular beliefs, Wahn concludes that there is a growing body of evidence that suggests that women tend to demonstrate the same or a higher level of organizational commitment than men—perhaps because there are fewer employment alternatives.

A study of 246 leaders and their immediate supervisors in a federal government agency found that the leaders' self-report of their initiating structure behaviors were related to their gender to a greater extent than their supervisors reported (Lewis and Fagenson-Eland, 1998). In other words, the leaders' perception of their own leadership style were more gender-sterotypic than their supervisors'. Male leaders described themselves as being higher on initiating structure behaviors than did female leaders. Inititating structure behavior was hypothesized to be more of a male style of leadership and consideration behavior to be more a female style, yet gender differences were not found on leaders' self-report of consideration behaviors.

The apparent discrepancy between the theoretical and the actual ethical behavior of most women administrators results from, we might conclude, the overwhelming influence of traditional organizational culture and structure. This hypothesis is consistent with literature within the public administration ethics field, literature highlighting the powerful impact of organizational environment on individual behavior (Denhardt, 1988; Cooper, 1990). Organizational reform appears to be critical if we wish to change individual administrative behavior.

In order for feminine reasoning and virtue to emerge among both male and female administrators, it is necessary, apparently, to alter the existing structures and cultures of traditional bureaucracies. Feminine morality may be, in Michel Foucault's terminology, a ''subjugated knowledge'' in American public administration. The feminine perspective will remain hidden and dormant within organizations dominated by the masculine ethic of competition, impersonality, abstraction, and self-reliance (Kanter, 1977). Women are powerless to effect meaningful change in authoritarian organizations; existent reward and punishment systems are simply too coercive. It is necessary, therefore, to turn to an analysis of the feminist critique of public bureaucracies and a description of alternative organizations supported by the feminist movement. The personal, feminists argue, must be connected to the political in organizations. Individual differences cannot emerge until new kinds of organizations develop in our society.

III. THE FEMINIST PERSPECTIVE ON ORGANIZATIONS

The feminist perspective addresses the structural and cultural components of organizational life that appear to powerfully influence individual ethical behavior. Rather than focusing upon gender-based differences in individual morality, feminists focus upon differences between male-dominated and female-dominated organizations. They argue that in male-dominated organizations, women are forced to adapt to masculine rules and norms. As Robin Derry writes:

> Look like them, talk like them, learn their games, and you will succeed in their world. Unfortunately, following those rules brought to women many of the unhappy consequences as well: emotional distance, isolation, loss of connection to other women, devaluing of family responsibilities, and the hollowness of pretending to be someone else for the dream of success. Women did not change the workplace by entering it in this way; they merely sacrificed themselves to it. (1990, p. 7)

The feminine voice is thus silenced in modern corporations, feminists assert. Critiquing both the hierarchical structure and the competitive culture of bureaucracies, feminists demand alternative forms of organizations. Only in alternative women's organizations, created and led by women themselves, can the feminine moral voice be heard.

A. Organizational Structure

Feminist theorists, beginning with Kanter (1977), have focused upon the role of hierarchical power in restricting the behavior of women. Traditional patterns of dominance and subordination are clearly gender related, with fewer and fewer women situated towards the top of the organizational pyramid. The organizational class (or perhaps caste) system divides employees, with the elite composed almost exclusively of men (Ferguson, 1984). Lower status employees are highly dependent upon recognition and rewards from elite managers. Subordinate women must learn to meet the expectations of their male superiors. They perforce adapt their behavior to the roles assigned to them by male bosses.

The behavior demanded of subordinate women can be either highly submissive or highly aggressive. In many organizations, women administrators are expected to be docile and cooperative—obeying orders and accepting the rules of the corporate game. As Ferguson writes in *The Feminist Case Against Bureaucracy*, "the political consequences of male dominance are such that women learn the role of the subordinate, and that the role can easily become self-perpetuating. The skills that one learns in order to cope with secondary status then reinforce that status" (1984, p. 94). Particularly in organizations where they are a token minority, women administrators may try to remain relatively invisible or may adopt the role of the "pet"—a cute amusing little thing . . . a cheerleader for shows of prowess" (Kanter, 1977, p. 235). In such situations, women may be forced to observe unethical behavior such as racial slurs, pornographic jokes, and sexual harassment and may feel powerless to respond.

As more women enter the ranks of management and as overt discrimination decreases, women increasingly are expected to "become one of the boys," to become as competitive, aggressive, and ambitious as their male colleagues. In a pattern one scholar has called "homosexual reproduction," men demand that their female subordinates become like them (Ferguson, 1984). Rather than challenging the masculine ethic, women adapt their behavior to it, often compensating for their relative lack of power by becoming even more ruthless than men. "Women entering the organization are usually required to put aside person-oriented values of women's traditional role in order to embrace the organization and prove themselves one of the boys" (Ferguson, 1984, p. 94).

Whether they become highly passive or highly aggressive, women without power learn to repress their caring and connective sides. Women who express feminine values are ignored, humiliated, or openly threatened (Derry, 1990). Acting in a feminine manner, for example expressing concern for the problems of a working mother, produces comments about "being too soft" or "not being the management type." Caring women are rarely rewarded or promoted. As one woman manager in Derry's study put it: "You don't talk about being a feminist in the workplace—you don't even raise notions of feminism, if you know what's good for you" (1990, p. 19). Women quickly learn that being successful requires complying with corporate norms (Kanter, 1977; Grant, 1988).

Following Ferguson, Camilla Stivers has provided a comprehensive and cogent critique of the masculine values of assumptions within the field of public administration (1993). Stivers argues that masculine bias is reflected in the "images of expertise, leadership, and virtue that mark defenses of administrative power" (p. 4). Further, she believes that the characteristic masculinity of public administration is systemic, that public administration contributes to the ongoing "power relations in society at large that distributes resources on the basis of gender" (p. 4). Public administration as a field discriminates against women (by limiting opportunities for advancement into the top ranks) and promotes inequity in the broader society.

Stivers' critique includes a wide range of issues that inhibit feminine values and qualities. First, she focuses on the claim of professional expertise that dominates the profession, finding four aspects that "contain gender dilemmas: its claim of scientific objectivity, its quest for autonomy, the hierarchical nature of the authority it seeks, and its implicit norm of brotherhood" (p. 37). She believes that the image of an objective, impartial, and authoritarian expert conflicts with women's tendency to be involved, caring, and respectful. There is dissonance between the professional expectations of objective, autonomous expertise and the feminine qualities of personalized "responsiveness, caring, and service" (p. 55). Stivers calls for "an idea of administrative discretion that is concrete, situational, experience-based, interactive, and grounded in perception and feeling as well as rational analysis" (p. 144).

The professional conceptions of leadership and virtue are also problematic for women, according to Stivers. She believes that, despite the emerging literature on women as effective leaders (such as Hegelsen and Rosener discussed in this chapter), the bias within the public administration field is still toward masculine images of leadership—images of "take charge" leadership. She is particularly concerned with emphasis upon visionary or charismatic leadership that implies a top-down approach (given the tendency of women to be more egalitarian and participatory in style). The focus on public virtue and administrative "heros" also raises gender dilemmas, because they imply that public administrators are elite guardians of the public good. Stivers states that the idea of public virtue is used to defend male-dominated administrative power. "The nature of public life is populated by independent, rational autonomous men (or women 'passing' as men), who protect the common good . . . and control the impulses of the people" (p. 99) which reinforces dominant power structures.

Stivers calls for a "new fabric" for public administration, acknowledging "the threads of womanhood." Male and female administrators need to resist the pressures "to appear technically expert, tough, and heroic" (p. 123). The feminine values of caring, benevolence, selflessness, and responsiveness need to be raised up. Administrators should work "with" as well as "for" the citizens. Greater respect for and connection to all members of our diverse society can enhance both the effectiveness and the popular perception of bureaucrats. Becoming a "whole person," both thoughtful and empathetic, both informed and inclusive, would promote the administrator's service. The gender dichotomies, therefore, need to be overcome if the field is to move forward.

The work of Lisbeth Schorr supports the importance of restructuring public programs, particularly in the social service arena. In a fascinating and influential analysis of successful family service programs, Schorr (1997) argues for human service management principles that are essentially feminine in nature. As she states, relationships are paramount in a "new form of professional practice," one often "at odds with more conventional ways of working" (p. 12). Successful programs are "comprehensive, flexible, responsive, and persevering," reflecting "caring, compassion, and especially patience" (p. 5). The managers of the programs were inclusive and participatory in style, building "strong relationships based upon mutual trust and respect" (p. 10). Interestingly, Schorr also notes that there is a strong spiritual dimension to the relationships that promote change. Leaders largely believed themselves to be connected to a greater life force. Spirituality was a vital source for both organizational and societal transformation—as it inspired connection, mutual trust, and respect.

Feminists believe that traditional power structures and hierarchies are fundamentally incompatible with feminine values (Ferguson, 1984; Stivers, 1993). Genuine caring and connection can only occur when there is mutual respect and trust between members of an organization. Feminism demands the elimination of domination and hierarchical power structures. Power, they argue, must be shared among all members of an organization. They view power as "infinite, unifying, enabling, facilitating, and democratizing; it is meant to be shared and is seen as a way of encouraging both self-reliance and collective determination" (Hyde, 1989, p. 155). Power should be "coactive" power, as Mary Parker Follett argued 70 years ago, not "coercive" power: "Coercive power is the curse of the universe; coactive power, the enrichment and advancement of every human soul" (1978, p. xiii).

Indeed, women managers and consultants, beginning with Mary Parker Follett, have frequently expressed a strong desire to share power; unfortunately, the existing power structures have rarely permitted such democratic behavior. Virtually all of Follett's work focused upon increasing genuine participation and promoting collaborative efforts. True power, she stated, is "power-with," not "power-over:" "Do we not see now that while there are many ways of gaining an external, an arbitrary power—through brute strength, through manipulation, through diplomacy—genuine power is always that which inheres in the situation?" (1978, p. 106).

Modern women managers appear to often share Follett's concern with democratic process, with open discussion and consensus building (Hyde, 1989; Helgesen, 1990, 1995). When empowered, women tend to create more egalitarian organizations. "In the relatively rare situations where women head up large organizations, they are able to establish new structures and patterns of communication which represent their values. These include organizational webs rather than hierarchies and meetings where careful listening, shared information, and frequent praise are expected" (Derry, 1990, p. 8).

Among the most powerful critiques of the traditional "control and command" management philosophy during recent years has been that of Margaret Wheatley (1998; see also, Wheatley and Rogers, 1996). Although not writing from an overtly feminist perspective, Wheatley challenges the old mechanistic value basis of male-dominated management. Wheatley uses the teachings of the "new sciences," the new theories in quantum physics and Gaian biology, to attack the basic assumptions and values undergirding Western organizational theory. As she states:

> The world we had been taught to see was alien to our humanness. We were taught to see the world as a great machine. . . . Because we could not find ourselves in the machine world we had created, we experienced the world as foreign and fearsome. Alienation spawned the need to dominate. Fear led to control. We wanted to harness and control everything. . . . But the world is not a machine. It is alive, filled with life and the history of life. (Wheatley & Rogers, 1996, p. 6)

The feminine principle, she contends, is the affirmation of life, the call to create organizations "worthy of human habitation, where life flourishes and creativity is a delight" (Wheatley, 1998, p. 83).

An astute management consultant, Wheatley teaches that life is "self-organizing" and that we can tap the natural process of order emerging from chaos. Organizations will naturally cohere around intentionality, around vision. "Identity is the source of organization. Every organization is an identity in motion" (Wheatley and Rogers, 1996, p. 58). She argues that organizing individuals should be about passion, about play, about creativity, about freedom, and, above all, about meaning. Organizations should enable humans to become fully human; they can enable us to nurture our passions and to connect through love.

Indeed, Wheatley argues that modern Gaian biology shows us that life on this planet is founded upon "two great organizing energies," the "need to create and the need for relationships" (1998, p. 87). Given the opportunity, individuals will naturally come together to improve their community, to enhance the common good. Individuals seek settings for self-fulfillment and service. In order for organizations to tap the capacities of the individuals involved, organizations must promote "love, purpose, soul, spirit, freedom, courage, integrity, meaning" (1998, p. 87). Leaders, therefore, must be flexible and open, allowing ideas to emerge from core purpose and empowering others to act spontaneously.

Too often, Wheatley believes, modern organizations stifle natural energy and creativity by putting people in boxes. Afraid of inevitable change, confusion, chaos, managers impose order that "destroys our desires." As she states, "We create an organization. The people who loved the purpose grow to disdain the institution that was created to fulfill it. Passion mutates into procedures, into rules and roles. Instead of purpose, we focus on policies. Instead of being free to create, we impose constraints that squeeze the life out of us. The organization no longer lives. We see its bloated form and resent it for what it stops us from doing" (Wheatley and Rogers, 1996, p. 57). Attacking the organizational "imperative," Wheatley argues for "a simpler way," a way more consistent with natural law.

Organizations should be, in Wheatley's vision, fully alive, changing, growing, learning in unpredictable ways. They should be communities of individuals linked in common purpose and passion with minimal formal structure. Organizing should be a verb, and structures should be fluid and dynamic systems. Organizations are linked through communicating information, developing relationships, and sharing common identity. "They are webby, wandering, nonlinear, entangled messes. How do we draw a dynamic process? A map can't capture its complex, coevolving, self-transcending relationships" (Wheatley and Rogers, 1996, p. 79).

Sally Helgesen uses the same metaphor of the web to describe "a new architecture for building great organizations" (1995). She states that the old hierarchical structure, "its emphasis on rank, boundary, and division, has outlived its usefulness as the metaphor by which we relate individuals to the institutions" (p. 13). What is needed is a flexible web that allows for an ongoing and never-ending process of linkage.

> The architect of the web works as the spider does, by ceaselessly spinning new tendrils of connection, while also continually strengthening those that already exist. The architect's tools are not force, not the ability to issue commands, but rather providing access and engaging in constant dialogue. . . . Thus the leader in a web-like structure must manifest strength by yielding, and secure his or her position by continually augmenting the influence of others. (p. 13)

Helgesen emphasizes that the web of relationships must be inclusive, must recognize the interdependence of all and the importance of each participant.

Organizations, when visualized as webs of connection, are constantly in flux. The structures are "continually being built up, stretched, altered, modified, and transformed"

(p. 20). Leaders must be flexible and responsive. Further, they must be comfortable "being in the center of things rather than on top," prefer "building consensus to issuing orders" (p. 20). Managers must forgo "symbolic perks and marks of distinction" and see themselves as co-equals, co-creators in the ongoing process of organizational work. Helgesen believes that women more naturally work in open and participatory organizations, "because the women who led the organizations labored continually to bring everyone at every point closer to the center—to tighten ties, provide increased exposure, and encourage greater participation" (p. 20). Focusing upon relationships rather than individual power or success promotes ongoing creativity, learning, innovation, and improvement.

In summary, feminists believe that feminine ethical behavior does not emerge in traditional bureaucracies where women remain relatively powerless. They blame hierarchical authority structures for abusive behavior. Unless women create alternative organizations or obtain much greater power in traditional organizations, the feminine commitment to care and nurture will not be translated into new modes of behavior. As management Professor Patricia Martin concludes:

> Women are less concerned than men with dominance and power plays and are more committed to diversity, inclusiveness, and openness. Women are also more committed to democratic processes. Yet, women who succeed in the "man's world" of work are forced to compete and to try to beat the next guy or gal. The presence of women in itself is rarely enough to change the masculinist values, practices and concerns of the typical work organization. (1989, p. 469)

B. Organizational Culture

In traditional organizational cultures, feminists contend, women and femininity are denigrated. The "masculine ethic"—being tough-minded, analytic, impersonal, unemotional, calculating, and hard-nosed—is the dominant value system (Kanter, 1977). Feminine values, such as caring, compassion, and connection, are ridiculed. Individual women are subjected to frequent harassment and humiliation. "Gendered relationships," placing women in subordinate positions, are reinforced by dominant corporate cultures (Mills, 1988). Women are made to feel vulnerable and weak—unable to assert their own personalities and convictions. They learn to adapt to the norms of organizational life, repressing their moral doubts and concerns.

Upon entering a traditional organizational culture, women rapidly recognize that females and femininity are devalued. To be accepted and included, they must participate in (or at least condone) sexist jokes and women bashing. As Kanter found in her study of a Fortune 500 company, "For token women, the price of being 'one of the boys' was a willingness to occasionally turn against the 'girls'" (1977, p. 228). Kanter observed female managers commonly laughing at disgusting sexual jokes or participating in derogatory discussions about women's incompetence. Such jokes and discussions continue throughout the workplace today. As the outpouring of support for Anita Hill during the fall of 1990 indicated, sexual harassment and denigration of working women is commonplace in the United States. One corporate lawyer in Derry's study, for example, commented:

> The reality of the workplace was . . . there existed a non-healthy view of women in general and then I heard and experienced many derogatory comments about women . . . And so, what I got was a sense of that was not something to be valued and I drifted

more toward being as much one of the boys as I could . . . I didn't appreciate what that was doing to me personally for a long time. (1990, p. 18)

In such a hostile environment, women learn to deny their femininity. Often overtly or covertly accused of being too emotional, too sympathetic, or too personal, they try to mask their true feelings (Mills, 1988). They observe that "caring" women are relegated to personnel or human relations jobs and avoid showing compassion lest they lose opportunities for career advancement. Female managers often distance themselves from other women, refusing to be identified with a second class group (Derry, 1990). Women, in other words, try to blend into the dominant culture, altering their behaviors and suppressing their feminine traits.

> The dilemma posed here for tokens was how to reconcile their awareness of difference generated by informal interactions with dominants with the need, in order to belong, to suppress dominant's concern about the difference. As with performance pressures, peer group interaction around the tokens increased the effort required for a satisfactory public appearance, sometimes accompanied by distortions of private inclinations. (Kanter, 1977, p. 229)

Successful image management often is achieved at great personal cost. Women express real emotional pain around "playing the man's game." They feel morally conflicted about their behavior. As Derry found, "Several women in my interview study indicated they were accepted most readily on projects when they modeled their behavior and communication after male colleagues. However, the same women also recognized that they were generally more comfortable with themselves if they acted consistently with their own values of sharing information, building trust with clients, and drawing co-workers into collaborative dialogue" (1990, p. 9). Women who become highly successful at repressing their feminine side can become suddenly aware of all that they have lost: "There were things, values and outlooks, that I did not even recognize I had in me because I would work so hard at being something else" (p. 18).

Feminine values and virtues only emerge in the rare situations where women in mainstream organizations have the skill, confidence, and power to assert their priorities. In such situations, women expose themselves to considerable personal risk and ridicule. Female managers in Derry's study expressed occasional success in making changes in the corporate environment. They were able to improve family-oriented policies, to increase collaborative efforts, to promote minority hiring, and to mentor other women. In implementing these innovations, however, the women experienced "significant threats and barriers. These women are not shaping their behavior entirely by the corporate reward systems, but implementing their own values in the face of strong disincentives and criticism" (pp. 30–31). Being true to oneself is obviously very difficult in traditional corporate cultures.

Perhaps the most famous woman manager in the world is Anita Roddick, co-owner of the "Body Shop" chain. In her autobiography (1991), Roddick advocates a distinctly feminist approach to management—emphasizing that principles and profits can both be achieved. She is determined "to create a new business paradigm, simply showing that business can have a human face and a social conscience" (p. 24). Her stores are famous for their commitment to social service; her company is exceptional in its social and environmental justice campaigns. She empowers front-line workers to pursue volunteerism and advocacy, to express their personal passions, to be guided "by the source of their own power." Her credo comes from Ralph Waldo Emerson's challenge: "to put love where labour is.'' Roddick fully realizes that she is often dismissed as an eccentric and emotional woman. She takes great pride in the commercial success of her enterprise that proves her critics wrong. ''They patronize our proselytizing, our environmental campaigning, our social welfare policies, our constant talk of putting love where our labour is. The big mistake they make is to equate our feminine values with weakness and inefficiency'' (p. 217). She asks, ''Why are we always called naive and innocent; why aren't we just right?'' (p. 217).

In conclusion, feminists challenge the dominant masculine culture of most organizations. Powerful cultures, as Derry (1989) contends, repress feminine behavior and virtue. The feminine voice is suppressed, silenced. Women lose touch with their fundamental understandings and values; they lose confidence in their moral reasoning and knowledge. Only in alternative settings, where feminine culture prevails and where women hold true power, can commitment to interpersonal responsibility and connection readily emerge. Let us turn then to an analysis of alternative feminist organizations.

C. Feminist Organizations

Given that feminists blame masculine power structures and cultures for the lack of feminine behavior within traditional organizations, it becomes important to inquire whether or not alternative feminist organizations actually reflect feminine values. Women, apparently unhappy with traditional corporations and bureaucracies, have been leaving their jobs at a record pace to start up their own small businesses and agencies. Unfortunately, to my knowledge, there have been no extensive studies of the managerial styles or values of these women entrepreneurs. There are, however, a substantial number of empirical case studies around alternative feminist service organizations—in both the public and non-profit sectors. As many of these feminist agencies have been in operation for two decades, they provide historical evidence of an alternative administrative framework based upon feminine morality, a framework that has, at least marginally, impacted upon public administration. As Patricia Martin states, ''Feminist organizations in the modern Western women's movements have proved to be extraordinarily prolific, creative, variegated and tenacious'' (1990, p. 183). They are living proof of the viability of the feminist administrative agenda and of feminine ethics within public administration.

Feminist service organizations, starting in the 1960s, have operated in a fundamentally different manner from traditional organizations, reflecting their commitment to the feminine values of caring, nurturing, and sharing. First, and perhaps foremost, feminist organizations promote egalitarian relationships, collaboration, and participation (Martin, 1990; Schwartz, Gottesman, and Perlmutter, 1988; Weil, 1988; Hyde, 1989).* Internal relationships are nonhierarchical and informal; all staff and volunteer workers are treated with respect. Although there may be formal leadership, all members are empowered to make operating decisions. Strategic decision-making is based upon extensive discussion and debate, with all employees included. To the extent possible, strategic decisions are based upon group consensus, with process as important as outcome. Goals, objectives,

---

* There are obvious similarities between the feminist approach and that of the so-called ''new public administration.'' The feminist agenda, however, is more radical—demanding the elimination of traditional bureaucratic hierarchy and rules. Issues of accountability to the voting public are generally not discussed within the feminist literature.

and procedures are constantly reevaluated and modified as needed. Further, organizational structure in feminist organizations is normally flexible and fluid, with teams created for particular tasks; formal leadership may be rotated or shared among team members.

Feminist organizations also endeavor to empower their clients. Clients are given as much information as possible in order to make informed choices and are encouraged to participate in self-help groups and to assist one another. Consciousness raising and political awareness are central to the feminist philosophy. The personal problems of women clients are linked to the political issues of the broader society; collective political action is encouraged around common issues (Hyde, 1989, Ferguson, 1984).

Diversity is valued within feminist organizations. The culture promotes the acceptance and inclusion of different ethnic, age, and racial groups (Hyde, 1989). Diversity and difference are considered a source of strength, as the participation of many women brings renewed energy and growth. All participants are welcomed, embraced, and treated with respect; all voices are to be heard.

In the women's health service arena particularly, non-profit feminist agencies have flourished and grown. The Elizabeth Blackwell Health Center for Women has been open since 1974. The guiding principles of the organization include the following statements:

> (1) The needs of the consumer should be the utmost consideration in organizing the delivery of health care . . . Consumers should be active participants in their personal health care and . . . participate in the decision-making activities of the health care system.
> (2) A feminist working environment recognizes the value of every staff member's contribution, guarantees the right of every staff member to participate in decision-making and encourages staff to expand their skills. (Schwartz, Gottesman, and Perlmutter, 1988, p. 7)

The Blackwell Center has successfully applied these principles—treating staff and consumers alike with remarkable dignity—and has continued to grow—expanding services to meet new needs. Particularly important are the "checks and balances on the accumulation of power," including staff participation in board meetings, direct staff access at all times to the executive director, rotation of key jobs, and staff committees that hire and fire all staff and set pay scales. Clients are also empowered and mobilized to participate in political advocacy on behalf of women's health and reproductive rights.

The Women Reaching Women Project, which opened in 1978 to help chemically dependent women, offers an example of feminist morality influencing public management (Kravetz and Jones, 1988). Although part of the state Office of Alcohol and Other Drug Abuse, the project retains considerable autonomy and flexibility. A statewide project in Wisconsin, the program is coordinated by only one paid project director; local agency coordinators are free to develop their own programs—with minimal supervision and bureaucratic constraint. Even volunteers "have significant input into program planning and priority setting" (p. 50). As one volunteer stated: "If you do not like something, you can complain about it, and do it openly. And if you want to take the initiative on yourself and change something, you can do that, as long as you stay within certain guidelines" (p. 51). Clients are provided with the support necessary to obtain appropriate services and are encouraged to participate in self-help groups. The local agencies have initiated grassroots lobbying and have a network available to influence legislators.

The Los Angeles County Department of Children's Child Sexual Abuse Program provides an outstanding example of "an alternative program with a collaborative, feminist-oriented organizational sub-culture within the structure and hierarchical culture of a massive bureaucracy'' (Weil, 1988, p. 69). The program was established in 1978 to ''treat and empower victimized children and their mothers.'' The organizational culture and structure is carefully constructed to empower both staff and clients. Flexible matrix teams are created for specific tasks, and the leadership of these teams is shared depending upon relevant expertise. For clients, there is an emphasis on self-help through participation in Parents United groups. Indeed, the Child Sexual Abuse Program shows us that even large traditional public bureaucracies can ''reframe their practice approach so that they function with shared decision-making responsibility, mutual participatory planning and problem-solving, and mutual dependence. Such restructuring requires a strong commitment to empowerment and mutual aid, for staff as well as clients'' (p. 80). Even within traditional public bureaucracies, feminist subcultures and organizations offer a humane and caring work environment.

In an outstanding collection of essays, Ferree and Martin (1995) bring together a wide range of feminist authors to describe ''feminist organizations'' throughout the United States and the world. They define feminist organizations as ''embracing collectivist decision-making, member empowerment, and a political agenda of ending women's oppression'' (p. 5). Looking at the case histories of these organizations, they conclude that ''working with women, for women, they encountered tensions and problems in their inevitable collisions and collaborations with what they called the 'male-stream' '' (p. 5). Nevertheless, these organizations have shown remarkable survival and growth over time.

Ferree and Martin believe that feminism continued into the 1990s, ''largely because of the number and variety of organizations it generated, nurtured, and influenced'' (p. 5). Feminist organizations are ''the places in which and the means through which the work of the women's movement is done'' (p. 13). They mobilize and empower women through collective action, primarily political agitation. They are concerned with broad scale societal change—as opposed to the enhancement and empowerment of individual women. Thus, the essays focus essentially on activist organizations (with direct service to women in need as perhaps secondary activities). They are particularly interested in the relationship of feminist organizations to the broader women's movement and the impact of institutionalization on the focus and agenda of activism. They also intentionally included studies that highlight the diverse ethnic, class, and age issues that are reflected in the breadth of these organizations—arising from local issues and conflicts in discrete communities throughout the nation.

Ferre and Martin conclude that there are a wide range of organizational types represented within the feminist movement. In specific, they recognize that although that the looser network and grassroots style may be more inherently challenging to the status quo, more institutionalized and bureaucratic style organizations may also be very effective change agents. ''Indeed, the most important outcome of any wave of social movement mobilizations may be the institutionalized resources'' (p. 11) that it garners and offers for future movements. In other words, there is no one style or model required to promote social transformation from the perspective of these authors. Political engagement can take many organizational forms, forms that, in fact, are not consistent with so-called feminine principles of caring and connection—an ethical conflict not directly confronted by the authors.

Because of the volume's focus on political activism, less attention is given to concrete management and leadership issues. In one interesting chapter, Joan Acker focuses on the challenge of nonhierarchical and participatory management (1995). She asks whether it is ''possible to remain true to the feminist ideals of collectivity, respect, and democracy and at the same time create or take enough power to make the changes in the society that are needed to meet feminist goals'' (p. 138). She argues that pressure toward hierarchy emerge as the organization seeks to become stronger and more effective. She concludes that certain factors do improve the likelihood for ongoing egalitarian participation: ''small group size, common goals (including the goal of equal participation), relatively equal knowledge and experience, individual members who are flexible and noncompetitive, and a benign organizational environment'' (p. 141). Acker also postulates that feminist organizing works best with women of similar race, ethnicity, class, and/or sexual orientation. Homogeneity of interest and background facilitates egalitarian participation; local networks and friendships lead to natural trust, cooperation, and shared power. Her conclusions, thus, are consistent with the editors—and pose interesting ethical dilemmas for the women's movement at large.

The question of whether a feminist structure and process is required within a feminist organization is addressed by the concluding author of the volume, Jo Freeman (1995). She argues that the ''plethora of organizations calling themselves feminist and pursuing feminist goals question the proposition that collective decision-making and participatory democracy are prerequisites to being feminist'' (p. 406). She concurs with the editors that the criteria should be whether or not the organization empowers women at large. The goal is ''to empower women as a group, not just individual women'' (p. 408). The outcome, not necessarily the structure or process, is the ultimate test of feminism.

Although the theoretical model informing this volume does not emphasize feminist process, many of the case studies do describe participatory organizations. One study of battered womens' shelters (Reinelt, 1995) describes the efforts to work ''toward eliminating professional hierarchies'' (p. 90), including hiring former clients and minimizing pay differentials. Reinelt emphasizes that these radicalized shelters came together collectively to embrace ''a politics of engagement'' (p. 85), uniting politically to fight for increased funding and tougher penalities. Another case study of community organizers in East Los Angeles emphasizes the collective nature of the groups (Pardo, 1995). The Mothers of East Los Angeles, for example, built upon ''existing networks within the community'' (p. 362), uniting a variety of ethnic groups in a common effort to protect their community from a state prison and from a toxic waste dump. The ''womanist'' groups worked together collaboratively, transforming ''family, friends, and neighbors into networks for collective action'' (p. 370) that successfully fought for the sanctity of their community. Other studies of relatively small, more discrete and local, organizations confirm that feminist organizing principles can effectively lead to systemic change.

In summary, this extensive study of feminist organization indicates that change and variety are the constants in the movement; feminism is a transformative process. As Reinalt concludes, feminism is ''guided by the values that include nurturance, democracy, cooperation, empowerment, inclusion, transformation, maximizing rewards to all, and ending oppression'' (p. 101). These values ''provide a moral framework,'' a way of being in the world, but do not require ''specific organizational forms or political strategies'' (p. 101).

Overall, it appears that organizational culture and structure can either suppress or foster feminine values and virtues among women. Women who work in traditional settings appear to adapt to the competitive, individualistic environment. In alternative settings, however, women can become more feminine in their behavior, nurturing their selves, their colleagues, and their clients. Whether men also can behave in a collaborative and cooperative manner within alternative settings is, at this time, unclear. (Unfortunately, none of the case studies of feminist organizations mentioned the presence or reaction of male employees.) The feminist agenda, focused largely upon the liberation of women, has enabled many women to discover new ways of organizing but has not yet created opportunities for male administrators to change their ethical behavior.

IV. CONCLUSION: LISTENING TO ANOTHER VOICE

Throughout this chapter, the feminine and masculine ethics have been treated as polar opposites. The feminine morality of responsibility, based upon a commitment to caring and connection, has been compared to the masculine rights position, founded upon abstract logic and universal principles of justice. Feminine virtues, including kindness, compassion, and patience, have been contrasted to masculine virtues such as courage and honor. The voices of women have been viewed as distinctly different from those of men.

In a similar fashion, alternative feminist organizations have been contrasted with traditional masculine organizations. The structures of feminist organizations are democratic and egalitarian while masculine organizations are hierarchical and authoritarian. Feminist organizations promote diversity and inclusion while masculine organizations encourage exclusion and competition. Male-dominated agencies, feminists argue, foster conflict and isolation while female-dominated agencies encourage cooperation and interpersonal relationships. Again, polar differences between the sexes are proposed.

In truth, scholars increasingly recognize that both men and women have the capacity to approach moral decisions from either the justice or the care perspective. Further, both men and women may act in a loving and nurturing fashion. Both ethical decision-making and ethical behavior may be as much context based as gender based (Derry, 1989; Gould, 1988; Helgesen, 1995).

As we have seen, men and women adapt to the competitive, individualistic culture and the hierarchical authority structure of mainstream organizations. When participating in alternative agencies, on the other hand, women (and probably men) act in a caring and nurturing manner towards colleagues and clients. Indeed, it is likely that men who belong to collectivist grassroots organizations are deeply committed to egalitaranism and connection—although an analysis of all alternative organizations was well beyond the scope of this chapter. Certainly, there are obvious parallels between feminist organizational theory, with its emphasis on participation, inclusion, and social change, and the new public administration theory articulated by (primarily) male scholars in the late sixties.

The feminine perspective is important to public administration, therefore, because it articulates and asserts an alternative approach to morality; it is significant "by theme, not by gender" as Carol Gilligan herself has recognized (1982, p. 2). It does not ultimately matter whether American men and women currently think or act in ways that are inherently different. What is crucial to the transformation of public bureaucracies is the recognition and acceptance of "a different voice." The care perspective radically challenges the presumed universality of the justice position. It represents the suppressed values of all those who have long suffered under the individualistic rights philosophy, including African-Americans, Native Americans, and women (Tronto, 1987; Ferree and Martin, 1995). It demands that interpersonal responsibility and connection be granted equal moral status with individual rights.

There is a clear need to move away from polarities and to move towards a constructive synthesis of the care and justice perspectives. Rights and responsibility are really countervailing philosophies that balance and restrain one another. As Friedman (1987) argues, given the increasing abuse and inequities within families, we should promote greater justice in the private domestic sphere. On the other hand, given the frequent demoralization and exploitation of workers, the feminine care perspective and feminine virtues are needed to humanize the public sphere of organizational life and to promote creative solutions to public problems (Helgesen, 1990, 1995). The potential of the care perspective to transform public bureaucracies is obvious; unfortunately, the structural and cultural barriers are equally obvious to most women administrators.

The challenge for public administrators is to successfully incorporate the feminine approach into mainstream organizations. As Friedman comments, we must recognize that ''the care/justice dichotomy is rationally implausible and that the concepts are conceptually compatible. This conceptual compatibility creates the empirical possibility that the two moral concerns will be intermingled in practice'' (1987, p. 97). Yet such integration within public administrative practice requires a willingness on the part of men in power to consider meaningful change.

Feminists have argued persuasively that integration is virtually impossible given ongoing sexual discrimination and bureauneurosis and have instead created alternative agencies. From the feminist perspective, the polar differences cannot be bridged, the different voice of women will always be silenced in male-dominated settings. The only option for women is to work apart from men, nurturing and empowering one another.

Personally, however, I retain hope that feminist organizations, on the whole successful and stable, provide models of alternative administrative behavior that can be incorporated into mainstream public administration. The feminine willingness to share power and to respond in a caring fashion to the concrete needs of others is sorely needed if our public institutions are to flourish. If we are to revitalize our demoralized public organizations, we must reduce the cultural and structural constraints on feminine behavior and create opportunities for enhanced interpersonal relationships—both within our bureaucracies and between these bureaucracies and the communities they serve.

Sadly, the voice of care is yet to be heard within mainstream public administration. Indeed, there has been remarkably little discussion of gender issues within the ethics literature. As our opening vignette illustrated, women who speak of cooperation, concern, or compassion are ridiculed; the feminine perspective is readily dismissed by scholars and practitioners alike. The women's voice is silenced and suppressed; feminine morality remains a subjugated knowledge. It is time, I believe, for both men and women in the field of public administration to listen with courtesy and thoughtfulness to the voice of feminine morality (Derry, 1990; Stivers, 1993). Let the dialogue begin.

REFERENCES

Acker, J. (1995). Feminist goals and organizing process (Ferree, M. and P. Martin, eds.), *Feminist Organizations: Harvest of the Women's Movement*, Temple University Press, Philadelphia, pp. 137–144.

Benhabib, S. (1987). The generalized and the concrete other: the Kohlberg-Gilligan controversy and moral theory, *Women and Moral Theory* (F. Kittay and D. Meyers, eds.), Rowman and Littlefield, New Jersey, pp. 154–77.

Betz, M., O'Connell, L., and Shepard, J. (1989). Gender differences in proclivity for unethical behavior, *Journal of Business Ethics*, 8(5): 321–4.

Chodorow, N. (1988). *The Reproduction of Mothering*.

Coles, R. (1977). *Eskimos, Chicanos, Indians*, Little, Brown, & Co., Boston.

Collins, N., Gilbert, S., and Nycum, S. (1988). *Women Leading*, The Stephen Greene Press, Lexington, Mass.

Cooper, T. (1990). *The Responsible Administrator*, 3rd ed., Jossey-Bass, San Francisco.

Denhardt, K. (1988). *The Ethics of Public Service: Resolving Moral Dilemmas in Public Organizations*, Greenwood Press, New York.

Derry, R. (1989). An empirical study of moral reasoning among managers, *Journal of Business Ethics*, 8(11): 855–62.

Derry, R. (1990). Feminism: how does it play in the corporate theater? Unpublished paper presented to Ruffin Lecture Series.

Eagleton Institute of Politics (1991). *The Impact of Women in Public Office*, Rutgers University Press, New Brunswick.

Eagly, A. (1987). *Sex Differences in Social Behavior: A Social-Role Interpretation*, Erlbaum, New Jersey.

Ferguson, K. (1984). *The Feminist Case Against Bureaucracy*, Temple University Press, Philadelphia.

Ferree, M. and Martin, P. (eds.) (1995). *Feminist Organizations: Harvest of the Women's Movement*, Temple University Press, Philadelphia.

Follett, M. P. (1951). *Creative Experience*, Peter Smith, New York.

Follett, M. P. (1978). *Dynamic Administration*, Harper and Brothers, New York.

Franke, G., Crown, D., and Spake, D. (1997). Gender differences in ethical perceptions of business practices: A social role theory perspective, *Journal of Applied Psychology*, 82(6): 920–934.

Freeman, J. (1995). From seed to harvest: Transformations of feminist organizations and scholarship (Ferree, M. and P. Martin eds.), *Feminist Organizations*: Harvest of the Women's Movement, Temple University Press, Philadelphia, pp. 397–410.

Friedman, M. (1987). Beyond caring: the demoralization of gender (M. Hanen and K. Nielsen, eds.), *Science, Morality, and Feminist Theory*, University of Calgary Press, Calgary, pp. 87–110.

Gilligan, C. (1982). *In a Different Voice*, Harvard University Press, Cambridge, Mass.

Gilligan, C. (1987). Moral orientation and moral development (F. Kittay and D. Meyers, eds.), *Women and Moral Theory*, Rowman and Littlefield, New Jersey, pp. 19–36.

Gould, K. (1988). Old wine in new bottles: a feminist perspective on Gilligan's theory, *Social Work* 33(5): 411–15.

Grant, A. (1988). Women as managers, *Organization Dynamics*, 16(3): 54–63.

Harding, S. (1987). The curious coincidence of feminine and African moralities (F. Kittay and D. Meyers, eds.), *Women and Moral Theory*, Rowman and Littlefield, New Jersey.

Held, V. (1987). Feminism and moral theory (F. Kittay and D. Meyers, eds.), *Women and Moral Theory*, Rowman and Littlefield, New Jersey.

Helgesen, S. (1990). *The Female Advantage: Women's Ways of Leadership*, Doubleday, New York.

Helgesen, S. (1995). *The Web of Inclusion*, Doubleday, New York.

Hyde, C. (1989). A feminist model for a macro-practice: promises and problems, *Administration and Social Work*, 3(4): 145–8.

Kanter, R. (1977). *Men and Women of the Corporation*, Basic Books, New York.

Katzenstein, M., and Laitin, D. (1987). Politics, feminism, and the ethics of care (F. Kittay and D. Meyers, eds.), *Women and Moral Theory*, Rowman and Littlefield, New Jersey.

Kittay, F., and Meyers, D. (eds.) (1987). *Women and Moral Theory*, Rowman and Littlefield, New Jersey.

Kohlberg, L. (1976). Moral stages and moralization: the cognitive-developmental approach (T. Kickona, ed.), *Moral Development and Behavior*, Holt, Rinehart, and Winston, New York.

Kohlberg, L. (1981). *The Philosophy of Moral Development*, Harper and Row, San Francisco.

Kravetz, D., and Jones, C. (1988). Women reaching women, *Administration in Social Work*, 12(2): 45–58.

Lenz, E., and Myerhoff, B. (1985). *The Feminization of America*, St. Martins Press, New York.

Lewis, A. and Fagenson-Eland, E. (1998). The influence of gender and organizational level on perceptions of leadership behaviors: A self and supervisor comparison, *Sex Roles: A Journal of Research*, 39(5/6): 479–502.

Martin, P. (1989). The moral politics of organizations, *Journal of Applied Behavioral Science*, 25(4): 451–70.

Martin, P. (1990). Rethinking feminist organizations, *Gender and Society*, 4(2): 182–206.

Mills, A. (1988). Organization, gender, and culture, *Organization Studies*, 9(3): 351–70.

Noddings, N. (1984). *Caring: A Feminine Approach to Ethics and Moral Education*, University of California Press, Berkeley.

Pardo, M. (1995). Doing it for the kids: Mexican American community activists, border feminists? (Ferree, M. and P. Martin, eds.), *Feminist Organizations*: Harvest of the Women's Movement, Temple University Press, Philadelphia, pp. 356–371.

Pateman, C. (1984). *Participation and Democratic Theory*, Cambridge University Press, Cambridge, Mass.

Powell, G., Posner, B., and Schmidt, W. (1984). Sex effects on managerial value systems, *Human Relations*, 37(11): 909–21.

Reinelt, C. (1995). Moving onto the terrain of the state: the battered women's movement and the politics of engagement (Ferree, M. and P. Martin, eds.), *Feminist Organizations*: Harvest of the Women's Movement, Temple University Press, Philadelphia, pp. 84–104.

Roddick, A. (1991). *Body and Soul*, Crown Trade, New York.

Rosener, J. (1995). *America's Competitive Secret: Utilizing Women as a Management Strategy*, Oxford University Press, New York.

Schorr, L. (1997). *Common Purpose: Strengthening Families and Neighborhoods to Rebuild America*, Anchor Books, New York.

Schwartz, A., Gottesman, E., and Perlmutter, F. (1988). Blackwell: a case study in feminist administration, *Administration in Social Work*, 12(2): 5–16.

Stewart, D., and Sprinthall, N. (1991). The impact of demographic professional and organizational variables and domain on the moral reasoning of public administrators, Unpublished paper presented to the Conference on the Study of Government Ethics, Park City, Utah.

Stivers, C. (1993). *Gender Images in Public Administration: Legitimacy and the Administrative State*, Sage, California.

Thumin, F., Johnson, J. and Kuehl, C. (1995). Corporate values as related to occupation, gender, age, and company size, *The Journal of Psychology*, 129(4): 389–400.

Tronto, J. (1987). Beyond gender differences to a theory of care, *Signs*, 12(4): 644–63.

Wahn, J. (1998). Sex differences in the continuance component of organizational commitment, *Group and Organization Management* 23(3): 256–266.

Weil, M. (1988). Creating an alternative work culture in a public service setting, *Administration in Social Work*, 12(2): 69–82.

Wheatley, M. (1998). Reclaiming Gaia, reclaiming life (Ryan M., ed.), *The Fabric of the Future*, Conari Press, Berkeley, pp. 82–95.

Wheatley, M. and Rogers, M. K. (1996). *A Simpler Way*, Berrett-Koehler, San Francisco.

27
Citizenship Ethics in Public Administration

Camilla Stivers
Cleveland State University, Cleveland, Ohio

The idea of citizenship has a long history in Western political philosophy, from the city-states of ancient times to the representative democracies of advanced capitalist societies. Citizenship connotes both a status and a practice. As *status*, it entails a set of formal relationships between individuals and the state, typically including important rights (the right to vote; freedom of speech, religion, and association) but few if any duties. As *practice*, citizenship involves a range of capacities, activities, and obligations constitutive of political life, such as participation in governance and the duty to consider the general good.

As an ethical anchor for public administration, the concept of citizenship has not been widely employed in comparison to a number of other normative frameworks, including many of those treated elsewhere in this volume. The clear outlines of a citizenship-based ethic for public administrators are nonetheless evident in the literature: preeminently in the work of Cooper (1991, 1984a, 1984b, 1980) but also in Frederickson (1991, 1982), Stivers (1996, 1991, 1990a, 1990b), and the articles in Frederickson and Chandler (1984). This chapter will set forth the major ingredients of a citizenship ethic in public administration, drawing mainly on authors within the field but amplifying the discussion with other sources as needed. The review proceeds by, first, rehearsing the ingredients of citizenship as status and practice; next, briefly tracing the development of citizenship thinking in public administration; then outlining the major features of a citizenship ethic in public administration as reflected in its literature to date; next, exploring the tension between citizenship and organizational values, especially as it has been heightened in recent years by calls to model administrative behavior after business practices (e.g., "reinventing government"); and finally, offering a few thoughts on the direction in which a citizenship ethic needs to develop in the future.

I. CITIZENSHIP AS STATUS

Citizenship fundamentally connotes a formal relationship between the individual and the state, one that grants the individual civil and political rights, such as those contained in the Bill of Rights of the U.S. Constitution. To the average person, these rights amount to *the* meaning of citizenship. Yet as Rohr (1984) notes, virtually all the rights (and in modern times, most welfare-state benefits) commonly associated with citizenship are also granted to noncitizens within the jurisdiction of the United States. Even the right to vote, which *is* restricted to citizens, is looked on as a means of protecting private interests rather than as a duty or opportunity to participate in governmental affairs. Perhaps because of this lack of substantive content, citizenship as status has not served as an important source of inspiration for administrative norms. In the public administration and political science literature, it is typically referred to as "weak" or "low" citizenship (e.g., Chandler 1984; Barber 1984; Flathman 1981) and contrasted with the "strong" or "high" citizenship that involves specific action opportunities and obligations. Cooper concludes that "The legal forms are important . . . but only as a means of focusing attention on the more fundamental evolution of a stream of values and principles which give essential shape and content to the role of citizen" (1991:47).

Yet if we are to have a full rendering of citizenship's significance, its sense as legal status should not be set aside entirely as a source of ethical precepts. This is particularly true since over the course of U.S. history (indeed, Western history in general) the extension of citizenship standing has raised important moral issues. For example, women have been a continuing anomaly in citizenship thinking over the centuries, generally treated as "citizens" in theory yet for long periods denied access to the most tangible distinction between citizens and others, the right to vote. The granting of citizenship status to African-Americans has been even more equivocal, from the time of the Dred Scott decision, which held that blacks had no rights that U.S. citizens need respect, to the continuing struggle since Emancipation to turn rights accorded in theory into substantive opportunities.

Shklar argues: "The struggle for citizenship in America has . . . been overwhelmingly a demand for inclusion in the polity, an effort to break down excluding barriers to recognition, rather than an aspiration to civic participation as a deeply involving activity" (1991:3). She reminds us that, by excluding people of color and women from the civil and political rights of citizenship, a society that professed to be democratic proved itself false to its own dearest principles. Shklar notes that historically the value of citizenship for white, property-owning men was derived primarily from the contrast between their status and those of excluded groups, a view that was clearly reflected in nineteenth century debates over the extension of the franchise. For example, for the delegates to the Virginia Convention of 1829–1830, the question of the vote was crucial "because it meant that they were citizens, unlike women and slaves, as they repeated over and over again. Their very identity as free males was at stake" (Shklar 1991:49; see also Morgan 1975). This perspective suggests that, even as *just* a legal status, citizenship is a more complex concept than might at first appear, since possession of it is so implicated in whether members of society are able not only to engage in certain practices but to develop a rich sense of self-identity, one that is not stunted by the experience of exclusion from public life.

On a related matter, Shklar and others have argued that a significant limitation on the notion of legal citizenship is its restriction to the realm of the political. In liberal philosophy, the idea of equality in citizenship does not extend to the economic realm, where liberty is thought to require the right to accumulate according to one's own interests and talents, making economic inequality inevitable. Yet it is clear that politics and economics are intertwined. The state does enforce contracts. Political—that is, policy—decisions enable and constrain market dynamics that directly affect citizens' lives; at the same time, economic conditions shape political opportunities and priorities, including not only which candidates citizens support but whether they are likely to vote at all. Shklar observes that in the early days of the United States the idea became established that citizenship actively entailed a certain economic status:

> Independent citizens acted in a republican economy in which each had an equal oppor-
> tunity to get ahead. . . . [T]his vision of economic independence, of self-directed "earn-
> ing," as the ethical basis of democratic citizenship took the place of an outmoded
> notion of public virtue, and it has retained its powerful appeal. We are citizens only
> if we "earn" (Shklar 1991:70).

Thus there is a further anomaly in the notion of citizenship: Our heritage is based on a vision of citizen virtue as the industrious pursuit of self-interest, yet the restriction of equal citizenship rights to the political sphere guarantees an economic system in which the accumulation of property on the part of some will inevitably restrict others—not only their ability to attain a sense of full membership in society but, given the strong correlation between economic status and voting, their likelihood of engaging in the most fundamental and important citizen right.

Based on this brief review, then, citizenship as legal status appears to have at least two significant moral questions to bring to the development of a citizenship ethic for public administration: (1) the idea of standing or inclusion, which arises from the gap between professed democratic principles and their actual enactment, and (2) the notion of full membership raised by the problematic relationship between economic security and political enablement. These issues are discussed later in this chapter.

II. CITIZENSHIP AS PRACTICE

As a practice or set of activities and capacities, the idea of citizenship has been marked by four key attributes: the exercise of decisive judgment on public matters, devotion to the public good, education or development, and community.

The classic vision of active citizenship is Aristotle's. He declared that mere residence in a place does not ensure citizenship nor does the possession of legal rights: "What effectively distinguishes the citizen proper from all others is his participation in giving judgment and in holding office" (1981: Sec. 1274a22). Citizens are those who take part directly in some aspect of governance: they rule and are ruled, in turn. Their authority may be limited, but with respect to the responsibility they are assigned, it is decisive. For example, in the Assembly of classical Athens, citizens had a right to decide about matters of public policy; in fact, as Held (1987) notes, the Athenian *demos*, or people, held the supreme authority in legislative and judicial affairs. Arendt has pointed out that the exercise of decisive judgment in public affairs distinguishes the citizen from the subject. The latter may have civil rights and attain the satisfaction of his or her private wants; but only the citizen is a participator in governing (Arendt, 1963: 127, 130).

What sort of authority do active citizens exercise? Schaar's treatment is instructive. He says that authority is legitimate power: "All theories of legitimacy take the form of establishing a principle which . . . locates or embeds power in a realm of things beyond the wills of the holders of power: the legitimacy of power stems from its *origin*" (1970: 287)—in other words, authority can be justified by its grounding in a constitution, divine law, immemorial custom, or other external foundation. In addition, Schaar suggests that authority is interactive in addition to being structural: "An authority is one whose counsels we seek and trust . . . who starts lines of action that others complete'' (pp. 291–292). Schaar's argument implies that the authority of active citizens is both externally grounded and acted out in relationships with others.

Finley's analysis of Athenian democracy makes it clear that, in this one state at least, ordinary citizens did exercise the kind of authority Schaar describes, that is, they made binding decisions that were both lawful and the outgrowth of interaction among peers. Finley points out that most Athenian citizens, while poorly educated, understood perfectly well the necessity for expert advice but still exercised final judgment themselves about what was to be done. Although there were leaders such as Pericles who were ''stars'' in Assembly debate and might therefore be considered an elite, their preeminence was personal rather than institutional—it was achieved and maintained by public performance rather than lodged in a formal status. Thus, as Finley says, citizen ''recognition of the need for leadership was not accompanied by a surrender of the power of decision'' (1985:25).

The judgment exercised by Athenian citizens was what Aristotle called *phronesis*, or practical wisdom, which is the ability ''to deliberate rightly about . . . what is conducive to the good life generally'' (1976: Sec. 1140a24). Practical wisdom is at once an intellectual and a moral capacity. The element of deliberation is crucial in distinguishing practical wisdom from science (*episteme*), or necessary knowledge—that which is demonstrated rather than deliberated about. Aristotle emphasizes that ''nobody deliberates about things that are invariable'' (1976: Sec. 1140b33 et passim). Thus the outcome of practical wisdom is knowledge that is relevant to the circumstances in which it is developed. It is also the result of exercising judgment about justice or the good, rather than of technical skill, which generates a tangible product. The practical wisdom of citizens enables them to judge rightly (that is, with the public good in mind) on particular public issues. As Arendt points out, such judging takes place without the aid of what she called bannisters (unarguable grounds) or yardsticks (firm measures such as we can apply to assess factual accuracy) (Beiner 1982).

Concern for the public good rather than narrow private interests is a major theme in the literature of active citizenship. Active citizens must be prepared to show that their decisions address the widest possible public interest. Wolin holds that ''the political'' per se signifies that which is general to a society; a citizen is one who is obligated to consider the common good. He observes that this capacity is crucial to integrating the multiple and conflicting demands that characterize pluralist societies (Wolin 1960:429ff.). Flathman argues that in modern times ''the public interest'' replaced the classical notion of ''the common good'' as a result of liberalism's concern for strengthening the political prerogatives of individuals. From this perspective, the assertion of an apparently objective ''good'' is a threat to individual interests. Yet the idea that a political authority (such as active citizens) should decide in the face of conflicting interests implies that these interests can be weighed in terms of some more general standard. Because policies are inevitably contextual, ''the public interest'' cannot be equivalent under all conditions to a single substantive value. Nevertheless, Flathman argues, a nonarbitrary meaning can be found in particular circumstances, through reasoned discourse that ''attempts to relate the anticipated effects of a policy to community values and to test that relation by formal principles'' (1966:82). Barber argues similarly that active citizenship is the starting point for working toward shared values, instead of needing such values as a prerequisite. He calls for a ''politics of mutualism that can overcome private interests'' (Barber 1984:198).

Another idea encountered in the literature is that by participating in governance citizens can develop capacities and skills important to the effective conduct of public affairs. The principle lines of argument have been, first, that human beings need the experience of wrestling with problems larger than their own private concerns in order to become full human beings, and second, that this ability to develop is what will ensure that a state run in some meaningful sense by citizens will be run well. Mill notes that even though modern government does not make possible the intensity of experience that citizens of Athens enjoyed, still such activities as serving on juries and in parish offices "must make them nonetheless very different beings, in range of ideas and development of faculties, from those who have done nothing in their lives but drive a quill, or sell goods over a counter" (1972:233). The key point for Mill is that public responsibilities constitute a moral education. The citizen "is called upon, while so engaged, to weigh interests not his own; to be guided, in case of conflicting claims, by another rule than his private partialities; to apply, at every turn, principles and maxims which have for their reason of existence the common good" (Mill, 1972:233). Along the same lines, Tocqueville argued that local political activity gave citizens an opportunity to practice what he called self-interest rightly understood. They would "attend to the interests of the public, first by necessity, afterwards by choice" (Tocqueville 1945:II, 112), and through this educative process initially self-interested participation would be transmuted to something approaching classical virtue.

One additional theme shapes the notion of active citizenship, and that is the idea of community. In fact, proponents tend to view the communal aspects of participatory activity as important support for its moral, functional, and cognitive dimensions. In ancient Athens, interaction among citizens was relatively easy, because the society was of a scale that facilitated face-to-face discussion and debate. The relationships that resulted from direct interpersonal experience generated consciousness of common destiny, shared myths and traditions, all of which then reinforced public mutuality. The sense of community underlying Athenian politics was not dependent, however, on unanimity of opinion. The factions that came to loom large for the framers of the U.S. Constitution were well known to the Greeks; but, as Finley points out, contention among factions has its good side as well as its dangers, because "conflict combined with consent . . . preserves democracy from eroding into oligarchy" (1973:72–73). Arendt goes even further: The inevitability of conflict is what makes the public realm viable. Public life depends on innumerable perspectives that have no common denominator. This is what makes being seen and heard by others—public speech and public action—significant: "[The] family 'world' can never replace the reality rising out of the sum total of aspects presented by one object to a multitude of spectators" (1958:57).

Tocqueville expresses a similar concern for binding members of a society together. Without opportunities for public-spirited association, he believes, each individual is isolated "within the solitude of his own heart" (1945:II, 106). By joining together in civil and political organizations for common purposes, citizens come to understand and appreciate shared endeavor: "The independence of each individual is recognized. . . . [A]ll members advance at the same time towards the same end, but they are not all obliged to follow the same track" (1945:I, 205). Similarly, Barber makes the point that the essence of politics is not preventing conflict but facilitating it; only through "strong democratic talk" can average citizens become "capable of genuinely public thinking and political judgment and thus able to envision a common future in terms of genuinely common goals" (1984: 197).

From the foregoing review of theory on citizenship as an activity or practice, we have extracted the following major elements:

The exercise of authoritative power, using sound judgment and relying on practical knowledge of the situation at hand;

Concern for the public interest, defined in particular contexts through reasoned discourse;

The development of personal capacities for governance through their exercise in practical activity;

The constitution of community through deliberation about issues of public concern.

In summary, active citizenship means participation in governance: the exercise of decisive judgment in the public interest, an experience that develops the political and moral capacities of individuals and solidifies the communal ties among them.

III. CITIZENSHIP THINKING IN PUBLIC ADMINISTRATION

The first appearance of citizenship in public administration thinking came in the field's earliest days, during the Progressive reform era of the early twentieth century. Middle-class reformers, concerned to rescue city governments from what they viewed as the depredations of machine politics, called for administrative practice based not on favoritism and party loyalty but on sound values and real skills. What started as an effort to "throw the rascals out" and replace them with "good men" quickly became a campaign to professionalize public administration by making it scientific and efficient. A key element in the rhetoric of this movement was an appeal to efficient citizenship. The idea was that a more knowledgeable and active citizenry could be an important ingredient in good government. To solve municipal problems, citizens would have to understand their causes and line up behind scientific and professional approaches. Municipal research bureau leaders such as Frederick A. Cleveland, William H. Allen, and others viewed an informed citizenry as a vital resource in the municipal reform effort. Allen declared: "Without . . . facts upon which to base judgment, the public cannot intelligently direct and control the administration of township, county, city, state, or nation. Without intelligent control by the public, no efficient, triumphant democracy is possible" (1907:ix).

The citizenship rhetoric of the municipal reformers has to be understood in its context, however. Their talk of "citizen participation" and "citizen cooperation with government" can reverberate a century later in a way they did not intend. The bureau men's faith in efficiency, science, and businesslike practices limited their understanding of who, practically speaking, could act as a citizen and what citizens should properly do. Progressives, themselves middle and upper-middle class educated people, understood "the public" not as the citizenry at large but as the third member of a troika that also included business and labor. The public consisted of "social workers, journalists, lawyers, educators, and other middle-class opinion makers" (Dawley 1991:154)—in other words, people like themselves who could speak on behalf neither of capitalists nor workers but of "the public interest." With few exceptions, municipal reformers believed that ordinary (that is, poor and working-class) people lacked, if not the intelligence, then certainly the time and energy to inform themselves about city government. If the common folk were to participate, bureau men expected them to line up behind scientifically demonstrated recommendations. They saw public opinion, properly guided by factual information, as a vast untapped resource to support municipal reform, professionally defined and led.

Interestingly, despite the fact that women did not gain the vote until 1920, they were deeply involved in municipal reform efforts and, like men, saw their work as a practice of citizenship. Carrie Chapman Catt's "Ready for Citizenship" argued, echoing Tocqueville, that involvement in municipal issues was educating women and helping them see the relevance of city problems to their own concerns: "City garbage collection is seen quickly to be a multiplication of many house garbage cans" (quoted in Andolsen 1986: 49). Along similar lines, Mary Ritter Beard declared: "In years gone by, women would have stood by the tub or faucet and thanked bountiful providence for water of any amount or description; but now, as they stand there, their minds reach out through the long chain of circumstances that connect the faucet and tub with the gentlemen who sit in aldermanic conclave" (1915:206).

In settlement houses established in poor neighborhoods, educated women—and some men—lived where city problems were greatest and sought to translate their lived experiences and those of their neighbors into tangible projects and policy proposals. Jane Addams of Chicago's Hull House said that settlement residents saw their work not as philanthropy but as fulfilling "the duties of good citizenship" (1981[1910]:10). The settlement workers' first-hand knowledge of neighborhood conditions made them somewhat less critical of machine politicians than were municipal researchers. They admired aldermen for the way they paid attention to the survival needs of the people of their districts: "Neighborliness is at the basis of even bad politics, and sound government can be built upon no other foundation" (Woods and Kennedy 1970[1922]:227; see also Addams 1902).

Among the bureau reformers, the surge of interest and faith in the average citizen's potential usefulness to administrative practice was short-lived. As Waldo has wryly observed: "'Bliss was it in that dawn, etc'! Gradually, in the public administration movement as a whole, research and facts have come to be regarded less and less as devices of citizen cooperation and control and more and more as instruments of executive management" (1948:43n.). The advent of scientific management and efforts to professionalize the public service transmuted "facts" from ammunition for efficient citizenship to the basis of increasingly specialized modes of public management. In addition, in the early part of the century male and female reformers interacted regularly and, though their activities differed, shared many of the same broad goals. But the professionalization process bifurcated the reform movement, with men clustering in public administration and women in social work. The social reformers' more participatory understanding of citizenship fell between the cracks of the two new professions (Stivers, 2000).

With the post–World War II onset of the behavioral frame of reference in the social sciences, it began to appear possible to many that scientific laws of administration might replace the rather naive precepts of earlier days, and writers like Simon (1945) argued that public administration should settle for no less. Notions like citizenship and the public interest fell into disuse if not disrepute on the basis that they could not be operationalized and subjected to quantitative empirical study.

Not until the 1980s did citizenship thinking reappear in public administration. It seems to have come about as one aspect of a general effort in the field to respond to two decades of "bureaucrat-bashing" with a concerted attempt to defend the legitimacy of the administrative state. Politicians traded on the perceived failure of the War on Poverty, swollen budget deficits and a series of government scandals by promising to reduce the size of the bureaucracy and clean up "waste, fraud, and abuse." Public administrators found themselves in need of a convincing rationale for the existence, in a representative democracy, of what the public considered administrative monoliths populated by tenured, unelected bureaucrats whose responsiveness could not be counted on. Numerous books, articles, special journal issues, and conference presentations aimed to validate public administration on such bases as the expertise of career public servants, the need for continuity of leadership in an era of complexity and rapid change, and the commitment of administrators to the public interest.

The first reappearance of the theme of citizenship came during this outpouring, in Frederickson's essay, "The Recovery of Civism in Public Administration." Frederickson's argument clearly reflects the sense of crisis in public confidence that marked the early eighties; it begins, "Something is wrong. Virtually all our institutions seem to be in trouble" (1982:501). Frederickson suggests that "effective public administration of the future should be intimately tied to citizenship, the citizenry generally, and to the effectiveness of public managers who work *directly* with the citizenry."

The next step in revivifying citizenship was the National Conference on Citizenship and Public Service in 1983, sponsored by the American Society for Public Administration, the Charles F. Kettering Foundation, and the National Academy of Public Administration. The conference proceedings, which explored a wide range of issues, were published as a special issue of *Public Administration Review* (Frederickson and Chandler 1984). The notion that public administrators have a responsibility to educate citizens about government was prominent in the presentations; for example, Gawthrop's call for professional administrators to "make government interesting once again to the citizenry" (1984:106) and the following suggestion from Rohr:

> Let the career civil servant work at broadening the base of the elite by encouraging as many members of the public as possible . . . to change from citizen as consumer to citizen participating in rule. The means for doing this is public instruction, not in the bookish sense of the schools but in the daily interaction between the citizen and the bureaucracy (1984:139).

Also at this conference, Cooper introduced what has proven to be a major contribution to the literature of citizenship in public administration, that is, the notion that administrators are themselves citizens and should use the citizen role specifically as an ethical anchor. Sounding most of the citizenship themes from classical political philosophy, Cooper argued:

> The ethical obligations of the public administrator are to be derived from the obligations of citizenship in a democratic political community. These obligations include responsibility for establishing and maintaining horizontal relationships of authority with one's fellow citizens, seeking "power with" rather than "power over" the citizenry. This attitude on the part of public administrators calls for engaging in activities which amount to an ongoing renewal and reaffirmation of the "social contract" (1984a: 143–144).

Thus public administrators as citizens are expected to use their authoritative expertise on behalf of their fellow citizens and to see themselves as operating under the sovereignty of the citizenry. Cooper and others, including the present author, have subsequently expanded on these ideas.

During the 1990s, however, relationships between the citizenry and public agencies apparently worsened. A 1993 opinion poll showed that only 25% of Americans believed they could trust government all or most of the time (Roper 1993), while a 1994 survey found that two-thirds of Americans picked big government as the country's gravest peril

(Zinsmeister 1995). Newspaper accounts regularly documented sporadic attacks on government workers.

There have been two types of responses to this new wave of anti-government feeling. A pervasive one has been the impulse to privatize government functions and generally to make government run more like a business. This impulse took on something like the status of a civil religion with the publication of *Reinventing Government* (Osborne and Gaebler 1992). The reinventing idea emphasized entrepreneurialism on the part of bureaucrats, based on the idea that what citizens want is not big policy changes or active involvement but "results." In much the way that early 20th-century reformers advocated scientific management in the name of efficiency, reinvention touted making government run more like a business in the name of getting things done. "Reinventing" and similar ideas suggested that public administrators could be ethical by treating citizens as taxpayers and customers. The Clinton administration set in motion a reinventing effort at the federal level, and states and localities mobilized similar projects.

The second type of response had a specific genesis. On April 19, 1995, a tragic watershed in negativism toward government was reached with the bombing of the Alfred P. Murrah Federal Building in Oklahoma City. A few days later, the American Federation of State, County, and Municipal Employees published an advertisement in newspapers around the country, showing rescue workers carrying the dead and wounded from the building. The ad said: "Isn't it time to end the constant attacks on the people who serve us? . . . Next time you hear someone viciously attack our government, and the Americans who work for it, tell them—STOP IT. THIS IS OUR GOVERNMENT." Inspired by the bombing, a group of public administrators and academics published *Government is Us* (King et al. 1998), a dialogue in the citizenship ethics tradition promoting collaborative relationships between "active citizens and active administrators."

To date, citizenship ethics continues to vie with customer service as the normative anchor for public administration. The following sections will attempt to suggest what is at stake in such a contest.

IV. THE INGREDIENTS OF A CITIZENSHIP ETHIC

Generalizing from the writings since 1982, in the following sections I outline what the literature suggests should constitute citizenship ethics, organizing the ideas according to the themes previously identified in this chapter.

A. Authoritative Judgment

Advocates of a citizenship ethic in public administration agree that citizenship thinking strongly implies as non-hierarchical and non-elitist an attitude as possible toward the exercise of whatever discretionary authority the administrator has. This emphasis is consistent with the classic idea that citizens are equals with one another, having equal access to the decision-making process and an equal right to speak and to be heard. Cooper's idea of horizontal authority, or "power with" relations, captures this theme: It promotes a collaborative rather than a chain-of-command approach to agency decisions. Both Frederickson (1982) and Stivers (1990a) have argued that horizontal authority relations are congruent with the complex tasks of modern agencies, which are poorly suited to the "command and control" mode of comprehensive rationality and instead require decentralization, tentative solutions, frequent feedback, and an artistic or creative process. Timney suggests that any gain in efficiency achieved by processes controlled by administrators in the name of efficiency is ''short-term at best. In the long run, building consensus on policy goals is far more efficient than the ongoing conflict and dissensus that can result from controlled administrative decisions'' (1998:100).

As Cooper (1991) notes, the details of horizontal authority as a public management strategy have yet to be worked out; it threatens to undercut the responsiveness to legislative oversight that agency hierarchy more clearly supports. Citizenship thinking would suggest, however, that hierarchy creates more problems than it solves, fostering inequality, an inappropriate mode of instrumentalism, and agency inattention to the needs of the community. Drawing on the work of Mary Parker Follett, Cooper suggests that

> ''Power with'' involves a collaborative integrating of desires among participants in a decision-making process, instead of a quest for dominance by some. It grows out of circular behavior in which participants have a genuine opportunity to influence each other. . . . Information, judgment, and advice flow back and forth around the circle of political authority (1991:140).

Cooper observes that sometimes the precept of horizontal authority may require administrators to resist or oppose public officials with whose understanding of the public interest or whose activities they disagree on principle.

The value of authoritative judgment can be expanded beyond the notion of horizontal authority relations in the abstract sense to include actual practices that foster citizen involvement in agency decision-making. For example, Stivers (1994) suggests that public administrators can improve their responsiveness by actively listening to citizens as well as actively seeking their involvement. The ''Government is Us'' group offers a number of concrete recommendations along these lines, including:

> Allocate [agency] resources to support participation efforts.
> Reward administrators for working with citizens.
> Create ongoing project teams of citizens and administrators that follow projects
>   through from conception to implementation.
> Hold meetings at more convenient times and places.
> Bring citizens in when the agenda can still be shaped.
> Have roundtable discussions instead of serial monologues.
> Avoid one-shot techniques like surveys (King et al. 1998:201).

Through such moves, citizens and administrators may be able to join together in a practice of active citizenship within the context of agency mandates and responsibilities.

B. The Public Interest

The public-spiritedness of citizenship thinking is another theme common to all the writers in this area. They agree that a public administration using the precepts of citizenship as an ethical guide will put the common good above any other consideration, including practical politics, professionalism, or cost efficiency. Hart argues that the fundamental obligation of the bureaucrat is to be a good citizen; professional obligations flow from and are shaped by this basic idea. Administrators look to regime values and strive for ''the best head joined to the best heart''—a notion that evokes the idea of practical wisdom, or phronesis, which Aristotle held to be the form of knowledge appropriate to public life (Hart 1984:114).

Stivers (1991) suggests that a citizenship ethic requires two important revisions in the notion of professionalism in public administration. These include (1) broadening the definition of expertise to take in the ability to interact effectively with as wide a spectrum of the public as possible and to involve them in agency affairs; (2) seeing leadership as less a matter of being out in front of a band of followers than being the facilitator of a collaborative effort.

Cooper draws on Tocqueville's concept of self-interest, rightly understood, for his notion of the public interest in public administration. Cooper argues that the American context and history make defense of classical virtue, with its renunciation of self-interest, a tall order. In his view Americans tend to see this sort of virtue as oppressive to individual liberty. He believes, however, that a revised understanding of "self," one that recognizes its communal aspects, can rescue self-interest from selfishness: "Enlightened self-interest . . . appears to be plausible as a form of civic virtue, but only when its latent 'other regarding' aspects are firmly and explicitly cultivated through community experience and supported by a theory of community" (Cooper 1991:157). Community tempers the idea of self-interest by adding the dependence of individuals on a network of associations and obligations to the more usual respect for individual rights. Ultimately, Cooper believes, the task is not to "banish" self-interest but to "humble it." He suggests replacing the idea of professionalism with the simple notion of "practice." This move expands the administrator's moral obligations beyond responsiveness to the legislature and the exercise of functional rationality to include acting as a fiduciary to citizens and upholding the exercise of enlightened self-interest.

C. Citizenship as Education

The perception that involvement in public life strengthens understanding of public affairs and enlarges devotion to the public interest has served as the basis for advocates of a citizenship ethic to call upon administrators to educate the citizenry. Mathews (1984:124) suggests that "[c]ivic literacy, the capacity of people to think about the whole of things, of consequences and potential, becomes education of the most crucial kind." Rohr argues that such education can and should occur in daily interaction between citizens and administrators. He thinks that the administrative hearing can serve as what Tocqueville called a "gratuitous public school" to help turn "consumers of government services into citizens in the classical mold" (1984:139).

Cooper believes that public-spirited action by citizens encourages them to understand how the satisfaction of their own wants are intertwined with more general interests: "Citizens must . . . not only be possessed of predispositions to serve the common good, but they must also be able to comprehend it" (1991:154). Box and Sagan argue that administrators must give citizens "the knowledge and techniques they need to deal with public-policy issues in an informed and rational way" (1998:169). Foley maintains that "Too often, government's role is seen as providing the expertise, with the community's role as giving feedback or input to the process" (1998:156). But recognition of the importance of deliberation in democracy means that administrators must move beyond seeking "input" to creating opportunities for dialogue about how issues should be framed.

Stivers suggests that only through involvement in governmental affairs will citizens come to see themselves *as citizens*:

> If they have the opportunity to see themselves as engaged in . . . the exercise of admin-
> istrative discretion, therefore in governance, with public administrators, rather than
> "involved" simply to the extent of petitioning administrators to satisfy their needs,
> they may be able to develop improved practices and make wiser judgments (1988:
> 110).

This perspective suggests that administrators have an ethical obligation to create opportunities for citizens to exercise active citizenship in order for them to develop their capacity
for political life in the highest sense.

D. Community

The value of community is also considered an important ingredient in a citizenship ethic
for public administration. Frederickson argues that reconstruction of community is the
most important issue facing America (and public administration) today and calls for the
"recovery of civism" (1982:504).

Two notions of community play an important part in Cooper's ethic of citizenship
for public administration. Community in the sense of covenant, social contract, and group
process is the fundamental source of horizontal authority relations Cooper sees at the
heart of citizenship thinking. Drawing on Robert Pranger's work, Cooper observes that
"citizenship becomes a kind of group dynamics involving friends and equals, a spontaneous 'field' . . . where collaborators create a common union" (1991:136). Community as
covenant calls on administrators to renew and reaffirm the social contract, engaging in
"regular readjustment or reconstruction of the mutual expectations of citizens" (Cooper
1984a:144).

Another sense of community is also important, in Cooper's view: "The citizen administrator bears responsibility for . . . supporting the existence of a community of communities that includes the [voluntary nonprofit], organizational economic, and political portions of the [public-private] continuum" (1984a:144). In other words, administrators must
not settle simply for partnerships between government and profit-making business, but
must nurture the associational sphere where much citizenship-building takes place. He
argues that administrative practice must be sensitive to the importance of voluntary associations in bridging the gap between the business firm's interest in profit and government's
responsibility for the common good.

Foley emphasizes yet another dimension of community: the issue of how community
is defined and how community representation is ensured in collaborative relationships
between communities and governments. Unless governments are willing to allocate resources to support adequate community involvement and to turn power over to community
members, the request for "input" will result in a hollow exercise: "Public administrators
need to ask whether policies and programs foster community as they are being designed"
or are simply aimed at winning "community acceptance." A citizenship ethic suggests
that administrators have an obligation to take communities seriously and work to include
them fully. Empowering communities entails creating structures and processes that will
integrate citizens into the governance process (1998:152).

Stivers (1990a:269) argues that ethical practice requires administrators to examine
"how the unacknowledged political-economic conditions surrounding administrative
practice shape and sometimes determine the level of citizen knowledgeability and capability to deal with policy issues." Similarly, Box and Sagan note that administrators are

often ''caught in the cross fire of [a] struggle between the values of the community as an economic marketplace and the community as a living space for people.'' This requires them to address the question, ''Whom do we serve, and for what purpose?'' Answering this question based on a citizenship ethic would lead administrators to help citizens achieve self-governance to the maximum extent possible (1998:167). To do so would require administrators to refrain from taking for granted the range of material interests their agency policies support and to use their discretion when they can to move the work of their agencies in more broadly democratic directions.

In summary, the literature of public administration offers the following ethical guidelines based on citizenship values:

> Maximize horizontal authority relations within agencies and externally with a wide range of constituencies; foster collaborative rather than chain-of-command decision-making; develop opportunities for active citizen involvement in agency agenda setting, policy formulation and implementation.
>
> Put consideration of the widest possible interpretation of the public interest ahead of all other considerations, including efficiency, professionalism, or practical politics; strive for knowledge of what is right given the circumstances; cultivate an other-regarding form of self-interest; act as fiduciary for the broad interests of citizens.
>
> Educate citizens about important public issues and the workings of government; create opportunities for substantive dialogue and activity among citizens and administrators.
>
> Foster community: not only a sense of covenant, friendship, and mutual regard among citizens and administrators, but more widely, through a critical sense of which community interests each agency supports or excludes; within existing legislative or regulatory guidelines, use discretion to foster equality among members of a democratic community.

A citizenship ethic for public administration requires administrators to act *as* citizens, practicing in light of the above precepts, and to act *with* other citizens, viewed as equals in what is ultimately a common endeavor.

V. CITIZENSHIP AND ORGANIZATION

The increasing application of business-derived ideas and standards to the workings of government agencies raises serious issues for a citizenship ethic in public administration. Market theories, as well as theories of how to structure and manage the private organization, are in fundamental tension with the political values that make up the notion of citizenship. In this section we will consider discrepancies, first between organization theories and ideas of citizenship, and second between democratic citizenship and the aims of the market, especially as reflected in the ''reinvention'' perspective.

A. Organizational Citizenship

As Chester Barnard (1938), the first theorist to define the nature of an organization, teaches us, organizations are instruments to induce cooperation on the part of a group of individuals toward the achievement of goals that are derived not collaboratively but by a relative few, the managers and leaders at the top. While there are more or less humane ways of inducing cooperation, when push comes to shove organizations exist to get things done, and those "things" take precedence over the preferences of individual members.

Within the goal-achievement structure of organization, citizenship values (for example, participation in decision-making) become instruments to induce greater cooperation and achieve organizational purposes. As instruments, their value is dependent on whether they promote organizational ends; if they do not, they must be abandoned. But one of the defining features of citizenship is that it is valuable for its own sake, as the expression of human aspirations and capacities that can be cultivated in no other way. Citizenship is an end in itself, not simply the means to other ends. It entails goods—justice, equality, participation, the public interest, community—that are to be addressed regardless of whether they foster efficiency, technical rationality, cost savings, profit-making, or the realization of organizational goals.

In some ways the tension between citizenship values and organizational aims is a reflection of the familiar politics-administration dialectic in public administration. From the citizenship perspective, however, one of the time-honored ways of resolving this tension is not viable: that is, by seeing efficiency as in the service of political ends determined externally (what Waldo has called "autocracy at work" as the "price for democracy after hours" [Waldo 1948:75]). The citizenship ethic holds that hierarchy in public organization as an instrument of political democracy is a contradiction in terms. If the polity values equal, active citizenship it must value it inside public organizations as much as it does elsewhere, even if this means the sacrifice of a measure (perhaps even a large measure) of efficiency and/or rationality. Thus the promotion of a citizenship ethic in public administration has to proceed with care, not to fall into the trap of selling itself solely on the basis that it will enable agencies to do their jobs better.

A growing literature on "organizational citizenship" envisions a form of management that mitigates hierarchy through collaboration, participation, and citizenship "behavior" within the organization, private or public. In contrast to the writings on citizenship ethics already described, virtually all of the organizational citizenship literature treats citizenship values instrumentally (see, for example, Parks and Conlon 1991; McAllister 1991; Organ 1990; Organ 1988). The flavor of this approach to citizenship in organizational life is captured in this typical excerpt:

> While it is generally acknowledged that OCBs [organizational citizenship behaviors] contribute to organizational performance, this relationship has, for the better part, been assumed to exist and left empirically unexamined. . . . There is some need, however, to reconcile [difficulty in measuring its impact on outcomes] with the realization that contextual considerations do modify this relationship—*performance suboptimization is likely when citizenship-type behaviors are engaged in inappropriately* (McAllister 1991:14; emphasis added).

In other words, citizenship "behavior" is tolerable only as long as it serves ("optimizes") organizational functions. Furthermore, much of the literature on organizational citizenship limits the notion to such values as loyalty, conscientiousness, sportsmanship, a willingness to go beyond what is strictly required by the job description. One central text styles this behavior "the good soldier syndrome" (Organ 1988).

On the other hand, Graham (1991) has tried to broaden the idea of organizational citizenship to take its political dimensions seriously. Participation, she notes, is controversial in the organizational context, for it raises the possibility that the good organizational citizen may have to dissent for reasons of principle: "Following unethical orders exemplifies poor citizenship at every level. . . . While sidestepping [power] issues by ignoring political participation as a category of citizenship behavior results in a picture of OCB that is extremely pleasant, it is nonetheless flawed as a result" (1991:32).

Focusing on public organizations, Golembiewski (1989) argues that membership in an organization, whether public or private, can be viewed as a form of citizenship. He presents a range of strategies for enhancing employee freedom and responsibility, group decision-making, and greater delegation of authority. He maintains that these methods will not only improve employee satisfaction and productivity but will lead to greater political efficacy and participation and thereby promote popular sovereignty (the paradigmatic statement of this argument is found in Pateman 1970).

In rejoinder, Stivers (1989) suggests that while participatory management is a good thing, it should not be thought of as citizenship. Not all public organizational decisions are clearly in the public interest. If we equate citizenship with involvement in organizational decision-making, that is, in serving organizational goals regardless of their relationship to the needs and wants of citizens, we are in danger of settling for involvement in organization and letting real (political) citizenship disappear.

B. Reinventing Government

The 1990s witnessed a concerted effort to improve public administration by drawing on business-oriented ideas and techniques. The central notion underlying this approach is that the bureaucratic paradigm of formal structure and control is obsolete. Instead of relying on professionalism to ensure that managerial decisions promote the public interest, government organizations should be "customer-driven and service oriented"—that is, "responsive, user-friendly, dynamic, and competitive providers of valuable services to customers" (Barzelay 1997:494–495). The most widely read expression of this viewpoint has been *Reinventing Government* (Osborne and Gaebler 1992). It argues that the problem is not *what* governments do but *how*, and promotes entrepreneurialism and creativity on the part of civil servants to maximize productivity and results.

President Bill Clinton took up the "reinvention" idea with fervor and appointed Vice-President Al Gore to head the National Performance Review (NPR), the reinvention effort at the federal level. Following Osborne and Gaebler, the NPR exclaimed that the main problem with government agencies was good people trapped in bad systems. Like Barzelay, it argued that bureaucratic thinking was outmoded in a world of rapid change and global competition. In the future, the key principles for government administration would be to cut red tape, put customers first, empower employees to get results, and find incentives so that public servants work better at less cost (Executive Office of the President 1993).

Advocates of business-driven ideas and practices insist either that their recommendations have no political implications or that the new methods will promote democratic values. Yet examined through the lens of a citizenship ethic, the entrepreneurial approach raises troubling questions.

First, thinking of and treating citizens as customers obviates any notion of sharing horizontal decision-making authority with members of the public. Many of government's "customers" have no choice about where to "purchase" the services they receive, let alone the power to affect what services are available or how they are delivered (Schachter 1997).

Second, in the reinvention perspective the public interest is treated as an outmoded concept. The idea that citizens could collaborate with administrators in the exercise of public-spirited judgment is obliterated by notions of managerial creativity and "results." But are managers the only ones with the potential for creativity? For all its talk of customer service, reinvention empowers managers, not citizens. By assuming that managerial decisions only deal with means, not ends, reinvention reasserts the old politics-administration dichotomy, and for the same reason: to strengthen executive and managerial power at the expense of political stakeholders, whether in the legislature or among the public at large. The Hamiltonian idea that what people want is not participation in governance but services that work well and do not cost very much strengthens the manager's hand and excludes citizens.

Third, business-driven government ignores the question of educating citizens in favor of "serving" them. Reinvention has nothing to say about how to inform citizens about public issues or how to create opportunities for substantive dialogue. It assumes that restoring the public's trust in government is a matter of simply delivering tangible goods, not enlightening citizens about the complexities of public decision-making or encouraging them to think beyond "getting mine."

Finally, reinvention lacks any attention to fostering community, friendship, or mutual regard among citizens and administrators. It treats citizens as anonymous units in a market mechanism.

In sum, the reinvention perspective presents public administration with an ethic that emphasizes efficient and effective performance, cutting through red tape, serving the customer, finding creative solutions to administrative problems, fostering teamwork within the agency and competition without, decentralizing, and leveraging change through market forces. All are strictly *organizational* rather than *political* recommendations, and in fact proponents frequently take pride in this. As far as relationships with the public are concerned, business-oriented reforms worry only about whether members of the public are satisfied—therefore supportive and quiescent—and not about whether they have a voice in decisions, as it is safer and more efficient if they do not.

VI. THE FUTURE OF CITIZENSHIP ETHICS

Future work on citizenship ethics in public administration will continue to be challenged by the tension between organizational (or business) and citizenship values. Continued expansion of market-driven approaches to the management of public agencies will require normative theorists to strengthen arguments for ethical frameworks grounded in democratic political values like citizenship. Themes of horizontal authority, the public interest, citizen education, and community will continue to shape the conversation in this area, but the danger that such ideas will be weighed within in business framework rather than a political one will remain ever present.

As far as potential expansion of citizenship thinking in public administration, two issues raised at the beginning of this chapter are worthy of note: the question of standing or inclusion and the question of the relationship between citizenship and economic status.

A. Inclusion

Advocates of citizenship ethics in public administration are faced with acknowledging that throughout U.S. history citizenship has both symbolized inclusion in a national community and been restricted in theory and/or practice to certain inhabitants. Certain "others"—women, people of color—have been and continue to be defined as different in order to rationalize substantive inequality among members of the polity. Supposedly innate differences justify unequal rights and public obligations, for example, women's "special" nature is used to bar women from certain combat duties or from the draft.

As a principle, the coherence of citizenship seems to require identical (i.e., "equal") citizens whose differences are politically insignificant; yet identical citizenship obliterates variations in life circumstance that come about because of the very characteristics (race, gender) that make certain people "different." Is there a way in which citizenship—membership in the polity—need not be based on wiping out difference? Citizenship thinking needs to confront this question (Stivers 1996). The gap between equality in principle and in actual circumstance suggests both its difficulty and its importance. The achievement of a political community that is both inclusive and diverse will require those whose membership has been relatively unarguable to begin listening faithfully and with great care to the views of those they perceive as "others." For public administrators, this process may begin with a lowering of barriers between themselves and the public at large, with particular efforts in the direction of those excluded on the basis of race, sex, or other ascriptive characteristic. A citizenship ethic based on true equality and diversity requires administrators to create practical communities of collaboration that are open and accessible to all.

B. Citizenship and Economic Status

In liberal citizenship theory, because of the primary of individual rights, political equality exists side by side with economic inequality. While theorists separate the economic and the political, it is clear that in practice the two spheres affect each other. Political rights safeguard the market economy, while the market enables and constrains political opportunities and priorities.

States that are both capitalist and democratic must therefore engage in an ongoing balancing act. Formal citizenship rights alone are not enough to change the power of investment wealth to shape how many and what kinds of jobs are available or to guarantee a minimum level of economic security for citizens. Nor, it is clear, does the market itself ensure the political conditions under which its continued operation is provided for. Capitalist economies are shored up by social services, income supports, and public regulation that have made most citizens comfortable and secure and therefore content with the status quo (Galbraith 1990:51).

The rise of democratic citizenship has failed to bring about economic equality or even an adequate living standard for all, and the continued theoretical separation between the political and the economic sets limits on what we as a society are able to envision doing. As Barbelet notes:

> Citizenship and class are based on opposing principles . . . ; one on equality and freedom, the other on inequality and domination. But the things to which the equality of citizenship refers are not the same as those which make up class inequality. It is for this reason that citizenship and social class can continue to exist together (1988:58).

The result is the system so familiar to us today, in which the granting of formal rights fails to create the conditions under which all citizens are able to order their lives to attain the minimal living standard that would make their participation in political life possible and meaningful.

If, as Shklar argues, "the source of the ideology of earning is not in the conditions of employment but in political perceptions," (1991:85) then citizenship entails not just formal rights but also the ability to be self-supporting. A citizenship ethic in public administration needs to explore the economic dimensions of citizenship and their moral implications for administrative practice.

Cooper (1991) leans in this direction when he expands the notion of community to consider structural relationships between governments, private businesses, and voluntary associations. Extending Cooper's argument might take us in the direction of a fresh look at ideas like "privatizing" and "contracting out." Administrators might analyze their workability not only in terms of offloading agency operations to increase efficiency but also in terms of the impact on community-based organizations. A citizenship ethic would require relationships between agencies and community organizations to meet political standards (inclusion, deliberation, judgment, education) as well as organizational ones.

Admittedly, these new directions for citizenship thinking, inclusion and consideration of economic implications, are controversial in that they question long-accepted dimensions of liberal political theory. But the moral issues they raise seem to me to be inherent in the idea of citizenship at its most admirable. And in light of the growing encroachment of business thinking in public administration, it may be necessary to develop deeper understandings of political ideas like citizenship if such values are to survive, let alone flourish.

REFERENCES

Adams, J. (1981[1910]). *Twenty Years at Hull House*. New York: Penguin Books Signet Classic.

Addams, J. (1902). *Democracy and Social Ethics*. New York: MacMillan.

Allen, W. H. (1907). *Efficient Democracy*. New York: Dodd, Mead.

Andolsen, B. H. (1986). *"Daughters of Jefferson, Daughters of Bootblacks:" Racism and American Feminism*. Macon, GA: Mercer University Press.

Arendt, H. (1963). *On Revolution*. Harmondsworth, UK: Penguin Books.

Arendt, H. (1958). *The Human Condition*. Chicago, IL: University of Chicago Press.

Aristotle. (1981). *The Politics* (trans., T. A. Sinclair). Harmondsworth, UK: Penguin Books.

Aristotle. (1976). *Nicomachean Ethics* (trans., J. A. K. Thompson). Harmondsworth, UK: Penguin Books.

Barbelet, J. M. (1988). *Citizenship: Rights, Struggle, and Class Inequality*. Minneapolis, MN: University of Minnesota Press.

Barber, B. (1984). *Strong Democracy: Participatory Politics for a New Age*. Berkeley, CA: University of California Press.

Barnard, C. I. (1938). *The Functions of the Executive*. Cambridge, MA: Harvard University Press.

Barzelay, M. (1997[1992]). Breaking through bureaucracy. In: *Classics of Public Administration*, 4th ed. (Jay M. Shafritz and Albert C. Hyde, eds.). Fort Worth: Harcourt Brace, pp. 491–513.

Beard, M. R. (1915). Women's work for the city. *National Municipal Review* 4:3(April), pp. 204–210.

Beiner, R. (1982). Hannah Arendt on judging. In: Hannah Arendt, *Lectures on Kant's Political Philosophy* (Ronald Beiner, ed.). Chicago, IL: University of Chicago Press.

Box, R. C. and Sagan, D. (1998). Working with citizens: Breaking down barriers to citizen self-governance. In: *Government is Us: Public Administration in an Anti-Government Era* (Cheryl Simrell King, Camilla Stivers and collaborators). Thousand Oaks, CA: Sage Publications.

Chandler, R. C. (1984). Conclusions: The public administration as representative citizen: A new role for the new century. In: *Citizenship and Public Administration* (H. George Frederickson and Ralph Clark Chandler, eds.). *Public Administration Review* 44 (Special Issue): 196–206.

Cooper, T. L. (1991). *An Ethic of Citizenship for Public Administration*. Englewood Cliffs, NJ: Prentice Hall.

Cooper, T. L. (1984a). Citizenship and professionalism in public administration. In: *Citizenship and Public Administration* (H. George Frederickson and Ralph Clark Chandler, eds.). *Public Administration Review* 44 (Special Issue): 143–149.

Cooper, T. L. (1984b). Public administration in an age of scarcity: A normative essay on ethics for public administrators. In: *Politics and Administration: Woodrow Wilson and Public Administration* (Jack Rabin and James Bowman, eds.). New York, NY: Marcel Dekker, pp. 297–314.

Cooper, T. L. (1980). Bureaucracy and community organization. *Administration and Society* 11 (February): 411–444.

Dawley, A. (1991). *Struggles for Justice: Social Responsibility and the Liberal State*. Cambridge, MA: Belknap Press of Harvard University Press.

Executive Office of the President. (1993). *National Performance Review*. Washington, DC: Government Printing Office.

Finley, M. I. (1985). *Politics in the Ancient World*. Cambridge, UK: Cambridge University Press.

Finley, M. I. (1973). *Democracy Ancient and Modern*. New Brunswick, NJ: Rutgers University Press.

Flathman, R. (1981). Citizenship and authority: A chastened view of citizenship. *News for Teachers of Political Science* 30 (Summer): 9–19.

Flathman, R. (1966). *The Public Interest*. New York: John Wiley and Sons.

Foley, D. (1998). We want your input: Dilemmas of citizen participation. *Government is Us: Public Administration in an Anti-Government Era* (Cheryl Simrell King, Camilla Stivers, and collaborators). Thousand Oaks, CA: Sage Publications.

Frederickson, H. G. (1991). Toward a theory of the public for public administration. *Administration and Society* 22(February): 395–417.

Frederickson, H. G. (1982). The recovery of civism in public administration. *Public Administration Review* 42(November/December): 501–508.

Frederickson, H. G. and Chandler, R. C., eds. (1984). Citizenship and public administration. *Public Administration Review* 44 (Special issue).

Galbraith, J. K. (1990). The rush to capitalism. *New York Review of Books* (October 25): 51–52.

Gawthrop, L. C. (1984). Civis, civitas, and civilitas: A new focus for the year 2000. In: *Citizenship and Public Administration* (H. George Frederickson and Ralph Clark Chandler, eds.). *Public Administration Review* 44 (Special Issue): 101–107.

Golembiewski, R. T. (1989). Toward a positive and practical public management: Organizational research supporting a fourth critical citizenship. *Administration and Society* 21(August): 200–207.

Graham, J. W. (1991). An essay on organizational citizenship behavior. Typescript furnished by the author. Published in *The Employee Responsibilities and Rights Journal* 4(4).

Hart, D. K. (1984). The virtuous citizens, the honorable bureaucrat, and ''public'' administration. In: *Citizenship and Public Administration* (H. George Frederickson and Ralph Clark Chandler, eds.). *Public Administration Review* 44 (Special Issue): 111–120.

Held, D. (1987). *Models of Democracy*. Stanford, CA: Stanford University Press.

King, C. S., Stivers, C., and collaborators. (1998). *Government is Us: Public Administration in an Anti-Government Era*. Thousand Oaks, CA: Sage Publications.

Mathews, D. (1984). The public in practice and theory. In: *Citizenship and Public Administration* (H. George Frederickson and Ralph Clark Chandler, eds.). *Public Administration Review* 44 (Special Issue): 120–125.

McAllister, D. J. (1991). Regrounding organizational citizenship behavior research. Presented at the Annual Meeting of the Academy of Management. Miami, FL. August 11–14.

Mill, J. S. (1972). *Utilitarianism, On Liberty, and Consideration on Representative Government* (H. B. Acton, ed.). London, UK: Dent/Everyman's Library.

Morgan, E. S. (1975). *American Slavery, American Freedom: The Ordeal of Colonial Virginia.* New York: W. W. Norton.

Organ, D. W. (1990). The motivational basis of organizational citizenship behavior. *Research in Organizational Behavior* 12: 43–72.

Organ, D. W. (1988). *Organizational Citizenship Behavior: The Good Soldier Syndrome.* Lexington, MA: Lexington Books.

Osborne, D. and Gaebler, T. (1992). *Reinventing Government.* Reading, MA: Addison-Wesley.

Parks, J. McLean and Conlon, E. J. (1991). Organizational contracts and citizenship behaviors: An experimental test. Typescript (June).

Pateman, C. (1970). *Participation and Democratic Theory.* Cambridge, UK: Cambridge University Press.

Rohr, J. A. (1984). Civil servants and second class citizens. In: *Citizenship and Public Administration* (H. George Frederickson and Ralph Clark Chandler, eds.). *Public Administration Review* 44 (Special Issue): 135–140.

Roper, B. W. (1993). Democracy in America: How are we doing? *The Public Perspective* 5(1): 3–5.

Schaar, J. H. (1970). Legitimacy in the modern state. In: *Power and Community: Dissenting Essays in Political Science* (Philip Green and Sanford Levinson, eds.). New York: Pantheon Books, pp. 276–327.

Schachter, H. L. (1997). *Reinventing Government or Reinventing Ourselves.* Albany, NY: State University of New York Press.

Shklar, J. N. (1991). *American Citizenship: The Quest for Inclusion.* Cambridge, MA: Harvard University Press.

Simon, H. (1945). *Administrative Behavior.* New York: The Free Press.

Stivers, C. (2000). *Bureau Men, Settlement Women: Constructing Public Administration in the Progressive Era.* Lawrence, KS: University Press of Kansas.

Stivers, C. (1996). Citizenship, difference, and the Refounding Project. In: *Refounding Democratic Public Administration* (Gary L. Wamsley and James F. Wolf, eds.). Thousand Oaks, CA: Sage Publications, pp. 260–278.

Stivers, C. (1994). The listening bureaucrat: Responsiveness in public administration. *Public Administration Review* 54:4(September/October): 364–369.

Stivers, C. (1991). Some tensions in the notion of "the public as citizen:" Rejoinder to Frederickson. *Administration and Society* 22 (February): 418–423.

Stivers, C. M. (1990a). Active citizenship and public administration. In: *Refounding Public Administration* (Gary L. Wamsley et al.). Newbury Park, CA: Sage Publications, pp. 246–273.

Stivers, C. (1990b). The public agency as polis: Active citizenship in the administrative state. *Administration and Society* 22 (May): 86–105.

Stivers, C. (1989). Organizational citizenships—a problematic metaphor. *Administration and Society* 21 (August): 228–233.

Stivers, C. (1988). Active Citizenship in the Administrative State. Unpublished Ph.D. dissertation. Blacksburg, VA: Virginia Polytechnic Institute and State University.

Timney, M. M. (1998). Overcoming administrative barriers to citizen participation: Citizens as partners, not adversaries. In: *Government is Us: Public Administration in an Anti-Government Era* (Cheryl Simrell King, Camilla Stivers, and collaborators). Thousand Oaks, CA: Sage Publications, pp. 88–101.

Tocqueville, A. de (1945). *Democracy in America*, 2 vols. (Phillips Bradley, ed.). New York: Vintage Books.

Waldo, D. (1948). *The Administrative State.* New York: Ronald Press.

Wolin (1960). *Politics and Vision.* Boston: Little, Brown.

Woods, R. A. and Kennedy, A. (1970[1922]). *The Settlement Horizon: A National Estimate.* New York: Arno Press.

Zinsmeister, K. (1995). Payday mayday. *The American Enterprise* 6(5): 44–48.

28

Administrative Ethics and Democratic Theory

John P. Burke
University of Vermont, Burlington, Vermont

The place of bureaucracy within a democratic political order is one of the most important issues in public administration. Most textbooks in the field contain at least one chapter that seeks to inform readers about the linkage between the administrative process and democratic governance, and most scholars who delve into normative assessment of public bureaucracy (and many do, either explicitly or implicitly) seek to connect it, in varying ways, to some conception of democracy. Yet discussion of the relationship between bureaucracy and democracy has been fraught with conceptual difficulty and has lacked consensus. As Dennis Thompson has observed, the tension seems to stem from their respective conceptual cores: "Many of the values we associate with democracy—equality, participation and individuality—stand sharply opposed to the hierarchy, specialization and impersonality we ascribe to bureaucracy" (Thompson, 1983: 235).

The problem compounds when we consider the relationship between administrative *ethics* and democracy. Here we not only find the familiar tension between bureaucracy and democracy but also the introduction of a third (and, possibly, further opposed) concept—ethics—which seems to connote a realm of personal morality and individual value judgment further at odds with the other two.

Yet conceptual difficulties notwithstanding, consideration of administrative ethics from the perspective of democratic theory raises a number of interesting issues. First, it forces us to examine what we mean by administrative ethics and what place such individual value judgments rightfully have within the administrative sphere. Second, democratic theory may offer useful insights into how administrative ethics may be substantively defined in ways that avoid conflict between the personal and political. Third, it may serve as an avenue of reconciling the oft-conflicting demands of bureaucracy and democracy. Let us consider each in turn.

I. ADMINISTRATIVE ETHICS AND DEMOCRATIC THEORY

That administrative officials ought to exercise ethical judgment in the carrying out of their various tasks and duties seems—at least on the surface—both indisputable and firmly in line with the aims of democratic theory. The protection of individual freedom is undeniably one of the central goals of a democratic political order and the free exercise of ethical judgment by democratic citizens is both historically and practically one of the most important expressions of that freedom. Most democratic systems can trace their origins to a felt need by citizens to establish a political order that would more fully secure liberties—especially those of conscience, religious practice, and personal association—that are most intimately linked to leading what might be termed "the freely chosen ethical life." And protection of such liberties—witness our own Bill of Rights—remains firmly enshrined as an important, if not the most important, aim of democracy.

It may also be the case that ethical action can further the goals of democracy. Whistleblowing and other practices of disclosure can reveal malfeasance in office and thwart unethical and illegal activities that detract from the pursuit of proper public purposes. Timely ethical action can protect the rights of others and otherwise ensure they are provided with the goods and services to which they are entitled. Ethics can even strengthen democracy, rather than just protect it from abuse, by providing information needed for informed political choice and by encouraging the fairness necessary to its deliberations (Burke, 1986: 64–78). Ethical behavior can also foster a more general ethos that not only can pervade officialdom in a positive manner but set an example for democratic citizenry at large.

Yet, on closer examination, the exercise of ethical judgment by administrative officials may raise problems for democracy. First, ethics generally has as its source personal moral judgments and principles. These values may be shared by others, but their use by persons who occupy positions in public service may set public goals to private ends and purposes. My ethical principles, for example, may tell me I have a duty to feed the hungry and provide shelter for the homeless, but use of the funds and power I have been entrusted with as a public servant for even these noble purposes may divert public funds and my attention from other projects I am expected to carry out. Ethics counsels one course, my duties of office another.

The problems are compounded by the fact that ethical judgments often vary greatly in how they might inform the actions of administrators; shared use of the term "moral" or "ethical" offers no guarantee that the substantive content of value judgments issuing from them gain common recognition. An administrator steeped in Catholic moral dogma, for example, might reach very different conclusions about whether government funds ought to be expended to finance the use of fetal tissue in medical research than would a Unitarian, an agnostic, or an atheist.

Even among those scholars who have restricted their attention to the administrative setting, ethical views and recommendations vary greatly. For Stephen Bailey, for example, "the essential moral qualities of the ethical public servant are: 1) optimism; 2) courage; and 3) fairness tempered by charity" (1965: 235–36). H. George Frederickson points to the central role of "social equity" in defining ethical behavior (1974: 1; 1990: 228–37), and elsewhere he and David K. Hart embrace the "patriotism of benevolence" (1985: 547–53) as a central normative principle. Louis Gawthrop rejects an ethics of civility that is incremental, mechanistic and pragmatic, and he urges administrators instead to follow an ethics of creativity and maturity, which, respectively, provide an ability to be critically honest to oneself and a sense of purpose in one's life (Gawthrop, 1984). Gerald Pops and Thomas Pavlak (1991: 3–6) regard justice as the "core value" in public administration, a view they share with Terry Cooper, who notes that "Justice defines the most essential political good; it is the fundamental ordering principle of democratic society . . ." "If that is the case," Cooper continues, "then fairmindedness, rationality, prudence, and courage are essential virtues for the practice of public administration" (1987:325).

Even within more established ethical traditions, moral insights and recommendations vary greatly. For example, both John Rawls' (1971) notion of "justice as fairness" and Ronald Dworkin's (1977) rights-based theory of "equal concern and respect" find their inspiration in Kant, yet the principles each derive from Kant differ significantly and lead, in turn, to very different insights about the justice of public policy. Similarly, moral philosophers who have argued in favor of a "common morality" underlying disparate theories of ethics and applicable both to personal and public life reach very different conclusions about the source of such a morality and its substantive implications. The common morality that Alan Donagan (1977: 172–209) seeks to distill from the Judeo-Christian tradition, for example, differs markedly from that which Stuart Hampshire (1978) embraces. Both claim the applicability of their respective theories across private and public life, but for Donagan the source of that morality is historically universal, while for Hampshire it is culturally and socially specific.

There is undoubtedly a realm of moral judgment that bridges both spheres of public and private; bribery, influence peddling and other corrupt practices, for example, are problems for public officials that seem to take their proper ethical cue from commonly held moral beliefs. But the great bulk of analysis in the field of administrative ethics seems more ambitious: to inform public officials about a wide range of discretionary action and to create a sense of "subjective responsibility" (Cooper, 1990: 71–76) or an "administrative ethos" that may variously embody, for some scholars, a commitment to Rawls' concept of social equity (Hart, 1974; Harmon, 1981: 87), allegiance to a "higher law . . . above and beyond both individual and government" (Waldo, 1980: 101), a "moral framework" applicable to both the public and private domains (Goldman, 1980: 71), or some notion of a "lasting moral order" (Denhardt, 1988: 39).

Such a "thick theory" of administrative ethics, in turn, raises a second problem for democratic theory. Even if we assume, for purposes of argument, that there was general agreement on a wide and inclusive range of moral principles, it may still not necessarily be the case that they ought to be applied by public officials, administrators in particular. Application of even widely shared moral principles may give insufficient weight (should they be in conflict) to the institutional obligations of administrators, obligations that may have moral weight in their own right and that may justifiably "trump" the claims of a morally inspired politics.

Even more problematic is the compromise to the basic democratic principle of collective—rather than individual—choice such a "thick theory" seems to apply. Particular moral or ethical theories may detect a wide range of social harms, inequities, and violations of individual rights that, while important from the perspective of one or another set of ethical principles, can fail to gain remedy or recognition by democratic politics (Burke, 1986: 100–141). Most democracies, however, generally limit the goods and services that government provides.

Liberal democracies, in particular, balance the provision of services through the public sphere against their provision through private economic and social activity. Indeed the preference—less so in European democracies but more so in the United States—is generally for the latter over the former; government is often thought to be the "provider of last resort" or at least an avenue that ought to be avoided whenever possible or if other alternatives are available.

Even if one believes that the public sphere ought to be favored over the private—one as, say, a strong democrat rather than a cautious liberal—a wide berth for ethical judgment may remain problematic: The notion of some type of *collective* decision-making process, which seems basic to most democratic theories, whose purpose is to arrive at general agreement in the face of differences on particulars might be at risk if the particular moral principles of persons who occupy positions of power are allowed free rein. Indeed, it seems anti-democratic to suggest that moral principles (which, as we have seen, are often themselves in conflict) ought to take precedence over political deliberations about what goods and services government should provide. Conversely, it may only be through democratic procedures that moral principles can find legitimate expression; as Dennis Thompson (1987: 3) concludes, "disputes in political ethics, even about fundamental principles, must be resolved finally or at least partly through some form of democratic process."

II. WHAT DEMOCRATIC THEORY?

Let us now, for purposes of argument, "assume democracy," as Paul Appleby (1952: 28) once put it, and ask how democratic theory might inform or otherwise define a theory of administrative ethics. Unfortunately, the problem that now arises is very much like the dilemma confronting administrative ethics that we discussed above: democratic theorists offer very different definitions of democracy and, accordingly, the role of administrative officials (and the definition of the scope and content of their duties and responsibilities) can vary greatly depending on the particular theory.

A. Classical Democratic Theory

Unfortunately, the various strands of what might be termed classical democratic theory—the "great texts" in political philosophy—are not much help. Writing before the advent of modern organizations, most did not anticipate the impact of political, social, and economic modernization in creating the need for a complex administrative state; thus there is little attention to bureaucracy much less the more delimited topic of proper conduct on the part of administrative officials. John Locke, for example, is deliberately silent on administrative matters, noting, in the *Second Treatise*, that of "the ministerial and subordinate powers in a Commonwealth, we need not speak . . ." (Laslett, 1960: 415). In *The Social Contract*, Rousseau states that the general will "solely directs" (Frankel, 1947:56). He does note, a few pages later, that "It is not good for the power that makes the laws to execute them," adding that it is not "proper that the body of the people should turn their eyes from general views to fix them on particular objects" (Frankel, 1947: 56, 59). But he fails to consider the duties of those officials who must so fix their attention on the particular.

Similar absence of attention to the administrative sphere prevails among the American Founders. In *Federalist No. 70*, Hamilton worries about the enfeeblement of the executive by republican government, but it is "enfeebled execution" that is his primary concern. In *Federalist No. 72*, he offers in passing the view that officials involved in the "administration of government" ought to be "considered as the assistants or deputies of the Chief Magistrate, and on this account . . . ought to be subject to his superintendence." As Ralph Clark Chandler observes, "It was clear . . . in *The Federalist* as well as in the debates of the Constitutional Convention, that political liberty and economic energy unavoidably engender some immorality, but that government can control it without the institutional consequences of preaching and being preached to'' (Chandler, 1983: 32). Although Madison recognized that men were certainly rarely angels, his general solution in *Federalist No. 51* of ''ambition countering ambition'' through means of a system of checks and balances was thought sufficient to curb the passions and interests of those who would threaten the public weal.

Thomas Jefferson takes a more democratic stance, viewing administration as largely subject to the dictates of popular control. In a December 10, 1819 letter to John Adams, he states that ''No government can continue good but under the control of the people'' (Dumbauld, 1955: 92). In a letter to Abbe Arnoux on July 19, 1789, he offers the classical solution, which can be traced to the practices of the Athenian polis, of rotation in office and popular participation in administrative matters: ''We think, in America, that it is necessary to introduce the people into every department of government so far as they are capable of exercising it, and that this is the only way to insure a long continued and honest administration of its powers'' (Dumbauld, 1955: 89).

Writing in the mid-nineteenth century, John Stuart Mill, in *Considerations on Representative Government*, begins to articulate concerns about participation, equality, and representation within a more complex state structure. We now find, for example, attention to the role of expertise as a guide for official conduct: ''the entire business of government is skilled employment; the qualifications for the discharge of it are of that special and professional kind which cannot be properly judged of except by persons who have themselves some share of those qualifications . . .'' (Mill, 1958: 199). But Mill, like his predecessors, remains chiefly concerned with issues relating to democratic control over the entire state apparatus, albeit within the framework of a more republican and institutionally structured—but still participatory—conception of government.

For the remainder of the nineteenth century and the early decades of the twentieth century, the general lack of attention to the place of bureaucracy within democratic government persisted among leading democratic theorists. The great bulk of speculation in democratic theory turned on issues of the quality of citizen participation and broader questions of democratic control (see Pateman, 1970; Thompson, 1970). The English pluralists, such as G.D.H. Cole, took up Mill's call for increased participation, expanding its applicability to a range of public and private associations. On the other side of the issue, ''democratic revisionists'' such as Michels, Mosca, and Schumpeter, while recognizing the emergence of bureaucratic organization, challenged the competence of the mass public and embraced in its place various schemas of elite rule. The empirical and normative debate over citizen participation, although important, overshadowed attention to the place of administrative conduct within democratic government, a condition that still unfortunately persists in political philosophy and empirical analyses of the requisites of democratic government.

Although offering only a ''thin theory'' of the administrative sphere, these classical democratic theorists did raise concerns that would be more fully developed with the emergence of public administration as a discrete field of scholarly inquiry. Most share a general view of bureaucracy as subservient to the direction of higher political authorities, thus implicitly anticipating the ''split'' between politics and administration that would be prominent in public administration through the first four decades of the twentieth century. Mill is a bit more prescient in his insights: his notion of the importance of skill and expertise anticipates the emphasis on professional responsibility that Carl J. Friedrich would later articulate in his famous exchange with Herman Finer. And Mill also recognized the educative effects upon citizens of participation in representative government—the development of moral intellectual faculties and a sense of "public spiritedness"—that would concern the New Public Administration movement beginning in the 1960s as well as contemporary writers on administrative ethics.

B. Formal-Legalism

It is only with the emergence of public administration, roughly at the turn of the century, as a discrete field of scholarly inquiry that we begin to find systematic attention to the question of how bureaucratic officials should conceive of their proper role within the administrative sphere. One school of thought that dates from this period, termed formal-legalism, was the reigning orthodoxy in public administration through, roughly, the first four decades of the twentieth century. Its origins can be found in such classic works as Woodrow Wilson's "The Study of Administration" (1887), Frank Goodnow's *Politics and Administration* (1900), and Max Weber's essays "Politics as a Vocation" and "Science as a Vocation," both in 1918, and the section from *Wirtschaft und Gesellschaft* on "Bureaucracy" published posthumously in 1922 (Gerth and Mills, 1958: 77–158, 196–240).

The central thread running through the formal-legal approach is that bureaucratic officials are passive instruments of "higher authorities." Administrators are not expected to be responsible, ethical, or even political in an active way. At most their responsibilities are passive and delimited: they simply apply those laws, standards, rules, and procedures that their organizational superiors or higher political bodies, such as legislatures or courts, deem appropriate. According to Woodrow Wilson, "administration lies outside the sphere of politics. . . . Public administration is detailed and systematic execution of public law." Administration, in Wilson's view, "is part of political life only as the methods of the countinghouse are a part of the life of society; only as machinery is part of the manufactured product" (1887: 210, 212). For Max Weber, the proper vocation of the civil servant requires that he "will not engage in politics. Rather he should engage in impartial 'administration'." Political leaders can "take a stand" and "be passionate," but the conduct of the civil servant is "exactly the opposite:"

> The honor of the civil servant is vested in his ability to execute conscientiously the order of the superior authorities, exactly as if the order agreed with his own conviction. This holds even if the order appears wrong to him. . . . Without this moral discipline and self-denial, in the highest sense, the whole apparatus would fall to pieces. (Gerth and Mills, 1958: 95)

In formal-legal approaches, then, the emphasis falls on the strict obedience of civil servants to hierarchy, the orders of superiors, and the explicit legal and administrative rules and procedures established by those political "higher-ups." In terms of administrative ethics, it is, for the formal-legal approach, moral to be amoral.

The neat split between politics and administration advocated by formal-legalism came under increasing challenge in the 1930s with the emergence of greater empirical study of the administrative process and the internal workings of public and private organizations (Herring, 1936; Barnard, 1938; Roethlisberger and Dickson, 1939). Formal-legalism was further challenged by the recognition of the need for bureaucratic responsiveness in responding to the economic difficulties of the Great Depression and Roosevelt's clarion call for an activist New Deal. Although most formal-legalists did not deny that discretion sometimes occurred within bureaucratic organizations, they claimed that it reflected legislative or executive inattention and laxity, not genuine bureaucratic need. This view came under both empirical and normative scrutiny (Leys, 1943). Empirically, bureaucratic discretion and activism was recognized as a "normal part" and "predictable behavior" within the administrative process, as were over-conformism and goal displacement (Merton, 1949), bounded rationality (Simon, 1957: 61–78), and organizational rigidity (Blau and Meyer, 1971: 51–52). Normatively, the general view was that such activity represented a positive contribution to the democratic state.

By the 1940s formal-legalism was in eclipse. Its contribution to understanding the place of bureaucracy within democratic politics, however, should not be underestimated. Despite its empirical shortcomings, its overly narrow prescriptive prohibitions against the exercise of discretion, and its view that strict adherence to organizational hierarchy and the dictates of political authorities was the chief means for ensuring a responsible bureaucracy, it did firmly uphold a central tenet of democratic theory: administrative officials are "instruments" of the people and that they should serve the public will as expressed, represented, or otherwise directed by those political authorities and institutions charged with its formulation and implementation (Thompson, 1975). The shortcomings of the approach, however, stemmed from its structural solution to the place of values within the administrative sphere: hierarchical control coupled with an administrative sphere passively transmitting the dictates of higher political authorities and bodies.

Yet those who ignore one of the general principles behind formal-legalism—that the rule of law should prevail—do so with some risk. As Roberts has recently pointed out, the Supreme Court has been increasingly attentive to laws governing administrative responsibility and public service ethics. The Court appears to be adopting an "individual responsibility model." While this differs from the traditional understanding of responsibility offered by the formal-legalists by placing a greater onus of responsibility upon the individual official, it upholds laws designed to make officials more individually accountable for their acts. According to Roberts, "Today public officials find themselves subject to an unprecedented level of scrutiny," and that scrutiny, in turn, "has been deemed constitutional by the Court" (1999: 21).

But, that said, such scrutiny can sometimes have unintended effects on the ability of officials to perform their duties effectively; surely an important goal of any reasonable theory of public ethics and accountability. According to Frank Anechiarico, anti-corruption efforts can lead to a number of bureaucratic pathologies: decision-making delay, defensive management, goal displacement, poor morale, barriers to cooperation, and managerial distrust (1999: 88–90).

C. Pluralist and Participatory Approaches

With the decline of formal-legalism, interest group pluralism and decentralized participation emerged as alternative understandings of the place of bureaucracy within democratic politics. Each approach, however, takes a different emphasis, with pluralism positing interaction with and accountability to group pressures and decentralized participation positing the devolution of administrative decision-making to local bodies and direct citizen involvement. Unlike formal-legalism, both stress a more informal process of interaction between the bureaucracy and its political environment as a guide to responsible conduct. They share the view that politics and the role of bureaucracy in that politics is a drama of competition, bargaining, and accommodation with diverse interests—whether groups or citizens—as participants. For administrators it is this process and the agreements that result that define the scope and content of public policy relevant to administrative activity. Decisions of elected representatives and political executives—central to formal-legal theory—are relevant to pluralist and participatory approaches only in the limited sense that they set the parameters within which this competition operates. Once established, however, it is the competition of interests directly confronting administrators that is relevant in determining their responsibilities. Both, however, share with formal-legalism a view of bureaucracy that is highly politically responsive and, generally, with little room for independent ethical judgment and action. They too offer a structural solution to the problem of linking democracy and ethical judgment, but redefine the nature of the political structure at the level of individual and group interaction.

In the years following the Second World War, interest group pluralism, in particular, gained acceptance among many scholars as a descriptively accurate and normatively acceptable account of American politics, bureaucracy included. It was later challenged both for its empirical claims and its normative implications, but it remains influential: the "incrementalist" and "partisan mutual adjustment" perspectives that pluralist theorists adopted in the 1960s and 1970s still offers a persuasive account of the workings of the policy process, especially at the national level (see Dahl, 1955; Lindblom, 1959; 1965: 88ff.; 1977: 314–317).

The pluralists' primary emphasis on the external competition of group interests, however, places the administrator in a largely passive role. In most pluralist theories, there is no independent standard separate from that of reflecting the accommodations and compromises of competing interests. Theorists such as Bentley (1908), Leiserson (1942), and Truman (1951: 443ff.) even seem to suggest that policy automatically results from the process of group interaction; that is, a "resultant of group forces" is passively registered and transmitted into policy.

Pluralist approaches especially face conceptual difficulty concerning the equity of the group process. At the stage at which individual interests are articulated into group interests, for example, incentives for collective action may be present in different degrees thus hindering the formation of some individual interests into group interests (Olson, 1966; Moe, 1980). Furthermore, those interests that are expressed politically may reflect the interests of elites within the group rather than those of individual members—Michels' "iron law of oligarchy." At the level of inter-group competition, it is not necessarily the case that all groups exercise the same amount of influence in particular policy areas, nor are groups that are excluded or otherwise underrepresented always able to seek relief through alternative political channels. Presence of "iron triangle" relationships, selective co-optation (Selznick, 1949) and "issue networks" (Heclo, 1978) can favor the representation of select interests and impede the entrance of new groups.

To be fair, there has been some discussion among some pluralist theorists of administrative guarantees of "standing," "due process," equitable representation, and other guidelines for officials in dealing with various individuals and groups (Long, 1962: 82; Vogel, 1980–81; Burke, 1986: 199–215); some of these concerns have found their way into laws, rules, and procedures governing administrative bodies that receive policy input from various public sources (Stewart, 1975; Pops and Pavlak, 1991: 32–47). However, even with this added tool, advocates are often nonspecific about the meaning of terms such as "due process" or the particular responsibilities officials incur to ensure it (Morone and Marmor, 1981; Burke, 1986: 204–206; Pops and Pavlak, 1991: 51–55). Officials thus continue to face vague charges about the occasions, nature, and extent of their obligations.

Similar difficulties beset decentralized participation. Most of the community action programs of the 1960s and 1970s were characterized by low levels of participation and were often dominated by elites of higher socio-economic status rather than the targeted groups (Moynihan, 1969; Altshuler, 1970). Participants were also likely to be self-regarding and narrow in their policy demands, thus potentially neglecting larger community-wide interests (Aleshire, 1972; Strange, 1972; Frieden and Kaplan, 1975; Cole and Caputo, 1974). One study of community action agencies, for example, found that the representatives from the community identified themselves as representatives of particular constituencies; in contrast, only one third of the noncommunity representatives identified themselves as such (Austin, 1972). More general studies of participation have found that it can be stressful for participants (Mansbridge, 1983), costly as a means for reaching consensus (Wilson, 1966), and often reflective of socio-economic inequality (Verba and Nie, 1972; Kweit and Kweit, 1981).

It is also difficult to square the logic of democratic politics with the political effects of decentralized participation. Democratic decision-making essentially requires that those affected by policy be given a chance to participate in its making or otherwise exercise influence in some way. Decentralized participation, while democratic in form, cannot always meet this test. The policies determined in decentralized settings, for example, may have "spillover" effects on and transferred costs to other constituencies that have had no say in their formulation. A tension thus exists with decentralized participation between, on the one hand, the interests of participants and the policy views that tend to result from them and, on the other, the interests of a broader public that may be affected by the actions taken in decentralized contexts (Fesler, 1965; Barnard and Vernon, 1975).

These problems notwithstanding, decentralized participation may foster a number of democratic goals. It not only may offer a political vehicle and mode of empowerment for heretofore marginalized sectors of the public (Stenberg, 1972), it can, under the right circumstances, enhance knowledge and information about politics, increase political trust and efficacy while reducing alienation (Smith, 1971; Cole, 1974: 113ff.), and otherwise foster "democratic character" (Hart, 1972; Abrahamsson, 1977). Community-based participation may be able to offer a better environment in which ethical behavior might flourish (Sembor and Leighninger, 1996). New types of client-bureaucrat relationships may also emerge. Cooperation between public and bureaucracy may be enhanced (Moore and Kelling, 1983; Levine, 1984; but also see Kweit and Kweit, 1981: 135–149), and participation may encourage officials to treat the public not as passive consumers or clients, but as constituents: as individuals having certain rights that entitle them to better and more equitable treatment (Miller and Rein, 1969). Overall, as Thomas McCullough concludes, "When the public is included in the policy-making process not simply as individuals seeking their disparate interests but as participants in deliberating about what is good for society, new possibilities emerge" (1991: 88). However, as King, Felty, and Susel have observed, for such a relationship to develop, "re-educating administrators" may be required, particularly in "changing their roles from that of expert managers towards that of cooperative participants or partners." But that, they concede, "requires a significant shift in the mainstream values about what it is that administrators do. Administrators typically are expected to manage, not govern" (King et al., 1998: 325).

D. Democratic Responsibility

Formal-legal, pluralist, and participatory theories posit a similar solution to the role of individual value judgment, including ethical judgment and the action, in the administrative sphere: they rely on certain political structures—be they bureaucratic hierarchy, group competition or citizen contact and responsiveness—for guidance and value definition. These structural solutions, however, are not the only means available: one can approach the issue of ethics and democratic theory by focusing on the individual value orientations of administrative officials and attempting to define them in ways that are consonant with the aims and purposes of democratic government. Speculation about *democratic responsibility* thus becomes the central task, and it has generated a rich debate in recent years among those concerned with ethics, democracy, and bureaucratic organization.

The advantages of this approach are suggested by the two elements in its label: democracy and responsibility. Its emphasis on individual responsibility establishes a clear linkage with the kinds of awareness and concerns to which ethics is attentive: What ought I to do? What are my duties in this situation? What is proper conduct here? The modifier "democratic" imparts a substantive definition that is attentive to the official nature of the administrator's role and its place within a democratic framework of government, that takes seriously the notion that public officials "act for us" not simply themselves.

The critical task, of course, is defining what we mean by democratic responsibility. One way a number of scholars have attempted to do this is by emphasizing certain core principles of democracy. For Paul Appleby, Michael Walzer, and Terry Cooper, for example, it is the concept of democratic citizenship that is foremost in this definition. According to Appleby, administrators should think of themselves as "especially responsible citizens who are officials" (1965: 335). For Walzer, "They are citizens in lieu of the rest of us; and the common good is, so to speak, their specialty" (1970: 216). And Cooper has written a whole book on the topic in which he argues that the tradition of ethical citizenship can provide "a viable normative foundation for the public administrator" (1991: 134).

For Harlan Cleveland, Fritz Morstein Marx, and Douglas Yates it is the post facto check of accountability in a democracy that ought to guide administrative behavior. According to Morstein Marx, "Infinitely more important than compelling administrators to live up to minutely defined requirements of control is their acceptance of an ethical obligation to account to themselves and to the public for the public character of their actions" (1949: 1134–1135). For Cleveland, it is the central question: "If this action is held up to public scrutiny, will I still feel that it is what I should have done, and how I should have done it?" (1972: 104). Douglas Yates makes a similar point but in a more developed way when he suggests that "bureaucratic policy makers owe citizens in a democracy a careful accounting of the reasons why they have decided to act, what public purposes they are pursuing, and what values they have emphasized as against reasonable alternatives" (1981: 40). Conversely, other theorists have argued that democratic guidance should precede questionable administrative activities. For example, in her book *Lying*, Sissela Bok argues that ethically questionable practices can sometimes be justified if they have been agreed to beforehand: "only those deceptive practices which can be openly debated and consented to in advance are justifiable in a democracy" (1978: 185).

Others have relied on a larger array of democratic principles and practices. James Freedman (1978) argues that the legitimacy of administrative action depends on four attributes: constitutionality, accountability, fairness, and effectiveness. Donald Warwick notes that there are five "signposts pointing toward the responsible and away from the irresponsible'': public orientation, reflective choice, veracity, procedural respect, and restraint on means (1981: 115–124). Emmette Redford proposes three ''democratic ideals'':

> The basic ideal is that persons are the units of value in social arrangements. . . . This is the individualist foundation of democratic morality. . . . The second ideal is that all men have worth deserving social recognition. . . . This is the egalitarian component of democratic morality. The third ideal is that personal worth is most fully protected and enlarged by the action of those whose worth is assumed . . . liberty exists only through participation either in decisionmaking or in control of leaders who make decisions. (1969: 6)

Dennis Thompson, on the other hand, turns to such common elements of democracy as citizens' ''opportunity to approve or disapprove,'' public accountability, consent, publicity and disclosure, and retrospective electoral approval (1987: 11–39). Democratic responsibility in his view is both a ''process of deliberation'' and a ''process of accountability.'' The former implies that an adequate conception of democratic responsibility should include a ''wide range of reasons that officials may give for their decisions,'' and thus should not be limited to formal-legal or technical issues. And the latter must ''provide a basis for identifying which officials actually make specific policies'' (1983: 236).

J. Patrick Dobel (1998) has recently pointed to the importance of political prudence as a central component of ethical leadership. According to Dobel, it ''focuses upon the obligation of a leader to achieve moral self-mastery, to attend to the context of a situation, and through deliberation and careful judgment to seek outcomes that are legitimate and durable.'' Seven principles, in turn, guide such prudence and provide standards for others to judge its proper application: (1) disciplined reason and openness; (2) foresight; (3) proper deployment of power and resources; (4) timing, momentum and direction; (5) the proper alignment of means and ends; (6) the durability and legitimacy of outcomes; and (7) building and sustaining community (1998: 74, 80). Larry Terry's notion of the administrative leader as ''conservator,'' while not framed in exclusively ethical terms, offers implications for the ethical leader. Conservatorship is directed at preserving the ''integrity'' of an institution and involves ''protecting from injury, destruction, or decay those processes, values and unifying principles that determine an institution's distinctive competence'' (Terry, 1995: 44–45).

These various attempts to bring together ethics and democratic theory within the rubric of democratic responsibility or a democratic morality, as it might also be termed, have marked a profitable line of inquiry in contemporary debate. In their generality they avoid the disagreement over specifics that is likely to ensue with more comprehensive and detailed statements of individual responsibility. But their differences also suggest some of the criticisms that have been lodged against purely ethical principles, namely that in their multiplicity and divergence it is hard to see which should be granted priority or otherwise gain recognition. To put the issue a bit more simply: How do officials know which general characteristic of democracy should be applied? Moreover, discussion of them is often at a general level in which the tension between particular principles is often unexplored. For example, in Warwick's (1981) schema, which should take priority: ''procedural respect'' (presumably to higher authorities and the rules and roles they have prescribed) or a more citizen-regarding ''public orientation''?

That said, however, the kinds of general concerns to which a democratically inspired conception of responsibility alerts officials may generate sufficient awareness of broader

"public interest" concerns to supplement their institutionally defined roles and obligations. Unlike the application of ethical principles in personal life, public officials already
have a web of official duties and obligations, rules and procedures in place that can serve
as a first step in helping them think about what they ought to do. These various conceptions
of democratic responsibility may, then, be sufficient in the way they supplement those
"normal" responsibilities or in the way they create a countervailing ethos that pervades
the organization.

E. Constitutional Inspiration

If it is difficult to agree upon what features of democracy we deem important in understanding the roles and obligations of public officials, then perhaps the authority of the
Constitution might be invoked to resolve the dispute. It is, after all, a blueprint for the
institutions and processes of American government and sets out the rights and privileges
of its citizens. It is based on the consent of the governed—"We the People . . ."—and
is subject to their change and amendment as they see fit. There is, in addition, a substantial
body of documentation and literature about the intentions of its framers, its interpretation,
and its evolution over time such that it may provide an authoritative text for understanding
the proper bounds of the policy process and the role of administrators within it. Furthermore, unlike the democratic approaches previously discussed, it has the advantage of recognizing the republican features of our system of government—e.g., shared powers,
checks and balances, and a framework of individual rights—which purely democratic
approaches seem to lack.

There is, of course, no question that the express powers and individual rights set
out in the Constitution ought to be binding, nor is there any question that the decisions
of the Supreme Court about the application and scope of those powers and rights ought
to be heeded; a reasonable observer of the administrative process would be hard put to
argue otherwise. But can the Constitution and its interpretation be used for a more ambitious end: informing a theory of bureaucratic ethics?

John Rohr has been the leading authority in arguing that it can. In his book *Ethics for
Bureaucrats* he explicitly makes the case that Supreme Court decisions articulate certain
"regime values" and instruction on those decisions can help fulfill the ethical obligation
of bureaucrats (Rohr, 1978: 4). He also argues that the system of separate but shared
powers spelled out in the Constitution can be usefully applied in understanding the proper
role of the bureaucracy in that institutional schema. This argument is more fully developed
in a 1986 work, *To Run a Constitution*, where he further fashions a normative theory of
bureaucracy that is modelled on the framers' view of the U.S. Senate as a balance wheel
counteracting the more popular tendencies of the U.S. House of Representatives.

Rohr's effort is undoubtedly useful pedagogy for students of bureaucracy and its
practitioners. But it is not at all clear that the Constitution and its interpretation through
decisions of the Court can fulfill the more ambitious project of informing a theory of
regime values. Several difficulties stand out. First, the Supreme Court often speaks with
many voices. Unanimous decisions are rare and its written decisions often contain concur-
ring opinions and dissenting opinions based on alternative constitutional reasonings. Second, Court opinions are usually complex with many strands of legal and constitutional
argument marshalled to support the eventual decision; they also sometimes turn on matters
of technical legal detail because the Court generally likes to avoid constitutional controversy whenever possible. Third, care must be taken in discerning philosophical coherence

and the presence of constitutionally inspired value judgments in the Court's rulings; political give-and-take in gaining a majority of the Court's members and concern for the wider political reception of a particular ruling also can influence the Court's thinking. Finally, opinions of the Court often change over time; this is especially true when the Court enters new, constitutionally uncharted waters where an initial ruling will be followed by successive cases that seek to define and refine legal and constitutional issues as they are applied to situations raising new facts or issues.

A similar set of interpretive issues confronts those who argue that the intentions of the framers of the Constitution ought to be taken seriously in crafting an understanding of the administrative role. This argument has not directly entered debate on bureaucratic ethics but it is an important strand of argument in constitutional interpretation among legal scholars and jurists, including some members of the current Supreme Court. The problem here would be two-fold: not only would there be difficulties in establishing regime values based on the Court's decisions—Rohr's argument—but those decisions, in turn, would be understood and informed by their adherence to what is presumed to be the intentions of the framers, an interpretive exercise of equal if not greater controversy.

F. Procedural Approaches

Another possible approach to defining the responsibilities of administrators from a democratic perspective looks not to the Constitution, various democratic principles or discrete features of democracy for its inspiration but to the obligations officials acquire that relate to the institutions and processes that define the administrative setting and the broader political environment in which it is embedded. The basic notion here is that the relevant political authorities possess the basic power to define official roles and basic duties, but, unlike the formal-legal approach, persons who occupy those roles must take on additional responsibilities.

Theodore Lowi's path-breaking critique of interest group liberalism in his 1969 work, *The End of Liberalism*, anticipated one of the central tenets of this approach, namely that higher-level political authorities, rather than administrators relying on their informal contacts with select groups of interest, should serve as the primary source of policy direction. In Lowi's view, interest group politics has weakened the legitimacy of formal rules and procedures and undermined the authority of the American state. Although Lowi's proposal for a ''juridical democracy'' to remedy the situation harkened back to formal-legalism and was based on the anti–New Deal rulings of the Supreme Court in the Schecter and Panama Refining cases in 1935, it laid the foundation for an understanding of administrative responsibility that would recognize the rightful claims of higher political authorities as an expression of democratic governance upon what transpired in the administrative sphere (1969: 287–341). It reopened a debate about the role of formal institutions and processes as a source of value guidance that would lead to more robust theories of administrative duty and obligation.

Kenneth Culp Davis, also writing in 1969, explored the question of discretion but with more attention to the role of bureaucracy and more subtlety in how the vexing issue of discretion might be handled. Davis rejected the formal-legal view of and prevailing practices in administrative procedure that administrative discretion should be eliminated or otherwise held in check by the judiciary or tighter legislative enactments. He proposed, instead, that administrators should exercise discretion but take care to limit, check, and structure it, especially through upholding standards of procedural fairness and openness.

In his view, higher political authorities remain the principal source of direction over administrative activity, but administrative officials have an active role to play in properly handling the policy discretion that they are sometimes given, especially in ensuring the integrity of the processes that they employ in reaching closure on policy judgments.

Pops and Pavlak develop the argument further by concluding that administrative justice must be regarded as the core value for public administrators, and they define that justice largely in procedural terms: "Administrative justice is distinguished from the broader concepts of justice and social justice by the constitutional-legal arrangements, laws, regime values, and specific roles that attach to bureaucratic positions and authority" (1991: 10). In their view, judgments about the justness of policy outcomes—distributive justice—"are normally beyond the bureaucracy's scope of authority" and "require that the administrator pursue the lawmaker's intent" (1991: 72–73). But bureaucrats can aid the implementation of that intent through such actions as ensuring that decisions are accurate, rationally related to policy objectives, and serve targeted client needs. In matters of procedural justice—the fairness of processes that produce and implement policy decisions—bureaucrats are generally more directly involved, and they must employ such criteria of fairness as equality of access, neutrality, participation and humaneness, and the right to appeal (1991: 85–92).

Burke (1986) offers another procedurally grounded conception of responsibility. Individual responsibility, at the most basic level, is "properly defined" by the "institutions and processes" of democracy, predominantly the constitutionally established "political" branches, at least in the American system (1986: 216). But there also is posited a broader set of responsibilities to the project of constitutional democracy, to the "ethos of democracy." Drawing on Dworkin's (1977) notion that persons who enter public service take on not only responsibilities for their explicit duties but a broader set of obligations to "the enterprise as a whole," he articulates a conception of responsibility that is directed at: (1) the actions of other officials; (2) enhancement of the integrity of a fair and informed process of policy choice; and (3) the effective and efficient implementation of policy choice within a context that is heavily influenced by the organization, dynamics, and behavioral patterns typical in public bureaucracies.

Albert Flores and Michael Kraft also rely upon a procedurally based approach. They argue that because there is no agreed-upon way to define "the public interest," administrators should seek public legitimacy for their actions (1988: 126). Procedural criteria, in turn, can provide such legitimacy, and Flores and Kraft propose that administrators consider such procedurally relevant questions as:

> Did the proposal receive majority approval in the legislature?
> Were significant minority perspectives on the issues considered?
> Did legislative consideration take place in an informed, open, and deliberative manner? . . .
> Was there an opportunity for interaction among participants and an effort to search for compromises? . . .

Approaches that are attentive to the dictates and workings of existing processes and institutions have an advantage over other conceptions of democratic responsibility in that they do not need to specify a particular conception of democracy or a particular interpretation of the Constitution to inform their basic principles. Obligation and proper conduct are directed at insuring (what might be termed) the "integrity" of existing processes and institutions rather than supplanting them with some alternative or rival conception.

Furthermore, as Ralph Clark Chandler has noted, the placement of the reconciliation of differing views at the level of political institutions and processes may be beneficial in a political and social order where a plurality of values exist and must be reconciled: "Proceduralism is necessary because . . . an article of faith must be that from the clash of opposites, contraries, extremes and poles will come not the victory of any one, but the mediation and accommodation of all" (1983: 33).

But what is gained at the level of first principles may be lost elsewhere: vagueness in determining how officials might respond to unfairness in legislative deliberations, for example, or lack of specificity in ascertaining how they might contribute to the project of informed, open, and deliberative policy choice or more effective policy implementation. More generally, as Chandler warns, there is no guarantee that a procedural approach will deliver on its promise of mediating and reconciling competing value claims: "The irony of the proceduralist position, of course, is that as the need for shared values in an increasingly factionalized and anomic society grows, adversaries who no longer find in their disagreements a basis for common norms are transformed from adversaries into enemies" (1983: 33).

Is the proceduralist's conception of democracy too narrow? The democratic task to which a procedural theory is attentive may require more effort and attention than just making the "system work." As Thomas McCullough notes, "The public interest is more than neutral, procedural policy making. It is deliberation by citizens about public values" (1991: 88). The proceduralist might respond, however, that a too generous embrace of democracy is ill-considered: it fails to recognize the republican and constitutional features of the American system and their legitimate role in setting the scope and content of public policy. Citizen deliberation of the sort McCullough and others favor may have some place in our politics, but it is one that must largely be mediated through existing institutions and processes or those avenues for direct participation they set out (Burke, 1986: 197–215).

Joel Fleishman and Bruce Payne pose a particularly difficult challenge. They argue that it is precisely when the democratic system is under strain that the most significant dilemmas of responsibility are likely to arise. Some procedural criteria enter into their assessment of such a circumstance—violation of the "constitutive rules of the political process," suppression of relevant information in policy debate, and policy-makers' "superior understanding of the long-run consequences." But when the latter arise, they conclude, it is not enough to look to the political process for guidance; the exercise of individual conscience and moral judgment may be required (1980: 20–21).

III. CONCLUDING OBSERVATIONS

Although scholars who have grappled with the place of individual responsibility and ethical action from the perspective of democratic theory have taken very different courses, it can at least be said that it has generated an informed and profitable dialogue in recent years. There is increasingly a shared realization that discussion of administrative ethics is not simply a task of encouraging moral calculation or applying some favored system of ethics but that it involves a more complex understanding of how politics, especially democratic politics, the place of bureaucracy within that politics, and the individual roles of administrative officials within that organizational structure must enter into any calculation or assessment of proper conduct.

A rich literature has emerged that is especially attentive to the two senses of responsibility that Terry Cooper outlined a number of years ago: "objective" responsibility to laws, procedures, and the dictates of organizational hierarchies and "subjective" responsibility to ethical values, shared experiences, and professional training. Most of the theories discussed above define the latter much more narrowly than does Cooper, but they all partake at least to some extent of both elements and that is to their credit. As noted in the introduction to this chapter, speculation about and proper definition of individual responsibility may make possible the conjoining of the seemingly disparate concerns of democracy and bureaucracy; the ability to link together both of these senses of responsibility seems especially important in the achievement of that end.

Democratic approaches are able to encompass these considerations because they emphasize the political reconciliation of competing value and belief claims and are attentive to institutional and procedural constraints on the definition of responsibility and conduct. But in so doing, one must also ask whether ethics is lost in the process. As I noted early in this chapter, some sphere of personal moral judgment seems necessary even if one recognizes the authority and claims of politics. Emphasis on democratic mechanisms cannot guarantee that the decisions that result are always right and just in some ultimate sense, nor can officials rest assured that those higher up in the organizational structure have faithfully adhered to the public interest.

Understanding where the proper boundary between public obligation and ethical duty should be drawn, thus, remains an uncompleted task in the analysis of administrative ethics. The recent work in analyzing democracy's claims upon responsible conduct have emphasized political and institutional constraints that have often been ignored in discussions of administrative ethics. But once these claims and constraints have been recognized, there still remains a need to revisit the domain of personal ethics and assess its role in the judgments and actions of public officials.

One topic that deserves further attention is whether there are ethical considerations that ought to "trump" democratic judgments no matter what. The Nuremberg principles are the best known example of this: prohibitions against conduct so heinous that they are beyond reasonable dispute. Are there other, perhaps less extreme but nonetheless important, ethical judgments of this type?

Dennis Thompson (1987: 3) has noted another way that ethics should enter into consideration. Although recognizing that "many of the disputes in political ethics, even about fundamental principles, must be resolved finally or at least partly through some form of democratic process," he argues that the democratic process "must satisfy certain ethical constraints," such as publicity. Are there others that must be satisfied so that, in his words, the democratic "process itself can be the source of ethical judgments?"

Ethics and the democratic process may also be relevant to different dilemmas of judgment that arise in the administrative sphere. Responsible conduct that draws for inspiration on personal morality, for example, may be more appropriate in those areas that involve individual conscience most intimately and where the individual official is the cause of wrong: lying, deception, and other personal misdeeds. Conversely, democratic approaches are likely to be more relevant when the question involves the exercise of policy discretion; here the scope and content of public policy is at issue and the political rather than the personal seems to be a more appropriate guide.

It may also be likely that democratic principles and personal moral judgments may be intermixed in particular cases. Peter French (1983: 135), for example, proposes that whistleblowing activities are justifiable if they meet four conditions: (1) established governmental channels have been exhausted before the matter is made public; (2) careful assessment has been made to determine whether procedural, moral, or legal bounds have been violated; (3) the action in question involves a demonstrable harm; and (4) the action in question is specific in nature, based on reasonable evidence and not simply some general complaint. Conditions 1 and 2 involve political and organizational considerations, condition 3 seems largely moral in nature, while condition 4 seems an intrinsic or categorical element of responsible action. Although one might quibble with the conditions French has selected, they seem generally reasonable and demonstrate the various considerations—moral, political, organizational, and categorical—that are probably relevant to the assessment of most situations of responsible conduct.

Finally, the guidance ethics provides in how to move from general principle to specific application merits further attention. One problem that Thompson has noted concerns the organizational nature of public office: not only do officials "act for us," they act "with others" (1987: 4). Bureaucracies are complex entities in which actions can be traced back to the partial contributions of many actors, and this in turn complicates an understanding of the particular responsibilities of any one actor (Thompson, 1987: 40–65). Second, ethical action, from whatever theoretical approach it is defined, requires a kind of practical wisdom to apply its general rules and provisions to concrete realities and in light of particular circumstances; as Terry Cooper notes, "It is important to assess the seriousness of a situation, consider the range of values at stake, and then act in proportion to these circumstances" (1990: 43). A proper understanding of administrative ethics must encompass not only a right definition of its governing principles but knowledge of the prudence and moral compromise necessary to its effective and proper application.

REFERENCES

Abrahamsson, B. (1977). *Bureaucracy or Participation: The Logic of Organization*, Sage, Beverly Hills, CA.

Aleshire, R. (1972). Power to the people: an assessment of the community action and model cities programs, *Public Administration Review*, 32: 428–443.

Altshuler, A. (1970). *Community Control*, Bobbs-Merrill/Pegasus, New York.

Anechiarico, F. (1999). Corruption control means bureaucratic pathology, *Public Integrity*, 1: 87–91.

Appleby, P. (1952). *Morality and Administration in Democratic Government*, Louisiana State University Press, Baton Rouge.

Appleby, P. (1965). Public administration and democracy, *Public Administration and Democracy: Essays in Honor of Paul Appleby* (R. C. Martin, ed.), Syracuse University Press, Syracuse, pp. 333–347.

Austin, D. (1972). Resident participation: political mobilization or organizational cooptation, *Public Administration Review* 32: 409–420.

Bailey, S. K. (1965). Ethics and the public service, *Public Administration and Democracy: Essays in Honor of Paul Appleby* (R. C. Martin, ed.), Syracuse University Press, Syracuse, pp. 283–298.

Barnard, C. (1938). *The Functions of the Executive*, Harvard University Press, Cambridge.

Barnard, F. M., and Vernon, R. A. (1975). Pluralism, participation, and politics, *Political Theory*, 3: 180–197.

Bentley, A. (1908). *The Process of Government*, University of Chicago Press, Chicago.

Blau, P., and Meyer, M. (1971). *Bureaucracy in Modern Society*, Random House, New York.

Bok, S. (1978). *Lying: Moral Choices in Public and Private Life*, Random House, New York.

Burke, J. P. (1986). *Bureaucratic Responsibility*, Johns Hopkins University Press, Baltimore.

Chandler, R. C. (1983). The problem of moral reasoning in American public administration: the case for a code of ethics, *Public Administration Review*, 43: 32–39.

Cleveland, H. (1972). *The Future Executive*, Harper and Row, New York.

Cole, R. (1974). *Citizen Participation and the Urban Policy Process*, Heath-Lexington, Lexington, MA.

Cole, R., and Caputo, D. (1974). *Urban Politics and Decentralization: The Case of Revenue Sharing*, Heath-Lexington, Lexington, MA.

Cooper, T. L. (1987). Hierarchy, virtue, and the practice of public administration: a perspective for normative ethics, *Public Administration Review*, 47: 320–328.

Cooper, T. L. (1990). *The Responsible Administrator*, 3rd ed., Jossey-Bass, San Francisco.

Cooper, T. L. (1991). *An Ethic of Citizenship for Public Administration*, Prentice-Hall, Englewood Cliffs, NJ.

Dahl, R. (1955). *A Preface to Democratic Theory*, University of Chicago Press, Chicago.

Davis, K. C. (1969). *Discretionary Justice*, University of Illinois Press, Urbana.

Denhardt, K. G. (1988). *The Ethics of Public Service: Resolving Moral Dilemmas in Public Organizations*, Greenwood Press, Westport, CT.

Dobel, J. P. (1998). Political prudence and the ethics of leadership, *Public Administration Review*, 58: 74–81.

Donagan, A. (1977). *The Theory of Morality*, University of Chicago Press, Chicago.

Dumbauld, E., ed. (1955). *The Political Writings of Thomas Jefferson*, Bobbs-Merrill, Indianapolis.

Dworkin, R. (1977). *Taking Rights Seriously*, Harvard University Press, Cambridge.

Fesler, J. (1965). Approaches to the understanding of decentralization, *Journal of Politics*, 27: 536–566.

Fleishman, J. L., and Payne, B. L. (1980). *Ethical Dilemmas and the Education of Policymakers*, Hastings Center, Hastings-on-Hudson, NY.

Flores, A., and Kraft, M. (1988). Controversies in risk analysis in public management, *Ethics, Government, and Public Policy* (J. S. Bowman and F. Elliston, eds.), Greenwood Press, Westport, CT, pp. 105–136.

Frankel, C., trans. (1947). *Rousseau's The Social Contract*, Hafner Books, New York.

Frederickson, H. G. (1974). Introductory comments: social equity and public administration, *Public Administration Review*, 34: 1–2.

Frederickson, H. G. (1990). Public administration and social equity, *Public Administration Review*, 50: 228–237.

Frederickson, H. G., and Hart, D. K. (1985). The public service and the patriotism of benevolence, *Public Administration Review*, 45: 547–553.

Freedman, J. (1978). *Crisis and Legitimacy*, Cambridge University Press, New York.

French, P. A. (1983). *Ethics in Government*, Prentice-Hall, Englewood Cliffs, NJ.

Frieden, B., and Kaplan, M. (1975). *The Politics of Neglect: Urban Aid from Model Cities to Revenue Sharing*, MIT Press, Cambridge.

Gawthrop, L. (1984). *Public Sector Management, Systems, and Ethics*, Indiana University Press, Bloomington.

Gerth, H. H., and Mills, C. W., trans. (1958). *From Max Weber*, Oxford University Press, New York.

Goldman, A. H. (1980). *The Moral Foundations of Professional Ethics*, Rowman and Littlefield, Totowa, NJ.

Goodnow, F. J. (1990). *Politics and Administration*, Macmillan, New York.

Hampshire, S. (1978). Morality and pessimism, *Public and Private Morality* (S. Hampshire, ed.), Cambridge University Press, New York, pp. 1–22.

Harmon, M. (1981). *Action Theory for Public Administration*, Longmans, New York.

Hart, D. K. (1972). Theories of government related to decentralization and citizen participation, *Public Administration Review*, 32: 603–621.

Hart, D. K. (1974). Social equity, justice, and the equitable administrator, *Public Administration Review*, 34: 3–10.

Heclo, H. (1978). Issue networks and the executive establishment, *The New American Political System* (A. King, ed.), American Enterprise Institute, Washington, D.C., pp. 87–124.

Herring, E. P. (1936). *Public Administration and the Public Interest*, McGraw-Hill, New York.

King, C. S., Felty, K. M., and Susel, B. (1998). The question of participation: toward authentic public participation in public administration, *Public Administration Review*, 58: 317–326.

Kweit, M., and Kweit, R. (1981). *Implementing Citizen Participation in a Bureaucratic Society*, Praeger, New York.

Laslett, P. ed., (1960). *Locke's Two Treatises of Government*, New American Library, New York.

Leiserson, A. (1942). *Administrative Regulation: A Study in Representation of Interests*, University of Chicago Press, Chicago.

Levine, C. (1984). Citizenship and service planning: the promise of coproduction, *Public Administration Review*, 44: 178–187.

Leys, W. A. R. (1943). Ethics and administrative discretion, *Public Administration Review*, 3: 10–23.

Lindblom, C. (1959). The science of muddling through, *Public Administration Review*, 19: 79–88.

Lindblom, C. (1965). *The Intelligence of Democracy*, Free Press, New York.

Lindblom, C. (1977). *Politics and Markets*, Basic Books, New York.

Long, N. (1962). *The Polity*, Rand McNally, Chicago.

Lowi, T. (1969). *The End of Liberalism*, Norton, New York.

Mansbridge, J. (1983). *Beyond Adversary Democracy*, University of Chicago Press, Chicago.

Marx, F. M. (1949). Administrative ethics and the rule of law, *American Political Science Review*, 43: 1119–1144.

McCullough, T. E. (1991). *Moral Imagination and Public Life*, Chatham House, Chatham, NJ.

Merton, R. (1949). *Social Theory and Social Structure*, Free Press, Glencoe, IL.

Mill, J. S. (1958). *Considerations on Representative Government*, Bobbs-Merrill, Indianapolis.

Miller, S., and Rein, M. (1969). Public participation: poverty and administration, *Public Administration Review*, 29: 15–24.

Moe, T. (1980). *The Organization of Interests*, University of Chicago Press, Chicago.

Moore, M., and Kelling, G. (1983). To serve and protect: learning from police history, *Public Interest*, 70: 49–66.

Morone, J. A., and Marmor, T. R. (1981). Representing consumer interests: the case of American health planning, *Ethics*, 91: 431–450.

Moynihan, D. P. (1969). *Maximum Feasible Misunderstanding*, Free Press, New York.

Olson, M. (1966). *The Logic of Collective Action*, Schocken Books, New York.

Pateman, C. (1970). *Participation and Democratic Theory*, Cambridge University Press, Cambridge.

Pops, G. M., and Pavlak, T. J. (1991). *The Case for Justice*, Jossey-Bass, San Francisco.

Rawls, J. (1971). *A Theory of Justice*, Harvard University Press, Cambridge.

Redford, E. (1969). *Democracy in the Administrative State*, Oxford University Press, New York.

Roberts, R. (1999). The Supreme Court and the law of public service ethics, *Public Integrity*, 1: 20–40.

Roethlisberger, F. J., and Dickson, W. J. (1939). *Management and the Worker*, Harvard University Press, Cambridge.

Rohr, J. (1978). *Ethics for Bureaucrats: An Essay on Law and Values*, Marcel Dekker, New York.

Rohr, J. (1986). *To Run a Constitution*, University Press of Kansas, Lawrence, KA.

Selznick, P. (1949). *TVA and the Grass Roots: A Study of Politics and Organization*, University of California Press, Berkeley.

Sembor, E., and Leighninger, M. (1996). Rediscovering the public: reconnecting ethics and ethos through democratic civic institutions, *Ethical Dilemmas in Public Administration*, (L. Pasquerella, A. Killilea, and M. Vocino, eds.), Praeger, Westport, CT, 161–178.

Simon, H. (1957). *Administrative Behavior*, 3rd. ed., Macmillan, New York.

Smith, M. (1971). Alienation and bureaucracy: the role of participatory administration, *Public Administration Review*, 31: 658–664.

Stenberg, C. (1972). Citizens and the administrative state: from participation to power, *Public Administration Review*, 32: 190–197.

Stewart, R. (1975). The reformation of American administrative law, *Harvard Law Review*, 88: 1667–1813.

Strange, J. (1972). Citizen participation in community action and model cities, *Public Administration Review*, 32: 655–669.

Tead, O. (1945). *Democratic Administration*, Association Press, New York.

Terry, L. D. (1995). *Leadership of Public Bureaucracies: The Administrator as Conservator*, Sage, Thousand Oaks, CA.

Thompson, D. F. (1970). *The Democratic Citizen*, Cambridge University Press, Cambridge, U.K.

Thompson, D. F. (1983). Bureaucracy and democracy, *Democratic Theory and Practice* (G. Duncan, ed.), Cambridge University Press, New York, pp. 235–250.

Thompson, D. F. (1987). *Political Ethics and Public Office*, Harvard University Press, Cambridge.

Thompson, V. (1975). *Without Sympathy or Enthusiasm: The Problem of Administrative Compassion*, University of Alabama Press, University, AL.

Truman, D. B. (1951). *The Governmental Process*, Knopf, New York.

Verba, S., and Nie, N. (1972). *Participation in America: Political Democracy and Social Equality*, Harper and Row, New York.

Vogel, D. (1980–81). The public interest movement and the American reform tradition, *Political Science Quarterly*, 95: 607–626.

Waldo, D. (1980). *The Enterprise of Public Administration*, Chandler and Sharp, Novato, CA.

Walzer, M. (1970). *Obligations: Essays on Disobedience, War, and Citizenship*, Harvard University Press, Cambridge.

Warwick, D. P. (1981). The ethics of administrative discretion, *Public Duties: The Moral Obligations of Government Officials* (J. Fleishman, L. Liebman, and M. Moore, eds.), Harvard University Press, Cambridge, 93–130.

Wilson, J. Q. (1966). The war on cities, *Public Interest*, 3: 27–44.

Wilson, W. (1887). The study of administration, *Political Science Quarterly*, 2: 197–222.

Yates, D. T. (1981). Hard choices: justifying bureaucratic decisions, *Public Duties: The Moral Obligations of Government Officials* (J. Fleishman, L. Liebman, and M. Moore, eds.), Harvard University Press, Cambridge, pp. 32–51.

29

Administrative Ethics in Nonprofit Organizations

Michael O'Neill
University of San Francisco, San Francisco, California

I. INTRODUCTION

Nonprofit organizations generally escape the kind of ethical scrutiny directed at government and business, presumably because nonprofits have neither the power of the state nor the economic self-interest of the market. However, recent scandals involving United Way of America, NAACP, Goodwill Industries, and other nonprofits have served as a reminder that ethics is an important issue for nonprofits as well as for other types of organizations. One could even argue that nonprofits, far from being ethically exempt, need ethics even more than business or government. While all organizations depend to some extent on constituency trust, nonprofits critically depend on their trust relationships with clients, volunteers, donors, and other constituents, especially since it is often difficult to measure the quality and effect of nonprofit services (religious, counseling, social work, health, education, advocacy). Hansmann (1980, 1987) argues that this "information asymmetry" helps explain why people seek such services from nonprofit providers, which have little or no economic incentive to reduce quality. Fundraising experts (e.g., Mixer, 1993) report that long-time trust relationships are essential to soliciting major donations.

Ethics is hardly new to nonprofit organizations. Health care, much of which is delivered by nonprofits, has given careful attention to ethical issues at least since the time of Hippocrates. Nonprofit human service and education organizations frequently deal with ethical challenges because of the relative vulnerability of their clients. Religious organizations attend to a wide variety of ethical issues, often expressed in a particular theological viewpoint. Advocacy and cause organizations focus on societal ethical issues such as the rights of minority groups. In spite of all this attention and involvement, however, nonprofits—perhaps absorbed with their service-oriented and idealistic missions—have generally not developed explicit internal ethical mechanisms such as written codes, as government and business organizations have in recent decades.

The lack of formal attention is especially true with respect to administrative ethics in nonprofit organizations. The dominant ethical concerns of nonprofits have been those of direct service providers such as doctors, nurses, teachers, religious professionals, social workers, counselors, advocates, and the like. Relatively little attention has been paid to ethical issues involving managers and board leaders of nonprofit organizations (for some exceptions, see Boris and Odendahl, 1990; Briscoe, 1994; Jeavons, 1992; Jurkiewicz and Massey, 1998; Koziol, 1998; and O'Neill, 1989, 1992, 1993, 1997). However, there has been some attention to administrative ethics in fields heavily populated by nonprofits, such as health care (Darr, 1991) and social service (Levy, 1982).

The rationale for giving special attention to nonprofit administrative ethics is based on the somewhat unique characteristics of nonprofit organizations and the special ethical challenges that face leaders of these organizations. While nonprofits are in many ways similar to business and government organizations, there are differences that have important implications for administrative ethics. The following are generally thought to be the most significant differences between nonprofit and other (especially business) organizations (see Billis and Harris, 1996; Mason, 1984, pp. 20–22; and O'Neill, 1998, pp. 1–4):

> *Basic purpose*: Nonprofits exist to provide some service, whereas business firms exist to make a profit. "One generates the money in order to do the job. The other does the job in order to generate the money" (Mason, 1984, p. 88). This fundamental difference in organizational purpose distinguishes nonprofit from for-profit groups and shapes much of the behavior in the two types of organizations.
>
> *Values*: Churches, cause organizations, private schools and colleges, and many other types of nonprofits are strongly value-oriented. While all organizations have some values, nonprofits are particularly likely to be value-driven.
>
> *Resource acquisition*: Business gets its revenue largely from the sale of goods and services. Government gets its revenue largely from taxes. While there are many different forms and strategies of revenue acquisition in these two sectors, the fundamental structure of the revenue acquisition task is relatively simple. Nonprofits, on the other hand, acquire revenue through a combination of the sale of goods and services, fundraising, government contracts, and ancillary "for-profit" ventures.
>
> *Bottom line*: Nonprofits do not have the same clarity regarding acceptable performance as that provided by the balance sheet for business and the election system for government. A nonprofit organization must proceed without clear bottom-line indicators and yet must continually persuade funders, clients, and other constituents that the agency's work is effective and efficient.
>
> *Legal constraints*: Nonprofits are prohibited from distributing financial surpluses to constituents (the central purpose of a business organization), are exempted from paying property or income taxes, receive tax-deductible contributions, and are prohibited from engaging in certain types of political activity.
>
> *Worker characteristics*: Nonprofits differ significantly from business and government organizations in the composition of their work force. Volunteers play a major role in most nonprofits, often constituting 75–90% of the work force. The demographics of nonprofit paid staff differ from those of business and government: two-thirds of nonprofit employees are female, and nonprofit workers are more likely to be well educated and professional, due to the industries in which nonprofits specialize.
>
> *Governance*: Nonprofits are governed by volunteers, usually appointed rather than elected, who act as trustees for the public interest and are prohibited by law from receiving any profit from the organization.

The partial uniqueness of nonprofit organizations underlies the partial uniqueness of nonprofit administrative ethics. Just as government administrative ethics is a special case due to such unique government characteristics as police power, taxation power, responsibility for the general welfare, and dependence on general elections, so nonprofit administrative ethics is shaped by characteristics that differentiate nonprofits from other kinds of organizations. The following examples illustrate how nonprofit managers, because of these organizational differences, face somewhat different ethical challenges than do their counterparts in business and government.

II. PROMOTING VALUES

Every organization has some value dimension, but values are not the dominant purpose of business or government whereas they *are* the dominant purpose of many nonprofit organizations including religious entities, private schools and colleges, and advocacy groups. Leading value-intensive organizations imposes unique demands on the leader. Such organizations demand that leaders behave in a manner consonant with the values that the organization is trying to foster. Novels such as *The Scarlet Letter* and *Elmer Gantry*, and reactions to recent scandals involving Covenant House and televangelist ministries, make the same point: when people assume a values-leadership role and then fail with respect to those values, their fall is a special kind of betrayal. Other examples would include a university administrator who plagiarized others' work, a manager of a civil rights organization who told offensive jokes about minorities and women, a head of a Quaker school who practiced corporal punishment, an executive director of a soup kitchen who took a six-figure salary, and so forth.

One of the few clear results from the thousands of empirical studies on leadership is that leadership is importantly shaped by the characteristics of the organization and the task (Bass, 1985). A value-intensive organization demands leadership that is clearly consistent with and strongly permeated by the values of the organization. Most nonprofit managers, leaders of what Alexis de Tocqueville called "moral and intellectual associations," have a special mandate to act in accordance with the ethical expectations of the organizations they head. To the extent that they neglect this organizational imperative, they become ineffective leaders and, in extreme cases, lose their leadership positions entirely if the organization perceives a radical discontinuity between their behavior and the organization's values.

The obligations, however, do not stop there. The manager of a value-intensive organization is expected not only to adhere to but also to create, shape, and articulate the organization's values in a special way. It is not enough for the preacher simply to get up and read the sacred text; he or she must also make it come alive, give it new and fresh meanings, apply it to new moral and social conditions. Similarly, the manager of an environmental or civil rights or free speech organization is constantly called upon to redefine and reapply the organization's basic values; not to do so is a failure of leadership in such an organization.

III. RELATIONS WITH STAFF, BOARD, AND VOLUNTEERS

Ethical theory since Plato and Aristotle has centered largely on questions such as justice, honesty, and fairness. All managers are ethically bound to be just, honest, and fair. This general responsibility has special implications for nonprofits because of their somewhat unique personnel characteristics. Managing professional workers is one example. Non-profits are heavily concentrated in several human service fields (religion, health care, education, social work, mental health care) that call for a high degree of discretion and judgment by direct service providers. In such agencies, frequent managerial overruling of professional decisions could be not only poor management but also unethical, since it could easily result in damaging the quality of the organization's professional services and harming the organization's clients. Barnard (1938, p. 276) noted that "an executive position is exposed to more and more moral conflicts the higher it is." Similarly, it is reasonable to assume that the manager of an organization whose principal work is morally complex—mental health care, for example—rather than non-complex, such as manufacturing rubber bands, will be more likely to face morally complex managerial decisions relative to the work and the workers involved.

Nonprofits differ dramatically from business and government agencies with respect to the role of volunteers. Business uses virtually no volunteer labor. Government uses relatively few volunteers and typically uses them in low-level roles such as playground supervisors, teachers' aides, and "candy stripers." Nonprofit organizations, by contrast, use tens of millions of volunteers (Hodgkinson et al., 1996), often in high-level and complex roles. Nonprofit volunteers do management work, fundraising, lobbying, sophisticated consulting (in marketing, computer usage, accounting, graphic design), public speaking, and a variety of other tasks that are handled exclusively by paid employees in the business and government sectors.

What is the fundamental relationship between nonprofit managers and nonprofit volunteers, and what—if any—is the ethical component of that relationship?

First and importantly, the relationship is *not* one of direct economic exchange. There is, in the volunteer-nonprofit relationship, no neat balance between work rendered and payment received. There are two other possibilities: either the labor donation is a "pure grant" with no semblance of mutual obligation or reciprocity, or the labor donation creates some form of non-economic mutual obligation. The latter, in fact, seems to be the case in many forms of volunteering. Volunteers donate their labor without expectation of personal remuneration, but they expect and assume that the organization will use their labor to achieve the stated goals of the organization. For example, if a dozen volunteers work hundreds of hours addressing and stamping envelopes for an environmental organization and later find that the organization has sold the results of their work to a commercial firm for advertising a non-environmental product, the volunteers would be outraged. They would intuitively understand that there was an implicit moral contract between themselves and the nonprofit organization: we give you our labor, you use our labor to achieve the stated goals of the organization. Nonprofit organizations and managers, by soliciting and accepting volunteer labor, create an ethical obligation to use that labor appropriately. Nonprofit organizations and managers are in this sense ethically accountable to their volunteers.

Nonprofit board members represent a special subset of nonprofit volunteers. They not only donate labor but also assume ultimate legal, fiscal, and societal responsibility for the organization. Drucker (1990) and others have emphasized the unique importance that boards play in nonprofit organizations, and Herman and Heimovics (1991) have produced empirical support for the importance of the CEO-board relationship in nonprofits. While this relationship is typically cast in technical terms, it has a clear ethical dimension. For instance, a board cannot fulfill its responsibility to the organization and the society without full and adequate information. In practical terms, it is virtually impossible for the board to have that information without the active cooperation of the executive director. One of the most common temptations of nonprofit CEOs is "to put the best face on things" even and perhaps especially with the board. This sometimes leads to the CEOs concealing or conveniently omitting negative information without which the board cannot do its job. Such information restriction, however humanly understandable, could at times be a serious ethical violation on the part of the CEO; for instance, when a CEO keeps from the board negative information on financial threats to the agency that might lead to staff layoffs, severe cuts in services, or even dissolution of the organization.

IV. RELATIONS WITH CLIENTS AND THE BROADER SOCIETY

Goodpaster (1984, p. 4) has noted that the ethically relevant behavior of executives falls into two broad categories: transactions with the external environment of the organization as a whole and transactions with the internal environment of the organization. Business examples of the former include product safety, environmental protection, truth in advertising, and honesty with government regulators. Again, these basic moral imperatives apply equally to nonprofit organization managers, although the specific applications will often differ greatly. However, two characteristics of nonprofit work suggest a somewhat different ethical context in relations with the external environment: (1) the vulnerability of many nonprofit clients, and (2) the high degree of societal responsibility that many nonprofits assume.

Although some nonprofit organizations (certain private clubs, schools, colleges, churches, arts organizations, foundations, and hospitals) deal primarily with privileged and powerful clients, nonprofit agencies commonly work with and for individuals and families who hold a relatively weak, disadvantaged position in society: children, people of color, immigrants, the poor, the physically and mentally ill, older people, low-paid and low-status workers, and so forth. Other nonprofits work for categories of vulnerable or potentially vulnerable clients: environmental organizations, civil and legal rights organizations, women's organizations, peace organizations, and biomedical research groups. Consequently, many nonprofits are much more likely than business organizations to be in a power relationship with their clients. The typical business client can buy a dress from Macy's, a computer from Apple, or a head of lettuce from Safeway and not be or feel at the mercy of any of those organizations, aside from routine considerations about product safety. Many nonprofit clients, however, are by definition in a position of weakness relative to the serving organization. Confucianism reminds us that any time power enters a human relationship, ethics must follow. The work of nonprofit organizations takes on a special ethical dimension precisely to the degree that the organization's work necessarily involves a power relationship with clients.

Ironically, this fact is probably the main reason so little attention has been given to nonprofit administrative ethics. The classic professions of religion, health care, and education, and newer professions such as mental health care and social work, have largely dominated nonprofit work. Since these professions have long had formal and informal codes governing the behavior of the direct service providers (doctors, teachers, counselors, social workers), it may not have seemed necessary to focus on the administrative ethics of organizations providing these services. However, the greatly increased size and complexity of nonprofit service organizations have made such attention to administrative and organizational ethics, as distinguished from service provider ethics, a clear necessity.

REFERENCES

Barnard, C. (1938). *Functions of the Executive*, Harvard University Press, Cambridge, MA.

Bass, B. (1985). *Bass and Stogdill's Handbook of Leadership* (3rd ed.), Free Press, New York.

Billis, D., and Harris, M., eds. (1996). *Voluntary Agencies: Challenges of Organisation and Management*, Macmillan, London.

Boris, E. T., and Odendahl, T. J. (1990). Ethical issues in fund raising and philanthropy. In: *Critical Issues in American Philanthropy: Strengthening Theory and Practice* (J. Van Til, ed.), Jossey-Bass, San Francisco, pp. 188–203.

Briscoe, M. G., ed. (1994). *Ethics in Fundraising: Putting Values into Practice. New Directions for Philanthropic Fundraising*, No. 6, Jossey-Bass, San Francisco.

Darr, K. (1991). *Ethics in Health Services Management* (2nd ed.), Heath Professions Press, Baltimore.

Drucker, P. F. (1990). *Managing the Non-Profit Organization: Practices and Principles*, Harper Collins, New York.

Goodpaster, K. E. (1984). *Ethics in Management*, Harvard Business School, Boston.

Hansmann, H. (1980). The role of nonprofit enterprise. *Yale Law Journal*, 89: 835–901.

Hansmann, H. (1987). Economic theories of nonprofit organization. In: *The Nonprofit Sector: A Research Handbook* (W. W. Powell, ed.), Yale University Press, New Haven, CT, pp. 27–42.

Herman, R. D., and Heimovics, R. D. (1991). *Executive Leadership in Nonprofit Organizations: New Strategies for Shaping Executive-Board Dynamics*, Jossey-Bass, San Francisco.

Hodgkinson, V. A., Weitzman, M. S., Abrahams, J. A. Crutchfield, E. A., and Stevenson, D. R. (1996). *Nonprofit Almanac, 1996–1997*, Jossey-Bass, San Francisco.

Jeavons, T. H. (1992). When the management is the message: relating values to management practice in nonprofit organizations. *Nonprofit Management and Leadership*, 2(4): 403–417.

Jurkiewicz, C. L., and Massey, T. K., Jr. (1998). The influence of ethical reasoning on leader effectiveness: an empirical study of nonprofit executives. *Nonprofit Management and Leadership*, 9(2): 173–186.

Koziol, K., ed. (1998). *Ethics in Nonprofit Management: A Collection of Cases* (2nd ed.), Institute for Nonprofit Organization Management, University of San Francisco, San Francisco.

Levy, C. S. (1982). *Guide to Ethical Decisions and Actions for Social Service Administrators: A Handbook for Managerial Personnel*, Haworth, New York.

Mason, D. E. (1984). *Voluntary Nonprofit Enterprise Management*, Plenum, New York.

Mixer, J. R. (1993). *Principles of Professional Fundraising: Useful Foundations for Successful Practice*, Jossey-Bass, San Francisco.

O'Neill, M. (1989). Responsible management in the nonprofit sector. In: *The Future of the Nonprofit Sector: Challenges, Changes, and Policy Considerations* (V. A. Hodgkinson and R. W. Lyman, eds.), Jossey-Bass, San Francisco, pp. 261–274.

O'Neill, M. (1992). Ethical dimensions of nonprofit administration. *Nonprofit Management and Leadership*, 3(2): 199–213.

O'Neill, M. (1993). Fundraising as an ethical act. *Advancing Philanthropy*, 1(1): 30–35.

O'Neill, M. (1997). The ethical dimensions of fund raising. In: *Critical Issues in Fund Raising* (D. F. Burlingame, ed.), John Wiley and Sons, New York, pp. 58–64.

O'Neill, M. (1998). Nonprofit management education: history, current issues, and the future. In: *Nonprofit Management Education: U.S. and World Perspectives* (M. O'Neill and K. Fletcher, eds.), Praeger, Westport, CT, pp. 1–12.

30

Military Ethics

Richard D. White, Jr.
Louisiana State University, Baton Rouge, Louisiana

> Warfare is almost as old as man himself, and reaches into the most secret places of
> the human heart, places where self dissolves rational purpose, where pride reigns,
> where emotion is paramount, where instinct is king (Keegan, 1993).

Mankind has waged organized war for 5,000 years. For much of that time, men have
attempted, with tragically little success, to create regimes that either abolish war or limit
its destruction and inhumanity. The dilemma mankind too often faces is to choose between
two conflicting moral realities: first, humans should not deliberately harm other humans,
and second, humans may sometimes engage in violence to protect themselves and others
from harm. Faced with this dilemma, the question of war itself—whether war should
indeed be fought—has been mostly the concern of philosophers, theologians, jurists, and
politicians, while military professionals have developed the ways of warfare. These basic
questions of war—when and how it is fought—are the essence of the study of military
ethics.

Military ethics is a unique and relevant branch of applied ethics that focuses on the
waging of war and professional soldiering. Military ethics literature has three general but
closely related perspectives, two institutional and the other individual. One institutional
perspective focuses on *when* war can be waged and what conditions justify the use of
force, while the other institutional perspective focuses on *how* war is waged and what
limits should be on the amount and types of force that may be used. The individual perspective, a more recent body of military ethics literature, discusses the morality and ethical
behavior of the soldier and sailor and has been termed the warrior ethos or more recently
the professional military ethic.

1. *JUS AD BELLUM* AND *JUS IN BELLO*

Since the earliest civilizations man has struggled with the morality of war, questioning
when war is, or is not, permissible (*jus ad bellum*) and questioning what is permissible
when war has begun (*jus in bello*). As early as the fifth century B.C., Chinese lords provide
one of the first known efforts of determining *jus ad bellum*, commanding that no war
should begin without just cause; that the enemy be warned of imminent attacks; that no
injury be done to the wounded; and that the rights of innocents be respected. Sun Tzu,

the fifth century B.C. Chinese soldier philosopher, provided early humanitarian standards for *jus in bello*, as do the ancient Egyptians and Babylonians. Around the fourth century B.C., the Hindus developed humanitarian rules for restricting warfare that are similar to many aspects of modern international laws of war. In the Aztec Empire, warring factions fought battles with fixed numbers of soldiers at set times on prearranged battlefields. Thucydides, in the *History of the Peloponnesian War* (431–404 B.C.), described negotiations between Athenian and Melian generals that debate the morality of the powerful Greek attack upon the island of Melos and the possible harm to innocent civilians (Christopher, 1999; Stromberg et al., 1982: 7).

Early attempts to codify the laws of war trace at least to the classical philosophers. In the *Laws*, Plato (1961) argued that wars are necessary evils to be fought to gain peace. Because wars are often unavoidable, he outlined restraints relating to *jus ad bellum* as well as *jus in bello*. Aristotle, like Plato, regarded war as inevitable and his rationales for waging war may be found in the strategies of his student, Alexander the Great. Ancient Rome also contributed to the evolution of the laws of war. In the first century B.C., Cicero used a natural law theory of civil and intersocietal politics to set forth his Stoic foundations for modern *Jus ad Bellum* in that: a war is never undertaken by the state except in defense of its honor or safety and as a last resort; no war is just unless it has been announced and declared by proper authority and unless reparation first has been demanded; the opponent must be notified of the declaration; and the opponent must be provided the opportunity to make a peaceful settlement prior to the launching of hostilities (Cicero, 1928: 211–213).

During the Middle Ages, European moral theologians developed *jus ad bellum* principles based on explicit concepts of theology and justice. In the fourth century, Saint Ambrose accepted the hierarchy of duties toward God, country, and family that Cicero describes in natural law. He deems morally justified, "that kind of courage which is involved in defending the empire against the barbarians, or protecting the weak at home, or allies against plunderers." Ambrose declared a soldier must protect the innocent based on the principle of brotherly love, defined justice as the fundamental and highest virtue upon which disputes are resolved, and distinguished the innocent from the guilty among the enemy (Ambrose, 1969).

A.   St. Augustine and St. Thomas Aquinas

Of all the Christian theologians, St. Augustine (354–430) is the most influential interpreter of the laws of war. Augustine's true genius is a synthesis of classical philosophy and Christian theology, with many of his ideas coming from Plato, Aristotle, and Cicero as well as from his own interpretations of the Gospel. Augustine accepted the Roman principles of *jus ad bellum* that war must be for just cause, declared by proper authority, and the final objective must be peace. Augustine also decreed that just causes for war include those ordained by God and where the divine forces of good combat the satanic forces of evil. Writing during a period when Europeans began to fear invasion from the Goths, Huns, and Vandals, Augustine provided the justification for Christianity, previously pacificist and militarily weak, to protect its lands, wage Holy Wars against the invading barbarians, and ultimately to spread the Gospel during the Crusades that began in 1095. Augustine's three principles of just war form the basis for ecclesiastical adjudication between warring factions until the Reformation (Christopher, 1999; Mays, 1997; Keegan, 1993: 382).

The influence of the church in defining *jus in bello* continues for centuries, with several notable attempts to limit the destruction of war. In 989 A.D., the edict known as the Peace of God prohibited warfare against monks, women, shepherds, cemeteries, and other groups. In 1027 the Truce of God restricted warfare to certain days of the week and certain seasons, while in 1139 the Second Lateran Council prohibited crossbows and siege weapons. LaCroix (1988: 68) argues, however, that the limitation on certain weapons such as the crossbow was not caused by a concern over their inhumanity, but rather the weapons could be used by soldiers in revolt against their own nobility and leaders. Nonetheless, the ban on crossbows did not last. By 1250, Hosteiensis issued a canonical opinion, already in practice, that all weapons are lawful in just war.

Saint Thomas Aquinas (1225–1274), inspired by Aristotle and Augustine, believed human reason is the sole arbiter between right and wrong moral choices. Whereby Augustine considered war inevitable, Aquinas held that war is prima facie against natural law and Christian virtue. He contributed a more utilitarian theme to *jus ad bellum*, arguing that human laws for the common good, justice, and the maintenance of order may compel the destruction of life, limb, and property and the denial of liberty. In his *Summa Theologica*, Aquinas (1957) followed Augustine and stipulated that for a war to be just it must be declared by proper authority, waged for just cause, and conducted with a morally right intention. Aquinas is the first to describe the concept of proportionality, that is, the good realized by war must be proportional to the evil that the war will cause.

Two centuries later, the Spanish clerics Francisco de Vitoria (1492–1536) and Francis Sua'rez (1548–1617) further refine the teachings of Augustine. Vitoria, who helped frame the imperial legislation for Spain's New World territories, was concerned with the inhumane treatment of Native Americans by the Spanish conquistadors. He wrote that Native Americans have rights because of their humanity and that all people belong to one universal society because of their natural abilities to socialize and communicate. He contributed to *jus in bello* with a commitment that deliberate slaughter of innocents is never lawful in itself and makes a powerful case for protecting innocents. Sua'rez, a student of Vitoria, translated much of the ecclesiastic war doctrine into the language of jurists. He contributed definitive work on the distinctions between combatants and innocents as well as describing war as a last resort (Coates, 1997; LaCroix, 1988; Christopher, 1999).

B. The Secularization of the Rules of War

The secularization of *jus ad bellum* began with the Dutch legal scholar Hugo Grotius (1583–1645), who consolidated a thousand years of moral and ecclesiastic principles into a single body of objective criteria. He created legal standards for states to follow in their relations with each other and organized his theories around the natural law theory of the Stoics and Cicero. Grotius insisted on natural laws that are binding on all people at all times and ''cannot be changed even by God.'' Grotius' primary objective was to prevent war; failing to prevent it, he sought to minimize its brutality. He listed six conditions necessary for *jus ad bellum*: just cause, proportionality, reasonable chance of success, public declaration of war, declared by legitimate authority, and waged as a last resort. Grotius argued that all members of a society are responsible for the public actions of the leaders. Declaration of war therefore requires the overt or tacit consent of the governed. Grotius established limitations on *jus in bello* in terms of who can be attacked, what means can be used to attack them, and the treatment of prisoners. Grotius' writings on just war still form the basic justification for modern peacekeeping missions (LaCroix, 1988; Mays, 1997; Christopher, 1999).

Ecclesiastic *jus ad bellum* principles remained influential until the eighteenth and nineteenth centuries and the gunpowder age when nation-states turned away from church teachings. During this period there was also a shift from natural law to a positivist view that the only functional rules for sovereign states are those to which they commit themselves. The dominant theory became Machiavelli's (1469–1527) secular view that state sovereignty provides all the justification needed to wage war. Machiavelli saw war as a means of defending the republican ideal from lawlessness, chaos, and corruption (Mays, 1997: 4).

C.   The Lieber Code and Modern Laws of War

In many ways the culmination of the movement to humanize war through the use of reason took place in 1863. In that year the U.S. Army published the Lieber Code, officially known as "General Orders No. 100, Instructions for the Government of Armies of the United States in the Field." The Lieber Code was a response to the expansion of the U.S. Army during the Civil War. The pre-war army numbered thirteen thousand frontier professionals and was small enough for junior officers to learn the basics of military law and the customs of war from more senior colleagues. In the war, however, the army expanded to a force of a million men led by thousands of inexperienced officers with little knowledge of legal issues ranging from court martials to the paroling of prisoners of war (Lieber and Hartigan, 1983; Carnahan, 1998). More formal, codified laws of war were necessary.

Abraham Lincoln, concerned with the maltreatment of prisoners, recognized the need for regulations to restrict the more immoral aspects of war and appointed the jurist Francis Lieber to draft the most detailed codification of the laws of war of that time. Lieber's most significant contribution to the modern law of war was the identification of military necessity as a general legal principle to limit violence. The code provided a positivistic and very specific treatment of military necessity, classifying all peoples in an enemy country as enemies, the only distinction being some were armed, some unarmed. Noncombatants no longer received automatic immunity. The Lieber Code is also one of the first documents to specify an ethical obligation of the individual military service member, stating that "men who take up arms against another in public war do not cease on this account to be moral beings responsible to one another and to God" (Lieber and Hartigan, 1983: 48).

Over the years, the influence of the Lieber Code spread beyond the ranks of the U.S. Army. In 1868, an international commission meeting in St. Petersburg, Russia, applied Lieber's provision of military necessity to a ban on the use of small-caliber explosive bullets because they cause unnecessary suffering. In 1870, the Prussian Army based its own comprehensive code on the Lieber Code that includes a range of battlefield scenarios such as marshal law, espionage, desertion, encounters with civilians, prisoners, wounded, armistice, surrender, and humanitarian issues (Mays, 1997). The Lieber Code also provided foundations for the Brussels Declaration of 1874 and the Hague Conventions of 1899 and 1907 (Lieber and Hartigan, 1983; Carnahan, 1998: 215).

Military officials continue to refine the interpretations of *jus in bello* over the years, as evidenced by the development of U.S. Army field manuals. The 1917 manual expresses the principle that, first, a belligerent is justified in applying any amount and any kind of force necessary for the complete submission of the enemy at the earliest possible moment and with the least expenditure of men and money. Second, the principle of humanity says that all kinds and degrees of violence as are not necessary for the purpose of war are not permitted to a belligerent (U.S. War Department, 1917). The 1956 field manual refines the restrictions of *jus in bello*, stating that the prohibitions of the law of war are not rationalized by military necessity justifying warfare as essential for the complete submission of the enemy as soon as possible. The 1956 manual rejects military necessity as a defense for acts forbidden by customary and conventional laws of war (U.S. Department of the Army, 1956).

Despite efforts to clarify the definition of military necessity over the years, the Lieber Code remains the most important and valid precedent for modern laws of war. By including some of the first humanitarian aspects into the laws of war, the Lieber Code is a primary resource for modern war doctrine and international protocols, including the Geneva and Hague Conventions and the United Nations Charter. The Geneva and Hague Conventions take great care to stress human rights and civility in the event of war and endeavor to balance each nation's right to self-defense with the need to regulate international conduct. Now somewhat enforceable under UN auspices, these conventions mandate: protection of immunity from attack for neutral countries; full protection of neutrality for hospitals, humanitarian aid stations, and their personnel; protection of civilians, cultural and private property, and merchant vessels; humane treatment of war prisoners; respect for fundamental human rights; fair trials for war crimes; and distinctions between belligerents and spies (Mays, 1997).

II. RECENT SCHOLARSHIP ON MORALITY AND WAR

Appreciation of military ethics and especially the ethics of war diminished in the first half of the twentieth century because of the opinion that the subject was beyond reform, subjective, and anachronistic. The doctrine of *inter arma silent leges*—during war the laws are mute—found general endorsement. Recently, however, and especially after the Second World War and Vietnam, the study of military ethics enjoys increased interest and some scholarly approval. While jurists have chronicled the laws of war for centuries, many aspects of the study of military ethics are much more current, yet emerging, and may signal a renewal in philosophical debate.

Of the more recent literature on morality and war, Christopher (1999) provides an excellent primer for those concerned with the use of force as an instrument of politics. He argues that centuries of just war scholarship provides an appropriate framework for resolving moral issues of when and how to wage war in the twenty-first century. His work focuses on several critical questions. Is it ever permissible to use violence to achieve political objectives? What are the moral and legal constraints on the types of weapons that combatants may use against one another? What precautions should military forces take to protect civilians during warfare? Beginning with the evolution of Grecian and Roman laws of war and Judeo-Christian teachings, Christopher explains the moral and ethical principles that form the justification for international laws governing the use of force and connects these to contemporary issues. These include a discussion of the moral and legal obligations of soldiers who believe a war to be unjust and considerations of using military force for humanitarian reasons.

LaCroix (1988) provides a treatment of the laws of war, describing authority, just cause, and right intention as requirements for *jus ad bellum*, and proportionality and discrimination as requisites for *jus in bello*. Drawing on examples from the Crusades to the present, Coates (1997) explores both the limitations and opportunities posed by the moral regulation of both *jus ad bellum* and *jus in bello*. He focuses on the question of just war, although acknowledging the moral ambiguity and mixed record of that tradition. The first half of his book compares the broad image of the just war with the rival images of realism, militarism, and pacifism. The second half examines the moral issues raised both by the resort to war and by its conduct, addressing concepts such as just cause, proportionality, last resort, treatment of noncombatants, and peacemaking.

Taylor's (1970) *Nuremberg and Vietnam: An American Tragedy* is a concise treatment of classic just war theory, war crimes, and the issues surrounding superior orders involving illegal or immoral activity. While defending the need for rules of war, Taylor takes the utilitarian approach in arguing that military necessity and completion of the wartime mission frequently may be sufficient reason to disregard *jus in bello*, such as the killing of prisoners and the suffering of innocents. He distinguishes between legal killing on behalf of the state, which he defends, from abhorrent killing done for selfish or emotional reasons. Like Taylor (1970), Ramsey argues that the military often has no choice but to override *jus in bello* on the basis of military necessity. Fotion (1990) also takes a utilitarian view, arguing for a powerful military and giving a limited moral argument for a large weapons arsenal. He attacks pacifism, or what he calls the "big argument," and suggests that in certain circumstances nuclear weapons, poison gas, and other weapons of mass destruction are morally permissible.

Walzer (1992) provides some of the more complete treatments of military ethics, including: a contrast of human rights arguments with utilitarian positions; historical examples illustrating which wars are, or are not, justified; a theory of aggression; issues of noncombatant status in modern war; the principle of double effect; and discussions of guerrilla war, terrorism, reprisals, and military necessity. He offers provocative guidelines for determining when military necessity justifies overriding the laws of war, writing that the laws of war must be obeyed "until the heavens fall" and that only in cases of imminent defeat by a heinous enemy may a nation set aside the principles of *jus in bello*. His reasoning is more restrictive and specific than the utilitarianism of Taylor and Fotion, arguing that military necessity may outweigh the laws of war only at the national and political level and only *in extremis*. For the soldier in the foxhole and the general at headquarters, the rules of war always apply and the humanitarian aspects of *jus in bello* are absolute (Walzer, 1992: 251–268).

While Walzer plays a prominent role in the renewal of interest in just war theory, his work is not without criticism. Coates (1997: 5) writes that Walzer's "excessive realism, his reliance at key points in his analysis on utilitarian augmentation, his apparent willingness to sacrifice a fundamental just war norm like noncombatant immunity to military necessity, his preoccupation with national sovereignty and territorial integrity, his inclination to moral particularism are all out of step with mainstream just war thinking."

A. Nagel and Criticisms of Just War Doctrine

Among the influential commentators on just war theory is Nagel (1976), who criticizes current restrictions on warfare for emphasizing legal grounds while the moral basis is often poorly understood and seldom explained. He attacks the present-day acceptance of military necessity as a valid justification for overriding *jus in bello*, offering a qualified defense of absolutism. His use of absolutism is not the more common pacifism where one may not kill another person under any circumstances, no matter what good would be achieved or evil averted thereby. Instead, Nagel's absolutism regards *jus in bello* to encompass two types of unwavering restrictions: restrictions on the category of persons at whom aggression or violence may be directed (noncombatants, medical personnel, etc.); and restrictions on the method of the attack (weapons of mass destruction, destruction of crops, etc.).

Nagel (1976) focuses on one of the more basic moral problems raised by the conduct of war: the problem of means and ends. He sees a fundamental conflict between two distinct categories of moral reason: utilitarianism and absolutism. To him, utilitarianism emphasizes what will *happen*, while absolutism emphasizes what one is *doing*. Utilitarianism says that one should try, either individually or institutionally, to maximize good and minimize evil. The absolutist focuses on actions rather than outcomes and sees the deliberate killing of innocent noncombatants as murder. The absolutist condemns outright the indiscriminate destructiveness of not only nuclear weapons but anti-personnel weapons, napalm, aerial bombardment; cruelty to prisoners; massive relocations of civilians; destruction of crops; and so forth. Not surprisingly, Nagel criticizes the widely accepted policy of attacking civilian populations in order to compel an enemy to surrender or to damage morale. Such policy is evidence of a mistaken moral conviction that the deliberate killing of noncombatants—women, children, old people—is excusable if enough can be gained by it.

Opposing Truman's decision to drop atomic bombs on Hiroshima and Nagasaki, the just war theorist Anscombe (1963) refines the definition of absolutism. She argues that pacifism is an untenable position: it simply does not take account of the fact that civilization without constraints is generally impossible. She does not deny that war is a great evil, principally because it tends to lead to the morally abhorrent killing of the innocent. But pacifism, she adds, tends to have a morally harmful effect. By ignoring the difference between spilling any blood and spilling innocent blood, pacifism tends to lead to an "anything goes" position once war begins. One is, furthermore, deceived if one believes that Christianity entails pacifism; such a position sees Christianity not, as in truth it is, a severe and practicable religion, but rather as a beautifully ideal and impracticable one.

Wasserstrom (1970), another critic of existing laws and conventions, writes that current doctrine does not attempt to embody a decent moral position, its provisions are determined by other interests, it is a doctrine in fact immoral in substance, and it is a grave mistake to refer to the current doctrine as standards in forming moral judgments about warfare. Tucker (1960) writes that in contemporary times the only morally acceptable condition for waging war is self-defense. While sympathetic to just war reasoning, Ramsey (1961) provides a discussion of a Christian approach to the classic conflict of war and morality. In a later work (1968) addressing U.S. morality in Vietnam, he argues that guerillas who fight within the confines of women and children are themselves responsible for innocent deaths, not the anti-guerilla forces who have no choice of battlefield.

Peters (1996: 104) argues that modern concepts of *jus in bello* lead to unnecessary violence. He writes that current Western war doctrine allows society to disguise psychologically the killing of human beings behind rationalized ideas, higher causes, and approved conduct. He faults ethics in war for shielding us from the graveness of our actions. To Peters, military ethics are ritualistic: "they rarefy and codify the darkness, implying a comforting order in the chaos and void.'' He cites the cause for the immorality in military ethics as the rise in technologies that distance killers from the killed, depersonalize and dehumanize modern warfare, and rationalize the killing of an enemy who has become faceless. The unexpected result of more distant weaponry, however, has been the increasing reluctance of Western society to kill those enemies who acquire faces and therefore identities. During the Gulf War there was little outcry to the slaughter of some 100,000 Iraqi soldiers while it was unthinkable to announce and carry out a threat to kill Saddam Hussein. Peters, like Nagel (1976) before, argues aggression should be aimed at its true enemy and attack must be *relevant* and *direct* to the issue. Peters argues that the current system amounts to ''punishing the murderer's neighborhood while letting the murderer go free,'' and calls for a rehumanization of warfare by aiming military technology directly at the responsible parties instead of the innocent masses. To do so, a drastically different ethic of war is necessary.

B. Anthologies and Case Studies

Several anthologies are useful additions to the just war literature. Wakin (1986) contributes a comprehensive volume of thirty-three articles on the morality of war by contemporary authors, including Huntington, Janowitz, Hackett, Telford Taylor, Wasserstrom, and Walzer. The articles in the first section underscore the ethical dimensions of the military profession, considering themes such as the conflict between military values and societal norms, the relation of the military to the state, and the concepts of loyalty, honor, and integrity. The second section addresses agonizing moral issues associated with warfare, especially modern warfare and weapons of mass destruction.

Wasserstrom (1970) provides another anthology containing eight major articles including essays by Anscombe, Ford, Walzer, Narveson, and Lewy. He provides William James' ''The Moral Equivalent of War,'' one of the more classic statements on this subject. James argues a society would be worthless if it lacks military virtues such as ''intrepidity, contempt of softness, surrender of private interest, . . . , discipline and honor'' (James, 1910).

Cohen, Nagel, and Scanlon (1974) edit a series of essays dealing with fundamental moral justifications for actions in war, as well as specific issues formed during World War II and Vietnam. Matthews and Brown (1989) provide an anthology of seventeen articles describing the aspects of just war, the ethical dimensions of military professionalism, a possible military code of ethics, and operational ethics. Rains and McRee (1980) edit the proceedings of the War and Morality Symposium held at the Military Academy and provide the remarks of Brandt, Nagel, Walzer, Lewy, and Taylor, among others, exploring morality and nuclear warfare, individual responsibilities in war, and the morality of military intervention.

Several military case studies involving major ethical incidents are relevant. Peers (1970) provides a detailed account of the My Lai incident. General Peers and his team of investigators carefully collect information incriminating American soldiers in the 1968 massacre of a large number of Vietnamese noncombatants. The Peers Report questions the competence of Army leadership at several levels and describes flagrant attempts to conceal information. The Peers investigation recommends investigations of several officers and enlisted men for serious violations of the law of war and the Uniform Code of Military Justice.

The writings of Stockdale (1993) are also pertinent. A naval aviator, Stockdale is shot down over North Vietnam in 1965 and spends the next eight years as a prisoner of war. He writes that his survival was due in part to his earlier education focusing on classical philosophy. To Stockdale, classical theory provides invaluable moral perspectives on his confinement. In particular, his application of the *Bible* and the *Book of Job* especially teaches him that life is not fair and the *Enchiridion* of Epictetus teaches him to concern himself only with what was within his power. He learns that integrity is far more important than physical needs. As a result of his experience, Stockdale recommends training in history and philosophy for professional soldiers. "In stress situations, the fundamental, the hardcore classical subjects, are what serve best."

Sheehan's (1971) *The Arnheiter Affair* is the real-life story of a naval officer that resembles the fictional events in Wouk's (1952) *The Caine Mutiny*. Both of these are intriguing case studies in military ethical conduct and contribute many lessons about careerism, officership, and the dilemma of moral decision-making in the military hierarchy. Both fictional literature and film provide some excellent portrayals of military ethics. *The Red Badge of Courage* (Crane, 1925), *The Cruel Sea* (Monsarrat, 1951), *From Here to Eternity* (Jones, 1951), *Mister Roberts* (Heggen, 1946), *The War Lover* (Hersey, 1959), and *Catch 22* (Heller, 1961) are just a few examples of military fiction providing vivid portrayals of war and the ethical dilemmas it creates.

III. OFFICIAL MILITARY ETHICS DOCTRINE

Since World War II, the military services and military scholars furnish a substantial body of literature discussing the moral dimensions of the military organization and the ethical behavior of military members. The military ethics literature differs on several counts from that of other professions such as medicine and law. First, there is no formal U.S. military code of ethics. Instead, a wide range of official documents, international and domestic law, internal military regulations, unratified conventions, bilateral agreements, semi-official creeds, and informal customs and tradition comprise the broad, loosely defined field of military ethics.

Military ethics also differs from other professional fields of ethics because the stakes are higher. The consequences of unethical behavior by military members can be catastrophic, as the lessons of Nuremberg and My Lai gravely illustrate and the threat of nuclear warfare forebodes. The military is the lone profession whose basic function is immoral. Military ethics is a paradox, attempting to connect the antithetical concepts of morality and killing. On one hand, American society requires military professionals to be of the highest moral character and to be prepared to make the ultimate utilitarian sacrifice of giving their life defending the nation. On the other hand, society requires the same highly moral military professional to carry out the most immoral of duties—the large-scale killing of other human beings. Military ethics deals with a most difficult question: How can an effective military, efficient in the killing of an enemy, also be ethical?

The military ethics literature suffers from its own unique problems. McGrath and Anderson (1993: 188), for example, criticize military ethics for being insulated from external analysis and deprived of the benefit of vigorous outside philosophical commentary. Although internal military journals frequently address ethical topics, there is little dialogue in traditional scholarly and philosophical journals. Written by former and serving soldier-scholars, much of the military ethics literature lacks sophisticated research, involves little empirical study, and overemphasizes officership at the expense of the enlisted soldier and sailor. Even with much of the military ethics literature centering around the just war question, no consensus theory of military ethics unifies the literature or points to a standard set of problems (McGrath and Anderson, 1993). Much of the literature omits important historical, philosophical, and theological precedents, such as Augustine and Grotius, or fails to acknowledge the legal underpinnings of military ethics, especially the absolutely essential role of the U.S. Constitution. Rice (1996) adds that current military ethics literature suffers from a polarized ethics of war debate: on one extreme, some theologians apply just war doctrine to make war anathematic, while at the other extreme military scholars use the doctrine to rationalize conflict, often after the fact. Between these philosophical extremes is an unfortunate void that lacks balanced scholarly debate. Despite these shortcomings, some exceptional military ethics scholarship is available, including the works of Hartle (1989), Christopher (1999), Coates (1997), Walzer (1992), Taylor (1970; 1986), and edited volumes by Wasserstrom (1970) and Wakin (1986).

While no formal code of ethics exists, the military services disseminate considerable internal, official material on military ethics that creates a broad patchwork of ethical guidance. Foremost is the U.S. Constitution, with Article VI requiring all officers to be bound by oath, and codified in detail by the U.S. Code and federal regulations. The Department of Defense publishes the *Code of the US Fighting Force* detailing the six articles of the Code of Conduct which specify behaviors while an American serviceman is a prisoner of war.

The Uniform Code of Military Justice (UCMJ), promulgated in 1950, provides substantial legal guidance to the military professional as well as proscribes immoral and unethical behavior. Article 133, for example, prohibits "conduct unbecoming an officer and a gentleman," and the courts have interpreted the article to make morally intolerable acts violations of military law. Likewise, military officials often apply Article 134, prohibiting "all disorders and neglects to the prejudice of good order and discipline," to cases of moral misconduct. Consequently, military officials and the courts interpret a wide range of infractions that fall within the proscriptions of Articles 133 and 134, rendering a military justice system possessing extremely high moral and ethical requirements. Many military infractions, such as the prohibited fraternization between officers and enlisted personnel, have no counterpart in civilian law. Indeed, military scholars consistently maintain that a higher moral standard is applied to military professionals when compared to society at large (Ficarotta, 1997; Fotion and Elfstrom, 1986).

Several professional military journals provide a forum for discussing military ethics, including: U.S. Naval Institute *Proceedings*, the Army Command and General Staff College's *Military Review, Air University Review, Naval War College Review*, the Army War College's *Parameters*, and the Air Force Academy's *Journal of Professional Military Ethics. Armed Forces and Society*, an interdisciplinary journal of the Inter-University Seminar on Armed Forces and Society, frequently addresses military ethics.

Three professional associations contribute to the academic and practical discussion of military ethics. The Hastings Center maintains materials on professional ethics and sponsors national workshops on professional ethics and includes military ethics as an important area of study. Ethics instructors from several U.S. armed services formally organized the Joint Service Conference on Professional Ethics (JSCOPE) in 1980. JSCOPE assists military ethics instructors with substantive materials and teaching innovations and provides a forum for dialogue on military ethics issues. JSCOPE publishes military ethics conference papers, case studies, and maintains a current bibliography. The Inter-University Seminar on the Armed Forces and Society, established at the University of Chicago by Morris Janowitz, provides another forum for military ethics. Its membership includes civilian and military scholars from many disciplines and from many countries. Under the society's sponsorship, Brown and Collins (1981) edit a collection of essays that discuss changes in the ethics of the military profession, the misuse of statistics, the moral attributes of professional competence, and the impact of technology on leadership and management.

Each of the military branches provides ethics instruction at service academies, advanced schools, and other instructional opportunities and each produces military ethics literature unique to its own service requirements. The Army, for example, periodically publishes *The Law of Land Warfare*, service-particular guidance on the laws of war, relevant treaties, the limitation of how wars are fought, and how to diminish war's evils by establishing rights of noncombatants, prisoners of war, the wounded, and the sick (McGrath and Anderson, 1993; Hartle, 1989). The Army also published *Ethics and Professionalism* (1981) containing a list of goals, an approach to moral decision-making, detailed lesson plans, additional instructor references, and ethics case studies. The Army War College published *Readings on Professionalism* (1980), an anthology of thirty-five articles on military professionalism, leadership and ethics, as well as the *Study on Military Professionalism* (1970) highlighting the perceived difference between the actual operating values of the Army Officer Corps and stated professional ideals. It makes several recommendations for institutional policies that bring actual conduct closer to ideal ethical standards. The Army War College maintains a comprehensive and updated bibliography of military ethics literature (Shope, 1997), as do other military academies and service schools.

IV. THE PROFESSIONAL MILITARY ETHIC

During the post–World War II period and especially since the moral controversies of Vietnam, a distinct body of literature emerges discussing the ethical behavior of the individual military professional and the creation of a professional military ethic. Huntington (1957), Janowitz (1960), Moskos (1970), Sorley (1982), Hartle (1989), Toner (1993, 1995), and others create a broad description of the military profession, the basic justification for its role in American society, its unique organization and culture, and its distinctive sense of morality.

The two classic studies by Janowitz and Huntington remain essential for understanding the military organization. Janowitz (1960) provides many insights into the values and future of the American military profession. His empirical sociological study describes the professional life, organizational setting, and leadership of the American military as it evolves during the first half of the twentieth century. In treating the military profession as an object of social inquiry, he creates an accurate and comprehensive assessment of its power position in society and its behavior in international relations. Janowitz stresses the military's need for understanding the principle of civilian control and a more realistic understanding of practical politics as distinguished from the "moralistic exhortations regarding ideal goals."

In describing the military profession, Huntington (1957) defines a professional military ethic that serves as a standard upon which the professionalism of any officer corps anywhere, anytime, can be judged. In Huntington's view, conflict is universal and violence is rooted in the permanent biological and psychological nature of man. Emphasizing evilness and selfishness, Huntington's view of the military professional is decidedly pessimistic and Hobbesian. While man has elements of goodness, strength, and reason, he is also wicked, weak, and irrational.

Huntington provides a rich cultural portrait of the military institution and the individuals who comprise it. To Huntington, the military is disciplined, rigid, logical, scientific; it is not flexible, tolerant, intuitive, emotional. He assumes two sets of attitudes to be characteristically military: bellicosity and authoritarianism. However, the military profession is not necessarily warmongering for it urges preparedness and cautions against starting war.

Huntington's professional military ethic emphasizes the importance of the group over the individual, as battlefield success demands the subservience of the will of the individual to the will of the group. To Huntington, the military ethic is basically cooperative in spirit, fundamentally anti-individualistic, and requires organization and discipline. For the profession to perform effectively, each level of the hierarchy must command the instantaneous and loyal obedience of subordinate levels. Without loyalty and obedience as the highest military virtues, military professionalism is impossible.

In Huntington's model, the military man is *a*political and not judged by the policies implemented but rather by the promptness and efficiency with which they are carried out. The apolitical nature creates a conflict, however, between military obedience and basic morality. The soldier remains a free individual who is morally responsible for his conduct. The soldier cannot surrender to the civilian the right to make ultimate moral judgments and must continue to be a moral individual. Huntington creates a dilemma for the military professional torn between the combat requirements of the organization and the moral requirement of the individual citizen. This dilemma, with no resolution in sight, continues as one of the central themes of the military ethics literature.

A.   The Modern Military Ethic

More recently, a movement in military scholarship has been toward the development of a distinctive, self-conscious, and individual-focused professional military ethic (PME). McGrath and Anderson (1993) provide a comprehensive survey of the PME literature and declare that the subject fails to receive the philosophical attention it deserves. Hartle (1989) contributes a discussion of the basic justification for the military role in American society and builds one of the more complete descriptions of the PME. Hartle argues that, first, there exists a fairly clear and morally coherent professional military ethic; second, this ethic is compatible with the fundamental values of American society; and third, the military professional has and deserves a "partially differentiated status." The last is a claim that the professional military has the right to violate an ordinary person's moral restrictions, a role which morally justifies actions that otherwise would be immoral.

Hartle asks how can military members follow a set of moral principles when the combat situations they face lie outside the rules of society. By applying the concept of role differentiation, he argues that the professional military ethic allows, and limits, the use of the military's dominant power in important ways. To him, the American PME is a combination of the moral implications generated by the traditional values of American society, the functional requirements of the profession of arms, and the laws of war. He recognizes that American national policy contains many inconsistencies that make it quite difficult for military members to act in a moral way.

Overbey (1996) expands on Hartle's notion of a professional military ethic by providing principles of right conduct for military forces and placing the PME within the larger context of society's moral framework and a common system of rules. Behaving morally, he concludes, is an integral part of being a professional in the U.S. military. Again, the professional military ethic does not stand alone but is one of many practical ethics that fit within the larger moral framework of society and is bounded by its common system of rules.

Sorley (1982) also strives for a clearer definition of the PME. He describes a public service ethic whereby certain professions, both collectively and individually, acknowledge their duties to serve the general interest. But the military goes beyond the traditional altruistic concept of public service. While the public servant has an obligation to serve the general interest *in addition* to self-interest, the military member in combat faces the ultimate obligation to serve the general interest *instead of* self-interest, including the sacrifice of one's life. To Sorley, it is this mortal aspect that underpins the distinctive professional military ethic.

In describing the professional military ethic, Toner (1993) suggests a trinity of military values: the first and highest is principle, second is purpose, and third is people. These three values closely parallel the traditional military obligations toward duty, honor, and country. To Toner, the value of a military member's own career comes in a distant fourth. In a more recent and comprehensive work (1995), he provides a thoughtful discussion of the PME and discusses topics such as civilian control of the military, military ethics training and education, and military codes of ethics.

Girdon (1980) provides a useful model for discussing the PME. He uses Rokeach's (1968) five essential value categories to examine the personal values of military officers through the writings of senior military leaders and scholars; analyzes those officers' perceptions of their organization's values; performs a content analysis of relevant military publications dealing with values, including those done on the values of military academy, ROTC, and OCS cadets; and summarizes findings concerning military values produced by a wide variety of nonmilitary scholars. Girdon concludes from these sources a consensus of nine ideal military values.

B. Critical Views of the Professional Military Ethic

The majority of the internal military scholarship extols the morality of the professional military ethic. However, other scholars, mostly from outside the military, provide a much more critical view of military ethics. While some argue that the military is a microcosm of the society that it defends and possesses the same moral values, critics suggest that the military organization, from an ethical standpoint, is dramatically different and possibly morally inferior when compared to society at large. As early as 1909, George Bernard Shaw, summarily dismissing military professionalism, provides the extreme view that, "There can no longer be any question of the fact that military service produces moral imbecility" (Toner, 1995). Galligan's (1979) Naval War College–sponsored study argues that the general ethical conduct of military professionals is deficient and does not meet the standards of professional military ethics. Gabriel and Savage (1978) speak of the "ethical deterioration" of the military, while Fotion and Elfstrom (1986: 70) also paint an uncomplimentary picture of military ethical behavior, writing:

Both sociologists and all of those who have been in a military uniform are familiar with the kinds of group behavior exhibited by young men in uniform. Such behavior can, and at times does, range on the negative side all the way from mild intimidation of others to rape and murder. In a group, these men will do things they ought not, which they would not do by themselves. The principle here seems to be that the whole is worse than the sum of the parts.

This observation supports evidence that the design and culture of the military organization may have a significant effect on the ethical behavior of military members. In general, organizational theory argues that members of rigidly structured, hierarchical organizations exhibit less autonomy and more heteronomous behavior such as overconformity, decreased innovation, groupthink, and at times pathological and illegal conduct when compared to society at large (Blau, 1955; Burns and Stalker, 1961; Argyris, 1964; Bennis, 1966; Thompson, 1965; Janis, 1982). The landmark studies of Milgram (1974) and Zimbardo (1975) suggest that under extremely tense conditions, organizations can create pathological, immoral behavior from even the most moral of individuals. While the research is clear on the impact of organizational design on overall behavior and productivity, it is less clear on the effect that organizational design may have on ethical behavior, and even less so on military ethics.

White's (1997) empirical study supports this notion that the rigidly hierarchical organization, of which the military is the epitome, may contribute to unethical and immoral behavior of its members. He compares the moral development of military members with individuals from less-rigid organizations. Using Kohlberg's (1983) moral development framework to operationalize moral judgment and Rest's Defining Issues Test as a measurement instrument, the study finds military members average seven points lower than a meta-sample from society at large, a statistically significant difference. The study also finds the scores of military members assigned to ships, where organizational hierarchy is most rigid, to be significantly lower than members assigned to less-rigid shore units. More research is needed in this emerging field to investigate the relationship between military structure and ethical behavior.

Gabriel and Savage (1978) criticize the professional military ethic in their examination of the differences between careerism and professionalism. Writing during the era of post-Vietnam discontent, they charge the armed services with ethical decline and identify "careerism" as one of the causes. Among factors allegedly leading to careerism is rapid rotation in the Army during Vietnam, with six-month combat tours allowing an officer to include combat service in his record. The authors claim that many officers seek preferment and advancement in the wrong way. Gabriel (1982) continues his critique of military ethics in a treatise on the antagonistic relationship between moral obligations and the military profession. To him, the loss of its "ethical compass" causes the military to experience an exponential growth of careerism. He argues that the all-volunteer force is a failure and contributes to the decline of military morality.

Gabriel argues that the military profession is qualitatively different from any other profession. However, this fundamental difference has been ignored since Vietnam when "business school" ethics initiated by the McNamara regime begin to undermine the age-old value system of the fighting man. The entrepreneurial ethic and the military ethic are fundamentally opposed, and the latter suffers badly from the invasion of the former. He supports Johnson's (1974) conclusion that several institutional forces lead to major ethical challenges from within the military profession. First, ethical relativism now dominates the moral culture of the military, allowing a widespread attitude that if something works and gets the job done, then it is right. Next, the loyalty syndrome leads to blind obedience of superiors in order to gain their favor and career support. Image is more important than integrity. This is true of both the military institution as well as the individual, careerist-oriented service member. Finally, the drive for success promotes careerism and a zero-defects attitude that creates unrealistic and cosmetic performance expectations.

C. The Need for a Military Code of Ethics

Since the 1970s, scholars have frequently proposed a military code of ethics (Lynn, 1971; Taylor, 1978; Gabriel, 1982; Diehl, 1985; Hartle, 1989; Zoll, 1989; McGrath and Anderson, 1993; Groll-Ya'ari, 1994). The ensuing debate over a proposed military code is split in two polarized camps: skeptics, many from within the military, attack proposed codes from many quarters, while idealists, many from outside the military, defend codes of ethics vigorously.

Skeptics who oppose a military code of ethics provide a range of objections. First, a code assumes men are bad and necessarily corrupt, an unacceptable notion within the proud military culture. Skeptics also argue codes are meaningless because one cannot teach ethics to begin with and ethical habits already are ingrained before one enters the military. Once ingrained, ethics therefore cannot be enforced from without. At the same time, a code might become a substitute for ethical judgment and allow codified minimums to become maximums. Also, a code describes ethical obligations in an ideal form that is empirically unattainable, while the range of alternatives offered by a code is impossibly large and difficult. To skeptics, codes are futile because they can be misapplied within the military community. A code does not guarantee compliance and could constitute a danger to military men by releasing them from all obligations of ethical choice (Gabriel, 1982: 182).

While resistance to a military code of ethics is formidable, there is significant discourse favoring a code, including a recommendation to establish a professional ethics board to create a code (Lynn, 1971) and an assertion that "every major study on the subject of ethics undertaken by the (military) profession itself sees a need for a code of professional ethics" (Gabriel, 1982: 120). Drisko's (1977) Army War College empirical study explores unethical conduct among officers, how the Army deals with it, the effectiveness of military ethics training, and the need for codes as a guide to ethical behavior. The study finds strong concern among all officers for military ethics, perceptions that better training programs in professional ethics are needed, and a two-to-one opinion favoring the development of a formalized military code of ethics.

Scholars note numerous persuasive reasons for establishing a military code of ethics. Fotion and Elfstrom (1986: 70) see the need for a military code because society requires greater moral constraints upon the military when compared to other professions such as medicine, law, and education. Gabriel (1982: 139) stresses that a code is necessary to create and preserve the values, habits, and practices traditionally associated with the military as "a special community of brothers who share special values and responsibilities." A formal code creates a "common ethical center" and unifies the military profession in its shared respect for common ideals (Taylor, 1978), as well as builds a foundation for a special trust between civilian society and the military establishment that has sworn to defend it (Sorley, 1982). A formalized code would show the civilian populace that the military does indeed possess a special sense of obligation and certain core ideals (Gabriel, 1982: 121).

What would a proposed military code of ethics look like? Title 10 of the U.S. Code contains some of what presumably would be included in a code of military ethics. Article 5947, titled "Requirements of exemplary conduct," requires all commanding officers and others in authority to show in themselves a good example of "virtue, honor, patriotism, and subordination; to take all necessary and proper measures to promote and safeguard the general welfare of persons under their command or charge; and to be vigilant in inspecting the conduct of those persons and to correct them when necessary." While Article 5947 explicitly applies to the Navy and Marine Corps, military ethicists extend its provisions to all officers (Hartle, 1989).

There are several possible explanations why the American military has never promulgated a formal code of ethics similar to those of other professions. Stromberg, Wakin, and Callahan (1982: 4) note the military exhibits a "particularly anti-intellectual dismissal of ethics" that poses resistance to a formal code. At the same time, the conservative, inflexible nature of military culture observed by Huntington (1957) suggests resistance to change. The creation of a formal code of ethics would be a significant change in military doctrine and, not surprisingly, faces stiff resistance from the senior rank and file.

V. CONCLUSION

The importance of military ethics is as important as any time in history. While technology continues to change the efficiency, lethality, and discretion of warfare, the basic ethical and moral issues remain the same for policymakers, philosophers, and military professionals to ponder. When should war be waged, and once commenced, how should it be fought? If there is a lesson from a study of military ethics, the lesson is that we have not learned our lesson well. One needs only to look at a host of regional and ethnic conflicts, the proliferation of nuclear weapons, and the relentless spread of international terrorism to concede that mankind has learned little in abolishing and minimizing warfare over the last 5000 years.

This failure, however, does not make the deliberation over military ethics any less essential. Indeed, the writings of Augustine, Aquinas, and Grotius provide strictures for warfare that are as appropriate today as when written centuries ago. They only need to be read, to be understood, and most essential, to be followed.

APPENDIX   THE CODE OF CONDUCT

ARTICLE I: I am an American fighting man, fighting in the forces which guard my country and our way of life. I am prepared to give my life in their defense.

ARTICLE II: I will never surrender of my own free will. If in command, I will never surrender the members of my command while they still have the means to resist.

ARTICLE III: If I am captured I will continue to resist by all means available. I will make every effort to escape and to aid others to escape. I will accept neither parole nor special favors from the enemy.

ARTICLE IV: If I become a prisoner of war, I will keep faith with my fellow prisoners. I will give no information nor take part in any action which might be harmful to my comrades. If I am senior, I will take command. If not, I will obey lawful orders of those appointed over me and will back them in every way.

ARTICLE V: When questioned, should I become a prisoner of war, I am required to give

ARTICLE VI:

name, rank, service number, and date of birth. I will evade answering further questions to the utmost of my ability. I will make no oral or written statements disloyal to my country or its allies or harmful to their cause.

ARTICLE VI: I will never forget that I am an American, fighting for freedom, responsible for my actions, and dedicated to the principles which made my country free. I will trust in my God and in the UNITED STATES OF AMERICA.

REFERENCES

Ambrose, Saint. (1969). *Duties of the clergy*, Bk I, XXIV, 115, in *Nicene and Post-Nicene Fathers*, vol. X (S. Schaff, ed.). Erdmans Publishing Company, Grand Rapids, MI.

Anscombe, G. (1963). War and murder, in *Nuclear Weapons and Christian Conscience* (W. Stein, ed.). Merlin Press, London.

Aquinas, Saint Thomas. (1957). Summa Theologica. In *The Political Ideas of St. Thomas Aquinas*, (Bigongiari, D., ed.). Hafner Publishing Company, New York.

Argyris, C. (1964). *Integrating the Individual and the Organization*. John Wiley, New York.

Bennis, W. (1966). *Changing Organizations*. McGraw-Hill, New York.

Blau, P. (1955). *The Dynamics of Bureaucracy*. University of Chicago Press, Chicago.

Brown, J. and Collins, M., eds., (1981). *Military Ethics and Professionalism*. National Defense University Press, Washington, DC.

Burns, T. and Stalker, G. (1961). *The Management of Innovation*. Tavistock, London.

Carnahan, B. (1998). Lincoln, Lieber and the laws of war: The origins and limits of the principle of military necessity. *American Journal of International Law*, 92(2): 213–231.

Christopher, P. (1999). *The Ethics of War and Peace: An Introduction to Legal and Moral Issues*, 2nd ed. Prentice Hall, Upper Saddle River, NJ.

Cicero, Marcus Tullius. (1928). *De Re Publica*, 3, XXIII (C. W. Keyes, trans.). G. P. Putnam, New York.

Coates, A. (1997). *The Ethics of War*. Manchester University Press, New York.

Cohen, M., Nagel, T., and Scanlon, T., eds. (1974). *War and Moral Responsibility*. Princeton University Press, Princeton, NJ.

Crane, S. (1925). *The Red Badge of Courage*. Modern Library, New York.

Diehl, W. (1985). Ethics and leadership: The pursuit continues. *Military Review*, 41: 19.

Drisko, M. (1977). *An Analysis of Professional Military Ethics: Their Importance, Development and Inculcation*. US Army War College, Carlisle Barracks, PA.

Ficarrotta, J. (1997). Are military professionals bound by a higher moral standard? *Armed Forces and Society*, 24: 59–75.

Fotion, N. (1990). *Military Ethics: Looking Toward the Future*. Hoover Institution Press, Stanford, CA.

Fotion, N. and Elfstrom, G. (1986). *Military Ethics: Guidelines for Peace and War*. Routledge and Kegan Paul, Boston.

Gabriel, R. (1982). *To Serve with Honor: A Treatise on Military Ethics and the Way of the Soldier*. Greenwood Press, Westport, CT.

Gabriel, R. and Savage, P. (1978). *Crisis in Command: Mismanagement in the Army*. Hill and Wang, New York.

Galligan, F. (1979). *Military Professionalism and Ethics*. Naval War College, Newport, RI.

Girdon, T. (1980). *Current Military Values*. Naval War College, Newport, RI.

Groll-Ya'ari, Y. (1994). Toward a normative code for the military. *Armed Forces & Society*, 20(3): 457–473.

Hartle, A. (1989). *Moral Issues in Military Decision Making*. University of Kansas Press, Lawrence, KS.

Heggen, T. (1946). *Mister Roberts*. Houghton Mifflin, Boston.

Heller, J. (1961). *Catch-22*. Simon and Schuster, New York.

Hersey, J. (1959). *The War Lover*. Knopf, New York.

Huntington, S. (1957). *The Soldier and the State: The Theory and Politics of Civil-Military Relations*. Harvard University Press, Cambridge, MA.

James, W. (1910). The moral equivalent of war. In *War and Morality* (Wasserstrom, R., ed., 1970). Wadsworth, New York.

Janis, I. (1982). *Groupthink: Psychological Studies of Policy Decision*. Houghton Mifflin, Boston.

Janowitz, M. (1960). *The Professional Soldier*. The Free Press, New York.

Johnson, K. (1974). Ethical issues of military leadership. *Parameters*, 4: 35–39.

Jones, J. (1951). *From Here to Eternity*. Scribner, New York.

Keegan, J. (1993). *A History of Warfare*. Alfred A. Knopf, New York.

Kohlberg, L. (1983). *Essays in Moral Development*. Harper and Row, New York.

LaCroix, W. (1988). *War and International Ethics: Tradition and Today*. University Press of America, Lanham, MD.

Lieber, F. and Hartigan, R. (1983). *Lieber's Code and the Law of War*. Precedent, Chicago.

Lynn, W. (1971). The military profession: What is it? *Army*, 3: 23–27.

McGrath, J. and Anderson, G. (1993). Recent work on the American professional military ethic: An introduction and survey. *American Philosophical Quarterly*, 30(3): 187–208.

Matthews, L. and Brown, D., eds., (1989). *The Parameters of Military Ethics*. Pergamon-Brassey, New York.

Mays, A. (1997). *War and Peace: Of Law, Lawlessness, and Sovereignty*. Paper presented to the Joint Services Conference on Professional Ethics, January 30, 1997, Washington, DC.

Milgram, S. (1974). *Obedience to Authority: An Experimental View*. Harper and Row, New York.

Monsarrat, N. (1951). *The Cruel Sea*. Knopf, New York.

Moskos, C. (1970). *The American Enlisted Man: The Rank and File in Today's Military*. Russell Sage Foundation, New York.

Nagel, T. (1976). War and massacre, in *Understanding Moral Philosophy* (J. Rachels, ed.). Dickenson Publishing Company, Encino, CA.

O'Brien, W. (1967). *Nuclear War, Deterrence and Morality*. Newman Press, Westminster, MD.

Overbey, B. (1996). *An Ethic for the Military: Establishing and Grounding a Professional Military Ethic for the Military Forces in the United States*. Unpublished doctoral dissertation, University of North Carolina, Chapel Hill, NC.

Peers, W. (1970). *The Peers Report*. Government Printing Office, Washington, DC.

Peters, R. (1996). A revolution in military ethics? *Parameters*, 26(2): 102–108.

Plato. (1961). Laws. In *Collected Dialogues* (E. Hamilton and H. Cairns, eds.). Princeton University Press, Princeton, NJ.

Rains, R. and McRee, M., eds. (1980). *The Proceedings of the War and Morality Symposium*. U.S. Military Academy, West Point, NY.

Ramsey, P. (1961). *War and the Christian Conscience*. Duke University Press, Durham, NC.

Ramsey, P. (1968). *The Just War: Force and Personal Responsibility*. Charles Scribner's Sons, New York.

Rokeach, M. (1968). *Beliefs, attitudes, and values: A theory of organization and change*. Jossey-Bass, San Francisco.

Sheehan, N. (1971). *The Arnheiter Affair*. Random House, New York.

Shope, V. (1997). *Ethics: A Selected Bibliography*. U.S. Army War College, Carlisle, PA.

Sorley, L. (1982). Competence as an ethical imperative. *Army*, 32, 8: 42–48.

Stockdale, J. (1993). The world of Epictetus. In *Vice and Virtue in Everyday Life* (C. Sommers and F. Sommers, eds.). Harcourt Brace, New York.

Stromberg, P., Wakin, M. and Callahan, D. (1982). *The Teaching of Ethics in the Military*. The Hastings Center, Hastings-on-Hudson, NY.

Taylor, M. (1978). A professional ethic for the military. *Army*, 28: 18–21.

Taylor, T. (1970). *Nuremberg and Vietnam: An American Tragedy*. Quadrangle Books, Chicago.

Taylor, T. (1986). Just and unjust wars. In *War, Morality, and the Military Profession* (M. Wakin, ed.). Westview Press, Boulder, CO.

Thompson, V. (1965). Bureaucracy and innovation. *Administrative Science Quarterly*, 10: 1–20.

Toner, J. (1993). Teaching military ethics. *Military Review*. 73, 5: 33–40.

Toner, J. (1995). *True Faith and Allegiance: The Burden of Military Ethics*. University Press of Kentucky, Lexington, KY.

Tucker, R. (1960). *The Just War*. The Johns Hopkins Press, Baltimore.

U.S. Department of the Army. (1956). *The Laws of Land Warfare*, Manual FM 27-10. Department of the Army, Washington, DC.

U.S. War Department. (1917). *Rules of Land Warfare*, Doc No. 467. War Department, Washington, DC.

Wakin, M., ed. (1986). *War, Morality, and the Military Profession*. Westview Press, Boulder, CO.

Walzer, M. (1992). *Just and Unjust Wars*. Basic Books, New York.

Wasserstrom, R., ed. (1970). *War and Morality*. Wadsworth Publishing Company, Belmont, CA.

White, R. (1997). *Organizational Design and Ethics: The Effects of a Rigid Hierarchy on Moral Reasoning*. Unpublished doctoral dissertation, Pennsylvania State University, Harrisburg, PA.

Wouk, H. (1952). *The Caine Mutiny*. Sears Readers Club, Chicago.

Zimbardo, P. (1975). *The Psychology of Evil: Or the Perversion of Human Potential*. National Technical Information Service, Springfield, VA.

Zoll, D. (1989). The moral dimension of war and the military ethic. In *The Parameters of Military Ethics* (L. Matthews and D. Brown, eds.). Pergamon-Brassey, New York.

31

Administrative Ethics in a Chinese Society
The Case of Hong Kong

Terry T. Lui
University of Hong Kong, Hong Kong

Ian Scott
Murdoch University, Perth, Australia

This chapter addresses the problems of public service ethics in a Chinese society. Taking Hong Kong—a Special Administrative Region of the People's Republic of China—as an example for discussion, the chapter will highlight the significance of contextual variables in understanding the role of administrative ethics in the process of government.

Context affects administrative ethics in two significant ways. From a *spatial* perspective, since public service ethics is an instrument for the attainment of accountable and responsible governance, it is bound to be conditioned by a number of factors peculiar to the environment of its application. These include, *inter alia*, the type of government, the relationship between the state and society, the role and functions of the bureaucracy in the political system, and the expectations placed upon public administrators by the community. Hence, in a democracy where sovereignty rests with the people, administrative ethics tends to be closely associated with the values of responsiveness, participation, and so on, because the bureaucrat is supposed to be a "servant" of the public. By contrast, in a highly paternalistic system of government in which decision-making power rests with an administrative elite, a responsible civil servant can be expected to assume a more proactive role in structuring values and engineering sociopolitical changes. Even among societies which can be broadly labelled as "democracies," differences in their political and administrative systems have often given rise to rather different conceptions of the nature and problems of administrative ethics (Chapman, 1993; Jabbra and Dwivedi, 1988; Kernaghan and Dwivedi, 1983; Rohr, 1989).

Context also affects administrative ethics in a *temporal* sense in that the setting of standards to guide the behavior of civil servants must be considered as a dynamic process. It must be responsive to the shifting nature of societal problems, the changing perception of the role and functions of the government, and the varying types and degrees of environmental factors which impinge on the capacity of the bureaucracy at different points in time. The stronger the capability of the bureaucracy and the higher the expectations on the government to solve problems in society, the more obligations there will be for the "morally responsible" public administrator; and vice versa. In the United States, these contextual considerations have contributed to the emergence and decline of New Public Administration. The general conception of public service ethics has also been changing as a result of evolving perceptions of the nature of the administrative organization, the administrative process, and the role of individuals in the bureaucracy (Denhardt, 1988, chapter 1).

The central theme in this chapter is therefore that any discourse on administrative ethics must address the problem of *relevance*. This concern for relevance has both practical and conceptual implications. On a practical level, it is important that norms of ethical behavior for civil servants be adjusted to suit the peculiarities of the circumstances. A code of ethics may work well in one situation but not necessarily in another. On a conceptual level, the consideration for relevance inevitably imposes constraints on the degree of generality which can be accorded to any "theories" of administrative ethics. This point is particularly significant at this juncture in the development of the subject, which scholars generally see as in a "chaotic" state (Rohr, 1990) and in need of a more soundly based theoretical framework (Denhardt, 1988). An awareness of the cultural and temporal limits of the assumptions underlying any attempt at theory-building is clearly important for a more refined understanding of administrative ethics. At the same time, progress in this area would help to provide a solid foundation for comparative empirical research.

Considering that an appreciation of contextual variables is essential to the proper conceptualization of public service ethics, the first task for the researcher is therefore to identify the crucial factors shaping ethical standards in any given frame of reference. In the sections to follow, we shall attempt to highlight these factors as they pertain to our analysis of administrative ethics in Hong Kong.

I. ADMINISTRATIVE ETHICS IN HONG KONG: THE POLITICAL DETERMINANTS

Viewed from a comparative perspective, the two most prominent features of the bureaucracy in Hong Kong which are of relevance here are: first, it was (until very recently) a colonial administration; and second, it is a system which has strong Chinese characteristics. Over the years, these two factors have interacted to produce a brand of administrative ethics which represents a curious mix of modern Weberian notions on the one hand and traditional Confucian values on the other.

Although administrative ethics in Hong Kong is shaped by its politics and culture, the political factor tends to predominate. This is mainly because the values of the bureaucracy are closely associated with the colonial legacy of the government.

Geographically, Hong Kong is a small territory situated on the south-east coast of China. It was historically a part of China, but was ceded and leased to Britain in three phases in the nineteenth century following China's defeat in military confrontations with foreign nations (Endacott, 1964; Wesley-Smith, 1980). When the British first colonized Hong Kong in 1841, the territory was rather barren and scarcely populated. There was already a primitive form of administration, but the British colonizers gradually began to establish their own system of government (Eitel, 1983) which consequently took on some characteristics of British colonial administration elsewhere. Britain formally relinquished control over Hong Kong on July 1, 1997, when the territory became a Special Administrative Region enjoying a "high degree of autonomy" under the People's Republic of China (Sino-British Agreement, 1984).[1] Nonetheless, given the long history of British rule, coupled with the fact that China has provided for the system of government in Hong Kong to remain more or less intact after 1997, many features of colonial governance have survived the change of sovereignty.

Among these features, one aspect that stands out most prominently is the hegemony of the administrative bureaucracy vis-á-vis other political institutions. Formally, there has always been a structural distinction between policy and administration in the territory. The Constitution of Hong Kong (that which operated under British rule, as well as that which came into effect on July 1, 1997) provides for the establishment of two councils, the Executive Council (which is a high-powered body of advisors to the Chief Executive and operates along the lines of a cabinet) and the Legislative Council (the formal legislative body in the territory). Policies are supposed to be made by the Chief Executive in consultation with the Executive Council, and by the Legislative Council with the Chief Executive's assent. In reality, however, most policies emanate from, and are even determined by, the bureaucracy (Lee, 1995; Miners, 1995). Senior administrators in Hong Kong do not simply coordinate or undertake the execution of public policies; they often formulate policies, provide the agenda for the political institutions, and, through their control of information, shape the outcome of the political decision-making process.

That public administrators are assuming an increasingly political role in the process of government is a well-documented fact in many countries (Aberbach et al., 1981; Kingdom, 1990; Suleiman, 1984). What distinguishes the Hong Kong case, however, is that the ascendancy of the bureaucracy is a product of deliberate political design. It appears that, from the very start, the British imperial authorities had decided that political powers should be vested in the hands of an appointed bureaucratic elite whose interests were closely intertwined with those of the British. The antecedent of the present Administrative Grade, which is the elite policymaking cadre in the government, comprised three cadets recruited directly from Britain in 1862 (Lethbridge, 1978). Over time, the membership of the bureaucratic elite became more localized,[2] but their support of colonial rule remained unchanged. They owed their powers to the Crown and their career opportunities were heavily dependent on the continuation of a British presence in the territory. Hence, a symbiotic relationship developed between the administrative elite in Hong Kong and their colonial masters in Britain. Neither party was willing to see any significant changes which might upset the balance of power in the polity.

The mutual dependence between the ruling political authority and the local administrative elite appears to have persisted beyond the change of sovereignty. From China's point of view, power concentrated in the hands of its appointed Chief Executive and a few hundred Administrative Grade officers who have an entrenched interest in the system is more readily subject to control from Beijing than if it were dispersed to semi-elected political bodies representing diverse groups in the community. For these reasons, the formal political institutions in Hong Kong have never been allowed to develop properly into autonomous decision-making agencies reflecting the aspirations of the local population. The concept of "representative government" did not find its way into the political vocabulary of the government until 1984, when it became clear that China would eventually resume sovereign rule over Hong Kong. Until 1985, there were no elected elements in the Legislative Council. To date, the Executive Council is still wholly appointed, and top civil servants retain their long-standing right as voting members in the Council.[3] Despite token gestures towards democracy since the mid-1980s, the system of government remains executive-led. The territory is still fundamentally an "administrative state" (Harris, 1978), a "bureaucratic polity" in which "the administrative bureaucracy . . . is the only significant political institution" (Lau, 1984: 26).

The political role that has been thrust upon the bureaucracy has significant implications for administrative ethics in Hong Kong. If power is to be centralized in a non-elected (and therefore potentially unaccountable) executive, the legitimacy of the regime would have to rest upon factors other than the degree of popular participation in the process of government. Bureaucratic performance, defined in terms of its capability to solve societal problems, has therefore become the key to the public's acquiescence to colonial, and subsequently, Chinese, rule (Lau, 1984; Miners, 1995; Scott, 1989). The Hong Kong government has always prided itself for the efficiency of its administrative machinery. This efficiency can be attributed to a number of factors. But an important explanation for the capacity of the bureaucracy to deliver services in a generally cost-effective and expeditious way is that Hong Kong has a very well-developed system of administration.

Many scholars have observed the close resemblance between the Hong Kong bureaucracy and the Weberian model of organization (Scott, 1984). The structure and modus operandi of the public administration are clearly founded on Weberian precepts. What is more important, the *values* that are definitive of the ethic of civil servants in Hong Kong are also strongly Weberian in nature. The entire personnel management system is geared to the maximization of one value, that of *administrative competence*. Staff are appointed into the civil service primarily on grounds of their qualifications and ability to perform designated tasks successfully. Training is principally designed for the purpose of enhancing job-related skills. The performance appraisal system is weighted heavily towards the individual's capabilities for the satisfactory fulfillment of his/her duties as well as his/her potential to contribute to greater organizational efficiency and effectiveness. In short, "responsible government" in Hong Kong has become synonymous with bureaucratic competence.

In other modern societies, bureaucratic competence is usually associated with specialization and professionalism. However, public administration in Hong Kong is generalist-oriented, in that top positions are dominated by officials who are not specialized in any profession, and who tend to move across functional borders delineating the different areas of government work. This generalist domination of the civil service system is partly attributable to the British administrative legacy (Scott, 1988a), but it is also an outgrowth of the government's philosophy in the early days of colonialism. This philosophy was that of minimal state intervention into society (Scott, 1989: 40–60). In the absence of clear policy goals to guide the governance of the territory, administration was conceived not so much in terms of the provision of public goods for the purpose of transforming society according to any preconceived ideal. It was rather a matter of maintaining a basic level of social and political order. Bureaucratic competence did not therefore hinge on officials' expertise in any specialized fields, but on their ability to balance and integrate conflicting forces in the polity. Since the 1970s, the Hong Kong government has become more interventionist. There has also been a corresponding increase both in the number and influence of specialists in the civil service (Scott, 1988a, 1988b). Yet the generalist tradition of administration persists and bureaucratic competence is still considered within the government as dependent on the capacity of senior administrators for political decision-making.

If competence is the primary value of public service, it is supported by two secondary values, namely, the value of *neutrality*, and the value of *loyalty to the hierarchy*. Civil servants in Hong Kong are neutral in three senses. First, they are "ideologically neutral," as they "are independent from political groups both left and right" (Lau, 1984: 28). Second, they regard themselves as neutral from politics (Scott, 1995). This is somewhat surprising since top-level bureaucrats are actually closely involved in the political process. However, according to the findings of empirical research, senior public administrators appear to believe that "politics is not their concern" (Cooper and Lui, 1990: 339). Other research into the views and attitudes of middle-to-lower-ranking civil servants toward political changes in the territory also shows a general feeling that politics is *external* to the administration, as a significant proportion of respondents expressed the fear that "future politics will interfere with the workings of the administration" (Cheek-Milby, 1988: 119). Although studies into the ethos of the civil service since the Chinese resumption of sovereignty are not yet available, there is evidence to suggest that political neutrality is still regarded as a key principle underlying the continued success of the administrative system.[4]

Finally, civil servants are morally neutral, in that they do not seem to espouse any ethical values beyond what the bureaucracy has inculcated in them. There is no clear ethics legislation to guide civil service conduct, and although rules and regulations abound in the Hong Kong government, they are largely designed to facilitate efficient organizational operations rather than to prescribe norms of moral behavior. There are civil service-wide as well as professionally oriented codes of conduct, but with a few exceptions they are not very well publicized, or they may be so loosely phrased as to be almost unenforceable (Lui, 1988). In recent years, attempts have been made by certain organizations, notably the Ombudsman and the anti-corruption body, the Independent Commission Against Corruption, to draw attention to the significance of administrative ethics.[5] However, these efforts are still at a nascent stage of development; their impact on the mentality of the public service is bound to be restricted. Individual virtue has yet to be recognized as an important aspect of ethical administration in Hong Kong.

The neutrality of civil servants predisposes them to accepting orders from their superiors in the bureaucracy. In this sense, neutrality and hierarchical loyalty are complementary values. Considering that the ultimate source of authority governing the Hong Kong administration has been alien to the bulk of civil servants,[6] the readiness of public administrators to comply with hierarchical order is remarkable. There are relatively few instances of insubordination, and whistleblowing is extremely rare.[7] Surveys undertaken in the lead-up to the transfer of the territory's sovereignty to China in 1997 have shown that civil servants at all levels were deeply concerned about their future (Lui and Cooper, 1990; Scott, 1988c; *South China Morning Post*, 1992). Moreover, there has been evidence to suggest that senior administrators were distrustful of the intentions of Britain and China towards Hong Kong (Cooper and Lui, 1990). In the midst of their misgivings, however, bureaucrats did not appear to have forsaken the value of hierarchical obedience.[8]

In sum, public service ethics in Hong Kong is largely the result of, and a perpetuating factor for, the type of bureaucracy which the British colonial authority created for the purpose of sustaining its political control over the territory, and which China has inherited for the sake of political expedience and administrative convenience. To the extent that the value of competence, together with the attendant values of neutrality and hierarchy, has served to enhance bureaucratic performance, administrative ethics has become a necessary instrument for the legitimatization of colonial as well as subsequent Chinese rule.

II. ADMINISTRATIVE ETHICS: CULTURAL INFLUENCES

Administrative ethics in Hong Kong has been shaped principally by the politics of the place, but it is also a reflection of the culture of the people. Demographically, Hong Kong is a predominantly Chinese society. Over 99% of the civil service, and as much as 93% of the population of 6.6 million in the territory, are Chinese. Over 60% of the residents were born in Hong Kong, while 32.6% were born in mainland China and subsequently settled in the territory (Census and Statistics Department, 1996). In terms of their ethnic and geographical origins, therefore, Hong Kong people are a fairly homogeneous group. Under these circumstances, one would expect that cultural factors should have a very strong influence over the ethos of the community.

Insofar as culture represents a system of shared values, perceptions, attitudes, and beliefs which characterize a community, a study of culture is definitely relevant to our exploration of the administrative arrangements and their attendant ethical implications for Hong Kong as a Chinese society. On the other hand, the importance of culture must not be overrated in this context. First, from an academic perspective, scholars still dispute the utility of culture as a framework for explaining political development and political behavior on a comparative basis (Thompson et al., 1990, Part Three). Second, even considering that Hong Kong is a Chinese society, it is a gross simplification to talk about a distinct set of cultural features which are quintessentially "Chinese." As Wang (1991) notes, China is a vast country with a long history (over 3000 years), so that "Chineseness" is by no means a single, unified quality. Third, and perhaps most important of all, the ethos of the Hong Kong Chinese is somewhat distinctive from the mainstream "Chinese culture." This is borne out of a study conducted by two academics in the mid-1980s. Through empirical surveys into the views of a select sample of Hong Kong people on such concepts as the individual, the society, the economy, politics, and the law, they concluded that a "Hong Kong identity" was emerging (Lau and Kuan, 1988). Whereas their analysis testifies to the lingering effect of Confucian values on Hong Kong Chinese, there is little doubt that modernization and Western influences have taken their hold on the mentality of the local population. Hence, to label Hong Kong as a "Chinese" society without qualification would be downright misleading.

These caveats are important in reminding us of the limitations that must be placed upon cultural explanations of administrative ethics in Hong Kong. Nonetheless, there is a considerable degree of congruence between Confucianism and the bureaucratic order in the territory. In that sense, culture may have predisposed the populace at large and the public administration in particular to embrace certain values which are concordant with the intentions of the ruling authorities.

Considering the vastness and complexity of the subject, it is not possible here to engage in a detailed analysis of Chinese civilization and its relationship with Confucianism.[9] Nonetheless, some salient characteristics of China as a Confucian state can be identified. Balazs (1964) once described China as "a permanently bureaucratic society." He remarked that

> When taking a bird's-eye view of the vast stretch of China's history, one is struck by
> the persistence and stability of one enduring feature of Chinese society that might be
> called officialism, the most conspicuous sign of which was the uninterrupted continuity
> of a ruling class of scholar-officials. (Balazs, 1964: 6)

Indeed, governance in imperial China had always been associated with the preeminence
of a literary elite who were selected into positions of power on the basis of their performance in open competitive civil service examinations. These examinations were designed
to test their knowledge of the Chinese classics, which in the Confucian scheme was taken
as a measure of the individual's suitability for political leadership.

There are therefore some interesting parallels between the tradition of government
in China and that in Hong Kong. In China, politics and administration are not clearly
separable. The mandarinate is the government, and the government is the only legitimate
source of political authority. This was the case in ancient times, and is still largely true
of the present political order under Communist rule (Pye, 1968, chapter 2). The dominance
of the bureaucracy and the bureaucratization of politics have been as much a feature of
governance in Hong Kong as it has been in China.

A second point of comparison relates to the generalist orientation of administration.
Under the imperial system of civil service selection, the mandarins were chosen on
grounds of their virtue and their ability. Virtue was of primary significance. Confucius
and his followers believed that the emperor and his scholar-officials should rule by educating and setting a moral example to their subjects rather than by coercion or the threat of
punishment (Koller, 1985; Pye, 1985; Yeh, 1969). Ability was also important. To ensure
the competent performance of the tasks of government, the rulers must identify and recruit
capable and talented individuals into public offices (Chang, 1980: 174; Chen, 1986: 526–
527; Rubin, 1976: 30). Hence, in an ideal Confucian state, the bureaucracy should be as
much a "virtuocracy" (Shirk, 1982) as a meritocracy (Wu, 1987: 60). But since "merit"
was assessed on the basis of the individual's literary knowledge of the Confucian classics,
the elite administrator in China was essentially a generalist (Yang, 1959).

This emphasis on the selection of public officials on grounds of general knowledge
and ability was closely related to the Confucian conception of the functions of the bureaucracy. For the Confucians, the primary purpose of the government was to maintain peace
and harmony in the country. The role of the scholar-officials in society was to manage,
to mediate, to settle conflicts, and to coordinate the activities of others. The bureaucrat
was therefore a political figure. In this sense, the generalist tradition of administration
in Hong Kong bears remarkable resemblance to the bureaucratic system in imperial
China.

Besides the dominance of the administrative elite and the generalist orientation of
the top officials, a third area of similarity between the Hong Kong bureaucracy and its
Chinese counterpart is that both systems are strongly hierarchical in the structure of their
authority. In the Confucian state, government was an institution comprised of individuals
of ascending moral understanding and achievements. At the apex of this ethical-political
order was the emperor, who was supposed to be the embodiment of ultimate virtue and
wisdom. The moral superiority of the government over its subjects provided the former
with the legitimacy to claim authority over the latter. This hierarchical ordering of institutions and individuals on the basis of virtue and wisdom extended beyond the political
realm to cover all aspects of social and familial interactions. In traditional China, it was

believed that harmony and stability could only be sustained if everyone observed his station in life. Given this strong adherence to the principle of differentiation in the Chinese culture, it is hardly surprising that formal powers within the bureaucracy have always been organized on a strictly hierarchical basis (Balazs, 1964; Pye, 1968).

There are, of course, differences between the political-administrative system in Hong Kong and that in China. Confucianism is founded on the idea that good government should depend on the kindness and wisdom of the emperor and his officials. It therefore advocates rule by man. The bureaucracy in Hong Kong is, in contrast, more legalistic in its orientation. It places greater emphasis on the rule of law. Furthermore, the role of morality in governance is also dissimilar in the two cases. For the traditional Chinese steeped in the Confucian philosophy, politics and ethics are inseparable; morality is the foundation of legitimate political authority as well as a necessary condition for the effective administration of public affairs. In Hong Kong, it is the ability of the officials that counts. Individual rectitude and responsibility are taken into consideration in the staff selection and management process. However, there are no universally accepted or systematically developed ways of comparing the moral qualities of civil servants in the different grades and departments within the bureaucracy.

In the final analysis, the ideologies that underlie the two systems are different. The Chinese bureaucratic tradition is characteristically Confucian; that in Hong Kong is more typically Weberian. For this reason, it would be misleading to carry the analogy too far. Nonetheless, the public service ethos in the two cases are comparable in some vital respects. The importance attached to bureaucratic performance in Hong Kong has a historical precedent in traditional China. The Hong Kong Chinese have therefore cherished the value of administrative competence no less than their former British colonial masters. Hierarchical loyalty is a virtue rooted in the Western Weberian conception of organizational life, but it is also deeply entrenched in the Chinese Confucian precept of human interaction.

To some extent, it is also possible to discern elements of political neutrality in the Chinese bureaucratic mentality. Confucius' disapproval of partisan politics is well-documented in the classics (Chang, 1980: 174–175; Yeh, 1969: 138). The monolithic and highly centralized nature of the political order in Confucian (and also Socialist) China, coupled with the total bureaucratization of politics, has meant that there could only be one source of political authority and one forum for political activities. Accordingly, private interests need not be represented in the political system; the rulers' sympathy and understanding of what is in the best interest of all would suffice to ensure against unfair discrimination against individuals or groups in society (Pye, 1968). Hence, although political neutrality is an administrative value which was implanted in the Hong Kong civil service by the British, the relative absence of partisan affiliations in the bureaucracy has a Chinese heritage of its own.

The consonance between politics and culture in Hong Kong has, among other factors, contributed to the relative stability of the administrative system and the integrity of its underlying values in the past. Yet, the sociopolitical milieu within which the bureaucracy operates has been changing rapidly. This raises questions regarding the adequacy of the prevalent norms of administrative behavior in preparing civil servants for the challenges ahead. In the next section, we shall examine the nature of the changes that are impinging on the bureaucracy and assess their impact on the ethos of competence, hierarchy, and neutrality.

III. ADMINISTRATIVE ETHICS IN A CHANGING ENVIRONMENT

To the extent that public service ethics should be relevant to the context of its application, standards of bureaucratic conduct must be constantly reviewed and updated to keep pace with changes in the environment. In the United States, academic response to the growing complexity and diversity of government tasks since the early part of the twentieth century has brought about a gradual evolution of the paradigmatic framework for understanding and analyzing public administration. At the same time, the normative values that inform public administration have also been subject to review. The most significant development in this respect has been the changed conception of the role of the bureaucrat in the process of government. Under the sway of the Weberian notion of administration, the bureaucrat was seen to be a passive implementer of public policies. By the 1930s, there was an increased awareness that the bureaucrat was very much an *actor* in the political process. The question of individual responsibility thus began to emerge (Friedrich, 1935, 1972 [1940]; Gaus, 1936) and has since dominated the discourse on administrative ethics (Bailey, 1965; Wakefield, 1976).

In recent years some scholars have attempted to provide a more objective basis for the cultivation of a public service ethos by relating it to the values of the regime (Rohr, 1978) and/or the values of citizenship (Cooper, 1991). Others have tried to refocus attention on the organization as a crucial factor shaping administrative ethics (Cooper, 1990; Denhardt, 1988). However, this emerging concern for the external environment of public administration has by no means displaced the importance of the individual as a source of responsible administrative behavior. The search for a more objective foundation of public service ethics has generally been guided by a desire to enhance, rather than to replace, the capacity of the individual for moral decision-making.

In Hong Kong, the conception of public administration and of public service morality has largely remained unchanged. The bureaucracy still operates as a corporate moral entity. The individual official remains a faceless, anonymous bureaucrat, a cog in a machine who has no moral identity outside his place in the collectivity. An "ethical" civil servant is one who abides by the norms of the organization and the orders of his superiors. In consequence, there is little place for moral autonomy in the Hong Kong administrative system (Lui and Cooper, 1997).

Compared to the United States, therefore, public service ethics in Hong Kong lags behind. The problem of anachronism would not have arisen had Hong Kong been a backward society. But Hong Kong is in many ways a modern society. The tasks and challenges confronting the government are no simpler than those of their counterparts in other industrialized countries. Hence, the level of social and economic development in the territory is in itself sufficient to justify a reconsideration of the appropriateness of the prevailing norms of administration. When politics is also taken into account, the case for reviewing the civil service value-system becomes even more compelling.

Since the commencement in 1982 of negotiations between Britain and China over the question of Hong Kong's future, the territory has been undergoing a rapid process of political change (Scott, 1989). The most significant development in this respect is the democratization of the political system. This has inevitably resulted in a relative decline in the authority of the bureaucracy. At the same time the Hong Kong government has been adopting a program of public sector reform since the early 1990s. This requires a process of adaptation which affects both the political capabilities of public servants and the conception of their political role. These developments have arisen directly or indirectly from the 1997 transfer of sovereignty. Together they contribute to a volatile political-administrative scene which is hardly compatible with the prevailing values of public administration. We shall examine these developments in turn.

A. Democratization of the Political System

In July 1984, two months before the publication of the Sino-British Agreement on the change of sovereignty, the Hong Kong government announced its plans to open up the Legislative Council to some form of democratic control. As a result, limited franchise and indirect elections were introduced into the legislature for the first time in Hong Kong's history (White Paper, 1984). In 1988, there was a minor increase in the number of elected seats (from 24 in 1985 to 26 of a total number of 57 seats) (White Paper, 1988). Universal franchise was, however, not granted to the Hong Kong electorate until late 1991, when 18 legislators (out of an enlarged Council comprising 61 members) were directly voted into public office. The franchise was further expanded in 1995 when the Legislative Council was, for the first time, wholly elected. Twenty members were directly elected, thirty members were elected through a (limited franchise) functional constituency system and a further ten were (indirectly) elected by a committee. The expansion of the franchise was achieved in the teeth of opposition from the Chinese government which claimed that the changes were in contravention of the *Basic Law* (the mini-constitution governing Hong Kong after the Chinese resumption of sovereignty) and vowed to reverse them after the handover in 1997 (Scott, 1996).

The real motive underlying the colonial government's decision to democratize the political system has never been entirely clear, but the anticipated transfer of sovereignty appears to have been a vital factor. Democratization was probably seen to be necessary to prepare the Hong Kong people for a high degree of autonomous self-rule after 1997 as promised in the Sino-British Agreement. There were also suspicions, however, that democracy might have been a sop to make the agreement more palatable to the people in the territory (Scott, 1989: 275) and to assuage the rising tide of domestic demand for greater representation. On the Chinese side there were concerns that democracy was a British plot to constrain the powers of the Chinese Communist Party in Hong Kong after the formal handover of sovereignty (Chan, 1991; Kohut, 1991).

Whatever the reasons, the process of democratization has had a rapid politicizing effect on the community. Interests which were previously unorganized began to emerge as potent political forces clamoring for a share of power. The process of political grouping and mobilization in turn heightened the awareness and democratic aspirations of the popu-lace.[10] By the 1990s, it was clear to the Chinese government that any erosion of democratic rights after the departure of the British would not be readily acceptable to the local people. However, this has not stopped China from changing the electoral system to its advantage. After the handover, the leadership in Beijing revoked the arrangements which had governed the 1995 elections. The elected Legislative Council was replaced by a Provisional Legislature whose members were in effect selected by the Chinese government. In May 1998, an electoral system was introduced which was designed to disadvantage the democratic parties through the use of a proportional representation "list" system in the directly elected seats and a restricted electorate in the functional constituencies. In the period immediately preceding the handover, the bureaucracy in Hong Kong came under mounting pressures (particularly from the elected members in the Legislative Council) to be more accountable and responsive to public opinion. In the post-handover system, the nature of bureaucratic accountability to the Legislative Council is not sufficiently specified in the *Basic Law*. This has provided some protection for senior public servants, who wish to avoid scrutiny in the Council, but it has done nothing to improve relations between the legislature and the executive (Lo, 1998; Miners, 1998; Scott, 1998). There are continuing demands for greater administrative accountability both from legislators and the wider public.

B. Declining Authority of the Bureaucracy

Democratic changes in the political system, however limited, inevitably result in a decline in the authority of the bureaucracy. Arguably, the seeds of this development were sown earlier, when the question of Hong Kong's future was first mooted. Until the early 1980s, the colonial administration was permitted to enjoy a high degree of autonomy vis-à-vis both Britain and China. However, the Sino-British negotiations over Hong Kong's future, and the subsequent publication in 1984 of the agreement, had a profound impact on bureaucratic hegemony. To begin with, China and Britain deliberately excluded Hong Kong representatives from the negotiations (Scott, 1989, chapter 1). This undermined the status and authority of the Hong Kong government. The process of the marginalization of the Hong Kong government was further reinforced by the Sino-British Agreement, which formalized the role of the British and Chinese authorities in the governance of Hong Kong in the build-up to the transfer of sovereignty. With the intrusion of Britain and China into the local political scene, senior administrators in Hong Kong increasingly found that they were unable to make decisions without consulting both their incumbent and future sovereign masters. Many internal affairs, ranging from political reform and infrastructural developments to the reorganization of the public sector, became politicized, to the extent that they had to be scrutinized and approved at a "higher" level, that is, through diplomatic exchanges between Britain and China. The administration in Hong Kong was effectively reduced to no more than a caretaker, a "lame duck" which had little control over matters of importance to the territory nominally under its charge.

Following the retreat of the British from the local political scene in the latter half of 1997, the Hong Kong government has sought to reassert its authority. The government is officially "executive-led" and both the *Basic Law* and the electoral arrangements introduced after the handover were designed to limit the role of the Legislative Council. The political executive, however, has not been able to exert effective control over the bureaucracy. The non-civil servant members of the Executive Council have little experience in dealing with the bureaucracy or, as they perhaps would like to do, in providing direction for it. For their part, the senior public servants have been required to occupy an uncomfortable power vacuum between a weak political executive and an occasionally interventionist Chinese government, on the one hand, and a hostile Legislative Council and a vibrant civil society on the other. Amidst these circumstances, the bureaucracy has not been able to reassert its former hegemonic rule because of factors which have detrimentally affected public perceptions of its performance. It has taken the brunt of criticism for hardships resulting from the Asian economic crisis and for a series of policy disasters including financial losses resulting from the premature opening of the new airport, ineptitude in dealing with avian influenza and red tide problems, and inaction in combating health-threatening air pollution. Its credibility has been consequentially affected with serious implications for its ability to introduce and implement new and appropriate policies.

C. Public Sector Reform

In the face of turbulence arising from the 1997 transfer of sovereignty, there has clearly been a need for the administration to reinvent itself. The significance of reform was not lost to the colonial government. Efforts to change the administrative system have also been endorsed and, to some extent, extended by the post-handover government. Essentially, these reform measures follow two mostly separate, but occasionally related, paths. The first takes its cue from conventional measures commonly recognized as New Public Management initiatives which have been adopted in industrialized democracies around the world. As early as 1989, the Finance Branch (1989) of the Hong Kong government issued a document, *Public Sector Reform*, outlining the rationale for organizational and procedural adaptation to maximize the efficient and effective use of resources. This was followed by the establishment of a special body, the Efficiency Unit, within the Government Secretariat in 1992 charged with the task of overseeing management reform in the public sector. Traditional government departments were transformed into trading fund bodies, public corporations, or quasi-governmental entities with increasing levels of participation from the private sector. Decision-making authority was delegated downwards so that it was closer to the points of service delivery. Management practices were supposed to become more flexible and outcome-oriented. Responsibility for personnel policies was decentralized, and these policies stressed core competencies under human resource management guidelines. The post-handover government, strongly influenced by private sector practices, has sought to extend these managerial reforms, especially in the fields of corporatization and privatization (Hong Kong Government, 1999:22).

In the last years of colonial rule, a second reform path centered on efforts to make the bureaucracy more responsive and more open (Huque et al., 1998:51–52). Performance pledges, designed to instill a new service culture where recipients of public services would be treated as customers rather than beneficiaries, were introduced in every department (Scott and Thynne, 1994). The powers of the ombudsman were strengthened. A Code of Access to Government Information was introduced and an Equal Opportunities Commission was created. It is difficult to assess the effects of these changes. Although they appear to have met with public approval, there seems to be little support for them in post-handover government circles. The term of the ombudsman, for example, who is widely credited with significant reforms in public service practice, was not renewed. Nor has there been much evidence of enthusiasm within the bureaucracy for extending the scope of freedom of information or equal opportunities legislation.

To the extent that administrative reform may strengthen the governing capacity of the bureaucracy and enhance the colonial goal of democratization, it can be seen as a substitute for genuine, radical political change. Putting aside the question of the motive of reform, the political dimensions of public sector reform in Hong Kong can also be analyzed in terms of its anticipated outcome. Unlike the experience in other Western countries, administrative reform in Hong Kong has not (yet) resulted in drastic cuts in public sector expenditure, massive redundancies, and their attendant problems of organizational uncertainties and low staff morale. However, the reform may have had the effect of breaking down the previously secluded nature of the bureaucracy. As the line between the public and the private sectors, between bureaucrats and citizens, becomes blurred, the public service is inevitably rendered less unified, more internally differentiated, and more vulnerable to external influences. Its role in governance and its relationship with other actors in the polity will also have to be redefined.

D. Impact on Administrative Ethics

Sociopolitical changes in recent years have engendered a host of problems for public administration in Hong Kong. In the long history of colonial rule, the government's typical response to any volatility in the environment was to strengthen the bureaucracy. However, in the present case, the administration cannot regard itself as being distinct from, and hence immune to, the turbulence in society. While public expectations for effective government are rising, the bureaucracy is yet to recover from an erosion of its hegemony in the years leading up to the 1997 transition. In the meantime, public sector reform has brought about an indisputable, albeit gradual, shift in the way administrative capabilities and the administrative role are to be understood.

Research into the mentality of public servants in Hong Kong has suggested that the bureaucracy is ill-equipped for meeting the challenges ahead. For example, a study of the relationship between administrators and politicians in 1993 indicates that although the top echelon of the civil service was adapting to the demands of democratic governance, there was still an element of distrust vis-à-vis the politicians (Cheng and Lee, 1994). Another survey, conducted in 1994, also confirmed that civil servants had a well-developed sense of bureaucratic accountability, but that their sense of political accountability remained weak (Leung et al., 1995). In short, public administrators in Hong Kong are *attitudinally* unprepared for change.

The realities, however, are that change is both necessary and inevitable. It follows therefore that the capacity of the public service to cope with the environment hinges first and foremost on its willingness to transform its culture. The existing values of bureaucratic competence, neutrality, and hierarchy are not entirely obsolete, but their relevance to the context of public administration is becoming increasingly questionable. The pursuit of competence as a standard of responsible behavior presupposes a fairly stable, or at least predictable, environment where goals can be defined clearly. It also presumes that the bureaucracy is relatively strong, that it is capable of mobilizing internal and external resources to achieve set targets. Finally, bureaucratic competence in Hong Kong has been used as a political legitimizing device. There is therefore the assumption that competent performance of the administration would suffice to ensure the people's confidence in, and acceptance of, the regime.

As we have seen, recent developments have rendered these presumptions problematic. In the first place, the situation in Hong Kong is volatile. It is hard to lay down clear policy goals which would satisfactorily address societal issues on a long-term basis. The difficulty in this regard is attributable to three causes. First, with the politicization of society, policymaking has inevitably become embroiled in conflicts among diverse groups whose interests and allegiance shift over time, and whose relative influence in the decision-making system waxes and wanes. The second consideration relates to the novelty of the political order under which the relationship between China and Hong Kong is still to be worked out in detail. It is not unreasonable to assume therefore that adjustments in various policy areas will have to be made against the backdrop of evolving values and expectations. Finally, the problem has been complicated by the Asian financial crisis which began in Thailand, Indonesia, and South Korea in early 1997 and which eventually hit Hong Kong later that year. To the extent that the crisis is regional, perhaps even global, in nature, the degree of control over which bureaucracy can exert over the economy in the territory is bound to be limited. Where policy goals are diffuse and imprecise, the administration is left with little guidance regarding what constitutes "competent" behavior.

The most important consideration, however, is that administrative competence is no longer an adequate guarantee of public faith in the government. With democratization and the attendant rise in societal aspirations, the people in Hong Kong are beginning to look beyond the bureaucracy for alternative sources of legitimate political authority. For some who believe in the importance of popular mandates, authority ought to rest with the legislature. For others who are more inclined to accept the constraints set by the *Basic Law*, the proper source of authority is to be found in the office of the Chief Executive.[11] In either case, an efficient civil service is a necessary but not a sufficient condition for sustaining the political legitimacy of the regime.

From an empirical perspective, there is little sign that the neutrality and hierarchical loyalty of Hong Kong civil servants have been compromised because of recent changes in the sociopolitical environment. Nonetheless, one cannot be sanguine that they can realistically remain as the guiding norms for the administration. The external milieu of the bureaucracy is no longer conducive to a management philosophy that is founded on Weberian precepts. Democracy, albeit stunted at the present moment, calls for a public sector that is flexible, responsive, humane, and committed to service to the community. The values of neutrality and hierarchy need not be entirely foresaken, but they could be relaxed to take into account the changing expectations and mentality of the population. Ideally, the new ethos of public administration should provide opportunity for a personal sense of responsibility to be developed, and a genuine concern for the welfare of the citizens to be entrenched. Reform along the lines of New Public Management may signify a step in the right direction. However, for a new culture to be established, the reform must go beyond the confines of management to address the *service* dimensions of public administration at an attitudinal level.

IV. THE POSSIBILITY OF A NEW ADMINISTRATIVE ETHIC IN HONG KONG

Thompson (1985) argues that administrative ethics in an organization is possible only if its members can exercise moral judgments and be subjected to the moral judgments of others. This capacity to judge and be judged is, however, thwarted in an organization which adheres to the "conventional" belief in "the ethic of neutrality" and "the ethic of structure." According to this view, members of an organization are not supposed to be independent moral agents. They should only carry out the orders of their superiors and should not therefore be held personally responsible for the negative consequences arising from their acceptance of organizational imperatives. Thompson expresses dissatisfaction with this conception of the individual's role in an organization on the grounds that it is neither realistic nor desirable. He calls for a rejection of the two "ethics" and a reorientation of our thinking of organizations to embrace the idea that administrative ethics is possible.

The targets of Thompson's attack are precisely the notions that have guided public administration in Hong Kong. Following Thompson's line of reasoning, it would appear logical that the first step to establishing a new administrative ethic in Hong Kong is to modify the "old" values of neutrality and hierarchy. Unfortunately, Thompson's prescription is easier said than done. Putting aside the problem of bureaucratic conservatism and the difficulties associated with changing deeply embedded values and perceptions at the organizational level, the political realities in Hong Kong do not readily lend themselves to the development of a fresh basis of public service ethics.

The obstacles to genuine reform are two-fold. The first consideration is that there is a general lack of political will to engage in value changes which might upset the balance of power in the political-administrative system. For China, the main concern is the maintenance of sovereign rights over Hong Kong. A strictly regimented command pattern within an administration which is committed to neutral competence would suit its purposes well. An alternative value-system that permits individual civil servants to exercise their reflective choice would be regarded as far too dangerous. On the part of the bureaucratic elite, there is also a reluctance to relax the requirements for observance of hierarchy and neutrality. In the wake of their weakened authority vis-à-vis society, the reassertion of their autonomy is seen to rest on an administrative system which is internally stable. New public management reform is about the only extent of change they would see to be appropriate. Although such a reform initiative coincides to some degree with the demands of a more flexible and discretionary public administration, it can still provide the elite with a set of standards for controlling the rest of the bureaucracy (Huque et al., 1998: 49–51). Any further reform which allows for personal moral judgment, an internalized sense of responsibility to substitute external, organizationally based, sources of authority or even the modest liberalising measures introduced in the last years of colonial rule, would undermine the top-down power structure so cherished by the bureaucratic elite.

A more formidable problem, however, is that there is no concrete basis upon which changes in administrative values can be founded. The bureaucracy in Hong Kong is a central political institution. Its legitimacy and capacity to participate in the process of government depend, among other things, on the degree of congruence between the values that inform public service ethics and the values of the wider society. Put in another way, public administration must be seen to be upholding the same set of values which are cherished by other members of the polity. At first sight, Rohr's "regime value" approach, as well as Cooper's emphasis on the notion of "citizenship" as a foundation of administrative ethics, could be immensely useful to Hong Kong. The crucial point, however, is that the search for a new basis of public service ethics along these lines presupposes the possibility of identifying a core set of values which are definitive of Hong Kong society.

Unfortunately, Hong Kong society is in a state of flux. The old values which the colonial regime has inculcated into the collective mentality of the people, and which have largely been compatible with the cultural dispositions of the Chinese, are gradually eroding. Meanwhile, a new set of values has yet to be put in place. This state of transition is reflected in Lau and Kuan's study of the ethos of the Hong Kong Chinese (1988), in which they found that the respondents' views on a number of issues were generally ambivalent and laden with inconsistencies. The *Basic Law* seeks to enshrine certain principles (for example, preservation of the capitalist economy and the sustenance of a form of government that is executive-centered and authoritarian) which may eventually provide the basis for the evolution of a new set of values in Hong Kong. But the *Basic Law* was drafted by the Communist Chinese and their sympathizers in Hong Kong. There was minimal input from the bulk of the population (Chan, 1991; Lau, 1988). It did not win the wide support of the Hong Kong people, and its acceptability to, and influence on, the populace has yet to be gauged.[12] In the absence of a popularly accepted set of societal values, it is hard to work out the "right" direction for reforming administrative ethics.

V. CONCLUSION

This chapter begins with an exposition on the importance of contextual variables to the understanding of administrative ethics. The Hong Kong experience is used to illustrate the relationship between the ethos of the civil service and the broader environment of public administration. Specifically, it is postulated that the ethical norms that guide the bureaucracy in Hong Kong have been closely correlated with the political concerns of the former British colonial regime, but they have also worked well in the past because of their conformance with Chinese cultural values.

Since the appearance of the 1997 issue on the political agenda of Hong Kong, the territory has been undergoing rapid and dramatic changes. This calls into question the relevance of the prevailing norms of administration to the sociopolitical milieu. Although the case for reforming the values of the bureaucracy is compelling, the development of a new ethic for public servants in Hong Kong appears to be infested with problems. These difficulties may not be insurmountable. Indeed, one would anticipate that they should eventually be resolved as a new sociopolitical order begins to emerge after the uncertainties and adjustments arising from China's resumption of sovereignty have been settled. In the meantime, however, Hong Kong is still groping for an identity. In the absence of this identity which could define the core values of society, the foundation for a new public service ethos could not yet be firmly established.

The problems of administrative ethics in Hong Kong are therefore peculiar to the territory's history and realities. Nonetheless, this is not to suggest that public service ethics is totally particularistic in nature. The search for responsible public administration is a universal concern. The difficulties encountered by different societies in this process of search may vary, but the solutions may be comparable. Hence, while Hong Kong society has to ultimately confront its own problems within the confines of its politics and culture, it can gain invaluable insight by looking outwards to the experience of others for possible directions of change.

NOTES

1. In 1984, Britain and China publicized the *Joint Declaration of the Government of the United Kingdom of Great Britain and Northern Ireland and the Government of the People's Republic of China on the Question of Hong Kong* (commonly referred to as the Sino-British Agreement). According to the Joint Declaration, Hong Kong would become a Special Administrative Region upon China's resumption of sovereignty on July 1, 1997. The "one country two systems" principle is supposed to provide the basis for Hong Kong to retain "a high degree of autonomy" under Chinese rule.
2. The colonial government had been following a policy of localizing the civil service since the late 1940s. By 1996, local officers comprised 99% of the total civil service strength of 182,675. See Civil Service Branch, Hong Kong Government (1997).
3. The pre-1997 Constitution of Hong Kong provided for a number of seats in the Executive Council to be reserved for senior civil servants. At the beginning of 1997, government officials made up more than a quarter of the Executive Council. See Hong Kong Government (1997b:

414). Under the current constitution, the *Basic Law*, the Chief Executive can appoint members of the Executive Council from among the senior officials (those at the rank of principal officials) in the government. See the *Basic Law* (1990: Chapter IV, Section 1, Article 55).

4. See, for example, a speech by Anson Chan, the Chief Secretary for Administration on May 21, 1998 at a seminar organized by the Independent Commission Against Corruption and the Civil Service Bureau. In that speech Chan identified six key principles guiding the civil service: ''Commitment to the rule of law; honesty and integrity above private interests; accountability and openness in decision-making and in all [their] actions; political neutrality in conducting [their] official duties; impartiality in the execution of public functions; and dedication and diligence in serving the community.''

5. In 1995, the Ombudsman (previously titled the Commission for Administrative Complaints) published an *Administrative Fairness Checklist*, which provides general guidelines for the fair and reasonable handling of the public by public servants. This was followed in 1997 by the publication of an *Administrative Ethics Checklist* which lays down some form of guidance on ethical administrative practices. Whereas the *Administrative Fairness Checklist* focuses primarily on procedural propriety (for example whether administrative procedures in any given public organization are user-friendly; whether channels of communication and/or consultation with the public are available and readily accessible; whether a system for reviewing the organization's structure and process is in place; and whether service standards are realistic and exhaustive), and as such departs little from the prescriptive approach to management, the *Administrative Ethics Checklist* places emphasis on the *public service* dimensions of public administration. The document stresses that the goal of ethical public administration is to promote citizen welfare, professes that its aim is to change some aspects of the old public service culture (which is essentially management and control-oriented), and, most interestingly, draws attention to the need to caution against over-standardization lest the *responsibility* of public officials would be eclipsed. The Ombudsman simultaneously published an internal Code of Conduct for its office staff, drawing on the general points in the *Administrative Ethics Checklist*. Other public organizations have been encouraged to follow suit. For detail, see Hong Kong Government (1997a). The Independent Commission Against Corruption has, since its establishment in 1974, been at the forefront of ensuring the probity of the public service in Hong Kong. Its focus and methodology are primarily prescriptive. Its emphasis is on legal and line accountability as the source of official integrity. In its quest for an ''ethical'' service, the commission has nonetheless played an important role in developing training and educational approaches aimed at changing the *culture* of the public service. In this respect, the significance of the internal, personal dimensions of responsible administrative behavior is not lost to the commission.

6. This statement applies both to the situation before and after the change of sovereignty. Before July 1997, the ruling authority was the British government, when 99% of the civil service comprised local Chinese. Since July 1997, authority emanated ultimately from the Central People's Government in Beijing, China, to whom the bulk of civil servants feel little sense of affinity for political, historical, and cultural reasons.

7. There are no exact figures covering cases of insubordination in the civil service, but the number of disciplinary offences among public officials is low, indicating that the enforcement of hierarchical compliance is generally not a problem. There has only been one known case of whistleblowing among serving officials in the recent history of administration in Hong Kong.

8. In the survey into the values and attitudes conducted by Cooper and Lui (1990), respondents were asked to express their agreement or otherwise with the statement that ''a civil servant should obey all lawful orders.'' Out of 234 responses, 206 either agreed or strongly agreed with the statement; 10 remained neutral and those who disagreed or strongly disagreed numbered only 18. A more recent survey into the public service by the same authors, conducted in 1994, produced similar findings. A total of 279 respondents were given a list of 21 factors which could inform their conduct in the workplace. They were asked to rank the relative

importance of these factors. A majority of them chose such factors as: respect for organization rules and regulations, the reputation of the organization, respect for the law, and duty to organization as of the most importance in guiding their conduct. In another part of the survey questionnaire, respondents were asked if they would resign or tell people outside their organization if their bosses insisted that they carry out some action that they strongly felt was wrong. A majority (51.3%) indicated they would not resign and a substantial proportion (43.7%) chose not to relate the incident to outsiders. Furthermore, respondents were presented with a vignette depicting an official who decided to follow a hierarchical order even though he considered the order to be morally unacceptable. A total of 61.6% of respondents expressed approval of the official's action. See Terry Lui and Terry Cooper (1996, 1997).

9. It is generally accepted that Confucianism has had immense influence on Chinese civilization for the past two thousand years. See Raymond Dawson (1981, chapter 7) and Lucian W. Pye (1985, chapters 2 and 3). Confucianism has often been referred to as the state doctrine in ancient China. However, the philosophical roots of Chinese moral and political thoughts can also be traced to Taoism, Buddhism, and legalism. See John M. Koller (1985, Part Three) and Charles A. Moore (1968).

10. An opinion poll commissioned by one of the local English newspapers, *Sunday Morning Post*, shows that Hong Kong people were overwhelmingly in favor of more democracy before 1997. See Danny Gittings (1992). Results of a study on the 1991 direct elections in Hong Kong have also borne comparable findings. See Kwok et al. (1992).

11. According to the provisions of the *Basic Law*, the government of the Hong Kong Special Administrative Region is executive-led. The Chief Executive is the head of the region. He or she is appointed by, and held directly accountable to, the Central People's Government in China. See the *Basic Law* (1990, chapter IV, Section 1).

12. To extend the point further, it can be argued that China itself is also in a transitional stage. While the leadership continues to pay lip service to communist ideals, the economic system has become characteristically capitalist. The Central People's Government is also struggling to balance the potentially conflicting demands of economic liberalization on the one hand and the observed need for tight political control over civil society on the other hand. The values defining China as a polity are therefore also in a state of flux.

REFERENCES

Aberbach, J. D., Putnam, R. D., and Rockman, B. A. (1981). *Bureaucrats and Politicians in Western Democracies*. Harvard University Press, Cambridge, MA.

Bailey, S. K. (1965). Ethics and the public service. In: *Public Administration and Democracy* (R. C. Martin, ed.). Syracuse University Press, New York, pp. 283–298.

Balazs, E. (1964). *Chinese Civilization and Bureaucracy* (A. F. Wright, ed.). Yale University Press, New Haven.

Basic Law of the Hong Kong Special Administrative Region of the People's Republic of China (1990). The Consultative Committee for the Basic Law of the Hong Kong Special Administrative Region of the People's Republic of China, Hong Kong.

Census and Statistics Department, Hong Kong Government (1996). *Hong Kong 1996 Population By-Census: Summary Results*. Government Printer, Hong Kong.

Chan, M. K. (1991). Democracy derailed: Realpolitik in the making of the Hong Kong Basic Law, 1985–1990. In: *Hong Kong Basic Law: Blueprint for "Stability and Prosperity" under Chinese Sovereignty?* (M. K. Chan and D. J. Clark, eds.). Hong Kong University Press, Hong Kong, chapter 1.

Chang, C. (1980). *Confucianism: A Modern Interpretation* (O. Lee, trans.). The Hwa Kang Press, China Academy, Taiwan.

Chapman, R. A. (1993). *Ethics in Public Service*. Edinburgh University Press, Edinburgh.

Cheek-Milby, K. (1988). Identifying the issues. In: *The Hong Kong Civil Service and Its Future* (I. Scott and J. P. Burns, eds.). Oxford University Press, Hong Kong, chapter 5.

Chen, L. F. (1986). *The Confucian Way: A New and Systematic Study of "The Four Books"* (S. S. Liu, trans.). KPI, London.

Cheng, J. Y. S. and Lee, J. C. Y. (1994). *A Study of the Bureaucrat-Politician Relationships in Hong Kong's Transition*. Department of Public and Social Administration, Faculty of Humanities and Social Sciences, City University of Hong Kong, Hong Kong.

Civil Service Branch, Hong Kong Government (1997). *Civil Service Personnel Statistics 1996*. Government Secretariat, Hong Kong.

Cooper, T. L. (1990). *The Responsible Administrator*, 3rd ed. Jossey-Bass Publishers, San Francisco.

Cooper, T. L. (1991). *An Ethic of Citizenship for Public Administration*. Prentice Hall, Englewood Cliffs, NJ.

Cooper, T. L. and Lui, T. T. (1990). Democracy and the administrative state: The case of Hong Kong. *Public Administration Review*, 50:332–344.

Dawson, R. (1981). *Confucius*. Oxford University Press, Oxford.

Denhardt, K. G. (1988). *The Ethics of Public Service: Resolving Moral Dilemmas in Public Organizations*. Greenwood Press, CT.

Eitel, E. J. (1983). *Europe in China*. Oxford University Press, Hong Kong.

Endacott, G. B. (1964). *A History of Hong Kong*, 2nd ed. Oxford University Press, Hong Kong.

Finance Branch, Hong Kong Government (1989). *Public Sector Reform*. Government Secretariat, Hong Kong.

Friedrich, C. J. (1935). Responsible government service under the American Constitution. Monograph No. 7 in *Problems of the American Public Service*, (C. J. Friedrich et al., eds.). McGraw-Hill, New York.

Friedrich, C. J. (1972). Public policy and the nature of administrative responsibility. In: *Bureaucratic Power in National Politics*, 2nd ed. (F. E. Rouke, ed.). Little, Brown, Boston. (Originally published in 1940.)

Gaus, J. M. (1936). The responsibility of public administrators. In: *The Frontiers of Public Administration* (J. M. Gaus, L. D. White, and M. Dimock, eds.). University of Chicago Press, Chicago.

Gittings, D. (1992). Pattern urged: stand up to China on democracy reform. *Sunday Morning Post*, Hong Kong, May 3.

Harris, P. (1978). *Hong Kong: A Study in Bureaucratic Politics*. Heinemann, Hong Kong.

Hong Kong Government (1997a). *Annual Report of the Ombudsman of Hong Kong*. Office of the Ombudsman, Hong Kong.

Hong Kong Government (1997b). *Hong Kong 1997*. Government Printer, Hong Kong.

Hong Kong Government (1999). *The 1999–2000 Budget*. Government Printer, Hong Kong.

Huque, A. S., Lee, G. O. M., and Cheung, A. B. L. (1998). *The Civil Service in Hong Kong: Continuity and Change*. Hong Kong University Press, Hong Kong.

Jabbra, J. G. and Dwivedi, O. P. (1988). *Public Service Accountability: A Comparative Perspective*. Kumarian Press, West Hartford, CT.

Joint Declaration of the Government of the United Kingdom of Great Britain and Northern Ireland and the Government of the People's Republic of China on the Question of Hong Kong (The Sino-British Agreement) (1984). Government Printer, Hong Kong.

Kernaghan, K. and Dwivedi, O. P. (1983). *Ethics in the Public Service: Comparative Perspectives*. International Institute of Administrative Sciences, Brussels.

Kingdom, J. E. (1990). *The Civil Service in Liberal Democracies: An Introductory Survey*. Routledge, London.

Kohut, J. (1991). Lu Ping attacks democracy calls. *South China Morning Post*, Hong Kong, October 9.

Koller, J. M. (1985). *Oriental Philosophies*, 2nd ed. Charles Scribner's Sons, New York.

Kwok, R. Y. F., Leung, J. Y. H., and Scott, I. (1992). *Votes Without Power: The Hong Kong Legislative Council Elections, 1991*. Hong Kong University Press, Hong Kong.

Lau, E. (1988). The early history of the drafting process. In: *The Basic Law and Hong Kong's Future* (P. Wesley-Smith and A. Chen, eds.). Butterworths, Singapore, chapter 6.

Lau, S. (1984). *Society and Politics in Hong Kong*. The Chinese University Press, Hong Kong.

Lau, S. and Kuan, H. (1988). *The Ethos of the Hong Kong Chinese*. The Chinese University Press, Hong Kong.

Lee, J. (1995). The civil service. In: *From Colony to Special Administrative Region*, (Joseph Y.S. Cheng and Sonny S.H. Lo, eds.). The Chinese University Press, Hong Kong, chapter 3.

Lethbridge, H. J. (1978). *Hong Kong: Stability and Change*. Oxford University Press, Hong Kong.

Leung, J. Y. H., Brewer, B. and Lee, G. O. M. (1995). Redefinition of roles: Hong Kong's politicians, civil servants and the general public. *Hong Kong Public Administration*, 4: 205–222.

Lo, S. S. H. (1998). The changing dimensions of executive-legislative relations: The case of Hong Kong. *Public Administration and Policy*, 7: 73–103.

Lui, T. T. (1988). Changing civil servants' values. In: *The Hong Kong Civil Service and Its Future* (I. Scott and J. P. Burns, eds.). Oxford University Press, Hong Kong, chapter 6.

Lui, T. T. and Cooper, T. L. (1990). Hong Kong facing China: Civil servants' confidence in the future. *Administration and Society*, 22: 155–169.

Lui, T. T. and Cooper, T. L. (1996). Bureaucracy, democracy and administrative ethics: A study of public service values in Hong Kong. *International Review of Administrative Sciences*, 62: 177–196.

Lui, T. T. and Cooper, T. L. (1997). Values in flux: Administrative ethics and the Hong Kong public servant. *Administration and Society*, 29: 301–324.

Miners, N. (1995). *The Government and Politics of Hong Kong*, 5th impression (updated). Oxford University Press, Hong Kong.

Miners, N. (1998). Executive-legislative relations. In: *Institutional Change and the Political Transition in Hong Kong* (Ian Scott, ed.). Macmillan, London.

Moore, C. A. (1968). *The Chinese Mind: Essentials of Chinese Philosophy and Culture*. University of Hawaii Press, Honolulu.

Pye, L. W. (1968). *The Spirit of Chinese Politics: A Psychocultural Study of the Authority Crisis in Political Development*. The M.I.T. Press, Cambridge, MA.

Pye, L. W. (1985). *Asian Power and Politics: The Cultural Dimensions of Authority*. The Belknap Press of Harvard University Press, Cambridge, MA.

Rohr, J. A. (1978). *Ethics for Bureaucrats: An Essay on Law and Values*. Marcel Dekker, New York.

Rohr, J. A. (1989). British and American approaches to public service ethics. *Public Administration Review*, 49: 387–390.

Rohr, J. A. (1990). Ethics in public administration: A state-of-the-discipline report. In: *Public Administration: The State of the Discipline* (N. B. Lynn and A. Wildavsky, eds.). Chatham House Publishers, Chatham, NJ, chapter 6.

Rubin, V. A. (1976). *Individual and State in Ancient China: Essays on Four Chinese Philosophers* (S. I. Levine, trans.). Columbia University Press, New York.

Scott, I. (1984). Introduction. In: *The Hong Kong Civil Service: Personnel Policies and Practices*. Oxford University Press, Hong Kong, chapter 1.

Scott, I. (1988a). Generalists and specialists. In: *The Hong Kong Civil Service and Its Future* (I. Scott and J. P. Burns, eds.). Oxford University Press, Hong Kong, chapter 2.

Scott, I. (1988b). The supply of professionals. In: *The Hong Kong Civil Service and Its Future* (I. Scott and J. P. Burns, eds.). Oxford University Press, Hong Kong, chapter 3.

Scott, I. (1988c). The Hong Kong civil service and its future. In: *The Hong Kong Civil Service and Its Future* (I. Scott and J. P. Burns, eds.). Oxford University Press, Hong Kong, chapter 9.

Scott, I. (1989). *Political Change and The Crisis of Legitimacy in Hong Kong*. Oxford University Press, Hong Kong; Hurst, London; University of Hawaii Press, Honolulu.

Scott, I. (1995). Civil service neutrality in Hong Kong. In: *Democratization and Bureaucratic Neutrality* (H. Asmeron and E. P. Reis, eds.). Macmillan, London.

Scott, I. (1996). Party politics and elections in Hong Kong. *Asian Journal of Political Science*, 4: 130–152.

Scott, I. (1998). Hong Kong's post-handover political system: Disarticulation and the re-emergence of bureaucratic hegemony. Paper delivered at the Contemporary China Centre, Australian National University.

Scott, I. and Thynne, I. (1994). Public Sector Reform: Ciritical Issues and Perspectives. *Asian Journal of Public Administration* (AJPA), Hong Kong.

Shirk, S. (1982). *Competitive Comrades: Career Incentives and Student Strategies in China*. University of California Press, Berkeley.

Sino-British Agreement (1984). See entry on p. 667 under *Joint Declaration of the Government of the United Kingdom of Great Britain and Northern Ireland and the Government of the People's Republic of China on the Question of Hong Kong.*

South China Morning Post, Hong Kong, April 18, 1992, p. 1.

Suleiman, E. N. (1984). *Bureaucrats and Policy Making: A Comparative Overview*. Holmes and Meier, New York.

Thompson, D. F. (1985). The possibility of administrative ethics. *Public Administration Review*, 45: 555–561.

Thompson, M., Ellis, R., and Wildavsky, A. (1990). *Cultural Theory*. Westview Press, Boulder and San Francisco.

Wakefield, S. (1976). Ethics and the public service: A case for individual responsibility. *Public Administration Review*, 36: 661–666.

Wang, G. (1991). *The Chineseness of China: Selected Essays*. Oxford University Press, Hong Kong.

Wesley-Smith, P. (1980). *Unequal Treaty 1898–1997: China, Great Britain and Hong Kong's New Territories*. Oxford University Press, Hong Kong.

White Paper (1984). *The Further Development of Representative Government in Hong Kong*. Government Printer, Hong Kong.

White Paper (1988). *The Development of Representative Government: The Way Forward*. Government Printer, Hong Kong.

Wu, T. Y. (1987). *The Confucian Way*. Institute of East Asian Philosophies, National University of Singapore, Singapore.

Yang, C. K. (1959). Some characteristics of Chinese bureaucratic behavior. In: *Confucianism in Action* (D. S. Nivison and A. F. Wright, eds.). Stanford University Press, Stanford, pp. 134–164.

Yeh, T. T. Y. (1969). *Confucianism, Christianity and China*. Philosophical Library, New York.

32

Constitutionalism and Administrative Ethics
A Comparative Study of Canada, France, the United Kingdom, and the United States

John A. Rohr
Virginia Polytechnic Institute and State University, Blacksburg, Virginia

This chapter presents a comparative study on the relationship between constitutionalism and public administration ethics in Canada, France, the United Kingdom and the United States. Careful observers of American Politics have always recognized the remarkable salience of constitutional considerations in our country's governmental affairs. Thus, in the opening pages of his probing work, *Bureaucracy*, James Q. Wilson reminds his readers that the main problems in American public administration have "little to do with limitations or inadequacies of individual bureaucrats and everything to do with the constitutional regime of which they are a part" (Wilson, 1988: 28). The same could be said of the study of any aspect of American government, including ethics in public administration. Elsewhere, I have developed in some detail the connection between ethics and constitutionalism in the United States (Rohr, 1989b). The present chapter takes a comparative approach to the same questions because I agree entirely with those comparativists who tell us that one of the best ways to understand our own government is to look at those of other countries.

I have chosen Canada, France, and the United Kingdom because each of these countries is sufficiently similar to our own to make comparisons meaningful and sufficiently different to make them interesting.[1]

I. INTRODUCTION

Ethics in American public administration falls conveniently into two major categories—the legally enforceable and the aspirational. The first deals almost exclusively with financial irregularities in such matters as bribery, conflict of interest, and financial disclosure. For the most part, these questions are governed more by statutory construction than by constitutional principle.[2] The second category goes beyond legal obligation and looks for practical ways in which civil servants might operationalize their oath to uphold the Constitution of the United States.

Aspirational questions forge a link between constitutional principles and matters of governance, both routine and spectacular. They do this in two ways.

First, there are questions of constitutional structure wherein public servants see to it—or at least try to see to it—that the cardinal constitutional principle of separation of powers does not incapacitate the government for action. At times this duty thrusts public servants into the midst of the highest questions of statecraft. Admiral Harold Stark, Chief of Naval Operations at the beginning of World War II, for example, was so deeply involved in the struggle between an isolationist Congress and an interventionist president that an exasperated Winston Churchill advised President Roosevelt of the British government's willingness to do whatever it could to satisfy the demands of "your law or your admiral" (Rohr, 1989a: 36). Ordinarily, however, the administrative statesmanship that keeps Congress and the executive on course goes on behind the scenes and deals with more routine matters. For instance, a career civil servant in James Watts's Interior Department took on the difficult and courageous role of "devil's advocate" in advising the Secretary of the negative reactions his policy innovations would likely engender in Congress and what sorts of compromises might be possible (Barth, 1991: 112–113).

Secondly, there are aspirational questions of individual rights wherein public servants of all ranks, from mighty political appointees to humble "street level bureaucrats," have an opportunity to shape the practical meaning of constitutional guarantees for both ordinary citizens and great corporations alike. Administrators frequently have significant discretionary powers that can be used creatively to put into practice the "regime values" that undergird our constitutional order. This is true both of policymaking officials in major regulatory agencies and of policemen, caseworkers, and school teachers as well.

The normative link between these two types of constitutional issues—separation of powers and individual rights—is the civil servant's oath to uphold the Constitution of the United States. In a pluralistic society, it is extremely difficult to agree upon a common framework for serious moral argument and discussion. The oath of office provides such a framework and thereby keeps the logic of pluralism within manageable bounds. When American public servants discuss right and wrong, they have a principled reason for taking their cues from their constitutional tradition. This is not to say the Constitution of the United States is an ethics handbook bristling with moral imperatives for governing the republic. The constitutional tradition is merely the starting point of moral dialogue not its conclusion (Rohr, 1989b).

Public servants in Canada, France, and United Kingdom do not take an oath to uphold the constitutions of their respective countries. Consequently, Americans should not expect that the constitutions in these countries will play as important a role in public administration ethics as the American Constitution plays in the United States. Nevertheless, by examining public administration ethics comparatively through the narrow lens of constitutionalism, we will expand our moral imagination and illuminate our understanding of our own institutions. Since most of those who read this chapter will be American citizens with a serious interest in public administration, I shall assume an overall familiarity with such matters on their part and touch upon American questions only in reaction to what we see in the administrative practices of the United Kingdom, France, and Canada. After examining these three countries, we will conclude this chapter with a review of what we have learned about our own.

II. CONSTITUTIONALISM AND THE UNITED KINGDOM

The relationship between ethics and constitutionalism in the United Kingdom (UK) is quite different from what we have seen in the United States (US). This is hardly surprising since the constitutions of the two countries are so different. The most obvious difference is, of course, that the American Constitution is written and the British is not; an obvious difference to be sure, but one that is perhaps overstated. To characterize the British Constitution as unwritten *tout court* is not entirely correct. Indeed, one knowledgeable commentator dismisses it as "absurd" (Wolf-Phillips, 1968:ix).

The British Constitution is unwritten only in the sense that there is no single document to which one can point as *the* Constitution. There are many important documents which, along with long-standing unwritten conventions, together form the British Constitution. Chief among these documents are famous statutes which address such bedrock issues as how one defines the precise nature of the United Kingdom itself, the power of the House of Lords, the status of the established church, the role of the judiciary, certain fundamental rights of citizens, the UK's relationship to the European Community, etc. (Norton, 1982: 4–5).

Common law principles expressed in important judicial decisions provide another written source of the British Constitution. The same holds for major scholarly treatises which, though not legally binding, enjoy a certain persuasive authority, not unlike that of *The Federalist Papers* in American constitutional law. One of the most important functions of these treatises is to explain and interpret the unwritten conventions which are, of course, themselves part of the British Constitution as a whole. Because the British Constitution is a blend of venerable written and unwritten sources that have never been formally organized into one coherent document, it can be best described as "partly written but unmodified" (Norton, 1982: 5).[3]

For our purposes, the constitutional principle of parliamentary sovereignty (Dicey, 1959: 39–40) provides the most important difference between the British and American constitutions. The American civil service reformers of a century ago were unreconstructed anglophiles whose emphasis on the distinction between politics and administration cried out in vain for a sovereign parliament. Woodrow Wilson was so unabashed in his admiration for parliamentary government that he even proposed a constitutional amendment to permit members of the president's cabinet to sit in Congress (Wilson, 1885).

The politics/administration dichotomy has, of course, been thoroughly discredited on empirical grounds in both the UK and the US—and this long before the delightful "Yes Minister" series graced our television screens. To stress the de facto participation (or even the dominance) of administrators in political affairs, however, misses the *constitutional* significance of the dichotomy which raises the crucial question for any constitution—"who's in charge?" In the UK the answer is clear in constitutional theory: Parliament is in charge. No such constitutional clarity exists in the US because of our constitutional principle of separation of powers which denies sovereignty to any single institution of government. The Congress and the courts are supreme in their respective spheres and the president is supreme in his; but the all-important qualification, "respective spheres," is but another way of saying none of the three is sovereign and therefore no institution is in charge.

This is why the politics/administration dichotomy has never made any sense—*even in theory*—in the US.[4] The theory of the dichotomy demands that the subordinate administrator carry out the will of the political master, but the American administrator has three constitutional masters who are not particularly notable for always agreeing among themselves. In the UK there is but one master, Parliament, from whose supremacy there flows logically the fundamental constitutional principle of British public administration—ministerial responsibility.

The crisp, conceptual clarity of ministerial responsibility is at its best when contrasted with the untidy American system of separation of powers; but, like a prophet in his own country, the venerable principle fares less well within the UK itself. In discussing both the individual and collective responsibility of ministers, Philip Norton acknowledges that, alas, "when it comes to definition and application neither convention is precise" (Norton, 1982: 55). This is because the principle did not spring full-blown from the minutes of a political science conference, but emerged only gradually and from exceedingly complicated historical circumstances that eventually produced the constitutional monarchy that has served the country so well for so long. Originally, ministerial responsibility meant "the legal responsibility of every minister for every act of the Crown in which he takes part" and, as such, was a simple application of the more general rule that the "action of every servant of the Crown . . . is brought under the supremacy of the law of the land" (Parris, 1969: 81).

Thus the principle of ministerial responsibility rests squarely on what no less an authority than Dicey maintained were "the two pillars of the Constitution: parliamentary sovereignty and the rule of law" (Norton, 1982: 5). The impeccable constitutional pedigree of the administrative principle of ministerial responsibility offers eloquent testimony to how smoothly public administration is integrated into the British constitutional order. The contrast with the US is both remarkable and instructive.[5]

The legal aspect of the principle of ministerial responsibility gradually gave way to the political aspect which means that the minister who loses the confidence of Parliament will lose his office as well (Parris, 1969: 81). The flip-side of this principle is civil service anonymity, for if the *minister* is responsible for what takes place in his ministry, he may not dodge the bullet by blaming his wayward subordinates when things go wrong. The full constitutional-administrative orthodoxy was stated with stark clarity in 1985 by Sir Robert Armstrong who was then the Head of the Home Civil Service:

> Civil servants are servants of the Crown . . . [I]n general, the executive powers of the Crown are exercised by and on the advice of Her Majesty's Ministers, who are in turn answerable to Parliament. The civil service as such has no constitutional personality or responsibility separate from the duly elected Government of the day. (Armstrong, 1985)

The ethical problems for British civil servants begin where the formal constitutional principles end. British civil servants, like civil servants throughout the world, play an extremely important role in governing their country. Indeed, because of certain well-known characteristics of the British personnel system, notably the remarkable role of the Permanent Secretaries, civil servants in the UK are far more significant actors than their counterparts in many other countries—especially the United States.[6] The undeniable fact that civil servants participate in governing the UK puts considerable pressure on the constitutional principle of ministerial responsibility. Richard Chapman reconciles practice with principle by de-emphasizing legal simplicities in favor of the de facto operation of the doctrine of ministerial responsibility which "permeates the day to day administrative work of all departments of state" (Chapman, 1987b: 54). Acknowledging "that in recent times no minister has resigned simply because of errors by his officials," Chapman nevertheless discerns practical effects of the principle of ministerial responsibility in departmental attention to the ever-present possibility of parliamentary questions and to "the arrangement for financial accountability" (Chapman, 1987b: 54). Other commentators, less generous to constitutional tradition, describe the interrelated principles of ministerial responsibility and civil service anonymity as myth or fiction—a singularly penetrating myth (Turpin, 1989: 69) and a very useful fiction (Parris, 1969:298), but myth and fiction nonetheless.

The heart of the matter is that an active role for civil servants in governance is ill at ease with the traditional constitutional norms of British public administration—and this is for two reasons:

1. To the extent that civil servants really govern, the principle of ministerial responsibility is in danger of becoming a morally vacuous formality. It follows the path of the old navy rule that the captain is responsible if the ship runs aground. Such a rule has a certain value as an instrument of naval discipline insofar as it guides a Board of Inquiry in fixing blame but it is of no moral significance if the guilty party was really a lazy operations officer.[7]

2. To the extent that civil servants really govern, the principle of civil service anonymity is at war with the contemporary demand for "open government" which regards as intolerable the notion that those who really govern are screened from effective accountability by a misleading constitutional doctrine.

The important moral dimension of the separation beween the principle of civil service anonymity and the exigencies of administrative reality came to light in the "Ponting affair," an ethical-administrative crisis in the aftermath of the Falklands War, which has received far too little attention in American public administration literature.

Clive Ponting was a senior civil servant in the Ministry of Defence during the Falklands War of 1982. On May 2 of that year, HMS *Conqueror*, a nuclear-powered submarine of the Royal Navy, sank the Argentine Cruiser, *General Belgrano*, an action that resulted in the death of 368 Argentine sailors. The action came at a time when Peru and the United States were still trying to find a peaceful solution to the crisis but the sinking of the *Belgrano* contributed substantially to the inevitability of war as the only solution to the conflict—and a marvellously successful war it was for the UK, the Royal Navy, and the Thatcher government.

Shortly after the *Belgrano* had been sunk, however, Opposition members of Parliament questioned the government closely on the precise circumstances that surrounded the event. Specifically the Opposition queried ministers as to whether the attack was consistent with Royal Navy Rules of Engagement that were in effect at the time. The official replies were uncertain, confused, and inconsistent. Once the war was over, the Opposition pressed the Ministry of Defence more closely on these matters, as government critics became increasingly convinced that the *Belgrano* had never been within the "total exclusion zone" declared by the Royal Navy's Rules of Engagement. As one wag would put it later, the Falklands War showed that Britannia rules the waves but does she also waive the rules? (Norton-Taylor, 1985: 96).

Further, there was growing evidence to challenge the government's claim that the *Belgrano* was on its way to rendezvous with an Argentinian aircraft carrier in order to attack ships of the Royal Navy. Indeed, much of the evidence suggested that the *Belgrano* was on its way home to Argentina when it met its unhappy fate.

As these troubling questions dragged on throughout 1983 and early 1984, the Ministry of Defence became increasingly uneasy, and for good reason, because its original version of the events had been deliberately misleading. Ponting, who had no part in the original deception was asked in March of 1984 to prepare a chronology of the events that would satisfy the government's critics. He urged a policy of openness that would put an end to the cover-up and thought that the Secretary of State for Defence, Michael Heseltine, had agreed (Ponting, 1985: 130–132). By the end of April, he realized that Heseltine had decided to deliberately mislead members of Parliament who were inquiring about just when and where the *Belgrano* had originally been sighted by the Royal Navy. As Ponting tells it: "I had never come across anything so blatant in my fifteen years in the Civil Service. It was a deliberate attempt to conceal information which would reveal that Ministers had gravely misled Parliament for the previous two years" (Ponting, 1985: 138).[8]

On April 24, he took the decisive action of anonymously leaking information to Tam Dalyell, a Labour MP, who had been particularly aggressive in challenging the official version of the *Belgrano* affair. The information was unclassified but of such a nature as to alert Dalyell to the fact that his questions were right on target. Meanwhile, the cover-up continued apace as the ministry escalated the deception to include not only individual members of Parliament but the Select Committee on Foreign Affairs as well. Ponting agonized over whether he should leak additional documents to Parliament which would surely expose the government's deception. He bares his soul as follows:

> Could I really bring myself to send the documents to Parliament? All my instincts after fifteen years in the Civil Service told me that my loyalty was to Ministers and the department. But then I realised that Ministers had broken their side of the bargain in attempting to evade their responsibilities to Parliament. If they could just simply shrug off their duties, refuse to answer questions, give misleading answers or refuse to correct false statements to Parliament how could there be any effective control over what the Government did? In the end Ministers had to be responsible to Parliament or the whole British constitutional system would break down. (Ponting, 1985:150)

In a word, Ponting seemed to think that it was his duty to alert Parliament to the fact that ministers were not fulfilling their constitutional duty of responsibility to Parliament.

Having mulled all this over, he once again anonymously leaked unclassified but seriously compromising documents to Dalyell. This time, however, he was identified as the source of the leak, arrested and subjected to criminal prosecution under the Official Secrets Act of 1911.[9] His trial began on January 28, 1985. As the Official Secrets Act was worded at that time, the only defense available to Ponting was that he had communicated the offending information "to a person to whom it is in the interests of the State his [the defendant's] duty to communicate it." The language is tortured but the legal point is clear enough. In order to be found not guilty of violating the sweeping prohibitions of the Official Secrets Act as it was worded in 1985, Ponting had to show that he had a duty "in the interests of the State" to send the documents to Dalyell, an Opposition member of Parliament. Clearly, the nub of the matter was the meaning of "the interests of the State." This, of course, is a point of law and, as such, it fell to the trial judge, Justice McGowan, to instruct the jury as to its meaning:

> What, then, of the words 'In the interest of the State'? Members of the Jury, I direct you that those words mean the policies of the State as they were in July of 1984 when Mr. Ponting communicated the information to Mr. Dalyell and not the policies of the State as Mr. Ponting, Mr. Dalyell, you or I might think they ought to have been. The policies of the State mean the policies laid down for it by its recognized organs of government and authority. (Norton-Taylor, 1985: 102–103)

In framing the issue in this way, Justice McGowan virtually directed the jury to convict Ponting. If the interests of the State are the interests of the government of the day, there was no way Ponting could claim to have acted in the interests of the State. Remarkably, however, after a very brief deliberation, the jury found Ponting not guilty.

As might be expected, this decision sent shock-waves through Whitehall. Within a fortnight, Sir Robert Armstrong had issued the statement noted above in which he restated emphatically the traditional doctrine that civil servants have no responsibility to Parliament, an opinion that echoed Justice McGowan's instruction to the jury.[10] The fact that the jury clearly disregarded McGowan's instruction may have been a meaningful indication of the state of public opinion on the implications of ministerial responsibility and its corollary principle, civil service anonymity.

The specific facts of the *Belgrano* affair put Ponting's flagrant violation of these principles in a rather favorable light. From a straightforward ethical viewpoint, it is hard to position Ponting anywhere but on the side of the angels. Nevertheless, his argument is somewhat unsettling when seen in a different light. Consider Defence Minister Heseltine's perspective on the Ponting affair as he stated it on the floor of the House of Commons shortly after Ponting's acquittal. In its enthusiasm for Ponting, the Opposition, according to Heseltine, was asking the House to support the proposition

> That the most trusted civil servants, in the most secure parts of our defence establishments, should be free anonymously to draft questions for Opposition back benchers to submit to Ministers on which the self-same leaking civil servants may then brief Ministers on the answers which they consider appropriate. (Drewry, 1985b: 208)[11]

As one of the Defence Minister's critics candidly concedes, ''Mr. Heseltine's rhetorical onslaught does contain an element of uncomfortable truth'' (Drewry, 1985b: 208).

Despite Heseltine's fears and Armstrong's efforts to maintain the traditional civil service orthodoxy, there are serious indications that the principles of ministerial responsibility and civil service anonymity are gradually undergoing considerable changes. Colin Turpin, for example, chronicles a good number of instances in which civil servants have been publicly blamed for their errors and other instances wherein they have openly admitted to their independent decisions and even to their personal views in politically controversial matters. He adds examples of permanent secretaries mentioning changes in staffing arrangements and administrative structures, an under-secretary acknowledging authorship of a minister's response to a parliamentary question and allows that ''officials may reveal that a minister's decision was based upon a prior judgment reached by themselves'' (Turpin, 1989: 66).

Even more significant was the revitalization in 1979 of the Select Committees of Parliament (as opposed to Parliament's Standing Committees which review prospective legislation). Senior civil servants appear routinely before these select committees which often examine the way the ministries conduct their affairs.[12] Since the rules governing what the civil servants may say to the select committees are quite strict, one knowledgeable observer maintains that their appearances amount ''to a dent rather than a gaping hole in official anonymity'' (Drewry, 1989).

As for ministerial responsibility, informed commentators maintain that no minister has resigned simply because of his subordinates' failings since the Crichel Down affair of 1954. ''Crichel Down'' refers to an area in which the government had acquired a tract of land for military purposes in World War II. The Ministry of Agriculture was accused of inordinate delays in returning the land to its rightful owners after the war. At the time, it appeared that the Minister of Agriculture, Sir Thomas Dugdale, had no knowledge of the failings of his wayward subordinates but felt, nonetheless, that the principle of ministerial responsibility demanded his resignation. Subsequent research has revealed that the entire affair was much more complicated than the diagrammatic simplicities of the case had originally suggested and that Dugdale may have been more personally involved than was thought at the time.[13] In any event, "Crichel Down" has been enshrined in the literature as shorthand for the last example of a pure case of a blameless minister resigning his office because of his subordinates' shortcomings.

Today Crichel Down is looked upon somewhat nostalgically as a relic of a bygone and simpler era. This may be true but, if so, this raises an interesting question that goes to the heart of the constitutional foundation of public service ethics in the UK:

> If Crichel Down is dead and Ministers are not accountable to Parliament for some actions of their officials, then who is? Not to put too fine a point on it, who ought to resign or to be penalized if mistakes are made? If it is not Ministers, it can only be officials. (Turpin, 1989:67)[14]

III. CONSTITUTIONALISM AND FRANCE

If ministerial responsibility is the guiding constitutional principle in British public administration, separation of powers plays this role in France. The Declaration of the Rights of Man and of the Citizen of 1789 proclaimed unequivocally that "[a] society . . . in which there is no separation of powers has no constitution." This explicit adherence to the principle of separation of powers would seem to highlight the similarities between the French and American constitutional traditions.

Similarities there are, but these are overshadowed by fundamental differences. First and foremost is the traditional French understanding of law as "the overt expression of the general will," a principle that is also announced in the famous Declaration of the Rights of Man and of the Citizen of 1789. Because the legislature makes law, it expresses the general will and therefore the French constitutional tradition has regarded it as superior to the executive and judicial authorities that perform ancillary tasks. In a word, there is a profound, perhaps an irreconcilable, tension in French constitutional history between parliamentary sovereignty on the one hand and separation of powers on the other (Marshall, 1992). This is not an issue in the American constitutional tradition wherein no institution is sovereign and where law makes no pretence to embody a general will, but simply the will of an ad hoc coalition of interests that forms a transient majority.

From the French point of view, however, the American version of separation of powers is seriously flawed. In 1958, for example, the founding fathers of the Fifth Republic debated the question of separation of powers at some length and found the American approach wanting because it is based on "an abstract and theoretical logic" (Documents: II, 218), which has led to harmful "excesses" (Documents: II, 222). Chief among these excesses—interestingly enough for our purposes—was the contemptuous attitude of American congressmen toward high-ranking executive officers (Documents: II, 220, 227). The founders of the Fifth Republic wanted none of this for France, a country that has traditionally held public administration in high regard.

The Constitution of the Fifth Republic links separation of powers to ethics and public administration in Article 23 which provides in part:

> The office of member of the Government shall be incompatible with the exercise of any Parliamentary mandate, with the holding of any office at the national level in business, professional or labor organizations, and with any public employment or professional activity.[15]

Thus, the very text of the French Constitution of 1958 addresses specifically the question of conflict of interest. Members of the government, that is ministers appointed by the president of the republic on the recommendation of the prime minister, are explicitly banned from certain types of remunerative activity. Subsequent statutory and administrative regulations spell out the specifics of the very general constitutional language (Céoara, 1987).[16]

The constitutional language itself, however, goes beyond questions of conflict of interest. Members of the government are also forbidden from being members of Parliament or civil servants. Thus professional, commercial, parliamentary, and civil service activities are lumped together and placed off limits to government ministers. How all this came about is an interesting story that illuminates an important constitutional dimension of French public administration.

The policy underlying all the prohibitions is the same: "to assure the independence of members of the government" (Céoara, 1987: 631). Originally, the prohibition concerned only members of Parliament. When the present constitution was being drawn up in 1958, an early version of what would eventually become Article 23 provided simply that "no one may combine a governmental function with a parliamentary mandate" (Documents: II, 574). This uncomplicated prohibition expressed an opinion that was of the greatest importance to General de Gaulle, the founder of the Fifth Republic.

De Gaulle attributed the fall of France in 1940 in large part to the incessant and petty wrangling among the political parties in the Parliament of the moribund Third Republic. For de Gaulle, the parties represented particular (usually selfish) interests, whereas the State stood for the good of all. One of the great tasks of constitution-making was to design a system that would empower the government to be sufficiently stable to serve the universal interests of the State. To do this, members of the government must be independent of Parliament and its political parties where particular interests abound. By banning parliamentarians from the government, de Gaulle hoped to diminish the temptation for parliamentarians to vote to overthrow a government in place in the hope of securing for themselves a ministerial post in a new government. Gaullists believed that parliamentarians had all too often yielded to this temptation and thereby contributed to the perennial governmental instability that had plagued French Republics. The prohibition on members of the government serving simultaneously in Parliament would reduce this temptation because if a parliamentarian should become a minister he would have to surrender his seat and, therefore, would have no safe haven to which he could return if his government were overturned.

Critics of this plan objected that it undermined the very essence of a parliamentary regime which demands that those who exercise the executive power, i.e., the government, be themselves members of Parliament (Documents: II, 539–548.)[17] General de Gaulle and his supporters responded that the integrity of the Parliamentary system was preserved as long as the government was *responsible* to Parliament, i.e., as long as Parliament could vote the government out of office. It did not demand that the government itself be comprised of ministers who are also members of Parliament.

De Gaulle himself defended his innovation explicitly on separation of powers grounds. Following the traditional French understanding of parliamentary supremacy, de

Gaulle argued that the legislature is the "controlling" power and the executive the "controlled" power. The same power cannot be simultaneously both controller and controlled and therefore members of the government (the controlled) cannot simultaneously be parliamentarians (the controllers) (Documents: II, 303, 755).

This argument may have been somewhat disingenuous because one ordinarily does not think of General de Gaulle as a champion of parliamentary control of anything; but within the French constitutional tradition of parliamentary sovereignty, a tradition that was seriously compromised by de Gaulle's constitution, it made sense—regardless of what the general himself really believed at the time of the founding of the Fifth Republic in 1958.

For comparative purposes, we might pause to note that the famous Brownlow Committee made a similar argument in 1937 when it laid out the case for enhancing the "administrative management" capacities of the president of the United States. The document was recognized then and now as a thinly veiled grab for power by President Roosevelt and his supporters. The core of the proposal was to concentrate power in the hands of the president. This was justified on the grounds that it would enable Congress to monitor more carefully the president's responsibility to itself and thereby to control him more effectively (Rohr, 1986: 135–153).

Needless to say, Franklin Roosevelt was not really looking for ways to help Congress control him. The Brownlow Committee was simply trying to provide rhetorical cover for the president's expansionist views of executive power. To support this idea of facilitating congressional control of the executive, the commission relied upon an analogy to corporate structure whereby management is accountable to a board of directors. This, of course, is a preposterous theory of the American Constitution. Aside from the impeachable offenses explicitly stated in Article II, the president of the United States is responsible only to those who elected him and most emphatically not to Congress.

In France, however, the traditional doctrine of parliamentary sovereignty made de Gaulle's distinction between controller and controlled at least a plausible theory if not a convincing statement of his personal beliefs.

Eventually, de Gaulle's point of view prevailed but only after his critics and supporters had joined forces to expand the list of activities prohibited to governmental ministers. It seemed only fair that burdens placed on parliamentarians should fall as well upon civil servants who became ministers (Documents: II, 541–543). At this point the high constitutional argument of separation of powers unraveled and civil servants-turned-ministers were required to resign their career positions temporarily on the rather pedestrian grounds that no man can do two things at the same time (Documents: II, 543).

From here it was but a small step to fret over commercial, financial, and professional interests exerting an unwholesome influence on government and soon debate focused on banning persons with such interests from the government.[18] One proposal would have required that men holding high positions in a broad range of business enterprises be prevented from becoming ministers for a period of five years following their resignation from their commercial activities. This would have amounted to a post-employment restriction in reverse—i.e., a pre-employment restriction! Indeed, at one point in the constitutional debates the list of prohibited activities had expanded so far as to prompt the exasperated outcry, "Somebody has to be able to be a minister" (Documents: II, 541). Fortunately, the excesses were curbed owing principally to the moderating influence of Michel Debré, de Gaulle's principal legal advisor (Documents: II, 627, 687).

There is an irony in the fact that France enshrines in her constitution an explicit concern with the evils of conflict of interest. In practice, French inattention to such matters is remarkable and perhaps even notorious (Mény, 1992: 29–59 and 142–162). Together, the constitutional statement of high principle and the relaxed enforcement in practice provide still another example to support de Tocqueville's shrewd comment on French political culture in general: "The rule is rigid but practice is gentle" (Mény, 1992: 17).

A very different aspect of constitutionalism and administrative ethics in France arose in the famous Greenpeace affair of 1985. Although many of the details of this unhappy event remain shrouded in mystery, enough reliable information has come to light to support the brief narrative that follows.[19]

In the harbor of Auckland, New Zealand on the night of July 10, 1985, two bombs tore open the hull of the *Rainbow Warrior*, a trawler belonging to Greenpeace, a well-known environmental group with an international following. The boat sank at once and a photographer working for Greenpeace was killed. The *Rainbow Warrior* had been on its way to a French possession in the South Pacific to protest against underground nuclear testing that was planned for October. A few days later, two French secret service agents travelling in New Zealand on false passports were arrested on suspicion of having participated in the bombing.

At first the French government denied any knowledge of the attack but eventually it became clear that high-ranking French military and secret service officers had planned it and that French frogmen had carried it out. Just why the French government undertook this unseemly project is still not entirely clear but it was surely related to the national interest in maintaining a free hand in testing nuclear weapons.

The sinking of the *Rainbow Warrior* launched a remarkable spate of ethical issues in public administration. These ranged from such obvious problems as the lies that had to be told at all levels to try to maintain a cover-up to the exotic and unfounded speculation that disaffected right-wingers in the secret service had deliberately botched the attack in order to embarrass the socialist government of President Mitterrand (Bornstein, 1988: 103).

While the cover-up was in full swing, the Prime Minister, Laurent Fabius, and President Mitterrand announced that they would appoint an "unimpeachable figure" to conduct a rigorous investigation that would get to the bottom of the matter. In the United States, we would probably turn to a retired federal judge to lead such a probe, but in France the political leadership turned to a renowned civil servant, Bernard Tricot. Such is the prestige of the civil service in France.

Tricot interviewed all the high-ranking officials who might possibly be involved, including the defense minister and top military advisers to the president of the Republic. He found nothing to implicate the French government and announced this finding to the press. His exculpatory statements, however, were laced with broad hints for ambitious journalists on just where they might look for further evidence if, perchance, they were dissatisfied with his findings. He even stated publicly that he would not exclude the possibility that the officials he had interviewed had lied to him.

Tricot's performance raises an endless series of ethical questions on how he discharged his responsibilities as he simultaneously absolved the government from guilt while sowing the seeds of further doubt. The issue is complicated even more if Tricot sincerely believed, as many thoughtful Frenchmen did, that Greenpeace presented a threat to the *force de frappe* which, again, many thoughtful Frenchmen believe was essential for France's national security.

Today it is clear that many of the officials Tricot interviewed must have lied to him. Indeed, two French journalists state flatly that President Mitterrand himself knew that the French government had planned the attack (Faligot and Krop, 1989: 294). Whatever the truth might be about "what the president knew and when he knew it," there seems to be considerable evidence to support the belief that Prime Minister Fabius did not know about it. If this is true, it raises a remarkable constitutional issue because the prime minister heads the French government and, as such, shares important executive powers with the president who is head of State but not head of government.

Articles 20 and 21 of the Constitution of the Fifth Republic provide that the prime minister "shall direct the operation of the government" and that the government, which he directs, "shall have at its disposal the administration of the armed forces." The prime minister himself is specifically designated as the officer "responsible for national defense." These impressive constitutional powers highlight the ethical significance of the entirely plausible speculation that President Mitterrand knew about the attack and Prime Minister Fabius did not. Where would this leave the public servants—civilian and military—who would be actively involved in carrying out a furtive but extremely important military operation that had to be kept secret from the constitutionally designated head of the French government? How would one sort out such divided loyalties?

A final ethical consideration from the Greenpeace affair goes beyond questions of public service and concerns what might be called the "constitutional climate" for the press in France. Stephen Bornstein's illuminating analysis of the Greenpeace affair contrasts the way the American press handled the Watergate scandal with the way in which the French press treated the sinking of the *Rainbow Warrior*. Nowhere is the contrast sharper than in the way in which the two national media establishments reacted once it became clear that the nation's president might possibly be involved. This news whetted the already voracious appetite of American reporters who tackled with vim and gusto the task of destroying a duly elected president. Not so, the French press. The prestigious *Le Monde* had taken the lead in exposing the scandal but seemed to back off after the defense minister had resigned. This was especially true after it had become "clear to the press and to the leaders of the opposition that any further efforts to expose the truth would likely lead to the Elysée Palace and the president" (Bornstein, 1988: 114).

There are several possible explanations for this curious contrast. One is purely political. *Le Monde* traditionally leans to the Left and, hence, had no desire to disgrace the first socialist president of the Fifth Republic. Richard Nixon, on the other hand, was no friend of the liberal *Washington Post* which played a major role in his downfall. There is probably some truth in this explanation but hardly enough to satisfy the serious scandal-watcher. To dismiss both Watergate and Greenpeace as purely partisan affairs is to miss the deeper significance of both events.

A second surmise is that French elites of both Right and Left feared a major presidential scandal might threaten the stability of the entire regime and France had seen too much of this to be willing to run risks along these lines. As responsible members of the French elite, the media establishment looked the other way.

At a less dramatic level, one might speculate that the French Right and Left closed ranks in the face of a threat to the nation's nuclear deterrent, a military initiative that commanded a broad consensus in French politics.

A final explanation, which I find more compelling than the others, is the absence of institutional support for an aggressive press willing to take on a powerful sitting president. Watergate is often hailed as a great triumph for American journalism and so it was. This is the truth but not the whole truth. How much success would the press have enjoyed if it had not benefitted from the support it received from such institutions of government as Senator Sam Ervin's Investigative Committee, special prosecutors Cox and Jaworski, Attorney General Eliot Richardson and his Deputy William Ruckelshaus, Judge John Sirica, the Supreme Court of the United States, the House Judiciary Committee that initiated impeachment proceedings against President Nixon and an assortment of grand juries throughout the land that looked into a variety of Watergate-related matters?

Bornstein cites as follows an unnamed adviser to President Mitterrand who said of anyone eager to press the investigation to include the president himself: "Whoever wants to go any further, will have to aim very high, strike very hard, and, above all, advance without any covering fire." This is a very telling comment and it captures nicely a crucial difference between the two countries. The American media aimed high and struck hard but, unlike their French counterparts, they knew they had abundant covering fire as they advanced on Richard Nixon's beleaguered White House. Most importantly, the covering fire was provided by institutions of the government itself. Watergate was not simply a triumph of press over government but of the press and two great branches of the United States government over a seriously delinquent president. Watergate and Greenpeace had different outcomes not precisely because the American press is more free than the press in France but because the American press benefitted from the vitality-in-action of the American constitutional principle of separation of powers.

IV. CONSTITUTIONALISM AND CANADA

As we turn to Canada, we discover that the great constitutional question is not separation of powers but separation itself. Canada was in the midst of a profoundly serious and potentially tragic constitutional crisis in May of 1992 when this chapter was first written.

For well over a century, the British North America Act of 1867 had served as the basic document in Canada's Constitution. The Constitution Act of 1982 replaced it amidst great fanfare that included the arrival of Queen Elizabeth in Ottawa to sign the document that severed the last legal ties between Canada and Great Britain. The signing took place on March 29, 1982, exactly one-hundred fifteen years after Queen Victoria, the present queen's great-great-grandmother, had signed the British North America Act. Conspicuous by his absence at the grand affair, was René Lévesque, the premier of the Province of Quebec and head of the separatist *Parti Québécois*.

Many citizens of Quebec found the Constitution Act of 1982 unacceptable because it failed to go far enough in recognizing Quebec as a "distinct society" within Canada. Although the Canadian courts have rejected the argument that Quebec alone could veto the new Constitution, the hold-out province has not yet been reconciled. Successive federal governments have unsuccessfully tried to heal the rift. In 1990, there were high hopes that an agreement styled the "Meech Lake Accord" would succeed, but last minute objections from the provinces of Manitoba and Newfoundland dashed these hopes and sent Canada into its present constitutional tailspin.

In a political climate of this sort, neither civil servants nor anyone else can look to an embattled constitution for normative guidance. Constitutional crises apart, however, Canadians would still have serious difficulties in deriving normative guidance from their constitutional traditions. This is because the North America Act, which was effectually Canada's constitution until 1982, had no Bill of Rights. It dealt almost exclusively with the allocation of powers between the federal and the provincial governments. All this changed with the 1982 Constitution which included a Charter of Rights and Freedoms where one finds important statements on individual and group rights. Although the Charter is controversial, it has already begun to play an important role in Canadian public law. Because it is so new, however, it is extremely unlikely that it will have a chance to shape the fundamental normative principles of Canadian civil servants. If Canadians can extricate themselves from this crisis, the Charter promises to contribute significantly to the development of Canadian constitutional history, a fascinating topic in itself and one which should be of interest to Canada's neighbors to the south.

The substance of what eventually became the North America Act was agreed upon during the American Civil War and considerably influenced by that dreadful conflict. John A. MacDonald, the most prominent architect of the Dominion of Canada, believed that the Civil War was caused in no small part by the excessive powers enjoyed by the states under the Constitution of the United States. In his determination to avoid a similar disaster for Canada, he and his collaborators designed a government with impressive federal powers—far more impressive than those of the United States Congress. Much of Canadian constitutional history centers on the story of how brilliant provincial politicians and jurists whittled this parchment giant down to what they considered more desirable proportions (Vipond, 1991).

Constitutional development in the United States followed the opposite path. A national government that was textually weak in comparison with its Canadian counterpart has come to dominate the states which, in principle, have far greater constitutional powers than the really powerful Canadian provinces. Administrative institutions played an important role in the contrasting constitutional development of both countries.

For the contemporary Canadian civil servant, the Constitution has become not a symbol of unity but a sign of contradiction. Civil servants, like all other Canadians, however, have an important stake in the outcome of this crisis. Indeed, within Quebec itself, an important issue in the sovereignty debate centers on how, in the event of separation, former federal civil servants might be repatriated to their new country and at what cost (Normand, 1990; Drouin, 1990). Prime Minister Mulroney has been quite blunt in trying to persuade would-be separatists that the cost to Quebec would be staggering. In a recent address, he warned against the danger of separation by reminding his listeners "that 50,000 Quebeckers now work for the federal public service, which makes the Canadian government the largest employer in Quebec after the government of Quebec" (*Toronto Globe & Mail*: April 29, 1992).

Personal costs to civil servants themselves could be considerable as well because separation might threaten the desirable status that is theirs today. According to a recent study by the United States Merit System Protection Board, federal civil servants in Canada presently enjoy substantially better pay and working conditions than their counterparts in the United States (U.S. MSPB, 1991).

At a more substantive level, Quebec civil servants have been playing and continue to play an important role in the ongoing negotiations aimed at overcoming the constitutional impasse. Former Quebec premier, Robert Bourassa, boycotted these negotiations after the collapse of the Meech Lake Accord in 1990. He did, however, send senior civil servants to these deliberations as observers.

In a perceptive academic paper, Jean Mercier, a professor of public administration, has suggested that the debate over sovereignty for Quebec should focus less on abstruse questions of constitutional law and more on the likely *administrative* costs and benefits of a definitive separation. This would mean looking squarely at such sober matters as military policy, the Quebec share of the present Canadian national debt, postal services, and mechanisms for settling post-separation disputes with Canada. Politicians may duck these questions but administrators should not (Mercier, 1992).

What is missing, however, in the abundant literature on this great constitutional crisis is a serious study of the attitudes of federal civil servants themselves, especially francophone federal civil servants from Quebec. In 1980 there was criticism of federal civil servants who were alleged to have violated the ethical standard of political neutrality by urging citizens of Quebec to vote "no" in a sovereignty referendum that was defeated in that year (Kernaghan and Langford, 1990). The climate of 1992 of course, precluded further study of such matters. The published results might have only heightened tensions. In happier times, however, when the crisis resolved, such a study might be safely undertaken. It would be interesting—and important, I believe—to know what civil servants think and feel about such soul-wrenching matters.[20] For the present, we must content ourselves with examining the less dramatic but still significant issue of the relationship between Canadian constitutionalism and conflict of interest. The Canadian experience in this area is particularly instructive because conflict of interest issues in the United States seldom raise constitutional questions. Thanks to the efforts of two Canadian political scientists, Ian Greene (1990) and Andrew Stark (1993), we can see the connection between the mundane questions of conflict of interest and deeper questions of constitutional law and governmental structure.

Ian Greene maintains that the high number of conflict-of-interest scandals in Canada "can be explained in part by the absence of a clear connection between the substance of the conflict rules and basic principles of the Canadian constitution" (Greene, 1990: 234). He notes the curious fact that more than 90% of the conflict-of-interest problems in Canadian government concern cabinet ministers at both the federal and provincial levels. This raises the question of whether there is something in the minister's role to explain this fact. To distinguish ministers from ordinary MPs on the one hand and from high civil servants on the other, one would have to note that ministers alone are *both* legislators and administrators.

The link between this dual role of ministers and their marked proclivity to embroil themselves in conflict-of-interest situations becomes clear if we recall that the reason we look askance at conflict of interest is because it undermines impartial decision-making by government officials. To take the simplest case, a "decision-maker cannot be perceived as impartial if he or she could derive a specific financial benefit from the decision" (Greene, 1990: 236). Impartial or unbiased decision-making is but a simple application of the common law doctrine of fairness which itself is derived from the broader principle of the rule of law. Mentioning the rule of law leads directly to the Constitution Act of 1982 whose preamble announces that "Canada is founded upon principles that recognize the supremacy of God and the rule of law."

Thus, conflict of interest scrambles to the high ground of the Canadian Constitution atop the solid principles of the rule of law, fairness, and unbiased decision-making. These principles are clear enough in themselves but their practical application is exceedingly complex, because they cannot have the same meaning for all officials. Again, to take an easy case, judges are quite properly held to a much stricter standard of impartiality than popularly elected legislators. Indeed, if representative democracy is to function properly, legislators *should* be biased in favor of their constituents. Their bias would be reprehensible only if it were exercised primarily for their own personal benefit rather than for the good of those they represent.

Ministers are somewhere between the relatively clear situations in which judges and legislators find themselves. As legislative leaders, ministers should be thoroughly partisan, i.e., biased in favor of their supporters. As men and women charged with applying the law, however, more even-handed norms are appropriate. We need not revisit the discredited politics/administration dichotomy to realize that it is not always easy for ministers to keep these two roles separate in practice. This is especially true when we recall that Canadian ministers, like high-ranking executive officers in every democratic country, carry out laws that often confer broad discretionary powers upon those who execute them. As Carl Friedrich put it over a half-century ago, a hallmark of modern government is that policy is made as it is being executed (Friedrich, 1940). All this, of course, serves only to confound the confusion of the minister's roles as legislator and executive.

Without denying the complexity of the minister's role, Greene attempts to illuminate the problem by distinguishing three types of bias in official decision-making: (1) bias created by personal financial gain for the decision-maker; (2) bias created by the decision-maker's effort to help persons with whom he is closely associated; and (3) bias created by the decision-maker's previously expressed views on the subject matter before him (Greene, 1990: 239).

The consequences that flow from the first and third types of bias are relatively clear. The minister should not make official decisions in order to advance his personal interests (type 1). He should not, however, be disqualified from making decisions on subject matters in which he has previously expressed his opinion (type 3). Such a rule would discourage politicians from discussing public affairs openly. It is the second type of bias—favoritism toward associates that is the most difficult to apply in practice.

Greene notes that a substantial number of the conflict-of-interest situations involving Canadian ministers concerns questions of favoritism toward political allies. This is obviously an area in which it is impossible to draw a bright line separating permissible from impermissible conduct. If the rule is too strict, the democratic political process is imperilled because part of this process demands that the winners reward their friends and punish their enemies. If the rule is too lax, the rule of law itself is threatened because ministers and their subordinates will distribute legal benefits and burdens on political grounds rather than on the principle of equality before the law.

Although this issue is at bottom intractable, Greene argues that some progress could be made if those who draft conflict-of-interest rules would keep in mind that the constitutional principle of the rule of law is central to their enterprise. He shows quite convincingly that such rules are usually drafted in hasty reaction to a particular scandal or irregularity. Little effort is made to examine or to explain the reasons behind the rules, which always treat conflict of interest as though it were exclusively a question of officials enriching themselves or their friends improperly. This narrow financial focus misses the more fundamental constitutional point of fairness and impartial decisions as corollaries of the principle of the rule of law. Consequently, ministers tend to regard conflict of interest rules ''as nothing more than cumbersome regulations which promote the same kind of search for loopholes and the same problem of differing interpretations that taxpayers confront when filing their annual returns'' (Greene, 1990: 234).

In a word, Greene argues that ministerial behavior will improve only if ministers have a clearer idea of *why* certain actions are prohibited by conflict-of-interest rules and if these rules themselves reflect more precisely the constitutional principles on which they stand.

Andrew Stark, like Ian Greene, links conflict of interest to constitutionalism but, in so doing, he presents an explicitly comparative study showing that the very different conflict-of-interest practices in the United States and in Canada can be explained by the different constitutional structures in the two countries; that is, by parliamentary government in Canada and by separation of powers in the United States (Stark, 1992 and 1993).[21]

For example, the United States Congress has traditionally imposed harsher ethical standards upon executive officers than upon itself. The Ethics Reform Act of 1989 has recently narrowed this gap but only after long and bitter executive complaints about a lack of parity in ethical demands. In Canada, however, the dominance of the cabinet over the legislative process has guaranteed that "Parliament has never been given the opportunity to consider conflict-of-interest legislation which treats the cabinet (including the Prime Minister) significantly more severely than it treats members of Parliament" (Stark, 1992).[22] According to Stark, constitutional structures also explain why the behavior of officials below cabinet rank is regulated by law in the United States but by more flexible non-statutory codes of conduct in Canada. In the Canadian parliamentary system, the cabinet dominates the legislative process and, hence, there is little opportunity for MPs to impose standards on executive officials at any level that would displease the highest executive officers, i.e., the cabinet. There is little opportunity for Parliament to act and little need as well; for if the cabinet decides a new conflict-of-interest standard should be imposed upon its subordinates, it can do so by executive action without invoking the cumbersome legislative process. In the United States, Congress is by no means dominated by the executive (to put it mildly!) and therefore can impose unwelcome conflict-of-interest restrictions at will on executive officers and employees at every level. It can do so, of course, only by law.

Post-employment restrictions in the two countries provide a particularly illuminating example of the influence of constitutional structures on conflict-of-interest practices. In the United States, high-ranking executive officers frequently come from the private sector and ordinarily return to it at a time of their own choosing or at least at a time that is predictable because of the fixed periods for elections in the United States. They seldom have trouble finding employment outside of government that is far more rewarding financially than their brief tenure in government service. Canadian ministers, however, tend to be career politicians who have worked their way up through the parliamentary system. Their departure from office can be more abrupt than is the case with American cabinet officers and they are far less likely candidates for lucrative positions in the private sector (Stark, 1992). Consequently, the post-employment restrictions of former high-ranking American officials are much stricter than those on former Canadian ministers. As Stark puts it, former senior-level executives in the United States "are commonly treated as if they are both more capable of surviving under a stricter post-employment regime, and more deserving of one" (Stark, 1993).

The rather severe post-employment restrictions imposed on former United States officials underscore the traditional American fear that private sector interests will corrupt the integrity of governmental decision-making. Quite consistent with this fear, American post-employment restriction laws place the burden of compliance on the former official himself.

The Canadian approach differs. Mitchell Sharp and Michael Starr, co-authors of an extremely influential report on conflict of interest commissioned by former Prime Minister Trudeau, maintain that if post-employment restrictions should be adopted in Canada, the legal responsibility for avoiding such contacts should rest on the *current* officeholder and not on the former official. This is true even for former ministers dealing with their former subordinates. Stark maintains this policy clearly implies that the current official "no matter how junior is still more powerful and protected than is his or her ex-ministerial boss, and should thus be considered capable of, and held responsible for, resisting the ex-minister's blandishments" (Stark, 1993).

A final contrast between the two countries' policies on conflict of interest appears in the way they handle the matter of legislators being influenced by financial interests outside of government. As noted above, Americans abhor this sort of thing and, consequently, have extensive and detailed safeguards against congressmen being on any payroll other than that of the United States. Indeed, when public debate focuses on whether congressmen should vote themselves a pay raise, one of the perennial arguments for higher pay is to preserve the financial independence of the members of Congress.

Canadians, like the British, see the problem quite differently. Because of the historical development of parliamentary institutions, the great fear has always been that MPs would be corrupted by the executive—originally by the Crown and, in more recent times, by an overbearing cabinet. Hence, historically, the British and Canadian traditions have been skewed "toward the idea that legislators who rely on income from private interests are relatively more likely to retain independence of mind and integrity of judgment" (Stark, 1993).[23]

In the United States, such an idea would fall on deaf ears but it is quite consistent with the long-standing British practice of MPs serving without salary—a practice that endured until 1911.[24]

An interesting variation on this theme surfaced in a debate in Canada's House of Commons in 1983 when Parliament was discussing the merits of post-employment restrictions on former ministers. Inevitably, someone raised the issue of the possible dangers of making such regulations too severe. When this issue arises in the United States, the danger that is always mentioned is that excessive harshness will deter competent men and women in the private sector from entering government service as presidential appointees. Canadian parliamentarians saw a very different danger. Excessively harsh post-employment restrictions might lead a cabinet minister to "cling 'inordinately' to office." That is, strict post-employment rules would make life outside government so unpleasant that the very prospect would sap the courage of ministers and weaken their resolve "to take the sorts of unpopular or impolitic action which could hasten their leaving office" (Stark, 1993).

V. CONCLUSION

To conclude our study, let us glance back briefly over the major comparative points we have discussed in the preceding pages. First, there is the notable fact that the United States alone among the four countries requires of its public servants an oath to uphold its Constitution. It is utterly obvious why there is no such requirement in Canada where the Constitution Act of 1982 is at the heart of a constitutional crisis. The British Constitution is surely revered in the United Kingdom but in its present "partly written but uncodified" form it is an unlikely object of an oath. The juror, no matter how patriotic, would not really know just what it is he swears to uphold. In France, the 1958 Constitution is relatively new—at least by American constitutional standards. It is not sufficiently venerable to be the object of an oath.[25]

Secondly, we have seen that both France and Canada have a much closer connection between their constitutions and questions of conflict of interest than is true in the United States. In France, the connection is textually explicit whereas in Canada the specific content of conflict-of-interest provisions flows from the parliamentary structure of the regime.

Thirdly, our study revealed very little about the connection between individual rights and constitutionally-based administrative ethics. To be sure, questions of individual rights are of the utmost importance in Canada, France, and the United Kingdom, but their link to constitutionally-based administrative ethics is not as apparent as it is in the United States where the oath to uphold the Constitution obliges the civil servant to look for ways to actualize the commitment to individual rights that is the bedrock principle of our constitutional order.

Finally, we have discovered the overwhelming importance of the constitutional principle of separation of powers in our effort to understand administrative ethics. No doubt we would make the same discovery in studying any question related to American government. Separation of powers helps to explain the remarkably aggressive behavior of American journalists during the Watergate affair, especially when compared with the French press and the *Rainbow Warrior*.

The most important differences in ethics policies between the United States, with its separation of powers, and the parliamentary regimes in Canada and the United Kingdom can be explained structurally, as Andrew Stark shows so well in his comparative study on conflict of interest. If the Clive Ponting case is contrasted with our own Iran-Contra scandal, we find a compelling illustration of the paramount importance of governmental structure in explaining political behavior. The Iran-Contra offenders faced criminal prosecution for lying to Congress and the same fate befell Ponting for telling Parliament the truth!

ACKNOWLEDGMENTS

I am pleased to acknowledge the considerable benefits I have drawn from critical comments on earlier drafts of this paper by Richard Chapman of the University of Durham, Terence Marshall of the Université de Paris X-Nanterre, and Andrew Stark of the University of Toronto. In acknowledging my gratitude, I grant the customary absolution for any errors of fact or judgment contained herein. I am sure this chapter would be much stronger if I had followed all their wise suggestions.

ENDNOTES

1. For a broader comparative ethics study, see Dwivedi and Olowu (1988).
2. For a potentially important exception, see *National Treasury Employees' Union vs. U.S.* United States District Court, District of Columbia, March 19, 1992. Civil Action #90-2922.
3. There is a lively debate within the UK on whether that nation should adopt a written constitution. See, for example, Lester, 1989. The European Court of Human Rights has had a particularly strong influence on the movement for the reform of British law. For a discussion of this

influence with particular reference to its impact on the exercise of administrative discretion, see Szablowski, 1992.

4. An interesting exception, however, is the development of the city manager plan in American local government. The politics/administration dichotomy makes good theoretical sense in this form of government because there is usually no separation of legislative and executive powers in those local governments that adopt the manager plan. Ordinarily, the city manager is accountable to a city council which, in theory, is his superior. The theoretical aspect of this arrangement is emphasized because in practice city managers often dominate their political masters. For this reason, the city manager may present the closest American parallel to the British parliamentary system. It is surely not by accident that the city managers organization is called the *International* City Managers Association. The movement represents a clear rejection of the traditional American notion of separation of powers.

5. For a comparative ethics study on "whistle blowing" with specific reference to the principle of ministerial responsibility in the UK, see Vaughn, 1981a, 378–382.

6. For an illuminating, in-depth study of the ethical and constitutional issues that faced Edward Bridges, one of the UK's most distinguished civil servants, see Chapman, 1988. In a more recent effort, Chapman has called attention to potentially far-reaching constitutional implications in the Civil Service Pay and Conditions of Service Code (Chapman, 1992).

7. For a careful analysis of the ethical aspects of the practice of holding superiors responsible for subordinates' mistakes, see Thompson, 1981.

8. My account of the Ponting affair relies heavily on Ponting's moderately self-serving book. The book is self-serving because of the self-righteousness and moral posturing to which the author occasionally succumbs. In fairness to Ponting, however, I hasten to add that the book is only moderately self-serving when one considers all that the poor man went through. The factual account Ponting presents seems to be consistent with the broad outline of other published accounts of his ordeal. See, for example, Norton-Taylor, 1985 and Drewry, 1985b.

9. The Official Secrets Act is one of the old chestnuts of British public administration. The literature on it is overwhelming and for the most part critical. The Act was substantially revised in 1989. For a discussion of the legal changes, see Thomas, 1991. For discussions of the Act shortly before its revision, see Hunt, 1987; Thomas, 1987; and Hooper, 1987.

10. For an extensive critique of Sir Robert Armstrong's position, see Ridley, 1985.

11. Drewry cites H. C. Deb., February 18, 1985, Volume 73, Col. 750.

12. For a full discussion of the significance of the Select Committee revival in 1979, see Drewry, 1985a. For a shorter discussion that focuses on constitutional issues, see Drewry, 1985b.

13. For a detailed analysis of the Crichel Down affair, see I. F. Nicolson, 1986. For opposing evaluations of Nicolson's book, see Delafons, 1987 and Chapman, 1987a.

14. Turpin cites as his source Seventh Report (1985–6) HC 92-I, para. 3.17.

15. For a commentary on this article, see Céoara, 1987.

16. For a pungent criticism of how conflict-of-interest matters are handled in France, see Mény, 1992:32–44.

17. On this point, see in particular the comments of M. David in Documents: II, 541.

18. Frequent criticisms were voiced of the American practice whereby presidents appoint businessmen as "ministers," i.e., as heads of the executive departments (Documents: II, 539–548). At the same time it was recognized that American businessmen who accept these positions are subjected to severe regulation of their financial holdings. However, some of the founders of the Fifth Republic had an exaggerated view on the severity of these rules (Documents: II, 543).

19. There is an extensive literature in French and in English on the Greenpeace affair. I have followed Bornstein (1988), Derogy and Pontaut (1986) and Faligot and Krop (1989).

20. I have not come across any studies of the federal civil service as an integrating force in Canada's present centrifugal political atmosphere. Outsiders might wonder if the world-renowned Royal Canadian Mounted Police could perform this function, but the role the RCMP played

in Quebec in pursuing the *Front de Libération du Québec* (FLQ) in the early 1970s makes this very unlikely. See Whittakee, 1988.

21. Two versions of Andrew Stark's manuscript are listed in the references—a shorter version which appeared in *Public Administration Review* and a longer one which appeared in a collection of essays edited by H. George Fredrickson.

22. These examples fit nicely into Stark's effort to offer a structural explanation for national differences in conflict-of-interest matters. He also acknowledges, however, that there is a principled argument for legislators treating themselves more leniently than they treat executive officers. This argument is grounded in the broad range of legislative activities as opposed to the more specialized areas of executive agencies. This point is also developed in Greene, 1990.

23. In discussing the influences of private sources of income, Stark confines his analysis to British and Canadian *legislators*. For a comparative study of outside income received by American and British Civil Servants, see Vaughn, 1981b.

24. The Constitution of the United States provides explicitly that members of Congress shall receive a salary to be paid out of the Treasury of the United States (I, 6). This provision along with other restrictions on members of Congress in Section 6 of Article I express the 18th century American response to the fear of executive control of the legislature.

25. Even if the constitution of the Fifth Republic does become venerable some day, it would be an unlikely object of an oath and this precisely because it is a *Republican* constitution. For a discussion of the incompatibility between oaths and republicanism in France, see Rohr, 1991.

REFERENCES

Armstrong, R. (1985). The Duties and Responsibilities of Civil Servants in Relation to Ministers. 74 H. C. Deb. 6s. Col 130-2 (February 26, 1985).

Barth, T. J. (1991). Administrative Statesmanship in a Government of Shared Powers (Ph.D. diss., Virginia Polytechnic Institute).

Bornstein, S. (1988). The Greenpeace Affair and the Peculiarities of French Politics. In A. S. Markovits and M. Silverstein, eds. *The Politics of Scandal: Power and Process in Liberal Democracies*. New York: Holmes and Meier.

Canada, Department of Justice. (1989). The Constitution Acts: 1867 to 1982. n.p.

Céoara, M. (1987). Article 23. In Francois Luchaire et Gérard Conac, eds. *La Constitution de la République Francaise*. 2d ed. Paris: Economica.

Chapman, R. A. (1987a). A View from Academe. *Public Administration* 65: 347–349.

Chapman, R. A. (1987b). Minister-Civil Servant Relationships. In R. A. Chapman and M. Hunt, eds. *Open Government*. London: Routledge.

Chapman, R. A. (1988). *Ethics in the British Civil Service*. London: Routledge.

Chapman, R. A. (1992). Ethics in Public Service. In Richard A. Chapman, ed. *Ethics in Public Service*. Edinburgh: University of Edinburgh Press; and Ottawa: Carleton University Press.

Delafons, J. (1987). A View from Whitehall. *Public Administration* 65: 339–347.

Derogy, J. and Pontaut, J. M. (1986). *Enquête sur trois sécrets d'Etat*. Paris: Laffont.

Dicey, A. V. (1959). *An Introduction to the Study of the Law of the Constitution*. 10th ed. London: Macmillan.

Documents pour servir à l'histoire de l'élaboration de la Constitution du 4 octobre 1958. (1987–1991). 3 tomes. Paris. La Documentation Francaise.

Drewry, G. ed. (1985a). *The New Select Committees: A Study of the 1979 Reforms*. Oxford: Oxford University Press.

Drewry, G. (1985b). The Ponting Case: Leaking in the Public Interest. *Public Law*. Summer: 203–212.

Drewry, G. (1989). Select Committees and Back-Bench Power. In J. Jowell and D. Oliver, eds. *The Changing Constitution* 2d ed. Oxford: Oxford University Press.

Drouin, M. J. (1990). Comment un Québec souverain pourrait-il recevoir 135,000 fonctionnaires de plus? *La Presse*. 5 avril.

Dwivedi, O. P. and Olowu, D. (1988). Bureaucratic Morality. *International Political Science Review* 9: 1(3–239).

Faligot, R. and Krop, P. (1989). *La Piscine: The French Secret Service Since 1944*. Trans. W. D. Halls. Oxford: Basil Blackwell.

Friedrich, C. J. (1940). The Nature of Administrative Responsibility. *Public Policy*: 3–40.

Greene, I. (1990). Conflict of Interest and the Canadian Constitution: An Analysis of Conflict of Interest Rules for Canadian Cabinet Ministers. *Canadian Journal of Political Science* 23: 233–256.

Hooper, D. (1987). *Official Secrets: The Use and Abuse of the Act*. London: Hodder & Stoughton.

Hunt, M. (1987). Parliament and Official Secrecy. In R. A. Chapman and M. Hunt, eds. *Open Government*. London: Routledge.

Kernaghan, K. and Langford, J. W. (1990). *The Responsible Public Servant*. Halifax: Institute of Public Administration of Canada.

Lester, A. (1989). The Constitution: Decline and Renewal. In Jeffrey Jowell and Dawn Oliver, eds. *The Changing Constitution*, pp. 345–369.

Marshall, T. (1992). Préface. *Théorie et Pratique du Gouvernement Constitutionnel: La France et les Etats-Unis*. Paris: L'Espace Européen.

Mény, Y. (1992). *La Corruption de la République*. Paris: Fayard.

Mercier, J. (1992). Bilan québécois du fédéralisme canadien: perspectives d'un administrativiste. In François Rocher, ed. *Bilan du Fédéralisme Canadien*. Montréal: V. L. B. pp. 177–195.

Nicolson, I. F. (1986). *The Mystery of Crichel Down*. Oxford: Clarendon Press.

Normand, G. (1990). Le PQ promet un ministre aux fonctionnaires fédéraux. *La Presse*. 6 décembre.

Norton, P. (1982). *The Constitution in Flux*. Oxford: Basil Blackwell.

Norton-Taylor, R. (1985). *The Ponting Affair*. London: Cecil Woolf.

Parris, H. (1969). *Constitutional Bureaucracy*. New York: Augustus M. Kelley.

Ponting, C. (1985). *The Right to Know: The Inside Story of the Belgrano Affair*. London: Sphere Books.

Ridley, F. F. (1985). Political Neutrality in the British Civil Service. In *Politics, Ethics and Public Service*. London: Royal Institute of Public Administration.

Rohr, J. A. (1986). *To Run A Constitution: The Legitimacy of the Administrative State*. Lawrence, K. S.: University Press of Kansas.

Rohr, J. A. (1989a). *The President and the Public Administration*. Washington DC: American Historical Association.

Rohr, J. A. (1989b). *Ethics for Bureaucrats: An Essay on Law and Values*, 2nd ed. New York: Marcel Dekker.

Rohr, J. A. (1991). Ethical Issues in French Public Administration: A Comparative Study. *Public Administration Review* 51: 283–297.

Stark, A. (1992). Public-Sector Conflict of Interest at the Federal Level in Canada and the U.S.: Differences in Understanding and Approach. *Public Administration Review* 52: 427–437.

Stark, A. (1993). Public-Sector Conflict of Interest at the Federal Level in Canada and the U.S.: Differences in Understanding and Approach. In H. George Fredrickson, ed. *Ethics and Public Administration*. Armonk, NY: M. E. Sharpe.

Szablowski, G. J. (1992). Administrative Discretion and the Protection of Human Rights: Public Servants Duty to Take Rights Seriously. In R. A. Chapman, ed. *Ethics in Public Service*. Edinburgh: University of Edinburgh Press; and Ottawa: Carlton University Press.

Thomas, R. (1987). The British Official Secrets Act, 1911–1939. In R. A. Chapman and M. Hunt, eds. *Open Government*. London: Routledge.

Thomas, R. (1991). *Esponage and Secrecy: The Official Secrets Act 1911–1989 of the United Kingdom*. London: Routledge.

Thompson, D. (1981). The Moral Responsibility of Public Officials. *American Political Science Review 74*: 905–916.

Turpin, C. (1989). Ministerial Responsibility: Myth or Reality? In J. Jowell and D. Oliver, eds. *The Changing Constitution*, 2nd ed. Oxford: Oxford University Press.

U.S. Merit Systems Protection Board. (1991). *To Meet the Needs of the Nations: Staffing the U.S. Civil Service and the Public Service of Canada*. Washington, D. C.

Vaughn, R. (1981a). The Role of Statutory Regulation of Public Service Ethics in Britain and the United States. *Hastings International and Comparative Law Review 4*: 341–398.

Vaughn, R. (1981b). Implications of the British Experience on Administrative Regulation of Conflicts of Interest in the Federal Civil Service. *American University Law Review 30*: 705–729.

Vipond, R. C. (1991). *Liberty and Community: Canadian Federalism and the Failure of the Constitution*. Albany: SUNY Press.

Whittakee, R. (1988). The RCMP Scandals. In Andrei S. Markovits and Mark Silverstein, eds. *The Politics of Scandal: Power and Process in Liberal Democracies*. New York: Holmes and Meier.

Wilson, J. Q. (1988). *Bureaucracy: What Government Agencies Do and Why They Do It*. New York: Basic Books.

Wilson, W. (1885). *Congressional Government: A Study in American Politics*. Boston: Houghton-Mifflin.

Wolf-Phillips, L. (1968). *Constitutions of Modern States*. New York: Praeger.

33

Administrative Ethics in an African Society
The Case of Zimbabwe

Jonathan N. Moyo
University of the Witwatersrand, Johannesburg, South Africa

This chapter examines administrative ethics in an African society using Zimbabwe as a case study. It should be pointed out from the outset that there is a paucity of specialized literature in this area of public administration in Africa.[1] This, however, is not surprising in view of the fact that administrative scholarship tends to be contextual, following the political environment of the country under analysis. In this regard, the subject of administrative ethics in Africa is better examined and understood in the context of the rapidly changing political experience of the Continent which, for better or worse, has been dominated by colonialism and neocolonialism. This domination has meant that Africa is yet to be understood in its own terms. Otherwise, since the decolonization process in Africa which started in 1957 with the independence of Ghana, most of what has passed as "administration" in Africa has been based on the administrative history of the colonizing countries, mainly Britain, France, Germany and Portugal.

It therefore does not come as a surprise that the dominant view of administrative ethics in Africa has tended to be "law and order" oriented. This is the essence of colonial administrative systems, including their postcolonial offshoots. Virtually throughout Africa, the colonial experience left behind administrative systems which were authoritarian, disciplinarian, and generally hostile to cultural and political influences from indigenous communities. In other words, because of the law and order orientation of colonial administrative systems which were later inherited in toto by independent African countries, the history of administrative ethics in Africa is a history of "imposed obligations,"[2] first by colonialism and later by African nationalism.

Imposed obligations emanate from *objective responsibility* which Cooper has defined in the following manner:

> All objective responsibility involves responsibility to someone, or some collective body, and responsibility for certain tasks, subordinate personnel, and goal achievement. The former is accountability and the latter is obligation. Accountability and obligation, responsibility to someone else for something—these are the dual dimensions of objective administrative responsibility.[3]

But, of course, externally imposed obligations are only one form of administrative responsibility. There is also subjective responsibility which arises out of the individual's own feelings of, and beliefs about, responsibility.[4] Typically, such feelings and beliefs tend to be rooted in the individual's definition of loyalty, conscience, and identification. Insofar as it is based on the individual's personal orientation toward ethical conduct, subjective responsibility is "developed through personal experience."[5]

Be this as it may, it should be obvious that personal experiences do not emerge in a vacuum. Personal identities are expressions of wider cultural and political contexts. For example, it is not possible to believe in being legal without having lived in an environment which values legality. Indeed, it is important to recognize that legality itself is a socially contrived experience. In this sense, objective responsibility and subjective responsibility are inextricably intertwined. They are not separate experiences which alternate or which precede one another.

The importance of subjective responsibility is that it underscores the value of the individual as a rational being capable of moral conduct beyond or outside what is socially imposed. In other words, subjective responsibility gives some room to voluntary action. Furthermore, the distinction between objective responsibility and subjective responsibility allows the student of administrative ethics, and indeed of political and administrative studies, to develop concepts which transcend the socially given. Ethics cannot be simply a matter of objective responsibility, there is more to it than that. Yet, and despite this qualification, it is also true that most societies have attempted to develop administrative systems which are based solely on objective responsibility with all the consequences which come with imposed obligations. This certainly has been the administrative experience in Africa. The case of Zimbabwe provides an instructive illustration of imposed obligations as an *exclusive* source of administrative ethics.

Against this backdrop, administrative ethics in Zimbabwe have been shaped by politics. Not that this in itself is a bad thing. Man is a political animal. The problem, however, is that the type of politics has not been the deliberative kind which allows the individual to exercise "subjective responsibility" along with "objective responsibility." Rather, it has been the kind of manipulative politics which is based on a corrupt notion of the public good, the notion that what is good for the ruling party is good for the public.

In this sense, the state of administrative ethics in Zimbabwe is not unique. It very much reflects the problems of creating and establishing administrative ethics in postcolonial African societies. This problem has several reasons three of which are examined in this chapter: (1) the lack of settled constitutional frameworks, (2) the one man presidential system, and (3) the lack of a fully elaborated administrative state. Countries with such problems, and there are many not only in Africa but throughout the Third World, do not have the presence of some kind of attention to administrative ethics. Before examining these issues in some detail, a history of imposed obligations in Zimbabwe is in order because it goes a long way toward explaining important sources of present day practices and problems in the country's administrative ethics.

I. ORIGINS OF IMPOSED OBLIGATIONS IN ZIMBABWE

Zimbabwe, called by various names at different times by assorted white settler governments, fell under British rule on October 29, 1889, when Queen Victoria granted a Royal Charter of Incorporation to Cecil John Rhodes' British South Africa Company (B.S.A.C.).

This royal charter followed the granting of what is known as the Rudd Concession of 1888 given to Rudd, Maguire, and Thompson by King Lobengula who later repudiated the concession. The King's concession provided, among other things, that "the . . . grantees, their heirs representatives and assigns" would have "complete and exclusive charge over all metals and minerals situated and contained in my kingdoms principalities and dominions."[6]

Queen Victoria's royal charter of October 29, 1889, thus gave blessing to the Rudd Concession, notwithstanding the fact that King Lobengula had by then expressed displeasure with the terms of the concession which he had repudiated by the time the charter was granted to the B.S.A.C. empowered by Queen Victoria to "govern the territory" which was previously under the jurisdiction of King Lobengula. Thus, the royal charter marked the beginning of British colonial rule in Zimbabwe which spanned 90 years from 1890 to 1980 when Zimbabwe became an independent majority ruled state. Right from its inception, the effect of this rule was to put in place an alien administrative system which sought to either wholly supersede traditional authority or to significantly weaken it. This was quite a serious problem because black Zimbabweans already had an extensive and intensive political and administrative history in their country prior to its occupation by the Europeans.

Against this background, two broad phases of the development of the public service in Zimbabwe can be categorized, namely, the colonial and the postindependence periods, with the former extending from 1890 to 1979 and the latter from 1980 to the present. The two periods can be further subdivided as follows.[7]

1. The Royal Chartered Company comprising the early administration under the British South Africa Company: 1890 to 1923;
2. Responsible government comprising (and including (3) and (4) below) all subsequent colonial administrations: 1923 to 1963;
3. The federal government which brought together Malawi, Zambia, and Zimbabwe between 1953 and 1963;
4. The Unilateral Declaration of Independence (UDI) by white settlers led by Ian Smith which lasted between 1965 and 1979 and;
5. The independence period from 1980 to the present.

Each of these periods had decisive influences on the development of the public service in Zimbabwe with far reaching implications on the cultivation of an administrative ethos. It is therefore useful to briefly examine some of the salient features of these periods and to assess their impact on the development of administrative ethics in Zimbabwe.

II. THE PERIOD BETWEEN 1890 AND 1923

It should be pointed out and emphasized here that, before 1889, Zimbabwe did not have a formal public service as it is known today. Generally, there was some kind of a semi-military administration as is typically found in periods of occupation and conquest. This co-existed with a type of administration which was based on traditional authority in the Weberian sense. As such, the civil service was *open*, anybody who was a subject of the King was good and qualified enough to be a civil servant. This open nature of the public service caused some serious problems for the first colonial administrator, Colquhoun, who was appointed because of his administrative experience in colonial India.

Colquhoun resigned within a few weeks of his appointment because he judged himself, "not well suited to working in conditions where all the public institutions had yet to be created on the basis of a legal fiction."[8] In other words, Colquhoun found that Zimbabwe was still under the imperative of traditional authority, and not a model akin to the legal-rational type of authority which he was expecting on the basis of his colonial experience in India. It was therefore not surprising that Colquhoun was replaced by an administrator, Jameson, who was "unversed in official routine, impatient of formality and always prone to take short cuts to achieve his purposes."[9] In a way, Jameson was sensitive to, or at least aware of, the predominance of traditional values in Zimbabwe. This sensitivity and awareness, which was probably by default, turned out to be an advantage to Jameson who apparently dealt expeditiously with the daily problems of the white settler community which was having difficulties settling down in an African society.[10]

Jameson's administrative style was, however, not acceptable to the B.S.A.C. which had been empowered to "govern the territory" by the royal charter. Cecil John Rhodes replaced Jameson and brought in individuals whom he considered to be experienced administrators from the Cape province in South Africa who "set up a permanent civil service on Cape lines."[11] These administrative experts were given the responsibility of general administration and the "dispensation of justice" working alongside white officials in the Native Department which "primarily dealt with African matters . . . assisted by Native Chiefs who drew a small salary, and whom the law regarded in the light of hereditary village constables devoid of judicial powers."[12]

Against the experience of this background, Government Notice No. 6 was promulgated on January 11, 1898 with the effect of establishing the very first regulations which defined the beginning of a formal public service in Zimbabwe. The notice declared that,

> The Civil Service of Rhodesia shall include and consist of all persons appointed by the Administrator who are continuously employed in the discharge of duties, other than purely police or military, in any department of the Public Service, not being Judges of the High Court or members of the personal staff of the Administration.[13]

What was significant about these regulations, especially in terms of their subsequent impact on the development of an administrative ethos in Zimbabwe, is that the authority in their interpretation and meaning rested in their origin in the Cape administration in South Africa. This was explicitly stated in Section 17 of the regulations which declared that,

> In the workings and interpretation of these Regulations, and of the rules and regulations framed thereunder, reference shall be made to the Civil Service Acts, Rules and Regulations of the Cape Colony, and, in all cases not provided for, the Administrator may follow the provisions of the said Cape Acts, Rules and Regulations.[14]

It is important to underscore the point that these regulations formed the basis of the development of the public service in Zimbabwe. For this reason, and having in mind the possible impact of the regulations on the development of administrative ethics, there are several problems which should be highlighted. In the first place, it should be noted that the regulations excluded the indigenous African population from meaningfully participating in the public service on racial grounds. This was somewhat of an irony because the regulations did not actually specify race as a factor in qualifying for employment in the public service mainly because the regulations were fashioned on the generally liberal tradition of the Cape province in South Africa. Black Africans were excluded in practice because of their lack of literacy which disqualified them from serving in the public service. This was because the regulations specified that the administrator could appoint to the fixed establishment of the civil service:

(a) Any person who has been transferred, at the date of passing of this Ordinance, to the Civil Service from the service of the trustees under the will of the late Right Honor able Cecil John Rhodes;

(b) Members of the British South African Police transferred to the Civil Service after not less than 3 years and not more than 10 years service in such Police;

(c) Persons transferred, at the date of the passing of this Ordinance, to the Civil Service from the non-administrative service of the British South Africa Company and;

(d) Technical officers, teachers, matrons, nurses, persons under agreement for fixed periods and temporary officers.[15]

These specifications which did not include race had a de facto effect of excluding Africans because none met the criteria for self-evident reasons. Therefore, right from the beginning, the development of the culture and values of the public service in Zimbabwe involved the systematic exclusion of the majority of the population. An imported administrative system, with colonial values from the Cape province in South Africa and a heavy dosage of British influences, was imposed in a wholesale fashion without regard to local values which were prejudicially considered to be either inferior or uncivilized.

Indeed, the regulations imagined black Africans to be prone to lawlessness. Hence, the regulations had a strong element of control, law maintenance, and tax collection which began with the 1894 "hut tax."[16] Thus, as far as black Africans were concerned, the colonial administrative system was about law and order maintenance and tax collection. This orientation gave the colonial public service a racial dimension which had no regard to the professional and moral development of the indigenous population.

III. THE PERIOD BETWEEN 1923 AND 1980

It should stand to reason that a company cannot run a country. The fact that the B.S.A.C. governed Zimbabwe between 1889 and 1923 is a historical oddity peculiar to Zimbabwe. By 1920 the B.S.A.C. had lost the capacity to govern the country not only because of challenges from the indigenous population but also from white settlers who had become politically assertive, demanding independence and a national identity. However, at the time, the more decisive pressures came from the white farming class which was emerging as a rural bourgeoisie seeking to be independent from South African capital and politics.[17]

The pressures on the B.S.A.C. eventually led to the holding of a whites-only referendum in 1923 to determine the magnitude of white opinion on the political status of the territory. The referendum asked whites to decide whether they wanted "their" territory incorporated as a fifth province of South Africa, or if they wanted the territory to be a self-governing colony with a "responsible government." The whites participating in the referendum voted by a margin of 60% in favor of a self-governing colony. Thus Zimbabwe, then called Southern Rhodesia, attained the status of a "responsible government" under Government Notice Number 2 of October 1, 1923. The notice, given under the authority of the British government, established six divisions of government, namely, the Premier, the Treasury, the Attorney-General, Mines and Works, Agriculture and Lands, and the Colonial Office. These divisions created a new form of government in Zimbabwe with far reaching implications on the development of the public service.

These divisions effectively ended company rule in Zimbabwe. However, this did not mean the end of white rule and the emergence of an all inclusive political system. Quite the contrary, the vote actually served to entrench white settler domination in Zimbabwe. In 1928, the "responsible government" established in 1923 undertook to review regulations and procedures on personnel administration in the public sector. The review produced a Civil Service Consolidated Bill which was enacted in 1931 as the Public Service Act. This act superseded all previous acts, ordinances, and regulations governing the public service. The act provided for a complete reorganization of the service including precise definitions of who qualified to be a civil servant.

As to who qualified to be members of the civil service, Section 8 (1) of the 1931 Act provided that,

> The service shall consist of all persons in the employment of the colony and included in:
> (a) the administrative and clerical division;
> (b) the schools division;
> (c) the professional and technical division;
> (d) the general division; (but shall not include any native or colored person).

What is notable about the 1931 Public Service Act is that blacks (referred to as natives) and people of mixed blood (referred to as coloreds) were openly excluded from serving in the public service. This was not surprising as it was a recognition of prevailing practice. Also, by 1931 there was already a formidable regime of legal instruments which discriminated against black Africans and other people of color. Specifically, racial relations had been blighted by a panoply of previous enactments, notably the Native Regulations (1898); the Hut Tax (1894); the Pass System (1895); the Order-in-Council reserving Native Reserves (1920); the Native Affairs Act (1928) and the Land Apportionment Act (1930).

By 1955, the public service had come under intense political pressures from African nationalists who were demanding majority rule. The pressures forced the government to set up a committee tasked to "report and revise the salary scales and conditions of service for African employees in the government."[18] When the committee got down to its work, it focused its attention on what it considered three fundamental factors:

1. African ability to assume service duties and responsibilities;
2. The attitude of the European population to African advancement of this nature and;
3. The socio-economic issues which were involved.

The first two factors deserve some brief review in order to underscore the racial values which have influenced the development of the public service in Zimbabwe. The committee defined African ability as "a compound quality" comprising intelligence and character "which latter in turn involves and demands honesty, loyalty, reliability, faithfulness and a sense of responsibility."[19] The committee argued that these were vital qualities needed in a good civil servant, conceding that the African could not be rated lower than the European if the educational opportunity were to be made available but the committee doubted the African character arguing that it could not measure up to that of the European.[20]

Arguing that the "European-type of character" was necessary to keep the standards and ethics of the public service which was dominated by whites, the committee maintained that the African was unable to acquire the "European-type character" owing to his ethnological background and behavioral characteristics.[21] To buttress its patently racial view, the committee claimed that experience throughout Africa had demonstrated that Africans "have been found too frequently to be unreliable and untrustworthy when placed in positions of even minor responsibility."[22] From this reasoning, the committee concluded that the African had to be precluded from employment in the public service on terms equal to those of whites.

Another controversial issue examined by the committee was the European attitude toward the possibility of African advancement in the public service. As expected, the committee concluded that whites would not accept Africans to be employed in the public service "in positions in which [the Africans] could direct the actions and activities of Europeans on an individualistic basis."[23] For example, the committee reported that it was particularly concerned about the prospect of white women sharing offices and common sanitary facilities with African women!

In 1959, when pressures for black majority rule were mounting not only in Zimbabwe but throughout British colonies in Africa following the independence of Ghana in 1957, Parliament in Zimbabwe passed a motion which declared that, "In the opinion of this House, the time has now come to admit non-Europeans to the Southern Rhodesian Civil Service."[24] This declaration was made with all sorts of assurances to whites such as that no African would immediately assume a high post in the civil service since such an eventuality would take at least 30 years. Other assurances were that no African would be assigned to work in European areas. A bill was eventually introduced in Parliament with provisions which accommodated these assurances. The bill was debated in emotional terms and with a lot of acrimony within the white community. In the final analysis, the bill was adopted and enacted into law on January 1, 1961, a date which is a milestone in the history of the civil service in Zimbabwe as it marked the first time Africans were allowed to serve in the fixed establishment.

This development triggered a white backlash which led to the defeat of the incumbent government in the 1962 whites-only elections. To make matters worse, the backlash which lasted for a few years coincided with the political independence of neighboring countries, Malawi and Zambia. The situation got worse when, on November 11, 1965, Ian Smith's Rhodesia Front party made a Unilateral Declaration of Independence (UDI), vowing never to surrender to African majority rule in a thousand years. Thus, the period between 1965 and 1980 witnessed entrenched racial conflict in Zimbabwe, resulting in a protracted armed struggle by African nationalists. During the struggle, more than 60,000 people were killed and several times many more were displaced and left homeless. The struggle finally led to Zimbabwe's independence on April 18, 1980 after the successful conclusion of the Lancaster Talks held in London the previous year.

IV. THE PERIOD FROM 1980

When Zimbabwe became independent in 1980, the new black-led government inherited a public service which had a white hierarchy. Previous regimes had systematically excluded blacks by law, as shown in the preceding sections of this chapter. What made the task of the new government formidable is that the new constitution had been a result of compromise which entrenched the protection of white settlers, especially officers in the public service. Among other things, the new constitution guaranteed:

1. The safeguarding of white settler economic interests in the name of ensuring continuity and efficiency in the public service;
2. The retention of managerial and technical staff to sustain confidence in the new government not only by the local white community but also by potential investors from outside the country;
3. Safeguarding of the pensions of those civil servants who chose to take early retirement with the guarantee that the pension could be remitted in foreign currency if the recipient so chose.

This scenario is typical of the emergence of the civil service elsewhere in African countries moving from colonialism to independence. There was a clear and present need for the redressing of the historical problems of racism in the public service. Cognizant of these considerations, the first president of Zimbabwe, Reverend C. Banana proclaimed a directive to the Public Service Commission which sought to promote African advancement in the public service.

The directive, given in terms of Section 75 (2) of the Zimbabwe Constitution agreed at the Lancaster Talks which ended the armed struggle for majority rule, first noted the following:

(a) The major tasks of the Government in resettlement, education, reconstruction and development will make great demands on the Public Service. It will be necessary to expand the service to discharge this growing range of tasks, and the African people of Zimbabwe must be afforded increasing opportunities of playing their full part in these developments.

(b) At present [1980] the great majority of senior posts in the Public Service are filled by European officers. The government continues to need the services of these officers to ensure a high standard of efficiency in carrying out these new and expanding programmes. The Government wants to assure all European officers that it will continue to protect their terms of service and support the Public Service Commission in its statutory duties, that it will maintain the integrity of the service, and that it is confident that the impending expansion of the service will offer them continuing prospects of satisfying careers.

(c) To achieve full African involvement in these developments by orderly steps the following general directions of policy are given to the Public Service Commission under Section 75 (2) of the Constitution of Zimbabwe:
    (i)   to recruit staff to all grades of the Public Service in such a manner as will bring about the balanced representation of the various elements which make up the population of Zimbabwe;
    (ii) to give more rapid advancement to suitably qualified Africans in appointments and promotions to senior posts in the Public Service;
    (iii) in carrying out these directions, to have due regard to the maintenance of a high state of efficiency within the Public Service and the need to satisfy the career aspirations of existing Public Servants and;
    (iv) to make an annual report on progress.

(d) The objective is the early creation of a balanced service fully representative of all elements of the population and with the skills appropriate to the country's needs. For this a greater training effort will be required.[25]

The preface of *The Presidential Directive*, (a) and (b) above, underscored the new direction of the public service in independent Zimbabwe. The new government had initiated programs in the areas of resettlement of families displaced during the war and had committed itself to massive expansion of educational and health facilities to cater to the majority of black Africans who had been previously marginalized during colonial rule. The chosen instrument for realizing these objectives was the public service which was going to be used to afford the African people of Zimbabwe "opportunities of playing their full part" in the government's programs.

It is also clear from its preface that *The Presidential Directive* served as a convenient platform for expressing the government's unhappiness with the fact that a great majority of senior posts in the 45,000 strong public service were filled by European officers. This observation was more important than the government's attempt to assure the European officers that their jobs were secure in an independent Zimbabwe embodied in (b) above. The assurance was a political statement without a basis in the facts of what was an impending overhaul of the public service promised under (c) above. The government was indeed in a hurry to bring about the "early creation of a balanced service fully representative of all elements of the population."

A major reason for the hurry was that the new government found itself unhappily relying on the services of the white officers who had served the previous colonial governments against black majority rule. There was a strong belief, real or imagined, that the white civil servants did not subscribe to the policies of the new government and that they were going to use every available opportunity to frustrate the new policies. The impact of this belief was quite real considering that out of a total of 10,570 established posts at independence only 3,368 (or 31.86%) were occupied by blacks who did not hold a rank higher than that of a Senior Administrative Assistant.

The black government which, like many others elsewhere in Africa at independence, professed to be committed to socialism and feared that the white civil servants were committed capitalists who would not have anything to do with implementing the government's socialist objectives.

V. THE NEW POLITICIZATION OF THE PUBLIC SERVICE

It should be obvious from the foregoing that the public service in Zimbabwe was, since its inception, highly politicized. Between 1889 and 1980, the politicization was done by successive white settler governments which employed the politics of race to influence the development of the civil service ethics as a white preserve. The postindependence period saw the emergence of a new era in which race was replaced by the politics of African nationalism accompanied by the euphoria of independence. One student of the public service observed that,

> Immediately after independence there appeared to be a serious commitment on the part of the civil servants to execute government programs with a zeal. The basis for this commitment was two-fold: First was the keenness to build a socialist society which the liberation movements had espoused during the struggle for independence. There was enthusiasm in reconstructing the country following years of white and minority domination. Many people wanted to play a part in building a new social order with new ethics and wanted to apply a new social theory in management and administration

. . . Second was the excitement that blacks could now rule themselves. The majority of people wanted to show the world that they were efficient in management of resources even if they had little experience.[26]

This enthusiasm to serve in the "new" public service was understandable. Zimbabweans expected the colonial and UDI attitudes which discriminated against the black community to change with the advent of independence in 1980. But this did not happen. Instead of rectifying the situation at independence, the ruling Zimbabwe African National Union-Patriotic Front (ZANU-PF) party sought to take maximum advantage of the un- and under-developed civil society within the black community by claiming that it was the sole legitimate representative of the people. Under this claim, the party declared itself as the umbrella organization of all social movements and went about destroying civil society in the name of the revolution which had defeated colonialism. All "legitimate" organizations, which would normally serve as outlets for competing moral values, were challenged to join the ruling party as a way of proving their revolutionary commitments.

Following its election in 1980, ZANU-PF declared 1981 as "the year of the consolidation of the people's power" which, according to the party's president who was then prime minister, Robert Mugabe, impelled his ruling party to "adopt a more comprehensive and a more generous view of Government embracing all these [pre-independence revolutionary] forces."[27] The need for such a comprehensive view of government was interpreted by the ZANU-PF leadership and supporters to mean the establishment of a one party state. Youth and women's brigades of the party held numerous demonstrations throughout 1981 calling for a one party state. At one of these rallies, Mugabe rhetorically asked the cheering crowd, "Smith declared UDI [unilateral declaration of independence]—why can't we declare a one party state?"[28] He argued that demands for a one party state should be preceded by the laying of a strong foundation of ZANU-PF support throughout the country. Earlier Mugabe threatened to ban Ian Smith's Republican Party (RF) in an angry reaction to a statement by a white member of Parliament who had said "a one party state was not in the interest of the country and could turn the government into a dictatorship."[29] Mugabe said:

> He [Dennis Divaris, RF member of Parliament] is averse to a one party state. What sort of rule have we had in this country from 1890 to 1980? Specifically from 1964 to 1979? . . . There was nothing preventing the government from banning the RF, and using the same tactics the RF had used against black nationalists parties while it was in power. But banning the party would give it prominence and it could pretend to be a democratic institution. . . . We [ZANU-PF] are still committed to the principle of a one party state but will not bring it about until the people of Zimbabwe desire it. The time will come when we can address ourselves to that question much more forcefully.[30]

On the eve of 1981 he told the nation that, "As Zimbabweans, our new nation now demanded of us either as individuals, or as groups or communities, *a single loyalty* that is a proper and logical manifestation of our national unity and spirit of reconciliation."[31]

By "a single loyalty," Mugabe meant loyalty not to the nation but to his ruling party. In effect, he was making a plea for a legislated one party state because in his words, "we are one state with one society and one nation, that is the political concept we cherish."[32] In essence, therefore, the ruling party was going to be the only source of single loyalty which would inform and shape the values of the public service which the new government had identified as the most viable instrument for transforming the country.

Those social groups which tried to resist ZANU-PF's tactic of exclusion by inclusion, under the guise of "one state, one society and one nation," were branded as sellouts bent on working for "the enemy" as the party publicly touted its commitment to a legislated one party socialist state. This had quite an impact on the development of administrative ethics in the public service as politicians openly called on civil servants to secure their jobs by joining the ruling party. Public statements were issued indicating that ZANU-PF was determined to ensure that civil servants are loyal to the ruling party to allow for effective implementation of the party's directives in economic, political, and social spheres. A ranking government minister who was then responsible for home affairs, Enos Nkala, complained about civil servants whom he accused of sabotaging government policies saying, "these civil servants' only qualifications are academic degrees and diplomas. They are not committed to the people oriented policies of the ZANU-PF Government. To redress this, there will be a political vetting of civil servants."[33]

Later, the prime minister, Robert Mugabe, supported this view telling Parliament that under a one party state, which his government was working towards, civil servants would have to "accept the complete ideological direction of ZANU or become non members of the public service."[34] Mugabe further argued that,

> We are proceeding to a one-party state. . . . Those we elect to top Government positions must be members who are conscious of the political policies of the party, those who espouse the views and the direction and ideology of the party. Otherwise it doesn't serve any useful purpose having a one-party state. In other words, *if we have adopted socialism as we have done, as the ideology of the country, we can't afford to have the luxury of members in the public service or in other institutions of Government whose views are opposed to the political ideology and the socio-economic direction of the country.* That would be a contradiction . . . [35] [emphasis added]

These pressures on the public service continued throughout Zimbabwe's first decade of independence. As late as 1990, leading politicians in government continued to call on civil servants who were not members of the ruling party to quit the civil service. For example, a former Speaker of Parliament, Didymus Mutasa, publicly challenged civil servants "who did not agree with the principles of the Government"[36] Mutasa argued that,

> Anyone who does not whole heartedly accept the principles of the ZANU (PF) Government should, quite honestly, not seek to work for it. What will he do in a government whose policies he does not believe in? . . . Shouldn't we really be rid of such subversive elements in our midst and shouldn't they, in fact, take their skills and apply them, quite honestly, in an institution and at a workplace where they are happy?[37]

This challenge to civil servants was repeated hardly a month later by the government's Minister of Home Affairs who was also the ruling party's Secretary for the Commissariat, Moven Mahachi, who complained that, "we do not want civil servants who do not want our policies, to be employed by us. They cannot effectively carry out and implement the policies they do not agree with."[38] A year later, Mahachi sparked even more controversy by calling on members of the ruling party to supervise civil servants.[39] Arguing that Zimbabweans owed their freedom and the country's independence to his party, Mahachi maintained, using banal arguments typical in one party state societies, that "the party is supreme to Government. . . . The Politburo supervises the Cabinet. The Central Committee supervises Parliament. So the party's provincial executive should also supervise the work of civil servants in their respective areas."[40]

These pressures on civil servants forced the Public Service Review Commission of Zimbabwe to conclude that the country's public service was under undue political influences. The commission reported that,

> Both members of the public and civil servants spoke feelingly about the problems arising from various forms of political interference in public offices and the confused relationship between politicians, public servants and the public. As for the influence of politicians on appointments, public servants described the public service as "warped with tribalism." They alleged that "Africanisation" of the public service at independence resulted in a "political service" to which unqualified people came in the name of the Party, leading to tribalism, nepotism, regionalism and favoritism.[41]

VI. THE ETHICAL CONTENT OF THE PUBLIC SERVICE

As pointed out at the beginning of this chapter, social scientists interested in studying administrative ethics in Africa immediately find that the field has a paucity of literature. This lack of literature is due to the fact that virtually all African countries are still more preoccupied with political questions of establishing new polities than those of administration. The reasons for this are not difficult to understand. African nation-states are still struggling entities largely because of political problems associated with their recent post-colonial history. With the exception of Ethiopia which did not experience much of colonialism, the majority of countries in Africa got their political freedom between 1957 and 1968. A few others, such as Angola and Mozambique, had to wait until the mid-1970s while yet others, such as Zimbabwe and Namibia, which got their independence in 1980 and 1989 respectively, had to wait even longer. In South Africa, serious talks aimed at ending apartheid rule only started in 1992.

By and large, and without basing this observation on a deterministic approach to politics, it is true that countries preoccupied with fundamental questions of political order tend to take administrative considerations for granted or to relegate them to a secondary level. Put differently, emerging states are more concerned with *genetic* questions of how to put in place a new republic than with *functional* questions about how to sustain the republic in administrative terms. An instructive parallel to this is found in the United States.

Between the period of the founding of the American Republic and the Civil War, the emerging United States body politic was chiefly concerned with framing a workable constitution, and less with running or implementing one. During this period, the role of administrators was either taken as a given or altogether ignored, as American society was moving from an agrarian to an industrial base. This ambiguity about the nature and purpose of the administrative role led to the spoils system, a practice in which the political party winning an election would reward its campaign workers and other active supporters by appointments to government posts. Until it was challenged by meritocrats, the spoils system encouraged political activity by public administrators in support of their party, and it thus involved the removal from office of employees belonging to a party losing an election so that a change in a party necessarily meant a change in the personnel composition of the civil service. The spoils system in the United States slowly disappeared as a predominant value as public attention shifted from worrying about framing a workable constitution to being concerned about implementing the constitution.

This shift brought administrative questions into focus with the attending interest in administrative ethics as the American society moved from a liberal state in the political sense to an administrative state. Concern about administrative ethics in the United States is thus linked to the rise of the administrative state run by a managerial elite which claims its legitimacy on professional as opposed to political grounds. It follows from this that questions of administrative ethics are better understood in the context of an operation theory of the state. That is to say, in order to understand administrative ethics, we must first examine the theory of the state in the particular environment of our concern. But, since our interest here is in administrative ethics, an understanding of the theory of the state which has informed administrative practice in Africa would be useful.

VII. THE STATE IN AFRICA

There is a consensus among students of African politics that the state in independent Africa is the engine of social and economic development. This consensus, however, poses a fundamental problem in that the African state is also known to be generally disorganized and without a requisite resource dowry to facilitate effective state involvement in national affairs. Part of the reason why the state in Africa plays a crucial role in the process of resource allocation is that in most of Africa, the arena of civil society, the social sphere outside the state, is characterized by wide and deep conditions of material deprivation. In fact, the scope of civil society in most African nations is much poorer than the sphere dominated by the state apparatus. As a result, there are no economic opportunities which exist outside the state.

The effect of this situation is that the state in Africa has an unrivalled position within its territorial boundaries and this fact alone gives the African state its preeminent political role. In his study of state politics in Zimbabwe, Jeffrey Herbst cites various commentators who have concluded that employment in the modern sector in Africa is often employment by government.[42] Control of the state apparatus brings the ability to reward and to coerce. Private wealth is scattered in most countries, and power and status frequently stem from a place in or access to the state apparatus. Elites in Africa derive their power from control of the state, not from private property or private large-scale organizations.

It is therefore not very surprising that, more often than not, the elite who take over power from colonial settlers tend to be prone to increasing the size of the state at the expense of the private sector, i.e., civil society. Thus, the expansion of the state sphere in Africa tends to generate the scourge of patronage politics with all its negative consequences on good governance, especially the ethical dimensions of administrative accountability and responsibility. This scourge has prompted some observers to conclude that the key to understanding state politics in Africa is personal rule defined as,

> A system of relations linking rulers not with the "public or even with the ruled (at least not directly), but with patrons, associates, clients, supporters, and rivals, who constitute the "system." If personal rulers are restrained, it is by the limits of their personal authority and power and by the authority and power of patrons, associates, clients, supporters, and of course, rivals."[43]

A telling affirmation of personal rule in Africa was provided by President Daniel Arap Moi of Kenya who astonishingly made the following proclamation in 1984,

> I call on all ministers, assistant ministers and every other person to sing like parrots. During Mzee Kenyatta's period, I persistently sang the Kenyatta tone until some people said: "This fellow has nothing to say except to sing for Kenyatta." Therefore you ought to sing the song I sing. If I put a full stop you should put a full stop. This is how the country will move forward.[44]

The system of personal rule in Africa, epitomized by the above quotation, has had a decisive impact on the possibilities for developing a stable public service with an independent professional and moral ethic. This is because the African presidential system poses a basic threat to the job security of civil servants. As one observer noted.

> The presidential system [has] not been accompanied by any changes in the parliamentary hierarchical structure of the civil service. The countries are operating White House type government with Whitehall type civil services. This is causing great strain and stress to the civil service. The greatest strain is the threat which the new political system poses to the integrity, authority and security of the service. In almost every African state, the installation of a new president is accompanied by a series of retirements or termination of the appointments of top civil servants. In 1975 over 1,000 public officers in Nigeria lost their jobs on the coming into power of a new Head of Government. . . . Outsiders and some relatively junior officers are usually appointed as replacements. Even when replacements come from within the service, they are appointed without due regard to civil service norms and procedures.[45]

While the argument of personal rule has had wide currency among students of African politics, and while it has indeed defined the conduct of politics throughout Africa, it nevertheless has some serious problems relating to its marginalization of, not only the historical background to the state in Africa but also, the institutional and structural dimensions of African states. This problem has been examined by many radical scholars who have sought to argue that state formation in Africa is influenced and shaped by the imperatives of international capital. Writing about this influence, a noted radical Zimbabwean political scientist, Ibbo Mandaza, observed that,

> The post-white settler state [such as Zimbabwe] is more than just a neo-colonial state. It is born fettered and historically constrained by the midwife of imperialism; and in growing, it has to contend with the former white settlers who, by their economic, social and political existence, also influence the nature and direction of the state.[46]

Mandaza's point deserves careful attention because of the tendency of many observers, especially the liberals outside Africa, to exaggerate the omnipotence of the state in Africa. While the state is obviously an important and indeed decisive social agency in Africa as it is elsewhere, this does not, however, mean that there are no equally or more powerful social forces outside the state sphere but within and beyond its territorial boundaries. The "political" should not be viewed and analyzed outside the "economic." Settler-states like Zimbabwe are characterized by the existence of a significant settler population previously associated with colonial rule. For obvious historical reasons, the settler community tends to be well organized, even better organized, than the state.

In some policy cases, the settler community tends to prevail over the state because of the former's sheer superiority in terms of organizational competence and capacity. This has certainly been the case in Zimbabwe where the autonomy of the state has been significantly structurally constrained by an externally negotiated constitution and situationally constrained by the settler white community which benefited during some 90 years of colonial rule between 1890 and 1980 and thus has more resources than the state in commerce, industry, and agriculture upon which the state heavily depends. Therefore, an examination of civil society in Zimbabwe, which ipso facto would be an examination of alternative value premises for administrators, must take account of the existence of relatively well organized and powerful economic forces outside the state sphere. With this understanding of the role of the state in Africa in mind, the following section discusses the politics-administration dichotomy as a most relevant concept for explaining administrative ethics in Africa.

VIII. THE POLITICS-ADMINISTRATION DICHOTOMY

The context of administrative ethics in any country is defined by that country's structure of the relationship between politics and administration. This relationship has been, following the history of the spoils system in the United States, conceptually defined by the politics-administration dichotomy. The dichotomy is an important pillar in the study of administrative ethics in particular and public administration in general. This is despite the fact that, in the United States, there is now almost a consensus that the dichotomy is a dead issue. The view that the dichotomy is dead has been based on the consideration that a major characteristic of the administrative state is the predominance of the exercise of administrative discretion by bureaucrats.

In the administrative state, it is usually argued by those who question the purpose of the politics-administration dichotomy, administrators have freedom to make choices which determine how a policy is implemented. This freedom results in a type of interaction between politics and administration which is radically different from that envisioned by the classical Wilsonian politics-administration dichotomy. As Terry L. Cooper has noted,

> In the modern administrative state the role of the career public administrator must be accounted for in some way. Since administrators are close to the problems, possess specialized knowledge and technical expertise, have ongoing relationships with their clientele groups, and tend to maintain longer tenure in government than most politicians, they appear to be essential participants in the democratic educational process.[47]

Research on administrative discretion has shown that as discretion increases, the scope and frequency of choice also increases such that the exercise of greater choice decreases the administrator's adherence to policy goals. This then gives rise to the need for an administrative ethic to "control" the exercise of administrative discretion in order to avoid goal displacement in the administrative state.

The significance of administrative discretion cannot be doubted. What is doubtful is whether its exercise necessarily renders the politics-administration dichotomy irrelevant or meaningless. Some thought should be given to the consideration that the significance of the dichotomy has less to do with the exercise of administrative discretion and more to do with the overall political environment within which administrators work. The political environment of the administrative state, which is dominated by questions of how to implement a particular constitutional order, is likely to lead to a situation in which administrators play a pivotal role. On the other hand, a political environment in which the body politic is concerned about framing a constitution is likely to lead to a situation in which politicians play a more pivotal role than administrators.

Therefore, the politics-administration dichotomy is more about indicating whether politicians or administrators play a *pivotal* role in a given political system. During the spoils system in the United States, politicians were pivotal for the simple reason that the American Republic had not settled down. Later on during the industrialization of the United States, especially from the 1920s onwards, the political environment demanded professional administrative attention as administrators increasingly played a pivotal role in sustaining the industrial society. It is this context which has given impetus to increased discretion among administrators in the United States with the consequence of raising fundamental questions of administrative ethics. In Africa, the situation has been radically different.

This is not to say that administrators in Africa do not exercise discretion like their counterparts elsewhere. They do. However, the difference is that administrators in Africa still operate under a heavy cloud of explicit and direct political influences similar to those which were common during the spoils system in the United States. It is one thing to exercise administrative discretion in a political environment seeking to frame a constitution and another to exercise it in a relatively stable environment, with entrenched "regime values," concerned about running a constitution. In either case, there is a whole lot of administrative discretion save for the fact that in the former, discretion is exercised toward a political direction while it is exercised toward professional administration in the latter case.

When Andrew Jackson was inaugurated as the seventh president of the United States in 1829, his defense of the spoils system was not a repudiation of administrative discretion but a plea for a *particular* kind of discretion which was politically inclined. It is in this context that Andrew Jackson argued that rotation of public office in accordance with electoral results would safeguard against the danger of public servants acquiring "a habit of looking with indifference upon the public interests and of tolerating conduct from which unpracticed men would revolt." The essence of this argument was that the spoils system is the only personnel system compatible with democracy and democratic government. Jacksonian spoilsmen maintained that basic principles of democracy demand that appointed officeholders should be subjected to elected officials who, in their turn, are responsible to the people. This is exactly the argument which has dominated the debate on administrative ethics in Africa.

But the argument is facing new challenges as African countries have come under the grip of the tide toward democratic transitions propelled by demands for radical economic reforms in favor of market economies. The challenges are likely to refocus attention from genetic questions, which are largely political, to functional issues, which are largely administrative. Administrators will then be properly viewed as governors in their own right, not just as pawns of ruling politicians as has been the case so far. This eventuality is likely to lead to an interest in administrative ethics never before seen in the newly independent African nations such as Zimbabwe.

ENDNOTES

1. For a general treatment of the subject see *African Public Services: Challenges and a Profile for the Future* [compiled by the African Association for Public Administration and Management] Vikas Publishing House, Pvt. Ltd., Sahibabad, India, 1984.
2. The notion of "imposed obligations" is derived from Terry L. Cooper's explanation of Mosher's concept of "objective responsibility," which he distinguishes from "subjective responsibility." See Cooper's *The Responsible Administrator: An Approach to Ethics for the Administrative Role* Jossey-Bass Publishers, San Francisco, 1990, pp. 59–71.

3. T. L. Cooper, *The Responsible Administrator: An Approach to Ethics for the Administrative Role* (3rd ed.), Jossey-Bass Publishers, San Francisco, 1990, p. 60.

4. T. L. Cooper, *The Responsible Administrator: An Approach to Ethics for the Administrative Role* (3rd ed.), Jossey-Bass Publishers, San Francisco, 1990, p. 71.

5. T. L. Cooper, *The Responsible Administrator: An Approach to Ethics for the Administrative Role* (3rd ed.), Jossey-Bass Publishers, San Francisco, 1990.

6. The following sections draw quite considerably from the "Report of the Public Service Review Commission of Zimbabwe," Volume 2, Appendices, Government Printers, Harare, May 1989, pp. 14–32.

7. See Note 6.

8. "Report of the Public Service Review Commission of Zimbabwe," p. 16.

9. "Report of the Public Service Review Commission of Zimbabwe."

10. "Report of the Public Service Review Commission of Zimbabwe."

11. "Report of the Public Service Review Commission of Zimbabwe."

12. "Report of the Public Service Review Commission of Zimbabwe."

13. "Report of the Public Service Review Commission of Zimbabwe," p. 16–17.

14. "Report of the Public Service Review Commission of Zimbabwe."

15. "Report of the Public Service Review Commission of Zimbabwe."

16. "Report of the Public Service Review Commission of Zimbabwe."

17. See Rukudzo Murapa, "Race and the Public Service in Zimbabwe: 1890–1923," (mimeograph), University of Zimbabwe, Harare, p. 3.

18. The author is grateful to Rukudzo Murapa for the following discussion on the committee set up in 1955 to review the conditions of service for Africans, see "Race and the Public Service in Zimbabwe: 1890–1923," pp. 8–13.

19. "Race and the Public Service in Zimbabwe: 1890–1923," p. 10.

20. "Race and the Public Service in Zimbabwe: 1890–1923."

21. "Race and the Public Service in Zimbabwe: 1890–1923."

22. "Race and the Public Service in Zimbabwe: 1890–1923."

23. "Race and the Public Service in Zimbabwe: 1890–1923," p. 11.

24. "Race and the Public Service in Zimbabwe: 1890–1923," p. 14.

25. See "The Presidential Directive," Government Printers, (Harare, Zimbabwe, May 22, 1980), pp. 1–2.

26. See S. Agere, "The Promotion of Good Ethical Standards and Behavior in Public Services in Africa," (unpublished manuscript with no date), University of Zimbabwe, Harare.

27. See "Consolidation of New Power" in *The Herald*. Harare, Zimbabwe, January 1, 1981.

28. See "Thousands in One-Party State Demo" in *The Herald*. Harare, Zimbabwe, September 21, 1981.

29. See "We can Ban RF, Says Mugabe" in *The Herald*. Harare, Zimbabwe, July 24, 1981.

30. See "We can Ban RF, Says Mugabe" in *The Herald*. Harare, Zimbabwe, July 24, 1981.

31. "Consolidation of New Power" in *The Herald*. Harare, Zimbabwe, January 1, 1981.

32. "No One-Party State Yet, Mugabe" in *The Herald* Harare, Zimbabwe, August 5, 1982.

33. See "Civil Servants Must be Loyal to Party—Nkala," *The Herald*. Harare, Zimbabwe, September 22, 1983.

34. "One-Party State means Zanu Public Service," *The Herald*. Harare, Zimbabwe, September 13, 1984).

35. "One-Party State means Zanu Public Service," *The Herald*. Harare, Zimbabwe, September 13, 1984.

36. See "Back Zanu (PF) or Quit the Civil Service—Mutasa," *in The Herald*. Harare, Zimbabwe, June 24, 1990.

37. See "Back Zanu (PF) or Quit the Civil Service—Mutasa," *in The Herald*. Harare, Zimbabwe, June 24, 1990.

38. See "Civil Servants Told to Back Policies or Quit," *The Herald*. Harare, Zimbabwe, July 4, 1990.

39. See "Zanu (PF) Members Should Supervise Civil Servants," *The Herald*. Harare, Zimbabwe, June 30, 1991.
40. See "Zanu (PF) Members Should Supervise Civil Servants," *The Herald*. Harare, Zimbabwe, June 30, 1991.
41. See "Report of the Public Service Review Commission of Zimbabwe" (Volume Two, Appendices), Government Printer, Harare, May 1989, p. 8.
42. Jeffrey Herbst, *State Politics in Zimbabwe*. Harare, Zimbabwe: University of Zimbabwe Publications, 1990, pp. 2–6.
43. Robert H. Jackson and Carl G. Rosberg, *Personal Rule in Black Africa: Prince, Autocrat, Prophet and Tyrant*. Berkeley, California: University of California Press, 1982, p. 19.
44. Quoted from *The Daily Nation*. Nairobi, Kenya: 14 September 1984.
45. See Chief J. O. Udoji, "The African Public Servant as a Public Policy-Maker," in *Public Policy in Africa*. Addis Ababa, Ethiopia: African Association for Public Administration and Management, no date, p. 31.
46. Ibbo Mandaza (ed.), *Zimbabwe: The Political Economy of Transition 1980–1986*. Dakar, Senegal: Codesria Books, 1986, p. 50.
47. Terry L. Cooper, see Note 5, p. 52.

SELECTED BIBLIOGRAPHY

Books

Adam, T. R. (1965). *Government and Politics in Africa South of the Sahara*. 3rd ed. (revised). New York, Random House.
Adamolekun, L. (1990). "Institutional Perspectives on Africa's Development Crisis." In *African Governance in the 1990s*. Atlanta, Carter Center.
Adamolekun, L. and Ayo, B. (1989). "The Evolution of the Nigerian Federal Administration System." Publius 19 (Winter): 157–176.
Ahiakpor, J. C. W. (1985). "The Success and Failure of Dependency Theory: The Experience of Ghana." International Organization 39, no. 3: 535–552.
Almond, G. A. and Powell, G. B., Jr. (1966). *Comparative Politics: A Developmental Approach*. Boston, Little, Brown.
Almond, G. and Sidney, V. (1958). *The Civic Culture*. Princeton, Princeton University Press.
Anyang'Nyongo, P. (1987). *Popular Struggles for Democracy in Africa*. London, Zeds Books.
Apter, D. (1966). *The Politics of Modernization*. Chicago, University of Chicago Press.
Arendt, H. (1965). *On Revolution*. London, Penguin Books.
Arendt, H. (1966). *The Origins of Totalitarianism*. London, George Allen and Unwin.
Arrow, K. (1963). *Social Choice and Individual Values*. New Haven, University of Connecticut Press.
Austin, D. (1978). *Politics in Africa*. Manchester, Manchester University Press.
Ayandele, E. A. (1971). *Making of Modern Africa*. London, Longman.
Ayo, B. (1988). "Social Policy" In *Nigeria's Second Republic: Presidentalism, Politics and Administration in a Developing State*, ed. V. Ayeni and K. Soremekun. Lagos, Daily Times Press.
Ayoade, J. A. (1978). "Federalism in Africa: Some Chequered Fortunes." Plural Societies 9 (Spring): 3–17.
Baker, E. (1942). *Reflections on Government*. Oxford, Oxford University Press.
Barkan, J. D. (1989). with Chege, M. Decentralizing the State: District Focus and the Politics of Reallocation in Kenya. Journal of Modern African Studies 27, no. 2: 431–453.
Barrows, W. (1976). *Grassroots Politics in an African State*. New York, Africana Publishers.
Beach, D. N. (1986). *War and Politics in Zimbabwe: 1840–1900*. Gweru, Zimbabwe: Mambo Press.
Bebler, A. (1973). *Military Rule in Africa*. New York.

Bradford, C. (1986). "East Asian Models: Myths and Lessons," In John P. Lewis and Valeriana Kallab, eds. *Development Strategies Reconsidered*. New Brunswick, New Jersey, Transitional Books.

Bratton, M. (1989). "Beyond the State: Civil Society and Associational Life in Africa." World Politics 41, no. 3 (April): 407–430.

Bretton, H. L. (1973). *Power and Politics in Africa*. London, Longman.

Brotz, H. (1977). *Politics of South Africa: Democracy and Racial Diversity*. London, Oxford University Press.

Busia, K. A. (1967). *Africa in Search of Democracy*. London, Routledge and Kegan Paul.

Cain, J. (1988). *Civil Society and the State: New European Perspectives*. London and Sweden, Verso.

Cardoso, F. H. (1973). "Associated-Dependent Development: Theoretical and Practical Implications." In Alfred Stepan, ed. *Authoritarian Brazil*. New Haven, Yale University Press.

Carter, G. M. (1962). *African One-party States*. Ithaca, Cornell University Press.

Claude, A. (1978). *Revolutionary Pressures in Africa*. London, Zed Press.

Cliffe, L. (ed.) (1967). *One Party Democracy: the 1965 Tanzania General Elections*. Nairobi, East African Publishing House.

Coleman, J. S. and Rosberg. (1964). *Political Parties and National Integration in Tropical Africa*. Berkeley, University of Press.

Cooper, T. L. (1990). *The Responsible Administrator: An Approach to Ethics for the Administrative Role* (3rd ed). San Francisco, Jossey-Bass.

Craig, F. W. S. (1974). *British Parliamentary Elections Results, 1885–1918*. London, Macmillan.

Curie, D. P. (ed.) (1964). *Federalism and the New Nations of Africa*. Chicago, University of Chicago Press.

Dahl, R. (1971). *Polyarchy: Participation and Opposition*. New Haven, Yale University Press.

Dahrendorf, R. (1958). *Class and Class Conflict in Industrial Society*. Stanford, Stanford University Press.

Damachi, U. G. (1976). *Leadership Ideology in Africa: Attitudes Towards Socio-Economic Development*. New York, Praegar.

Davidson, B. (1978). *Africa in Modern History: The Search for a New Society*. London, Allen Lane.

Dewy, J. (1972). *The Public and its Problem*. New York, Henry Holt & Co.

Diamond, L., Linz, J., and Lipset, M. S. (1988). *Democracy in Developing Countries. Vol. 2: Africa*. Boulder, Colorado, Lynne Rienner Publishers.

Downs, A. (1957). *An Economic Theory of Democracy*. New York, Harper and Row Publishers.

Dunn, J. (1986). "The Politics of Representation and Good Government in Post-Colonial Africa." In *Political Domination in Africa*, ed. P. Chabal. London, Cambridge University Press.

Ehrmann, H. W. (1965). *Democracy in a Changing Society*. London, Pall Mall Press.

Elster, J. (1989). *The Cement of Society: A Study of Social Order*. New York, Cambridge University Press.

Fortes, M. and Evans-Pritchard, E. E. (eds) (1970). *African Political System*. London, Oxford University Press.

Gicheru, H. B. N. (1976). *Parliamentary Practice in Kenya*. Nairobi, Transafrica Publishers.

Giddens, A. (1987). *The Nation-State and Violence: Vol. Two, A Contemporary Critique of Historical Materialism*. Berkeley and Los Angeles, University of California Press.

Ginsberg, B. and Stone, A. (1986). *Do Elections Matter?* New York, M. E. Sharpe, Inc.

Gitonga, A. K. (1988). "The Meaning and Foundations of Democracy." In *Democratic Theory and Practice*, ed. Walter O. Oyugi, E. S. Odhiambo, Michael Chege, and A. Gitonga. Portsmouth, NH, Heinemann.

Gonzalez-Vega, C. (1986). "The Fear of Adjusting: The Social Costs of Economic Policies in Costa Rica in the 1970s." In Donald E. Shulz and Douglas H. Graham, *Revolution and Counterrevolution in Central America and the Caribbean*. Boulder, Colorado, Westview Press.

Goran, H. and Bratton, M. (eds.) (1992). *Governance and Politics in Africa*. Boulder, Colorado, Lynne Rienner Publishers.

Gupta, A. (1975). *Government and Politics: A Comparative Survey of Political Processes and Institutions*. Delhi, Vikas Publ. House.

Haggard, S. (1986). "The Politics of Adjustment: Lessons from the IMF's Extended Fund Facility." In Miles Kahler, ed, *The Politics of International Debt*. Ithaca, New York, Cornell University Press.

Haggard, S. and Kaufman, R. (1989). "The Politics of Stabilization and Structural Adjustment." In Jeffrey D. Sachs, ed. *Developing Country Debt and Economic Performance*. Chicago, Chicago University Press.

Harris, P. B. (1970). *Studies in African Politics*. London, Hutchinson.

Hapgood, D. (1975). *Africa: From Independence to Tomorrow*. New York, John Wiley & Sons.

Hatch, J. (1974). *Africa Emergent: Africa's Problems Since Independence*. London, Sector & Warburg.

Helleiner, G. (1986). "Policy-Based Program Lending: A Look at the Bank's New Role." In Richard E. Feinberg, et al., eds. *Between Two Worlds: The World Bank's Next Decade*. New Brunswick, New Jersey, Transaction Books.

Herbst, J. (1990). *State Politics in Zimbabwe*. Harare, University of Zimbabwe Publications.

Hermet, G., Rose, R. and Rouquie, A. (1978). *Elections Without a Choice*. New York, John Wiley & Sons.

Herzog, D. (1989). *Happy Slaves: A Critique of Consent Theory*. Chicago, University of Chicago Press.

Hodgkin, T. (1961). *African Political Parties: An Introductory Guide*. Harmondsworth, Penguin Books.

Huntington, S. P. (1968). *Political Order in Changing Society*. New Haven, Yale University Press.

Jackson, R. H. and Rosberg, C. G. (1982). *Personal Rule in Black Africa: Prince, Autocrat, Prophet, Tyrant*. Berkeley, California, University of California Press.

Janowitz, M. (1964). *Military in the Political Development of New Nation: An Essay in Comparative Analysis*. Chicago, Chicago University Press.

Jaspers, K. (1976). *The Origin and Goal of History*. Westport, Connecticut, Greenwood Press Publishers.

Joseph, R. (1987). *Democracy and Prebendal Politics in Nigeria*. New York, Cambridge University Press.

Katzenstein, P. (1985). *Small States in World Markets: Industrial Policy in Europe*. Ithaca, New York, Cornell University Press.

Jennings, I. (1963). *Democracy in Africa*. Cambridge, University Press.

Kaushal, I. (1972). *Political Ideologies in Africa*. Delhi, Indra Kaushal.

Kriger, N. J. (1992). *Zimbabwe's Guerrilla War: Peasant Voices*. Cambridge, Cambridge University Press.

Legum, C. (1979). *Africa in the 1980's: A Continent in Crisis*. New York, McGraw-Hill.

Lewis, W. A. (1965). *Politics in West Africa*. London, Allen & Unwin.

Lijphart, A. (1968). *The Politics of Accommodation*. Berkeley and Los Angeles, University of California Press.

Lijphart, A. (1985). "Non-Majoritarian Democracy: A Comparison of Federal and Consociational Theories." Publius 15 (Spring): 3–15.

Lindblom, C. (1977). *Politics and Markets*. New Haven, Connecticut, Yale University Press.

Lindblom, C. (1977). *Politics and Markets, The World's Political-Economic Systems*. New York, Basic Books Publishers.

Lofchie, M. F. (ed) (1971). *State of the Nations: Constraints on Development in Independent Africa*. Berkeley, University of California Press.

Mackintosh, J. P. (1966). *Nigerian Government and Politics*. London, Allen & Unwin Ltd.

MacPherson, C. B. (1988). *Democratic Theory: Essays in Retrieval*. Oxford, Clarendon Press, 1979 and *The Political Theory of Possessive Individualism*. Oxford, Oxford University Press.

Mandaza, I. (1986). *Zimbabwe: The Political Economy of Transition, 1980–1986*. Dakar, Senegal, Codesria.

Markovitz, I. L. (1970). *African Politics and Society: Basic Issues and Problems of Government and Development*. New York, The Free Press.

Moore, B. Jr. (1966). *Social Origins of Dictatorship and Democracy*. Boston, Beacon Press.

Morgan, E. P. (1974). *Administration of Change in Africa: Essays in the Theory and Practice of Development in Africa*. New York, Dunellen.

Mutiso, G. C. M. and Rohio, S. W. (eds) (1975). *Readings in African Political Thought*. London, Heinemann Educational Books Ltd.

Nelson, J. (ed.) (1990). *Economic Crisis and Policy Choice: The Politics of Adjustment in the Third World*. Princeton, New Jersey, Princeton University Press.

Neuman, W. R. (1986). *The Paradox of Mass Politics: Knowledge and Opinion in the American Electorate*. Cambridge, Massachusetts, Harvard University Press.

Nkrumah, K. (1970). *Class Struggle in Africa*. New York, International Publishers.

Nwabueze, B. O. (1974). *Presidentialism in Commonwealth Africa*. London, C. Hurst & Co.

Nyangoni, C. and Nyandoro, G. (1979). *Zimbabwe Independence Movements: Select Documents*. London, Rex Collins.

Nyerere, J. K. (1973). *Freedom and Development: A Selection from Writings and Speeches 1968–1973*. Nairobi, Oxford University Press.

O'Donnell, G., Schitter, P. and Whitehead, L. (eds.) (1986). *In Transitions from Authoritarian Rule: Comparative Perspectives*. Baltimore Maryland, The Johns Hopkins University Press.

Olorunsola, V. A. (1986). "Questions on Constitutionalism and Democracy: Nigeria and Africa." In *Democracy and Pluralism in Africa*, ed. Dov Ronen. Boulder, CO: Westview Press.

Oyediran, O. (ed.) *Nigerian Government and Politics under Military Rule*. 1966–1979.

Piven, F. F. and Cloward, R. A. (1988). *Why Americans Don't Vote*. New York: Pantheon Books.

Polanyi, K. (1945). *The Great Transformation*. London, Victor Gollancz.

Polanyi, K. (1971). *The Great Transformation*. Boston, Beacon Press.

Pollock, N. C. (1971). *Studies in Emerging Africa*. London, Butterworths.

Potholm, C. P. (1972). *Swaziland: The Dynamics of Political Modernization*. Berkeley, University of California Press.

Potholm, C. P. (1979). *Theory and Practice of African Politics*. New Jersey, Prentice-Hall.

Ramos, A. G. (1985). *The New Science of Organizations: A Reconceptualization of the Wealth of Nations*. Toronto, University of Toronto Press.

Ranger, T. (1985). *The Invention of Tribalism in Zimbabwe*. Harare, Zimbabwe, Mambo Press.

Ranger, T. and Bhebe, N. (1992). *Zimbabwe's War of Liberation*. University of Zimbabwe Publications and James Currey Publishers.

Rook, P. J. (1967). *Wind of Change in Africa*. London, Blackie.

Ronen, D. (ed.) (1986). *Democracy and Pluralism in Africa*. Boulder, Colorado, Westview Press.

Rowley, C. (ed.) (1987). *Democracy and Public Choice: Essays in Honour of Gordon Tullock*. New York, Basil Blackwell.

Rupert, E. (1971). "The Prospects for Democracy in Africa." In Lofchie, M. F. (ed.) *The State of the Nations—Constraints on Development in Independent Africa*. Berkeley, University of California Press, pp. 239–266.

Sabine, G. H. (1959). *A History of Political Ideas*. London, George G. Harrap and Co. Ltd.

Schon, D. (1971). *Beyond the Stable State*. New York, Random House.

Schumpeter, J. (1942). *Capitalism, Socialism and Democracy*. New York, Harper and Row.

Scott, W. G. and Hart, D. K. (1979). *Organizational America*. Boston, Houghton Mifflin Company.

Shaw, T. M. and Herd, K. A. (eds.) (1979). *The Politics of Africa: Dependence and Development*. London, Longman.

Shapera, I. (1956). *Government and Politics in Tribal Societies*. London, C. A. Walts & Co. Ltd.

Shivji, I. G. (1976). *Class Struggles in Tanzania*. London, Heinemann.

Shivji, I. G. (1988). *Fight my Beloved Continent: New Democracy in Africa*. Harare, Sapes Trust.

Shulz and Douglas, H. G. (1986). *Revolution and Counterrevolution in Central America and the Caribbean*. Boulder, Colorado, Westview Press.

Sklar, R. (1986). "Democracy in Africa." In *Governing in Black Africa*, eds. Marion E. Doro and Newell M. Stulzt. New York, Africana.

Sklar, R. (1987). "Developmental Democracy." Comparative Studies in Society and History 29, no. 4:686–714.

Social Sciences Today Editorial Board. (1984). *The Ideology of African Revolutionary Democracy*. Moscow, USSR Academy of Science.

Staunton, I. (1990). *Mothers of the Revolution: The War Experiences of Thirty Zimbabwean Women*, London, James Currey Publishers.

Todd, J. (1987). *The Right to Say No: Rhodesia 1972*. Harare, Zimbabwe, Longman Zimbabwe.

Vereker, C. (1967). *Eighteenth Century Optimism*. Liverpool, Liverpool University Press.

Voegelin, E. (1975). *From Enlightenment to Revolution*. Durham, North Carolina, Duke University Press.

Wallerstein, I. (1961). *Africa: The Politics of Independence*. New York, Vintage Books.

Weber, M. (1978). *Economy and Society Vol. 1*. Edited by Guenther Roth and Claus Wittich. Berkeley, California, University of California Press.

Weiner, M. and Huntington, S. P. (eds.) (1987). *Understanding Political Development*. Boston, Little, Brown.

Weisskopf, W. A. (1957). *The Psychology of Economics*. London, Routledge and Kegan Paul.

Weitzer, R. (1990). *Transforming Settler States: Communal Conflict and Internal Security in Northern Ireland and Zimbabwe*. Berkeley, California, University of California Press.

Welch, C. E. (ed.) (1970). *Soldier and State in Africa: A Comparative Analysis of Military Intervention and Political Change*. Evanston, Northwestern University Press.

Wiseman, J. (1990). *Democracy in Black Africa: Survival and Renewal*. New York, Paragon House Publishers.

World Bank. (1989). *Adjustment Lending: An Evolution of Ten Years of Experience*. Washington D.C., World Bank.

Journals and Articles

Adam, M. M. (1980). "The African Soldier in Politics." New Africa, August, No. 155, pp. 11–17.

Anglin, D. G. (1964–65). "Brinkmanship in Nigeria; The Federal Election of 1964–65." International Journal, vol. 20, No. 2, Spring, p.180.

Arnold, G. (1981). "New Directions for the 1980's." Africa Report, Vol. 26, No. 3, May-June, pp. 58–61.

Born, W.-R. (1980). "Democratic Republic of the Sudan under Nimeiry." Aussen Politik, Vol. 31, No. 2, pp. 210–34.

Chandhoke, N. (1983). "The Prospects for Liberal Democracy in Zimbabwe." Indian Political Science Review, Vol. 17, No. 1, January, pp. 52–64.

De Ashweinitz, K. (1954). "Industrialization, Labour Control, and Democracy." Economic Development and Cultural Change, Vol. 7, No. 4, July, pp. 385–404.

Decalo, S. (1973). "Military Coups and Military Regimes in Africa." Journal of Modern African Studies, Vol. 11, No. 1, March, pp. 105–127.

Emezi, C. E. and Nwosu, H. N. (1971). "Problems of Democracy in New African States." Research Review (Inst. of African Studies, University of Ghana), Vol. 7, No. 3, pp. 48–65.

Feit, M. and Evans-Pritchard, E. E. (1968). "Military Coups and Political Development: Some lessons from Ghana and Nigeria." World Politics, Vol. 20, No. 2, January, pp. 179–193.

Frederickson, H. G. (1991). "Towards a Theory of the Public for Public Administration." Administration and Society, Vol. 22 No. 4, February, pp. 395–417.

Freedman, R. (1960). "Industrialization Labour Control and Democracy." Economic Development and Cultural Change, Vol. 8, No. 2, January, pp. 192–196.

Gellner E. (1991). "Civil Society in Historical Context." International Social Science Journal 129, August, pp. 495–510.

Goldsworthy, D. (1981). "Civilian Control of the Military in Black Africa." African Affairs, Vol. 80, No. 318, January, pp. 49–74.

Gray, W. H. and Mkafa. (1981). "Major Policy Issues for the 1980's." Africa Report, Vol. 26, No. 2, March–April, pp. 22–26.

Grundy, K. W. (1968). "Conflicting Images of the Military in Africa." (Makerere University College Dept. of Political Science and Public Administration Short Studies & Reprint series No. 3) Nairobi, East African Publishing House.

Gupta, A. (1979). "Africa in the 1980's." India Quarterly, July–Sept., pp. 309–328.

Herskovits, J. (1979–80). "Democracy in Nigeria." Foreign Affairs, Vol. 5 8, No. 2, Winter, pp. 314–335.

Koehn, P. (1981). "Prelude to Civilian Rule: The Nigerian Elections of 1979." Africa Today, Vol, 28, No. 1, pp. 17–45.

Kraus, J. (1979). "From Military to Civilian Regimes in Ghana and Nigeria." Current History, Vol. 76, No. 445, March, pp. 124.

Laitin, D. D. (1976). "The Political Economy of Military Rule in Somalia." Journal of Modern African Studies, Vol. 14, No. 3. September, pp. 449–468.

Lawson, R. M. (1967). "The Distributive System in Ghana." Journal of Development Studies, Vol. 3, No. 2, January, pp. 195–205.

Lewis, A. W. (1965). "Beyond African Dictatorship: The Crisis of the One Party State." Encounter, Vol. 22 No. 2, August, pp. 3–18.

Lijiphart, A. (1985). "Non-Majoritarian Democracy: A Comparison of Federal and Consociational Theories." Publius 15. Spring pp. 3–15.

Lipset, S. M. (1959). "Some Social Requisites of Democracy: Economic Development and Political Legitimacy." American Political Science Review, March.

Lofchie, M. F. (1967). "Representative Government, Bureaucracy and Political Development: The African Case." Journal of Developing Areas, Vol. 2, No. 1, October, pp. 37–55.

Mackenzie, K. (1981). "Nigeria's New Democracy." The Round Table, Issue 283, July, pp. 258–263.

Mazrui, A. A. (1973). "The Lumpen Proletariat and the Lumpen Militariat: African Soldiers as a New Political Class." Political Studies Vol. 21, No. 1, p. 1–12.

Melennam, B. N. (1973). "Armed Forces and Political Power in Africa." Africa Quarterly, Vol. 13, No. 2, July–September, pp. 131–135.

Morrison, D. G. and Stevenson, H. M. (1972). "Cultural Pluralism, Modernization and Conflict: An Empirical Analysis of Sources of Political Instability in African Nations." Canadian Journal of Political Science, Vol. 5, No. 1, March, pp. 82–103.

Moyo, J. N. (1992). "Prospects of Democracy in Southern Africa: Three Stumbling Blocks." Journal of Asian and African Affairs.

Msekwa, P. (1978). "The Doctrine of the One Party State in Relation to Human Rights and the Rule of Law." Utafiti, Vol. 3, No. 2, pp. 397–413.

Nehru, B. K. (1980). "Western Democracy and the Third World: A Further Comment." Third World Quarterly; Vol. 2, No. 1, January, pp. 126–30.

Nursery-Bray, P. F. (1980). "Tanzania: The Development Debate." African Affairs, Vol 79, No. 314, January, pp. 55–78.

Nyerere, J. K. (1963). "Democracy and the Party System." Africa Quarterly, Vol. 2, January–March, pp. 263–282.

Ogigbo, A. O. (1972). "On the Advantages of Non-Party State." Journal of Modern African Studies, Vol. 10, No. 1 May, pp. 122–127.

Ogueri, E. (1976). "African Nationalism and Military Ascendancy." Owerri, Conch Magazine Limited.

Ola, O. (1973). "Economic Foundation of the Crisis of Parliamentary Democracy in Africa." African Studies Review, Vol. 1, No. 2, September, pp. 233–254.

Polmer, D. S. and Palmer, C. D. (1978). "Political Participation Under Military Rule." Africa Quarterly, Vol. 17, No. 4, April, pp. 87–109.

Pralt, C. (1978). "Democracy and Socialism in Tanzania: A Reply to John Saul." Canadian Journal of African Studies, Vol. 12, No. 3, pp. 407–428.

Rothchild, D. and Gyimah-Boadi, E. (1981). "Ghana's Return to Civilian Rules." Africa Today, Vol. 28, No. 1, pp. 3–16.

Rustow, D. A. (1970). "Transitions to Democracy: Toward a Dynamic Model." *Comparative Politics* Vol. 2, No. 3, April, p. 337.

Salamone, F. A. (1980). "Indirect Rule and the Reinterpretation of Tradition." The African Studies Review, Vol. 23, No. 1, April, pp. 1–44.

Schacter, R. (1961). "Single Party System in West-Africa." American Political Science Review, Vol. 55, No. 2, pp. 294–307.

Sklar, R. L. (1983). "Democracy in Africa." African Studies Review, Vol. 26, No. 3/4, September/December, pp. 11–24.

Slovo, J. (1978). "A Critical Appraisal of the Non-capitalist Path of the National Democratic State in Africa." Utafiti, Vol. 3 No. 1, pp. 245–276.

The Stockholm Initiative on Global Security and Governance's Common Responsibility in the 1990's. Stockholm, Sweden, Gotab Printers, 1991.

Valpy, M. (1984). "One Party State African Tradition." Globe Mail, Toronto: Canada, March 23.

Verner, J. G. (1981). "Legislative Systems and Public Policy: A Comparative Analysis of Developing Countries." The Journal of Developing Areas, Vol. 15, No. 2, January. pp. 275–296.

Wallerstein, I. (1971). "*Left and Right in Africa*." Journal of Modern African Studies, Vol. 9, No. 1, May, pp. 1–10.

Wiseman, J. A. (1980). "Elections and Parliamentary Democracy in Botswana." World Today, Vol. 36, No. 2, February, pp. 72–78.

Welch, C. E. (1974). "The Dilemma of Military Withdrawal from Politics: Some Considerations from Tropical Africa." Africa Studies Review, Vol. 17, April, pp. 213–228.

Welch, C. (1978). "Military Intervention in Africa." Vol. 8 No. 4, pp. 40–42.

Weitzer R. (1984). "In Search of Regime Security: Zimbabwe Since Independence." The Journal of Modern African Studies, Vol. 22, No. 4, pp. 529–557.

Newspapers

The Herald, Harare, Zimbabwe, January 1, 1981, "Consolidation of New Power."

The Herald, Harare, Zimbabwe, September 21, 1981, "Thousands in One Party State Demo."

The Herald, Harare, Zimbabwe, August 5, 1982, "No One-party State Yet, Mugabe."

The Herald, Harare, Zimbabwe, December 5, 1989.

The Herald, Harare, Zimbabwe, July 16, 1990.

The Sunday Mail, Harare, Zimbabwe, May 28, 1989.

The Nambian, June 2, 1992.

The Weekly Mail, Johannesburg, South Africa, June 4, 1992.

34

Public Service Ethics in Australia

John G. Uhr

Australian National University, Canberra, Australia

I. AN AUSTRALIAN REGIME?

This chapter reviews the main threads making up the pattern of developments in public service ethics in Australia. As used here, "public service ethics" refers to the ethics of career officials in merit-based systems of public employment with norms of non-partisanship, providing loyal service as policy advisers and program implementers to whatever political party holds office as the government of the day. The Australian system of public service was derived in the late nineteenth century from the evolving British system, with important Australian innovations designed to strengthen the political independence and official impartiality of public servants (see Caiden 1965; Finn 1987). Now a century later, Australia is going through a fundamental overhaul and streamlining of the public sector, with a breakdown in traditional responsibilities of public and private sectors that poses an uncertain future for the concept of a career public service (Mulgan 1998; Keating 1998).

The intention of this chapter is twofold: to report on the main initiatives taken by Australian governments in their responsibility for public service ethics, with emphasis on the public policy issues identified as particularly relevant to administrative ethics; and to review the main analytical frameworks which are emerging as policy analysts attempt to help governments evaluate and improve ethics-in-government programs. Of necessity, the focus here is on formal policy frameworks as distinct from informal organizational behavior. Some attention will be paid to the place of ministers and legislators but the primary focus here is on the situation of career officials. As will be apparent, there is considerably more enthusiasm within government for ethics programs than there is confidence outside government about appropriate ethics policies. Ethics regulations abound, despite quite fundamental policy disagreements over the appropriate place of administrative ethics in the Australian policy process.

It is not just the pace of economic restructuring that makes the Australian case interesting. Australia is also an example of a nation going through a process of redefinition of national identity. This process is a significant political feature, comprising a formal agenda of regime change from a constitutional monarchy to a republic, as well as a less formal agenda of values clarification in relation to multicultural citizenship. Although Australia is one of the most enduring of modern democracies, the centenary of the national constitution in 2001 has been prefaced by a remarkable series of public debates over the changing nature of Australian "regime values" to use John Rohr's phrase (Rohr 1989). One effect of this process of redefinition is the loosening of significant structural supports for the traditional Australian ethos, including the ethos of public service and administration. This wider process of change entails major restructuring of traditional policies and practices of social as well as economic protection, calling on individuals to take greater responsibility for their own well-being and not to rely on the welfare state. This change makes it increasingly difficult for commentators to speak with clear authority about the general nature of Australian social and political values or about the specific character of core values shaping the Australian public service.

Two illustrations of this change in regime values deserve brief attention. First, the community debate over constitutional change to establish Australia as an independent parliamentary republic, which is in form if not in substance a major alteration to the executive branch of Australian government; and second, the community debate over multicultural citizenship, which is one of a number of significant debates over various attempts at national statements of Australian core values. The republic debate is the more pressing of these two policy areas but in many ways the debate over a multicultural identity for Australia represents the deeper level of community concern.

First, a comment on the formal values in the national constitution. The Australian constitution of 1901 establishes the Commonwealth of Australia as a constitutional monarchy with the British monarch as the Australian head of state, represented in Australia by the governor-general who is appointed by the British monarch on the advice of the Australian government. Australia has a parliamentary system of government, with the governor-general in possession of potentially great legal authority as the formal holder of executive power, exercised in practice by the prime minister and cabinet. The constitution grafts the democratic norms of representative government on to the pre-democratic norms of a foreign monarchy.

From an ethical perspective, it is interesting that the formal terms of the constitution provide no real guide to the responsibilities and accountabilities of those who hold executive power. Public servants reading the constitution are asked to see themselves as servants of the crown since the government of the day is barely acknowledged. But in everyday reality, public servants appreciate that they are in the first instance servants of their minister. The crown continues in the form of the governor-general who delegates executive power to ministers, while retaining a role as circuit breaker or constitutional umpire in the event of a deadlock between the two houses of parliament. This role is routinely in evidence when determining the merits of governments' requests for dissolution of both houses of parliament; but it is used in its most extreme form when dismissing a government facing parliamentary gridlock, as was the sorry fate of the Whitlam government in 1975 (Barlin 1997: 54–59). Not surprisingly, much of the momentum of Australian republicanism dates from 1975.

One important democratic norm of the constitution is that no formal constitutional change may take place except through popular referendum. November 1999 saw Australians vote down proposals to replace the monarchy and governor-general with a new office of president: a head of state appointed by the prime minister and confirmed by parliament but dismissable by the prime minister alone. Australia would have been an independent republic by virtue of having its own head of state. But the president would continue with tradition as the formal holder of executive power, with important national responsibilities for commissioning governments and dissolving parliaments. Students of political morality should take note: such a situation would test the durability of unwritten conventions relating to the political impartiality of the constitutional umpire and to the unwritten norms regulating the respect by governments for the moral authority of the head of state.

A related issue is the debate over a new constitutional preamble. The movement for a republican head of state brought forth calls for a new preamble to the constitution with a fresh declaration of national values to begin the second century of nationhood. The agenda of issues requiring recognition was set by the 1998 Constitutional Convention which devised the program of constitutional change for determination through the 1999 referendum. Subsequent political debate has made it far from clear whether either the government or the community now supports the recommended ensemble of preamble values: ranging from "Almighty God," "the rule of law," "our federal system of representative democracy," acknowledgement of indigenous "original occupancy and custodianship of Australia," through to "Australia's cultural diversity." The lead up to the 1999 referendum saw many competing model preambles, but the only common element was their united opposition to the set of very traditional values proposed by the government in its preferred model preamble. This is not surprising given that the prime minister was publicly opposed to the basic change to a republic and so ensured that the preamble on offer at the referendum was appropriate to the traditional political system.

The second realm of uncertainty over regime values relates to multiculturalism. The 1999 debate over the values to be declared in a preamble draws on earlier debates over statements and charters of Australian citizenship which reflect deeper community anxiety over Australia's regime values. The Labor governments of Hawke (1983–1991) and Keating (1991–1996) secured bipartisan support for a "national agenda for a multicultural Australia" as a basic declaration of the Australian social consensus. This declaration developed into a carefully balanced statement of the civic rights and obligations associated with the privilege of Australian citizenship. The agreed set of core values began with a clear and unambiguous acknowledgment of "the obligations that all Australians should have to an overriding and unifying commitment to Australia," including acceptance of "the basic structures and principles of Australian society—the Constitution and the rule of law, tolerance and equality, parliamentary democracy, freedom of speech and religion, English as the national language, and equality of the sexes."

This policy in favor of multiculturalism has impacted on the Australian framework for public administration. Under the former Keating government the reigning policy was one of "productive diversity" explained in terms of harnessing the diverse skills and experiences of a multicultural workforce to contribute to the country's economic prosperity (PSC&OMA 1995). The Australian emphasis of multiculturalism has always been on equality of rights of access to common public services, in contrast to the strategy of some other nations where the emphasis has been on diversity of services to different social groups. A classic illustration is that a majority of Australian government programs called "multicultural policies" relate to English language training, designed to promote the rights of individuals to participate in society and the economy regardless of linguistic background.

Under the successor Howard government this emphasis on multiculturalism has been maintained in practice if not in policy rhetoric, with the public service experimenting with many new approaches to enable greater participation in mainstream activities by non-mainstream individuals and groups. The 1998 release of the *Charter of Public Service in a Culturally Diverse Society* reflects widespread intergovernmental consultation over a national framework designed to integrate into mainstream service "planning, delivery, evaluation and outcomes reporting" (DIMA 1998). This charter covers seven principles of effective public administration in a multicultural context, with fresh approaches to such core activities as program accountability as well as the expected emphasis on access and equity. The intent is that the charter will be supplemented by agency-specific plans which will vary according to program and community.

But while the words describe challenging new values, the conduct of government tends to retreat from the rhetoric. The reason behind the retreat is the fear of "white backlash." The difficulties associated with a national commitment to values of diversity were highlighted by the mid-1990s eruption of right wing populism in the form of the "One Nation" political party (Manne 1998). Multiculturalism was one of the main targets of the new protest party which won electoral support from segments of the lower skilled workforce who somehow saw themselves as victims of globalization and multiculturalism. This new party took support away from the established conservative parties and caused the Howard government to look more critically at the formal agenda of multiculturalism, thereby adding to the uncertainty over the scope of rights and obligations expected of Australian citizens.

What evidence is there that these worries over words tell us anything about Australian regime values? The answer is provided by two telling indicators of the fractured accord on national values. First, the 1996 debate over the passage of bipartisan declaration of racial tolerance reaffirming parliament's commitment to "maintaining Australia as a culturally diverse, tolerant and open society" (Uhr 1998: 229–230). Second, the slow and painful reappraisal of the 1989 national agenda on multiculturalism began in mid-1997 (NMAC 1997). Both indicators point to the instability of Australian regime values and highlight a difficulty facing government agencies intent on anchoring their ethic of public service in a commitment to core Australian values. The very existence of the unique 1996 parliamentary declaration on core values of tolerance and respect highlights the fragility of the social consensus once taken for granted and the responsibility taken by parliament to try to restore eroding standards of civility, within and without the parliamentary arena. The repeated delays in the release of the national inquiry into the revision of the 1989 national agenda highlights the divisions within the ranks of the government's policy advisers and the reluctance of the government to exercise moral leadership for fear of getting too far ahead of the tail end of community opinion (NMAC 1999).

II. THREE ETHICS PERSPECTIVES

Readers should be warned that the Australian situation is changing quite rapidly and that many of the details of institutions and regulations in any report will date quickly. The three reports dealt with here achieved excellent coverage of their subject, but the remarkable differences among these reports give a graphic indication of the changing political and legal landscape which confronts recorders of what passes for the Australian way of treating public service ethics (Hughes 1980 and 1991; Wiltshire 1989; Jackson and Nelson 1991). The tone runs from legal definition of ethics, to confrontations over accountability among competing political institutions, finally to acknowledgments of systemic corruption in government, reflecting in no small measure the regime's criminal origins as a convict colony. The trend in academic coverage has been from the legal to the moral: from an initial attention to the regulation of conflicts of interest, then a widening of focus to include the political requirements for the ethics of accountability, and more recently to the moral makeup of the Australian polity. As successive Australian governments try to manage public service ethics, they excite successively deeper doubts about the political morality of aspects of the Australian regime.

At the beginning of the 1980s, Hughes (1980) published his pioneering survey of administrative ethics in Australia, noting that concern over financial interests provided the initial excuse for a steadily widening scope, with ethics guidance tending to become more expansive even if less prescriptive. Australian governments seem to sense that the tradition of case-by-case regulation required supplementation through statement of general ethical principles. Hughes noted with some relief that such general statements were not intended strictly to be part of the law of the land (Hughes 1980: 198–200).

At the end of the same decade, Wiltshire (1989) published his survey of institutions of accountability in Australia and their major contribution to public service ethics. In examining the operations of accountability in Australian governments, Wiltshire emphasized that many of the core institutions served an ethical rather than legal function associated with establishing community standards by which to judge official behavior. Australian governments had a tendency to proclaim statements of exacting public accountability for officials, then to complain about the expanding web of external scrutiny which blocked the managerial discretion of officials. Tensions began to arise within the Australian system of responsible government over the competing ethical demands of the many accountability agents examining official responsibility. The concentrated ministerial interest in responsive administration, with its more focused requirement of executive confidence and accountability to the government of the day, increases the risk of confusion over the place of wider public trusts and accountability (Wiltshire 1989: 115–119).

Finally, Jackson and Nelson (1991) published a more recent comparable survey of the Australian scene. Paradoxically, their report offers the bleakest prospects of ethical administration, despite all the anti-corruption initiatives which they cite. They contend that the scope for moral integrity in public office is severely constrained by the ways in which the Australian political culture of ''anti-authoritarianism and materialism'' encourages ''complacency about corruption and ethics.'' The political system combines some of the worst features of British administrative secrecy and American purchase of political influence. Especially under the influence of the so-called ''new managerialism''—an Australian term used to contrast the newer practices of results-oriented public management with traditional administrative process-orientations—Australian public organizations are affected by a ''disregard for procedures,'' with increasing tensions ''between the vocation of the public service and the norms of business management.'' The odd combination of political executives committed to what is described as a managerialist ethic, and accountability agents suspicious of the ethical costs of risk management, has established ''a new set of potentially conflicting loyalties'' which ''muddies the old set lines of accountability'' (Jackson and Nelson 1991: 126, 136, 139–140).

III. ETHICS AS IT IS: CONFLICTING LOYALTIES

A 1990s case-study illustrates Australian trends in administrative ethics and highlights the important and unresolved public policy issues associated with them. New South Wales established the Independent Commission Against Corruption (ICAC) in 1989 as the chief policy instrument in a set of initiatives directed against fraud and official misconduct in government. Mr. Greiner, the state premier, or chief political executive, headed a recently elected government brought to office in no small measure through his election promise of an ICAC-type body to combat fraud and corruption in government. The premier introduced a wide-ranging ethics program into the state's aging and rusty public administration, which was reformed along orthodox public management lines of organizational efficiency and political responsiveness.

Three years later, soon after being returned to office only with the formal support of a small number of independent legislators, Mr. Greiner was declared "corrupt" by ICAC. The allegation focused on his offer of what his opponents described as a bribe of a public service job to a former party colleague who had become one of the independents and a prominent critic of the government (ICAC 1992: 46–47, 58–59; Page 1992: 27). The ICAC cleared the premier of the bribery charge, but reported that he was still "corrupt in terms of the ICAC Act" for his "partial exercise" of his office in bypassing established appointment procedures protecting the merit-system of public service. The ICAC, which only took up the reference upon formal direction by the parliament, declined to recommend any further legal prosecution, leaving it up to parliament to determine the political fate of the premier—but finding that there existed, under the strict terms of the ICAC Act, "reasonable grounds" for the premier's dismissal (ICAC 1992: 72–76). Mr. Greiner quickly resigned as leader and later, together with another minister named in the report, also from parliament. The governing party quickly elected a new leader who, with the support of parliament, became the new premier, only to lead his party to defeat at the next election.

Many elected politicians, including a number of nationally prominent party opponents of the ex-premier, spoke out against the bureaucratic monster which had turned against its creator. The ICAC had faithfully applied the remarkably strict test of official corruption found in the ICAC Act: including that very open test as to whether official actions were "partial"—understood in this case as partial compliance with the requirements of the merit-based system of public service. Within a few months the state appeals court overturned the ICAC finding in a 2–1 decision, although their doubts were directed to the ICAC's subjective test of the grounds for dismissal from office, rather than the initial finding of "partiality."

The case reveals much more about administrative ethics than might be apparent from the publicly reported preoccupation with corruption. The law includes, as a leading category of corruption, conduct which involves "the partial exercise . . . of any official functions." The ICAC law stipulates that in making findings of corruption, the commission must satisfy itself that the partial actions are of sufficient magnitude that, in the words of the act, they could constitute a criminal offense, or a disciplinary offense, or constitute at the very least reasonable grounds for dismissal. The ICAC used only the reasonable-grounds case against the premier, arguing that his conduct threatened his continued hold on the office of chief executive: parliament could well have reasonable grounds to cause his dismissal by withdrawing its confidence in his administration. As the ICAC emphasized, whether parliament actually caused his dismissal was a matter for parliament alone. The superior courts declared this to be wrong in law as an unreliably subjective test.

Political critics were outspoken in their criticism of so-called "ethics police." Former Labor prime minister Bob Hawke, for example, after conceding that the premier had seriously misjudged the political risks of the job offer, raised what he termed a "profound question of public policy" in warning against any trend to confuse "a lack of wisdom, mistakes of judgment or plain bloody stupidity with corruption." Similarly, Queensland state premier Mr. Goss protested against the trend represented by the ICAC finding of casting politicians' behavior "only in dark and self-interested terms": judging actions according to such an elevated impartiality test is politically naive because "seeking a party advantage" is "what politicians do each day at the office." The ICAC report had anticipated this, even to the extent of quoting from the premier's own explanation of the needlessly high standards of what the premier called the fearsome "disinterestedness" standard, under which elected politicians may "act only in what they consider to be the national interest" (ICAC 1992: 92). As Mr. Greiner clearly recognized, successful enforcement of standards of disinterestedness would require the expulsion of partisanship, parties, and party government from Australian political life.

Of great interest here is the debate over the value of merit and the fear of political manipulation of the merit system of public service. The ICAC report reveals two related ethical dangers embedded in the Australian political system: first, a corrupt tendency for politicians to act *partially* by, second, influencing officials to act *improperly* in unethically bypassing the procedural conventions of the merit-based public service. In the opinion of the ICAC, the premier "failed the test of impartiality" (ICAC 1992: 73). He attempted to appoint to a permanent public service position a political opponent on the partial grounds of the political advantage of the government, and not on the properly impartial grounds of the individual's merit. The ICAC quite carefully distinguished appointments to the merit-based career *public* service from those to *government* service, such as boards of public enterprises, diplomatic posts and politically sensitive agency headships. This partiality test presumes that one can reasonably distinguish career public service cases from routine political appointments by governments to public offices, which are conventionally accepted as being within the gift of executive governments. Being part of a conventional government service, they are therefore not protected by statutory provisions stipulating appointment solely on the basis of merit, as in the case of the senior executive position established under the state's Public Sector Management Act examination (See ICAC 1992: 58–59, 69, 75, 93). Ministers brought pressure to bear on the official head of the state's career public service to apply the appointment provisions of the Public Sector Management Act "in a positively partial fashion" which, if not strictly unlawful, was improper in the opinion of the ICAC (ICAC 1992: 78–79, 88).

The ethical agony of public service life is illustrated in the situation of the administrative chief of the state system of public service, the secretary to the premier's department, who had been put "in a most invidious position" by the government (ICAC 1992: 87). His practical problem was how best "to exercise a discretionary power in highly unusual circumstances." This involved the dilemma of balancing his obligations to his minister, the premier, and his statutory obligations to care for the professional public service. In finding that the most senior official had acted improperly, the ICAC reported that he had done the bidding of the government and was party to the positively partial process in which there was "no genuine merit selection" (ICAC 1992: 88–89).

The ethical test of proper use of powers cannot be reduced solely to a legal one without exhausting ethics of any moral meaning. The policy task is to identify the appropriate bodies with responsibility and capacity for auditing the ethics of official discretion: the two extremes of ministerial and judicial bodies each pose tests of form which too easily abstract from the substance of the public interest. The alternative of closer legislative oversight, which suggests itself as the unexplored remedy, suffers from Australian uncertainty as to the constitutional credibility of a legislative body controlling executive officials. Some of this uncertainty has been met by the welcome developments in the ethical reorientation of the state legislature of New South Wales in the wake of the Greiner Affair.

One of the most significant institutional developments to come out of the Greiner Affair is the articulation of legislative ethics. For present purposes, the developments in the state of New South Wales can stand as representative of legislative ethics trends in the larger Australian scene, although different jurisdictions will be a little ahead or behind the trends reported here (see Uhr 1998: 170–176). Australian public servants frequently find themselves in professional dilemmas, caught between their organizational duties to their ministers who direct the activities of their agencies and their countervailing obligations of accountability as public employees to parliamentary oversight committees. Hence it is useful for all concerned when parliamentary institutions set out the standards of appropriate conduct against which elected representatives want to be judged (Preston and Sampford 1998).

Consistent with this, the ICAC Act has been amended to ensure that the state parliament put its own house in order. Three subsequent developments reflect the rather sudden arrival of ethics within the legislative sphere in Australia. First, the two houses of the state parliament each established specialist ethics committees based on an overhaul of the traditional, rather self-protective, committees on parliamentary privileges. The inquiries and reports of these committees are now important sources in the Australian policy literature on public sector ethics (see Burgmann 1998; Smith 1998). Second, both houses have agreed to a code of conduct declaring the standards which the community had a right to expect of its elected representatives. Typically for Australian parliaments, there was initially no agreement between the two houses on the content of such a code: the lower house favoring a vague aspirational code and the upper house preferring a very detailed set of guidelines on misconduct. In 1988 the state premier released a model code which eventually obtained parliamentary consent. This code is short and legalistic, full of must-dos, reminding members that under their general duties as trustees of the public they must: declare conflicts of interest and declare gifts; resist bribery; refrain from using confidential information for private gain. An important parliamentary addition to the premier's code is the public acknowledgment that "organised parties are a fundamental part of the democratic process." The implication here is that party loyalty is not to be understood by ICAC or other external scrutineers as a form of partiality inappropriate to the parliamentary sphere.

Third, both houses moved towards the establishment of an ethics commissioner, styled a parliamentary ethics adviser. Each step here is small and tentative. The federal legislature has no such ethics officer and like most of the state parliaments relies on the skill and prudence of the privileges committee. Australian legislatures acknowledge that their credibility as agents of public accountability now depends on their ability to demonstrate their own ethics of accountability. The New South Wales upper house ethics committee has signalled that this demonstration should proceed through internal training rather external policing and has undertaken to produce a novel casebook on legislative ethics as an adjunct to the work of the ethics commissioner (Burgmann 1998).

IV.   ETHICS AS IT SHOULD BE: PUBLIC TRUST

Developments in the state of Queensland illustrate many of the boldest policy measures that have emerged in recent years in Australian public service ethics. At around the same time that New South Wales experienced a newly elected conservative government establishing the ICAC, Queensland experienced a liberal government experimenting with alternative policies to combat fraud and corruption in government. Whereas the ICAC model is, as its name implies, geared up *against* invasive and negative elements which corrupt the integrity of government, the Queensland model attempts to promote positive standards of ethically appropriate official practice. Following the main outlines recommended by the 1989 Fitzgerald Inquiry which effectively brought to an end over two decades of secretive conservative rule and increasing public cynicism about public life, the new liberal government established, among other anticorruption institutions, an Electoral and Administrative Review Commission (EARC) to advise government on best policies and practices for rebuilding public confidence in government (Prasser et al. 1990; EARC 1992: 1–6; Solomon 1998; Whitton 1994).

EARC existed from 1989 until it completed its series of systemic reviews of state governance in 1994. Among EARC's many inquiries and reports is that of 1992 on codes of conduct for public officials, which was published around the time of the ICAC inquiry referred to above (EARC 1992: 192–204). This was EARC's primary contribution to ethics in government, and it broke ranks with many traditional Australian approaches to the regulation of public office. EARC was unconvinced of the public policy merits of the conventional view about administrative morality which holds that officials are neutral instruments of the government of the day, with no professionally independent role in the policy process; and further that trust in government referred principally to the confidence which ministers have a right to expect of their loyal officials. Focusing on the duty of trusteeship as the primary orientation for public officials, EARC reported that the need for new policies and practices on administrative ethics was urgent now that administrative discretion was being accepted as an inevitable element of the public policy process in systems of responsible government (EARC 1992: 34–56).

But the mere articulation of public trust concepts is, as the EARC knew full well, insufficient, for there is "no settled view of the ethical standards" appropriate for "public officials in a democratic system of government." EARC saw its role as including that most basic of public policy tasks: drawing together the core elements of the absent consensus on administrative ethics. Where other review bodies have attempted to define the substantive moral responsibilities of the ethics of public office, EARC mapped out new ground by attempting to define what one might call the process framework of obligations of public accountability. This is the framework regulating the ways in which officials' ethical discretions are, if so required, publicly justified. EARC's distinctive approach to the ethics of office was to focus on the concept of public office as the primary category, with the stated aim of devising "a set of distinctive relationships inherent in our society's concept of 'public office' . . ." The result is a refreshing reappraisal of the relevance of the constitutional framework of the Westminster-derived tradition of responsible parliamentary government, which has in practice shown great "potential for conflict between the public and private loyalties of public officials" (EARC 1992: 9, 11, 15, 16–28; Solomon 1998: 14–17).

EARC recognized a systemic defect in Australian constitutionalism: the exclusion of appropriate checks and balances under the political fiction that public officials can and should act as neutral, technocratic instruments, unbiased by value distractions relating to their wider public interest obligations (EARC 1992: 16–17). In contrast to many other ethics reviews, that by EARC went beyond the common initial steps of identifying flaws in the orthodox doctrine of neutrality and called for recognition of a values dimension to public office. Such a generic call for values (surprisingly unspecified in many cases) is the easy part of administrative ethics; the hard part is devising institutional environments that invest in ethics within public agencies. EARC in contrast saw the importance of providing an institutional dimension to this search for values-based public administration, and it turned to constitutional structures to provide a legitimate grounding for administrative ethics.

The proposed solution was the challenging constitutional doctrine that public offices are positions of public trust, which involve a balance of *policy* responsibilities and *process* accountabilities. Officials exercise power over public policy through their administrative discretion in advising on, implementing, and evaluating government programs. In contrast to most ethics regimes which attempt to specify the values with which proper public administration should comply, the EARC approach puts to one side the principles of motivation while paying greater attention to those of public justification. This implies that there is a zone of acceptable ethical values which is defined and ordered by the tests of justification imposed by the agents of accountability. For public officials, the basic test of being ethical is meeting the tests of open, public justification of results as constitutionally required by the structures of accountability. This approach is not simply an institutional one but a constitutional one that locates appropriate regime values in the core political institutions which constitute the system of democratic governance.

Not all have been convinced that constitutionalism thus understood gets us far enough beyond the limitations of role ethics (Preston 1996; Corbett 1997). One understandable fear is that this route might reduce administrative morality to compliance with the endless demands of the agents of accountability for more and more information about administrative process, regardless of whether the public interest is being served by program management. When push comes to shove, trusteeship becomes responsiveness to political demands made in the name of, but not necessarily in the service of, public accountability.

The EARC response is that the constitution of accountability provides the essential processing structures within which administrative discretion is examined. Further, examination by accountability agents must itself meet certain compliance standards, the aim being to relate the two parties in an audit of the trustworthiness of the officials under examination. Like ICAC, EARC accepted that their new standards might be regarded as too demanding for public life. In practice, much depends on the working relationship between the office of public trust and official actions respecting the "duty to act in the public interest." Public trust notions might work most effectively as inhibitors on self-interest, reminding officials that their powers will be judged according to a benefits test, with a critical eye to the possibility of official self-interest or partiality. Trust thus understood serves as a check on the irresponsible use of public office for private gain. But EARC opens a door to another mode of managing the ethics of office, in which the concept of the public interest serves as a positive goal against which actions will be judged by the agents of accountability. In this alternative mode of official ethics, the appropriate standard is not the negative one of avoiding self-interest, but the more exacting one of promoting the common good or public interest (EARC 1992: 22–25).

EARC itself raises all the usual warnings about the difficulty of finding practical definitions of the public interest and adds to the potential mischief of any such standard by detailing the conventional subdivisions of public interest theories into the two camps of utilitarianism and deontology. Their proposed solution is to accept that the notion has an unavoidable elasticity due to the "three overlapping criteria" derived from the set of three legitimate perspectives on what is in the public interest as judged by executive government, professional standards, and personal ethics (EARC 1992: 25).

Life after EARC measures up remarkably well against the demanding EARC standards. Ethics features prominently in two spheres in the newly reformed public sector in

Queensland. First, the place of administrative ethics in the newly articulated professional ethos of career public servants; and second, the surprising turn to legislative ethics as an important supplement to the emphasis on the public accountability of officials. Other jurisdictions are reshaping their own ethics regimes along generally similar lines, if at a slower pace of reform.

In relation to administrative ethics, the general Queensland framework is regulated through the state's Public Service Act and the specific ethics regime is established by the Public Sector Ethics Act. The latter is the immediate product of the government's response to EARC and the former is an interesting consequential rewrite of the basic legislative provisions for core public employees. The basic legislation states that state public service exists "as an apolitical entity responsive to Government needs" and committed to "a spirit of service to the community." This establishes the formal declaration of a *public* as distinct from a *government* service. The basic law also stipulates the core principles of public service management, nicely captured in the duty to implement government policies responsively and responsibly. So too official conduct is acknowledged as a public trust such that officials are expected to carry out their duties impartially and with integrity.

Who is responsible for making this happen? Interestingly the law recognizes that the ultimate responsibility of the state premier or chief political executive, working normally through the public service commissioner whose own functions must be performed "independently, impartially, fairly, and in the public interest," thereby modelling the qualities of bureaucratic chief executives generally. Under this legislative umbrella, the Public Sector Ethics Act establishes the specifics of the ethics regime. This law lists five core ethics principles which it declares as fundamental to good public administration: respect for the law and the system of government; respect for persons; integrity; diligence; economy and efficiency. From these core principles an extensive set of ethics obligations flows, with each of the five principles attracting a package of "should" and "should nots." For example, the principle of integrity requires that officials should "seek to maintain and enhance public confidence in the integrity of public administration; and to advance the common good of the community the official serves"; and therefore should not allow personal interests to interfer with their official duties.

How can such admirable principles and obligations become administrative realities? The policy answer is through the promotion of codes of conduct as instruments of ethics. The law outlines the general character of codes of conduct and then identifies the preparation of agency-specific codes as a responsibility of the relevant chief executive—with the final public approval resting with the appropriate minister, thereby making the political executive equally responsible alongside the bureaucratic leadership for the carriage of codes. After that point, agency employees must comply with the duties as codified and chief executives must ensure that appropriate education and training are provided to employees about their rights and obligations.

As with New South Wales, the renovation of legislative ethics has been less forthcoming. But the system of governance can not overhaul administrative ethics in the absence of greater appreciation by elected officials of their own ethical obligations. Once again, the incentive rests with EARC which called for new efforts to devise a scheme of legislative ethics. The various detours and eventual achievements since that original plea in 1992 are recorded in the 1998 parliamentary report which devised and recommended a draft code of legislative ethics (E&PPC 1998). Among the proposed innovations is a statement of commitment for newly elected members and a substantially upgraded program of induction and training.

V. ETHICS AS GOOD MANAGEMENT: CODES

The merit of codes of ethics and conduct is the transparency they bring to public expectations of official conduct. But even the most ardent proponents of codes know that codification is not all there is to ethics. Public credibility requires proof not only of official compliance with proclaimed standards but also of external scrutiny and review to ensure that standards are both fair and feasible (Uhr 1999). Recent Australian experience has highlighted a number of limitations of the code-centered approach to public service ethics. Two issues stand out: legislative uncertainty over what governments accept as fair and feasible; and political conflict over the adherence of ministers to their proclaimed standards as leaders of public administration. Both instances surfaced early in the life of the Howard government elected in 1996.

The case of legislative uncertainty surrounds the thwarted parliamentary passage of the most recent government bill to overhaul the operations of the Commonwealth public service (CBPA 1997). The Howard government's long-awaited 1997 rewrite of the Public Service Act was not passed by the Senate, forcing the government to introduce a number of its changes by way of regulation. The parliamentary debate clearly indicated considerable political uneasiness over several ethics-related proposals. Of particular importance was the opposition of nongovernment parties to the proposed new statement of public service values. Instead of any reference to the public interest one finds the description of the public service as "apolitical," which is at best a negative definition of service values. Critics feared that this negative approach meant that governments might be tempted to subvert traditional values of public interest impartiality by substituting value-free instrumentalism in its place.

Interestingly, the most hotly debated provision related to the qualities appropriate to policy advising, which is a sphere of public service activity that is becoming more prominent as many spheres of program implementation are being hived off to contract providers (Uhr and Mackay 1996). The Howard government proposed a set of values including one that identified a standard relating to the provision of "accurate and timely" advice. Critics feared that this declaration fell far short of the standards of public interest advocacy which the community is entitled to expect from their public servants.

What is equally revealing is the extent of the government's dogged but vain opposition to the change that was eventually made under sustained public pressure: rewriting this core advisory value in terms of the provision of "frank, honest, comprehensive, accurate and timely advice." The parliamentary debate over this statement of values provides a rare and fascinating insight into the importance attached to words identifying the core values of public servants (CBPA 1997). As it now stands, the new legislation has made its way on to the statute books, prominently displaying the new core values and public service responsibilities.

The case of ministerial compliance with their code of conduct is even more complicated. During its first term (1996–1998), the Howard government found itself impailed on the sharp point of the prime minister's welcome but demanding code of conduct (Uhr 1998: 194–196). The government was taken by surprise when eight ministers or parliamentary secretaries (i.e., ministers in waiting) were forced to resign for various lapses of official conduct. Three ministers have gone for breaches of conflict of interest and the rest for various travel scams which breached related guidelines as well as the spirit of the new code. Another minister had the public support of the prime minister against charges of conflict of interest but, weary from the burden of repeated public justification of his apparent if not real conflicts of interest, eventually retired from ministerial office after the 1998 election.

Most of the immediate commentary related to the prime minister's reluctance to force strict ministerial compliance with his code. But just as important is the very existence of the code. While earlier prime ministers have had rules requiring ministers to file statements of financial interests, John Howard is the first Australian prime minister to establish a public code stipulating standards of ministerial conduct. The Commonwealth public service had done its policy development and had provided the former government with an important statement on accountability in Australian government which identified the place that ministerial ethics should play in setting the tone for responsible government in Australia (MAB 1993). To an extent, the bureaucracy had taken the initiative and gone some considerable way towards providing whoever was the government of the day with two companion documents: an emerging report which identified the important place of values and ethics in Australian public administration, and a working draft of a set of standards for ministers. Soon after his election in March 1996, John Howard published both documents: first his version of the ministerial code and then the public service report on bureaucratic ethics (Howard 1996: MAB 1996: Uhr 1998: 194–209).

The so-called ministerial code is not really a code or legal instrument but a public declaration by the prime minister. The document is not a law or regulation and it does not even have any formal parliamentary authorization. There is nothing to stop the prime minister as author of the document from using his authority to alter or amend it or to interpret it as he sees fit—and nothing to stop a new government from starting all over again with a new code. As critics have argued, this is very much an informal conduct code.

Ministerial misconduct should be understood in terms of its context, within the rules of the game of parliamentary government. Even after acknowledging the formal authority of the governor-general as head of the federal executive council, the Howard code notes that even though the cabinet is not mentioned in the constitution, it really is "the central organ for collective consideration of issues by ministers." The code usefully identifies three leading principles of collective ministerial responsibility which effectively define the operating ethic of cabinet government in Canberra, which is one of player loyalty to the captain/coach: first, all cabinet decisions "bind all ministers"; second, all ministers "must give their support in public debate to decisions of government"; third, ministers must "refrain from public comment" on matters before cabinet or its committees "until endorsed by the full cabinet." So who really is in charge of our national system of collective or cabinet government? Who sets the terms for collective confidence? The code is very clear on this point: it is the Prime Minister who decides both the agenda of business and the means of determining cabinet decisions (Howard 1996).

When the code finally comes to section five on ministerial conduct, the opening theme is that it is vital that the conduct of ministers not "undermine public confidence in them or the government." As in real life, public confidence in government should depend on evidence of trustworthiness by government. But frequently when governments demand our confidence all that they are really doing is asking us to take them on trust. This theme of retaining public confidence can be taken in two senses; first, in a high-minded sense of public trustworthiness introduced by the prime minister's foreword when referring to ministerial observance of the highest standards of public trust which the Australian people "have . . . as their entitlement;" there is also a second sense which is less high-minded and relates to the public credibility and electoral reputation of the government in power. Public confidence thus has at least these two meanings: a positive public faith in the trustworthiness of the ministry and a negative sense that the ministry has not yet lost community confidence and deserves to remain in office, pending final electoral judgment. The path of honor places a burden on the prime minister to take positive responsibility for promoting and reinforcing public confidence in the trustworthiness of the ministry. But the path of convenience puts the burden on individual ministers not to rock the boat, either by speaking out against questionable conduct by colleagues or by disclosing personal details which might somehow undermine public confidence (Howard 1996).

But the code also notes that ministers must also ensure that whatever they do "that their conduct is defensible." To many, a defensible course of conduct falls short of conduct that is more openly justifiable. Defensible conduct is akin to getting off with an unproven verdict as distinct from a full exoneration. This test of defensibility could be reduced to a minimalist one of avoiding conduct that is not capable of a public defense against charges of impropriety. This falls short of a strict ethical test of reassurance and trustworthiness. On the other hand, perhaps the code is taking a fair account of the relevant court which is *political* rather than *judicial*. Parliament is a political forum in which the opposition parties can be expected to remain unconvinced even of the most reasonable evidence in a minister's favor. The code in effect alerts ministers to the need to think ahead and ensure that their conduct, even in such minor matters as periods of leave while on overseas business, must be clearly defensible (Howard 1996).

The code takes a remarkably strong line against private use of public office for personal gain. It silently draws on advice given to the former Fraser government in the influential report of the Bowen inquiry into *Public Duty and Private Interest* (Bowen 1979; Barlin 1997: 163–164). Bowen's proposed code of conduct rested on the principle that officeholders "may be required by the nature of public office to accept restrictions on certain areas of their private conduct beyond those imposed on ordinary citizens" (Bowen 1979: 31). Such restrictions are more than simply obstacles to self-interest and should be understood as evidence that public officials are to act, in the best of worlds, as moral exemplars of public service.

The Howard code is especially useful in drawing attention to the appropriate relationship between ministers and public servants. The code recognizes that ministers will encounter areas of unclear responsibility in their work with their "permanent secretaries"—as their departmental heads were once called, before the former Labor government turned them into "departmental secretaries" employed by the government of the day on limited tenure. The code notes that both ministers and public servants have complementary roles in maintaining the trust upon which their public partnership rests. The ethical foundation of the career public service working under the general direction of departmental secretaries is their professional commitment to political impartiality. The code recognizes that ministers have very limited rights over the employment of career public servants and that they must not do anything "which could call into question their political impartiality" (Howard 1996: 13, 15; cf Howard 1998). Merit-based employment in the public service is about many things, but particularly about safeguarding the public service against politicization.

This is a two-way street with professional obligations binding ministers and public servants into a public partnership. The code notes that the high standards expected of the public service in relation to their "honesty, integrity and conduct" demands of career public servants that they provide their ministers "frank and comprehensive advice" and "party-political impartiality." The code is equally clear that ministers have no obligation to accept public service advice, although they do have an obligation to ensure that public service advice be "considered carefully and fairly" (Howard 1996: 13).

VI. ETHICS AS IT COULD BE: COMMENTATORS

The Australian ethics literature is small but growing. The field was originally the preserve of political scientists, most of whom have directed their contributions to the debate over the policy merits of the so-called "new managerialism" (Corbett 1997; Hood 1998; Pusey 1991). To the limited extent that Australian ethics-in-government literature has had any policy effect, it is as a participant in the often polemical dispute over the fate of equity and social justice under "new public management." The initial issues in debate have been; first, whether equity has been a casualty of the recent efficiency drives; and second, whether the professional ethic of career officers has been politicized through a form of "asset stripping" in which political executives have neutralized the public service's capacity and will to act as an independently accountable institution of government. These two issues are about the *social values* of policy and policymakers. There is, however, a third and (at least in my view) regrettably minor issue relating to the *institutional virtues* of public servants which also deserves comment here (Uhr 1990:25–26; cf Mulgan 1998).

The traditional pre-managerialist perspective is ably represented by R.S. Parker, whose reflective accounts of practical dilemmas in administration formed the major Australian chapter in the dismantling of the influential politics-administration dichotomy (Parker, 1993). Parker's interest was in administrative ethics as a political issue affecting the operations of interrelated institutions in the system of responsible government. As a public administration scholar, his contribution stopped short of advocating particular social outcomes, or even advocating systems of administration conductive to particular social outcomes. This is to do less than full justice to Parker's energetic rejection of managerialist models of public organization and the professional ethic of administrators.

On the first issue, those nongovernment policy analysts closely involved in the debate over public service ethics have tended to be severely critical of the insiders' claims that the managerialist reforms to the organization of public services have enhanced social justice. Representative scholars include Anna Yeatman, Marian Sawer, and Martin Painter. The model of ethical administration at work here is one adapted from the "new public administration" literature. The research task has been to identify the social pattern of winners and losers under managerialism, and to assess the ways in which the policy design shaped by economic rationalism has adversely affected the equal opportunities of vulnerable groups. By implication, much of this research work suggests that officials have an ethical duty to act in government on the basis of their sense of social responsibility. This segment of the ethics literature focuses on the social outcomes of government, and tends to see officials as potentially influential participants in the policy process, who should act with a commitment to equity and socially beneficial outcomes.

Typical of this group is the rather angry exchange between the external analyst Considine and the agency head Paterson over the federal government's equity credentials (Considine 1988, 1990; Paterson 1988). As a contribution to Australian public policy development, this and the associated literature mark an important turning point in the treatment of ethics. The equity literature fixes on the organizational relationship between processes and outcomes, and laments the managerialist preoccupation with private sector

styles of organizational management, in which a range of social goods traditionally produced by government is marginalized. Although strongly rejected by many senior officials,
the anti-managerialist critique has served to keep the ethics of office to the force, and
might even have forced the architects of managerialism to rein in some of the risky components of the risky management package.

On the second issue relating to personal rather than social responsibility, the relevant
Australian policy analysts contend that the professional ethic being cultivated amid managerialism is basically instrumental and devoid of officers' individual commitment to independent moral standards. The model of ethical administration here is allied to moral theories of personal responsibility, and is close to that devised by John Burke and Terry Cooper
in the United States. The ethical perspective is that officials have a duty to act with a
sense of personal responsibility for the processes of public administration. This segment
of the ethics literature includes the whistleblowing research, mainly written by its advocates who argue that individual officials have a personal responsibility to see that the
process is structured so that the truth wins out (Corbett 1997; Hood 1998; Pusey 1991).

Typical of this segment of the ethics literature is the influential research of Jackson,
which has turned the bright spotlights of morality on to public administration, in an attempt
to identify its weak ethical foundations (Jackson 1987, 1988). Where many others confine
their attention to professional ethics, Jackson reminds us that adjectives such as professional before ethics tend to confine and stifle the place of genuine morality in office.
Jackson's treatment of administrative ethics focuses on the personal moral responsibilities
of decision-makers, as they weigh contending versions of the right thing to do. Drawing
on Aristotle's robust political science, Jackson represents the important view that the ethics
of office can not be reduced to pragmatic functionalism, in either its lowly managerial
mode or its more lofty constitutional mode. Here the interest in administrative ethics is
not limited to the network of institutional responsibilities linking officials to their accountability agents, but reaches out to the higher responsibilities which officials must observe.
These higher duties include an interest in ensuring that the network operates to satisfy
not simply the interests of the institutional stakeholders but more fundamentally the interests of justice. Administration is a political component within a larger social and economic
whole, with a bias towards system maintenance. Administrative ethics must include the
consequences of bureaucratic power for the enhancement of the moral opportunities of
all.

On the third issue of what I have termed institutional virtues, much excellent research is being done in Australia, without as yet great effect within government (see the
chapters by Kellow, Finn, and Saunders in Power 1990). The view of the relevant policy
analysts is that the overlooked area of ethics is that of the institutional basis of official
responsibilities (Sampford and Preston 1998). The model of ethical administration here
is close, despite the absence of a public service oath to uphold the constitution, to that of
Rohr's constitutional officer who balances the responsibilities of office against the legitimate interests of the other core institutions of government (Rohr 1989; Uhr 1988). The
aim here is not to identify a set of appropriate social values fit for official implementation,
or even, like Jackson, a theory of justice which could elevate the moral dimension of
decision-making. Instead, the interest in this segment of the literature is to replace the
search for right social values with a map of duly-constituted responsibility centers, in
which different administrative offices and institutions would fulfill their policy responsibilities in line with the broad constitutional responsibilities of the office, as delegated to
offices or institutions by the duly-constituted policy-authorizers. In contrast to the former

treatments of *social* and *moral* trusts, here the core ethical idea is that of the duties of *public* trust which acts as one of the primary fetters on the official exercise of discretion. The perspective being developed here is that of the institutional responsibility of officials, understood in terms of their quite specific duties attached to their particular responsibilities of offices.

Typical of this segment of the ethics literature is the research by Paul Finn, which has addressed as the most urgent policy requirement the need to obtain greater clarity of the basic constitutional morality appropriate to the different types of public office (Finn 1990, 1991, 1993). Finn's work represents the viewpoint that effective operation of the ethics of office presupposes a constitutional ordering of offices so that the accountability agents can know what range of legitimate purposes are appropriate in assessing official use of public power. Whereas the social justice and the moral responsibility groups have identified an external standard of ethics relevant in assessing government performance, the constitutionalists have made their most telling mark with the admittedly negative argument that Australia lacks an inner constitutional doctrine of public service. The language of public trust is all very well as identification of the category of ethical responsibility, but where does it find a home in Australian political institutions? Paradoxically, then, it is not the existence of external standards but the poverty of Australian forms for their institutionalization which stands in the path of an agreed ethical regime for Australian public service. The task for analysts of public sector ethics is not to shop around the ethical markets in search of models of morality, but to reconstitute the public sector so that officials can know the constitutional roles for which they have specifically accountable public trusts (Uhr 1990: 26–27).

The latest wave of research on public sector ethics has included a formidable body of work on what is termed institutional ethics. This takes the ethics of role as a starting point for a fresh inquiry into the capacities of differently placed public officials to bring ethics to bear on public policy and administration. Typical of this trend in research are Charles Sampford and Noel Preston who have built on the practical achievements of Howard Whitton—one of Australia's leading ethics advocates within the public service (Whitton 1994; Sampford and Preston 1998; Preston and Sampford 1998). It is probably an advantage that no one school or approach to ethics has anything like market dominance. Cynics would argue that all three approaches are marginal to the mainstream focus on managing for results, with its surprising devaluation of traditional process-ethics. Current developments within Australian governments and bureaucracy indicate something of a retreat from earlier levels of acceptance of the basic form of democratic ethics—the ethic of accountability. The following sections describe these latest trends and attempt a provisional evaluation of their alternatives.

VII. THE ETHICS OF ACCOUNTABILITY

Finally, it is important to stand back from the welter of changing political policies and try to identify any deeper principles that might resonate with a search for stable regime values. Australia is unusual in that the system of public administration has generated its own remarkable articulation of values. We conclude with a brief look at two of the most impressive and enduring accounts of public service ethics that have done so much to define the ethic of career service in Australia. The alternative vision in new public management of the contract state with its rejection of traditional careerism has yet to generate a comparable values-based vision.

The best place to find Australian benchmarks for administrative ethics is still the 1976 *Report* of the Coombs Royal Commission on Australian Government Administration (Coombs 1976; Uhr 1998: 164–170). For our present purposes, there are two main reasons for paying attention to the Coombs *Report*: first, it redefined the concept of Australian responsible government to include more direct public accountability for officials; and second, it rounded off its redefinition exercise with a prominent argument against codes of conduct, opting instead for a balance of external accountability mechanisms and renewed attention to internal sources of responsibility such as professionalism in public management, including training in the ethics components of public management.

The arrangement of the balance follows from the underlying theory of government. The Coombs Commission and *Report* spent some considerable time trying to define the core political concepts of the Australian system of government and to identify the constitutional place and formal responsibility of officials. The *Report's* challenging argument holds that Westminster is no longer relevant as the appropriate standard for describing and evaluating Australian political practices. In addition to the obvious existence of federalism and bicameralism, two key reasons adduced are: (1) the truncation of *ministerial responsibility* through the formal declaration by ministers that they are not liable to be held to account before parliament for all the administrative malpractices and policy failings of their officials; and (2) the corresponding development of *administrative responsibility* with an increased burden of open, public accountability on officials.

The *Report's* path from ministerial irresponsibility to administrative ethics ran as follows. In the Coombs' view, ministers have good and bad reasons for rejecting the traditionally onerous standards of strict ministerial responsibility. The bad reasons are associated with self-interested flight from parliamentary responsibilities. Under the strict view of individual ministerial responsibility, which might appear to be an essential requirement of genuine parliamentary government, ministers are liable before parliament for all administrative actions performed in their name by their anonymous officials. From this perspective, bad faith could account for ministerial noncompliance with their obligations to wear their public responsibilities as chief executives. The good reasons flow from the recognition of the political facts of life, especially those of: steadily increasing bureaucratic power, with officials exercising ever wider-ranging administrative discretions; the reluctant recognition that official discretion is not only entrenched but necessary for good government and effective public policy; and the need to supplement ministerial responsibility and oversight with new protections against irresponsible uses of administrative powers.

Coombs sensibly looked to the inner checks of responsibility before resorting to the external checks of accountability. Discretion is directed by political processes but is driven by personal values. Almost by definition, discretion is intended to be exercised at the outer limits of the law: procedurally consistent with the law but substantively beyond the capacity of the law. For Coombs, discretion thus understood could be investigated and reviewed—and an account made of its responsibility—but it could not very effectively be codified or regulated. In moving beyond Westminster, Coombs trampled on and collapsed that useful fiction, the policy/administration divide (Coombs 1976: 11–13, 22–27, 65–67).

The *Report* called for policy guidelines on the appropriate practical response of public officials to parliamentary committees—guidelines designed to clarify the existing convention supporting answers to questions on "matters of fact" but not with such irresponsible independence as "to express opinions for or against government policy" or to comment "on the merits of a ministerial or government policy." The commission conceded that it is proper for *some* officials *sometimes* to comment on policy: for instance, in the cases of officials either (and it is a big "either") in positions of responsibility in statutory authorities or otherwise established to "exercise independently" their legal authority and provide government "with independent and publicly stated advice" (Coombs 1976: 114–117).

In defending their regime of accountable management for officials, Coombs warned that "the tradition of the supremacy of Parliament requires that the lines of that accountability should lead ultimately to Parliament" (Coombs 1976: 13). Discussion of the responsible use of discretion inevitably results in arguments over accountability hierarchies and institutional loyalties. The Coombs' examples illustrate that ethics is a political as well as a moral issue. Indeed, the most characteristic conflict situation giving rise to ethical dilemmas is that of a conflict of *duties* as distinct from *interests*—a conflict of institutional loyalties and obligations, as distinct from conflicts of financial or other corrupt forms of self-interest.

Ethics comes in through this front door of administrative responsibility and is always likely to be shown out again through the back door of public accountability. The internal institutions are (1) codes of ethics, which as Coombs understood them are primarily forms of professional self-regulation; and (2) the ethics components in management training and guidelines for official conduct. The external checks are (1) parliamentary oversight and (2) those other forms of administrative review of official decisions Australians now associate with "the new administrative law" (Uhr 1998: 192–194).

In 1979 the federal public service commission produced its initial response to Coombs: the *Guidelines on Official Conduct of Commonwealth Public Servants* (Hughes, 1980: 195–200). The *Guidelines* have been since revised several times under the responsibility of the Public Service Commissioner and are "intended to ensure that public confidence is maintained in the Australian Public Service" by articulating a set of three root principles. First, that officers should, "with professionalism and integrity," efficiently "serve the Government of the day"; second, that officers should observe fairness and equity; and third, that officers should avoid "real or apparent conflicts of interest" (PSC 1995: 1).

The *Guidelines* frankly recognize that public employees are part of the political system and that standards of conduct are affected by the political role which officials play in managing the public business. Within the first two pages of the *Guidelines*, one reads that the desired model of "a professional and scrupulous public service" can not be quarantined from political conflicts over public power, especially those disputes between legislative and executive politicians over the accountability obligations of officials, which helps to explain the purpose of the companion *Guidelines for Official Witnesses* before parliamentary and related inquiries. Accepting the potential for disputed ownership of the bureaucracy, the *Guidelines* state the main responsibilities of officials as the provision of honest and frank policy advice—in contrast to advice that is given simply to curry favor—and the implementation of government programs "conscientiously and with full regard for government policy" (PSC 1995: 2–3, 12).

Commendably, the *Guidelines* reject any professional image of neutral instrumentalism: both major responsibilities require judgment which itself calls upon "a public servant's own values." Such enlistment of personal values is legitimate except where those values "supplant those implicit in government policy." The *Guidelines* offer quite practical advice on professional ethics even if that term is not in fact used. A section on how agency heads ought to manage policy and value disagreements with ministers helps set a tone of responsible political management, which contains a recognizable professional ethos even where ethics are not explicitly part of the theme. Officials act in ways which are "the result of compromise and conflict between different perspectives, interests and values." Officials are not neutral in that they make value judgments; they ought to be only as neutral as is consistent with acting "inside Government policy"—although "equity should be a goal and commitment in making those judgments" whatever the policy of the government of the day (PSC 1995: 3–5, 63). Equity thus understood can be regarded as a basic constitutional or regime value, part of the vital value consensus within which political dispute is contained.

The professional character of the public service is particularly evident in two aspects of officials' responsibilities: their duty of public comment and their commitment to equity. Their positive duty to contribute to public policy debate is restricted to "reasoned public discussion," not so much on the policy merits of proposals as on their "factual technical background" (PSC 1995: 14–17). Restrictions do apply, principally where public comment might undermine public confidence in the professionalism and integrity of the public service. As for the meaning of professionalism, the *Guidelines* note that its nature varies with employment positions, although "skill, care, diligence and impartiality" are among its common elements (PSC 1995: 52).

The *Guidelines* conclude on the second theme of the equity commitment. This involves responsibilities to "fairness in decision-making and equity in program administration." Fairness here relates to the observance of the rules of natural justice; equity relates to the discretion exercised by officials who have a responsibility to try to honor a range of competing objectives—to the policies of the government, to efficiency, to the law, to equity—and on occasion "those responsibilities will conflict with one another." The principle of reconciliation is the obligation to act within government policy (PSC 1995: 58–63).

CONCLUSION

Australia is entering its second century as a nation-state. The contemporary Australian experience provides an interesting example of a democratic state with an evolving set of regime values. The political turbulence associated with the national debates over republicanism and race is difficult to interpret. The emerging character of national regime values can be seen as either open-ended or severely fractured. The allied set of changes to traditional public sector structures, including the core public service, must be seen in this wider context of social change. This note of caution is not to deny the prospect of innovative institutional redesign of the public service. The job ahead is to retain the best of the old world of career public administration while trying to meet the challenges of the promised new world of "new public management," as government ministers have clearly identified (Kemp 1998; Howard 1998). At least all concerned agree that ethics is central to that task, even if there are disagreements about the ideal political framework for a renovated system of public administration.

ACKNOWLEDGMENTS

My thanks go to Terry Cooper, Del Dunn, and John Rohr, whose generous but critical comments greatly improved the original edition of this chapter.

REFERENCES

Barlin, L. ed. (1997). *House of Representatives Practice*, 3rd ed. Canberra: Australian Government Publishing Service.

Bowen, N. (1979). *Public Duty and Private Interest: Report of Committee of Inquiry*. Canberra: Australian Government Publishing Service.

Burgmann, M. (1998). Constructing codes. In Preston and Sampford, eds., *Ethics and Political Practice*. Sydney: The Federation Press, pp. 118–126.

Caiden, G. (1965). *Career Service*. Melbourne: Melbourne University Press.

CBPA (*Canberra Bulletin of Public Administration*) (1997). Special Issue on Public Service Bill, No. 86, December.

Coombs, H. C. (1976). *Report, Royal Commission of Inquiry into Australian Government Administration*. Canberra: Commonwealth Government Printer.

Considine, M. (1988). The corporate management framework as administrative science. *Australian Journal of Public Administration*, 47/1: 4–18.

Considine, M. (1990). Managerialism strikes out. *Australian Journal of Public Administration*, 49/2 (June): 166–178.

Corbett, D. C. (1997). Serving the public. In G. L. Clark, E. P. Jonson and W. Caldow eds. *Accountability and Corruption: Public Sector Ethics*. Sydney: Allen and Unwin, pp. 15–35.

DIMA (Department of Immigration and Multicultural Affairs). (1998). *Charter of Public Service in a Culturally Diverse Society*. Canberra.

EARC (Electoral and Administrative Review Commission). (1992). *Report on the Review of Codes of Conduct for Public Officials*. Brisbane: Government Printer.

E&PPC (Ethics and Parliamentary Privileges Committee). (1998). *Report on a Draft Code of Conduct*. Brisbane: Legislative Assembly of Queensland.

Finn, P. (1987). *Law and Government in Colonial Australia*. Melbourne: Oxford University Press.

Finn, P. (1990). Myths of Australian public administration. In J. Power, ed., *Australian Public Administration*. Sydney: Hale and Iremonger, pp. 41–56.

Finn, P. (1991). Integrity in government and the law. In K. Wiltshire, ed., *Do Unto Others*. Brisbane: RIPAA and EARC, pp. 88–95.

Finn, P. (1993). The law and officials. In R. A. Chapman, ed., *Ethics in Public Service*. Edinburgh: Edinburg University Press, pp. 135–145.

Hood, A. Public officials, government and the public trust. *Australian Journal of Public Administration*, 57(1): 99–114.

Howard, J. (1996). *A Guide to Key Elements of Ministerial Responsibility*. Canberra, Prime Minister's Office: April.

Howard, J. (1998). A healthy public service. *Australian Journal of Public Administration*, 57(1): 3–11.

Hughes, C. A. (1980). Administrative ethics. *Australian Journal of Public Administration*, 39/4 (September/December): 192–201.

Hughes, C. A. (1991). Codes of conduct. In K. Wiltshire, ed., *Do Unto Others: Ethics in the Public Sector*. Brisbane: RIPAA and EARC, pp. 54–63.

ICAC (Independent Commission Against Corruption). (1992). *Report on Investigation into the Metherell Resignation and Appointment*. Sydney.

Jackson, M. (1987). The eye of doubt: Neutrality, responsibility and morality. *Australian Journal of Public Administration*, 46/3 (September): 280–292.

Jackson, M. (1988). The public interest, public service and democracy. *Australian Journal of Public Administration*, 47/3 (September). 241–251.

Jackson, M. W. and Nelson, H. G. (1991). The forbidden city: Ethics in Australian governments. *Corruption and Reform*, 6/2: 123–146.

Keating, M. (1998). The role of IPAA. *Australian Journal of Public Administration*, 57(2): 3–5.

Kemp, D. (1998). Public administration in the new democratic state. *Australian Journal of Public Administration*, 57/2 (June): 6–11.

MAB (Management Advisory Board). (1993). *Accountability in the Commonwealth Public Sector*. Canberra: Australian Government Publishing Service.

MAB (Management Advisory Board). (1996). *Ethical Standards and Values in the Australian Public Service*. Canberra: Australian Government Publishing Service.

Manne, R. (1998). *The Way We Live Now*. Melbourne: Text Publications.

Mulgan, R. (1998). Politicisation of senior appointments in the Australian public service. *Australian Journal of Public Administration*, 57/3 (September): 3–14.

NMAC (National Multiculturalism Advisory Council). (1997). *Multicultural Australia: The Way Forward, An Issues Paper*. Canberra: Government Printer.

NMAC (National Multiculturalism Advisory Council). (1999). *Australian Multiculturalism for a New Century*. Canberra: Government Printer.

Page, B. (1992). The Metherell affair. *Current Affairs Bulletin*, 69/3 (August): 27–28.

Parker, R. S. (1993). *The Administrative Vocation*. Sydney: Hale and Iremonger.

Paterson, J. (1988). A managerialist strikes back. *Australian Journal of Public Administration*, 47/4: 287–295.

Power, J. ed. (1990). *Public Administration in Australia: A Watershed*. Sydney: Hale and Iremonger.

Prasser, C., Wear, R. and Nethercote, J., eds. (1990). *Corruption and Reform: The Fitzgerald Vision*. Brisbane: University of Queensland Press.

Preston, N. (1996). *Understanding Ethics*. Sydney: The Federation Press.

Preston, N. and Sampford, C., eds. (1998). *Ethics and Political Practice*. Sydney: The Federation Press.

PSC (Public Service Commission). (1995). *Guidelines on Official Conduct of Commonwealth Public Servants*. Canberra: Government Printer.

PSC&OMA (Public Service Commission and Office of Multicultural Affairs). (1995). *Productive Diversity in the Australian Public Service*. Canberra: Government Printer.

Pusey, M. (1991). *Economic Rationalism In Canberra*. Melbourne: Cambridge University Press.

Rohr, J. (1989). *Ethics For Bureaucrats*. 2nd ed. New York: Marcel Dekker.

Sampford, C. and Preston, N. eds. (1998). *Public Sector Ethics*. Sydney: The Federation Press.

Smith, R. (1998). Strange distinctions In N. Preston and C. Sampford, eds. *Ethics and Political Practice*, pp. 41–51.

Solomon, D. (1998). *Coming of Age: Charter for a New Australia*. Brisbane: University of Queensland Press.

Uhr, J. (1988). Ethics and public service. *Australian Journal of Public Administration*, 47/2 (June): 109–118.

Uhr, J. (1990). Ethics and the Australian public service: Making managerialism work. *Current Affairs Bulletin*, April: 22–27.

Uhr, J. (1998). *Deliberative Democracy in Australia: The Changing Place of Parliament*. Melbourne: Cambridge University Press.

Uhr, J. (1999). Institutions of integrity: Balancing values and verification in democratic governance. *Public Integrity*, 1/1: 94–106.

Uhr, J. and Mackay, K., eds. (1996). *Evaluating Policy Advice*. Canberra: Federalism Research Centre and the Department of Finance.

Whitton, H. (1994). The rediscovery of professional ethics for public officials. In N. Preston ed., *Ethics for the Public Sector*. Sydney: The Federation Press, pp. 39–59.

Wiltshire, K. (1989). Accountability in the Australian public service. In J. G. Jabbra and O. P. Dwivedi, eds., *Public Service Accountability: A Comparative Perspective*. West Hartford: Kumarian Press, pp. 101–121.

Index

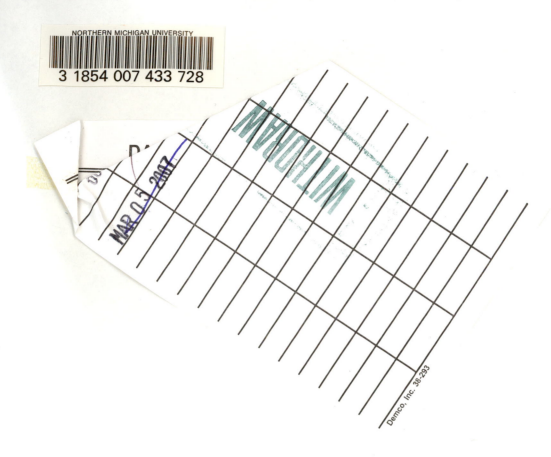

MAR 0 5 2007

Demco, Inc. 38-293